BELCHING
OUT THE
DEVIL

To Jenny

BELCHING OUT THE DEVIL

MARK THOMAS

EBURY
PRESS

1 3 5 7 9 10 8 6 4 2

Published in 2008 by Ebury Press, an imprint of Ebury Publishing

A Random House Group Company

The Random House Group Limited Reg. No. 954009

Addresses for companies within the Random House Group
can be found at www.randomhouse.co.uk

A CIP catalogue record for this book is available from the British Library

The Random House Group Limited supports The Forest Stewardship
Council (FSC), the leading international forest certification organisation.
All our titles that are printed on Greenpeace approved FSC certified
paper carry the FSC logo. Our paper procurement policy
can be found at www.rbooks.co.uk/environment

Mixed Sources
Product group from well-managed
forests and other controlled sources
www.fsc.org Cert no. TT-COC-2139
© 1996 Forest Stewardship Council
FSC

Printed in the UK by CPI Mackays, Chatham, ME5 8TD

ISBN 9780091922931

To buy books by your favourite authors and register for offers visit
www.rbooks.co.uk

Contents

An Admission

Globalisation can claim to have won on the day elderly grandparents started wearing trainers. Somehow it just seems wrong that a generation who fought and defeated the Nazis with sacrifice, ration books and allotments should endure the graceless experience of Footlocker. At that moment this very generation who had endured wars, created welfare states and could mend radios and bikes changed into consumers. It was around the same time that someone decided that instead of selling things with guarantees it was more profitable to sell the goods and then sell the guarantee too.

My own grandmother lived to ninety-eight and was no role model for sobriety or chastity. Her name was Margaret Isabel and she had more lovers than her family will ever know. She was small but got into fights because she hated bullies. And when I went to stay with her as a boy she would bounce me on her knee, sing Geordie folk songs and entrance me with the smoke rings she could blow. She could also flip the lit end of the cigarette into her mouth, blow smoke through the now protruding filter and then pop the lit end out again, using only her tongue. I utterly adored her. She was a unique woman, who took pride in her family's shoes being polished. I'm glad she never wore a trainer. But I cannot smell Coca-Cola without thinking of her. That is my admission. I used to love drinking Coca-Cola. Moreover, whenever I held a glass of just poured Coca-Cola to my lips and felt the bubbles popping under my nose, I would think of my nan. It was a Pavlovian response. When I stayed with her, every day began with the two of us making a trip to a coffee shop. She would have an Embassy and a coffee and I would have a Coca-Cola and a sticky bun. It is one of my favourite memories.

To this extent I was a classic Coke drinker. It was a treat when I was young. I'd drink Coke all the time in my twenties and Diet Coke in my thirties. I even dabbled with caffeine-free Diet Coke, which is about as pointless as consumerism can get. Coca-Cola is essentially sugar and caffeine and water, so take out two of the main ingredients and really I was just buying chemically treated water with a nice logo. But I fell into the ultimate Coca-Cola advertising trap when I started associating an intricate part of my life, the memory of my grandmother, with their product. Weaving their drink into our lives has been Coke's greatest advertising feat. Why am I telling you this? The fact is that before I looked into the Company I enjoyed their drink. Immensely. And Fanta, too. All I am saying really is: my name is Mark and I'm a recovering Coca-Cola drinker...one day at a time.

PROLOGUE

'The Coca-Cola Company is on a journey. It is a bold journey...fuelled by our deep conviction that collectively we can create anything we desire...Ultimately, this journey will be propelled by unleashing the collective genius of our organisation...it is our very nature to innovate, create and excel. It is who we are.'

The Coca-Cola Company, Manifesto for Growth[1]

am not that great a traveller. I may like to think of myself as mix between Hunter S Thompson and Michael Palin but in reality I am a middle-aged fat dad with asthma, trudging around the world with half-eaten bars of Kendal Mint Cake and a six-pack of Ventolin inhalers.

I'm fond of neither airplanes nor airports, believing them to be the secular limbo of the badly dressed. No one wears their best clothes to fly in and as a rule, the larger the flyer the more likely they are to be decked in sportswear. Thus creatures the size of sea mammals trawl departure lounges in clinging tracksuit bottoms that serve only to highlight the disparity between sporting aspiration and achievement. I know: I'm one of them. I'm a man who has seen too many airports in too few hours; my eyes are glazed, my pallor is pasty and I'm starting to look like my police picture. Atlanta is my seventh airport in five days. I have been propelled to 36,000 foot in metal tubes so many times that my ears pop if I walk up a flight of stairs, and after 4,207 miles of recycled air and microwaved food my breath tastes like someone else's fart.

There is no greater reminder of the reasons, need and urgency for reducing air travel than airports and spending time in them. I wince at the carbon footprint I am going to leave, though it occurs to me that no one pointed the carbon footprint finger at the United Nations Climate Change Conference and that was in Bali – an island in the Indian Ocean, a location which enabled only Balinese delegates to reduce emissions by walking or getting the bus. Everyone else had to fly. I decide there is a corrupt UN official in charge of such conferences who collects air miles.

Such is the mental state of my meanderings. I have stood in too many queues with my shoes in my hands over the past few days. Only half an hour ago I saw an elderly couple, with cardigans and travel sweets, shuffle to the front of the line at the metal detectors. They respectfully asked, 'Do we have to take our shoes off?'

'Yes, ma'am. Shoes off and into the tray,' said the member of staff who had obviously excelled at brusqueness training school.

'Shoes...' They looked at each other and shrug.

'Shoes and belts please,' he barked

'Belts...'

'Belts and jackets, please into the tray.'

A large young black woman turned to them confidently and said, 'It's the same all over, you wanna go anywhere these days you gotta get half-naked, honey. That's the truth.' Then, staring directly at the security guard, she yelped, 'Come on. Let's get them off.' And she begins to disrobe in a manner that can only be described as hostile.

I smile at the memory and traipse through a row of the terminal gift shops looking for something to read and a present to take home for my children. This isn't shopping, this is Groundhog Day. Another airport, another baseball cap; same cap, different city, just a matter of changing place names and animals. And so the Chicago Bears become the Miami Dolphins, who become the Washington Pandas, who in turn morph into the Georgia Head Lice or some other sporting mascot. The hats are on stands placed strategically around the newsagent's cash register and sweet display, while the walls are packed with magazines ranging from *Home & Garden* to *Guns & Ammo*, shelf loads of glossy front covers featuring cars, bridal dresses, computers and Britney Spears. There are hundreds of magazines here. To paraphrase Sir Winston Churchill: never in the history of consumerism have so many been offered so much of so little.

On one display stand alongside the hats is a pyramid of shot glasses, little tumblers for downing spirits in a gulp. These glasses have I ♡ OUR TROOPS over a khaki background so while the troops are living under fire some patriotic stay-at-home is getting drunk on their behalf. Next to the glasses is a pile of teddy bears, little soft toys full of Styrofoam beans or some such stuff. Each is decorated in the US army desert camouflage kit, complete with Stars and Stripes on its chest and a plaintive stare on its little face. It is as if the bear is saying 'I've seen some things out there man. Things a bear shouldn't see.'

'Who buys this crap?' I think. Tired idiots with a misfiring sense of kitsch value, I conclude, slouching into a moulded plastic seat, sweaty and glazed with a soldier teddy bear on my lap.

I sit, pale and tired, watching the display boards and listening for flight information on Colombia, my next destination being Bogota. My journey is seven airports, five days and four cities old and now I'm heading off to the cocaine capitol of the world with a teddy bear dressed like a US marine...

Oh God, what have I done...

* * *

At this moment in time you may well be asking yourself three questions: 'Where has Mark been, why is he going to Colombia and more importantly, have I kept the receipt for this book?'

To which the short answers are: the Coca-Cola museum, to meet a Coca-Cola deliveryman and I don't know.

You find me at the midway point of a trip to the US and Colombia. This is the first of a series of journeys to try and find the reality behind the PR image of the world's most famous brand, Coca-Cola. Quite why I set myself this task needs some explanation and to fully understand you need to grasp one fact: I have been a paid egotist all my working life. I started out as a comedian in the mid-1980s in London. Back then you didn't have to fuck a footballer or eat kangaroo penis on a reality show to appear on TV. No, back then any half-decent comic could get their own series on Channel 4, and being half-decent, I did. The shows ran from 1996–2002, 45 episodes over six series and a string of one-off documentaries. Some of the shows were crap, so bad I have not been able to watch them and I never will. Some of them were good and actually worked – the government tightened up tax laws on the back of two shows I did. A large company changed their policies and practices, some of the stories I covered made the front pages of the national press and Amnesty commended my work. By this stage my ego was robust enough to shield entire towns from most forms of attack (with the possible exception of kryptonite to which I have always been vulnerable). If I were to do a graph of my ego's peaks and troughs you would find the high spikes of my vanity and self-belief coincided with the decision to take on Coca-Cola. At the pinnacle of my narcissistic faith in my abilities, a series of events conspired that led to me being here.

Back in 2001 I was writing a column for the *New Statesman* magazine, a left-of-centre weekly with circulation figures that were the envy of every other British left-wing journal. It is sold in many cities and was once spotted in a petrol station rack. It is a crotchety old rag that is owned by a New Labour millionaire, runs adverts for the arms dealers BAE Systems and gives out Tesco gift vouchers as prizes for its competitions, but somehow it manages to host really good columnists from John Pilger to Shazia Mirza. I loved working for it and after one column was left a message from a chap called Professor Eric Herring, offering to help me by providing academic research and data. After the initial shock of realising that some academics have social skills and can conduct a conversation without the need for footnotes and peer review, a world of wonderfully brainy folk opened up to me. It is not that the academic world is closed to outsiders it is just insular, very insular. So it is essential to have a guide through this world, someone like Professor Eric Herring. If he was unable to help with an issue he would invariably pass me on to another academic who could. It was like Mensa meets the Masons but without the aprons and David Icke pointing the finger

One day Professor Eric Herring left a message saying, 'Really good column, nice analysis but you need up-to-date examples, you need to talk to Doug, one of my research students. He'll tell you about Colombia.' And what he told me about Colombia was the shocking figures and facts about the number of trade union organisers and leaders killed by paramilitary death squads. Thousands killed for the audacity of challenging sackings, wage cuts, intimidation, coercion to work longer hours, unsafe conditions and trying to halt the wave of casualised jobs – temporary jobs with no security or protection – that has swept over Colombia.

As one of the academics was connected to the Colombia Solidarity Campaign it was only a matter of time before I came into contact with them and their campaign on Coca-Cola, as trade union leaders working for the Coke bottlers had been killed by death squads: one of those was killed inside the bottling plant.

Misfortunes seemed to rain upon the Company around this time. Coca-Cola were getting some considerable attention on the issue of obesity from the Parliamentary Select Committee on Health[2] and the story of Plachimada in Kerala hit the international airwaves after the Coca-Cola bottlers there faced massive protests accusing the Company of exploiting the communal water resources. So depleted was the water supply that the Company was forced to bus in two tankers of water a day for the villagers.[3]

Then one afternoon I was talking to the man who used to produce my TV work, Geoff Atkinson. He is a quirky British chap, a large man with curly blond hair and a habit of wiggling his thumbs to signify excitement and contentment. In effect he has shrugged off years of evolution and relegated his prehensile thumb to the role of a dog's tail. Geoff was drinking a bottle of Coca-Cola and as we started to discuss New Labour I had pointed at the bottle and said , 'That is New Labour. Good packaging, lots of sugar and otherwise worthless.' Half an hour later I had formalised my obsession with the Company. There followed two months of internet trawls, late-night phone calls to anyone who was still awake and long meetings with non-governmental organisations and journalists, all of which culminated at the start of 2004 with me standing outside the Coke bottling plant in Southern India clutching a borrowed camera from Geoff pondering the subjects of globalisation, democracy, and wet wipes.

Over the next year I wrote and toured a stage show about the company, had numerous columns about Coke in the *New Statesman* (to the extent of the editor telling me 'You really can't do them three weeks running') and I co-curated an exhibition, with artist and friend Tracey Moberly, that invited anyone to submit drawings, pictures and Photoshopped images mocking the company's adverts.

All of us have psychological ticks and mine is that I find enemies easier to work with than friends. Broadly speaking you know where you are with an enemy and there is always the faint possibility of redemption; friends are altogether more complex and require much more attention. In the voyeuristic car-crash TV world of agony aunts and life coaches we are often told of the value of 'moving on', of walking away from trouble and getting on with our lives. But there is little joy to be had in avoiding trouble and people who don't bear grudges frankly have not got the emotional stamina for the job.

Friends who still wanted to speak to me asked, 'Why Coca-Cola, why are you going after them?' And the answer I most frequently gave was that The Coca-Cola Company is a relatively small company that makes syrup – they don't actually make much pop themselves. They franchise out the pop production, getting other companies to make it. Admittedly they own some of those companies, they have major shareholdings in others and some are what are called 'independent bottlers' –but they are all franchisees. They operate under what the company calls 'the Coca-Cola system'. The Coca-Cola Company (or TCCC) controls who gets the franchise, they control the distribution of concentrate (the syrup with which to make Coke), the production method, the packaging and they even coordinate marketing and advertising with the local bottlers. They have an enormous level of control over the bottlers yet will often claim they have no legal or moral responsibility for the actions of their bottlers if it involves labour rights or environmental abuses.

The one thing The Coca-Cola Company does have is a whopping great enormous brand and that is what they sell. Coke epitomises globalisation: a transnational worth billions that actually produces very little and yet is known the world over.

And that is truly part of the reason. But it is not the whole answer. There are two other reasons why I wanted to look at Coca-Cola and the first is simple: I don't like Pepsi. I never have and I never will. Coca-Cola is what I used to drink every day and, like many everyday things, I never really questioned it. In a similar way, I look at my watch but I have never wondered who first quantified units of time. Then one day sitting with Geoff I just looked at the bottle and thought, 'What actually is it I am drinking?' And I wasn't looking at just the physical ingredients, but the ingredients of the brand and the company. Like many, I did not buy South Africa goods while Mandela was jailed, as they were contaminated by the apartheid system; so what battles were going on in a bottle of Coke? I just wanted to know – and considering that every year they spend billions of dollars on advertising, I reckon a few of those dollars were spent on me. As far as I'm concerned they came after my custom, so they started it.

The first reason is specific to me; the second is global. When George Mallory was asked why he wanted to climb Mount Everest he said 'Because it's there.' Why do I want to write about Coke? 'Because it's everywhere.' You can't escape it.

And sitting here in Atlanta airport the impact of that statement was just beginning to hit me. The gulf between self-image and reality can be an ego-crushing chasm. I like to think I have a competent grasp of the basic concepts of globalisation, human rights and social movements, but realistically I know on a bad day I'm about as incisive and cutting as a Haribo.

Like most big-heads I believe my abilities to be greater than they are, but even I have moments of clarity. This morning I visited the Coke museum which is a testimony to the Company's history and its advertising blitzkriegs, and as I look around I realise I am witnessing a skirmish in one of those battles right now. In the immediate vicinity of my seat in the the airport lounge is a man-sized Coca-Cola fridge packed with Company products, an authentic Mexican diner serving drinks in Coke glasses, a massive Coca-Cola vending machine, a bottle of Coke sticking out of a seven-year-old's rucksack, a 30-something in a Coca-Cola T-shirt and numerous bottles of Dasani, Coca-Cola's brand of bottled water, being slurped by a school sports team that have arrived in tracksuits. Leaning back on the seat I can capture this entire scene within my field of vision. I am the odd one out, the exception to the Coke-drinking norm.

Coca-Cola is the biggest brand in the world, they have a greater global reach than a flu virus, they have lawyers who excrete spare IQ points and I am a dad sitting in an airport holding a teddy bear and an asthma inhaler muttering, 'Oh God, what have I done...'

1

THE
HAPPINESS
FACTORY

Atlanta, USA

'Coke is like a little bottle of sparkle-dust.'

Inside the Happiness Factory, The Coca-Cola Company 'documentary'

Everyone tells stories and a good story is a sleight of hand, distracting where needs be and discerning in its revelations. But the craftiest storytellers can tell you a tale without you realising it's being told. They are called advertisers – though some prefer the word 'twat'. Every product they sell has a tale to tell and an audience in mind to tell it to. They can tell a story with a phrase, a picture and sometimes with a single pencil line. Without them transnationals would become extinct because in order to sell they have to tell stories. They have to tell them to survive. Without adverts, brands do not exist and without brands modern corporations crumble.

No company spends money unless they feel it is for their financial benefit, so consider the estimated total global advertising budget for 2008: it is US$665 billion[1], or to use its technical term a 'gazillion'. With that amount of money you could run the UN and its entire operations for 33 years[2]. Or you could finance a totally new 'War on Terror'[3]: the US could invade North Korea and Cuba and still have change for a fair crack at France. For lovers of traditional forms of statistical comparison, the global advertising budget is Liberia's GDP for 600 years[4].

In the battle of the brands Coca-Cola are king. In 2007 news spread across the globe's financial networks that for the sixth year in a row Coca-Cola had been ranked as the world's top brand, beating well-known competition from Microsoft, McDonald's, Disney, IBM and Nokia to the title[5]. *Business Week*/Interbrand annual ratings and its evaluations are based on a distinct criteria: the belief that brands can be intangible assets, ie, something that doesn't physically exist yet can nonetheless have a financial worth. The value of a brand is calculated through surveys, which essentially measure the goodwill felt towards a company. Now I'm not an expert on high finance but the day that the trader or banker came up with the idea that you could put a price on...er...nothing tangible – well, that day must have ended very late at night with a taxi driver helping them to the front door.

Interbrand valued the Coca-Cola brand at $65.324 billion, which is a lot of goodwill. And the company must fight for every penny of it. For take away the brand, the image, the red and white colours and iconic script, take away the shape of the bottle, the advertising, the polar bears, the lights in Times Square, the Santa ads at Christmas, the Superbowl commercials, the sponsorship of the Olympics and football leagues, take all that away and you are left with the product: brown fizzy sugar water. And brown fizzy sugar water with no packaging, no logo and no built-in aspirations concocted in advertising land is not something any of us really need. Asa Chandler, Coke's first proprietor, knew this and set to conquering the world with a simple philosophy: advertise everywhere and make sure the drink is always available.

But there is one crucial thing about storytelling, as any narrator knows: the details that are left out of a story are as important as those that are left in. I am about to be reminded of this as I head for the World of Coca-Cola, a smooth silver building, with metal curves and a gleaming tower, half-corporate HQ, half-Bond-villain lair. It is essentially the Coke museum, the repository of the official Coke story, but this corporate autobiography leaves out some of the more uncomfortable truths.

* * *

The morning is cheerfully cold, a lovely Southern winter's day in Atlanta; the sun makes not one bit of difference to the temperature but it shines bright across the clear blue sky. A few police officers stand around Pemberton Park in the city centre, coats zipped up and wearing hats with earmuffs that dangle down each side of their heads, gently reducing them from figures of authority to parodies of Elmer Fudd. They drink coffee, smile and nod as I wander past. This is the entrance to The World of Coca-Cola and somewhere discreet loudspeakers are playing Coke's most memorable advertising jingle, 'I'd like to buy the world a Coke'.[6] Which may explain the earmuffs.

I like to think the company plays this song as a hymn of thanks to the Atlanta Development Authority who gave them $5.4 million to help pay for the park landscaping and the entrance plaza,[7] or the City Council who scrapped $1.5 million worth of sales tax for the company,[8] or indeed the property tax worth $2 million that the Atlanta city fathers decided they didn't want Coca-Cola to pay.[9] Coke might be worth billions but they are not averse to sticking out their hand for loose change, especially when the loose change has six noughts at the end of it.

In pride of place in the state-subsidised Pemberton Park stands a six-foot four-inch bronze statue of the area's namesake, the founding father of Coca-Cola, pharmacist John Pemberton. Officially he created the drink in 1886 and sold it from Jacob's pharmacy;[10] now, over 120 years later, his noble image stands facing the park, one hand on a small Victorian table at his side. In his other hand he holds up a glass of Coca-Cola, partly in celebration, partly inspecting it, his impassive face considering his drink and offering it out to the world. It is the image of a pioneer, a scientist hero and benefactor to humanity. Sir Alexander Fleming wouldn't have minded having a statue like this and he discovered penicillin. The statue portrays Pemberton as thinner than the photos I have seen of him, where he looks a tad chubby. This apparently is not the only factual discrepancy. According to Mark Pendergrast, one of the most respected authors on the company, John Pemberton returned from the American civil war addicted to morphine.[11] So Coca-Cola's founder was a chunkie junkie, though in fairness, who would erect a statue of a fat druggie outside a family tourist attraction – with the exception of the Elvis Presley estate?

So for the greater good of the corporate image ol' morphine Pemberton loses a few pounds and gets clean. And inside the historical revisionism continues; bizarrely there is no mention of one of the drink's original ingredients, cocaine, which with hindsight is hardly the greatest sin, as there were other beverages of the late nineteenth century that contained varying quantities of Colombia's most famous export. Admittedly it's a slightly messy fact: one minute you want to teach the world to sing, the next you want to teach the world to talk really quickly and rub its gums with an index finger.

It is these 'messy facts' that the Company seem to have an almost pathological desire to try and hide. They are deviations in the Company narrative, grit in the PR grease. And Coca-Cola do not like grit in the grease.

The World of Coca-Cola's image control even extends to their choice of neighbours. Right next to it sits the Georgia Aquarium; in 2002 Coke gave nine acres for the aquarium. In 2006 Coke set aside two and a half acres for a civil rights museum – for an attraction that would celebrate Atlanta as the cradle of the movement, with plans to house some 7,000-odd pages of Dr Martin Luther King Jr's writings. Thus corporate and civic history entwine together in one single downtown location, so we can remember the fight for human dignity and visit the fish.

Coke's new neighbours may or may not choose to display details of Dr King's last-ever speech, made the day before he was killed. In it he called for African Americans to withdraw their economic support of companies if they 'haven't been fair in their hiring policies', that is, favouring white workers over black workers. One of three companies that was targeted for boycotting that night was Coca-Cola. Dr King's exact words were, 'we are asking you tonight, to go out and tell your neighbours not to buy Coca-Cola in Memphis'.[12]

Likewise there may or may not be mention of the lawsuit bought against the company by hundreds of Coke employees, accusing them of discriminating against black workers in pay and promotion. The Company made no admission to these charges, but in November 2000 announced they were paying $192.5 million to settle the case.[13] If you're measuring racism by the buck, that's a fuck of a lot of racism.

Another little story the Company are not fond of is linked to the Olympics. Coca-Cola's relationship with the Olympic Games began in 1928. But Coke downplays its sponsorship of the 1936 Games, the Berlin Olympics, where a certain psychopathic painter and decorator launched a PR drive to promote his Nazi state. The Coca-Cola Company are happy to mention that one of the US 1936 Olympic rowing team went on to become their chairman. They are also proud to point out that sprinter Jesse Owens advertised Coke – though this was years after he won four gold medals in Berlin, somewhat spiking the Aryan master-race theories of his host. The Company are keener to place themselves alongside those who are seen as 'fighting' the Nazis or promoting the 'Olympic ideal', rather than display themselves as a backers of the Olympic platform given to Hitler. And frankly, who wouldn't be?

But the Company have a few other Nazi items in the attic. Consider Max Keith, the managing director of Coca-Cola GmbH, Coke's bottler in Germany, during World War Two. As the war progressed the supply of ingredients to make Coca-Cola dried up, so Max invented a new drink to quench the German thirst. He named it Fanta. Now there's a strap line for an ad. Fanta: The Reich Stuff!

Company historians note that Max Keith never joined the Nazi Party but he did exhibit Coca-Cola GmbH at a trade fair organised to embrace the concept of the German worker under the Fuhrer. In another instance Max Keith decorated his Coca-

Cola stand with Nazi flags. This has been confirmed by The Coca-Cola Company which said: '[Max] Keith at a bottler convention displayed swastikas and ended with a salute to Hitler. [This] would not have been out of place in the US if it were reversed and the podium had an American Flag and the proceedings began or ended with the Pledge of Allegiance.'[14] I'll leave you to be the judge of that.

What I do know is that The Coca-Cola Company archives have pictures of the stand at the trade fair 'that depict swastikas used as decor'[15] under the Coca-Cola banner. It is merely a guess on my part that the archivist would rather burn in hell than release those photos for public viewing

It's fairly safe to say that these stories are not going to generate greater sales for Coca-Cola, with the exception of the odd Klan customer. None of these facts, whether it is Pemberton's naughty needle, Fanta's dodgy parentage or King's condemnation, tell the story Coca-Cola want us to hear and it is the story *they* want to tell that sells their drink.

* * *

To hear the Coca-Cola story, it is a $15 admission charge for adults, $9 for kids aged between three and twelve. But before you are tempted to visit the World of Coca-Cola ask yourself one question: what is on show here? They make fizzy drinks and advertise all over the world in order to sell them; all they have are bottles and adverts – they can't make a museum out of that, can they? Yes, they can. That is exactly what the World of Coca-Cola is: Coca-Cola, Coca-Cola adverts and a giftshop selling Coca-Cola merchandise.

The first gallery you come to is the misnamed 'Loft', situated on the ground floor. Essentially this is an open area in front of two display cases, with the capacity for about two hundred people standing. The room is wall-to-wall banners, bottles and posters, pictures of American footballers urging them – and therefore us – to 'Play Refreshed'. Another has a boy holding up a six-pack of Coke in the old-fashioned design: 'All Set at Our Home' it reads. Coke clocks, bold and bright shine from high up on the loft rafters, next to art deco leaded-glass lampshades, with stained-glass pictures of the company script. A huge banner reads 'Live on the Coke Side of Life', though it is not as if there is any other option around here. Even the lighting has a red hue, and my retinas are beginning to ache slightly from over-exposure to the Coke colours: everywhere is red and white.

The glass cabinets hold Coke memorabilia as if it were treasure from the time of the pharaohs: toy delivery trucks, Christmas decorations, a pair of promotional hip huggers from the Seventies and the jewellery Raquel Welch wore on a Coke modelling shoot.

In front of the cabinets, a young woman dressed like a zookeeper in boots, long trousers and a red collared T-shirt, is addressing the crowd with a hand-held cordless mic. She's probably a perfectly nice girl, but she has all the emotional intonation of a flight stewardess. She must have repeated this spiel countless times leaving her over-familiar with the lines and distant from any meaning they might have. But she musters all the gusto she can and launches into the company schtick one more time.

Running through the lines like a chore best done quickly, she says, 'You'll be in this room for just a few minutes then the doors either side of me will open and you will be allowed into the,' she pauses for theatrical effect before proclaiming,

'Happiness Factory.' The trouble is she loses interest before she finishes the phrase, so it sounds like 'HAPPINESS Factory.' She gulps down some more air before charging on in near-monotone 'In the Happiness Factory is an approximately six-minute-long animated documentary based on our 2006 Superbowl commercial and it gives you a little glimpse of all the magic that goes into each and every,' she pauses, 'Coca-Cola.'

I manage to hang on to a couple of facts that she reels out: there are four hundred brands and the logo of the white swoosh on the red background is called the Dynamic Ribbon. Then I hear that our time in the Loft is 'just a prequel to the rest of your day here'. Frankly, I don't know which is more alarming: the prospect of staying here for a whole day or the use of the word 'prequel' to describe waiting in a room. Next time you're on hold at the end of a phone waiting for an operator to become available, just remind yourself you are not in a queue but experiencing a prequel.

Carla, the woman with the mic, continues by drawing our attention to the fact that the lights have just dimmed, which is the signal that 'our audio artefacts have cued up, which are basically eighty years' worth of Coca-Cola jingles. Feel free to sing along to them if you know the words.' I raise an eyebrow in concern as snippets of ads get blasted at us. The second eyebrow goes up as a mum in tracksuit bottoms starts mouthing 'Can't beat the feeling', while she wanders past the Rachel Welch jewellery. People are joining in, a group of thirty-something men who told me they're from Florida start on 'Always Coca-Cola'. I just know that if they play 'I'd like to teach the world to sing...' the whole room will burst forth in harmony. Oh fuck, I'm in a cult – this is what the Hari Krishnas would be like if they took sugar in their chai.

The doors to the cinema open and I move rather too quickly through them and into a large auditorium with raked seating. There about twenty-five of us dotted around the empty space facing a big cinema screen, in front of which a tour guide called John stands grasping a microphone. 'I'm here to welcome you to Happiness Factory and living on the Coke side of life, and having fun is what it's all about,' he says, adding 'Now I understand we have a birthday in the house', at which one of the Florida thirty-pluses delivers a half-hearted cheer. 'So let's all sing happy birthday after three. One. Two. Three . Happy Birthday to you...'

The audience, such as we are, mumble through Happy Birthday, while John throws himself into his mirthless task. If by bizarre chance anyone were ever to ask me, 'What do you think it would be like to be taken hostage by Ronald McDonald?'

   I can reply, 'I have a vague idea.'

'OK,' shouts John, 'How many of you have seen the commercial "Inside the Happiness Factory"? A show of hands? A couple of you. It was actually shown last year during the Superbowl and it was the second-highest rated commercial and because of that we turned it into a documentary. So, how many of you have wondered what happens every time you put a coin into a Coca-Cola vending machine, anyone wondered that?'

   A lone and slightly strangled voice yelps, 'Yes.'

   'Let me tell you what happens,' says John. 'Everyone say a little bit of love, let me hear you say 'Love'. '

   'Love' croak six or seven of us.

   'Magic' he gleefully urges.

   'Magic', reply even less than the first time.

   'Magic *and* Happiness!'

'Happiness' I find myself saying almost alone.

'And that is what goes on inside the vending machine. Enjoy the show.'

The lights go down and the advert begins. If you have a TV you'd recognise it. A young man puts a coin in a Coke vending machine, but as the money rolls down the chute the advert becomes an animation with a sub-Tim Burton soundtrack. A small swarm of huge insects, overweight maggots with helicopter blades strapped to their backs, fly in an empty Coke bottle, which a mechanised decanter promptly fills. A track-suited figure with a gold tooth and a plume on his helmet, half-knight half-pimp, is catapulted – holding a bottle cap – on to the top of the bottle. A gang of fluff ball lips are released from a cage, ambush the bottle and frantically kiss it. Then penguins in goggles throw a snowman into a large fan that blows the flakes from the now decapitated snowman on to the bottle. Finally the drink is led down a parade ground by a band, with cheerleaders and a fireworks display, before being dropped into the trough at the bottom of the vending machine for the young man to collect.

As ads go it is actually a very good one, but it is odd that the company guides keep referring to it as a documentary, which it isn't. It is no more a documentary than Snow White is an academic study of interpersonal relationships within polygamous communities. But as the ad finishes the 'documentary' element begins. Various Coca-Cola employees were interviewed, their words re-voiced by actors and assigned to different cartoon characters from the commercial. So the majorette, all blue hair, lips and eyelashes has a voice of an All American Mall Girl, whose words at least are a real worker's testimony.

'Are we rolling?' she asks in true behind-the-scenes

documentary style. 'Hi I'm Wendy, I'm single...and it's my job to keep everybody happy,' the coy cartoon trills. How would she describe Coca-Cola? 'Coke is like a little bottle of sparkle dust.'

Later the maggot with the helicopter blades (who upon closer examination looks like he has nipple rings or piercings of some kind) says in a deep husky voice, 'It's a relaxed atmosphere, it is not like some jobs that are tense when you get [t]here, it is a good working environment.'

These, remember, are the words of Coca-Cola employees, recorded and revoiced. According to these real employees, Coke is a great place to work, so it must be true. It is such a good environment that all sorts of creatures line up to testify, including a blue, long-necked chimera, a weasel salamander in a hard hat with a monkey wrench held over his shoulder. He speaks in a gruff ol' southern voice 'I smile ten minutes before I go to bed and ten minutes before I wake up every morning...It is people like me an' Eddie who make this company, the fact that we have been here and stayed here, to me that is the heart and soul of Coca-Cola.'

And as if that wasn't enough a shy Hispanic woman tuba player, demurely whispers, 'What have I given to Coca-Cola? My loyalty and my love. I give that.' She pauses before adding, 'Don't make me cry.'

Is she glad to work for the company? 'We are lucky to be one little piece of this wonderful company.'

The room momentarily goes dark as the feature finishes, people begin to shift in their seats, when the music suddenly swells louder. I turn to the noise just as the auditorium lights come on and catch the cinema screen swiftly gliding upwards, to reveal a secret corridor behind it. Guides are now on their feet, arms outstretched, beckoning us to leave our seats, descend the stairs and enter the tunnel, leading us to the next part of our tour, while a voice booms 'Welcome to the Happiness Factory.'

* * *

There are seven more rooms in the Happiness Factory and with the exception of the miniature bottling plant they all contain yet more adverts, Olympic ads, sports ads, ads in Arabic, German, French...on rolls the Happiness Factory with its TV screens blasting even more ads...onwards to the Perfect Pauses Theater, a small movie screen where you can watch Coke ads on an endless loop – and people do! Couples sit arm-in-arm watching adverts together. If by some perverted act of sabotage a film started to play in the middle of the ads the audience would get up and walk out, bored and confused. The final chamber, The World of Coca-Cola's colon if you will, is the tasting room, where dispensers pour Coca-Cola products from around the world for all to sample. It is packed with kids on a school trip, shouting over the music and tearing from tap to tap with plastic cups, while the teachers look on powerless to stop the sugar-rush tsunami that is heading towards them.

Naturally the exit is via the gift shop. And equally naturally every item on sale is covered in Coca-Cola logos, thus turning customers into walking adverts. The school kids from the tasting room will pass through here soon and at that thought I silently offer up a prayer to the god of small shoplifters.

* * *

'What did you expect Mark?'

Well, that is a good question and I am glad you asked it. It is hardly surprising that the company self-promotes to the point of nausea. It is the company's showcase attraction – a fizzy-drink version of Disneyland. Actually it is more Chessington World of Adventure, but you get the point. The attraction is unlikely to be a thorough critical examination of the Company's business practices. By now you might be thinking: 'Lighten up Mark, it is a Coke fun house, there is free fizzy drink, a working bottling plant which is vaguely educational and kids can get their picture taken with a polar bear! What more do you want?' Or you may think, 'It employs thousands of people around the world, it sponsors some worthy projects, surely that is a good thing?'

It'll come as no surprise that PR is designed to show companies in the best possible light and this will always be different from cold reality. But consider this: the animated majorette from the Happiness Factory commercial just called Coke 'a little bottle of sparkle dust'. Consider the disparity between eight teaspoons of sugar in each can of Coke and 'sparkle dust'. Frankly, it would be nearer the truth if the huge maggot with the strapped on helicopter blades were to appear crying, 'I'm so fat because I drink this sugary shit everyday! Now I need to get my stomach stapled!' There can be a wind-blown plain of tumbleweed between the image a transnational promotes and the reality of working for them or having them as a neighbour.

This is a globalised economy, where goods and money move with ease to the cheapest work force and some of the cheapest labour is found in some of dodgiest countries with poor human rights records and little or no environmental standards. And just as transnationals move in and out of tax havens, labour markets and emerging economies, so their critics have found an emerging world of dissent. If the familiar jingle of the Coca-Cola crates bouncing on a delivery truck can be heard in the furthest reaches of a mountain track, then a phone can get there too, or an internet connection and a camcorder, even an old camera will do. If your company gets caught dumping toxic materials in a village stream then it only takes one photo and a send button for your logo to be wired up to a world of trouble.

Coca-Cola say they strive 'to enrich the workplace, preserve and protect our environment and make a positive difference and effective contribution to our shared world.'[16] They say that they have 'long been committed to using our resources and capabilities to help improve the quality of life in the communities where we operate.'[17] But it is not the company tale I am concerned with. I'm interested in hearing from those who deal with the Company every day – the villagers, farmers, workers and shopkeepers. These are the people I want to find, these are the people I want to talk to, these are the stories I want to tell.

In the World of Coca-Cola, not only have folk paid $15 to watch, celebrate and have a chance to purchase the company's adverts, Coke have even found a way for their visitors to contribute to the company's PR machine. Up on level two the Pop Culture Gallery houses some kitsch retro-style furniture, a few Andy Warhols and a large Perspex display filled with handwritten letters. The identical writing paper and legibility of the script suggests that these are not the originals, but the content at least is written by Coke's customers. A sign reads 'Whether it's a childhood memory, a moment of refreshment far from home, or a recollection of good times with friends, Coca-Cola touches the lives of millions of people. Do you have a favourite Coca-Cola story? Share your story with us...' Which is exactly what I am doing. Going around the world, hearing stories from people whose lives have been touched by Coca-Cola and its bottlers.

For there is one missing detail from the tale of Coca-Cola's brand value. It is true that company profits have risen, they have bought other brands and sold more Coca-Cola and it is also true that the Company was rated the world's top brand for the seventh year in a row. Yes, the brand value is estimated at $65,324 billion.[18] Yes, that is a huge sum of money. But the missing detail is that this figure of $65,324 billion is actually a drop in value. In 2006 the figure was $67 billion,[19] in 2005 it was $67,525 billion.[20] Which means the company has lost $2.2 billion in brand value, that's $2.2 billion of goodwill the company has lost in the past couple of years. Something is beginning to make people like Coca-Cola less.

It is a small irony, given Coke's original ingredients, that the company's current PR problems started in Colombia. The murder of a trade unionist working for Coca-Cola's bottler and the subsequent campaign has inspired students, campaigners and activists around the world to challenge the company and has brought the mighty drinks giant up against a stark fact: if you are a transnational at the forefront of globalisation, then opposition to your practices can be globalised right back at you. So that's why I'm sitting in an airport waiting lounge bound for Colombia. I am going to hear just how some of those billions of dollars worth of 'sparkle dust' started to turn to dust.

2
GIVE 'EM ENOUGH COKE!

Bogota, Colombia

> *'Everyone has the right to peaceful assembly and association.'*
>
> **UN Declaration of Human Rights Article 20, 1**

The lighting in the hotel lobby is dim and so is the porter. The lift is tiny, room enough to fit one person and a bag. I go to get the lift. But I don't. The porter takes the lift. I take the stairs. He leaves the bag. I take the bag. He takes the tip. Hmmm. They must have a different definition of dim around here...

The city of Bogota is situated on a plateau approximately 8660 feet above sea level, thus making its altitude the second-most likely thing to give you a nosebleed in Colombia. It is not uncommon for travellers to suffer from altitude sickness, which for me takes the form of being tired and clumsy, not to mention tipping dim people who turn out to be clever.

The room is two floors up on the corner of the building overlooking the police station. Its stone frontage is picked out of the night by lamps around the arched doorway, under which a young man in uniform stands, stamping his feet wearily against the chill. Drawing the curtains forces my attention back to my immediate surroundings, a cold, small room with dark wood panelling and a reinforced doorframe. The reinforcement is only vaguely reassuring as it looks as though someone has tried to prise open the door with a large screwdriver, so I am glad to have company. Watching me slowly unpack are Emilio and Jess. Emilio is a Spaniard by birth and a Colombian by marriage; this will be the second trip to Colombia where he has translated for me. Jess, a London photographer doing a feature on firefighters, has stayed on past her assignment to photograph some of the people I hope to meet. The altitude sickness has given me the mental agility of an ex-boxer who has turned his talents to sports commentating. So I am currently holding my toothpaste in my hand while looking frantically round the room for it.

Emilio notices the teddy bear in a US Marines outfit propped up on the bedside table.

'Wha' the fuck is that?'

'That is a kitsch *memento mori*.'

'A wha?'

'A reminder of death. *Memento mori*, it's Latin, for reminder of death,' I say, cheerfully spotting the toothpaste in my hand.

Emilio furrows his brow and says, 'I don' think you need that here in Colombia, no?'

Which is true. More than forty years of conflict between governments, paramilitaries, drug cartels and left-wing guerillas has left the country with a well-deserved reputation for violence. It is the most dangerous place on earth for trade unionists caught between employers eager to be rid of them and barbaric paramilitaries who are quite capable of doing just that.

Across the world trade unions have traditionally been at the forefront of the great battles for democracy, education and decent working conditions and as trade union membership has gone down since the start of the Nineties, it is worth remembering that the right to belong to a trade union is a fundamental human right, enshrined in the UN Declaration of Human Rights.

In Colombia, the attacks on human rights are not limited to labour rights violations. 2004 saw 1440 people kidnapped in Colombia:[1] one person every six hours. That was the year I first visited Bogota with Emilio, accompanied by another friend called Sam, who was a good two stone heavier than me. And this weight difference is significant because before arriving in Bogota I took the precaution of learning key Spanish phrases from Emilio, the most important of which was *Dispara el gordo primero*: shoot the fat one first. Fortunately I only needed to use it once. This is what happened.

The dub sound-system night took place in a club that inhabited the top two rooms of a building accessed by knocking on the door nicely and ascending some long and narrow stairs. What the place lacked in fire exits it made up for in atmosphere and the friendly squatter-chic decor, though without the chic. The club was full of swaying bodies and a small serving hatch produced cans of beer from a mountain of trays visible over the shoulder of the barman.

Leaning against a wall wet with condensation was a tall chap wearing a brown leather coat and, with what I now know to be a chemically assisted smile. Turning to face me he said, 'Your first time in Colombia?' in impeccable English.

'Yes.'

'How do you like it?'

'Great, people are very friendly here,' I shouted over the bass lines rattling from the speaker.

'Very friendly...' the decibels increased. 'Yes, friendly!' he yelled, then he nodded to his hand, which had not left his side, 'Would you like?' He was holding a glass bullet-sized chamber with a plastic nozzle, full of cocaine.

'No thanks,' I said.

'No?' He seemed flabbergasted.

Perhaps it was his reaction which prompted me to forcefully add: 'I have just spent the day listening to trade union leaders talking about the hundreds of their members that get killed by paramilitaries – who are funded by cocaine. I don't buy Nestlé products because of their baby milk, so I'm certainly not going for that.' I shouted over the music jerking my thumb at his container.

'No, no, no, this is okay,' he said, genuinely upset, 'This Is FARC cocaine – left-wing cocaine. Not paramilitary. This is fine.' A smile crept up one side of his face, and his eyes glinted.

Sneeringly I declared, 'Sure it's fine, it's probably Fairtrade, right.'

And as quick as it came the smile left his face, in fact he looked quite cross and started to lean towards me. At that point it dawned on me that it may be unwise to pick an argument in a Bogota nightclub with a drug dealer. With hindsight I think a polite 'no' would have sufficed.

'Your first visit,' he shouted over the music, with a blank menace. 'First time, right?'

Sam suddenly loomed from the dance floor, sweaty and clutching a can of beer. He slouched on to the wall with a bump and a smile, 'All right?'

And for some reason the next words I said were, *'Dispara el gordo primero.'*

There was a pause, the man looked at Sam, Sam looked at me, I looked at the man, the man stared back, Sam looked at the man, the man turned to Sam, Sam turned to me, then turned to the man and with an innocent grin yelled, 'All right?'

The man in the jacket shook his head and walked away.

* * *

Nearly four years and one good night's sleep later Emilio guides Jess and I on our walk through the rundown side streets, Downtown Bogota may proclaim itself a modern city with skyscrapers and a financial centre, but the world of international commerce seems far away as we pass old men selling cigarettes from trays. There are no smart suits and briefcases as we wander by the small and cramped shops, where stock spills out of the doorways and hangs into the street. Half in and half out, overflowing packs of chewing gum on cardboard strips, sweet tubes of mints, boxes of matches, plastic toys and plasters. Here glass cabinets perch on stands, full of brown glazed buns, small dumplings, primped and crusty, cornbreads, *arepas* with melted cheese filings that sit drying on the heated racks. The coffee shacks have radios that tinnily grate out songs while groups of men smoke in doorways and sip coffee from little white plastic cups, that bulge out of shape with the heat of the drink. Carefully we pick a thread through the potholes that litter the roads like concrete acne and dodge the rasping roar of trail bikes and the nasal splutter of mopeds that scythe the thoroughfare.

In minutes we have moved from the morning havoc of the back streets into Teusaquillo, an area where the roads are slightly wider and the craters fewer. Trees periodically dot the pavement and white walls and grilles harbour little gardens of yuccas and palms. The terracotta roof tiles give each home an air of stability, while the buildings themselves are set back a little from the road. The well-to-do used to live here but they moved on long ago, leaving it inhabited by human rights lawyers, civic groups and non-government organisations.

We stop at a house with a low brick wall. The front garden consists of one patch of grass, one patch of concrete and two oil stains. It is the kind of place that back home in England would have a disused caravan parked in one corner. Here the front doors of the building are large, wooden and nondescript, and give little clue as to the identity of the occupants. Especially since the old graffiti that used to read 'Death to trade unionists!' has been painted over. Now there is nothing to announce that this ordinary house is home to Sinaltrainal (*Sindicato Nacional de Trabajadores de la Industria de Alimentos* – The National Union of Food Workers). They are the biggest trade union in the 'Coca-Cola system' in Colombia, representing over half the organised Coke workers, though after over a decade of attacks and intimidations the membership isn't as big as it was. In fact, with a current membership in the Coca Cola plants of only 350 it is fair to say they have been decimated, but (and the but in this case is enormous) this is the group that started Coca-Cola's current woes. This is the union that has seen its members and leaders murdered. This is also the union that took on one of the biggest companies in the world. These two things are not coincidental.

This building is where we meet two men, Giraldo and Manco. They arrive on different days and subsequently give their testimonies separately but they tell the same story and they both tell it from an old table in the middle of a union office covered in campaign posters. The propaganda slogans demand boycotts and justice. The images are of handguns painted in the company colours of red and white. The names and pictures of dead trade unionists are everywhere. Giraldo and Manco knew these men, they were friends and relatives, and now they sit under the watch of the dead as they speak of how they died.

* * *

On a Saturday morning Oscar Alberto Giraldo Arango (Giraldo) walks into this office. He is forty-two but he carries a few more years on his shoulders. His shirt is as thin as his face, worn and frayed too, his cheeks look like they are down to the last layer of skin. Hunched and with an old black cap on his head ready to be pulled down, he sits looking out of big dark eyes, void but for an impassive watery stare.

The first time I met the men at Sinaltrainal they told me, 'To be a trade unionist in Colombia is to walk with a gravestone on your back.' I initially took this as a reference to the fact that Colombia is the most dangerous place in the world for trade unionists: since 1986 2,500 trade unionists have been killed, that averages two a week. But the men I met looked weary – as if they had physically borne their stone.

Giraldo sits down, looks up, takes off his cap, stiffly rubs the top of his head with his hand and begins. He was born and breed in Carepa, Urabá , in the north-west of the Colombian countryside near the Panama boarder. He started work for Coca-Cola in 1984 at the Bebidas y Alimentos de Urabá bottling plant – which translates as Drinks and Foods of Urabá. When he told his friends of his new employers they congratulated him, 'Well done, that's great! You got such a good job!' and it was too. The union had done well for the men, securing bonuses, overtime and health benefits. But this was not to last. Graffiti announced the paramilitaries' arrival in Carepa in 1994. 'We are here!' it declared. Shortly after the graffiti arrived so did the bodies. The first Coca-Cola worker and trade unionist in Carepa to be assassinated was José Eleazar Manco in April 1994. The second was killed days later on the 20 April. He was Giraldo's brother, Enrique.

In the mornings Enrique travelled to work on the back of a friend's motorbike. There is only one road to the bottling plant and that morning three men emerge from the side of it. They stand in the middle of the road and aim guns at the bike forcing it to stop. Enrique is dragged from the publicly exposed lane, into the trees and bushes with the armed men. As the paras disappear they shout to the driver –'Go!'

News travels fast and when Giraldo gets to work everyone is talking about what has just happened. The shock of Enrique's kidnap circles the plant, disbelief and confusion growing with the telling. The deliverymen, production-line workers – all of them try and grasp the facts and speculate on why Enrique was picked up in this way. But the gossip quickly turns to mourning. Another man arriving for work has seen Enrique's body dumped at the side of the road.

THE PARAS

'We are the defenders of business freedom and of the national and international industrial sectors.'
Carlos Castano, leader of the AUC paramilitaries[2]

The Colombian paramilitary groups were spawned in the conflict between the state and revolutionary guerillas. In 1982 officers under General Landazabal, the Defence Minister of

Colombia, worked with multinationals and cattle ranchers to organise and fund 'defence groups'. Ostensibly they were to fight left-wing insurgent groups but increasingly the paras, as they are known, became entwined with the drug cartels and the army, often leaving it difficult to see where one group finishes and another starts.

Spreading out countrywide, the paras grew steadily into the AUC (in Spanish this stands for the *Autodefensas Unidas de Colombia*, its English translation is the United Self-Defence Forces of Colombia). They quickly became known as death squads, attacking and killing anyone considered to support the left-wing guerillas – basically anyone working in human rights or trade unions. It is a common refrain amongst the establishment and security forces that the guerillas and trade unionists are one and the same. As if to illustrate this point Colombia's President Uribe as late as 2007 said 'Either carry out union organising or carry out guerrilla warfare, but this wicked mixture does much damage to Colombia.'[3]

The paras have a bloody history of working with the security forces. Human Rights Watch published a report in 2001 called 'The Sixth Division'. The title comes from the fact that there are five army divisions in Colombia but so great is the level of collusion between the army and the paras (sharing equipment, information and personnel) that the paramilitaries are often called the Sixth Division.[4]

Carlos Castano, the charismatic leader of the paras, claimed that 70 per cent of his organisation's funding came from the cocaine industry. However, he was also an ardent supporter of neo-liberal economic policies and of multinational investment in Colombia. Castano said of their relationship with the AUC, 'Why shouldn't national and international companies support us when they see their investments limited...We have always proclaimed that we are the defenders of business freedom and of the national and international industrial sectors.'[5] Perhaps not surprisingly for a group so committed to multinationals, the paras developed their own logos, branding almost, and one of their logos was crossed chainsaws – the preferred tool of choice when carrying out massacres.

In a newspaper interview Carlos Castano was quoted as responding to the accusation that the paras attacked indiscriminately by saying, 'Blind attacks? Us? Never! There is always a reason. Trade unionists for example. They stop the people from working. That's why we kill them.'[6] Given that statement it's perhaps not surprising that Colombia is the most dangerous place in the world to be a trade unionist. The International Trade Union Confederation (ITUC) puts the conviction rate of trade union murderers at 1 per cent,[7] although even that figure is considered a little on the high side by those on the ground. Certainly President Uribe has shown little inclination to rectify this situation. His public statements on the matter include, 'There are no assassinations of workers in Colombia'[8] but there are 'rotten apples' in the trade union movement.[9]

Perhaps the most startling statistic with regard to violations of international humanitarian law is the dramatic escalation in the direct role played by the Colombian State. When President Uribe assumed office in 2002, the State was responsible for 17 per cent of all human rights violations. Four years later – at the end of Uribe's first term – the State was responsible for 56 per cent of human rights abuses; with the paramilitaries and FARC accounting for 29 per cent and 10 per cent respectively.[10]

Giraldo has lived with the story of his brother's murder for twelve years and betrays little emotion when he says, 'they contacted the body collectors in the area who went in search of the body.' No one was charged with Enrique's murder. He was dragged from the motorbike and executed, his body left at the side of the road, and as far as the authorities were concerned that was that; it was an unpleasant incident that generated a little paperwork. 'There wasn't very much of an investigation,' says Giraldo. But a definite pattern emerged when almost a year to the day another Sinaltrainal leader working at the Coca-Cola plant in Carepa was killed. His name was Enrique Gómez Granado and on the 23 April 1995 he was shot on his doorstep in front of his wife and children. It seems almost indecent to mention the end of this man's life and the searing horror endured by his family in so brief a sentence. But it is with brutal ease a man's life becomes a statistic. So Enrique Gomez became the third Sinaltrainal leader murdered in just over a year, leaving the unavoidable link between union organising at the Coke plant and being killed.

When the surviving union leaders were threatened and intimidated it became blindingly obvious that there was a campaign against the union at the Coca-Cola plant. These men were followed as they left work, cards and letters delivered to their homes that read 'Go now or face death!' The entire union leadership opted for the first option and fled to Bogota en masse, which left the workers with no effective union in the Carepa plant, a situation that appeared to suit the management just fine. Giraldo claims that, 'some of us had been working for the company for nine or ten years but the company would call us in one by one and say to us, "Come on, look, the union has fallen...the union doesn't exist any more so you need to do what the company tells you to do".' As the union was attacked and its leaders murdered, managers at the plant were making it crystal clear that they intended to take full advantage of this situation.

So the workers remaining in Carepa meet in secret. 'We agreed to set up a new underground union,' says Giraldo. The president was Luis Hernán Manco Monroy (Manco). A few days after talking to Giraldo at the old table in the Sinaltrainal office in Bogota, I speak to him. At 1.9 metres he is a tall man with receding black hair and a maroon coat that looks like a battered driving jacket. But the thing that catches your attention when you meet Manco is the way he holds himself. He has a cautious swagger, his whole frame seems to bob slightly, like a boxer. He is sixty years old but has the awkward twitch of a man who expects to be hit.

As president of the newly formed union leadership he helped draw up a collective agreement, the terms and conditions they wanted the company to negotiate over. Then the union came out into the open. 'We informed Coca-Cola that we had new leadership and so we started having meetings with the management at the Coca-Cola plant.' The manager at the time was a man called Ariosto, who, they allege, not only knew but socialised with the paramilitaries. On one occasion, Manco said Ariosto sat drinking with the local paramilitary commanders outside the plant. 'There was a meeting with Cepillo and Caliche [the commanders] at the kiosk, they were drinking with Ariosto and he said that if he wanted to end the union, it would be very easy.'

Giraldo recalls another instance when Ariosto said, '"The union exists because I let it exist, if I don't want it here, that will be the case", but we didn't think about this because we didn't know how bad it would get...'

They didn't have to wait long to find out. On 6 December 1996 Carepa's darkest day begun.

* * *

The body of Isidro Gil lay inside the plant. The first bullet had hit him between the eyes. The remaining five shots were fired out of spite or anger or bravado – who knows, perhaps it was just a way of saying 'We are here!' But he died where he fell in the courtyard. No one touched him until his brother Martin arrived. Crying, he held Isidro in the courtyard as the Coke workers looked on until the police came to take them away. It was just after 9am, and he was the fourth Coca-Cola union leader to be killed in Carepa.

The two paras who killed him had arrived on a motorbike and gone to the security hut by the main gates, where Isidro was working. As he opened the large iron gates to allow a delivery lorry to leave the paras saw their chance, slipped past the office, through the gates and shot him. Giraldo 'was 10 metres away from him when they shot him, and then I ran inside because I didn't know what...' His voice trails off. 'When I heard the first shot, I was walking nearby the entrance. Those of us who were nearby ran off.'

Manco looked up when he heard the first shot. 'the machine that I was working on was quite near the door...When I heard the shots, I looked behind me because the door was behind me, and Isidro had already fallen to the ground.'

Aristo the manager had disappeared and was nowhere to be found. So without knowing what to do or directions from the company the men hung around the plant. 'We didn't know where to go and we were waiting for [the police] to come and take the body and tell us that we could leave,' said Giraldo.

Even when the men were finally told to go home they didn't. 'The production line stopped,' said Manco, 'but we stayed there in the afternoon because we were too scared to leave...not working, just waiting there.'

Eight hours after Isidro had been killed the men finally left the plant to go home. They were right to be fearful. One of the worried men was a trade union organiser called Adolfo Luis Cardona, nicknamed El Diablo. El Diablo was a local footballer of some renown, a former champion in fact. He too had seen Isidro killed and that afternoon, while his friends and workmates waited in the plant, he went to Carepa. The paras spotted him and called out that the local para commander Cepillo wanted to see him, 'Come with us, Cepillo wants you...Come, nothing will happen. Get in the lorry we will drive you there.' But this lorry was of some local infamy. It was said people got into it but did not return alive. 'Come and get in we will take you to meet the Cepillo,' the paras insisted.

There and then El Diablo made the most important decision of his life. He ran. He took off running down the village street screaming *Van a matar a mí!* They are going to kill me! He ran and ran and ran towards the police station four blocks away. There were few cars but the road was full of people, fetching, carrying, hustling, bustling, shopping, walking, working people. Into the oncoming crowd he ran, dodging anything that came towards him, twisting his body to avoid a collision, his legs churning and scuttling to keep upright. On he ran through the narrow streets crying, panic filling every part of him as he screamed to onlookers, 'They are going to kill me! They are going to kill me!' Behind him the paras gave chase, one on motorbike the rest on foot charging after him, all pretence of normality thrown away. They were hunting him down in broad daylight. The bike weaved its way through the traffic of people as the foot soldiers bumped and jostled those in their path. No one said anything. No one did anything. What could they do? How could they stop the paras stalking a man in broad daylight? But the assassins lacked the adrenalin of a condemned man and the instincts of a footballer. El Diablo burst frantically into the police station begging for protection and sanctuary.

The police all but shrugged: 'What can we do?'

This is what they managed to do: they escorted El Diablo home, waited while his family packed and then drove them to the airport. There they went first to Bogota and then on to the USA, where El Diablo lives today. In this case Colombian justice was no more than a taxi service into exile.

The morning had seen the murder of Isidro Gil, the afternoon the attempted abduction of El Diablo and that night saw the final event. Sinaltrainal's offices in Carepa were firebombed. Metal bars had smashed the doors apart, files and papers were scattered around the building, joining the litter of the broken tables and chairs. And then the entire building was burned to the ground. A blazing beacon shone out in the night as the union office crackled and smoked in the flames, a warning beacon, to which the message was clear: your union is finished, go or die!

Manco had gone into hiding but the following day the para leader, Cepillo, sent out messages that he wanted to talk to the union men, to hold a meeting with them. Manco's world had been destroyed, his certainties had vanished, the only coping mechanism he had left was fear. In order to survive in abnormal situations we need to make abnormal reactions and fear helps us make them. Manco certainly reacted abnormally... he agreed to see the paras, persuaded by another union man that he should go.

The meeting was to be held at the paras' local hang out, an ice-cream shop in Carepa, called La Cieba. Two other union men arrived with Manco to find Cepillo at a table with a group of paras. The killers' commander was a chubby man, aged about 25, wearing jeans and a short-sleeve shirt. The shutters were rolled down, the shop was closed. Manco sat opposite the chubby leader. There were no pleasantries, no one drank, no one smoked, there was none of the usual Hollywood paraphernalia you might expect with such a scene, just an ice-cream shop with armed killers at a table.

'Cepillo said that they had killed Isidro, and they said it was them who burned down the headquarters. And they said that the union was over, that the union was the guerrillas,' said Manco. As they sat in the shuttered shop the paras calmly issued their orders for what was to follow. 'We could have killed you all today,' said Cepillo, 'but we can be reasonable.'

The following morning the killers' version of being reasonable was unveiled for all to see, at 9am they assembled all the Sinaltrainal members at the Coca-Cola bottling plant. There the paras made them to sign letters resigning from the union. The letters were prepared by 'Rigoberto Marín, who worked for the company...He gave them out one after the other, like "here's yours, here's yours",' said Manco.

The union in Carepa was smashed. The leadership was in hiding and exiled – they had fled or were dead. The members, cowed by guns, threats and intimidation, had signed away their rights. Meanwhile the managers of the Coca-Cola bottling plant surveyed the wreckage of the union and promptly introduced a pay cut to the workers. According to Sinaltrainal the wages dropped from between $380 – $450 a month for experienced workers, to $130 a month: Colombia's minimum wage. When asked about this drop, Coke failed to respond. Given that they would have met resistance to this if Sinaltrainal was still there, it is fair to say that, from the point of view of company profits, murder and arson did have an upside.

* * *

B ack in the union office sitting at a table littered with empty coffee cups and grains of sugar, Manco and Giraldo finish their tales as all exiles do, by talking of the life they fled to. They lived for six months in the building they now tell their stories from – the union office – there was nowhere else for them to go. Both men were in the office when the paramilitaries' package arrived containing the letters of resignation they had made the union members in Carepa sign. The paras even included blank copies for Manco and Giraldo to sign. Eventually Giraldo's family left Carepa to come and join him in Bogota and he moved out of the union office. He has not had a full-time job since. 'I haven't been able to earn much. I have just been doing odd jobs with three- or four-month contracts...sometimes days go by here where we have no food, because sometimes there's work and sometimes there's not, it's not like it was.'

I asked Manco if he has stayed in Bogota since leaving Carepa.

'Yes, of course, but it's horrible. I don't always get food here, I lost my house, my family, and everything.'

'Your family?'

'They didn't want to come so they stayed there, the mother took the children there. And of course I can't go there, I haven't been there.'

I watch Giraldo leave. Instinctively and without display he stands by the front door of the building with his coat zipper pulled up tight, tugs his collar around his neck, opens the door, looks across the street and then along it. He steps out through it glancing both ways and then slips away, a hunched silhouette heading to a home in exile, to wake to a dawn of few certainties. Where work may or not be found, where bellies may or may not be empty; where dead friends' faces haunt posters and memories of home are full of longing. And if you ask 'Why did he fight so hard and take so many risks to be in a trade union?' The answer is this: so he would not have to live the life he does now.

COCA-COLA TRADE UNIONISTS KILLED IN COLOMBIA

AVELINO ACHICANOY ERAZO
Worked at Embotelladora Nariñense SA – COCA-COLA (Nariño Bottlers Ltd) in Pasto. Killed on 30 July 1990. Sintradingascol leader (Colombian National Union of Fizzy Drinks Workers).

JOSÉ ELEASAR MANCO DAVID
Worked at Bebidas y Alimentos de Urabá SA – COCA-COLA (Drinks and Foods of Urabá) Carepa. Killed 8 April 1994. Sinaltrainal member.

LUIS ENRIQUE GIRALDO ARANGO
Worked at Bebidas y Alimentos de Urabá SA – COCA-COLA, Carepa. Killed 20 April 1994. Sinaltrainal organiser.

LUIS ENRIQUE GÓMEZ GRANADO
Worked at Bebidas y Alimentos de Urabá SA – COCA-COLA, Carepa. Killed 23 April 1995. Sinaltrainal regional union leader.

ISIDRO SEGUNDO GIL
Worked at Bebidas y Alimentos de Urabá SA – COCA-COLA in
Carepa. Killed on 6 December 1996. Sinaltrainal leader and
negotiator. ALCIRA DEL CARMEN HERRERA PEREZ, Isidro's
wife, was murdered on 18 November 2000 in Apartado.

JOSÉ LIBARDO HERRERA OSORIO
Head of Technical Maintenance at Bebidas y Alimentos de
Urabá SA – COCA-COLA in Carepa. Killed 26 December 1996.
As a manager he had been very supportive of Sinaltrainal.

ADOLFO DE JESÚS MÚNERA LÓPEZ
Worked at Coca-Cola plant in Barranquilla, Atlántico
department. Killed 31 August 2002. At the time of the killing
he had been sacked but had been reinstated after legal
process. Sinaltrainal union leader.

ÓSCAR DARÍO SOTO POLO
Worked at Embotelladoras Román SA – COCA-COLA (Román
Bottlers) Montería plant killed on 21 June 2001. Union leader of
Sindicato Nacional de Trabajadores de la Industria de las
Bebidas en Colombia (Colombian National Union of Drinks
Industry Workers) 'Sinaltrainbec'.

Source: Andy Higginbottom at the Colombia Solidarity Campaign

3
SERIOUS CHARGES

New York, USA

> *'Serious charges demand a serious response...we take accusations regarding labour rights violations seriously...'*
>
> **Neville Isdell, CEO The Coca-Cola Company**[1]

'Serious charges demand a serious response,' said the company CEO Neville Isdell, referring to allegations of abuse by Coke's Colombian bottlers, in what seems a reasonably appropriate statement; though in all honesty he was hardly likely to say, 'We lost a couple of Latinos, who gives a fuck.' However, serious statements deserve serious evaluation. According to Sinaltrainal, the murders at the Carepa plant were part of a countrywide campaign against the union. These are the serious charges they make:

- A worker is killed inside the bottling plant, six other union leaders are killed by paramilitaries, many are killed during, or approaching, negotiations with the bottlers and during industrial action. The bottlers are alleged to have contracted with or directed the paramilitaries.

- Bottlers are accused of union busting, intimidation and harassment of workers.
- The security manager at the bottler company's Bucaramanga plant falsely accused union leaders of terrorism, resulting in the workers being imprisoned for six months for a crime they did not commit; one was tortured.
- Paramilitaries operated from within the Barrancabermeja plant at a time when attempts were made on the life of the union leader. It is alleged that this was with the knowledge of a plant manager.

These would, by most people's standards, qualify as serious charges. So what was The Coca-Cola Company's serious response? Did the Company itself investigate the allegations of collusion between plant managers and the paramilitaries? The answers are: not much and no.

The Company website proudly displays the first and only public audit by The Coca-Cola Company into their bottlers in Colombia.[2] This was conducted in spring 2005, over eight years after Isidro Gil was shot dead. Intriguingly, the audit conducted by the Cal Safety and Compliance Corporation does not examine or investigate any charges of collusion or paramilitary activity in the plants. Focusing on the plants compliance issues, the report does however note several health and safety breaches, including:

- the absence of a protective guard on a syrup container at one plant
- the incorrect number of fire extinguishers at two plants
- incorrect documentation for an employee at one plant[3]

Fortunately there is no need to get up a petition or start a letter-writing campaign, as I am happy to report that the appropriate remedial action has been taken so as to comply with health and safety regulations. However, reassuring as it is to know that a protective guard now covers the syrup container in the Bogota plant, there still remains the outstanding 'serious charges' to be addressed by the company. To this day The Coca-Cola Company has not investigated the alleged links of Colombian bottling plant managers with the paramilitaries, despite a man being shot dead under their logo.

From the outset the first line of defence coming out of Atlanta was the denial of 'any connection to any human-rights violation of this type' and to distance themselves from the bottlers saying, 'The Coca-Cola Company does not own or operate any bottling plants in Colombia'.[4] This is the standard use of the 'Coca-Cola system' operating as an entity but claiming no legal lines of accountability to The Coca-Cola Company. TCCC does not own the bottling plants, the bottlers operate under a franchise. But the case here is similar to that of Gap and Nike in the 1990s. In these particular instances the clothes giants had outsourced their production to factories in the developing world that operated sweatshop conditions. It was not Nike or Gap who forced the workers to do long hours for poor pay, it was the contractors. However, campaigners insisted the companies should have enforceable human rights standards applied throughout the supply chain, compelling the companies to take action. The argument was then, and is now, that no matter where the human rights abuse occurred, if it's your name on the label then you're responsible for sorting it out. In The Coca-Cola Company's case the argument is made more compelling by the fact that, although they franchised Coke production to Bibedas y Aliementos and Panamco, they held 24 per cent of

Panamco's shares[5] – a controlling interest. Which gives them considerable clout in how the business is run.

This view of the Company's responsibilities is shared, in particular, by Councilman Hiram Monserrate from New York City. He represents a large Latino community and through some of his constituents became aware of the situation. Appalled, he took up the matter and has investigated Coca-Cola's response to the events. And so I visit New York for the first time, to talk to him.

* * *

I love New York. I nearly bought the I ♡ NY T-shirt but for adhering to the only rule of fashion that I know: namely don't buy things worn by people you don't like. Walking around the place I keep pointing and shouting, 'That's where *King of Comedy* was filmed...see, that's the bridge in that scene from *Saturday Night Fever*...if that's Ben Stiller let's heckle him...'. The city is a vast historic map of films and music. I get a coffee on the Bowery hoping that the Ramones once sat here before appearing at CBGBs. Lexington gets me singing the Velvet Underground and Central Park has me quoting Woody Allen.

Tall apartment blocks are dotted with white air-conditioning units sticking out of the windows, as if a swarm of flying fridges have just crashed straight into the side of the building. And the sight of them is suddenly wonderful. The plethora of pointy water towers stuck on rooftops like fat fireworks on stilts is amazing. I'm happy enough to gaze idly at hanging traffic lights suspended over the streets or fire escapes and ladders that criss-cross entire blocks. I am a fan. So much so that when I wander past a blue wooden police barrier outside a mosque, presumably ready to corral anti-Islamic demonstrators, I instinctively squeal, 'Oh look bigotry...they have that here too.'

My visit coincides with Super Tuesday, the big day in the US Primaries when Democrats and Republicans vote to decide who will be their presidential candidate. It is the Democratic race between Hillary Clinton and Barack Obama that focuses New York. Stickers on cars proclaim 'I'm backing Billary!' and Obama's face decorates Brooklyn windows.

I'd gone into a deli to eat and the primaries were the talk of the lunch queue. Now, being English, I'm a little baffled by the number of decisions required to get a sandwich: you have to choose your bread, spread, filling, dressing, condiments, extras and opt out of getting a pickle. Essentially you have to tell them how to make the bloody thing, leaving me momentarily resentful and wanting to shout, 'I'm not Jamie Oliver, all I want is a sandwich!'

As I ponder on rye or sourdough a man behind me strikes up a conversation. He's on a wheelie Zimmer frame, has a face like a tomato with stubble and is dressed in a green jacket. He looks like he should smell of alcohol, though he actually doesn't.

'Yew voted today?' He says as I catch his eye.

'No, I'm not eligible to vote, I'm English.'

'Yew want me t'vote for yew?' he says in a kindly manner, 'I'll vote for yew. Who yew want me t'vote for?'

'No, I'm all right, thank you.'

'I voted twice already today, I did it for my friend here,' he says, gesturing to a man beside him in a black pleated leather jacket and a bobble hat. 'They didn't recognise me,' he continues.

'They didn't?'

'Nah, one time I went in backwards.'

New York City Councilman Hiram Monserrate represents District 21 in Queens. Queens is across the East river from Manhattan Island, but on his side of the river the houses and salaries are much, much smaller. Queens is dirty and quirky. It is essentially a working-class area, you can tell this by the significant increase in 'Beware of the Dog' signs. Households tend to sit on the side streets off the main road, expressways tend to sit over the main roads and the traffic from LaGuardia airport sits on top of it all.

Just off East Elmhurst, on one of those side streets, sits Councilman Monserrate's office, opposite a parking bay for school buses. It has a sign in the glass front window, *'Por favor registrese para votar hoy'*, a polite reminder to his Latino electorate: don't forget to vote, folks. Inside, some plastic chairs and a sofa provide a waiting area for his constituents. The rest of the office is small and open plan by necessity. Six staff members sit at desks, handling casework, phoning housing departments, debt agencies or whoever needs to be called off or brought in. Councilman Monserrate's office is tucked away at the back.

The councilman does not appear to be a typical corporate critic, if indeed such a thing exists. Monserrate served in the US Marine Corps for four years, spent twelve years in the NYPD and to be honest he looks like his CV. He is stocky and strong-jawed, with a neck you could moor tugboats to; and I'd bet if you were able to snap him in half you'd find the word COP running all the way through his body, like a stick of Brighton rock. His politics is that of a Queens Democrat, a combination of liberalism on issues like immigration mixed with a strong populist streak. He appeared on breakfast TV pitching a notion that New York should be nicknamed Gotham City, as he was inspired to fight crime by his boyhood hero Batman. The idea has all the political rigour of renaming London Beanotown, but in terms of political PR it underlines his police credentials and 'record of public service'. So in the context of American politics he is not yet part of the establishment but boy, does he want to be.

Despite this, the councilman has been a persistent critic of The Coca-Cola Company since 2004. He worked with New York City's pension fund about how they might use their stockholding in Coke to influence the company, tabling critical resolutions at shareholders' meetings. He has spoken out against the company on US campuses, with students subsequently boycotting Coke.

'So you want to talk about Coca-Cola...' he says as he drops his black overcoat across one chair, scrapes another across the floor and leans back in it.

The councilman was introduced to Sinaltrainal's officials in New York in 2003 and found their tale compelling enough to help organise a delegation to Colombia in 2004. 'My initial impulse: I wanted to know more. At the very least it seemed to me there had to be some truth in what the workers were telling me. That labour reps and workers were being killed.'

While planning for the delegation, Councilman Monserrate decided he ought to invite The Coca-Cola Company along too. 'We have to have some fairness,' he explains, 'they were invited to participate. They were invited to visit the plants with us. They were invited to join the meetings and join in the discussions. They could have been a partner in this delegation: they refused.'

Whether he asked them out of a political desire to be seen to be fair or a genuine sense of fair play, I don't know, but nevertheless the Company declined the offer. 'I wasn't trying to malign Coca-Cola or FEMSA[6]...I'm not a socialist revolutionary.

I am an elected official from New York City.' He says this as if one might harbour a notion the breeding grounds of Trotskyism are to be found in the US Marines and New York Police Department, two bodies not noted for their adherence to dialectical materialism. In truth it is precisely because of his relative orthodoxy that I want to talk to him about what the delegation found out and why he seems to be picking a fight with the company that is so symbolic of America.

Councilman Monserrate's 2004 report on the Colombian allegations found not only a distinct lack of action by The Coca-Cola Company and the bottlers but an alarming laissez-faire attitude to the charges levelled against them. Although the delegation was denied access to Coke's bottling plants, Coca-Cola/FEMSA representatives Juan Manuel Alvarez and Juan Carlos Dominguez did meet with them. The delegation asked outright what they had done to investigate the allegations of ties between plant managers and paramilitaries. At first 'these allegations were vigorously denied,' the report states, but it continues, 'Alvarez and Dominguez acknowledged that Coke officials had never undertaken any internal or external investigations into these assertions, nor into any of the hundreds of human rights violations suffered by the company's workers.'[7] That is, the Colombian bottlers themselves admit that these serious allegations were not taken seriously at all.

In his office Councilman Monserrate leans forward, puts one hand in between his legs, grasps the seat of the chair and hauls it closer to the table. 'Isidro Gil was killed inside the bottling plant. That alone, to me, puts the onus on The Coca-Cola Company to say, "Hey we have a problem here and we have to deal with this problem one way or another".' He nods his head and stares at me, like he's Robert De Niro. 'There's a causal relationship between the trade unionists' deaths and working at Coca-Cola. So at the very least the company in Atlanta has an obligation to try and get to the bottom of it... Coca-Cola, just like any other major corporation, has a responsibility to be responsive corporate neighbours. You can't just chalk it up to the politics of the country. You're Coca-Cola and your logo is worldwide and it started here in America.' His forefinger taps the table pointedly, as if the company is in the room and he is telling it off. 'I mean we wouldn't accept it in America. Could you imagine it if in a Coca-Cola plant in the USA, a worker was killed because he was part of the union – what kind of outrage there would be!' His mobile phone rings, he looks at the caller's number before pushing it to one side.

And as he sits with his back to the office wall which is covered in honorary degrees, citations, community awards and other such chaff of public office, it dawns on me that it's the councilman's patriotism that has put him in the fight with Coca-Cola. American patriotism often entwines love-of-country with love-of-country's-economic-system. The councilman seems to fall into this category. 'They do represent American Capitalism,' he says in such a way as to put capital letters on both words. 'And American Capitalism should never be about allowing your workers to be subject to violence or death because they are organising to defend their rights. What does it say about America?'

The Carepa murders were the starting point of a new saga of violence and intimidation for the union and though these were the worst cases they were a long way from being the only human rights violations. Sinaltrainal alleged a campaign of murders, intimidation and harassment against trade unionists working at Coke bottling plants across Colombia. But so far The Coca-Cola Company had shown little, if any, interest. So the union responded by doing three things:

- They brought a lawsuit against The Coca-Cola Company and its Colombian bottlers in July 2001 in the USA
- They initiated a call for an international boycott of Coca-Cola products in 2003
- They went around the world telling as many people as they could about the first two things

This got the Company's and the bottlers' attention. So what did the company do? Was there finally a moment of corporate self-reflection and realisation? No, the bottlers took the union to court claiming that in bringing the US lawsuit the union had libelled and defamed them. I'll repeat it for those of you who might be distracted picking your jaw from off the ground: the bottlers said the union had libelled them by taking them to court in the US. The bottlers even went after 500 million pesos in damages, until the case was dismissed as being without merit in 2004.[8]

Councilman Monserrate discussed the case with Coca-Cola FEMSA representatives in Colombia and he reports that one of the men 'characterised these criminal charges as a "consequence" of the ACTA case [ie, the US lawsuit], which the delegation interpreted to mean that the company intended the charges as a direct reprisal.'[9]

So according to the bottlers, when the victims of violence and intimidation seek legal remedy they become criminals. Which I would suggest is akin to Union Carbide suing the inhabitants of Bhopal for inhaling their property without permission.

In his office in Queens the councilman is flabbergasted. 'They were facing criminal charges because they filed a lawsuit in the US...this is outrageous! This is ridiculous, this is worse than ridiculous!'

He leans forward in his chair, furrows his brow and purses his lips. With the phone ringing and meetings stacking up around him the councilman has little time, so he seems to be gathering his thoughts and momentum for a final verbal assault. And it comes.

'My question to The Coca-Cola Company,' he pauses, 'is: are you saying this is just the cost of doing business or is this the business that you are in? Which one is it, because either one is not a good choice. Right? Are you saying this is what Coca-Cola does by design or is it just complacent and allowing these things to happen? Either option is bad.'

THE ALIEN TORT CLAIMS ACT AND SINALTRAINAL'S CASE

The legislative spectrum in the USA varies from the progressive – their Freedom of Information Act, for example, is light years ahead of the UK – to the bizarre: in Alabama it is illegal to play dominoes on a Sunday. However, the Alien Tort Claims Act is one of those laws that actually elicits a genuine expression of 'God Bless America'. This bit of legislation also deserves a further cheer, as President George W Bush tried to 'reform' it and failed. Which is always worthy of a quick hurrah!

The Act allows for companies and individuals to be taken to court in the USA for complicity in the crimes of kidnap, torture and murder committed outside of the USA. The Alien Tort Claims Act of 1789 was not widely known or used for that matter until the 1980s when the Filartiga family used the act to sue an Inspector General of Police from Paraguay, who was visiting the USA. They claimed he tortured and killed their seventeen-year-old son Joelito in Paraguay in retaliation for his father's political activities. The courts found in favour of the Filartiga family and awarded them over $10 million and although the family never received any money they did finally get some form of justice. Their case had been denied in Paraguay and when national legal systems fail to deliver justice then one of the only avenues left is ATCA.

Increasingly, human rights' advocates are using the Act to bring multinationals to the courts. In 1997 suit was filed against the oil company UNOCAL for alleged human rights abuses in the construction of its oil pipeline in Burma. In 2004 the company went for an out-of-court settlement, paying an undisclosed sum in damages.[10]

Another case relates to Chinese dissident Wang Xiaoning, who used a Yahoo! email account to post pro-democracy articles anonymously. Yahoo! complied with a request by the Chinese authorities for information on the account which lead to the arrest detention and torture of Wang, the lawsuit filed against the company claimed. Yahoo! also settled for an undisclosed sum out of court.[11] Wang Xiaoning remains in custody serving a ten-year sentence.

Currently Firestone, Exxon, Shell and Wal-Mart have suits filed against them under the Alien Tort Claims Act.[12]

Pro-corporate lobby groups have sought to limit the scope of the law. Senator Dianne Feinstein introduced a bill to do just that. She said her bill was 'designed to balance the interests of US companies and human rights groups.' She also received $10,000 that same year for her re-election fund from Chevron[13] – another company with a pending case against them. She shortly after had a change of heart, and withdrew her bill, 'in light of concerns raised by human rights activists'.[14]

Given that the law can be applied to acts of kidnap, torture and murder, attempts to limit it or reduce the law's effectiveness in order to balance US interests seems to imply that US multinationals can't compete in the global marketplace without the odd incident of complicity in murder, kidnap and torture.

SINALTRAINAL

July 2001, the United Steelworkers of America union and the International Labor Rights Fund filed an Alien Tort Claims Act (ATCA) suit on behalf of Sinaltrainal in the US Federal Court in Miami. The suit, claiming $500 million compensation for the plantiffs, alleges that the bottlers Panamerican Beverages (Panamco) and Bebidas y Alimento 'contracted with or otherwise directed paramilitary security forces that utilised extreme violence and murdered, tortured, unlawfully detained or otherwise silenced trade union leaders,' and that The Coca-Cola Company as the parent company bore indirect responsibility. The Colombian bottlers deny the charges.

The Coca-Cola Company argued the Colombian bottlers were separate companies and The Coca-Cola Company had no case to answer, stating 'We deny any wrongdoing regarding human rights or any other unlawful activities in Colombia or anywhere else in the world' adding that, 'The Coca-Cola company do not own or operate any bottling plants in Colombia'.[15]

The union's legal team argued The Coca-Cola Company exerted control over its bottlers by way of a legal agreement, called unimaginatively – 'the bottlers' agreement'. The argument went thus: The Coca-Cola Company licences the production of their drinks, they provide the syrup with which to make them and dictate the types of bottles, cans, industrial processes, adverts and promotions that the bottlers are to use. Thus they exert a degree of legal and economic control.

Furthermore, The Coca-Cola Company not only possessed 'a controlling 24 per cent interest' in Panamco's stock, but had two seats on Panamco's Board.[16] And whilst Bebidas y Alimentos, was owned by US citizen Richard Kirby, the union's lawyer claimed that The Coca-Cola Company had such an influence on the company that it refused to agree to their request to sell the business in 1997.[17]

The case is being brought by the International Labor Rights Fund, supported by the United Steelworkers of America on a no-win no-fee basis (though this does not apply to any money settled on for the victims of violence).

March 2003 In an landmark ruling, District Court Judge Martinez ruled that the case against the bottlers Panamco and Bebidas y Alimentos can go ahead – the first time a US judge has allowed a case against a company for alleged human rights violations committed overseas to be heard under the ATCA.[18]

But the judge dismissed the case against The Coca-Cola Company on the grounds that the 'bottlers' agreement' did not give the Company explicit control of labour issues over the bottler.

2006 District Court Judge Martinez reversed his previous decision and dismissed the case against the bottlers, now arguing that the case can't be brought in the US because of 'lack of...jurisdiction'.[19]

2008 Sinaltrainal lawyers submitted an appeal on both rulings on 31 March 2008[20] and a result is expected by the lawyers in 2009. If successful it means the case can be heard and Sinaltrainal will have their day in court in the USA with The Coca-Cola Company and their bottlers.

3.5

THE HUSH MONEY THAT DIDN'T STAY QUIET

'We envisage a world in which ...we improve lives in every community [we] touch.'

TCCC Strategic Vision[1]

Neville Isdell, the Chief Executive Officer (CEO) of The Coca-Cola Company from 2004–2008 and current chairman of the Board of Directors, is a tall balding man whose hair leans to ginger and is cropped short in the way soldiers and men of a certain age prefer. His body is trim but his face is baggy and craggy; its shape is that of Charlie Brown, the Peanuts cartoon character, but with the muscle tone of Keith Richards. In short, he looks like a typical upper management man – and I mean that in a pejorative sense. At the 2005 Annual Meeting of shareholders, Isdell stated, 'there are no threats or attempts by management to attack or intimidate workers for being affiliated with a union or for being a union organiser or for being a union official.' He went on to say that, 'the people employed by our Colombian bottling partners work in facilities where their labor and human rights are respected and protected.' It was a noteworthy event, as the CEO of the world's most popular brand felt compelled to defend the company but the true significance of his robust public pronouncements can only be measured by what the company was doing in private.

In Colombia the pressure on Sinaltrainal was immense: the intimidation of workers by the paras was relentless, and the company's drive to casualise the workforce was driving down union membership. 'Every time we recruit new workers and members they get sacked,' said Carlos Olaya, the union's researcher. Indeed Councilman Monserrate's delegation claimed that Coca-Cola FEMSA, 'continually pressured workers to resign their union membership and their contractual guarantees. Since September 2003, they have pressured over 500 workers to give up their union contracts in exchange for a lump-sum payment.'[2]

Across the world the boycott met with mixed results. In Ireland Trinity College and the University of Dublin voted to 'Kick Coke off Campus' and refused to stock their products in student-run facilities. They were joined in the UK by Sussex, Manchester, Middlesex and the School of Oriental and African Studies, and in the USA by New York University and Michigan University. Even though the contracts with US universities are usually worth millions, kicking Coca-Cola off campuses is unlikely to dent the balance sheet of a company that made $5.98 billion profit last year.[3] But the accompanying media attention and headlines like 'Is Coke the new McDonald's'[4] in the *Guardian*, and *The Nation* calling Coke 'the new Nike'[5] must surely be part of the reason Coca-Cola has lost billions from their 'brand value'. Something had to be done.

Publicly the company's attitude to the Colombian issue was not hostile nor was it dismissive, it was both. Coke increasingly described the lawsuit brought by Sinaltrainal as an 'out of date' allegation[6] or 'an old story'.[7] But this is not the full picture and behind the scenes the Company was involved in negotiations with the union to settle the case.

Timing is everything – from boiling an egg to having sex to deciding it is time to talk with the trade union taking your company to court. The US lawsuit was going nowhere fast but that all changed when District Court Judge Martinez dismissed the case against Coke's bottlers on 4 October 2006. It might have looked as if the Coca-Cola system had been exonerated in court but the judge had opened up a world of potential pain for the Company. Crucially the court decision was *not* the hearing of the case itself, instead it was to decide if the US courts were the correct venue for the trial. And once District Court Judge Martinez decreed the US courts did not have jurisdiction this left the union lawyers free to launch their appeal, bringing The Coca-Cola Company back into the dock to face the whole thing one more time.

If the union lawyers were successful in their appeal then the case would go to full trial and The Coca-Cola Company would face the legal procedure of disclosure, forcing them to hand over internal documents detailing their relationship with the bottlers. I can't speak for the company but I would imagine this prospect was about as appealing as syphilis. Timing is everything – and six weeks before Judge Martinez cleared the way for the union to get the Company back into court The Coca-Cola Company began to negotiate with Sinaltrainal on 19 August 2006.

When I asked The Coca-Cola Company about these talks they portrayed them as 'fruitful and informative'[8] as if remembering the biscuits served. They went on to describe the negotiations as 'warm and buttery', 'sweet and moist' and 'chocolaty on the top'.

The purpose of the talks the Company said was 'to assess whether a mediated resolution of the parties' differences could be achieved.'[9] In short they were looking to settle out of court and with a settlement like this comes money...a lot of money. How much money? A barrow full. Although I can not disclose the exact sum offered to Sinaltrainal and the plaintiffs in the lawsuit it is my understanding that it had six noughts at the end of a dollar sign and a couple of digits in between. For those working in the British coin of the realm it would the same number of noughts but a single digit in front of the pound sign. For those working in the Zimbabwean Dollars, I am afraid the world has run out of noughts.

If the Company was offering money what were the conditions attached to it? I spoke to Ed Potter, The Coca-Cola Company's Global Workplace Rights Director, a man with intimate knowledge of these negotiations. I said to him that the company had history in this department, 'financial settlements are reached, but part of that financial settlement is that you don't criticise us again, you shut up, you go away.'

Ed Potter replied, 'All I will say as a general matter is we've had several different resolutions...you've described one of them.'[10]

Whereas Coke describe the talks as 'fruitful and informative', Sinaltrainal use an altogether different set of words. 'We were in a process that lasted almost a year and a half where we talk and talk and talk with them in order to find a solution to the conflict...and it didn't give us any result at all,' said Edgar Paez, the union's International Officer. He is sitting in his office, by the same table Giraldo and Manco gave their testimonies from. Edgar, is a man prone to smiling, with a touch of a South American George Michael to his unshaven appearance, but throughout our conversation he remains grim-faced. The only reason Coca-Cola negotiated according to him was, 'because they don't want us to keep reporting them [campaigning]...What the Company wanted was to buy the silence of the people involved. They give some money to the victims in order not to denounce the problem.'

The negotiations broke down in early 2008. Coke said ' no final resolution was possible. An impasse was reached and no further discussions are anticipated at this time.'[11] Arguably, the impasse was the conditions of the settlement – Coke would pay millions of dollars but anyone working for Coca-Cola FEMSA and involved in the lawsuit had to leave their jobs, they could no longer work at Coke. But more than this they would be legally bound never to criticise Coca-Cola ever again. According to Edgar Paez this would apply 'not only in Colombia but everywhere in the whole world. They wanted us to sign an agreement that no one would denounce Coca-Cola any more, for the rest of their lives.' In effect, the agreement, if signed, would prevent them from campaigning against any multinational that Coca-Cola had business with. From the moment they signed until they day they died.

The end result of key members of the union leaving Coke and unable to criticise or organise against the company from the outside would effectively mean the union would be finished. Sinaltrainal would cease to exist in the Coca-Cola plants. That is, after all, what is meant by my phrase 'you shut up, you go away'.

The money was on the table and all Sinaltrainal had to do was agree and take it. So the men and women who had fought for the right to be in a trade union would become silent. Their right to free speech and freedom of association would be gone for ever. All they had to do was take the money and sign the paper. For men like Giraldo and Manco the prospect of compensation was money they literally could only dream of.

The union refused to sign. They refused to be silent. Leaving The Coca-Cola Company with an 'old story' that would not go away.

4

'CHILE'

Bucaramanga, Colombia

'There are no threats or attempts by management to attack or intimidate workers for being affiliated with a union or for being a union organiser or for being a union official.'

Neville Isdell, CEO, TCCC Annual Meeting 19 April 2005

This is the story of the first time I stayed with a man called Chile, a Sinaltrainal member who lives in Bucaramanga, to the north of Bogota. The city sits in the basin of a plateau ringed by hills, a packed urban island sprawling over its convex foundations and is surrounded by terracotta soil and the ripe light green of the trees. It's the seventh biggest city in Colombia – the English equivalent would be Leicester or Coventry.

Given that most Catholic countries draw the line at evoking cooking spices at christenings it should come as no surprise that Chile is a nickname. Though the name derives from the spice, here folk spell it after the country. His real name is Luis Eduardo García, and he earned his moniker after a particularly heated argument with a manager at the local Coca-Cola bottling plant. I met Chile in 2004 on a fact-finding mission, which is how I came to be on a bus travelling through Bucaramanga with a crowd of trade unionists, leftists, Christians and human rights' campaigners. Each day we would set off to visit displaced people, families of murder victims, NGOs and lawyers, listen to their stories and then head off to our next destination – a sort of human rights coach trip.

The bus is knackered. Very knackered. You may be familiar with the type of American bus that Evel Knievel used to jump over on his motorbike. Well, our bus looks like the one that he accidentally landed on. Inside it is incredibly hot: were we to be parked in England, someone would be checking the back seat to see if the dog was still alive. There is little respite from the heat. The windows come down only a few centimetres at the top of the frames. In the absence of a breeze to force the air around a little I am trying not to come into contact with the seat's back, lest I stick there – though given the lack of suspension on this vehicle it is unlikely that any of us are going to sit anywhere for long.

On board we divide up into our various gangs. Near the front are Pax Christi, a Christian peace outfit, made up of elderly Germans who have traipsed around the fact-finding trip with grim faces and even grimmer clothes. They have an air of concerted concentration and gloom, giving them the appearance of someone trying to digest an espadrille. Everywhere we go they appear with notebooks and pencils ready to catch every misfortune. They are the stenographers of the apocalypse.

Just a few seats back are the two male Swiss trade unionists, who never sweat and have duty-free breath mints in their rucksacks. They gently nudge, natter, whisper and giggle together: I wouldn't be surprised if they had a password and a tree-house in their garden back home. Around them are the Americans, who subdivide into those from Brooklyn and those not. Those 'from' are loud, brash and, despite the fact that they have never been to Bucaramanga in their life, are prone to shouting directions at the bus driver. He in turn ignores this advice.

Chile has a square build. His black hair is receding, his T-shirt bulges around his gut and no one save a Krankie could call him a tall man. But he has a confident and determined presence and must have been quite a catch 25 years ago. He stands by the driver, hanging on to the rail up by the front door, and gives a running commentary as we drive past sites of local oppression. It is essentially a historical battlefield tour, except the history is recent and the tour guide personally knows the dead.

As we pass a large prison, one of the Colombians shouts out. 'Here!' he points at the building we can see through the window. 'Here! This is where they put Chile!'

The passengers crick their necks in unison to see the jail, the prison cell bars visible from the street. Others join the loud chorus, shouting, 'There is the prison where Chile was jailed!'

The man in front of me has both of his arms in the air, almost appealing for sanity. 'That is where Coca-Cola sent him!'
   'They locked him up because of Coca-Cola's lies!' shouts another.

'It is true,' says Chile to the German heads that are now bent over their notebooks, scribbling frantically. His admission serves only to unlock further floodgates of communal anger and it seems everyone has to shout

'There is where they torture him!'

'There is where they abused him!'

'There!' screams the loudest voice of all, bellowed from one of Chile's closest friends, 'There!' he shouts along the suddenly silent bus, declaring to the fixed faces turned to him. 'There ...is where Chile lost his virginity!'

And he promptly erupts into raucous laughter, undercutting the sombre and angry mood in a deft moment. The whole bus laughs. Chile laughs hardest of all. He is bent double, slapping his thigh and looking like he might choke.

By the time we finish the day's journey and return to Chile's home it is late, everyone is tired and no one has thought about supper. So Esmeralda, Chile's partner, gets a Chinese takeaway and for a few moments there is only the sound of cutlery on tin trays and the background hum of the family fish tank. Away from the bravado of the bus Chile drops his nickname and returns to being Luis Eduardo. Assisted by Esmeralda, their daughters Mayela and Laura, and their son Alexander, he tells a less rumbustious tale of how he become a plaintiff in the USA courts accusing the Coca-Cola bottlers of engineering his wrongful imprisonment.

Luis Eduardo started work for the Coca-Cola bottling plant in Bucaramanga in 1988, working his way up from a cleaner to the position he currently holds, assistant to José Domingo Florez, his best friend who drives a huge red Coke truck. Luis Eduardo is the crate shifter and stacker for the truck. This tale has a familiar start. Initially there was respect for the union but that changed in the mid-1990s when the manager of the plant accused the trade unionists of being 'guerillas' and employees' medical insurance was suddenly cancelled. This provoked a strike, led in part by Luis Eduardo. Then events took an altogether more conspiratorial turn. After the strike the head of security at the Coke plant, José Alejo Aponte, contacted the police accusing Luis Eduardo, Domingo Flores and Álvaro González Pérez, another trade union organiser, of planting a bomb in the bottling plant. The three men went to prison in March 1996 to await trial and spent the next six months there.[1]

'Coca-Cola employees publicly accused us, before the authorities, that we were terrorists,' says Luis Eduardo illuminated by the glow of the fish tank. As proof of the terrorist plot, 'The boss of security in the firm, he took a packet, a metal box, put it beneath his arm and he ran around the plant saying that it was a bomb, it was a bomb!' Luis Eduardo shakes his head in wonderment that any sane individual might walk around holding a real bomb under their arm. And, more than this, that the authorities might credulously believe the word of a man who claims he has a bomb tucked under his armpit. Not content with finding a fictitious bomb the company then said it had actually gone off. Where was the damage then? Ah, those cunning terrorists had cleaned it up afterwards. Obviously following a new insurrectionary trend: tidy terrorists, terrorists your mother could like – they may blow up buildings but they always leave some potpourri in a bowl by the smouldering rubble.

'The company [security manager] says that the bomb exploded but there was never any damage inside the company,' says an incredulous Luis Eduardo.

Indeed the Regional Prosecutor shared his view, finding that not only were the men innocent of plotting to plant a bomb but that no such bomb existed in the first place.[2]

'We managed to prove our innocence and Coca-Cola had to return us to our jobs,' says Luis Eduardo

But by then the damage had been done, as they had spent six months in prison awaiting trial. Domingo Flores, Luis Eduardo's best friend arrested alongside him, claims he was tortured by the police. And if it was tough for the men it was even worse for the families.

'For the kids it was really hard,' says Esmeralda, her arm draped casually around Mayela as they sit on the sofa.

Luis Eduardo nods in the direction of Laura, 'My youngest daughter – I had to remove her from the school because her friends said to her that her father was a delinquent and a terrorist.'

'Because it was all on the TV news and in the newspapers,' adds Esmeralda. So the nine-year-old Laura would demonstrate outside the prison gates, banner in hand, demanding the release of her father. 'The girls would visit their dad once a month,' she continues, but the official visits were not enough. 'They wanted to see him, they'd wait outside the prison and he would see us through the window and throw us a note.'

'In prison in order to communicate with your family, you have to write a note,' Luis Eduardo explains, so he would wrap the note around a sweet or something he could hurl through the bars of the open cell window, over the wall. Nothing too personal was ever put in it in case it fell into unintended hands. The contents would read, 'I am OK. Don't worry, the lawyer came and it's going OK.'

Except it was far from OK. With no wages for six months Esmeralda battled to keep the bank from taking their home and had to resort to begging to get by.

It was far from OK for Luis Eduardo too. He and Domingo Flores were placed in the highest security wing of the prison alongside the paramilitaries, the people who were trying, and often succeeding, in killing trade unionists. Both men avoided showers and toilets for fear of being attacked, and Luis Eduardo's face displays his revulsion as he revisits the stench of the cell, the humiliation of being forced to piss in bottles and shit in bags. And so they lived in the stench and the fear for six months, throwing notes wrapped around sweets to his children in the street.

'Coca-Cola bottlers were involved in this conspiracy because the ones who denounced us were administrators within the company, managers of the company,' he says. So alongside the family of Isidro Gil the names of Luis Eduardo García , José Domingo Flores and Álvaro González Pérez were added to the suit filed in the USA, under the Alien Tort Claims Act. The court documents allege the Coca-Cola bottler, Panamco Colombia,[3] 'brought charges against the aforesaid Plaintiffs in retaliation for their trade union activities. Their resulting prolonged unlawful detention and accompanying torture was therefore the result of Panamco Colombia's malicious prosecution.'[4]

The Coca-Cola Company have never apologised for the bottlers' actions or sought to investigate them, preferring to stick to their original defence, namely that The Coca-Cola Company does not own the bottlers in the 'Coca-Cola system'. When questioned on this the company replied, 'TCCC have *discussed* [my italics] the matter with the bottler and understands that the bottler's employees gave truthful statements to the Colombian government investigators…Messrs García and Flores were compensated for their time away from work [back pay], provided additional security and protection and have remained employed by the bottler.'[5]

And that just goes to show how caring the bottler is: having made accusations that the men were terrorists the bottlers kindly gave the men their jobs back when the claims turned out to be bollocks. Though the men were not actually paid any compensation for being falsely imprisoned by the security manager's 'truthful statements', they were 'compensated for their time away from work' and I imagine the men felt that they were compensated merely to be back in the caring bosom of their employer. Though they have not expressed that.

With unintended irony TCCC have described the lawsuit brought by Sinaltrainal against them as 'aggressive'.

Over the past couple of years The Coca-Cola Company have taken great pains to promote themselves as a union-friendly company, which 'respects our employees' right to join, form or not to join a labor union without fear of reprisal, intimidation or harassment.'[6] In fact they say 'the Company have shared the Policy [for respecting trade union rights] with our independent bottling partners and is committed to working with and encouraging them to uphold the principles in the Policy.'[7] You don't need a degree in semantics to see that a dead worm could wriggle through the gaps in this. Seldom has the word 'encouraging' been used in such an unencouraging manner – this state of affairs also applies to the words 'committed and 'principles'. It is a mini masterpiece in stating the bloody obvious, as they have 'shared the Policy with our independent bottling partners'. They are 'committed to working with and encouraging' the bottlers to respect workplace rights. Frankly I know nursery school teachers with better discipline policies than that. So what form will Coca-Cola's encouragement take? Praising the good and ignoring the bad? So if no paramilitaries shoot Coke workers, do the bottlers get a sticker? Essentially we can paraphrase the statement as: We'll ask them to be nice but don't blame us if it goes tits up.

* * *

It was time to visit Luis Eduardo aka Chile one more time. It has been seven years since he and the union launched the court case in the USA in 2001, five years have passed since the call for an international boycott and four years since I last visited him. I wanted to find out how his family and the union had faired under Coca-Cola's new-found respect for employees' rights, what had changed for them?

'We'll find some examples of how they [the bottlers: Coca-Cola FEMSA] respect our rights.' Chile told me, so once again he is taking me on a tour of Bucaramanaga, though this time on foot. As the morning sun has yet to rise to the humid midday prime and the traffic pollution hasn't had time to build up a head of fug, it is the perfect time to bustle through the city. We pass the market carts piled high with star fruit, pineapples and grapes, dusty from the orchards and the city dirt. The juice sellers lounge by their stands, pausing after the rush-hour surge, chatting and cleaning the fresh pulp and pips from the blades of their blenders. Occasionally people call out his nickname, 'Chile!' and wave as we march through. The market bingo hall is just getting started, and those who can't play watch from the street as the numbers are called in a rapid-fire monotone by a man who mistook hair oil for charisma. On the pavement a patchwork of vendors sit on their haunches beside rolled out mats decorated with random wares, from small packs of screwdrivers to hair dye, pens to lighters, duct tape to yo-yos and nail clippers to radio batteries. They are laid out in a deliberately random fashion, like objects in a memory test. Unified by nothing but cheapness, I marvel at the world of possibilities this incongruous mix of goods represents. A world where someone might stop to pick up some industrial gloves and while they are at it impulse-buy some joss sticks.

Onwards we stride, searching for a specific man. The trouble is that we don't have the man's name, we don't know where he lives and he doesn't know we are coming to see him. All of which sounds rather unprepared; after all, the key to any quest is to know what you are going in search of before you start. I doubt Jason would have found the Golden Fleece were he to have set out with a vague idea of getting some duty-free knitwear. Nevertheless, there are two facts that will help us in our endeavour: one, Chile's certain that he knows the district the man lives in and two, the man we are after was recently knocked over by an out-of-control police car. Of all the things that might mark a man out in his community, being run over by the cops is definitely a distinguishing feature: misfortune is the satnav of a community. So we have only to end up in the right district, approach a local and say, 'We are looking for the guy who was waiting at the bus stop for work when for no reason whatsoever a cop car ploughed into him' and in theory they should know where to find him...and they do.

In a back street where old men sun themselves in fold-out chairs and unemployed dads gather round the underside of a broken-down van, while their children help them work, Chile approaches a guy in an oil-covered vest holding a hammer. He says words to the effect of, 'I'm looking for the guy the cops fucked up...' and the oily dad lifts his arm, hammer still in hand, and points out directions.

The road bends where it starts to run up the hill. This is where Carlos Maldonado Anaya rents a room in a bungalow. Behind it palm trees grow and their wilting leaves hang over the roof, under the shade of which sits Carlos in a wheelchair. He shoots a brief smile when he sees Chile, recognising him from other days, and leads us cautiously inside. The cool small front room is the lounge, the dining area and the parlour. The room is three steps long, with a kitchen to the rear and two bedrooms to the side. What it lacks in size it fails to make up for in decor: the doors are plain unpainted plyboard affairs, with bolts rather than handles to keep them shut. Old faded photos of children long grown and gone decorate the wall, a solitary china cat sits on a shelf. Positioning himself opposite a cheap print of the Last Supper, Carlos tells us he is fifty, but in poverty years this translates as about seventy-five, he's skinny enough to evoke the word 'wretch' and sits in a raggedy pair of shorts and a shirt. The most eye-catching thing about him though are his legs, thin and brown with silver metal tubes and pipes sticking out from the flesh. The pins holding his bones together emerge from his skin and run at angles down his leg, like a homage to the Pompidou Centre.

Before the police ran him over Carlos was a *fletero* – literally translated the word means transporter or porter. He worked in the dense streets of Bucaramanga where the lanes are sometimes inaccessible to a truck, where the crowds flow down the narrow capillaries of the city, so crates of Coca-Cola have to be delivered by hand. Weaving amongst them shouting warnings of his presence Carlos hauled crates of Coca-Cola to the shops and cafés for twenty-five years.

The system worked liked this: the company supplied the stock, Carlos provided the manpower, 'they give me the product so that I can distribute it,' he says. Using a sack barrow that can balance fifteen crates on its iron frames he would deliver during the day and return to do the paperwork at night. Carlos said, 'I have had to work almost eighteen hours, in previous seasons. I used to work from 6am and sometimes until 11pm or 12pm' his fingers arc through the air to show the passage of time. As you might expect his earnings were far from great. 'The last year I worked I earned the minimum wage. The minimum. I was earning around 360,000 pesos a month.' That's about £100.

Carlos explains the set up, 'The company gives us the job, but from that job we had to to pay the warehouse.' This is often just a small lock-up with a roll-down shutter where you can stack crates of pop. The Coca-Cola trucks come round and deliver the crates of soda to the warehouse. They tell you how many crates you have to deliver. They tell you what drinks each order needs, where you have to deliver them to, the routes. They make you wear a Coca-Cola uniform. They tell you who you can hire as an assistant and they sometimes say, 'Sack so-and-so they're no good.' Effectively the Coca-Cola bottlers control their working lives, which sounds remarkably like the role of an employer, but the job of a *fletero* is a sub-contracted one, hired by contractors, not directly by the company, so they do not appear on Coca-Cola's books. 'No, I don't have any contract, nothing signed at all, never, I have never signed any document with the company.' This means that he can be fired any time.

Given this precarious state it is perhaps not surprising when Carlos spoke of the wish to unionise and spoke about this with his fellow workers, 'but the problem is that we cannot join our union because of the fear that when the company realise that you belong to the union they will sack you. They will say that you know that the company does not allow you to join a union. Then they say "no, you have become a trade unionist there is nothing else for you to do here".'

So to sum up the relationship: Coca-Cola bottlers don't employ Carlos, but they do tell him when to collect the stock, where to go, what to deliver, who to deliver it to and when to do it, what to wear, who to hire and who to fire and threaten him with the sack should he join a union. None of which sounds like the declarations The Coca-Cola Company have made to respect workplace rights.

Carlos has kindly given us the name of another person who used to work delivering Coke so we set out to search for him, though having the name of the person we are looking for feels slightly like cheating. Leaving the bungalow we cut back through the side streets to the centre, squeeze past the cattle trucks parked up on the kerb side, dodge buses as they lurch out of the station and wander against the lunchtime market crowd of shoppers, where shoulders hunch with the weight of bags, jaw chomp on snacks held in napkins and feet tango through the surge of fellow humans. There are wide-eyed chickens stacked high in wire boxes with guinea pigs and geese as neighbours. We pass stalls selling cutlery, crockery, lace and knives as we head out of the market, along the main roads and on to the quieter roads. Here Ivan works in a kiosk, a small café selling sweets, beer, hot food and cigarettes, with a few tables and chairs outside. The boundaries of this establishment are an ambiguous affair, as the pavement runs into the dining area and visa versa. This is the epitome of Colombian café culture: a café, a street and a complete absence of culture.

Ivan only has two customers – a young man in denim with a proprietary arm draped around an even younger woman whose crop shirt allows her puppy fat to gently lollop over her tracksuit bottoms. Ivan leaves the counter when he sees Chile, and nods a friendly smile. He is twenty-nine years old, with a baseball hat pulled back on his head and a grin that collapses to hide an overreaching top set of teeth. He's as eager to talk as Carlos was cautious, but constantly checks the couple drinking beers lest they want another round.

Ivan was a delivery assistant. 'I had to go with the lorry and deliver the bottles.' These were long days, 'to be honest we started at quarter to six in the morning and we finished around 7, 8, 9pm.'

Like Carlos he too talked to Sinaltrainal about joining the union, but Coke said 'that if we join a trade union we would have been sacked'.

In one single motion Ivan lets out a little 'hmmph' through his nose, his head twitches to one side, eyebrows raised and he pulls his lips tight together in an expression of disgust.

Just to be absolutely clear I ask again, 'So they would sack you if you joined the union?'
    'Yes.'
    'Is that a common occurrence?'
    'Nowadays it is happening…The project, the plan the company has, is to end the union.' He explains, slightly perplexed that the question was even asked.

Under the bottlers' system of subcontracting, which is referred to simply as contracting in Colombia, Ivan was employed by four different subcontractors. In this kind of environment the possibility that workers might have some kind of job security is non-existent.

'There was an indefinite contract,' Says Ivan

'Could they sack you at any point?'

'They sacked us because the company gave them the order to do it...' he shrugs matter-of-factly. 'There was a verbal agreement contract, there wasn't any signed contract. It was kind of indefinite.' According to Ivan it was the bottlers who decided who was hired and fired; if the bottlers didn't like you 'then they called one of the men and they said 'we don't want to see this man any more. He cannot work for you any more.' Ivan hmmphs with increased vigour and as if to prove his point adds that in 2006 he became ill with tuberculosis. 'They sacked me, I never had any help from them...they turned their back and they didn't help me, not even five pesos.' Hmmph.

His head twitches with a sideways tilt as he adds, 'Lastly I want to clarify that I want the trade union to carry on its duties. And to carry on fighting as they always have done.'

With that, right on cue, a denim-clad arm appears in the air behind him to order another beer, Ivan turns instinctively, says 'Thank you' and politely returns to serving beer.

So far our morning tour of the city has found two men who claim to have had their right to join a union denied them; Chile thinks there is another nearby and it turns out there is. His name is Jorge Santana Acostaho. The metal doors open inwards from the bright light of the sun into the shadow-dim world of the lock-up. A step down leads to the bottle bunker. It is a maze of narrow walkways created by stacks of crates with room enough to fit a small sack barrow. God knows how far back the place goes, there are endless crates, red ones, yellow, brown ones too. Stacks of Aguila beer, Coca-Cola, Pepsi, Gatorade, 7Up and Crystal. A small workbench is to one side by the wall with a desk lamp on it and above it, on the brick, a calendar features the obligatory woman in a swimsuit. This is very much a man's world. The place has the faint whiff of fresh sweat and pride. Jorge Sanatana leans with one hand on his desk, the collar on his shirt open, revealing a red V where the sun has caught him over the years. His face is hard and his hair is short and greying. Now maybe I am just a soft hand-wringing middle-class Englishman abroad and maybe all the men are like this around here, but I swear to whatever God you want that I don't think this man is capable of standing up without looking defiant.

Jorge worked for three years on the delivery lorries and for nine years in the warehouse. Back then the bottlers were more reliant on the *fleteros* not just delivering the drinks but for drumming up the orders too. 'Coca-Cola gave me an area and said I had to find the customers, so I got two or three people to go and find them. They told me to sell 200 crates a day. They used to call saying you have to sell more...So Coca-Cola pressured me and I had to pressure the employees.' According to Jorge Santana the pressure to sell that number of crates was so intense that, 'sometimes I would cheat and buy the crates myself just to make up the numbers.'

As with the other testimonies 'They used to tell me "this guy is no good, sack him". And I have to sack them.' Coca-Cola ended up sacking him for arguing, and Jorge Santana set up as an independent *fletero*. He is happier now, but 'Coca-Cola won't sell to me directly. I have to buy Coca-Cola on the black market as they refuse to sell to me.'

So far none of this paints a picture of 'respecting workers' but at this juncture I should mention my relationship with The Coca-Cola Company, which is this: I ask them questions about their practices, a PR person prevaricates on answering, waits until after my deadlines expires, then sends over a wodge of PR guff last thing Friday and buggers off on holiday for two weeks so I can't ask a follow-up question. It would be sad but for the fact that the company accidentally sent over their lawyer's notes on how to answer my questions [see Appendix B].

Trying to get TCCC to answer a question directly is like trying to run a quiz night in an Alzheimer's care home. So I have taken the liberty of imagining what they might say were they to imbibe the original recipe and get a little talkative. The Coca-Cola Company could say that I had merely spoken to disgruntled former employees, people with a grudge against the company. To which I would reply, 'That is most surely true, they do indeed have a grudge.'

The Coca-Cola Company could also say that I have spoken only to people known to Chile, a Sinaltrainal member who is in dispute with the company and that the views expressed are not representative of the workforce. Which makes the next person I talk to all the more significant.

We leave Jorge and walk through the alleyways in the hot afternoon, skipping across to the shady side of the street to avoid the sun. I become aware that we are walking, purely by chance, behind a Coca-Cola deliveryman – a *fletero*. The red shirt with the Coca-Cola logo on it is the first clue. The enormous metal frame on wheels that he is pushing, the second. The large crates of Coca-Cola merely confirms my suspicions. So ambling at his side I whisper to Chile,'Do you know him?'

'No.'

'Can we talk to him?'

'We can ask.' And with that Chile strikes up a conversation, the result of which gains me a five-minute audience in the *fletero's* warehouse – on the condition he remains anonymous. Hiding your identity for fear of reprisal is one thing but denying yourself a name seems a bit too impersonal, so I have taken the liberty of giving this *fletero* a false name: Pemberton, after Coca-Cola's founding father.

No doubt the daily delivery of 300 boxes containing 9,000 bottles of drinks has helped keep Pemberton trim, unlike his historically lard-arsed namesake. He stands legs akimbo with one hand on his hip, like an action hero, and with his other hand holds a clipboard at his side. Just like the other *fleteros* Pemberton says he is told what to deliver, to who, in what amounts and at what time, as well as what to wear by the bottlers, 'You have to buy this uniform from Coca-Cola,' his hands now motion to his clothes, a red T-shirt, with a green collar to match the green company approved trousers. The T-shirt bears the words COCA-COLA FEMSA on the breast.

Pemberton is matter-of-fact and businesslike even when he tells of the precarious nature of his employment. 'They can get rid of me whenever they want. I have no job security at all. I have been working [here] for ten years and I have no security for those [years]...So I have to do whatever they ask and agree to everything.' He looks to his assistant and whistles out a call, pointing at some crates stacked tightly together at the side of the lock-up, which the assistant starts to load on a barrow. Pemberton turns unsmiling and continues, 'Coca-Cola say I can only employ one other person to help me.' But he explains there is too much work for the two of them so he has to break the rules and employ two assistants. Running with the theme I ask, 'Has the bottler ever mentioned who you should or should not employ?'

'Yes, two years ago they told me to sack someone.'

'Who told you?'

'The Coke Supervisor.' Mimicking the supervisor, Pemberton says, '"This guy is useless, get rid".' Shrugging he adds, 'What can I do? If they ask me to do it I have no choice.'

'What about joining a union?'

He laughs and shakes his head with a mild contempt. Joining a union is simply not an option.

It was not always like this, Chile says the Coca-Cola deliverymen – like the *fleteros* used to be unionised, 'In 1992 80 per cent of the distribution workers were fixed contract workers and unionised. Today in Bucaramanga there are only two workers in distribution who are on fixed contracts,' himself and his driver Domingo Flores. For Chile, sub-contracting is one of the main causes for the decrease in Sinaltrainal membership, 'In 1992 there were 282 Bucaramanga workers in Sinaltrainal, and in Bucaramanga today you will only find sixteen.'

Meanwhile The Coca-Cola Company proudly boast of their good employee relations, 'In Colombia, a country where 4 per cent of workers are unionised, 31 per cent of the employees of Coca-Cola Colombian bottling partners belong to unions.'[8] So why are the *fleteros* telling such a different story? The answer lies in the statistic...oh yes, my friends, statistics: the thinking man's lie. Calculating a statistic is similar to normal counting but with different rules and when dealing with an entity like a transnational corporation it is important to remember that statistics are facts that have been shaped to fit the story. So, is the Coca-Cola statistic accurate? Let us suppose for a moment it is and consider the implications. The rest of Colombia has only 4 per cent union membership, yet the Coca-Cola bottlers have created such an employee positive environment that union membership is up nearly 800 per cent on the national average. If true the appropriate response has to be *Viva Coca-Cola! La Lucha Continua Hasta La Victoria Siempre con Coca-Cola!*

Meanwhile, back on my planet, logic dictates that this surely cannot be the case, how can Coke bottlers be so pro-union in such an anti-union environment? The answer is they are not. Coke's calculations are based on the number of *permanent* employees they have working for them, and as for the casual labour, or the sub-contracted workers – they are simply not included in the figures. Neither Carlos, Ivan, nor any of the other *fleteros* I spoke to are counted as employees.

A few days earlier in Bogota I had spoken with Sinaltrainal's researcher Carlos Olaya, who told me that since the Nineties Coke bottlers have taken full advantage of a change in the law,[9] which enabled them to remove swathes of workers from their books as direct employees and push them into casual contracts. Huge sections of the bottlers' operations were sub-contracted out – hirings, delivery, maintenance services (like canteens), security, accountancy; all of it was outsourced. 'Now the Coca–Cola bottlers have about 9,000 workers but only about 1,850 are directly or permanently employed, of that figure about 600 are in a union – about 32 per cent.' Which is close enough to the company figures of 31 per cent. 'However, when you include the other 7,150 workers, the true figure is about 6.5 per cent of the workforce are unionised, higher than the national average, true, but still ridiculously low.'

So Coke can say, 31 per cent belong to a union , because the rules they use only count every fifth worker employed under the Coca-Cola logo. Now I am not saying that this special counting method is necessarily bad; there are times when it would be nice to count five as only one, *Die Hard* movies for example.

The *fletero* testimonies raise some serious issues. If the

Coca-Cola bottlers do not employ these workers, why do they keep insisting that these workers cannot join a trade union? Answering this question TCCC's global workplace rights director responded by saying, 'Colombia has unique labour laws in that contract workers are not allowed under Colombian law to belong to industrial unions...it's a unique law in the world...'[10] Implying quite clearly that the 'Coca-Cola system' was just obeying the law on the issue. This is somewhat disingenuous.

Colombian law, according to the Colombian Trade Union Federation 'recognises the right of association only to the workers who have a labour contract [permanent employment]'.[11] This means temporary or casual workers are being denied one of their basic human rights – the right to freedom of association.

So is Coke merely an innocent party here? Is the Pope a lesbian? According to Sinaltrainal, in 1990 75 per cent of workers under the Coca-Cola system in Colombia had permanent employment and 25 per cent casual employment. Today that figure is basically reversed, 80 per cent of workers in the 'Coca-Cola system' in Colombia are casual labour. The 'Coca-Cola system' has subcontracted its workforce at an incredible rate thus denying them the right to join a union and keeping wages low and work hours high.[12]

* * *

I wake up the next morning at Chile's house to find that the family rush hour has just kicked in. Amidst the washing and dressing, shouting and shushing, beating and stirring, sweeping and feeding, homework and cleaning, Esmeralda is showing me how to make *arepas*, a flat round griddled cornmeal patty stuffed with cheese. Frankly, this is the last thing she needs and after tasting my efforts it is the last thing the family need too. Laura is finishing her homework while glancing urgently for her breakfast. Mayela feeds the baby while trying to ignore the smoke from the griddle tray. The baby's attention is caught by the smoke and so hangs open-mouthed over the bottle. Esmeralda is making dough balls, coaching me, doing up a child's shirt while serving as a human clock by periodically shouting out someone's name and the time. Jess leans over the table to snap the scene with an enormous camera, Laura's college friend is eating eggs and ducking to miss Jess's lens. Someone is in the shower upstairs shouting 'What's burning!' Emilio stands blankly in his underwear and Luis Eduardo frantically searches for the latest batch of death threats he has received.

'Luis Eduardo aka Chile' is what the paramilitaries call him in their death threats, that and 'you trade unionist son of a bitch.' Luis Eduardo collects death threats like my mum collects parking tickets.

It's a trivial point, but considering the nature of death squads and their primary purpose, namely killing people, they rarely come up with catchy names for themselves. The old Colombian paramilitaries were called the Autodefensas Unidas de Colombia (AUC) which translates as The United Self-Defence Forces of Colombia. The new paras, both nationally and in Bucaramanaga, have opted for the Águilas Negras – The Black Eagles, which doesn't sound that threatening, evoking as it does, the name of a Goth Folk band.

What isn't so trivial is that they regularly send death threats to prominent Sinaltrainal members. This one was sent to Chile in February 2007: 'The Paramilitiaries of Magdalena Medio, The Black Eagles, call on the terrorist Coca-Cola trade unionists to stop bad mouthing the Coca-Cola Corporation given that they have caused enough damage already. If there is no response we declare them military targets of the Black Eagles, and they will be dealt with as they prefer: death, torture, cut into pieces, coup de grace. No more protests!'

There are a number of significant points about this threat: 1) The Black Eagles target Luis Eduardo because of his work as a Coca-Cola trade unionist and clearly object to the campaign against Coke. 2) They insist that trade unionists are terrorists. 3) They bizarrely offer a menu of physical assault, as if murder à la carte is somehow classy.

This particular threat came shortly after the vice-president of Colombia, Francisco Santos, made some particularly unhelpful remarks. In a thinly veiled reference to Sinaltrainal, Vice-President Santos called on those agitating against 'Coca-Cola, Nestlé, and other private companies' to stop their campaign, adding that this was fuelled by interference from 'sectors of the extreme left, radicals infiltrated into trade union sectors that are generating absolutely absurd campaigns against the corporations.'[13]

'It was after the State's version of the events that the threats started coming through to the trade union leaders...the security situation became much worse in 2007,' says Chile.

'How many death threats have you received in a year?' I ask, expecting a rough estimate.

'Eight threats,' he says precisely, as it dawns on me that death threats by their very nature are not likely to be forgotten. Death threats rarely illicit the response of, 'Oh Lord, I've been that busy I've lost count of them.'

Alongside the eight threats came a visit to the family home. Two men got past the security hut, crossed the wide courtyard in the middle of the blocks, passed the grocery shop with a tray of eggs on the counter, then turned left through an archway that goes under an apartment, emerging quickly into the cool shaded walkway that nips and tucks between the homes. Small iron fences balance on top of low brick walls where little front patios are littered with clutter – kids' plastic toys, spades, garden chairs and lots of pots sprouting firs, ferns, palms and red-leaved lilies. At the end of this is a home with bigger railings, with proper locks on them. Laura, the youngest daughter says, 'I was inside, on my own...I came down when they knocked on the gate.' She curls up on the chair. 'They said they wanted my father.'

'It's really bad and we're really scared,' says Esmeralda.

While Coca-Cola might call this an 'old story' it is a crucially current one for the family and the familiar chaos of breakfast belies the strain. A couple of years ago their eldest child Alexander had to jump from a moving bus to escape two men who clearly knew who he was and seriously threatened him. Alexander has moved well away with his wife and child and now manages a restaurant. Esmeralda spends most of her week working for him there and returns home when she can. Laura is receiving counselling as the recent visit by the paras has triggered memories of her childhood exclusion from school while her father was in jail.

The Coca-Cola Company says that the bottler, Coca-Cola FEMSA, has given assistance to workers threatened by the Black Eagles, including:

- 'Paid leaves of absence from work.'
- 'Loans to install security cameras at the homes of affected workers.'
- 'Set flexible working schedules for those workers upon their return to work.'

- 'Provided individual transportation for those workers to and from work.'[14]

Which sounds reasonable, but let us balance the books – what is in the credit column and what is in the debit column? In the debit column we have The Coca-Cola Company whose bottlers have been accused of collaborating with paramilitaries and they themselves have been accused of making little or no effort to redress the situation despite an employee being killed in the bottlers' own plant. In the debit column the bottlers' security manager falsely accused union members of terrorism, for which they are wrongfully imprisoned for six months, while their families have to beg to survive. Those bottlers have made no effort to redress that wrong. In the debit column Coke wanted rid of the union, which was the logical outcome should a settlement have been reached. In the debit column the bottlers have subcontracted workers so they do not have to give them permanent employment and refused to let them join a union. The bottlers are accused of undermining Sinaltrainal while The Coca-Cola Company claims to respect their rights.

And so on to the credit column. This entry in the balance books is not quite as long as the previous column. In the credit column is: when workers receive death threats the company lends them some money for a camera, gives them some time off and provides them with a lift to work. It is a list you could sum up as: a day off, a taxi and a loan...

Luis Eduardo has by most standards led an eventful life. There was an attempt on his life, when a para appeared with a gun while he was delivering Coca-Cola. He was saved by a shopkeeper pulling him into the store. On top of the false imprisonment on trumped-up terror charges, he has been on hunger strike for better conditions at work. Paramilitaries visit his house and his children have been threatened. His friends are either dead or carry pistols, tucked inside their shirts. Yet paradoxically I feel totally safe in his home. Perhaps my sense of security is the result of rationalisation, namely: the paramilitaries are more likely to kill Luis Eduardo than they are to do anything to me and it is a reasonably good bet that they are not going to kill Luis in front of a foreigner with a press card. Ergo, as long as I stay with Luis Eduardo, everything will be fine...it is when I leave that the problems will start. I reckon Jackie Kennedy had similar feelings, figuring that 'no one is going to bother shooting at me when they can shoot at John.'

* * *

Leaving, under the cloud of this calculation, is an unsettling affair.
'This is a little thank you.' I say handing Luis Eduardo a bottle of single malt whisky.

'This is for you' says Esmeralda, handing me a rolling pin and an *arepa* mould, 'But you must promise to make them when you get home.'

'Thanks, that is really kind of you and thank you for putting up with me,' I say.

'These are for you,' says Luis Eduardo, handing over a bundle of photocopied death threats. Not a traditional parting by any means, but I don't think he had time to get me a presentation tin of regional quality biscuits.

5
THE DAYS OF THE GREAT COKE PLEDGE

Istanbul, Turkey

'Coca-Cola acknowledges that Coca-Cola workers are allowed to exercise rights to union membership and collective bargaining without pressure of interference. Such rights are exercised without fear of retaliation, repression or any other form of discrimination.'

Joint Statement issued by The Coca-Cola Company and the International Union of Foodworkers on 15 March 2005[1]

Everyone is a mere six phone calls away, so says the theory of six degrees of separation. It works like this: you can contact anyone in the world merely by phoning someone you think might be able to help track down your target and creating a chain of contacts until you reach your goal. Admittedly, anyone who has used NHS Direct at a weekend would beg to differ. But, for example, if I wanted to reach Vladimir Putin I would try and find someone who in turn knew someone else in the Russian Embassy and go from there. Admittedly, in Putin's case you would only have to make a couple of calls before he came looking for you, probably with a plate of sushi with a half-life of a few million years, but you get the point.

In practice though, this is far from foolproof. One unforeseen consequence of attempting to utilise the 'six degrees' theory is that once you start the ball rolling, people come back with all sorts of unrequested information. You might start out looking to track down Eddie Murphy and end up getting through to Aleister Crowley's cousin.

And so it was that I had set out for Istanbul with the intention of talking with ex-Coca-Cola workers sacked for joining a trade union, and ended up nattering to a host of other, unexpected folk, including the man who wrote a history of Coca-Cola in Turkey. Someone I knew knew someone, who knew someone, who thought it might be interesting for me to meet with a Coca-Cola obsessive. Partly out of curiosity but mainly out of a desire not to appear rude I said, 'Sounds great.'

Which is why I am sitting in a patisserie just off Taksim Square fighting to keep a polite smile from turning into jowl cramp. The writer opposite me is slouching across the table. In fact everything about him slouches, his sixteen-stone frame slouches in the chair, his black driving jacket slouches, his shoulders slouch, even his thick-rimmed glasses slouch on his nose. He doesn't so much sit at the table as nearly melt over it. If I were him I would be worried in case the Buddhists are right and in the next life he comes back as an ice-cream.

He's a knackered guy in his mid-forties but has the glint of a young believer in his eyes. The front half of his head is bald and the back full of black curls, flecked with the odd grey. These same colours are sported by his stubble, making his chin look like a badger recovering from chemo.

Our man here has written a history of Coca-Cola in Turkey. Naturally he orders a bottle of the stuff, while I opt for the traditional Turkish apple tea. He slugs, I sip and I feel the better man for it. His book has not been officially 'authorised' but is currently 'with Atlanta' awaiting a decision. There have been a few hoops to jump through too as, according to our fellow, the company doesn't like any mention of their cocaine history – of all the C words to take offence at, it seems that 'Cocaine' tops the Company's list. I imagine it must be quite a task, writing a history of a product with Coca in its name and not actually mentioning cocaine. But our slumped fellow avoided this pitfall by reference to alkaloid compounds throughout the book to avoid the dreaded 'cocaine' word and is hopeful that he will get it published.

On mentioning that I am researching communities and groups who have found themselves in conflict with the company, his reaction is livelier than his posture belies.

'There is no story here,' he says in good English, 'there is no story about Coca-Cola in Turkey.' Pausing to looks at me directly 'The only story here...' he spreads his hands out across the table top, palms up, Jesus-style '...is of a miracle drink...'

his eyes widen in wonder '...the miracle of Coca-Cola. The drink that unites people across the world.'

I don't mention the Istanbul Coke deliverymen I've just met who would probably interpret 'uniting people across the world' in a slightly different fashion, seeing as they were sacked for joining a union. For the time being I'm not uttering a single word, as I have an unnerving feeling that if he's interrupted he'll go back to the beginning and start all over again. Blinking, I focus on what he has to say. 'I was involved in one of the bridge projects, it was partnered by a Japanese firm and at the end of it there was a party to celebrate.' He leans forward in the way that racists do when they are about to say something they know they shouldn't. 'The Japanese...' he says on cue, 'served up this food...' his face is full of disgust, '...that soup with seaweed, really disgusting, you can't drink it,' he informs me as if this is scientific fact. 'Then these vegetables and rice, it smells disgusting, like vomit, you know what I mean.' He looks around and finding no disagreement, sneeringly spits out the word again, 'Vomit. No one could eat this shit. But all of us...' his faces smiles at his conclusion '....we could all drink Coca-Cola.' And he toasts the sky with his bottle.

This fellow is a zealot, Coca-Cola to the core, you could cut him and he would spill fizzy brown blood, possibly with a slice of lemon. His feelings towards Coca-Cola are intense enough to border on love, although this kind of love is the type one normally associates with restraining orders. I find his obsession fascinating, indeed it is almost an asset as it gives him a certain gauche charm. I do not, however, have much like for him.

It's not his physical appearance at fault, because to be honest I am at best only five years behind him. Nor do I dislike him because he idolises Coke so much; life is too short to hate someone over a fucking fizzy drink. Believing Coca-Cola to be the greatest thing in the world is neither a crime nor an affliction. I actually don't even mind pushing cake around a plate, while he tells me all about his collection of Coca-Cola memorabilia – a topic that is as endless as it is dull. Nor do I dislike him because his obsession has led to the suspension of any critical faculties he must have had. No, all of these things are kinks and quirks, the odd strand of DNA that defines who we are as people. No, I dislike him for the simple fact that he is a bigot.

'Coca-Cola has brought only good to this country.' He explains that he and his wife visited the east. As the south-east is the Kurdish region I wince in anticipation. 'We went into a shop and the grocer used disposable gloves to cut the cheese.' He holds his hands up in wonder and mimes putting on the gloves. 'Those people have never been able to understand basic personal hygiene...' In this particular instance the subtext is more 'text' than 'sub' and the message is quite clear: 'Kurds are filthy'. 'And do you know who taught them about hygiene? Coca-Cola. I talked to the shopkeeper and he told me how Coca-Cola had taught him about hygiene in classes...Their hygiene was terrible, no one could do anything about it, not even the government could teach them. But do you know who taught these people? Coca-Cola taught those people.'

If I have interpreted this correctly Coca-Cola are great because they and only they have managed to teach the Kurds to wash their hands. It is fair to say that logic plays no great part in our man's analysis. He sees a world where Coca-Cola brings western values and civilisation to the heathen hordes, where the company are missionaries travelling the globe for converts. It is a cap-doffing vision of 'our betters' doing their bit to improve us, one drink at a time.

I finish the Turkish apple tea, and as I get up to say good bye it dawns on me that our man here is one of those rare people whose Ralph Steadman portrait would actually look prettier than the subject.

Yet while sitting in judgement, like some south-London Solomon, I have been equally delusional. I have gently sipped the sweetness of my tea and appreciated its fine apple aroma. I have dangled my tea glass by its rim between my finger and thumb, gesticulating with it like a contemplative sophisticate. Yet it turns out this traditional Turkish apple tea is neither, tea, apple, nor indeed traditional; it is made of a bright pink powdered concoction, that was invented by a pharmaceutical company and marketed to tourists. Indeed, it is Turkish only in the sense that powdered milk is traditionally English. More than that, the tea has enough sugar in it to make my man boobs go up a cup size at the mere thought of it. In short this Turkish apple tea is about as natural as ketamine, as healthy as a sherbet dab and I would be shocked if real fruit has been anywhere near the production process.

And to cap it all, do you know how I found this out? The drummer from Turkey's entry in the 2008 Eurovision Song Contest told me! I have been tutored in cultural authenticity by a man who aspires to be liked by Terry Wogan. Oh the post-modernism of it all...

* * *

It came about because Jess the photographer was to ply her trade, photographing an interview with a Turkish rock band called Mor Ve Otesi. Unfortunately the journalist who was to do the interview dropped out at the last minute.

'You should do it,' she said.

'I don't know who they are.'

'So? They'll tell you who they are.'

'Why interview a band I know nothing about?'

'Because they were going to perform at RocknCoke....'?

'What?'

'Big festival. The biggest in Istanbul, sponsored by Coca-Cola and they pulled out of it.'

'Oh great. I can see the headline, "Obscure Rock Band Snub Sponsor Shock!"'

'No the point is that...'

'Or maybe "Coca-Cola hardly notice as Turkish band don't take their money sensation!"'

'No, there is more to it than that.'

And then she told me that the group who turned down Coca-Cola's gig were none other than Turkey's entry for the 2008 Eurovision Song Contest. The Cliff Richard of Istanbul, the Turkish Brotherhood of Man, the Katrina and the Waves of the Orient turned down Coca-Cola's moolah...And that extra sequin, well that puts a whole different set of goggles on the story for me.

* * *

On arriving at their office the band are far more hospitable than a bumbling ignoramus deserves.

Lead Singer, a balding, skinny thirty-something in a white jumper asks, 'Do you know who we are?'

'No.'

'Have you heard our music before?'

'No.'

'Do you know anything about us?'

'No.'

'Would you like a drink?'

'Yes, that would be lovely.'

Drummer, who has cropped short hair and a goatee that can only be described as jazz-wizard style, says 'I'll get some albums for you to have.'

He disappears for a moment then re-emerges with Bass Player, who is suitably adorned with floppy hair, and is clutching a fistful of CDs for me.

We drink and chat, and I learn that Mor Ve Otesi have been around for a few years, are a respected rock band, with a string of albums and whose members work on the Turkish anti-war organising committee. Not your normal Eurovision fare but as Lead Singer points out, 'Turks take Eurovision very seriously.'

'Which is not something I understand coming from Britain,' I say, 'we just put anything up for it.'

'We noticed,' he replies.

I also learnt that the first RocknCoke festival in Istanbul was held in 2003 and the line-up included the Pet Shop Boys, Simple Minds, Suede and the Dead Kennedys.

'And just a few Turkish acts...' said Drummer.

'...Four Turkish acts, and we were asked to be one of them. We said "why not?"' adds Lead Singer.

The band were touring at the time and on returning to the capital, 'We heard that there was a global campaign that started with what happened in Colombia,' says Lead Singer, 'we decided not take part in this festival and we decided to take part in Rock for Peace.'

'That was seen as a big success for the alternative festival,' says Drummer, 'as we were perceived as a band coming from the other side.'

So I promise to listen to the music, thank them for having me and put my notebooks in the rucksack. Drummer kindly waits to see me out and while we head to the office door I mention that it seems fitting that Coca-Cola, the outriders of globalisation, should reap global disapprobation. If the image of a brand can travel from Atlanta to Istanbul, then criticisms of it can likewise arrive from Bogota. As the brand travels the world, negative stories can stick to the logo. So, I conclude, when people ask how can I challenge a brand as big as Coke, we can reply that it starts by individuals learning to look past the PR image.

Drummer nods, standing at the open door and as we exchange pleasantries he politely enquires, 'What else have you got planned for your trip?'

'Well, the one thing I do need to do is to find some traditional Turkish Apple Tea to take home.'

'Erm...You do know...' he begins.

* * *

The Coca-Cola Company are but one of a multitude of companies that shape the image of their brands to suit their marketing needs and in the case of apple tea I am but one of a multitude of consumers prepared to suspend reality. But the statement from our man in the patisserie that 'there is no Coca-Cola story in Turkey,' is a suspension of reality too far. I tracked down the ex-Coke workers I had originally come here to see and I set out for the offices of the Transport Union of Istanbul, to hear their allegations of how Coca-Cola bottlers drove down their wages with sub-contractors, sacked them for unionising and then colluded with the police who attacked them and their families. The union's name is Nakliyat-Is, pronounced knack lee yat – eesh.

Alpkan, the man who is going to act as my interpreter, is a lecturer. As a native of Istanbul, he told me that 'The union is easy to find from where you are staying, just head across the bridge and up the hill…' Directing someone to walk up the hill in Istanbul is a little like saying, 'Oh, just follow the canal' in Venice. In Istanbul it is impossible not to walk up a hill. Here the streets are narrow and steep, and halfway up every single hill seems to be an old man pushing a cart with an unfeasibly enormous load. I'm beginning to suspect that it is a legal requirement for steep inclines to have an old man on them.

Fortunately the union offices are on a main road that runs under the slightly more eye-catching landmark of a huge and ancient aqueduct. Some 500 yards away uphill (naturally) is a five- maybe six-storey structure which seems to make up the entire block. Every apartment, office, warehouse, shop and storerooms exists in one extremely large building. It has the look of a Soviet construction from the 1960s, though the sight of shops stocked with actual goods for sale spoils that particular illusion. At pavement level the block's entrance is tall wooden doors, a garland of nameplates and buzzers at their side.

On the other side of one of these doors lies a circular stairwell encased in frosted glass, tinted a light brown with nicotine and age. The echoes of our footsteps rush up the stairs before us to the second-floor landing. Here, through what looks to be an apartment door, lie the offices of Nakliyat-Is. The meeting room is a small place with a low ceiling but about sixty seats have been packed tightly together, forming five rows of chairs which all face a desk at the front of the room. Behind the desk, hanging from the wall is a red banner with yellow letters declaring, 'Organised labour will defeat the forces of capital!' It is as if someone had set up a union hall in a council flat living room. I wouldn't be surprised if halfway through lively meetings there was the sound of banging from the other side of the wall and a shout of 'Keep it down in there! I can't hear the bloody telly!'

The union came into conflict with Coke in May 2005, just two months after the company in Atlanta had issued a suitably foot-shooting statement. On 15 March 2005 The Coca-Cola Company made the Great Coke Pledge and said, 'Coca-Cola acknowledges that Coca-Cola workers are allowed to exercise rights to union membership and collective bargaining without pressure of interference. Such rights are exercised without fear of retaliation, repression or any other form of discrimination.'[2] Exactly sixty-six days after the Great Coke Pledge Turkish deliverymen were sacked for organising a union. The four men sitting in front of the red banner are going to tell me the story.

Let me introduce you to them. Behind the desk sits President Küçükosmanoōlu. My translator explains that even Turks have problems pronouncing his name and so he is more often than not just called President K. He looks constantly determined and has a glare that could make a statue blink. Such is the force of his stare that I would not be surprised if there is a scientific gauge for measuring its magnitude. Today it is turned on a low setting – which would be about 2.5 on the Ayatollah Khomeini Scale. President K is a smart man, who sports a side parting and a moustache that is a classic of the region. His suit informs the room what his words confirm, that he has been in negotiations all morning. Sitting next to him is Fahrettin Takici, a lean and trim forty-nine-year-old with hair cropped close to his scalp; hunched over his chair, legs apart with his forearms leaning on his thighs. He is dressed all in black: black roll-neck sweater, black leather jacket, black trousers, all of which combine to give him the air of a loyal lieutenant. Next to him but sitting to the side of the desk is the oldest-looking man in the room, Ahmet Gakmak, whose suit is as grey as his hair. Under his jacket is a V-neck jumper with a brown and purple diamond pattern, but this description gives this garment more colour than it deserves, as it blends into the suit with an effortless ease borne of penury. Ahmet has poverty teeth, where the gaps between them tell of a life of thin wage packets. In complete contrast in front of him sits the last and youngest member of the quartet, Erol Turedi. His hair is pure Tony Curtis, his shirt crisp, his tiepin tidy, his enamel badge of the Turkish flag perfectly positioned on his lapel and his black zip-up boots are straight out of Austin Powers. And when he flashes you a cheeky smile it is the kind of grin that deserves its own theme music.

Erol, Ahmet and Fahrettin worked for Coca-Cola Icecek, the Turkish bottling company jointly set up by the Anadolu Group in Turkey and The Coca-Cola Company in Atlanta. Coke now owns 20 per cent of CCI shares.[3]

Their story starts in a manner similar to the *fletero* in Colombia. Originally the deliverymen worked directly for Coca-Cola Icecek and considered it a good job – then they were subcontracted, they ceased to work for Coca-Cola directly, and everything changed.

Their new employer, the sub-contractor, was called Trakya Nakliyat Ve Ticaret Ltd STI (Trakya). The wages went down, overtime money went down and they were forced to resign from their old union, Oz-Gida Is in 2000 on the insistence of the management. The one thing that did not change was the job itself, as Erol points out, 'We were driving the same trucks, wearing the same Coca-Cola shirts, we changed our clothes in the same place.' In fact, according to Erol, the managers they were working under remained the same too, so not even the personnel changed. 'They were absolutely the same people.'

President K reiterates this point in his deep voice, 'The relationship between [the sub-contractors] and Coca-Cola Icecek is only a bureaucratic relationship, the whole management is lead by Coke managers, [the decisions of] who to hire and who to fire were all taken by Coke managers. Coke choose the route, what brands, how much, when it was to be delivered. Everything went from Coke, even the receipts, even the paperwork was on Coke papers. The only issue that Trakya appears on is on the workers security payments [that is, the national insurance].'

The four men telling this tale have a curious unity. They're all distinct personalities yet they speak as one. An odd ensemble – I was going to call them a Greek Chorus but this being Turkey it's probably best to leave the Greeks out of it. However, there is something beyond the normal workplace camaraderie here, as they finish each other's sentences and join in together on certain refrains and sayings. It is the nearest I have seen to barbershop storytelling.

You can see this in action when the men discuss one aspect of the story, which is that The Coca-Cola Company says that 'the labour dispute does not directly involve the [Turkish bottlers] CCI.'[4] President K starts to explain why he thinks the sub-contractors are used. 'Consider the law in Turkey,' he says. 'Coca-Cola can divorce itself from any problems with the subcontractor...'

Ahmet chips in, 'Trakya was set up to decrease wages and stop any attempt at unionising.'

Erol fills in some detail, 'when we were working under Coca-Cola the wages were four times more than when we worked for the subcontractor...' he throws his hand away in unconcealed scorn '...and the working conditions used to be better.'

Ahmet starts to say, 'When we went to the management for a wage increase the management said...'

But Fahrettin jumps into the tale and along with Ahmet, they chant in unison the words of the manager told them, 'Get off the job, many people would work here in these conditions.'

Erol says nothing but his head bobs sagely and he stares at me as if to affirm the truth. President K adds a comment too, he lights a cigarette and his stony impassive face raises an eyebrow in a rare emotional outburst.

So with pay down and overtime squeezed they quietly began to unionise the deliverymen at two of Coke's plants in Istanbul, Dudullu and Yenibosna. Ahmet had the first clandestine meetings with President K preparing the legal work they would need to comply with. When these meetings began 'a maximum of five people in each plant initially knew of the plans...' confides Erol '...we were very careful and very secret.'

Their caution was borne out of concern of how the management would react. They were right to be worried. On 19 May 2005, sixty-six days after the Great Coke Pledge was made public – six days after announcing their intention to form a union, they were sacked. Without any indication or warning the five union organisers were laid off. Erol and Fahrettin arrived for work at the Dudullu plant and were informed along with the three other men that they were being sacked for poor performance.[5] Considering Fahrettin and Erol had recently been rewarded by the company for their good work this seems an odd reason. 'I have many awards for being a good worker,' Erol insists, 'Awards the firm gave me, presents and certificates, for Best Driver.'

Which just goes to show how complex business really is these days. Those of us not involved in the corporate world would think that the best driver would be the last driver to be sacked for poor performance. How wrong we would be. Indeed a quick study of the bonus and share options for the world's top business executives illustrates how the system works: the more the Chief Executive Officer runs a company into the ground the more they are rewarded.

To the untrained eye it might appear suspicious that the five men sacked for poor performance just happen to be the five main union organisers. Indeed, Erol alleges that on the day they were sacked, 'Coke management agrees to have a meeting.' He sits bolt upright as he continues, 'And I stress this is the Coke management not Trakya...They meet the five of us and they say, "Why are you doing this? You have brought this action upon yourselves but still let's talk".'

'We have unionised.' says a friend.

A manager replied, the delivery men could '[go] on working by resigning from the union.'

According to court documents submitted in the US the union also alleges that one of the managers went on to say, 'We, as The Coca-Cola Company, shall let no members of the union work for us.'[6]

The next day, 20 May, another fifty deliverymen are sacked at Dudullu; all but a couple were members of the new union, though these non-members joined swiftly afterwards.

Five days later on 25 May the unionised deliverymen at the Yenibosna plant were sacked too – another fifty men. Within sixty-eight days of signing up to protect and respect trade union rights Coke had overseen the sacking of over one hundred workers for joining a union. At this point I fear the gap between pronouncement and reality is so great that only the likes of Heather Mills dare brook the chasm.

Every country in the world has its own customs, some old, some new, some cultural, some religious and some just for the tourists, but perhaps Turkey's most enduring tradition has been the random use of excessive force at public gatherings. Though this societal norm is not exclusive to them the Turkish authorities do excel at it, thanks to the notorious police rapid deployment force called the Çevik Kuvvet. It is at this point in the union's saga that these same police enter the story. Now, according to human rights groups the Çevik Kuvvet is responsible for about 80 per cent of the accusations and reports of torture and abuse committed by the Turkish security forces.[7] According to Nakliyat-Is 'Coke arranged for the Turkish Çevik Kuvvet to attack, gas, beat and arrest the union members and their families' so as to terrorise them into accepting 'mass terminations without further protest'.

The events took place 97 days after Coke signed its pledge to respect union rights. Up until then the deliverymen had been busy campaigning for their reinstatement. From May to July they had marched, rallied, petitioned, lobbied and protested, becoming quite a cause célèbre on the way. But after two months there was still no prospect of Coke giving them back their jobs. So the union planned a demonstration for 20 July at the Dudullu plant – the operational headquarters of Coca-Cola Icecek.

* * *

This plant at Dudullu is ringed with black ornate iron railings. Inside, there are trimmed hedges and lampposts placed just so to mark out the pathways and borders, while a concrete walkway sweeps to the administrative office. This is a long building, wider than it is high, with a domed tower in the middle of it, like a town hall clock. Except this building has no features to speak of and appears to be made entirely of dark reflective glass. If Lego made their blocks out of Ray-Bans and Nihilists designed shopping centres, this would be the result. Or if you fancy, imagine Corbusier had rebuilt Trumpton.

Beyond the iron railings on the street lies a less precocious construction, the union's protest shelter, erected by the men to keep the heat of the sun at bay while they continue their vigil. The shelter resembles the summer self-assembly shades that crop up in south-London back gardens, long-poled affairs with all the stability of Amy Winehouse, under which entire families sit clutching paper plates while fathers in shorts ritually turn meat into charcoal.

The morning of the demonstration finds the men from Dudullu under this same protest shelter, though half of the gathering consists of their wives and children who are with them for the day. The plan is to start the demonstration just as soon as their friends and colleagues arrive from the other Coke plant at Yenibosna. They do not have long to wait. At about 10am a coach draws up alongside the shelter, screeching to a halt with its air brakes hissing. The Dudullu families are instantly up and out of their chairs to welcome the newcomers. Women in headscarves and coats, kids in T-shirts and jeans are climbing off the coach with their fathers in their white Coca-Cola delivery shirts, now adorned with slogans scrawled in marker pen. No sooner have the first protestors got their feet on the ground than a shout goes out, then another, an arm is raised and motions the protestors forward. Suddenly and with no further ado a group of men cross the few metres to the perimeter of the plant's iron railings and start to scramble over them. Hands go up to steady the climbers before they launch themselves from the top. Hollers and whistles rise as they jump off into the plant. Quickly both groups, those inside the railings and out, start towards the main gates and in an instance they are prised open. Then with a slight look of disbelief at their own audacity 200 people stroll into Coke's plant. Older children hold the hands of the younger ones, women hold bags and banners, men wave flags as they wander past the trimmed hedges. Just for a moment they pause under the Coca-Cola logo that sits above the main entrance of the black-mirrored building. A few kids glance around with a look of 'Oh blimey, what have we done', then turn back to the entrance and everyone simply walks on in.

A handful of police in white T-shirts appear at the door. They were supposed to keep an eye on the demonstration but have been taken completely unawares; frankly, in this situation, a lollipop man would have more authority. Powerless to stop the crowd from walking in, one policeman tries to halt the crowd's progress before a protestor pins the officer's arms to his side and moves him out of the way, lest he hurt himself. As they stride past the stunned constabulary the workers urge, 'Keep out of this.' And on they go, into the corporate reception area of the main atrium. This is an open-plan and air-conditioned large glass box, placed squarely in the middle of the building – a box within a box. Around its glass walls run corridors and offices. An escalator whirrs to the other floors, while a balcony overlooks the vista of a reception desk and a floor dotted with pot plants – the corporate equivalent of flowers bought from a petrol station. Ceramic and metal basins stuffed with an unimaginative selection of greenery mix with genteelly roped-off sculptures of Coke bottles. This place is bland, grand, almost featureless and easy to wipe clean. It is what I imagine a waiting room looks like in a Swiss euthanasia clinic.

And into this antiseptic lounge surge the protestors, twisting and turning to take in their surroundings, craning their necks, holding hands, shouting 'Our goal is bread!' and 'Reinstate the dismissed workers!' clapping, cheering and embracing each other.

In their midst President K motions them to sit down on the floor. They have made it into Coca-Cola's Turkish operational headquarters, they want to speak to the Coke managers about getting their jobs back and they are not going to leave until President K negotiates with Coke.

Coca-Cola say that the protestors 'illegally broke into the facility'.[8] Which is true. Though there is a certain innocence to their intentions. 'This was not an occupation, it was simple: we wanted our jobs back and we wanted to talk to the managers or whoever is responsible,' the President tells me.

Erol flicks his hair and elaborates, 'We never declared this an occupation or anything like that, we said – you did an illegal act, we came here to talk about this issue and find agreement.'

As the general manager for the entire Coke operations in the region had his office in the Dudullu plant it made complete sense for the families to walk into the place. In their eyes they were simply knocking on the door asking for justice.

Most of the white-collar workers had been sent home leaving only key management in the building. Messages were sent up to them and for a while the atmosphere stayed relatively calm. There are a few arrests, but the presence of the children and women (one woman pregnant and some elderly) keeps everyone on good behaviour. The cops even bring in some food and water for the families. 'At first we didn't eat it,' I am told later by one of the protestors who was there on the day, 'as this was from Coke and the police...but then we got hungry.'

Both the union and Coke describe a relatively peaceful interim period. Coca-Cola say that 'No action was taken to remove the protestors for ten hours...and several meetings were held between CCI management and the protestors to try and resolve the situation peacefully.'[9]

That charity was over by 3pm. TV cameras set up at the gates on the street. Police buses park outside the main entrance. Istanbul's second most senior policeman appears at the plant to oversee operations. But the biggest development was the arrival of 1,000 police drafted in to cope with the 200 protestors. The Çevik Kuvvet – 'robo cops' in full body armour – mass outside and are deployed into the building in groups. They fill the corridors. They occupy the balcony. They take the floor above the workers. Hundreds of police appear in the atrium, with riot shields and batons at the ready. The police charge nets six arrests and forces the protestors into a corner, the women and children huddled at the back by the walls. The men stand in front of them. They have linked arms together in an effort to protect themselves and their families, but when the assault finally comes their efforts are proved to be instinctive rather than practical. In front of them are 1,000 police and behind them the children have started to cry.

Finally Coca-Cola's managers agree to talk to the union. So while the police corner the families downstairs President K and the union lawyer go upstairs for talks. It is late afternoon when they gather in a meeting room, which is small. Around a table, which is large. Alongside the managers, which is essential. And next to the police...which is baffling. Why were the police sitting in on reinstatement negotiations? Riot police are rarely, if ever, known for their roles as conflict resolution facilitators. I tend to think the words, 'Perhaps you could express your thoughts and feelings,' would ring hollow when uttered from behind a reinforced Perspex visor. It just wouldn't foster confidence in the non-violent aspect of mediation.

The union had no say as to whether the police were present or not. 'We obviously didn't want the police there,' says the President, as the cops 'said that they would attack the workers at any moment. So the meeting was very tense...On one hand we're talking to the managers and we are near an agreement but the cops are intimidating and abusing the workers.'

Despite this the talks seemed to be more fruitful than might be imagined. According to Coca-Cola, the bottlers CCI tried to 'resolve the situation peacefully, asking the police to delay action'.[10] Indeed the union thought they were going to reach a positive outcome. 'The meeting with Coke gave me the impression that we were close to agreeing to the demands,' President K recalls. 'In the meantime the police are constantly pressuring us in the meeting, "Time is late. You must stop." We said to the police "You can see we are close to an agreement, please wait a little more".'

In fact it is curious that Coca-Cola's managers did not address this anomaly. 'They could have said, "please leave now because we are close to an agreement or do not increase tensions".' The fact that the company did not do this 'implies that Coke are happy with the police behaviour,' says President K. Perhaps the Coke managers in Turkey were just too busy subcontracting workers into lower wages to read that The Coca-Cola Company (owners of 20 per cent of their shares) respected the rights of trade unions to 'collective bargaining without pressure of interference'.

If events were going badly upstairs, events downstairs took an expected turn for the worse. On the frontline Erol looked out at the police – 'they just pulled down the gas masks and that was when we knew.'

Two years later, listening to the men describe these events it is obvious that neither the outrage nor indignity has left them. Erol is on the edge of his seat, Fahrettin and Ahmet are out of theirs as they describe the whirling chaos as the canisters spun furiously, spurting out chemical clouds. Their arms shot into the air in improbable directions to show how it engulfed them. Their eyes widen as they tell of stumbling into each other in panic and blindness, gasping for breath. They curse the police as children were separated from their parents and the men beaten with riot sticks. And they hold out their hands when they talk of being bundled into the police wagons outside, of reaching up to the small windows to gasp for fresh air – only to be sprayed in the face by the police.

After finishing their story the men relax, stirring sugar into their glasses of black tea and lighting cigarettes. Alpkan the translator has not seen these folks for a while so he catches up with the gossip about their families, lives and work. Union staff who up until now have stayed out and left us alone now feel able to wander into the room. A few papers for the President to sign are informally dropped on the desk. Fahrettin has to be dragged away from his mobile phone as we just have time to pose for photos. Erol and I grin madly with our arms around each other's shoulders, and the while place feels like a post-show dressing room. Though in truth the story is not quite finished...

In the aftermath of the attack the union continued its campaigning. 'Originally it was about getting jobs back,' continues President K after the break is over. 'When we said this to Coke, they said "we have changed the transportation system and can't give you back your jobs". After that point we talked about money.'

So they started working on compensation and five months after it all started Trakya settled with the union in October 2005, paying out for the dismissals. Shortly after settling Trakya suddenly and strangely ceased to exist. Though the agreement once again forbids disclosure of its contents, it is understood the payment was approximately £500,000. This was divided amongst the 105 sacked men giving an average of £4,760 per person – about a year's pay on the minimum wage. However, this settlement was for the dismissals, not the attack by the police at Coke's HQ, for which Coke has always denied any responsibility.

Turkey is not a country noted for its access to justice or respect for human rights. For example, under Penal Code 301 it is an offence to even mention the Armenian genocide, hampering any inquiry into such a matter, as it is illegal to describe what happened. So as a trade union, especially one banned by the Generals after the military coup in the 1980s, Nakliyat-Is believed they stood a better chance of pursuing their claims through the USA. So they followed the Colombian route, bringing a case against The Coca-Cola Company and Coca-Cola Icecek in the States under the Alien Tort Claims Act. Nakliyat-Is claims in court documents that the Çevik Kuvvet 'attacked them with a particularly lethal form of tear gas that under international standards is not permitted to be used indoors, and then brutally beat the workers and their family members with clubs. Most people were paralysed from the gas, and when they were felled by the clubbing, they were kicked repeatedly.'[11] The writ alleges that the police were acting with the 'agreement' of the local Coke managers.[12]

The Company has a different interpretation of events saying, 'the Public Prosecutor made the decision that the situation could not be allowed to continue. The Coca-Cola system respects the rights of people to hold peaceful protests and regrets that a peaceful resolution to the illegal occupation of the CCI building could not be achieved.'[13]

They have also described the situation as a 'local issue' that has been 'resolved'. But once again, while they are publicly dismissive they are privately concerned. In a parallel manner to the way in which Coke handled the Colombian trade unionists, the Atlanta company has been involved in talks to reach a settlement out of court with Nakliyat-Is. As both cases were being brought by the same lawyers, it is my understanding that The Coca-Cola Company decided to tie the labour issues – both Colombian and Turkish – into the same negotiations, enabling them (were an agreement to be reached) to staunch their PR misery regarding trade unions. It is also understood that a figure close to $1 million to settle with Nakliyat-Is was being discussed when Sinaltrainal pulled out of the talks and the Company ended any further discussion on the case. The failure to resolve the issue has left the court case ongoing.

* * *

The following morning sees me hunched on a wooden seat at the side of a ferry, clutching a coffee in one hand and in the other a bread ring covered in sesame seeds. The ship's engine makes a low thrumming sound, harbour air smells of diesel and I'm off to Asia in a minute. The Bosphorus Strait divides the city of Istanbul, leaving part of the city in Europe and the other part of it in Asia.

With a slow blast of the horn the ferry leaves Europe and heads for the declared cultural centre of the Asian shore, the district of Kadikoy, from where the next income bracket down is but a bus ride away and is followed by a car ride literally to the edge of a residential development area. Here fresh builders' rubble splashes across the grass expanses between the housing blocks, casual litter in the shape of paint pots, timber, copper wire and sacking. The windowpanes in the new builds still have X-shape tape stuck on them and unconnected wires hang from lamp fittings. Beside one such unoccupied set of apartments, opposite a lone cherry blossom, is a modest three-storey affair where Mr Pomba, an ex Coca-Cola deliveryman, lives with his family. He is going to tell me about his experiences inside the plant on the day the police attacked.

He a quiet and gentle man, wearing what looks to be his 'for best' V-neck navy blue jumper, with a Windsor knot tie under it. He is older than the other workers and silver hair sits happily on top of his head. Bowing slightly he holds out his arms beckoning me to sit on the sofa. Opposite is his chair, part of a suite, and between us snugly fits a coffee table, with a glass top and a scented bowl of plastic flowers placed precisely in the middle. Two framed texts from the Koran hang opposite a wooden cabinet that is a shrine to his daughter's passion for Besiktas football club, anything in the team colours of black and white is placed here: scarves, shirts, rosettes, teddy bears and even photos of her in black and white face paint, with the club initials drawn on her cheeks.

Mrs Pomba and her daughter Ebru quietly enter the room, their heads shyly bent and covered with headscarves, carrying a large shiny metal samovar on a tray. This is for the Rize tea, Turkish black tea –cay – it heats the water and brews the cay which comes out of a small tap at the base.

'Please make yourself at home,' Mr Pomba says with a slight clearing of his throat.

The plastic flowers are removed and the samovar is carefully laid on the coffee table. Saucers soundlessly appear with their white rims dotted in red paint like petals and small thin glasses stand in the saucers like daffodil flutes.

'I wonder if we could start with talking about working at Coke?' I say.

Mr Pomba's reply leaves me uncertain as to whether he said 'yes' or 'let us wait until after tea', he says, 'Please.'

Not knowing what to do...I begin. 'Others have said it was a prestigious job to be working at Coke...'

'Yes it was. It was job number one.' He says smiling slightly, 'I really loved my job.'

Ebru produces photos of her father receiving a gift from one of the managers. 'The present they are giving him is this clock,' and from the other side of the coffee table she produces a metal encased carriage clock. Smack bang in the middle of the face is the famous script of the Coca-Cola logo. The arms are frozen still as the clock no longer works, but Ebru still carefully places it in a box to return it to safe keeping.

Mrs Pomba in her big dark housecoat puts a plate on the table. It's the best china. A perfect ring of royal blue on each plate's border is overlaid with golden threads of vines and leaves.

'After you were dismissed did you go to the protests outside the plant?'

'Every day. I was going on a daily basis. As if I was going to work.' He clears his throat softly, 'I was going there at 8am and was leaving at 6pm' He motions to his daughter Ebru and she comes and sits on the chair next to him. Her face flushes as she looks up and places her folded hands on her lap. She was on the demonstration with her father and two younger sisters. 'I wanted to get my father's job back,' she says tucking her chin into her chest.

'We had a lot of hope, expectation of getting our jobs back,' Mr Pomba explains, 'we were very joyful when we went there.'

Silently, neatly folded triangular serviettes and tiny dessert forks are put on each plate, just as Mr Pomba reflects on how close they were to getting reinstated when the police attacked. 'The head of the union was just about to get a deal with the company. We probably needed another ten minutes and we would have got a resolution.'

He smiles and offers his hand to table indicating I should take some food. There are plain puff pastries on serving plate. I have been given the best food in the house. I unfold my serviette and slowly pick apart the layers with the dessert fork.

Hot black tea is poured into my glass and two cut-glass sugar bowls added to the table, the sugar in each one piled into a perfect mound. Opposite me Mr Pomba continues. 'Then they start spraying gas at us and attacked us...they were beating us and putting whoever they caught inside the police vehicles. My youngest child's eyes have been affected by the gas....she had to have an operation.'

Ebru was there when this happened, she too was gassed and so I say, 'How did you feel when all of this happened?'
    'Don't even remind her,' says Mr Pomba, shaking his head.
    Ebru cannot look up, 'I am upset even now, with my father just talking about it...'

She stops and silence takes over and I notice the steam rising gently from our glasses. Alpkan stirs some sugar making a small sound with his spoon. Ebru's head stays firmly down. Her father looks to her. Then her mother, the nigh invisible tea lady suddenly screams across the living room, 'I would kill those police!' She explodes with unrestrained rage. 'I'd shoot them now if they were here!' We're staring as her fists beat the sky, declaiming to the heavens. 'The dogs sprayed gas in my people's eyes! Like you see on TV – the Israeli police and the way they treat people! They are like them!'

And then she catches herself and with a flutter of her hands to fidget herself calm, she is quiet. Her voice is gone as quickly as it came. She shakes her head, collects herself, Mr Pomba clears his throat and his wife pours another glass of black tea.

For this family there is no doubt, 'Coke is responsible. They are responsible for the whole thing. They made the police attack us.'

I genuinely don't know if they did or did not, but I ask 'Do you really think Coca-Cola could have stopped the police attacking you?'

'Yes, they could have if they had wanted to,' he sighs and forces a smile on to his reddened face.

Some things did change after the great Coke Resistance, here is a list of them:

1) Mr Pomba and Fahrettin Taciki both got new jobs as drivers with different companies, though on lower wages.

2) Erol Turedi now is a salesman for Nestlé.

3) Ahmet Gakmak has not worked since being dismissed for unionising, he insists this is because he has been blacklisted.

4.) Mor Ve Otesi came seventh in the final of the Eurovision Song Contest with the song 'Deli'. They scored 138 points, receiving one maximum 12 points from Azerbaijan.

Legendary broadcasting phenomena Sir Terry Wogan was very encouraging of them. The UK song came last in 25th place, receiving only 14 points.

5) To the best of my knowledge no book has come out on Coca-Cola in Turkey.

6) President K recently won the world glowering competition.

7) After the mass sackings, the campaigns, the protest shelter, the gassings and the settlement, the Turkish government, sensing the need for reform and change, grasped the nettle and acted decisively. The erection of protest shelters without permission is now illegal.

8) Coke has allowed the trade union Oz-Gira-Is back into the plant. Eagle-eyed readers will remember this is the union that workers were forced to resign from in 2000. So it is nice of Coke to let them back...

9) The Nakliyat-Is court case brought in the USA against The Coca-Cola Company and Coca-Cola Icecek is ongoing. The case is currently pending in the 11th Circuit USA.

6

MAY CONTAIN TRACES OF CHILD LABOUR

El Salvador

'Any child labour allegation is a very serious issue that we fully investigate.'

The Coca-Cola Company[1]

I t's early morning and it's hot. Long palm leaves lollop over the country lane, dark and shiny in the warm coastal mist. Few appear to be about at this hour, save the odd delivery van for the hotels or night watchman finishing a shift. But along one otherwise deserted stretch of road, a small gaggle of elderly Miami joggers wearily pounds its way up the incline. They comprise mainly of women, with one gasping male in their company. Their lungs are greedy for air, their heartbeat races, though they do not. You can practically see Death on their shoulder, taunting cynically, 'Whoa there, this one's a quick one!' You may well ask how I know they are from Miami? Well, it's a series of deductions. Firstly when Salvadorean women get old, they don't jog, they sit. They sit on benches, on rugs in the streets, in doorways, by churches and always in the shade. But jogging, no. Clue number two is the brightly coloured wrist and headbands, which just seem to scream the words 'Florida Retirement Community'. However, the final give away is their security guard. Striding lightly behind them is a Salvadorean man in his mid thirties, wearing a brown company shirt and matching baseball hat. He has a massive pump action shotgun, hanging from a strap around his neck while one hand holds the handle and his forefinger rests over the trigger guard. There can't be many people in this area other than Miami tourists who'd have armed security accompany them for a jog. Though in all honesty I'm not sure if he was there to protect them or to step in at the first sign of a coronary and administer the mercy shot.

I pass them in a van driving from a place called La Libertad on the El Salvador coast. It's a popular holiday haunt where the waves pull in large groups of surfers and the beaches are big enough for everyone else to avoid them. My destination is north to the Department of Sonsonate and its eponymous main city. This city is essentially one long high street packed with car-repair workshops, fast-food bars and strip joints. However, it is the journey to the city that takes us through sugar cane country. The place is packed with plantations. The sugar is why I am here – sugar and children.

Sugar comes second to water as the main ingredient in a can of Coca-Cola, and with nearly eight teaspoons in each 330ml can,[2] the sugar gives the water a good run for its money. It is sugar that has left a bitter aftertaste for the company in El Salvador, as the sugar Coke uses is tainted with child labour.

In 2004 Human Rights Watch (HRW), an NGO with considerable experience documenting and campaigning in the area of child soldiers and child labour produced a report criticising Coca-Cola for not doing enough to prevent child labour in its supply chain. The report, 'Turning a Blind Eye, Hazardous Child Labor in El Salvador's Sugarcane Cultivation' said:

- 'The Coca-Cola Company buys sugar refined at the Central Izalco mill.'
- 'At least nine of the twelve children Human Rights Watch interviewed in the Department of Sonsonate worked on four plantations that supply sugarcane to Central Izalco. These children ranged in age from 12 to 16. Their testimonies and the accounts of adult workers on those plantations confirmed that those plantations regularly use child labor.'
- 'Coca-Cola's guiding principles apply only to its direct suppliers, who must not 'employ' or 'use' child labor.... Coca-Cola can itself turn a blind eye to evidence of human rights abuses in its supply chain as long as its direct suppliers do not themselves use child labor.'
- 'In Coca-Cola's case, child labor helped produce a key ingredient in its beverages bottled in El Salvador. In that sense, Coca-Cola indirectly benefits from child labor.'[3]

Not surprisingly Coca-Cola was not pleased to have such practices associated with its products. They get in enough trouble over their drinks being too sugary for kids, without the public finding out that children are helping to supply the sugar in the first place.

Surely for Coke there are two essential questions: if there is child labour in the supply chain for our drinks, are we content for that to be the case or are we not? And if we are not, what are we going to do about it?

Coke says 'any child labour allegation is a very serious issue that we fully investigate'.[4] But they were less adamant when

they said to the *Washington Post* that their ability 'to assist in
addressing these fundamental issues of tradition and norm
that surround rural poverty is limited.'[5] It is an interesting use
of the word 'tradition' in relation to child labour. To my mind
traditions should be warm and pleasant things – brass bands
and summer fetes, rather than stuffing kids up chimneys. It is
also historically and morally flimsy to defer to tradition,
tradition is subject to change. After all, slavery was traditional,
as was burning witches, indeed child labour in America was
traditional; some even eulogised its beneficial nature, like
Coca-Cola's first proprietor Asa Chandler who said, 'The most
beautiful sight that we see is the child at labour. As early as
he may get at labour, the more beautiful, the more useful does
his life get to be.'[6]

'BEAUTIFUL' CHILD LABOUR IN EL SALVADOR

There are approximately 5,000 children harvesting and a
further 25,000 children 'helping' their parents on the harvest
in El Salvador.

Some children will get up at 4.30 in the morning in order to
walk to the cane fields. Harvesting is hazardous and classified
as one of the worst forms of child labour by the UN. Children
are vulnerable to injuries from the machetes used for cutting,
the cane sap can cause rashes and irritations, a significant
proportion develop respiratory problems and a working day
from 4.30am to 1pm leaves no time for school.[7]

On a more positive note The Coca-Cola Company inspected the sugar mill Central Izalco, stating that 'we again verified that it [the refinery] and its supplying mill had sound policies against employing underage youth.'[8] Laudable as this inspection is, there was never any allegation that the mill employed child labour, HRW doesn't say the problem lies in the sugar refinery, but rather it says child labour is rampant in the harvesting on the plantations. It often helps in an investigation to look in the right place and the right place in this instance is in the fields.

It can't be that difficult to check for child labour, all you have to do find the fields, turn up and look. And that is exactly what I am going to try and do: turn up and look for child labour. I'm making a programme for Channel 4 and I want to find out if, three years after the report, child labour is still in Coke's supply chain and if it is, how commonplace is it?

* * *

The crew is international, coming from the States, New Zealand and El Salvador and we have to gain entry to the plantations, film what is going on and hope the gang masters don't get too angry when we arrive unannounced. The challenge to find a way on to the fields proves to be more difficult than we thought as most of the plantations lie behind a curtain of trees and villages unseen from the road. Which is why Armando, our Salvadorean translator and driver, has taken to stopping at roadside stalls and quizzing locals as to where the crops are being harvested. The first attempt is unsuccessful, as is the second and the third too. Asking folk at random if they can help us in our search yields but one fact, which is this: the phrase, 'We're looking for working children' just sounds bad in any language.

David the American cameraman curtly says, 'Someone has got to know what the score is. Pull up and ask again.'

'I'll ask we need to be more direct.' I'm worried that Armando might just be a tad too polite to his fellow countrymen and women.

So I lean out of the front window at the next stall. Two old men in buttoned-up shirts and leather strap sandals stand staring at the empty road. They appear as if their whole purpose in life is just to stand there and collect furrows on their faces. And they are not doing too badly at it. I ask, in my admittedly imperfect Spanish and with help from the others, if the good gentlemen might know of any plantations cutting today that have a reputation for employing child labour?

They both shake their heads with one slow and barely discernible twist of the neck.

'*Gracias, señor*,' I say, turning back inside the van. 'Let's try again at the next stall, Armando.'

He swings the van off the dirt and back on to the tarmac, leaving the men to continue the wrinkle harvest. We drive in silence for a minute before Armando nonchalantly says, 'You are aware that you just told those people that we were 'hunting' children.'

'What?'

'You said to them 'we are hunting down children, can you help us?''

'Oh God...'

My head hits my hands. Here we are trying to investigate one of the blights of the developing world and I have made us look like the Child Catcher in *Chitty Chitty Bang Bang*.

Field one

There is one place we know for sure will be harvesting today, as we visited it last night to watch the foreman burn the crop ready for harvest. The sugar grows higher than a man and close together too, with big dry leaves and debris bunched in with the cane, making the job of harvesting all the more difficult. The simplest method of clearing this is set it alight.

The foreman is a young guy with not an ounce of fat on him and a metal plate over his front teeth. Last night he was happy for us to film the burning and even introduced his wife and child who have wandered over to watch the palavar of a film crew. He used a long dry leaf as a taper, lit it, inserted it deep into the detritus that litters the forest of tall cane, then stepped back. The flames jumped ten feet high with a low rushing rumble and a loud cackle that sounded as if the fire were chewing through the field. Left in its wake was black and dry earth and the prized cane, burnt on the edges, still hot to touch, scorched but standing in the drifting smoke ready for the next day.

The foreman had not expected to see us this morning and he does not smile this time. He just nods and snorts before turning his back and getting on with his work. Filming the burning is one thing but now there are children working in the fields and he is deeply suspicious of our presence.

'Hola, bueneos días,' I call, cheerfully and ineptly.

But he just looks blankly and continues grabbing the long cane with one hand and swinging the machete with the other. In a single motion he chops the stalk at the base, twists it free, cuts off the shoot end, clipping the remaining leaves and throwing the cane at a pile, where it lands with a rustle.

Nearby is a ten-year-old boy with his father who's cutting the cane. The boy's name is Jonathan, this is his first year working on the sugar cane harvest, he tells me. His job is to collect and stack the cane.

'You've come to earn some money?' I ask Jonathan.

He laughs and so does his dad. This work is piecework so a family needs as many helping hands as possible to earn a wage. Jonathan is one of the 25,000 child 'helpers'.

The kids are uneasy with our presence, so after a quick chat there is little need for us to stay and even less of an invitation to do so. But our first search has found two children working on a small six-acre site. If we are to find if the practice is commonplace or not we will need to look in other locations.

Heading back to the main drag we pass the company transport parked at an angle on a bank of earth just by the field. It's an old American-style yellow school bus, with Transporte de Personal Agrícola Ingenio Central Izalco (transport for the agricultural staff working for Central Izalco) written on the destination plate above the driver. Central Izalco the sugar mill has driven the workers down here to the fields, as they often do. Given the reputation for child labour in the area I wonder if the use of a school bus is an act of corporate irony.

As we bump along the narrow mud track, dodging dogs and grunting pigs, at one point we slow right down and inch past a homestead on the roadside. It consists of a sloping shelter made of palm leaves. The roof nearly extends to the ground at the rear and the two side walls are almost triangular. In the shaded light we can make out a wooden framed couch. To say there is no door on this shelter would be to miss the point, as there is no wall on which to hang it. Standing in front of it is a young mother washing bowls and she smiles as we pass. Her kids have all got thick scruffy morning hair, they look up too, while a chicken scuttles round their legs. They were all standing in the kitchen. But the use of the word kitchen in this instance leaves the word straining and groaning at the seams of its own meaning. The kitchen is an area in the dirt that has been swept. One sheet of corrugated iron stands upright to support a board and a bowl. In the middle of the orderly dirt is a table, with a couple of chairs and a single piece of wire runs around the whole area at waist height – tied to a tree here and a stick in the ground there – it is a boundary, just so we all know where the 'kitchen' actually is. I have wandered into this world without walls carrying a simplistic set of values picked up off the Fairtrade shelf, where kids working = bad. And I curse myself. I have forgotten that there is another equation here in this place where a piece of wire marks out a room, and this is as true as the first one and it is this: kids not working= really bad.

HRW clearly identifies the kids working/not working equation as they recommend that the sugar mills 'should never take actions that would deprive child laborers of their livelihoods without ensuring that children and their families are receiving programs and services designed to provide them with alternatives to hazardous labor.' It is better that children do hazardous work than go hungry. But, in an environment where the only options open to these children are starvation or hazardous labour, then The Coca-Cola Company has only one option, which is to make sure it isn't responsible in any way for either.

Field two

Barely minutes later along the highway we happen upon another harvest. Slowing as we approach we peer out of the van window. David the American squints, 'I can't tell how old these people are, they must be 200 metres away...'

At that moment a young man pops up and looks at us from the field. He was bent over cutting thus making it impossible to see how old he is, but straightening reveals he must be all of 13 – though David is right, it is hard to get an accurate age. Regardless of his exact age this young man is definitely too young to be working here. We know this because as soon as he sees our van with the camera, he runs rushing into the uncut cane and disappears. We have had only seconds to catch the look of panic on his face before he is swallowed by the dense green and brown stalks and hidden from sight.

The original HRW report had said, 'Plantation foremen turn a blind eye to the fact that children as young as eight cut cane.'[9] Since its publication I had heard that the foremen were now concerned not so much with using child labour, but with being *seen* to use child labour. Perhaps that is what the boy was doing. Trying to make sure the plantation was not seen to be using child labour.

Field three

Another ten minutes down the way and my suspicions are aroused again. This time a young lad, machete in hand, trims cane. Having learnt our lesson from the first incident we don't slow down, we drive on. Once out of sight, we turn around, head back and stop. The child is out in the open field when the van brakes suddenly, men near to him shout and he breaks for the refuge of the sugar cane, his legs splaying awkwardly as he hops over the stumps and stalks protruding from the ground. He disappears momentarily but can only have gone a few feet into the dense wooded canes, as he pokes his head out to take a quick peak, catches sight of us, and then vanishes once more.

Barely moments later a white jeep arrives on dirt track by the side of the field, carrying three officials from the Ministry of Labor. This looks like a spot check of some kind and they dismount the vehicle with considerable officiousness. Civil servants they may be but their walk is pure Sweeney. Or at least a version of the Sweeney that works out. Wearing smart short-sleeve shirts and even shorter necks, the body-building bureaucrats start to go through paperwork with the plantation foreman. Coca-Cola say the Ministry of Labor 'has labor inspectors whose only task is to detect child labor.'[10] Could we be witnessing the authorities clamping down on child labour? How will they find the lad who has just hidden? What will happen to him and the foreman?

Actually, nothing happens. Their inspection seems to be just checking papers. It might appear brusque but it is short, sweet and painless. As they get back into the jeep I run over with Armando translating and say, 'I wonder can I grab a few quick questions? My name is Mark Thomas from the UK.'

Sitting in the front passenger seat an official turns to me. His expression is that of a man who can't quite be arsed to be menacing, like a bouncer with a minor case of ennui. He rolls his shoulders and blankly says 'Hello' – though I am sure his shoulders just told me to 'fuck off'.

'I'm making a programme for TV in Britain and it looked like you were making an inspection and I just wondered what you were doing?' I say, all breezy and blasé.

He replies with a mixture of boredom and aggression, 'What the ministry does is check for children working here and for illegal immigrants.'

At this stage I realise I might as well be standing before him in plus fours with a 12-bore under my arm, spouting like a toff, 'I'm on a child hunt don't you know...'

Nonetheless I plough on, asking, 'Oh...is there much child labour here?'

'Here? No.'

'None at all?'

'Not here...' He says through rigid lips.

'None?'

'Not on this plantation.'

'You've checked for children working here illegally have you?'

'There is none here...at the moment...none.'

He rolls his shoulders at me. Twice.

* * *

Solving the problem of child labour involves a lot of different groups of people, including the Salvadorean Ministry of Labor. The HRW report highlights the complexity of the problems and is clear that it is not just the problem of one organisation. The solution, they say, will involve people from UNICEF, the Salvadorean Government, the Ministry of Education and the Ministry of Labor, as well as the sugar industry and Coca-Cola. The problem is that Coca-Cola seem to be taking a back seat on this particular example of problem solving. The HRW report made a series of recommendations that The Coca-Cola Company should adopt to play its part in eradicating child labour. Though there is no compulsion for the company to adhere to these recommendations it is worth noting that TCCC has not implemented a single one of them.

COLA-COLA'S REPORT CARD
DID THEY DO ANYTHING THE REPORT RECOMMENDED?

2004 HRW Recommend that Coca-Cola adhere to UN standards on child labour (which they do) and that they 'should require suppliers to do the same throughout their supply chains.'[11] This would mean insisting the sugar mill in turn insists that the plantation does not use child labour and this should be a contractual condition.

2008 Coca-Cola says in its Supplier Guiding principles that as a 'minimum' the 'Supplier will not use child labor as defined by local law.'[12] But does not require the supplier to enforce this through the supply chain.

They therefore do not meet that recommendation.

2004 HRW Recommend that Coca-Cola 'adopt effective monitoring systems to verify that labor conditions on their supplier sugarcane plantations comply with international standards and relevant national labor laws'[13]

2008 Coca-Cola says it is eradicating child labour by being 'part of a multi-stakeholder initiative *working towards hiring* [my emphasis] social monitors to work with the co-ops to monitor against child labour.'[14] So no one has been hired then...

2008 Mark Thomas is currently working towards a positive reaction to the above comment. Coca-Cola do not meet that recommendation.

2004 HRW Recommend 'In cases where plantations fall short of such standards, Coca-Cola and other businesses should assist their supplier mills in providing the economic and technical assistance necessary to bring plantations into compliance.'[15]

2008 The company says, 'Coca-Cola is eradicating child labour by being a part of a multi-stakeholder initiative *working towards hiring* social monitors...to provide education and income streams in collaboration with government and NGOs to divert youth from hazardous work in the harvest.[16]

2008 Mark Thomas is engaged in a multi-stakeholder dialogue that is working towards the eradication of derision of such corporate statements.

There is no evidence that Coca-Cola have met this recommendation.

2004 HRW Recommend 'In particular, Coca-Cola and other businesses should support programs and services that offer children and their families alternatives to child labor, publicly reporting the status of such efforts at least on an annual basis.'[17]

2008 Coca-Cola 'has partnered with TechnoServe, a local NGO working with targeted co-ops to find alternative sources of income for youth 14-18 years of age.'[18]

2008 Mark Thomas asked 'What is the nature of the partnering of TechnoServe? Was there any financial assistance involved? Have there been any assessments made of the results of the partnering and if so, by whom?'

2008 Coca-Cola replied 'We partnered with TechnoServe to financially support the programs that aid children through educational opportunities in El Salvador.'[19] Er, that is it...

The Company have not provided any details of the financial support it gives to TechnoServe, nor have they shown that the work they partnered with TechnoServe is addressing the specific issue of children in sugar cane harvesting. Nor do they show if the children TechnoServe are working with are being offered alternatives to child labour. And they just ignored the question regarding annual assessment.

Therefore, Coca-Cola have not fully and properly met the recommendations made by the Human Rights Watch Report.

Sitting in the front of the van and leaning on the side window, the sound of the wheels' low continuous rumble on the road is comforting and I turn to itemising the day. So far this morning has yielded child labour working on the three fields we visited, two of the boys have tried to hide from us to avoid being seen to work and the Ministry of Labor seem uninterested, at best, in doing anything today. But what this all amounts to I simply don't know. Does what we have seen make child labour on these plantations commonplace? Perhaps what we are seeing represents progress? The only thing I know for sure is that running around plantations filming child labour doesn't make you friends. I couldn't be less popular if I were the UK entry for the Eurovision Song Contest. In fact an outbreak of chlamydia in a nunnery would be greeted with less hostility.

My road-trip meditation is broken as we brake sharply to let a truck out of some gates and on to the highway. This is a *rastras*, a sugar cane lorry, which is essentially a truck with an enormous metal container coupled to it. These containers are almost literally huge rust buckets, 40 to 50 foot long perhaps and when they are piled high with cane they are easily 18 to 20 feet high. They lumber along the narrow roads, swinging from side to side, with odd sticks of cane falling from the uncovered top. So monstrous and unique are these mechanical beasts that it is a small wonder that *Top Gear* hasn't raced them across a conservation area yet.

'Where do these go?' I ask.

'They go to the sugar mill,' says Armando, 'they load up with cane on the plantations and then take it to the mill to be refined.'

'So that lorry has just come out of a plantation then...'

Field four

The gates to the plantation are tall and iron and come with a gatekeeper, an old man in a battered straw hat who is in charge of the padlock and chain. As another truck comes out we act as if we are expected and go through. He shuts the gates behind us and we are in, on a dirt track surrounded by tall green sugar cane, taller than the van it leans over the pathway forming a shady lane. This is all plantation land, behind the gates and away from prying eyes. No one expects to see a film crew in a van cruising around these tropical pathways and their expressions of surprise prove to be unnerving. The first harvest we come to has a group of about five or six children standing with machetes. They are young children. Maybe eight years old. One awkwardly puts the machete down when she sees us, holding it by their side and then cautiously dropping it, as if she had been caught doing something naughty. She looks at us and then runs to her parents working further away. Turning down a fork in the track we stop alongside a boy who is standing just off the road cutting. We are so unexpected that he looks up to find the van practically next to him. He too is underage. Through one corridor of cane a group of kids on bikes appear, catch sight of us, drop their heads, lift their backsides out of the saddle and pump their legs in panic, cycling madly to get as far away from us as they can get.

Further still we arrive at the main harvesting field to find a vision of seething toil. The men's vests and T-shirts are patched with sweat already and the sun is still far from its midday prime, their hands are black with soot and their faces smudged with ash too. Predictably the sad regularity of the scene unfolds. A young boy in a white shirt is in the cropped area, exposed for all to see, including the foreman who stands watching with his machete in a leather sheaf decorated with tassels slung over his chest. His older and legal workmates shout to him that we are here. He turns in utter confusion and starts to run, but not towards the dense cane that can hide him, but across the cleared field. He throws a long handled shovel to the ground. Someone shouts for him not to panic, 'Pick it up! Act normal!' they must have bellowed. In his chaos he picks up the shovel again but starts to run. 'Don't draw attention to yourself!' Someone must have shouted, as he slows down and walks to the edge of the field. Trying to gently let go of the long-handled shovel as he goes. He has made it to the path, where older workers are watching. He puts his head down, his hands in his pocket and walks away from us. He goes to turn around but seems to hear an older voice nearby, saying 'Just keep walking kid, just keep walking.'

Through it all, the foreman just stands there with one hand holding the machete sitting on his fat stomach. He has not even bothered to turn a blind eye to it all. He watches the whole thing, down to the kid disappearing into the plantations pathways. Along the pathway at the side a few workers stand watching, and it looks like the owner has arrived, or at least someone with money enough to ride a horse around the plantation with a pair of cowboy boots and a posh cowboy hat. No one talks to us directly, but you could cut the atmosphere with a knife and there are plenty of those around here. They stare at us with poker faces. Then turn back and as one group of men does this one of them spits. I couldn't say if it was out of necessity or with contempt. But what I hear next is definitely shouted for our benefit, as one of the *caneros* in the field yells, 'Come and look at the animals! Come watch the animals!'

Oh Christ, look at us, chasing children as they flounder and flee. Charles Dickens would have loved to have seen us in action, 'the kid hunters', caring beadles with compassionless hearts, terrifying youngsters so they can have a better life. We've been tracking kids like Fairtrade perverts. No wonder the cutters hate us. They hate our presence. Perhaps the landowners do too, but the landowners won't lose one moment's sleep over our visit; we've caused them neither distress nor loss. We have not even reprimanded them nor the plantation managers or the foremen either. But our very presence reprimands the cutters, the families and the children. Just standing by the field, we judge them, our presence alone says, 'you shouldn't be letting your children work on the cane harvest'. But what are they to do, go without money? So we judge them for having to work like this. We judge them for being poor. Intentionally or not, that is what we do. They did not asked us to come, they did not want to tell their story.

For all our discomfort, which is nothing compared to the discomfort of actually having to work in these fields, the fact remains that child labour is obviously present on an unacceptable scale. Our film crew, none of whom know the area, or have had any experience of harvesting cane, have in one morning managed to bumble through cane fields and found, by our reckoning, at least 15 children working. Which goes some way to showing that child labour is still commonplace, and on the plantations that provide the raw materials for Coke's sugar.

It would be glib and wrong to say The Coca-Cola Company don't care about this issue. They do – they say so on their website. 'We care about the plight of these children,'[20] they say. They also say. 'We firmly oppose the use of child labour.'[21] Yet despite this and their multitude of codes and practices there is a glaring loophole. The Coca-Cola Company has a

Global Workplace Rights Policy that says, 'The Company prohibits the hiring of individuals that are under eighteen years of age for positions in which hazardous work is required.'[22] OK, that's fine. They have Supplier Guiding Principles, for direct suppliers like Central Izalco, which state that the 'Supplier will not use child labor as defined by local law.'[23] But some countries do not have adequate laws. Nothing compels either The Coca-Cola Company or the sugar mills to investigate, take responsibility or prevent children harvesting cane on the plantations – no matter what happens further down the supply chain, it is simply not their problem. And until they make it their problem they will be open to the charge of not trying to solve it.

Last night as we filmed the foreman burning the dry leaves in the cane field, cutters told me that the Central Izalco engineers will tell the plantation owners which cane to cut, where, when and how much. The *rastras* have to know where to come to pick up the cane to take it to the mill and the cutters are often driven in company buses to the crops. HRW found that 'Central Izalco directly administers some of its plantations and provides technical assistance to those it does not administer directly.'[24] It is impossible for Central Izalco not to know about the child labour happening under their eyes. But such are the loopholes that a manager from Central Izalco could find children cutting sugar cane literally outside the mill, walk past without batting an eyelid and still comply with all of Coke's codes of conduct and principles. And this is what we witness next.

Field five

Leaving the plantation we tuck behind one of the large *rastras* as it heads to the sugar mill – Central Izalco. There is no other mill in the area but we should double check that the cane cut here is going to Coke's sugar supplier. So we settle into the whirr of the wheels on the road and the warm sun on the forearms that dangle out of the window alongside the van. The lorry sways along the road as it heads to the mill with the cane that children helped cut.

The *rastra* turns off the main highway onto a dirt track that leads to the sugar mill. The truck churns the ground into dust under the weight of its sweet load. The huge lorry turns tightly into an even tighter tunnel that goes under the road it has just left. There is only just enough room to get through and our van follows into the darkness and swirling clouds of dirt, missing the chance to wind the windows up and emerging into the sunlight with an added layer of grime. The truck continues to the mill, while we stop. Just next to this dirt track is a field being harvested, right under the Central Izalco water tower, which is shaped like a turnip on stilts and painted in red and white with the company name in bold: it is impossible to miss. As are the children working in the field below it. Three children, one as young as ten, are working harvesting cane, one cutting, another tying, they all look sheepish and pull baseball hats low over their eyes at the sight of us. And all of this is within view of the sugar mill. If a manager cared to look out of a window they would see the children working outside their mill, right under their noses. You would have to stick pokers in your eyes to miss it. How much more obvious can it get? Outside the fucking company office! For all their codes and PR guff the mill's managers can sit watching the kids hacking cane all day and would still be in total compliance with Coke's 'principles' if they did absolutely nothing. And from what I can see here this is exactly what they are doing.

The Company say 'we have made tremendous progress' on child labour, claiming to have been involved in the removal of 9,000 children from the sugar cane fields.[25] Let us assume this claim stands up to scrutiny: if you have sorted out 9,000 kids, how come there are children are working in broad daylight outside the sugar mill Coke use, and no one does a thing? Not one thing. Coca-Cola – were you so busy with the 9,000 you missed the ones outside the mill? Until the children are out of these fields and either in school or in legal non-hazardous work then every bottle and can coming out of El Salvador should be labelled: May contain child labour.

THREE THINGS COCA-COLA HAS DONE ON CHILD LABOUR

On its website, The Coca-Cola Company lists ways in which it is helping eradicate child labour in the El Salvador Sugar Industry. Warning – may contain corporate speak. For lovers of the nonsensical, whet your whistles here.

1) 'On Coca-Cola's recommendation, Fundazucar (the Salvadorean Sugar Association) engaged a social compliance auditing firm that helped the Association determine how to detect and control child labour and associated issues.'[26]

Coca-Cola have essentially said – 'oh you should do something about that,' and then listed this as a contribution in the fight against child labour. I repeat: the company didn't actually do anything themselves, they recommended someone else do something. And the something they recommended someone else to do, was hire another someone, to advise the first someone on how to detect child labour.

I would like to recommend that if they want to detect child labour, they look out of the window at Central Izalco. They can have that one for free.

2) 'Coca-Cola has publicly supported the proposal, authored by the World Bank and Business for Social Responsibility, to help position El Salvador as a responsible-sourcing country.'[27]

Oh, publicly supporting a proposal...is that like a petition? Did they sign a petition to end child labour? Hurrah! Now can I put a marker down for ending apartheid? I distinctly remember buying a 'Free Nelson Mandela' badge back in the 1980s...Actually come to think of it I signed a petition against the Indonesian occupation of East Timor and the bastards haven't thanked me yet...

3) 'Nine thousand children have been removed from the sugar cane fields in El Salvador over the last three years through our efforts with the UN and the Sugar Association.'[28]

That is more like it; 9,000 kids out of child labour! Well done. I have asked Coca-Cola how many of those 9,000 were removed from plantations that provide cane for Central Izalco? What was the nature of the work they did with the UN that has led to this?

The Coca-Cola Company replied, 'We have also participated in multi-stakeholder dialogues that have included the International Labor Organisation of the UN to understand and address the root causes of this serious issue in El Salvador.'[29]

7
DODGE CITY

London, UK

'It is not just Corporate Responsibility, it is doing the right thing.'

The Coca-Cola Company[1]

The afternoon sun is hitting the diesel fug in Central London and I am sitting in the visitors' cafeteria of the House of Commons when a woman from Coca-Cola's Human Resources looks at me across the table with earnest eyes and asks one of the best questions I have ever been asked. She says, 'Why are you picking on us?'.

There are few other people in the tearoom and the clink of cutlery being collected just nudges above the low hum of the chiller units that hold the sandwiches and yoghurts. In this setting and with a plastic tray placed on the table between us, the question has a strangely domestic tone to it. Almost as if the woman from Coca-Cola's Human Resources department is going to tug her chair closer to the table and say in a lowered voice, 'You've been seeing other multinationals, haven't you?'

It is a chance encounter, both of us have arrived early for a debate, decided to get a cup of tea and being the only people waiting at the till had got chatting. Her name is Clare, she is in her early thirties and I assume her question refers to past articles I have written along with a TV documentary I had presented all of which were critical of the company. Though I never imagined that investigating them might amount to 'picking on' Coca-Cola. It is tempting to reply, 'Why am I picking on a $67 billion transnational that sponsors the Olympic Games, the Football League and can summon US ambassadors to do its bidding? I guess I am just a bully...'

But actually I am slightly stunned by the question, because the words 'picking on' imply that the company is an innocent victim, blameless in fact; and more than that, not only are my questions to the company intimidatory but I am a flawed person for even asking them.

This is the second occasion where a Coke employee has accused me of picking on them, the first coming in the form of an anonymous email, sent by someone who claimed to work for the company. He also accused me of being a liar and hoped the company would take me to court. So I wonder, is the company's internal response to certain critical coverage to label it as the usual suspects- 'picking on us'? I don't know the answer and in the cafeteria my thoughts are not quite this cogent as I stammer out a response to Clare, 'I don't think I am picking on Coca-Cola, is questioning a company picking on them?'

'No, I mean why us?' she says with a tight face, 'why don't you pick on Pepsi?'

This is indeed an entirely reasonable question to ask, especially were it to come from anyone not associated with Coca-Cola.

'They simply do not have the same amount of human rights allegations lined up against them,' I reply.

Pepsi are certainly no paragon of virtue, they were criticised along with Coca-Cola in India over pesticides found in their products,[2] likewise Pepsi and Coca-Cola were fined over painting adverts on the Himalayas in a conservation area.[3] But while Pepsi may parallel Coke in some instances they come a resounding second in amassing form.

'I suppose we are just an easy target,' she continues, managing to keep a sneer out of her voice, but only just.

'No, you're not an easy target, you're just a big one,' I reply.

At this point a friend who is also attending the debate comes into the cafeteria and my chance encounter with Clare from Human Resources ends, the stairs beckon to the cavernous Great Hall of the Palace of Westminster and from there the committee rooms. It is time to go, we shake hands, smile politely and lie to each other.

'Nice meeting you,' we both say.

* * *

The debate in House of Commons committee room is on multinationals, labour and human rights and it features one of the stars in Coca-Cola's fizzy firmament, a man called Ed Potter who is their Global Workplace Rights Director. He is a cornerstone in the company's Corporate Social Responsibility programme. Let me explain a little. Fashion and fads afflict us all, none of us are truly immune from collective stupidity and corporations are just as prone as the rest of us. Management trends might be more rarified but they are equally humiliating. There was, for example, the mimicking of Japanese company methods, where employees had to endure doing morning exercises with their boss and sing anthems to productivity. The next boardroom fad was the New Age Executive. They never wore a tie to work, played Frisbee during brain-storming sessions and insisted everyone call them by their first name, thus ensuring everyone called them 'tosser'. There was also the obsession with team cohesion and group motivation, this was where managers increased their output as a result of an epiphany during paintballing and accountants bonded by building rafts out of dead okapis, or some such nonsense.

The latest fad is Corporate Social Responsibility where companies construct a series of programmes, projects, charitable pledges, codes of conduct and impact assessments, to show the beneficence of the company. No one working for a multinational listed on the stock exchange can buy a copy of the *Big Issue* without boasting of a contribution to society. For some it is nothing but a PR tool to convince doubters that multinationals are good corporate citizens. However, there are those with a genuine belief in Corporate Social Responsibility who argue that multinationals and transnationals are hugely powerful entities that have the capacity to improve social conditions through the workplace. Globalisation and neo-liberal economics are not just a reality but the dominant consensus amongst politicians, corporations and ruling elites. Thus, supporters of CSR argue, there is a potential for consumers to pressure companies to change, as governments seem disinclined and unable to legislate against corporate excesses. For some Corporate Social Responsibility is the only game in town.

Regardless of your perspective most CSR programmes will invariably do two things. Firstly, it will devise a code of conduct. In turn this will underline the company's aim not to discriminate against their employees on the grounds of race, religion or gender. Considering that it is illegal to do any of the above in the UK, these declarations essentially say, 'It is our policy not to break the law.' And when a company feels the need to publicly promise not to engage in criminal acts, I for one do not feel reassured. Nonetheless, codes of conduct are ubiquitous features on the business landscape and everyone seems to have one. Even the trade association of the Adult Entertainment Industry in America has a draft Code of Ethics for porn makers in which they acknowledge their commitments to employees stating that 'Adult performers are the backbone of the adult entertainment industry.'[4] Surely a fact beyond dispute.

The second item of the company CSR plan will be a pledge to 'go green'; just about every multinational has declared their intent to join in and do their bit to save the planet. BAE Systems, the arms dealers, are seeking to reduce carbon emissions on their munitions, so as 'to impact as little as possible on the environment.'[5] Hurrah! I can hardly wait for a computers-for-schools voucher with every 'precision' weapon! Meanwhile the oil giant BP is 'committed to the responsible treatment of the planet's resources.'[6] Of course they are, who would think anything less. It is now only a matter of time before Hell itself converts to solar power.

One of the central tenets of CSR is the workers' right to join a union and back on planet Cola allegations of union busting have been stacking up against the company. Alongside the Colombians and the Turks, trade union organisers from Pakistan and Indonesia claimed to have been sacked and mistreated for their union membership. Not to mention Russia.

Not surprisingly The Coca-Cola Company embraced the world of Corporate Social Responsibility with vigour and vim: pledges were made, policies and guidelines written, reports commissioned, websites were set up and a new position was created within the company: Global Workplace Rights Director. The chap who got the job was Ed Potter – the man speaking in the debate today. American Ed Potter is an ex-lawyer with a background in international labour and employer issues. He reports directly to The Coca-Cola Company board on 'workplace rights' and oversees the company programme. It is Ed Potter who is responsible for Coke's 2005 pledge to respect trade unions' rights. So he's the man to answer the questions on Coca-Cola and trade unions. Stuck away in Atlanta and with a heavy travel schedule it could prove difficult to engineer a meeting with him. So it is fortuitous that Ed Potter is here in London to address these issues.

The term progressive is a relative term, when governments claim to be progressive they mean out of touch, when musicians claim to be progressive it means they are so skilled and clever that no one actually likes them, and when think tanks claim to be progressive it means they will take funding from anyone. The debate in the House of Commons was hosted by the Foreign Policy Centre, a progressive think tank. Their slogan is 'Progressive thinking for a global age.' They have Tony Blair as a patron and have accepted 'generous support' from British Nuclear Fuels plc, BP, GKN, Nestlé and British American Tobacco. Today's debate is sponsored by The Coca-Cola Company, who join the illustrious names listed above.

The committee room is typical of the House of Commons, but for the fact that it is packed with people. The windows are leaded glass, the wallpaper decorated with heraldic lilies and roses, the ceiling is carved wood and the seats have the portcullis embossed in gold, but all of this merely serves to emphasise the fact that no one does grandeur quite so dully as the British. Somewhere a clock ticks loudly in agreement.

The place continues to fill up with a disparate mix of folk. Students and journalists rub shoulders with company executives, policy wonks and MPs' researchers, who in turn sit alongside non-government organisations and trade unionists, not to mention the smattering of over-qualified graduates hoping for a job. Most of the people from the rarified world of CSR are here, from the great and the good to the average and poor, there are no curious bystanders in this room. Everyone has a view and if you listen carefully, above the clock and the low hubbub you can distinctly hear the sound of axes grinding.

Arriving to the near-capacity crowd someone hands me a programme and I am gently propelled by a series of polite interns towards one of the few remaining seats, which is right in the front row, directly opposite Ed Potter who is sitting at the speakers' table with a little name card in front of him.

The woman chairperson sits in the middle of the four male speakers. At one end of the table is Peter Frankental from Amnesty International sporting a smart jacket and tie and looking like an RE teacher. Next to him is Michael Blowfield who is a real teacher at the London Business School and is a senior associate with the University of Cambridge Programme for Industry. His grey suit is either just from or just going to Oxfam: you don't need a good suit if you're really clever. On the other side of the chairperson is Brendan Barber, who like all previous TUC leaders, manages to wear a good suit badly. Next to him is Ed Potter in a tailored black suit with white pinstripes, a light grey shirt, a darker grey tie and black leather shoes. He has the best suit in the room, anything less would be unacceptable. If you represent the most powerful brand on earth you are not going to show up in tweed and leather elbow patches. It is just not done; it would be like the Pope getting a cock-ring.

The chair, one of the think tank, welcomes us to 'a series on Corporate Social Responsibility in emerging markets, in association with Coca-Cola Great Britain. This programme seeks to explore the issue of Corporate Social Responsibility in developing markets focusing on multinational corporations. It will examine the impact of multinational businesses on the workplace, marketplace and the environment as well as explore how well-designed CSR practices can contribute to economic social and environmental progress in newly industrial countries...' Somewhere a Business Studies student accidentally snaps the lead point of their pencil on their notepad in tense anticipation. The rest of us settle into our seats.

Ed Potter is trim, with thinning grey hair cut close to his scalp, thin-rimmed glasses and a few liver spots on the back of his hands. He must be in his late fifties or early sixties but I couldn't guess exactly. He is pleasant, polite and not prone to over excitement. He is careful and low key as he stands at the podium and outlines what needs to be done to improve 'global workplace rights'. Not long ago talk of workers rights would be wreathed in the oratory of struggle and sacrifice, today Ed Potter tells us they rely on 'a commitment to global and local stakeholder engagement.' In the word of Corporate Social Responsibility the real battle against worker exploitation needs a 'focus on aligned common business approach' and a 'commitment to get out in front of issues that are systemic in nature.' In the hushed tones of the room I'm sure I hear another pencil lead go...But it might have been the sound of a neck cricking as a slumped head jerks itself into the upright position.

Soft-spoken and mannered Ed Potter might be, but you don't get to be a lawyer in international law and employment for twenty-three years without having a hard streak somewhere.

So when Brendan Barber of the TUC mentions that there are 'unresolved issues in Colombia' Ed Potter doesn't flinch. When Peter Frankental from Amnesty International says 'Coca-Cola has been tainted by association of human rights abuses in Colombia,' Ed Potter seemingly registers nothing. Frankental continues, 'Coca-Cola were exonerated by the district judge in Miami in 2003 on the grounds that its bottling agreement with Panamerican Beverages and Bebidas Y Aliementos did not give the company explicit control over labour issues in Colombia. However, the fact that a company is exonerated by the courts does not mean that it has no moral responsibility.' Surely this is a gauntlet of sorts, thrown at Coke's feet for Ed Potter to pick up. He has to comment on this, doesn't he?

I take a good look at Ed Potter, a mere arms' length away. He is slowly doodling a large picture of a Coke bottle on an A4 pad, complete with curve lines and a passable imitation of the classic script.

Finally the floor is thrown open to queries, observations and comments. Someone from British American Tobacco asks about the forgotten plight of poor farmers in developing countries. And is taken seriously...If ever you want a measuring stick for CSR then this might be the moment, when a representative from British American Tobacco asks about workplace rights and security for farmers and doesn't get laughed out of the room.

The interventions continue apace. Journalists from the *Independent* and *Corporate Age* ask about the effectiveness of CSR and how to improve it. Points are made from the floor about the increasing feminisation of poverty and questions raised about the relationship of neo-liberal globalisation to CSR.

But Ed Potter is still attracting flak and is heckled by members of the Colombian Solidarity Campaign, keen to question The

Coca-Cola Company's response to the murders of trade
unionists in Colombia. We are about to learn that Ed Potter's
twenty-three years' experience as an American lawyer has
made him a blackbelt at avoidance. He deftly draws a line
between the bottlers in Colombia and The Coca-Cola Company
in Atlanta, the way the Company has always done. 'The
situation to which you are describing is one that involves our
independent bottlers in Colombia,' he says, that is an issue that
Coca-Cola FEMSA [the current Colombian bottlers] can address.'

Amnesty's man picks up this particular point when it is his
turn to respond to questions, arguing that human rights and
labour rights should be treated as a quality-control issue.
If a bottle was contaminated by the bottlers in Colombia,
distributed around the world and affected people's health,
'would Coca-Cola have tried to distance themselves from the
responsibility? Would they say that it is not their responsibility,
it is that of their franchise bottling plants? I don't think they
would say that. And they would not be allowed to.' So argued
Amnesty's man adding, 'any products we consume that have
human rights' violations in their making should be seen as a
defective product.' In essence, if Coca-Cola can treat
contaminated product as its responsibility then they should do
the same for human rights abuse.

And this must apply to everyone The Coca-Cola Company
works with, from the bottlers, to the distributors, to the sugar
refineries, to the plantation workers – every single man,
woman and subcontracted jack of them. It is not enough, said
Amnesty, to be 'committed to working with and encouraging
them [that is, the independent bottling partners] to uphold the
principles in the policy [i.e., workplace rights]'. Amnesty argue
that all parts of Coke's supply chain should regard human and
labour rights as 'a compliance issue and [there] has to be

sanctions against their suppliers, just as there would be if there were any technical defect in the product.'

This seemed like an appropriate point to jump in and try and muscle an answer out of Ed Potter, so I ask 'When are you going to introduce codes of conduct for subcontractors and what measures are you going to bring in to enforce it?'

Ed Potter looks through his thin glasses directly at me. His soft voice gets a rasp around its edge. He stops still and slowly says 'The question you are asking is a question that keeps me up at night.' He said it in such a way that I would not have been shocked if he had pulled put an acoustic guitar and sung his reply Johnny Cash-style. Then in true lawyer fashion he promptly ignores my question and asks the question he wants to answer, namely, 'What is the most effective way that a company can address workplace rights issues not only for ourselves but our independent bottlers and in the supply chain?' And how does Ed Potter answer his own question? He doesn't! He waffles evasively and manages to even dodge his own question. He must have been one hell of a lawyer.

As politicians and celebrities will concur, the distance between the finish of a formal occasion and the start of the car journey home, is measured not in minutes or metres but mishaps. It is in this arena that punches and eggs are thrown, knickers and ignorance shown and questions and answers improvised. Here you are not limited to asking one question and waiting for a morsel of a reply, here be dragons, arguments, oaths and curses. Any fool can wander into this unscripted landscape and they frequently do. So as the debate closes and the chair reads out the details of the next event over the sound of scraping chairs, the PR minders are on the alert. Ed Potter stands to pack his briefcase, inserting the doodle of a coke bottle, kept safe for a possible framing at a later date. Or maybe when the board ask him, 'What got done in London?' he can just hold up the picture with a smile.

Ed Potter already has a couple of people vying for his attention

'Mr Potter,' I interrupt, ' I wonder is there any chance we could arrange a time to have a quick chat about some of the issues?'

'Um...well...' he says looking over my shoulder seeking assistance from a minder, 'Well...I...er'

He is interrupted by a woman in her thirties, with long dark hair and a slightly clipped Home Counties' accent. She is Communications Director at Coca-Cola Great Britain and she is professionally polite, by which I mean she is wary, motivated and undoubtedly the product of numerous management training programmes.

'Can I help?'

'I just wanted to try and get five minutes with Ed Potter.'

Her answer is sure-footed and rapid fire, 'I can see if we can sort something out. It might be possible...' she says flicking her hair, first one way and then the next, all the while keeping intense eye contact, giving her the appearance of a barn owl advertising shampoo. Then quickly changing tack, almost urgently she says, 'Look, what do you want, Mark?'

'Pardon?'

'What do you want? What is it you want us to do? I mean you are looking at a company that is trying to change. They want to change!'

'Do they?'

'You are pushing at an open door.'

'Well, the company could try answering my questions to them...'

Another minder is moving towards us, Ed has extracted himself from the gaggle and is heading to the door with one of Coke's PR/security people in tow, but they have been momentarily distracted by one of the crowd and peel off from Ed Potter. Seeing him leaving I blurt, 'Excuse me' and lunge after him.

'Mr Potter I wonder...'

'I have to go...I have a plane...' he says pointing to the door.

I press on, 'You'll be at the company annual general meeting in Delaware in April?'

'Er...Yeah. Yeah I will.'

'Well I'm coming to the States for that too, so maybe we can grab five minutes for a chat?' On his own and with no minders in earshot maybe, just maybe he will say yes.

'Well if it was up to me...you know, back when I was a lawyer I would have said yes...but er....' he motions with his hand at the incoming group of PR closing towards us. They push past chairs, in their immaculate dark clothes, with speed and stealth.

'In principle would you mind?' I hurriedly say to Ed Potter.

'In principle, no, I don't mind...'

'Well, if you don't mind in principle it is just a matter of logistics isn't it?'

The question hangs in the air for a second before a woman with bundled hair and a US accent says, 'Talk to Lauren about it. We'll see if we can sort something out.' She takes Ed Potter's elbow. Two other Coca-Cola people have appeared at his other side, 'He has to go,' says one of them.

The hair flicker appears behind me. 'We'll try and sort something out. Here let me give you my number.'

I turn back and Ed Potter is almost out of the room in a phalanx of Coca-Cola employees. And in the confusion I thought I saw one of the Coke people in a suit and shades talk into the sleeve of his jacket...But I could be making this bit up.

POSTSCRIPT

Ed Potter and Coca-Cola declined a formal interview.

When I returned home after the debate my wife Jenny was helping our daughter with her homework. I interrupted them, telling Jenny of my meeting with Clare from Human Resources and her comment that I was picking on Coke because they were an easy target. My wife looked up briefly from a page of equations and said, 'If they are worried about being such an easy target tell them they shouldn't be so crap.'

8
LET THEM DIG WELLS

Nejapa, El Salvador

'We are commited to working with our neighbors to help build stronger communities and enhance individual opportunity.'

The Coca-Cola Company[1]

The second leg of my visit to El Salvador is far from the sugar plantations and the coastal tides, but it does find the film crew and I once more ensconced in a hire van currently traversing a four-lane intersection somewhere in San Salvador – the capital. All of us are screaming, braced against the seat in front and are wide-eyed with panic as we are just experiencing a 50-mile-an-hour near collision with a six-foot portrait of Jesus. In El Salvador there are few rules of the road and even fewer observances of them. The only traffic regulation that everyone seems to obey is the strict ban on any kind of signalling. Thus it was that a large municipal bus abruptly changed lanes lurching in front of our speeding van with all the calm precision of a drunk staggering for the toilet. The bus is one of the old US school-style buses, it's dented, rusty and looks like it has just escaped from a Fabulous Furry Freak Brothers cartoon, it is also covered in religious iconography, prayers, crucifixes and a life-size Jesus painted in blue on the back of the bus

Suddenly finding ourselves inches away from Jesus and imminent death we all scream 'Fuck!!!!!!!' directly at the Son of God. The van brakes in a haze of tyre-shredding smoke and the battered bus pulls ahead. Jesus looks at us, standing in his robes, hands spread at his sides, almost shrugging, as if to say, 'What can I do about it?' And as the adrenalin begins to subside and we begin to extract our fingers from seat-rests the irony of dying in a collision with the Lord begins to sink in. It occurs to me that in this highly religious country it must be strangely comforting if a pedestrians last thoughts are, 'I've just been run over by Jesus.'

Prior to my arrival all that I knew about El Salvador had been learnt from a T-shirt. Back in the 1980s T-shirts were a major source of information, especially for the Left. If there was a subject you didn't understand, all you had to do was to turn up at a demonstration and read the appropriate garment. Every social movement in the world had a shirt. It seemed as if revolutionaries had given up on seizing radio stations and at the first whiff of rebellion would storm the local flea market and surround the 'Your name or picture printed here' stall.

The particular T-shirt I'm referring to was owned by a supporter of the El Salvador solidarity campaign. Printed on it was a map showing El Salvador to be in Central America, somewhere under Mexico and above Panama. Given that most countries in Central America have been subject to US intervention of sort, it was almost inevitable that the accompanying slogan was 'US OUT OF EL SALVADOR'. So I imagined the place to be full of armoured cars, goose-stepping soldiers and generals in dark glasses with a penchant for putting jump leads on opponents' genitals. Which at one point it was. The civil war lasted twelve years and ended in 1992. According to the CIA out of a population of just under 7 million, a total of 75,000 people lost their lives in the war.[2] Others put the number at 300,000 killed, though no one gives a figure for how many of these deaths were caused by buses.

Driving through the city Armando, our translator and driver, is lecturing us on its dangers. 'We have so many gangs here and so many guns. It is terrible. You have to be careful of the gangs it is a real problem. Seriously, this is the most violent problem...' Then as we circumnavigate a roundabout he stops mid flow and says 'I hate this place!'

He is referring to what appears to be a memorial, a plinth and possibility the tallest flagpole I have ever seen, it must be at least five stories high at least and dominates the whole area. 'What's written on the plinth?'
   '"Patriotism Yes, Communism No." It's a very famous quote made by Major Roberto D'Aubussion' He navigates the roundabout pausing briefly 'This guy, D'Aubussion he was the father of the death squads here.'

Roberto D'Aubussion was a charismatic leader for the right wing, and his nickname was 'Blowtorch Bob'. The clue is in the name. Can anyone think of a civil rights leader or progressive figure that has a nickname based on building tools? 'Pliers Luther King'? No. 'Gandhi the Mallet'? No. Basically if your moniker is linked to anything sold by Black and Decker then it is more than likely that you are a cunt. This is a hell of a monument to erect to so recent a war criminal.

Armando sighs and continues, 'So the gangs, a lot of them are armed....'

The one thing for sure about The Coca-Cola Company is that it never knowingly undersells itself. It can't have passed your attention that Coke does love to wrap itself in the cloak of its own benevolence, and one of its proud boasts is the company's commitment to working in sustainable communities. 'As the world's largest beverage company...' so starts Neville Isdell, former CEO of Coke '....we have a presence in people's lives that reaches beyond that magical moment of providing that simple moment of refreshment...'[3] Wow, who would have thought a fizzy pop salesman could have that much self-worth. Neville Isdell continues 'We're also an employer, a business partner, part of the community, a global citizen; and I believe we must play our role in supporting sustainable communities.'[4] Who knew Coca-Cola had so many roles, the only one he left out was 'whore in the bedroom'.

To find out what kind of a role Coke plays in a sustainable community I am visiting Nejapa, a rural town some ten miles drive from the city. I would describe it as having one main street but that is typical of my tendency to exaggerate. Other towns and cities have main arteries to traverse, Nejapa...well let's just say the van jostled along the main capillary. The street is lined with single-storey squat houses, once painted in bright colours that are now bleached by the sun. The shops are essentially people's living rooms containing a few shelves, packs of biscuits, batteries and a Coke fridge. Next to a mural of Che a middle-aged woman sells lunch from an aluminium pot perched on a table. Downwind of her an older woman squats by a rug full of lemons laid out in the street. Opposite and under the shade of an improvised awning boys in black sleeveless T-shirts, baggy shorts and baseball caps listen to Latin hip hop. The speakers sit outside trailing wires across the street through a front door.

The town square is a cultural mix. It has the classic simplistic charm of any decent Western combined with the utilitarian finesse of a 1950s' British housing estate. So opposite an evocative white-walled church with a bell tower and brown wooden doors lies a kids' playground with some creaky swings and a slide. A toddler rocks back and forth on a scuffed plastic chipmunk which is nailed into the ground on a bendy spring, while a father looks on. If Ken Loach ever remade *For Few Dollars More* or Sergio Leone ever remade *Kathy Come Home*, this would be their location. Old men in straw hats sit on benches watching the square while women in shawls head to church. As for the handful of street dogs that stumble in the heat, they look good for nothing but swerving a car around. If I said that not much happens here I would be lying. It is less than that. Or at least that is how is seems, because this is the place that Coca-Cola forgot to sustain but this community fought back. And won.

The Mayor of Nejapa is a wily fellow and with having won four elections, he's popular too. His name is Rene Canjura and his office is just by the municipal gardens in the square. He is short, fit and dresses like a trade unionist on a Saturday night out – smart trousers and a casual checked button-down shirt. Rene loves football. His office is full of cups and trophies of little silver footballers. But the heart of the room are two pictures on his wall. One of them is the obligatory framed Che Guevara print. Every left-winger in Latin America has one. It's almost religious. I wouldn't be surprised to find pictures of him surrounded by candles and incense, a shrine to Che, patron saint of beret wearers. Next to Che is a framed black-and-white photo. Nine young men, unshaved and smiling, pose for the camera, they are guerillas dressed in khaki and jeans standing amidst tropical palms and plants. One wears shades, one a Che beret, another an army combat hat. They all have guns, some held upright pointing at the air. The biggest man of the group sports a large moustache and has a great metal buckle on his jeans, he holds a belt-fed machine gun on a stand. The confidence of the group is unmistakable. They are happy and defiant.

'These are my comrades' says Rene.

'FMLN?' I ask, using the acronym for the revolutionary front that fought the government in the war.[5]

'Yes.'

This was Rene's guerilla unit. This was Rene at war, these are his friends and it is virtually impossible that they are all alive today. I have a mechanism of dealing with complex emotional situations, especially ones about which I know absolutely nothing and that mechanism is to blurt out ill-considered suburban responses. Today is no exception.

'Gosh. Do you ever have reunions?'

Rene the Mayor keeps his eyes on the photo.

'They are mainly dead. There are only two living now. One is me and the other,' he says pointing a finger at one of the men, 'he lives in America.'

'Right...well...sorry to hear about that...'

'It was the war,' he says with a shrug that seems to cast aside a brief and monumentally crushing sadness.

'Shall we chat about Coca-Cola?'

Rene the Mayor turns from the picture and says, 'Come,' ushering me to a chair.

And there on the wall hang these two photos, one of Che and one of the smiling guerillas – the ideal and the reality. Right next to 'brand Che', the logo of the revolution, is the actuality of the revolution: seven of the defiant men are dead.

* * *

In the run-down world of Nejapa the Coca-Cola bottlers must have ridden into town like a cavalcade. The council were delighted they wanted to open up a bottling plant. 'We welcomed them,' explains Rene, as he places a cup of coffee in front of me. His eager reception of the company is not the predictable response of a gun-toting ex revolutionary footballer but times and needs change. The reason he welcomed Coke was simple.

'Jobs,' says Rene the Mayor sitting down behind his desk. 'It's a poor region, most people here are working class and their economic level is quite tough.'

I tentatively enquire, 'Did it seem odd to you, with your history, to now be working with Coca-Cola?'

'Well...' he says resting his hands on his lap with just the tips of his fingers touching, '...a little. I came from the war. They were a strong company. They had the idea that we couldn't do business. But we got past that stage and as a council we were able to give them permission, even though sometimes they were not meeting all the requirements. As a demonstration of our goodwill we said "Come." Because we wanted the employment they offered the community.'

He flicks a piece of lint from his button-down shirt and sits back.

Nejapa really wanted those jobs, the problem was that the Coke bottlers Embotelladora Salvadorena (Embosalva) did not have a spotless public record when it came to community relations. The previous plant in Soyapango, a working-class area a few miles to the east of San Salvador, was shut down amidst allegations the company had over exploited the area's water supplies whilst residents only had tap water for eight hours of the day.[6] So when Coke's bottlers, Embosalva, came to Nejapa the council had a few conditions. Rene the Mayor explains that the company were told 'There are four conditions you must agree to before opening up here: provide jobs, pay your taxes, respect the environment and provide some funding for the local amateur football team.'

If the company met these conditions it would indeed be fitting for Coke to boast of playing a role 'in supporting sustainable communities'.

So how well did Coca-Cola manage to comply with these conditions? Did they fund the local football team? No. Though as Rene says, 'lately they have taken up the issue again. I hope that it works this time.'

OK. Did they provide employment for the community? Rene says, 'they didn't employ anybody in Nejapa.'
    'They have employed no one?' I question.
    'No, no one. Absolutely no one.'

Though to be absolutely fair to the company, I later heard a very strong rumour that one person from Nejapa was employed at the new plant...as a part-time gardener. Though this is unconfirmed.

To find out how the company managed with one of the other conditions Mayor Rene has arranged for me to meet Councillor Carlos in the town square at midday. And in a manner befitting the time and place, Councillor Carlos appears with the sun behind him. Middle-aged, trim and sporting jeans, polo shirt and a quiff that any elderly fan of Bronski Beat or

Bros would be proud of, Councillor Carlos has been tasked with two jobs. Firstly to take us to the community he represents, who rely on the stream running downstream from the Coke bottling plant. This hopefully will provide some insight into how Coke works with sustainable communities. His second job is to act as our minder. It transpires that Armando's earlier worries about gangs are not unfounded. The Coke bottlers are supposed to protect the environment and the councillor is to protect us. I hope he does a better job than the company.

We are given directions to the community. The van is to turn right at the top of the town, follow the road for about five minutes, keeping an eye out for a dirt track on the right, it should be obvious as it is directly after a pile of old fridges lying on their side in a field. Then onwards down the dirt track, until we reach a standpipe, turn sharp right and we will have arrived. It is obvious we are not going to the salubrious end of the neighbourhood. Any explanation of how to get to someone's home, that involves the directions 'turn right at some abandoned fridges', tells you the person you're visiting is pretty much fucked.

By the standpipe lies Councillor Carlos' constituency, a narrow lane, with overhanging leaves and palms cutting out the light. The sides of the lane are banked high with dirt and debris forming walls to create a tunnel wide enough for the van but not its mirrors. These walls are where roots and scrub entwine with junk and litter, held together with packed mud. Gnarly branches are meshed into an old mattress frame, its springs knotted through with crawlers, which is all propped up by a tyre set in soil and baked hard. Into these walls of litter and grime are steps cut in the dirt and the steps lead to homes. This is the Gallera Quemada Canton of Nejapa.

Kids in shorts crouch on their haunches at the top of the steps. From up there they look straight into the van windows, our faces just feet away from each other. As we slowly rumble down this tunnel of hovels people stop what they are doing, adults stop cooking, girls stop hanging clothes out, kids stop playing; they stop and stare at us.

David our American raises his eyebrows and softly says, 'This is *Apocalypse* fucking *Now*, man.'

Except that it isn't. A foreign documentary film crew has just turned up with a camera that's worth more than three year's wages, so the locals are hardly likely to quip, 'Not another polemic on globalisation, well, there goes the neighbourhood.'

Getting out of the van Councillor Carlos greets a few of his constituents with a nod and a word or two. 'The people here make a living when it's the rice or sugar cane season, they get some building work too,' says Councillor Carlos
  'How much do they get paid?'
  'About $40 a month,'

But the one thing they had in their favour was access to clean water. The stream runs past the community and feeds into the San Antonio River. 'Originally the stream had more water flowing through it and everybody could use it to water their flocks. Within the stream we still had wells and people could use this water.' Poor yes, but with drinking water for themselves, their animals and for washing, they at least had that.

As we walk Councillor Carlos refers to the water in two distinct time zones, Before Coke and After Coke. 'Previously,' he says implying the time Before Coke, 'the water wasn't polluted. People would come and wash and children would get into the stream to have a swim; then as time went by the children would come out of the water with some kind of allergy on their bodies. They were sent to the clinic and that's when they found out it was because of the contamination of the water.' He pauses as we glimpse a field beyond the lane, with one solitary thorny tree and some small grey breeze-block homes in the distance made colourful with the laundry drying in the sun.

'We no longer use the water in the way we used to…People coming to the stream no longer use it for drinking water.'

Two men appear and smiling take the councillor to one side, say a few words and then Councillor Carlos explains that we should leave the area and that he will take us to a quieter location where we can continue the interview. The local gang is on their way down here to rob us and take the camera equipment. Apparently they are going to finish their drinks first, then come and get us. Great. Not only are we to be mugged, but we have to give the gang drinking-up time too. Armando the driver fumbles the gear stick gently muttering 'Fuck. Fuck. Fuck.'

'Have we got a security situation?' David the American cameraman asks, adding, 'I want a guard with a shotgun and I want one fucking now.'

Everyone ignores him, the engine revs and we leave. We have been saved by the universal phenomena of a bloke in a bar saying, 'You can't leave that, that's still half full.'

We drive for a further 15 minutes in glorious and valiant retreat; in situations like this there is nothing finer than the nobility of cowardice. We have followed the stream and charted a course deeper into the countryside, there is no one is sight and we are quite alone. Out here the water sashays along flat plains hemmed in by distant hills and against the backdrop of a clear blue sky. It is easy to forget this countryside is contaminated.

'The gangs will not come here,' says Councillor Carlos as we walk to the stream to set up the camera equipment. 'We are safe here,' he says. But nobody asks how he can be sure of this, no one says 'What if the gang had a car?' or 'What if they drove down the track they saw us leave on?' Or being a rural gang, 'What if they had a horse?' Tattooed gang members trotting along doing a twos-up on a horse might not seem a possibility but this is the countryside – an unfamiliar place in my own land let alone another continent. For all I know the gangs round here could use pigs as pitbulls and pimp tractors. We are in the middle of nowhere, a little shaken up and in need of some reassurance.

The sound of a motorbike revving in the distance is not reassuring. Nether is the vision of the solitary bike heading towards us down the hillside, with billowing dry earth blowing up behind it. A black cop car then screeches to a halt on a ridge, three men step out into the swirling dust, silhouetted in the dirt clouds. The red and blue lights mounted on the roof flash a dull light in the haze. They wait, looking on, as the lone cop on the motorbike drives towards us. The dust and roar gets nearer until the rider guns the engine, brings the bike to a stop, flicks out a stand and dismounts all without taking his gaze off us. He wears reflective shades and is dressed head to toe in black, laced paratrooper boots, combat trousers, short-sleeve shirt, gun belt and holster. Even his jungle hat is black. Perhaps it is a nervous reaction but I get an overwhelming urge to say, 'Fuck me it's a paramilitary goth.' But the words come out as, 'Hi, there.'

We have no idea if we are breaking the law, if we need permission to film here, if he will take exception to foreigners making films that might be critical of his country. He stands tall, legs astride, one hand resting on his belt. Councillor Carlos explains we are filming for a programme about water contamination. The cop removes his shades looks at us and says, 'I'm pleased, especially in view of what's going on.' Then he continues in a deep, serious and sincere tone, 'As a rural police officer we're involved with everything to do with the natural world and the environment. The other forces work within the city, within the urban areas. We ourselves are here for the well-being of the natural world, the rural areas.'

Oh my God, we've just meet our first genuine green cop. He's tough, rides a motorbike, looks as sexy as hell and wants to protect his local eco system. Does he have any idea of how many boxes he ticks? I have women friends who would ovulate at the sight of him...men too.

As if this isn't enough he initiates a brief and succinct critique of multinational corporations. 'Most of the companies, like Coca-Cola, for example – it's a very obvious example, isn't it? – these companies, the waste products which they produce: the only outlet they find is here in our scanty resources.' He gestures to the stream, smiles and says, 'I'm really pleased that groups like yourselves are concerned about rescuing the few natural resources we enjoy today.' And with that he touches the tip of his hat, nods his head, mounts his bike and roars off to fight wrongdoers, hug trees and break hearts.

It's a hard act to follow but Councillor Carlos returns to the matter in hand, telling us the final episode of his saga. The story so far: the Coca-Cola bottling plant dumps waste in the water, kids get rashes, fish die and are found floating belly up, the mayor and the council can't leave the community without water. Carlos says, 'We obtained water tanks...[everyone] gets their water from the water tanks.'

'Where does the water come from?'

'There is a well where the water comes from which by means of piping feeds water to the tanks...so the well water supplies these water tanks for the benefit of the community.'

'Who pays for it?'

'We as a community pay for it. If we get a bill for X amount and 50 people use the tanks then we divide up the bill by 50.'

So the company that was supposed to bring employment to the community doesn't employ anyone, pollutes the stream and causes people earning about $1.50 a day to pay out more money for their drinking water.

Carlos shrugs, 'We fought and struggled so that Coca-Cola would pay for the water tanks, so that they would pay for the consumption of water that we have. Unfortunately Coca-Cola, like the huge company they are, merely came here to take over the resources...'

The question that worrying me is a simple one: how can a company that makes fizzy pop produce waste that kills fish and pollutes drinking water? They are making Coca-Cola in there, they are not Dow Chemicals or British Nuclear Fuels, and to the best of my knowledge they are not the final hiding place for The Mythical Weapons of Saddam Hussein. So how is this pollution happening?

Chemical engineer Daniel Martinez, has agreed to meet me to explain. He's a chubby, clean-faced man with an innocent friendliness. A Salvadorean by birth he trained in Canada. 'I used to work for City Hall and was in charge of monitoring how Coca-Cola was handling waste products,' he says while we scramble down to the stream. We are looking for the Coke bottling plants' waste pipe and find it halfway down the bank side protruding on to a brick overflow that cascades into the stream. The pipe leads straight to the plant and is easily big enough for a man to crouch and walk in, Tom Cruise could probably get in standing upright and would do too, especially if you told him L Ron Hubbard was in there.

Daniel stands by the constant flow of water coming out of the pipe and explains how the waste is produced. 'There are two processes, one is the actual production and the other is when they wash the bottles. They use caustic soda to wash the bottles and detergents, that's what gives the water the high PH. The other contaminant is from the process itself, that's sugar mostly.'

Science admittedly isn't my strong point but if sugar is being dumped into the water don't the inhabitants just face very sweet water, surely their problem is calorific at this point?

Daniel develops a habit for dealing with my stupidity, namely he giggles then ignores me.

'The main problem is the biowaste contains too much nutrients. And they are all biodegradable but to be biodegradable they absorb the oxygen in the water.'

Somewhere in my mind a light bulb goes on.

'OK, so when people told us that the fish died when Coca-Cola moved here, it is because this stuff uses the oxygen and there is nothing left in the water.'

'Exactly,' he flashes a quick encouraging smile, 'they suffocate, they drown. When you have these multiple species dead, it's because Coca-Cola had a problem with the plant and they had a dumping...they just opened the gate,' he says referring to the pumps and sluice gates that release the waste, ' and the problem goes away.'

'Except it doesn't go away.'

'Except it comes to the community.'

THE CURIOUS CASE OF CLEAN WATER

Daniel Martinez, the chemical engineer who worked for the council, found curious results when the Coca-Cola bottlers tested the wastewater. He said 'They are supposed to test the water because of the quantities they manage, they have to test daily.' So who conducts these daily tests? The Coca-Cola bottlers, that's who, in their own labs. However, once a month, 'They are supposed to send samples to be tested in another lab outside of plant, independent laboratories.... That will help them compare the results with their own results and that will help them to see if their own lab is running properly or not.'

As the man employed by 'City Hall' to monitor Coca-Cola's waste results Daniel saw the lab results. So did he see anything unusual? What was coming out of the waste pipes at the Coke plant? According to Daniel the company's results said what was coming out of the pipe was 'almost drinkable...It was pretty amazing, unbelievable, the wastewater was so clean...it was pure clean drinking water.'

'But,' I ask, 'couldn't that be the case? Might it be that the wastewater is drinkable?'

'Look at the colour of the water,' Daniel jumps in, 'look at how people are feeling, look at the discussion about the dead fishes, how can that be clean water?'

Daniel doesn't know how the results came to show this level of water purity but what he does know is that the results on paper do not match the results in the stream. He looks resigned and matter of fact when he says, 'Remember, El Salvador doesn't have the laws that exist in Europe and the US and developed countries. As a matter of fact we don't even have a law regarding wastewater. It is a guideline still...I live in a country that doesn't have the policies to protect the environment and that means big companies can do whatever they want.'

With no resolution in sight it was at this stage that the council took the extraordinary move of taking the company to court over the non-payment of the council taxes. Daniel furrows his forehead and raises his eyebrows, 'To get the taxes they had to go to the Supreme Court to make them pay.' He shakes his head slightly almost in disbelief and smiles, 'I don't know how City Hall won that case, but they did, they actually made them pay.'

Back in the mayor's office, sitting with another cup of coffee, Rene the Mayor reveals how the company fared on its last condition to pay its council taxes. 'They also broke their promise to pay their taxes to the municipality.'

'What were the taxes for?'

'Rubbish collection, for electricity and other things' says Rene.

'Would the taxes include water rates as well?'

'No, the water, they are not paying anything for the water and they should.'

So the council took the Coca-Cola bottlers to court to get their taxes, and the council won.

I ask Rene the mayor and erstwhile revolutionary how he feels to have won in court against such a large company. 'Happy,' he says. Though he isn't displaying a huge amount of that particular emotion at the moment. 'To win against a company of this nature is not easy. They were thinking logically, "well we owe them two hundred thousand dollars, we'll pay one hundred thousand to a good team of lawyers and we'll save half the money and we'll win". They were wrong.' He shrugs the shrug of a stoic.

'After two years we won. They paid us two hundred thousand dollars, and it was a shame that we had to go to court to get them to pay us an amount which is not much for them, but for us it is a lot of money.'

So The Coca-Cola Company's assertion that they have a role to play in helping communities become sustainable is bogus in this case. The water was polluted. The poorest people in town now have to pay for their water. The football team got no support. No jobs came to the town, save the near-mythical part-time gardener. The company did not pay its taxes. Yes, the council won but as Rene says, 'we had to go to court to get them to pay us something which by law...they should have paid.' Which may be why he is so resolutely un-celebratory in this victory.

The ex-revolutionary mayor who welcomed Coca-Cola into town sighs, spreads his hands out and explains how it could have been. 'If you go and live in an area the best thing you can do is get integrated with the local population, look after them, so the place where you live is the best. But they have not done anything...they go to a place, they exploit all the resources and when there aren't any they leave, and they leave the people in the place with the problem.'

Before the *Dispatches* programme was broadcast in November 2007, I put these allegations to Coke. They said they had a certificate to show they met international enviromental standards.[7] They are also keen to promote their water stewardship efforts in Nejapa – which runs to providing two schools with clean water.[8] Which I wouldn't really want to criticise save for the fact that it doesn't really address the concerns raised. But maybe I'm just picky...

* * *

Returning to the capital from the stream at Nejapa the evening track turns to road and the road spreads out from one lane to many. The emerald trees and brilliant pink and peach of wild climbing flowers give way to roadside expanses of dust, inhabited by stalls offering pyramid piles of green coconuts. The open space of the country starts to brim with city clutter. Makeshift bars, handcarts and barrows vie for custom selling sweets and drinks, while people crowd around buses with prayers painted on the doors. The massed throng is as transitory as the dusk that surrounds them. Pick-ups swirl with farm workers who climb on board the back of the truck, and grab hold of anything vaguely stable before speeding off. Barking clouds of black diesel fumes disappear as quickly as they came and the familiar smell of wood smoke haunts the air, promising the dream of home and the distance yet to travel.

As the lanes turn to highways so the twilight turns to night and we glide into San Salvador, where the central strip casts off the mantle of a Central American country, throws its identity to the wind and revels in a downmarket version of LA. Blacked-out windows on Land Cruisers, blasting music, rev at the lights. New model cars compete with each other as to who can cram the most smoking teenagers on the back seat. Here the night sky is torn with a bright glare as every conceivable fast-food outlet proclaims its wares in retina-shrinking light. The mighty yellow buns of Burger King compete with McDonalds' golden arches and the glow fight spills over into the forecourts of Subway and Wendy's. A cartoon chicken waves a friendly cowboy hat from an illuminated plastic shop front – Pollo Campero – 'Howdy partner,' it seems to say, 'I'm cheap, tasty and happy as hell to be eaten!' But KFC outshines them all, it's a two-storey building in the shape of a KFC bucket. Neon strip lights run along the edges of the structure: a bucket glowing in the night. That is what identifies this restaurant, not the food but the receptacle it is served in, a bucket. Didn't anyone at the planning stage of this venture say, 'Isn't using an image of something you can throw up in, a bad idea for the food industry?'

'People here love fast food' says Armando in a resigned voice too old for his twenty-four years. 'Pollo Campero that's the favourite, but everyone likes fast food.'

'Is that because so many Salvadoreans fled to America in the civil war that people are really comfortable with US-style junk food?' I ask

'Some people are getting some dollars in their pockets, maybe they spend them here?' ventures Eduardo our minder.

'This, my friends,' I say, declaiming with indignation, '...this is the sharp end of globalisation. This is the future of everywhere.' I slump and sigh in the seat.

'Maybe,' says David the American, 'maybe they jus' like the taste, dude. Ever fuckin' thought about that?'

INTERLUDE: CONNECTING

I feel that Customs Officers do not need to know the ins and outs of my life. A brief who are you, do you match to photo in the passport, when are you leaving and then a quick check in the bags for Semtex, smack or bush meat: job done. So I am not at my most forthcoming turning up at US Customs when I arrive to get a connecting flight from El Salvador. I step up from the line to see the officer has all the visual requirements he needs for the job, a crew cut and no visible contours twixt head and neck.

'OK, sir,' he grunts, scanning the passport with some kind of blip gun. 'What was the purpose of your trip?'

'In El Salvador?'

'Yes sir, in El Salvador.'

'I was filming, working on a film.'

'You're an actor?'

'Of sorts'

'What kind of film was it?'

Not wanting to say I'm making a programme about child labour, pollution and one of your country's most esteemed companies, I say, 'A drama documentary.'

Without missing a beat he replies, 'What's that, sir? A feature film?'

'Well, sort of, it's live-action drama in real-life situations,'

I say attempting not to stray somewhere close to the truth.

'What is the name of the film?'

'Fizz.' I say, which is genuinely the working title of the documentary.

'Fizz.'

'Yes, Fizz.'

He lowers the passport, cocks his head conspiratorially towards me and in hushed tones says, 'You're not a porn star are you?'

'Sorry?'

'Are you a porn star?'

'No, no. I am not a porn star.'

He smiles and looks at me and says in a slow drawl, 'I think you are.'

'Well, no, erm, I'm flattered that you think I could be but I am not.'

He raises his eyebrows and in a monotone says, 'Of course not, sir.' Smiles, then snaps to officious mode, 'Thank you very much, sir.'

I head off thinking that if I can be mistaken for a porn star, then Coca-Cola is not the only industry that needs to review its standards.

INDIA: A PREQUEL

'The Coca-Cola Company exists to benefit and refresh everyone it touches.'

Coca-Cola Statement to BBC Radio 4's *Face the Facts*, 2003

In the Seventies, while the rest of the world was being taught to sing in perfect harmony, to grow apple trees and honey bees, the Indian government was busy with a new piece of legislation, the Foreign Exchange Regulation Act. The Act required foreign companies to ensure 60 per cent of their shares belonged to Indians in order to 'Indianize' these companies. In 1977, the Indian Government gave Coke two options – sell 60 per cent of your stake or leave. Coke decided to go. It wasn't quite the corporate equivalent of fleeing in helicopters from the rooftop of the US embassy in Saigon but American symbols were poignantly departing from the east. It would be sixteen years before the company could persuade the authorities to let them back in.

In 1993 after several failed attempts, Coca-Cola returned. Its triumphant re-entry should have marked a new chapter in its troubled relationship with the country but Coke was dogged by controversy almost from the beginning and remains so to this day. In the first decade back in India, Coke had three substantial complaints laid at its door:

'Where have the shares gone?'

Coke's re-entry into India through a wholly owned subsidiary, Hindustan Coca-Cola Holdings (HCCH) was under certain conditions, one of which was that HCCH would sell 49 per cent of its shares to resident Indians and was given the not insubstantial timeframe of June 2002 to do so. Did Coca-Cola agree to this mandatory requirement? Clearly. Did Coca-Cola comply with this mandatory requirement? Do bears use bidets? No. In fact, according to Indian news reports at the time, they co-opted the US Commerce Department and the US Ambassador to apply pressure on the Indian authorities.[1] Something clearly worked, because the Indian government agreed to let Coke sell the 49 per cent to private investors and business partners with a small percentage sold to employees' trusts.[2] But most crucially, and rather uniquely, these 'Indian' shares came with no voting rights because the company argued that would be 'substantive and onerous'.[3] So not only did they sell their shares to 'friendly' investors, what they sold was more of an accumulating gift voucher than a share as we might know it.

'Where's the water gone?'
Coca-Cola has shut down two bottling plants in India

In 1998, Coca-Cola bought 35 acres of land around
Plachimada, a village in Kerala, Southern India and started
building what was to become the most controversial plant in
Coke's Indian history. On 22 April 2002, villagers, concerned
about the serious drop in water levels and the quality of water
in their wells picketed the factory establishing a permanent
protest camp.[4] In 2003, the local Panchayat refused to renew
Coke's license to operate, citing 'public interest'.[5] And so the
David and Goliath battle, as it became characterised, between
this small, rural community and the most well-known
company in the world was on.

The problem was the very essence of Coke's business – water
extraction. Its plant was extracting water from the underground
aquifer at the rate of half a million litres a day according to the
only official figures there are.[6] Water levels in the area dropped
dramatically though Coca-Cola argued that 'the rainfall has
been well below average for several years'[7] and therefore the
water depletion was not their fault. And although rainfall was
indeed below average for several years, it is well known that
Plachimada is in a 'rain-shadow' area of Kerala which means
that its rainfall is always below average, somewhat limiting the
ability of water extracted to be recharged naturally.[8] Not
necessarily the best place to locate a water-intensive plant,
although the generous subsidies Coke received 'for having
invested in a backward area'[9] may have helped in that decision.

When I visited the protest camp in 2004 it was a low shelter
made of wood and straw and decorated with banners
demanding that Coca-Cola leave. Most of the people
protesting that day were women, as having to get the water,

they were the ones most affected. And a drive through the surrounding villages echoed this point. In each village by the side of the road a line of pots would appear, sometimes fifteen to twenty of them bulbous plastic pots for collecting water. The lead pot sat under the village standpipe and the women sat opposite, waiting for the water to be turned on for an hour or so. Coke's response to the villagers' concerns was to challenge the Panchayat's legitimacy. The leader of the Panchayat, Mr Krishnan, explained to me that the company argued the local Panchayat had the right to issue a licence but did not have the right to refuse to renew it. They effectively took the villagers as well as the protestors to court. They also asked for police protection...

As the legal battles raged on, the water levels continued to drop, so much so that Coke was forced to bus in tankers of water for the surrounding villages. In 2003, BBC Radio 4 broadcast their investigations into the plant on *Face the Facts*[10] and Plachimada became a cause célèbre both nationally and internationally. The programme makers tested both the water in the village well and the sludge from the factory that Coke gave away free to farmers to use as fertiliser. The water unsurprisingly was found to be unsafe to drink but the real controversy was in the sludge. It contained 'dangerous levels of toxic metals and the known carcinogen, cadmium'.[11] Britain's leading poisons expert, Professor John Henry said:

'The [test] results have devastating consequences for those living near the areas where this waste has been dumped and for the thousands who depend on crops produced in these fields.

'Cadmium is a carcinogen and it accumulates in the kidneys. Repeated exposure can lead to kidney failure. Lead is particularly dangerous to children and the results of exposure can be fatal. Even at low levels it can cause mental retardation and severe anaemia. What most worries me about the levels found is how this might be affecting pregnant women.'[12]

Sunil Gupta, Coca-Cola India's vice-president said, 'It's good for the farmers because most of them are poor...We have scientific evidence to prove it is absolutely safe and we have never had any complaints.'[13]

The complaints did come and the company was forced to treat its sludge as exactly what it was – hazardous waste. By March 2004, the company, were forced to stop production, later blaming the continued legal wrangling on 'certain misinformed campaigns'.[14]

As to the future, there are serious concerns over Plachimada's water level and it remains to be seen if the aquifer will recover. In 2005, a Indian lab report on water from a well in the village found that it was so acidic that if consumed, 'it would burn up your insides. Clothes could tear in such water, food will rot, crops will wither'.[15]

Coca-Cola's future, however, is altogether more promising – it has offered to relocate to another site, provided the company is adequately compensated. In 2005, it wrote to the Ministry of Industry regarding its offer, saying (I have provided a running translation from the corporate to plain English in the text): 'relocating to the new site would also incur substantial expenditure by us, [*it'll cost us to move*] we request to be provided appropriate compensation in the form of continued and increased sales tax incentives to offset the expense [*so a few subsidies wouldn't go amiss*]...We would like to request that the relocation to the proposed site would entail a confirmed resolution for meeting the infrastructure needs of the company such as water and electricity along with an amicable environment devoid of the problems as have been faced in

Plachimada [*keep the protestors the fuck away from us in future*]. Further, the Company may be allowed to continue with its sales tax incentives and other applicable beneficial schemes for the remaining period [*we're passing round the bowl please give generously*].'[16]

And Plachimada is not the only plant that has been shut down following protests. Villagers in Ballia in Uttar Pradesh launched a campaign against the plant alleging affected water levels and misappropriated community land, as well as calling on the Central Pollution Control Board to investigate chemical waste dumped on agricultural land. According to Coca-Cola, the 'Ballia plant was a co-packing facility owned by a franchise bottler. As part of business restructuring and consolidation, the production at Ballia was discontinued from 26 June 2007.'[17]

'Where's the pesticides...?'
...in the bottles of Coke and Pepsi

In 2003, the Centre for Science and Environment, an independent Indian public-interest organisation conducted a series of tests, firstly on bottled water and then on soft drinks. The Centre was concerned about the lack of regulations in the food industry and hoped its research would start a debate that would eventually lead to India adopting standards for water quality. On 5 August 2003 it published the results into its soft drinks study[18] and indeed sparked a debate – although not only in India but worldwide. For the CSE had found levels of pesticides in bottles of Coca-Cola and Pepsi to be between 30-36 times higher than would be permitted in the EU.[19]

It is fair to say that all hell broke loose and nothing in the world could have prepared CSE for the backlash. Within hours of the report being published Coca-Cola and Pepsico held a joint press conference to denounce the findings and question the methodology – which is a bit like Iran and Iraq uniting to say 'the Isle of Wight is picking on us' . Pepsico immediately slapped a writ on CSE which it later withdrew.[20] And a Joint Parliamentary Committee (the equivalent to a Public Enquiry conducted by Parliament) was convened – only the fifth in India's history. Not to consider pesticides in India's food chain but to see if CSE's findings are correct. Talk about shoot the messenger. In the eye of the storm, life was pretty hard for the CSE – although they expected a fight, they 'had not anticipated...the sheer power and the virulence of the attack'.[21] India's secret service even paid them a visit – just to let them know that anyone who had ever worked for the organisation was being investigated.[22] Their methodology and motives was all questioned, their reputation savaged but the CSE held their ground and in February 2004, the JPC upheld their findings.[23] They concluded, 'the Committee...find that the CSE findings are correct on the presence of pesticide residues...The Committee also appreciate the whistle blowing act of CSE in regard to alerting the nation to an issue with major implications to food safety...and human...health...The Committee note with deep concern that the soft drink...industry with an annual turnover of Rs 6,000 crores[24] is unregulated.'[25]

But despite this and their recommendations, little changed. So in August 2006 CSE conducted the tests again, this time using even more up-to-date equipment. It found Coca-Cola and Pepsico products contained pesticides on average 24 times over the prescribed limit.[26]

Coca-Cola's response was to conduct its own tests. Oddly, the samples provided by Coke showed no signs of pesticides above EU standards.

So not a great start to buinsess back in India.

I was about to find out how Coke's second decade was shaping up...

9
KURIJI

Kaladera, India

'If you want to know the truth about The Coca-Cola Company: Ask the farmer in India.'

The Coca-Cola Company, 2007¹

I do like it when companies write stuff like this. 'Ask the farmer in India...' they say, as if inviting all and sundry to drop whatever they are doing, travel to India, drive out to the farmer's place and ask if he will vouch for Coke. Assuming you did mange to get to India with this in mind, you would then face an added hurdle as the company weren't terribly specific about which farmer they meant. That's if they actually did have someone in mind, and hunting representational composites is fiendishly difficult. But I am in India surrounded by farmers and seeing as The Coca-Cola Company did invite me to ask them, I did.

The farmer I chose to ask is Mr Rameshwar Prasad Kuri who is sixty-four and comes from Kaladera in Rajasthan. It is common for Indians to use the suffix 'ji', adding it to a person's name when addressing an elder and wishing to show respect. So Mr Kuri is called Kuriji. This particular linguistic custom was explained to me by an Indian student, who after imparting this knowledge asked, 'What do you have in England like this?'

'Pardon?'

'What do you do to show respect for elders in England?' he earnestly enquired.

'We don't put them in a home,' I replied.

The comment is meet with incomprehension.

I met Kuriji in a village called Mehdiganj, the nearest city to which is Varanasi on the banks of the River Ganges, famous for its ghats and funeral pyres. The ghats are the long wide steps leading down to the river where pilgrims flock to absolve themselves of sin. So sacred is the Ganges for Hindus that here in Varanasi you can rent out rooms to die in, so your cremated ashes can be put straight into the river. A friend told me he once saw a tourist sign reading 'Come to Varanasi: a great place to die.'

It bustles with life, markets, crowds and the usual theatre of everyday Indian existence. Indeed, it is not a bad place to die, though my preference would be a violent heart attack in the British Library, just so the last thing I hear on the planet is SHHH!

It is from here that I set out, leaving the city and heading into the countryside for the village. The quick and easy way to get there is by motorised three-wheeler, a kind of tuk-tuk, if you were in Thailand. And travelling for forty minutes in a motorised three-wheeler in India is about the most fun you can legally have outside of Alton Towers. It stops, starts, jumps, revs and swerves its way though a jaw-dropping and beautiful world.

I love these forty minutes. The hot air rushes about you and the driver manhandles the steering like he is in a rodeo. Men scoot past on motorbikes with women riding sidesaddle on the back, clutching their saris demurely. Every village we drive through has a bike repair shop, a cow in the road and if you are early enough a bloke washing from a steel pan outside his home, wearing nothing but a wrapped tight lungi and a lot of soap suds. Temples and schools sit alongside peasant huts, where dung patties shaped like Cornish pasties sit drying in the sun. Top-heavy palm trees and pan wallah shacks sit next to roadside garages where trucks are serviced in the dust, stacked up on bricks while skinny engineers crouch under giant steel frames.

As the three-wheeler twists sharply to avoid imminent oncoming-overtaking-tractor-death, I remember that in India there is a special competition played on the roads called Who Can Transport the Most Improbable Object in a Vehicle. Today's contenders include a very old cyclist with legs like a plucked chicken wing. He carries two very large red Calor gas bottles, one balanced on each handle, and rides unconcernedly on the dual carriageway alongside speeding lorries. He is up against another cyclist doing a sharp left in traffic while carrying half a dozen 30-foot industrial steel rods balanced on his handlebars. It is as if the India's Heath and Safety Executive is run by Wile E Coyote.

As we drive past the hand-painted adverts which decorate walls, houses and shop fronts I marvel at the way the English language here is laced with the nuances of 1947, the time the British left. Back in Delhi buses have slogans on the side of them proclaiming 'Propelled by hydrogen!' What a wonderful word 'propelled'! and how brilliant it is that bus loads of Indians can be propelled. And wouldn't you look forward to

your commute every morning if you were propelled? Saris are
not sold in retail outlets or boutiques but in 'Emporiums'. And
out in the countryside adverts, painted on end walls, picture
Y-fronts and T-shirts, with the slogan 'Shirts, vest, panties,
drawers.' Oh, that we could advertise drawers and panties
instead of briefs and thongs. But my favourite word is used to
describe the activities of the farmers opposed to the Coca-Cola
bottlers, they are not a 'movement' or a 'campaign' nor do
they 'lobby'- they take part in an 'agitation'. And that is
exactly what they have done, a small group of people has truly
agitated Coca-Cola.

The only thing that marks out Mehdiganj from so many other
villages is the Coca-Cola bottling plant at one end of it. Apart
from that it is an ordinary village that sits on the side of a dual
carriageway and collects dust. Which it does very well. I turn
down the road that runs between two teashops where the
smoky wood fires lazily turn the air blue under the low eaves of
the bungalow roofs. The chai wallahs serve up clay cups of
scalding milky brew and small plates of home-made sweets.
I stand for a moment and see the road snake into the open
countryside. Then walking past the open doors of family homes
and a tiny shop with boxes of hair colouring pinned to the wall
I come to a glade that spreads out to the side of village, on the
edge of the fields. This is a natural meeting place, an opening
ringed with trees and a low canopy that casts a dappled shade.
This is the venue for National Right to Water Conference and
Protest against Coca-Cola, to give it its full title.

Over three days hundreds of farmers and villages from the
various corners of India gather to share their experiences of
what it is like to have Coca-Cola as a neighbour, as well as to
organise how to close those plants that remain open. There are
four Coca-Cola bottlers with local agitations running against

them. Plachimada in Kerala in the South and Ballia to the East have been shut down. The other two are Kaladera to the West and here in the village of Mehdiganj itself. The glade is set to swell with hundreds of people from these places – villagers, farmers and a smattering of activists and press. Some women and children are literally carted in to attend, on bright red metal trailers hooked up to large clunking tractors with black funnels decorated with gold and pink tinsel garlands. The conference is quickly packed and long trumpet-shaped loudspeakers are hung in the trees, tied up with string and wires run through the branches, so everyone can hear speaker after speaker stand at a podium to decry the company. This is the place to ask a farmer about Coca-Cola.

I spoke to a lot of them. I met Raj Narayan Patel, a fifty-five-year-old from Mehdiganj, a stocky man, with grey hair, black rings round his eyes and orange teeth that comes from chewing *paan*. He insisted I look at his well, a brick-lined circular pit level with the ground that descends to a puddle, some mud and a few stones. He pointed avidly at rings in the well, watermarks at various depths, to indicate the depletion. I asked him if he knew of a farmer who might be able to say a good word for the company. He gently led me to a seat in the shade and went off to fetch me a glass of water.

I met Siyaram Yadav, a bearded farmer with five children who, along with his father, sat with us under an awning. While he talked of failed crops and water shortages we shared brown balls of unrefined sugar that he passed around. I called it 'Bootleg sugar'. He too insisted I see his well, which looked like a wishing well that had been in a fight, and had a rudimentary cranked windlass to pull up the water, should any appear.

I met Baliram Ram from Ballia, he was dressed in a matching purple shirt and slacks and had a milky, dead eye where a goat had kicked him as a child. He was straight out of a Tom Waits song. His well is 180 km away but if I wanted he would take me to it. I politely turned down the offer; there are only so many empty wells a man can see. So instead he told me that Indian farmers should be sent to Kashmir to settle the issue, as 'Indian farmers will never give up one inch of land!' Later I retold this to friend who was also at the conference. He said, 'Mark, what you have to understand is that Indian farmers are not like British farmers.'

'Do they copulate sober?' I enquire.

'Most people in this country live on the land,' he continues, pointedly ignoring me, 'For them the land is everything, it is their worth, their life, their dignity, everything.'

Now I'll confess straight away that I know little about farming. And by little I mean nothing. In Britain most city dwellers tend to love the British countryside but hate the people who live there, leaving a large gap in our knowledge of matters agricultural. Fortunately some of the farmers here were very happy to talk me through the subject and demonstrated as much, if not more, patience in explaining their work as I did in listening about it. And after all their discourse on agriculture it comes down to these two simple facts:

- Farmers need water for crops and villagers need water to survive.
- Coca-Cola's main ingredient is water.

The Coca-Cola Company own and control The Hindustan Coca-Cola Beverage Pvt. Ltd (HCCBPL), which in turn own and operate the Kaladera plant near where Kuriji lives. The plant started running in January 2000 not far from Kuriji's farm and the fundamental problem with the plant is that, well, it's been built in a drought zone. To suggest the community have problems with water is an understatement. Kaladera is in the district which has been in drought for 50 of the past 106 years – 47 per cent of the time.[2] In 1998 the water in the area was deemed to be over-exploited by the Central Groundwater Board.[3]

However, someone at Coke in India decided it would be a good idea to open a water-intensive industry in a drought prone area. For some reason the word that springs to mind is 'D'oh!'

KALADERA AND THE TERI REPORT

I did ask Coca-Cola India if I could visit Kaladera. I also asked them for an interview. They didn't seem very keen. In fact, what they actually said was, '[g]iven the history of biased reporting about our operations by Mark Thomas, most recently in the *Dispatches* programme on Channel 4 that contained outdated and inaccurate allegations, we have decided not to have any involvement in this latest Mark Thomas project'.[4] I took that as a no. But we do know a little bit about how the plant is run from a report by The Energy and Resources Institute (TERI) and it is worth explaining a little about this report. It was commissioned after the University of Michigan suspended its contracts with Coca-Cola in response to student concerns that the Company's actions in Colombia and India violated the University's ethical trading policy. Coke finally agreed to an 'independent' third party study and it chose TERI to conduct that investigation.[5] Finally published in

January 2008 the report, however, did give some interesting information about the operation of the plant in Kaladera, including the following facts:

- The plant pays virtually nothing for the water it uses.
- The plant has four bore wells sunk to a depth of 330 feet that can bring up at least 120,000 litres of water an hour.
- There is a very small charge for the dumping wastewater: approximately Rs 0.2 per 1,000 litres (the equivalent of about £0.0024 per 1,000 litres).
- The average amount of water extracted in May (peak production month) between 2004-2006 was just under a million litres of water a day, to be specific, 953,333 litres a day.
- During the eight years that Coke has been operating, the water tables have gone down by more than a metre each year and about three metres in 2003/04.
- On average it takes 3.8 litres of water to make 1 litre of pop.[6]

Did I mention they pay virtually nothing for the water?

The conference in the glade is in full swing. Speakers are in full cry, the crowd cheer appreciatively and if there are any gaps in the programme the local band jumps in to perform protest songs – ripping out the lyrical innards of popular ballads and replacing them with a more suitable polemic. So Kuriji and I look for a quieter place to sit and have a chat. We cross the road and smile at the barber who has set up shop under a telegraph pole, walk through the mango orchard and out on to the fields, coming to rest at the edge of a grove of trees.

Even for a farmer Kuriji is a self-contained man. Balding and grey he is not a large person, either in height or weight, and he carries himself with the gentle gravitas of age. Two ballpoint pens are clipped into the top pocket of his shirt. His family have farmed in Kaladera going back to 'my great-grandfather's grandfather,' he said. His wife and son ran the family farm when he worked as a civil servant for the state government of Rajasthan. As the assistant director of agriculture, his job was to find ways that farmers could practically apply the latest research into farming methods and would tour farms explaining and helping. On retiring in 2002 he took to working full-time on the farm and in turn agitating. Sitting, he produces a large notebook, this is his journal of Kaladera's struggle for water, detailing each twist and turn in the saga, including each journalist he has ever spoken to on the subject. I suppose you can take a man from the civil service...

Kuriji begins with Coca-Cola's arrival, 'As soon as it started, the water level went down drastically. This is the main problem. Second problem, earlier we used a three-horsepower motor. But immediately after Coke arrived we had to replace it with a five-horsepower motor.'
    'Is this because of Coke?'
    'Yes. The water level went down. We had to dig the wells deeper and to pump water from such depth, five-horsepower motor was needed.'

He might well have the civil service knack of itemising the issues, but he has a farmer's concerns. Having listed depleted well water and pumps, he comes to 'Thirdly, earlier we could irrigate around fourteen–fifteen acres of land with the water available but now the water is sufficient for only ten-twelve acres of land. The fourth problem is that yield also reduced. Water is required for a good harvest...'

It is only after working his way through pumps, yields and irrigation he comes to the fifth and last problem, at the bottom of the priority pile. 'Fifth problem was that water for the hand pumps dried up. In some parts they have stopped working, have become dry. There is no water.'

Problem number five means that people in the village have no drinking water from the local pumps.

'People realised that it was because of the plant. The villagers started getting together. The people were involved not just farmers. So in February 2003 we started this agitation.'

Kuriji and others visited other villages in the five-kilometre radius of the plant, organising and campaigning, urging people to agitate. They did everything they could from demonstrating to writing to the state government of Rajasthan and members of the legislative assembly. 'Through this agitation we are trying to tell the government that the plant has used up all the water and there is a shortage and want the plant to shut down, so we can have sufficient water.'

As the agitation got under way Kuriji found himself approached by Coca-Cola. According to him they had asked, 'Why are you wasting your energy in this, you support us, we'll do a lot of good work if we're together.' I put it to him that this was a sign that the company wanted to work with its critics but Kuriji disagrees: 'they asked me whether I need a hand pump or a tube well, I told them I already have a tube well, why do I need you to make me a tube well?'

'When the Coca-Cola people came to you offering to install a new hand pump or tube well did they saying anything about stopping the struggle or supporting them?'

'Yes, that was the main thing that they talked about.'

The term Kuriji gave to describe Coke's offer to him was 'manage': Coca-Cola wanted to 'manage' him. He was not the first that the company sought to 'manage' either. A close relative of one of the campaigners was suddenly offered a job working at the plant, and that particular campaigner dropped out of the agitation.

The leader of the Panchayat (village council) was a slightly more spectacular turncoat, according to Kuriji and the agitation organisers. He had taken an oath in front of them vowing to fight Coke, 'He took some water in his hand and promised he would remove the plant from the village. He said that if he became the Sarpanch [leader of the village council] of this village, he would support us and try to do his best to remove the plant, and then what happened? He became the Sarpanch and within fifteen days he changed completely.'

Coca-Cola uses letters from the Sarpanch on their website to indicate the level of support they have within the Kaladera community.

Out by the grove, with the music and speeches of the conference wafting in the background, we chat for a hour or so. About how the police create a three-kilometre exclusion zone around the plant on demonstration days, about local politicians politicking and the shenanigans of local skullduggery but mainly about Kuriji's farm.

'If you come to Kaladera I will show you.'

'Thank you, that would be great.' I say.

'I will even show you the empty land in my farm.'

'Fantastic,' I say, hoping the language of raised eyebrows is not international.

It is not often that I get invited to someone's home to see an empty field. I suspect that the invitation is just an excuse, he wants to get me to the farm and then he'll do what all the farmers do around here: show me his empty well.

* * *

Four days later Kuriji leads us through Kaladera, a village by Indian standards but with a population of 12,000 to 13,000 people it would constitute a small town in the UK. This is a farmer's village to be sure, every other stall is piled with fruit and veg and every other shop sells sickles, similar to the old Soviet flag-style ones but much straighter. One trader has theirs laid out on a table next to the hair grips, and I envisage a shopper holding up some rupees tonelessly saying, 'Just the sickle and the hair grips, thanks love.' Here the cattle seem to aimlessly lollop down the roads, their hides as parched as their soft bellows, lethargic and thin they have more ribs on show than London Fashion Week.

In the centre of the village cool narrow alleyways bustle with shoppers and traders, where the milk-sweet sellers pick pieces of *barfi* from stacks piled on trays and hot fresh pastries are scooped out of pans of bubbling oil. Chai sellers and pan wallahs line the outskirts of these pathways where men sit spinning an eternity out of a tiny cup.

Kuriji chivvies us along, worried we are late. He looks old and smart today in his white pressed shirt and grey slacks. We arrive at a white building that looks like a small fort complete with mini battlements, the kind of place the Oompa Loompas might billet in times of war.

'Come. They are waiting.' Kuriji points to the door, clutching his ever-present notebook. The entrance is a shaded archway beyond which lies a small courtyard, partially covered with a low awning of metal sheets, propped up in the middle by a single pole. This is the local primary school, and the rug laid in the shadow of the awning is where the children sit for lessons, taught out in the open and out of the sun. Classroom charts and pictures are pinned to the back wall next to a blackboard with spellings hand written in Hindi and English and an adult-size bench sits at the front. Today the school doubles as a meeting place for the village resistance to the Coke bottling plant and twenty farmers sit waiting patiently on the large rug as we arrive. The farmers greet us with smiles and deference to Kuriji. These men form the Committee for Struggle, which is exactly what it is – a committee engaged in a struggle; an entity that marries India's twin loves of social movements and bureaucracy.

After tea, Kuriji sits to one side of the assembled group, notebook at the ready. It is not merely for my benefit that the men are gathered here, there is to be a planning meeting after I have chatted to them. In the meantime one of the farmers decides that the best introduction to the assembled group is a story, which he proceeds to tell. Kaladera has just celebrated Holi the festival of colour, where people mark the occasion by painting each other with coloured water. It is, I am told, advisable to wear old clothes around festival time as no one is immune and the administering can range from a polite face smearing, to throwing coloured water to using super soakers full of paint. The bolder and brighter the colours the better: reds, purples, greens, all collide leaving an end result that can be a tad LSD. With this in mind the farmer begins, 'We had a programme called Holi Milan here in Kaladera,' explaining this is traditionally a party where grudges and ill will are set aside. 'And for this Holi Milan, all the people contributed some money. We made arrangements for food and drinks for everyone. The manager of Coca-Cola, he was also there. Since it was open, anyone could come.' He pauses and looks around the gathering in the courtyard. They smile knowingly, already anticipating the punchline. 'The villagers thought that everyone would contribute, have some good food and have a nice get together... but the villagers had a problem. The villagers' biggest enemy had come to be a part of their celebrations. Everyone was furious.' What were they to do? They couldn't ask the Coca-Cola manager to leave as it would be impolite but he was spoiling the party by being there. So as it was Holi 'one of the oldest members of the committee he took some photocopying ink in his hands and applied it on the manager's face. He blackened his face.' Amidst the bright colours of Holi the Coke manager stood covered in jet-black ink and left shortly after that. The farmer telling the story pauses, looks around at his friends and then to me before saying, 'There has been a lot of tension since then.'

This story is carving its way into village memory already, everyone seems to know it and have probably told it themselves. And the farmers smile, happy to hear the tale told once again. Its ending is my cue to ask the question I have asked in countries halfway around the world: 'What was it like before Coca-Cola came?'

Mukut Yogi, squats leaning against a side wall half, he's thirty-six, with a pink shirt, a neat side parting and a moustache.
  'We were all self-sufficient in those days,' says Mukut.
  And when Coke came?
  'It was only when the water level fell, that we realised what was going on.'

His younger brother Mahesh, shakes his head ruefully, 'You could never imagine the speed at which the water level fell.'

'Earlier,' says Mukut talking of the time before Coke, 'there was water at a depth of thirty-five feet. Water could be pumped into the fields using a motor of three horsepower.... Now the water has to be pumped out from a depth of 125 feet. It is done with the help of a ten or fifteen horsepower motor.'

The farmers don't have an exact measurement for the water loss (amongst other factors the water level varies with the seasons) but they do know they have to dig their wells deeper and get stronger pumps to bring the water up. You don't need a tape measure to know the well is dry.

Everyone acknowledges the water situation here is bad, and it depends on who you are as to how you describe it: Coke call it 'a highly water-stressed area', the farmers call it a crisis. Water is being drawn out of the ground at a rate that is at least 35 per cent greater than what is being recharged by rainfall.[7] It's a Doomsday scenario. The impact has left farmers unable to grow their crops as they once did and leaves them fearful for their futures.

'People are unemployed now,' says Mukut

'Financial condition has worsened,' his brother adds.

Crossed-legged and leaning forward Mukut calmly explains, 'People from this village now go to other cities in search of work. There is no water here. A person cannot do farming. He has to look after his children. What will he do? Many villagers have gone to the cities.'

Few would argue that Coke is solely to blame. And Coke is right when it says 'agriculture remains the most significant use of water in the watershed'.[8] But by agriculture they mean the men sitting in front of me, the small farmers and their families. Here between 60-80 per cent of the population lives on the land, so by agriculture the Company means Indians growing food. Not surprisingly, when I put the Company's statement to them the agitators get very agitated. At the front of the group is Sudher Prahash, the thirty-year-old teacher at the school and a farmer with just under a hectare of land. Sitting on his haunches and with the eager disposition of a pupil he nearly leaves the ground in outrage at Coke's suggestion. 'I can explain this in a minute. In every man's life, there are a few basic necessities like eating food. What will the people of this country eat? If the farmers consume water, it's for growing crops. It is for sustaining life. But what are these people doing? You will neither live nor die by drinking a bottle of Coca-Cola.'

Perhaps the most surprising criticism has come Coke's own report. The TERI report, published in January 2008, does something quite incredible, Coca-Cola's own report suggests that Coke should consider shutting the plant down!

It is not often a company like Coke hires a consultant tasked with giving them the once over and the consultant says 'you're so shit you should think of shutting' – though the report didn't actually use these exact words.

The report examines the Coke plant's activities saying, 'the water withdrawals by the HCCBPL [Coke], Kaladera, need to be viewed in the context of the already overexploited condition of the aquifer.' The impact of the Coke plant on the water is such that TERI say 'the plant's operations in this area would continue to be one of the contributors to a worsening water situation and a source of stress to the communities around.' To this end TERI concludes:

'TCCC has to evaluate its options for HCCBPL, Kaladera, such as:

- Transport water from the nearest aquifer that may not be stressed (could be at quite a distance from the existing plant)
- Store water from low-stress seasons (may not exist!)
- Relocate the plant to a water-surplus area
- Shut down this facility.'[9]

Please note the whole of that statement is in quotation marks...

So let's look at the options. As Jaipur is a drought-prone area the chances of an nearest aquifer under no stress and with a population willing to let Coke grab is about as slim as the chances of storing enough water without rainfall. Thus eliminating the first two options. Leaving option three 'Relocate the plant to a water-surplus area.' Or take option four, 'shut down this facility.' The only viable options the plant has is to: shut down and move or shut down and not move. The company chose to continue its operations in Kaladera. Referring to the TERI report, Deepak Jolly the company Vice President said, 'It doesn't blame us even once,' adding 'It blames the farmers and agriculture.' In fact Mr Deepak Jolly goes on to say, 'It also does not even once suggest that we should pack up and leave those areas. It says that there are four or five options for bring up the water levels and if nothing is possible then alone we should go. Anything but closure.'[10] Deepak Jolly is also the holder Public Relations Council of India's 2006 award for Communicator of the Year.[11]

* * *

In the school that looks like a fort the farmers prepare for battle, sitting on the rug and planning how to persuade one of the biggest multinationals in the world to take option three or four. It is time for my questions to end and the meeting to start. Speaking nineteen to the dozen in Hindi, Kuriji explains the TERI report and its significance, that Kaladera's case was so strong the report couldn't help but condemn the current running of the plant. His audience listens rapt as Kuriji sits upright on his knees, notepad in hand resting on his lap. Sudher the teacher is still at the front, keen-eyed and coiled. Mukut leans against the wall with his brother next to him.

In the Land of Ignorance my knowledge of Hindi is infinite, in reality it is nil, all I know is that Kuriji has lowered his voice in dramatic significance when my mobile phone rings. My body assumes the 'oops' position as I reach hurriedly for it. With my hand cupped over the mouthpiece I whisper 'Hello?'

A friend from home wants to know if I can come to a party.
  'I'm in India,' I hiss.
  'Oh sorry, is it Coca-Cola?'
  'Yes.'
  'Oh, you poor thing it must be horrible for you.'

Speaking as a person who has said so many stupid and inept things in my life that I stand a good chance of being elected Mayor of London, I like to think my friend said that out of surprise and shock. But instead of uttering the hissed mantra of the inappropriate phone interruption, 'Call you back later, bye', I impulsively reply, 'I am in the middle of a meeting of farmers who are plotting how to take on one of the biggest multinationals in the world – it's not horrid at all, it's brilliant. Call you back later, bye.'*

Guiltily I lift my head, pocketing the offending technology. No one has noticed my blathering, they are listening as Kuriji

---

* *This conversation really happened.*

finishes with a flourish. They nod emphatically and murmuring breaks out. I edge over and ask one of the crowd, 'What did he just say?'

'He said "Are you ready to agitate?"'

* * *

Kuriji's son Mahendra jumps from his cot where a second before he had lain unaware of the impending visitors. Patting down his hair he hurries into the house and emerges moments later with a jug of water and a low bow. The first thing a farmer does when guests arrive is offer water – the second thing he does is show them the well. Groups gather around it, peer into darkness, point to old tidemarks on the wall and tut. In good years a farmer might have shown a guest his cattle or full crops, but these are dry years, so everyone comes to the well with a quiet lamentation, to plead, curse, and sigh. Farmers show their wells like bruises, as evidence of injury.

'Here,' says Kuriji gesticulating with an outstretched arm. Mere metres from of his home lies the dry and dead well. The top courses its brickwork have been exposed to the elements and are blown and puffy with erosion. 'Initially it was thirty feet deep. So where the pigeons are sitting, that was the depth of the well.'

Leaning precariously, holding the top of a metal ladder that descends into the well, I can see a circular shelf of concrete that is home to the birds; four nesting pigeons who inhabit the ledge, cooing in the shade amidst the caked bird crap and feathers.

'That was the depth of the well, dug in 1990,' says Kuriji enunciating the numbers so there is no confusion. From where the pigeons sit another smaller hole drops into total darkness, this was the second well, that went down to 80 feet.

'Dried. Dried.' he says, with a tilt of his head. 'I have this tube well after this,' he points to a couple of pipes that run across his yard to a metal cylinder which houses the pump. This tube well was dug in 2002 and goes down to 205 feet. That is the depth he brings the water up from.

'It cost me 1 lakh rupees.' Which is about £1,200. And as if this were not indignity enough, he can use the pump for only a few hours a day. The state decided to allow farmers four hours of electricity every twenty-four hours thus limiting the amount of water they can bring up. A decision that has caused considerable bitterness as the bottlers are not subject to the same measures. Coke can pull up water when it likes.

We walk along the side of a barley field that is home to a small temple, a stone affair with a peaked roof barely a metre in height. This is a temple to Hanuman, the monkey god who owns and protects the well. Not a task the primate god has excelled at in this instance. Before us is a large field that remains unplanted, the promised empty field. It is stark in its absence of plant life, it is a large patch of tilled earth. Where the blackish trunks of the trees are set out against the insipid brown of the earth. Kuriji speaking in English explains slowly, 'Out of seven hectares two fallow.'

'Why is this left fallow?'

'Due to lack of water, sufficient water is not available for us, that's why.'

We turn back to face the planted land, opposite the barley is the small family vegetable patch where white bulbs of garlic flowers sit on thin green stalks and coriander bunches grow close to the ground.

'Usually we cultivate all the land, it's all irrigated but now because of the scarcity of the water...two hectares are left.'

'So nearly one third of the farm is gone?'

And with that we walk back to the home away from the barren dirt in silence.

* * *

Before I leave I ask, 'Can we take a photo of you and your grandchildren in front of your home?'

'Yes. Of course.'

He calls for his two grandsons, Subham and Nishant, who are seven and ten, and they stand under the porch in front of the wooden cot their father had lain in as we arrived. The grandsons stand quietly, impassive and polite. Mahendra, their dad suddenly remembers he is wearing only a vest. He rushes inside and comes out doing up the buttons on his shirt. The children's hair is sorted with swift parental hands and someone must have said, 'Tidy yourselves up,' as the two boys tug their shirt bottoms and brush down their sleeves. Then with a herding shuffle and one arm gently around each child, Kuriji allows his chest to swell a little. They stand straight and confident, looking at the camera with a happy pride and I ask, 'Kuriji, do you hope that one day your grandsons will inherit this land?'

'Yes. They will. Automatically.' He answers instantly, without a second's hesitation, not taking his eyes away from the camera. He seems so sure. So painfully sure.

10
GAS

Kaladera, India

'The Coca-Cola Company
has invested more than
US $1 billion...[and]
employs approximately
6,000 local people...indirectly,
our business in India creates
employment for more than
150,000 people.'

The Coca-Cola Company[1]

The Company's ability to take credit for positive news is monumental. In fact it is inversely proportionate to their ability to distance themselves from the negative. Not surprisingly they talk up the jobs they create and the benefit they bring to a community. TCCC say they employ 6,000 people directly and 'indirectly, our business in India creates employment for more than 150,000 people.' Which sounds intriguing, who are these 150,000 people who benefit from the Company largesse? When pressed Coke said their 'positive economic impact is multiplied by the employment generated through our chain of distributors and retailers, through our vendors...[and] point of purchase.'[2] So the Company are taking credit for shopkeepers and street vendors who stock Coke...Now I have dealt with quite a few Coca-Cola PR and press people over the years and under these rules I would just like to make it clear that I am indirectly responsible for the creation of those people's jobs.

To put Coke's economic benefit to India into perspective, consider the Company's claim to have invested over $1 billion in just over a decade. The money that comes into India from foreign transnationals comes under the category of Foreign Direct Investment. But another source of money coming into India is remittance flows: very simply, this is workers leaving the country, working abroad and sending money home. The economist and analyst Kavaljit Singh estimates that, 'In India, remittance flows are nearly four times larger than FDI flows.'[3] This means that hard-working ordinary folk looking for a better life for their family and sending the money home put significantly more money into the Indian economy that foreign-based transnationals like Coca-Cola. And by significantly I mean four times as much money. Every year.

* * *

A potent image of the benefit the company has brought to Kaladera was shown to me early on in my visit and it happened before I went to Kuriji's farm and met the farmers' struggle committee. The day started with an encounter that was as sudden as it was unexpected and it began in a fertiliser supply shop in the village. This is the place I was to meet up with Kuriji; it is off the main drag, past a row of barbers in wooden huts lathering customers' chins and on a corner of a network of tight alleyways stuffed with traders. The shop is very small, with two doors, one opening at the front, the other to the side street. Instead of walking around the corner of the shop, you could walk in one door and out of the other and cut an entire second off your journey time. But somehow the place is packed with sacks, barrels, boxes, bottles, a couple of toilet seats to one side and a smell of ammonia that indicates the organic movement has yet to gather strength here. Pride of place in the shop pinned to the wall is the Indian flag covered with the slogan 'Pepsi Coca-Cola out of India!' Hanging a foot away by some seed packets, is its polar opposite: a Coca-Cola calendar with a picture of a chipmunk drinking Coke through a straw.

Helping me out with the translating is Amit Srivastava from the Indian Resource Centre, an NGO that has worked a lot with grassroots groups on the issue of Coca-Cola. Amit is an Indian non resident and a US citizen, so working on Coca-Cola's practices in India means he can attack the rapacious standard bearer of American capitalism and visit his mum in Delhi at the same time. He is about my age and has a West-Coast style ponytail, which is two years past its wear-by date.

'Good to see you. Hello,' Kuriji greets Amit and myself in English. 'Here please. Sit,' he says ushering me to a fold-out chair in the one remaining bit of space.

'Water?'

A copper metal pot with a spout is passed round, Amit holds it away from his lips and the pours water straight into his open mouth.

'Chai? For you?'

'Yes, yes please.'

I sit back and Kuriji explains today's itinerary. 'I will take you to my farm. And you will meet the farmers who are organising the agitation to talk with them. This afternoon I have arranged it.'

And with the business part of the morning over we get down to the hard work of sipping tea. I must have been there all of three minutes when an old man, with cracked NHS glasses and goggly eyes appears in front of me. Wearing a traditional big red turban dotted with tiny yellow and green flowers, his magnified black eyeballs hold me in his gaze, as he unleashes a torrent of Hindi gushing from him nonstop, as if gasping for breath might prove lethal. The village grapevine must be on broadband, because he had heard I was in the shop. It is me he has come to see. Well, not me exactly, he had heard a foreign journalist was here and how was he to know any better?

When he finally comes up for air Kuriji explains, 'He wants to show you something.'
    'Show me something?'
    'A well,' says Amit.
    'Oh.'
    'He wants to show you a well.'
    'A Coca-Cola well!' adds Kuriji.

The old man tilts his head and looks at me. Through the lenses his pupils look so large that if he ever took MDMA his eyes would end up bigger than his face. He cocks his head one way and then the other awaiting a response.

Taking a deep breath I say, 'Right then,' before reluctantly and unknowingly stepping off into an unscheduled revelation.

The old man leads us through the market, down the shaded alleyways and out of the centre of the village, out past the stalls and homes, out to where the shacks and shanties stack up in rickety regularity. This is a *basti*, a slum, home of the landless labourer, the Dalits, the lower caste. Out here the roads are wider, the tarmac thinner and the dust thicker.

The old man arrives at the edge of the *basti*, excitedly turns to us, refocuses, declares 'Here. Look!' and presents a large pothole with an outstretched arm. I've never seen a pothole get such a build-up and introduction. I should give it a round of applause but I'm a tough audience when it comes to potholes. I live in Lambeth, south London, we're connoisseurs. We classify potholes as something that an Invacar can't climb out of, anything less is a divot.

Amit, Kuriji and I stare at this metre-wide hole with a bit of tubing poking out above the soil.

'This what he wants to show you,' says Amit.

'A hole?'

The old man with the bushbaby eyes smiles in triumph, his one skinny arm outstretched waving at it like a tourist guide.

'A hole?'

He grunts and points again. I remain singularly unimpressed. But the crowd forming a circle around us obviously views this with slightly more significance.

People seem to gather easily in India. Even in the smallest village an argument over parking can over draw many more spectators than the average English County Cricket match. The throng here has assembled quickly, it's three deep already with kids pushing past grown-ups to get to the front and getting slapped on the head for their trouble. Already there is shoving at the back and shouted comments – this is a proper crowd, a mere scapegoat away from a rabble. Someone screams the words, 'Coca-Cola!' which is the trigger word for the old man to begin.

'This is the well Coca-Cola built for us,' he says with a flourish. 'Coca-Cola came. Coca-Cola drilled this well.'

'Useless,' shouts a man from the crowd.

'Not deep enough,' says a man in a grey T-shirt in the front row. 'They don't drill deep enough.'

The old man shakes his finger in the air and shouts to regain his position as chief storyteller, 'Soft soil! They only drill in soft soil not to rock.'

'Too shallow,' says grey shirt.

'It fell in,' the old man says.

The well had worked fine for a few months but once the moisture in the surrounding soil was gone it dried up and Coke's well collapsed in on itself and died. However the cave-in had only occurred at the bottom of the shaft, thus allowing one of the less sure-footed village goats to tumble down it and die too.

The old man starts, 'When the goat died, the community thought this is dangerous and a child will fall in and die too...'

'So we filled in the rest of the well,' says grey shirt nipping in to finish the story.

The old man glowers at him then turns to the hole. And for a moment the old man, grey shirt, the crowd, Amit, Kuriji, and I stand over the small crater of detritus that once was a well in respectful silence. Had I a lily about my person I would have cast it at that moment.

'The public of this colony are all distressed because of the shortage of water,' says the old man.

Wonky well aside, the bigger issue is the scarcity of water. It is normally women who bear the brunt of this, as they are the ones who have to fetch it. There's a group of women in the crowd so I try striking up a conversation by saying 'Hi' and holding out my hand. At the front of the group a small lean woman sticks a hip out, one arm folded and the other pulling her yellow and green headscarf across her face. She glares at me and there is no need for a translator to know that she's saying, 'Who does he think he is?'

Amit shoots me a prompting stare, brings his hands together and mouths 'namaste' at me.

'Namaste,' I say bowing slightly awkwardly.

With a tiny movement she pulls her chin up in contempt. Someone declares, 'He's a reporter.'

She retorts to the crowd while holding me in a hostile gaze. 'It's not going to bring any difference to our situation. The water problem will remain.'

I do what I do best in these situations, which is smile and bumble, and she agrees to speak though will not give her name. I nickname her The Stare.

The lack of water here has many consequences. Drawing it from the hand pump can take a long time and there may not be enough for the 200–250 families here. If a woman wants to make sure her family has enough water she has to work harder.

'What time do you get up for water?'

'We get up at four in the morning.' She replies, in a slightly less hostile manner.

'How long is the queue?'

'It is as crowded as it is now.' Which is very crowded. 'A lot of women end up with bruises. The children end up fighting.'

This is quite common as others confirm. A second woman in a green skirt joins in, telling of how she and her son go to collect water in the morning. 'Sometimes we end up fighting.' To avoid this her son 'goes on a bicycle to a different place to get water…it's very far away.'

Women and children are literally fighting for the remaining water.

Over a series of questions and curt answers The Stare explains she has to draw water for fifteen people in her extended family and five cattle. Then she makes breakfast, walks the three to four kilometres to work, fetching stones from eight in the morning until five in the evening. When she gets home there is no water. 'I have to fill water in the evening. By ten o'clock we have our meal.'

One of the kids, maybe five or six years old, takes her hand and looks up at her. The Stare has let her headscarf fall from her face and has tossed it over her shoulder.

'It's because of the shortage of water that my child looks like this. I don't even get time to bathe them.' She says pulling at her daughter's jumper to show that there is neither water nor time to wash their clothes.

   This is not the only impact on the children either, the woman in a green skirt says. 'We have four daughters and one son. All of them have stopped going to school because of the water.'

Because both parents are out working the children have to fetch the water and the shortage means they don't have time to get water and go to school. Green Skirt's youngest daughter Neetu is eight years old and she appears on cue.
   'Namaste,' I say to Neetu.

Embarrassed at having been spoken to she tucks herself into her mother's skirt and then peaks from the folds to flash a grin Hallmark could sell a million cards on.

'When there is no water she stays back,' says her mother, one hand around Neetu. Her son is a few metres away and she nods towards him. 'Because of water, even our son has stopped going to school. If there is water he will go to school tomorrow.'

So the women get up early, fight for water, have no time to bathe their kids and the children are taken out of school so they can get water for the family. What was it like before the Coca-Cola plant came? A voice from the crowd responds, 'There was a lot of water then.'

'So do you ever buy water?'

'We don't have money to buy water,' says The Stare.

The voice from the crowd calls back, 'No, we never bought water before.'

'Then, there was so much water here,' says The Stare and with that she tugs her headscarf firmly over her face and moves away.

A group of men stand by the collapsed Coca-Cola well, the older ones are in their late twenties, the younger ones are barely out of their teens and some are clearly not. They lounge with easy familiarity, leaning on each other's shoulders and dangling their arms around a friend: a vision of a stage gang in a West End musical. They all clearly have something on their minds, though it might be a dance rendition of 'Greased Lightning'. They lazily follow our activities and as the women walk away a male voice calls. 'Workers are always crying for employment. They are not given any jobs. Coke gives them employment.' This is no defiant cry, this is a sad statement of fact.

So I ask, 'Is there anyone who works for Coke?'

Nudges and looks are exchanged and then, 'Yes, I have,' says a young man.

'Yes,' adds another.

'I worked for three years,' says a confident voice. He's in his early twenties with swept-back hair and in a thin jumper with equally thin stripes. He stands in the middle of the group, framed by two lads behind one resting on each of his shoulders. The confident voice belongs to Rahis, he worked at the bottling plant, though he was employed as a casual worker by the contractor.

'They never made us permanent. One day you are working the next day you don't have a job. It is not just me. They do this to everyone.'

The group don't say a word but nod quietly as Rahis continues, 'Sometimes they take us, sometimes they don't. At times they remove us from the job. We are all troubled by this.' He says, indicating the crowd around him.

'How do you know if you have work that day?'

'At times they give us a phone call. Sometimes we go and stand in front of the gate. They chase us away, asking us to come the next day.'

It is a relatively common complaint of the temporary worker that the contractor holds out the promise of a permanent job if they do longer hours. And by Rahis's account this plant is no exception. 'They used to always say that we would be made permanent. They used to tempt us and make us work even harder'

This time the nods are more emphatic. It dawns on me that they all seem to have some experience of working there, so I ask if there are any more Coke workers in the crowd. They nod and put their hands up. About eight have worked at the plant at one time or another, though some like Rahis no longer do so.

'Has anyone got a permanent job?'

The 'No' that comes from the crowd is more confident now and the youngest-looking of the group pipes up, 'When the contractors are in need of workers, they make all kinds of promises,' he says, ' they promise but they chase the workers away after a while.'

The cocky member of the group is a young lad in a vest with chains around his neck and an Elvis mini-quiff. He stands leaning on his mate's shoulder, who is the drabber of the two in a plain brownish shirt and a scruffy mop top. They look to be best friends. Elvis Quiff nudges Best Friend, and says something to the group who burst out laughing. Best Friend drops his head, when he lifts it up a moment later his face has reddened, this proves even more hilarious to the group who laugh even louder. Best Friend laughs too and shrugs; Elvis Quiff pats him on the shoulder. It is obvious they are somewhat of a double act.

Amit explains to me that Elvis Quiff had told the story of how his best friend had been working in the water treatment plant – this is where the water is purified and cleaned ready to be used in drink production. Best Friend had passed out with the fumes of the chlorine, this, Elvis Quiff had joked, was because Best Friend was weak-brained, thus prompting the laughter and minor moment of shame. But when they stop giggling others acknowledge they have suffered too.

'While you were working was a lot of chlorine fumes emitted?'

'Yes, in huge amounts.' says Best Friend 'They never did anything for our safety. If people from audit came over they would give us something for our safety just to show them and took it back when they left'

'What did they give you?'

'Safety clothing.'

'What kind of safety clothing did they give you?'

'Something to cover our face,' reports Best Friend.

'Masks?'

'Gas masks,' says Elvis Quiff joining his friend.

'Gas mask. Gloves,' adds Best Friend.

'Could you describe the masks?'

'There were strings to tie it to the back of the head...but this was only to show them they never did give us these masks.'

'What did they make you do?'

'They gave us chlorine,' shrugs Best Friend.

'They used to give us chlorine,' Says Elvis Quiff backing him up.

'There were people to give us instructions and we used to do accordingly...they used to tell is what to do.'

'What did they chlorine look like?'

'It looked like white powder, it came in sacks,' explains Best friend.

'Plastic sacks,' says Elvis Quiff, who for some reason, probably mischief, points to the boy who looks like the youngest in the group and says 'He still works for Coke, he still works in Water Treatment.'

'Yes,' Youngest says looking at the ground and holding his folded arms high to his chest.

'Do you mix chlorine with water?'

'Yes,' Youngest replies.

He is a temporary worker like all of them and he gets 86 rupees for an eight-hour day.

'Did they give you anything for safety?'

'They have only given us this T-shirt,' Youngest scoffs lightly, indicating the dark blue collared T-shirt he is wearing.

'Yes, just a T-shirt,' joins in Elvis Quiff, 'Show him your T-shirt'

'No,' says Youngest giggling and hunching, pulling his arms to him covering something on the breast of his shirt.

'It's a Coke shirt,' laughs Elvis Quiff and one of the group playfully pulls Youngest's arm away to revel the Coca-Cola logo on his shirt, the shirt that will protect him from the chlorine fumes. And they laugh.

With this I sense they have said what they wanted to, so I ask one final question. 'When you are working, when you see the result of what Coca-Cola does, when you see the water going here. Does that make you feel conflicted?'

'It is necessary to fill our stomachs. We have no choice. We need to meet the expenses of our family,' says Youngest.

'If we don't go, they will bring workers from other villages,' Best Friend states with a shrug, and for once Elvis Quiff doesn't chime in.

* * *

So the men will line up outside the gates waiting for a chance to work in the chlorine fumes for a company which is pumping millions of litres of water out of the ground while the women fight each other for pots of water and the children are taken out of school. Like Coca-Cola's well this village is falling in on itself as the water runs out. The question that keeps recurring is the simple one, why did Coca-Cola set up in a drought-prone area? Surely when the company conducted its environmental assessments before opening up a plant, problems with water levels would have been identified? Surely any report would have shown that there was not enough water for them and the community? Exactly why the company chose to open there is a mystery. Who knows, perhaps it was the result of drunken chief executives playing dares: Exxon had to spill oil on the Alaskan coast, Enron had to turn the lights out in California and Coca-Cola had to open up in the worst possible place for bottling their product.

While no one but Coke knows the full reasons why they built their plant in Kaladera, we do know two key facts thanks to Coke's own report by The Energy and Resource Institute (TERI). Unsurprisingly, as they were conducting an assessment of Coke's plants, the organisation asked to see various documents, including the Environmental Due Diligence reports for the plant. These would show Coke's appraisal of the water situation before starting production and might shine a light on how the company thought they could operate in India's driest state. Stunningly, Coca-Cola simply refused to hand them over, 'due to reasons of legal and strategic confidentiality'[4] thus denying the assessors vital data with which to complete their work. But TERI did manage to elicit one vital piece of information. The TERI report states 'in response to queries from TERI, Coca-Cola representatives explained that the company's requirements do not explicitly necessitate the assessment of the effects of HCCBPL, Kaladera, bottling operations on groundwater in the region of operation but focused on ensuring a sustained supply of water for business operations.'[5]

TERI describes this situation by saying the 'focus of TCCC... is on business continuity – community water issues do not appear to be an integral part of the water resources management practices of TCCC.'[6]

In lay language this means the company only checked if there was enough water for its own use. Coca-Cola did not consider at any point if there was enough water for the plant *and* the community. They simply didn't give a fuck.

11

THE FIZZ
MAN'S BURDEN

India

'We are a user of water in a highly water-stressed area, and the burden of proof is on us to demonstrate that we can reconcile our operations with local community and watershed needs.'

The Coca-Cola Company, 2008[1]

I have simple rules for my life that apply to wherever I am and whatever situation I am in, but in particular they apply to India, and the rules are: I don't do joss sticks, chanting or naked. Yoga, yogis, gurus and inner journeys can fuck themselves as far as I am concerned. And the same applies to anything in the vicinity of the word 'tantric' – I can't think of anything worse than an hour-long orgasm – it sounds exhausting, pointless and showy. I do not want to find my inner self – I've found more than enough of myself already and what I've found so far is distressing enough. Furthermore the answer is 'no' to the question 'Do I need a fat bloke with a beard selling me meditation tapes and mantras?' Nor do I want anyone helping me reach enlightenment by teaching me breathing exercises. I have been breathing for forty-five years without a single lesson. Frankly when I want to expand my consciousness I'll read a book, thank you very much.

Having stated these simple rules, believed in them and indeed led my life by them I am somewhat bewildered to find myself in a Gandhian ashram in the middle of the desert having spent the early part of the evening sat on a rug at the top of a mountain having tea with a 'Holy man' dressed in a longi.* Frankly it has all gone a bit *Donnie Darko*. Furthermore I am not calmed by the fact that it is midnight, a thunderstorm is breaking overhead, the lightning has brought down the electricity, the place is in total darkness while the window shutters slam and bang and there is no one else in the

---

* *I had trekked up to the top of a mountain to see a dam that had been built by villagers to conserve water for the wildlife. The holy man lived in a tent at the top of a ridge. It was a tiring trip and he had offered a cup of tea. Sitting on the rug with him it had seemed rude to ask, 'so what are you about then?' So I did a lot of grinning, and bowing. His tent had grabbed the best spot, as it looked out across the long valley, green and lush from the dam water, and this scene rolled back as far as it was possible to see with the human eye. I did at one point say to the holy man,'you've gt yourself a lovely view here, haven't you,' but somehow as the words came out of my mouth it sounded like I was talking about Littlehampton.*

dormitory. If it were not for the two frogs and one mouse I would be completely alone. The bed is wooden with a straw mattress frame and the pillows have so many sweat stains that I wouldn't like to guess at how much DNA is soaked in them. I am sitting under a mosquito net that has been deployed more out of a need to erect a barrier of some kind between me and whatever else is out there than to stop me from getting bitten. I'm all for protecting the environment and minimalising our reliance on industrial-based consumerism but I am currently inhabiting a world that has never smelled the simple chemical pleasure of pine-fresh cleaner and I am not sure I like it. So holding a Maglite between my teeth and writing in my notebook I try and make sense of the past 48 hours and how I got to be here.

It started as usual with The Coca-Cola Company. The Company gave little credence to the fact that their own report recommended serious consideration be given to shutting down the plant in Kaladera. It had been the threat of a boycott by the University of Michigan that had led to Coke commissioning TERI, so when the report was finished Coke sent a copy to the university. In the seven-page covering letter Coca-Cola failed to mention that TERI had suggested the Kaladera plant be shut down. Instead they claimed the plant in Kaladera was responsible for putting *more* water into the ground than it took out,[2] despite the farmers, the workers and Coke's own report saying the opposite. I am not suggesting this is a comparison but if I ever get caught shoplifting my defence is going to be, 'Actually I was putting stuff on the shelf!'

Kaladera, like most of Rajasthan, relies on groundwater – getting water from a well. Coke claim that they are replenishing (recharging) the groundwater using 'rainwater harvesting schemes...In Kaladera the rainwater harvesting systems we have installed have the potential to recharge about fifteen times the amount of water the plant uses currently...Even in recent years when rainfall has been below average, *actual recharge has been more than five times the amount of water used for production of our beverages*[3] [my emphasis].' This appears to be an amazing assertion; it is not often you hear of water-intensive industries putting five times the amount of water they use back into the ground. And considering Coke normally charges for its water, I have to say nice of them to donate for free too.

The next line of the Company's letter to Michigan does qualify it somewhat, 'we will install measuring devices that will verify the amount of water recharged'. Now some might sneer at the fact that the Company can make such specific claims without bothering to actually measure and record the quantities of water involved. But I say shame on you naysayers! We are witnessing the birth of a new scientific era where companies can state facts without having to fall back on the outdated and tiresome concept of collated scientific data.

When I pressed Coke on this technicality, they told me that 'The company, along with community/NGO, tries to take water table readings before and after monsoon, keeps historical data, conduct community interviews, facilitate media visits to understand the efficacy and impact of such projects besides site visits by its own high-ranking officials'.[4] Oh where to begin...Firstly, I ask the Company how they monitor their scheme and they reply saying the company 'tries' to measure water. Secondly they say they keep historical data but of what? Old train tickets are 'historical data'. An Enron financial report is historical data. A stalker's trophy cupboard is 'historical data'. Thirdly the company say they 'facilitate media visits', so how does this relate to monitoring the schemes, am I to assume that the paparazzi finish with Brad and Angelina and then nip over to Kaladera with their hydrology kits? Fourthly, the company says they get visits from 'its own high-ranking officials'. Well done – your boss looked at it. So to conclude: The Coca-Cola Company, the company that put their own products in space with a device that enabled astronauts to drink their fizzy pop in zero gravity, when asked how they monitor their own rainwater harvesting schemes replied, 'We do try...I've got some cuttings...the boss looked at it and a photographer took a photo.'

Assuming Coke's claim is based on a paper calculation let's make one of our own. According to Coca-Cola the Kaladera plant extracted nearly 88 million litres of water in 2007.[5] If Coke's statement were to apply to this data then the company would need to be putting at least 440 million litres of water into the ground through their rainwater harvesting structures to replace the 88 million it took out. I wanted to find out how and if Coke are putting these amounts of water back into the ground, which is how I ended up at the ashram.

To be honest, I know a little more than nothing about rainwater harvesting but substantially less than anything of worth. If we were measuring ignorance in units I would assess mine to be about a *Daily Express*'s worth of stupidity; despite which I have a very strong negative opinion of rainwater harvesting. I have judged it to be a little tie-dye and lurking near the borders of pseudo-science. However, if Coca-Cola are basing their continued existence in Kaladera on a claim to be a net contributor of water in a drought-prone area, based on their rainwater harvesting projects...well it makes sense to try and understand a bit about it. Which is why I made contact with the man credited with pioneering water management and community rainwater harvesting schemes in Rajasthan, Rajendra Singh. He is referred to as the Rainwater Man and knows enough about the subject for Coca-Cola to try and get him on board for their schemes. Something he took exception to.[6]

* * *

Rajendra Singh is staying in Delhi at the Gandhi Peace Foundation.

'Have you been before?' asks the taxi driver as we weave for dear life.

'No, never.'

'Do you know anything about it?'

'Well it's run on Gandhian principles...it's educational and they have rooms you can stay in...other than that the only thing I can tell you is I would be surprised if they have a mini-bar service.'

'You are meeting Gandhi followers, yes?'

'Yes, though I wouldn't recognise a Gandhian if they hit me in the face...'

This was apparently a faux pas.

The driver resumes talking when he stops to ask for directions at the next lights and we re-enter the fray of Delhi's traffic with a firmer sense of where we are going. At one point a big banner on the side of the road reads 'Make every day safety day. 37th National Safety Day 8 March.' At least I think it was the eighth, it was hard to tell as we were swerving to avoid a cow in the middle lane. I have chewed my nails in many cars around the world but Delhi beats them all for sheer fear, here a driver's horn will wear out quicker than the brake pads; the experience is like playing Grand Theft Auto with four million people connected to the same console.

The front of the Gandhi Peace Foundation is a big building that looks like a university done in the style of a Soviet apartment block but without the frills. The walls used to be white and the strip lights used to work without flickering. Rajendra's room is bare save three camp beds with slim mattresses, two painfully hard wooden chairs built by comfort-hating carpenters and a portrait of Gandhi. Undoubtedly Gandhi was one of the most important political leaders of the twentieth century but he could have encouraged his followers to accessorise just a little bit. Frugality may well be the moral cornerstone of their philosophy but they manage to make the Amish look decadent.

Rajendra Singh leads me to the seat and smiles. He is nearly fifty with a black beard and a face that runs with emotion, his expressions letting you know the tone of the next comment before he opens his mouth. Shifting the folds of his kurta that hangs loosely on his stocky frame he sits on the seat, with an easy and relaxed manner that belies the austerity of the chair. And with a wave of his hand to signal the start of his story, he smiles, leans backs and says, 'I started this work in 1984 in Rajasthan in a place called Gaoloura village, in the Alwar District. This area is semi-arid with hardly any rainfall annually.'

He had originally gone there as part of an educational programme but became immersed in creating rainwater harvesting structures when a village elder taught him about the traditional ways of capturing water. Rajendra smiles as he tells me about the physical work he did. The first structure he made was a *johad*, a concave pond, he worked on it by himself and it took four years to make. Which probably explains his ability to luxuriate in the wooden chair; after spending four years navvying on your own I would imagine he could nap on concrete.

'In '88 we had very good rainfall, which collected and recharged the underground aquifer. You can see water in the wells that were old and dry before.' Though his English is infinitely more advanced than my Hindi it occasionally requires minor mental adjustments to get the flow of it. 'So in the beginning,' he says, 'it is a little hard, because in the beginning nobody believed, nobody trust it, but when you can show some visual impact, people come...and the next year thirty-nine villages start rainwater harvesting structures.'

Over 4,000 rainwater harvesting structures have now been built with this region, with the help and inspiration of Rajendra Singh and the non-government organisation Tarun Bharat Sangh. The work is done on the Gandhian principle, shunning development money, government aid and grant assistance, preferring instead on community work and self-reliance. 'In my country the water is not the asset of the government, it is not the asset of any one person...the responsibility for the drinking water, for agriculture, for industry is the community responsibility.'

It was when Rajendra and his structures started to make old rivers run again that people began to notice him outside the district. I ask him about this story.

'The river come after twelve years, the river was dry, and river come back in '98.'

'What was the name of the river?'

'Arvari river.'

'So this river was once dry...'

'Dead and dry.'

'And it is flowing?'

'The river is perennial.'

Using a series of dams built by villages along the length of it, the river started to flow again. Not surprisingly he began to attract press attention, articles appeared and awards quickly followed. Rajendra became known as the 'Water Man of Rajasthan'.

I am not exactly sure of how rainwater harvesting works, from the sound of it, you build dams and ponds in a place where water can collect and then it seeps into the ground. But maybe I am oversimplifying it and more to the point if it works and he can do it, can Coca-Cola? But this question is given short shrift, 'I am saying they can't give back to the region, the water they are taking is from the underground water. They can't, they are not doing recharge water.'

'But their publicity says "look at the rainwater harvesting we're doing", they're in the papers yesterday saying we will be water neutral by the end of the year, what do you make...'

'This statement, is a big lie, this is not possible, I can say that they are not doing what they are saying.'

'OK,' I say uncertainly.

'It is impossible. They can't do the water harvesting because they have no right on the water, so they can't do. The water can only be harvested through the community. They can't do it.'

'You saying that technically they can't do it?'

'I'm saying technically they can't do. '

But I have heard nothing that proves this point and I worry that Rajendra's Gandhian ideal of community self-reliance has become too dogmatic. I don't quite understand why Coke can't do what he has achieved? So I press the question home again, but he replies 'My dear friend, we have a community doing water conservation, water harvesting and water management. I request you tomorrow go there and see where the community is doing these things. You will understand.'

'Great.'

And with that I take the next step towards the ashram.

* * *

Twelve hours later the car wheels whirr with the familiar dry sound of motion along a fair to middling tarmac. The low noise leaves me feeling contented, it is the sound of connections having been made, people met and a journey underway. It is the sound that all is well. Quickly the trappings of the city fall behind us. The ashram is three hours' drive north of Jaipur and its famous Red Fort.

Lumbering lorries grinding through the highway to the desert replace the congestion of cars. The garish billboard hoardings hawking perfumes, burgers and pop stars gradually fade, and as their number diminishes so the number of camels increase. Nearly all of them have patterns shaved into their flanks, angular cuts in their coats creating a kaleidoscope pattern of flowers near each camel's backside. Intentionally or not this is the ultimate act of optimism, to stick such a scented image so close to a camel's arse.

Devayani Kulkarni sits in the front passenger seat. She works with Tarun Bharat Sangh, Rajendra Singh's NGO. She's a small wiry woman of about forty with long black hair in plaits, jeans, gappy teeth and a cough, she is taking me to visit rainwater harvesting projects. Sitting in the back next to me is Kanhaiya Lal Gurjor dressed in a neat, pressed kurta, trousers and a set of glasses that make him look like a Fifties jazz intellectual. Kanhaiya worked on his first rainwater harvesting structure in 1989, a check dam: a traditional dam used for rainwater harvesting.

'How many structures have you worked on since then?'

'Forty,' says Kanhaiya, answering the question as if he had just been asked how many combat missions he had flown.

Gazing out of the back window I try to pick out distinguishing marks in the scrubland. 'This is all semi-arid,' says Devayani, indicating the surrounding landscape. Semi-arid is an understatement, I never knew there were this many shades of light brown.

Although he's not driving, Kanhaiya keeps his gaze fixed firmly on the road as he explains how the state's annual rainfall can fall in just three days. 'In Rajasthan sometimes you can get ten centimetres of rainfall in one hour.'

'What? Ten centimetres an hour? That is huge!'

'Sometimes it happen,' says Devayani leaning over the front seat to tell me. 'If we don't construct any check dam or rainwater harvesting structure that rainfall goes. It does not go inside the ground, it goes...' and with that she shoos imaginary water away with her hand, '...when we arrest this water with a check dam the groundwater recharges and that goes in the wells.'

So that is all there is to it, build a dam in a strategic place which stops the water, the water then soaks into the ground and this fills up the wells.

Stopping halfway up a hillside we step out on to a scrubland that is called Darugula Ka Bandha. The hills climb behind us with a few bits of brush over the slopes, and these knotted little skirmishes seem to be the only plant life in sight. It is only when Kanhaiya shows me, 'There. This is where the water comes,' that I begin to notice the gullies. They are cut into the earth, lightly scarring the ground and streak downwards. At a second glance tiny signs of life become a bit more obvious, piles of stones dislodged by once rushing water have tumbled down only to re-lodge at a lower point, making untidy altars where they gather. 'Water comes down quickly, here and here and here,' he says pointing. Then smiling for the first time he says, 'Shall we see the structure?'

A short walk downhill leads to a dam made of earth about five metres high, its sloping sides and flat top make it look like a Toblerone that has had its tip filed off. 'This fills with 3.5 metres of water when it rains,' says Kanhaiya pointing at the dry pit behind the dam. Then he strides along a pathway on top of the earthen mound. As we follow him Devayani explains that the villagers collect money for the materials but use their own labour to build each pond or dam. We catch up with Kanhaiya looking downhill, and with small gesture of his hand points us to the other side of the dam and a wooden hut, a well with upright supports and a winding rope but most remarkably a garden – a vegetable garden. In the middle of a landscape Neil Armstrong would feel at home in there are tomato plants. Kanhaiya and Devayani point in turn.

'Mustard.'

'Wheat.'

'Black gram.'

And to crown the scene a young papaya tree stands upright in defiance of its surroundings.

The rest of the day is full such moments but my favourite was the village of Palpura, where the local rainwater harvesting structures culminate in a pond area. Climbing over a low wall we set off towards clumps of bright green tall grass.

'This is elephant grass,' laughs Devayani.

'Elephant?'

'Yes, because it is tall enough for an elephant to hide in.'

Kanhaiya is ahead of us again and, turning into the grass, he disappears. We find him walking carefully along an overflow, slippery with algae and a slight but steady cascade of water. Walking out after him on to the concrete I look up the pond, about a hundred metres long and maybe forty wide in places. Gulls swoop on it. Egrets emerge by the bullrushes, dragonflies hover and fish peep from under small lilies. A white temple sits on one bank where a troop of monkeys roam under the sound of the peacocks yowl.

'Sorry, what was that?' enquires Devayani standing next to me on the overflow.

'Oh, it's just an expression. It's very colloquial, very hard to translate. It means this is very beautiful.'

I had not realised she was quite so close behind and had overheard my muttered words of awe, 'Fuck me I'm in a Yes album cover.'

As we stand on the overflow, listening to the burbling water I decide to mention the C word and say, 'Coca-Cola claim they put more water into the ground than they take out, is that possible?'

'How much they take out?' says Devayani.

'Well it varies but a million litres a day at some points.'

'Does the company protect the water that much every day?' she says in contempt and disbelief that the company can put an equal amount of water back into the ground.

'They say they do...'

'That is not possible, it is impossible.'

'Why?'

'Because you don't get that much rain every day.'

'But they say they do put more water in than they get out...'

'Only a local community can protect, maintain and manage water resources properly. If you hand over water resources to a big company they could not think about the local situation, of how to protect these resources. So if any company construct a rainwater harvesting structure it is not enough for conservation.'

Undoubtedly Kanhaiya and Devayani have performed small miracles and I am looking at one right now, but there is just not enough science in their answer.

* * *

I am not sure where these past days have led in regard to Coca-Cola. Everyone has said Coke can't recharge the amount of water they claim to, but no one has proven this. No one has factually explained their claims. So have Coke's critics got it wrong? I don't know. The only thing I know for sure is I started as a sceptic, believing rainwater harvesting to be a pseudo-science and find myself lying on an old mattress in an ashram with a sense of genuine wonder. I curl up and sleep the sleep of a convert.

Having managed to stay here without being reborn, changing my name, getting a henna tattoo or even playing hacky sack with Dutch travellers recovering from dysentery, I bid farewell to the two-frog chorus in the dormitory; whom I have grown rather fond of and have nicked named Paul and Linda. Travelling south to Kaladera I arrive with genuine trepidation at Coke's rainwater harvesting structures.

'Hindustan Coca-Cola together in Development' reads the wind-blown sign by the side of the track, announcing we have arrived at one of Coke's much-vaunted projects. 'Kaladera a dream', it reads, sounding more ambiguous than the company's statements on the matter. If my dad had seen the sign he would have said it was 'on the piss' as it leans heavily to one side. However, according to the information on the board Coke has dug seventy filtered boreholes to a depth of 103 feet to recharge the local water supply. Apparently this benefits not only the farmers but the local area as well. This sounds simple and practical: rainwater trickles down through various thicknesses of gravel in the hole and percolates into the groundwater, instead of running off or evaporating.

These holes are laid along an old dry riverbed in the middle of an expanse of barren scrubland, where the sandy soil crunches underfoot, clear and crunchy like walking on stale crisps. A few trees make the effort but I've seen more flora and fauna in a builder's yard. It is hot, dusty and virtually featureless, exactly the kind of place you'd bump into Ray Winston while filming a Costa del Crime caper. The first borehole is a metre wide concrete circle, about half a metre deep before the first layer of gravel starts. It is surrounded by a few bits of rubble and a plastic bottle. The second hole is every inch as glamorous as the first, except this time a three-course brick circle has been built around the hole. Someone later took exception to it and kicked some of the bricks over. Possibly fans of the first hole gripped by inter hole rivalry.

There are another sixty-eight to go...

Across the way is a concrete road leading to the home of one Kaladera's politicians, an ex-Panchayat leader. They must have got along very well with Coke as the company has installed a metal hand pump just outside their home, for the community obviously, though in this case the community seems to be mainly the Panchayat leader's family. A man from the village emerges from a palm leaf shelter by the side of the old Panchayat leader's home and offers to crank the groaning handle up and down to illustrate the pump in action. After five minutes he is hotter and thirstier than when he started. 'It's useless,' he says, 'sometimes you can get water but it can take half an hour to bring it up.' It is Coca-Cola we have to thank for this thirty-minute wait, after all they have alleged they are a net contributor to the groundwater, so without their help there would be even less water and it would take even longer to draw the water. The villager walks back to the shade of the shelter muttering – possibly a hymn of praise to Coca-Cola.

The TERI report – Coke's commissioned work – noted that field visits to randomly chosen external recharge shaft sites 'revealed that all the shafts were in a dilapidated condition.'[7]

From what I can see out here I would agree. The place is dilapidated. Frankly, Pompeii looks in better condition and that was buried under volcanic ash. Coke claim they do the maintenance work just before the monsoon.[8] I suppose it doesn't matter what it looks like if it does the job, though at this stage I am convinced of nothing.

* * *

Someone has to know something about the veracity of Coke's claim and that someone might well be Professor Rathore, a Senior Fellow at the Institute of Development Studies in Jaipur, whose data is quoted in the TERI report. The professor specialises in water resource management and the fine academic tradition of vertical filing systems. Stacks of reports, articles, notes and statistics form tall ordered blocks around the room. So prominent are these piles that if ever a map were to be drawn of it, this would be the first study to require contour lines. The walls are covered in hydro porn, pictures of large bodies of water, bare-arsed reservoirs and cheeky lakes. And stuck in one corner a board has term information, phone numbers, timetables and official pronouncements tacked on with drawing pins. I find the room strangely reassuring, it smacks of the twin pillars of academia: obsession and overwork.

The professor sits behind his desk between two more literal pillars. He is somewhere in his fifties, and has (like many Indian men) innate trust in his ink pen's durability and craftsmanship, as it sits neatly in the top pocket of his spotless white shirt. He peers over his glasses before taking them off and exudes the demeanour of an educator, that is an air of quiet and calm exasperation, a man who has had to explain the obvious too many times.

'It is the rainfall pattern of Rajasthan which is important,' says the professor. 'If the rainfall is low, then the withdrawal is much more than the water that is being recharged through the rainfall. So it's a perpetual depletion of the groundwater.'

This much everyone seems to agree on. What I want to know is can Coke put up to fifteen times the amount of water they use in production back in the ground, so I start to ask my question, 'The company are saying that they are using rainwater harvesting projects to recharge…'

'It doesn't work,' he says shaking his head sadly.

'But,' I begin again, 'one of the rainwater harvesting projects which they've got is on a dried riverbed, they've got seventy bore holes—'

'That's the wrong thing,' He interrupts flicking his hand dismissively.

'Why is that the wrong thing?'

'Ask them how many times that river flowed, you will be shocked to know that in a year, in five years…OK, I'll have to show you something.' And with that he rummages in a pillar and plucks out a single piece of paper, showing the number of times the Jaipur area has been in drought. These are the figure that shows that the area has been in drought for 47 per cent of the last 106 years.

Jaipur district frequency of occurrence of drought and its intensity since 1901-2006
Number of years district of Jaipur over past 106 years

- 56 years normal
- 10 years light drought
- 17 years moderate drought
- 12 years serious drought
- 11 years very serious drought

Source: Professor Rathore, Institute of Development Studies Jaipur

After staring quietly at the piece of paper I look up at his expectant face and say 'So there is not enough rain...'

He affords a brief smile, 'There is no run off,' he says, referring back to the dry riverbed that won't run without rain, 'So you build a structure and it doesn't work. It will work only when there is a run off. OK? That run off only takes place one or two years, and how much is that? Very small, so these rainwater harvesting structures are to bluff people, and the state.'

'And it doesn't work because the riverbed...'

'Because of these reasons: the rainfall is very meagre; rainy days are very limited; droughts are a perpetual phenomenon, and where is the run off? Where is recharge? Where's the water going to come from?'

The professor makes the simple point that you can't do rainwater harvesting without rainwater. But I still can't quite believe Coke's credibility rests solely on this, so I try and sneak in one more attempt. 'Is there a way the company could do rainwater harvesting in a meaningful way in the area?'

'No, it's just not possible, it's not possible.' He holds his hand up and sighs. 'Coca-Cola also have a right to do business, we don't contest that but we contest that you can spoil the lives of so many people. You may have Coca-Cola or any brewery industry, but the source of water should not be groundwater, it should be surface water.'

Then looking out from between his two pillars of statistics and reports, unprompted he says, 'If I am chief minister in charge of this, I will stop today the industry, and ship it from that place. I will give them choice. Go to Kota Barrage, go to Indira Gandhi Canal, or quit, there's no other choice. Go to Namada, if you want, but not here, don't have groundwater as your source.'

* * *

So I'm left with Coke's claim that 'even in recent years when rainfall has been below average, actual recharge has been more than five times the amount of water used for production of our beverages.'[9]

I asked Coke if they would show me their figures and assumptions on which they base that claim. After a bit of a wait, they sent me a document compiled by a retired chief engineer that detailed each structure and its expected annual groundwater recharge. And unsurprisingly, it calculates that with normal rainfall the structures can recharge ten times what Coke takes out. In the case of less rainfall, that figure drops to five times. Which is still very impressive, and surely worthy of a little celebration. But before the corks are popped it is worth remembering that these figures are not verifiable.

There are no measuring devices. And around here no one's celebrating. Not the farmers, not Rajendra Singh, not the people who made the river flow again in Alwa and not Professor Rathore. Even TERI say, 'Water contingency measures as adopted by the plant seem to rely heavily on rainwater recharge structures, which in turn depend on rainfall in the region. Since the rainfall is scanty, the recharge achieved through such structures is unlikely to be meaningful.'[10] Everyone except Coca-Cola and their retired engineer says, 'no rain, no recharge'.

Perhaps it's too obvious a solution that maybe Coke could just actually measure the water its collecting, rather than merely 'trying' to do so. So I offer a different solution: if, Coca-Cola, you are so very sure in your historical data and attempted measurements that you harvest so many times more water than you use, why not just use the water you harvest instead of extracting it from the aquifer? You could store your harvested water and extract it at your leisure. Then, when you give back the five, ten or fifteen times more than you need, everyone will see exactly what great guys you are.

I agree with The Coca-Cola Company when they say the 'burden of truth is on us', their trouble is no one around here believes them.

* * *

Professor Rathore smiles politely and looks at his watch, by way of ending our chat, fortunately I am socially inept so I plough on.
   'If it carries on, what will happen, what do you think will happen?'
   He raises his eyebrows in concern and says, 'Very soon they'll realise that industry has to close. It cannot survive, not

more than four, five years definitely. Because the water quality will deplete, it will be so bad they cannot use it.'

Of all the answers I did not expect, this was about the most unexpected.

'So you're saying that industry has got four or five years here, and then it's finished?'

'Yes, it's definitely finished,' he says stretching slightly.

'What happens then to the communities?'

'Ruined...There'll be no drinking water available to them.'

INDIA:
A POSTQUEL

When I asked the Hindustan Coca-Cola Beverages Pvt Ltd if I could come and see their plant in Kaladera they refused saying I was 'biased'.

I reply using The Coca-Cola Company method of issue resolution and advanced rebuttal techniques.

'We are proud of the Mark Thomas system of objectivity and are appalled by these unfounded allegations levelled against him. Only recently Mark Thomas became the proud winner of the prestigious Emerald Eagle Award for Unbiased Reporting, the judges cited his even-handed dealing with The Coca-Cola Company as a case in point. But perhaps more importantly Mark Thomas has launched a bold and innovative truth harvesting and trading scheme initiative, where journalists in truth deficit can purchase unused truths on the open market, with exciting possibilities in the expanding markets in truth developing regions of Russia, Italy and the *Daily Express* news desk.

'Even in "truth drought" regions he has managed to recharge the equivalent of five times the amount of falsehoods extracted.

'It is a journey, he is not there yet, but it is one that Mark Thomas is committed to making and he aims to become completely bias neutral by 2011.

'Mark Thomas's book will create over 10,000 indirect jobs.'

12
SECOND FATTEST IN THE INFANTS

© Tracey Moberly

Mexico

'You know the bottom line is that we welcome competition... if the Pepsi company didn't exist we would have to invent them...but we welcome the increased competition because the voice behind the industry is, y'know, a rising tide floats all ships.'

Neville Isdell, The Coca-Cola Company Annual Meeting 2008

Mexico is *the* Coca-Cola country. This is what the landscape looks like when Coca-Cola invades and occupies a country, this is the view as the smoke clears from a marketing blitzkreig. Mexicans drink more

Coca-Cola products than anyone else on the planet, on average over 135 litres of stuff every year. Per Person.

And it is beginning to show. Mexicans are among the fattest people on the planet and are piling on the pounds at a rate that would alarm even Robbie Williams. In 1989 less than 10 per cent of Mexicans were overweight.[1] That figure is now over 68 per cent and rising.[2] Perhaps it is no coincidence that in the last fourteen years, the consumption of soft drinks has increased by 60 per cent;[3] it is also perhaps no coincidence that Coke spends a fifth of its global advertising budget in Mexico alone.

But despite controlling over 70 per cent[4] of the $6.5bn Mexican soft drinks industry,[5] Coca-Cola wanted more. This is the story of how Coca-Cola and its aggressive marketing were exposed by the determination of one working-class shopkeeper who wouldn't be bullied.

* * *

Arriving in Mexico City I start by visiting a man who I hope can explain the basics of why Mexico is plumping up. His name is Alejandro Calvillo and he founded El Podor del Consumidor – the Power of the Consumer – which runs a campaign called Dump the Soda. He has spent some time and thought trying to answer the question 'how did they get to be so big?' The 'they' in this case refers both to Coca-Cola and its drinkers.

Alejandro operates out of a shared building set in a quiet cobbled alleyway along the road from a squat church. Other NGOs work here too and Alejandro has his office set in the communal garden. He used to work for Greenpeace before leaving to form his own campaigning group, taking the compulsory environmentalist beard with him – though it is trimmed enough to reveal a lean and kind face. When he started El Poder del Consumidor he went back to basics. 'We began with a review at the office of information. We had a shock. It's terrible what's happening in Mexico. We found Mexico is the second-highest country in the world for obesity.'

But it isn't just the adult statistics that are alarming. More worryingly, the number of children between five and eleven who are obese or overweight has increased by 40 per cent in seven years. And El Podor del Consumidor lays the blame for Mexico's obesity problem on the soft drinks industry, 'Sodas have become the main source of refined sugar intake among the Mexican people and therefore the main responsibility for the current intake that has lead to overweight problems and obesity.'

'So what we've seen here is a quite big explosion, ' I say.

'Yes.'

'In quite a short time.'

'Yes...and in this panorama Coke sell 12 per cent of all their world sales in Mexico.'

And Mexico makes up just 1.65 per cent of the world's population.

Alejandro explains that one of the factors in the popularity of solft drinks is Mexico's lack of clean available drinking water, 'water fountains in schools in particular. If children can't have water they buy sodas.' And this is a country where 80 per cent of schools have no drinking water.[6] For the majority of children, soda consumption isn't a choice.

Coke's dominance of this market might be...well, how can I put this sensitively...it can't hurt to have the ex-President of Coca-Cola Mexico as the President of Mexico. Vicente Fox was the man who did that very thing, rising through the Coca-Cola system before branching out into non-drink-based politics.

FOX FACTS: From President of Coca-Cola Mexico to President of Mexico, Coca-Cola Country

President Fox's six-year term was between 2000-2006. According to Coca-Cola's own figures Coke sales increased 56.5 per cent between 1997 and 2007 – a period that coincides with Fox's Presidency.[7] It's not conclusive proof that he helped the company but he was seen selling cans of Coke during toilet breaks in the Mexican Parliament.*

During the Fox administration several things 'happened' that might be seen as beneficial to the company.

The first involves an artificial sweetener called cyclamate, banned from use in the USA and Mexico as it had been linked to cancer. One of the last acts of Fox's administration was to lift the ban on its use. Coke appeared to jump at the chance to use cyclamate as it is massively cheaper than aspartame and launched Coke Zero containing the sweetener in Mexico almost immediately after the ban was lifted. A massive backlash followed – led by El Podor del Consumidor and Alejandro – and the Ministry of Health even issued warnings over its consumption. Coke bowed to consumer pressure and removed cyclamate from the ingredients.[8] It is a well-known fact that during toilet breaks in the Mexican Parliament President Fox was seen using unsold Coke Zero containing cyclamate to clean the toilets.**

The other major helping hand Coke received during Fox's tenure was a change in the law that allowed Coca-Cola to bag generous twenty-year fixed-rate water concessions from the National Water Commission (CONAGUA). The man appointed to head up CONAGUA is an ex-Coca-Cola man Cristobal Jaime Jaquez.[9] Fox exchanged these concessions for cigarettes in the toilets in the Mexican Parliament where he smoked, a habit he kept secret from his wife.***

But the big reason Coca-Cola has got such a hold here is the combination of advertising and aggressive marketing practices. Coke spends a fifth of its annual advertising and marketing budget in Mexico alone,[10] or if we 'do the math', that's USD$4.54 for every Mexican man woman and child to persuade them to consume kilos of sugar every year. Let us pray heroin dealers never get an advertising budget.

Just as Coke's advertising budget is huge, so its sales teams are trained to work aggressively – to the extent of illegality. The Coca-Cola Export Corporation (a wholly owned subsidiary of the Atlanta-based Coca-Cola Company) and its Mexican bottlers have been found guilty of unfair monopoly practices by the Mexican Federal Competition Commission and fined the maximum penalty thanks in large part to a small shop owner called Raquel Chavez and a cheeky newcomer into the Mexican cola market, Big Cola.

When Peruvian drinks company, AjeGroup launched its star product in Mexico nobody, least of all Coca-Cola, predicted its success. An explanation for which can be found in its name, Big Cola – it was sold in really big bottles for a similar price to its smaller rivals and was a cola. Two things that were bound to appeal to a cash-poor, sugar-hungry people. Within two years, it had captured 5 per cent of the market. Not a killer blow for Coke and in actuality more threatening to Pepsi but Coke's response was to hit back and hit back hard. And one of the things they did was cut off the supply of Coca-Cola to shop owners if they dared to stock their Peruvian rival, which

---

* This is apparently not true but only in the sense that I have no facts to prove it
** This is absolutely true in the lying sense of the word.
*** Once again a truth waiting to happen...but technically a lie

is what they did to Raquel Chavez and her small shop. However she took the company to court and won, and along the way exposed a vicious national campaign of intimidation and coercion.

The lawyers from Big Cola have agreed to chat about the case so I head out to their offices in a newly developed business district – although the rate of development in Mexico City is so fast by the time you read this, it will probably be referred to as 'the old town'. Around the sculpted plains of these high-rise business parks there is a competition among companies to see who can put the most people into ill-fitting guards' jackets and place them around the building entrance. Here the parking lots seem full of black company cars still smelling of their new paint parked alongside enormous 4x4s, which for some reason all contain a single sports bag in the boot. But despite the conspicuous company culture the more lumpen branch of entrepreneurialism is evident all around, as along the street the irrepressible food stalls have sprung up like a crop. These makeshift wooden frames and their tarpaulin coverings are held together with bull clips big enough to trap a poacher, and under them Calor gas burners roar and frying pans the size of car tyres smoke with oil. Delivery boys and secretaries huddle around to stare into pots heating purple black beans and at grills turning corn breads brown. A police van has pulled up too, the cops get out, order *toastas* wrapped in napkins and then eat them leaning forward away from their uniform, for fear of dripping chilli sauce.

In one of these new company high-rises is a meeting room belonging to La Arena Trevilla Hernandez Y de la Torre, a legal firm who represented Big Cola. The room has the type of intense air-conditioning that can induce nosebleeds, and the walls hold a plasma TV and a presentation screen. To the side of a long desk, by the best chair in the room, is a pentangular conference call phone, with a big light underneath that flashes when it rings – it looks like a plastic electric starfish bought in a pound shop but it passes for flash around here.

Seated on the other side of the table is a lawyer, he might represent the people who sell big cheap cola but he sips small expensive bottles of water. He has requested that I do not name him, somewhat bizarrely given that his work has hitherto not been anonymous, so let us refer to him by the pseudonym 'Dan'.

Dan leans back in his chair and says, 'In Mexican culture a person who goes to buy a soft drink will never go to a big shop, they will always to got the corner shop...small shops where the owner is a family and the whole family depends on that shop to make ends meet.' There are 700,000 such shops in Mexico and 80 per cent of all soft drinks are sold through them. 'In mid 2002 a new soft drink called Big Cola was introduced. It started in the market offering a product, which is cheaper, and of better quality,' continues Dan, 'the company got 3 per cent of the market share in a year.'

In the lucrative soft drinks market this represents a major prize and one that Coca-Cola was not willing to give up easily. Dan explains that by April 2003 'Big Cola started to realise that the small shops had stopped buying their products.

'Why?'

He pauses.

'Because Coca-Cola were using their muscle to stop the small shops selling it...' I say answering the question that wasn't intended for me to answer.

'In mid-2003 Mrs Rachel Chavez together with other five shops denounce Coca-Cola to the Federal Competition

Commission because Coca-Cola had stopped selling Coke to her.'

'So they stopped selling to her because she sold Big Cola?' I chip in.

He nods.

The FCC found that Coke had been conducting a widescale campaign against Big Cola and so 'concludes that these are monopolistic activities which are aimed at removing Big Cola from the market. The authority imposed the biggest fine ever known in Mexico of $50,000,000 on Coca-Cola. This is the first time that a fine like this has ever given in the country...Everything was started thanks to Raquel Chavez.'

'Did you represent Raquel Chvez?'

'No, I was the lawyer of Big Cola. Mrs Raquel Chavez and the others did not have a lawyer. They are very poor people.'

We chat about the case and he gets some papers for me, but it is Raquel Chavez I want to see. I have been having problems trying to track her down. So I ask the lawyer if he knows has a current address for her.

'Have you got an address for Raquel?' I ask.

'She lives in Itzapalapa.'

'Oh, I should go and see her, she sounds great!' I say, reigning in my over-enthusiam for meeting Raquel that is clearly not shared by the present company.

'It is very difficult to get there and it is very dangerous, ' says Dan, though the assessment of danger by a man thus cloaked in anonymity might not be the most accurate.

Dan's parting gift had been a telephone number for Raquel Chavez, so all I had to do was phone her to arrange a visit to her shop and a chat. Unfortunately the line is dead and no pleading with the operator will bring it back to life. A journalist working in Mexico City says he has another phone number for her, different from the first. But that too does not work. So as I head towards the Metro station I call all the contacts I have once again to see if any of them have any new leads in my hunt for this elusive woman. The messages I leave on these poor people's answer machines are increasingly desperate – a mixture of begged favours, twisted arms, and promises I can't keep. But someone must have a a working phone number for her. As I descend the stairs I can only wait and hope it comes through.

* * *

I am getting to that age where I find travelling by foreign public transport to be quite exciting. I actually believe there should be an intermediary Freedom Pass for people like me, who are not technically in retirement but have adopted some of its attributes early. Nonetheless I love the fact that the Mexico City Metro stations not only have a station name but they also have their own pictoral representation – an individual logo for illiterate travellers to guide themselves by. Which also has the incidental benefit of enabling ignorant tourists to use them too. On one journey I boarded the train at the station of the 'jug of water with wavy lines' then zipped past the 'wasp' changed at the 'two snakes wrapped around a sword', stayed on as we went by the 'white cross' and then the 'cannon' too, finally getting off at the 'silhouette of an army bloke'.

Charles Dickens would have loved the Metro, all forms of urchin life are here. The carriages are packed but somehow the tide of hawkers runs a path around the cramped bodies: men selling peanuts, women waving packs of Chiclets chewing gum, a line of blind beggars and a woman selling Superglue. Who would have thought that there was a commuting market for Superglue? But here there must be.

My favourites are the home-made CD compilation sellers, playing their tracks on a portable player wired into a loudspeaker strapped to their chests- they look like jihadist DJs. One minute the carriage is filled with the sounds of salsa, the next it is dance music; one man's CD was so good I nearly missed the 'two snakes wrapped around a sword' and only just made it through the doors in time. On the platform the station's own speakers forlornly played 'I'd rather be a hammer than a nail' on pan pipes.

While feeling a tad despondent that no one had called me with Raquel Chavez's phone number, something rather remarkable happened. I got a source. Someone from inside Coke, willing to talk on condition of anonymity and this time there really was good reason not to name this person. Woodward and Bernstein had 'Deep throat'; I have 'Coke Throat'.

What can I tell you about Coke Throat? Well, essentially not a huge amount except that I was passed a piece of paper with a phone number and a time to dial it. I waited and dialled. A voice answered and asked me 'Are you having a good time in Mexico Mr Thomas?'

I said, 'Getting a stranger's phone number is often the way a good time starts.'

Coke Throat laughed but only just.

'I think you might want to talk to me.'

And that was the beginning of a beautiful friendship.

Coke Throat sung loud and long. So did Nana Mouskouri. But this stuff wasn't Greek to me.

Coke Throat knew all about the big trouble with Big Cola and was keen to tell me how it started. Instead of using sales staff, distribution warehouses and a fleet of delivery trucks, Big Cola opted for a more innovative distribution method and caught

Coke on the hop. The Peruvians simply said anyone who has a truck or even a car can come to the warehouse, pick up crates of drink and go and sell it on commission to the 'Mom and Pop' stores. These 700,000 'Mom and Pop' stores account for 80 per cent of soft drink sales in Mexico, so Big Cola were able to simply bypass the normal practice of setting up a sales force and delivery system and still get their product into the market. According to Coke Throat, the sudden arrival of Big Cola in these stores, 'gave them a huge massive presence that Coke never expected so that, combined with the nice pricing they have, almost 40-50 per cent cheaper than us, was why a lot of low-income consumers switched their preference to Big Cola and it started to hit us...we underestimated that product and it came and hit us in the face.'

Mexico offers soft drinks companies an extremely lucrative profit margin and with so much money at stake Coca-Cola decided something had to be done. 'The idea was to start blocking them at the point of sale,' Coke Throat explained. 'It was like that at the very beginning.' Coke assembled its sales force with the simple tactic. 'The name of the game is availability, if Big Cola was available, Big Cola has a winning formula that can sell. So the idea was to remove them, and if you are a salesman and if you have a hundred stores you should not have more than five stores selling Big Cola [in your area]. That was the benchmark.'

The operation against Big Cola even had its own name, 'The ABC plan – Anti Big Cola plan.' Local comedians were hired to appear in training videos for the sales forces, 'training them how to remove Big Cola from the point of sales and the consequence of not doing that. So less income, less job security and not having their nice house in at retirement.'

Coke's assault was a well-coordinated strike at the 'Mom and Pop shops' that stocked Big Cola, Coke Throat called it 'the red wave' and they used a variety of tactics.

'There was the direct change of Big Cola products for Coca-Cola products.'

'You take Big Cola out of the shop physically?' I enquire.

'Physically, yes.'

'You swap it bottle for bottle...'

'Bottle for bottle...I'm the salesman I see this Big Cola bottle I switch it for a Coke and throw the other to the garbage or throw it in the street so the shop doesn't sell it now.' In some cases the sales force would empty Big Cola down the drains in front of the shop.

'But why would a shop swap?'

'You offer two for one.

Coke Throat goes on to describe how the sales force would issue a 'direct order to remove Big Cola from any Coca-Cola cooler in the shop. [They would tell the store owner] that they would be losing the cooler if they have one Big Cola available either in the cooler or even in the store.'

Just to be clear I go over it again, 'So you would say to them if you have Big Cola in the fridge here, it's a Coca-Cola fridge, get the Big Cola out or I'm taking the fridge.'

'Exactly, or get Big Cola out of the store or I won't supply you with Coca-Cola.'

It all sounds slightly Al Capone with carbonation, going round to stores and intimidating or cajoling shopkeepers to get rid of Big Cola and I say, 'That's almost like Mafia tactics isn't it? '

Coke Throat affords a smile, 'Well, let's just call it protecting my market share.'

The big question is who sanctioned this?

'Very clear, from top to bottom, it was a well-organised army going into war.'

'So was this the Mexican bottlers...' I begin.

'It was Coca-Cola who coordinated it with bottlers, [we're] the brain power and the mastermind behind everything...we bring a lot of practices from other countries, we put them on the table and we find strategy with local knowledge, that might be the bottlers, we define it and then we go to war.'

'We wanted to get out of this saying to people "we do not sell Coca-Cola and we didn't do anything, we just sell concentrate" but the reality – and that's why the competition commission brought us down – was that we have the brainpower and are the money behind everything and we are the ones that make everything work in a synchronised way.' The FCC investigation visited various shops to examine the claims against Coca-Cola and found that Big Cola was either not available or was placed way at the back of the shop, away from the Coca-Cola fridges at the front, in 500 instances that they examined. The 'red wave' had struck across Mexico.

* * *

On 4 July 2005 the CFC fined the 'Coca-Cola system' $157 million pesos (approx USD$13 million) for monopolistic practices, as Coke's conduct contravened Article 10 Part IV of the Federal Law of Economic Competition. The fine was levelled at the bottlers and distributors FEMSA, Contal, Grupo Peninsular, Grupo Fomento Queretano as well as The Coca-Cola Export Company (Mexico) which is a subsiduary of The Coca-Cola Company. They were also ordered to immediately stop putting conditions on the sale of Coke products. The decision was appealed by Coke. But on 17 November 2005, the CFC ruled upheld the earlier decision and threw Coke's appeal out.[11]

As for Raquel Chavez the search was not going well, the six degrees of separation theory – that we are all but six phone calls away from the person we need to reach, the very theory that had worked its bizarre charm in Turkey – was failing to find her. True, it had turned up some interesting and charming folk along the way, including a former guerilla, a workers co-op and someone who knew someone who knew someone that could summon up the ghost of Leon Trotsky, but no Raquel Chavez. Not even an address for her shop. I trawled the internet looking for clues and found a couple of pictures of her from when she won the case. She was forty-nine in 2005 and photographed sitting in her small shop amidst its grilles and crates. She had black shoulder-length hair and a flowery top – that was all I could make out.

The part of town she lived in was called Itzapalapa and it quickly developed the status of a desolate moor, as every time I mentioned the place in the presence of a Mexican – be it a receptionist at a hotel or local folk I was meeting up with – they would pause significantly, adopt a Cornish accent and say, 'You don't want to go up there sir, not on a night like tonight.'

'Why?' I would ask.

'Why sir, the last tourist that went up there by 'em self never came back...though they do say on a dark moonless night you can hear the pages of a Rough Guide book a'rustlin' in the breeze.'

I was beginning to think somehow I missed the boat. Everyone I asked seemed to know someone who might know how to get to her but then never did. And time simply ran out. Or it nearly did. A telephone number was found at the last minute and although I didn't get to see her I did finally speak to Raquel Chavez over the phone.

She does indeed live in Itzapalapa and it is indeed a tad...
er...Moss Side. Some have called it impoverished, others worse
but Raquel says 'We are a working-class area. This is a
difficult area,' then adds, ' as everywhere is.'

'I wanted to meet you personally but I have only just got
your phone number,' I explain, ' all the numbers I had for you
were dead.'

'I had to change all the telephone numbers. After I won the
case against Coca-Cola people thought I had won thirteen
million dollars. But the fines go to the judicial system I had
not won any money. So people phoned. I got death threats, I
got blackmail attempts, people phoned up just wanting me to
give them money. But what could I do with all these people
threatening me? I had to make ends meet I still have to go to
work – I just had to change the phones.'

Then she told me her story. Raquel wanted what many
working-class parents want: for her children to have a better
life than her own. 'My biggest dream was to give them a
professional career and get them to go to university. I was in a
economic bind, so I started the shop and I started with all my
energy and enthusiasm in 1992.' It was on the corner of mall
but it was a 'Mom and Pop shop'.

Then in 2002 her Coke salesman came by and politely
asked 'Why don't you swap your Big Cola bottles for Coca-
Cola? I will give you two bottles of Coke for every one bottle of
Big Cola you give me.'

Recounting the moment to me she explained, 'If I accepted
they would give me the Coca-Cola and would take away the
Big Cola but the condition was that I could not sell Big Cola
any more.'

'What did you say to the Coke salesman?'

'I said "No. My shop is free. Even if it is only one customer who wants Big Cola I have to offer him the best service." He were very upset and annoyed.'

The Coke salesman had obviously seen one of the training videos that Coke Throat described, as Raquel's initial refusal didn't deter him. But Raquel kept saying no.

One day the salesman came into her shop and started again, 'Mrs Chavez, come on, I will give you two bottles of Coca-Cola for every bottle of Big Cola you give to me.'

'No,' said Raquel ' Not even if it is ten bottles of Coke to one of Big Cola will I do it.' And the salesman left.

A little later he came round again, this time arrogant and cocky, 'OK,' he said 'We will give you ten for one – I will give you ten bottles of Coca-Cola for one for Big Cola.' I suspect he even afforded himself a little knowing smile. He simply did not expect Raquel to say 'No. I won't let you buy me.'

So it began. At first they refused to give her any promotional presents or offers; the other shops had them, but not hers. Then they wanted to only allow Coke products in the Coke fridge in the shop. She said to the salesman, 'You can take your fridge away. I can buy one myself.'

The Bank Holiday in March is a big day and lot of drinks get sold. So Raquel placed her orders with 'Pre-sales – there is a person who comes round the day before and asks what we need and the following day the truck comes and brings the drinks. But they didn't bring any to my shop. They left me during that important Bank Holiday without a bottle.'

The following day when the truck came around she rushed out and gave them a new order on a handwritten note.

'Why didn't you deliver my order?' She said and started back to her shop.

The manager came after her holding her order in his hand and waving it in the air.

'Are you going to bring my order now then?'

But he kept waving the paper in the air. Smirking.

'You are not allowed any of our products any more,' He said.

'What? Why not?' She said, dumbfounded.

'Because you don't support us and because you won't stop selling Big Cola.'

'This is unconstitutional!' said Raquel, not knowing if it was or it wasn't.

'No,' he said, 'Coca-Cola does what they want...You can do whatever you want. Coca-Cola has too many lawyers and too much money. No one can touch them.' He waved her order in the air, 'If you want this you know what to do.'

'No, thank you,' she replied.

And with that they stopped bringing the products for good.

The trouble is people drink a lot of Coca-Cola in Mexico and if the shop doesn't have it then that shop loses a lot of custom.

'People are too used to buying Coke so people stopped coming to my shop and I didn't see them any more. I was completely alone. I had to start to work long hours into the evening and try to recover what I hadn't sold during the day. I lost a lot of money, I think I lost 50 per cent of my income at that time. Fridays and Saturdays I shut the shop at 2am,' she sighs. 'Too many hours for too little profit. Even my husband was upset with me.'

'How dare you do that against them,' he had said. 'You know they are very powerful, they will ruin us.'

On one rare day when she was away from the shop she asked her husband to mind it and on that day the Big Cola salesman came around. Her husband promptly cancelled the Big Cola orders. They did not stay cancelled for long. Raquel returned to her shop, and just as promptly reordered the Big Cola. Her husband simply didn't understand, he kept asking, 'What is it you want? What is it you want?'

Finally Raquel went to Federal Competition Commission to denounce Coca-Cola and ask them to investigate. 'I asked them "What can I do?"'

'What can we do?' they retorted.

'You are the Federal Competition Commission!'

'What can we do when no one will denounce them? When there are more people in the same situation I will talk to you.'

So Raquel went and found others.

Her husband became unhappier still. 'He kept putting a lot of pressure on me because of The Coca-Cola case.' But Raquel said to him, 'I would prefer to close the shop, and go and wash clothes in other people's houses in order for my children to have an education, but I won't let Coca-Cola humiliate me. I will never let them humiliate me.'

And she didn't. The FCC found The Coca-Cola Export Company, a direct subsidiary of The Coca-Cola Company in Atlanta, guilty along with the bottlers and fined them in November 2005. As Raquel said she gets no money as the fines go to the state. So why did she do it?

'Although economically I didn't win anything I wanted to have the pride of winning. My motivation was my pride... Raquel Chavez will always be a sour name for Coca-Cola and it will always be like that. I am very proud of myself.'

* * *

Recently a student came to visit Raquel and she lent him the papers from her case, showing the verdict in her favour. He was doing a new course on monopoly practices in business and wanted to study her case. There is a certain joy that a woman who fought so hard for her children to go on to higher education should finally have her story being taught at university.

13

BELCHING OUT THE DEVIL

San Cristóbal, Mexico

'San Cristóbal is my Tara of Gone With the Wind. It's a place I go back to. It's the place where you get strength, where you get strong.'

Vicente Fox, Interview with *Larry King Live*, CNN, 8 October 2007

I t was the city of San Cristóbal in the southern Mexican state of Chiapas that hosted the unlikely relaunch of the balaclava. Who would have thought a fashion comeback was ever on the cards? I for one thought its long association with peeping toms and the IRA had finished it off but it bounced right back into the limelight with Subcomandante Marcos of the Zapatistas when he boldly started to accessorise standard revolutionary army fatigues. Out went cigars and berets and in came balaclavas* and tobacco pipes. Through

---

* Balaclavas are referred to as ski masks in the USA but there is a major difference between these two items – namely, a British grandmother would never knit a ski mask.

the power of the internet Subcomandante Marcos, the enigmatic spokesman and poster boy for the Zapatistas Army of National Liberation or EZLN (Ejército Zapatista de Liberación Nacional), became a world-wide phenomena. The Zapatista 1994 uprising was primarily the indigenous Mayan people's struggle against poverty and racism but they became synonymous with anti-globalisation and opposing neo-liberal economic changes. And for a while the picturesque city of San Cristóbal became the epicentre of Zapatista activity and it was to this city that the solidarity groups, sympathisers and curious lefties flocked to witness the struggle. These supporters became quaintly and quickly know as Zapatouristas.

San Cristóbal is somewhat quieter these days. The town square has a gentle pace to its colonial colonnades, the narrow side streets in pastel shades are lined with gift shops, all seemingly packed with crystals and small animals made of wood, sold to the tune of non-stop Manu Chau. It is the only place in the world I have been comfortable enough to wear my WOMAD T-shirt in public – an act I wouldn't normally do, even at WOMAD itself. The local artisans' market is predictably rammed with things made out of brightly coloured woven thread, hammocks, belts, wrist bands, bags, hats, plant pots – probably driving jackets and slacks too. Rows of stalls covered with canvas sheeting to keep the sun at bay, offer rugs, jugs and shoulder purses on string, next to necklaces and woollen reptiles, not to mention the endless array of small percussion instruments, flutes, pan pipes and wooden armadillos with a shaky tail. You can even get a balaclava with EZLN, the Zapatista acronym, sown in red over the brow – which must be the anarchist equivalent of a Kiss-Me-Quick hat.

The place is stuffed to the gills with arts and crafts crap – or as we like to call it in our house – 'ethnotat'. There are even

Zapatista dolls on sale, small woollen figures wearing balaclavas, riding donkeys and armed with rifles.

'Who buys this sort of shit?' I ask Laura, an American friend who lives here.

'Probably the same people who buy the Subcomandate Marcos pipes,' she says, then pointing to a display of carved beasts and metal trinkets, warns, 'Don't buy anything from that stall. All that stuff is made in China.'

These days even handcrafted, locally produced indigenous produce seems to be subcontracted. Later I wander past two cooing German tourists bent over the Chinese goods and I sneer in superiority, before heading home clutching my two Zapatista dolls and a pipe.

* * *

Laura is a twenty-four-year-old American student living in San Cristóbal. She is tall, with short black hair and very clever. She is working on a master's degree and her thesis is on the local Coca-Cola bottling plant: together we form a Coke obsessives' support group. Friends of hers find us huddled in cafés hunched over laptops, swapping documents and data or chuckling over an in joke about borehole capacities and water extraction rates. The pair of us are a research paper short of an identifiable dysfunctional condition.

The situation here is unlike India. To the best of my knowledge Coca-Cola has not opened up a plant in a drought-prone region of Mexico (although if anyone knows different please write). Chiapas is water rich; what it lacks is not rainfall but publicly available clean water.

The local bus service is a fleet of white battered combies with wooden seats in the back and a couple of rails to cling to when it gets too cramped – using these and the odd taxi Laura and I set off on a whistlestop trip around San Cristóbal.

Our first stop is San Cristóbal's water board, where I ask the receptionist if there is any chance that I can talk to someone about the city's water situation. She mutters in a phone while nearby a fan on a stand rattles loudly as it manfully loses the battle with the hot air. From behind an office door a head pokes out and beckons to us to enter. Jorge Mayorga is a cheery chubby chap with an obligatory moustache and dressed in a pale blue water board shirt.

'Please,' he says, pulling out chairs. Sitting behind his desk, hands clasped together, Jorge beams a smile in anticipation, waiting to be asked a question. He is either someone working for an organisation that wants to promote its activities to foreigners who might pop in with a few queries or he doesn't meet many people interested in his work. He is so impulsively friendly that within five minutes he is offering to give us a tour of the water pumping stations and treatment rooms in the area.

'I just wanted to get an overview of the city's water situation,' feeling my inner nerd flinch at his awesome power.

'OK,' he says and starts to explain that part of the cause for the city's problems. 'There has been a big increase in the population of San Cristóbal.' He points out that back in 1991 the water board had 13,867 families on its books, now they have 34,900 families- and these are just the one connected to the water supplies. He gets out a data sheet to illustrate the increase and even helps me understand the water distribution by drawing concentric circles in my notebook. The inner circle represents the centre of San Cristóbal where the hotels and bars are – in the tourist area tap water is available twenty-four hours a day – the middle circle represents households that get water for twelve hours a day and finally the outer circle have their taps working for six hours a day.

'That's a very good day if they manage that, ' says Laura, 'I live in the area that should get water twelve hours a day and often that water doesn't come on at all, and when it does you have to boil it for at least twenty minutes before you can drink it.'

'When do you know it is OK to drink?'

'You get this white powder, really fine grains that falls to the bottom. God knows what it is but it ain't water. So when that falls to the bottom I know I can drink the stuff on top of it.'

'What happens if you don't boil it?'

'You don't want to find out.'

Two days later I didn't and she's right – you don't.

* * *

San Cristóbal's Coordinator of Epidemiology in Sanitary Jurisdiction No. II of the Highlands Region of Chiapas has an office that is only marginally bigger than his title. His name is Cuauhtemoc Zapata Cabrera and he is another eager and smiling official. The building he works out of is just by the abattoir, which is a bit too open-air for my liking. The less brutal environs of his cosy office, are cluttered with papers, books, folders and kids' toys, which I assume is to make them as happy as the physical state that drew them here allows. Over the next half hour he explains that gastroenteritis is one of the top five sicknesses in the highlands of Chiapas. In his district in 2006 there were 9,998 cases involving intestinal amoebas, intestinal non-specific organisms, giardia, paratyphoid, food poisoning due to protozoa and the like. The infection rates are higher in the indigenous communities and there is a focus on teaching the importance of boiling water and how to soak food in iodine and chlorine.

The lack of water, clean or otherwise, is a common story too. We bump into a friend of a friend of Laura's, a Spanish teacher called Yasmina who lives with her husband and children in an area that should get water six hours a day. In reality they get it 'Two or three times a week and maybe for three hours, sometimes four...We never know when it is going to come on, so we have a storage tank.' The next day her water went off and didn't come back on for two weeks.

And actually Laura and Yasmina are both relatively well off when it comes to water. Consider the situation the Comunidad 5th de Marzo, (5th March Community) found themselves in. The community squatted on an area of land, which was to have been developed into a hotel golf course, and for that alone they will have my undying love. As far as I am concerned the situation could only have been bettered if a Bush family member had been playing a few rounds at the time. Although initially a Zapatista community, it opened its doors to all comers and has expanded over the years. The water board, after refusing to run taps into homes, charged people instead for the standpipes they ran in. Javiar, one of the community's inhabitants said, 'They didn't give us even public fountains...and because we didn't pay they say "well we are not giving you any water".' So in a land that is water rich and in a culture that relies on taking water from springs, rivers and wells this refusal to pay for the second rate was met with petty punishment. In 2007 the water board issued locks for paying customers – so they can slip the small metal cap over the standpipe and padlock it after they are done, to ensure no free water for these golf-hating ingrates.*

The community are running their own water project with the help of Berkeley College to create a water system independent of the water board and without need of stand pipes.

Meanwhile the Coca-Cola plant sits on top of the best water source around, the Huitepec aquifer. The plant has a twenty-year lease to extract water and is legally entitled to withdraw 500 million litres of it a year.[1] And in academic research conducted with the anonymous assistance of a senior plant official it was revealed that in 2003 the company extracted 240 million litres of water and paid $320,000 Mexican pesos- about 1p per 150 litres – which is not bad for a main ingredient.[2] The concession at Huitepec is one of twenty-seven that Coca-Cola has negotiated with the CNA Comission Nacional del Agua (the National Water Commission)[3] – the body run by the ex-Coca-Cola man Cristóbal Jaime Jaquez, who had been appointed by another ex-Coca-Cola man, President Vicente Fox.[4]

Up on Huitepec mountain above the Coke plant one of the community representatives or agente municipal, says the water level has gone down, He sits in his zip-up mauve jacket and flicked-back greying hair like an elderly member of the Soprano family about to take a driving test, 'There has been a lot of depletion but that is understandable. There are more of us, there is global warming so we have less water and obviously as water flows underground Coca-Cola has an effect.' Further along the hill Martin, an ex-agente municipal and farmer is wearing split shoes and no socks. He has worked on the land so long that his huge, gnarled hands look like something could take root on them. His hands tell the story behind his impassive face. When I ask says about the well water on his land, 'Yeah it has gone down,' he says and then adds, 'The thing is they [Coca-Cola] have a very deep well that sucks up a lot of water.' The situation is not critical in terms of supply but he worries for the future.

There is no allegation that Coke is directly responsible for the lack of clean available water through San Cristóbal, but this is the situation they operate in and one they can take advantage of. Even the guidebooks say 'Don't drink the tap water, buy bottled water' – such as Coke's water brands. As Yasmina says 'It is the worst thing...There is a shortage for basic needs, no electricity, no water but everywhere Coca-Cola.'

When I ask Martin what he would say to the CEO of Coke in response to the company claim that they support sustainable communities he said 'Really, he should realise, instead of helping, how much Coke helps fuck communities over.'

Perhaps it is not surprising that there is some bitterness felt towards the company and later that evening when Laura and I sit among her friends in a café in the centre of town, they laugh as they tell the tale of Coke's gift to the community. Each year the company donates a thirty-foot high plastic Christmas tree covered in baubles decorated in the Coca-Cola logo and topped off with a large silver star. It stands in front of the church and under the tree is the classic nativity scene, Joseph, Mary and a large Coca-Cola polar bear – the type used in their adverts. In fact it is quite close to the baby Jesus, perhaps not surprisingly Joseph stands further back and Mary is behind him, there is absolutely no sign of the three wise men. Though the bear has a smirk on its face – a smirk and a resentful demeanour, as if to question its Arctic presence in Mexico.

A few years ago in the middle of the night miscreants, set fire to the tree, its thirty-foot plastic leaves momentarily shooting a pillar of fire under the star of Bethlehem. In the morning a sharp odour of molten plastic lingered in the air and a pile of black shrunken gunk was all that was left of Coke's gift to the community. The local businesses condemned the act, some blamed the Zapatistas, others blamed troublemakers and some blamed drunks – though a polar bear was spotted fleeing the scene.

But it takes more than a burnt Christmas tree to intimidate the Coca-Cola bottler and the very next year a new plastic tree rose from the ashes in all its majesty. And the baby Jesus was placed in its hallowed and traditional place under the Coca-Cola bauble. Mary and Joseph had obviously received some trauma counselling as they too stood strong under the protective plastic boughs. Though this year, the tree did have barriers around. And an armed guard. To enforce peace on earth.

* * *

Back in Mexico City right at the start of this trip, Alejandro from El Poder del Consumidor had said, 'I think Coke is inside the consumer habits of a great part of this society, and it's stronger in the indigenous communities and with the worst case in Chiapas, Coke is part of the rituals.' Which is why Laura and I are on a tourist bus bound for Chamula – a Tzotzil Mayan town, where the indigenous community allow visitors in to see their religious ceremonies. Here they use Coca-Cola to help remove bad spirits and nightmares by way of a gaseous emission. Now I have heard of Coca-Cola being used for many different purposes from a misguided anti-spermicidal douche to the LAPD using it to wash blood away at the scene of car crashes, but I have never before heard of Coke being used in an exorcism.* So there are a host of anthropological and cultural reasons to go and witness this event, there are questions to ask of the company regarding their marketing practices, as well as an appraisal of the economic and nutritional consequences. Though I have to admit a significant part of the appeal is the

---

* This is an urban myth.

sanctified burping in church. Why they do it and quite how Coca-Cola managed to muscle in on an ancient tradition, are important addendums, but the assault on the mannered orthodoxy of the church by the release of belly air at the altar is too alluring to miss.

Bizarrely this is one of the things that got Laura researching Coca-Cola. As an anthropology graduate she lived in the Highlands of Chiapas and became fascinated by the way the drink had become so ingrained in the religious life of the community. Laura explains her research and interviews with indigenous Mayans on the subject. 'Basically people say that Coke came to the Highlands, the indigenous communities, when it came to San Cristóbal in the 1950s. It was very much the advertising of the time, they used promotions, free gifts, they sponsored film shows in neighbourhood squares or had loudspeakers on a cart which went around town telling everyone to drink Coke.'

Laura told me the first man to run a Coke concession in Chamula started in 1962 and brought the bottles into the Tzotzil Mayan town on a horse. His wife recalled that no one really knew of Coca-Cola but Coke's businessmen said they could sell their product and they did very well doing just that. Indigenous people would come here from communities as far as forty kilometres away to buy it.

The tour bus potters through the mountain splendour, leaving the city centre of San Cristóbal behind us in the distance. And as we get nearer to Chamula our tour guide, a thirty-something bearded fellow, runs through the dos and don'ts of the trip like a flight attendant:'You must respect the traditions of the indigenous people. You must not take photographs unless I say. You must not give money to child beggars, it encourages them stay from school. You must not stare at the people in the church. Remember this is a mix of ancient beliefs – the worship of the sun and the moon and the earth fused with Christianity. It might seem strange too that they drink alcohol in church, indeed some people may be a little drunk but this is their religion and you must be respectful.'

I chime in wanting to demonstrate my understanding nature, 'Well, the Catholic church serve up wine at the communion rail, so they accept the principle, it's just the size of the glass that is at issue here...'

But the bearded man turns to me for a second in blank disapproval, then turns back to the group in the bus and starts again, 'You must respect the traditions...'

* * *

The population of Chamula is Tzotzil Mayan – it is an indigenous town, whose peaceful surroundings are constantly pierced by the loud screeching bangs of home-made fireworks and rockets that are set off as part of the religious rituals. And glancing around the surrounding hillsides and the stark blue sky you can see puffs of black smoke popping in the distance before the speed of sound catches up with a crack. Pitched on one side of the square the church of San Juan dominates the town, it has a high bell tower and large wooden doors – the kind that hunchbacks can gratifyingly bang on while calling for sanctuary.

'Stick close to me please,' says our bearded guide as we enter.

From the bright light of the cloudless sunny day we pass into the dim church. There are no pews or seats but there is an intense smell of smouldering resin and scattered fresh pine needles that cover the ground. It is a big spacious building but

296 belching out the devil

already the grey smoke has filled its entirety. Groups of worshippers clear a space of the green needles to sit, and drip wax on to the floor to stand their rows of burning candles upright. Some sit at the altar, some in the knave, some by the walls where row upon row of glass boxes house effigies of the saints. Some have a small band of drummers, guitars and singers with them.

'When you walk around, do not intrude on the worshippers,' says the guide.

'Is that a chicken in the bag there?' asks one of the tour party pointing.

'Yes, that is a live chicken which will be sacrificed for a healing ceremony.' Then, turning to the group, he says, 'Please, a few of you can walk around.'

'But don't stare, right?' says one of the group.

'Do not stare, just be quiet and if you are lucky you may see a chicken being killed for the sacrifice.'

There are plenty of Coca-Cola bottles, and Pepsi too, set out on the floor, and their metal caps mingle with the pine needles, as families and friends gather in groups sitting, drinking, lighting candles, praying and singing. One family sits with bottles around them and a wicker bag, while the mother and father pray, a grandmother holds a small child on their lap with a bottle of Coke in front of her. This is an image I particularly warm to and think of the memory of my own nan smoking and singing songs.

Wandering here it occurs to me that the Pope has about as much control here as he has over the Presbyterians and the sense of individual ownership here is quite moving. The models of the saints are gaudy and slightly disturbing – as they should be in a Catholic church – but the figure of Jesus is jaw-dropping. In a glass cabinet near the altar the prone figure of Christ is being borne down from the cross by his followers. But Our Lord is not wearing the traditional loincloth. Our Lord is wearing a spangled powder blue glitter flower frock that comes up to just under his nipples, making Jesus look like a Thai transsexual fainting at a wedding.

And no matter how much I want to respect the Tzotzil families here, I find it hard to feel comfortable amidst high camp, low poverty and liberal tourists trying to sneak a peak at a chicken having its neck wrung.

* * *

Searching for a line of enquiry that involved a little less poultry and voyeurism we follow the curves and crumpled hillroads back to San Cristóbal. From the tourist centre of the postcard homes and tiled roofs, we step from the raised pavements away from the bars and hotels, past the markets and the stalls of Zapatista dolls, out on to dust tracks that all seem to have a single Toyota pick-up truck lunging from side to side as it trundles in a cloud of dirt; and then on to narrow lanes lined with ditches and weeds, where bulrushes sprout by wasteland ponds and plastic bottles collect around them at the edge of the mud. Out in the sun we wander to the shanty towns through the packed soil corridors and alleyways of wooden boards, with lone standpipes and packs of barking dogs, past the open family huts and homes, on to a long car-less street where children play chase in its empty lanes, twisting and turning from each other's flailing arms, while their parents sit by stalls watching and waiting for customers. And above, looking down on us from the distance are the newly built mountainside hovels, a hill of blossoming shacks and sheds on stilts. These are the newcomers fresh from the frontline of penury sprawling across to spread to the upper reaches, searching for a foothold to cling to, searching for a moment's respite.

Under this gaze we arrive on the outskirts of San Cristóbal at the Mayan Medicine Museum. The compound houses not only a museum but is also home to the Organizacion de Médicos Indigenas del Estado del Chiapas (the Organisation of Indigenous Doctors in the State of Chiapas). Where, amongst other things, they organise Mayan midwives for the communities in these hills. The front steps of the museum are under the cool shade of a porch which proves a tempting place for folk to squat and chat. This is where I meet Miguel, a member of staff who works on the committee for the indigenous doctors as well as in the museum as a youth worker. He is going to talk me through the significance of the Coke in the Tzotzil church.

'You can see Coca-Cola being used in the rituals and ceremonies of traditional doctors as it happens in San Juan in Chamula. But these happen everywhere, in communities, in small chapels, here in this museum...' In the religious healing ceremonies each component represent an element: the candles represents fire, pine needles the earth, prayers represent air and Coca-Cola symbolises water. 'In this case the ritual process – the drink has another element, the gas,' he says, explaining that burping throws out the 'bad energy, negative energy'.

  'Some people say it is throwing out bad spirits?'
  'It's all the bad energy, the ghosts, the nightmares, everything bad in that spiritual part.'

Considering parts of these ceremonies go back hundreds of years, it begs the question how did Coke muscle in on an ancient ritual?

'Before the famous soda was introduced there was atole which is made of corn. You have to leave it to ferment for eight days. After that you grind it and you make sour atole.'

This was the original burp juice. However, people began to realise you could get the same effect with Coca-Cola or Pepsi, and you didn't have to ferment corn for eight days. According to Miguel, 'Step by step Coca-Cola has started to be involved in religion and the indigenous communities and it started at the beginning with very cheap prices [for a bottle of Coke].'

This is a practice that carries on today: the price of a Coke in an indigenous community is half the price it would be in San Cristóbal, because in this poor community they can only buy what they can afford. Miguel looks up at the shantytown on the side of the mountain. 'Even in the small shops on the tops of the hill – they transport it up by donkeys.'

Some of the men sitting on the porch have listened to us talking and take this opportunity to pipe up, 'You can have a healing ceremony conducted for you here.'
'Oh really?'
'Yes, if you want,' says Miguel.
'A healing ceremony,' repeats one of the men.
'I'm sure it is very good but there is nothing physically wrong with me.'
'That is what you think but this heals your spirit.'
'Do you think my spirit needs healing?'
There is silence. Then the man nods. 'Yes – you will see how much better you feel after it.'
'OK, then, I would like to do this...' I clap my hands together and smile awkwardly while mentally rationalising, 'It's all OK. It would be rude not to. I should respect this culture and after all what is the worst that can happen?'

I turn expectantly to Miguel, who says, 'First you will need to buy some big bunches of basil and an egg.'

* * *

Fifteen minutes later a shaman is instructing me how to order the rows of lit candles on the floor while he places the egg and a cup of water next to them. Our spiritual guide for this particular healing journey is a stocky small man with a paunch and cropped hair, dressed in a blue denim shirt. Although I didn't have a fixed image of a shaman in my mind, I somehow did not expect him to look like a night watchman at a Parcelforce depot.

This ceremony does not involve Coca-Cola and burping, so my bad spirits are staying put, but a couple of local folk are having the same healing ritual and tell me as we line up in the small chapel that this is a protective healing ceremony. Figures of the saints inhabit the alcoves, including the Virgin of Guadeloupe in crown and gown, Saint Anthony looking lost in the corner and John the Baptist with his head still on his shoulders. There is one figure that stands out from the rest, a cross, chubby man holding a stick in the air wearing a frock – though it could be a toga – and I wonder if John Belushi has been canonised.

The stocky shaman sits upright on a small stool, rocking back and forth with his hands on his knees, intoning place names and saints in a sing-song monotone. Rising with a laboured breath he motions for me to come forward and he starts walking the length of the chapel chanting in Tzotzil, brushing the basil against the saints, evoking their names each in turn, before arriving at the corner where I wait by my egg and candles. The stocky shaman stands before me, coming up to my nose in height and as he intones his prayers he brushes

the swatch of basil over my face, first once, then again. Then he taps my shoulders with basil, first one side then the other – all the while continuing his chant. Next my stomach and sides are hit, each time harder than the first. Bending down he starts working on my calves whacking them with such force that he is beginning to pant with the effort of the blows and the chanting. The air is now thick with a peppery smell and as he returns upright he starts all over again, with even greater energy – smacking my shoulders with such vigour that leaves begin to fly off the branches. As he hits my stomach the air becomes a blizzard of basil and I want to shout, 'This isn't healing, this is seasoning!' but I am speechless in the face of the serious conviction held by everyone in the room.
Suddenly he stops and stares as leaves flutters to the ground. Stooping he picks up the egg waves it over my body, breaks it into the cup of water which he holds to the light to examine the floating yolk. Then he says: 'All the jealousy people have towards you is gone – you will return to San Cristóbal one day.' And with that he motions it is over and I to return to my seat.

Outside one of the local folks walks with me back to the city centre.

'Well?' he asks expectantly, breathing in deeply to show his own contentedness 'Did you see the way the plant turned black?'

'The basil?'

'Si, it turned black. It is the plant taking your bad energy. Some things science cannot explain.' He nods wisely, breathes another deep sigh of contentment and says, 'So, how do you feel?'

'I feel like I have been beaten up by pesto.'

* * *

As an atheist son of a family of preachers I have a bastardised version of the supposed Christian credo, 'Love the sinner, hate the sin', namely 'Love the religious, hate the religion'. It is impossible for me to fault anyone for wanting to buy a bottle of Coke over brewing maize for eight days, and believing basil takes away bad energy is no more bizarre than thinking a wafer turns into Jesus' body when it hits your tongue. But Coke and Pepsi have managed to inveigle their way into a ceremony that is an intrinsic part of these people's identity. They have once again become woven into the fabric of ordinary lives and special memories and I wonder if the children in the church will remember drinking Coke with their grandparents on the pine-needle floor. In these circumstances it is entirely possible to 'Like the drink, loathe the company'.

14

WE'RE ON A ROAD TO DELAWARE

Wilmington, USA

> *'If the communities we serve are in and of themselves not sustainable, then we do not have a sustainable business.'*
>
> **Neville Isdell, The Coca-Cola Company, 2008**[1]

The city of Wilmington in the state of Delaware is about ninety minutes and three decades south of Brooklyn. The best thing about the place is that it is effortlessly forgettable. This is not where I envisaged ending my journey. Having stood on the banks of an oasis in the desert of Rajasthan, watched cane fields of fire turn the sky orange in El Salvador and marvelled at the mountain mist tumbling down the steep hillsides of Bucarmanga and into bustling streets of the city itself; Delaware is not the geographical dénouement I was hoping for. I have travelled thousands of miles, through squalor and splendour, meeting people with courage and tenacity searching for the political equivalent of what Spalding Gray would have called a 'perfect moment'.

If I was on daytime TV I would call it 'closure', if I was a lawyer
– a 'resolution', I suppose I want to know what the fuck this
has all been about and I have a niggling feeling that
Wilmington is a resolutely 'epiphany-free zone.' I am not doing
down Wilmington, I just didn't know that IKEA did a flat-pack
town. And as soon as someone finds that Allen key this place
will tighten up just nicely.

The Coca-Cola Company has its annual meeting of stock
holders in Wilmington because the company is registered not
in its southern home of Atlanta but up here in the north in
Delaware, along with half the Stock Exchange who take
advantage of this on-shore tax haven. The meeting is to take
place in the Hotel du Pont 'the best hotel in town' a policeman
tells me, which may be the case but a hotel owned by DuPont
– the second-largest chemical company in the world – just
doesn't conjure an image of pampered luxury. To be fair it
does look like the kind of place that hosts a lot of corporate
events, a place where managing directors pick up industry
awards and trophy wives.

Back in London I had taken Coca-Cola's PR people up on their
offer to try and arrange an interview with Ed Potter, the
company's Global Workplace Rights Director, who I had seen
at the House of Commons. The likelihood of the company
sanctioning such a meeting was never high, still I went
through the process with the same grim lack of expectation
with which my mum buys her lottery tickets every week –
knowing it is not going to happen but still being slightly
disappointed when that turns out to be the case. 'It's a No
right now' said the mail from the company, as if this were only
a temporary state of affairs.

Nonetheless this is the only chance I will have had of seeing the corporate titans of the world's most famous brand and I'm curious how they will handle the criticism levelled at them. But more than this I wanted to see if the company was changing, if all these campaigns and lawsuits struggles and fights were having an effect. In the House of Commons debates one of the PR people had said, 'You're looking at a company that wants to change.' And if that is the case here's the place to see.

* * *

Ray Rogers has been described as a 'legendary union activist' and has been campaigning against Coca-Cola since 2003. He founded and runs the Corporate Campaign Inc who coordinate Stop Killer Coke.[2] Ray is making the now-annual pilgrimage to Delaware to challenge the company at the annual meeting. With him is Lew Freidman, a retired teacher who coordinates the websites, and the pair of them gave me lift from Brooklyn. Arriving at Wilmington, Ray runs off ahead of us while Lew and I chat as we amble over to the protest line opposite the hotel. This comprises primarily of clean, well-groomed, polite people in their early twenties who look a bit like market researchers for a Bible college as they smile and hand out seditious balloons with anti-corporate slogans on their innocent oval shapes.

'Mark!' shouts Ray as he runs across the road, momentarily disappearing behind a large truck. 'Mark!' he shouts again. Passing, the truck reveals Ray running toward a smartly dressed man who stands on the wrong side of the hotel's covered colonnade, adrift from the mass of shareholders milling towards the meeting. And I suddenly realise that Ed Potter has been caught in open ground.

When properly motivated I can multitask like a motherfucker. By which I mean I can cross a road, extract a digital recorder, turn it on, check the sound levels right, pop a pre-interview breath mint, grab a blast of Ventolin and reach Ed Potter before he can get to cover. Behind Coke's Global Workplace Rights Director a group of scaffolders work overhead, with mandatory hard hats and obligatory work belts, a few wear high-visibility orange vest and the place is covered in safety signs and warnings. It is under the appropriate sound of their hammering and sawing that I manage to interview Ed Potter. He smiles wanly as I wave the digital recorder at him and dive straight away into the case of the Indian workers in Kaladera being forced to work in dangerous conditions without the proper safety equipment.

'How are you going to sort it out?' I enquire.

'I don't know the circumstances of India so I can't really comment directly on that but just like other issues that are, what I'll call systemic issues, we're working to resolve those,' he says.

Ed Potter's voice is slightly thin, pitched at the tone of a man trying to clear his throat, so every now and again he has to go up a decibel to be heard above the building noise.

'How would you deal with it?' I press.

'If you email it to me we will definitely look into it.'

'Is there a procedure that you have for looking at this?'

'Do we have a written down procedure?' He repeats, eyebrows raised with his voice, 'No...if you bring me a situation and location x, depending on what it is, we would put in an audit team...'

'...But they say the only time we get given gas masks and gloves to work in the water treatment plant is when the auditors come round.'

'You know,' he says shaking his head ruefully, 'we have the

same challenges as any national government will have with respect to people who may want to manipulate the outcome.'

But the real issue is not just tracking down these abuses but how the company acts to solve them, so I ask what the sanctions are for bottlers who commit this kind of labour rights' abuse.

'Well, in the case of the supplier, a supplier who fails to take corrective action is subject to not being a supplier any more, that's the sanction.'

Assuming that this is the case, that bottlers have their franchise removed, how will it work in this instance? Coca-Cola is the bottler. Or at least it is a direct subsidiary – the Hindustan Coca-Cola Beverage Pvt Ltd is owned by The Coca-Cola Company.[3]

From under the hotel covered entrance a Coca-Cola man has spotted Ed Potter talking alone and unguarded and has come over to keep an eye on things. The man introduces himself as 'Tom, Head of Public Affairs'. To be fair to Ed Potter he stays and answers the questions, his thin hair blowing slightly. I am keen to get some action taken on the situation in India and press Ed Potter once more on the course the company will take.

'These guys are going in, and not working with the proper safety equipment, is this serious enough to investigate?' I ask.

'Well, of course! Health and safety is one of our...things.'

'So if I come to you and say this is happening here...'

The Public Affairs man nods firmly, 'We'll go and look.'

'You'll go and look.'

'Yeah, of course,' says Ed Potter.

* * *

Days later I emailed Ed Potter asking how we might proceed on this issue. The reply I got reads:

Ed Potter has referred your email to me. You can find information about our workplace practices on both cokefacts.com and on www.GetTheRealFacts.co.uk.

Sincerely,
Kari Bjorhus

Which seems a long way away from the response of 'we'll go and look'.

* * *

Overhead the casual yells and hollers of building work continue as metres away the shareholders start to gather around the hotel entrance while police officers with Secret Service earpieces watch over them. So before time wears our encounter to a close and we too must herd inside I say, 'Colombia. Isidro Gil. I spoke to people who saw him killed – someone was shot and killed on Coca-Cola's property.'
Tom from Public Affairs says 'We understand that.'
'We get it,' joins Ed Potter.
'We understand that he was an employee. We understand that he was shot there...It's a very difficult area, it was a very difficult time. If we can come to some resolution, we'd like to help that family and move on.'

But it quickly descends from that compassionate line into the usual company statements, hiding in the mire of the 'Coca-Cola system'. Ed Potter describes the dead as men who 'were not current or ever Coca-Cola employees'. He parrots the company mantra, seemingly oblivious to the fact that the refusal of the Company to acknowledge they have a responsibility over 'the Coca-Cola system' is the very thing that gets them into so much grief. People don't much care for the lawyerly lines of separation between legal entities – if your name is on the label you have got the responsibility.

When I mention the breakdown in negotiations between the company and Sinaltrainal, Ed Potter takes a breath and realigns the furrows on his brow. 'All I will say is, and this is a personal opinion – I honestly don't believe they want to resolve this.'

'You don't think that Sinaltrainal wants to resolve it? Why not?' I say incredulously.

'That's something I...It's a personal opinion, I frankly...I mean as soon as it goes on that recorder...' He nods at the digital recorder, implying he doesn't want to talk of this publicly. But it seems that Ed Potter thinks a group of people who collect death threats like Nectar points and have been specifically targeted for organising workers in Coca-Cola bottlers want to prolong the situation.

Alongside other campaigners, Ray Rogers of Stop Killer Coke has caused the company some considerable discomfort. To Ray, arguing comes as natural as breathing and the idea of just allowing Ed Potter to get past without lambasting him is just too much for Ray to bear so he strides over to us, calling out 'The ILO investigation is a scam!'

Let me explain the back story here. The International Labor Organisation is a UN body that exists to promote labour and human rights. It is made up of representatives from government, employers and trade unions.[4] After coming under pressure from the University of Michigan student body (the folk who put pressure on for the TERI report in India) Coca-Cola agreed to approach the ILO with the International

Union of Foodworkers to ask that they conduct an assessment of workplace practices in Coke's bottling plants in Colombia. The ILO announced their intention to do so on 24 March 2006.[5]

The problem with this is that the Company have somewhat used the promised ILO assessment as a fig leaf to hide behind when questions are raised about the assassinations, when in fact the ILO is only assessing *current* labour practices and will not consider the assassinations or any of the allegations of complicity by the bottling plant managers. Which is why Ray is claiming, 'The ILO investigation is a scam. You know it, I know it, The Coca-Cola Company knows it.'

'I absolutely disagree' says Ed Potter emphatically.

'It's a scandal,' decries Ray raising his hands to the heavens, oblivious to the fact that the passing shareholders are turning to stare at him. 'There is no investigation being done.'

Ed Potter replies, 'Well we've never represented that the ILO was going to do an investigation.'

This is an unfortunate thing to say, as inside the annual meeting, just metres away from where we are standing, staff are issuing a printed company statement on Colombia, in which The Coca-Cola Company describes the ILO assessment as an 'investigation' on three occasions in five lines of text. This, they claim is 'fulfilling our commitment to an independent, impartial third-party investigation and evaluation,' though it fails to mention Ed Potter is the US Employer Delegate on the ILO. The body that just happens to be conducting this particular 'independent and impartial' assessment.[6]

Unfortunately Ed Potter is also contradicted by his boss the current chairman and former CEO, Neville Isdell, who said at the Company Annual Meeting for shareholders in 2006:

'We have a document. From the ILO signed by the ILO...We have a document. We have an agreement and they are going to investigate past and prior practices...We think we have gone to the most credible people that can possibly be found in this world to look at what has happened in Colombia.'[7]

Just to further clarify matters I talked to the General Secretary of the International Union of Foodworkers , Ron Oswald – this is the person who negotiated with Coke and then the ILO to get the assessment. Ron reacted to Neville Isdell's statement saying, 'Well, he was wrong, and they know he was wrong, but clearly once that cat's out the bag, that cat's out the bag. Our proposal to the ILO was very clear: we did not ask them to do an investigation into criminal or murderous events in the 1990s...I don't think they've got the competence to do that, frankly.'

In case there is any lingering doubt Ron Oswald says 'there are still calls for Coke to agree to an independent investigation of those incidents and that's something we thought Coke should have agreed to many years ago.' So obviously the ILO assessment is not that 'independent investigation'.

There was never going to be an investigation into past practices of Coke bottling plants in Colombia by the ILO. So I asked Coca-Cola if they would publish or let me see the document Neville Isdell alleges the ILO had given the Company, to see how such a such a prominent captain of industry could be so confused. After all it is probably not a good idea to tell untruths and give false information to shareholders at an annual meeting. To my surprise the Company reacted positively to my question to see the ILO letter and invited me to their HQ in Atlanta providing a private jet with in-flight entertainment from an acoustic set by Joni Mitchell...OK, I'm making it up, but they started it. They ignored my question.

* * *

Mood music is piped into the Hotel du Pont rendering the lobby's grand piano as just a symbol of good taste. But saunter past this soundless wooden box of strings and hammers, past the check-in desk, between the pair of welcoming signs and their attendant police officers, and at the bottom of the carpeted stairs and their polished handrails stands the company fridges in all their glory, lit up like a petrol station at night. These are the new HFC-Free fridges, which the company calls Climate Friendly Coolers. Each is packed with Coca-Cola products in branded blocks and shareholders are invited to enjoy the company's produce. I don't want to take anything out of their fridge, though I do wish I had a bottle of Big Cola to put in there. The meeting hall is cavernous and ornate, with two chandeliers, all brass and glass, hanging from the ceiling. The columned walls are painted with flowers, flutes and fat cherubs dancing and the alcoves house gilt-framed mirrors; around these edges staff and plainclothes police officers stand in an obvious display of authority.

Walking into the hall I immediately bump into the friendly smile of B Wardlaw. B Wardlaw dresses in grey tracksuit bottoms, trainers and a driving jacket which, along with his scarecrow grey crop and Southern gentleman-style goatee beard, give him the appearance of Colonel Sanders with a hangover. But despite his appearance B Wardlaw is heir to a large number of Coca-Cola shares which he uses to help finance a homeless shelter in Atlanta: 1,000 people drop by in the day, 600 sleep there at night. The homeless repay this charity by giving B fashion advice, which he appears to have accepted today. He comes from an old Atlanta family and his grandfather was involved in the financing of The Coca-Cola Company so B knows many of the board and the Atlanta elite.

The first time I met B was outside of Washington. I had heard of him through a network of anti-Coca-Cola campaigners, who helped set up our meeting. I had been told to get a train to Tacoma Park and phone his number.

'Hi is that B Wardlaw?'

'Mr Thomas?' I heard a Southern gentleman's drawl.

'Yes.'

'Walk along the platform. Come down the escalator not the elevator. Walk through the barrier...'

'And...'

Almost in a parody of southern manners he said, 'Ah will make myself know to you.' And then he hung up.

I did was what I was told and on leaving the station B popped out of a coffeeshop doorway and shot a wave at me. He was dressed much like he always does and was wearing a sweatshirt emblazoned with the slogan 'Celebrate Freedom: Read a Banned Book!' During that first meeting I asked him what he thought The Coca-Cola Company should do to address the many issues it faced and he had replied in his charming drawl, 'Stop making Coca-Cola.' He was serious, 'I don't think it is a good product and we shouldn't be conditioning children to it.'

'But this is the source of your money which goes to the shelter...'

He shakes his head with a smile, 'I know it's a paradox,' then with mock seriousness he confides, 'I call myself the Coca-Cola anarchist.'

'Seriously, what should the Company do?'

'Well, when I mentioned the Colombia issue to people involved in the...er, shall we say, upper echelons of the company,' he said with an edge of irony in his voice, 'they said "we just sell the syrup – it's the bottlers".'

'That is the standard line...'

'Well, we should take responsibility or we should not do business.'

* * *

B Wardlaw is here in Delaware to propose a shareholder motion that the company should create a Board Committee on Human Rights, which would consider and advise on the consequences of its actions on these issues, including sponsoring the Olympics in China.

'Do you mind if I sit next to you?' I ask.

'I would be honoured,' he says.

A company's annual meeting is one of the rare times activists and opponents of a company get the chance to question the board and all they have to do is buy one single share to gain admittance. So the room is beginning to feel like the gathering of the clans, just behind me is an official from Amnesty International who wants to second B's proposal; next to him is a representative from Reporters Without Borders. Ray Rogers has entered with Lew Freidman, though they spilt up and sit in different sections of the room as they stand more chance of both getting called on to speak if they are apart. Behind Ray is a contingent of Tibetans who have just seen the brutal repression of democracy demonstrations by China, the host nation for the Olympics and Coke's most precious emerging market. Teamsters walk into the room smartly dressed but still managing to swagger like they are part of Rocky Balboa's training camp. There are Campaign for Corporate Accountability folk dotted around, plus the environmental and human rights groups like the Polaris Institute and Canadian water rights campaigners. Amit Srivastava is back from India and looks suitably unimpressed by his surroundings, though he nips over to say hello with a hug. There are even a couple of nuns who have come along to protest Coke's policies.

Most meetings of this sort start with a chairman clearing his throat, welcoming the room and calling the session to order. Coke's begins with a hymn, the lights go down and they play one of their adverts – the ultimate song of praise to the product. A video screens the commercial in which enormous inflatable figures from a parade break away from their tow ropes and a cartoon toddler and a superhero dog do battle in the skies for the prize of a large inflatable bottle of Coca-Cola. B Wardlaw tucks a conspiratorial head in my direction and in his Southern lilt chuckles, 'They would appear to be over-carbonated...too much gas.'

The ad finishes, the lights come up with the applause of the room and Neville Isdell, the outgoing CEO, rises to the podium.

In the world of CEOs some are born elegant, some achieve elegance and some have elegance thrust upon them. Isdell falls into the latter category. Strip him of the suit and he would look like a balding referee at a Sunday morning football match. 'Good morning, and welcome to The Coca-Cola Company's 2008 annual meeting...'

Isdell is the model of competence, delivering his opening remarks and then introducing the board members who are up for re-election. These folks sit at the front of the meeting in a cordoned-off area for executives with the riff raff kept firmly at bay, a sort of mini Dubai. As Isdell calls out their names in turn they stand and wave to the assembled mass behind them. There is a director of Delta Air Lines brandishing his hand in the air like it doesn't quite belong to him, the President of Hearst magazines graciously gesturing and a chap touted as the outsider for the vice-president's slot on the Obama ticket grinning like he has messed himself.

Muthar Kent,[8] the incoming CEO, sits next to his outgoing counterpart. As Isdell is tall and lean, so Kent is squat and square, between them they possess the classic shape of a double act.

Muthar Kent takes his turn at the podium and says as CEO elect he is 'humbled' and 'honoured to be part of this great legacy...' and thunders that we all have 'good reason to be excited' in the future of the company. 'I believe,' he cries from the podium, 'there is no better packaged goods consumer business to be in, today or in the future, than the non-alcoholic ready-to-drink beverage industry.' It is noticeable that he never refers to Coca-Cola as 'pop', 'fizzy pop', 'sodas' or even 'carbonated sodas' – Muthar Kent describes Coca-Cola as 'sparkling beverages'.

His speech is littered with sentences like 'Our sparkling beverage growth is achieving its highest rates in almost a decade!' and 'Sparkling beverages are the oxygen of our company.' In fact he uses the phrase 'sparkling beverages' eight times so he obviously isn't taking the 'golden stream'. It is out with the old soda or pop with its image of sugar-laden fizz and in with the calorie-free phrase 'sparkling beverages.'

But it is Isdell's speech following Kent's, that proves to be the more intriguing, and he begins by saying, 'We're transforming our business very simply because the world in which we operate has changed. Our planet and its resources are facing increasing pressures.' As an opening it is standard fare for business leaders to stress changes they are bringing to keep the company at the top of its game, but he continues, 'We have a presence in people's lives that reaches beyond that magical moment of providing that simple moment of refreshment. We're also an employer, a business partner, a part of the community, a global citizen; and I believe we must play our role in supporting sustainable communities.'

Having just seen some of those communities that have not been sustained by Coke, I crane my neck around the room searching out other small scowls of disbelief. However, it becomes clear that alongside the business journalists, the investment fund managers and the vested interest groups there are ordinary shareholders here, not rich people just folk with a few dollars and a will to invest. Behind me sits a family on a day out. On one side of the family group sits the father, in a green check shirt, his back bolt upright with his hands on his knees. At the other end of the line a twelve-year old-boy wearing a baseball hat sits slumped dangling his rucksack between his knees. In between them is the mother, in her forties, knitting a red, white and blue jumper.

'Last year,' says Isdell, 'we set a very aspirational target: a goal of becoming entirely water neutral in our operations on a global basis…In the past, some of you have expressed some concern about our business in India that primarily revolved around water and water use. I can tell you not only have we listened, but we've taken action. For starters, there are over three hundred rainwater harvesting structures across seventeen states in India.' This is Isdell in full CEO as Indiana Jones mode, leading a company that faces criticism and triumphs. From here he deftly moves through the emotions of contrition, struggle and hope.

'People have talked about our transparency in India, so

we agreed to an independent assessment of our water management [by TERI],' says Isdell, underlining the idea that the company has risen to the charges of its critics. 'There were some areas that they identified where we can make some improvements; these were just recommendations, and of course we will proceed with those.' Without scrutiny this looks like a company that have looked deep into their corporate soul admitted imperfection and embraced change. The knitting mum is still working on patriotic woollen wear but the checked shirt dad is nodding vigorously in appreciation at the scale of Coke's challenge.

However, with scrutiny Isdell's comments reveal a sleight of hand and quite a good one too. The improvements the company is going to make are small ones, relating to waste water improvements and compliance issues. These may be necessary but they are not the major recommendation of the report, which is to shut the plant down. So the inclusion and acknowledgment of some of the TERI report's criticisms is a masterly stroke, humbly admitting to minor errors while ignoring the major indictments.

Isdell lunges into the climax of his speech. 'The challenges facing our planet are too urgent and complex for governments alone, business alone, or NGOs alone to solve. Working together, we can create a multiplier effect that helps build sustainable communities and addresses the issues of our planet.' He is a man with a mission going beyond the mere niggles of a few critics and now set to solve the problems of the world. 'All the efforts I have talked about are "nice" things to do, but we are not doing them just because they are nice. We've done them because they're the steps that we must take to earn a profit and to return a profit to you, our shareholders.'

And thus he has faced down his critics, mended the ways of the company, embraced social change, shouldered the burden of world leadership and wrapped it all into a corporate philosophy: you make money if you are seen to do good.

The board in front of Isdell lead the appreciation of their captain of industry. Behind me the woman has put down her knitting to join the applause. But the dad is holding his hands to his chest clapping wildly. He is a fan. Had he spare underwear to throw it would be in the air by now and Isdell would be whispering to his roadie 'That one to my dressing room.'

As the applause starts to dip B Wardlaw turns to me and says, 'Wow, that's the impact you folks have had, you wouldn't have heard that speech three years ago.' And I believe B, it has been the activists, union members, villagers, shopkeepers and students that have forced the Company to look at the issues. We would not have heard that three years ago, the speech was totally about Corporate Social Responsibility.

But it is also evident that the Company's old ways are resolutely at the helm. They remain wedded to their mantra that 'we only make and sell concentrate and are not responsible for the bottlers or suppliers' when it is clear that the 'Coca-Cola system' is controlled by The Coca-Cola Company, both in terms of the franchise and The Coca-Cola Company's share ownership. It is also evident that the company has not addressed the specific issues.

The story told here is the story of a company going through the growing pains of Corporate Social Responsibility and emerging a changed and mature business leader working for a better world. But any storyteller knows that what you leave out of a story is as important as what is kept in. And Coca-Cola's omissions are the uncomfortable specifics.

- Isdell talks of 'communities lack of public access to clean water,' but doesn't mention Kaladera, the farmers or the women from the *basti* fighting at the pumps.
- Isdell talks of 'creating economic empowerment everywhere we do business,' but blanks out the *fleteros* in Colombia working with no job protection, with long hours and low pay.
- Isdell talks of how creating jobs 'helps alleviate poverty in the communities we serve,' but skipped the children working the fields for Coke's sugar who are not alleviated but condemned to poverty.
- Isdell talks of a workplace 'free from violence, harassment, intimidation and other unsafe or disruptive conditions due to internal or external threats' but dropped the page that mentioned the Indian workers passing out in unsafe conditions and the Turkish deliverymen sacked for wanting to join a union and then gassed in a Coke plant with their children.
- Isdell says, 'If the communities we serve are in and of themselves not sustainable then we do not have a sustainable business' but didn't have time to mention the unpaid taxes to Nejapa and the slums where local people pay for water since Coke came.
- Isdell talks of the company being a 'functioning part of the local community,' but the name of Raquel Chavez has slipped his mind.

Campaigners have forced the company to respond and the company has responded with PR. It seems to be their pathological response. Ron Oswald, the leader of the International Union of Foodworkers, a man who regularly meets with the company, said 'When you build that whole thing around a product that nobody needs, that product is pure image...so the communications people inside Coca-Cola accumulate huge amounts of power over many years...they see issues of substance and they interpret them as issues of communication and then they try to communicate the solution, instead of dealing with the issue.'[9]

* * *

The shareholders' resolutions are next on the agenda and the outcome is predictably in favour of the company. Isdell's responses to questions are by now so prepared, prepacked and ready to go that you can practically hear the microwave bell ping before he opens his mouth. Polite and orderly, he controls the meeting like a teacher in a slightly rowdy class. Ray Rogers shouts 'Point of order' and jumps out of his chair at every possible opportunity. Amit tells Isdell he is insulting. B says 'I have worked out that with about 1,500,000 shares in the company and an hour to question the board that gives each share about 0.00024 seconds' worth of time, so I will be as quick as I can' before putting his idea of a board committee for human rights.

Isdell bats away the questions with his trusty PR shield and gets a few shareholders making supportive statements too, one shareholder compares Isdell to a 'gifted athlete', making leadership look so easy. Someone else congratulates the company on advertising on family-friendly TV like *American Idol*...But the meeting closes with a gentleman being called from the front executive enclave, he has thick glasses and is reasonably elderly.

'My name is Herbert Pinkus,' he says, looking as if he had been well named. 'I control around 10,000 shares, I personally own around 6,000 shares. I want to congratulate the board and thank them for the fine job.' Then he turns to face the rest of the room, 'And I also want to say a word or two to the naysayers here. The Coca-Cola Company is not the conscience of the world, The Coca-Cola Company is not the policeman of the world. The mission of The Coca-Cola Company is to enhance shareowner value and I think they do a terrific job in that.' He starts to get a round of applause but carries on over it raising his voice, ' and I have another personal message for the naysayers.' He pauses for good effect, 'Sell your shares and get out of the way. Thank you.'

The executive enclosure erupts and claps heartily and so do I. For all the talk of sustainable communities it is refreshing to hear an honest opinion, red in tooth and claw. B nudges me, 'I am glad you had an opportunity to see that attitude in action. America love it or leave it!' And he smiles, despite having had his proposal to set up a human rights committee within Coke defeated by 91 per cent of the shareholders.

The meeting closes and the lights are raised. The executives start to stand in their remarkably uniform bespoke suits, stretching their legs and slapping each other on the shoulder. A small group of big men assemble around Neville, and when the prerequisite number are fore and aft they set off down the side of the room, with Isdell in the middle, through the shareholders and the crowd. I remain seated, surrounded by the noise of scraping chairs and the litter of discarded order papers, thinking through what I've just heard.

This is the problem. You can call it sparkling beverages as many times as you want and you can talk of magic moments of refreshments but Coca-Cola is fizzy pop. You can talk of consumers inviting you into their lives and you can treasure secret formulas but all you are selling is essentially sugar and water: fizzy pop. No one actually needs Coca-Cola and no one would die if it disappeared off the planet tomorrow.

And that is my realisation. The brand is the most important thing the Company has because put aside the concentrate and that is all they have left to sell. The brand is what transforms fizzy pop into Coca-Cola, that intangible bundle of images and feelings held within people's minds and kept alive on a $2.4 billion advertising budget.[10] Coca-Cola is more image than product and as such exists as a mental construct within each and every one of us. Except my image of Coca-Cola is no longer linked to polar bears, Santa ads, iconic script and bottles. When I think of Coca-Cola now I think of Luis Eduardo in jail throwing notes wrapped in sweets out of the windows to his daughter on the street. On other days I think of a child disappearing into forest of sugar cane and sometimes I think of Raquel Chavez winning against the company or the protestors who shut down the plants in India.

There have been some significant successes in the struggles against the Company and there are campaigns and solidarity groups that anyone can take part in. Yet despite this there is an aching question of 'what can I do, they are one of the world's biggest companies?' But the one thing the Company has taught me is that stories matter. How much do they matter? The Coca-Cola Company does not want people seeing a bottle of Coke and not hearing the story they have spent US $2.4 billion telling. The last thing the Company wants is consumers thinking about their product rather than associating it with memories or feelings, things that do not sit well with awkward questions. The stories I have heard on these trips challenge the corporate narrative. The bundles of stories on scribbled notes and Edirol recordings matter, and they matter to the Company as much as to the people who told them. Each time they get told it is another chip away at the brand value. Sure, the Company will continue making profit, but they won't make as much as they could do...and believe me that really hurts them.

As epiphanies go this one lacks the dramatic gesture of being struck blind on the way to Damascus but it does mean I can make it out of the hall without stumbling for help.

It is time for me to go. I take leave of B Wardlaw, wave goodbye to Amit and search out Lew to try and get a lift back to Brooklyn. As I get to the top of the steps one of the Company staff stops me.

'Sir.'

'Pardon?'

'Have you got your shareholder's card?'

'Er...no...'

She tuts. 'Doesn't matter, you have one anyway. You should hand over your shareholder's card to receive one but it doesn't matter. There you go.'

Conspiratorially she hands me a thin cardboard box. 'Here you go, sir,' she says winking.

'Thank you.'

Heading to the hotel entrance I open the box. Inside is a slim silver metal commemorative Coca-Cola Company pen, a gift to the shareholders. 'Wow,' I think, 'they even give me the ink with which to write.'

POSTSCRIPT: BRAND LOYALTY

'Over the last thirty years, the employees in the Drogheda plant have made a very valuable contribution to the Coca-Cola business.'

Hugo Reidy, General Manager, Drogheda Concentrates, 29 August 2007[1]

Jerry Farrell is travelling to a football match with his brother and their children when his mobile rings. Jerry is in his early fifties and works as a line manager at Drogheda Concentrates where he oversees about eighteen workers. The plant, north of Dublin, is where The Coca-Cola Company makes the syrup and concentrates for their drinks. Jerry is a union official there for SIPTU (Services, Industrial, Professional and Technical Union). He is also the Co-Chair of the Coca-Cola Communications Forum. It is a grand title but essentially this is where managers and workers discuss how the company's long-term plans will affect employees. But today the business of work is relegated to its proper place and the matter in hand is football. Tomorrow Drogheda United will play against Helsingborg in the UEFA Cup in Sweden and the most important thing is to get to the hotel.

The mobile rings again, showing a number he isn't expecting. Not today leastways, today is holiday time. The voice on the end of the line is Coke's General Manager in Ireland.

'Jerry, sorry to disturb you, I know you are away at a football match, but I have to tell you there is an announcement being to be made in under an hour.'

'About what?'

'We are going to shut the plant in Drogheda.'

It is 29 August 2007, the day before Drogheda lost to Helsingborg 3–0. There are about 200 fans travelling to see the match, out of which fifty work at the plant. Jerry hangs up and goes to give them the news.

The plant employs 256 workers, probably 350 when you include the contract staff, the canteen, security and cleaners. As Jerry is the Co-Chair of the Coca-Cola Communications Forum the company informs him of the closure an hour before it is announced publicly; the call, says the General Manager, is out of respect.

Eleven months after that phone call and the plant is all but closed. 'Respect...' Jerry shakes, his head as he tells the story, 'an hour before they make the announcement and they call it respect.' Most workers left for the last time on 27 June 2008, leaving the plant to be run down for good by the end of August. By the time you read this it will be shut.

I had phoned SIPTU a few weeks ago and they had put me in touch with Jerry, so this is the first time I have meet him. Jerry is fifty-two, dresses well but not too flash, has a wife, two kids: he's a typical working-class guy. But the thing that defines him today is his anger and resignation, he exudes a kind of fuming fatalism. In his car he talks non-stop during the forty-five-minute drive from Dublin to Drogheda along the motorway, then on through the quieter lanes, following the lush riverbanks. 'This is where they fought the Battle of the Boyne' he says, pointing at a gateway, 'the tourist folk have done it really nicely.'

As we head through Drogheda he explains that they call it a 'Bed and Breakfast town, so many people work in Dublin and commute.' But driving through the industrial area is a different story. We seem to pass rows of disused warehouses and industrial units. Jerry nods at each and starts every sentence with the words, 'This was the place where the so and so factory used to be...' or 'This is the site of the old so and so place...' Row upon row of empty factories and businesses, the stillborn pups of the Celtic Tiger.

Sitting in a near-empty hotel bar just by the river we drink tea and natter for two hours while waiters in standard black shirts and white aprons glide around the room to the sound of discreet hotel tunes, 'lobby house music' or a compilation that is probably on sale at reception.

Jerry explains the significance of the plant, 'Seven out of every ten of Coca-Cola's drinks drank around the world on any given day start in Ireland, the concentrate is made in Ireland.' Given that 1.5 billion servings of Coke's products are consumed every day – that's a lot of concentrate.[2] This is the hub of Coke's operations.

Different drinks require different types of 'beverage base' some are liquid concentrates, some are powder, the various mixes leave the plant in various forms and head off as far afield as Australia. 'The flavourings come over from Sidcup in the UK,' says Jerry explaining that The Coca-Cola Company's secret ingredient called '7X' is manufactured there. 'But the main ingredient that goes into Coke for concentrate is caramel. Then you have things like phosphoric acid and obviously the 7X and then you have all these little flavours. So in a batch of Coke there are probably ten ingredients.' As there is little automation in the plant Jerry says the process of making the concentrate is quite skilled. 'It tends to be people weighing out ingredients into tanks, it is very, very manual. So it is very hands on, so that is why they rely so much on experienced operators knowing what they are doing cos if you make a mistake in any of this and it is not picked up by the labs and it goes out to the fields...' He shakes his head.

I am curious about the concentrate business. 'How much did the plant make?' I ask.

'Drogheda would make about 8 million units of concentrate a year,' Jerry replies.

'And how big is a unit?'

'For Coca-Cola a unit is a US gallon.'

'How many drinks would you get out of a unit?'

'Depends what it is, it varies from drink to drink.'

'Coca-Cola...'

'I think it is about two units make 100,000 or somewhere around there.'

'How much does a unit cost to make?'

'Drogheda made it for about $3.67.'

'So roughly $3.67 is enough for about 50,000 drinks...'

'The $3.67 is for the ingredients and labour costs to make it.'

I believe my next word is 'Fuck...'

According to Jerry the cost of concentrate was even lower in Ballina, 'US $2.60 a unit,' he says. The differences in production costs was used by the company, 'so if Drogheda didn't get down to Ballina's level the company shift work from Drogheda to Ballina. What they have is an internal competition going on. The company create a very competitive internal environment.'

The company might say they had overcapacity in Drogheda but the lure of cheaper concentrate could have played a part in the decision to shut down the plant here.

Drogheda Concentrates is owned by Atlantic Industries, which is registered in the Cayman Islands and is a direct subsidiary of The Coca-Cola Company. There is a distinct whiff of 'tax efficiencies' in the air. And by a 'distinct whiff' I mean 'stink'. For most of its history, Ireland has been a predominantly agricultural economy but in the Seventies it made some radical changes to its tax system to encourage investment. Corporation Tax for some industries was slashed to 10 per cent and it now stands at 12.5 per cent, offering one 'of the most beneficial corporate tax environments in the world'.[3] It is not surprising therefore that Ireland was by 2004, the world's most profitable country for US corporations.[4] (Though for lovers of irony and gossip the anti-poverty campaigner and musician Bono moved his music publishing company to the Netherlands after Ireland scrapped a tax break on royalties.[5])

According to Jerry, 'Coca-Cola came here purely for the taxes. Nothing else.' And logically he has a point, why else would a company establish its operations in Ireland and send 'seven out of ten' of its concentrates around the world from there?

Coke Throat in Mexico had explained that the concentrate for Coca-Cola made in Mexico came from Ireland, 'Well, we have a huge manufacturing facility here in Mexico that used to supply all the concentrate, we have the capability, the problem was that producing it here, and paying taxes here was less attractive than the full incentive of bringing it from Ireland and shipping it on a ship, on a freight to Mexico...it's just accounting.' For the Company it is a way of ensuring large profits remain in low tax regimes. As Coke Throat said, 'that way you reduce jobs in the country your bottling plants operate and you reduce tax paying, and this transfers all the benefits to Coca-Cola.'

Indeed, The Coca-Cola Company's annual report for 2006 says, 'Our effective tax rate reflects tax benefits derived from significant operations outside the United States, which are generally taxed at rates lower than the US statutory rate of 35 per cent. Our effective tax rate of approximately 22.8 per cent for the year ended 31 December 2006.' That year the company profits were US $6,578 million. By putting their business in tax havens the Company's declared tax paid that year was US $1,498 million. Had they paid tax in the US at 35 per cent the Company would have contributed approximately another US $804 million. So Coke Throat is right in the sense that is does indeed 'benefit Coca-Cola'.

* * *

Back in Ireland there were three plants that made concentrates, Drogheda in the east, Ballina in the west and a small plant in Athy to the south of Dublin. According to the company, Athy and Ballina 'are sufficient to meet the current and future demand for concentrate and beverage base supply from Ireland'.[6] So Drogheda was shut because of overcapacity and Drogheda's work was moved to Ballina. But according to Jerry there is another agenda going on here, Drogheda is totally unionised and Ballina is totally non-union.

The reason for Ballina being non-union is historic. 'In the Seventies they had a Japanese plant there and the union there had a strike,' Jerry tells me. 'Now the company said "If you don't report for work on Monday we will shut the plant down." And everyone said "Oh yeah, that's what they always say." But come Monday the plant shut and the company left...'
'And because of that the community is anti-union...'
'They blame the union for losing the jobs.'
'So is SIPTU going to try and form a branch in Ballina?'
'It is very difficult to get into Ballina...I have spoken to managers and supervisors, the normal people you would expect to talk to about it. They tell you the same thing. "Not interested, Jerry, not interested, Jerry..."'

When I talked to Ron Oswald from the International Union of Foodworkers, a man who deals with Coca-Cola a lot, he was quite blunt about Coke's operations in Ireland. 'We think there are sophisticated human resource practices inside these operations which essentially is designed to squeeze the space out from where unions can operate.'

The feeling that the company's moves were motivated by a degree of antipathy towards the union was compounded by what happened next. The workers from Drogheda finished their final shift on Friday 27 June 2008. On the following Monday morning, 30 June, it was announced that Coca-Cola was to open a new plant in Wexford in the south.[7] 'By which stage it was too late to try and negotiate moving the Drogheda workers to Wexford.' That chance had gone, and you wouldn't need to be a cynic to think that the timing of the announcement about the Wexford plant was deliberately chosen to come after Drogheda had closed. Jerry says, 'There is one reason and one reason only why they do not want Drogheda people there, they do not want a union over there.'

In their defence Coca-Cola point to the fact that the new plant in Wexford is a flavourings plant, which is different from a concentrate plant. But Jerry says 'Well, if you are trained in one side of the business it won't be too difficult to train for flavourings.' Surely retraining experienced Drogheda workers would be preferable from starting with people with no knowledge at all.

There are rumours that the Wexford plant will make 7X the company's secret ingredient and Coca-Cola management are reported to have said that the company never allows a union into a 7X plant, apparently fearful that if they have a dispute in the flavour plant the worldwide system goes down. So with Drogheda gone the only union members are in Athy. 'You have about fifty union members, and that is about it for the concentrates side of it, for the whole of Ireland.'

When the closure of Drogheda was announced SIPTU organised demonstrations, Ireland's national media covered the issue and the union even developed its own rescue package that would save the company some 10 million euros in voluntary redundancies and changes in overtime patterns. None of which had any effect. But as Jerry points out 'We failed to get the local community on our side, the local community sees Coca-Cola workers as extremely well paid... So was there a lot of sympathy for them? Probably not.' According to Jerry folk around here have not yet grasped the implications of the plant going, 'This town does not realise the devastation. That plant brought about 30–40 million euros into the local economy. That is gone.'

Jerry comes from a trade-union family, his father was a union man, his brother Ollie is a shop steward. So, during a family holiday when the three of them were sitting up talking late one night, it came as a surprise when his father questioned him. Jerry's father had asked, 'Do you think the company shut the plant down or is it the union that shut the plant?'

'It took me a while to realise what he was getting at,' says Jerry, 'he is a well-known fella about the town, he knows what is going on.' His father's question was not so much a question at all but a gentle nudge as to what the town was thinking.

After taking advantage of the tax regime – and it is a fair bet to say that should the tax rate increase to an unfavourable level the company would shift its operations quicker than you could say 'Is Bono here too?', after 'assistance' from the Irish Development Agency to set up its plants, after reducing the trade union to the margins and after making nearly $6 billion in profit The Coca-Cola Company leaves Drogheda with the community wondering if it was the union that lost the jobs.

Welcome to the World of Coca-Cola.

Acknowledgements

A heartfelt salute goes to Susan McNicholas who agreed to research this book. She was an inspiration to work with and a loyal friend.

Thanks also must go to Conor McNicholas, and Rian too, who put up with my endless calls to Susan at all hours of the night and day.

Martin Herring – who went above and beyond the call of duty, came to India filmed it, never got paid and remains a true friend.

Thanks to:
Nicky Branch who was transcript queen, Jess Hurd the comrade photographer, Emilio Rodriguez, Alpkan Birelma. Amit Srivasvta, who has been an enlightening presence and friend, Andy Higginbottom at Colombia Solidarity Campaign, Geoff Atkinson who oversaw the *Dispatches* documentary on Coca-Cola for Channel 4, Joan, Phoebe, Carrie, Amber, Sally Friedman, Kathy Haywood, Sarah McDonald at Uproar, David Lom, Armando, Eduardo, Sophie, Saroj Dosh and Alice Wynn Wilson at Action Aid, Peter Hirst and the Red Shed, Karen at Travel Matters, Olaf Christiansen, Kerim Yildiz, Mustafa Gundogu, Mel Alfonso, Tracey Moberley, Helen Waghorn, Bipasha Ahmet, Claudia, Lynn Sardinha, Sumita Joseph, Amanda Jordan. Lew Freidman and Nancy Romero – special thanks for looking after my family in Brooklyn, Ray Rogers, Jerad, Bernardo, Liam and Jaime for extended Brooklyn support, the Polaris Institute, Mariela Kohon at Justice for Colombia, Arife and Ronnie, Bijoy, Sandeep Panday, Nandlal Master, Santosh, Anita Komanduri, Kavaljit Singh, Nick Hildyard at the Corner House for advice and late-night support, Pablo Leal without whom stuff would not have happened, Alejandro Calvillo, Octavio, Joy and Damaso, Antonino García, Laura Jordan, Jason Parkinson, Guy Smallville, Tony Pletts, Ed Smith, Matthew Harvey, Amy Hopwood, Jeff and the list, Wendy, Andrea, Catherine Strauss and Michael Cummins who are bound to have helped somewhere along the line, Steve Mather and Charlie Allen at Hands Off Venezuela. Hannah MacDonald and Ken Barlow at Ebury Press, Justine Taylor for patient copyediting, Amanda Telfer for smoothing out the legal wrinkles and Sarah Bennie for waving at me on the M5.

As always CB, IJ and Gan Gan xxx

Appendix A: Endnotes

Prologue

1   Manifesto for Growth, The Coca-Cola Company website, www.thecoca-colacompany.com/ourcompany/manifesto_for_growth.html
2   Obesity Report, House of Commons Health Committee, www.publications.parliament.uk/pa/cm200304/cmselect/cmhealth/23/23.pdf
3   The Coca-Cola Company Press Center, www.thecoca-colacompany.com/presscenter/viewpoints_india_situation.html

Chapter 1: The Happiness Factory

1   'Another Trim In Spending', *New York Times*, 27 June 2007
2   Global Policy Forum
3   US Congressional Budget Office, Testimony before the Committee on the Budget, US House of Representatives, 24 October 2007
4   www.cia.gov/library/publications/the-world-factbook/print/li.html
5   Best Global Brands 2007, Interbrand/*Business Week*
6   The song was later re-recorded and the brand name removed to create 'I'd Like to Teach the World to Sing'
7   Atlanta Development Authority Quarterly Report, 18 May 2005, www.atlantada.com/media/1Q2005.pdf
8   'Business As Usual, Unfortunately', *The Atlanta Journal-Constitution*, 29 March 2005
9   'City Oks Bond Issue', *The Atlanta Journal-Constitution*, 9 June 2005
10 www.coca-cola.co.uk/Company_History/
11 Mark Pendergrast, *For God, Country, and Coca-Cola*, London: Weidenfeld & Nicolson, 1994
12 Martin Luther King, 'I've been to the Mountaintop', 3 April 1968, Mason Temple, Memphis
13 'Coke Settles Bias Lawsuit for $192.5 million', *USA Today*, 17 November 2000
14 www.gettherealfacts.co.uk/docs/gmbh.pdf
15 ibid
16 www.globalwaterchallenge.org/partners/partners.php
17 ibid
18 Best Global Brands 2007, Interbrand/*Business Week*
19 Best Global Brands 2006, Interbrand/*Business Week*
20 Best Global Brands 2005, Interbrand/*Business Week*

Chapter 2: Give 'Em Enough Coke

1   www.alertnet.org/printable.htm?URL=/db/crisisprofiles/CO_DIS.htm

2   'Colombia Paramilitary Chief Says Businesses Back Him', *New York Times*, 7 September 2000

3   www.amicustheunion.org/default.aspx?page=8139

4   www.hrw.org/reports/2001/colombia/1.htm669C8B63. Readers should note that the Colombian army now has created a 6th Division, so if the report were written today I would imagine it would now be entitled the 7th Division

5   'Colombia Paramilitary Chief Says Businesses Back Him', *New York Times*, 7 September 2000

6   Congressional Testimony on Violence against Trade Unionists and Human Rights in Colombia, Human Rights Watch, 28 June 2007

7   www.tuc.org.uk/international/tuc-13722-fo.cfm

8   'Colombia's Uribe ends Washington visit with fate of free trade agreement still uncertain', *International Herald Tribune*, 4 May 2007, www.iht.com/articles/ap/2007/05/04/america/NA-GEN-US-Colombia.php

9   www.amicustheunion.org/default.aspx?page=8139

10 Distorted perceptions of Colombia's conflict, Garry Leech, *Colombia Journal*, 1 June 2008, referencing Adam Isacson, 'CINEP: Colombia's Conflict Is Far from Over,' Center for International Policy, 10 April 2008, www.reliefweb.int/rw/RWB.NSF/db900SID/KKAA-7F89EE? OpenDocument

Chapter 3: Serious Charges

1   *Workplace Assessment in Colombia*, Cal Safety Compliance Corporation 2005, www.cokefacts.com/citizenship/cit_co_assessmentReport.pdf

2   ibid

3   ibid

4   'Coca-Cola sued over bottling plant "terror campaign"', *Guardian*, 21 July 2001, www.guardian.co.uk/world/2001/jul/21/julianborger

5   SINALTRAINAL v THE COCA-COLA COMPANY, news.lp.findlaw.com/hdocs/docs/cocacola/clmbiacocacola72001.pdf

6   Coca-Cola FEMSA is the Mexican multinational that bought Panamco in December 2002 creating the world's second- largest Coke bottling company, behind Atlanta-based Coca-Cola Enterprises

7   'An Investigation of Allegations of Murder and Violence in Coca-Cola's Columbian plants', The New York City Fact-Finding Delegation on Coca-Cola in Colombia, January 2004 killercoke.org/pdf/monsfinal.pdf

8   ibid

9   ibid

10 'Energy giant agrees settlement with Burmese villagers', *Guardian*, 15 December 2004

11 'Yahoo Settles With Chinese Journalists', *New York Times*, 14 November 2007

12 www.socialfunds.com/news/article.cgi/2353.html

13 'Feinstein Fights McCain on Burma Tax Break for Big Oil', *New York Sun*, 6 June 2008, www.nysun.com/foreign/feinstein-fights-mccain-on-tax- break-for-big-oil/79452/

14 www.earthrights.org/campaignfeature/senator_feinstein_ puts_breaks_on_anti-atca_bill_s._1874.html

15 'Coca-Cola sued over bottling plant "terror campaign"', *Guardian*, 21 July 2001, www.guardian.co.uk/world/2001/jul/21/julianborger

16 fl1.findlaw.com/news.findlaw.com/hdocs/docs/cocacola/ clmbiacocacola72001.pdf p. 14

17 ibid, p. 15

18 news.bbc.co.uk/1/hi/business/2909141.stm

19 www.cokefacts.com/facts/facts_co_court_new.pdf

20 'Dismissal Of Coke Lawsuit To Be Appealed', *International Business Times*, 3 November 2006, www.ibtimes.com/articles/20061103/ apfn-colombia- coca-cola-lawsuit.htm

Chapter 3.5: The Hush Money That Didn't Stay Quiet

1   www.thecoca-colacompany.com/citizenship/strategic_vision.html

2   The New York City Fact-Finding Delegation on Coca-Cola in Colombia, January 2004, killercoke.org/pdf/monsfinal.pdf

3   www.thecoca-colacompany.com/ourcompany/ar/financial overview.html

4   www.guardian.co.uk/media/2006/aug/18/marketingandpr.business

5   www.newsdesk.org/archives/004005.html

6   www.gettherealfacts.co.uk/index.html

7   Ed Potter interview with author

8   Email from The Coca-Cola Company to author

9   ibid

10 Interview conducted by author

11 Email from The Coca-Cola Company to author

Chapter 4: 'Chile'

1   fl1.findlaw.com/news.findlaw.com/hdocs/docs/cocacola/ clmbiacocacola72001.pdf p. 26

2   ibid

3   The defendant is listed as Panamco Colombia (d/b/a Embottellador de Santander, S.A.). Panamco was bought by Coca-Cola FEMSA in 2003. In turn, The Coca-Cola Company owns 31.6 per cent of Coca-Cola FEMSA, www.b2i.us/profiles/investor/fullpage.asp?f=1&BzID= 994&to=cp&Nav =0&LangID=1&s=0&ID=1940#COCACOMPANY) although it 'indirectly owns 39.6% of our capital stock, representing 46.4% of our capital stock with full voting rights.' www.b2i.us/ profiles/investor/fullpage.asp?f=1&BzID=994&to=cp&Nav= 0&LangID=1&s=0&ID=1940#COCACOMPANY

4   fl1.findlaw.com/news.findlaw.com/hdocs/docs/cocacola/ clmbiacocacola72001.pdf, p. 28

5   Email from The Coca-Cola Company to author
6   Coca-Cola's Global Workplace Rights Policy, www.thecoca-cola
    company.com/citizenship/workplace_rights_policy.html
7   Coca-Cola's Global Workplace Rights Homepage, www.thecoca-cola
    company.com/citizenship/workplace_rights.html
8   www.cokefacts.com/Colombia/facts_co_keyfacts.shtml
9   'The Political Economy of Labor Reform in Colombia', Background
    paper prepared for the World Development Report 2005,
    www-wds.worldbank.org/external/default/WDSContentServer/
    WDSP/IB/2005/01/31/000090341_20050131101310/Original/314340
    Echeverr14WDR05obkgdo1public1.doc
10 Interview conducted by author
11 *Labour Rights and Freedom of Association in Colombia*, Colombian
    Trade Union Federations, October 2007
12 I asked the Company what was the ratio of permanent to casual
    labour but they ignored my question completely. However, the
    figures Sinaltrainal give do reflect a nationwide trend in Colombia to
    put an increasingly large number of workers into casual or
    temporary employment
13 www.scottish.parliament.uk/business/businessbulletin/bb-06/
    bb-12-22f.htm
14 Get The Real Facts, The Coca-Cola Company website,
    www.gettherealfacts.co.uk/workplace/workplace.html

Chapter 5: The Days of the Great Coke Pledge
1   The Facts: Coca-Cola and Colombia, Coca-Cola website
    www.cokefacts.com/Colombia/facts_co_colombia_fact_sheet.pdf
2   ibid
3   www.cci.com.tr/en/index.asp
4   Coke Facts: The Truth About The Coca-Cola Company Around the
    Globe, Coca-Cola website, www.cokefacts.com/facts/facts_aw_
    keyfacts.shtml
5   lrights.igc.org/projects/corporate/coke/turkeycoke_complaint_
    part_1.pdf page 10
6   lrights.igc.org/projects/corporate/coke/turkeycoke_complaint_
    part_1.pdf
7   Kurdish Human Rights Project
8   Coke Facts: The Truth About The Coca-Cola Company Around The
    Globe, Coca-Cola website, www.cokefacts.com/facts/facts_aw_
    keyfacts.shtml
9   ibid
10 ibid
11 lrights.igc.org/projects/corporate/coke/turkeycoke_complaint_
    part_1.pdf page 13
12 ibid

13 Coke Facts: The Truth About The Coca-Cola Company Around the
    Globe, Coca-Cola website, www.cokefacts.com/facts/facts_aw_
    keyfacts.shtml

Chapter 6: May Contain Traces of Child Labour
1 Coca-Cola website, www.gettherealfacts.co.uk/workplace/
    workplace.html
2 Coca-Cola website, www.letsgettogether.co.uk/ListQuestionsOf
    Topic/TopicId=24/
3 El Salvador Turning a Blind Eye, Hazardous Child Labor in El
    Salvador's Sugarcane Cultivation, June 2004, hrw.org/reports/
    2004/elsalvador0604/elsalvador0604simple.pdf
4 Coca-Cola website, www.gettherealfacts.co.uk/workplace/
    workplace.html
5 'El Salvador Scarred by Child Labor', *Washington Post*, 10 June 2004
6 *Children for Hire: The Perils of Child Labor in the United States*, Marvin J.
    Levine, Greenwood Publishing Group, 2003
7 El Salvador Turning a Blind Eye, Hazardous Child Labor in El
    Salvador's Sugarcane Cultivation June 2004, hrw.org/reports/
    2004/elsalvador0604/elsalvador0604simple.pdf
8 The Coca-Cola Company Response to the Human Rights Watch
    Report on Child Labor in El Salvador, 13 June 2005, Coca-Cola
    website, www.thecoca-colacompany.com/presscenter/viewpoints
    hrw report.html
9 El Salvador Turning a Blind Eye, Hazardous Child Labor in El
    Salvador's Sugarcane Cultivation, June 2004, hrw.org/reports/
    2004/elsalvador0604/elsalvador0604simple.pdf
10 Email from The Coca-Cola Company to author
11 El Salvador Turning a Blind Eye, Hazardous Child Labor in El
    Salvador's Sugarcane Cultivation, June 2004, hrw.org/reports/
    2004/elsalvador0604/elsalvador0604simple.pdf
12 Coke Facts: Supplier Guiding Principles, Coca-Cola website,
    www.cokefacts.com/AroundTheWorld/cit_aw_supplier.shtml
13 El Salvador Turning a Blind Eye, Hazardous Child Labor in El
    Salvador's Sugarcane Cultivation June 2004, hrw.org/reports/
    2004/elsalvador0604/elsalvador0604simple.pdf
14 Get The Real Facts, Coca-Cola website, www.gettherealfacts.co.uk/
    workplace/workplace.html
15 El Salvador Turning a Blind Eye, Hazardous Child Labor in El
    Salvador's Sugarcane Cultivation, June 2004, hrw.org/reports/
    2004/elsalvador0604/elsalvador0604simple.pdf
16 Get The Real facts, Coca-Cola website, www.gettherealfacts.co.uk/
    workplace/workplace.html
17 El Salvador Turning a Blind Eye, Hazardous Child Labor in El
    Salvador's Sugarcane Cultivation, June 2004, hrw.org/reports/
    2004/elsalvador0604/elsalvador0604simple.pdf

18 Get The Real facts, Coca-Cola website, www.gettherealfacts.co.uk/
workplace/workplace.html

19 Email from The Coca-Cola Company to author

20 Get The Real facts, Coca-Cola website, www.gettherealfacts.co.uk/
workplace/workplace.html

21 ibid

22 Global Workplace Rights Policy, Coca-Cola website, www.thecoca-
colacompany.com/citizenship/workplace_rights_policy.html

23 Coke Facts: Supplier Guiding Principles, Coca-Cola website,
www.cokefacts.com/AroundTheWorld/cit_aw_supplier.shtml

24 El Salvador Turning a Blind Eye, Hazardous Child Labor in El
Salvador's Sugarcane Cultivation, June 2004, hrw.org/reports/
2004/elsalvador0604/elsalvador0604simple.pdf

25 Get The Real facts, Coca-Cola website, www.gettherealfacts.co.uk/
workplace/workplace.html

26 ibid

27 ibid

28 ibid

29 Email to author

Chapter 7: Dodge City

1 www.thecoca-colacompany.com/citizenship

2 Centre for Science and the Environment website, www.cseindia.org/
misc/cola-indepth/cola2006/cola-index.htm

3 'Coke, Pepsi Pay Himalayan Fines', BBC News Online, 17 September
2002, news.bbc.co.uk/1/hi/world/south_asia/2263917.stm

4 Best Practices in Adult Video website, bpav.org/bp.html

5 'Watch out, Sarge! It's environmentally friendly fire', *Sunday Times*,
17 September 2006, www.timesonline.co.uk/tol/news/uk/
article641494.ece

6 BP 2006 Environmental Statement, www.bp.com/liveassets/
bp_internet/globalbp/STAGING/global_assets/downloads/V/
verfied_site_reports/N_Amer ica/Whiting_2006.pdf

Chapter 8: Let Them Dig Wells

1 Our Economic Impact, The Coca-Cola Company website,
www.thecoca-colacompany.com/citizenship/economic_impact.html

2 CIA Factbook: El Salvador, www.cia.gov/library/publications/
the-world-factbook/geos/es.html

3 Speech by Neville Isdell, Coca-Cola Annual Meeting 2008,
www.thecoca-colacompany.com/presscenter/viewpoints_
isdell_annual_meeting_2008.html

4 ibid

5 FMLN – Farabundo Marti Liberation Front (*Frente Farabundo para la
Liberation*)

6 Ashveille Global Report 2003, www.theglobalreport.org/issues/212/
environment.html

7   Get the Real Facts, The Coca-Cola Company, www.gettherealfacts.
    co.uk/environment/environment.html
8   www.thecoca-colacompany.com/citizenship/pdf/cwp_011608.pdf

India: A Prequel
1   'To deny voting rights to Indian shareholders – Coke knocks at FIPB
    doors', 30 January 2003, www.thehindubusinessline.com/2003/01/
    30/stories/2003013002590100.htm
2   Multilateral Investment Agreement in the WTO, Kavaljit Singh, July
    2003, www.wto.org/english/forums_e/ngo_e/multi_invest_agree_
    july03_e.pdf
3   To deny voting rights to Indian shareholders – Coke knocks at FIPB
    doors, The Hindu BusinessLine, 30 January 2003, www.thehindu
    businessline.com/2003/01/30/stories/2003013002590100.htm
4   'Kerala's Plachimada Struggle', *Economic and Political Weekly*,
    14 October 2006, C R Bijoy
5   Poison Vs Nutrition, Centre for Science and Environment,
    www.cseindia.org/misc/cola-indepth/poison.pdf
6   Minister of Water Resources reply to Lok Sabha (lower House of
    Indian Parliament) starred question No.2 on 5 July 2004 as cited in
    Poison Vs Nutrition, Centre for Science and Environment,
    www.cseindia.org/misc/cola-indepth/poison.pdf
7   www.coca-colaindia.com/water_management/approach-to-
    water.asp
8   'Coke may wreak havoc in Plachimada: KSSP', *The Hindu* 9 February
    2003, www.hinduonnet.com/2003/02/09/stories/
    2003020905340400.htm
9   Letter to Shri. V.K Ebrahim Kunju, The Minister for Industry in Kerala
    from the Hindustan Coca-Cola Beverages Pvt Ltd, 28 November 2005
10 *Face the Facts* Coca-Cola Update Transcript transmitted 2 January
    2004, www.bbc.co.uk/radio4/youandyours/yy_20040102.shtml
11 '*Face The Facts* investigates Coca-Cola plant in India', BBC Press
    Release, 24 July 2003, www.bbc.co.uk/pressofficepressreleases/
    stories/2003/07_july/24/face_facts.shtml
12 ibid
13 ibid
14 Letter to Shri. V.K Ebrahim Kunju, The Minister for Industry in Kerala
    from the Hindustan Coca-Cola Beverages Pvt Ltd, 28 November 2005
15 'Coca-Cola Don't Poison My Well', *Outlook* 16 May 2005, cited in
    'Kerala's Plachimada Struggle', *Economic and Political Weekly*,
    C R Bijoy, 14 October 2006
16 Letter to Shri. V.K Ebrahim Kunju, The Minister for Industry in Kerala
    from the Hindustan Coca-Cola Beverages Pvt Ltd, 28 November 2005
17 Email to author
18 Analysis of Pesticides in Soft Drinks, Centre for Science and
    Environment, 5 August 2003, www.cseindia.org/misc/cola-indepth/
    cola2006/pdf/labreport2003.pdf

19 ibid
20 'HC orders govt to test Pepsi products', *The Tribune India*, 11 August 2003, www.tribuneindia.com/2003/20030812/nation.htm#1
21 'The Street Fight', *Down to Earth*, 15 August 2006, www.downto earth.org.in/cover.asp?foldername=20060815&filename= news&sid=70&page=1&sec_id=9&p=1
22 Interview conducted by author
23 'JPC report upholds CSE findings', *Hindu Business Line*, 5 February 2004
24 One Indian crore is a unit of measurement equivalent to 10 million. So the soft drink industry turnover is Rs60,000 million (or US$1.4 billion)
25 Report of Joint Committee on Pesticide Residues in and Safety Standards for Soft Drinks, Fruit Juice and Other Beverages, parliamentofindia.nic.in/ls/jpc/jpc-prsfb.htm
26 www.cseindia.org/misc/cola-indepth/cola2006/cola_press2006.htm

Chapter 9: Kuriji
1 Coca-Cola website, www.gettherealfacts.co.uk
2 Author interview with Professor Rathore, Institute of Development Studies, Jaipur
3 'Independent, Third Party Assessment of Coca-Cola Facilities in India', TERI Report, www.teriin.org/coke_files/FReport.pdf, page 123
4 Email sent to the author
5 www.vpcomm.umich.edu/pa/key/coke_qa.html
6 'Independent, Third Party Assessment of Coca-Cola Facilities in India', TERI Report, www.teriin.org/coke_files/FReport.pdf
7 ibid, p. 124
8 Letter to the University of Michigan from The Coca-Cola Company, 11 January 2008, www.cokefacts.com/PressCenter/TERI_Michigan_Letter.pdf
9 Independent, Third Party Assessment of Coca-Cola Facilities in India', TERI Report, www.teriin.org/coke_files/FReport.pdf, page 22
10 Coke Gets CSR Award Amidst Protests, Business Standard, 19 February 2008, www.indiaresource.org/news/2008/1013.html
11 Deepak Jolly Conferred Communicator of the Year Award, Company News, 21 March 2006, www.afaqs.com/news/company_news/Corporate/13108.html

Chapter 10: Gas
1 Coke Facts: The Truth About The Coca-Cola Company Around the Globe, www.cokefacts.com/India/facts_in_keyfacts.shtml
2 Email from The Coca-Cola Company to author
3 Interview conducted by author

4   'Independent, Third Party Assessment of Coca-Cola Facilities in India', TERI Report, www.teriin.org/coke_files/FReport.pdf, page 128
5   ibid, p. 128
6   ibid, p. 128

Chapter 11: The Fizz Man's Burden
1   Letter to the University of Michigan from The Coca-Cola Company, 11 January 2008, www.cokefacts.com/PressCenter/TERI_Michigan_Letter.pdf
2   ibid
3   ibid
4   Email sent to author
5   ibid
6   Interview conducted by author
7   'Independent, Third Party Assessment of Coca-Cola Facilities in India', TERI Report, www.teriin.org/coke_files/FReport.pdf
8   ibid
9   Letter to the University of Michigan from The Coca-Cola Company, 11 January 2008, www.cokefacts.com/PressCenter/TERI_Michigan_Letter.pdf
10   TERI report

Chapter 12: Second Fattest in the Infants
1   'Mexicans living fat, almost like Americans', *Oakland Tribune*, 24 March 2008
2   World Health Organisation, www.who.int/infobase/report.aspx?rid=114&iso=MEX&ind=BMI
3   'Mexicans living fat, almost like Americans', *Oakland Tribune*, 24 March 2008
4   www.ustr.gov/assets/Trade_Agreements/Monitoring_Enforcement/Dispute_Settlement/WTO/Dispute_Settlement_Listings/asset_upload_file565_6449.pdf
5   'In Mexico, Taking Fizz Out of the Cola Giants', *Los Angeles Times*, 28 December 2005
6   'Pepsi tackles childhood obesity with videogames in Mexico', *Guardian*, 2 January 2008
7   www.thecoca-colacompany.com/ourcompany/ar/percapitaconsumption_latin_america.html#mexico
8   Controversial Sweetener Dropped from Mexican Coke Zero, Cox News Service, 18 March 2008
9   fox.presidencia.gob.mx/en/cabinet/?contenido=18150
10   Coca-Cola Refuses To Cut Advertising Spending In Mexico, Internet Securities, April 2001
11   Interview conducted by author with Big Cola lawyer

Chapter 13: Belching Out the Devil

1 *Huitepec, the Mayan Hill of Water*, Coca-Cola's Raid on a Sacred Mountain, John Ross 7 September 2007, www.counterpunch.org/ross09072007.html,
2 Author interview with Antonino García
3 Cola Wars in Mexico, Beverly Bell, In These Times, 6 October 2006, www.inthesetimes.com/article/2840/
4 fox.presidencia.gob.mx/en/cabinet/development/?contenido=18150

Chapter 14: We're On a Road to Delaware

1 www.thecoca-colacompany.com/presscenter/viewpoints_isdell_annual_meeting_2008.html
2 Information on Ray's campaign can be found at: www.killercoke.org
3 Coca-Cola Annual Report SEC Filing 2007, www.secinfo.com/d14D5a.t18P7.b.htm
4 www.ilo.org/global/lang—en/index.htm
5 University of Michigan, Press and Media Relations Department, Questions and Answers re: Coca-Cola, Updated 11 April 2006, www.vpcomm.umich.edu/pa/key/coke_qa.html
6 'The Facts: Coca-Cola and Columbia', The Coca-Cola Company
7 events.streamlogics.com/pmtv/coke/apr19-06/auditorium/index.asp at 29:56
8 www.thecoca-colacompany.com/ourcompany/bios/ bio_76.html
9 Interview conducted by the author
10 'Make Your Mark With Branding', *Ocala Business Journal*, 21 April 2008, www.ocala.com/article/20080421/OBIZ/117317226/1357/obiz&title=Make_your_mark_with_branding

Postscript

1 'Coca-Cola to cut 256 jobs in Drogheda', *The Irish Times*, 29 August 2007
2 The Coca-Cola Company Press Release, 2 April 2008, www.thecoca-colacompany.com/presscenter/nr_20080402_timing_of_first_qtr_earnings.html
3 www.idaireland.com/home/index.aspx?id=659
4 www.finfacts.ie/irelandeconomy/usmultinationalprofitsireland.htm
5 'Bono, Preacher on Poverty Tarnishes Halo with Irish Tax move,' 6 Oct 2006, Fergal O'Brien, Bloomberg, www.bloomberg.com/apps/news?pid=20601109&sid=aef6sR60.DgM&refer=home
6 'Coca-Cola to move production to non-unionised plant', www.eurofound.europa.eu/euro/2007/09/articles/ie0709079i/htm
7 'Shock over Coca-Cola investment in Wexford', 2 July 2008, *Drogheda Independent*, www.drogheda-independent.ie/news/shock-over-cocacola-investment-in-wexford-1431032.html

Appendix B: Coke Q&A

Initially I expected the company not to respond to any of the questions I put to them. I had chased Ed Potter, The Coca-Cola Company's Global Workplace Rights Director. I had even negotiated with company personnel about 'potentially answering questions' but all of this faded to nothing and they returned to silent mode. However, Coke did resurface responding to a critical comment piece [by the NGO War on Want] in the *Guardian* newspaper by way of the letters page. As all other avenues of communication with them had been closed to me, I decided to write to the *Guardian* too.

> *Guardian*, Saturday 10 May 2008
> Interesting to see Lauren Branston defending Coca-Cola against 'alleged misdeeds in the past' (Letters, May 8). Especially as I visited India last month to research the current accusations levelled at the company. Lauren and Coca-Cola have not been able to reply to these serious questions about their business practices. So here are a few of them, in the hope that I can get a reply now. 1) Didn't Coca-Cola formally sponsor the TERI foundation, which carried out the 'independent report' Lauren refers to? 2) Despite this potential conflict, the report noted the company's refusal to give crucial documents and data needed for a proper assessment of the company; are you going to make this data available? 3) The report says the company's efforts to deal with the water crisis in Kaladera rely on rainwater harvesting – the company's much-vaunted solution to its water consumption problems. However, the report also notes that rainwater harvesting relies on rainfall, so can you tell me where this rainfall comes from in a drought-prone area, ie, a place with not much rainfall? Even the report concludes the company's efforts are 'unlikely to be meaningful'. 4) The report lists possible options to address the water crisis in Kaladera – one of those is to shut the Coke plant down. Any chance you will follow the report's advice? 5) Should I send other questions for Lauren to answer via the *Guardian* letters page?
> **Mark Thomas**
> London

The company did not respond to the *Guardian* letter, however, after a series of emails to the company detailing questions for them, they agreed to provide some answers. You can get a flavour of the correspondence between us from the two emails below.

Dear Mark,

Thanks for your email with another set of questions, which I would like to reassure you that we are working on. I am happy to come back to you once, to all your questions and will endeavour to meet your deadline of the 8th of July, however, I hope you understand that this involves a lot of work, pulling together answers from questions directed to our operations in many different countries around the world on important, and complex issues.

Moreover, I have to tell you that when you say 'these are all the questions I have at the moment', I have to say to you – we will not continue to answer your questions ad nauseam. I would suggest that if you have any further questions you submit them now (and we will let you know how quickly we can come back to you with answers, which will most likely be later than the 8th of July, at this stage).

Best wishes,

Lauren

Dear Lauren

Thanks for your mail. I understand you're very busy and that you will need to contact your colleagues abroad for some of the answers. I appreciate your efforts to find these answers. If I do have any other questions I will send them to you in the hope that you will be able to do your best with them.

Moreover, I should remind you that the Company has responded to precisely none of the questions for the book, some of which were submitted well over a month ago. Thus the use of the term ad nauseam, meaning a sickening or excessive degree, might be more appropriate for example in a phrase like, 'The Company prevaricated ad nauseam'.

Kindest Regards

Mark

Eventually the Company sent over their responses. Here are their answers reproduced word to word with my questions included. There is one unexpected bonus: when the Company sent over their replies to the allegations about Colombia, they accidentally included their lawyers' strikethroughs and comments – so you get a chance to see how they finessed their answers and spot the odd line the company deemed unfit for public consumption. Enjoy...and a hearty thank you to whoever left them in.

Colombia

~~CONFIDENTIAL ATTORNEY-CLIENT PRIVILEGED WORK PRODUCT~~
~~AND COMMUNICATION~~

Note: Since our bottlers are separate companies that are not controlled
by The Coca-Cola Company, the responses below are necessarily based
on information available to The Coca-Cola Company and our subsidiary
in Colombia. W~~and we~~ do not purport to speak for the independent
bottlers.~~:~~

**1) Has The Coca-Cola Company *itself* ever issued any public
statements or taken out any advertising defending the right to
unioni̶z̶e and/or to denounce the violence directed against
SINALTRAINAL? If so, may we see a copy of these statements?**
Representatives of The Coca-Cola Company in Colombia meet regularly
with Vice President Francisco Santos and members of the Human
Rights Office of the Vice Presidency, to keep them informed of our
challenges and initiatives, to reiterate the Company's strong support of
efforts to eradicate violence of any kind, including vio~~oi~~lence directed at
union organizers, and to request ~~their~~ the Government's assistance in
~~the~~ protecting~~protection of~~ union leaders in ~~the Coca-Cola~~ bottling
plants and ~~, as well as~~ the timely and thorough investigation of any
incidents of violence reported by the trade unions. Company
representatives ~~have~~ also have met regularly with the Minister of Social
Protection (Labor) and the Defensor del Pueblo (Ombudsman) on
similar topics, and with the Minister of the Interior, who manages the
government's protection program for union leaders (with funds from
Plan Colombia).
    The Coca-Cola Company~~[I understand that TCCC,~~, in conjunction
with setting-up the Colombia Foundation, itself specifically advertised
its support for union rights an opposition to violence. ~~(PL would know~~
~~the answer to this I assume.) I also believe that the press release~~
~~advertising the existence of the now defunct settlement talks specifically~~
~~referenced TCCC's strong opposition to trade union violence. JNH will~~
~~check my records and revert. These examples would more directly~~
~~answer the question.]~~

**2) Has The Coca-Cola Company's bottlers in Colombia ever issued
any public statements or taken out any advertising defending the
right to unioni̶z̶e and/or to denounce the violence directed
against SINALTRAINAL? If so, may we see a copy of these
statements?**
Throughout the years the independent bottlers of Coca-Cola ® brand
products in Colombia ~~The independent Coca-Cola bottlers in Colombia~~

have frequently and publicly denounced violence against union members in Colombia. See attached advertisement for example.

The largest of such bottling enterprises, Coca-Cola FEMSA, ~~has~~ also has informed us that it is their practice immediately to notify the appropriate authorities as soon as management is made aware of threats against union members. Coca-Cola FEMSA supplies notification and information to, among others, the Minister of Social Protection (Labor) and the Defensor del Pueblo (Ombudsman), as well as the Minister of the Interior, who manages the government's protection program for union leaders.

3) Has The Coca-Cola Company *itself* ever investigated or engaged an independent third party to conduct a comprehensive investigation into the allegations of ties between bottler management and paramilitaries? And if so, what were the conclusions?
In the spring of 2005, The Company commissioned an independent assessment of bottling plants in Colombia by the internationally respected and certified social compliance auditor Cal Safety Compliance Corporation to look into current workplace rights practices of the bottlers in Colombia. The assessment, which included interviews of hundreds of employees throughout Colombia, confirmed that workers in ~~Coca-Cola~~such plants enjoy freedom of association, collective bargaining rights, and a work atmosphere free of anti-union intimidation.

Assessments by other unions in Colombia and elsewhere have likewise found no evidence of wrongdoing by the Company or its independent bottlers. In an open letter to the National Union of Students, the UK trade unions explained the Company's lack culpability as follows:

> Since the first call to boycott Coca-Cola over Colombia was issued in 2003, the UK trade union movement has investigated and monitored the situation closely. We have sent delegations to Colombia to speak to workers' representatives there. We have kept in close contact with trade unions in Colombia and have continued to raise issues of importance to them by taking up their cause with workers, politicians and the media here in the UK. We have taken the lead from the CUT [Colombia's United Workers Confederation] . . . the democratic umbrella organization for Colombian trade unions, as well as from the IUF (the International Union of Foodworkers), the relevant global union federation. ~~Since 2003, no evidence has been provided to link Coca-Cola to the assassination of its workers in Colombia.~~

(March 21, 2006 joint letter to the National Union of Students from three UK trade unions, Amicus, T & G and GMB). ~~(emphasis added)~~.

In addition, the Company and its independent bottlers welcome efforts by other international organizations, including the International Labor Organization, to verify the Company's internal assessments.

4) When did The Coca-Cola Company become aware of the murder of Isidero Gil in the Carepa plant? And what was the Company's immediate response?
[JNH: Will need Ben Garren or Ed Potter to opine. My understanding is that W~~w~~ithin days of the murder, the Company was alerted to the situation and gave its full support to all staff and employees of the Carepa facility, the vast majority of whom (employees and managers alike) were forced to relocate from the territory.]

5) What is the current status of the promised ILO investigation and evaluation of Coca-Cola bottling operations in Colombia and what is the new timetable?
The political situation in Colombia has become more complicated since the assessment requests were made to the ILO. In particular, the ILO has placed a priority on addressing the issue of impunity, resolving the inconsistencies between the ILO standards that the Colombian Government has ratified and existing labor and employment law, and assuring that the historic tripartite agreement reached in June 2006 under the auspices of the ILO is fully implemented. To address these political complexities, in particular to be certain that there is overall government, business and union support for the procedures and methods of the ILO assessment, the Director General of the ILO, has required that each of these constituencies sign off of the assessment protocol before it begins.

For its part, The Coca-Cola Company fully supports the ILO initiative and investigation and remains willing and ready to cooperate in whatever reasonable form the ILO requests.

6) What is the ~~remit~~ scope of the promised ILO investigation?
This is an independent investigation that will be conducted by the ILO, therefore we do not know the full ~~remit~~ scope and process of the assessment. ~~They~~ The ILO has ~~have~~ informed ~~us~~ the Company that the assessment will include a ~~scope will be primarily a~~ review of current workers' rights ~~at~~ in the workplace, ~~including~~ conditions of work, health and safety, labor relations and social security.

7) Can The Coca-Cola Company confirm its claims that if the ILO investigation does get underway, it will investigate both past and present labour rights abuses in the Coke bottling plants in Colombia?
~~The ILO assessment is of current workplace rights at independent Coca-Cola bottling facilities in Colombia.~~

~~[FG: Suggest we attempt to address the ILO's non-investigation of past~~ ~~incidents this way:~~ "By mandate, the ILO assessment team is concerned with ensuring the implementation and maintenance of progressive labor practices in member countries. Accordingly, the assessment function traditionally does not investigate specific allegations of past labor abuse, which is a task performed by a separate arm of the ILO charged with evaluating formal complaints made by union members. In fact, SINALTRAINAL recently has filed complaints with the ILO, who is considering the charges and whether to conduct a further inquiry into the allegations.~~"~~

8) If that is the case, can The Coca-Cola Company explain how the ILO can investigate past labour rights abuses within a company (in this case The Coca-Cola Company bottlers – Panamco and Bebidas y Alimentos) when the ILO has a remit to investigate only on a countrywide rather than company specific basis and can only investigate current labour rights abuse?
As noted immediately above, t~~T~~he ILO assessment ~~is~~ concerns~~of~~ current workplace ~~rights~~ practices at the independent ~~Coca-Cola~~ bottling facilities in Colombia. The ILO has relevant experience monitoring labor practices in the garment industry which we believe will be helpful in this investigation. And as set forth above, the ILO has a separate arm to investigate complaints by union members.

9) Will The Coca-Cola Company publish or show the contents of the letter/agreement Neville Isdell claims the company has from the ILO stating the organization will investigate past and present labour rights abuses in the Coke bottling plants in Colombia?
The ILO assessment is of current workplace rights at independent ~~Coca-Cola~~ bottling facilities in Colombia. As set forth above, the ILO has a well-established procedure for investigating formal complaints by union members.

10) Has The Coca-Cola Company taken any action against its bottler for the false allegation made by a bottler security manager in Bucaramanga that lead to the wrongful imprisonment of Luis Eduardo García and Domingo Flores amongst others?
The Coca-Cola Company does not own or have the right to unilaterally punish or sanction the employees of the independent bottlers within its system. The Company does, however, seek to promote progressive labor rights within its bottling system and supply chain, and has established an office within the Company headed by Ed Potter that is charged with liaising with local bottlers to resolve any issue that may arise.
In the case of Messrs. Garcia and Flores, TCCC has discussed the matter with the bottler and understands that the bottler employees gave

truthful statements to the Colombian government investigators. This was the extent of the involvement of the bottler involvement in the case. The Company understands that following the Government's investigation, Messrs. Garcia and Flores were compensated for their time away from work, provided additional security and protection and have remained employed by the bottler.

11) Does The Coca-Cola Company share the view of its bottlers that in bringing legal action against the Company, SINALTRAINAL had libelled and defamed the company? And did the Company agree with the defamation suit brought against SINALTRAINAL?
~~TCCC~~ The Company has not~~never~~ filed any official action against SINALTRAINAL in the case. ~~Coca-Cola~~ Local bottlers in Colombia ~~Panamco~~ have denounced the ~~defendants'~~ certain actions – including incidents such as the painting of graffiti on bottling plant walls and barricading of plant entrances – to authorities based on ~~its~~ reasonable concerns for the safety of the Company and its ability to continue operations. In particular, the union's careless accusations that the bottlers somehow conspire with or support paramlitaries endangers the lives of the bottlers' management and personnel, who themselves are targets for violence, including at the direction Colombia's notorious guerilla insurgency. ~~T~~~~Regardless, regarding the circumstance of the incident, but~~to our knowledge, the bottlers have not ~~did not~~ filed any separate official action against SINALTRAINAL or its leaders.~~; rather, the company relied on the government's investigation of the crime, which resulted in the arrest and later release of some of the union members.~~

~~For its part, The Coca-Cola Company believes that the allegations in the law suits – and the law suits themselves – not only are intentionally false, but are part of a well-funded effort by U.S. labor interests, including the United Steelworkers (whose counsel assisted in bringing the lawsuits), to use the Coca-Cola ® brand to undermine free trade and the interests of foreign employers. [FG: I assume that we would prefer not to take potshots at the Steealworkers not sound like we are favoring foreigners of any stripe over the U.S. I wouldn't push this beyond saying that the lawsuits are intentionally false and part of a coordinated effort to use the Coca-Cola brand for their own political purposes.]~~

12) Did any Coca-Cola ~~Femsa~~ FEMSA bottling plants pay money for SINALTRAINAL members to give up their trade-union membership? If so how any many trade union members did the Coca-Cola FEMSA bottling plants pay to the trade-union members? How many trade-union members were given money to give up their membership? Over what period of time did this occur?
We ~~cannot respond on behalf of Coca-Cola FEMSA, however it is the case that in any company, some employees are are terminated for~~been

~~fired with legal cause (such as absenteeism, non- or under-performance, or violation of workplace rules). During an economic downturn or restructuring, other employees – some union members, some not – also may seek to retire and accept due to different reasons- and accept early retirement packages as part of restructuring of the bottlers' operations. The presence of unions in the local bottling plants of Coca-Cola ® brand products in Colombia remains strong.~~have no information to indicate that Coca-Cola FEMSA has ever paid money for SINALTRAINAL members to give up their trade union membership. The independent bottler guarantees the right to freedom of association and collective bargaining and has multiple agreements with multiple unions- and in a country where 4 percent of workers from unionizing, 31 percent of Coca-Cola bottler employees belong to unions.

13) Why did negotiations between The Coca-Cola Company and the plaintiffs in the ATCA suit break down earlier this year? What conditions did The Coca-Company put on any settlement?
In 2001, SINALTRAINAL, with the assistance of U.S. labor interests, filed ~~The ATCA~~ Alient Torts Statute lawsuits ~~were filed in 2001 by the Colombian union Sinaltrainal~~ against The Coca-Cola Company and ~~two~~ several entities affiliated with independent bottlers of Coca-Cola ® brand products in Colombia~~bottlers~~. The Coca-Cola Company was dismissed by the United States District Court for the Southern District of Florida from the case in 2003, which held that the Company possessed no control over or liability for the alleged conduct of third parties in rural Colombia. In October 2006, ~~the two~~ the remaining defendants ~~Coca-Cola bottlers in Colombia~~ also were dismissed from the case. ~~Sinaltrainal's motion to bring The Coca-Cola Company back into the lawsuit was denied and the judge has ordered that the cases be closed. Sinaltrainal has appealed the dismissal of the case and the appeal is pending.~~

Despite having secured its dismissal from the lawsuits, the Company ~~TCCC~~ sought – as it has throughout this dispute – to engage~~d~~ in ~~extended direct~~ constructive dialogue with the plaintiffs — both to better understand their concerns and also to assess whether a mediated resolution of the parties' differences could be achieved.~~in the litigation and the plaintiffs' representatives but the dialogue reached an impasse.~~ The parties' talks were fruitful and informative, although no final resolution was possible. An impasse was reached and no further discussions are anticipated at this time. ~~No further dialogue is anticipated related to the allegations of the lawsuit.~~

The Coca-Cola Company wishes to underscore that it is innocent of the charges brought by the plaintiffs in the dismissed litigation. However, ~~TCCC~~ the Company is sympathetic to the underlying concerns about violence against any member of Colombian society, including union members – which is one of the reasons why the Company helped fund and sponsor the Colombia Foundation, whose work continues to remediate the effects of violence in the country.

El Salvador

14. Is it still the case that Central Izalco is the sole supplier for Coke bottlers in El Salvador? If not, who are the other suppliers?
El Salvador is a controlled market and as such we buy from a marketing agency, who in turn assigns the volume to a qualified source. Central Izalco and El Angel are the two mills (out of 8) that meet our quality requirements and have been approved for use by our system in that country.

15. Your website states, *'We only buy from sugar mills that adhere to our standards and we constantly monitor for compliance. If we find a supplier is not meeting our standards, we take immediate action. We care about the plight of these children and are serious about helping them'* – could you explain how often and what form the constant monitoring takes place for Central Izalco and/or any other suppliers?
Our Company TCCC routinely utilizes independent third-parties to assess suppliers' compliance with our Company's Supplier Guiding Principles (SGP). The SGP are a vital pillar of TCCC's workplace accountability programs. They contain requirements that our direct suppliers must comply with regarding freedom of association and collective bargaining; prohibition of child labor; prohibition of forced labor and abuse of labor; elimination of discrimination; work hours and wages; provision of a safe and healthy workplace; and protection of the environment. If a supplier fails to uphold any aspect of the SGP requirements, the supplier is expected to implement corrective actions. The Company reserves the right to terminate an agreement with any supplier that cannot demonstrate that they are upholding the SGP requirements and has done so.

16. Your website states that you are *'working towards hiring a monitoring system for plantations'* – has the multi-stakeholder initiative yet hired a monitoring system? And if so, what is its remit, how often does it report, how is it funded and what results have been found so far?
The multi-stakeholder initiative, led by the Ministry of Labor and the El Salvadoran Sugar Association, has put into place several social monitoring systems for the plantations.

Ministry of Labor Work:
- During the harvest the Ministry of Labor has labor inspectors whose only task is to detect child labor.

- Those cooperatives found to have child labor are subject to economic sanctions.

El Salvadoran Sugar Association Work:
- The Sugar Association employs 10 social workers who implement the industry's social responsibility programs.
- Every morning during the harvest those 10 social workers visit the cane farms looking for evidence of child labor.
- If a child is found cutting cane he or she is immediately removed.

In addition, every engineer from the sugar mills who works at the sugar cane farms has the obligation to report child labor. Failure to report child labor, would result in the termination of the engineer's contract.

17. Your website refers to *'Nine thousand children have been removed from the sugarcane fields in El Salvador over the last three years through our efforts with the UN and the Sugar Association.'*
a) Can you explain how the figure of 9,000 was calculated and by whom? How many of those 9,000 were removed from plantations that provide cane for Central Izalco?
All figures quoted have been determined by the International Labour Organizations' International Programme on the Elimination of Child Labor. More information about IPEC can be found at:
http://www.ilo.org/ipec
b) What is the nature of the work that The Coca-Cola Company has undertaken through the UN that has led to this? Has the company sponsored or paid for practical programmes or are you referring to company support / lobbying for the establishment of UN norms and standards?
Our Company has publicly supported a proposal, authored by the World Bank and Business for Social Responsibility, to help position El Salvador as a responsible-sourcing country in conjunction with UN norms and standards. And we have funded the multi-stakeholder initiative working towards hiring social monitors to work with the co-ops to monitor and address child labor, led by the Ministry of Labor and the El Salvadoran Sugar Association.

We have also participated in multi-stakeholder dialogues that have included the International Labor Organization of the UN to understand and address the root causes of this serious issue in El Salvador.

18. Your website states, *'On Coca-Cola's recommendation, Fundazucar (the Salvadoran Sugar Association) engaged a social compliance auditing firm that helped the Association determine how to detect and control child labour and associated issues.'* **What is the name of the social auditing firm? How often have they reported and what were their recommendations?**
The social auditing firm is the internationally respected and certified

social compliance auditor, Cal Safety Compliance Corporation. The audits have taken place during the 2004–2007 harvests.

19. Your website states, 'Coca-Cola has partnered with TechnoServe, a local NGO working with targeted co-ops to find alternative sources of income for youth 14–18 years of age'. What is the nature of the partnering of TechnoServe? Was there any financial assistance involved? Have there been any assessments made of the results of the partnering and if so, by whom?
Techno Serve is an NGO dedicated to the development of businesses who work in the agricultural field. We partnered with Techo Serve to financially support the programs that aid children through educational opportunities in El Salvador.

20. The Human Rights Watch report, Turning a Blind Eye, recommends, 'In particular, it [Coca-Cola] should incorporate the UN Norms in its contractual arrangements with suppliers and should require its suppliers to do the same throughout their supply chains'. Are there any plans to do this and if so, what is your timetable?
Our Company's Supplier Guiding Principles (SGP) communicate to direct suppliers our values and expectations and emphasize the importance of responsible environmental and workplace policies and practices that comply, at a minimum, with applicable local laws and regulations. Our SGP is consistent with the key elements of the International Labor Organization of the UN's core labor standards (freedom of association and collective bargaining, forced or compulsory labor, child labor and discrimination).

India

21. According to the Company website, 'indirectly, our business in India creates employment to more than 150,000 people'. a) Of this figure, how many is casual or outsourced labour working within the plants? b) Can you break down this figure into categories? Does this figure include street vendors, outsourced workers, delivery drivers etc?
The Company and its bottling partners provide direct employment to more than 10,000 people in India. In addition, soft drinks being a seasonal business in India, the Company and its bottling partners also employ nearly 10,000 contractor's workmen during the peak season (summer season). This positive economic impact is multiplied by the employment generated through our chain of distributors and retailers, through our vendors and suppliers, through the transporters, signage painters, point of purchase and other marketing material designers and

manufacturers etc. As per an estimate by National Council of Applied Economic Research (NCAER) the soft drink industry generates an overall employment of 1,300 for every 1 million cases sold.

22. What financial benefits – tax incentives/subsidies/ infrastructure payments etc – were given to Coca-Cola for building their plant in Kaladera?

In order to fuel economic development in remote areas, the governments of all states set up Industrial areas to encourage industries to invest in economically undeveloped/underdeveloped areas. The government gives financial incentives such as tax exemptions of 5-7 years etc. as per the policy. The Coca-Cola plant at Kaladera was given sales tax exemption as per the Industrial policy of the Rajasthan State government.

23. How much ground water has Coca-Cola extracted each year for its plant in Kaladera for the last five years?

Year	Water Extraction in Kilo litres
2003	139156
2004	211173
2005	90660
2006	84074
2007	87977

24. What on-going relationship regarding rainwater harvesting do Coca-Cola and the Rajasthan Ground Water Board have?

Coca-Cola in India has undertaken a range of water conservation and awareness programs across the country. These programs are undertaken in partnership with Central Ground Water Authority, State Ground Water Boards, Resident Welfare Associations, Market Welfare Associations, Schools and Colleges, Industry Associations, NGOs and local communities. In Rajasthan also the Company has undertaken a range of water conservation initiatives like revival of traditional water bodies, installation of rainwater recharge shafts, rooftop rainwater harvesting projects etc. These projects have been undertaken under the guidance of Rajasthan State Ground Water Board. Thus, while there is formal relationship that exists between Rajasthan State Ground Water Board (RSGWB) and the Company, RSGWB focuses on initiatives that could enhance groundwater levels and hence have provided guidance to our rainwater harvesting initiatives in the state and have also assessed them periodically.

25. Specifically, how many rainwater harvesting shafts does Coca-Cola have in its rainwater harvesting scheme in Kaladera? And over what area?

The Company has installed 143 recharge shafts in Kaladera and surrounding areas spread over an area of 17 sq. KMS

26. How does Coca-Cola monitor its rainwater harvesting scheme?
The RWH schemes are monitored through defined protocols. For any location, before establishing any Rainwater Harvesting (RWH) system, studies are done with respect to area available for recharge, average annual rainfall, the type water harvesting area (to determine the coefficient of recharge) and any assumptions/considerations made in site selection. The site selection would depend on ground water situation, infiltration capacity of the local hydrogeology, and need for RWH intervention, including the ownership of such intervention. The established technical feasibility is vetted by local government or research agency involved with water resource management and the designs are finalized. The structures are executed by expert agencies and its completeness is verified by the competent technical experts. Usually, the executing agency is a local NGO group and would have responsibility to maintain the developed structure for period of three years initially. We have also developed a monitoring protocol to maintain the structures on annual basis to understand its full functionality and usefulness. Each year the incident rainfall data is obtained from nearest government meteorological observatory at the end of the year and the estimated recharge potential is revalidated by inserting the appropriate value of rainfall.

In addition, the Company undertakes regular maintenance of most of the structures with help of NGOs/ environmental groups. The Company, along with community/NGO, tries to take water table readings before and after monsoon, keeps historical data, conduct community interviews, facilitate media visits to understand the efficacy and impact of such projects besides site visits by its own high-ranking officials.

Besides the above, rising water level, non requirement to re-drill the borewells, functioning of defunct borewells, higher agriculture yield etc have been reported by communities across the country which serves as the community's own assessment of the impact of RWH.

27. What size are the rainwater harvesting shafts? And from what area (measurement) of land do they collect from?
The recharge shafts provide a pathway to the collected rainwater to flow into the ground through a reverse filter system and recharge the ground water. Each shaft has a diameter of 2 feet and average depth of about 105 feet. While the catchment area is different for different locations, each shaft receives water from approximately 10-15 hectares. Each shaft goes to a depth of over 100 feet below the ground and is filled with filter media to enable quick recharge of the ground water.

28. How much rainwater does the Coca-Cola Company estimate has been recharged by its rainwater harvesting shafts in Kaladera annually for the last five years? How is this monitored? Is it independently verified?

Our rainwater harvesting through recharge shafts started in 2004. In Kaladera, the rainwater harvesting systems that the Company has installed have the potential to recharge about 15 times the amount of water the plant uses currently, assuming normal rainfall (560 mm/year). Even in recent years when rainfall has been below average, actual recharge has been more than 5 times the amount of water used for production of our beverages. (See attached report by the former Chief Engineer of Rajasthan State Ground water Department)

Besides the Company's efforts at monitoring the RWH projects in partnership with NGOs etc as mentioned above, senior hydrogeologists of State Ground water department have been independently monitoring the RWH initiatives. A former chief engineer of Rajasthan State Ground Water Board had independently assessed potential of the same (copy attached). Need this report [sic] Most recently TERI has assessed our water management practices including RWH projects in Kaladera area.

29. How much rainwater does The Coca-Cola Company estimate has been recharged by its rainwater harvesting scheme on the two school roofs in Kaladera annually for the last five years? How is this monitored? Is it independently verified? What is the coverage area (measurement) of the roofs?
In fact there are four educational institutions are covered under roof water harvesting in Kaladera locations. The total roof area covered is about 6,400 square metres and the design RWH potential at average annual rain fall is about 3,400 cubic metres.

The monitoring activity is detailed under question 8 [sic] above.

30. What are the specific calculations that led Coca-Cola to claim its rainwater harvesting structures in Kaladera recharge five times more water than it uses even in drought years, and furthermore has the potential to recharge over 50 core litres of ground water annually at average rainfall?
There are accepted norms as adhered by Central Ground Water Board, UN agencies, Govt. bodies for estimating RWH potential from different surfaces. While for roof top a coefficient between 80-85% is well accepted (given that recharge pit/well/shaft is designed to receive that quantity of water) and for surface water coefficients between 10-20% are accepted, depending on land use/topography, intensity of rainfall, nature of soil etc.

Even with most conservative estimate for catchment of 0.1 sq KM for each shaft and a coefficient of 10%, these shafts would receive over 850 million litres of water.

31. What is the Company's response to the TERI report assertion in its plant specific recommendations for Kaladera, regarding Coca-Cola's rainwater harvesting structures, that 'since the

rainfall is scanty, the recharge achieved through such structures is unlikely to be meaningful'?

The TERI report notes that the Company is a relatively small user of water in Kaladera, tapping far less than one percent the area's available water. In Kaladera, the rainwater harvesting systems Coca-Cola has installed have the potential to recharge about 15 times the amount of water the plant uses currently, assuming normal rainfall (560 mm/year). Even in recent years when rainfall has been below average, actual recharge has been more than 5 times the amount of water used for production of our beverages. Coca-Cola has reduced its water use ratio within the plant by more than 40% over the last five years. The Confederation of Indian Industries (CII) has recognized the Hindustan Coca-Cola Kaladera plant as a 'Water Efficient Unit' across industries at the National Awards for Excellence in Water Management. The Kaladera plant also has won the 'Innovative Project Award' for its contribution towards reduction in specific water consumption.

32. What controls and monitoring have been put in place regarding treated wastewater through land application at Coca-Cola's Kaladera plant?

The wastewater is treated at the wastewater treatment plant at the manufacturing facility prior to use of treated wastewater for irrigating developed greenbelt at the plant premises. The treated wastewater complies with both the company and local standard on the wastewater treatment and disposal. The wastewater treatment plant is designed to treat 1000 m3/day wastewater, while average wastewater generation does not exceed more than 120 m3/day on an average. The overcapacity of the wastewater plant, resultant of the water conservation measures taken by the plant over the period ensures the consistent quality of the wastewater from the treatment plant.

The treated wastewater is monitored in-house as well as external laboratory as per below mentioned frequency

- Routine monitoring of about 8 parameters at in-house laboratory (Biological Oxygen Demand (BOD), Chemical Oxygen Demand (COD), Total Dissolved Solids (TDS), Oil and Grease (O & G), TSS (Total suspended solids),PH, Sulfates and Chlorides.)
- Monthly check of 9 parameters required by pollution control board from Ministry of Environment and Forest (MOEF), India approved laboratory.
- Quarterly monitoring of wastewater as per Coca-Cola standards.
- The monthly monitoring of wastewater report is submitted to state pollution control board for their records.

33. What controls and monitoring are there of the groundwater within the application area of treated wastewater at Coca-Cola's Kaladera plant?

The Company's bottling plant at Kaladera plant uses groundwater (borewells located inside the plant) as source of water. The groundwater within the plant is monitored on annual basis which has hardly shown any deterioration in quality over the period of time. External borewells at upstream and downstream are being monitored (since last 2 years) pre monsoon and post monsoon for quality of groundwater which has shown hardly any deterioration in the quality.

34. What controls and monitoring have been put in place to ensure that the soil's carrying capacity should not be exceeded within the application area of treated wastewater at Coca-Cola's Kaladera plant?
An area of about 40,000 sq. metres has been developed as greenbelt in the plant. This consists of about 10,000 sq. metres of lawn area and about 1,600 numbers of trees. The greenbelt is irrigated by the treated wastewater by means of sprinkler system. This prevents any run off and water-logging in the greenbelt. On an average about 120 cu. metre/day wastewater is used to maintain greenbelt of 40,000 sq. metre (4 hectare) which is well within the standard of 134 to 180 m3 of water / hectare prescribed by the state pollution control board for sandy loamy soil.

35. When did the Coca-Cola bottling plant in Ballia last produce beverages? What is its current operational status?
Ballia plant was a co-packing facility owned by a franchise bottler. As part of business restructuring and consolidation, the production at Ballia was discontinued from June 26, 2007.

36. When did the Coca-Cola bottling plant in Plachimada Kerala last produce beverages? What is its current operational status?
The bottling plant at Plachimada in Kerala has not been operational since March 9, 2004.

37. What is the current status of negotiations regarding the relocation of the plant in Kerala?
We are continuously engaging with all stakeholders to ensure a win-win solution for all.

Appendix C: The Non-Answers of Ed Potter

Ed Potter is the Coca-Cola Global Workplace Rights Director and is in charge of labour issues. After the company blocked my formal attempts to communicate with him I managed to secure an interview from the time-honoured method of 'bumrushing', namely, I spotted him in the street and ran at him with a recorder [Chapter 14: The Road to Delaware]. He assured me that allegation of misconduct and labour issues would be investigated seriously, so alongside other questions that arose from our chat, I emailed him. This is the summation of our all too brief exchange.

Sent: 05/01/2008 06:54 PM CET
To: Ed Potter
Subject: From Mark Thomas in the UK
Dear Ed

Good to see you at the AGM in Delaware the other month and I hope you are keeping well. I was wondering about some of the statements you made and wanted to follow up a few points.

Firstly, on Colombia, I asked if the union that replaced Sinaltrainal (SICO I believe) negotiated a pay cut following the events in Carepa where Sinaltrainal was driven out of town and had their offices burnt down. You said you didn't know, but would it be possible to find out?

Secondly, you said there was good relations with twelve other unions, what is the number of members in each of these unions and what percentage of the workforce does this represent?

Thirdly, you have said previously that CUT do not support the boycott call from Sinaltrainal. I was under the impression that CUT did support the boycott call, could you clarify this and provide the source for this statement?

Fourthly, you said that casual workers in Colombia were not allowed to join an industrial trade union, I wonder if you might point out the law which you refer to?

Fifthly, you said 31 per cent of the workers at Coca-Cola bottlers in Colombia were unionised, does this include casual labour? If it does not, what percentage of Coke workers are unionised if you were to include the casual workers into the equation?

On the subject of India, I was reading in the *Nation's* letter pages that you said that The Coca-Cola Company and its bottlers 'indirectly create employment for 125,000 more [workers] in related procurement supply and distribution roles'. I wonder if you might break down the 125,000 figure for me? Does this figure include panawallahs and juicewallahs (people who sell Coca-Cola products from their stalls)?

On the issue of passing on claims to you regarding the treatment of workers in developing nations, I wonder if you might spell out to me what measures would be taken to investigate the matters or indeed if you have initiated any measures? I look forward to hearing from you.

Best Wishes

Mark Thomas

Subject: response to the email

Ed Potter has referred your email to me. You can find information about our workplace practices on both cokefacts.com and on www.GetTheRealFacts.co.uk.

Sincerely,

Kari Bjorhus

Director, Public Affairs

The Coca-Cola Company

Appendix D: Death Threat

This is a copy of a death threat sent by the Black Eagles, naming Luis Eduardo aka Chile [Chapter 4: 'Chile']. This death threat was sent in February 2007.

> The Black Eagles call on the terrorists in the trade union of Coca-Cola – Javier Correa, Luis Garcia AKA El Chile, Domingo Flores AKA El Gordo, Nelson Perez – to stop the backlash against the Coca-Cola company – You have already caused enough damage – Stop this campaign against the employers of Santander who are supporting the downtrodden of this country – We declare that the military objective of the Black Eagles – how do you prefer death – torture – cutting up into pieces – coup de grace – in the style of Magdalena Medio and this is how you terrorists define it – So stop your campaign, the backlash – Remember Commander Mancuso doesn't like a fuss.
>
> This isn't just a threat, we will carry it out. We will do it. The day will arrive.

Contents

PART TWO

The Spiral of Ideology, 1920s–1969

PART THREE

Issues of Identity, 1960s–2000s

List of Illustrations

Every effort has been made to trace the copyright holders and we apologize in advance for any unintentional omission. We would be pleased to insert the appropriate acknowledgement in any subsequent editions.

List of Maps

Map 1 The regions of France

Map 2 **French** *départements*

| 0 | 100 | 200 km |
| 0 | 50 | 100 miles |

PAS-DE-CALAIS
NORD
SOMME
SEINE-MARITIME
AISNE
ARDENNES
OISE
MOSELLE
BAS-RHIN
MANCHE
CALVADOS
EURE
MARNE
MEUSE
MEURTHE-ET-MOSELLE
ORNE
Paris
EURE-ET-LOIR
AUBE
HTE-MARNE
VOSGES
HAUT-RHIN
CÔTES-D'ARMOR
ILLE-ET-VILAINE
MAYENNE
SARTHE
LOIRET
YONNE
HTE-SAÔNE
BELFORT
FINISTÈRE
MORBIHAN
LOIRE-ATLANTIQUE
MAINE-ET-LOIRE
INDRE-ET-LOIRE
LOIR-ET-CHER
CHER
NIÈVRE
CÔTE-D'OR
DOUBS
JURA
VENDÉE
DEUX-SÈVRES
VIENNE
INDRE
ALLIER
SAÔNE-ET-LOIRE
AIN
HTE-SAVOIE
CHARENTE-MARITIME
CHARENTE
HAUTE-VIENNE
CREUSE
PUY-DE-DÔME
LOIRE
RHÔNE
SAVOIE
ISÈRE
CORRÈZE
HTE-LOIRE
ARDÈCHE
DRÔME
HTES-ALPES
GIRONDE
DORDOGNE
CANTAL
LOZÈRE
ALPES-DE-HTE-PROV.
ALPES-MARIT.
LOT
AVEYRON
GARD
VAUCLUSE
VAR
LOT-ET-GAR.
LANDES
TARN-ET-GAR.
GERS
TARN
HÉRAULT
BCHES-DU-RHÔNE
PYRÉNÉES-ATLANTIQUES
HTES-PYRÉNÉES
HTE-GARONNE
AUDE
ARIÈGE
PYRÉNÉES-ORIENTALES

HAUTE-CORSE
Ajaccio
CORSE-DU-SUD

Départements of Paris region

VAL-D'OISE
HAUTS-DE-SEINE
SEINE-SAINT-DENIS
Paris
YVELINES
VAL-DE-MARNE
ESSONNE
SEINE-ET-MARNE

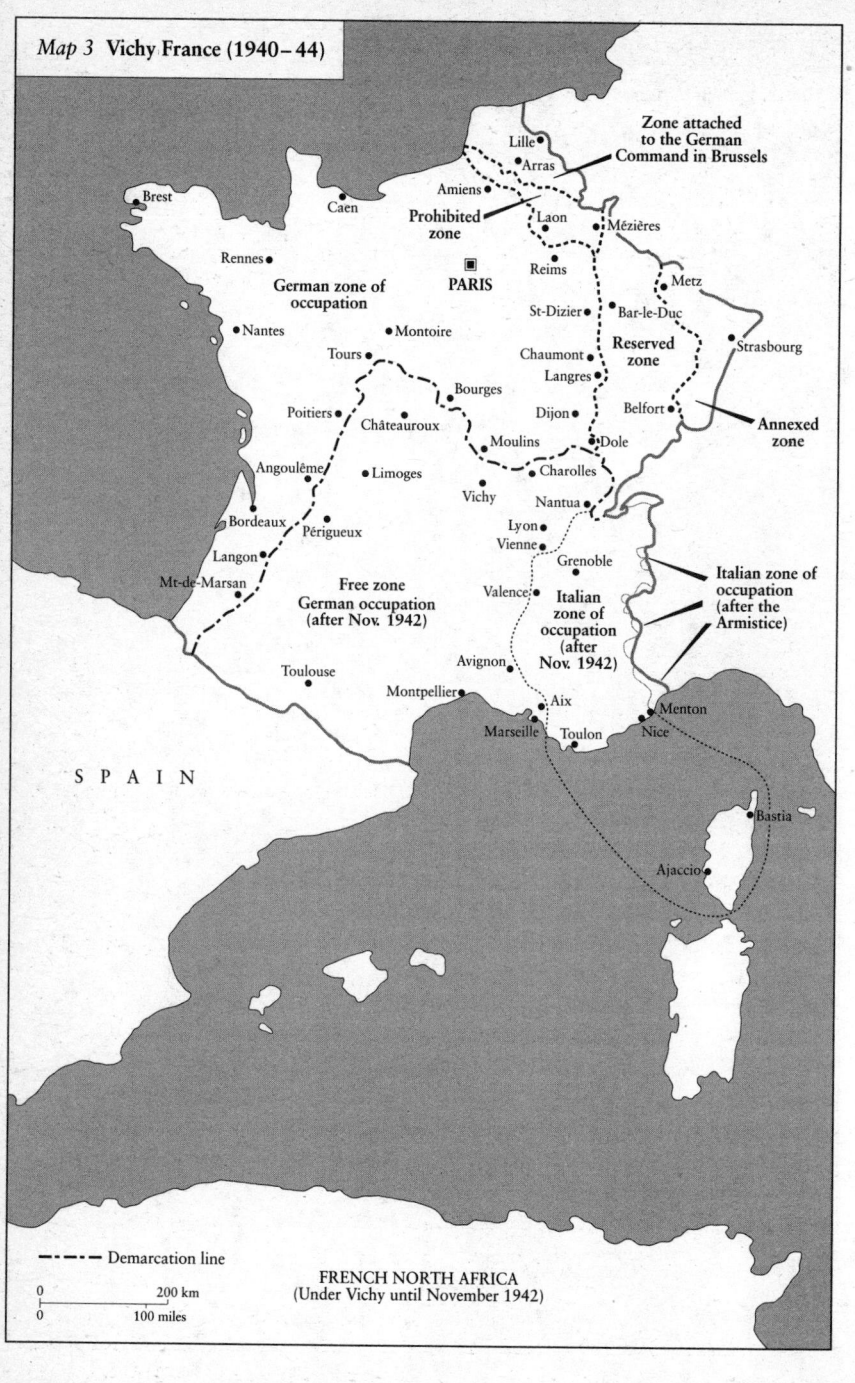

Map 3 Vichy France (1940–44)

Zone attached to the German Command in Brussels

Prohibited zone

German zone of occupation

PARIS

Reserved zone

Annexed zone

Free zone German occupation (after Nov. 1942)

Italian zone of occupation (after Nov. 1942)

Italian zone of occupation (after the Armistice)

S P A I N

Brest
Caen
Rennes
Nantes
Lille
Arras
Amiens
Laon
Mézières
Reims
Metz
Strasbourg
St-Dizier
Bar-le-Duc
Chaumont
Langres
Belfort
Montoire
Tours
Bourges
Dijon
Dole
Poitiers
Châteauroux
Moulins
Charolles
Angoulême
Limoges
Vichy
Nantua
Bordeaux
Périgueux
Lyon
Vienne
Grenoble
Langon
Mt-de-Marsan
Valence
Toulouse
Avignon
Montpellier
Aix
Menton
Marseille
Toulon
Nice
Bastia
Ajaccio

FRENCH NORTH AFRICA
(Under Vichy until November 1942)

–·–·– Demarcation line

0 _____ 200 km
0 _____ 100 miles

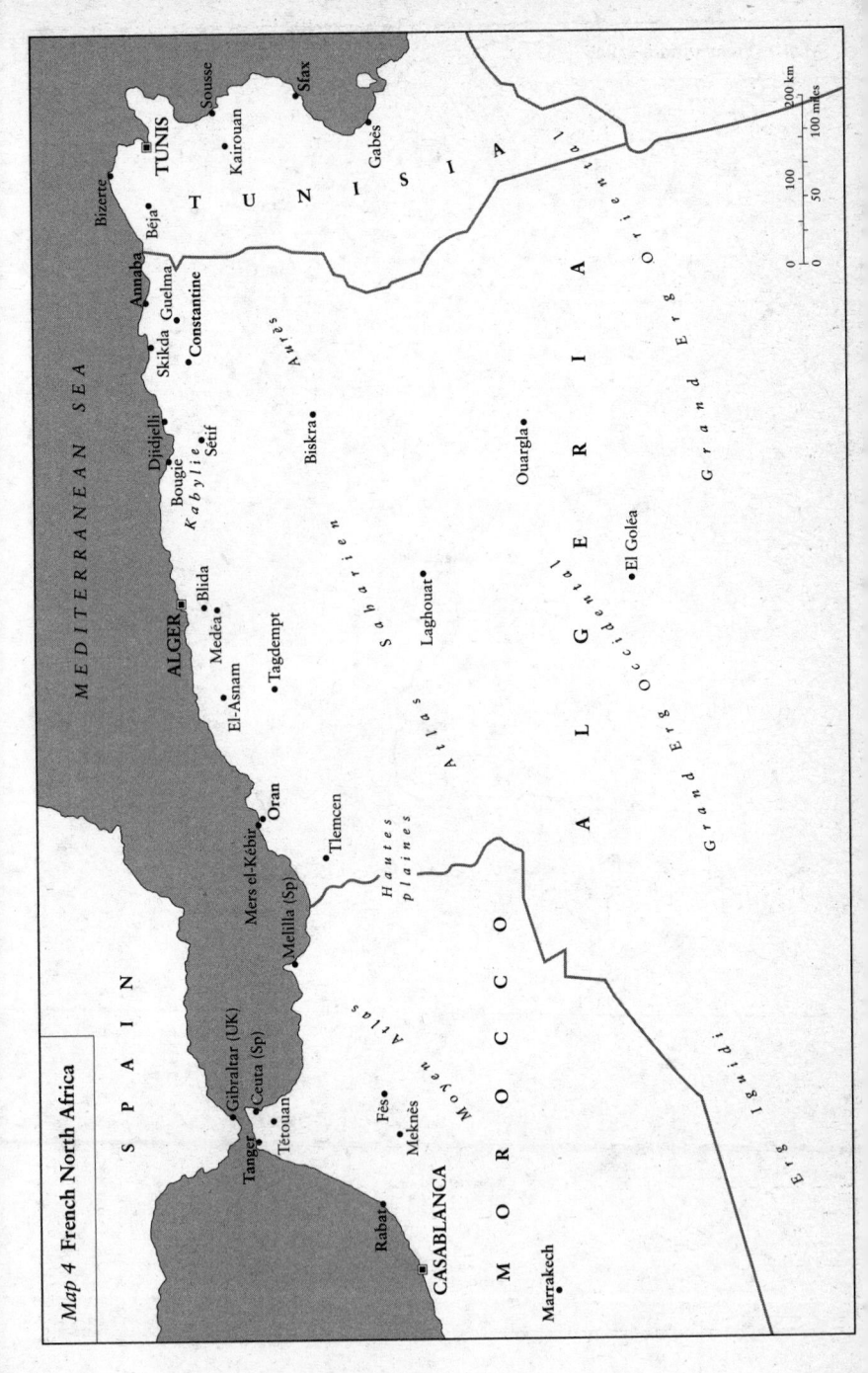

Map 4 **French North Africa**

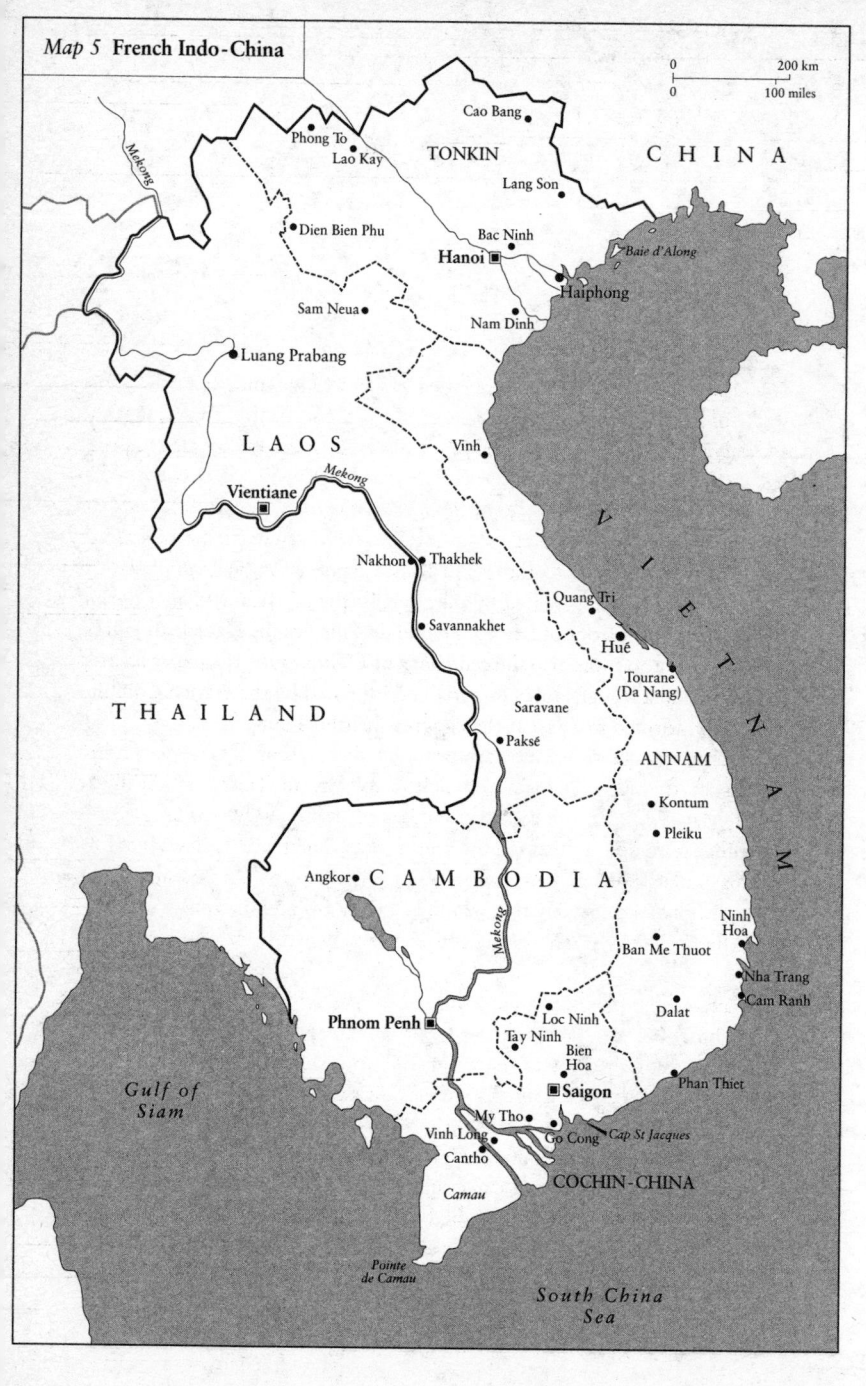

Map 5 French Indo-China

0   200 km
0   100 miles

Mekong

Phong To
Lao Kay
Cao Bang
TONKIN
CHINA
Lang Son
Dien Bien Phu
Bac Ninh
Hanoi □
Baie d'Along
Sam Neua
Haiphong
Nam Dinh
Luang Prabang
LAOS
Vinh
Mekong
Vientiane □
Nakhon
Thakhek
V I E T N A M
Savannakhet
Quang Tri
Hué
THAILAND
Saravane
Tourane (Da Nang)
Paksé
ANNAM
Kontum
Pleiku
Angkor
C A M B O D I A
Mekong
Ninh Hoa
Ban Me Thuot
Nha Trang
Cam Ranh
Phnom Penh □
Dalat
Loc Ninh
Tay Ninh
Bien Hoa
□ **Saigon**
Phan Thiet
Gulf of Siam
My Tho
Go Cong Cap St Jacques
Vinh Long
Cantho
COCHIN-CHINA
Camau
Pointe de Camau
South China Sea

Preface

On a late summer's day in September 2004 I found myself in the Loire town of Tours. Banners and *tricolore* flags in the centre proclaimed the sixtieth anniversary of the Liberation of France, and concurrently the centenary of the neo-Renaissance town hall designed by Victor Laloux, architect of the Gare d'Orsay in Paris. In tandem, the town hall and the railway station had mounted a display of photographs to celebrate the Liberation of Tours itself on 1 September 1944 and the genesis of the local paper, *La Nouvelle République*, created by the Socialist deputy Jean Meunier during the Resistance. In front of Laloux's Hôtel de Ville lies the Place Jean Jaurès, and the year 2004 was also the centenary of *L'Humanité*, the paper created by the Socialist leader Jaurès in 1904 and inherited by the French Communist Party, formed in 1920 at the congress held in Tours.

All anniversaries provoke comments on the present. The sepia photographs of the Allied destruction of the railway in Tours on the night of 21 May 1944, in the raids which preceded the D-Day landings, gave prominence to the civilian deaths and to the ruined streets devastated by bombs which missed their target. A discreet caption under one of the photographs read: 'Today this would be called collateral damage'.

Earlier in the year I had attended the Franco-British ceremonies of the centenary of the Entente Cordiale, and there were billowing banderoles proclaiming the Entente still in place in Beaulieu, close to Nice, when I was there shortly after Tours. The sixty years since the D-Day landings and the Liberation did not displace the ninetieth anniversary of the declaration of war in 1914, nor the fifty years since the fall of Dien Bien Phu in Indo-China and the outbreak of the war in Algeria. Away from wars the women's magazine *Marie-Claire* celebrated fifty years since its relaunch as a monthly in October 1954, and in a special issue stressed its persistent aim to enhance the lives of women through fashion, health, exercise, labour-saving devices and a happy house and home, but also its commitment to contraception and legal abortion, and its role in lifting the taboo surrounding female

homosexuality. Here, in this special issue, there was not only an anniversary but an intriguing set of narratives. No less was true for all the other commemorations which tumbled over one another during the year.

Rituals of everyday life and obituaries of public figures carried other narratives of custom, place, and people. On the same visit to Nice I heard as usual the cannon shot which echoes round the Baie des Anges to signal *midi* (noon) on working days. It expresses, like the few surviving factory hooters elsewhere, a threatened but resilient narrative of the long midday closure, a cultural fact, or remnant of a way of life, which still characterizes much of contemporary France. Deaths in the summer and autumn included the great photographer Henri Cartier-Bresson who died on 3 August, while on 24 September the death was announced of Françoise Sagan, born Françoise Quoirez, author of the record-breaking first novel *Bonjour Tristesse* in 1954. On 8 October it was the brilliantly original philosopher, Jacques Derrida, who died. The specific narratives evinced by the obituaries triggered countless others: everyone with a camera knew what Cartier-Bresson meant by 'the decisive moment'; it seemed that most people remembered the exact place in which they read *Bonjour Tristesse*, and admirers of Derrida rehearsed their own ways in which they had adapted his ideas of deconstruction to open up new layers of meaning in literature, everyday speech and even history.

It probably seems indulgent on my part to evoke these selected moments of 2004 but I have a good reason for doing something of the kind, whether for 2004 or any other year. It is a way of setting out the inescapability of different narratives which constantly coincide in history, in this case the history of France and the French since 1900. Narratives which overlap or compete are the substance of this book, and I have tried above all to disentangle the overlapping political layers. I hope to give some idea of the vitality of French political cultures and their chequered narratives, in which meanings attached to the past reverberate through every action of the present.

The border created between politics on the one hand and society and culture on the other has always been a dubious construction, but it was perpetuated until comparatively recently in different branches of historical research and writing. The wholesale crossing of this border finally became the norm of history in the last four decades of the twentieth century, and in those crossings the role played by collective memory and commemorations has been particularly significant. It goes without saying that the bicentenary of the Revolution in 1989 was a major cultural event not just for its celebrations but for the passionate re-examination of revolution as both an ideological and a cultural force. The expansion of the realm of

culture, in this sense as ideas, customs, myths and behaviour, has transformed the domain of political history.

Narrative too has moved. It is still a way of telling a story, whether fact
or fiction. It is also a set of ideas moving in a particular direction, an
agenda, a discourse of meaning. When John Berger wrote his compelling
short stories, *Pig Earth* (1979), as the storyteller of a French Alpine village,
the narrative infusing the separate stories was the meaning of peasant and
village life and what he called its 'surprising range of the possible'. As a
historian I have tried to show that France as a whole since 1900 has an
equally surprising range of the possible in its multiple narratives. A history,
and a title, which did not do justice to surprise or provocation would be
unrepresentative of the past, let alone the present.

The *tricolore* of blue, white and red (*bleu, blanc, rouge*) dates from the
Revolution and was provocative throughout the nineteenth century. By the
end of the twentieth it had long ceased to be disputed as the emblem of
France and Frenchness. Using just the colour blue as a shorthand for all
things French stems from sport and borrows from song, and I have adopted
'*la vie en bleu*' from the expressions of euphoria in France at times of
singular sporting success. I use it here as a title to suggest the wider singularity of French political and social life, while arguing throughout that
'Frenchness', however singular, cannot be a single narrative. The idea of
'*la vie en bleu*' is evocative: it is also in turn provocative and ironic. It
registers illusions no less than realities. It hides as much as it reveals. As an
affirmation it must be approached for what it also blocks and denies.

I could not have begun to trace the history of conflict and convergence
across a whole century without the ideas of stimulating colleagues at the
University of Sussex, and the originality of fellow historians and writers
throughout universities and French historical circles in the UK, France,
Australia, the USA, Canada and Ireland. My reliance on their scholarship
and pioneering research makes me enormously grateful to them all. I hope
they can imagine that this Preface thanks every one of them individually.

Several ways of writing French history initiated by close friends and
colleagues have set wholly new standards which I greatly admire and
would love to have been able to emulate, none more so than the multiple
integration of women into political history by Siân Reynolds in her many
articles and in the strikingly original approach of her *France between the
Wars: Gender and Politics* (1996). I cannot thank her enough for her
inspiration and her unerring pointers to the ways in which one worthy
history can obscure another. Equally, the originality of John Horne's social
and cultural studies of the First World War and its aftermath has opened

up entirely fresh dimensions of the period's history. He has been a constant exemplar of excitement and rigour in all our long, enjoyable discussions.

The insights of graduate students over many years have been the epitome of innovation. Writing this book gives me a chance to say how much I have learnt, and continue to learn, from Karen Adler, Dave Berry, Jackie Clarke, Hanna Diamond, Martin Evans, Daniel Gordon, Simon Kitson, Miranda Pollard, Scott Soo and Susan Trouvé-Finding, all of whom have brought new understanding to vital realms of France and the French. My thanks go to each of them, and to Patrick Leech and Glenda Sluga in related fields, for the warmth of their friendship and for the stimulus of their perceptions, approaches and theories. For the same sharing of old and new encounters with France I also thank my good friends and colleagues, Maurice Hutt and Nancy Wood, Hilary Footitt, Martyn Cornick and Julian Jackson.

I am continually grateful for the work, example and wisdom of mentors Douglas Johnson and Theodore Zeldin, and I treasure the many times when Richard Cobb shared his intimate knowledge of place and people in the parts of France which feature so vividly in his autobiographical writings. In Brighton, Martin Evans kindly read some of the later chapters and suggested several improvements from his specialist knowledge of the French Empire and the Algerian war.

The specific French interests of many friends have made me acutely aware of the aspects of France which I have not been able to include. I can only apologize to them, not least for all the possible titles to the book which they imaginatively invented. Stimulus came as ever from the friendships of Jean Gordon in Paris, Paulette and Philémon Pouget in Montpellier, Bill and Agnès Power in Geneva, John and Barbara Jacobs in Lewes, and Antony Copley who was already an expansive influence when we first confronted the mysteries of research in the Paris of 1961. He still commands a breadth of knowledge and understanding that I can only envy. At Penguin, Simon Winder has been the best possible editor, enthusiastic and full of suggestions, and I also thank Christine Collins and Helen Campbell for their sensitive and responsive copy-editing, and Richard Duguid and Elisabeth Merriman for their expertise and care. At home, ideas have flooded in from the family with huge amounts of support, encouragement and humour. Our times in France have forged intricate personal and shared memories which are vital to all our lives, and have left us always waiting to return. To Carol, Joshua and Jessica this book is dedicated with all my love: it owes more to them than I can possibly say.

Rod Kedward,
Brighton, October 2004

Introduction

Notions of Frenchness

Conflicting definitions of France and the French have been persistently advanced throughout the period covered by this history from 1900 to the present. They exhibit the obsession and passion with which national identity has been arrogated to, or claimed by, a particular set of ideas, political party, movement or personality. Conflict appears to dominate.

There have also been definitions which held consensus approval for a number of years only to be discarded later by common agreement as outmoded or dysfunctional. Once abandoned, they were often reinstated or reinvented.

Over the last 100 years, governments and the diverse forces of opposition constructed their own categories of Frenchness which were exclusive and excluding, while at the same time the struggles for inclusion created new definitional boundaries. It seems to some observers a paradox that a political culture which extols the rational, orderly mind should also value the power of dissent so highly, but the paradox is really a consistency, since it stems from an all-pervading involvement in disputing the conflictual merits of 'for' and 'against'.

Parallel to conflict there has been a repeated emphasis, not just in Marcel Proust's classic novel, on the act of seeking (*à la recherche* . . .) as a creative end in itself, a pursuit of the ideal. French creativity is frequently said to have a certain indefinable quality, a '*je ne sais quoi*' ('I don't know what') which gives it its distinctiveness. Alain-Fournier's novel of 1913, *Le Grand Meaulnes*, was immediately characterized both inside and outside France as having an elusive, evocative quality which stands for Frenchness in almost archetypal terms.

Much of French cinema is regarded in a similar way. The instinctive sense of pace, the unforced intellectual presence, the local settings and personal nuances of films from Marcel Pagnol and Jean Renoir to Agnès

Varda and Mathieu Kassovitz have encouraged historians to look for comparable forms of story-telling elsewhere in French culture. They have been located, for example, at the traditional evening gatherings (*veillées*) in rural France. At these *veillées* a threatened oral heritage, highly pictorial and distinctively local rather than national, was kept alive for more than half of the twentieth century before the universalizing impact of television. Perceptive comparisons are now made with the localized stories conveyed in the urban language, visual images and musical rhythms of rap and hiphop culture, where the definition of 'Frenchness' is yet again both specific and elusive.

The fluctuations between rural-centred and urban-centred perspectives have made for a shifting mosaic of social identity, while the intellectual notion of French 'exceptionalism' came to enshrine the tacit belief in a distinctive history, culture and society. For most of the twentieth century different forms of 'exceptionalism' were claimed by totally opposing political camps, and promoted in contradictory ways. Only in the last three decades was it narrowed down to a set of definitions and portrayed by many as a negative and regressive feature of political life. At that point its end was vigorously advocated or proclaimed. Yet it was precisely the promotion as well as the rejection of diverse elements of French distinctiveness which continued to provide much of the political debate in the 1990s and in the early years of the twenty-first century.

Political themes

Three themes of the recent and continuing history of France and the French are explored in this book, under the rubric of 'Republic', 'Ideology' and 'Identity'. The themes were present at all times in the twentieth century but each also had its own years when it held the centre stage, with particular impact on opinion and action, and each forms its own part of the book's political narratives. Other historians, to whom the whole book owes an enormous debt, have identified their own themes and their own ways of dividing the century. History as pattern-making is as subjective as any art form, but the patterns are not arbitrary. They are constructed from written and oral sources and the interpretations of others, as the past has always been. In the process historians become acutely aware of the bewildering number of patterns that were created during the past itself, and not just in retrospect. Events and conjunctures of events, the formative role of place, the significance of time, all patterned the fabric of experience and ideas. The imperative of dealing with the abundant historiography of France

means that there is a plethora of pattern-makers behind any new history, some of which stress the clarity of creating separate categories of experience in the tradition of Enlightenment and Encyclopedic thought, while others follow Jules Michelet and see history as a huge totality.

Concepts of 'The Twentieth Century' were already there in 1900 or even before, and were reconstructed endlessly thereafter. How to date the century's beginning has been repeatedly disputed. Should it be said to have begun with the economic depression of the 1880s, or with the arrest and conviction of Alfred Dreyfus in 1894? Or did it not begin until the outbreak of the war in 1914? A good case can be made for any of these and several other watersheds. But there is also a case for taking the literal start of the century, and I have taken 1900 out of interest in the ways in which formalized beginnings, as well as ends, pattern self-awareness. Anniversaries, commemorations, festivals and set days of national holiday do the same. They act as ritualized conduits for expression and discovery: they are the rites of time.

In the first thirty years of the century there was a particular awareness of 'the Republic'. In the last thirty years, as 2000 approached and the importance of 'end' and 'beginning' was accentuated by the notion of a new millennium, there was an obsession with 'Identity'. These two themes of Part One and Part Three certainly owe something to the awareness of opening and closure. Was there equally a concept of 'being at the heart' of the twentieth century, in the middle of it all? I found this concept less apparent, but there was no way of missing people's awareness of the power of ideology which seemed at the time to characterize the heart of the century, and for many historians epitomizes the whole. Exploring the undergrowth as well as the overgrowth of ideologies means that Part Two has a longer time-span than the other two parts. It is presented as a spiral to emphasize its dynamic and conflictual momentum, but this is not to suggest that the politics and events in the earlier and later parts of the century were in any way static.

In all three parts the dominance of political themes cannot do justice to the complexity of people's lives and the richness of social and cultural history. Yet political history, often narrowly defined in French discourse to mean only party politics, and only the politics of the top and the centre, also involves the margins, the outsiders, the subjugated and the minorities, and the base is invariably social and cultural.

Even with a range of different political narratives it is none the less difficult to do justice to the attitudes of those who appear to be unruffled by events. A comic sense of the shrugged shoulders was given by Ray Ventura in one of the great popular songs of the century, 'Tout va très bien,

Madame la Marquise'. At the core of the ideological years of the 1930s, in the early days of gramophone and radio, the song gave voices to servants speaking on the telephone who present the incredulous and horrified Marquise with one disaster after another which have occurred in her absence. Each catastrophe is reported by a different servant, in a kind of afterthought, as a mere nothing (*un petit rien*). The absurd escalation of the death of her favourite mare in the fire that destroyed the stables which caused the death of her husband who caused a further fire which destroyed the château, is punctuated by the repeated assurance at each disaster, 'Apart from that, everything's fine' (*à part de ça tout va très bien*).

The mordant humour of the song, the laconic acceptance of disasters falling on the absent aristocracy, reach back into the social comedy and satire of the eighteenth century and the world of Beaumarchais, but the song also acted as a foil to the turbulence and disasters of the twentieth. The refrain was much quoted as a form of resilience at several points in the following decades, whenever disaster piled on disaster, and it has even been used as a commentary, or query, on the European twentieth century as a whole. Apart from wars, inhumanity of all kinds and genocide, was everything fine?

By whatever ironic route, the song leads to consideration of daily life and the significant social and material changes in France. When, where and for whom does '*tout va bien*' typify the experience of daily life in the century? And were claims of well-being despite, or because of, the political events which captured the headlines? And what of the dissatisfaction equally often expressed, and the reservations about the nature and effect of change?

Old, new, and meanings of 'modernization'

Persuasively behind this book there is the presence of the major analysis presented by the American and French team at the Center for International Affairs at Harvard University in the 1960s, an analysis which both derived from and affected French historiography. Stanley Hoffmann and his colleagues preferred to offer not a triad but a duality, one of 'change and tradition'. It is seen to comprise a paradox of French politics, which shifted into a different gear through the massive clashes of the middle years of the century, resulting in a new France of modernization and planning, in which Jean Monnet is central. Their claim was that both Vichy and the Resistance helped produce this shift, breaking with the stalemate and equilibrium society of the 'republican synthesis' in the first part of the century.[1]

Like many others I long ago accepted this perceptive analysis with gratitude for its clarity and I seek to use it by continuing to stress the constantly shifting amalgam of old and new, the process of keeping an old France while creating modernity, a theme in which 'old' means trusted and essential and comes to include the 'republican synthesis' and the unitary republican tradition set out in the early years of the century. In this perspective there is good reason for solving the question, 'When did the twentieth century start?' by saying that the old France is still very much in place until the huge shifts in mid-century, and that 'the new France', which has been the title of countless books, dates from the mid-century onwards.

I would add the Popular Front to the analysis of Hoffmann and his colleagues as an acceleration point towards the recognizable France of today, and I have devoted the bulk of the pages in this book to the sixty-five years since the mid-1930s, without actually proposing that 'the twentieth century begins in 1936'. Such a bald statement would look provocative by any criterion. There could never be any understanding of twentieth-century France, or Europe, which did not place the trauma and dynamic of the First World War somewhere at the nerve centre of the century's subsequent history.

By the end of the century 'old' has ceased to refer to the bygone pre-revolutionary age mourned by the anti-republican movements such as Action Française. It refers to something within personal memory, identified with pre-1940 or pre-1936, which remains visible in French life, landscape, society and cultural attitudes. It is still seen by many as relevant, and is not dismissed as archaic. By including the Popular Front in the mid-century seismic shift, I have also proposed that 'change' and 'modernization' should cover not just the technology and rationalization of a market-driven liberal economy, but also the Jaurès-inspired quest for greater humanity within society. Social justice and human rights as parallels, correctives or rivals to the normal meaning of 'modernization' come into their own at many points of the century's history and ultimately envisage a multiplicity of cultures, even though the word 'multicultural' turns out to be highly problematic in the last years of the century and is still controversial today.

Polarities and diversity

However updated, the underlying themes of change and tradition, new and old, as dialectically engaged with each other, indulge the love that historians have for paradox and complexity. I can see complexity and ambivalence in twentieth-century French history in each era of its politics, but I am also

very aware of the stark polarities of so many of the actors and the actions which made that history. If the book gives an extra stress to these polarities it is to avoid the truism of today which argues that everything in French history is too complex to be reduced to questions of 'for' and 'against'.

Besides the three themes already stressed, the themes of unity, diversity and difference make up another triad in the book. The key of diversity was used continuously throughout the century to unlock problems of identity, and it had a prime role in the ways the century was imagined in retrospect, in the outpouring of memory. It is there as the main player in the final chapter.

Throughout, I have tried to stress that identities in politics are constructs, always evolving despite their apparent or assumed permanence. This is especially important for gender and race, but no less for class, nation, republic, and all 'isms' such as socialism and Catholicism. Ideology and 'isms' in the mid-century tended to see themselves as constant, creating a form of mythology which denies the mutations of history. Roland Barthes drew attention to this in his *Mythologies* of 1957, a penetrating, cultural insight into ideological codes. Ultimately towards the end of the century the emergence of post-isms, such as post-Gaullism and post-socialism, recognized the mutation of certain ideologies in response to time and events.

As far as possible I have tried not to personify and mythologize a single 'France', although I emphasize that the concept of a unitary French Republic and culture was a dominant factor, a major actor, in the national history. I prefer to see France as a plurality of histories, while stressing that a unitary France was volubly asserted throughout the century and is still prevalent in French politics today. If there is a paradox right from the start, that is surely the one.

The Primacy of the Republic, 1900s–1931

Introduction to Part One

In his controversial attack of 1927 on the departure of intellectuals from the realm of pure thought, reason and truth, the critic and essayist Julien Benda represented their descent into the worldliness of polemic as a betrayal (*La Trahison des clercs*). He castigated in particular the writers and thinkers who had thrown themselves into the politics of nationalism, dynamism, class struggle and the cult of violence, notably Maurice Barrès, Charles Péguy and Georges Sorel, and outside France, Nietzsche, Marx and D'Annunzio, all of whom he mentioned by name in a short trailer to his book two years previously.[1] The intellectual, according to Benda, should defend the eternal and the universal and not be dragged down into baser causes in which passion and prejudice disfigure thought. His models were Erasmus, Kant and Renan, and he absolved Émile Zola from launching his epic defence of Alfred Dreyfus in the letter *J'accuse . . .* of 13 January 1898, on the basis that Zola was interested only in truth.

What made Benda's arguments so representative of a dominant strain in politics, as well as thought, was his conviction that the French republic equated with reason, and France with universalism. When war broke out in 1914 he declared that France, and France alone, incarnated the highest values of truth. His political passions as an unapologetic Jacobin were, in fact, demonstrable throughout his life, and the way he rationalized his own beliefs as free from the 'betrayal' he found in others still invites controversy and a certain incredulity.

The assumptions about the republic as 'true' and 'universal', giving France a civilizing mission in the world, linked the fervent republicans of 1900 to the Jacobin leaders of the Revolution. The ongoing campaign for secular values and the defence of Alfred Dreyfus polarized them from counter-revolutionaries, from the bulk of the Catholic hierarchy and from traditionalists in the army. A pure form of republican thought and practice

was believed to be attainable through secular state education as created by Jules Ferry in the early 1880s. Establishing the primacy of the republic was the drive to see these values triumph, in France, in the empire and internationally.

Later in the century, in the bicentenary year of the Revolution, the intellectual friend and committed colleague of Che Guevara, Régis Debray, who became an adviser to the Mitterrand government in the 1980s, defined the republic as a particularly French ideal which lifted it above the conventional ideas of Western democracy. It could always do with more democratic structures, he agreed, but it was essentially different from democracy itself. The difference lay in its embodiment of reason, justice and the will to carry out enlightened policies.[2]

The question, which was an anguished one at the time of Debray's article, was the extent to which the primacy of the republic was in reality the primacy of the state. Did the legacy of Jacobinism and the achievements attributed to republicanism in effect establish the supremacy of the state (*étatisme*) and the supposed benefits of state intervention (*dirigisme*)? Was there already in the first thirty years of the century a particular structure of beliefs and political behaviour that is later defined in the 1980s as 'French exceptionalism'?

It is not really anachronistic to ask this question of the early part of the century, since it is precisely in this period that the modern values attached to both the republic and the state were deeply scored into the political history of twentieth-century France. These values constituted an ideology, of that there can be no doubt, and it was pitted against other determined ideologies of both religious and political nature. Its primacy, which amounted to a real hegemony of ideas and structures, was grounded in the widespread conviction that the republic was the regime, in the words of Adolphe Thiers, first President of the Third Republic in 1871, which divided people the least, and was the modern inheritor of the Enlightenment. This in no way stopped people from exposing its serious deficiencies and fighting for major structural reforms. Nor did it stop governments from arrogating to themselves powers which only their confirmed political supporters could equate with enlightenment, reason or justice.

I

The Use and Abuse of Reason,
1900–1906

1. Republicans and reason

Images of reason: Buisson in Tunis

Crossing the Mediterranean to Tunisia in April 1903, the 62-year-old Sorbonne professor Ferdinand Buisson made one of his many speeches in praise of secular education. Buisson had been one of the main architects of the educational reforms carried through by Jules Ferry between 1879 and 1886, which had initiated free and compulsory primary education for all children up to the age of thirteen, most of whom would be taught in a local, secular school, *l'école laïque*. Tunisia, outpost of the old Ottoman Empire, had been a French protectorate since 1881. French administration of this Muslim country was accompanied by French culture. Secularism, Buisson proclaimed, is ready to continue its triumphal progress in 'this African extension of the soil of France'. In Tunis, as in France, he concluded, 'the aim of education is to establish human dignity, to elevate the individual into a sacred and invulnerable being, whom no one in the world will be allowed to oppress or suppress'.[1]

France and its empire in the early twentieth century represented nearly 10 per cent of the world's land surface. French schoolchildren were quickly made familiar with this fact. They were rarely instructed that the colonies within the empire had cultures and histories of their own which pre-existed, and struggled to survive, the French imperial presence. The Third Republic was thirty years old on 4 September 1900 and its new education system, the most self-consciously centralized in Europe, taught all children the benefits of Frenchness, regardless of origin or belief. France entered the twentieth century with its global mission from the Revolution still intact. Its republican self-image was one of 'reason' and 'civilization'. Both concepts were the product of the specific history of France but they were raised into absolutes of universalizing power, occluding and obscuring the history and culture of colonized peoples.

Images of reason:
dissolution of the Prémontré monks in Nantes

While Buisson was speaking in Tunis, a handful of monks, belonging to the order founded in 1120 by Norbert of Prémontré and living in a small monastic house in the Atlantic port of Nantes, received a government order to dissolve themselves and leave their monastery within fifteen days. The militant anticlerical Émile Combes had become Prime Minister in 1902 and his Radical government immediately tightened every sinew of state power in a confrontation with the hierarchy of the Catholic Church, which had thrown its dwindling, but still influential, moral authority against Alfred Dreyfus, the Jewish army captain falsely accused of treason in 1894. With the Dreyfus Affair still potent as a motivating force in politics, the Radicals, who emerged as the largest party from the 1902 elections, projected themselves as the embodiment of Dreyfusard values of justice and the individual. In forming a programme to articulate these values they decided as a matter of urgency that the Church should be formally removed from the centre of French society, and its influence devalued and marginalized.

In Nantes the population divided for and against the beleaguered monks. In the streets on the way to their first appearance in court on 4 May 1903, the monks, dressed simply in their habits, presented themselves as victims. People appeared at overhanging windows to throw them flowers, and at the house itself, where the monks withstood a siege for over a year, there were fights between defenders and detractors. It was an ideological and social conflict, re-enacted in many parts of France, where traditional loyalty to monks and nuns who were rooted in the community challenged the right of the government to dictate local cultural practices. It was another restaging of that visceral confrontation between 'reds' (pro-Republic) and 'whites' (pro-Church) which filtered down to children's games, as Pierre-Jakez Hélias vividly recounted in his evocative memoirs of a Breton village in the *pays bigouden* in the early years of the twentieth century.[2]

Were the enforced evictions of Catholic orders the fruits of justice and reason which Buisson had extolled, or the very oppression from which he had proclaimed the individual would be protected? They were both. Reason under Combes was an offensive weapon, and specific ideas of justice were aggressively applied. The justification given for wholesale evictions was that the republic had been, and still was, endangered by superstition and reaction.

Images of reason: Jaurès in Albi

Reason, justice and humanism had their most eloquent secular defender in the Socialist deputy Jean Jaurès, a fervent Dreyfusard with a historian's overview, a lawyer's meticulous eye for details of proof and a journalist's flair for communication. In 1903 he spoke at prize-giving in the lycée at Albi in south-west France where he had once been a philosophy teacher, some forty kilometres from his birthplace at Castres with its locally important textile and tanning industries. The republic, he told the assembled pupils, had become 'the definitive form of French life, and still more, the form towards which all the democracies of the world were slowly evolving'. But now, he continued, the proletariat had made it clear that this republican form had to be applied not just to politics but to economic and social relations: 'The workshop, work itself, production, property: these must be organized according to republican principles.' His exhortation was clearly addressed to the government in Paris no less than to the youthful scions of the Albigeois middle classes. Jaurès put forward a confident vision of a vast republican venture in social co-operation, which would 'reconcile freedom with the rule of law' and would enable people to 'fight for their rights without tearing each other apart'.[3] The idealism was palpable: it was a pinnacle of rational expectation. It was also a warning. By invoking the spectre of civil war as the alternative to social co-operation, Jaurès warned the dominant republican élite of the price of failure.

Reason and identity

All sectors of politics were affected by republican reason, by its uses and abuses and by the ideological debate over its meaning and desirability. The powerful ideology which claimed to have made republicanism and reason into interchangeable terms also claimed to inherit the new century, and its combativeness was a consequence not only of the Dreyfus Affair, which had been a major catalyst for numerous tensions in French society, but also of the 1898 and 1902 parliamentary elections, when ideological divisions on the future of society were deeply felt and bitterly disputed, not just at the ballot-box. Women were excluded by men from the vote, but their public presence was evident in a whole range of activities from textile strikes in the northern towns of Lille and Roubaix to the feminist daily paper *La Fronde* in Paris. As the new century opened, the electoral and legal claims of women were to be one of the rational demands which continued to be blocked in the name of reason. The double standards employed by

politicians to restrict the electorate to men were starkly evident to political women at the time. Similarly the arguments which rationalized social injustices in the lives of working men and women could seem only the denial of reason to those who were degraded in lives of meagre subsistence. Over 100 years after the Declaration of the Rights of Man, political consciousness of how these rights should be extended was widespread, challenging the complacency of conventional politics.

By 1900 those at various levels of power who determined the meaning and politics of reason, and those who prescribed the nature of civilization, were a middle-class male élite, but not a dictatorial clique or an oligarchy, and they were scrutinized by the most diverse and independent press in Europe. The revolutions, coups d'état and century-long battles to work out a viable regime for post-revolutionary France had created a plethora of parties and movements, which represented considerable political diversity. But because each government in the nineteenth century had traditionally been identified with a regime, whether republic, monarchy or empire, there was no concept, even in the thirty-year-old Third Republic, of a 'loyal opposition'. Political opposition was suspected of seeking the overthrow not just of the government of the day but of the regime itself, and much of the anti-Dreyfusard agitation in the late 1890s had confirmed this suspicion.

The response of the republican élite was to maximize the wide-ranging powers of the bureaucracy, instituted by Napoleon; to increase the range and effectiveness of centralized state authority; and to repress or outmanoeuvre not only ideological opposition, but also any centrifugal force which demanded independence, the structural reform of society or greater delegation of power. The governments of the 1900s insisted that republican reason was essential to any definition of French civilization on the world stage.

2. Defining civilization: colonized and colonizers

The French protectorate in Tunisia was twenty-five years old in 1906 when the first organized movement of 'Young Tunisians' started a campaign for independence. The most recurrent resentment among the Tunisians was the ease with which a select band of French landowners had used their parliamentary connections to cover the acquisition of vast lands and fortunes at the expense of the indigenous population. Two years later 'Young Algerians' formed a movement which was apparently similar. In fact it was more accepting of the benefits offered to those who became naturalized

French citizens, and demanded the right to both traditional Muslim law and French citizenship. Algeria had been assimilated into the political system of mainland France and male French settlers voted for deputies to the National Assembly in Paris. French citizenship had been decreed for Algerian Jews in 1870 by Adolphe Crémieux, but nothing resembling civil or legal equality had been granted to the Arabs and Berbers in Algeria nor to other indigenous peoples colonized in the second wave of imperialism, whereas in the old colonies (*vieilles colonies*) dating from the seventeenth and eighteenth centuries citizenship had been extended to the local populations in 1848. In Indo-China, from 1906 onwards, protests at the French presence were particularly virulent. Underground organizations led by Phan Boi Chau and Prince Cong Lê, with a base in Japan or China, staged mutinies, killings and raids on French property and institutions. Even in one of the old colonies in the Caribbean, Martinique, the century had begun with a protest demonstration in February 1900 which was bloodily suppressed by the French authorities.

It is possible to argue that Buisson's secular sermonizing in Tunis remained at the level of high-minded words and historical references. Ferry had decided that his educational reforms should apply to the colonies, so that primary education was more widely available, but the anticlericalism which decimated the power of the Catholic Church in French education was not rigorously exported to the colonies, and Catholic missionary schools were largely untouched. Nor did the secular French state attempt any co-ordinated offensive against Islamic religious practices either in the protectorate of Tunisia or in Algeria. It was rather that French culture and traditions of almost any kind, republican or otherwise, secular or Christian, were paraded as the epitome of civilization. Colonialism was universally projected in France as an epic adventure in the realization and growth of French identity. This did not make French imperial arrogance significantly different from the norm in Britain, Belgium or Russia, but the level of tacit agreement achieved on colonial matters in the period 1900–1914, and well beyond, was itself a rare facet of French political life. It had not been the same in the 1880s. But by 1900 imperial expansion was accepted as inevitable, and widely endorsed as desirable.

The colonial lobby

As a political pressure group the colonial lobby gained its strength from several different benches in the Chamber and Senate. In the person of Eugène Étienne, deputy for Oran, it manipulated parliamentary politics to

prevent any concessions to the indigenous Algerians. By the law of 13 April 1900 colonial budgets were made autonomous and were directed to be self-sufficient, so that government expenditure was minimized, and largely confined to the Ministries of War and the Navy. The republic wanted colonies but at no extra expense. Paul Doumer, in 1900 Governor General of Cambodia, Laos, Cochin-China, Annam and Tonkin, which made up French Indo-China, returned to France in 1902 as a powerful colonial apologist within the Radical Party. Before leaving he had secured highly favourable investment terms for a railway project to the north of Tonkin, which delighted the banks involved and still more the iron and steel industry. The secret of the colonial lobby's economic power was to have accepted that the colonies would not be a priority area of state expenditure and to have created a loose network of businesses which could exploit the opportunities of budgetary autonomy. Outlets in the press, such as André Tardieu in *Le Temps*, assured that their enterprise was well presented.

By such means at least nine deputies and eight senators acquired vast personal domains in the colonies in often highly questionable circumstances. At the same time, humanitarian concern at what was perceived as 'backwardness' was a spur to colonization by administrators, doctors, nurses, missionaries and teachers who went out expressly to alter conditions through structures of health care and education and the imposition of Christianity. By the twentieth century, economic investment in the colonies was firmly located under the umbrella term of humanitarian improvement, and budgetary autonomy gave it an extra justification. It was not a question of urgency for public opinion to know what happened to the profits, nor to monitor the incidence of land expropriation or the level of indigenous wages. Assurances were sought that the colonies were responding to 'progress' and were not a burden on the metropole, and that was as far as most enquiries went.

The most recent calculations show that trade with the colonies, both import and export, was almost as high in 1913 as trade with Germany, which was second only to trade with Britain. A third of cotton textiles, over 40 per cent of metal tools, 31 per cent of iron and steel and over 65 per cent of sugar and soap were exported to the colonies. From North Africa imports included phosphates, non-ferrous metals, wine, olives and corn; from Indo-China zinc, lead, pewter, rice, coffee, tea, rubber and wolfram; from West and Central Africa cotton, bananas, coffee and groundnuts, and from New Caledonia chrome and nickel. The important raw materials were produced but not processed in the colonies, leaving the processing and manufacture to jealously protected industries in France. The

figures of buoyant trade contradict long-held theories which portrayed French colonialism as an economic mirage, and lend conviction to the arguments of the 'parti colonial' at the time that colonial investment was lucrative for the metropole. The return on shares in Indo-China in distilleries and mining varied from 50 per cent to over 120 per cent; dividends from shares in the Compagnie Française de l'Afrique Occidentale grew strongly after 1905, and savings with the bank of Indo-China raced ahead of most banks within France itself. Loans to Russia, which took the lion's share of financial investment overseas, were more profitable but carried greater risks. The colonies were a dependable source of income, and this goes some way to re-establishing, if not the primacy of economic gain in theories of imperialism, at least a recognition of its substantial role in the consolidation of colonial rule.

Algeria was the primary scene of settler colonization, followed by Tunisia and Morocco. A few thousand French gradually took up residence in Indo-China, New Caledonia and Madagascar, but beyond North Africa it was sometimes said that the only French presence, besides the military and the administration, was the lone trader, the missionary and the dentist. North Africa was different.

North Africa

The incoming *colons* in Algeria established settler villages in the fertile coastal plains and European *quartiers* in Algiers and Oran. They were the radial centres of a dominant authority and an invasive culture. The discourse of a France stretching from the Channel to the Sahara began to affect the definitions of French identity. The decline of the Algerian population in the mid-nineteenth century even led some experts to prophesy, with overt neo-Darwinist confidence, that there was a natural law determining the disappearance of 'backward' peoples. By 1900 this looked distinctly suspect, even in statistical terms, as the Algerian demographic curve moved upwards and the French steadily downwards.

The societal norms of the complex North African society, with its primary division into Arabs and Berbers, were ones of collectivity and customary rights, based on the Koranic law, which had little or nothing in common with the rationale of the Napoleonic code or the liberal cult of individualism which lay behind the *Droits de l'Homme*. The individualist culture and economics of the new 'infidels' from France could not be embraced without a loss of traditional roots and structures, though this is what naturalization into French citizenship, offered individually and selectively, involved. The

17

vast majority of the colonized North Africans kept their cultural distance, and nurtured varying degrees of bitterness at the special corpus of administrative laws, fines and penalties, the *code de l'indigénat*, by which they were governed. This code underwent a slow evolution towards more tangible rights for the indigenous peoples in all the recently colonized territories, and there was always the inclusive relationship with the *vieilles colonies* as a model of assimilation. In the early twentieth century this gave way to a more pluralist policy of association, endorsed by Étienne Clémentel, the Minister for Colonies in 1905, and practised by Albert Sarraut in his first spell as Governor General of Indo-China from 1911 to 1914. Theoretically, differences of cultures were to be openly recognized and forms of coexistence promoted, but whereas progress towards this ideal was made in Indo-China, in Algeria the discourse of French unitary culture and assimilation remained the dominant one.

For acceptance of French rule amongst the indigenous population the colonial lobby pointed to the small number of *évolués*, particularly in black Africa, who 'evolved' into the French way of life without a total surrender of their own culture and roots. Their social mobility through the use of the French language and education made them the subaltern class of colonial authority, though eventually, in many cases, they became leaders of their country's aspirations for independence. By the second quarter of the century they recognized the greater internal cohesion of their lands achieved by French military 'pacification', by transport development and by a unitary administration: there was more consistent good health and access to medical care, and a very small male minority gained access to secondary education and training to become lawyers, francophone writers and doctors. Before 1914 this degree of mobility between cultures was almost invisible, and much more striking in Algeria and Tunisia was the physical mobility forced on the scattered rural population whose lands had been allotted by French decrees to the expectant *colons*. Dispossessed and often dislocated from semi-nomadic patterns of agriculture, rural Algerians were faced with survival in more restricted and less fertile rural space or an internal exodus to the congested slums of the big towns.

The *colons* gradually produced their own identity, one which measured its distance as much from the metropole as from the indigenous Algerians. Without sharing power or promoting equality with those subject to the *indigénat*, they nurtured pride in their own rootedness of many generations. The writer Robert Randau coined a new expressive term in the title of his novel of 1911, *Les Algérianistes*, which articulated the sense among the French and other Europeans in Algeria of having created a distinctive

culture. Still more assertively the novels and other writings of Louis Bertrand, from *Le Sang des races* of 1899 onwards, portrayed the French settlers as the rightful inheritors of ancient Roman civilization in Algeria, and the Arabs as the interlopers. 'We are the true Africa,' he wrote in 1922, 'we the Latins, we the civilized.'[4] The claims of the *colons* to have inalienable historical rights which existed independent of the mainland and pre-dated the power politics of colonialism played a major role in the brutal struggle to retain the colony in the mid-twentieth century, over 100 years after the prolonged violence of the military conquest.

There were *évolués* in the other direction, though never described as such. The 'evolution' of Marshal Hubert Lyautey into a close identification with Muslim civilization may seem unrepresentative since he was neither a *colon* nor a lifelong resident of any single colony; but as the most notable commanding officer in the colonies after General Galliéni, whom he served in Tonkin and in Madagascar, his undisguised preference for the company of Muslim intellectuals and his revulsion against colonial arrogance brought his military rule in the protectorate of Morocco closer to the ideal of association than any other comparable administration.

The conflict for Morocco

French influence in Morocco was accepted across the political spectrum in France as the logical extension of colonial dominance in Tunisia and Algeria; necessary, even, to avoid rebel incursions from the disputed lands of the Atlas Mountains and the high plateaux which bordered the southern region of Oran and the Sultanate of Morocco. The colonial lobby had campaigned vigorously since 1898 for a protectorate, though aware that the British presence in Gibraltar and the escalating German interests in the raw materials of Morocco would call for delicate negotiations alongside military and economic pressure. The financial desperation of the Sultan for a massive loan accelerated events from 1902, as rival banking and industrial syndicates disputed the right to make the lucrative transfer of capital. On 8 April 1904 the Foreign Minister, Théophile Delcassé, reached a wide-ranging settlement with Britain, known as the Entente Cordiale, which gave Britain the freedom of manoeuvre in Egypt in exchange for French ascendancy in Morocco. The French bank Paribas, which had secured its position in Morocco, had close links with certain British banks, and it was the complementarity, rather than the rivalry, of British and French colonial interests which was celebrated in the Entente, a veritable watershed in international relations.

At the time Lyautey was commanding officer in southern Oran, where, from 1903 to 1911, he perfected the mix of armed strength and cultural sensitivity which he went on to practise for thirteen years as military Resident General in Morocco after the protectorate was finally established in 1912. His exploits became the stuff of colonial romance, flaunting the conservatism of Paris where his nonconformity to the *colon* model was viewed with alternate tolerance and despair. Lyautey in Morocco fashioned a cult of colonial dedication, which had been evident in the humanitarianism attendant on the history of colonialism, but which had seemed a rebuke of military rule until the two were apparently reconciled in the personality of Lyautey and the heterodox beliefs which were more or less accurately ascribed to him.

Morocco was also the stage on which international players with far more power than Lyautey practised their roles of bluff and belligerence, which convinced many in France and elsewhere that the aggressive pursuit of colonial status and gain was a major threat, not so much to indigenous peoples and their cultures as to European peace. The Entente Cordiale had European consequences very much in mind when it settled the colonial disputes that had brought Britain and France close to conflict at the end of the nineteenth century. From 1904, Franco-German suspicion and hostility over Morocco took their place.

The close interweaving of European nationalisms and the development of colonialism made each the necessary context of the other. Jaurès, a constant critic of the 'parti colonial', saw this as clearly, though with different conclusions, as Delcassé or Kaiser Wilhelm II, whose bellicose speech at Tangiers on 31 March 1905 dramatically raised the stakes of German involvement in the exploitation of Morocco. The Chamber of Deputies, fearful of imminent hostilities, demanded the resignation of Delcassé, who had interpreted the Kaiser's intervention as a hollow threat and had urged the Sultan even more strongly to concede a French protectorate.

Jaurès was prominent in the critical response to the Moroccan imbroglio, but as he refined his own position he showed the extent to which he acknowledged that colonialism was a norm of both European capitalism and diplomacy. He endorsed the efforts of the international conference on Morocco which met at Algeciras in the first months of 1906 and which pronounced more in favour of French financial 'rights' than German. From 1906 to 1912 he expressed approval for any sign of Franco-German cooperation, rather than rivalry, in the exploitation of Morocco, while writing more reflectively at several points on the eventual inevitability of colonial independence and the cultural importance of Islam, China and India. In

their own ways the maverick right-wing Lyautey and the socialist humanist Jaurès were both important forces in a minority struggle against colonial arrogance, hysteria and excess, Jaurès because he was in the thick of European politics, Lyautey because he was not.

Dissident attitudes criticizing the whole imperial ethos were rare, but invariably pungent and outspoken. In *L'Assiette au Beurre*, the most famous satirical review of the decade from 1901 to 1910, different cartoonists indulged their passions against the police, the conniving politician, the Church and the colonial enterprise. The *colon* in Africa was lampooned as an idle, hard-drinking sadist who spread syphilis to the indigenous populations: the Moroccan policy was denounced as a giant swindle, and the capitalist was shown to exploit not only the colonized but also the French workers who tried to escape unemployment through emigration. The most expressive cartoonist, Jules Grandjouan, was a militant of the revolutionary left, and in May 1903 produced a drawing entitled 'Algeria for the Algerians': a young woman in a white tunic represents the Algerian people in their bid for freedom, while in the background a military officer representing the mother country holds the people of Senegal and Martinique in chains. It was exceptional for its time, not specifically for its anti-colonialism, but more for its positive image of an assertive indigenous nationality. The norm in *L'Assiette au Beurre* was to register the colonized as victims; poor, ragged and passive. In 1910 the review closed; Grandjouan met Isadora Duncan and travelled to Egypt with her for a year, sketching her dancing, and distancing himself from French politics. By 1912 the anger of his earlier cartoons was echoed in caustic newspaper articles for *Le Populaire du Midi* by Paul Vigné d'Octon, an ex-Radical deputy for the Hérault who had joined the Socialist Party in 1910. Vigné roundly condemned the *code de l'indigénat* as a rapacious tyranny under which the indigenous people were expected to smile. Scathing towards the colonial lobby, he nevertheless stopped short of rejecting all colonialism out of hand. In this he endorsed the position that the Socialist Party had adopted in its congress at Nancy in 1907. More often than not among its political critics, colonialism was clearly and simply one of the consequences of capitalism. It remained, however, low on the agenda of party meetings.

3. Citizenship, rights and religion

The recognition that a new century should be boldly announced was embodied in the opening of the first line of the Paris métro on 19 July 1900 from Porte de Vincennes to Porte Maillot. With the brass door locks slamming down miraculously into place, the grinding sounds of metal on metal, the vaulted roofs and the dragonfly *art nouveau* entrances designed by Hector Guimard, it was a functional and artistic success. It was open from 5.30 a.m. until midnight, the long hours registering its determination to serve both ends of the working day and a full evening of entertainment. Three months before, the Universal Exhibition in Paris had opened its gates, with the second of the new era Olympic Games also staged in Paris at the same time. Particular local satisfaction was registered with the victory of an all-Paris team of rugby players who defeated both German and English teams from Frankfurt and Moseley in a three-nations invitation tournament, prompting Pierre de Coubertin, the Olympic initiator, to order gold medals to be struck for each of the winning French players. It was something of a final all-Parisian flourish, as the veritable heart of rugby was soon acknowledged to be the south-west.[5]

At the Universal Exhibition, the themes of technical innovation and human achievement in both science and the arts were intended to prove that France was the centre of progress. The exhibition's promise was rewarded by an attendance of over 50 million visitors during the course of the year. Paris was architecturally enriched by the Grand and Petit Palais and by the Pont Alexandre III, but by comparison with the euphoric welcome given to the Eiffel Tower and the atmosphere of scientific intoxication in 1889 the newspapers were not as impressed by the displays of 1900 as they expected to be, and the exhibition appeared to some to mark the end of the age of progress, or at best a confused hiatus, rather than a new beginning.

Transport and travel, however, provided new metaphors for an age of speed and dynamism. There was an infectious feeling that 1900 could be celebrated in terms of a revolution in mobility, not only in the Paris métro, but also in the success of the automobile industry. Produced since 1885 by Panhard, Peugeot, Bollée, de Dion and Levassor, almost 3,000 vehicles were registered in 1900. A limited automobile tour of the country was organized in 1899, anticipating the launch of the cycling Tour de France in 1903, which became one of the century's most potent symbols in the imagery of modern France (see Chapter 22). In August 1900 the Michelin rubber industry, located in Clermont-Ferrand since 1889, produced its

first *Guide*, distributed free to owner-drivers. Outreaching the bicycle, the 'auto-mobile' incarnated the same sense of independence and individual freedom, the bicycle from parental control, and the automobile from the restrictions of the railway system. Michelin spread the functional and psychological virtues of 'riding on air' with its inflatable tyre, symbolized in its cartoon character Bibendum, made up of inner tubes and associated from the start with a discriminating appetite, devouring the kilometres and gourmet meals in style.

In general, the expectations of the dawn of a new century were high, and nowhere more so than in the realm of citizenship and rights, where recognition of the individual's worth was expected to be the climax of rational thought and the 'irresistible' march of enlightenment.

Women's suffrage

One visitor to Paris in 1900 who openly proclaimed these expectations was May Wright Sewall, who came as an American official representative, but whose primary concern was to attend the women's conferences in Paris which coincided with the Universal Exhibition. As founder of the International Council of Women, Sewall was concerned to enrol a number of French women's organizations. At Versailles, the Conseil National des Femmes Françaises (CNFF) was launched, the largest federation of women's movements in France with 21,000 members. Initially its leaders, including the president Sarah Monod, were involved with the expansion of women's philanthropic work among industrial workers. They had not come together to campaign for women's right to the vote.

However, a petition which did call for women's suffrage was laid before the Chamber of Deputies in 1900. It comprised 3,000 signatures of women and men and was the product of Hubertine Auclert's suffrage drive which had started in the late 1870s. Daughter of a landowning family in the Allier and a rebel against her convent education, she centred her movement on Paris where she used every means to give real meaning to the term 'universal suffrage' which was the misleading term used for the electoral system since 1848. 'With the existing suffrage, restrictive and unnatural as it is,' she wrote in 1908, 'the voter has only the illusion of sovereignty. But with universal suffrage, women as well as men, the elector will be given the substance of sovereignty itself.'[6]

Hubertine Auclert's campaign exposed the inconsistencies in women's civil position. She refused to pay taxes or fill in the census until citizenship was completed by the vote. Increasingly ready to organize street

demonstrations and insistent on trying to register at every election and even stand as a candidate, she carried the suffrage message to the heart of politics, while remaining dependent on the male initiative of Jean Gautret from the Vendée to present a bill to the Chamber of Deputies. Gautret's project was ignored by the Chamber and never discussed. This was not the bold opening to the new century which suffragists had envisaged, although their own activity was strengthened by the decision of the pioneer women's organization, the Ligue Française pour le Droit des Femmes, to campaign for suffrage, a new departure which was soon vigorously pursued by the young lawyer Maria Vérone, who had worked her way up through the state education system to become one of the first women to be allowed to practise as a barrister.

Women's organizations which converted to women's suffrage in the early 1900s were often hesitant at the start and frequently no more than receptive in principle. Monod and other pioneers of the CNFF shared none of Auclert's history of suffrage agitation. A surprising move in favour of votes for women by liberal Catholics led by Marie Maugeret seemed a rebuke to the republican, Jewish and Protestant members of the CNFF, and in 1906 they moved stutteringly towards their own suffrage support, inviting Hubertine Auclert to be president. In the first six years of the century, therefore, a tiny minority of Catholic women and a still small, but larger, proportion of Protestant and Jewish women had joined demands for women's suffrage, which had originated in a disaggregated form within middle-class, largely free-thinking, and mainly Parisian, circles.

Socialist women had considerable problems in accepting that the activity of middle-class feminists and well-connected suffragists could be liberational. The issue of class cut across gender to such an extent that the gulf between bourgeois and proletarian women seemed unbridgeable. Louise Saumoneau, a poor seamstress in Paris, consistently warned working women against pursuing the purely bourgeois political goal of placing suffrage first, while the more individualistic Madeleine Pelletier, though demanding the vote, made her name as the most uncompromising feminist of the 1900s partly through her contempt for the mainstream activity of women suffragists. In 1908 she joined Hubertine Auclert and Caroline Kauffmann in storming a town hall in the Paris municipal elections of 1908, where Auclert smashed a voting urn to the floor, and a week later Pelletier threw stones through windows when prevented from entering a polling station, acts which became legendary. For Pelletier they were acts which she located more firmly in the context of social revolution than within the evolutionary growth of suffragism.[7]

The issue of integration

At a time when the Radicals boasted a flagrant individuality and a critical mind, the generality of their hostility to women's suffrage forms a singular strand in the history of left-wing politics. There were women republicans who shared their position. Among the most loyal and expressive champions of Dreyfus and the cause of justice, the newspaper of Marguerite Durand, *La Fronde*, was unique. The only daily paper run, written and produced by women with feminist convictions, it nevertheless refused to embrace a pro-suffrage position, seeing this as incompatible with its support for the anticlerical Dreyfusard republicans, who helped to form the moderate government of Waldeck-Rousseau in 1898 and who triumphed in the elections of 1902. The Radicals argued, with gestures to reason and empiricism, that if women were allowed to vote they would follow their priest and assure the permanent victory of the forces of clerical superstition and reaction. In short, they concluded, there would be no integration of women into the republic through women's suffrage; the opposite would prevail.

Combes, Clemenceau and the majority of the Chamber of Deputies took no account of the reasoning of Ferdinand Buisson, the respected elder of secularism, who repeatedly told his colleagues that citizenship and voting rights were inseparable. On the contrary, they replied, the defence of the republic, the *raison d'être* of the Radical ideology, was a defence against priests and women seen as political accomplices. 'If the right to vote were given to women tomorrow,' wrote Clemenceau in 1907, 'France would all of a sudden jump backwards into the middle ages.'[8] Ironically, politicians of the conservative, Catholic opposition were equally convinced that working women would all vote socialist, or, still worse, vote differently from their husbands.

The anticlerical offensive: Radical dominance

The culture of Radical republicanism which underpinned Combes and his government, elected in 1902, was more than a broad, popular acceptance of the idea of progress, reason and the rights of the individual. The monopoly of such values and the mantle of the Revolution, worn successively by Gambetta and Ferry, had to be continually justified and reasserted if the rival socialist claims to the revolutionary inheritance were to be outmanoeuvred. The danger that the Radical Party would lapse into political immobility and a stultifying social conservatism was clearly a reality once it had affirmed itself as the defender of private property and small and

medium-sized business. It therefore made political sense to relaunch the party in 1901 and base it on secular militancy in the small provincial towns which were barely affected by socialism and where radicalism could still claim to be the energetic public face of the revolutionary tradition, locked in a clash of ideals and personalities with the local representatives of the Catholic Church. Secularism was a political cause of apparently unlimited scope, and given the tenacity of Catholicism in protecting its historical and customary place in society, a polarizing conflict could be assured. Socialists were fervent apostles of secularism, but did not give it the most important role in their ideology. The Radicals did. It gave them new life in the new century.

The anticlerical offensive mounted by the Radicals mobilized an impressive array of cultural, social and political forces. The party announced itself as composed of committees, leagues, unions, federations, intellectual groups of freethinkers, newspapers and propaganda units, and municipal councils. In class terms these represented a middle and lower bourgeoisie of mainly provincial property-owners, teachers, lawyers, doctors, artisans, white-collar workers, and the cohorts of local *fonctionnaires* (civil servants) whose jobs were an index of the echelons of state, departmental and municipal authority and the expanding areas of public policy. The social politics of the conservative Senate and those of the Radicals in the Chamber gradually became closely, if sometimes awkwardly, intertwined, a far cry from the purist demands for a single legislative body which had marked the earlier days of the republicans and the strident rhetoric of Georges Clemenceau. Émile Combes was himself a senator for the Charente, and Clemenceau, the very embodiment of constitutional radicalism, entered the Senate in 1902 for the Var, in what could only be seen as a trading of principle for political opportunity nine years after his electoral defeat in 1893. It was to be the first of his surprising political personas in the new century.

From Delacroix's emblematic vision of *Liberty Leading the People* (1830) to the small figure of Combes in a frock coat, 'le petit père', leading the battalions of republicans against the Catholic enemy, the sense of embattled republicanism had the same visceral pull. The cry of Léon Gambetta of 'No enemies to the Left' in the defence of the Republic held the parliamentary majority together as the Bloc des Gauches. Socialists, whose beliefs had been officially denounced in the Syllabus of Errors proclaimed by Pope Pius IX, had little problem in following the Radical lead on an issue for which there was such vociferous left-wing enthusiasm at local level. Collectively, the Radicals and Socialists underlined the popular antagonism to clerical power in much of the Paris region, in Burgundy, the Limousin, the centre of France, the Rhône valley, the Bordeaux region, in

Provence and the Languedoc. Even in these regions there were signs of the spiritual revival which was widespread elsewhere in the first decade of the century, but the government was confident that a permanent decline of belief would follow the dissolution of the religious orders (*congrégations*).

From June 1902 to July 1903 Catholic communities, such as the Prémontré monks of Nantes, were dissolved and closed down in bulk, affecting over eighty female and fifty male *congrégations*. On 7 July 1904 all teaching by religious orders was banned. In republican areas the notable figures of doctor, lawyer and schoolteacher, personifying the rational convictions of positivism, vividly dramatized by Roger Martin du Gard in his novel *Jean Barois*, were now more firmly than ever entrenched in local power. Mayors had been elected since 1884, and in small *communes* it was not just the mayor, but the mayoral secretary, *le maire adjoint*, a post held usually by the village schoolteacher, who came to represent the triumphalism of *laïcité*. When the new Pope, Pius X, appeared to counter the Combist measures by a show of diplomatic aggression, the conflict moved into a final showdown: weight was now given to the preparation of a bill which would disestablish religion entirely.

Ironically the anticlerical campaign insisted that Catholicism was a unified body of thought and practice just when it was showing signs of diversification and pluralism, however reluctant the papacy was to recognize the fact. There had been a few eminent Catholic Dreyfusards, not least the well-known Paris preacher the abbé Frémont, and the abbé Brugerette whose critical book on Catholics and the Dreyfus Affair was published at the height of the Combist legislative programme. 'Modernism', as the term was first known in pre-war France, referred to ideas among Catholics which sought to bring democracy into the running of the Church and open up theology and Christian scriptures to debate and historical research, as a response to the challenges of 'modern times'. Pius X denounced all aspects of religious *modernisme* in an encyclical of 1907, which Alfred Loisy, a priest and theologian at the Catholic Institute in Paris, well known for his writings on the Christian New Testament, refused to accept. Loisy was excommunicated by Pius a year later. The clash between 'modernism' and orthodoxy within Catholicism was not in substance a close parallel to the furore caused by the avant-garde within literature, art and music. Catholic modernism was an opening towards the rational world of enquiry, while modernism in the arts was a distinctive break with rational convention, logic and 'normative' expectations (see Chapter 6). What they had in common in their separate areas was the very considerable ability to offend traditionalists.

Even as Brugerette was writing, Marc Sangnier, later acknowledged as the founder of Christian Democracy in France, was controversially activating the Sillon movement which thrived from 1902 to 1910 when it was banned by Pius X for its increasingly secular-style activities. Sangnier combined impressive organization and imaginative rhetoric. He refused the polarization of Combism, fully accepted the Republic, claimed an essential link between Christianity and socialism, and recruited young Catholic intellectuals, students and workers into vigorous social welfare activities. The Sillon heavily influenced the history of left-wing Catholicism in the twentieth century.

Separation of Churches and State

Émile Combes had originally trained, unsuccessfully, for the priesthood and still nurtured a residue of spirituality. The combination of religious training and conversion to an opposing set of beliefs was thought to be the secret of both his rigour and his insensitivity. He was far from alone in his determination to ban the religious orders *en bloc*, and it was not Combes in person who hurried to advance the Separation of Churches and State which had been on Radical and Socialist agendas since Gambetta's Belleville programme of 1869. Napoleon's Concordat had given control of priests' salaries to the state, as also those of Protestant pastors and Jewish rabbis. The Combist legislation against the religious orders maximized the controlling and interventionist power of government. Separation would mean the surrender of that measure of control over the churches and might therefore entail a diminution of state power. Combes vacillated. It was the logical arguments of certain Socialists, including Jean Jaurès through his newspaper *L'Humanité*, that played a crucial role. They made separation appear as the inevitable climax of secularization. Among the meticulous drafters was the astute Protestant civil servant Louis Méjan, and by the summer of 1905 a bill was ready. On 3 July 1905 the skilful advocacy of the ex-Socialist deputy and lawyer Aristide Briand secured the acceptance of a version which enabled the Catholic Church to reapply for legality and use of its property as an independent network of *associations cultuelles* (associations for religious practice) but which firmly disestablished it from all state subsidy and protection.

The Separation bill was finally enacted on 11 December 1905 and enshrined the principle of freedom of conscience. Most Catholic leaders in France, though outraged at the losses and humiliation inflicted by over four years of the anticlerical offensive, were inclined to stay within the law and

apply for the new status of the *associations cultuelles*. Pope Pius X refused to allow them to do so. French bishops already spent much of their time negotiating with prefects, but now they were told by Rome not to compromise. Two encyclicals laid down the papal line. Of all the results of the Separation this was one of the least expected. Gallicanism, a coveted but contested form of French Catholic independence from Rome, was forced into retreat, no less than the educational role of the Church. The papacy and the secular French state both emerged strengthened in their own spheres of influence, while at the level of the village *commune*, wrangling and angry confrontations ensued in many areas where republican councils exercised their right to draw up inventories of Church property and treated all Church activity as illegal. Elsewhere there were many examples of new kinds of co-existence: reason tempered by custom.

In 1906 the balance in the Catholic–secular antagonism shifted towards a more or less uneasy truce, and in 1907 towards widespread compromise, due largely to the conciliatory policy of Briand. Nevertheless there was little doubt that the Catholic Church as an educational force and owner of substantial property continued to suffer huge losses and reversals: at least a third of Catholic schools which remained in 1905 were closed by 1913. The notion of martyrdom was encouraged by a Catholic society formed to 'liberate youth from the yoke of atheistic teaching', and in 1910 it issued some 8,000 Joan of Arc medals to pupils who defended their faith to the point of exclusion from the *écoles laïques*. There was no republican sympathy for their individual predicament. Memories, particularly among women schoolteachers (*institutrices*), of intolerant treatment at the hands of clerical opinion were still rife: Francisque Sorcey's dossier of teachers' experience contained a wealth of references to the abuse thrown at the impoverished women teachers who had replaced the nuns, and the refusal of Catholic shopkeepers to sell them bread, milk, butter and vegetables.[9]

The series of moves from Ferry to Combes to create and protect a norm of educational practice and experience independent of all religious faiths was clearly popular with over three-fifths of the population. Secularism was firmly established as the central pillar of the twentieth-century republic. In the 1906 elections the Catholic cause, allied to the traditional political right, lost heavily: the republican majority of 1902 was reinforced, and by the end of the year Georges Clemenceau, to many the epitome of demagogic anticlericalism, was Prime Minister. But beyond the theme of *laïcité* the unity on the left dissolved, and Clemenceau was now identified with quite another form of intransigence.

2

New Forces: Socialism and Syndicalism, 1900–1909

1. *Workers and working lives*

Demography and jobs

In the early and mid-nineteenth century France had experienced urbaniz-ation without industrialization. At the *fin de siècle* there were both. Exodus of rural people into the towns had accelerated with the great depression of the 1880s and the ravages of phylloxera across the vineyards of the south. A 10 per cent increase in urban numbers between 1881 and 1911 drew attention to industrial mechanization and the spreading tentacles of the towns. Yet within the definition of 'urban' lay every French *commune* with more than 2,000 inhabitants, forming a category which was as diverse as the rural and regional tessellation which still made up the habitat of 56 per cent of the population. In 1906 over half of the industrial workforce was still working in small and medium-sized businesses with fewer than five employees, and only 10 per cent in factories with more than 500 workers.

The nature of internal migration changed more conspicuously than its tempo. The newer and younger migrants, especially to Paris, had no skills to trade and were forced to seek jobs in the unqualified labour market. As mechanization spread, deskilling of the old workforce was rife, as experi-enced in Carmaux, a small town in the Tarn with mines and glassworks where the introduction of mechanical glass-blowing shattered the work practices of a close-knit community. Other threats hung over different industries. A specific recession hit the textile industry of Roubaix, Tour-coing and Lille in the Nord for the first seven years of the new century, intensifying the degradation of life in the cramped, insanitary courtyards (*courées*), and the insecurity and hazardous nature of work in the mills which employed a combined workforce of over 130,000, almost a third of whom were women. Here was an underclass, a proletariat, a mass of labour whose appalling conditions of life and work stunned the hardened journalist Marcelle Capy who investigated the plight of the working classes for *La*

Bataille syndicaliste. And yet there was 'a rich community life' centred on the *courées* and the small cafés (*estaminets*), on musical activities, popular clubs and music-halls, which all adapted to the ideas and expressions of socialism.[1]

In the vineyards of the south economic depression and natural disaster struck at one and the same time, but as replanting of new strains of vines, resistant to phylloxera, was seen to be successful, the small peasant proprietors of stricken vineyards in the Var embraced the socialism of co-operatives, the practical solution to their dire economic predicament. The economics of collective peasant production, the traditions of Provençal sociability and the humanistic ideals of socialism merged into a specific local politics.[2] In the vine-intensive plains of Languedoc it was the landless agricultural workers, suffering from low wages and the continued precariousness of work in the vineyards, who formed a substantial part of the emergent socialist movement in the Hérault, alongside miners from the coal basin at Graissessac where industrialism and rural patterns of life were interlocked, a distinctive feature of the French economy in the first half of the twentieth century until the third industrial revolution of the 1950s.

The expansion of urban industry might well have been far greater in the early part of the century had the demographic curve been upwards and the pressure for work correspondingly higher. But the opposite was the case. Labour was comparatively scarce. French population figures in 1906 give 38,962,000 for the metropole. Population growth was already seen as the weakest in Europe, and markedly inferior to Germany and Britain. France became aware of itself as a country where immigration was fast becoming a demographic necessity. The first census to distinguish foreigners was in 1851, and from 1888 foreigners resident in France had to declare themselves to the local town hall. The geography of immigration was initially along the borders with Italy, Spain and Belgium, but by 1891 the larger industrial towns of Paris, Lyon and Marseille, as well as the border towns of the Nord and Pas-de-Calais, were the main reception areas for European immigrants. Their arrival was organized by state conventions with Italy and Belgium in 1904 and 1906, and eventually with Poland in 1919 and with Czechoslovakia in 1920. Not all left their homes for economic reasons. By 1914 there were close to 40,000 Jewish refugees from Russian pogroms, many of them living in penury and miserable conditions in the Marais district of Paris. From 1898, after severe repression of revolts in Milan, there was a diaspora of Italian revolutionary organizations, with political refugees in Marseille contributing substantially to the expansion of socialist organizations. A hierarchy of immigrants began to form in the official mind with assimilation

as the goal. At the top were Belgians, who were portrayed as solid and safe and were welcomed even by the nationalist movement of Action Française.

Public anxiety about the population figures was already evident in 1896 when a doctor and statistician, Jacques Bertillon, formed a National Alliance to campaign for the increase of French population. Its most unexpected recruit was Émile Zola, whose fictional exposé of a brutalized mining community in *Germinal* (1885) had done much to spread images of teeming workers living on the edge of survival. It was in his later novel *Fécondité* (1899) that he turned to extolling the virtues of the family, implicitly favouring a pro-natalist policy.

From the workers' point of view the demographic statistics were far from a disaster. Labour shortages gave them greater bargaining power and in many areas a chance of mobility between different jobs. The mining industry, located within a diffuse number of urban and rural areas, each with its own local culture, experienced a universal instability of labour, with a sufficient deficit by 1907 for the mine-owners to call for an instant drive to recruit 15,000 workers to replenish a tenth of their entire labour force. At Blanzy, a small mining community in the industrial complex of southern Burgundy, close to Montceau-les-Mines, it appears that many mining families deliberately limited the number of offspring in order to allow them to take advantage of other jobs and the new educational possibilities.[3] In 1914 open propaganda for birth control was still permitted and socialist posters could be seen in Paris stating that more children would bring impoverishment, and that 'Every worker's child is a future rival to its parents and to others'.

This positive interpretation of the population statistics points away from the much-quoted underdevelopment of French industry. It removes the focus from demographic decline and redirects it to the survival of small to medium-sized businesses, the resilience of the rural economy and the interpenetration of rural and urban patterns. It also stresses the element of mobility through the labour market, through education and through the expanding opportunities for the lower grades of clerical workers and *fonctionnaires*.

In this more nuanced interpretation of social trends, the lasting images of squalor and misery go side by side with a labour history which underlines hope as well as despair. The unification of divergent socialist parties in 1905, the confident independence of trade unions (*syndicats*), the proliferation of strikes and labour revolts, all testify to a climate of ideological expectation.

2. Representing the workers

The Radicals entered the twentieth century believing that they incarnated all that was enlightened and pragmatic in the revolutionary tradition: they claimed to be the voice of the people. The term 'radical-socialist' used by the relaunched party in 1901 was intended to span social as well as political radicalism, and in Léon Bourgeois the Radicals had a social thinker whose ideas were laid out in *Solidarité* in 1896 in which he sought to combat the excesses of capitalism. The doctrine of Solidarism was an attempt to create a synthesis of Marxism and liberalism: it rejected class struggle, the fundamental tenet of socialism, and proposed a fusion of classes and the practice of fraternity in social relations. The rivalry of socialism, however, could not be contained by Radical politics, and Solidarism as a programme made no inroads into workers' culture, practice or understanding of themselves. Far more effective as a nursery of social practice outside the ranks of socialism was the École de Nîmes, animated by Charles Gide, a professor of political economy from a Protestant background at Uzès in the Gard, where Protestantism was rooted in the middle classes of Nîmes and in the mining communities of the Cévennes. He favoured consumer co-operatives in the form of friendly societies (*mutualités*) which he defined as socialist in principle. They thrived on the fringes of mainstream socialism, and Jean Jaurès acknowledged their significance.

The voicing of workers' needs had long been the aim of social Catholics, identified most notably in the well-established good works of the Société de Saint-Vincent-de-Paul and the movement of young workers' circles founded by the military aristocrat Count Albert de Mun in 1871. Thirty years later the same aim was vigorously cultivated in the workers' allotments movement (*jardins ouvriers*), enthusiastically pioneered by the abbé Jules Lemire, who fought the Separation bill in the Chamber of Deputies with the fear that capitalists would infiltrate a disestablished Church. The candidates for the subsidized vegetable gardens were carefully screened for family and religious virtues, and the experiment was on a very small scale, but such was their success on the outskirts of Paris that the Socialist mayor of Ivry, Jules Coutant, joined abbé Lemire in 1909 to inaugurate new gardens within the *commune*, which had gained a reputation as the typical industrialized suburb with all its attendant miseries. The Sillon movement of Marc Sangnier with its youthful *élan* and acceptance of democracy and modernity expressed the most controversial Catholic commitment to social equality, marked by the co-operative structure of its journal, *L'Éclair*

démocratique, in 1905 and ever-increasing use of insights and language which bordered on socialism. The papal ban on the Sillon meant that contact between Catholicism and workers was restricted in many industrial areas to the paternalist gestures of charitable industrial magnates.

The welfare of women workers, and especially their moral welfare, was high on the Church and paternalist agenda. Communities of nuns (*Petites Soeurs*) worked closely with the employers in many industries to minister to the sick and provide religious and moral instruction: they were a permanent facet of management, and a recourse for many workers: dechristianization of labour had been extensive but far from universal. It was against the close partnership of employers and Church that *La Femme socialiste* employed its most vituperative language in its year and a half of existence. It was founded in March 1901 by Louise Saumoneau and the 54-year-old Élisabeth Renaud, once a governess, who was widowed at thirty with two children and survived by running a boarding-house. Saumoneau was a dour combatant, Renaud already an exceptional survivor, which gave her authority. Life expectancy in France in 1900 was forty-nine for women and forty-five for men; it was still less for workers. Their small, vocal and autonomous Groupe Féministe Socialiste identified the cause of women workers with the class struggle of all workers, but their group lost much of its freedom and its separate identity in a confident socialist and syndicalist world in which women were frequently allotted a theoretically equal position but where gender discrimination against them was ingrained.

A united Socialist Party

In the Chamber of Deputies Jean Jaurès epitomized the parliamentary road to socialism, still more so Alexandre Millerand, whose acceptance of a ministry in 1899 in a non-Socialist government became a test case for all political socialists. Expectations of his influence had been high among reformists, but Millerand stood condemned by Jules Guesde's Parti Ouvrier Français, not least for entering a government in which the Minister of War was General Gaston de Gallifet, infamous in all revolutionary eyes for his brutal repression of the Paris Commune. By 1904 it was increasingly obvious that Millerandism as a symbolic contract between Radicals and Socialists had no depth of socialist support. The Congress of the Socialist International, meeting at Amsterdam in August 1904, put pressure on the different French movements to unite into one party, capable of defeating the Radicals, and in 1905 Jaurès rallied to the Guesdist position on Millerand, facilitating the creation of a single Socialist Party, the Section Française de

l'Internationale Ouvrière (SFIO), which declared itself to be 'not a party of reform but a party of class struggle and revolution'.

At the outset the new party had 33,000 members, of which under 3 per cent were women. In parliament the SFIO initially grouped together thirty deputies, while a further twenty-one opted to remain independent, protesting at the revolutionary definition of the party. The Guesdist movement appeared to have taken over the party, but in fact it was a coalition of Jaurès and Édouard Vaillant, the old Communard whose mentor had been the revolutionary Auguste Blanqui, who formed the nexus of the party and held the centre ground. To their right, Albert Thomas led a small group still favourable to the Bloc des Gauches, while on the left of the Guesdists were the insurrectionists and anti-militarists of Gustave Hervé and his explosive weekly paper *La Guerre sociale*, whose revolutionary cause was joined by Madeleine Pelletier before she moved towards the anarchists. By 1914 the party had won 103 seats in the Chamber, with 17 per cent of the national vote: its membership had expanded to 90,000, but although it remained the only party formally open to women the percentage of women members had not increased. This could not be blamed equally on all the local federations. Diversity operated here as in all aspects of French politics. The Socialists of the Isère had a strong commitment to women's rights, mandating Angèle Roussel as a representative at national level. In 1910 they agreed that Élisabeth Renaud should fight the national elections in villages close to the Rhône valley town of Vienne, and gave her every backing. Renaud improved the SFIO vote sensationally in an unwinnable seat and drew large rural crowds to hear her campaign speeches.

A triumphant audience of 15,000 greeted Jaurès and celebrated unity at Béziers on 30 April 1905, five days after the formation of the new party. The town was one of the centres of the southern wine industry, and more than one participant spoke of the final recovery of a long-lost Languedoc identity through the voice of socialism. Agricultural *syndicats* were there in number and every speaker emphasized a different aspect of socialism which had merged into unity. The powerful popular orator and publicist Marcel Cachin, whose father had been a peasant turned gendarme and who himself had been a fervent Catholic until his adolescence, stressed that it was the break with both the clerical and the Radical bourgeoisie which marked the modernity of the party.

Syndicalists and anarchists

Selling for ten centimes, Gustave Hervé's popular manuals of social revolution published in 1902 contained an account of future life under socialism, in the form of a dialogue between a disbelieving, laconic peasant and a patient, instructive socialist. Hervé allows the socialist to give pride of place in the organization of an ideal society to the labour exchanges, the Bourses du Travail. As important to the culture and lives of working people in many areas as the secularized schools were to education as a whole, the Bourses du Travail used municipal grants to provide a location for workers to meet, mutual insurance, a number of libraries and training classes, and propaganda for trade unions. Radical town councils, often the providers of a local Bourse during the 1890s, rarely refused to make premises available, but tough controls on policy and action were commonplace. Socialist municipalities were more permissive, but recurrent discord between political socialism and syndicalism reflected acute differences of strategy. Unity of the trade-union movement in the Confédération Générale du Travail (CGT) had preceded socialist unity by ten years, and independence was jealously guarded. The self-sufficiency of workers' action and their education within the Bourses du Travail made the world of parliamentary politics and party organization both alien and irrelevant, and on 13 October 1906 at the congress of Amiens, a new CGT charter (*Charte d'Amiens*) sealed the separation of syndicalism from the SFIO by asserting that the class struggle was at the workplace, not in parliament.

Within the CGT there was a reformist wing, stressing wage claims, but there was also a sense of immediacy, of a socialist future that was close. Militant syndicalists rehearsed the imminence of a revolutionary general strike. The theory behind it was associated in the minds of intellectuals with Georges Sorel. In *Réflexions sur la violence* in 1908, Sorel, self-appointed prophet and philosopher of the general strike, made it into a 'mobilizing myth'. He saw workers responding to the 'myth' of a general strike in the same way as early Christians had responded to the 'myth' of the return of Christ. The 'Sorelian myth', defined as a causal force in history but located in the future, became a key concept in the twentieth century. But his writings were little known and rarely discussed in the Bourses du Travail; he remained aloof from any experience of strikes and had no wish to be involved. By 1910 he had lost all hope and interest in a general strike in France. He was later enthusiastic for Russian Bolshevism and died shortly before the Italian Fascists' March on Rome, apparently more and more sympathetic to Mussolini.

Anarchists, repudiating the individual act of the Ravachol era, gave syndicalism much of its revolutionary and libertarian mentality. Émile Pouget, once the scurrilous voice of *Le Père Peinard*, who in 1900 took over responsibility for *La Voix du Peuple*, the organ of the CGT, wrote from prison in 1908 that 'Direct action is the worker's strength at its most creative, the strength which gives birth to new rights, to social justice.' This was not the mentality of all the unions, least of all the printers' union, which, under Auguste Keufer, was never anarcho-syndicalist but represented the reformist wing of the CGT. It was also openly misogynist, boasting of its determination to block women's access to the heart of the profession. As late as 1913 Emma Couriau, a typesetter like her husband Louis, was denied membership of the Lyon branch of the printers' union by 300 votes to 26. The decision was denounced by Alfred Rosmer in the leading syndicalist newspaper *La Bataille syndicaliste*, but there was no hiding the very low level of women's integration into workers' *syndicats*: in 1914 there were only 89,364 women out of a total membership of 1,026,302 at a time when women constituted 34 per cent of the industrial and artisanal workforce and 40 per cent of those in the tertiary service sector: in textiles women constituted two-thirds of the workers.

The accent on the workplace led to a far greater consciousness of a worker's identity, but one which was unsure of its relationship to the Republic and to other issues of citizenship, such as gender roles and the problems experienced by immigrant labour. Focus on the workplace clarified the practice of class struggle through the strike, but left the next move unclear. It gave the false impression that French workers did not have a political mentality, whereas strikes were the politics of direct action in the barricade tradition of the June days of 1848 and the Paris Commune, recruiting the locality as well as the workforce. The drawings of strikes in *L'Assiette au Beurre* in 1906-8 show women in all strikes fighting equally alongside men, often in the front line, the whole working-class family involved in the struggle. These images are endorsed by eye-witness accounts, not least from the police.

Rituals made strikes into cultural events: the flags, pipes and drums; the time-honoured revolutionary songs, 'L'Internationale' by the Communard Eugène Pottier and Pierre Degeyter, 'Le Temps des cerises', popular during the Commune, and the 'Carmagnole' dance from 1792; the appropriation of music-hall songs and burlesque of the day; the hats taken round by strikers' children; the community organization of soup-kitchens, and the totemic identification of places, buildings, squares and marching routes as an inversion of religious processions. Within the economic desperation and

the violence of action there was a dimension of customary festival, an intimation of a new and better social order, which made the arrival of troops and the shooting of strikers all the more shocking.

3. Strikes and social conflict

In March 1906 a fire broke out in the coal-mine of Courrières in the Pas-de-Calais. It was not a rare event underground: old wooden supports in disused tunnels not infrequently caught fire. The company did not halt production, preferring to brick up the fire. Complaints by the miners of insufficient renewal of air at the coal-face had been repeatedly made and regularly disregarded. A build-up of noxious gases from abandoned coal seams began to leak into the working galleries. Early on Saturday morning, 10 March 1906 a vast explosion ripped through the mine, killing 1,200 miners from the villages of Méricourt, Sallaumines, Montigny and Billy-Montigny who had just taken the morning shift. It was the worst mining disaster on record, exceeding by far the 800 killed in 1896 in a Silesian mine, and the miners' families and unionized miners were convinced that it had been avoidable. Shock and grief were followed by anger and protest. By 16 March 40,000 miners were on strike. Ten days later, Georges Clemenceau, the scourge of authoritarian governments in the past but now assuming power for the first time as Minister of the Interior, promised the strikers at Lens that the right to strike was equal to any other civil right and that there would be no deployment of troops, providing the rights of property and persons were duly respected. The strikers' anger was not appeased: demonstrations and violence against local authorities and mine-owners multiplied. The demand was for the punishment of the 'assassins of Courrières' and a recompense for the families. In mid-April Clemenceau sent in the cavalry.

A widespread miners' strike in 1902 had been a union failure, and a new, rival union was created, personified in the figure of Benoît Broutchoux and given forceful articulation in the columns of Pierre Monatte in *Les Temps nouveaux*. In the violent climate of March and April 1906 it carried majority support among the miners, but it was the old union which patched together a compromise return to work after the confrontation with the troops. Broutchoux was twice imprisoned, and Monatte temporarily discredited by a Byzantine insinuation that he had been paid 75,000 francs by a maverick Bonapartist to spread violence throughout the north-east. Counter-insurgency tactics of infiltration, *agents provocateurs*, spying and

false evidence were quickly ascribed by syndicalists to Clemenceau's ministry, and eventually to his entire government style when he became Prime Minister later in the year.

The mainstream campaign by the CGT in the early months of 1906, even as the Courrières explosion dominated the headlines, was for an eight-hour day for all industrial workers, to replace the norm of ten to twelve hours exacted by employers. The strategy was to implement the eight-hour day by workers' action on 1 May 1906, either by an unlimited strike until employers conceded, or by ceasing work every day after eight hours. In Paris the government left nothing to chance: the Prefect of Police besieged the streets round the Place de la République with cavalry and dragoons. Hundreds of arrests severely curtailed the marches and festivities, but examples of significant stoppages or absenteeism included most of the ports, the military arsenals of Toulon, the building industry, the mines of the Massif Central, and the glassworks of the Nord. The eight-hour day was not achieved, but the six-day working week, with the right to a full day's rest on Sunday, was passed in the Chamber on 13 July 1906. It was a major gain, though whether from syndicalist pressure or from parliamentary reformism was fiercely contested.

Vineyards, 1907

In June 1907 the wine-growing areas of the south broke into open revolt. Economic desperation of peasant proprietors and vineyard workers had grown due to over-production of basic wines, the high quantities of sugar used by wholesalers to produce wine cheaply and a saturation of the market with watered-down wines. The first epicentre was the *commune* of Argeliers in the Aude, where a defence committee of *vignerons* (wine-growers) and workers was set up in March 1907 with its propaganda sheet *Le Tocsin* ringing out a message of hunger: 'We can't sell our wine or our labour: we are in debt . . . we are those who love the Republic, those who hate it or couldn't care a damn about it: we are radicals, conservatives, socialists and reactionaries but we all have a stomach.' The president of the committee was a peasant smallholder, Marcellin Albert, thin, serious, with a fixed stare, who moved as if chosen for a sacred mission. A prophet rather than a political leader, he addressed meetings with an earnestness which brought him the nickname of 'The Redeemer' (*Le Rédempteur*). Large gatherings in small *communes* escalated to the meeting of 45,000 on 5 May in Narbonne. By 9 June there were 500,00 gathered at Montpellier. Refusal to pay taxes was accompanied by violence. A participant, Jules Rivals, spoke

of the 'extraordinary role of women in 1907, at the head of the demonstrations, wearing red scarves, always in the vanguard, the most relentless of the activists. When the tax collectors were chased out of Coursan and Baixas it was they who struck the first blows: they were the revolutionaries.'

Clemenceau, Prime Minister since October 1906, took little notice of the risings at first. His frequent, but unpredictable, resort to force conflicted with his reforming instinct. He had created a Ministry of Labour, and the ex-Socialist René Viviani accepted the post. Viviani and Briand, the Minister of Justice, created an ambience of negotiation. But in mid-June Clemenceau went on to the offensive once again. Troops were sent in against the barricades in Narbonne. On 19 June they opened fire. An ex-official of the Bourse du Travail, Ramon, was killed, his daughter seriously wounded. In an explosion of anger the crowds turned on the police, and across the whole region there were insurrectionary gestures. In Perpignan the prefecture was stormed and set on fire. On the night of 20–21 June the 17th regiment of infantry, drawn from local men, mutinied and entered Béziers with the butts of their rifles in the air. The reception was tumultuous. Albert was summoned by Clemenceau to Paris, his triumph already mythical, but there he was outmanoeuvred, his rough charisma lost in the formalities of government etiquette, his innocence sullied by his acceptance of money for a return ticket. On 29 June the government hurried through a settlement with stipulations on the disclosure of wine harvests and a surtax on the use of sugar; troops were withdrawn, the mutineers amnestied, prisoners liberated and unpaid taxes left uncollected from the poorest families. It appeared a victory for 'the red south' (*le Midi rouge*), but economically the settlement failed to issue in viable long-term solutions to the problem of over-production.

The image of the red south dated from the widespread southern resistance to the coup d'état of Napoleon III in 1851. It was a 'red' image which incorporated the struggle of Protestants against Catholics, so that Protestantism was seen to ally with anticlericalism against the Catholic 'whites' (*les blancs*), but also a 'red' tradition which was part of a long-standing mentality of village sociability, favouring democracy and popular equality, rather than 'red' in the more recent and specific sense of Marxist and internationalist. Cultural as well as political, the events and personalities in the south were widely interpreted in Paris and the north as high in folklore but low in national importance. The Midi was the butt of northern witticisms that Gascony had been under the *ancien régime*. And yet it was in the Midi that the majority of the first eighteen Bourses du Travail were created, and where co-operative socialism in the Var had its own ideological

rationale. Although the revolt of 1907 was not explicitly an ideological battle for either syndicalism or socialism, a key political player had been the Socialist Dr Ferroul of Narbonne, and agricultural *syndicats* emerged strengthened with the right to go to law. Most of the Socialist municipalities had rallied strongly to Marcellin Albert.

Gravel-pits, 1908

Workers in the building industry were at the forefront of the agitation for an eight-hour day on 1 May 1906: over 1,000 masons were arrested in a bitterly contested strike. For two years conflict in the industry was endemic. In May 1908 strike action was taken by those working the quarries and gravel-pits of the upper Seine, south of Paris at Draveil-Vigneux and between Corbeil and Villeneuve-Saint-Georges. Employers had demanded higher productivity of raw materials for the building of the underground métro in Paris: the new Sunday rest-day was regularly refused by the Société des Sablières de la Seine, and hazardous working conditions of waist-high water and moving sands underfoot made the imposition of piecework all the more detested. A brigade of gendarmes took on strikers in their café headquarters at Draveil-Vigneux and in the assault and struggle on 2 June 1908 two workers were shot dead. The gendarmes had exceeded their orders, but it was Clemenceau who was held responsible. A poster from the CGT denouncing 'The Government of Assassins' had spiced the propaganda war, and the situation now deteriorated even further. On 30 July fighting across barricades at Villeneuve-Saint-Georges between the army and strikers left four workers dead and numerous soldiers and workers wounded. All the main leaders of the CGT were immediately arrested in what looked like a panic measure. It was widely asked if Clemenceau, now reviled universally by syndicalists and socialists alike, had lost his head. An attempt at a 24-hour general strike on 3 August was not a success, but the repression seemed set to continue when Clemenceau offered to send in the army to control an electricians' strike in Paris three days later. The employers declined, fearing permanent damage to installations. They recognized the severe limitations of Clemenceau's confrontational tactics.

The criterion of social justice

The speech made by Jean Jaurès at Albi in 1903 did not foresee the divisions of theory and strategy which would affect socialism and syndicalism after 1905. It pre-supposed a universalist ideal of social justice which would

enrich the rational humanism of the republican tradition. His words were designed to convince the political Radicals that they should warm to the opportunity of social reform in order to preserve their very claims to a universalist ethic. This opportunity was missed.

Radicals pointed to a failure of workers and their representatives. The violence of the theories and practice of social revolution, whether socialist or syndicalist, was given as a reason for the alienation of Radicals, and their reluctance to give priority to social reform during their eight years of dominance from 1902 to 1910. Workers' demands were described as inflexible and strikes as counterproductive: actions against persons and property were outlawed by Clemenceau not just as illegal but as irrational. Socialism and syndicalism in their period of rapid growth were accused of doctrinaire rigidity. What was missing from this critical perspective, however, was the sheer plurality of workers' actions, demands and hopes, the taxonomy of which was complex and relativist. Differences within the syndicalist movement were due to a multitude of working practices, but they were also relative to the degree of intransigence among the employers. Ideological entrenchment was not a feature of the majority of strike actions, many of which ended in settlements in which workers accepted an advance, if only marginal, in their conditions of work and standard of living.

Debates in the Chamber over the confrontations were fierce, and a minority of Radical deputies were dubious of Clemenceau's tactics. In dialectical diatribes of mutual power, elegance and rhetorical passion, Jaurès accused Clemenceau of betraying his whole political creed and Clemenceau indicted Jaurès for supporting social violence. Positively Clemenceau laid claim to important social reforms: the six-day working week; the Ministry of Labour, and the law of 13 July 1907 giving married women the right to dispose of their earned income and wages. His record also included the passing of the first income tax bill through the Chamber, only to be blocked by his fellow senators, and the first acceptance of retirement pensions for urban and rural workers. This became law in the next government on 5 April 1910, but was derided by the CGT as the charter of the dead, since only a small minority of workers survived to the stipulated retirement age of sixty-five. It was not an insignificant list of reforms, but they were offset by Clemenceau's devious use of police informers and by his recurrent recourse to armed force. Against his own self-image he identified his government with the authoritarian confines of repressive power and narrow economic interests.

Clemenceau failed to meet the challenge of Jaurès launched at Albi. Radical and republican universalism suffered critically as a result. In 1909,

the third year of his reflex opposition to syndicalism, he refused all trade-union rights to postal workers, teachers and other employees of the state, and sacked and arrested public service strikers *en bloc*. At this point his strategy can only be fully understood within a value-system in which the breaking of strikes in the name of law and order was increasingly bound up with issues of Nationalism and patriotism.

3

New Forces: Nationalism and Patriotism, 1900–1914

1. Reformulations of Nationalism

The voice of Paris 1er

The first district of Paris (*premier arrondissement*) stretches along the right bank from Châtelet to the Place de la Concorde, enclosing Les Halles, the Palais-Royal and the Place Vendôme. For the general election of 1902 its trees and walls were fly-posted with a Nationalist poster proclaiming 'It's a fight between the two Republics: Vote for the true Republic, the French Republic'. The Nationalist candidate, Edmond Archdéacon, left no doubt of the poster's meaning in his electoral declaration: 'I am an antisemitic republican. As a Nationalist I demand respect for our French and military traditions. I am a declared opponent of internationalism. As an antisemite I demand that the 150,000 Jews and their lackeys, the 25,000 Freemasons, stop oppressing and ruining 38 million Frenchmen.' After the 1900 municipal elections in Paris the Nationalist councillors made up the largest group, with their strength mainly but not exclusively in the wealthier districts of the capital, and in 1902 the Nationalist candidates for the Chamber did well in Paris, winning fifteen seats, while failing badly in the rest of France. Archdéacon was elected with the support of the right-wing leagues that continued to express the visceral anti-Dreyfusard and anti-Jewish polemic of the 1890s. Déroulède's Ligue des Patriotes, heavily subsidized by the wealthy Archdéacon, Jules Guérin's over-inflated and corrupt Ligue Antisémitique, and Jules Lemaître's well-endowed Ligue de la Patrie Française were all involved in the Paris electioneering. Archdéacon spoke for all of them when he declared that his republic would also be a populist one (*plébiscitaire*), a direct reference to the way in which the charismatic but fallible General Boulanger had aroused popular emotions and secured a mass following in the series of elections in 1888–9. Nationalism declared itself as the voice of the French people.

The enemy within

That Paris should be atypical in the 1902 elections was not surprising. The Dreyfus Affair had divided the capital more deeply than the rest of the country, and it was in Paris that the dynamic of the Affair as a shift of rhetoric into popular agitation was most keenly experienced. The press played a major role here, but so too did students, forming rival gangs of Dreyfusards and anti-Dreyfusards which disputed cafés, university buildings and whole sections (*quartiers*) of the capital with such commitment that Charles Péguy had no difficulty in evaluating the Affair in *Notre jeunesse* (1910) as primarily one of youth. After 1899 the anti-Dreyfusards were forced on to the defensive. Nationalism offered the beleaguered right a prospect of renewal.

Antisemitism was at the core of this reinvigorated right-wing response, the Jew being imaged as the archetype of the enemy within. The whole ragbag of paranoid fantasy which Édouard Drumont had launched with *La France juive* in 1886, persistently revived through his newspaper *La Libre Parole*, and the conspiracy theories behind the forged *Protocols of the Elders of Zion*, were adopted consciously as the collective programme of the Paris Nationalists in 1902. Graffiti on Parisian walls, mentioned in police reports, called starkly for 'Death to the Jews' (*Mort aux juifs*), and were scrawled either by student members of the Jeunesse Antisémite et Nationaliste, whose membership figures for Paris can approximately be put at 200–300 in 1902, or by shopkeepers, whose move to the right during the Dreyfus Affair had been marked.[1] The central concept of the Jew as outsider and traitor was reanimated in 1902 by Maurice Barrès in *Scènes et doctrines du nationalisme* in which he claimed that Dreyfus 'had sweated treason' in the dock at Rennes, and that the racial question was now at centre stage, with 'dire consequences for certain people'. The new Nationalism, largely articulated by Barrès, was one of an organic French society with a dominantly rural culture and a respect for ancestry (*la terre et les morts*) as opposed to what was preconceived as the rootlessness of urban, industrialized society and its materialist preoccupations. These polarities were given a conceptual simplicity in the terms '*le pays réel*' and '*le pays légal*', where *réel* was equated with natural, and *légal*, meaning imposed by legislation, was rejected as artificial. It was the French version of the German *Gemeinschaft* and *Gesellschaft* defined by Ferdinand Tönnies in 1887.

Nation and 'Patrie'

Fractious and riven with inconsistencies, Nationalism as a distinct political movement disintegrated in Paris with remarkable rapidity after the 1902 elections. Antisemitism did not grow into a viable political programme. Elsewhere it was clear that it had failed to establish the very rootedness of which it boasted. The anti-Dreyfusard right failed in its bid to monopolize national sentiment.

Against its claims to be the people's voice stood the greater popularity and strength of republican patriotism and its ritualized identity with the revolutionary tradition, to which the political heirs were the very Radicals and Socialists who formed the Bloc des Gauches and who launched the anticlerical offensive in the name of that tradition. In the wake of the Affair the right tended to describe themselves as *nationalistes* and the left as *patriotes*, but the historic dispute over the nature of France and Frenchness, waged untiringly since 1789, was not in any way resolved by the distinction. What the Nationalist movement achieved from the margins was a pressure on republican patriotism that caused it to be even more self-consciously assertive.

In Camille Pelletan, appointed as Minister for the Navy by Combes, the Nationalist fringe denoted all that they held to be corrupt and degenerate in the republican government. Pelletan's programme of democratization involved a shift of emphasis from the hierarchy of the Admiralty to a more open recruitment from the ranks, a relaxation of the harsh military discipline imposed on naval and arsenal workers, and the development of a navy of small, mobile ships, torpedo-boats and submarines which would defend French coasts more adequately than the large, prestigious cruisers commissioned by his predecessor. From outside the Chamber Pelletan was smeared as dishonest and drunken, Drumont's *Libre Parole* one among many Nationalist publications to accuse him in 1903 of taking money from the infamous fraudsters Thérèse and Frédéric Humbert, a calumny of which he was cleared, but not without damage to his authority. The case against him seemed to his detractors to be proven by contamination, when General André, the Minister of War, with similar democratizing aims, fell victim to an exposé in October 1904 which showed him secretly and crassly employing informers and members of the Freemasonic lodges to discover and discredit Catholic officers in the army. The army files affair (*affaire des fiches*) forced André's resignation, and its lingering effects eventually brought the resignation of Combes and the end of Pelletan's ministry, but Radical confidence was not affected. The military verdict on Dreyfus was

finally quashed after a review set up by General André, and Dreyfus himself was decorated with the Légion d'Honneur at a full ceremony at the École Militaire on 22 July 1906. By then Clemenceau was Minister of the Interior, his whole past personifying the republican patriotic tradition.

Nationalist but not republican: Action Française

There was no doubt in the mind of Charles Maurras that the Nationalist movement identified mainly with Déroulède, Barrès, Lemaître and Drumont had made one crucial mistake. Maurras, the literary critic, poet and political writer from Martigues in Provence, combined a sanctimonious nationalism with atheism and doctrinaire positivism; he had been almost completely deaf since adolescence and hated the impenetrable noise of argument and urban life; he had defended the forgery of Colonel Henry in the Dreyfus Affair and proclaimed his suicide as martyrdom, and in 1900 had published his enquiry into monarchism and his conviction that only an authoritarian and hierarchical monarch could rescue 'true France' from the grip of 'anti-France', whom he defined as Jews, Protestants, Freemasons, Socialists, Radical Republicans and, for good measure, the *métèques*, a word for 'stranger' in Greek city-states, used as a term of xenophobic abuse. Nationalism, proclaimed Maurras, must be monarchist or it will fail. Its readiness to preserve some form of republic, he argued, had been the reason for its eclipse after 1902.

Little known outside the intellectual circles of the anti-Dreyfusards, Maurras, the positivist, presented his views not as opinions but as facts. He took from Auguste Comte not only a methodology but the obsession with dissent as chaos and anarchy. When he ventured into the streets of Paris he collected shopkeepers' and professional names containing letters of the alphabet which he claimed were factually not French. His *pays réel* was similar to that of Barrès, but in his monarchist canon the preference for rural culture carried a further rationale which insisted on the end of republican *départements* and the restoration of the ancient provinces of pre-revolutionary France.

On 21 March 1908 the fringe right-wing movement of Action Française, which Maurras had converted to monarchism almost from its beginning in 1899, launched a newspaper of the same name. *L'Action française* was sold on the streets by young members of the movement who took the name Camelots du Roi, literally 'the King's street-vendors' with the connotation of political vanguard, fighter, zealot and martyr to the cause. Largely students from the Parisian bourgeoisie and Nationalist *quartiers*, the

Camelots were organized by Maurice Pujo and led by a twenty-year-old art student, Maxime Réal del Sarte, a descendant of the Florentine painter whose family had been in France since the time of François I. For del Sarte, as for Nationalist students before him, the symbolic national figure, with her statue in Archdéacon's Paris constituency, was Joan of Arc. Regular patrolling of her statue and a keen watch on her treatment by critics, historians and sceptics in university circles quickened into violent disruption of lectures given by a Professor Thalamas, who questioned the divine mission attributed to her. For several weeks in the winter of 1908–9 the Latin Quarter of Paris was once again the scene of violent student clashes in which this new radical right-wing Nationalism paraded its total opposition to the Republic.

In their readiness to entertain alliance with any anti-republican force the leaders of Action Française, Maurras included, courted the self-styled prophet of syndicalism, Georges Sorel, and set up a Proudhon Circle animated by Georges Valois to develop a strategy for Nationalist–syndicalist co-operation, an echo of the attempts by Maurice Barrès in the late 1880s to create a union of Nationalism and socialism. Both used the equation of capitalists and Jews as a unifying device, and both failed to make any impact on the development and direction of either socialism or syndicalism. The version of Nationalism, refined in the doctrinal columns of *L'Action française* and spread from aristocratic students to a truculent and nostalgic squirearchy in the provinces, became known as integral, one based on a complete exclusion of everything defined as anti-France. It was highly significant in the reformulation of the radical right, but of negligible importance in the direction of national politics between 1900 and 1914, both internally and in the field of foreign affairs.

2. *Republican nationalism/patriotism*

Social defence

The policies of Combes and Clemenceau were carefully monitored by social conservatives for any sign of concessions to the forces of labour or to the proponents of income tax. The solid resistance of Clemenceau to syndicalism established a broad social base for republicanism within the business bourgeoisie and the middle classes which largely defined mainstream French nationalism in the twentieth century. This broad base was established with more state intervention than classic economic liberalism ostensibly favoured, and what eventually made France conspicuously different from

Britain and the USA at many points in the century was the extent to which a politics of *dirigisme* (state interventionism) was accepted.

As the Republic's social roots spread and deepened within the heterogeneous classes of property, ownership, business and management, it became increasingly apparent that successive governments were performing a successful balancing act between political radicalism and social conservatism. In a decade of street jugglers and acrobats there were few tightrope acts more symbolic of the time than the faltering steps towards and away from a progressive income tax. This long-overdue fiscal reform was particularly associated with the career of Joseph Caillaux. Descended from Protestant bankers through his Norman mother, and with a railway engineer and administrator as his father, Caillaux was Minister of Finance in the Clemenceau government from 1906 to 1909, and it was on 3 March 1909 that the deputies finally voted for an income tax bill. The Senate, guardian of social conservatism, carried out its role, and the bill was stopped. For years it was tossed between the Senate and the Chamber, as opposition to it grew dramatically outside parliament, revealing the very considerable strength of organized business.

Employers had responded to the organization of labour in the CGT by creating federations and unions to co-ordinate their own response to strikes and to social and fiscal reform. The powerful metal and mining interests of the Comité des Forges and the Comité des Houillères, dating from the Second Empire, came together to form the Union des Industries Métallurgiques et Minières in 1900, with its secretary, Robert Pinot, a professional technocrat, disseminating ideas which reflected the continuing importance of the Social Catholicism of Frédéric Le Play. Modernization was seen as best promoted through paternalism, so that the Schneider metalworks at Le Creusot near Autun and the Michelin universe at Clermont-Ferrand were seen as models of good business and caring employment, with workers' housing and provision for insurance and savings combined with a robust social defence against syndicalist encroachment. The term 'social defence' took on nationalist overtones to the point that state force against strikers and paternalist control within manufacturing became seen as joint strands in protection of the nation's economy. The two were fused in the training and outlook of the Republic's new management vanguard, the professional engineers (*ingénieurs*) with their historic prototype Gustave Eiffel, and their contemporary exemplar the Schneider director Émile Cheysson, educated at the École Polytechnique, one of the many *polytechniciens* who formed an élite of professionals in both military and civilian service.

The Republic's credibility in business circles was further advanced when Aristide Briand, Clemenceau's successor as Prime Minister and initially a practitioner of 'social harmony', reacted to a threatened railway strike in October 1910 by decreeing a 28-day mobilization of 15,000 railway workers into the army and the arrest of the entire strike committee. Railway workers were now subject to military discipline should they disobey orders. The strike collapsed. Briand's tactics of social defence, a legislative version of Napoleonic methods 100 years before, sealed his total break from the Socialists, whom he had left in 1905 for a career with no party attachment. Caillaux, Prime Minister and Minister of the Interior in 1911, announced that he was there to create a government which would govern against the forces of social disintegration, but in 1911 social defence and national defence, political radicalism and social conservatism, the future of income tax and Caillaux's public image were all reshaped by the exigency of foreign affairs. Germany sent a gunboat to Agadir.

A nationalist foreign policy

The fall of the Foreign Minister, Théophile Delcassé, on 6 June 1906 was interpreted in the Foreign Office and in a diffuse spread of national newspapers as an unnecessary concession to German sensitivities over Morocco. Without serious self-questioning a climate of single-minded anti-Germanism took root in the country, eclipsing the anti-British sentiment of colonial rivalry and giving a new bite to the habitual patriotism of school classes, in which children routinely, but abstractly, remembered the lost provinces of Alsace-Lorraine and sang, as everywhere in nationalist Europe, *Mourir pour la patrie, C'est le sort le plus beau* ('There is no finer end than to die for one's country'). School maps ritually coloured Alsace and Lorraine in violet, the colour of mourning. The drama of the *affaire des fiches* and the fate of General André was symptomatic of a nervousness about the army's role in society, which a more focused sense of international tension with Germany did much to dispel.

The inheritance of Gambetta was ubiquitous and pervasive. The references back to his aspirations for France after the Franco-Prussian War proclaimed him as the guide and mentor for patriots in general and the Foreign Office in particular. The aim of all policy was to prevent a second humiliation at the hands of Germany. Harbouring deep suspicions of Germany's intentions in the Mediterranean, Delcassé was an early percipient of Germany's drive for world power (*Weltpolitik*). He was an avowed follower of Gambetta, as were his ambassadorial team, notably Paul

Cambon in London, his brother Jules Cambon in Madrid and later in Berlin, and Camille Barrère in Rome. They respected and even rivalled Delcassé in his passion for secrecy, codes and ciphers, and helped to create a culture of independence for the diplomatic corps which made the French Foreign Office at the Quai d'Orsay one of the most autonomous in Europe. In Berlin Jules Cambon, a key player in Franco-German relations, was motivated by the concern that the test of French strength would be its ability to avoid another war with Germany, the most pacific version of Gambetta's legacy. His influence was marked by an economic agreement with Germany in 1909 which envisaged mutual co-operation in areas of financial and commercial rivalry, notably in Morocco, but he was soon accusing the Foreign Office officials of sabotaging his efforts at détente and removing all substance from the agreement. Their obsession with staying one move ahead of Germany, he believed, was not without influence in the decision in April 1911 to occupy Fez, the old Islamic cultural centre of Morocco, which broke French undertakings to Germany. It provoked the Germans into retaliation. On 1 July 1911 the German gunboat *Panther* arrived at the Moroccan port of Agadir. No one underestimated the crisis.

Caillaux as the succeeding Prime Minister faced not only a rampantly assertive Germany but also the strength of nationalist fervour among the established circles of the republic. It was apparent just how solid was the mainstream nationalism of Foreign Office officials, the Colonial Lobby, the industrial and financial magnates and the influential press headed by *Le Temps* and the *Journal des débats*. Throughout the late summer he worked to improvise a settlement which would defuse the crisis. On 4 November 1911 a Franco-German agreement was signed, by which a substantial portion of French colonial conquests in the Congo was traded to the Germans in exchange for their acceptance of the long-conceived French protectorate over Morocco. The Quai d'Orsay stiffened the final clauses relating to Morocco. The population of the Congo and the people of Morocco were not consulted, as anti-colonialists were quick to point out, but it was certainly not this which prompted the outrage of Nationalist voices in parliament and the press: they accused Caillaux of underhand methods and the sacrifice of French colonial possessions. He countered with the plausible claim that his actions had prevented war.

It was not immediately apparent that 1911 was a watershed in French politics, but a year later it was far clearer that something fundamental had changed. The elections of 1910 had seen a dilution of the meaning of Radicalism. Seats were lost to Socialists on the left and conservative republicans on the right, but the left-wing majority was still intact. It was the clear

sense of purpose of the Bloc des Gauches of 1902 to 1906 which was missing. Radicals on the left, such as Caillaux, still believed in a Radical and Socialist alignment, and the declared backing for income tax by many of the Radical candidates made such an alliance feasible, but they were shackled by the way in which the recent governments had permanently alienated the Socialists. A reformulation of the Bloc des Gauches was never close to realization. Instead, the choice of the moderate, liberal republican Raymond Poincaré as Premier in 1912 and as President of the Republic in 1913 was an expression of the new dominance of social and national defence. In December 1912 *Le Matin* carried an advertisement for Michelin, denouncing German rubber teats as dangerous for French babies. It was a telling sign of what had become normative nationalism. Poincaré seemed a safe choice to embody this mainstream. Already seen as a non-partisan, national figure, his ministerial declaration opposed both income tax and social reform. His foremost priority was 'to give the country the feeling of security'.

A pacifist alternative?

Nationalism did not command ubiquitous allegiance. Within the Socialist Party and the CGT an international mode of political thought and action shaded into anti-militarism and pacifism, and within the more historic tradition of republican patriotism there were eloquent voices raised for peace. Exactly spanning the first fourteen years of the century, Charles Péguy's review, *Cahiers de la Quinzaine*, allowed a rare glimpse of pacifist and anti-pacifist ideas presented as dynamic alternatives. They were two sides of Péguy's own intellectual ambivalence, but it was significant that his anti-militarism at the time of his youthful socialism during the Dreyfus Affair seemed to him to have been superseded not so much by a change of heart as by events.[2] His reactions to the first Moroccan crisis of 1905, expressed in his work *Notre Patrie* (*Our Fatherland*), seemed to tell him that there was now a necessity for nationalist fervour, but he gave space for Gustave Hervé to elaborate his contrary title and ideas, embodied in *Leur Patrie* (*Their Fatherland*) of the same year. Hervé had been a history teacher at the lycée in Sens to the east of Paris, and he was soon to be known as the country's most outspoken anti-militarist. Fired from his teaching post, he moved on to being a barrister in Paris, only to be revoked from the bar as his journalism scourged the capitalists, the army, colonialism and patriotism. At the height of the syndicalist offensive, he set the scathing insurgency of his newspaper *La Guerre sociale* against the

police and military tactics of Clemenceau. He preached to the cathedral dignitaries at Sens that Christianity commanded that 'You shall not kill'.

The opinions of Jean Jaurès were also given expression in the *Cahiers* and although his voice was constantly raised in defence of internationalism and pacifism he took issue with Hervé over the negative meaning he gave to patriotism. The socialist agenda for Jaurès meant bringing the workers to the fore of national politics and using patriotism as a spur to social progress. Jaurès saw the revolutionary tradition as a patriotism for peace, and in his critical work on the theory of patriotism published in 1911, *L'Armée nouvelle* (*The New Army*), he refused to put the *patrie* above the human person or above human rights. On the question of the 'lost provinces' of Alsace and Lorraine he preferred to try to negotiate their autonomy rather than risk any military confrontation with Germany.

The voice of the Socialists in foreign affairs was almost entirely that of Jaurès, but this was not equivalent to actual power in the decision-making process. On most foreign issues between 1905 and 1914 the Socialists were outvoted in the Chamber, and their integration in the Second International alongside the German Social Democratic Party meant that it was comparatively easy for Nationalists to equate them with pro-German sentiment. Of all the many political crossings in the wake of the Dreyfus Affair, that of journalist Urbain Gohier from virulent anti-militarism to an equally passionate defence of the army gave the Nationalists extra venom against Jaurès, in what became a campaign of personal vilification. Gohier accused Jaurès of conspiring to provoke the threatened railway strike of 1910 as a paid agent of Germany, and several newspapers of the right took to labelling him Herr Jaurès.

From 1910 anti-militarists found themselves faced by a cult of youthful energy which glorified action and the romance of war and promoted the philosophy of Henri Bergson, an old friend of Jaurès and Péguy from Dreyfusard days, whose treatise of 1907, *L'Évolution créatrice*, discerned a dynamic life-force (*élan vital*) at the centre of the natural world which reached its highest realization and self-consciousness in human behaviour. Bergson's philosophy was both cause and effect of a move away from the rationalism of the early years of the century. The fact that Bergson was Jewish gave the antisemitic Nationalists an ideological problem, but at a time of renewed middle-class interest in religion, saints, the occult and all forms of spiritualism it was easy for them to appropriate his mystique of vitality for militarist action. In its idolization of the army the cult revelled in the strong-arm tactics used by Clemenceau, and its discourse was aimed at middle-class male youth, as yet untried in physical hardship or national

service. The army promised little to working youths who had seen at close hand the repression exercised by Clemenceau, but after 1910 the syndicalist wave began to ebb, due partly to the successes of reformism, partly to a marginal but cumulative improvement in the standard of living, and partly to the illusory nature of the revolutionary strike. A general strike was declared for 16 December 1912 at the height of the Balkan crisis, but it did not happen, except in the Ardennes, in Lyon and in certain mining areas. At the same time the intoxication of Nationalism turned individual heads and lives. In the most astonishing conversion of the period Gustave Hervé between 1910 and 1914 progressively abandoned his anti-militarism for its opposite, identification with the army. Péguy's litanies of Nationalist rhetoric were now punctuated by visceral attacks on his old friend Jaurès. On 7 March 1913 2,000 youths prevented Jaurès from speaking in Nice against the increase in national service from two to three years, and it was on this issue that sides were most bitterly divided in the aftermath of Agadir.

The three-year bill

The key to the giant moral and political stature of Jaurès, beard thrust forward and upward, short arms gesticulating fiercely, was his capacity for working out alternative solutions. He was no mere antagonist: he overshadowed all other politicians by the sheer drive of his positive proposals. He was a breaker of moulds, not so much a negotiator as a visionary without the usual attendant dogmatism. He could imagine clearly how legislation, policy, attitudes could be different. He sustained socialism within republicanism, pacifism within patriotism, and internationalism within a deep identity with his native Tarn and its specific history of struggle by Cathars, Protestants, and now miners, glass-blowers, small-town social-ists and the workers in his birthplace, Castres. Idealistic, optimistic, anti-militarist, he even had a positive plan for the army. On 14 November 1910 he presented a project to the Chamber for a democratized officer corps and a restructuring of national service to produce an effective and enlarged citizen army in the reserves. Article 16 contained words which defined all war as criminal unless it was self-evidently defensive, and on these grounds he defended patriotism in *L'Armée nouvelle*. By contrast, the High Com-mand of the army was increasingly geared to an offensive strategy, one of quick and decisive attack, dramatically imagined by Colonel Grandmaison of the War Ministry and solidly endorsed by General Joffre, head of the General Staff. In 1913 the arms race with Germany quickened with the German plans for massive military growth, which would take the German

standing army to 850,000 as against the French numbers of 480,000. Given the negative population ratio of 60:40, the rapid, offensive strategy became all the more convincing to army leaders as the only viable French answer. Such an offensive would require a larger standing army and an increase in the length of military service.

In fact, for secrecy reasons the offensive plans of the High Command were not announced as the reason for the three-year bill, a project presented to the Chamber early in March 1913 by Eugène Étienne, the War Minister in a Briand government. The fears of Socialist opponents, volubly expressed at all levels of debate, parliamentary and public, were hardly calmed by the right-wing press of *La Patrie*, *Le Gaulois*, *L'Écho* and *Le Figaro* which recommended the extension to three years as an extra opportunity for the discipline of the barracks to destroy the democratic and disrespectful sentiments of the average republican conscript. In mid-May riots against a third year briefly flared among conscripts already enlisted in various garrisons including towns close to the Alsace-Lorraine border, Toul, Nancy and Belfort, and critical reaction to these, possibly more than the whole campaign of the Nationalist right, swung doubters in the centre of the Chamber behind the bill. On 19 July 1913 the bill was carried by 358 to 204.

Far from secondary to the issue of numbers was that of finance. Who would, or should, pay? Caillaux's return to the Ministry of Finance in December was a reminder that the Radical left had not been sidelined by the debate. He saw this clearly as the time to step up the pressure for Senate to accept the progressive income tax voted by the Chamber four years before. The arguments for the tax had featured prominently in the public debates on the three-year bill. Once the bill was passed, acceptance of income tax seemed inevitable to Caillaux and to Jaurès, but the opposition of the social defence lobby was still entrenched. *Le Figaro* sank into gutter politics. Its editor, Gaston Calmette, had laid his hands on Caillaux's love letters written to the Minister's new spouse Henriette while he was seeking a divorce from his previous wife. He threatened to publish them. On 16 March 1914 Henriette Caillaux, in a sensational *coup de théâtre*, arrived at the offices of *Le Figaro* and shot Calmette dead. For all her justifications and her acquittal at the end of July, it marked a catastrophic descent of personal outrage into murder. Caillaux was forced to resign, yet another opportunity for a Caillaux–Jaurès alignment was lost, and the pressure on the Senate was temporarily lifted. Throughout the three-year debate and the Calmette–Caillaux affair, Poincaré appeared to enshrine national stability and internal reconciliation. It was Poincaré who stepped still

further into centre stage when the Archduke Franz-Ferdinand was assassinated on 28 June 1914 in Sarajevo.

Politics and the Presidency, June–July 1914

In the 1914 elections, supporters and opponents of the three-year bill were
roughly equal in numbers. There was a noticeable left-wing drift to the
Socialists, particularly in the first round of voting, and they increased their
seats from 74 to 103. It was not evident that the bill was the major factor
in voting behaviour in all areas, although in many constituencies it gave an
added focus to already existing social tensions. In the Var, for example,
several months of fervent and physical opposition to the bill certainly
helped the Socialists to win all four seats for the first time. The SFIO gains
were a vote for social reform, of that there is no doubt, and the voters as a
whole were far from bellicose. They remained steadily convinced that the
Chambers of 1906 and 1910 contained the republican forces necessary to
serve their interests, and there was no move towards the Nationalist right.

Among the organizations of those who were not allowed to vote, pacifism
had been a constant feminist position, combined with expressions of patriotism. In the face of pro-natalists such as Fernand Boverat, who declared
in 1913 that women should give their country at least four children or
be considered 'no better than deserters',[3] most feminists concentrated
on demanding improved maternity rights and care. In this they were increasingly successful, with a law of 17 June 1913 creating compulsory paid
maternity leave for all women workers. Only a few feminists such as
Madeleine Pelletier and Nelly Roussel rejected the social primacy of motherhood, but there were no signs that either women or men in any meaningful
numbers were influenced by calls for an increased birth rate for 'the good
of the nation'. Nevertheless the very notion that motherhood was a national
duty could only reinforce the overwhelming logic of women's right to full
citizenship. During the elections of 1914 the campaign reached a crescendo,
with feminists organizing their own concurrent poll of women, asking them
whether or not they wanted the vote. It brought in over 500,000 votes for
women's suffrage and only a handful against. Suggested by Gustave Téry,
editor of the major daily *Le Journal* which had promoted votes for women,
the runaway success of the poll was followed by the largest street demonstration so far achieved in the history of the movement for women's rights,
when between 5,000 and 6,000 women gathered in the Jardin des Tuileries
in Paris on 5 July 1914 for a march across the Seine.

The destination of the march was the statue of Condorcet, the Enlighten-

ment pioneer of political rights for women. Hubertine Auclert had died in April 1914, but several years previously she had proposed a ceremonial honouring of Condorcet. It still did not reconcile the socialist feminist Louise Saumoneau to the suffrage movement, which she continued to see as a middle-class cause, but she had her own triumph on 9 March 1914 when the first rally in Paris to celebrate International Women's Day attracted over 2,000 women and men. On 29 July, the day after Austria's declaration of war on Serbia, Saumoneau produced a tract which rejected the 'murderous barbarism' of war and called on all women comrades to recognize that their sons, brothers and husbands would be fighting their comrades from beyond the frontiers: 'Will you allow this monstrous massacre to take place?'[4]

In the intricate mix of internal politics and the increasing threat from external affairs it is still difficult to discern exactly who in mid-1914 allowed what to happen. The disarray of the Radicals during the three-year bill and their fragmentation into a politics of individualities made it difficult for them to arrive at a collective voice, even though they were still technically the largest grouping in parliament: the Socialists were united and stronger than ever but still refused to play an executive role in any non-socialist government, while a coalition of the right would fail to gain a majority in the Chamber. As a result Poincaré's Presidential role as national figurehead became steadily more political as the international crisis deepened. Historians, in their search for 'responsibility' in 1914, have naturally followed this shift in the balance of power away from political parties and parliamentary figures towards the Presidency. For a period in the 1920s and 1930s Poincaré was attributed with a crucial role after Sarajevo in hardening French nationalist attitudes and stiffening Russian resistance to Austria-Hungary, but as more and more national archives became available, research in the late twentieth century began to discount him as a dynamic force in the making of war.

Raymond Poincaré's appointments to his cabinet when he was Premier in January 1912 were highly revealing of his political personality: Aristide Briand, the moderator of anticlericalism on the one hand and the mobilizer of striking railway workers on the other; Alexandre Millerand, the first socialist to accept a government position in 1899; Léon Bourgeois, the theoretician of class co-operation and *solidarisme*, and Théophile Delcassé, architect of the Entente Cordiale with Britain and consistently wary of German expansionism. As a boy of ten in a traditional republican family Poincaré had experienced the humiliation of the Prussian occupation of his home town, Bar-le-Duc, in 1870–73, while his training in law had grafted

professional concepts on to his personal sense of injustice at the German annexations of Alsace and large areas of his native Lorraine. The French claim to these provinces was taken for granted by Poincaré, as it was by the vast majority of the population. The political right, who voted for him *en bloc*, welcomed a President who came closer to being a strong national leader than any President of the Third Republic since the late 1870s. Poincaré, however, was fully aware of the left-wing strength of the Chamber and although he came close to overstepping his constitutional position, and was described by Jaurès in *L'Humanité* as having inclinations towards dictatorship, he drew back from anything approaching an irreparable collision.

In June 1914 a power struggle between President and Chamber looked possible at any moment. No such struggle occurred. Poincaré's knowledge and calm in foreign affairs countered Premier Viviani's singular unease and lack of inside information, which became apparent during the state visit to Russia and Scandinavia which began on 16 July. Three days before, Senator Charles Humbert had brought internal disarray by startling revelations in his commissioned report on the state of supplies and equipment in the French army. Clemenceau launched one of his most blistering attacks on the failures of government, which he now accused of leaving France undefended, while in Germany Humbert's disclosures were greeted with concealed delight by those intent on launching an offensive as soon as the military and diplomatic situation was at its most favourable. That precise moment was now seen by German decision-makers to be imminent, and while Poincaré and Viviani were out of the country decisions were taken in Vienna and Berlin which were intended to precipitate war.

Viviani, partly through ill-health on the journey, allowed Poincaré to assume full control on the Russian visit, a voyage planned to last a full fortnight and not postponed after Humbert's disclosures, in itself suggesting that the French Foreign Office and Presidency did not envisage a rapidly escalating crisis. There is no convincing evidence that Poincaré encouraged belligerence by Nicholas II or Sazonov, the Russian Foreign Minister, beyond the necessity to stand firm against provocation. He was as concerned as he had been since 1912 to avoid allowing France to be dragged into war by an intemperate Russian act. His support for Russia remained conditional, and far from being provocative he was always one step behind events after Austria's ultimatum to Serbia. This left him in a moral position of defensive innocence: he avoided the mistake of 1870 when Napoleon III fell into Bismarck's trap and was provoked into declaring war. In July 1914 Poincaré may be said to have allowed the war crisis to develop, but only in

the secondary sense that he was responding to decisions taken outside France and did not produce a radical diplomatic initiative for peace.

Last rites

Even Jaurès, pursuing his hopes for a détente with Germany right to the end, told the Socialist International in Brussels on 29 July that the French government wanted peace and was working to preserve it. He appealed to socialists of all countries to bring about 'the unchained revolution' and secure peace and justice. On 26 July Léon Jouhaux and other leaders of the CGT, who had largely followed the political initiatives of the SFIO during the three-year bill, used the columns of *La Bataille syndicaliste* to reiterate the syndicalist call for a revolutionary general strike in the event of war, and on the following day Parisian workers responded positively to a call for an evening of street demonstrations in favour of peace, resulting in several clashes with the police, and a government order which banned further peace meetings. It seemed a sign of the confusion of the Socialist leadership that these demonstrations were given only sparse coverage in *L'Humanité*, with the inference that Jaurès himself was now anxious not to antagonize the government and risk losing the influence for peace he still possessed.

On his return from Belgium Jaurès was faced with the news that the government had ordered troops to take up defensive positions from Luxembourg to the Vosges, but to stay ten kilometres from the frontier. It was tantamount to a partial but cautious mobilization, and Jaurès went straight to Viviani to check that the intention was truly defensive and to discover whether syndicalists and socialists on the police file known as *Carnet B* were about to be arrested in a state of emergency. Viviani mixed conciliation with evasion, but it was clear from the reactions of the CGT leaders that the threat of arrest had had its effect. The tone of *La Bataille syndicaliste* softened, and on 31 July the national committee of the CGT met in the evening and agreed to do nothing to endanger the efforts of the Socialist politicians for peace. At the time of the meeting Jaurès was eating with his close journalist colleagues at the Café du Croissant in the rue Montmartre. He never heard the decision of the CGT leaders. At 9.40 p.m. he was shot twice by a half-deranged assassin, Raoul Villain, who made no attempt to escape. Villain told the police that Jaurès was a traitor who had to be killed. The news sped overnight across the country. The reaction was the same everywhere: 'They've killed Jaurès.' It had been predicted many times in the previous few years: the hate campaign in the right-wing media had cast

him as a paid German agent, subversive, treacherous and anti-French. His assassination was a permanent possibility. On 17 July 1914 *Paris-Midi* contained the words, 'Any general on the eve of war who orders four men and a corporal to put Jaurès against a wall and shoot him will surely have done no more than his most elementary duty.' It was not a lone voice, but even Jaurès's arch-enemies were stunned by the act which their nationalist fervour had done so much to promote. The whole press condemned the killing, including *L'Action française.* Among his supporters and all those who still wanted peace the last hope seemed to have gone. In all communities of workers the sense of loss and anger was deep: Jaurès was loved as a personal friend. It was a powerful and ubiquitous emotion which could not be left without focus. The last tragic irony of July 1914 is that it was channelled into a fatalistic acceptance of war. The death of Jaurès was conscripted for the cause of national unity. On 2 August the full mobilization order was resisted by only 1.5 per cent of those called to arms. The army's High Command had forecast a refusal rate of 13 per cent.

Swift letters of condolence from Poincaré and the government's immediate identification with the grief of the Socialist Party had much to do with this appropriation of the stature and reputation of Jaurès for national defence. Poincaré watched Socialist reactions almost hour by hour in the first two days and found them positive. Within a day, working-class anger had found its target in German autocracy and military aggression. Avenging the death of their leader was sublimated in defiant expressions of patriotic duty. The trend of turning hostility inwards was reversed. The internal enemy who had killed Jaurès was externalized. German belligerence and Villain's vile act were conjoined. 'They', the perpetrators, were threatening the republic: the response was 'Vive Jaurès, vive la France'. It is tempting to conclude that this was entirely the result of skilful manipulation from above, but this would be inaccurate. From below, ordinary workers and peasants allowed it to happen, and the leaders of the CGT and the SFIO failed to create a viable practice of pacifist action. It can even be said that Jaurès himself with his recognition of the citizen army as the ultimate defence of the republic had prepared his own metamorphosis into a symbol of patriotic unity. His relentless campaigning for international socialist solidarity, his years of investment in Franco-German co-operation and understanding, and his passionate opposition to the three-year bill should not be eclipsed, but at many levels the leaders and the militants of socialism allowed action against war to crumble away, leaving only the rhetoric of peace.

Germany declared war on Russia on 1 August and continued to demand

that France should declare its hand. Joffre had not ceased to argue that the ten-kilometre decision put French mobilization at least two days behind that of Germany, with the terrifying calculation that this would mean an immediate loss of twenty kilometres of French territory the moment that hostilities were formally engaged. The government conceded that full mobilization should start on 2 August, but still without advancing into the ten-kilometre zone whose importance was seen by Poincaré as a guarantee to Britain of French defensive intentions. With Sir Edward Grey equally unwilling to decide on war, the Germans had to formalize their offensive. On 3 August they declared war on France and demanded unrestricted passage through Belgium, which the Belgians refused. Confident in the reactions of the Socialists whom he had monitored so closely since the death of Jaurès, Poincaré built his message to parliament round his central political theme of national unity in the face of the enemy, transformed into the phrase *union sacrée*. Grey spoke in the House of Commons in favour of intervention on the side of France, and on 4 August the Germans invaded Belgium, defying the British to act. Poincaré's message was read to the Chamber and Senate and was greeted with unanimous enthusiasm and emotional applause. The Socialist deputies joined in voting the war credits. At midnight of 4 August both Britain and France were at war on the side of Tsarist Russia. Earlier in the day the mourners at the funeral of Jean Jaurès had listened to an unscripted oration given by the leader of the CGT, Léon Jouhaux, who, according to one reconstructed version, exclaimed, 'It was not his fault, or ours, if the cause of peace has not triumphed . . .' The responsibility for war lay with 'imperialism, the savagery of militarism . . . and the bloody face of despotism'. He declared that he, like others, was heading 'towards a massacre' and in such words he reassured the rest of France that the CGT was not engaged in a different direction. They were the last rites of Jaurès, peace, and the syndicalist alternative to war.

4

Total War, 1914–1918

1. The war of movement

From *commune* to *commune*, from household to household, the reaction to the general mobilization and the outbreak of war varied from shock and pessimism to stoical acceptance. The *union sacrée* proclaimed by Poincaré did not manifest itself in villages or towns in a ubiquitous show of spontaneous enthusiasm. The men were conscripted: they did not have to volunteer, though a certain number of fathers, reprieved because of age or the size of their families, did so. The change came with the actual departure of the soldiers for the front. At train stations all over France emotions broke into the open. Tears, painful separations, high spirits, expressions of enthusiasm and bravado, patriotic songs and declarations of imminent victory were noted by individuals in their diaries and by schoolteachers, instructed by the Minister of Education, Albert Sarraut, to keep a record of public response and behaviour. Resignation yielded to a more extrovert assertion of confidence. Signs of collective refusal were palpably absent.

What was also absent was any clear understanding of what the war might involve beyond the epic notions of heroism and sacrifice. It was thought that only those who departed had gone to the war: it was barely envisaged how far the war would be a civil and not just a military experience, nor was there any intimation of how mass and technology would affect the nature of warfare. The uniforms of the infantry were symptomatic. The blue tunics and the scarlet trousers, the red-and-blue hats belonged visibly to the military culture of the previous century. Many of the first letters home heightened the illusion: there was an impatience to make an individual impact on the enemy. The young Anatole Castex, from Mirande in the Gers, who was made an officer in early September, wrote to his wife on 19 August, 'I am sure that you also would rather that I were close to the enemy and that I had played my part in winning a victory.' By the end of August, after his first encounter, there is a rueful pointer to the mechanical

realities: he wrote to his sister, 'On the whole the men held up well, and we kept our positions for the whole day, despite our considerable losses and 20,000 German shells.'[1] The attempt at quantifying experience signals a new language of mass, size and number. As thousands of trains arrived from all corners of France into the terminus stations of Paris, press commentary was staggered by the masses of soldiers disgorging in the capital. In the first mobilization, reservists up to the age of forty-eight were recalled; the provincial barracks were full; in all over 4 million men were under arms. Industry everywhere was initially paralysed. The first sign of total war was the realization that there had to be more to logistics than entraining heroic individuals to meet the enemy.

The full impact of this realization was delayed by the hopes placed in a decisive victory at the front, despite the fact that the Germans secured a territorial advantage by the invasion of the north-east. This initial period of German advance and occupation pushed the discourse of war into hyperboles of patriotism, and dehumanized the enemy. It silenced the residual doubts about French war aims, which were now all too obviously geared to driving out the invader and defeating German 'barbarity'. This justification was not permanently undermined by any subsequent event.

Human losses on an unparalleled scale were already in evidence to the military authorities when 40,000 French soldiers were killed between 20 and 23 August in futile and largely theoretical attempts to realize General Joffre's strategy of aggression through Lorraine and the Ardennes. They advanced defiantly upright in their colourful uniforms and were shot down before they could establish a forward position. The so-called Battle of the Frontiers brought instant retreat which might have become a rout, and indeed the Germans reached a front line within forty kilometres of Paris, but Joffre finally demonstrated a strategic understanding and a cool-headed sense of realities which could not have been safely predicted a month earlier. His organization of a Franco-British counter-attack on the Marne maximized the railway network close to Paris, which he understood as an engineer who had once been an expert in railway work. The people of Paris had sunk into despair and panic at the unexpected news of the retreat, and thousands of the wealthier inhabitants had left for places of safety, the government following them with an evacuation to Bordeaux on 2 September. The military governor of Paris, General Galliéni, paraded an extra army across the capital, and the population galvanized itself to defend the Marne. Some 4,000 men were ferried to the front by Paris taxis, a civil–military co-operation which was seen immediately as a further episode in the long republican saga of the citizen army.

On the critical days of the Battle of the Marne, from 6 to 9 September 1914, the French and British soldiers recovered fifty kilometres of territory over an extended line from the river Oise to Verdun, with horrendous losses, the French alone losing 25,000 men, drawn from all over France. Their deaths were instantly sanctified as a martyrdom which saved Paris, and there was talk in the newspapers of a decisive victory. Joffre even used such terms in mid-September, just as the Germans had done at the end of August, so quickly had the situation appeared to have changed. But appearances were cruelly deceptive. The German armies embedded themselves in strength in the north-east, and in a series of horrific battles in Picardy and Flanders the so-called 'race to the sea' was in reality the first stage of an increasingly immobilized and unyielding defence of a front line which now stretched from Switzerland to the Pas-de-Calais. By the end of the year the grandiose military designs of the German Schlieffen plan and the French plan XVII were no more than the pencil markings which had scored the large-scale maps of command posts comfortably away from the front. Anatole Castex in the area of Verdun reported to his sister as early as 4 September that they were digging trench after trench and surrounding them with 'a sea of barbed wire'.[2] The French deaths after five months totalled 300,000, and there were 600,000 wounded. It was as if the entire populations of both Lyon and Marseille had been killed or wounded. But the figures were not made public: all statistics of the escalating carnage were kept secret throughout the war. The experience of loss remained essentially at family level, or at most became the shared knowledge of the rural *commune* or urban *quartier*.

Author of the novel *Jean-Christophe*, which revolved round the friendship of a young German and a young Frenchman, Romain Rolland reacted to the first weeks of the war with a declamatory essay entitled *Au-dessus de la mêlée (Above the Conflict)*. It described the war fever which had broken the international solidarity of socialism as a demented passion, engulfing the entire intellectual world. No one, he declared, had resisted the contagion: reason, faith, poetry and science had enlisted unanimously in the regiments of destruction: European civilization was tearing itself apart. Rolland was neutral by conviction and location: from his home in Switzerland he castigated German militarism in particular for having launched the war, but the whole élite of Europe for having sacrificed itself at the shrine of nationalism. His language was bitter and his sense of isolation acute.

Towards a war economy

The needs of the millions of soldiers could only be met by requisitions of food and animals from every rural area. Payment was rarely immediate, and often took the form of government bonds, with interest assured at 5 per cent. Incredibly, it seemed, despite the loss of so much male labour, the autumn harvests of grain, fruit and wine were secured through mutual help between farms, and long hours of extra work by women and children. The collective solidarity of *communes* was the subject of immediate and widespread comment, as was the allocation of roles within the depleted family. As the harvests gave way to winter ploughing, the prefect of the Yonne, in a *département* which borders on the south of the Marne, spoke of the recurrent sight of women guiding the plough and of horses led by ten-year-olds.[3] For many urban authorities, and indeed for the schoolteachers who furnished reports, it was the first time they had scrutinized patterns of rural labour so closely. There is admiration and incredulity at the extent of women's agricultural role but also a recognition of its normality.

Admiration jostled with resentment in some rural areas. The separation and child allowances paid to women whose men were mobilized were, alongside the requisitions, the first sign of a specific war economy. Authorized by a law of 5 August, the allowances could improve the standard of living of women and families previously dependent on the very low wage of a male labourer or on his intermittent work. Some wives of such workers were perceived by neighbours to live better than before the war, a perception expressed with indignation that war should bring providential social opportunities.

In the towns the industrial paralysis was slowly easing by the end of 1914; unemployment stood at 35 per cent in October and was still at 20 per cent in January 1915, although the figures were over twice as high for women workers in textiles and clothing. The recovery led by the rapid expansion in war-essential sectors of the economy led to a redistribution of both male and female labour. Shortage of labour in key war industries began to determine the nature of the war economy. No less than family allowances, the selective economic upturn could easily be read as a basic inequality of both sacrifice and reward. It was simpler to fall back into recriminations within civil society than to mobilize a concerted response to the war. An intensified polarity between country and town was evident in 1915 as the demand for munitions grew and industrial workers were recalled from the front, totalling 500,000 by the end of the year. The

groundswell of rural resentment was directed not against the war but against the privileges of industry.

Defining the enemy

Given the social and political divisions of the decade before 1914, it was not at first obvious how the *union sacrée* would work, if at all. It was therefore something of a surprise for the authorities to find how easily the anti-German emotions of the autumn acted as a form of social bonding. Patriotism thrived on the increasingly virulent images of the invader and accomplices which made up the unacceptable 'other', the cultural and political opposite of everything that France was believed to stand for. As the Germans advanced, spies and traitors were rumoured to be active and ubiquitous. Close to the frontier with the lost provinces of Alsace and Lorraine, Anatole Castex wrote to his sister: 'This area abounds in spies.' A local mayor, he reported, had been shot for giving information to the Germans, and such betrayals were quickly associated with the staggering retreat at the end of August.[4] It was not only at the front that the obsession with spies was manifest. Evidence from all parts of France, including Saint-Étienne, Brive, Tulle and Nice, suggests a mentality of fanatical accusation which swept the country; anyone with a suspicious accent, or still more anyone taking photographs or simply carrying a tripod, might well be arrested or brutalized by the crowd.[5]

Obsession with spies gave way in late 1914 to stories and rumours of German barbarity in the occupied territories of Belgium and north-eastern France. The facts of German atrocities against civilians are still being established and disputed. The Belgian government started investigating the stories immediately, and the French set up a committee of enquiry on 23 September 1914. The testimonies it heard were then added to evidence drawn from the diaries of German soldiers captured after the Battle of the Marne, leading to official reports in 1915 on 'acts committed by the enemy in violation of Human Rights'. An eminent philologist, Joseph Bédier, quoted at length from the German diaries in his impassioned pamphlets of 1915 which spread the conviction that atrocities of all kinds had been perpetrated on an innocent population, including the severing of children's hands, widespread rape of women and girls, the mass shooting and mutilation of civilian hostages and the burning of buildings, most notably churches. Later in the war, the details of trench warfare overshadowed these early images of bestiality, and war itself became the atrocity, while in the inter-war years the stories were largely explained as the excesses of

propaganda. In the climate of official recognition of war crimes at the end of the twentieth century it became clear that the German archives contained other diaries of the war which substantiate those captured in 1914, if not the polemical use which was made of them. The aim of recent researchers has been to contextualize the brutal acts by showing how terrified the German army was of civilian resistance, but the demand by German commanders that the population should passively accept the invasion of their lands still excites incredulity. It was the last symptom of a past military ethic in which war was the exclusive concern of regular troops. They knew this was now archaic, but did not know how to adapt. Kurt Riezler, private secretary to the German Chancellor Bethmann Hollweg, also knew that the executions of civilians in Belgium which he recorded in his diary 'marked a terrible tragedy in the war, perhaps also in the destiny of the German people'.[6]

The dominance of number

The mutilations most evident to some French people at the start of the war were those caused by shells on the bodies of the injured who were evacuated to hospitals far from the front. In Narbonne on the Languedoc coast a first frisson of public curiosity quickly gave way to indifference, wrote Louis Barthas in his diary, one of the outstanding personal and literary chronicles of the war. The 35-year-old cooper from the village of Peyriac-Minervois in the Aude was a corporal throughout the war, and with remarkable insight and sardonic humour he described the everyday experiences of the ordinary soldier (*poilu*) in the most appalling and yet commonplace situations of trench warfare. He had been a militant socialist alongside Dr Ferroul at the time of the revolt of the wine-growers in 1907 and was a close follower of Jean Jaurès. His immediate captain, Léon Hudelle, was a fellow socialist from the same area who showed him instructions from his superiors. It allowed Barthas to document his belief that individual soldiers were consciously sacrificed in a strategy in which more and more men were thrown into the assaults with the conviction that sheer numbers would prevail. In mid-December 1914 he was shown an order which he describes as 'barbaric': 'Attack, no matter what it costs. Pay no attention to losses.'[7]

The attacks ordered by Joffre in 1915 were vain attempts to continue the war of movement. He launched the infantry (*la biffe* in military slang) over and over again in Artois and Champagne against merciless machine-gun fire, incessant shelling and an impenetrable thicket of barbed wire. Léon Sebelin, one of only 800 men left from the original 3,000 of the 155th

Infantry Regiment from Commercy in the Meuse, wrote to his wife on 25 June: 'It's a miracle I am still alive . . . We have been 30 hours without food or drink . . . we have been bombarded with every size of shell, mines, bombs and asphyxiating gas . . . I have thought so much about you.'[8] Joffre clung obstinately to his conviction that the number and *élan* of the attackers, supported instantly by reserves, would break open the German defences, and he was not deterred by repeated failure or by the insignificance of an advance which only measured a handful of metres. It indicated a level of obduracy which historians have criticized even more harshly than Louis Barthas. The attacks were little short of organized massacre, the number of dead mounting to a further 300,000 during the year without any compensation of territory gained, but the French command refused to countenance a major change of tactics. They merely planned a bigger movement for the spring of 1916 to be launched on the Somme. The German command, by contrast, decided that the French could not be broken by the movement of infantry but only by artillery attrition at a point where the French lines, protruding towards Alsace, were exposed from the sides as well the front. The German aim of 1916 was the encirclement and seizure of Verdun, the most advanced position of the French armies.

With the incidence of death and injury so high at the front, the logistics of getting more men under arms and more workers into the munitions factories also raised the question of equity. Who should be mobilized for what became a central issue in 1915, and with it emerged the popular definition of shirkers, the *embusqués*, those who were given jobs away from the front. It was an undiscriminating category, and was used by many to deride all those recalled from the front for factory work, or all those kept in Civil Service positions. Pressure groups formed solely around the issue, but no resolution to the competing demands of the army and industry was found.[9] In the light of this dispute the industrial mobilization of women and immigrant labour was seen as a necessary solution. From 18 May 1915 the Socialist Albert Thomas was at the crux of all munition supplies, first as Under-Secretary of State in the War Ministry with particular responsibility for artillery, then as Minister of Armaments from December 1915 until September 1917. The definition of 'total war', which came into popular usage in 1917, largely derived from the ways in which he and other politicians organized production and confronted its social implications.

2. Defining the nation

On 22 October 1916 Alexandre Millerand, Minister of War from August 1914 to October 1915, gave a lecture at Versailles called 'The War of Liberation' in which he praised 'la résistance française'. Almost all the discourse of managing the home front was already in place: praise for the noble endeavours of both sexes, the admission of past mistakes, the reference to the wider war, the realism, the need for government control, and the moral imperative of patriotic good against evil. Only the promises for the post-war were missing and these would be added abundantly in 1917–18.

The war of 1870 had lasted only a few months. The speed and finality of the Prussian victory had profound effects on the way the French viewed themselves. In 1914 urgent reconsiderations of national identity were not left until the end of the war: they followed immediately after the assassination of Jean Jaurès and the outbreak of war. All three major strands of political identity, republican, nationalist and socialist, were involved. Poincaré's *union sacrée* was the first attempt at a new definition, heavily backed by Catholics and the political right. When Socialists, including the fervent Marxist leader Jules Guesde, entered the coalition government, this sealed an emergency pact between long-term adversaries, and in the first few months of war the definition of the enemy as autocratic, predatory and barbarous had dialectical implications for any assessment of national identity. The process of defining the nation, openly divisive before 1914, became abruptly more inclusive.

Political expression and union rights

Millerand's admission of failures came from the bitter experience of being held responsible for neglecting the artillery in 1914–15 and for being too subservient to military General Headquarters. The Chamber and Senate had been adjourned by President Poincaré for the duration of hostilities, but members insisted on their recall. The President and the government of René Viviani had returned to Paris from Bordeaux on 10 December 1914, and from the following January they faced a Chamber regularly in session but depleted by the 220 deputies who had been mobilized to the front. Patriotic speeches were the staple diet of deputies and senators until the insufficiencies and military stalemate of 1915 rekindled parliamentary opposition, notably from Georges Clemenceau, who had already attacked the inadequacy of medical services and the shortfall in munitions at the end

of 1914, incurring censorship of his newspaper *L'Homme libre*, which, in retaliation he renamed *L'Homme enchaîné*. In 1915 he pursued both Millerand and, more savagely, Joffre, for whose tactics and command he had little but contempt, despite, or perhaps because of, Joffre's continuing popularity in the country.

The negotiator and organizer *par excellence* in 1915 was Albert Thomas. His contribution to updating the artillery, whose field-gun, the seventy-five, was limited by its flat trajectory, resulted in the massive provision of heavy guns and mortars. Supply of labour was now determined by the insatiable demand for shells. The armaments industry, as moulded by Thomas but dominated by big private companies, eventually employed over 1,700,000 workers, and the take-off in numerous small war industries, producing everything from mess-tins to military clothing, enabled Thomas to achieve a rapport with labour which brought Léon Jouhaux as leader of the CGT into a wary but effective co-operation with government.

Although working quite separately, the actions of Clemenceau on the one hand and Thomas and Jouhaux on the other did much to shape two of the earliest aspects of national inclusion during the war. There would be political opposition and there would be a role for the unions. An authoritarian reaction to the emergency situation of autumn 1914 would have insisted on the opposite, but it was here that the definition of the enemy as autocratic acted as a brake. Freedom of expression and freedom for union activity were thus critical elements of French identity which the war initially affirmed, but the limitations on these freedoms were also part of the definition process.

The war of 1914–18 was the first total war for many reasons, not least in the sense that information and propaganda were inextricably entwined in the management of both front and rear. Rudimentary at the time of mobilization, the control of information by the Minister of War was exercised through a press bureau which determined what news should be made available to the press and by the press to its readers. This control was unseen, whereas censorship of written articles or editorials left blank columns in the newpapers and enabled determined journalists such as Clemenceau and Gustave Hervé to portray themselves as victims. Prefects were given extended powers of political censorship, finely attuned to local circumstances. There were no war correspondents: the press was forced to rely on the scant or bland communiqués from military authorities.

Descriptions by individuals of the nature of the fighting were largely anecdotal, but one work stood high above all others. Forty-year-old Henri Barbusse, socialist, humanitarian and pacifist before the war, had volun-

teered in 1914 as a simple soldier. After months in the trenches of Artois and Picardy he was too ill to continue and was moved from hospital to hospital in search of a cure. During this period he wrote *Le Feu* (*Under Fire*) which first appeared in instalments and then in 1916 as a full novel, eventually crowned with the Prix Goncourt, one of the more surprising acts of inclusiveness at the height of the war. The novel was a realistic portrait of the horror of the trenches, with personalized and terrifying images, but with an image of peace and resolution at the end. The brutality and senselessness of war are there, but so is the gentler side of soldiers' fraternity and the sensitivity of suffering. The final scene of hope is conjured out of the fragments of a discussion emerging from the flooded trenches, voices which recognize that ordinary soldiers have the capacity for deciding their own future: ' "All the masses ought to agree with each other" ... "All men ought to be equal". Their eyes are opened. They are beginning to make out the boundless simplicity of things. And Truth not only invests them with a dawn of hope but raises on it a renewal of strength and courage ... And a soldier ventures to add to this sentence, though he begins it with a lowered voice, "If the present war has advanced progress by one step, its miseries and slaughter will count for little." '[10]

Barbusse received immediate letters from the front confirming his picture of the war and expressing gratitude, more than balancing the attacks from the right-wing press. On 2 November 1917 he joined with three socialist colleagues to form the Association Républicaine des Anciens Combattants (ARAC), with its egalitarian slogan 'For equal wounds, equal pensions. A general's leg is not worth more than the leg of a simple soldier'. By November 1918 *Le Feu* had sold almost a quarter of a million copies. Barbusse's account was both popular and enlightening, but despite its success the public at large was still uninformed of the numbers of dead and injured even as the war came to an end, and it has been consistently argued by war historians that ignorance of the horrors of the front played a crucial part in keeping the French people at war.[11]

The limitations to trade-union inclusion came from above and below. Partnership with government and private management was uncharted territory for the unions: Jouhaux's positive response to Thomas and to the Minister of Public Works, Marcel Sembat, also a Socialist, was rejected by some syndicalists as class collaboration. The revolutionary and pacifist leader of the metalworkers' union, Alphonse Merrheim, stayed in Paris with other leaders of the CGT in August 1914 when Jouhaux accompanied the government to Bordeaux. The co-operation of the metalworkers' union was essential for the rapid growth of munitions: it was far from subservient,

but equally far from subversive. The attitudes of Jouhaux and Merrheim were palpably conflictual, but in terms of union rights to represent the workers and bargain for better pay and conditions their policies were complementary, Jouhaux using his position to secure government agreements and Merrheim unyielding in following through the logic of his union's manifesto of 1 May 1915: 'We have a historic mission to fulfil; the atrocious war that we are undergoing should not make us forget it.'[12] In early September 1914 the CGT agreed to join with the Socialist Party in an Action Committee to protect the interests of the workers, and most notably to tackle problems caused by the effects of loss and injury. In the Paris region solidarity with the victims of war was particularly marked in the building unions, in printing and railways: the typographers' union created a 'war tax' which it levied on its non-mobilized members. With the flight of the richer Parisians in late August, the capital seemed to many to have regained some of the idealistic dimension preserved in socialist memory of the Commune of 1871.

Women's paid labour

The greater inclusion of a female industrial workforce into the national identity was clearly a feature of the war, though the trend had been upwards before 1914. By 1918, 20 per cent more women were employed in industry and commerce than before the war. They eventually constituted 25 per cent of the munition workers. In some other sectors the change was more total: from 124 female workers on the Paris métro in 1914 the numbers rose to 3,037 by 1918, over 75 per cent of the workforce. The range of women's work broke almost all the gender taboos on female labour, with only the army holding out against women office workers until the end of 1916. For three years the young urban woman was more independent, with new professional opportunities grasped by many from the middle classes, and working-class women more visibly autonomous at work and at leisure. But the reality of inclusion was ringed with qualifications. The CGT and the Action Committee were vocal in their opposition to the recruitment of non-unionized labour at lower wages. Logically this would involve unionizing women workers and advocating equal pay for equal work. Private employers, however, who dominated the armaments industry would not surrender the discriminatory wage levels which were so manifestly to their advantage.

Two new bodies from unions and government addressed themselves forcefully to all issues of female labour: an Inter-Union Action Committee

against the Exploitation of Women, set up in July 1915 by Gabrielle Duchêne, a 45-year-old activist on all issues of women's domestic labour, and a Committee of Female Labour initiated by Albert Thomas in April 1916, with ten women members and thirty-five men. Duchêne had been at the forefront in pressing for safeguards and standards in domestic work before the war, backed by a range of caring interests from doctors, religious bodies and trade unions. Her Action Committee was launched a few days after seeing a law adopted by the government which imposed a minimum wage for domestic labour, affecting over 1.5 million women. Outrage at factory conditions also brought new controls, and Jouhaux presented a report in 1916 which called for equal pay, but there was no long-term union commitment to the acceptance of women workers in industries previously monopolized by men. Unevenly, women's wages in the war industries did increase. Men were always paid more for equal work, but the discrepancy had lessened by 1918. This, along with every other aspect of female labour, was put into long-term perspective by the post-war backlash, already latent in the notion of wartime as exceptional.

Verdun

No ordinary soldier who lived through the Battle of Verdun, which the Germans launched on 21 February 1916, has described it in terms other than pitiless, brutalizing slaughter. The pulverized dead strewn in all directions, the gassed and asphyxiated injured buried alive, the dismembered bodies piled in mounds of rotting flesh and clothing, the choking sulphurous smoke of incessant explosions, the hail of mechanized fire: five months of unrelieved carnage in a crescent of churned and flooded makeshift trenches round the fortress town, leaving an estimated 650,000 dead, 350,000 of them French, and 300,000 Germans. The battle was famed for its ferocity, endurance and courage well before the outcome was decided. Louis Barthas writes of some attacks by both sides with instructions that no prisoners should be taken, of stretcher-bearers shot, of wounded and their carers deliberately killed, but he also specifies moments of fraternization and praises some 'brutish' officers for their personal courage and others who refused to detail men to carry out some of the more suicidal orders. Replacement units, he wrote, arrived with haggard, drawn and terrified faces: they were sheep led to the slaughter, the difference being that 'sheep do not know for certain what slaughter awaits them'. It may have looked the same from a position of command, but the letters of Captain Anatole Castex do not betray it. He wrote on 26 February 1916, 'All are in good spirits and

do their duty, even though they have not slept for nights on end.' Later he registers 'an incalculable deluge of shells' which killed 106 of his men in a few days but interprets it as the steely triumph of French resilience and notes that 150 replacements had immediately arrived. It was this ceaseless turnover of men which made the supply of Verdun as legendary as the infernal experience of its fighting.

At the start of 1916 Joffre had not thought an attack on Verdun was likely and the High Command had ordered a dismantling of the outlying forts in order to reorganize a defence in depth. The German attack was launched before this was ready. The defenders ringing the town were caught with nowhere obvious to go, with fortifications incomplete and orders just to hold on. The forts of Douaumont and Vaux were quickly lost, the former abandoned, the latter ferociously defended. Joffre did not want to take men away from the Allied push planned for the Somme and what he again believed would be a decisive victory. The defenders were told to manage. The supplies were deficient; starvation was rife in the flooded holes which passed for trenches: everything was improvisation. Piles of dead bodies gave a new meaning to man-made defences. Incredibly the Germans found that their advance was stopped. In the public mind, however ill-informed, the siege took on the emotional tension of the highest drama, the suspense lasting from February to July. Psychologically both front and rear knew that holding Verdun would give an epic meaning to the French war effort: losing it would be catastrophic at all levels. The commanding general, Philippe Pétain, who had long predicted that defence would be the essence of the war and was known already for his sensitivity to the ordinary soldier, realized that Verdun could only survive by limiting the soldiers' time at the front and by the constant relief of the fortress by new men, supplies and weapons. The Germans had cut off the main rail link. Only a poorly built, winding road to Bar-le-Duc in the rear was usable, though constantly under bombardment. Pétain, from his headquarters on the road at Souilly, organized massive repairs to the road and the single-rail track which adjoined it, and ordered a chain of perpetual supply to the fortress and non-stop movement of troops in both directions. Day and night 6,000 vehicles circulated, a slow and painful convoy carrying 90,000 men and 5,000 tons of supplies every week. Almost three-quarters of the entire French army was sent at some point to Verdun. Some units were sent back three or four times into the same inferno.

The siege was lifted. Verdun was not taken. Pétain moved to the Somme, leaving General Nivelle in command of the counter-attack, which succeeded with fewer losses. The retaking of Douaumont brought celebrations across

the whole country, and established a deceptive reputation for Nivelle. By 18 December 1916 the Germans had been forced back to their original lines. They had gained nothing. Their war of attrition had only intensified the unutterable hell of combatants' lives. By a law of 30 December 1923 the supply road was the only national route to be given a name and not a number: it appears that Maurice Barrès originated the name 'Voie Sacrée'. Verdun came to epitomize the French at war: it too defined the nation.

Indigenous recruits

The defence of Verdun and the break-out were an entirely French affair, the regiments from the colonies subsumed within the national category. This further evidence of inclusion was never less than ambivalent. It is estimated that during the whole war about 820,000 men in the French colonies and protectorates were raised, or forcibly conscripted, for military service. Over 600,000 of these were transported to France, almost 450,000 of them as soldiers. In Algeria there was the obligation of military service, even without political rights, and in the so-called old colonies (*vieilles colonies*), French citizenship carried the duty to armed service. This did not exist in Madagascar, Morocco, Tunisia, Indo-China or black Africa where the *code de l'indigénat* by which the indigenous populations were governed carried no such status. The code was therefore suspended in July 1914 to give the government greater freedom to levy indigenous troops, but without creating new citizens. Nevertheless the eminent West African deputy for Senegal, Blaise Diagne, saw his active recruiting role as an assured way of extending his own enfranchised status to all Africans. The army, he told recruits, would be the way to integration.

For decades after the war the historical picture of the role of colonial troops within France remained purely episodic and impressionistic: the first uniformed Senegalese or Moroccans landing at Sète or Bordeaux in 1914 were greeted excitedly as an exotic spectacle; in December 1914 Tunisians on the Flemish front were paralysed by the cold and unable to move when the order to advance was given: ten of them were shot as an example on the orders of General Foch; at Verdun in the last days of February 1916 units from the Army of Africa were thrown into counter-attacks to relieve the decimated defenders, gaining an immediate reputation for bravery and sacrifice; Somalis and Moroccans distinguished themselves under Generals Nivelle and Mangin in the taking of Douaumont on 24 October 1916; and in 1918 the mass levy of indigenous troops gave rise to the belief that they were being cynically used as cannon-fodder.

The picture is now more detailed. Scholarship since decolonization has shown that conscription in the colonies was resisted by scattered individuals in all colonial societies, but was without serious incident except in Algeria in late 1916 when the Chaouïas people of the Aurès led a revolt in south Constantine and proclaimed a republic of Algeria. The repression lasted for five months with troops and aviation diverted from France and deployed under General Deshayes de Bonneval. The rebels' habitat and crops were systematically destroyed and between 200 and 300 rebels shot. Lesser revolts occurred among the Bambara, Somba and Touareg peoples of equatorial Africa, while in Madagascar the indigenous movement Vy, Vato, Sakelika (iron, stone and branches), which started amongst the educated élite in the capital Tananarive, spread protest and refusal across the rural areas in 1915. Throughout the colonies there was a complex mix of submission, individual escapes into the fastness of the interior or over the borders, and collusion in recruitment by local chieftains, notables and mandarins, who were offered a *per capita* incentive.

Once at the front the losses among the indigenous forces were no higher than those suffered by French troops, but equally appalling, one in seven being killed either in France or in the Dardanelles and Salonika. The losses were highest in the first month after arrival in France in 1914; the early contingent of 4,000 Moroccans was reduced to only 800 after the Battle of the Marne, a carnage approached again in April 1917 when Senegalese battalions launched on the Chemin des Dames suffered losses of 45 per cent.[13] The general accusation of cannon-fodder, however, is no longer commonplace, though it is agreed that the military authorities saw the fighting strengths of the black Africans and the Arabs and Berbers from North Africa as ones of attack, and used them effectively as shock troops on several occasions to raise morale in the trenches. By contrast, the merits of the Vietnamese were seen as implacable fortitude and endurance in defence; they were attributed with the technological skills to manage the artillery and were widely deployed as military engineers. In such ways racial stereotypes were hardened in the perceived attributes of war, foreshadowed by General Mangin's work *La Force noire* (1910) in which he had portrayed the French empire as a vast reservoir of men equipped by nature and history for feats of arms.

Given the extremities of suffering, it is perhaps surprising that some of the experience of the indigenous troops in France was a positive one. In letters written by a small minority it was frequently mentioned that they felt included in the propaganda image of a civilized France and its empire confronting German barbarism. The levelling experience of the front and

the tolerance of fellow soldiers and French civilians were seen to be in stark contrast to the arrogance of the colonial settlers and the humiliations of the colonial system. After 1914 Africans in the army were sent for part of the winter to barracks in Fréjus, Arles and other specially created centres in the south of France where the food injunctions of the Islamic code were observed. Postcards of a Moorish café behind the lines or posters advertising 'Army of Africa Day' spread the visual images of the colonial troops into all areas; the soldiers often met with marked admiration and respect, and the injured were normally treated with equality in the hospitals. In their lives away from the front they were heavily restricted, but less segregated than the black soldiers who arrived with the American armies in 1917.

Against this evidence of relative acceptance stood the blatant racial inequalities of promotion to officer status, reserved almost exclusively for whites, and the insufficiency and surveillance of leave. War oppressed but offered glimpses of change. It gave first-hand experience of French military failures which effectively undermined the notion of imperial invincibility; white soldiers were seen as vulnerable to emotion and despair, and there were the lessons of military technology and tactics which future nationalist leaders took from the war. It was the French who failed to see the potential effects of the war on movements for colonial autonomy: for most mainland French people the inclusiveness of the war kept the empire firmly within the national identity, and enhanced the significance of its resources.

3. The limits of endurance

With the French fully extended at Verdun, it was mainly the British soldiers who were mown down in their thousands in the Battle of the Somme, launched on 1 July 1916. On 12 December that year a new government was formed by Briand, who carried out the recommendations of a secret Senate committee and removed Joffre, who was held responsible for two years of failed offensives but whose inseparability from the Battle of the Marne earned him elevation to Marshal of France, the first since 1870. General Robert Nivelle, superficially clever and amenable to civilians, was given the High Command, with General Lyautey, recalled from Morocco, as Minister of War. General Headquarters was moved from Chantilly closer to the front at Beauvais, and Nivelle planned a breakthrough for early 1917 which he expected to take only forty-eight hours. It was to be located on the Aisne near Soissons, with a pincer movement at Arras by the British, giving the opportunity for a main thrust through the centre of the German

lines to the south of Péronne at Roye. For the first time the French would use the latest in modern weapons, the assault tank, pioneered by the British in September 1916.

The Germans gained advance knowledge of the French intentions. Their new commanders, von Hindenburg and Ludendorff, carried out a scorched-earth retreat on the Somme from Péronne to Saint-Quentin and strongly fortified a new line of defence from Arras to Soissons. En route to this Hindenburg line the German army carried out orders to destroy defence works, bridges and railways, to cut down fruit trees, mine the countryside, poison wells and devastate farms. Nivelle's tactics were negated by this retreat. Snow and bitter cold made Mangin's plan to use black troops as at Douaumont a cruel impossibility. Nivelle was advised to wait for better weather. Pétain was doubtful that the offensive could be realized. Nivelle refused to listen. On 9 April 1917 the British and Canadians carried out the first offensive from Arras and captured Vimy Ridge, but failed to get to Douai and Cambrai as planned. On 16 April the French, including African troops, reached the plateau of the Chemin des Dames between Reims and Soissons but ran not only into a prepared German defence but also into the mist, cold and mud which disrupted the rapid movement of artillery and immobilized the infantry. The offensive failed. Nivelle's inability to face facts and rethink revealed him to be a disastrous appointment. The breakthrough which he had promised had not occurred, but he ordered the fruitless attacks to continue. In two weeks 40,000 French soldiers were killed and 90,000 wounded. It was a level of inhumanity and obstinacy which even Joffre had not attained.

Weariness and discontent

From the beginning of 1917 outbreaks of social discontent and urban strikes placed extra pressure on Nivelle's offensives: a breakthrough was desperately needed for the morale of both fronts. The prospect of a third full year of war deeply depressed public opinion and demobilized social solidarity. The right-wing press of *L'Action française*, the heroic drawings in the weekly *L'Illustration* and the high diction of war in the writings of Maurice Barrès continued the illusion of a war of chivalry at the front and of 'jaunty lads' at home, but most public attitudes to the war had become grim and unsmiling.[14] The upturn in optimism with the capture of Douaumont had been followed by a winter of despondency, not least in the countryside, where the high prices of agricultural products failed to offset the decimation of families, the absence and loss of labour and the serious

decrease in cultivation: over a third of fields were unworked at the end of 1916. The war now clearly meant unrelieved personal suffering, war regulations and war shortages, though for some, war profits.

The current of pacifism identified with Romain Rolland persisted as a reference point, but little more. *Au-dessus de la mêlée* was finally available in France in the middle of 1915, but his main defender in France, the trade unionist Alfred Rosmer, acknowledged that his followers in the CGT amounted to only a handful. The continued presence of the Germans on French soil, and solidarity with dead and wounded comrades, stood against calls for peace at any price. Anti-war tracts dated March 1916 were circulated from Socialist pacifists in Limoges to the rest of the SFIO but their impact was small: the party continued to be represented in the war coalition reshuffled by Briand in December 1916. In fact the level of Socialist Party activity did not increase with growing frustration at the stalemate on the front: on the contrary, it suffered a decline with the spreading war weariness of 1917. Local meetings were poorly attended; political motions were infrequently put.

Pacifist agitation among a small minority of feminists was marginal to most of public opinion, but produced individual moments of public drama. Gabrielle Duchêne chaired a clandestine group at her rented house in the rue Fondary in the 15th *arrondissement* of Paris, alongside the socialist Jeanne Halbwachs, Marcelle Capy and Marguerite Thévenet who smuggled Romain Rolland's text from Switzerland into France. Duchêne's group caused a stir with its pamphlets in 1915, attracting police searches and provoking Duchêne's exclusion from the Conseil National des Femmes Françaises, and in 1916 Rolland provided a preface for Capy's own pacifist testimony, *Une Voix de femme dans la mêlée*, while in 1917 the schoolteacher Hélène Brion published a feminist and pacifist call to women entitled *La Voie féministe*. Brion as a pacifist was seen by the authorities as subversive, mainly because of her trade-union activity. She was arrested in November 1917, and tried before a war tribunal in March 1918 for defeatism. The witnesses in her defence read like a series of entries in her own feminist encyclopedia which she began to compile during the war, and included Marguerite Durand, Madeleine Vernet and Gabrielle Duchêne. She was found guilty, but her three-year sentence was suspended, the military president of the Paris tribunal declaring, 'We are no longer in the age of Dreyfus.'[15]

It was Paris that saw the first strike of 1917 on 8 January when women workers in two clothing workshops demanded a rise in wages, a female militancy which marked the whole of the year, 75 per cent of strikers being

women. Male and female munitions workers on strike in January were met by a government injunction from Albert Thomas which fixed a minimum hourly wage but imposed compulsory arbitration procedures. Purchasing power had declined by about 10 per cent since the beginning of the war. On May Day a much larger crowd than anticipated attended an anti-war meeting of the CGT minority. The strikes extended outside Paris. In May, action in forty fashion houses brought out 10,000 strikers; on 1–2 June over 400 striking workers marched through Nîmes, and on 13 June 5,000 women workers in the gunpowder factory of Toulouse downed tools and stayed out for a week. Every strike affirmed the moral and physical exhaustion of the workforce: their demands were economic and were, on the whole, quickly met, at least by compromise. It was the absence of co-ordinated pacifist action, in fact the absence of a political agenda altogether, which received most comment in official accounts. The strikers were a small, if vocal, minority, but there was no doubt that the series of strikes, which also affected railway workers, banks and public services, was the most negative revelation of civilian morale since 1914. Some news of the strikes filtered through to the front, but it was the failure of the spring offensive and Nivelle's heedless pursuit of a breakthrough which broke the morale of the French army.

Mutinies

It is still difficult to detail how individual soldiers, faced daily with the machine-gun fire, the shells, the shrapnel, the cold, floods, mud, lice and rats, held on to any semblance of life in the trenches. That they did so produced an admiration but also an incredulity which marks all the literature and histories of the war. How and why did they endure? The different answers are all partial: they were heroic; they had no choice; they were too shell-shocked to care; they found meaning in a letter from home, a dry corner of a dug-out, extra alcohol, a practical joke, sexual anecdotes, comradeship, a stolen chicken: 'Since killing was a duty, a holy thing to do,' wrote Barthas, 'then stealing was surely no more than a peccadillo.'[16] The incessant nightmare created its own rituals and reality: leave and home often brought a sense of unreality and failures of comprehension. In the fall-back lines, trench newspapers were put together, theatrical revues were staged, cinema booths were erected. Demand was insistent for the latest Charlie Chaplin. At Commercy, five kilometres from the front on the river Meuse, a covered market was transformed into a cinema and music-hall for the troops and extended into a cycle track, football pitch and boxing

rings, the whole known as 'Poilu's Park'. Initiated by Major Rehm, a specialist in collective psychotherapy, the centre concentrated on diversion without apparent moralization, on therapy through laughter, on breaking with monotony, but geared to the production of a higher patriotic morale, conducive to effective soldiering.[17] Figures for seats at the cinema suggest some 4 million soldiers passed through the Park during the war.

The Chemin des Dames tipped the balance of endurance. On 17 April 1917 some soldiers refused to obey orders. During May and June the mutinies just behind the front spread to some 40,000 soldiers and affected nearly half the divisions of the entire army, if only in part: whole companies refused to move up to assault positions, though very few soldiers actually abandoned the front lines: it was the High Command's mindless devotion to offensive at any cost which was rejected. A few officers were jeered at, insulted and rough-handled where they failed to listen to the men's demands for better and more regular food and for guaranteed leave. Men bleated like sheep to register the ways in which they were herded into battle. But restraint was as marked as despair. No guns were turned on the military hierarchy. There was no drive towards revolution, though spontaneously red flags were run up to the strains of the 'Internationale' and there were shouts and collective declarations for an end to the war, even in one sector for a march on Paris. It was essentially a series of military strikes for better conditions, which a few officers, often with civilian backgrounds in law or politics, endorsed.

The army was one of citizen-soldiers: that was the republican boast, the Jacobin tradition. 'The revolt,' claimed Barthas, 'was about rights and justice.' It began in his regiment in the last week of May at the village of Daucourt, close to Sainte-Menehould on the Aisne, the ancient capital of the Argonne, when a corporal in the village square began to sing not the usual drinking songs but words of revolt against the sad life in the trenches, words of adieu to loved ones, words of anger against those responsible for the infamous war and contempt for the rich *embusqués* who let the poor do the fighting. Hundreds of voices took up the refrain, clapping loudly at the end, with shouts of 'Peace or Revolution! Down with the war! We want leave.' The recent Russian Revolution furnished a language and reference of revolt, and Barthas was proposed as the men's choice to head a Russian-style soviet. 'Of course I refused. I had no wish to find myself facing a firing squad just for the sake of apeing the Russians.' But he helped to draw up a manifesto demanding regular leave. It was that particular injustice which had broken the discipline of the most hardened troops. Close to the Chemin des Dames, at Soissons and neighbouring Villers-Cotterêts, Coeuvres,

Fère-en-Tardenois and Missy-aux-Bois, the mutinies were a more serious threat to the military authorities, but even there the revolts were mostly acts of direct democracy which allowed the reasonable claims of soldiers to be heard.[18] It was this that the mutinies achieved. They were a courageous assertion of citizenship by citizen-soldiers who had been pushed beyond acceptable limits. Several officers acknowledged this by their reluctance to escort mutineers, whom they knew to be responsible soldiers, to face trial.

Even before the scale of the mutinies was known to the government, Nivelle was forced to suspend his offensives, and on 16 May 1917 he was replaced by General Pétain, who had nurtured the armies at Verdun. He was determined that military justice should assert itself by the discovery of leaders, or those who could be designated as such. Trial by court-martial led to 3,427 sentences, 554 carrying the death penalty, of which forty-nine are known to have been carried out. By High Command standards this was a show of leniency, but given the peaceful behaviour of the mutineers and the moderate nature of their demands, the death penalties were yet another sign of the inhuman levels of violence which the war had produced. What still remains a haunting question in many minds is why the whole army did not mutiny, either in 1917 or before. The possibility was not far from Pétain's consciousness. He met it by ordering better food and regular leave for the soldiers, and he praised benevolent attitudes of commanders to their men. As the new commander-in-chief he turned French tactics round and postponed further assaults until the Americans, who had entered the war against Germany in April, were fully in place. In the eyes of many *poilus* it was due to Pétain's insight into the meaning of the mutinies that the French army continued to function at all. He tried to keep the civilian authorities from what he saw as interference in the war, but he met the ordinary soldier half-way. The bleating died away, even where the sheep-like behaviour enforced by military discipline was seen to continue. The main area of speculation is what might have happened had the Germans discovered the extent of the mutinies. In a war so full of spy stories it remains extraordinary that they never discovered the facts of the situation. Neither, of course, did the home front.

4. War to the end

Pétain's policy of defence with only intermittent assaults gave the army the opportunity to restock and update its artillery, develop its aviation and reduce the vulnerability of the tanks whose power had been neutralized all too easily in the spring offensives, with the result that the German command badly underestimated their capacity when they were re-employed in 1918. The months of comparative calm in the French lines contrasted sharply with the waterlogged nightmare to which the British soldiers were subjected at Passchendaele in pursuit of Haig's illusion of a decisive breakthrough to Bruges and Zeebrugge from the Ypres salient. The violent and unremitting engagements in Flanders from July to early December were repeatedly edged from the headlines by the situation in Russia, which was closely followed. The March Revolution had been enthusiastically received by a wide spectrum of French opinion, but during the summer anxieties grew that the Russian military disasters heralded defeat and withdrawal from the war. The reversal of pro-Russian attitudes was dramatic and largely preceded the October Revolution, news of which arrived shortly after the crushing Italian defeat at Caporetto on 24 October. The international dimensions of the war were more intensively debated than at any time since the July crisis of 1914.

The range of conclusions drawn from the events of 1917 was vast. At one end of the spectrum there was the pacifist pamphlet issued at the end of May by the Charente section of the union of primary-school teachers. It refused to accept that teachers should indulge in war propaganda and spread evidence of German atrocities. The tract argued that there had been horrific French massacres in the colonies, especially in Madagascar in 1897: 'Poor Belgium, yes, but the crimes committed in the Congo in the name of King Leopold should also be remembered.'[19] The argument that France and Britain had shameful histories of their own, and that the working class had been gulled into supporting a war of profiteers, became the open language of a range of left-wing publications, heavily censored and with a small readership.

In complete contrast, the year's events led to the recall of the 76-year-old Clemenceau to government and an all-out campaign to wage war more intensively than ever. Pacifism was marginalized still further; the hunt for traitors and spies was accelerated and promises of post-war changes and reforms abounded. France was galvanized, pressured and constrained to wage war to the end.

There was nothing inevitable about Clemenceau's return to power. Following the army mutinies, which Clemenceau could not publicly mention, his diatribes in *L'Homme enchaîné* had turned against the Minister of the Interior, Louis Malvy, whom he accused of protecting defeatists. When Malvy was slow to investigate the German funds which were found to be subsidizing the anti-war paper *Le Bonnet rouge*, Clemenceau denounced Malvy in the Senate on 22 July in an onslaught of accusations. Two weeks later Almereyda, the arrested editor of *Le Bonnet rouge*, was found dead in prison, his death interpreted by the right-wing press as suicide testifying guilt. Malvy resigned on 31 August, and the net of accusation widened to enmesh anyone who, with reason, in hope, or with illusions of various kinds, believed that the war could only be settled by a negotiated peace. All such initiatives foundered on the German refusal to return Alsace and Lorraine, but the search for alternatives to the unending horrors of the war was variously defended as morally necessary. One report discussed by the General Staff put forward a negotiated peace as the only way of avoiding social revolution.[20] Clemenceau rejected it as commensurate with treason. The fiery old maverick of the Radical left, mayor of Montmartre at the time of the Paris Commune, defender of Dreyfus, was now the unlikely toast of polemical right-wing journalists of *L'Action française*, whose exclusive and strident nationalism had re-emerged after two years of uneasy truce within the *union sacrée*.

Socialists and trade unionists had good cause to believe that if Clemenceau became premier he would reactivate the social repression of 1908. Poincaré, the President, was mistrustful of Clemenceau's temperament and judgement. Few senators, and still fewer deputies, had reason to believe that Clemenceau could hold together a majority, given his crude, spontaneous and autocratic style and his unapologetic defiance of collective politics. Nor did he claim to be a tribune of the people, although his tough defence of his right to expose incompetence and weakness chimed well in 1917 with public anxieties about drift and indecision in government. When the third government of the year fell on 13 November, Poincaré appointed Clemenceau, his mistrust assuaged by a positive meeting at which they agreed fundamentally on the intensification of the war. Already nicknamed 'le Tigre', and once a feared duellist, Clemenceau threw down the gauntlet to the Socialists who refused *en bloc* to join his ministry, and was backed by 418 votes against 65, the enthusiasm mostly coming from the right of the Chamber.

In the circumstances the appointment was a gamble. A decisive move to explore the possibilities of a compromise peace would also have been a

gamble. Poincaré and Clemenceau did not wreck a negotiated peace: it was not on offer. But they made any further explorations impossible. Jouhaux, the CGT leader, had admitted in September 1917 that 'Unless ... peace can be made by free peoples wars are bound to continue.'[21] The German workers, by his criterion, were not free. With Clemenceau's return to power the argument intensified on the left about the degree of freedom that would be left in France. Would his policies precipitate revolution?

'Je fais la guerre'

Curiously enough, the decision of the revolutionary Bolsheviks to end the war caused more dismay than admiration within the French labour movement. A year before Brest-Litovsk, Alphonse Merrheim, while still keeping a critical distance from the Jouhaux majority in the CGT, dismissed the very notion of a separate peace between Russia and Germany, and when it happened few trade unionists and socialists could resist the reaction that it had jeopardized a negotiated peace and came close to a betrayal of French soldiers and workers. This was a crucial response because it came after two months of protests by workers who looked not only to revolutionary Russia but also to the notion of a peace without annexations, adumbrated in Woodrow Wilson's Fourteen Points of 8 January 1918. The iron and steel works of Firminy in the Saint-Étienne basin was at the centre of the protests, and the leaders were confident enough at the start of the year to add demands for peace to the struggle for union rights which they had waged in late 1917. On 28 January, the departure of conscripts from Saint-Étienne was opposed by a large crowd of demonstrators denouncing the war and demanding peace, while the most prominent local syndicalist leader, Clovis Andrieu, originally from Picardy, took the arguments to a public meeting at Roanne to challenge Albert Thomas. The prefect reported that the widespread singing of the 'Internationale' and the occasional slogan for a workers' soviet expressed an atmosphere of revolutionary pacifism. though it was noted that Merrheim, during a tour of the area, had not endorsed the revolutionary use of industrial action to disrupt the flow of either men or munitions to the front. Brest-Litovsk strengthened his hand. It played equally into the hands of Clemenceau.

The pacifist protests flared again in May 1918, with the Loire industrial area once more raising the prospect of revolutionary action. Over 100,000 munitions and aircraft workers in the Paris region declared a strike on 13 May which lasted for five days. The momentum was taken up by Andrieu and other local leaders in the Loire. On 18 May a strike 'until peace is

achieved' spread across the basin and news on 21 May arrived from Roanne that conscripts had fraternized with the strikers.[22] Yet by 28 May the strike was over. Clemenceau had sent troops but also entrusted his personal envoy Théophile Barnier to show discretion and diplomacy. Arrests of the leaders only took place when support was starting to collapse across the region. The unexpected moderation of Clemenceau is seen as evidence of his residual radicalism, and some historians argue his fidelity to constitutional forms.

The military context of the strikes was all-important to their outbreak and their failure. The first German offensive on 21 March broke through the British lines on the Somme and threatened Amiens; the second on 8 April pushed into Flanders, and the third on 27 May took the French by surprise on the Chemin des Dames, captured Soissons and reached the Marne within sixty kilometres of Paris, a nightmare repeat for the French armies of the situation in 1914. In the face of these severe defeats public and political opinion swung between despair and resilience. Recriminations against the government threatened Clemenceau's *raison d'être* as war leader. 'Je fais la guerre' had been his slogan pounded out in the Chamber on 8 March, but by mid-April this had an ironic ring. Yet at the same time it was palpably clear that peace in such circumstances would mean a more decisive victory for Germany than in 1917 or at the start of the year. Ultimately, refusal to accept such an outcome outran revolutionary ideals. With German heavy artillery finding targets in the heart of Paris, 'Je fais la guerre' found a widespread echo, even in strike areas, in a grim and sour determination to hold on (*tenir*).

'Tenir'

The relief of Verdun in 1916 had been based on the intensive reorganization of military supplies and resources. The ability to hold on and respond to the German offensives of 1918 was made possible by an extension of state organization, including sweeping powers of rationing, control of the merchant fleet, massive recruitment and deployment of immigrant workers, and the securing of American loans. The production of artillery from 1917 to 1918 was doubled, and new tanks and aircraft were produced in sufficient numbers to be used *en masse* for the first time, giving the Allies an entirely new dimension of power.

Success came in a counter-offensive on 18 July in the forest of Villers-Cotterêts, planned by General Mangin under the direct instructions of General Foch, who had been nominated supreme commander of the Allied forces on 14 May and was made Marshal of France on 7 August. Surprised

by the power of the French tanks, the Germans were forced back over the Marne, and for the first time General Ludendorff was faced with the impossibility of victory. The spectacular thrust of the Allied counter-attack in the Amiens sector on 8 August brought the end suddenly closer. Offensives over the whole front at the end of September sealed the German defeat, but although the Germans were in constant retreat into Belgium, there was no rout and little disorder in their ranks, and Allied progress was slow. On 5 October the Germans requested an armistice. The request was made to President Woodrow Wilson and his Fourteen Points were accepted. The war was effectively over, but the fighting went on.

The comments by Louis Barthas on the delay between the German request and the end of the war affirm the deeply held anti-militarism of his *Carnets de guerre*, and express some of the final frustrations of soldiers at the front: 'What did it matter if there were a hundred thousand more dead, two hundred thousand, and several more months of unimaginable suffering? Did any of that matter to those who were far from the thick of the fighting?'[23] In fact the authorities were themselves in sharp disagreement, beyond their shared indignation at Wilson's monopoly of the negotiations with Germany. Foch was against making more demands on the exhausted troops. Lloyd George and Clemenceau objected to being forced to accept the Fourteen Points, but once they had vainly registered their views with Wilson they endorsed the message to the Germans that an armistice was ready.

On 19 October Clemenceau visited the liberated towns of Lille, Douai and Lens. He had made regular inspections of the front since returning to power, assuring the troops of victory. This was now a celebration. His speech to the Chamber on 5 November announcing the terms of the Armistice with Austria-Hungary was even more so. But the final rituals of the war had still to be observed. Railway tracks led into the interior of the forest of Compiègne, where the generals mapped out their tactics in carriages hidden from enemy aircraft. On 11 November in the very early morning the German military delegates arrived by one line and were transferred to Marshal Foch's carriage in the clearing of Rethondes. The Armistice was signed. It came into effect at 11 a.m. Church bells carried the news. The streets were full. People wept with joy, danced and sang. Patriotic speeches were made. All remembered the dead. No one knew just how many there were.

5

The Republic at War and Peace, 1914–1920s

1. *The meanings of the war*

Well before the ceremonies which unveiled war memorials at the heart of every *commune*, the history of the war had become inseparable from the process of memory and representation. No other event since the Revolution had produced such a universal public intertwining of history and memory. Whether at individual or collective level, representations of the war gave meanings not only to the immediate past but also to policies, hopes and prejudices which shaped the post-war present and the future. There was no single meaning.

War as enemy occupation

In April 1916 the German commandant of Lille, Graevenitz, signed an order deporting civilians to work in the fields behind the German lines. A notice in the Grand-Place declared that the order was irrevocable and advised the population to co-operate in their own interests. For four years the Germans pillaged the town and requisitioned its goods, down to the mattresses of the poorest families. At the end of the war one of the first Allied journalists to arrive described Lille as almost a dead city, where gaunt and filthy wretches survived only on charity or credit, a city without industry or transport.[1] The deportation of 1916 was not, however, typical of the day-to-day spoliation of the town and its inhabitants. It went much further. Women were the main target, in a ratio of three women to every man, young women above all. Over 10,000 were deported from their homes and forcibly subjected to lives of heavy labour in the fields of the Aisne and the Ardennes. The action violently contravened the Hague Convention of 1907.

In towns and villages elsewhere in the German occupied areas, the experience was invariably one of humiliation, shortages and the surveillance of

labour, although the degree of suffering inflicted depended on the character of the local German commander. A report on the Occupation written in December 1918 by Jeanne Macquart, village schoolteacher at Dun-sur-Meuse, specified the relentless labour for all from age nine to sixty, directed entirely to German needs and demand. Her report, and those from other schoolteachers in the Meuse, detail subjection to a German presence which was more or less intolerable.[2] Metaphors of prison abound. The meaning of the war for those behind the German lines kept alive the early image of the rapacious enemy.

War as obliteration at the front

The *commune* of Chiry-Ourscamp in the east of the Oise fell to the invading German army on 30 August 1914. With the onset of trench and attritional warfare, Chiry became the last village occupied by the Germans on the road to Paris via Compiègne. It was ringed with fortifications to make sure that it remained in German hands, and the château, church and the ornate nineteenth-century folly, the Mennechet tower, were used as look-out positions. The French artillery targeted all three. On 15 February 1915 a French shell set fire to the Ourscamp textile mill, destroying the main livelihood of the community. Two years later the Germans withdrew to the Hindenburg line, after destroying the houses and wells with dynamite. The French found a pile of smouldering ruins when they retook the village on 17 March 1917. Heavily shelled in March 1918, it was re-evacuated, this time in the French direction, before it fell again to the German infantry on 9 June. The final liberation began on 20 August, by which time the ruined village had been nominated a 'commune martyre'.[3] In the north and east, ten *départements* were totally or partially affected by the remorseless destruction at the front: over 11,000 schools, town halls and churches, and at least 350,000 houses, had been destroyed; over 2.5 million hectares of agricultural land were devastated; 62,000 kilometres of roads, 1,800 kilometres of canals and more than 5,000 kilometres of railways needed rebuilding. At Chiry-Ourscamp, 1918 became known as 'zero year' from which all life had to restart. A miniature of the vast battlefield in eastern and northern France, the meaning of 1914–18 for this *commune* lay in the indiscriminate obliteration and ravages of war.

The lost generation

Adjustment to the human carnage of the First World War affected the rest of the twentieth century. It was not just the horrific statistics of death, loss and mutilation; it was the question of justification. What had it all been for? The question was framed well before the final victory but it was not an easy question to ask immediately after 1918 in the face of family grief and the national commitment to mourning and memorialization. The keyword was 'sacrifice' as a self-willed act: the dead were memorialized as heroes who had given their lives for France and the Republic. This gave reason to dying; it sanctified not war in general but the specific war of 1914–18, 'a war to end wars' (la der des ders). Sacrifice to that end was heroic on a grand scale. The heresy was to use the word sacrifice but to turn it round to suggest that the dead had been sacrificed against their will or interests, whether by state, politicians, military authorities or ruling class. This was the last wry comment of Louis Barthas in February 1919, as he saw monuments planned which would claim that the victims 'had made the voluntary sacrifice of their lives'. He added, 'as if the poor sods had any choice, or could have done anything else'.[4]

If reasons for the dead were disputed, there was unanimous agreement that they should be collectively and individually respected. Bereaved families had received notification of the dead and the missing, but it was the bodies which they now reclaimed, particularly in regions where religious or family burial rites had a strong tradition. Anguished relatives demanded the freedom to look for the bodies of their dead, and entrepreneurs were quick with offers to dig them up and transport them at a price. In June 1919 the government decided that private exhumations in the war zones should not be allowed, but clandestine disinterments and distraught family pressure led to a reversal of policy a year later. Everyone was now entitled to rebury their dead, transported to their locality at state expense. Some 40 per cent of identified bodies eventually made this journey.[5]

Number had been a major theme of the war: in peace it did not diminish. The national statistics gradually revealed that over 1,400,000 had been killed in battle, were missing or had died after the war as a result of injuries, including 81,000 of the 600,000 indigenous troops. At the very end of the century in 1999, a further 550 names were added by military historians after eighty years of blocked research into those executed for military offences, including shell-shocked victims who were accused at the time of desertion or refusing to attack.

The demographic calculations also included the deficit in births over the

four years of the war, estimated at a further 1,400,000, those killed on the home front, and the 200,000 who died in the influenza epidemic of 1918. In total the population loss of the war years reached 3 million, only partially offset by the 1.9 million in Alsace-Lorraine who returned to French citizenship. Two-thirds of those killed at the front were from rural occupations. Peasant communities were decimated. Arriving at a village *monument aux morts*, it is still a traveller's first reaction to find the number of names inscribed there unbelievable. Most monuments were constructed and ceremonially unveiled between 1920 and 1924, some speeches deliberately stressing the comparative nature of the statistics. One of the later ones was at Ajaccio in Corsica in May 1926, where the veterans' president proclaimed that no other *département* of France had suffered greater losses: a quarter of those enlisted in the island had been killed. In France as a whole one in every six men enlisted was killed, the toll rising to over a quarter of those sent to the front.

The 'génération du feu'

The survivors of the front were the living, or partly living, witnesses of a hell which others could only struggle to imagine. The number of injured has never been exactly known, but it exceeded 3 million. The nature of the wounds varied considerably, as did the condition of lungs and eyes, but over a third of the injured were registered as permanently disabled, including 300,000 *mutilés* who had lost one or more limbs or suffered severe facial deformity, some of whom were kept permanently from public sight in special hospitals such as the Invalides in Paris.

Associations representing the claims of the wounded and the discharged had been formed during the war. The Union Fédérale (UF) tended to gravitate towards the political left, the Union Nationale des Combattants (UNC) to the right. Demobilization was spread over more than a year, revealing a combination of grandiose projects and petty meanness. Veterans scorned the Abrami civilian suit initially offered to each demobilized soldier, and ridiculed the alternative handout of 52 francs.[6] Their protests were effective. In March 1919 a fairer system of demobilization premiums was established by the government, and a moratorium was declared on taxes which had accumulated during the combatant's period of enlistment. The 'génération du feu' was acknowledged to have inalienable rights over the rest of society. The day-to-day symbol, still visible in the 1980s, were the seats reserved on buses and the Paris métro for the *mutilés de guerre*.

The war of the 'poilu'

Agricultural work accounted for roughly 43 per cent of the working population in 1906: three-fifths of all men in this sector were mobilized, totalling 3.5 million. Almost all served in the infantry. The public image of the *poilu* was heavily coloured by this rural predominance, and one of the most lasting national constructions of sacrifice was of rugged young sons of the soil returning heroically through death to the earth from which they had come. The cycle was so complete and so open to religious and secular mysticism that it was difficult for the surviving *poilus* to break the spell it exercised over public opinion and to insist on the appalling nature of both death and life at the front. At the heart of national memory lay an idealization of battle and the symbolic status given to the ultimate battlefield, Verdun, in which the *poilu* was transfigured by legendary stories carried by illustrated magazines in 1916 and developed into all-pervading myths in the post-war years. Alongside them a more realistic memory was enshrined in the awesome Ossuary at Douaumont, constructed over ten years and not fully inaugurated until August 1932, in which the bodies and bones of the battlefield were placed and the experiences of the battle shared by *anciens combattants* who organized their own pilgrimages to the site.[7] Slowly the words and memories of the *poilus*, collected largely by local historians for anniversaries and memorial events, allowed some understanding of the front to penetrate the aura of national symbolism and elevated rhetoric, but there was never a clear-cut division between myth and history. The *poilu* as national icon was central to both.

War of profiteers

Hub of national communications, military transit zone, stopping-place of hundreds of thousands of troops on leave, *ville tentaculaire* of arms production and heavy industry, formative index of public opinion, political nerve-centre of the war, Paris saw the greatest concentration of soldiers and civilians together in one place. Parisians nurtured the republican idiom of the citizen-soldier and they saw in 1914 and again in 1918 the direct effect of the 'levée en masse' in two decisive battles of the Marne. Codes of acceptable behaviour were constructed, and in the category of the unacceptable it was the construct of the profiteer which came to dominate.

The image of the profiteer included the entrepreneur and employer who conspicuously made a profit from war-linked enterprise, the middleman or hoarder who pushed up prices, and the property-owner who tried to avoid

the moratorium on rent rises. These constructs had variably firm foundations in reality, but relied on moral judgements and a stock typology. They
were one way in which the social dimension of the war was kept in the
public eye, preventing the *union sacrée* from turning into social passivity.
The denunciation of profiteers which accompanied most industrial disputes
put the strikers on firm moral ground.[8]

The urban nature of the campaign was underlined by the frequent
addition of the peasant farmer to the stock of profiteering images, carrying
the inference that rural greed made a fortune out of urban needs, an
accusation countered from rural sources by the image of the industrial
worker as an *embusqué* (shirker).

The persistence of these constructs powerfully affected long-term conflicts of an ideological nature. The profiteer was defined as the rapacious
enemy on the home front, the language of war adapting easily to social
resentments.

War as a forcing-house of social change

The polyvalent meaning of the war was epitomized by the widespread
expectation of social change. To say that every group expected something
different would exaggerate the fractious nature of French society but it
would underline the sense of opportunity which greeted the end of the war,
alongside the recognition of sacrifice. Government, management and labour
had experienced a form of partnership, however unequal and contested it
had been. For those whose working lives had been improved by this realignment of previously hostile forces, the war established the possibility of a
permanent change for the better. The CGT reformists led by Jouhaux,
and the Socialists close to Albert Thomas, were determined to seize the
opportunity for labour to gain an even greater share in the economic
organization of peace.

At the same time private industry had seen the benefits of intensive
methods of production. Renault exemplified the possibilities. The war and
the automobile industry were inextricably linked, from taxis at the Battle
of the Marne to tanks in the final breakthrough of 1918. For the company
the war was diversification, expansion and prosperity. Under government contracts, cars, lorries, armoured cars and tanks rolled off the production line. At its head Louis Renault was both tyrant and inspiration, a
man of action and achievement, the exacting and inventive *patron* of his
factories at Billancourt, south-west of Paris, Lyon, Bourges and Bordeaux, a
pioneer of new technology, an epitome of the successful entrepreneur, and

collaborator of Albert Thomas and his successor Louis Loucheur. The end of the war was the opportunity to continue the process which had been so productive, but without the interference of the state, a proviso expressed in the emotive notion of a 'return to normalcy', whereby pre-war norms of economic independence would once again predominate.

Against both labour reformists and private enterprise stood the expectations of change derived from the major international by-product of the war, revolution. For an effective minority in the CGT and a growing majority in the Socialist Party, the war had forced the pace of revolutionary change in a syndicalist or Marxist direction. With inflation still high, food supplies failing to meet people's needs in the larger towns, the memory of strikes in 1917–18 still fresh, and a febrile excitement at events in Russia and Germany, there seemed to many to be a revolutionary opportunity in the spring of 1919. The war itself was seen as a symptom of capitalism in crisis.

Change was also expected to follow from the vital incursion of women's labour into male domains; the recognition of women's suffrage and other civil rights appeared imminent; peasants expected a new prosperity to flow from the national reliance on their productivity at home and their sacrifice at the front; and immigrant labour, with few rights and without a collective voice, was established by the war as a permanent presence and necessity in French society.

War accelerated the expectations of change, but in a multitude of specific and contradictory directions.

A war to protect wives, home and family

Letters home written by soldiers during the war reveal an idealized attitude to women and family which gave a strong impetus to the continuation of traditional gender relations once the war was over. The 'return to normalcy' had a heavily gendered meaning.

For most combatants the main motivation for remaining hopeful at the worst stages of the cold, mud and slaughter at the front was the belief that they were fighting for wives, girlfriends and families. A photograph of wife or girlfriend was a talisman, signifying a private emotional and moral contract between soldier and home. Anxieties about infidelity were expressed in uneasy jokes and erotic fantasies. Failures of understanding between soldiers and civilians, the subject of constant comment throughout the war, were frequently expressed in gender terms, pitting a 'male' fighting front against a 'female' home front, and yet, despite this, images of mothers

and wives as devoted and loyal still predominate in all trench literature. Positive and negative, idealized and demonized, the two ways in which women were represented by men had long been complementary. The power of these images was now heightened by the experience of war, and given a new moral authority by male deaths and suffering on the battlefield.

Despite the apparent overturning of conventional roles for women on the home front, it was the consolidation of traditional male roles at the fighting front which was far more influential. The rights of the 'génération du feu' carried over into the domestic sphere. They re-established norms of safe and familiar family roles with the woman as wife and mother. Pro-natalists enjoyed new-found status. Legislation in 1920 and 1923 made abortion and contraception illegal, and throughout the two decades after the war a gamut of ideas for strengthening the family were regularly discussed by parliament, making Fernand Boverat, the leading pro-natalist, into something of a political fixture. His proposals included: taxation and pensions to benefit parents of large families and penalize the wilfully child-less; extra family votes at elections (*vote familial*), and recognition that 'an honest and hard-working immigrant who is also a father would do our country a great service by accepting our nationality'.[9] The underlying ideology is one of duty to the nation, which is held to take precedence over individual freedoms. The pro-natalist lobby elevated family values into a discourse of natural patriotism which stigmatized the 'modern' single woman and the man who refused to marry as emblems of moral delinquency, social decadence and, finally, unpatriotic behaviour.[10]

Salient facts of demography and cultural change questioned and destabilized this constructed world of 'normal' male–female relationships. The war made 600,000 wives into widows, many of them still very young; the imbalance of numbers between men and women at the end of the war meant that thousands of women would always be single; changes in women's work and lifestyles during the war increased the sense of what women, by themselves, could achieve. The necessities and consequences of the war had thus created a significant area of women's experience and ideas which lay alongside or outside the 'norm'.

Victory for the Republic

On 10 November 1918 Jacques Peirotes proclaimed the French Republic in Alsace, in front of the statue of Kléber, the symbol of France in the centre of Strasbourg. On the same day German soldiers, workers and sailors led by Charles Frey converged on the Place Kléber to proclaim the revolutionary

German Republic. A dual-language council of thirteen members was led by 'Comrade' Rebholz. In the confusion which dominated in Alsace from 6 November, the inhabitants of Benfeld led by the butcher Joseph Bieth forced the German guards to open the gates of the local prisoner-of-war camp, freeing 300 French prisoners. All paraded in Benfeld the following day, 11 November, no one knowing that the Armistice had been signed. All doubt evaporated with the arrival of the French army at Mulhouse on 17 November and at Strasbourg on the 22nd. The French had retaken Alsace and Lorraine, a feat which Charles Maurras and his royalist movement, Action Française, had proclaimed was beyond the capacity of a republic.

In Paris, from the Porte Maillot to the Arc de Triomphe, and from there through the Place de la Concorde to the Bastille, the victory march of 14 July 1919 featured Maréchals Foch, Joffre and Pétain, contingents from all the Allied armies, and every French regiment represented by its flag, an officer, a sergeant and four corporals or privates. It lasted twelve hours, and at the end the vast crowd broke into the march, embracing and lifting the *poilus*, seizing a cap here and a badge there as souvenirs. It was 'le jour de gloire' of the 'Marseillaise', sung passionately as a defiant republican symbol, if no longer, for the majority, as a call to revolution. Victory was celebrated as an epic justification of the Republic, consolidating its primacy within French society.

Conclusion. A national memory?

Of all these meanings the two which created something akin to a national memory were firstly the war of the *poilu* and secondly the victory of the Republic. Fused into one, they provided an image of the war which was remarkably resistant to alternative meanings throughout the twentieth century. The identity which they gave to post-war France had a base of support far wider than those previously constructed as left-wing or right-wing identities and based on differences over the Revolution and its inheritance.

No one took issue with the status of the fighting soldier. Verdun was the symbol of, and for, all *poilus*, and what made the battle supremely representative at a national level was that a new image of the soldier-peasant, utterly aceptable to the political right, to regionalists and to ruralists, had merged with the older republican tradition of the citizen-soldier, identified with the political left and with Paris. This meaning of the war, the war of the *poilu*, dominated all others.

2. Peacemaking

The process which led to the Treaty of Versailles on 28 June 1919 was a secret, difficult and at times acrimonious compromise between the Allies, unable to agree on how to control or eliminate the power of Germany. The French demanded that the Germans should pay full cash reparations for the war they had caused, and that the map of the Rhineland should be redrawn to make the west bank at the very least into a buffer zone, occupied by the Allies. For Clemenceau, now immensely popular and nicknamed not only 'le Tigre' but also 'Père-la-Victoire', the peace process, staged in Paris, was the final act of war leadership. He initially favoured the ideas of Foch who argued strongly for making the Rhine itself into the new Franco-German frontier, but this would have meant annexation of the Rhineland, which was against Clemenceau's better judgement. Forced to compromise by Wilson and Lloyd George, Clemenceau left Foch angry and powerless in the sidelines. A limited period of Allied occupation was eventually set at fifteen years.

Parallel to Foch as a hardliner on the reparations issue was André Tardieu, foreign affairs editorialist on *Le Temps*, volunteer at the outbreak of war, wounded in 1915, and in 1919 one of Clemenceau's closest advisers. His arguments, backed by his impeccable *ancien combattant* credentials and the unrealistic financial calculations of Clemenceau, succeeded where Foch's had failed: the massive reparations bill finally imposed on the Germans paid little attention to Germany's ability to pay. On both issues the question close to the surface throughout the negotiations was whether to return to war if Germany refused to agree.

Peacemaking was uppermost in the calculations of the millions awaiting demobilization, manifesting itself in widespread opposition to any continuation of warfare, whether against a recalcitrant Germany or the perceived threat of Bolshevism. Ephraïm Grenadou leaves no doubt in his recorded memoirs that he and fellow soldiers connived by every means to resist further military engagement in the early months of 1919. Indiscipline was an increasing problem for the officers.[11] In April 1919 a mutiny of sailors in the Black Sea, led by André Marty, effectively ended the notion of military intervention in the Russian civil war. A revolutionary link between mutiny at the front and social unrest at home had excited anti-war socialists and haunted government circles since 1917, and four months into the peace there was every sign that this was not an impossible scenario.

Peacemaking was foremost also on the agenda of feminists, socialists and

trade unionists. International meetings, parallel to the peace conference, were held in Paris, in Zurich and in Berne. In Paris the French suffragists, represented by Cécile Brunschvicg, joined with other Allied suffrage movements to call for women's full representation in the peace process, a case to which President Woodrow Wilson appeared to be responsive, although the outcome was rhetoric rather than action. In Zurich four French women attended a meeting of a feminist anti-war movement which took the name Women's International League for Peace and Freedom. The French section grew into a vocal pressure group for internationalism under the presidency of Gabrielle Duchêne. The struggle for a settlement which would have meaning for individuals as well as nations continued to inspire women's involvement in peace movements throughout the 1920s and 1930s.

The socialists at Berne thrashed out a number of principles which were sent to Clemenceau. They rejected any separation of the Saar or the Rhineland from Germany, and proposed that Germany's colonies should not be the only ones to become mandated territories under the League of Nations: all colonies, they argued, should be similarly treated. This was one of the very few examples in 1919 of serious thought about the global nature of colonialism. At their separate meeting trade unionists called for the inclusion of a far-reaching Labour Charter in any peace settlement, to maximize the new inclusiveness which governments had conceded during the war. All these proposals had a collective rationale which was inimical to Clemenceau. In May he was joined by Lloyd George and Woodrow Wilson in refusing to receive a socialist delegation to the Paris peace conference.

A month before the Armistice, the Socialist Party (SFIO) had affirmed its shift towards an anti-war position. The minority, led by Jean Longuet and counting Louise Saumoneau as one of its fiercest defenders, had become the majority, with interest in the Bolshevik success gaining momentum at every meeting of the new executive. On the streets passions were inflamed in March by the inexplicable acquittal of Raoul Villain, the assassin of Jean Jaurès, who had been held pending trial throughout the war. The court's decision provoked angry demonstrations in Paris and in all socialist strongholds.

Independently, but in parallel, the trade-union movement (CGT) had its own pro-Bolshevik wing animated by Pierre Monatte, originally from anarchist circles, and editor of the syndicalist paper La Vie ouvrière, but the majority, still led by Léon Jouhaux, remained in control. It took credit for a sensational increase in trade-union membership, which it was careful not to jeopardize by inaction. Strikes called in January and February 1919

among transport and railway workers were therefore backed by the leadership, even though revolutionary aims were expressed by a minority of the strikers. With the peace settlement unresolved and a government ready to use its wartime powers, the situation was explosive. Eyes turned towards May Day 1919, the first post-war demonstration of workers' hopes and demands.

Clemenceau's measured handling of strikes during the war conditioned his response. He had told Jouhaux after the Armistice that he favoured an eight-hour industrial workday, one of the long-standing demands of organized labour. This he now conceded in a law of 23 April 1919, while banning all May Day marches in advance.

The new eight-hour day still needed to be confirmed by individual employers, but did the government's concession indicate a willingness to push for a far-reaching social peace? The law was a substantial victory for urban workers and their confidence was high as they refused to accept Clemenceau's ban on the May Day demonstrations. The numbers who marched on that day made it a workers' overture to the national victory festivities of 14 July. But the possibilities of a peacetime working alliance between government and labour rapidly faded. Against the revolutionary rhetoric of the labour left, the forces of management paraded liberal economics as the only way to guarantee peacetime stability. The government of Clemenceau endorsed the management position, and the two sides of industry became locked in a language of class war.

The loser was social justice and reform. The Treaty of Versailles created an International Labour Organization (ILO) but without any firm guarantees of an international charter of workers' rights: within France such a pact was effectively excluded from the post-war settlement by the time elections were finally called for 16 November 1919.

3. Post-war power struggles

1919 elections

'The right to vote,' wrote Maria Vérone in *La Française* on 25 October 1919, 'is not a reward, but the means for us to better fulfil our duties towards our children, our families, our country, to humanity. We would maintain the Union Sacrée. We should vote as much for men as for women, without distinction of religion or political party . . .'[12] The Chamber of Deputies had passed a motion in favour of integral political rights for men and women on 20 May. Powerful speeches in favour of women's suffrage

by René Viviani and Aristide Briand produced a huge majority of 329 votes to 95, suggesting that all opposition had been rendered anachronistic by women's role in the war. Their right to vote was now, finally, supported as rational and logical in the best republican tradition.

But this tradition was far from seamless. Republican values were wheeled out in the Senate to oppose it, views passionately held and argued with no sense of self-parody. Women, stated the Radical senator Alexandre Bérard who drafted the Senate's response, had insufficient civic education for political rights; the 'Catholic mentality' of the majority of women, he continued, would lead to a clerical backlash against the republic; their suffrage might lead to a new Bonaparte and another military defeat as in 1870; nature, he argued, had given women a different role from men; women were creatures of sentiment and tears, their hands 'were not for ballot papers but for kisses'. These arguments in Bérard's report, satirized as his 'Fourteen Points' by Le Droit des Femmes, allowed the Chamber's motion to languish in the lumber-rooms of Senate business until November 1922, when it was finally debated and rejected.

Radical senators were the guardians of constitutional stasis. With their fiefdoms in small towns, mindful of Émile Combes's warnings against clerical reaction, and keen not to upset the electoral map by any extension of the suffrage, they were the main force in blocking women's voting rights. Had Poincaré, eminent supporter of women's suffrage, thrown his weight into the Senate debate in November 1922, the result might have been different. But too many politicians in too many positions of authority allowed their opinions to go by default: they did not see the issue as a priority.

The elections marked a sizeable swing to the right, loosely grouped in many areas into a Bloc National, which proposed itself as the inheritor of the union sacrée and architect of victory. Led by Alexandre Millerand, it claimed support in the centre ground and some from the Radicals. The Socialist Party, identified with a pro-Bolshevik stance, made substantial gains in numbers of votes, but due to the new electoral system of voting for lists rather than single candidates, lost 34 of the 102 seats it had held since 1914. Millerand's electioneering speech of 7 November in Paris capitalized not only on his association with the recovered territories of Alsace-Lorraine where he had been Commissaire de la République for eight months, but also on his vision of 'our admirable colonial empire which, during the war, in service at the front, in workers and in goods, has so copiously repaid its debt to the mother-country'. This notion of the empire as indebted to the metropole, rather than the other way round, reinforced

the Bloc's claim to represent the national achievements and potential of the Republic, which, it was argued, would be jeopardized by the internationalist left. The success of the Bloc located mainstream nationalism as the major inheritor of the war, just as it had been the main progenitor, and it was now unimpeachably republican. In January 1920 Millerand led the first government of the Bloc National. Eight months later he was elected President.

Clemenceau outmanoeuvred

The post-war elections brought an end to the long and volatile career of Georges Clemenceau. On 4 November 1919 he made a fighting speech in Strasbourg, not as a candidate but still as the head of government, determined to achieve the toughest application of the reparation clauses of the Treaty of Versailles and simultaneously defining Bolshevism as 'the bloody dictatorship of anarchy'.

This was the veteran breaker of strikes and war leader in full cry, and there was nothing in this speech which made Clemenceau unacceptable to the post-war nationalist consensus, except, for some, his attachment to the anticlerical tradition. His insistence on the same toughness at home as in the pursuit of reparations abroad made him central to the supremacy of centre-right republicanism. When Poincaré's term as President expired in January 1920, Clemenceau believed he was the obvious national leader to replace him. But in terms of personality his pugnacious individualism typed him still as a maverick. He was elected to the Académie Française, but he was sidelined from politics. He retired into the comparative solitude of his country house at Saint-Vincent-sur-Jard on the coast of the Vendée, enjoying the continued friendship of Claude Monet, whose first paintings he had strenuously and perceptively defended. He returned to intellectual writing on philosophy and science, spicing his own memoirs with contempt for those he claimed had failed to win the peace by refusing to cripple Germany permanently by retribution. Monet died in 1926, Clemenceau in 1929, aged eighty-eight.

Socialism: the great divide

The war and the Bolshevik revolution had changed the whole backdrop to ideological discussions within the SFIO. Lenin's launch of the Third, or Communist, International (Comintern) in March 1919 brought the backdrop to centre stage. He called on all socialists who had co-operated in

their country's war effort to acknowledge that they had been wrong. With every meeting that followed Lenin's challenge, an irrevocable split among socialists seemed increasingly likely.

It was not just a simple clash of revolution and reform. The belief that the working class would liberate itself from below was fundamental to all Marxian socialists. Mistrust of any alliance with liberal forces was rife. The war had not destroyed that mistrust but it had provided clear opportunities for advancing working-class aims by means which maximized workers' power and organization and forced the state and employers into a policy of inclusion. The war could not have been won without their co-operation. Reforms could be seen to lead to the very social goals which socialist revolution envisaged. To many socialists it was no contradiction to be a revolutionary and to have backed the war effort.

But the post-war collapse of inclusion suggested strongly that it had been no more than a temporary concession by state and employers, a response to the exigency of war. There was a flood of new members into the Socialist Party. What was not clear was whether it was the inclusiveness of the war, or its collapse after the war, which had so raised the expectations of the workers, artists and intellectuals who now identified the future of France and of Europe with socialism.

The socialist debate was profoundly affected by the consequences of two strikes by railway workers in February and May 1920. In March the strikes gained the support of miners in the Nord and Pas-de-Calais. Millerand's government reacted with a force that had not been deployed a year earlier. Arrests and searches of strikers produced serious clashes between workers and police. Employers took on anyone, including students, who were willing to drive trains and break the strike. Impressed by the vigour of the strikers, Jouhaux surprisingly decided to take over the campaign for a general strike, and proposed that it should start on 1 May and spread throughout industry. The response from workers was poor, and by the end of the month the CGT was forced into a humiliating climbdown. The backlash of employers and government was as severe as the police repression and over 15,000 *cheminots* were sacked. Despite, or rather because of, the threat of unemployment, the labour movement had failed to turn the high cost of living and poor working conditions into a convincing platform for action. The attempt to bridge reform and revolution had failed. Strikers remembered May 1920 as a tragic missed opportunity or as a fiasco.

Rival socialists were not slow to use the May events as confirmation of their different theoretical positions. Evidence from two delegates sent to

Russia, Frossard and Cachin, argued in favour of adherence to the Third International. The terms of membership, issued as Lenin's Twenty-one Points, insisted not only on a break with wartime reformism but on the adoption of methods similar to those of the Bolshevik Party. The vigour and decisiveness of Lenin's programme were its main attractions, and it gained still more from its rejection of colonialism. There was an idealism about Bolshevik achievements which was in direct proportion to the frustration within France. To others, however, the dogmatic assertiveness of Bolshevism called for a defence of the revolutionary tradition identified with Jaurès, whose commitment to democracy had never been in doubt.

The split came in December 1920 at the Party Congress in the Loire city of Tours. Among the powerful speeches was one from the 48-year-old Léon Blum, whose academic brilliance and fervent support for Dreyfus had marked him out in the pages of *L'Humanité* as the intellectual heir to Jaurès. With a subtlety of theory and historical reference he defined the revolutionary ideas and practice of the Socialist Party as incompatible with Bolshevism. It was a powerful performance, but the dramatic coup of the congress was the appearance of the German revolutionary Clara Zetkin, who defied a French exclusion order and appeared on the platform to deliver a passionate appeal to join the Comintern. With a majority of over 67 per cent, the congress voted to adhere to Lenin's model and movement. The party was renamed the Section Française de l'Internationale Communiste (SFIC), soon known as the Parti Communiste Français (PCF). By virtue of its majority status it kept the party's newspaper *L'Humanité*, founded by Jaurès but now edited by Marcel Cachin. The minority of delegates vowed to preserve the existence of the Socialist Party (SFIO), still insistent that they represented the heart and the tradition of the French working class. A year later the CGT split along the same lines, although the majority and minority were reversed.

The institutional fracture of French socialism remained unhealed for the rest of the century. There was little to match the rivalry of these close political neighbours. Attempts to overcome that rivalry involved most socialists and Communists in the twentieth century at some point in their political career. The primacy of the Republic was not affected. The gravitational pull was now towards the political centre.

4. *The politics of peace, 1919–1929*

Alternatives to nationalism

Post war attitudes had a Janus-like quality which defined the politics of peace in the 1920s. Public opinion no less than political leadership fell into binary opposites; either returning to pre-war structures or building new ones; either making Germany pay or creating a new Franco-German understanding; either stressing nationalist values or searching for internationalism. A pendulum swing from one to the other seemed to many at the time, and to many historians since, to be in the nature of the post-war predicament. People came together in village and town squares to commemorate the dead, only to divide ever more passionately about the policies which should follow.

Two of the most recurrent meanings of the war continued to affect public opinion and government policy: the image of the rapacious enemy and the reality of obliterated towns and villages in the battle-scarred zones of the north-east. The force of these was reflected in the votes and results of the 1919 election. The parliament, nicknamed 'bleu-horizon' after the uniforms of the *poilus*, sustained over three years of nationalist government intent on bringing an evasive Germany to account. Pressure was exerted to extract the maximum of financial reparations from Germany to finance reconstruction of the devastated zones. In addition, German mines in the Ruhr were expected to provide coal and coke to enable France to build the strongest European steel industry in the Lorraine. All demands for reparations and deliveries in kind were backed by the threat of military occupation of the Ruhr.

And yet, despite the pride in victory and the election of a nationalist Chamber, despite a continuation of high military expenditure, despite the role of French military experts in Romania, Czechoslovakia and Brazil and despite the military entanglements in the Middle East arising from the French mandates over Lebanon and Syria, it is the surprisingly low level of militarism within post-war French society which calls for comment. No military leader came to power. The body of an unknown soldier, disinterred from Verdun, was buried under the Arc de Triomphe with military pomp and ceremony on 11 November 1920, but the overwhelming atmosphere of the local commemorations of those killed in the war was one of civic rather than military pride. Only a small handful of monuments explicitly condemned war, but equally few glorified it. The ritual observation of 11 November, decreed as a national *fête* in 1922, converged with the period

of *Toussaint* (All Saints), the traditional Catholic season of respect for the dead, and gave the day a sombre rather than celebratory aspect.

In a parliamentary debate on the length of military service in March 1922, the Socialists Paul Mistral, deputy for the Isère, and Joseph Paul-Boncour, lawyer and deputy for Paris, set out the stall of a new universalism in terms which confronted the Bloc National on its own ground, the organization of national defence. Mistral, on the left of the SFIO, argued that Europe was already a 'confederation of states' in which purely national questions were taking second place to international ones. The reparations issue, he declared, could only be solved at international level and he proposed that the League of Nations should be given real power and military resources to accomplish its peacekeeping role. The League he envisaged would be a kind of United States of Europe, still more a United States of the World. Paul-Boncour, more to the right of the party, hinged his speech round Jean Jaurès, and in prodigious detail outlined a plan for national defence based on integrating a new, popular army with industrial mobilization, involving the whole nation as citizens.[13] The two speeches, published together, evoked republican patriotism and universalism as a unified tradition, and Mistral's idealism of a world confederation was echoed by a study group within freemasonry which concluded that a Congress of Humanity should be set up by the League of Nations, elected by men and women from all countries. Internationalism was a regular topic for lectures and speeches in Free-masonic lodges during the mid-1920s: Pierre Parot argued to the Grand Orient on 17 February 1925 for the economic necessity of Franco-German and Franco-Russian co-operation, 'however much this shocks timorous people'.[14]

Patriotic feminists from the main suffrage movement, including Marie-Louise Puech, Cécile Brunschvicg and Germaine Malaterre-Sellier, formed the Union Féminine pour la Société des Nations in 1920 to promote the cause of peace without any loss of national identity. A year later the Ligue des Femmes contre la Guerre was founded by Madeleine Vernet, a libertarian educator who had run a co-educational workers' orphanage before the war and who dedicated her monthly paper, *La Mère éducatrice*, to the 'unknown mother of the unknown soldier'. Her league attracted women close to the Communist Party as well as the pacifist feminist Hélène Brion who had no doubt, either before her trial or after, that war was an entirely male creation; Vernet herself was difficult to pigeon-hole either in political terms or as a feminist and placed the struggle for peace above everything else, incumbent on all mothers.[15]

The moral force of Communist internationalism far exceeded the

Communist Party's membership. Socialist ideals flourished in post-war society as an antidote to war and social inequality, and there was an alluring logic to the Leninist argument that capitalist nations could never make peace among themselves since they were driven to compete for profit and resources. The rationale was strong but the effect was sectarian: all peace initiatives within the capitalist structure were discounted as useless. This included any moves by the Socialists of the SFIO, condemned as permanently compromised with capitalists and war, even though the speech of Paul Mistral was applauded by Communist deputies in the Chamber.

Occupation of the Ruhr

Fears that the Bloc National would pursue reparations at the risk of another war were widespread in 1920–23, although there was every sign that a majority of public opinion agreed that Germany should be made to pay. Aristide Briand, a friend of President Millerand and fellow traveller in the odyssey from socialism to the moderate right, became Premier and Foreign Minister in January 1921 at a critical stage in the post-war confrontation with Germany. He adopted the Bloc's strong line on German payments but behind the rhetoric lay a subtlety of diplomacy which Millerand did not possess. Briand could see that Germany benefited from Franco-British disagreements. America had withdrawn from the League of Nations and from any commitment to French security, but had refused at the same time to cancel the war debts incurred by Britain and France. Briand understood that Britain also needed a settlement of the reparations issue, though not at the level demanded by his predecessors. In London at the end of April 1921 he agreed to limit the demand to 132 million gold marks, roughly half the figure previously floated by France. The German government, faced by this unexpected unity, was forced to accept.

The settlement could be read as the success either of coercion or of compromise. Briand's subsequent behaviour confirmed it as a move towards international conciliation. In keeping with his pre-war diplomacy he officially reconciled the Republic with the papacy by sending an ambassador to the Vatican. Pursuing Franco-German issues, he met his British counterparts in Cannes in January 1922 and outlined a conference to entice Bolshevik Russia into agreements with the capitalist world and to secure German recognition of French frontiers in return for still further reduced reparations. On this issue he had no mandate. The majority of the Chamber was scandalized. Millerand had not been consulted and refused to back his Premier. Briand resigned. Poincaré was appointed in his place and hardened

the French position. Germany and Russia made common cause in an out-siders' treaty at Rapallo and within a year Franco-German relations deterio-rated and collapsed. On 11 January 1923, when German deliveries were once again in default, Poincaré carried out the threat of military enforce-ment. French and Belgian troops occupied the Ruhr.

Technically the occupation met with success. Inter-Allied commissions to run the factories and mines to the west of the Rhine were activated. Tens of thousands of German officials were expelled and plans to take over the railways were well advanced. The passive resistance of German workers excited international sympathy, but was called off as the German mark plummeted on the exchanges and inflation reached astronomical heights. From 1 October German businesses in the Ruhr re-established relations with the occupiers on the basis of renewed payments. Poincaré seemed to have the situation under control, but lost it in the last months of 1923. He surprisingly backed a dubious Rhineland separatist group, yet paradoxi-cally agreed to an American offer to discuss the reparations issue where he had previously refused to negotiate. The Dawes plan was the result, propos-ing a limited period of German payment, a reduction in the total and a loan to Germany. In the autumn, investors and speculators turned on the franc. Between December and March 1924 it lost almost 50 per cent of its value against the pound. Poincaré took urgent fiscal measures and the recovery of the franc was as impressive as its fall, but despite his victory in what was billed as a financial Verdun, confidence in the Ruhr operation had evaporated. In May, the French electorate, faced with a rise in taxation to pay for the franc's stability, gave a majority vote to the opponents of the Bloc National.

Briandism, apogee of peace

The electoral results of 1924 registered the failure of the moderate right to preserve the positive image which nationalism had gained in 1918–19. Repressive refusals of social change in 1920 followed by a blustering assert-iveness in foreign policy gave it a reactionary edge, ill-suited to expectations that post-war France would build constructively on its victory. The occupa-tion of the Ruhr created more questions than it solved, not least how to withdraw without losing face. A pact between Radicals, Socialists (SFIO) and smaller left-wing groups formed a loose Cartel des Gauches, and voters responded to its promises of reform at home and negotiation abroad.

There was no thought of an unconditional retreat from the Ruhr, but that is almost what it became. The new government under the Radical

leader Édouard Herriot embraced negotiation with a mixture of trust and enthusiasm which made him vulnerable to hardened and hostile British diplomacy. Mayor of Lyon since 1905, Herriot's brilliant academic career had led to Radical politics in the universalist spirit of the Ligue des Droits de l'Homme. A large man with an expansive nature, musical talent and more time for intellectual discussion than bureaucracy, he epitomized the kind of outgoing republicanism that the self-promoting Millerand and the efficient but cold Poincaré appeared to have left behind. Eyes turned to Herriot, with his exuberant readiness as negotiator, to settle the question of the Ruhr, but he fumbled his case badly in London despite, or perhaps because of, his sincerity, and he was forced to compromise in all directions, accepting not only the evacuation of the Ruhr but reduced assurances on payments from Germany and an end to economic exploitation of German resources. His own belief in reconciliation survived. Symbolic acts to confirm the new direction at home and abroad followed quickly. In October the government recognized the Soviet Union and in November the ashes of Jean Jaurès were conveyed to the Panthéon. Both were headline material, but what caught the imagination of a whole generation was the project for peace, initiated by Herriot's government to promote 'arbitration, security and disarmament' and adopted by the League of Nations in October as the Geneva Protocol.

The French representative in Geneva was Briand. He was not an originator of the Protocol, but he saw immediately that its universal ideals needed localizing in a pact for European security with Germany as a full member of the League. His proposals were carried in the Paris paper *L'Europe nouvelle*, run by Louise Weiss whose influence for peace as the rationale of a new Europe was recognized and harnessed by Briand when he once again became Foreign Minister. His return to the Quai d'Orsay followed the collapse of Herriot's government in April 1925 but indicated that Herriot's new brand of foreign policy would be continued. It was soon defined as Briandism.

In three years Aristide Briand took the Republic to the pinnacle of internationalism. Having started his political life as a young Breton in Paris, living in bohemian style with anarchist friends and expressing vigorous anti-militarist ideas, Briand had moved through anticlericalism and socialism to a moderating role in Church–state relations, the military conscription of striking railway workers in 1910 and the promulgation of the three years' military service bill in 1913. Political leader of France at war from 1915 to March 1917, he then seemed to veer towards negotiation. Denounced in September 1917 for rumoured peace initiatives, he was

excluded from all power by Clemenceau. In return he was influential in keeping Clemenceau away from the Presidency before making his own re-entry into government in 1921. With his drooping moustache and swathe of dark hair, inspirational oratory and careful cultivation of a growing number of followers, he cut a charismatic figure in the salons of Geneva. Back at the Foreign Ministry he refused to be dismayed by Britain's rejection of the Geneva Protocol and instead forged a close working relationship with the new Foreign Secretary, Austen Chamberlain. Both mirrored the constructive flexibility of Gustav Stresemann in Berlin. The achievement of all three was the Locarno Pact of 1925 by which the post-war borders of Germany with France, Belgium and Luxembourg were guaranteed, although to arrive at this point Briand reluctantly suspended efforts to reach a comparable deal on Germany's frontiers to the east. This left Poland and Czechoslovakia with nothing but insecurity, though a year later this seemed less of a fatal flaw when Germany was admitted to the League of Nations, a logical consequence of the Locarno Pact. Briand, Stresemann and Austen Chamberlain were collectively awarded the Nobel Prize for Peace.

Locarno was met by a barrage of nationalist criticism. Speaking at Auxerre to a meeting of the Ligue des Patriotes, the local president, General Lafontaine, declared that every detail of the pact was to Germany's advantage. The Germans, he argued, were masters of camouflage: they appeared to have withdrawn their claws but only to gain concessions and lull the French into a false confidence. Then at an opportune moment they would strike again. Peace, he stated, could only be secured through national strength and the maintenance of a powerful army on the Rhine, and he accused the government of betraying the memory and sacrifice of the dead.

Lafontaine's language showed that Briandism did not start with a monopoly of the word 'peace', and yet this is exactly what it came to possess. Internationalism as aspiration and fact dominated the mid- to late 1920s. The years of commemorating the dead had emphasized not only memory but also the activating force of anniversaries. From 1924 to 1929 the public was continuously alerted to the tenth anniversary of some major event between the outbreak of war and the Treaty of Versailles. In 1927, as the Communist Party prepared to celebrate ten years of Soviet Russia, Briand was reminding America of its entry into the war and effectively into European alignments. After Locarno he was encouraged by the French ambassador to the United States, the poet Paul Claudel, into making new overtures to Washington. Such was the pervasive effect of universalism that the American Secretary of State was able to avoid a specific commitment to European peace by diverting the talks into an unprecedented declaration

outlawing all war. This became the Briand–Kellogg Peace Pact, signed in Paris and endorsed by fifteen nations. It was August 1928, ten years after the Allied push to end the war which would 'end all wars'.

The pact gives more than a glimpse of how the rest of the twentieth century might have been different. The depth of Briandism was profound.[16] At the Quai d'Orsay there was a well-informed and effective League of Nations section; the head of the Foreign Office, Philippe Berthelot, is now credited with much of Briand's perseverance and a healthy scepticism which kept the idealism of the Geneva salons in perspective, and Claudel's imaginative influence was more than matched by a fellow poet as political director at the Quai d'Orsay, Saint-John Perse, working under his real name Alexis Léger. In society at large a wealth of organizations, personalities and publications pursued the politics of peace. The teacher and philosopher Alain, *nom de plume* of Émile Chartier, formed pacifist mentalities among candidates for the École Normale Supérieure; the primary teachers' union, the Syndicat National des Instituteurs, worked with German colleagues to try to create a genre of schoolbooks without the bellicism of pre-war texts, while contacts with Germany which preoccupied various intellectual and economic journals came to a climax in 1926 in a Franco-German Committee of Information and Documentation, animated by the prolific publicist Pierre Viénot and a powerful industrialist from Luxembourg, Émile Mayrisch, who promoted a Franco-German steel cartel. A more complete list would take us back to the examples from feminism, socialism and freemasonry with which this section began. There was a circular but cumulative recurrence of peace initiatives throughout the 1920s.

Few personalities were more central to Briandism than Louise Weiss and it was her New Europeanism which surfaced in Briand's last initiative of the decade, a call to an astonished League of Nations in September 1929 to accept the political and economic federation of Europe. Alexis Léger's hand is visible in the memorandum which followed and there were clear echoes of the visionary pan-European Union, pioneered in 1923 by the Austrian Count Coudenhove-Kalergi: there was also the direct influence of the coal and steel entente hatched by industrialists from France, Germany, Belgium and Luxembourg in 1926. These antecedents would be recognized by Europeanists twenty-five years later, but in 1929 the ideas of Weiss and Briand were soon dismissed as misconceived and unrealistic, not least by Britain, with its preference for imperial trade. Ramsay MacDonald's suspicions of France had survived intact from his first government of 1924 and there was little Europeanism in London in 1929. With or without the crash on Wall Street the British reaction might have been the same.

Nor could Briand's vision ignore the growing threat of fanatical German nationalism. At the heart of all relations with Germany this was already causing division. Circumstances which had favoured Briandism were changing. He did not advocate an unthinking acceptance of all things German, but hindsight largely dictates historical judgements and Briand is still judged by the twist which the rise of Nazism gave to his policy of reconciliation with Germany. He was continuously in office from 1925 to January 1932, entrusted by a sequence of premiers including Poincaré. He was not responsible for the appeasers of Nazism in the 1930s and 1940s who claimed to be his inheritors, and yet Briandism as an attitude of mind has to be seen as an important reference point for those seeking peace through appeasement in the decade which followed his death in March 1932. In person, however, he belonged to the hopeful decade of 1919–29 when his idealism reinvented the possibility of a permanent peace. It was the great lost cause of the post-war world.

6

A Distinctive Society, 1920–1931

Pride in the victory of 1918 permeated most of French society. It gave the *poilu* prestige and expectations, especially in rural areas. It also co-existed with pacifist intentions for the future or even strong feelings of anti-militarism. Looking backwards and forwards at the same time was the most salient characteristic of society in the 1920s. A belief that France had triumphed because of its political ideals and social structure made for complacency. The contrary belief that the war had shown the vital necessity of social and political change made for a sense of permanent unrest. It was easy to oscillate between the two. The immediate result can be seen as ambivalence and indecision on the big, but ill-defined, questions of reform and modernization. There is also a longer perspective which shows a distinctive society emerging, partly by intent, partly by default. Whether due to calculated policy, obstinacy, invention or inaction, much of the fabric of life which distinguished France in the twentieth century was created or preserved in the 1920s.

1. Ruralism and the peasantry

France carried over from the nineteenth century a wide diversity of rural occupations. There was a huge disparity between the 33,000 farms with over 100 hectares and the 4 million farms with less than five hectares each. The government of Méline had protected French agriculture from the explosion of market forces in the 1890s. A basic living from the land and related rural professions still sustained roughly half of the population in 1914, an amazing statistic in industrialized Europe. It did not mean that patterns of rural life were unchanging. The war can be read as a climax of peasant acculturation. The forces of modernization analysed by Eugen Weber for the period 1871 to 1914 were basically three: transport, education and military service. In his striking aphorism of 1977 they turned

'peasants into Frenchmen', a shift of emphasis away from archaic regional and local culture to a more national consciousness.[1]

Modernization, however, was slow to penetrate the countryside and a steady stream of peasants made their way into the towns. The rural exodus was acknowledged by everyone to be a sign of the times, and yet in the post-war climate of a 'return to normalcy' it was equally apparent that there was a strength in the depth and diversity of rural life which gave France its uniqueness, resistant even to a war of mass mechanization. Recent scholars have detailed a complex regional mosaic of the pre-modern and the modern to modify Weber's thesis. Several million farms at the end of the war were still practising polyculture; there was still ancient solidarity at times of harvests, collective hunting, traditional rituals and specific village identities. The self-image of the peasant was adapted to encompass new realities: it was not abandoned as an anachronism.

In the ten years after the census of 1921 a further 600,000 people migrated to the towns, mostly from farms with poor soil, from rural habitations at high altitudes in the Massif Central and from precarious livings on steep hillsides. By 1931 for the first time the majority of people lived in towns. The number of the smallest farms had dropped by almost half, a massive reconfiguration of life in the countryside. Protecting agriculture and rural life became an evangelical cause, pursued in grandiose plans, election manifestos and parliamentary speeches. Literary works simplified and dramatized the issues, encouraging an ideological discourse of ruralism and regionalism, much of it unrelated to the specific economic needs of the peasantry.

'Retour à la terre'

Méline had followed his protective tariff of 1892 with a rational defence of rural life in *Retour à la terre* (Return to the Land), published in 1905. It was a title to become heavy with ideological baggage in the next forty years. A call for the return of the population to the land and the soil was more than a defence or celebration of rural values: it became a strident denunciation of urban and industrial culture, politics and society. In 1919 a little-known writer, Gilbert Stenger, wrote a novel also called *Le Retour à la terre* in which a young peasant, Antoine Daudat, sets out to find urban wealth but discovers instead only misery, squalor and trade-union violence. Beaten up when he refuses to go on strike, he returns to his *petit pays* in the Bourbonnais and rediscovers the happiness, good sense and strength of village relationships.

The value structures in the novel were, during the 1920s and 1930s, common coinage. More eminent writers than Stenger had set up similar scenarios. Maurice Barrès had fantasized a rural world of unchanging meaning which preserved the heritage of 'true France'; Charles Péguy was lyrical about peasant virtues and their spirituality. They were the literary mentors of a dominantly right-wing perspective which arraigned peasant women as responsible for giving in to the decadent seductions of urban life. Women were exhorted to return to the role of natural earth mother round whose skirts children would play and chicken contentedly feed. The cult of Jeanne d'Arc, not only as virgin warrior but as peasant heroine, epitomized the links between peasantism and nationalism. The folklore surrounding her knew no limits during the war, and the recovery of her natal province of Lorraine in 1918 reasserted her symbolic status as liberator. In 1909 she had been beatified and in 1920 the Pope announced full canonization. A long-term object of popular piety in rural Lorraine, Sainte Jeanne became the dominant allegorical figure in the region's memorialization of the dead.[2] Barrès was also from Lorraine. His classic formulation of *le pays réel* continued to express the certainties of assertive ruralism.

But it was also more complicated than that.

Peasantry and republic

Méline's active concern for the rural economy was shared by the civil servants and politicians in the Ministry of Agriculture throughout the Third Republic. Radical deputies relied on peasant votes. Radical senators cultivated their power base in the countryside. There was a depth of republican commitment in many rural *départements* in the south which rivalled that of the socialist urban strongholds in the north. The rural *commune*, endearingly satirized in Gabriel Chevallier's popular novel *Clochemerle* in 1934, had for decades been the site of ideological conflict between schoolteacher and priest, between democracy and hierarchy. Where these differences were minimal it was because of the dominance of one over the other. Such was the diversity of the rural political scene that the defence of rural life could not be assumed to belong to the anti-republican right.

The state spread agricultural agencies (*offices agricoles*) throughout the *départements*, while a network of elected agricultural bodies (*chambres d'agriculture*) was finally deployed in the 1920s after decades of prevarication. The former tended to promote bureaucracy and the latter to empower rural notables. Small producers had little political clout at any level except at grass-roots demonstrations, although there were local excep-

tions. In Brittany in the late 1890s a subversive cleric, the abbé Trochu, organized local peasant syndicates and sources of credit in the area round Saint-Malo, and in the teeth of opposition from his Church superiors created a new and successful local paper, *L'Ouest-Éclair*, as the voice of the peasantry. After the war in 1920, another priest, the abbé Mancel, backed by Trochu's paper, grouped the syndicates together to form the disciplined and effective Fédération des Syndicats Paysans de l'Ouest. He was no more part of a right-wing ruralist discourse than Trochu but rather replicated in rural form the social Catholicism of Marc Sangnier and the Sillon.

More traditionally from the political left, Renaud Jean, a socialist from a family of Gascon peasants, unexpectedly won a parliamentary by-election at Marmande in the rural Lot-et-Garonne in late 1920. Jean had been wounded at the Battle of the Marne, had become a pacifist and anti-militarist and as such accepted the majority verdict at the Congress of Tours. He thus became the first elected Communist deputy, and even more importantly the first to be elected on an assertively rural programme. Between 1878 and 1914 the Lot-et-Garonne had lost 15 per cent of its population: a further 10 per cent was lost during the war. It was a typical area in need of its own rural defence. Over the years Jean was to experience as many problems from the party leadership as Trochu from the Catholic Church, but initially he was given the editorship of the party newspaper aimed at the peasantry, *La Voix paysanne*, and in 1929 created a trade union of small peasants. His argument, which fell largely on deaf ears, was that the economic situation of the small peasantry and agricultural workers made them a proletariat no less worthy than the industrial working class.

Much non-aligned writing on rural matters followed the example of Émile Guillaumin in the Allier who had emphasized not the romance of village life but the stark facts of hardship in his influential rural portrait of 1904, *La Vie d'un simple*. It roundly criticized the Republic for neglect. The losses in the war, the low birth rate (except in rural Brittany) and the haemorrhage of the rural exodus were visible to the traveller in endless abandoned buildings, and the weekly magazine *L'Illustration* serialized the emotive photographs of Ludovic Nadeau who toured the deserted villages during the 1920s.

Other facts told a different story which accounts for much of the complacency of urban policy-makers. The demand for agricultural products during the war had kept prices high; inflation in 1918 allowed many rural proprietors to pay off their debts; many benefited from low land prices at the end of the war to increase their holdings, encouraging the agricultural

expert Pierre Caziot to propose to parliament a massive extension of peasant ownership which would put a brake on rural departures. It came to nothing, but the family farm was held by urban opinion to be a prosperous long-term concern. Fuelled by the official policy of immigrant labour, agricultural productivity slowly returned to pre-war levels. It was thought not to need money or intervention from the state.

In 1920 a Radical administrator, Louis Tardy, designed a bill which set up a national network of agricultural banks, the Crédit Agricole. It financed the electrification of villages throughout the 1920s and 1930s, and its achievements were associated with the energetic initiatives of the Radical Henri Queuille, mayor of Neuvic, a small market town overlooking a lake in the Corrèze. Deputy for the Haute-Corrèze since 1914, Queuille was an emblematic republican defender of rural life. His war experience as a doctor at the front who had served at Verdun and been decorated assured him the loyal support of *anciens combattants*. Regularly appointed to the Ministry of Agriculture in the rue de Varenne, he was popular in the countryside but sidelined in government priorities. In 1927 he proposed a huge state subsidy to equip every rural area with technical expertise and trained agronomists. Like Caziot's grand design it was thought to be logical but was too much for a financially cautious Chamber. The opportunities for agricultural modernization were not consistently seized.

The gap between urban and rural incomes widened throughout the decade. The indecision of deputies and senators festered in the farmyard (*basse-cour*) and on the small arable plot. Small farms were having to sell up at a loss. There were huge differences between regions and between peasants themselves. Talk of the peasantry as a single unit was always artificial, but allowed politicians of all colours to ignore the discrepancies. By the start of the 1930s it was apparent that agriculture could not adequately sustain the lives of all its workers and peasant proprietors. It was this reality that allowed the political right in the 1930s to build on its *retour à la terre* ideology and pose as the only friend of the peasantry. The Third Republic appeared to have failed its own rural heartland.

2. *Immigration*

Second only to the haphazard but distinctive nature of rural development in the 1920s was the singular effect of immigration. The policy of importing male workers had been vital to the war economy. From 1915 the ministers in charge of armaments and agriculture recruited, placed and controlled

foreign workers, and monitored their work, their social relationships and their reactions. The control went furthest for the workers brought from the colonies and from China, the Africans in particular subjected to military discipline and increasingly to housing in guarded barracks away from the French population. Almost all were shipped back to the colonies at the end of the war. More numerous were Spanish workers who came and went mainly according to seasonal opportunities in agriculture and general labouring, though armaments firms tried to assure a more specific recruitment of Spanish labour. Smaller, but important, contingents came from Greece and Portugal, while Italians and Belgians who had formed the largest two sectors of immigrants in 1911 mostly returned home in 1914, less than 10 per cent remaining as workers or refugees during the war. They re-entered France in their hundreds of thousands after 1918.

As part of the wartime understanding between government and the trade-union movement, wages paid to immigrants were theoretically equal to those of French workers, but practice fell way short of theory. CGT leaders were acutely sensitive to workers' anxieties about losing their jobs to cheaper labour from abroad. It was in the interest of the CGT to see immigration regulated to keep the demand for labour high: xenophobic protests and local clashes between French and foreign workers occurred at all times of economic crisis and unemployment in the post-war decade. Employers had opposite interests, and throughout the 1920s took more and more initiatives in recruiting immigrant workers, in deliberate defiance of what they saw as protective practices of the French labour force. The governments of the 1920s abandoned much of their wartime intervention and allowed private companies considerable leeway in recruitment. But immigration was always more than a question of who controlled it. It had it own political, social and cultural dynamics.

In the autumn of 1923 fourteen Italian families arrived in the Lot-et-Garonne in the south-west to work as share-croppers. They arrived on foot and in carts, with a contract to work on abandoned land. They were the vanguard of some 20,000 who eventually settled in this depopulated *département*, home to Renaud Jean, but more relevantly to an Italian journalist, Luigi Campolonghi, who welcomed the first immigrant families on to their land. Small declining villages such as Montignac-de-Lauzun and Castelculier were repopulated and each became known as a 'little Italy'.

The same description was given to Villerupt in Lorraine. By 1927 some 70 per cent of the 45,000 iron-ore miners in Lorraine were Italians. In 1926 there were 40,000 Italians working in the Parisian area, and by the end of the decade 30,000 in the Nord and Pas-de-Calais. It was not just the

numbers that were significant, but the diaspora and the range of jobs. In the 1920s Italians expanded from work as tailors, shoemakers and dockers in Marseille into agriculture in the south-west, iron and steel work in Lorraine, carpentry in the Faubourg Saint-Antoine in Paris, and building and construction work in the devastated areas of the north. By the time of the census of 1931 the figure of 808,000 Italians in France was probably a substantial underestimate. They represented approximately a third of nearly 3 million immigrants who made up 7 per cent of the total population of France.

The forging of identities

The stories and group photographs of Italian immigrants in the 1920s are scored with political agendas. For thousands of poor and landless Italians France represented a land of opportunity second only to the United States. Italian socialism had flourished in Marseille at the beginning of the century. After Mussolini's march on Rome in October 1922, and still more so after the Matteotti affair, immigration and political refuge were closely interwoven. Syndicalists and political opponents of Italian Fascism swept into Nice, Marseille and increasingly Paris, and it was they in particular who became known as the *fuorusciti* (literally 'those who went outside'), a proud title of political commitment to anti-fascism. Campolonghi in the Lot-et-Garonne contributed to the republican daily *La Dépêche de Toulouse*, while in Agen his colleague Oreste Ferrari launched *L'Attesa*, published in Italian and French, describing it as 'a political, anti-fascist, literary, scientific, agricultural and news weekly'.[3] The rural Italians of the south-west were conspicuously more integrated into the local French communities than their compatriots in Nice and the south-east, where an aggressive French nationalism had thrived since the cession of the area by Piedmont in 1860. The political *fuorusciti* were seen in Nice as provocation.

Singular identities were formed by other immigrant groups. Ten thousand Russians were taken on by Louis Renault to meet labour shortages at Billancourt: they kept themselves intact from pro-Soviet workers in the Communist trade-union movement. Armenian refugees from the Turkish massacres began arriving in 1923 and formed their own distinctive communities of silk workers. They found work in rundown silk factories at the villages of Décines and Saint-Maurice-de-Beynost to the east of Lyon. Life was reanimated at Décines, the workers opening their own school, café and Armenian church.

In the north and east private companies were the most assiduous in the

drive for immigrant recruitment. Committees from coal-mining, the steel industry and agriculture came together to form the Société Générale d'Immigration (SGI) in 1924 and in the next five years brought half a million workers into France under contracts which earned the SGI the reputation of a slave market. Polish workers were the targeted group, already anticipated in a convention signed by the government with Poland in September 1919. This afforded paper protection to the workers but in reality placed few constraints on the mining employers of the north-east, who sent them on piece rates to mine the poorest seams. Their retaliation was the creation of a national identity on French soil, more separatist than any other immigrant community, resisting the assimilating forces of republican education and the French language. Polish identity was preserved in a separate Catholicism, sporting clubs and choral societies and through a thriving press of thirty-seven Polish publications. In contrast, a small minority of the immigrants from Poland, including Jews, who had arrived individually and not through the SGI, made their way into trade-union and left-wing politics.

Distinctive cultures

During the war cultural difference associated with immigration had been identified with the presence of black workers from Africa, labelled 'exotic'. Difference was seen as problematic, but it was thought to have been solved by careful surveillance and segregated accommodation. This control was extended to the relatively few North African immigrants in the 1920s, who were sent to the industrial areas of Marseille, Lyon, Paris and Lorraine according to specific labour needs. Algerians were not strictly immigrants, being French subjects, but were treated as obviously foreign. Their difference was interpreted in derogatory terms: they were accused of suspect morals and criminal tendencies, and it was assumed that their Muslim religion ruled out any cultural integration. The response of a substantial minority of the Algerians was to forge their own nationalist identity. In 1926 an Algerian member of the French Communist Party, Hadj Abdel Kader, formed the Étoile Nord-Africaine, a nationalist movement among Algerian workers in Paris, identified two years later with the charismatic Messali Hadj, a shoemaker's son from Tlemcen, close to the Moroccan border.

The practice of cultural difference was never the intended result of immigration policy. Economics determined recruitment and little thought was given to the diversity of culture. Republican education was expected to take

immigration in its stride through a process of cultural assimilation assumed to be the desired goal of immigrants themselves. It frequently was. The career of Ivo Livi, a young Italian immigrant in Marseille, became a model: 'At school we were all the children of immigrants . . . racism meant nothing concrete, nothing meaningful or threatening, since all my friends were Italians, Armenians, Greeks or Spanish . . .'[4] He later became Yves Montand, singer, film star and icon of left-wing France in the 1960s. By 1931 the French working class, alongside the world of the arts and the intellect, was the most cosmopolitan in Europe. The ethnic mosaic, like the distinctive mix of rural and urban occupations, was at its best an impressive cultural feature of a buoyant society. But it did not signal a move away from the concept of a unitary republic. Despite their rich array of cultural expression, over 3 million adult immigrants retained the single identity of foreigner; it carried no vote and no security. It was distinctive because it was precarious.

3. Divisions of labour

Deserted villages were one graphic illustration of the demographic issue: workers' housing in the towns was quite another. Hastily erected shacks and chaotic suburban development registered the acute problems of overcrowding as 2 million new workers were added to the industrial workforce between 1906 and 1931, producing a massive expansion in certain sectors of industry. The boom was registered in the sensational take-off in mechanical engineering and car production, the expansion of the iron and steel industry, the output of electricity from huge hydro-electrical stations, the accelerated supply and demand in chemical products, and the steady increase in the building and cement industries subsidized by money for post-war reconstruction. Due to these sectors the rate of French industrial growth outdistanced Germany and even the USA by the end of the 1920s. Taking a base of industrial production in 1913 as 100, it had dropped to 57 in 1919 but by 1929 it had reached 140, a figure which was not achieved again until the 1950s. Statistics in these profitable industries show full employment, and this enabled many workers to move jobs with relative impunity, though this sideways mobility often masks the social control exercised through shift work, by which management (*le patronat*) observed the eight-hour law of 1919 but kept production turning, twenty-four hours out of twenty-four.

New patterns and concepts of work

At the end of the nineteenth century the concentration of labour at the Schneider metalworks at Le Creusot in the Saône-et-Loire was one of the very few exceptions to the dominance of small workshops employing fewer than ten workers. War production intensified the move towards concentration, and throughout the 1920s the image of the large factory and industrial complex took on a potent social significance which resonated with the debate about modernization, referred to indiscriminately as the rationalization of labour, mass production, Fordism, Taylorism and the Bedaux system of payment by results. Essentially a method of dividing production into its component parts, with assembly lines and single, repetitive tasks performed by otherwise unskilled workers, rationalization came to be negatively equated with dehumanization, and seen as American and un-French. Had this been its only image in the labour force it would not be easy to explain why trade unionists in the CGT were far from united in opposing it. Léon Jouhaux at the head of the CGT listened closely to the advice of Hyacinthe Dubreuil, a psychologist within the trade-union movement, who encouraged optimism towards rationalization. From the middle of the decade an acceptance that productivity could be usefully boosted by technological innovation was written into the CGT's programme, in return for which the worker would expect shorter hours and higher wages.

In the huge Renault factories at Boulogne-Billancourt, more than 53 per cent of the work in 1925 was unskilled repetition on assembly lines by ironically named *ouvriers spécialisés* (OS, specialized workers), with a large and diffuse contingent of immigrant labour from Russia, Poland, Italy, Armenia and Algeria. Once hired as an OS there was little chance of further training. 'All I know,' said one worker, 'is that I'm an OS and I shall die as an OS, no matter what work I am able to do.'[5] On the island between Billancourt and Meudon, the Île Seguin, the vast new Renault works with its own power station symbolized the rigour and the profit of mass production (*travail à la chaîne*) where the belt was never allowed to stop moving and the severest discipline cracked down on any defaulter.

This mechanical pattern of working was increasingly introduced into the naval workshops at Saint-Nazaire, into armaments production, chemicals, the rubber factories of Michelin at Clermont-Ferrand and in many larger factories in the expanding metal-processing industry. In coal-mining there were companies, such as those at Anzin in the Nord, which introduced all aspects of rationalization by closing the smaller pits and employing mostly immigrants in strictly separate, timed, and repetitive tasks.[6] Time and

motion studies associated with the American engineer F. W. Taylor were used at Anzin but were not universal even where assembly lines dominated, but they attracted much of the heat of the debate, alongside clocking on and off and the Bedaux system, all such practices given a modern, rational allure in the initials OST (Organisation Scientifique du Travail).

Mechanical patterns of work fragmented labour, in many factories exploiting and intensifying the segregation of French and immigrant workers. In the newer industries it also broke the male monopoly of factory work which had existed outside textiles. Women were present in light metal components work, inside or outside automobile factories; in electrical assembly; in chemicals, leather-working, rubber goods and food-processing. The status of the woman factory worker was still seen as inferior by the male workforce, and rewarded with piece rates and lower wages by management. Women were allotted to separate assembly functions, and while production boomed they were not seen as undercutting the male worker. Many were straight from the countryside and it was ruralists who provided most of the adverse comments on their employment. Rationaliz-ation notably increased the scope of women's work opportunity outside the home. This wider choice did not reduce the numbing effects of repetitive labour. The *Journal d'usine*, written by Simone Weil about her factory work in 1934–5, describes the alienated nature of component work, which was true for both female and male workers, and the strictly limited horizon open to women machinists. Mechanization was a distinct force on its own, leading to advanced maintenance skills, but these were almost entirely closed to women. The servicing of machines became a new profession, and the experienced worker with technical *savoir-faire* remained and thrived in most industries as a male élite.[7]

Textiles always had been and remained different in its intensive female workforce, but comparatively it was declining in its share of the labour market, though the paternalist nature of its management in the Lille–Roubaix area, with provision of crèches, youth groups, family allowances and leisure activities, continued to be a striking feature of the industrial scene, with similar patterns at Schneiders, Michelin and at the major steel-works in Lorraine, the Aciéries de Longwy. This was not replicated by the newer industries where the accommodation and social life of the worker were considered to be of no concern to the *patronat*. Their political and union affiliations were another matter. Stories abound of the ubiquitous Louis Renault marshalling his factory spies and rooting out anyone thought to be a militant. Through such controls rationalization gained an extra reputation for producing a submissive workforce.

The high-density slum dwellings which housed the new and migrant workers in the suburbs of Paris and Lyon expressed much of the rootlessness of post-war labour. Bobigny and Saint-Denis outside Paris and Vénissieux outside Lyon saw staggering, unplanned development of insanitary, disease-ridden dwellings with no privacy and little or no furniture except for the bed in which everyone slept according to the factory shifts. No traditions of popular culture existed as they did in the equally degrading but established housing provided by the older industries; no equivalent to the pigeon-raising in the north, or the *pétanque*, bull-fights and rugby of the south. There were a few allotments, growing spectator presence at football matches, and a residue of rural customs in the popularity of fishing. River banks, canals and ponds were lined on Sundays, mostly by men, but here and there by whole families.

The visible prosperity of the later years of the decade brought certain new products and better food within the range of working families. But there was never more than a fractional distribution of profits to the work-force, even though real wages at Renault increased by 40 per cent over the decade. The children of workers had virtually no access to secondary or higher education, while primary schools were as overcrowded as the suburbs themselves, alleviated only through truancy. It was against this harsh daily reality that the trade-union pressure for paid holidays was set, encouraged by the pioneer summer holiday camps for children (*colonies de vacances*), run by religious or secular authorities, which grew from pre-1914 origins in a philanthropic, educational and scouting framework to become the pride of working-class municipalities. In Ivry-sur-Seine in the south-east suburbs of Paris the electorate returned a Communist council in 1925 and it was in the commitment and euphoria of the election that officials first used abandoned army buildings on the Channel coast and then refurbished an old farm at Les Mathes near Royan on the Atlantic, building extra accommodation to take over 200 children in 1929, rising to 600 a decade later. The existing Catholic holiday camp run from Ivry already provided the model for a lively child-centred *colonie*, with play a central element. 'Both Catholic and Communist pedagogues thus strove to direct the spontaneous activity of children . . . toward the development of a resilient autonomy.'[8] For adult workers the dream of liberated escape from the factory grind was a formative image in town–country polarities, drawing strongly on childhood glimpses of freedom. The film-maker René Clair captured the essential pull of this image in his 1931 satire of a robotic factory system, *À nous la liberté*, a fertile source for Charlie Chaplin's *Modern Times* of 1936.

The wider picture: older traditions

New work, boom industries and rationalization provided the headlines of the 1920s, but heavily concentrated industrial work affected only 20 per cent of the total workforce. The full picture of workers' lives is less dramatic, and in its mix and diversity it corresponds closely to the heterogeneity of rural society, to the plurality of immigrant experience, and indeed to the disparity of situations within the middle classes. In 1931 almost 60 per cent of workers were in firms with a workforce of less than 100, and 34 per cent were in the smallest units with under ten. In these small workshops, skills were still acquired and handed down in traditional manner, and the techniques which fired the apostles of Americanization barely penetrated.

The strong element of continuity in working practices must help to explain the survival of a working-class tradition which to some commentators seemed in abeyance during the 1920s after the strike failures and repression of 1920 which caused a massive fall in trade-union membership. The major split in the movement which followed that of the Socialist Party seems ostensibly to have weakened the force of labour still further, and the decline in number of strikes throughout the decade appears to substantiate this. The CGT lost its most revolutionary members to the breakaway minority which called itself the CGTU, the added word *unitaire* signifying the presence of the anarcho-syndicalists who refused to accept that the labour movement could ever be divided. The CGTU joined the Communist trade-union International and made some inroads among immigrants and the new workforce, particularly in the Paris suburbs, although it failed to become a mass movement, losing membership steadily throughout the decade. Its revolutionary propaganda and optimism in the potential of the labour movement was, however, effective in keeping a combative mentality alive.[9] At the same time the CGT, now an unquestioned reformist movement, maintained a steady membership after the fall in 1921, and attracted the newly unionized public-sector workers, notably the teaching unions and postal workers. It influenced government policy at several points of the decade. It helped to persuade the Radical Édouard Herriot to set up a National Economic Council in January 1925 which the labour movement had been demanding since the war and which gave the unions at least a nominal role in the discussion of economic policy.

Reformist advances jostled with revolutionary discourse for the mind of the workforce. Together they preserved a disaggregated but effective commitment to the memory and ideals of labour activism. It is true that the vast majority of new workers appeared passive: it is noticeable that

collective activity was highest in the more traditional industries like textiles in the Nord and among well-established workers in medium-sized metalworking industries. The much-quoted memoirs of Georges Navel, which he published himself in 1945 as *Travaux*, are as fertile a source for defiant individualism as the war journal of Louis Barthas. Navel moved from one job to another in search of satisfaction at work, finding not just appalling conditions whether in mechanized factory work or navvying jobs outdoors, but also the expectancy that the worker should be an unthinking and unprotesting robot, while the management lived in comfort and complacency. It would be naïve to take Navel as a summary of working-class mentalities: it would be misleading not to see him as indicative.

4. *Affinity with modernism*

The multiple currents of modernism in literature and the arts contributed forcefully to the distinctiveness of French history in the first decades of the century. The close affinity of a minority in society with the avant-garde movements was one which threw into sharp relief the significance of independent publishers, printers and engravers, and the existence of far-sighted or maverick dealers whose pockets and enthusiasm provided individual patronage in an art world wary of investment in 'the new'. The diversity of the press and avant-garde journals was already a subject of international comment during the Dreyfus Affair. The ideological dimensions of republican politics in the wake of the Affair reflected a widespread readiness to advance programmes through intellectual channels: Jaurès was a philosopher and historian, prepared to write on 'social theatre'; Clemenceau a passionate journalist in the defence of freedom of expression, and a champion of the art of the Impressionists. There was never any shortage of media attention to the arts. Within politics there was alacrity to debate their relationship to society.

News of artistic assault on tradition was regarded as front-page copy. The incomprehension of bourgeois connoisseurs was interpreted among the writers and artists themselves as the desperation of an easily shocked middle class whom they scorned for using culture for social status. As the avant-garde artists in Paris attracted coverage for 'scandalizing the bourgeoisie', anarcho-syndicalist sources promoted their own cultural 'avant-garde' in the anti-bourgeois projects of the Bourses du Travail, not just in Paris, but in all the main working-class towns. In Marseille a Social Theatre (*théâtre social*) run by the local Bourse du Travail mounted shows

from 1900 to 1914 to inspire workers' consciousness and dramatize struggles with the police, army and political authorities. Stock characters gave the performances the familiarity of *commedia dell'arte*: it was stylized polemic, censored by the police for its anti-militarist sketches, but otherwise gaining a wry acceptance by the local authorities that the theatre was an effective organ of political propaganda.[10]

In his home town of Bussang in the Vosges, Maurice Pottecher founded a People's Theatre (*Théâtre du peuple*) at the end of the 1890s which outlived many other such projects in Paris. He himself wrote many of the plays that were performed, originally in the open air with the mountains as backdrop, and his aim was to expand the vitality of popular festivals. He was far less political than the anarcho-syndicalists of the Bourses du Travail and was avant-garde only in the sense of being at the forefront of popular theatre, with a firm belief in integrating art and social reform. The novelist Romain Rolland, politicized by the Dreyfus Affair, sought to co-operate with Charles Péguy in setting up a viable popular theatre in Paris, which he believed could harness the Europeanism of the French socialist movement, and build on the short-lived success of his revolutionary drama, *Le 14 Juillet*. Staged in the winter of 1902 by the successful actor and director Firmin Gémier, and dedicated to the people of Paris, it staggered critics with the bravura of the tumultuous crowd scenes, but soon found itself playing to dwindling houses; it never attracted a working-class audience. Neither Rolland's schemes nor the Popular Theatres in working-class Belleville and in the mixed area of the Avenue de Clichy, could induce the governments of the 1900s to subsidize independent socialist projects.

Rolland was delighted to find the Belleville Popular Theatre had an audience which was 'entirely popular: not one bourgeois apart from himself'.[11] In fact the Parisian working class did not have the leisure time, money or interest to enable these pioneer popular theatres to thrive. Without their intended audience, without state funding, and regarded as only marginally relevant to class struggle by Jaurès and other socialist leaders, these ventures in the capital mushroomed and disappeared. The republican governments saw their own way to providing popular culture through initiatives in schools, by staging popular galas, and in 1920 creating the state-run Théâtre National Populaire (TNP), entrusted to Firmin Gémier. Known for his production of Alfred Jarry's absurdist aperitif to modernism, *Ubu roi*, in 1896, as well as Rolland's *Le 14 Juillet*, the talented Gémier strode between new work and the revival of popular dramas and festivals.

No structural aims bound popular theatre to modernism in the arts, but across the diffuse scene of artistic initiatives there was a confidence that the

post-Dreyfus republic was open to cultural experimentation. Inventiveness and creativity within the avant-garde were also seen to be encouraged by the sociability of café life and the tradition of small, private galleries in which new work was passionately discussed. Paris and the larger towns were sites of street performance by theatrical troupes, acrobats and jugglers, who could still exhibit an artisan craft. Street artists provided free entertainment and in their precarious situation brought pathos to poverty and a comment on urban disorientation or 'anomie' as defined by the sociologist Émile Durkheim.

It was to this heroic pathos and the urban struggle of artistic life that the bohemian artists of the mid-nineteenth century had been drawn. In the early twentieth century, 'bohemia' was an inherited romantic myth, but it was still a lifestyle which was thought to indicate the artist's dedicated search for originality. In Paris, cheap rooms to rent and local access to bars, cabarets and night-clubs made first Montmartre, scene of much of Communard history, into a haunt of artists with individual agendas and sociable lifestyles, and then established the Montparnasse area on the Left Bank as the artistic hub of Paris, to which modernist writers and artists from all countries made an obligatory pilgrimage during the 1920s. The hill (*butte*) of Montmartre retained a village atmosphere until 1914, with its nocturnal café life centred on Le Lapin Agile. Its pre-war appeal was conveyed years later as authentically bohemian by the memoirs of Roland Dorgelès, the writer who made his name with *Les Croix de bois* in 1919, with its vivid depiction of the war which had ended what he called his second birth in the artistic circles of Montmartre. Unlike others, he was comfortably subsidized by his parents.

Freedoms of perspective, time, and expression

The identity of the pre-war years as 'La Belle Époque' was a selective emphasis. For the vast majority of the people it was a hard and bleak period, summed up in the etching of the wine-growers' revolt in *L'Illustration*, with its social observation, 'So much wine, but no bread to eat'.[12] The term signified a nostalgic memory of stability by the moneyed and social élite, and yet there was another identification of the pre-war years as ones of excitement at the pace of technical change with its major impact on leisure, travel, and ways of seeing; it signified the avant-garde. The revolutionary movements in painting, identified with the expressionist colours of the Fauves and the construction of multiple perspectives in Cubism, radically transformed the horizons of art and artists. Concepts of abstraction in art,

the pursuit of pure form, a relativity of perception and a synthesis of primitivism and modernity, allowed the Parisian avant-gardes to shock and excite the entire art world. Their legacy was adopted and further revolutionized by the anarchic wit and imaginative absurdities of Dada in the last stages of the war and by the merging of art, revolution and the unconscious in Surrealism in the 1920s.

Literary modernism revolutionized concepts of time, and explored the subjectivity of memory. Time as relative to different functions of the mind preoccupied the philosopher Henri Bergson, whose distinction in 1896 between the memory which enabled the individual to repeat behaviour, and the inner remembering of images and events from the past, established the relativity of memory. It was to underline the dynamism and creativity of this inner life that he wrote *L'Évolution créatrice* in 1907, itself the expression of a rich imagination, in which he suggested that a creative force, which he called *élan vital*, operated in the process of natural evolution and was more accessible to intuition than to rational analysis. If this resembled and revitalized various religious explanations of creativity, Bergson's insights into time and memory also coincided with the inspiration behind Marcel Proust's seven-volume novel *À la recherche du temps perdu* (literally 'In search of time lost'), which he was still reworking at his death in 1922. Sensitive, witty, suffering continuously from ill-health, and unpredictably affected by his homosexual loves and disasters, the upper-middle-class Proust showed the influence of his father's interest in psychology and the intimacy of his mother by creating a world of relationships in which the glittering surface is contrasted with a deeper inner life and its sudden, involuntary memories, evoked by the taste of a *madeleine* or a host of other sensations. It is this inner memory which creates an alternative time, lost and regained, and provides an often intensely pleasurable sense of personal continuity.

Notoriety in the world of avant-garde art was won less by Alfred Jarry, Henri Matisse, Pablo Picasso, Georges Braque or Marcel Proust than by the musicians and ballet performers from Russia, the Ballets Russes, choreographed by Sergei Diaghilev and the leading male dancer, Vaslav Nijinsky. Their performance of Igor Stravinsky's *Le Sacre du printemps* (*The Rite of Spring*) at the recently opened Théâtre des Champs-Élysées on 29 May 1913 provoked a riot of indignation and protest. The audience hurled abuse at the musicians for what was resented as 'strident cacophony', and at dancers for their 'half-naked sexual gyrations'. The outrage ensured the fame of the event and intensified the avant-garde conviction across Europe that modern art and music were inexorably separated from the vast majority of the bourgeois public.

In 1924 René Clair directed a short Dadaist film, *Entr'acte*, which was close to being the perfect summary of the inventiveness of pre-war and post-war avant-gardes. Ways of linking the two decades which had been sundered by the war preoccupied artists, writers and film-makers, as well as politicians intent on the 'return to normalcy'. Shock was only one element in the minds of the Dada artists who made and acted in *Entr'acte*. The inspiration it took from the pre-war years and the distinctiveness it contributed to post-war French culture was one of whimsical humour and fantasy, shot through with an acute sense of parody and burlesque.

The pioneers to whom it paid homage were the Lumière brothers, originators of cinema in the mid-1890s, and Georges Méliès, who famously explained his discovery of film-editing (*montage*) by saying that it was by chance that his camera broke down while filming in the Place de l'Opéra: after a few seconds he restarted and found that 'when the bus emerging from the boulevard des Capucines reached the boulevard des Italiens it was a hearse'.[13] Like the photomontage of the Dada movement, the effect of film-editing was to undermine realism by realism itself. René Clair and Francis Picabia in *Entr'acte* developed this inversion of realism, gave centre stage to a runaway hearse, and enabled the coffin when it finally fell into a field to burst open, to the horror of the exhausted mourners who appeared to have chased the hearse across Paris and through the Luna Park rollercoaster. Out of the coffin steps the corpse, very much alive and dressed in the clothes of a magician. With a wave of his wand he makes each of the astonished mourners disappear.

Shot partly in the same Théâtre des Champs-Élysées of *Rite of Spring* fame, and featuring the hearse of Méliès, *Entr'acte* embodied pre-war creativity, and its screenings were directed to be accompanied by the quirky, innovative music of Erik Satie. It was also a parody of a funeral at the height of the post-war commemorations of the war dead, a reminder that one strain of Dada had originated in Zurich in 1916 among artists estranged from the nationalist excesses of the war. In the *Manifeste Dada 1918*, written in French by the Romanian poet Tristan Tzara, the nihilism of a set of bizarrely creative individuals was uppermost. To critics of the war their message indicated that if the inhuman slaughter of the war made sense to a rational world, then the world turned upside down and dedicated to non-sense would ensure a better future for humanity. In *Entr'acte* the body emerging from the coffin was taken by some to be a reference to Abel Gance, whose film *J'Accuse* (1919) had pictured the war dead rising up from their graves and returning to haunt the victory parades with the human tragedies of the war.

Film was firmly established as popular entertainment by the time of *Entr'acte*, but its equal identity as a revolutionary art form kept innovative artists within reach of the public, producing a French cinema of nuance and sensitivity as well as plot and melodrama. Montage freed the film from the constraints of time and the linear sequence of events, a freedom which the commercial cinema also exploited, carrying one of the main aspects of modernism, the relativity of time and perspective, to the widest of publics.

In a break with Dada, André Breton, an ex-medical student turned writer and poet, made himself into the theoretician of Surrealism and issued his *Manifeste du surréalisme* in 1924. Surreality was defined by Breton as a fusion of dream and reality, and the Manifesto put forward the creative power of automatic writing, defying reason and logic. The Surrealists saw that the freeing of time in film brought the cinema close to dreams, as interpreted by Sigmund Freud, or states of intoxication. In *Entr'acte* the artists Man Ray and Marcel Duchamp are seen playing chess on a rooftop, an irrelevance to the 'narrative' of the hearse. But for the Surrealists nothing was really an irrelevance, since even the most fantastical image could be understood as an expression of the unconscious. To make this point Luis Buñuel's and Salvador Dali's Surrealist film of 1928, *Un Chien andalou*, opened with the slicing of an eye by a razor, allowing the inner eye of the unconscious to express itself in the sexual and anticlerical images which followed.

Cosmopolitan strengths; assimilating the exotic

Dada and Surrealism brought together experimental writers and artists from a multitude of countries inside and outside Europe. The diffuse international composition of modernist movements reflected and promoted the cosmopolitanism of Paris, enhanced by the migration of intellectuals throughout Europe and from America. The new forms of internationalism, whether the League of Nations or the Communist International, and the demographic movements of people from repressive or poverty-stricken areas of Europe, made the mixing of nationalities a distinctive feature of artistic creativity as much as of industrial production.

Art and industry co-existed with little interaction, although the architecture, drawings and paintings of the Swiss-born Charles Édouard Jeanneret, known as Le Corbusier, sought to integrate architecture and the urban world of work, symbolized by the interpenetration of spaces in his buildings and his use of the recently developed material of concrete. The painter Fernand Léger pictured the forms and colours of people and machines at

work, and he was one of several modernists who were drawn to identify with the working class and join the recently formed Communist Party. The Surrealists as a group led by Breton and Louis Aragon subscribed to the Communist Party in the mid-1920s, which was receptive at that stage to intellectual affiliation. The group's Freudian concepts and notions of revolutionary art stretched the Marxist-Leninist doctrines of class-based revolution, and although they were eventually experienced as incompatible the Surrealists brought anti-colonial passion and their own celebrity to the party. The unlikely conjuncture of these different revolutionary idealisms flourished initially through the literary journal *Clarté*, founded by Henri Barbusse in 1919, but expulsions and resignations ended the group's Communist saga by the mid-1930s. Louis Aragon was the one literary recruit from Surrealism drawn ever closer into the party. He became the companion of the Russian writer Elsa Triolet in 1928 and continued to promote the Soviet Union in intellectual circles throughout the shifts and turns of the following forty years.

The poet Guillaume Apollinaire, advocate of Cubism, was credited with the invention of the term 'Surrealism' in 1917. He used it to describe radical discontinuity in language, tone and substance. Born in Rome to a family of Italian, Polish and Russian extraction, he died in 1918, aged barely thirty-eight, as a result of the flu epidemic and the effects of a war wound. Apollinaire's poetry exploited the ambiguity of words and made them into objects in themselves, disrupting conventions of syntax and normative meanings. His reputation for originality in literature and insight into Cubism was dented by a critical response from Breton and Picasso and there were accusations of plagiarism from Blaise Cendrars, his equal in poetic invention, but his dynamic life and promotion of the avant-garde made him into a modernist icon. He was far from alone. There were other promoters, many of them incomers to Paris, not least the American Gertrude Stein, an experimental writer whose work anticipated many elements in James Joyce and Samuel Beckett and who bought early canvases of Picasso and Matisse, and the German art critic and dealer Daniel Kahnweiler, who established himself as a buyer of the Fauves and Cubists. Above all there was the representation of Paris itself.

The climate of prolific and diffuse invention in Paris made artistic society in the French capital a legend in its own time. Constantin Brancusi, sculptor of abstract birds in space, of totemic shapes and heads reduced to their essence, was widely rumoured in the 1920s to have walked to Paris in 1904 from rural Romania. In the set of squalid studios known as La Ruche (The Beehive) in Montparnasse, the expressionist painter from Lithuania, Chaïm

Soutine, painted bleeding carcasses of meat as seen in the nearby slaughter-house; the Russian artist Marc Chagall, in a separate studio, gave the animals back their life and painted them in vibrant colours, floating above the roofs of Paris and the streets of his native home of Vitebsk. Jewish folk art was integrated into modernism as were the African and Polynesian masks which had inspired Picasso. Jazz and its black musicians had arrived with the American army during the last stages of the war: the musicians returned to Paris in the early 1920s. They were followed by the cabaret dancers of the *Revue Nègre* in 1925 which opened to sensational applause, with Josephine Baker its fabulous star and Sidney Bechet its exuberant saxophonist. The term 'exotic', already widely used to describe Senegalese soldiers during the war, came to indicate a particular cultural identity ascribed to black jazz, but also to much of modernism. By extension it was applied to a whole ethos of cultural and social life in Paris.

The construction of this exotic identity was often reduced to the sensuous aspects of the exotic body, in which a dominantly male fascination was evident, redolent of colonialism. It was perceived in the odalisque paintings of Matisse, while the sensation attributed to the voluptuous dancing of Josephine Baker brought men to queue for the *Revue Nègre*. It was noted, however, that fashionable white Parisian women went in equal numbers to the rue Blomet to dance with young black men from the French colonies of Africa and the Caribbean, and that the sensuousness of the exotic worked its fascination for both sexes. It was present also in the cult of the Greek lyric poetess Sappho in avant-garde lesbian circles in Paris.

The interest in the primitivism of Marc Chagall's paintings, the inspiration to Cubist form provided by ritual masks, the place of the strange and unexpected in Dada and Surrealism, and the whole reception of jazz, revealed a more complex relationship to exotic cultural forms. Those who most vigorously promoted jazz in the 1920s did so because it was both primitive and modern, exciting bodily expression in dance but also spreading through the latest technology of wireless and gramophone. They insisted on its black authenticity, *le jazz nègre*. By the 1930s this was rendered as 'hot jazz' (*le jazz-hot*), to emphasize its accentuated rhythms and syncopation, and in 1932 Hugues Panassié, one of the main promoters in the 1920s, launched Le Hot-Club in Paris which achieved international jazz status for France in the importance of its performances and recordings. Black jazz, it was said, had colonized Paris.

Assimilation, as applied to the integration of immigrants or the aims of colonialism, was understood as bringing foreigners into the orbit of French institutions, language and culture. Much of modernism and the enthusiastic

adoption of jazz were forms of assimilation in reverse. They involved the adaptation of French musical and artistic ideas to forms, colours, expression, rhythms and dance which were the culture of others, notably racial others, and celebrated as such. The writer, artist and film-maker Jean Cocteau was a self-confessed paladin of jazz, accepting the reputation for promoting it in all its forms, as Parmentier had done for the potato.[14]

In parallel, or rivalry, there were attempts to divorce jazz from its black origins and to re-establish the norms of assimilation by implying that 'French jazz' was an adaptation of the new musical genre to the refinement of French music and taste. Jazz *à la française* was advanced by some pundits in national terms which implied a demotion of *le jazz nègre*. The two streams were publicized as different, but among players and audience alike a lasting plurality in the jazz scene was established in the 1920s. It enabled Louis Armstrong to comment that he felt at home among both American and French musicians when he came to relax in Paris in 1934, playing the occasional concert.

In the militant nationalist pages of *L'Action française* modernism was resisted as a subversion of French tradition: the positive words 'hot' or 'black' associated with jazz were made negative and ascribed to decadence. Debates over cultural identity were a central feature of the ideological struggles which increasingly defined the years beyond the late 1920s. The world economic depression made all cosmopolitan structures vulnerable to nationalism and xenophobia, and it became starkly evident that modernism was a minority taste. Black and foreign musicians were denied employment. Traditional schools of painting had been promoted in Paris by the exhibition 'Poussin to Corot' at the Petit Palais in 1925. In countless journal articles during the depression the lyrical themes of nature and the countryside were juxtaposed to the jangling disturbances and 'alien' origins of modernism.

The conflict at the time was frequently reduced to a simple one between the traditional and the new. It was always more complicated than that. New cultural experiences were not limited to the modernist avant-garde. A sense of cultural discovery and difference marked many of the intensive encounters with the rural regions and colonies in the 1920s. Popular photography, travel and cinema stretched the horizons. Nor was tradition set in stone. The cosmopolitan influx and the recognition of 'other' cultural forms as vital to creativity decisively contributed to the long-term character of twentieth-century France. Surviving the outrage and the rival forms of art and thought, modernism set up traditions of its own, with Paris recognized as its international atelier.

5. Structures at the centre

Structures do not normally make news, but in the 1920s they began to make history. In 1929 Marc Bloch and Lucien Febvre, Professors of History at the University of Strasbourg, threw off the orthodoxy of positivism and political history to launch a new journal, the *Annales d'histoire économique et sociale*, which integrated history and the social sciences in studies of underlying structures and long-term themes. Looking at demography, economic factors, social strata and cultural mentalities in a comparative way, the ground-breaking journal solidified as an intellectual movement simply known as the Annales school, with its concept of the *longue durée* making short-term histories look trivial and ephemeral. It was little interested in politics, but short-term structures could be comparatively long-lived, and the polarity of left and right was structural to political mentalities in the twentieth century: voters, towns, villages and regions were all described at some point in one of these terms; publishers, newspapers and intellectuals equally so. Some issues and policies moved from one side to the other: Briandism was acknowledged to be a left-wing foreign policy at the end of the 1920s, but Briand's legacy was eventually identified with the right in the 1930s. Regionalism was on the right for the first half of the century, but steadily lost this identity in the 1960s, although the old associations lingered on. In many ways the left–right polarity seemed to dominate the 1920s, but structurally it was also the more elusive identity of the centre which was laid down, in layers of attitudes which were highly formative.

Left–right polarity

In the autumn of 1924 Herriot set out the programme of the Cartel des Gauches which aimed systematically to revoke the internal policies of the Bloc National. It was a moment of apparent political clarity when the two sides faced each other item by item. Wartime pacifists accused of relations with the enemy (but who were not traitors) were to be amnestied; striking railway workers, sacked *en masse* in 1920, were to be reinstated; civil servants were given the right to unionize; Jaurès was elevated to the highest national status in the Panthéon; concessions to religious sensibilities in Alsace and Lorraine were to be withdrawn and the French embassy in the Vatican to be dismantled. All the proposals caused an uproar on the right of the Chamber and Senate but all were carried through except for the anticlerical measures; these were met by immovable popular opposition in Alsace-Lorraine and

a highly vocal campaign by Catholic organizations to assert their position in society, which the war had done much to reconfirm. Herriot was forced to concede. Anticlericalism would continue to inform the left's defence of a secular republic, but after 1924 there was no major renewal of the legislative onslaught associated with the heyday of Émile Combes.

Alarmed at the left's political measures, investors withdrew their holdings in government bonds. This triggered a fall in the franc, which had been vulnerable to speculation since the war and had only recently been stabilized by Poincaré's remedial action in March, funded by a major loan from the New York Morgan Bank. Socialists led by Blum proposed a wealth tax to boost the dwindling government funds and to begin a structural redistribution of wealth throughout society. Although totally unacceptable to the Radical Minister of Finance, Étienne Clémentel, Blum's proposal was positively received by Herriot. The ministerial disarray was manifest. The run on government stocks accelerated, with the privately owned Banque de France heavily committed to blocking Blum's proposal. Its tactics carried the Senate, and Herriot was forced to resign in April 1925. Over a year of financial sniping and recrimination saw a sequence of governments come and go. The pickings for currency speculation grew and the franc fell against the pound sterling from 100 in the spring of 1925 to 174 at the end of June 1926 and 235 by 21 July. Panic now seriously affected the more conservative Radicals. Poincaré was proposed as premier and on 27 July 1926 his financial solutions were accepted by the Chamber. The Cartel des Gauches had lost its hold on power, outmanoeuvred, quipped the right-wing press, by 'the plebiscite of bond-holders'.

The national left–right confrontation of 1924 focused for a brief moment on a local event which stole the headlines. For the first time a government intervened in a strike in the private sector, not with police repression but with material support for the strikers. Workers in the fish factories in Douarnenez, on the Finistère coast in Brittany, had mounted a strike for better pay which took over the whole community. The workers were mostly girls and women aged twelve to seventy-five from peasant, Catholic backgrounds, constrained to work a seventeen-hour day when the fish arrived, and even three or four consecutive nights. Conditions were primitive and unhealthy and the pay for women was eighty centimes an hour, a fraction of the average working wage. The strikers demanded one franc an hour for the women. By 21 December the strike was solid among all local factory workers, fishermen and lorry-drivers. The prefect suspended the Communist mayor, but local elections brought the Communist list an increased majority. The employers gave way and agreed to the strikers' demands.

The government's decision to offer arbitration and to subsidize a fund for the strikers' families represented something of the social action demanded by those on the left of the Cartel des Gauches. The unprecedented nature of the action was reflected in the outrage of the employers' national body, the Confédération Générale de la Production Française, now even more convinced that the economy could not be entrusted to the left. Ernest Mercier, the electrical industrialist, was the foremost organizer of business reaction to the Cartel. He formed a technocratic movement called Redressement Français in 1925 with 200 experts advocating industrial concentration. By the following year he had secured an impressive list of 10,000 adherents who contributed to a vast campaign in the press for an American-style economy. The conflict over the franc in 1925–6 was given extra bite by the determination of business and investment to make government by the left an impossibility, whatever their electoral majority might have been. In this they succeeded.

Capital values

Within a few days of returning to power Raymond Poincaré had re-created confidence in the franc, with a government of 'national union' (*union nationale*) to signify his own mix of secular and nationalist republicanism. Aged sixty-six, his reputation as the architect of the *union sacrée* was underpinned by his bearing as an archetypal wise old man with his white goatee beard and aloof manner. A mixture of spending cuts, small increases in taxation and a high bank rate attracted foreign investors. By December 1926 the franc was trading at 122 to the pound. This was still far below its pre-war value of 25.5 to the pound, but the level represented its real purchasing power since the war. Two years of currency stability followed, and this convinced Poincaré that the depreciation was permanent. After national elections had reversed the results of 1924 he decided he had the mandate to consolidate the franc at this level. On 25 June 1928 the 'Poincaré franc' was officially established at a fifth of its pre-war value.

The elections of 1928 saw a slight majority of votes for the left, but a comfortable majority of seats for the right who claimed Poincaré and his policies as their own. Poincaré did not lurch back to the aggression of the Ruhr, however; seeing that Briand had fashioned a workable and popular internationalism, he kept him at the Quai d'Orsay. He was reassured in this by the strategy adopted by the army high command under Marshal Pétain, whose conviction that defence was the permanent lesson of the war had spawned plans for a line of immense concrete defences along the

Franco-German frontier, named eventually as the Maginot Line after André Maginot, Under-Secretary of War in 1913–14 and Minister of Defence first in 1922–4 and then at the crucial stages of construction in 1929–32. The heavily fortified 'wall of France' was voted through in July 1927 and work began first in the areas most exposed to German invasion in the region of Metz on the borders of Alsace and Lorraine.

Together, Poincaré's franc and Briand's foreign policy made up a composite which was not as easily defined on the right–left scale as the politics of the early and mid-1920s. There were policy links with the Cartel des Gauches as well as with the Bloc National. The notion of a centre which avoided the excesses of right and left took root during Poincaré's regime, and it can be argued that it represented a kind of consensus at the heart of French society on the nature of 'good government'.[15]

If it did represent a centre it was a socially conservative one, buttressed by industrial growth and a liberal market economy, but in particular by the continued prominence of small and medium-sized businesses at the structural core of private enterprise. Small firms and many of the older industries based on traditional family ownership did not exalt the boom culture and there was a distinct hostility towards speculators, opulence and conspicuous consumption. There was a wide resistance of small employers to any increase of costs through social security. Wages were kept low in an effort to combat the inflation that had diminished the value of rents and inherited wealth. The weaker franc, on the other hand, had been good for exporters, although in the labyrinthine retail world of small commerce the suspicion of new wealth was expressed in campaigns to block the new chains of Monoprix and Uniprix which had begun to exploit the potential of mass marketing.

New boom or old resilience, it was the values and interests of capital which dominated over those of labour. The notion of a government of the centre was, however, reinforced by the law of 5 April 1928 which began to structure a welfare system of social security for workers, funded not only by deductions from earnings but also by employers' contributions. Two months later the Minister of Labour, Louis Loucheur, set out the government's intention to counter the severe housing shortage with 200,000 apartments at low rent, a measure endorsed by the new majority of the Chamber after the elections.

The measures did not signify the end of right–left polarity. Within the year the Radicals had left the government on an issue of anticlerical principle, and Poincaré's next cabinet signalled a move to the right. He resigned due to ill-health in July 1929, retired to write his memoirs, and died in

1934. Symbolically, for an impeccable secular republican who nevertheless personified the *union sacrée*, he was given funeral rites in both civil and religious ceremonies.

Colonial cul-de-sac

Colonial policy in the 1920s was conducted as if it was consciously mapping the centre ground of politics, raising the flag in an area of irrefutable consensus. The image of President Millerand, dressed in topi, bow tie and frock coat, pinning medals on white-robed and hooded Moroccan leaders, was one of the illustrations which circulated during his visit to North Africa from March to May 1922. Millerand returned via Corsica in an arc from Morocco, Algeria and Tunisia which formally drew the two sides of the Mediterranean together. On the first day over the Moroccan border into Algeria, the record states that 'despite misleading information which classifies the inhabitants of Algeria by different religion, origin and race, they are all one people in the process of becoming French'.[16] This confirmed what had become almost a platitude in public attitudes towards the colonies: that all indigenous peoples of colonized North Africa would, by the process of assimilation, become part of the history of France. It was tantamount to declaring that Muslim North Africa had no living history of its own, only a dead past. And even this past was denied legitimacy by the French settlers who identified themselves as 'Algerianists' and claimed to have inherited Algeria from the Romans.

Millerand's grand tour was staged a year after the Minister for Colonies, Albert Sarraut, had proposed an ambitious project aimed at realizing the potential worth (*mise en valeur*) of the colonies. Loans, with interest guaranteed by the state, were to be designed to allow the colonies to develop their own social, economic and educational infrastructure to a point where they would become net contributors to the national wealth. The plan from the ex-Governor of Indo-China, now a Radical minister in the Bloc National, was rejected by the Chamber as too expensive, but it survived as one central ideal of policy-makers throughout a decade of colonial display which reached its apotheosis in the lavish Colonial Exhibition of 1931.

In April 1925 it was the political left which was in power when Emir Abd el-Krim, leader of the Rif communities in the mountains of northern Morocco, extended his military campaign into French-held territory, claiming national status for the Rif and entry into the League of Nations. Compared by some with the Swiss struggle for independence personified by William Tell, the Emir's cause was seen by the insecure governments of the

ailing Cartel des Gauches as a revolt to be quashed. Marshal Lyautey, still Resident General in Morocco, advised negotiation. It was quintessential Lyautey strategy, combining military presence with political flexibility. Marshal Pétain was sent with reinforcements and accused Lyautey of playing at politics. He urged an all-out war against Abd el-Krim, with bombardment from the air and heavy artillery. It was a strategy which notably conflicted with his preference for defensive tactics against potential enemies within Europe. He received backing from Paris, and Lyautey resigned in protest. In May 1926 the offensive was launched but turned into something more like a military parade. Abd el-Krim surrendered and was deported to the French Pacific colony of Réunion with forty of his family and entourage.

Later a figure of romance and myth, Abd el-Krim was passionately supported at the time by the CGTU and the Communist Party, which called on all French troops to fraternize with the fighters from the Rif. It was a call to mutiny, backed by references to the mutineers of the Chemin des Dames and the fact that their leaders had been shot on the orders of Pétain. This specific association of Pétain with repression and not pacification in 1917 was to remain a Communist theme throughout the shifts and changes in party policy over the next fifteen years.

If there was a direct sequel to the Rif war it was the stimulus it gave to independence movements among young Moroccan intellectuals who formed an action committee in the early 1930s. Resistance by the Berbers to the extension of French rule in the Atlas mountains continued until 1933–4.

In France the emphasis on the civilizing benefits of railways, hospitals and schools was redoubled as the great Colonial Exhibition was prepared. When it finally opened on 6 May 1931 in the Bois de Vincennes, Marshal Lyautey was the iconic figurehead of empire and Albert Sarraut the embodiment of visionary policy. The centrepiece of the Indo-China section was Angkor Wat, the twelfth-century Vishnu temple in Cambodia, reproduced as a full-scale replica remarkable for the exactness of its detail. Over 33 million visitors brought a profit to the whole event. Exoticism was the motif but colonialism was the substance. It had a cul-de-sac quality, leading back on itself, a self-reflexive statement, less about the colonies than about how the colonial powers thought of themselves. It was a paradigm of the way in which the French vision of colonial life and culture was mounted, as a mosaic of diversity within a unitary frame. It is crucial to understanding the cultural fantasies which underpinned the determination after the Second World War to hang on to the colonies, long after the concept of empire was discredited. Away from Vincennes, satirical counter-exhibits were

provided by Surrealists in the Communist Party, who issued a tract headed 'Don't visit the Colonial Exhibition' denouncing colonialism as brigandage and claiming that all colonial people shared the same struggle as the proletariat.[17]

There had been some movement over the decade. Assimilation, deriving from Enlightenment and Jacobin principles, had never been extended in practice to all colonized people. For many French settlers the egalitarian aims of assimilation seemed preposterous and dangerous, such was their ingrained belief in the 'inequality of races', claimed as a scientific fact by a stream of popular racist literature stemming from Gobineau and Gustave Le Bon. It was common for French officials, teachers and missionaries to meet these rooted prejudices half-way and concentrate on assimilating only an accepted élite. Assimilation was therefore failing in its grand design, though it remained present in French colonial thinking throughout the 1920s and beyond. Alongside it developed the alternative policy of association, as initiated by Sarraut in Indo-China before the war, by Lyautey in Morocco, and by the authorities in Senegal. The indigenous cultures, schools and practices allowed to co-exist with French institutions carried inferior status, but it could be publicly argued against critics of colonialism that they were a pathway to independence.

Association and control appeared incompatible at many junctures. The Colonial Exhibition opened just after a period of ruthless repression of dissident and insurrectional movements in Vietnam. As a precaution against disruption of the exhibition, Nguyen Van Tao, student leader of the recently formed Communist Party of Indo-China, was arrested in Paris and deported. Nevertheless, in Saigon, Vietnamese culture was promoted alongside French, and the fact that Angkor Wat should be the showpiece at the exhibition reflected the respect of certain French colonial architects, notably Ernest Hébrard, for the pre-colonial heritage of Indo-China. The pinnacle of control, whether through assimilation or association, was the opening of selective aspects of higher education within France to indigenous élites.[18] What was only partially recognized, even after the deportation of Vietnamese students from Paris, was that their exposure to French republican concepts primed liberational ideas and resentment at colonial inequality and injustice.

Republican routes

In 1872 Adolphe Thiers had stated, more as policy than as prophecy, that the republic would be conservative or it would not exist. Nearly sixty years later there was little doubt that the republic existed and was indeed socially conservative. The primacy of the republic was solidly established by the end of the 1920s, though it was still only a democracy in the making and had never possessed the monopoly of reason that had been claimed for it in the wake of the Dreyfus Affair.

From a comparatively narrow base, first under Combes as anticlerical and then under Clemenceau as strike-breaker, the republic had broadened under the impact of the war not just through the concept of the *union sacrée* but through the practical inclusion of socialists and trade unionists in government projects, and nationalists in the politics of 'war to the end'. The victory in 1918 was as much a sign of internal cohesion as of military achievement.

But there was no seamless narrative of ever-widening inclusion. Radical senators refused to contemplate the rational case for the inclusion of women, and generally there was no single way of interpreting the diffuse meanings of the war. The unprecedented destruction over four years made reconstruction the key word of peace. It was as much the reconstruction of an imagined past as the construction of the future, and the opposition of these two created much of the dynamic of the post-war years. Both right and left now firmly existed within the republic and both reconstructed their own exclusive agendas: for the Bloc National it was getting rid of the interventionist role of government and state in the economy, and this involved returning to conflict with socialists and the trade unions; for the Cartel des Gauches it was overturning the tolerance for nationalists and Catholics, and this meant an attempted return to the anticlerical certainties of the pre-war years.

In the conflict between the two, a mixed and increasingly diverse society began to emerge. There was a stubborn resilience of sectional interests, and (perhaps the most positive sign of the primacy of the republic) an internalization of the notion of rights and a conviction of the justice of defending any threatened point of view or way of life.

Symbolically, intellectuals were increasingly profligate in their attachment to a diversity of political causes, provoking an astringent warning from Julien Benda of the threat they posed to themselves. The generic term of 'intellectuals' had emerged during the Dreyfus Affair. Émile Zola's letter, *J'accuse* ... carried in the newspaper *L'Aurore* on 13 January 1898, was

followed by a letter signed by writers and academics, with Zola and Anatole France at their head, demanding a revision of the trial of Dreyfus. On 1 February Maurice Barrès referred to it in *Le Journal* as 'the protest of the intellectuals'. It was not a compliment. The pro-Dreyfus 'intellectuals' were pictured in anti-Dreyfus cartoons as a minute fragment which had broken off from the organic whole of the nation. By the beginning of the 1920s it was apparent that the nationalist writer Charles Maurras, and Barrès before him, might also be labelled 'intellectuals'. The term was effectively adopted by nationalists in 1925 at the time of the Rif war in response to the denunciation of French Moroccan policy by Henri Barbusse and left-wing intellectuals in, or close to, the Communist Party. Printed in *L'Humanité* as a collective protest of 'intellectual workers' (*travailleurs intellectuels*), it provoked a nationalist rebuttal in *Le Figaro* from 'intellectuals on the side of the *patrie*' who defended the French troops fighting in Morocco in the cause of 'law, civilization and peace'.[19]

The early presumption that a republican, left-wing bias defined the 'intellectual' did not disappear, but in 1927 the austere and egoistic sixty-year-old Julien Benda, who had been a Dreyfusard, qualified this entire inherited image by taking scholars and intellectuals to task for abandoning what he maintained was the upper sphere of pure thought and reason and descending into the worldly domain of political polemic and passion. In his high-minded treatise, *La Trahison des clercs* (*The Betrayal of the Intellectuals*), he berated nationalists and Marxists for their betrayal of 'the universal' and the ideal of truth. He objected fundamentally to the philosopher Henri Bergson for promoting intuition, flux and dynamism at the expense of reason. Benda saw no betrayal in his own rejection of the pacifism firstly of Jaurès in 1914 and later of Romain Rolland, and he unquestioningly embraced the republic as the embodiment of reason and 'the universal'.

Benda tried to create an ideology, or moral economy, of the intellectual, making the definition and role of the intellectual into a system of ideas which could stand on its own, in defiance of other systems. His treatise and his inconsistencies became a reference point throughout the century. When intellectuals contributed forcefully to the spiral of political conflict in the 1930s he was credited with having sounded the first alarm, but his 'universal' was open to relativist definition, and unsurprisingly he had produced no absolute definition of truth. His ideology of the intellectual was rejected by other ideologies which had already placed the realm of thought in a quite different relationship to politics.

Schoolteachers were included in any colloquial definition of intellectuals. In 1919 Anatole France addressed a pacifist message to state schoolteachers

in a conference at Tours and told them to 'Make people hate war . . . it is a new humanity you have to create, new intellects you have to awaken if you want to stop Europe from falling once again into imbecility and barbarism.'[20] Romain Rolland and Henri Barbusse both emphasized that teachers had the mission to regenerate France in a pacifist and revolutionary direction. At local level, whether the handful of Communist teachers in the peasant villages of the Alpes-Maritimes or large numbers of socialist teachers in the mining communities of the Pas-de-Calais, the *instituteurs* and *institutrices* were the intellectuals, sons and daughters of peasants or miners who had gone on to teacher training but remained rooted in their class and locality. They were expected to be politically engaged. Marxist intellectuals were insistent in pointing to Benda's lofty ideal as expressing the interests of the ruling class. The young writer Paul Nizan, who joined the Communist Party in 1929 at the height of its rigid reaffirmation of class conflict, reiterated the Marxist suspicion of anyone who appeared to separate thought from action. Against the concept of 'the intellectual' as idealized by Benda he defended 'the revolutionary' as someone, in Marx's own terms, who set out not only to understand the world but to change it.

Benda's treatise was a robust but fallible attempt to regulate attitudes and behaviour in his own world. Other categorical formulations or fears were as powerfully expressed and just as subject to divergent outcomes. Modernization in industry did not become the all-devouring Moloch of Fritz Lang's film *Metropolis*; tradition in workshops and on small farms did not disappear. Scores of villages were left moribund and deserted by the *exode rural*, but a certain autonomy of peasant life survived, increasingly insistent on its interests. Strikes were not outlawed, neither did they cease altogether in the 1920s, and one government set a precedent for specific aid to strikers. Attachment to the victorious nationalism of 1918 did not prevent the flowering of internationalism, under first Herriot and then Briand. The royalist movement, Action Française, was weakened by the denunciation of its atheism by Pope Pius XI in September 1926, which prompted a further rallying of right-wing Catholics to Poincaré's conservative republic. And yet the right-wing legacy from the Bloc National did not determine all the options taken by Poincaré in 1926–8. Modernism was assertively international: traditional landscape painting assertively national and provincial. One seemed outward-looking, the other inward: but provinces too needed rediscovery.

It was one sign of the enjoyment of peace that increasing numbers of mainly wealthy or mechanically-minded urban dwellers set off on the roads of France to discover the provinces. A car was the property of an élite,

organized into the Touring Club de France since 1890, with 137,000 members by 1913. The provision of tyres was monopolized by the Michelin industry at Clermont-Ferrand, designed as a model environment for workers and their families. The *Guide Michelin*, created by André Michelin in 1900 and offered free to car-owners until 1920, was followed by the firm's production of detailed maps of France, town plans, and hotel and restaurant details, and by the inclusion of road numbers on road signs, which the government made obligatory in 1919. The visibility of France in map form owed much to the impact of the war. Locating the fighting, understanding where the soldier son or husband might be, were popular demands, despite the fear of spies. The need to visit the scenes after the war was no less a dynamic. Michelin provided maps and guides to the battle-fields, with dramatic photographs of towns and villages before and after the devastation. The regional guides developed and satisfied curiosity about regional diversity, while the acculturation of Lyautey to Moroccan culture was given Michelin's benediction in its guide to the protectorate, which established Lyautey as 'the creator of tourism in Morocco'.

If on the large historical stage the politics of the war saw the republic successfully in pursuit of the nation, the years of peace saw the republic-nation in pursuit of its geographical and cultural identity. Extending to the provinces as well as the colonies, the discovery of diversity was a route taken by writers and cultural specialists of all kinds, by curators of new museums and by ethnologists. The routes provided picture postcards, products of a mechanized craft in its golden and most creative years, which dispersed images not only of unfamiliar places but also of the people of a region or colonized country, their dress and habitat. The film made of André Citroën's mid-1920s automobile expedition to Central Africa, *La Croisière noire* ('The Black Cruise') was a box-office success, praised in the press for its portrait 'of all those mysterious races' and celebrating the triumph of French technology in the colonies. It distracted attention from the cancellation of a massive travel project across the sands of the Sahara, in Citroën cars to be equipped with caterpillar tracks, announced with flamboyant publicity but taking little account of realities.[21] The self-conscious postcard, film and touring industries were miscrocosms of the countless organizations in the Republic bent on mapping and displaying 'unity in diversity'. The theme, embedded during the 1920s, contested and constantly redefined, outlasted the entire twentieth century. For staunch republicans, French roots and routes carried a unitary but at the same time culturally diffuse meaning of Frenchness: France singular and plural.

The diversity of the 1920s was not a plurality of equal parts. There were

too many inequalities, too many exclusions; too many failures to modernize as well as excesses; too many dysfunctional traditions as well as resilient survivals. But at a very real level of experience and of emotion, whether pride, grief or anger, the war had included all of society. In itself this was a fact of watershed significance.

PART TWO

The Spiral of Ideology, 1920s–1969

Introduction to Part Two

At the end of the 1920s the political clashes of the previous three decades were familiar to the point where they began to seem to many to be tired and lifeless. The diversity of the distinctive society which emerged against the backdrop of reconstruction and the memorialization of the war dead came under fire for complacency and social stagnation. Demands for renewal and the pressures of economic crisis set off a spiral of ideology.

The influence of Nietzsche has been widely perceived as dominant in the attraction of an irrational dynamism which pervades literature and thought, identified with both ends of the political spectrum. No single influence or cause can possibly account for the range of ideas which assume committed ideological form. Communists express themselves in the apocalyptic language of imminent revolution, which draws on 1789 and 1871 as well as the Bolshevik revolution of 1917. Ideals of fascism are not so much imported from Italy, Spain or Germany as home-grown in radical developments from ideas and movements dating back to the early years of the century. Every kind of ideology is thrown into the arena, affecting clashes over rural policy, over immigrants and refugees, and over the fundamental consensus for peace.

The issues of secularism against clericalism, identified with the conflictual era of Combes, are pushed into the wings of a political stage vastly increased in size. The streets and the workplaces are contested in a climax of social confrontation, which exudes festivity and humanism as well as bitterness. Invasion from outside accelerates the spiral, producing in 1940–44 the most impassioned conflict of French against French since 1871. The contest for running the state had taken on a much more overt ideological colour, to the point where its historic republicanism is actually repudiated in 1940, leaving only the state. The war is barely over when post-war governments

of a restored Republic tragically refuse to separate the primacy of the republic from colonialism.

The leadership of Charles de Gaulle and his presence in politics across almost thirty years shifts the identity debate about Frenchness from one centred on the republican tradition to one centred on the nation. Putting a concept of the nation first had always been the contention of nationalists. De Gaulle's ideology of the nation was announced in the first sentence of his memoirs as 'une certaine idée de la France' but his defence of the republic and the sequence of policies that he pursued in power also had a certain idea of pragmatism and adaptability which made it difficult for his followers to define Gaullism with any exactitude.

The question of what caused the intense ideological conflicts of French against French, replicated in the student revolt and the general strike of 1968, has been posed as a European, or Western, issue, and not just one of internal French politics. People tend to rise in hope rather than despair, so that repeated confrontations are not automatically the sign of a country, or groups within it, reduced to chaos or desperation. It was nevertheless increasingly apparent that there was a specificity about Franco-French conflicts (*les guerres franco-françaises*) which suggested another element of 'exceptionalism'. It was not until the spiral of ideology lost its momentum after the revolt of 1968 and de Gaulle retired in 1969 that the two 'exceptional' aspects, the primacy of the republic-state and Franco-French ideological violence, began to be analysed together.

Throughout the heightened period of ideological conflict, some but not all of the pressures for the modernization of society and the economy were fervently ideological, though many of the massive changes in the thirty years after the Liberation were experienced as incremental rather than eruptive. It was a central political issue to decide just how revolutionary the changes were, and whether or not they 'improved' the lives of ordinary people. It was around this issue that much of the creative as well as disruptive thought of 1968 coalesced.

7

Manipulating Crisis, 1920s–1934

1. Calls for renewal

'We are in a period of enormous material progress,' wrote Henri Barbusse in 1927, 'yet also one of bankruptcy.' He saw disillusion and anxiety everywhere. Intellectuals, like the whole of society, were searching for direction: 'They are searching for something new. They feel that a huge change is in the air, but they don't know what it is.' He was arguing for a new social consciousness among fellow intellectuals, a realization that there were not two levels of truth, one theoretical and the other practical, but only one. Manual workers and intellectuals should work together to fight the established order, which, he claimed, masked its reactionary politics with the bland proposition that 'whatever is, is normal'. Only together would they 'open up the future'.[1] This was the particular agenda of Barbusse to attract young intellectuals into the Communist Party, but in fact the call for thought and action to move as one, and the diagnosis of 'change in the air', were widespread across the political spectrum.

Part of the passion for new ideas was an impatience with the growing complexity of life and politics in the 1920s. What made it so complex was the increasing part that government of some kind was beginning to play in moulding the context and direction of most people's lives. The theories of mass society which emerged in the 1920s were adamant that the state was eroding people's individual rights, and yet in an undramatic but structural way the notion that government would inevitably have an impact on everyday lives was slowly implanting itself as acceptable in the post-war decade. The rise of the civil servant, the *fonctionnaire*, occasioned biting satire and political outrage from libertarians of left and right, with ready reference to the comedies of Georges Courteline at the turn of the century ridiculing the bureaucratic mentality. On the other hand the range of jobs held by *fonctionnaires*, which included primary-school teaching and postal work, represented modest but widespread aspirations of

social advancement for those who had most to gain from universal education.

Whether from boredom, paranoia, petulance or frustration, the attacks on officialdom were carried by bodily metaphors such as myopia, sterility and impotence, a reflection of the obsession with demographic decline and the ageing nature of the population. No less than bureaucracy, politics was increasingly seen as a system, tired, lifeless and moribund, or as a game played at the people's expense. Jokes about the age of republican leaders multiplied, summarized in the ironic question and answer, 'Why is France ruled by seventy-year-olds? Because the eighty-year-olds are dead.' To the antinomy of left and right was added the polarity of young and old, only this cut across all political boundaries and was far from a simple opposition. In the language of Barrès, age-old tradition could indicate permanent youthfulness. But 'young' did imply action of a type generically different from everyday politics and administration: it signified idealism before it became mired in petty regulations and lost its dynamic potential. Péguy's 'Tout commence en mystique: tout finit en politique' ('Everything starts as mystique: everything ends as politics') was widely quoted as prophecy, proverb, truth and warning.

Allusions to Péguy multiplied when Pope Pius XI in 1926 condemned the atheism and absence of spirituality in Action Française and put the writings of Charles Maurras on the index of forbidden books. Long considered as the natural home for Catholics hostile to the Republic, the royalist movement did not collapse, but the dichotomy between its politics and the aims of the Catholic Church deepened with the successes of Catholic Action initiated by the Pope in 1922. It was the papal answer to the vexed question of the role of Catholics in contemporary politics: no model for a specific Catholic party but rather a co-ordinated campaign to carry the social teachings of the Church into every aspect of society through action by lay, and particularly young, Catholics. Carried forward by the Association Catholique de la Jeunesse Française (ACJF), Catholic Action formed specific organizations of students and of young workers in both industry and agriculture. The Jeunesse Ouvrière Chrétienne (JOC) was formed in 1926 with parallel groups for women workers (JOCFéminine) and the rural Jeunesse Agricole Chrétienne (JAC and JACF) in 1929. Jocistes in the workplace embodied the revived sense of mission that many Catholic intellectuals were expressing in passionate denunciations of the materialism and mechanization displayed throughout society.

Catholic practices and belief during the war claimed to have unified industrial communities where syndicalism had been divisive. Class struggle

was rejected, but the specific claims of workers were recognized. Expressing this ambivalence, a Catholic trade-union structure was launched in 1920 and opened to Protestants whose strength in Alsace-Lorraine was immediately visible. The Confédération Française des Travailleurs Chrétiens (CFTC) was rejected by the two main union movements as a device of the *patronat*. This was too simple. Its support did emanate from areas where Catholicism was traditionally strong in both popular culture and paternalist industry, notably the north, Alsace-Lorraine, Paris, the Lyon area and towns such as Nantes in the west, but throughout the 1920s and still more the 1930s it provided a focus for office workers, bank employees, technical staff and white-collar employees, whose collective material interests marked them as hostile to the liberal economics of the *patronat*. There was some parallel action to the CGT at several moments of widespread social confrontation. In politics the attempt to register the particularity of Catholics was equally problematic. The Parti Démocrate Populaire (PDP) formed in 1924 was the uncertain creation of a mix of Catholic democrats and social Catholics, and cautiously echoed some of the aspirations of the pre-war Sillon movement. It gained eighteen seats in the 1928 elections and had its own weekly newspaper, *Le Petit Démocrate*, but Pius XI did not suggest that Catholics from Action Française should transfer to the PDP. It was unable to establish itself as the authoritative political voice of all Catholics, and the vacuum was filled by scores of small movements, intellectual reviews and spiritual manifestos.

Jacques Maritain followed the Pope's injunction and broke with Maurras, affirming the primacy of the spiritual domain with a book of that title in 1927. It was a seminal influence on Catholic intellectuals who engaged in intense discussions at his home in Meudon, bordering the forest south-west of Paris.[2] But the royalism of Action Française did not lose all its Catholic followers. In a stirring little monarchist book written for Christmas 1930, the Catholic novelist Georges Bernanos, who had joined Action Française before the war, attributed to a young boy he met in Lorraine the wisdom and innocence necessary to recognize a king as a fearless hero mounted on a horse, the stuff of royalist mythology and the culture of the *ancien régime*: 'Our dear old Péguy, republican as he was, would have been very happy.' The book rails against the stuffy pedantry of republican education and calls for the replacement of Durkheim's 'soulless books' by the great military legends, in which the Marne, the Yser, the Somme and Verdun are added to the battles of Malplaquet and Rosbach.[3] In the same year, 1930, at the opposite end of the political spectrum, the socialist ideals which had influenced Péguy's youth were evoked by Louise

Saumoneau, who had not joined the Communist majority at Tours but who sought constantly for a revival of socialism as 'a pure and life-giving force. That is what socialism was in the past. May it be the same tomorrow.'[4]

The need for revival, renewal and a recaptured idealism was seen to be starkly evident in the electoral campaign of 1928. This was the judgement of Albert Thibaudet, regular political commentator in the *Nouvelle Revue Française (NRF)*. Synonymous with younger literary writing, the *NRF*, launched by André Gide and Jean Schlumberger in 1909, had acquired a reputation for radical thinking and Radical politics. It was specifically Radicalism that needed revitalizing, argued Thibaudet. He discerned a serious lack of ideas in the party: it was too passive, and he argued that it needed to confront the challenge of class analysis by active dialogue with the Socialists.[5] Within the Radical Party the most vocal expressions of unease came from an inchoate group of self-styled Young Turks, some of whom argued for closer links with the Socialists and others for a celebration of the political centre.

The urgency for a new activism was sensed precisely at the time when France was emerging from its period of mourning and the memorialization of war. The revivalist ideas of the late 1920s signified the end of the *après-guerre*. The trauma of the war and the local co-operation of different political and social forces in the creation of the *monuments aux morts* had acted as a palliative for several years, tempering the divisiveness of both action and ideas, though by no means suppressing them altogether. A release of pent-up energy lies behind the restatement of ideals and the call for action.

Class against class

Nowhere was identity more radically subject to renewal than in the volatile doctrines of Communism. Identity implies difference. Thibaudet's awareness that class difference had to be confronted reflected its heightened use and new sectarian thrust by the eight-year-old Communist Party. The party had been accused by three of its own ruling committee, Pierre Monatte, Alfred Rosmer and Victor Delagarde, of 'living in a state of permanent crisis'. That was in November 1924 in an open letter to members of the party in which the three attacked its growing authoritarian structure. They discerned a military-style imposition of discipline under the cover of 'bolshevization', a cascade of orders from the top to the bottom: 'Soon the bureaucracy of the party will leave that of the French state well behind.'[6] Their expulsion was announced shortly afterwards in *L'Humanité*, which

claimed that the party's influence was visibly increasing among the masses.

Such claims were in inverse proportion to the party's declining membership. In 1927–8, under Henri Barbé, a caricature of rigidity, it carried through the new Stalin-inspired doctrine of exclusivity, known as 'class against class', under which the Socialists were denounced as bourgeois enemies of the proletariat and as 'social fascists'. The narrow appeal of the doctrine was on view at the 1928 elections. It reduced the party's seats from twenty-six to twelve and drained its membership by 1932 to a low of 25,000. It was little more than a small sect in the national political field. Rigidity, however, was also clarity and identity: the vaunted proletarian tradition was now not so much the old and diffuse pre-war legacy of Jaurès and Guesde shared by the Socialists, as the embattled experience of those who had followed the Soviet example. Militants formed at the end of the 1920s remained in strategic party positions until the late 1940s and beyond. In 1931 the new Secretary-General was thirty-year-old Maurice Thorez, from a working family in the Pas-de-Calais, and he remained in charge until his death in 1964. He had a militant Guesdist grandfather and had initially opposed the imposition of 'class against class' before accepting its necessity. Eugen Fried assured the all-important regular links between the redefined party and Moscow. As leader, Thorez was frequently described as little more than a colourless bureaucrat. But he promoted himself as 'le fils du peuple' (son of the people) known simply by his first name as Comrade Maurice, a workerist familiarity which made an impact on the rootless new working-class communities in the suburbs of Paris.

Despite its marginality in electoral politics, the Communist Party managed to project itself vividly in *L'Humanité* as locked in 'daily conflict with the bourgeois state'. This was more than polemic. Sackings and arrests for Communist activities were commonplace. Étienne Fajon, who joined the party at the age of twenty-one in 1927, was a primary-school teacher in the rural commune of Aniane at the centre of the Hérault vineyards. The local secretary was the village *pâtissier* and together they staged the singing of the 'Internationale' after the 'Marseillaise' on 14 July. The mayor called for Fajon's dismissal, which he successfully avoided, but two years later he was refused access to any teaching post after distributing party tracts in the Mediterranean fishing port of Sète and spending fifteen days in gaol.[7] Prison as an apprenticeship to the party was a norm. The earlier actions of the party against the occupation of the Ruhr and the Rif war had brought a string of convictions for provoking disobedience in the army, a constantly renewed charge which put party leaders Marcel Cachin, Jacques Duclos and Paul Vaillant-Couturier in prison in January 1928.

The accusation of social-fascism brought Communists and Socialists to blows in local meetings but what most abused the rival Socialists was the charge that they were actively seeking power within the bourgeois structure of society. They were certainly well set to do so. The Socialist rump at Tours had become the dominant of the two Marxist movements within a few years, turning the tables on the initial Communist majority. They marked their electoral dominance in 1924 with 104 deputies and reaffirmed it in 1928 by losing only four seats when Poincaré's policies won the elections for the parties of the right. The process of political bargaining in the Republic had always exercised a pull to the right, known as *droitisme*, and increasingly in the 1920s it was expected that the Socialists would be unable to resist it. The SFIO had a militant revolutionary wing in the Seine, but the consolidation of unionized white-collar workers and *fonctionnaires* within the party gave it a core of small-town, non-industrial and rural supporters, notably in the middle of France from the Haute-Vienne, through the Allier to the Saône-et-Loire, and across the Languedoc to the south of the Massif Central. The attraction was a party which was democratic in its organization, in which a collective belonging to the idea of revolution could co-exist with practical programmes of social reform.

With this wide base the Socialist Party was always eligible for power according to the social norms described by the Communists as bourgeois: over 25 per cent of the Socialist deputies in 1928 were lawyers or doctors, and less than a third were workers.[8] But participation in a government run by non-Socialists was specifically rejected by the party. Class struggle for Socialists still meant the classic Marxist formulation of the whole working class against the bourgeoisie, and they countered the Communist slur of 'social-fascism' with bitter accusations that the Communists were merely puppets of Moscow and were dividing the labour movement against itself.

Mystique of action

Before the clamour for renewal at the end of the 1920s there had been a spurt of new activity on the nationalist right in 1924. A call to combat came from a nationalist deputy for Paris, Pierre Taittinger, a prosperous industrialist who owned hotels, shops and *brasseries* throughout the city. The Communists had staged an assertively independent march through Paris on the day that Jaurès was elevated to the Panthéon. Taittinger announced the 'horror of revolution' on the streets and revived the passion of Déroulède's Ligue des Patriotes by the formation of young action groups of national defence, the Jeunesses Patriotes, who adopted as uniform the

blue raincoats fashionable in bourgeois circles, and the Basque beret. The baptism of fire for the Jeunesses Patriotes was a clash with Communists demonstrating against the Rif war in the rue Damrémont in Paris. Outnumbered, four were killed. 'They died,' wrote Taittinger in *La Liberté*, 'protecting with their breasts the peaceful citizens whom they had sworn to defend.'

In the spring of 1925 other nationalist legions were launched which were transformed symbolically on 11 November into Le Faisceau, to consummate a new awakening by Georges Valois, the economic specialist on *L'Action française*. His movement claimed to renew the spirit and collectivity of those who had fought in the war, 'which had been for all of us,' said Valois in 1921, 'our earliest and greatest school'. The revelations of the war experience were stirred together with syndicalist ideas from the nineteenth-century anarchist Pierre-Joseph Proudhon, whose vision of workers' federations Valois had adapted within Action Française to offer a nationalist alternative to Marxist socialism. Across the Alps he saw a similar synthesis of anarcho-syndicalism and nationalism in Mussolini's plans for a Corporate State. He made a personal visit to Il Duce in 1923, but the Faisceau came from his own hotchpotch of ideas put forward in his publication *Le Nouveau Siècle* where a form of national-syndicalism was promoted as the key to resolving the class struggle and outflanking the forces of the left.

The Faisceau effectively collapsed in under two years. Valois broke with Charles Maurras, and his militants clashed at meetings with the Camelots du Roi. Increasingly disillusioned by the patriarchal power of Action Française, he became more and more populist and his ideology moved to the left. He turned back towards the anarchism from which he had started in the early 1900s, but not before he had formed collectives of veterans, producers and heads of families, the latter specifically including widows who had taken over from their men: 'In this sense,' ran the movement's doctrine in 1926, 'the Faisceau incorporates feminism.' The paramilitaries of the movement sported a uniform of blue shirts, and *Le Nouveau Siècle* expressed the fascist mystique of action and the cult of the new. As such it attracted the largesse of the perfume magnate François Coty, impresario of action squads with illusions of grandeur.

Coty was ready again with money for a new departure in November 1927. A veritable sign that the co-operative period of the *monuments aux morts* was finally over, the writer Maurice Hanot d'Hartoy, author of *La Génération du feu*, announced an élite association of *anciens combattants* geared to action, the Croix-de-Feu. The name represented soldiers cited for

bravery at the front and the object was to constitute what d'Hartoy later called 'a great anti-revolutionary and anti-defeatist force of incomparable moral and military standing'.[9] Yet another call for renewal, it found immediate echo at the offices of *Le Figaro* which was owned by Coty. But the context was significantly different from that of 1924–5. In 1927, in full Poincarist euphoria, there was no threat from the left which called for new measures of social defence. The formation of the Croix-de-Feu was a luxury of nationalist revivalism, a product of *ennui* and frustration, a flexing of muscles against the dominant pacifism and normative lives of the bulk of the war veterans. It was an idea of combat looking for an opportunity.

2. *World depression, French crisis*

A sense of political crisis and a readiness to manipulate it were endemic at the end of the 1920s. It was in the realm of ideas and political behaviour that the problem was diagnosed, but it was not widely recognized as real or urgent throughout society until the economic crisis from America began seriously to affect people's lives. The Wall Street crash of November 1929 did not immediately impinge on French society, but the consequences were felt gradually from 1931 and intensely from 1933. When the effects were clearly evident, the 'crisis' of ideas and the calls for renewal from both left and right became substantive. In the terms announced by Barbusse, the theoretical and the practical were brought shudderingly together.

Failure to modernize?

The economist Charles Rist declared in a report in 1931 that the depression was due to an event exterior to the economy of France. The particular mix of industry with its core of small workshops revolving round the local economy, and the relative prevalence of the agricultural sector with its bastion of peasant self-sufficiency, undoubtedly cushioned France from the knee-jerk deflation which followed the American crash. Within two years, cuts in the workforce in Britain put 2.7 million men and women on the dole; in Germany 4.6 million and in the USA 8 million. The corresponding French figures for 1931 showed 55,000. This was strikingly out of line, even though it was an underestimate firstly because it only showed those on relief payments and secondly because the first victims of cutbacks were immigrant workers who were not counted in the statistics. There was escalation after 1933, and in the five years from 1931 it is estimated that

between 1.1 and 1.4 million jobs were cut, mostly in textiles and the metalworking industries. By the beginning of 1936 the number of jobless receiving relief had risen to 465,000, but the real total of unemployed was double that number. Throughout, the figures were substantially lower than those in comparable industrial countries. And yet France failed to turn round economically in 1935 when Britain, Germany, Italy and the USA all showed recovery. In 1938 industrial production was still well below that of ten years before. It seems reasonable therefore for recent historians to propose that if the crash did indeed come from outside, the delayed recovery on the other hand was due to structural, or political, deficiencies within France.[10]

This distinction between a world depression and a French crisis contains a particular model of modernization which determines the analysis. According to this model, France was ill-equipped in both economic thinking and political willpower to face the lack of competitiveness in world markets due to outmoded, archaic habits and structure, including a mistrust of expansion based on credit. This lack of dynamism was initially a protection from the stock-market crash which plunged the most modern economies into a headlong fall, but it was precisely this protective shield which became a liability when recovery demanded a major shake-up of the 'backward' sectors. Immobility was heightened by the obsession with a strong franc, and a refusal to devalue even when sterling was devalued on 20 September 1931 and the dollar in April 1933. French exports were now doubly crippled and the cycle of uncompetitiveness was reinforced. While exports were shackled and home demand remained limp, there was no path to recovery.

This analysis was already fully formed in the assessment of the centre-right deputy Paul Reynaud in 1934, who provoked the rage of extreme nationalists by calling for devaluation. Battered by accusations of being a traitor and a Judas, he wrote in 1936: 'The French are totally obsessed with keeping the franc as it is; they wrap it up in the *tricolore*.'[11] A fear of inflation was buttressed by a suspicion of borrowing which ran through much of French society. Dependence on credit carried an atavistic image of unscrupulous and foreign moneylenders, and this produced a particular form of anti-capitalism to which much of the world of small and medium-sized business, local commerce and shopkeeping was prone.

In the countryside, action by peasant farmers in 1928 already announced a rural perspective which would become deeply embedded as the depression affected the viability of small-scale agriculture. On 9 December several thousand Breton farmers converged on Vannes, the *chef-lieu* of Morbihan

on the Atlantic coast, to demand the withdrawal of the law recently passed on social insurance and its replacement by a voluntary system. The anger was over the compulsory employers' contributions which they claimed would severely reduce their income or force them to cut the number of their farmhands. Similar protests came from shopkeepers and small businesses through the Fédération des Contribuables (taxpayers). On 2 January 1929 Henri Dorgères, director of a small publication, *Le Progrès agricole de l'ouest*, printed on green paper in Rennes, organized a Comité de Défense Paysanne on this issue. Within a year it had started a vociferous campaign against the trusts controlling cereals and nitrate fertilizers, accused of riding roughshod over peasant interests. Protests escalated with the depression, for which large business, urban interests and politicians were held directly responsible. This perspective as a general attitude held a monopoly in most rural areas, but only some backed the specific solutions of Dorgères as he developed more violent and ideological tactics of active peasant defence.

3. Public projects, scandal and riot

Tardieu experiment?

André Tardieu was neither an eighty- nor a seventy-year-old when he became Premier in the same month as the Wall Street crash. A youthful fifty-four, he had been one of Clemenceau's closest advisers, and something of a maverick reputation was later ascribed to Tardieu. His willingness to spend public money was in direct contrast to the deflationary cuts by which his successors tried to stem the mounting economic crisis.

Was he an instinctive Keynesian *avant le mot*? It seems not. He later showed no support for either Keynes or Roosevelt's New Deal. His expenditure was more a continuation of the public projects which he had backed under Poincaré as investment in national prosperity. The social insurance announced in 1928 was confirmed in a new bill of 1930, which most of Tardieu's majority opposed but could not bring themselves to vote against. Work continued on a 1929 initiative by Louis Loucheur to set up a public system of child benefits (*allocations familiales*) which reached the statute book in March 1932. In 1930, for the first time in republican history, a limited amount of free secondary education was introduced. Road-building schemes over five years and the further extension of electricity into the countryside set up a rolling programme which ensured that electricity was one of the industries which suffered no decline during the 1930s. Salaries of the *fonctionnaires* were increased, which occasioned ribald criticism, but

this was offset by a popular retirement scheme for *anciens combattants* and payments for those injured in agricultural work.

Tardieu was not personally in favour of every measure adopted by his government. As the depression began to bite in 1931 the programme of expenditure looked irresponsible. Tardieu was replaced, and it became orthodox 'good' government, practised by the centre-right first under Pierre Laval and then under Tardieu himself in a second ministry, to balance the books by economies in public spending. Outside parliament the CGT openly advanced the benefits of higher public expenditure, and codified their demands in a campaign for a forty-hour working week, followed with some hesitation by the Socialist Party. The right attacked the left as potentially dangerous spendthrifts in a visceral campaign mounted for the 1932 elections, but the Radicals, who returned to power on the wave of left-wing victory at the polls, continued with deflation from 1932 to 1934, and this was accentuated by right-wing governments in 1934–6. By then it was clear that the first Tardieu ministry was pre-crisis; it was not a reflationary experiment. Like Tardieu himself, it is difficult to categorize. The left could not use it as a precedent because Tardieu had given it right-wing credentials, but historically it holds a place, however ambivalent, in the slow gestation of a welfare state.

Victory but no unity on the left

From the rue Amelot in Paris, Henri de Kerillis, of lesser Breton nobility and the son of an admiral, set up what he called 'the most powerful propaganda organization against socialism and Communism'. In 1928 he claimed to have fly-posted 25,000 towns and *communes*, and for 200 francs he guaranteed to keep any locality under constant propaganda and to intervene in every sensitive by-election. He envisaged a vast political *rassemblement* on the model of the British Conservative Party, with electoral tactics which would back the Jeunesses Patriotes in some situations and Radicals in others, depending on how best to defeat the 'revolutionary' candidate. With a regular outlet in the nationalist daily *L'Écho de Paris* he claimed credit for the victory of the right in 1928, and in 1932 set out his own electoral stall in the 7th *arrondissement* of Paris. He was defeated.

The electoral tactics of the left proved superior. Successful Radical deputies numbered 157 and Socialists 129, once again making the Communists look marginal with only 12. With a million fewer votes, the right numbered 259. The majority of voters had rejected the right as incapable of protecting jobs, wages and standard of living. Édouard Herriot returned as Prime

Minister, far more centrist than in 1924 and favourable to deflation. Economies of every kind dominated the scene.

It was under this renewed Radicalism that immigrants, officially numbering 2,715,000 at the 1931 census, but unofficially considered to be close to 3 million, were the first to be collectively victimized. The move pre-dated the elections but the decisive immigration law was enacted on 10 August 1932. Frontiers would be tightly controlled; employers would not have the freedom to take on immigrant labour as they wished; numbers for any profession or region would be centrally decided. When it came before the Chamber in December 1931 no one voted against: the Socialists and the Communists abstained. The creeping malaise was xenophobia. In a satirical reversal of the Colonial Exhibition, immigrants were depicted in the rightwing press as the colonizers, turning France into 'an immense Tower of Babel'.[12] It was at this point that modernism in the arts was most widely seen as alien: foreign artists, like immigrant workers, were forced on to the defensive, their lives blighted by insecurity and poverty.

Almost hand in glove, the campaign intensified against women in the workplace. The return of women to the home (la femme au foyer) was proposed in a number of high-minded Catholic publications as an even more urgent answer to unemployment than the repatriation of immigrants. Charles Rist, an eminent academic friend of women's suffrage, surprisingly set the moral agenda for the campaign in Le Matin in November 1931 by suggesting, in the interests of both family and the unemployed, that women's duty now lay in a return to housekeeping and childcare.[13]

There was no robust counter from the Radical governments of 1932–4 to this pervasive slippage from management of the crisis to scapegoating. A policy of non-interference in industry combined with cuts in expenditure failed to stem the rise in unemployment, and a rapid turnover of premiers fed into anti-parliamentary cynicism. The Communists kept up a parallel denunciation of Radical and Socialist politicians as lackeys of capitalism, and while the Radicals kept socialist policies at arm's length, the Socialist Party itself continued to block the possibility of sharing power in a Radical cabinet. The left was a forceful construct as an attitude of mind, as an electoral tactic and as a block of votes in the Chamber: as a strategy for government action in the crisis it did not exist.

In 1933 the issue exploded within the Socialist Party. Participation in government was debated at the July congress with new ideological twists. Response to unemployment was framed by reaction to the dramatic accession of Hitler and the Nazis to power. The revisionist ideas of the Paris deputy Marcel Déat, published as Perspectives socialistes in Novem-

ber 1930, were central to both questions. As a respected theorist of socialism Déat rivalled the intellectual leadership of Blum. He argued that the state did not have to be seen as the product of capitalism but could be used by socialists to control it: state action would protect what he saw as the joint interests of workers and middle classes. It followed that entry into government was a necessity. For Blum and the majority of the party this was all too close to the fascist ideology of the state, a direction which Adrien Marquet, one of Déat's followers, appeared to confirm at the congress with the slogan of 'order, authority, nation'. Déat's group of 'Neo-Socialists' were expelled from the party shortly after the decisive debate. It was a victory for party orthodoxy but yet more evidence of the inability of the left to work out a common approach to the depression.

Mounting xenophobia

Events in Germany also impacted immediately on the right. Primed by the passing of the immigration law of 10 August 1932, the nationalist press seized on the arrival of Jewish refugees to denounce the left as colluding in a Bolshevik invasion. At the most extreme were François Coty's newspapers *Le Figaro* and *L'Ami du Peuple* and the propaganda of Action Française. On 8 March 1933 *Le Figaro* carried an article urging the necessity for concentration camps in France to be erected to contain the 'Jewish Bolsheviks' and protect French society from contamination. Unceasingly antisemitic and anti-German since the Dreyfus Affair, *L'Action française* used every hyperbole of prejudice to illustrate its royalist contention that the Republic was a foreign regime in the grip of German Jews. The government did not concede to the mounting xenophobia by withdrawing the right of asylum (*le droit d'asile*) but ringed the refugee status with restrictive conditions.

Most of the 35,000 Jews who crossed from Germany in 1933 were young men, few of them workers, many with professional qualifications. Refugees seeking asylum had no right to work and professional middle-class bodies within France, notably in medicine, law and dentistry, closed ranks and vehemently opposed their employment, an opposition which intensified in 1934–5. Although trade-union leaders were largely sympathetic to the refugees, there was growing xenophobia at local meetings when members argued that their jobs would be lost to foreigners on lower wages if they were given permission to work. Antisemites manipulated the events of 1933 to reinforce their particular form of nationalism. From the margins they moved to the centre of political agitation.

Stavisky affair

Investment did not collapse entirely during the depression. Safe investment was all the more urgently sought by small-time savers. The safest seemed to be municipal credit. Towns were known to be careful when lending money. Loans secured by items of value were a sound proposition. In 1931 the deputy-mayor of the Basque port of Bayonne, famed for its ham and captured from the English in 1451 after a 'miracle sign' in the sky, agreed with Alexandre Stavisky to set up a municipal pawnbroking business backed by jewellery. Bonds were issued to investors. It was one of several municipal swindles engineered by Stavisky, then aged forty-five, whose Jewish family came originally from Kiev, and who had already spent seventeen months in prison in 1926–7 for fraud. The jewels were non-existent or their value entirely inflated, the bonds were ultimately worthless, the fraud extravagantly effective. By the end of 1933 Stavisky had amassed almost 300 million francs. In December the Ministry of Finance discovered irregularities in Bayonne. Arrests followed quickly, including that of the deputy-mayor on 7 January 1934. The following day Stavisky was found dead in the snow resort of Chamonix in the Alps as the police came to arrest him. Suicide was the inconclusive verdict.

Two recent affairs of rampant fraud associated with Marthe Hanau and the financier Oustric had led to accusations of corruption in high places, and as the extent of the Bayonne fraud unravelled, charges of collusion with Stavisky implicated several politicians, newspaper editors, lawyers and personalities at the heart of Radicalism. The extreme nationalists celebrated a new miracle in the sky of Bayonne. The scandal allowed them to capture the moral high ground and present themselves as protectors of the hard-won savings of the ordinary citizen. Insinuating that the government of Camille Chautemps had hired a killer to get rid of Stavisky, Léon Daudet in *L'Action française* described Chautemps as a leader of thieves (*voleurs*) and assassins. 'À bas les voleurs!' echoed across the country. Chautemps resigned. For the Communist *L'Humanité* the affair was an indictment of the whole bourgeois political system. For all extra-parliamentary leagues and nationalist paramilitaries it was a golden opportunity to take to the streets and force the left to surrender. Action Française brought out 2,000 protesters against 'foreigners and thieves' on 9 January, the day that the Chamber reassembled; 4,000 demonstrated on the 11th. Solidarité Française was out in force on 26, 27 and 28 January. Numbers of police were injured, but the Paris Prefect of Police, Jean Chiappe, appeared sympathetic to the cause of the leagues. His political bias was clear when he reacted

with a quite different severity against a trade-union march of *fonctionnaires* on 22 January protesting at cuts in their allowances. Chiappe became the toast of the right. Édouard Daladier, the newly designated Premier, decided to reassign him as Resident General in Morocco. Chiappe refused to be moved and on 3 February was relieved of his post. The tinderbox in Paris was alight.

6 February 1934

Daladier was due to present his government on 6 February in the Chamber of the Assemblée Nationale, the Palais-Bourbon. In the corridors André Tardieu co-ordinated the opposition. In *La Liberté* on 4 February he accused Daladier of giving the Socialists the head of Chiappe in exchange for their support. On the same day Léon Blum, speaking in Clermont-Ferrand, denied any bargaining, but the Socialist paper *Le Populaire* welcomed the departure of Chiappe as a liberation of Paris from dictatorship. The street disorder of the nationalist leagues intensified: newspaper kiosks were set on fire and police were attacked with pick handles; there were calls to rush the Chamber and death chants against foreigners, Jews, the left, Blum and Daladier. Orders went out to demonstrate on the 6th, in uniform with full regalia, ready for confrontation. In what seemed like a deviant gesture the Croix-de-Feu assembled on the evening before, simulating a siege of the Ministry of the Interior and the Élysée Palace. This was the decision of Colonel François de La Rocque, the movement's leader since 1931 who had reorganized it with military flair, opening its ranks to the sons and daughters of the Croix-de-Feu and to national volunteers, and forming a combative vanguard known as *dispos*, available at all times for action. But on the 6th he held these forces aloof.

Massing all day at various assembly points, the Jeunesses Patriotes, Action Française, Solidarité Française and militants of the Union Nationale des Combattants formed the bulk of the 20–30,000 regimented demonstrators who converged on the routes to the Chamber. A few thousand communist *anciens combattants* were mobilized a short distance away, uneasy about where to stage their own riot. Police, armed and mounted, barred the way across the bridge from the Place de la Concorde. In the gathering dark and with no military plan, the right-wing leagues stormed the barriers, expecting the police to give way. A bus, benches and barricades were set on fire, shots from the crowd brought a fusillade in reply; some police fired into the air, others into the crowd. In the smoke, dark and confusion hundreds were injured on both sides. There was a second round

of shooting, with charges and countercharges throughout the night. One policeman was killed and fourteen rioters, all from the extreme right. Two more died later. Over 1,400 were injured, the wounded police numbering more than those among the assailants. The barriers were not breached. Inside the Chamber, against a tumult of insults and shouts, Daladier received his vote of confidence. Dawn revealed a blackened urban battle-field. It was the most violent of clashes in Paris since 1871.

8

Confrontations, 1934–1936

1. The making of ideological conflict

'In the grey light of winter 1934,' wrote Gilles Martinet, 'the two political traditions of France [*les deux France*] which had never renounced their old passions, revolutionary or counter-revolutionary, once again confronted each other. I don't think they were unhappy about it.'[1] Martinet was seventeen in 1934 and had recently joined the Communist Party. Later in the 1930s he denounced the Stalinist trials and moved away from the party but stayed on the socialist left and founded what eventually became *Le Nouvel Observateur*. This was his comment on the watershed of 6 February, written sixty years after the event.

The interlocking activism of the street and the effects of the depression created acute instability across the country but also a sense of opportunity at both extremes of the political spectrum. It produced the most dramatic conflict of political ideas since the Dreyfus Affair.

The politics of the street: 6 and 12 February

Martinet's comments on 6 February went on to acknowledge that the revolutionary tradition of the left was bitterly divided at the time of the riots. The young fascist writer Robert Brasillach remembered the weaknesses of the right. He looked back nine years later on the leagues of 6 February, and saw only fractious leaders unable to form a coherent movement.[2] Fragmentation is the dominant memory of 6 February, and the recurrent interpretation is that the riots carried no risk of a seizure of power. It was not so clear on the morning after.

The first reaction in the corridors of power was a prediction that the army would have to be called in. To avoid this, most Radical ministers urged Daladier to resign. Blum encouraged him to resist, and this was also the message dispatched from the CGT. It arrived too late. Isolated from

his own party, Daladier remembered the army's violence against strikers at Villeneuve-Saint-Georges in 1908 and the mutiny of the 17th regiment in the revolt of the *vignerons*, and was unwilling to run the risk of similar military action against civilians. He visited the injured police in hospital on the morning of the 7th and then, reluctantly, resigned. The extreme right had brought about the withdrawal of the Daladier government, the first objective of the rioters and the fifty right-wing municipal councillors from the Seine who had joined the demonstrations early on 6 February, incensed by the removal of Chiappe.

The politics of the street achieved on 6 February 1934 what the campaign of banks and investors had achieved in 1926. A government which represented the democratic majority of the left was once again forced to give way to one supported by the parliamentary minority, still styling themselves as the *union nationale*. This time there was no Poincaré, no Briand, no prosperity and no welfare measures. There was, however, the genial figure of 71-year-old 'Papa' Gaston Doumergue from the wine-growing region of the Gard, ex-President of the Republic from 1924 to 1931. He proclaimed a political truce but accelerated deflationary cuts in public expenditure and attempted, without success, to initiate a reform of the state towards a stronger executive and a weaker parliament.

In effect the government of Doumergue was a compromise for the activist leagues who had appeared to be demanding something or somebody much more extreme. They offered no alternative leader. Charles Maurras, the deaf, vitriolic ideologue of Action Française, devotee of classicism, romantic versifier, atheist and positivist, racist and paranoid, was the royalist alter ego of much of conservative France, but totally lacked any capacity for assuming political power. He had spent the evening of 6 February at his home writing poetry. The disciplined Colonel de La Rocque had disappointed insurrectionary militants by his absence from the streets at the crucial moment of confrontation: he disliked the volatility of crowds and did not want to be seen as a conspirator against the republic. Marcel Bucard, a self-declared fascist, who had belonged to every other extreme-right grouping before forming his own uniformed movement, Francisme, in September 1933, had just 1,500 supporters and was never more than a scheming, opportunistic failure. Taittinger and Coty were both too closely identified with a capitalism in crisis. Henri Dorgères, instigator of rural protest and subversion, was virtually unknown in Paris. He did not create his greenshirted peasant activists until 1935. The violent protests of 6 February were planned and orchestrated, but there was no strategy or even vision of a coup d'état, and no leader waiting to take power.

The limitations of the extreme right were evident in retrospect. At the time, however, the threat to the Republic seemed all too real, not just in Paris but elsewhere. In Lyon, where there had been a strong gathering of the Jeunesses Patriotes, the Camelots du Roi and the Croix-de-Feu in the Place Bellecour, the Prefect suggested that the leagues enjoyed an unprecedented popularity.[3] The newspaper of the CGT, *Le Peuple*, had no doubt of the nature and seriousness of the riots. Its coverage on 7 February declared: 'The fascists of Paris have mobilized their troops.' Blum also spoke of royalist and fascist shock troops, and the Communist *L'Humanité*, while indicting the Radical and Socialist Parties for a 'regime which has dirt and blood on its hands', stated that it was 'fascist leagues' who were trying to manipulate discontent. Very quickly a left-wing consensus on the fascist nature of the threat took hold. The Communist Party organized a counter-demonstration in Paris on 9 February at the Place de la République: the numbers who responded exceeded expectations; four were killed in violent clashes with the police. Before this, on 7 February, the CGT had called for a one-day general strike on Monday the 12th. One by one the CGTU, the Socialists and the Communists all decided to call for national action on the same day. All were conscious of the risk of failure and backlash. The precedent of 1920 was still an uncomfortable memory.

In effect, the day of strikes and left-wing action on 12 February 1934 made instant history no less than the riots of the 6th. The spiral of ideology was propelled by the events of these two days. Remarkably, when the CGT's instructions reached the provinces on the evening of 7 February, a spontaneous unity formed between members of the two rival trade-union confederations in at least eleven towns including the naval dockyard and foundries of Saint-Nazaire which had been a barometer of working-class attitudes during the war. Smaller urban centres were in the vanguard of unity. It was celebrated in the truffle and pâté centre of Périgueux by a CGT official: 'The working class of our town has understood that, faced with the threat of fascism, internal quarrels should stop . . .'[4] This became the passionate motif of the widely successful strike and demonstrations on the 12th. In places where unionization was strong the response was considerable. In the port of Le Havre, for example, most of the factories were forced to shut down, 70–80 per cent of the workforce was on strike and the demonstrators numbered 10,000. In neighbouring Rouen, however, where unions were semi-clandestine if they existed at all, police reported that factories were working normally, though over half of the customs and postal workers were prominently on strike. For the first time the CGT had brought out white-collar and blue-collar workers together, and in some

places it was even seen as a day belonging to the *fonctionnaires*, directly hit by the cuts in public expenditure. Some local Communists and Socialists appeared on the same platform, though sectarian divisions persisted in several towns, including Lyon and Saint-Étienne. In Lille Communists and Socialists fought each other. The concept of a united anti-fascism and a hint of festivity were the creative elements of 12 February. The activist response to the events of 6 February was the first cause in a rapid sequence of events which led the leaders of the Socialist and Communist Parties to contemplate new parameters of political action.

Hardship: backdrop and motivation

For more than two years the politics of the street fought to dominate both space and opinion. A wave of demonstrations energized the conduct of politics on both the left and the right throughout the country. Only a small handful of *départements*, Meuse, Haute-Loire, Lozère, Hautes-Alpes and Tarn-et-Garonne, were relatively unaffected. Alongside the explicitly political events were the marches, strikes, open-air meetings and active protests which pursued economic claims and which were frequently contemptuous of political parties and the promises of politicians.

The political activists of 6, 9 and 12 February 1934 did not give primacy to the depression, but by the middle of the year unemployment and hardship, both urban and rural, increasingly framed all political statements and action. It was both the backdrop to political conflict and a motivation in itself. By 1935 miners from Doumergue's region of the Gard had to fill twelve trucks with coal to earn twenty-eight francs, whereas in 1929 they were paid thirty francs for six. In Rouen, the leading French port in volume of trade, the number of dockers had already been reduced to a third by rationalization in the 1920s, and the wages of those that were left were reduced every month from November 1930. Only 200 out of an original 4,000 in 1913 had regular work. The textile factories in the town and in the valleys to the south employed 80 per cent women, mostly rural migrants. The factories were small family firms where the employees were largely dependent on the charity of the *patron* and were denied all unionization. Unmechanized and uncompetitive, half the textile factories of Rouen closed, throwing the women back on rural scarcity. Their poverty was dire. In all approximately 350,000 women workers across the country were laid off by 1935. Most of these were textile workers. In areas of heavy industry over a third of immigrant workers were expelled. In the spring of 1934, 7,000 immigrant miners brought in by the northern companies in the

1920s were sacked, 6,000 of them Poles. In the mines of Leforest in the Pas-de-Calais this led to a bitter strike in August, after which the expulsions intensified. Trains were loaded with immigrant families under heavy police guard. The novelist Saint-Exupéry described them as reduced to 'no more than half human beings, shunted from one end of Europe to the other by economic interests'.[5]

The pages of the local papers have to be closely scrutinized for the full impact and diversity of the depression. Street protests were carried in headlines, but inside pages also carried details of the municipal dole, charity aid, soup-kitchens and public projects. The image is of local resources stretched to the limit and increasingly subsidized to over 40 per cent by the state. Claimants had to wait for the fourth day of unemployment before payment, which in all cases was less than half of the previous wages and paid consecutively for a limit of thirty days. Unemployed women who lived with their husbands were ineligible and are absent from all statistics, as is the washing, mending and cleaning work which they took on for a supplementary pittance. Time and motion, payment by results and deskilling all increased. The belief that monopolies, profit and an unregulated market were the cause of the hardship produced a massive surge of support for trade-union action. A banner on the hunger march from the Lille area on 18 July 1934 read, '5,000 men and women on the dole in Calais: the whole population affected': the faces in the photograph register grim despair. There were also photographs and reports with a more political message; a positive expectation that the whole edifice of capitalism was collapsing.

Stringent cuts in public expenditure by Doumergue in 1934 and Laval in 1935 were carried out by decree-laws. Supporters backed the emergency legislation in moral as well as economic terms. Deflation appeared to justify the charges during the Stavisky scandal that the government was profligate and corrupt in its spending; the cuts reduced the national debt and lowered the need for taxation. All this was acceptable to shopkeepers, small retailers and small to medium-sized businesses, so long the matrix of social and economic values in the conservative Republic, who lost heavily as the depression deepened. Radical and right-wing deputies pointed out that small businesses paid a large proportion of the country's taxes and were the real victims of the depression, a claim buttressed by the figures of bankruptcy which soared in 1934–5 to 1,250 per month. Deflation, however, was double-edged. It benefited cut-price stores like Prisunic, Fixprix, Monoprix and Priminime, which offered an ambience of light, warmth and modernity to those with little money to spend. Independent retailers launched vigorous protests at every new store of this kind. In 1934 almost

the whole Chamber backed a bill to abolish discount stores, only to see it rejected by economic liberals in the Senate. The stores survived and flourished. The closures of small businesses intensified. It was not a simple cause and effect, but it was seen as such by the Croix-de-Feu with its ideological rejection of both big capitalism and socialism.

Staggering effects of the depression were felt in the rural areas where deflation was never seen as an obvious remedy. Grain prices in 1935 were 50 per cent lower than in 1929 and between those dates the average income of the peasant farmer fell by at least a third, with many facing ruin and enforced sale of their goods and land. Migration to the towns was no longer a viable option and the *exode rural* slowed down for the first time in decades. The scale of the crisis was countered by expectations that it would be short-lived. It was not. Peasant farmer Ephraïm Grenadou, in the region west of Chartres where Péguy had eternalized the virtues of the soil, found he no longer made a living: 'No money! I was making nothing! For four or five years I had to cut down on everything. I couldn't put by a single sou, but I was working as hard as it was possible to do.'[6] There was no point in threshing his corn since he could sell none of it. Good harvests in cereals in 1932 and 1933 and over-production of wine only pushed agricultural prices lower. André Tardieu as Minister of Agriculture in 1931 set a new benchmark for state intervention by regulating the output and replanting of vineyards and taxing over-production. In December 1934 a further measure offered subsidies to those willing to uproot their vines. Deputies wrangled over endless schemes of protection, without coherent result. Socialists argued that Wheat and Wine Offices should be set up as state regulating bodies which would also act as marketing agencies, but their proposals were blocked by Radicals in the Senate. In response, there was anger among most peasant farmers that the politicians of the Radical Party had failed to translate their dependency on rural voters into consistent economic priority for agricultural needs.

Anti-fascism

The anti-fascism of 12 February seized the initiative on the streets and tightened its hold throughout the following two years. The restrictive Communist ideology which tarred Socialists as social-fascists came under severe pressure from the PCF's own rank and file. Dramatically, one of the rising stars of the leadership, Jacques Doriot, formed a local front in the northern Paris suburb of Saint-Denis, where he was deputy and mayor. In keeping with the surge of opinion on 12 February he invited Socialists and members

of the CGT to join. He was arraigned for indiscipline but stood firm against both Moscow and the party's secretary Maurice Thorez. In early June he was expelled from the party. Ironically, in the same month Stalin took the Comintern into a new phase of policy, abandoning the sectarianism of the previous six years and commending an anti-fascist front against the evident threat posed by Nazism in Germany. This resulted in a Franco-Soviet pact in 1935 signed by Pierre Laval, while the PCF adopted a policy of left-wing unity at its Ivry congress in late June 1934. Doriot had unacceptably anticipated Stalin, but it was also his individualism and personal power in his fief of Saint-Denis which had raised doubts, and the party was to see its suspicions justified when Doriot created a new party of his own in June 1936, the Parti Populaire Français (PPF), which quickly established itself as the most overtly fascist movement in France.

The change of Stalinist policy was soon referred to as the turning point (*le grand tournant*) in the making of Popular Fronts across Western Europe, most effectively in Spain and France, and in the realignment of Communism behind policies of national defence which it had rejected since 1917 as imperialist. It was policy dictated from the top but it merged with movement from below. The impromptu anti-fascism of 12 February was immediately popular among workers and *fonctionnaires*. Its potential to transcend political divisions was evident. On 15 March 1934 an Intellectual Anti-fascist Vigilance Committee was formed in Paris. Its manifesto was issued on 18 May as a call to all workers to fight as comrades against fascism. It was signed, as a portent of alliances to come, by the anthropologist and socialist Paul Rivet, by Paul Langevin, a professor of physics close to the Communist Party, and Alain (Émile Chartier), the writer and philosopher, an *éminence grise* of the Radicals. Throughout the country the depression made for links at the workplace which frequently took the two left-wing parties by surprise. Policy from above and below converged in agreement between the Communists and Socialists on 27 July 1934 to set up a Common Front. In Paris on 29 July a combined demonstration marched from the rue Saint-Jacques to the Panthéon to commemorate the assassination of Jaurès. It blatantly encroached on the right-wing territory of the student *quartier*.

Right-wing leagues

The manifesto of Rivet, Alain and Langevin declared that the fascism of 6 February was dressed 'in the colours of a national revolution which presaged a new Middle Ages'.[7] Taittinger had repeatedly referred to the need for a national revolution, and joint marches by Solidarité Française,

Jeunesses Patriotes and Action Française were organized as a 'national front', formed to combat the 'red front' of Communists and Socialists. As fervent nationalists they were ambivalent about their debt to the success of Mussolini in Italy and Hitler in Germany, and historians have scrupulously debated whether or not to label them fascist. The argument is complicated by whether or not to claim that France had already established its own fascist, or proto-fascist, tradition in the ideas of Maurice Barrès at the end of the nineteenth century, which flaunted a youthful mix of nationalism and socialism and promoted antisemitism. Within this tradition the movement and ideas of Action Française had provided an activist dimension through its student-based Camelots du Roi, and a hardening of xenophobic and antisemitic positions.

The traditionalism, royalism and social conservatism of Action Française distinguished it from the radicalism of early Italian Fascism and much of Nazism of the 1920s, and a single definition of fascism became even more elusive in the 1930s with the differences across Europe between movements in power and those that remained in opposition. It is now mandatory for historians to talk of fascisms in the plural to accommodate national variations. But despite all the differences there were generic similarities of rhetoric and style, a dynamic stress on action and regeneration, the cult of leadership, and a populism which denounced parliament and political parties as out of touch with an imagined 'real' national community. The right-wing leagues exhibited all these characteristics in the confrontations which polarized French society in 1934–6.

Progressively the conflict radicalized the leagues, accentuating their populism which rejected any submission to the established élites of the parliamentary right. The Croix-de-Feu emerged as the most powerful nationalist movement, eclipsing the impact, though not the long historical pedigree, of Action Française. Its membership expanded from under 40,000 before 6 February to over 225,000 by August 1935 and was estimated to have reached 400,000 or even 500,000 six months later.[8] Its marching core was composed of *anciens combattants*, but its street activists were also drawn from younger men, often from families in small-to-medium businesses, and patronized by larger employers who used them as a counterweight to the organized forces of labour. Women were significantly present, initially as daughters of the decorated veterans, but increasingly with their own function, organized as propagandists and running soup-kitchens for the unemployed, hostels and leisure centres. The national and family values of the Croix-de-Feu's social programme were enshrined in Colonel de La Rocque's political testament, *Service public*, issued in 1934. It allowed the

movement to recruit in depth among right-wing Catholics who had heeded the Pope's injunction against the atheism of Action Française in 1926. In the practising Catholic areas of the textile industry in the Nord, its popularity threatened the independence of Catholic Action groups, notably the successful Jeunesse Ouvrière Chrétienne (JOC) which had a monopoly of spiritual, educational and relief work among young male and female Catholic workers. Cardinal Liénart of Lille issued a national warning against this trespass on to Catholic territory in October 1935.

Openly hostile to a parliament which it denounced as decadent, the Croix-de-Feu was authoritarian, with a corporatist ideal to transcend class struggle, and a paramilitary force which vastly exceeded the cohorts of all the other leagues. Its newspaper, *Le Flambeau*, berated the growing unity of the left as Communist-inspired, praised the achievements of Italian Fascism, but kept a cautious distance from the racism and rabid nationalism of Nazi Germany. La Rocque denied that the movement was fascist, but in Paris and other urban centres its aggressive bravura made it the epitome of the fascist threat as perceived by the left. It showed its strength in mobilizations to commemorate the Battle of the Marne and in marching manoeuvres as if it was training for a decisive moment, frequently referred to by La Rocque, and Georges Valois before him, as 'Heure-H'. What this H-Hour might be was never clear, but the spectacular displays and motorized sorties of the Croix-de-Feu into working-class districts were staged as intimidation. The 'dispos' were put on regular alert.[9] The Croix-de-Feu appeared to be set on an imminent coup d'état. Repeatedly, though, it declined from a frontal assault on the state, and did not even try to take over the town halls in the areas targeted by its motorcades. Despite their differences, the Croix-de-Feu and the AF both gave a fascist image to extreme nationalism, but remained rooted within a more conservative tradition.

In the Breton area of Rennes and in the neighbouring Maine-et-Loire, the activism of the extreme right was inspired by Dorgères. In 1927 the Parti Agraire et Paysan Français had been formed in the Auvergne by an ex-schoolteacher, Gabriel Fleurant, in an attempt to unite all peasant farmers regardless of previous political allegiance. It prefigured the peasant front (Front Paysan) which formed as a coalition of interests in July 1934 but whose politics were firmly on the right. For Dorgères the peasant front was too passive. He formed combative peasant defence committees and made a tactical alliance with the imposing Union Nationale des Syndicats Agricoles (UNSA), animated by the young Jacques Le Roy Ladurie, whose vigour, oratorial skills and inherited family hostility to the republican left made him a formidable leader of agricultural conservatives throughout the

1930s and 1940s, moving between his Normandy château and the rue d'Athènes in Paris. Where Dorgères was demagogic and activist, prepared to go to prison for inciting the withholding and falsification of taxes, Le Roy Ladurie took the high road of pressure group politics, eventually distancing himself from direct action.[10]

In 1935, the worst year for farm prices, the action groups formed by Dorgères staged a series of militant actions. They were composed largely of peasant producers whose dependence on price stability in local markets brought them into direct conflict with wholesalers forcing down prices for urban consumption. They created their own form of rural fascism, with greenshirted uniforms, fighting songs and slogans, oaths of obedience and a cult of violence against the forces of the left and the parliamentary republic. The Greenshirts, in the rhetoric of Dorgères, were the heroes of folklore, the avenging knights of a dispossessed peasantry. At their height in the summer of 1935 Dorgères claimed that they represented a single peasant France, with a nod to regional diversity admitted in their songs: the 'Bro Goz Ma Zadou' of the Bretons, the 'Lorelei' of Alsace, the 'Vivat' of Flanders and the 'Coupo Santo' of Provence.[11] This national base was wishful thinking. The extent of their power was limited to the west and north with an outpost in Algeria, where they threw imported grain into the sea. Irruptions south of the Loire by Greenshirts only served to highlight the rural strengths of Socialists, the influence of Renaud Jean in the southwest and the fresh implantation of Communists in the Corrèze and the Dordogne.[12] Established historical patterns of left and right died hard in rural areas. They marked the varied typology of the peasantry no less than patterns of landholding and husbandry. Some actions were common to both Greenshirts and rural Communists: tax strikes, the disruption of farm sales and the blocking of distraint. Both expressed the depth of rural anger, but there was no single 'peasant nation' as imagined by Dorgères.

Momentum for a Popular Front

On 19 May 1935 the photographer David Seymour, nicknamed 'Chim', captured the changing face of the anti-fascist demonstrations at the annual commemoration of the Commune at the Mur des Fédérés in the Père Lachaise cemetery. Communist and Socialist leaders were there together; banners carried slogans for bread, peace, work and freedom, and it was the presence of families with their children and the confident salute of the clenched fist which more and more marked the image of the united left. Cries for a Popular Front gave the ideology of anti-fascism an electoral

focus. The informality made local demonstrations expressive of everyday life and pushed the uniformed displays of the right into a more belligerent and menacing mould.

The turn of the Communists towards mainstream national politics heavily influenced the Radical Party, guardians of the centre ground. Their fragile hold on town hall dominance was exposed in the municipal elections of 1935, when they were forced to depend on Socialist and Communist votes in the second round. The gains of the Socialist Party were impressive. Herriot's willingness to hold office under governments of the right was increasingly challenged by the left wing of the Radicals, now led by Édouard Daladier, and it was he who joined Léon Blum and Maurice Thorez at the head of the enormous celebratory march in Paris on 14 July 1935. Alfred Dreyfus, a quietly retired old man, died in the same month, and Blum published his evocative *Souvenirs de l'Affaire* in 1935 to accentuate a Dreyfusard and republican tradition reinvented as anti-fascism and Popular Frontism. The Ligue des Droits de l'Homme was there on 'le quatorze', Phrygian bonnets were worn, a solemn oath was sworn, penned by Jean Guéhenno and André Chamson. Unity had also been won by trade unionists. On 24 July the leaders of the CGT and the CGTU issued a joint declaration as a preamble to reunification, and at local level this began in the autumn. It was confirmed at a joint national congress in March 1936. The name of the CGT was retained, its autonomy from political parties was reasserted, and Léon Jouhaux remained at its head.

Communists provided the main thrust towards unity at both political and trade union levels: their gains in membership and credibility were immediately apparent. The party slogan in 1935 was 'la main tendue' (the outstretched hand) towards not only Socialists but also Radicals and Catholics. From October Thorez repeatedly declared that the Young Communists had no hard feelings towards those Jocistes (Jeunesse Ouvrière Chrétienne) who were working for social change in their own way, and argued that totalitarian fascism was the enemy of all nonconformist movements, even those of a religious character. This was the language of his radio broadcast on 17 April 1936, which made 'la main tendue' the party's official stance in the general election. It built on local initiatives. Already, for example, the Communist municipality of Clamart, south-west of Paris, had set up an unemployment relief committee with the local Mother Superior of the Sœurs de Saint-Vincent-de-Paul, three parish priests and a Protestant pastor.

For waverers on the left the support of the right-wing leagues for Mussolini's invasion of Abyssinia on 3 October 1935 rekindled the acute sense of

an international fascist threat. The Prime Minister Pierre Laval favoured conciliation with Mussolini rather than the policy of sanctions decided by the League of Nations, and hatched a scheme with the British Foreign Secretary, Sir Samuel Hoare, conceding two-thirds of Abyssinia to Italy. The plan was leaked and the outcry in both Britain and France cut short its diplomatic passage. Laval's clear preference for an alignment with Mussolini and his piecemeal dilution of the pact he had negotiated in May with Stalin, prompted the Communists to pin national defence even more assertively to their ideological masthead. Radicals who had not demonstrated on 14 July felt forced to choose. At the end of October 1935 the adherence of the Radicals to the Rassemblement Populaire was endorsed by the party conference. A Popular Front was now a reality, and the electoral campaign of 1936 was launched as the climax to a long ideological struggle largely fought out on the streets.

Changes in Paris suggested what the outcome of this struggle would be. The nationalist right had always asserted an ownership of the centre of Paris, with its support from medical and law students in the Latin Quarter who ruled the Boulevard Saint-Michel, its ritual gathering places at the statue of Jeanne d'Arc and the Palais-Royal and its claim to the Champs-Élysées and the Arc de Triomphe as the marching ground for its formations of *anciens combattants*. Socialists and Communists had their own clearly delineated spaces in the east of the city, in the marching route of the Cours de Vincennes and the rue du Faubourg Saint-Antoine, in the popular squares of Nation, Bastille and République, and at 'le Mur' in the cemetery of Père Lachaise. As the political fronts formed, the skirmishes between extreme left and right occurred mainly where the space dominated by the right was disputed. On 11 November 1935 the shift of power was confirmed by the presence of Communists at the tomb of the unknown soldier under the Arc de Triomphe. *L'Action française* had declared it unthinkable that 'the reds' should be seen there. In response *L'Humanité* on 12 November claimed that 'The Unknown Soldier has been finally reunited with his comrades'.[13]

Action Française found it no less scandalous that Léon Blum, a Jew, should be the leader of a party contending for national responsibility. On 13 February 1936 at the time of a funeral ceremony for the historian and royalist writer Jacques Bainville, Blum's Citroën 4 was spotted on the Boulevard Saint-Germain. The Socialist deputy Georges Monnet was driving: Germaine Monnet and Blum were in the back. The royalist crowd was incensed by his proximity to the funeral. To shouts of 'It's the Jew Blum! Do him in!', Blum was pulled from the car by members of the Camelots du Roi and badly beaten, before being bundled to safety by nearby scaffolding

workers. In the shock reports the following day it was recalled that Maurras had attacked Blum on 9 April 1935 with the words, 'This is a man to be shot: in the back.' Known to be guilty of the street assault, the league of Action Française was immediately dissolved by the government, even before the elections which brought Blum to power.

Polarity and votes

The innovation of the electoral campaign of 1936 was the publication of a common programme by the allied parties of the left. There was an agreement not to stand against each other at the second ballot. For a small minority of the candidates involved this was the only credible meaning of the Popular Front: an electoral device. Promises were couched in general terms, leaving each party to issue its own manifesto. The compromises came mostly from the Socialist Party which had a strong programme of nationalizations. These were minimized in the common text due to the tacit accord of the PCF and the Radical Party, neither of which for different reasons wished to antagonize the middle classes. Gone were the Communist calls for soviets, peasant collectives and the rule of the proletariat.

The common programme elaborated the official trilogy of the Rassemblement Populaire, 'Pain, Paix, Liberté', unequivocally denouncing deflation and the decree-laws of Laval and promising a reduction of the working week without loss of earnings, pensions for retired workers, a national unemployment fund and expansive public works. Control of the private Banque de France was to be removed from 'the economic oligarchy' of the leading shareholders, a reference to the '200 families' believed to hold the economic destiny of the country in their hands, but financial orthodoxy was guaranteed with a continued refusal of devaluation, the most salient assurance given to those who had lost their savings at the time of the first Cartel des Gauches. There was no language of social revolution.

Politically the intentions were equally clear and moderate in tone, although they registered the passion of the street confrontations in a section headed 'Against the fascist leagues' in which there was a pledge to dissolve all paramilitary organizations. The particular pressure experienced by women fighting to save their jobs was recognized in a guarantee of women's right to work, alongside a general defence of trade-union rights and secular education, a promise of a free press, purged of its capacity to libel and blackmail, and a guarantee of equality of political access to state radio.

The defence of peace was to be pursued through the League of Nations, a commitment to disarmament and the nationalization of all weapons

industries, outlawing private commerce in arms. A parliamentary enquiry was promised into the political, economic and moral situation in the colonies, notably in North Africa and Indo-China: it was the vaguest of undertakings, but nevertheless one which indigenous movements would repeatedly interpret as a commitment to long-overdue reforms.

There was no promise or even mention of women's suffrage. The omission was deliberate. No reform of the state or the constitution was envisaged: pressure in that direction had been monopolized by the Fédération Républicaine on the right, by Tardieu and Doumergue and the anti-parliamentary leagues. In the conflict of ideology the left had seen the demand for changes to the constitution as a fascist threat. Women's suffrage was a victim of this polarity. Although it was the one change in the constitution that a majority of Socialists and Communists in the Chamber had supported, candidates were left to make their own statements on the issue.

Women suffragists had not been absent from the streets. Louise Weiss, the high-profile Europeanist of *L'Europe nouvelle*, arrived on the suffrage scene in 1933, recruited by Cécile Brunschvicg and Marcelle Kraemer-Bach of the Union Française pour le Suffrage des Femmes (UFSF) to inject vigour into the campaign. She created a new organization in October 1934, Femme Nouvelle, and threw herself into direct action to capture the news through press, cinema and radio. Her tactics deliberately echoed the pre-war agitation of Pelletier, Auclert and Kauffmann, and won new militants to suffrage reform, but seemed to others, including the disappointed Brunschvicg, derivative and gratuitous, ill-fitted to win over the undecided in parliament. Weiss argued that her action was no more than the urgency of the issue demanded. Publicity was instantly achieved. Most successful was her campaign during the Senate elections of 1935 in the region of Poitiers where she pilloried the senator of the Vienne, Raymond Duplantier, whose recourse to lewd and salacious verbal assault in the Senate had earned him a few cheap male laughs but widespread female contempt which Weiss conveyed effectively to the voters. He was not re-elected.

Feminist urns, installed by Femme Nouvelle at the polling booths in the municipal elections of the same year, were removed by the police, but surfaced in cafés where support was registered in tens of thousands. But despite over three decades of agitation and persuasion, the recent co-option of women to a number of town councils, the presence in 1931 of Kraemer-Bach as head of a ministerial mission appointed by Henri Queuille, Minister of Public Health, and the leading role of Gabrielle Duchêne in international peace and anti-fascist movements, women were still politically ignored by the Rassemblement Populaire, as they were by the majority of those on the

other side of the ideological divide. In this respect the elections of 1936 saw no struggle between left and right.

In all other respects the divide was sharpened by the very unity of the Popular Front. The right found no equivalent combination to present to the electorate. Neither of the two parties of the centre right, the Alliance Démocratique and the Parti Démocrate Populaire, nor the staunch right of the Fédération Républicaine, published an electoral programme. They found a common voice only in portraying the Popular Front as the work of Moscow, a propaganda device whose claim to reality was grounded in the dramatic shift of Communist policies since 1934. To this was added the role of Jacques Duclos as a Comintern envoy to Spain, and his success in persuading Largo Caballero to join the Frente Popular. By the time of the French elections the Spanish Popular Front was riven with internal conflict, which Henri de Kérillis, still co-ordinating anti-revolutionary tracts, exploited with the slogan that a vote for the Popular Front in France would be a vote not only for Moscow and for revolution but also for war. Images of anarchy and social chaos were the negatives: order, national union and a strong executive republic were the positives, and the major economic appeal went to rural societies who were promised a restoration of agricultural prices.

It was a viable economic programme which most eluded the right. They had tried deflation. It had failed. This record of failure was the biggest asset to those on the left whose solutions had not yet been tried. It also helps to explain the move of votes within the left away from the Radicals, many of whom did not even mention the Popular Front in their campaigns. They too had conspicuously failed to find a formula for recovery.

The results were startling. The Communists almost doubled their vote in the first round on 26 April. The second round on 3 May confirmed this shock advance of the PCF. They emerged with 72 deputies where before they had only 10. The SFIO gained an extra 49 to make them the largest party with 146 seats, and the Radicals fell back from 159 to 116. The combined votes of the right were only 70,000 less than in 1932, so that there was no sign of a major swing in public opinion to the left. The discipline of the Popular Front at the second ballot was the determining element, creating a new Chamber where the parties of the Rassemblement Populaire held 376 seats against 222 on the right.[14] In all these figures the Radicals are placed within the left, according to the party's decision in 1935, but in several areas the local party or candidate was hostile to the Popular Front and there the vote in their favour was often higher than elsewhere. What could not be hidden in local variations was the overall

decline of the Radical Party as the main bastion of republican politics: that role was now assumed by the Socialist Party, and its leader Léon Blum became the first Socialist Prime Minister in the history of France.

The Communist successes had far more than numerical significance. They gained heavily in certain major industrial areas: in the suburbs of Paris most notably; in the mining but not the textile areas of the North; in the ports of Marseille and Toulon in the south-east and in the mining communities of Alès in the Gard on the edge of the largely Protestant Cévennes. Many of these gains were at the expense of the Socialist Party which could no longer claim that it had retained the primary allegiance of the industrial working class. More surprising to contemporaries was the penetration of the PCF into rural areas other than the stronghold of Renaud Jean in the Marmande area of the Lot-et-Garonne. The Corrèze and the Haute-Vienne were also areas of relative success, and to a lesser extent the Dordogne. Individual Communists had emerged, like Renaud Jean before them, to fashion a network of sociability, an attitude of defiance against the rich and powerful, and a politics of social justice which appealed to a minority of small peasant proprietors in polycultural holdings, rural artisans and villagers hit hard by the depression years, and acutely conscious that rural sacrifices in the war had brought them nothing.[15]

Overtaken as an industrial force, the Socialists advanced strongly in the rural south where the image of the Radical deputy as the natural patron of individualism, of market towns and village aspirations had little political tradition and no cultural depth. The memory and ideals of Jaurès and of the *vignerons* of 1907 were consecrated among southern Socialists as a social and regional justice which Radicals had signally failed to add to their concepts of political liberty and democracy.

It was the whole of economic liberalism which really suffered, from the Radicals across to the centre-right parties within the Alliance Démocratique. The signs of a consensus politics of the centre which had marked the high days of Poincaré and Briand were lost in the polarities of 1934–6. By contrast the impact of the right-wing leagues who by ideological choice stood outside and against parliamentary politics can be glimpsed in the successes of the staunch and often independent nationalist conservatives on the far right of the Chamber. Their geographical heartland was the largely Catholic west of the Vendée, interior Brittany, the Maine, Anjou and Normandy, but the combined right was also rooted in the rural areas of the Pas-de-Calais and the Nord, and in traditional Catholic and nationalist areas of Alsace and Lorraine. Almost isolated in the south was the fiercely independent right of the Basque country, while in most of the largest

towns there was a wealthy *quartier* which voted reliably for the right, protecting its own cultural and historical difference.

The elections of 1936 inherited the bitter and violent conflict of the streets. There was now a France of the Popular Front and it faced almost half the country who had a different France in mind: it was bound to be divisive, no less than the France of Combes, of the Bloc National or the Cartel des Gauches. But division and conflict do not necessarily endanger democracy. They can also lead to a wider definition of democratic institutions which has long been blocked. The nature of the victory won by the united left showed an eagerness of the majority of the electorate for long-overdue social reforms. The accession of the Popular Front to power marked a historic swing of the republic away from a purely political definition. It was also a stunning victory for anti-fascism, remarkable enough in itself given the plethora of dictatorships and political reaction which had triumphed in Europe. The vote of 1936 in France rejected this European trend.

9

Popular Front, 1936–1938

Images of festivity

Festivity in 1936 affected attitudes in and towards politics for years to come. It was not simply a colourful extra; it was a prime component of what was widely experienced as a triumph over established social and political hierarchies. It celebrated new possibilities. It harnessed the old tradition of carnival, a reversal of cultural norms, a world turned upside down for a prescribed period, before a return to everyday life. Much of this euphoric sense of inversion and *charivari* invaded the demeanour and slogans of demonstrators in 1935, and continued to do so in the early months of 1936. In the victory of the Popular Front the transience of carnival appeared to give way to a permanent inversion.

Not everyone was caught up in the euphoria. It was apparent to those who marched with fists defiantly clenched that almost half of the electorate was bitterly opposed to them, and it was expected by workers and trade unionists that employers would resist the reforms pledged by the Popular Front programme. This opposition had to be outmanoeuvred: the electoral victory had to be turned into action. Even before Léon Blum was endorsed as Prime Minister, a wave of strikes swept across the country. They were a new and different kind: workers occupied the factories; they kept out the *patrons*; they brought in food and blankets; they made the work space into a place of leisure. A confident festivity reigned. They counted on the collusion of the new government and they grasped the opportunity to expand their aims within and beyond the social programme.

Photographers in particular were quickly aware that something out of the ordinary was happening. The occupations carried the street conflicts over space to new dimensions. It was a seizure of workspace, privately owned, in the name of the workforce. As red and *tricolore* flags were planted on factory roofs and out of windows it looked like scenes from the Russian Revolution, of which everyone, on both sides of industry, had a

forceful image, positive or negative. Amateur and professional cameras captured the expressions of festivity: a group of workers playing cards or cooking inside the factory; baskets of food hoisted over the factory gates; machines lying idle but not vandalized; irrepressible smiles which could be read as triumph or insolence. In Poitiers snapshots were taken of carnivalesque scenes inside the gas factory: workers dressed in the top hats of management, men in women's clothes, parodies of priests and feats of athleticism. Symbolism was rife. The decree-laws of Laval were ceremoniously buried under a pile of coke.[1] Outside Paris, the gigantic Renault factory at Billancourt, employing 30,000, was totally occupied by the workforce. The young philosopher Simone Weil who had worked there in 1935 went back to describe the atmosphere of the strike and wrote of it in festive terms as the moment when workers dared to take control and assert their humanity over both the employers and the rationalization of work.[2]

The form of the strikes ensured maximum publicity. Poorly unionized sectors were often in the van of the movement. The action of women strikers in big department stores, including Galéries Lafayette in Paris, made a huge impact on shoppers, faced for the first time with personal accounts of their low wages and the petty tyranny of the shop managers. Women were low or non-existent in the executive ranks of the trade unions, but their solidarity in industrial disputes was the subject of much contemporary comment. For the opposition press it was the image of games and idleness among men and the presence of women in the occupations that led to accusations that the 'joy' of the strikes noted by Simone Weil was about debauchery and not social reforms at all. This was fantasy. Where the workforce was mixed, the gender control exercised by men on the strike committees gave women conventional support roles and enforced their return home at night.

What was not fantasy was the realization by both supporters and opposition that the strikes were actively changing the landscape of industrial relations, but for how long? The atmosphere in the occupations was ebullient but not carefree: there was also well-justified fear that retribution would follow.

1. *The summer of reform*

A revolutionary moment?

The strike wave of May–June was larger than any previous ones in French history. Close to 2 million workers were involved in over 12,000 strikes, and occupations occurred in over 75 per cent of the disputes. They were almost all in the private sector. Public employees felt they did not need to take action against a government overtly sympathetic to their needs. In this perspective the strikes were industrial disputes against owners and management and not political. But this is a misleadingly narrow definition. The political import of the factory occupations was seismic. It occasioned Marceau Pivert, leader of the Trotskyist tendency within the Socialist Party, to voice his belief that 'Tout est possible', a specific claim that all the Marxist revolutionary aims were now within the grasp of the proletariat. Such a clarion call to revolution was widely expected on the right to be the next stage in the policy of the Communist Party, fresh from its electoral breakthrough. The leaders of the PCF ruled it out. Without joining the government they guaranteed full support for the Popular Front programme, and rejected calls to revolution as premature, indicting Trotskyists and anarchists within the strike movement as counter-revolutionary agents playing into the hands of fascism. The origin of this indictment was Stalin's demonization of Trotsky which acted as a brake on revolutionary action throughout the long period of Stalinist ascendancy within French Communism.

Communist trade unionists were a minority in the newly reunified CGT, and concentrated on strengthening their hold on the workforce with which they were closely associated, notably in the belt of metallurgy and car plants round Paris and in the mines of the North. The strikes were many things but they were never less than the scene of an internal battle for local position and control. The anarchist paper *Le Libertaire* claimed that there was a 'popular front of the streets and not of the politicians' which was ready for revolution. Certainly membership of the Union Anarchiste and readership of anarchist papers increased spectacularly during 1936 with the anticipation of revolution spreading from Spain.[3] In contrast, a revolutionary scenario was never on the PCF's agenda.

Nor was it even close to the pragmatic political thinking of Prime Minister Léon Blum or Léon Jouhaux, leader of the CGT. Blum's ideological rhetoric since 1920 had kept the Socialist Party in touch with its Marxist origins, but he had defined the process of governing through a coalition of the left

as the exercise of power not as a conquest. He insisted that the broad electoral support would be betrayed if the Socialists tried to foment a revolution. A social programme of major social reforms endorsed by the electorate was already revolutionary in the sense of overturning social injustice. His mentor Jean Jaurès would have settled for this. It was not Marxism but it was humanist and feasible. For Léon Jouhaux this was not the moment to risk the prospect of substantial union gains for the mirage of revolution. His position was reinforced when the representatives of the *patronat* agreed to meet the CGT leaders at the Prime Minister's residence, the Hôtel Matignon, on Sunday, 7 June, with the strike movement in full flood.

What might normally have taken two weeks of delicate negotiation took only one afternoon. The elections and the strikes had so altered the balance of power that the employers could carry no argument against the collective force of electorate, strikers, unions and government. They accepted the five main points of the union demands: recognition of the right of workers to join or form a trade union; acceptance of collective bargaining; acceptance of union representation in management policy towards the workforce; a 15–17 per cent increase in wages, and finally, no penalty for strike action. Furthermore, the government agreed to proceed instantly to legislate for a forty-hour week without loss of pay, and promised to bring in the obligation for employers to concede two weeks of annual paid holidays (*congés payés*) for their workers.

The Matignon agreements propelled labour relations with industry into a new age. Long overdue, they demonstrated that the economic climate was only one factor in the equation. Although unemployment was still relatively high, theoretically giving the employers the whip hand, they had been forced to acknowledge the strength of grass-roots action backed by union solidarity and government policies. Workers' affiliation to the CGT rose by hundreds of thousands, but the unprecedented defeat for employers did not immediately ensure a return to work.

Much to the surprise of both CGT and government, the strikes continued. Among small groups of workers there was renewed revolutionary intent. Within four days a climate of apprehension within the parties of the Popular Front prompted the PCF leader Maurice Thorez to intervene on 11 June with an instruction, which rapidly became historic, that the workers 'should know how to end a strike' once satisfaction of their grievances had been obtained. On the same day the government introduced legislation to fulfil its promises made at the Matignon talks, and on 12 June the metallurgical industries of Paris secured an agreement with the employers on the

basis of the Matignon accord. The return to work accelerated, although some 300 factories were still occupied at the end of July. The role of Thorez in the closure of the strike movement underlined the conviction of rival Marxists and revolutionaries that the PCF and Stalin had betrayed the cause of revolution in the West. The proliferation of groups competing for revolutionary purity became a permanent feature of the extreme left.

Focus on government

The Matignon agreements threw parliament into an intense round of legislative action. Major reforms were enacted in the same spirit that had enthused the elections and the strikes. The opposition could only look on with growing incredulity and warnings of imminent disaster. Laws enforcing collective bargaining, the forty-hour week without loss of earnings and a fortnight of paid holidays, were passed on 11–12 June; the paramilitary leagues including the Croix-de-Feu, Solidarité Française and the Francistes were dissolved on 18 June, and the reform of the Banque de France was voted six days later. In the next four weeks the school-leaving age was raised to fourteen and the armaments industries were nationalized, while on 4 July the much-heralded commitment to create stability in grain production was given substance in the form of a Wheat Office (Office du Blé) with market prices increased by 75 per cent for 1936 and by a further 50 per cent for the following year.

This was government interventionism on a scale not seen in peacetime. It was clear that it embodied not just practices of power but a coherent set of ideas. It answered many of the revivalist calls of the late 1920s. Indifference or neutrality from intellectuals gave way to commitment. People were involved. Government mattered.

It was important that Léon Blum was at its head. Under other leadership the exercise of power might have slipped into narcissism or autocracy. The 64-year-old Blum came from a comfortable bourgeois family of Alsatian Jewish descent. In his student days he was a fervent Dreyfusard, a friend of Péguy and Bernard Lazare, and drawn into socialism like so many others by the librarian at the École Normale Supérieure, Lucien Herr. As a close confidant of Jaurès, Blum developed an essentially moral attachment to socialism, which his acute intelligence and legal mind sharpened into a social democracy of humanist conviction. Being a socialist, he had written in 1919, was like having a blind spot removed from the process of rational thought. It was akin to a spiritual revolution.[4] Looking back over his government, he would claim that he had tried to bring inside the door

those who for too long had been forced to wait outside. His rhetoric had impressed at the Congress of Tours and in the 1930s he became a confident and eloquent orator, straining his weak physique to register the emotion. He was often caught on camera falling back exhausted with the effort. It looked like a mannered gesture, and indeed there was a certain reserve and fussiness about his manner which did not draw him easily into the southern sociability of his Narbonne constituency. His eyes behind round-rimmed glasses were sharp and his drooping moustache counteracted his smile. It gave him an ironic air. He was always conscious of the extra twist in the argument: it made him, in the opinion of his left-wing critics, over-scrupulous.

Opening the door to those outside had to be more than a gesture if it was to constitute change and reform. Blum's government appointments surprised parliament in their inclusion for the first time in French political history of three women as junior ministers. Suzanne Lacore, appointed to child protection within the Ministry of Health, had been a primary-school teacher at Ajat in the Dordogne and had backed Louise Saumoneau in 1913 in keeping socialist women distinct from middle-class feminists. Class struggle, she had declared, was 'a hard fact it would be puerile to deny'.[5] She had remained an activist inside the national committee of socialist women after Saumoneau's resignation in 1930. Irène Joliot-Curie, daughter of Pierre and Marie Curie, was a more recent recruit to the SFIO from close to the Communist Party. She was joint winner in 1935 of the Nobel Prize for Chemistry with her husband Jean-Frédéric Joliot-Curie and was nominated to research within the Ministry of Education, to which Cécile Brunschvicg, the eminent suffragist and member of the Radical Party, was also attached, with responsibility for welfare. Joliot-Curie left the government in the autumn to return to academic life, whereas the other two remained background but respected figures throughout the length of the government, Lacore involved in significant improvements in protecting children at risk.[6] Their role exposed the artificiality of gender barriers in politics but there was no attempt by Blum to use their obvious acceptability as a lever for women's suffrage or other civil rights. In July a unanimous vote in the Chamber for women's suffrage was blocked again by the Senate, but the government did not pursue the matter. Full of the promise of reform, the presence of women ministers and the focus given to them seemed in the end to be little more than tokenism. They were not reappointed when Blum's government fell in June 1937. It had been a symbolic breakthrough, but women still remained outside the door.

Refugees

Literally seeking admission, Jewish and non-Jewish refugees from Nazi Germany and Eastern Europe were incomers just at the time when employers were cutting back on labour and expelling immigrant workers.

The plebiscite in the Saar, overseen by Pierre Laval in January 1935, took the industrial zone back to Germany with a 90 per cent vote for reunification. Among those who were against integration into the Nazi regime were the region's Jewish population, numbering about 5,000, many of whom had already fled to the Saar from other parts of Germany. Rumours grew in France that some 40,000 refugees were hammering at the doors, a grossly inflated figure which brought calls from the right for an immediate closing of the frontiers. Eventually, with plans to provide a majority with transit to Latin America and close scrutiny of visas, most of an estimated 9,000 refugees were reluctantly received in France, joining over 35,000 Jews and non-Jews given refuge since 1933. After the Nuremberg Laws of September 1935 there could be no lingering doubts about the structural nature of Nazi antisemitism. Refugees continued to turn to France, aware of the tradition of asylum going back to the Revolution and even beyond.

Those accepted into France were constantly reminded that political refugees, unlike immigrant labourers, had no right to work, and further restrictions on the employment of foreign artisans made up one of Laval's decree-laws on 8 August 1935. Jewish relief agencies would have collapsed had it not been for aid provided by the American Joint Distribution Committee. As it was, Jacques Helbronner, vice-president of the Jewish Central Consistory and prominent in the national relief committee, argued consistently for restrictions on the influx of foreign Jews. There were fears throughout the Jewish establishment that the recurrent backlash of antisemitism would engulf the long-assimilated community of French Jews. The main Jewish paper, *L'Univers israélite*, under its editor Raymond Raoul-Lambert, was more openly sympathetic to the refugees. The fact that there were divisions within the French Jewish community did not deter the significant actions of the International League against Antisemitism nor undermine the strong support for the refugees from the Ligue des Droits de l'Homme.

Léon Blum had consistently pointed to the absurdity of granting people asylum without employment, and while in opposition the Socialist Party had been in the forefront of support for the refugees against the restrictive controls and the hardening of antisemitism in the right-wing press. The

pressure of refugee organizations was very much on Blum to turn these sympathies into legislative reforms, but no bill to give existing refugees the right to work was presented to parliament, and the Popular Front did not offer an open-door policy to any future refugees from Nazi persecution. Nevertheless, actions taken by the Socialists Roger Salengro as Minister of the Interior and Jean Lebas as Minister of Labour and by the Radical Marc Rucart at the Ministry of Justice improved the lives of refugees already in France. Almost at once the government endorsed the League of Nations Geneva Accord to give identity certificates to those who had been given refugee status from Germany. This protected them from arbitrary expulsion. Issued as a Presidential decree on 17 September 1936, the measure also offered the same recognition to those who had entered the country illegally.

The three ministers gave flexibility to existing regulations over entry and work. The arguments of professional overcrowding used by lawyers and doctors to block the employment of foreigners were rejected, and the process of naturalization was overhauled and accelerated, so that from 1936 to 1938 the number of foreigners who became French citizens increased from just under 29,000 a year to over 46,600.

Roger Salengro, vilified by the right for his leading role in the Matignon agreements and the dissolution of the fascist leagues, and attacked as the instrument of the Geneva Accord, was an increasing object of lies and abuse throughout the summer from *L'Action française*, *Gringoire* and *L'Écho de Paris*. His short detention in August 1914 for his part in a demonstration against the three-year law on military service and his later capture by the Germans were twisted into a fabricated history of desertion, ignoring his courage in the front line. The campaign against him became a sport for the political right. Salengro was dragged down by its relentless victimization and on 18 November 1936 committed suicide. The huge crowd that followed his cortège in Lille recalled the Parisian protests after the near-lynching of Léon Blum. The refugee commission, of which Salengro had been a liberal member, called him 'a sincere friend of the Germans who have sought and found asylum in France'.[7]

'Congés payés'

As mayor of Lille, Salengro had also been represented in August 1935 at a congress in the town on the necessity of holidays and open-air activities. The congress was confident that paid holidays would soon be recognized as the best way of combating obesity, tuberculosis, arthritis and other

physical ill-effects of workers' lives. A score of manuals from the Catholic youth organizations for workers and students had also been urging the benefits of the open air and youth hostelling, claiming spiritual regeneration, particularly in the mountains where 'far from the world, close to God, high above the valleys of anxiety and pettiness, one is really free'.[8] Legal studies were made of the feasibility of holidays as an obligation on all employers. In 1918 working wives had been given paid holidays to be with their soldier husbands on leave from the front, and in the 1920s further initiative had been taken by a few private employers, particularly Catholic *patrons* in Alsace-Lorraine. Civil servants and white-collar workers had enjoyed some right to holidays since the beginning of the century. Though much discussed in the CGT, obligatory *congés payés* were not expected to be one of the main ingredients of the Matignon agreements, but once promised they swiftly became the most universal symbol of Popular Front commitment to social reform.

The government resources given to popular culture and sport signalled the seriousness with which the forty-hour week and *congés payés* were seen as permanent departures in social organization. Léo Lagrange, aged only thirty-five, was appointed to a department of sport and leisure within the Ministry of Public Health, and epitomized the whole ambience of popular culture through his youth, his skill at public relations and his personal advocacy of scouting, youth hostelling, sport and theatre. By sheer persistence he persuaded the privately owned railways to introduce 40 per cent reductions in individual holiday fares and still more for family tickets. The first Paris workers to benefit on trains going south faced the cameras waving the 'Lagrange ticket' in the air and calling out 'Vive la vie' and 'Merci, Blum'. In the early years of the century, novels by Paul Bourget, Gyp and Colette had described Paris as empty in August. It was a bourgeois Paris that was taken for the whole. Now, on 31 July, the socialist *Le Populaire* called on all workers to make their absence felt: 'For too long you have watched the others leave on holiday. It's now your turn to get away from the grind and the heat.'

There was a certain amount of contempt for the *congés payés* from the right, but no major campaign of opposition. The special trains put on to the Côte d'Azur were satirized as 'les trains rouges'; there were jibes at the Lagrange 'Ministry of Idleness'; many shops and hotels in Nice put up signs 'Closed to workers on paid holidays'; some local people treated poorly dressed holidaymakers as tramps, and someone everywhere took moral exception to young women in shorts. The right-wing press protested at the politicization of holidays typified by the Socialist scouts, the 'Red Falcons'

organized by Georges and Germaine Monnet: their camp at Cap Breton was divided into four villages, three of which were called 'Espagne rouge', 'Frente Popular' and 'L'Europe libre'. The Catholic-inspired League of French Youth Hostels (Ligue Française des Auberges de la Jeunesse (LFAJ)) also objected to Communist campers who sang the 'Internationale' while mixing the salad.

The LFAJ had been founded in the late 1920s by the ex-Sillon leader, Marc Sangnier. By 1935 it had opened seventy-five hostels and twelve *gîtes*, distinguishing itself carefully from the rival Centre Laïque d'Auberges de la Jeunesse, founded in 1933 by the CGT. Lagrange favoured the secular organization but diplomatically so, paying a visit to Sangnier to discuss co-operation and setting a joint target of 1,000 hostels, which was still far from being realized three years later.[9] Many urban workers were able to stay with their families in the countryside but in 1936 the majority were too poor to be able to afford even the 'billet Lagrange': they remained within their home area, fishing and relaxing on canal and river banks, evocatively captured by the photographer Henri Cartier-Bresson.

Taken as a whole, the politics of leisure introduced by the Popular Front were blatantly assertive. The Lagrange initiatives, however diplomatic, were yet another variant of the 'conquest of space' evident in the demonstrations and strikes. The government, and the PCF outside it, presented leisure as something to be grasped, and encouraged a new level of participation in the common national culture, while at the same time a distinctive workers' culture was to be given its own space and time to breathe. One version of it had already been savoured in the annual festival of the PCF, the Fête de l'Humanité. At Garches to the west of Paris in 1933, 80,000 Communists had enjoyed a day of sport, dance, theatre and gymnastics, with music from Metz and Strasbourg as well as bands from the Parisian suburbs of Ivry and Villejuif. This cultural celebration was inward-looking in 1933: in 1936 the mood was for discovery and expansion. There was no mistaking the tone of the literature made available by the CGT and the PCF to workers going on holiday. It was 'their' France to discover. This was an image of social inclusion, to be realized from below. At its height the Popular Front was cultural recuperation on a grand scale, with the government as an enabling but not controlling force. Lagrange and Blum both stressed the democratic nature of the opportunities, as distinct from the leisure schemes of Fascist Italy and Nazi Germany.[10]

Rural France: nostalgia and modernity

'Un p'tit village, un vieux clocher/ Un paysage si bien caché/ Et dans le nuage le cher visage/ De mon passé' ('A small village, an old church tower/ A hidden landscape/ And in the clouds the dear face/ of my past'). The words of a Charles Trenet song during the German Occupation of 1940–44 encapsulated a ruralist nostalgia which took a profound hold in the mid-1930s. It crossed politics, but as an ideological position it was almost universally identified with the right, and often with clerical and monarchist extremes. The rural successes of the Popular Front in the elections could not efface the assumption that the Socialist government was an urban and industrial achievement, with ingrained urban prejudices. The strikes appeared to confirm this, especially for the militant Greenshirts of Dorgères who regarded the Popular Front as the enemy incarnate. The Greenshirts were not dissolved with the other leagues and their militancy continued throughout the period of Blum's ascendancy. But far from neglecting rural issues, Blum made it a priority area by appointing his close friend Georges Monnet to the Ministry of Agriculture.

If anything, interventionism was as pronounced in agricultural policy as in matters of industry. Monnet fought a prolonged battle with the Senate to get the Wheat Office established. He eventually held the trump card with the threat to return to the disaster of an uncontrolled market economy. It was a bitter defeat for the agricultural élite within the Union Nationale des Syndicats Agricoles (UNSA) to have to accept government nominees on a regulatory body which they argued should be left to the farmers themselves, and the Wheat Office never freed itself from the ripple effects of being called a soviet-style device aimed, in the words of Pierre Caziot, now a Breton deputy, at making peasants into slaves. Caziot, with his grand design in the early 1920s for protecting the peasant economy, could not, however, fully dismiss the positive impact of the Office. Helped by relatively poor harvests in 1936 and 1937, grain prices rose considerably, and there were signs that peasant producers accepted for the first time that governments could control the price fluctuations which had caused widespread rural bankruptcy. Complementary to the workings of the Office was the promotion of producers' co-operatives, a tradition of rural socialism which now made increasing economic sense for small and medium farms, ensuring in many areas the very peasant survival that Caziot had championed.

The Popular Front put forward a rural France which would and should embrace modernization as a *sine qua non* of survival. The context of its rural policies was the ongoing processes of electrification, education and

medical care which were slowly but steadily transforming the life of the countryside. To these Monnet added a system of family allowances for farm labourers, and with the enthusiastic support of Renaud Jean in the Chamber tried to get collective marketing established for all branches of agricultural production. This was refused by the Senate, as were plans to give relief to farm debtors and the protection of tenants against unfair rents.

As a list of initiatives and intentions it was impressive, but it did not bring contentment to the countryside. The Matignon agreements made the hours of work and wages in the towns attractive, and the rural exodus once more accelerated. From 1936 to 1939 roughly 300,000 peasants, men and women in equal measure, moved from the countryside. In 1938 the Independent-Socialist deputy Ludovic-Oscar Frossard, Minister of Propaganda in Blum's short-lived second government, published *Le Désert au village*. 'Yes,' he argued, 'the peasants I talk to admit that things are better: they are pleased with the Office du Blé . . . but they all look enviously on a stable income and retirement, and nowadays when you travel through a village you see only old men and women . . . it is sad and dismal. Ruined buildings are everywhere.'[11]

No major change in the countryside was achieved by the Popular Front, but images of how a modern peasantry might look underlined the fact that the government had the rudiments of a ruralist vision. They were on show at the 1937 International Exhibition, mounted on the banks of the Seine inside Paris between the purpose-built Palais de Chaillot and the Eiffel Tower. The brashly assertive confrontation between the Soviet and the Nazi pavilions announced that this World Fair was about more than national identity: ideologies were combatively engaged, and the Popular Front was accused by the opposition of making a national event into a polemical display of its own values. It was precisely this that was revealing.[12] The exhibition showed that the Popular Front did not abandon the tradition of the peasant farm: at the annexe at Porte Maillot, a constructed rural centre took as a paradigm the medium family unit of ten to fifty hectares, with a harmonious degree of mechanization. At the same time the exhibition showed that the Popular Front sought to confirm the cultural diversity of the regions, with displays and conferences on the artefacts and folklore of the *petit pays*, but always within the unifying identity of the single nation.

2. Roots, regions and nation

The prominence of regional culture at the 1937 exhibition was an act of definition: acceptable regionalism was cultural; the unacceptable was political. Much has been written about the provincial peasantry 'becoming French' from the end of the nineteenth century, but at the same time the urban working classes were also gaining nationhood and Frenchness. Socialists and Radicals were both inheritors of urban Jacobin centralism; the Communists adopted the nationalist discourse of the Republic from 1934. The nation-state and the dominance of Paris were not undermined by the Popular Front.

An accumulation of geographical studies gradually informed Parisians that it was an absurdity to use the term 'provincial' to nullify differences between the regions but the habit and prejudice persisted, allowing François Mauriac to present a book of witticisms called *La Province* which opens with the statement that 'Paris is populated solitude: a provincial town is a desert without solitude' and goes on to declare that *la province* stultifies, blocks universalism, narrows the vision, condemns conversation and social mix, and prevents self-analysis. On the other hand it cultivates a sense of belonging, family, youth, the seasons, weather and virtue. Mauriac's own circle was one of fashionable literary society and it was exactly on such *mondain* aphorisms that the dialectic of Paris and provinces thrived. The Popular Front government was conscious of its strategic position in the enlargement of national consciousness, but it aimed to render regional differences as cultural variations, not as aberrant or counter histories. The dominant perspective of the centre was preserved.

Autonomy and separatism

Focus on the lost provinces of Alsace and Lorraine before the war had been political and military and their reincorporation into France a highpoint of national pride. Their particularity as frontier regions, the bilingualism of the area, the tragedy of localities torn in opposite directions by the war, all these were marginalized by the importance attached to reassimilation into French history and culture. Any kind of political autonomy within France, beyond the recognition of a special religious status, was ruled out by successive governments throughout the 1920s, to the point where regionalist groups felt they were faced with a Parisian diktat.

Autonomous movements in Alsace found local resentments easy to mobil-

ize, crossing divisions between left and right. The Communist Party was responsive to autonomous ideas as an expression of working-class discontent, and in 1929 the Communist deputy Hueber was elected mayor of Strasbourg with the support of right-wing autonomists and clericals. In 1926 the Heimatbund formed as a broad-based political league to press for autonomy within France, while the abbé Haegy was the most influential publicist of the Catholic Union Populaire et Républicaine (UPR) which sustained a large regional press and gained nine deputies in the 1932 and 1936 elections. There was no change of policy from Paris: all autonomous activity was treated as separatist and was met with repression, which peaked in 1928 with a trial of autonomists in Colmar, accused of conspiracy against the state. A sub-spiral of ideological conflict pushed the state and regionalists into irreconcilable positions, the autonomist Landspartei spawning a paramilitary force, the Jungmannschaft under Hermann Bickler with brown uniforms which echoed the Nazi SA and recruited among Lutherans in the Bas-Rhin. Parallel to it was the Bauernbund or Union Paysanne d'Alsace, animated by Joseph Bilger with its green uniforms and fascist salute, influential on the movement of Dorgères, not least in its claim to have enrolled 6,000 members from the Catholic milk and wine producers of the Haut-Rhin. The anti-fascism of the Popular Front was pitted no less against these movements than against those directly responsible for the riots of 6 February. The PCF abandoned its sympathy for autonomy at the *grand tournant*, leaving a rump of dissident comrades in Alsace, and what was lost in the ideological escalation of the mid-1930s was the moderate voice of political regionalism arguing for decentralization within the nation-state.

In Brittany comparisons were made with Ireland or Poland. Breton nationalists built on a history of resistance against centralism both before and after the Revolution, on the distinctiveness of the Celtic language, on a popular cultural tradition and on a combination of religion and folklore which assimilated pre-Christian and Druidic practices. The cult of local saints allotted each a separate function in everyday life and gave Breton Catholicism its renowned unorthodoxy. Doubt, animalism and superstition were woven into the fabric of Breton belief: in the area of Pont-l'Abbé to the south-west of Quimper the *chienne du monde* (world bitch) was the respected and feared cause of personal misfortune. Defying the educational ban of Breton as even a co-language in schools, the publishing house Gwalarm, run by a teacher of English in Brest, Roparz Hémon, adapted the language to modern and educational usage with stories, sagas and scientific texts in Breton, providing unquestionable evidence of cultural

regeneration, shaped into political form after the war by the journal and movement *Breiz Atao* (Brittany Forever).[13]

Cultural and economic arguments for an autonomous Brittany were bypassed by a more strident political separatism. Led by Michel Debauvais and Olier Mordrel, the Parti Nationaliste Breton (PNB) of the early 1930s urged complete independence from France. The leaders were momentarily upstaged by an activist segment called Gwenn Ha Du (Black and White) in reference to the nine black-and-white stripes which represented the nine *pays* of Brittany. In 1932 it achieved notoriety at the 400th anniversary of the merging of Brittany and France by blowing up the Rennes monument which figured Anne de Bretagne kneeling before the French king. Political agitation fed on the polarities after 6 February, and in the 1936 elections the 'Breton front' secured fifteen seats, a highly vocal expression of regional frustration which was ascribed unthinkingly by the left to inveterate right-wing and clerical reaction. In 1938 Debauvais and Mordrel were arrested as plotters against the state and their Breton Nationalist Party was banned. On the outbreak of war in 1939 they proclaimed neutrality and in 1940 their eyes turned to the invading Germans as a liberating force.

The cultural route

The Popular Front government might have exposed the very real divisions of opinion within both Alsace and Brittany by concessions to the regional language and some degree of self-rule. It was prevented from doing so not only by its own Jacobin heritage but also by the right-wing monopoly of ruralist and regionalist discourse. Decentralization was at the masthead of *L'Action française*; it signified the *ancien régime*. The Popular Front could not negotiate with the nationalism of Maurras: even less could it entertain the reborn, apocalyptic visions of separatists, increasingly tinged with fascism. New routes between nation and regions in the mid-1930s were blocked by these decisive considerations.

The pathways which offered some form of mobility were cultural, signposted by the very different regionalism of the south. Although there was regionalist pride in the wine-growers' revolt of 1907, and political reality in the concept of a 'Midi rouge', the cultural idea of Occitanie prioritized poetry and folklore. The lyrical poet and linguist Frédéric Mistral, the inspiration behind the Provençal circle of the Félibrige, had died in 1914 after winning the Nobel Prize for Literature in 1905. The circle was populist, prophetic and well to the right in political terms, providing the Provence-born Maurras with a lifelong model which he believed was invul-

nerable to republican influence. He was wrong. The legacy of Mistral, like his statue in Arles, proclaimed a romance of Provence and the Languedoc which younger poets, novelists and film-makers in the 1930s merged with the aspirations of peasants and workers in the south to form a specific cultural version of the Popular Front. Charles Camproux, a foremost poet writing in the *langue d'Oc*, created a new Provençal Party to follow the example of Catalonia which had gained substantial autonomy under the Second Spanish Republic. Camproux made his vision of Occitanie essentially anti-fascist.

The novels of André Chamson, redolent with the Protestantism of his Cévenol background, and the plays and films of Marcel Pagnol celebrating the characters and landscape of Marseille and Provence began to create a canon of work recommended to the holidaymakers of the Popular Front. With Jean Guéhenno, originally from Fougères in eastern Brittany, André Chamson edited the influential left-wing periodical *Vendredi*, many of whose essays suggest the potential of an alternative ruralism and regionalism, freed from the associations of the Barrèsian *pays réel* and the 'true France' of Charles Maurras. In eastern Provence, François Morénas set up a youth hostel near Manosque which he called 'Regain' in tribute to Jean Giono's novel *Regain* of 1930 which had given the saga of 'a return to the land' its most classic evocation as a study of roots and obduracy. Young socialist men and women who came to the hostel set about rebuilding a ruined village, a project modelled on the rural restorations initiated by Giono.

The requisition of regional culture for the 1937 exhibition could not, however, free itself from accusations of Parisian arrogance and autocracy, levelled by representatives not just from Brittany but also from Normandy, Provence and the Savoyard region. Regional artefacts and artisans were chosen by the government's nominees on the Regional Commission, often in defiance of the regions themselves. The exhibition returned persistently to the theme of co-option: 'the diverse cultures of provincial France were proudly reclaimed as France's national patrimony' making 'the regionalist cause into a nationalist one'.[14] The paradox was a conscious attempt by the Popular Front to make apparent opposites compatible, a process which typified a huge range of intellectual and political practice in the 1930s, not least the body of thought known as nonconformity.

3. Popular Front and nonconformity

Reconciling opposites: modernization 'à la française'

When first Jean Touchard in 1960 and then Jean-Louis Loubet del Bayle in 1969 focused on a certain 'spirit of 1930' which they believed defined an epoch, they gave centre stage to an inchoate body of young thinkers who were self-styled nonconformists, a term first applied by Emmanuel Mounier. Caught up in the intellectual sense of crisis which began to pervade French thought at the end of the 1920s, the nonconformists were part of a generation in revolt, but they were not seeking to regenerate existing political parties. They believed that revolutionary thought was an affirmation of life stretching beyond the parameters of right, left and centre. The nonconformists refused the materialism of both capitalism and Communism. Péguy, Bergson, Heidegger, Jaspers, Nietzsche and Kierkegaard, pioneers of a distinctive European mind, were plundered for a spiritual dimension which the nonconformists believed the world needed and they could provide.[15]

The monthly journal *Esprit* did most to try to reconcile the humanist aims of socialism with Maritain's 'primacy of the spiritual'. Its Catholic editor, Emmanuel Mounier, though only twenty-seven at the time of the journal's first appearance in October 1932, was already convinced that the temporal and the religious should be brought together. This was not to throw Catholicism back into the arms of the political right which exploited Péguy's nationalism, but on the contrary to follow through the implications of Péguy's anti-materialism and the innovative social thought which had inspired the Sillon. *Esprit* engaged with the ideological issues which dominated the period, and created a focus for left-wing Catholic thought. Mounier endorsed the Popular Front, while yet working towards an ideology of personalism, centred on the human person as a social being with both a material and spiritual existence.

Reconciling opposites was a central feature of nonconformist thought, and there was a constant interest in movements which challenged the two hegemonic structures, liberal economic thinking on the one hand and Marxism on the other. This brought several nonconformists within the orbit of fascism, whose rhetoric also claimed a youthful and dynamic synthesis of opposites. Had nonconformity as a whole succumbed to the fascist temptation, it would have held only passing interest. Its importance was to have explored similar ideas and yet to have created an intellectual space in which a number of different solutions could emerge. It demonstrated alternatives.

Ordre nouveau, at first a friendly rival to *Esprit*, was launched in May 1933. Its directors, Robert Aron and Arnaud Dandieu, had already caused an intellectual stir in 1931 by the title they gave to their diagnosis of crisis, *La Décadence française*, in which they bemoaned the decline of patriotism and pilloried, like Bernanos, the desiccated rationalism in French thinking. In the same year they stigmatized Americanization of French culture and industry as a cancer, enlarging the dystopic account of America given by the novelist Georges Duhamel in *Scènes de la vie future* (1930), and giving it a philosophical depth which made Duhamel seem modish and superficial by comparison. In 1933 they produced what was hailed as a seminal work of nonconformity, *La Révolution nécessaire*, in which a number of young intellectuals, engineers and social planners discerned an economic way of thinking which was modern but neither American nor Marxist, and a vigorous French tradition which was not mired in the royalist anachronism of Action Française. Among those influenced by the book were the social theorists in the group X-Crise animated by the engineer Jean Coutrot. Modernization *à la française* became the major theme in his social and industrial thinking and he envisaged the rationalization of labour in such a way that the worker would enjoy all the work-satisfaction of the traditional French artisan.[16]

It is not difficult to show how ideas of 'modernity with a French face' overlapped with the social reforms of the Popular Front and the plans for workers' leisure. Much of the government's social innovation and the mix of modernity and tradition in its rural policies suggest parallels with nonconformist thought. There were also just as many dissociations: *Ordre nouveau*, unlike *Esprit*, kept its distance. But the intellectual reach of the Popular Front far exceeded the sum of its political forces: many Christian Democrats, friends of the journal *Sept* from 1934 to 1937 and central to French politics ten years later, and a wealth of committed existentialists, all looked back to the Popular Front period as their departure point.

Intellectuals, moral authority, cinematic commitment

Not just from personalists but from Marxists, anarchists, ideological pacifists, nationalists and self-proclaimed fascists came the objection that Julien Benda in *La Trahison des clercs* had made a false dichotomy between the world of the intellect and the 'real' world. The 'vanity of the intellectual' and the 'false freedom' of pure thought were repudiated by the scholars, thinkers, experts and academics who signed a proliferation of manifestos and petitions in the forty years of ideological confrontations which characterized France

in the middle four decades of the twentieth century. If anything, Benda had made it imperative for intellectuals to couch their political interventions in concepts of high principle, increasing their apparent wisdom and moral authority.

It is doubtful whether such moral authority would have been claimed or publicly acknowledged without the impact caused by the drive for renewal at the end of the 1920s. As political parties were criticized as lifeless, and government after the Stavisky affair as corrupt, the accent on a reinvigorated politics brought pressure on the realm of both action and ideas. The Popular Front actualized the role of ideology in political renewal. Blum himself was an intellectual at the heart of politics. The conflict between secular and religious values, which had come to a head in the early years of the century, had already thrown open the category of moral leadership. Intellectuals made up a motley secular priesthood: they were mandarins, though not a coherent caste. They assumed the mantle of public conscience while insisting on their own individuality.

The arguments over modernism, socialism, nationalism, fascism abounded in abstract concepts and questions of principle, and posed major issues of identity. Intellectuals took people beyond the specific to the abstract, while arguing that the abstract could be located in the specific. In such ways Charles Maurras claimed to have his positivist feet in the world of hard facts while dealing in abstract notions of the organic nation, and the novelist André Malraux in *La Condition humaine* (1933) addressed the human condition through the specifics of an attempted Communist revolution in Shanghai. The question of whether intellectual integrity was compromised by involvement remained, but it had not been solved by Benda. The passions aroused by the Spanish Civil War swept his advocacy of intellectual detachment into the backwaters.

Artistic detachment was not Benda's cause, but it was through the involvement of creative film-makers that many of the central ideas of the Popular Front were further popularized. The leading director of the 1930s, Jean Renoir, son of the Impressionist painter Auguste Renoir, committed himself to the cause of social revolution with *La Vie est à nous* (*Life Is Ours*), made in the political heat of 1936, using working-class actors and commissioned by the Communist Party, while his last film of the decade, *La Règle du jeu* (*The Rules of the Game*), made in 1939, portrayed a corrupt aristocratic world of love, caprice, compromise and deceit, interwoven with its mirror world of servants and gamekeepers. Overtaken by the change of public mood, it was a disaster at the box office, but was later seen to have presaged the collapse of social structures which played exclusively by their own rules.

Renoir's films fused cinematic realism and social commitment, but retained much of the avant-garde inventiveness evident in the earlier social critique by the anarchist and surrealist director Jean Vigo whose contrast of poverty and luxury on the Côte d'Azur in *À propos de Nice* (1930) was followed by his dreamlike parable of revolt in *Zéro de conduite* (*Nought for Conduct*) in 1933. As a medium of revolutionary ideas, the potential of cinema had famously been recruited by Lenin in Soviet Russia but it was not only on the left that its power was recognized. While small left-wing cinema clubs in Paris screened the early films of Sergei Eisenstein, and the Marxist critic and historian Georges Sadoul was researching his history of film, the pro-fascist writers and film historians Robert Brasillach and Maurice Bardèche were compiling their own critical version of the cinema, based on their image of film as the perfect embodiment of the mobile dynamism which they discerned in fascist politics. There was a potent romance of the cinema on both sides of the ideological divide.

4. Peace, anti-fascism and Spain

In the festivities of 14 July 1936 slogans for peace and anti-fascism made a joint statement. By the end of 1938 they seemed intractable opposites, and yet vast numbers of people from all walks of life continued to believe, and still do, that the achievement of one would have automatically ensured the success of the other. The justifications for this belief became increasingly intricate and dense; many have said hollow. Keeping the two together was the most fractured conciliation process of the 1930s. Anti-fascism implied a readinesss to go to war for ideological reasons. Peace came to imply peace on any terms.

Something of this contradiction surfaced in 1935 in the November congress of the Rivet, Alain and Langevin committee of anti-fascist intellectuals. Members loyal to Langevin adhered closely to the anti-German stance adopted by Stalin, and defined anti-fascism in Soviet Russia's new language of national defence as well as the old one of working-class revolution. This was problematic for those who continued to believe that national defence had been a prime cause of war in 1914 and still constituted a threat to peace. In June 1936 the Langevin group broke ranks and started a move away from the committee, accusing their colleagues of pacifist extremism and pandering to German demands. In 1938 Rivet also left in protest at the ultra-pacifist tendency. It was a far cry from the unity of May 1934.

Gabrielle Duchêne took the French section of the Women's International

League for Peace and Freedom, founded in 1915, in the same direction as Langevin's breakaway group. Increasingly caught up in the shifts within the PCF, though not formally a member, she had been to Russia with Communist trade unionists in 1927 and now faced attacks from within the section on her acceptance of the Stalinist *grand tournant*. Her colleague Camille Drevet made one of several withering comments: 'To see Marxists justify the national defence of a capitalist country really surpasses everything.'[17] But unlike Langevin, Duchêne did not break away from her organization, but forced her critics to do so, facing down taunts of autocracy and insisting that the incessant struggle against fascism was the only way to peace.[18]

On 18 July 1936 Spanish generals launched a rebellion in Morocco against the republican Frente Popular and invaded mainland Spain. Initially the insurrection did not appear to pose a foreign policy problem for France. Blum expected the democracies to support the constitutional Spanish republic against the rebels and was responsive to appeals from the Spanish republican government. His willingness to send aid was leaked and was met by an orchestrated campaign of outrage in the right-wing press. It put forward the spectre of French involvement in an ideological war on behalf of Spanish communists and anarchists which would leave Stalin as the arbiter of Western Europe. The allegation in the pages of *L'Action française* and *L'Écho de Paris* that the Frente Popular was a bloody revolution obscured the fact that it was the Spanish right who were the rebels and that both Mussolini and Hitler had hastened to support the rebellion. A passionate and influential article by François Mauriac in *Le Figaro* declared Spain to be indivisible and that aid to the republic would make the French Popular Front into gangsters, collaborating in the massacre of the peninsula.

Blum hesitated. Yves Delbos, the Radical Foreign Minister, argued against any involvement, visibly affected by the scenario of the right. There was talk of Blum resigning, but Spanish representatives in Paris argued that such a move would in no way help their cause. Delbos and an agonized Blum went to London where they succumbed to the spectre of potential European conflagration. Blum suggested an international pact of non-intervention. The British accepted with alacrity, and were later accused by many in France to have outmanoeuvred Blum. Within his own cabinet, Pierre Cot, Minister of Aviation, Vincent Auriol, Finance Minister, Léo Lagrange and Roger Salengro were among the ministers hostile to the pact, but an equal number were in favour. No one was more ambivalent and distressed than Blum himself: his divided self has been variously described in words which range from hypocrisy to tragedy. During August some

twenty-six nations signed the agreement not to intervene. Among them were Germany, Italy and Russia, even as the first two stepped up their military intervention, countered in October by Stalin's active supply of arms and material to the republic.

By the end of the year the Communist Party and the CGT, the revolutionary sections of the Socialist Party, the Trotskyists and anarchists, all accused Blum of a betrayal which seemed to them inconceivable after two years of anti-fascist rhetoric. Throughout August, however, Blum was not completely isolated from the left of the Popular Front. On 6 September he made an impromptu visit to an open-air meeting at Luna Park near Porte Maillot, organized by the Socialist federation of the Seine which was openly backing aid to Spain. Heckled and booed at first, Blum turned round the audience by admitting personal responsibility for a difficult decision and arguing that peace and the dignity of France demanded the full observance of the pact. He challenged them by his very presence to say that he lacked courage or loyalty to his party. His speech was spontaneously applauded and ended with shouts of 'Vive Blum' and the singing of the 'Internationale'.

Stalin's move to intervene came at the end of September, redoubling the pressure on Blum. Maurice Thorez now openly attacked the policy of non-intervention, but stopped short of bringing the government down. On the extreme right this confirmed the Communists as warmongers, while on the left it questioned the government's commitment to anti-fascism. It looked ominous that at the first real test in foreign affairs it should have backed away. Its emphasis on avoiding another European war was now its main line of defence: it was a *de facto* acceptance that the twin causes of peace and anti-fascism had been torn apart. The heady days of summer gave way to a long winter of self-justification and ambivalence for the Popular Front.

'Passion and death'

It has always been calculated that a prompt supply of arms would have enabled the Spanish republic to crush the rebellion, but it was the unknown effects of such a move within France that weighed most heavily with Blum. The mirror image of the Spanish and French Popular Fronts was too exact for comfort. Would aid to Spain precipitate another 6 February, but this time with a leader? There was talk of the eighty-year-old Marshal Pétain as a possible candidate, but this was mainly the wish-fulfilment of Gustave Hervé, the old anti-militarist turned nationalist, who published in 1936 a utopian scheme for entrusting France to his war hero, *C'est Pétain qu'il*

nous faut (It's Pétain We Need). The book has the same infantilism as the royalist brochure of Bernanos in 1930, an image of the French people as squabbling children needing a folk hero and father-figure to protect them from themselves. Fairy tales, folklore and hero worship made up a genre of political thinking on the extreme right in this period. The adulation for the USSR and Stalin played a similar fantasy role on the extreme left. Reactions to the Spanish Civil War were conditioned by this climate of make-believe. It was both the apogee and the nemesis of Péguy's *mystique* which had so dominated ideas of revivalism across the political spectrum since the late 1920s.

August was the month of *congés payés*. It was also the month when André Gide, the most widely known novelist with sympathies for Communism, returned from a high-profile visit to the USSR with his illusions in tatters. Stalin's dictatorship and paranoia were blatant. The 67-year-old Gide confided to friends that 'Communism no longer exists in Russia: there is only Stalin.' He was encouraged to speak out. The journal of Chamson and Guéhenno, *Vendredi*, eloquent in its advocacy of the Popular Front but independent of the PCF, was opened to Gide. On 6 November it published his introduction to what became *Retour de l'URSS*, which went on sale on the 13th. Its impact on ideological certainties cannot be overestimated.

At exactly the same time the young and successful anti-fascist writer André Malraux was heavily preoccupied with his own mix of fantasy and reality which led in the opposite direction. Half Gide's age, Malraux shared the restlessness for ideals which marked the end of the 1920s. He won the Prix Goncourt for *La Condition humaine*, which featured both committed revolutionaries and metaphysical anguish, and he was a regular contributor to Gide's *Nouvelle Revue Française*. He rallied immediately to the republican cause in Spain, which he visited in a small plane piloted by Édouard Corniglion-Molinier at the end of July. With the collusion of Pierre Cot, Minister of Aviation, and a young administrator, Jean Moulin, they made a number of planes available and set about recruiting a volunteer force to pilot them. Malraux's commitment was energizing and the squadron *España* was formed, though its efficacy has been doubted in the memoirs of the Spanish head of the republican airforce, Ignacio de Cisneros. What was not in doubt was the significance of Malraux's intellectual aid to the republican cause, and his advocacy of disciplined action in his novel and film of the civil war, *L'Espoir*. His first preferences had been for what he called the 'illusion of lyricism' which he identified with the Spanish anarchists. He ended by backing the organization and *savoir-faire* of the Communists. Revolutions cannot survive on idealism, he argued, but only through

structures, a thesis almost the contrary to that of Gide, and the exact reverse of Péguy.

Idealism was everything in the eyes of Robert Brasillach, the young editor of the weekly *Je suis partout* which grouped together writers indelibly marked by Action Française, but disclaiming any ideology, a disingenuous pretence which could not survive its emotional involvement in fascism and support for General Franco. Brasillach was receptive to instant tales of heroism in the Spanish struggle to defeat 'Muscovite barbarism'. With Henri Massis, a close colleague of Charles Maurras, he extolled the bravery of the Catholic military cadets of Alcazar who were believed to have held Toledo against a superior number of republican troops and merciless bombardment until relieved by a nationalist force. The story was inaccurate but it allowed Brasillach and Massis to interpret the rebellion as an epic Christian crusade. Their account diverted attention away from the massacres perpetrated by Franco's forces at Badajoz on 15 August, which crushed the moral certitudes of François Mauriac and led him to a public repudiation of support for the nationalists. Equally Catholic and equally influential, Georges Bernanos also refused to accept atrocities in the name of the Church and broke decisively with the politics of the royalist right.

French anarchists were among the first volunteers in 1936 to cross into Spain. 'The Spanish revolution is ours,' claimed *Le Libertaire* on 31 July. In September a fighting unit was named after the anarchist Sébastien Faure, composed mainly of French and Italians, but the message from Spanish anarchists was more for the French to work within their own communities to create solidarity. Stalin's aid carried a more political aspiration in terms of influence among the leaders of the republic, reflected at the grass roots in the tightly organized recruitment and control of volunteers by the Communist Marcel Cachin. A quarter of the 30,000–50,000 fighters within the International Brigades were French, but far more were recruited by the PCF within France among anti-fascists from all over Europe. Cachin was accused by non-Communists of ruthless partisan measures to turn the Brigades into a party militia, but their reputation on the left as martyrs for 'the great cause' was instantly established. By contrast, French volunteers for the nationalists numbered only a handful. Brasillach went as an observer in 1938, and in April of the same year Charles Maurras, Pierre Gaxotte and Pierre Daye made what *Je suis partout* called a triumphal visit to Seville. The journal designed a celebratory issue for the second anniversary of the rebellion, dedicated to the 'glory of Spain'.

Six months later, at the height of winter from January to March 1939, 500,000 Spanish refugees, in acute fear and desperate states of hunger,

illness and cold, fled from the nationalists in Catalonia towards border crossings in the eastern Pyrenees. To the west some 40,000–50,000 had already escaped by sea in 1936 to 1937 from the Basque region, but in 1939 the Daladier government, no longer the Popular Front, was totally unprepared for the scale of the exodus at the end of the Civil War. Makeshift, insanitary and underfed camps just inside France on the windswept beach at Argelès, at Saint-Cyprien and Barcarès 'concentrated' the first mass of the refugees, dividing families by segregating men from women, before transfers to other internment camps in the south, including Gurs near Pau, Le Vernet in the Ariège and Les Milles across to the east in the Bouches-du-Rhône.

Anarchist and ex-republican minister Federica Montseny was one of the refugees, with two young children and a mother dying of cancer. Her memoirs, entitled *Pasión y Muerte* (*Passion and Death*) narrate the tragic end of the Spanish Republic on the beaches of republican France where only a few of the 12,000 sick and wounded were provided with treatment. The government used the term 'concentration camp' to describe the huts on the beach at Argelès and emphasized that internment would be temporary, especially for the 300,000 men from the republican militias who had at first been refused entry into France and then had to surrender their weapons at the borders. Stripped of their military identity, they found themselves ringed with barbed wire in what was remembered more as a prison than as a refuge. Some few thousands were enlisted in the French Foreign Legion, or were accepted by Mexico and South America. For the bulk of the others forced repatriation was tried but gradually gave way in 1939 to government labour schemes, still under close surveillance. Women, children and old men, numbering over 200,000 at first, were moved on to hundreds of small centres in the southern *départements* before the intensive effort to repatriate them took over in the second half of 1939. By the end of the year there were still over 140,000 Spanish republicans in France. As refugees they were not met with universal acceptance. But in most localities, committed members of the political left and certain religious centres collected money, clothes and food for them. It was a gesture of solidarity and compassion, which often conditioned individual reactions to the catastrophe which transformed French lives in 1940.

5. Counter-offensive

The elections of 1936 drew stark attention to the disarray of the parliamentary right. The Matignon agreements were a humiliation for the big employers. To the economic and political crisis of the early 1930s was now added a social crisis of élites. The capitalism of big business was widely blamed by medium and smaller firms for the rout of May and June. The middle classes of small employers, shop owners, artisans and independent professions, salaried employees, small rural proprietors and traders, had been divided by the electoral campaigns, many allowing their social conservatism to yield to a burst of political radicalism which caused them often to vote for Socialists rather than the Radicals whom they saw as having severely mismanaged the economic depression. According to the census of 1931 the *classes moyennes* made up almost half of the population entered as 'active'. They shared with the *fonctionnaires* many similar views on social advancement, but jealously guarded their individuality and independence from the state. Their belief and trust in the republic had given the regime its solidity and a central core of social conservatism; their politics, however, were volatile and could register, as they did in 1936, a profound distance from the bourgeois élites.

Hopes within these middle classes that the Socialists had an answer to the depression lasted for several months until it was clear that the government was facing serious financial difficulties. In an economic recoil by high finance and big business, investments had been moved out of the country, while internally the extra costs of the forty-hour week were passed on in price rises. Production increased during the summer, but slipped back in the autumn as employers argued that there were not enough specialist workers to mount extra shifts to compensate for the loss of working hours. Blame was attached to the government for bringing in the forty-hour week too carelessly for purely political motives. The middle classes found this argument increasingly persuasive.

After the summer, pressure on the franc and a rapid decline in gold reserves created the problem which had haunted all left-wing governments since 1924. To reassure savers, Blum had ruled out any change in the franc when he took power but in September, after negotiations with Britain and the USA, he was forced into a devaluation which left the franc at between 25–35 per cent less than its previous value. It was the devaluation Paul Reynaud had been calling for since the depression began, but it was now too late to do more than momentarily halt the slide away from the currency.

Middle-class support disintegrated. Alarm among Radicals in the government, already exacerbated by Spain, grew steadily. Inflation continued to mount, eating away not only at savings, but also at the increases workers had gained in June. Strikes broke out to protest at this loss, ascribed by workers to employers' sabotage of the reforms, an argument which the Socialist leader might have openly endorsed earlier in the year. Instead Blum put forward a bill to curb the rash of labour stoppages by imposing arbitration prior to a strike, and in January 1937 he talked of a pause in the rate of social reform. This was publicly announced to the nation in a broadcast on 13 February, halting, in particular, progress on pensions for elderly workers. The right sensed a major ideological retreat, and in June the Senate reasserted its power by refusing the government new emergency powers to tackle the financial issues. Blum treated it as an issue of confidence. On 21 June he resigned. The new government led by the Radical Camille Chautemps included Socialists, and Blum himself, but it marked a swing towards the Radicals who gradually reasserted themselves as representatives of social conservatism.

—

How real was the fascist threat?

Had Blum continued in power, might the Popular Front have provoked an alliance of big business with a populist party and a fascist leader as had happened in Italy and Germany? It was a possibility much discussed at the time and the very question suggests that the Popular Front in 1936–7 faced an even greater threat of a fascist takeover than the Daladier government had done in 1934. Much of this was illusory, but to what extent is difficult to quantify.

The ban on the leagues had brought an abrupt end to paramilitary pretensions: any that remained had to go underground, literally as it soon emerged. Rumours in 1937 of a military conspiracy involving hooded men, Cagoulards, planning a coup d'état through the Paris sewers and catacombs, led to arrests and a bizarre trial at the end of the year which did little to establish whether or not the Cagoule was a real force, but much to remind fascist-style organizations that the authorities were not prepared to turn a blind eye. The government did not, however, prevent the extreme right from organizing new political parties and it was in this guise that the Croix-de-Feu transformed themselves in June 1936 into the Parti Social Français (PSF). At the same time the ex-Communist mayor of Saint-Denis, Jacques Doriot, launched the Parti Populaire Français (PPF) with anti-Communism as its main *raison d'être*.

Doriot was not acting alone. In 1935 he was already in contact with Pierre Pucheu, Paul Baudouin and Gabriel Le Roy Ladurie, all highly placed representatives of financial and business interests. Once founded, the PPF was subsidized by several Parisian banks, by certain steel magnates, car manufacturers, mining and textile groups in the Nord, and business circles in Marseille and Algiers. Its first militants were drawn from expelled or renegade Communists, loyal to Doriot, and as it expanded it drew increasingly on resentful individuals from all classes and on social racketeers such as those organized with brazen panache by Simon Sabiani in Marseille. It gained roughly 50,000 adherents and twice that number at its peak in 1937, but always claimed far more. Its aims, ideas and style, and the demagogic leadership of Doriot, made it recognizably fascist by any European comparison.

The novelist and political essayist Drieu la Rochelle was at the town hall in Saint-Denis at the birth of the PPF. An intellectual who juggled with every contemporary idea, Drieu was an internationalist, a Nietzschean, contemptuous of bourgeois decadence, dismissive of Marxism but admiring of Communist methods. In 1934 he had defined his fascism in *Socialisme fasciste*. He wanted no variant of reactionary nationalism, which he despised, but looked for a dynamic leader who could revolutionize not the proletariat but the bourgeoisie. He saw his man, physically and politically, in Doriot. For three hours Doriot harangued a packed audience in his shirtsleeves. 'He is large, fat and strong; he sweats a lot . . . There are still hefty Frenchmen who can control events.'[19] The romantic accolade given to Doriot by Drieu and other credulous intellectuals encouraged his illusions of political power, but the PPF never became a mass party to compare with Italian Fascism or German Nazism. In the spring of 1937 Doriot tried, but failed, to group together all the extreme right in a 'Front de la liberté'. It seems certain that the resignation of Blum reduced the urgency for Doriot's backers to provoke a political showdown outside parliament. The PPF lost its subversive edge and drifted into a defeatist form of pacifism. It forfeited the support of its intellectuals. By the end of 1938 it was in sharp numerical decline.

The morphology of the Croix-de-Feu is a history of increasing moderation, with occasional reminders of its coup d'état potential. As the PSF it remained for the left the supreme emblem of French fascism, but in reality the party's gradual move towards caution and conservatism made it parallel, not to the PPF, but to the long-established right in the Chamber, the Fédération Républicaine. Within two years of its formation the PSF had probably a million members, making it a mass party, and in the region of

Lyon it was the largest party that the area had ever seen.[20] Authoritarian and populist, the PSF appealed to small businesses, equally in the country-side and the towns. Its nationalism, fierce anti-Communism and its mystique as a unifying, orderly movement made significant inroads in the same rural societies that Dorgères had mobilized, promising a new order under the Croix-de-Feu's triptych, 'Travail, famille, patrie', but stoutly republican. In 1935 La Rocque had asserted that the peasantry had always been lied to: he would tell them the truth and 'expel the parasites who squeeze our soil dry'.[21] In pursuit of this policy the PSF showed only glimpses of direct action. Instead it developed its family and corporative profile and sedulously prepared for the general elections due in 1940.

Both Doriot and La Rocque were hailed by various expectant journalists as 'the French Mussolini'. Doriot postured as such to little effect; La Rocque avoided the comparison. Neither came even close to a revolt. Vis-à-vis the fall of Blum, it can be argued that the return of Radical ministers to political ascendancy reassured business interests, but if this amounts to saying that there might otherwise have been a fascist coup it is essential not to exaggerate the power of the PPF, nor to underestimate the steady move of the PSF towards parliamentary politics.

Disillusion

Spain was the first issue which broke the festive unity of the Popular Front; inflation and the loss of earnings were the second. Others followed in quick succession. Blum criticized union irresponsibility and restricted impromptu strikes. Gide's revelations about the USSR were the most publicized but far from the only denunciations of Stalinism from within the intellectual circles of the Popular Front.[22] Then out of the blue a series of blunders brought tragedy to the streets. The PSF had announced a meeting at the Olympia theatre in the Paris suburb of Clichy on 16 March 1937. The left-wing local council wanted it banned, but the government decided that La Rocque was not breaking the law. A determined counter-demonstration of Communists and left-wing Socialists converged on the theatre, defying a large force of police sent by Marx Dormoy, the Minister of the Interior. A street battle ensued between police and Popular Front sup-porters, unthinkable several months earlier. Shots were fired and five of the demonstrators were killed. A sixth died later in hospital. At the massive funeral for the victims, feelings of anger and betrayal ran deep. Blum took responsibility and was devastated by the shootings.

The Popular Front was never the same after Clichy, but it did not immedi-

ately disintegrate. Even after Blum's resignation in June, the combined left still had its majority in the Chamber, and at the annual congress of Young Communists from 10 to 14 July 1937, Raymond Guyot's official party report made no mention of problems, but gave a positive image of the Popular Front, rehearsing its successes and claiming Communist inspiration, particularly in the training of youth in modern skills such as radio, telegraphy and aviation.[23] The 1937 *congés payés* involved far greater numbers than in 1936, and on 31 August the state and private railway companies were merged by the government into the first version of the SNCF (Société Nationale des Chemins de Fer), for decades to be the standard-bearer of successful state enterprise. Trade-union membership, which had soared to 4 million, stayed high throughout much of 1937. Most industrial communities sustained an expansive range of new organizations. Only in the winter of 1937–8 was there the start of a disillusioned retreat by workers from union involvement.

Disillusion was total for one collective voice in the Rassemblement Populaire, the Étoile Nord-Africaine, the movement which embodied the demands of a number of Algerian immigrants for major reforms to the whole edifice of colonialism. Its leader, Messali Hadj, backed the Popular Front and had high hopes of the anti-imperialist record of the Communist Party. The government set up the colonial enquiry promised in the common programme, but not with any rigour. Blum took up the 1931 proposal of Maurice Viollette, an ex-Governor General of Algeria, to extend political rights to the indigenous male Algerian élite without affecting their personal Muslim status, and together Blum and Viollette in December 1936 announced a proposal to promote some 21,000 Algerians in this way. It heralded more extensive citizenship but made no mention of independence. A cautionary measure of reform, it went too far for the French *colons* in Algeria whereas for Hadj it missed the fundamental issue altogether. In *El Ouma*, the journal of the Algerian nationalists, he had put forward ideas of a constituent assembly leading to an Algerian parliament which he had expected the Popular Front to promote. It failed to do so, and positions were radicalized in January 1937 when the government dissolved the Étoile Nord-Africaine under the same law that suppressed the right-wing leagues. It numbered some 5,000 members, mostly in the Bouches-du-Rhône, Paris and Lyon, and it had already been denounced as sectarian and divisive by Ben Ali Boukhort, the Secretary-General of the Algerian Communist Party. Two months later Hadj laid the grounds for a new movement, the Parti du Peuple Algérien (PPA), but on 27 August 1937 he and several of its other leaders were arrested. By then the PPA had crossed the Mediterranean, a

significant move of nationalist organization away from immigrants within France into Algeria itself. In March 1939, speaking in Algiers, Maurice Thorez officially separated the Communists from Hadj and the PPA's programme of independence by the cautious formula that Algeria was not a nation but only 'a nation in the process of formation'. Meanwhile the Senate had quashed the remnants of the Blum–Viollette project.

Immobility and repression were to be the memories of the Popular Front among Algerian nationalists, but the readiness for reforms within colonialism had been there. What had swayed many of the discussions was the high profile that North Africa was given in the context of renewed German assertion and the fragile security of France. The reliance on the resources of the greater France of the Empire was symbolized by the new label, 'France d'outre-mer'. At the end of the 1930s the colonies were more popular in public and political opinion than they had ever been.

Daladier's decisive break

In the declining economic climate of 1937–8, with the franc sinking, public debt increasing and business confidence low, the clarity of political aims and alignments within the Popular Front disappeared. A struggle was discerned between the forces of labour hanging on to the gains of 1936, and forces of management and government looking for ways of stepping up production. Trade unions were now easily cast as immovable conservatives, refusing to look reality in the eye. Management called for the removal of the forty-hour week as the only way forward to greater productivity. Blum was returned in March 1938 for a second ministry, which he set up with a Keynesian programme of government-led investment, exchange controls and a wealth tax. The Senate was unimpressed, foreseeing yet more socialist experimentation, and forced him out after only a few weeks. The shift of Radicals to the right would now only permit a government which would throw itself firmly into economic growth on management terms. Édouard Daladier provided this.

Target of the rioters on 6 February, committed partner in the Rassemblement Populaire, Vice-Premier under Blum in 1936, the 54-year-old Daladier personified the middle-of-the-road republic. Son of a small-town baker, he had early identified with the Dreyfusard cause, had fought with distinction at Verdun, had become mayor and Radical deputy of Carpentras, north-east of Avignon, and left-wing leader of the party in 1927, sympathetic to the Young Turks' revivalism of Pierre Mendès France, Jean Zay and Pierre Cot. In his role as Minister of National Defence under Blum he was ambiva-

lent about Spain, but became convinced of the need to accelerate arms production within France as a secure grounding of anti-fascism. More than anyone, he accepted the argument that productivity had been shackled by the forty-hour week. He spoke on the radio of his 'common-sense' approach which would 'get France back to work', and his skill with words and ease of manner brought him a huge popular following. The Senate fell in line with his decision to govern by decree-laws, which he justified by the seriousness of the international situation: he came to power in April 1938 just after Hitler's Anschluss with Austria.

By the autumn, economic and foreign policy were inextricable. Daladier needed the security of peace for his economic revisionism. He favoured a strong democratic front between Britain and France against the threat of the Rome–Berlin axis, but like Blum in the Spanish crisis of July 1936 he was forced by Hitler's demands on Czechoslovakia in September 1938 to choose between appeasement and resistance. The Nazi pressure on the Czechs and threat of invasion triggered a war crisis and a partial mobilization of the French reserves. Avoidance of war was as near to a consensus position as any in a period of intense ideological confrontation. France was committed to standing by Czechoslovakia, but the fear and human costs of another war were widely felt to be the determinants in the crisis, despite the warnings from anti-fascists of Hitler's megalomania. Daladier went to Munich quite unprepared for the enormity of the concessions he finally made, but conscious of being no more than a second player to Neville Chamberlain and his own Foreign Secretary Georges Bonnet. On his return from Munich he exhibited none of the triumphalism of Chamberlain in London; his sense of guilt made him astonished at the popular acclaim that he received and the overwhelming support in the Chamber. Only the Communists voted as a party against the Munich Agreement. Internally it gave Daladier the confidence to marginalize the Socialists and break decisively with the Popular Front. Backed by Paul Reynaud, his new Finance Minister, he embarked on a series of decrees which effectively abolished the forty-hour week, energized production in the defence industries and brought investments back into France. An attempted general strike on 30 November was a dismal failure: counter-measures by police were effective and the unions miscalculated their militant support.

In 1939 a popular Daladier prorogued parliament, exuding a sense of dependability and personal strength, living up to his nickname as the 'bull of the Vaucluse'. The economy under Reynaud registered renewed growth, and confidence among the employers. Workers saw their weekly workload exceed forty and then forty-five hours. The social collapse of Popular Front

assertiveness made the search for extreme political solutions by the *patronat* unnecessary. The fortunes of Doriot's PPF visibly declined. Observers from abroad who had been critical of the ideological conflicts began to talk of the Third Republic as stable and well governed. In mid-summer, Daladier gave a family identity to his authoritarian republic, dubbed his 'dictatorship' by opponents. The decree-law of 31 July instituted a pro-natalist code (*Code de la famille*) which increased family allowances for the third and subsequent child, paid mothers to stay at home (*la mère au foyer*), and gave extra tax advantages and assistance to peasant families to keep them on the land. State loans to young peasant couples would be written off after five children.

The Code also hardened the 1920 law against abortion and the punishments for advertising contraception. Madeleine Pelletier had just been arrested for performing abortions. She died a few months later in a mental institution. Behind the Code lay a new government committee on population, studded with experts on demography such as Alfred Sauvy and passionate advocates of pro-natalism including the tireless campaigner Fernand Boverat whose reports throughout the 1920s had argued the 'higher' reason of national duty against the 'selfish' reason behind small families.[24] There were no women members on the committee. The language of the Code was one of traditionalism, but also of reform. It vastly increased public expenditure and it lay on the chequered path towards the welfare state. It was accepted across the political spectrum. *La Terre*, rural voice of the Communist Party, welcomed its defence of the small peasantry.

The integrity of the family was inseparable in much public opinion from the integrity of the nation, seen by the right to be threatened by refugees. Jewish refugees, seeking political asylum, pressed on the frontiers after the Anschluss, Munich and Kristallnacht. They were fewer than the refugees from Spain. But Spanish republicans were a tragedy of a civil war that was past: German and Eastern European Jews were a tragedy of a European war that they, already the victims, were accused of unleashing. The triple accusation – Jew, Communist, warmonger – was daily coinage in much of the extreme right-wing press, led by *L'Action française*. It was flanked by the biological racism of publications like *Le Bonnet jaune*, which published the names of Jews in all walks of French life and described them as mosquitoes, venomous bearers of plague.[25]

There was nothing vague about this level of race-hatred. It was the active province of a small minority, but it echoed across a substantial range of opinion. It was exceeded only by the most discussed of all antisemitic pamphlets at the time, the *Bagatelles pour un massacre* by the literary

maverick Louis-Ferdinand Destouches who wrote under the name of Céline. Published in December 1937, it repeated in virulent language every demented facet of antisemitism since Drumont's *La France juive* of 1886, and honed in on Léon Blum as 'the worst enemy' to whom Céline said he 'would prefer a dozen Hitlers'. The scandal caused by his pamphlet was all the more intense as there were many in the literary world who insisted it must be a clever parody. It was not. If anything, Céline's loathing of Jews increased with the war crisis over Czechoslovakia, and he published *L'École des cadavres* shortly after Munich to extol an agreement with Germany which alone, he stated, could avoid the slaughter of another war. For many in France the language of massacre, corpses and slaughter was precisely the vivid imagery in which the cause of peace had to be presented. But in the context of the Jewish refugees it cut viciously both ways, intensifying dehumanization.

On coming to power, Daladier broke immediately with the fluctuating help given to refugees by the Blum government. During 1938 he and his Radical Minister of the Interior, Albert Sarraut, used a series of decree-laws to try to close the borders and crack down on illegal entrants, while maintaining that France was still the country of asylum. The pretence was thin: the Daladier government was alone among the democracies not to condemn the Nazi pogrom of Kristallnacht. But by the beginning of 1939 it was clear that the harsh measures were neither effective nor the best use of human resources at a time when every newspaper was underlining the dramatic imbalance of population between France and Germany.

Popular Front proposals to create agricultural and colonial settlements for the refugees re-emerged, and five rural centres began to receive families, though progress was painfully slow. In April 1939 military recruitment of foreigners was given priority for labour on urgent tasks such as building fortifications, and the Minister of Justice, Paul Marchandeau, gave his name to a measure which outlawed religious and racial defamation in the press, though he sought to minimize naturalizations. The overall shift was a small one towards pragmatism, in which Louise Weiss assumed yet another influential public role as the persistent advocate of a rational system of refugee employment. She argued at the highest level that the influx of so many remarkable people was a windfall for France.[26] The Chambers of Commerce in Paris, Lyon and many other towns were incensed. Refusing competition, and swept along by the currents of xenophobia, they did everything to block initiatives. It was here, and in the medical pressure groups, that the protectionism of sectional interests claimed to speak for much of society.

Protection of the nation was the *raison d'état* of Daladier's rule by decree and his extensive appointment of technocrats to ministerial posts. He ignored parliament. He took emergency constitutional powers, confident in the social base which the counter-offensive against the forty-hour week had created. He was either blamed or credited for burying the Popular Front. He increased productivity and rearmament. His record on these issues gained him a reputation for decisive leadership, but he was not incapable of altering his policy. The refugee issue demonstrated an initial reflex for repression, but then showed a certain capacity to rethink. In foreign policy he found the national interest elusive. His non-confrontation with Hitler at Munich made for many continuities with Léon Blum's non-intervention over Franco's rebellion. Despite his resolute break with the Popular Front, Daladier was caught in the same ambiguities that avoiding another war entailed.

IO

Not Another War? Shattered Illusions,
1930s–1940

1. The tangled ideologies of peace

Multiple idealisms

Dismantling the cultural and moral scaffolding of war had begun seriously at many levels of society in the 1920s. The work had reached a peak of activity, idealism and initiative under Briand, and his name and policy were in everyone's mind when Jean Renoir's film, *La Grande illusion*, opened in 1937. Renoir was closely identified with the Popular Front: he headed the Ciné-Liberté group and had worked with the Communists in making *La Vie est à nous*, a title which captured the assertions of working people during the heady summer of 1936. 'Life is ours' was no less the humanist moral of *La Grande illusion*, its life-affirming portrait of human relations across national divides making it the most powerful peace film of the 1930s. As Norman Angell had argued well before 1914 in his famous predictive book, *The Great Illusion*, the purpose, benefit and rationale of war were illusory. *La Grande illusion* was acceptable to the bulk of the war veterans who, ten years before, had felt enabled by Briand to relate the horror of their experiences and to seek out ex-combatants from other countries to exchange ideas for a permanent peace. Renoir, who had been wounded twice during the war, portrayed heroism, humour and sacrifice, but transposed it from the trenches on to the lives and escape of prisoners of war, and made reconciliation with the enemy a sign of emotional wholeness. But there were arguments among peace groups as to how far the critique of the film extended: it did not contest the Jacobin and revolutionary tradition of war embodied in the patriotic words of the 'Marseillaise'.

The dystopia of the First World War was the subject of Jean Giono's novel of 1931, *Le Grand troupeau* (The Great Herd), a passionate reference to the bestial predicament of the men in the trenches, and an echo, for those who wanted to hear it, of the protests of the mutineers of 1917. Giono, in full revolt against his own war experience and exposure to gas, had returned

to his birthplace in Manosque in Haute-Provence, and had made an international reputation with his tough, poetic rural novel, *Regain*, of 1930. In
1935 he took young admirers of his work on a hike to the plateau of the
Montagne de Lure, and started a series of retreats and artisan labour at the
partly ruined village of Cantadour. The peasant values, poetry, music and
folklore of Cantadour were underscored by Giono's visceral hatred of war
and his commitment to pacifism. In 1937, the same year as *La Grande
illusion*, he published writings whose title announced his own refusal to
obey another summons to war (*Refus d'obéissance*). Where Renoir's film
was seen to fall within the compass of the Popular Front's idealism, Giono
passionately criticized the Popular Front for not going far enough and not
endorsing the totality of pacifism. It was both a justification of desertion
and a refusal of the new Communist Party line on national defence. He
broke his links with Chamson's and Guéhenno's periodical *Vendredi*, but
continued to theorize war as the inevitable product of capitalism.

In a series of writings from Cantadour, Giono invited peasants, in the
event of war, 'to destroy the stocks of corn which they possess and only
cultivate the soil to feed themselves', rejecting the inhuman order of a
civilization which, he argued, would continue to herd them to the slaughter-
house.[1] He opposed the concept of mass, the forces of industrialization and
the pull of partisan politics, and although his guru pretensions alienated as
many as they attracted, he stood out as an influential agitator for peace as
a philosophy of life, linking the Greek mythology of Pan with anti-
modernization.

The inadequacy of the left-wing critique of militarism and war, premise
for Giono's refusal, had been the basis for the integral pacifism of the
journalist Victor Méric, an anarchist and socialist in the 1900s, briefly a
Communist in 1920, then once again a maverick socialist after 1923.
Méric's writings gave substance to public fears that another war of aerial
bombing and gas warfare would finally destroy civilization, and in 1931
he launched the Ligue Internationale des Combattants de la Paix (LICP),
which became the largest non-party pacifist movement in France by the
time of his death in 1933. The numbers were small, reaching at most 12,000
members in France, but the ubiquity of the movement was sufficient to
provoke wild talk in some circles of substantial desertion in the event of
war. The integral pacifism of the LICP, stronger in the provinces than in
Paris, placed peace above all other social and ideological objectives; it was
critical of the weakness of the League of Nations, and repudiated both
national defence and left-wing concepts of a revolutionary war. Among its
most effective speakers on the provincial circuit was Marcelle Capy, whose

warmth and directness made an instant impact on war widows and *anciens combattants* alike.

Ideals of peace were kaleidosocopic in the 1930s: events shook them into new patterns and shapes and unplanned relationships to one another. Hundreds of separate groups and associations disputed the morality of war: individuals of all classes and situations felt urged by 'life itself' to state their position, sign declarations, attend meetings and pressure politicians. Women, still excluded from the political process, underlined the absurdity of their exclusion by politicizing war and peace in as rich a complex of alignments and policies as any parliamentary debate or electoral campaign, responding as organized representatives to the multiple opportunities for international solidarity.

Ambitious targets for peace were set in 1932, the year of the disarmament talks at Geneva and a Congress against Imperialist War in Amsterdam. It was also the year in which Briand died, his work immediately commemorated in the development of a garden city within Suresnes in western Paris, laid out as a peace neighbourhood, with the central axis of the Boulevard Aristide Briand intersecting with that of Gustave Stresemann, and a home for old people called the 'Maison Locarno'. The Amsterdam Congress brought together intellectuals and activists from the European left, and was followed by a congress against fascism at the Salle Pleyel in Paris in 1933. The ensuing Amsterdam–Pleyel movement against both war and fascism, with Communist leadership and eminent peace credentials in Romain Rolland and Henri Barbusse, was something of a colossus, bestriding the other peace groups in its bold rejection of nationalism as incurably belligerent. The movement was seen as almost a definition of oppositional pacifism until the PCF changed its line in 1934–5 to one of peace through, and no longer against, national defence.

The massive international petition sent to the Geneva talks by women's peace groups brought publicity for their conference at the Ligue des Droits de l'Homme in Paris at the end of April 1932, at which 600 women pressed for peace through disarmament. Madeleine Vernet headed the secretariat, and went on to form a permanent disarmament commission. Gabrielle Duchêne, also active in the conference, as at Amsterdam, described her combination of feminism, pacifism and anti-fascism (see Chapter 9) as 'realistic' pacifism to distinguish it from 'integral' or 'doctrinaire' pacifism. She denounced the indulgence towards Nazi Germany shown by the integral pacifists of the LICP, and threw herself into aid for the anti-fascist refugees and action for an economic boycott of the fascist regimes. Duchêne made no apology for her partisan politics when compared to Vernet and Capy.

All three epitomized distinctive relationships between feminist and pacifist ideals, contributing powerfully to the miscellany of peace aspirations in public opinion.

In 1936 the umbrella role of the Amsterdam–Pleyel movement was paralleled by the Rassemblement Universel pour la Paix (RUP), the broadly based popular movement which grew out of the British Peace Ballot and whose French section was headed by the Radical Pierre Cot, French delegate to the League of Nations in 1933, Air Minister under Daladier in 1934 and again under Léon Blum in 1936. Cot broke fundamentally with Daladier over Munich. Peace and anti-fascism as a duality either stood opposed to Munich or hung its head in what Blum acknowledged as 'guilty relief'. The LICP, however, after four years of declining membership under the impact of anti-fascism, was optimistic at a surge of support provoked by Munich. It was short-lived, and in March 1939 the LICP was swept aside by the current of national reassertion at the German occupation of Prague, revealing just how much of a backwater unaligned pacifism had become. In the context of Hitler's mounting aggression, the effort of integral pacifists to argue the necessity of peace 'for its own sake' was marginalized. Still more unhappily for the movement, the desperate arguments of many in the LICP brought them closer to those who ideologically called for co-operation with Nazi Germany. Their innocence was lost.

Obsession with the internal enemy

Without too much exaggeration, it seemed as if the nation and the republic had become indissolubly one on 11 November 1918, and still more so in the victory parade of 14 July 1919. The premise of such an eventuality lay in the *union sacrée* of 1914 against Germany as the agreed enemy, and it was finalized by the victorious outcome of the war and the epic role ascribed to the *poilus*. Patriotism and nationalism still retained some of their pre-war distinctiveness, but the combined entity of nation and republic was embodied in the thousands of *monuments aux morts*, and it even looked as if Briandism had created a specific foreign policy for the nation-republic, with idealism and reason projected into a form of pragmatic internationalism.

The coherence in Briandism was fractured at home by the intensive political search for 'renewal' at the end of the 1920s followed by the ideological effects of the depression across Europe. The spiral of ideology that took hold in France whirled the meanings of war and peace into a vortex of ever-greater complexity. The events and sequel of 6 February 1934 on the one hand and the Popular Front on the other were critical.

People on all political sides referred to their eyes being opened. Obsession with 'the enemy within', identity mark of the new brand of nationalism which had entered European history at the end of the nineteenth century, became a general psychosis.

The change in Communist policy in 1934 to support for national defence issued in regular articles in *L'Humanité* by Gabriel Péri, the Communist voice on foreign affairs in the Chamber. The articles consistently addressed foreign policy in the name of France as well as of the party and the proletariat. The day after Nazi Germany's Anschluss with Austria in March 1938, Péri warned that Czechoslovakia was the next target on the Nazi list, and that Europe would pay in blood for its 'tragic error' in minimizing the fascist threat. The last hopes of peace, he claimed, lay in producing a government which would 'rigorously pursue a democratic and French foreign policy'.[2]

The national rhetoric in Péri's journalism had a popular resonance: the surge of patriotic recruitment to the PCF continued throughout the Popular Front. For the party's opponents on the political right, and many on the left, the Communist effusion about France and Frenchness was opportunist and hypocritical, masking what they saw as the PCF's craven submission to Stalin's Russia. The criticism only encouraged Communists and their sympathizers to reimagine the nation even more assertively as a republic in the Revolutionary tradition, and to cast the right-wing leagues and pro-German business interests as the enemy within, ready to do a deal against the interests of France and its working people.

In the exact context of the Anschluss Péri was also urging that foreign policy should be French and not British. As elsewhere in anti-fascist writings, appeasement of Nazi Germany was seen as a British import keenly consumed by the French bourgeoisie. Appeasement, argued Péri, would lead inexorably to the war for which Nazi Germany was actively preparing. It was this conviction which established Péri and the PCF in 1938 as a cogent voice warning simultaneously against both Nazism and war. Péri promoted the concept of peace as dependent on a popular and national resistance to the forces of fascism, in close identity with the Soviet Union.

Not far from the PCF in its reaction to the events of 6 February 1934, the anti-fascist Vigilance Committee of Rivet, Langevin and Alain broke apart under the stress of reconciling its anti-fascist propaganda with equally strong pacifist sentiments derived directly from the First World War. This stress, common to most left-wing movements in Europe in the mid-1930s, only grew worse as the threat from Hitler increased. It was the source of bitter feuding on the left at the time of Munich. Despite Hitler's withdrawal

from the League of Nations and the disarmament conference, all three founders of the Vigilance Committee managed to sign a pacifist brochure in March 1936 arguing that war was not inevitable, but it did acknowledge that in three years' time Germany might be strong enough to impose itself through war.[3] The cracks in the movement's solidarity widened into ruptures in 1938. Whereas Rivet and Langevin took the path of anti-fascism against Munich, Alain and a rump of the Vigilance Committee backed Munich by arguing persistently that war itself was fascist and that avoidance of war must therefore be interpreted as anti-fascism. They were accused by those who broke with the Committee of whistling in the wind.

Much of the pro-Munich sympathy among the remaining members of the Vigilance Committee was due to concerns that anti-fascism had been hijacked by the PCF. This was also the argument advanced by the pacifist wing within the Socialist Party (SFIO), led by its general secretary, Paul Faure. Acutely suspicious of the volte-face in Communist policy and its endorsement of national defence, Faure and the socialist pacifists denounced the PCF for its denial of Stalin's tyranny and egomania. Paul Faure's recipe for peace was anti-Communist and pro-disarmament, with a readiness to negotiate with Nazi Germany in the interests of economic and international co-operation. Faure, at one with the pacifists of the Vigilance Committee, argued potently in 1938 that any increase in the military build-up of the French state would benefit internal fascist tendencies. The support for this position among trade unionists who had always seen the military state as an internal enemy strengthened Faure's bid for supremacy over the party leader, Léon Blum. In December 1938, however, his tendency was outvoted at the party congress by a majority which preferred Blum's call for a firm stand against Hitler. Faure nevertheless remained as the party's secretary-general, his pacifism too widely shared for it to be rejected altogether.

Among socialist pacifists of the Paul Faure tendency, the nation was reimagined as part of a greater international community, towards which the League of Nations and Briandism had pointed. The military Jacobinism of the republican tradition was downplayed, and the internationalism of the pre-1914 socialist movement was merged with the anti-war convictions which had reached a more assertive level of popularity in the late 1920s. Within the trade unions, the primary-school teachers and the postal workers were the most pacifist, with many student teachers at the training colleges (*écoles normales*) refusing to enter for the extra military courses leading to officer status.

The Faurists were flanked outside the party by the integral pacifists

of the LICP. Technically above politics, the LICP's civil dissent on the fundamental issue of peace made its scattered pockets of militants into radical critics of a republic which could still sanction the resort to force. One of its prominent publicists, Henri Jeanson, tried to rouse members in March 1938 to look mainly inside France for motivation. He countered demands for a new *union sacrée* against Hitler by decrying it as a diversion from the essential fight against the internal destroyers of a free and peaceful republic: 'Our enemies are not outside. They are within.'[4]

On the political right, fringed at the extremes by the nationalist ideologies of Action Française and the Croix-de-Feu, politicians had long thrived on the identification of 'enemies within'. There was little change in their imagined nation during the late 1930s, except in intensity: their anti-Communism was even more rife, and the continued appetite for antisemitism fed avidly on the 'threat' perceived in the influx of refugees fleeing from persecution. Yet the nationalism of the right was radicalized in reaction to the success of the Popular Front, to the point where the enemy of 1914–18 was almost entirely replaced by 'the enemy within'. The danger from Nazi Germany was minimized.

The anti-Germanism of the political right had castigated governments throughout the 1920s for failing the victors of 1918. By the mid-1930s personalities on the right were showing respect for German achievements and a barely disguised fascination with the personality of Hitler. Sympathy for Franco and Salazar, and a broad agreement on the need for reappraising Germany, set the right against the perceived 'warmongering' of the anti-fascist left. The shift in attitudes of Pierre-Étienne Flandin was not untypical. Situated on the moderate right as deputy for Avallon in the Yonne, Flandin had a seven-month spell as Prime Minister in 1934–5, and was Foreign Minister early in 1936, pragmatically supporting the Franco-Soviet pact negotiated by Laval in 1935 despite his own anti-Communism. Flandin's aim was to contain the military ambitions of Hitler starkly displayed in the remilitarization of the Rhineland in 1936 and Germany's repudiation of the Locarno Pact. To this end he exercised his pro-British charm to try to persuade London to back an armed response to Hitler's military moves in the Rhineland. He failed, and withdrew his proposals. They were the last sign of the 'old' Flandin. In reaction to the Popular Front he moved radically towards appeasement of Germany, calling on the French people to send anti-war petitions to Daladier when the Czech crisis erupted in September 1938. Ecstatic at the Munich agreements, Flandin sent a personal telegram of congratulation to all the signatories, including Hitler.

In his pre-Munich press campaign Flandin referred to 'occult forces'

dragging France towards war, an undisguised reference to Jews and Communists. In the papers closest to fascism, support for the Munich agreement was articulated openly as a refusal to go to war for the 'Judeo-Bolshevik' refugees, accused of seeking a war of revenge on Nazi Germany. The cartoon by Charlet in the weekly *Gringoire* portrayed the political leaders of the PCF and the SFIO, including Blum, shouldering each other to stick up posters for a military mobilization. The argument that peace should be made with a strong Germany as a bulwark against Soviet Communism and the internal forces of the left, found a receptive audience throughout all the political parties who had opposed the Popular Front. The slogan 'Rather Hitler than Blum' echoed down the corridors of the parliamentary right. It was a choice of ideologies, a recipe for a specific kind of peace, not an invitation to the Nazi Führer to invade.

Not all of the right took Flandin's path. As dramatic evidence of the anti-German convictions which remained, it was a Parisian barrister, Jacques Renouvin, a fervent anti-German and recent member of the Action Française vanguard, the Camelots du Roi, who objected most actively to Flandin's telegram to Hitler. He struck Flandin across the face in full view of dignitaries assembled under the Arc de Triomphe.

The lead in Franco-German initiatives was taken by the Comité France–Allemagne (CFA), set up in 1935 and inspired by interviews with Hitler as Chancellor, the first of which had been accorded in November 1933 to the journalist Fernand de Brinon. Collaborative youth programmes were enthusiastically reported in Jean Luchaire's newspaper *Notre Temps*, featuring the enterprise on the German side of Otto Abetz, a Francophile in the 1920s who had rallied to Nazism and was central to the burgeoning cultural projects of the CFA. The writers, journalists, war veterans and politicians attracted to the Comité made up a set of notable pro-German personalities, described on the left as 'pacifists of the right'. They secured the backing of Pierre Laval, Prime Minister in 1935, and the CFA was not repudiated by subsequent governments, even those of the Popular Front.

During 1935–9 the previously unthinkable became commonplace, but never ceased to surprise: Communists were urging a foreign policy of national defence, and politicians of the right were arguing for negotiation and co-operation with Germany. This was an astonishing and acrimonious reversal of accustomed positions, though there was little public alarm that the nation might be made vulnerable by the in-fighting. The pursuit of peace was seen to be conflictual but not necessarily debilitating. Even as the Czech Sudetenland was conceded to Hitler at Munich, there was extensive confidence that the defence of France was in good hands.

Defensive military policy

The relationship between the tangle of peace movements and the makers of military policy was fraught but not always hostile. However contradictory the programmes for peace, the depth of public feeling against war kept governments committed to a defence policy that was genuinely defensive, spurning any military planning or foreign policy that would set off another conflict. Blum's decisions on Spain were critical in this respect. In return, the defence measures sanctioned by successive governments since the end of the occupation of the Ruhr, and associated most publicly with the name of André Maginot, provided a bedrock of defensive constructions which allowed peace groups to attract support from those who might otherwise have been worried about national security. Briand had pioneered this two-pronged approach: his peace initiatives and support for the Maginot Line co-existed.

The strictly defensive planning advocated by Marshal Pétain expressed the country's determination not to return to the blood-letting of the war. A public update of demographic figures in 1935 reminded society that 1.4 million had been killed in the war and 3.2 million had been injured. Over a million were living as war invalids and 3.2 million people were dependent on war pensions, including 700,000 war widows. On top of this there was the severe deficit in the birth rate compared to Germany. 'Sparing the blood of France' was a phrase taken up by the civil authorities in their agreement with the defensive lead given by the military. Where iron was the long-established material of war, concrete was the newly invented material of peace. Fortifications as a genre took on a fashionable appeal; eminent visitors and endless photographers made the 400 massive concrete case-mates of Maginot's 'wall of France' into policy statements of peaceful intent. The living quarters underground were furnished with conspicuous comfort: shelves of books, armchairs and carpets in the officers' rooms envisaged long periods of occupation, and the labyrinth of tunnels, rails and electric cables was revealed in illustrated magazines as stretching end-lessly into the distance in bright artificial light. In 1937 a film, *Double crime sur la ligne Maginot*, gave it mystery, while Roland Dorgelès, popular novelist of the First World War, wrote of his amazement at the subterranean splendour. Time and again comparisons with the hell of the trenches ended with the statement that defence was now about concrete and not human flesh.

André Maginot had survived as a sergeant in the war. He died of typhoid fever on 7 January 1932 as Minister of War. The Ministry was renamed

the Ministry of Defence. By 1935 the Maginot defences, with one section supplied by artificial flooding, ran from the Swiss frontier along the German edges of Alsace and Lorraine to Montmédy just past the end of the Luxembourg border. There the line stopped. The Belgian frontier where the Meuse wound through the heavily wooded hills of the Ardennes was only lightly defended. In 1934 Pétain declared that the Ardennes were impenetrable, and subsequent military commissions sent to inspect the site of the Prussian victory at Sedan in 1870 decided that even if some German tanks got through the Ardennes they would falter at the width of the Meuse, allowing the French army time to reinforce the river's defence. There was no persuasive military or political dissent from this conclusion. Further north it was agreed with Belgium that French troops would move forward to advanced positions on the Belgian-German frontier should Germany threaten an attack.

In 1936 this co-ordinated strategy was undermined by the declaration of Belgian neutrality. It was Belgium's response to Hitler's military build-up and was indicative of the concern of all countries confronted with Nazi Germany to avoid a war. An urgent priority for defence spending was announced by Léon Blum's Popular Front government. Rearmament had restarted in 1934 after the failed conferences of 1932, but the programme of arms expenditure launched in September 1936 and boosting the production of tanks was a quantitative leap. Another heavy commitment was made in March 1938 after the Anschluss. In neither case was there a rethinking of the basic defensive mentality.

Daladier inherited and continued defensive planning, and if Munich was thought by some to have endangered the security of France there was the reassuring ministerial presence of Georges Mandel, Clemenceau's aide in 1917–18, and Paul Reynaud, nicknamed 'Reynaud-la-guerre' by the extreme right. Reynaud agonized over whether or not to resign over Munich, but his decision to stay and accept promotion to the Finance Ministry sent out a message that a government policy of peaceful negotiation was not incompatible with funding renewed measures of defence. Reynaud, aged fifty in 1938, a right-of-centre deputy for the 2nd *arrondissement* of Paris, had signalled his support for an unyielding foreign policy in 1935 when he had advocated a resolute stand against Mussolini.

Small, neat, energetic and businesslike, Reynaud appealed in his election campaign of 1936 to the youth of France with a pamphlet asking what kind of France they wanted (see Chapter 7). Repeating Herriot's comment that there were far too many political fronts and not enough thought, he rejected comfortable visions of the past and what he saw as the atavistic

remedies of left and right. His language was tough, rational, economic and technical. He argued for a strong Anglo-French alliance and he urged the creation of a professional, mechanized army as the only way to defend the modernized, liberal economy that he believed would create an outward-looking nation. He accused the French of an obsession with staying as they were, cocooned in their nostalgia.

Reynaud took his ideas on the army directly from a lieutenant-colonel attached to the defence administration, Charles de Gaulle, whose little book, *Vers l'armée de métier* (*Towards a Professional Army*) published in 1934, convinced Reynaud that the technological modernization he was urging on industry should also be applied to the army. He argued the merits of de Gaulle's proposals in parliament, but saw them rejected by a consistent majority who perceived no need to tamper with the defensive strategy and the system of conscription on which traditional military thinking was based. The left still regarded the people as the citizen army, while politicians on the right argued that Marshal Pétain knew what was needed.

The passion for fortifications and the idea of a fully professional army were both influenced by the lack of population growth. In their opposing ways both were strategies for dealing with the dearth of men of fighting age. Apart from its defensive strengths, the Maginot Line would free soldiers to fight on the Belgian front, while a mechanized army would also use numbers more sparingly. The dearth was accentuated in 1934 at the start of the 'hollow' years, twenty years after the outbreak of the war. Military service was raised from one year to two in 1935 to compensate for the shortfall, but not as a move towards an aggressive strategy. The military leader who had succeeded Pétain as Chief of General Staff in 1930 was General Maxime Weygand. The proposals from the barely known Colonel de Gaulle coincided with the term of Weygand's leadership. They each conveyed a personal romance with the army which made them suspect to the republican left. Weygand was openly on the reactionary right, warning of Communist infiltration in the army ranks, and bitterly resenting the left's anti-militarism. He retired in 1935 but had made no attempt to move the army on to the offensive. His successor, General Maurice Gamelin, intellectual and ultra-cautious, perpetuated the search for ways of permanently avoiding another war on French territory, and despite Belgian neutrality kept open a secret line with his Belgian counterpart, confident that French troops would still be invited to fight on Belgian soil if Germany attacked.

The interweaving of defensive policy with the multiple strands of pacifist idealism identified French society of the 1930s with a fundamental concern

to avoid war. The profound, if discordant, humanist aspirations behind much of this avoidance were not always subsequently acknowledged. It was easier retrospectively to focus on the blinkered ideologies. Contrary to Renoir, it became obligatory to point backwards to the illusions, not of war but of peace. Yet for ten months after Munich there was an atmosphere of sober realism which did not abandon the emphasis on defence but adjusted the sights of peace, marginalizing the integral pacifists and rendering the appeasers desperate.

The Nazi-Soviet pact of August 1939, and the German invasion strategy in the spring of 1940, threw everything from the 1930s into turmoil.

2. What kind of war?

Daladier's realignment

An opinion poll in October 1938 concluded that a larger percentage of the public (37 per cent) was hostile to Munich than the vote in parliament suggested, where 553 deputies were in favour and only 75 against, 73 of whom were Communists, plus a lone rebellious Socialist, Jean Bouhey, and the conservative individualist Henri de Kerillis, made famous ten years before through his flamboyant propaganda organizations. A large proportion of those who voted in favour privately expressed concern at the betrayal of Czechoslovakia, and it was partly guilt at the failure to honour international obligations which caused people in 1939 to reconsider the momentum for peace and accept that no further concessions should be made.

Daladier noticeably began to move in this direction once he felt secure in his break with the Popular Front and registered the unlikelihood of a further trade-union challenge after the fiasco of the general strike in November 1938. Knowing that he could not be accused of sympathy with the internal policies of the PCF and the Socialists, he felt free to be assertive in foreign policy whereas at Munich he had been pliant. He backed increasingly urgent rearmament programmes after Hitler's occupation of Prague, and reacted with anger when in the same month Mussolini demanded colonial concessions from France. Daladier riposted that France would not hand over a single acre of territory, nor surrender an iota of its colonial 'rights'. His own realignment continued at the end of April in response to Hitler's threats against Danzig and the Polish corridor. Daladier stepped up efforts to renew the Franco-Soviet pact which had been signed by Pierre Laval in 1935 and which reflected orthodox diplomacy towards Russia emanating from the Foreign Office (Quai d'Orsay) since 1894.

It was in just such national, and not ideological, terms that Daladier represented his shift away from Munich, though he retained Georges Bonnet as his Foreign Minister, possibly because he thought he would be less trouble inside the government. Bonnet had made a virtue out of shelving the commitments made to Czechoslovakia, Romania and Yugoslavia in the 1920s. His vigorous appeasement of Germany was based on the belief that the First World War had largely been caused by the rigid system of alliances. He showed no enthusiasm for renewed overtures to the Soviet Union, nor did Pierre Laval outside the government, who valued his own attempts to appease Mussolini much higher than his negotiations with Stalin. Laval, a caustic critic of party politics, never forgave the democratic system for having allowed his planned concessions to Mussolini to be rejected. His pacifist urgings in 1939 persisted with the accusation that irresponsible democracy had thrown away the one opportunity of keeping Mussolini and Hitler apart.

The diplomacy in Russia was promoted by Daladier on the basis that it would promote the cause of peace, regardless of the issue of Bolshevism. He made this point to London at the end of May, but Britain was reluctant to commit high-level officials. On 4 May the pacifist and neo-socialist Marcel Déat, expelled from the SFIO in 1933, wrote an article in his paper *L'Œuvre* entitled 'Mourir pour Dantzig?' ('Die for Danzig?') claiming that French peasants would never be prepared to sacrifice themselves for the Poles. The article was a dramatic formulation but elicited very little media sympathy. It quickly disappeared from public discussion, as popular views hardened on the need to confront Hitler over Poland. The change in government attitudes was marked internally by the orders sent out to prefects to carry out the conscription of refugee labour for specific manual tasks including military constructions. By the end of August some 20,000 Spanish refugees had been enrolled in companies of foreign workers, subject to military discipline but rewarded by allowances and benefits. It was a first, if tentative, rupture with the sterile mentality of internment camps.

The little news of the diplomatic front in Russia that reached the French press was interpreted by many as a sign that Daladier's shift of policy had belatedly justified opposition to Munich. With parliament suspended, there were no debating opportunities for the Communist deputies to claim that Daladier was effectively acknowledging that they had been right, but this was the triumphant tone of Péri in *L'Humanité* at the height of the summer, alongside the PCF's calls for the army and the diplomatic service to be cleansed of elements opposed to a firm policy of anti-fascism.

On 23 August 1939, as the Nazi threats to Poland intensified and the

war crisis of September 1938 was vividly re-created, the army leaders signalled to the government that France had no choice this time but to stand by its commitments, in this case to Poland, which, they added, preceded the reopening of relations with the Soviet Union. The news of the Nazi-Soviet pact was just breaking.

Nazi-Soviet pact: outbreak of war

In the last week of August 1939, writers and diarists all over Europe expressed a heightened sense that a world of negotiation and patched-up peace was coming to an end. It seemed unlikely that another crisis would be resolved, unless Hitler himself stepped back from war. This was the outside hope of most people. What seemed more likely, and to some even preferable, was that Nazi moves against Poland would provoke a show-down with the Soviet Union and a suicidal clash of the two ideological systems. No one predicted the Nazi-Soviet pact of non-aggression which Ribbentrop and Molotov made public on 23 August.

It was a Russian Munich, carrying some of the same justifications: an avoidance of war, time gained for Russia to rearm and strengthen defences, a calculated concession in the 'higher' interests of peace. But it went much further. Within a week it was clear that it was a pact of predators, both determined to dismember Poland. Its secret clauses envisaged military and economic co-operation. The British and French failure to give serious pur-pose to their diplomacy in Russia seemed to some to have provoked Stalin's about-turn, but this was not the widespread reasoning in the indignant outpourings of the press. The Nazi-Soviet pact scandalized opinion by turning everyone's ideological certainties on their head. The Communist Party itself had no way of understanding it. The moral highground claimed by Péri before and after Munich was swept away. Self-righteous moralism now exuded from a near consensus of anti-Communist opinion.

The PCF struggled initially in its isolation to hang on to its credibility. For two days *L'Humanité* and the rest of the Communists' seventy regular publications were silent. On 26 August they were banned by Daladier before they could openly reappear.

On 25 August Britain broke its pattern of appeasement by committing itself to Poland. Daladier was urged by Bonnet to explore a way out by responding to Mussolini's call for a revisionist conference on the Treaty of Versailles. Secure in the Nazi-Soviet pact, Hitler gambled on British and French indecisiveness. Having already massed his troops on the Polish frontier, he issued the command to invade. The German army and airforce

crossed into Poland on 1 September in a devastating Blitzkrieg operation, based on mechanized mobility and land-to-air co-ordination. Daladier rejected the Italian ploy as a diversion and decreed a general mobilization of the French armed forces. He recalled the two Chambers of the National Assembly on 2 September, and declared that there was nothing ideological about the confrontation with Germany. He succeeded in gaining a unanimous vote for the necessary war credits. The Communist deputies voted in favour.

On 3 September separate ultimata were sent by Britain and France to Germany, instructing Germany to withdraw from Poland. The mentality of Munich had been reversed. There was only disdain from Ribbentrop. Several hours later, first Britain and then France declared war. Maurice Thorez, on behalf of the PCF, had said on 25 August that Communists, called to the ranks, would defend their country.

The initial resilience of the PCF's policy of national defence in the face of the devastating Nazi-Soviet pact evaporated during the last two weeks of September. An autocriticism was undertaken by the leadership at the insistence of the Comintern. Plans were drawn up for the clandestine publication of the banned party press. The war against Germany, accepted by the PCF in its vote of 2 September, was now denounced in the underground edition of *L'Humanité* on 6 October as 'a war of capitalist brigands'. Slowly Leninist theory was reworked to conclude that the Soviet Union was pursuing peace and that the war was 'an imperialist war' in which the proletariat could have no role, except as victims, a premise familiar to party militants who had joined the party in the 1920s or had agitated against the war of 1914–18. The about-turn of 1934, which had brought a massive increase in PCF membership and a popular marriage of the 'Internationale' with the 'Marseillaise', was negated in the wake of the Nazi-Soviet pact. Thorez deserted from the army, slipped out of the country on 4 October and made his way to Moscow. Communists, accused of warmongering from 1935 to 1939, were vilified as shabby renegades and dangerous defeatists.

Before the full reversal of PCF policy was apparent, Daladier and his Minister of the Interior, Albert Sarraut, decided on a strategy of repression. The party was declared illegal on 26 September, and known militants were arrested if they gave any evidence of political or trade-union activity. Sarraut called it an essential national purge (*épuration*). Many of the arrests were clearly retrospective, in retribution for activism over the previous years, and affecting many who were neither defeatists nor socially subversive. Those arrested had few doubts that it was an act of ideological revenge.

Local members had no party newspapers to consult during September and there was scepticism towards the account of the pact in the non-Communist press. Workers and intellectuals who saw the Soviet Union as the promise of the future found it difficult to believe that Stalin had also invaded Poland on 17 September. By May 1940 the number of imprisoned Communists reached 6,000, the sequel to more than 15,000 police investigations and raids on individual homes. On 20 March 1940 thirty-five Communist deputies, out of forty-four indicted, appeared in court accused of acting on behalf of the Comintern. They were sentenced to five years' imprisonment.

It is arguable that Daladier's repression did not take account of the acute demoralization of the PCF in the country at large. In the mining town of Alès in the Cévennes where the PCF was well established, the authorities reported that the dissolution of the party 'had been followed by no reaction whatsoever'.[5] The pact decimated membership and thirty deputies left the party. The chain of direction from the centre to the periphery was severely disrupted. It can only be speculation that a different policy from the government might have increased the disarray of the PCF rather than drive it underground, but there is certainly evidence that the persecution gradually hardened the resolve of many party activists that the PCF should survive, accompanied by resentment and a sense of political injustice.

It remains difficult to estimate what the reaction of Communists would have been to Stalin's invasion of Finland on 30 November 1939, had they themselves not been subject to repression. For some fervent anti-Communists, however, who had fully endorsed the measures against the PCF as more important than support for Poland, the Soviet aggression against the Finns opened up the possibility that the strange war which France had pursued since 3 September might be redirected and given a new sense of purpose. Daladier may have said on 2 September that ideology was not at issue, but it could not so easily be discarded.

'Drôle de guerre'

There was no *élan* in the mobilization nor in the declaration of war. How could there be? Years of determination to avoid another war had been sustained by the belief that no one could possibly want a replay of the carnage and destruction of 1914–18. The call-up was answered with resignation, the word used in every prefectoral report. Almost 4.5 million were drafted into uniform, in both France and the colonies. There were very few cases of refusal, statistically no more than in 1914. Pride in the victory of 1918 was still present among the bulk of the *anciens combattants* who

were recalled. It was transferred to the younger classes. A firm resolve was observed by the reports, and a confidence that France was well protected. The reason for declaring war needed little elaboration: it was understood by the population as another classic war of balance, preventing Germany from dominating Europe, although amateur theorists quickly pointed out that France had forfeited the goodwill of Eastern Europe and lost that of Russia so that containment of Germany would no longer be based on encirclement. For that reason it was seen as vital not to alienate Italy: anti-fascist language was blatantly absent from all official communiqués.

In the battle areas of 1914–18, reconstruction was still a day-to-day discourse and activity, and the arrival of the British soldiers who took up positions in the Nord and Pas-de-Calais in mid-September brought comments of a waking dream. British columns traipsing through the rain in villages near Arras were said to be treading in the very ruts of the soil where their blood had recently run. There were warm welcomes from local families in the 840 *communes* in which they were stationed, and waves from children to the British planes. The authorities in Lille proclaimed civilian morale high at the end of October, and commented on the sympathy displayed for Poles from the mining areas who had joined units of the Polish army constituted locally.

Only the inadequate supply of gas masks caused concern. Air-raid drills were practised with variable intensity across the whole of the north of France. The term 'civilian mobilization' had been popularized in 1938 with 600,000 copies of a short guide to civil defence (*défense passive*), and the recall of the National Assembly on 2 September coincided with the first air-raid warning in Paris. Thousands of volunteers joined the civil corps which became a practical way of perpetuating the peace drive of the decade. Valued monuments and buildings were piled high with sandbags, and windows shuttered. Close to the Belgian frontier, digging out shelters linked civil defence to military preparation. From the Channel to the Ardennes, troops of the 7th, 1st and 9th Armies were employed in manual construction of trenches and casemates, along what became known as 'the Daladier Line'. There was sidelong envy for the 3rd Army encased on the Maginot Line.

If there was any common expectation on how the new war might be fought, it was in terms of expectation that impenetrable French defence and an economic blockade of Germany would be determinant. Pétain contributed to this by writing to the Commander-in-Chief, General Gamelin, in September to say that he hoped he would not be foolish enough to launch an offensive. Gamelin had carried out a very limited movement

into the Saar from 7 to 12 September but showed no intention of repeating it, and for several weeks showed a preference for the least advanced line of defence inside Belgium, should the Germans show signs of attack. Chronicler and novelist of war Roland Dorgelès visited the front lines in October and commented in *Gringoire* that 'war was not funny [*drôle*], but it was certainly a funny war [*une drôle de guerre*]'. The term rapidly gained currency, embroidered by every detail of inaction, immobility and lack of conflict. Other rival words such as *curieuse* and *mystérieuse* were used but it was the sense of oddity in the word *drôle* that made it so applicable. It was not initially so much of an indictment as the English word 'phoney', and at times it was almost reassuring, as if it was really *une drôle de paix*. The Soviet invasion of Finland at the end of November acutely affected its usage.

The Finnish war unleashed an intensity of anger and polemic. The 'suffering' of the Finns and the 'savagery' of the Soviets were the recurring words in striking reports and images of the snow-bound 'winter' war. Anti-Communism had burst its ideological confines at the news of the Nazi-Soviet pact. It now carried a popular moral incitement to action. The most discussed project was to use air bases in Syria and Iraq to bomb Russian oilfields in Baku. By February 1940 General Weygand had quite a different message for Gamelin than Pétain's in September. Sharing the outrage of Charles Maurras, most bellicose of the extreme right, he told Gamelin that 'For my part I believe it is essential to break the Soviet Union in Finland and elsewhere.'[6] Sarraut reiterated the need for a complete purge of Communists, and prefects responded with reports on 'foreign influences' to indicate any Communist activity in their area. The Communist clandestine tracts which circulated in very few hands argued that more 'French workers' were in prison than 'German soldiers', making the war really *drôle* (in the 'phoney' sense) because, they insisted, it was not against Germany at all but was an ideological war of the French bourgeoisie against the PCF, termed 'the party of peace'.

The tangle of war and peace ideologies had re-emerged. The nationalist right arrogated a 'pure form of patriotism' to its cause, as summarized forcibly in *Gringoire* on 18 January 1940 by the right-wing Catholic deputy for the Gironde, Philippe Henriot: 'Whoever is a follower of Stalin is a follower of Hitler.'[7] The equation was much quoted and there is little doubt that the temporary effect of the Finnish war was to prompt ideas of how both the Soviet Union and Nazi Germany could be undermined at once. At the same time attention on maps of Finland and Scandinavia swivelled more practical minds in the government towards the economy of war and

the importance of iron ore to Germany. *Paris-Match* on 7 December 1939 showed the critical iron ore and timber routes running from northern Sweden through Narvik in Norway into the North Sea, the alternative to the Baltic route, frozen over in the winter. Cutting the German supplies via Norway was an active challenge which dovetailed with the overall defensive strategy of the war. It did not have to indulge the fantasies of General Bergeret of the École de Guerre, who spoke excitedly of France mounting a vast pincer operation on Moscow from the Caucasus to Finland.

Daladier belatedly seized on the iron ore plan as an answer to the public concern over 'the gallant Finns'. He was also faced with the growing problem of boredom in the front lines and a widespread discontent among industrial workers over the hours of work which reached sixty and even seventy in a week, the benefit of overtime wages lost in the inflationary food prices. Military reports showed that a number of reservists had not returned to the army after the Christmas break. Officers on the border with Belgium were said to be installing wives and girlfriends in local hotels. Muted criticism of indiscipline was growing more insistent. An expedition to Norway would show initiative. The British were thinking cautiously along similar lines. They were baulked by the armistice signed by the Finns and Soviets on 13 March, leaving Daladier exposed to accusations that he had not taken the Finnish war seriously. On 20 March he resigned as Premier and was replaced by Paul Reynaud.

Reynaud's greater air of purposeful action raised expectations of a change of policy. He set out to galvanize the country, but in essence the defensive strategy remained intact, and Daladier was retained as Minister of Defence. The spring brought an upturn in morale at the same time as a forceful injection of realism. Impressive war production under the technical brilliance and energy of Raoul Dautry, Armaments Minister since mid-September, was recognized in the increased number of tanks and planes arriving at the front lines, bringing renewed confidence. Workers' standard of living and work conditions improved, as industrialists toned down their offensive which had been rampant since the failed strike of November 1938. The realism came from Scandinavia. On 9 April the Germans astonishingly trumped the dilatory Allied plans by seizing Norway in a lightning strike on towns from Oslo to Narvik. The vaunted Allied control of the seas had to be reappraised. Recognition that an attack from Germany might be imminent was squarely faced.

Neither military nor political decomposition accompanied the *drôle de guerre*. Restlessness was more marked than complacency. It was represented quite differently in retrospect.

3. The débâcle of May–June 1940

Not on the fields of Waterloo

The Nazi war machine was unleashed on Holland and Belgium at dawn on 10 May 1940. It looked as if the historic fields of Waterloo and Charleroi would once again be the scene of an epic European battle. Gamelin ordered the French armies to move forward into Belgium with the British Expeditionary Force. But Hitler had chosen to listen to General Erich von Manstein who convincingly proposed that the main German assault should be through the Ardennes. Unaware, disbelieving, unprepared for the depth and speed of General Guderian's Panzer divisions, the French 2nd Army of General Huntziger on the Meuse was unable to counter the audacity of the German strategy. French bombers, like the bulk of the army, had been directed into Belgium. They might otherwise have destroyed the German tanks before they reached the Meuse. Reconnaissance photographs of the German progress along the forest roads had been discounted as a decoy. When planes did arrive they were too late and suffered huge casualties, the British losing forty-one bombers out of seventy-one. The decoy was in Belgium. On 13 May the Meuse was crossed at Sedan and French defences breached. In the first week of the 'real' war, before the French and British armies in the north were even engaged, the Allied military leaders had been so outmanoeuvred by Guderian's motorized tactics that historians tend to describe the defeat of France as an event essentially decided by the breakthrough at Sedan.

It is difficult to resist such a conclusion, for the course of the German victory over the five weeks which separated the crossing of the Meuse from the final capitulation of the French army on 17 June was so unchecked by any major Allied counter-offensive that it seems as if there was only one decisive moment in the entire battle of France. This was not how civilians saw it on 13 May, for the folk legend of Valmy and the living memory of the Battle of the Marne allowed hopes to flourish of a solid retrenchment and defence of Paris. As the Panzers seemed set for the capital, newspaper articles fell back on references to Dumouriez and Kellerman in 1792 and Joffre in 1914, and wheeled out pictures of the Paris taxis which had carried volunteers to the front. But there was no immediate battle for Paris, heroic or otherwise. On 17 May the German tanks were set on their course to the west, heading towards the Channel. With Holland defeated and the Belgian defence disintegrating, the German pincer plan to cut off the bulk of the Allied troops in an indefensible corner of Flanders was turned into reality.

It was beyond French and British capacity to mount a counter-attack from this predicament. There was only retreat.

On 15 May Reynaud used the phrase 'We have lost the battle' when reporting events on the Meuse to Churchill. But over the next three days he produced a show of determined resistance, taking over the Ministry of Defence from Daladier, and strengthening his cabinet by the inclusion of Marshal Pétain, the incarnation of defiance at Verdun, and the promotion of Georges Mandel to Minister of the Interior in evocation of Clemenceau. In the military sphere Gamelin had been a brilliant second to Joffre, but his limitations as supreme commander in his own right were evident by the time of the German breakthrough. He appeared constantly behind events, geographically a long way behind. So at crucial moments were other senior officers, repeatedly called away from the front for high-level talks which were too often ill informed and unco-ordinated with the British. General Weygand, one of the architects of the victory of 1918 and highly prized by Foch, was recalled by Reynaud from Beirut to replace Gamelin. By the time he was in post, Guderian's tanks were at Abbeville in the Somme, heading north towards Boulogne, Calais and Dunkirk. They had covered over 320 kilometres in less than ten days.

Cut off from the south, the retreat of the Allied troops from Belgium into a bridgehead at Dunkirk was eventually a combined operation, but the British did not tell Weygand at once that they planned to evacuate their army, a move which started on 26 May. On the day before, quite separately, Weygand had alerted his colleagues in the French cabinet to the prospect of admitting defeat. From Dunkirk 338,000 troops, a third of them French, were evacuated, but in the first phase of the operation it was unclear whether or not French soldiers would be embarked. There was a short gap of several hours before Churchill ordered the boats to take both British and French alike. It was enough of a delay to allow a story to grow that the French had borne the brunt of the bridgehead while the British scuttled back to their shores. The desperate hunt for people to blame rapidly took over the press, deprived of reliable information. Even the Belgian capitulation by King Leopold III on 28 May was kept secret at first, in order not to alarm civilians. When it broke, the public anger in government circles set the tone. Blaming the Belgians was the response, from Reynaud downwards. In a radio broadcast he declared that 'there has never been such a betrayal in history'.[8] On the roads, the blame went much wider.

'Exode'

The arrival of German tanks and planes across the Meuse precipitated a flight of the civilian population from the north and east which echoed the official policy, already enacted, of evacuating civilians from the war zones, including Alsace and Lorraine. By its spontaneity, desperation, panic and helplessness, the flight (*exode*) was a totally new phenomenon. Frequently columns of refugees fleeing south arrived at villages through which German troops had already passed. They were randomly machine-gunned by German Stuka planes as they struggled along the unprotected roads. In a countryside crossed by a succession of large rivers, the bridges were of critical military importance for a retreating army which might well have destroyed them after crossing. With hordes of civilians dependent on the bridges for a safe exodus, an obvious military tactic became a profound human dilemma. More often than not they were left intact.

Across the plains of Picardy and Champagne the war graves of the First World War aggravated the refugees' fears of German atrocities which the deadly Stuka fire confirmed. Memoirs underlined the catastrophe of modern war for civilians by evoking the stench of humans left as corpses with horses and dogs on the side of the road. The Germans, faced only with the remains of the French army on the line of the Somme and the Aisne, pierced the disaggregated French defences on 6 June, opening the routes to Paris. Knots of French soldiers, overtaken but not as yet made prisoners of war, roamed across fields, noting sourly the absence of British planes in the skies.

The weather was hot, the Germans used the main roads, their soldiers often stripped to the waist (*les torses nus*). News of the advancing troops and their invincibility spread images of a superhuman force, the phrase '*les torses nus*' echoing down the newspaper reports in a matter of hours as far as the Pyrenees. The contagion of flight spread across into Normandy, down into Paris and well beyond. Between 8 and 10 million people took to the rail and roads, continuous lines of women, children and old men, frightened, hungry, dirty and tired, dragging animals, carts and wheel-barrows, or filling lorries and cars, piled high with furniture and mattresses. Few vehicles had self-starters: they were pushed aside into the ditches, or pulled along for a few more kilometres by horses. The aim was to cross the Loire into imagined safety and plenty on the other side, fantasies nurtured on the folklore of rural self-sufficiency in the heart of France. Parallels were made with the irrationality of the Great Fear (*Grande Peur*) of the summer of 1789 at the rumoured return of the aristocratic landlords, but there was no equivalent social violence. It was more an immense tragedy of fears,

hopes, loss and illusion in which a few historians later discerned a foretaste of resistance in the refusal to be taken by the enemy.[9]

Less than a quarter or even a fifth of the people stayed in their homes in the northern towns, including Paris, reduced from 2.8 million inhabitants to about 700,000 by the time the German army arrived. By contrast, Brive and Tulle in the Corrèze received over 230,000 refugees and over 200,000 people slept on the pavements of Limoges. Cahors in the Lot, and Pau, much further down towards the Pyrenees, saw their population temporarily increase almost sixfold. But the mass of refugees on foot never reached the proximity of the Loire. On the roads out of Paris, hundreds of children were separated from their families; smoke from burning oil depots fuelled the certainty that Paris was burning; spies and the imagined Fifth Column of traitors were thought to be everywhere, identified mostly with stray motorcyclists; cars which sped past the trudging columns were believed to be driven by wealthy Jews; antisemitism prospered in the resentment. Anger was provoked by mayors and councillors, like those of Versailles, who abandoned their responsibilities and fled, leaving the population to cope. Blame was turned relentlessly against government and officialdom.

The government itself left Paris on 10 June and made its broken way south, ending up at Bordeaux. It learned, en route, that Mussolini had seized the opportunity of the French collapse to declare war, keen to share the spoils of defeat. French troops on the Alpine border did not, however, cede any territory. For them the very short war against Italy was a history of successful defence, but the achievements of the Chasseurs Alpins could not affect the outcome against Germany. Weygand declared that Paris would not be defended, a political as well as military decision by a passionate anti-Communist fearful that the history of the Paris Commune of 1871 might be repeated. Individual Communists had called for the people of Paris to be armed, but there was never any shred of substance to rumours of a planned uprising. On 14 June the German army entered Paris and paraded in triumph down the deserted Champs-Élysées.

Humiliation

Reynaud and Mandel were not excluded from worries about a Communist takeover in Paris. Pressured by Weygand and Pétain who argued that the government should admit defeat and call for a cease-fire, Reynaud cast around for places in which a last-ditch stand could be made, Brittany or North Africa. The speed of the German advance made a 'Breton redoubt' impractical. Mandel favoured North Africa. It was opposed by the majority

of the cabinet in anguished, ill-tempered sessions in Bordeaux. Reynaud was linked to the British in London by his appointment of Charles de Gaulle as Under-Secretary to the Ministry of Defence. Surrendering to Weygand's insistence that the politicians and not the military should take responsibility for the defeat, Reynaud sought the British response on 15 June.

The reply the following day was an astonishing proposal from the British government for a merger of the two nations 'at this most fateful moment in the history of the modern world' into a single Franco-British Union. It had gone through the British cabinet, and Churchill, after initial doubts, had helped it on its way by his call for an imaginative initiative. Its last two sentences conveyed its purpose: 'The Union will concentrate its whole energy against the power of the enemy, no matter where the battle may be. And thus we shall conquer.' Much later it was noted that Jean Monnet and René Pleven, key players in the first stages of the post-war European Common Market, had been among the creators of the scheme. No less intriguing was the contribution of de Gaulle, who was party to the project and made the telephone call to Reynaud.

The scheme was dismissed out of hand by the pro-Armistice majority in Bordeaux. It disappeared, almost without trace on either side of the Channel, as a moment of collective fantasy. Late in the evening of 16 June Reynaud resigned, handing power to Pétain. On 17 June the 84-year-old Marshal Pétain announced to the nation that he had agreed to head a new government and that he was asking the Germans for an armistice. He called on the French forces to lay down their arms. His sympathy went out to the refugees on the roads, and in religious terms he offered his person as a gift to France to attenuate the country's deep misfortune. The reaction to the broadcast was one dominantly of relief and emotional gratitude, which gave Pétain a personal ascendancy which was barely touched by incredulity that he, of all people, had surrendered. The Germans were already well south of Dijon and pressing down the Atlantic coast towards Bordeaux. By the time the Armistice was signed on 22 June they were in Clermont-Ferrand and close to Grenoble. A total of more than 1.6 million prisoners of war were rounded up into makeshift camps, half of that number in the week following Pétain's broadcast. They were cynically promised a free rail ticket home by the German army. It seemed that only Pétain's words relieved the crushing humiliation. Very few heard the BBC broadcast from London by de Gaulle on 18 June, insisting that the cause of France was not lost and that 'the flame of French resistance must not and shall not die'.

Hitler insisted on the same clearing in the forest of Compiègne as the scene for a ritualized reversal of the French victory of 11 November 1918.

The short Armistice of twenty-three articles imposed many of the same conditions as the Allies had done at Versailles, including a reduction of the army to 100,000 men. The Occupation costs were set as astronomically high as the reparations of 1919. France was divided into several different zones, and a demilitarized zone along the Italian border was given to the Italians to police. The Germans were to occupy Paris, the north and the west, separated by a heavily guarded demarcation line from the unoccupied zone of the south. The French navy was to be deactivated. The colonies were left in French hands. Hitler had already been filmed in Paris, looking from the Palais de Chaillot at the Eiffel Tower, slapping his knee with delight.

In the two historic broadcasts by Pétain and de Gaulle, it was the much younger, little-known, junior officer, provisionally promoted to General during the fighting in Belgium, who summarized the reasons for the military defeat with most accuracy. Pétain spoke of the 'magnificent resistance of the army' against an enemy 'superior in number and in arms'. De Gaulle declared that it was the enemy's mechanized forces on the ground and the air, and the tactics of the Germans, 'far more than the fact that we were outnumbered' that provided the element of surprise and 'forced our armies to retreat'.[10] Military historians have agreed with de Gaulle's instant analysis and have shown that the French were not inferior in arms, except in the number of divebombing planes. There was even a rough equation of numbers of tanks, with the medium weight French Somua S35 superior in quality to its German equivalent, although the German heavy tanks could fire more rapidly than their French counterparts. It was the distribution of mechanized armour that made all the difference, and the strategic importance allotted to the German offensive through the Ardennes. The French scattered their tanks thinly across the infantry and artillery lines of defence. The Germans concentrated the Panzer divisions with emphasis on assault, strike power and speed. The same was true for the use of the airforce.

Aggression and superior strategy, not defence, decided the outcome of the battle of France in only six weeks. It was an Allied disaster, but it registered as a French débâcle. The Maginot Line did not have to prove itself: it was bypassed and taken from the rear. The campaigns for peace and the defensive strategy of France were turned into shattered illusions by the determination of Nazi Germany to wage war and the nature of the catastrophic defeat. It was quite another matter to rewrite the illusion into symptoms of moral collapse and political decadence, and to see national decline in the pursuit of a forty-hour working week. The new Pétain government began this rewriting of the 1930s as it moved from Bordeaux and

took up residence in Vichy, a fashionable thermal spa in the Auvergne with enough hotels to house all the Ministries in a certain degree of comfort.

Pétain's agreement to a separate armistice was given a *raison d'être* on 3 July in what was seen as the ultimate perfidy of the British. Churchill and the British Admiralty were not convinced that the French navy was safely beyond the reach of the Germans. They instructed Admiral Somerville to issue an ultimatum to Admiral Marcel Gensoul, commander of a substantial portion of the French fleet at anchor in the Algerian port of Mers el-Kébir. He gave the French various options which amounted to an acceptance of British instructions. Gensoul had previously received orders from the head of the French navy, Admiral Darlan, not to allow his ships to fall into German hands, and believed that should be sufficient for the British. He was authorized to refuse Somerville's terms as humiliating. Somerville felt he was constrained to open fire. A rapid bombardment sank or immobilized most of the ships in the harbour and killed 1,297 French sailors. It was described in the French press as an unprovoked massacre. The ensuing anglophobia which gripped the country was a bonus to the occupying Germans. At Vichy it provided the ideal context for the government of Pétain to elevate the isolation of France into yet another rationale for sweeping emergency powers, leading to a new regime.

Occupied France (1). Vichy and Collaboration, 1940–1944

1. *Living under Occupation*

The occupied

The distress of the civilians on the roads as they first fled from their homes and then tried to return brought an acute awareness of place, which marked the whole period of German Occupation from June 1940 to August 1944. The specificity of each locality and the particularity of every event and development in what were subsequently called *les années noires* (the dark years) accentuated the relativity of people's lives and resulted in a complex multitude of different experiences and responses. The aim of millions in the *exode* to get beyond the Loire has its subsequent parallel in those on the run trying to cross the demarcation line from the occupied north to the unoccupied south. Imaginings of what life was like 'elsewhere' were fed by endless rumours and reports throughout the Occupation of places to hide, places to find food, places submissive to the Germans, places of resistance, any of which could be a single farm or café, or a whole region, urban *quartier* or village.

The government which emerged from the ruins of defeat in the spa town of Vichy extolled the particularities of the old provinces and encouraged the practice of local rites and customs. Submersion in what was locally familiar; interest in regional culture, in places of pilgrimage and historical sites; a passion for archaeology and local mythology, all can be read as an avoidance of the issues of the Occupation but they were also an accessible way of reaffirming an unbroken identity. The response to the *exode* was of that nature. For weeks or even months, places south of the demarcation line coped with the destitution of the refugees, a local achievement which was offset against the national disaster. Clutching at a semblance of pride had no inevitable political agenda. It primed the cult of Pétain, the dedication of local administrators appointed by Vichy, and even certain local forms of co-operation with the Germans. It also primed motivations of

refusal, resistance and revolt. Affirming something tangibly French came down to exploiting what was immediately available.

Adaptation to the Germans brought anything from personal accommodation to their presence by a few individuals in a small provincial town to the raucous enlistment in Nazi ideas and practices by a plethora of fascist-style groups in Paris. Resistance to the Germans started as a disconnected set of ideas and actions at the base of society, strongly conditioned by personality and the possibilities of specific towns: its later expansion into armed struggle brought a range of highly differentiated rural locations into play.

Place was never entirely deterministic: there were too many other variables, personal, social and ethnic, which shaped the outcome of people's lives. Jews were persecuted just for who they were, not for where they lived. But it was significant for the history of choice as well as experience that, for example, the Nord and Pas-de-Calais had strong pro-British sentiments from the shared history of the First World War, that the Breton coast allowed small boats to leave and arrive undetected, that the Cévennes had its own Protestant history of revolt, that the village of Le Chambon-sur-Lignon had a history of refuge, and that pathways through the Alps and Pyrenees were too numerous to police.

The Germans used curfews to control and confine urban populations, which compelled people into a greater awareness of their homes. Marshal Pétain urged people to turn inwards towards their domestic and family lives. Specific basements, attics and even belfries entered history as places where Resistance tracts were printed and radio messages sent. Torture in the last years of Occupation brought a terrifying reputation to specific buildings, such as the Gestapo headquarters in the rue des Saussaies in Paris or that of the local French Milice at the Caserne de Lauwe in Montpellier. Escape routes were roofs, interconnecting alleys and railway shunting yards, making knowledge of the topography of the home and the geography of the neighbourhood into priorities. The process of getting back home, avoiding checkpoints, was the initiation of the occupied into ways of outwitting the restrictions of the situation as well as the authorities.

The ubiquitous search for food highlighted the differences of town and country, but still more between soil where anything would grow and the monoculture of terrain in the south, yielding only citrus fruits, wine and olives. Parks and public gardens in Paris and the northern towns were dug up and planted with vegetables. This was not possible in the squares of Nice and Marseille.

Regardless of place, improvised ways of coping with shortages (*la disette*)

were known everywhere as the *système D*, from *débrouiller* (to manage). Hours of fruitless queuing and the struggle to outwit the Ministry of Provisions (*ravitaillement*) were common to most people's lives. Rabbits were bred on town balconies, old recipes were rediscovered, coffee was made of everything, especially chestnuts. Bicycles were essential for foraging into the countryside. Such was the importance of securing extra food, for survival, pride and identity, that the complexity of the Occupation was often collapsed into two national images: the alien, strutting Germans and the French finding food on the black market (*marché noir*). They are both there in the classic opening of the sombre film on the Resistance, *L'Armée des ombres* by Jean-Pierre Melville in 1969. A puppet-like German military band marches round the Arc de Triomphe in a deserted Paris. An abrupt cut takes us into the rain-soaked countryside. A police van splashes through the ruts of a deserted road. It stops at a farmhouse. A gendarme in the back justifies the stop to the man sitting opposite: 'We're getting provisions. We all have to look after ourselves these days.' 'Naturally,' replies the man in a dark coat. The camera slides down to his handcuffs. The driver emerges from the farm with two baskets of provisions. In these few deft strokes Melville evoked the whole period. It was almost an obligatory formula.

The *marché noir* was a major symptom of the ambiguities among the occupied. On the one hand, there was a form of dealing which declared itself 'patriotic' by keeping goods out of German hands and allowing underground organizations, and eventually the maquis fighters in the woods, to feed and equip themselves, often through promises of payment after the war. Much of the small trafficking secured the complicit or reluctant nod of local Resistance leaders. On the other hand there were extensive networks of opportunists who worked for anyone if the price was right, and were largely infiltrated by the Gestapo and the Vichy Milice, who used the illegal economy as a way of securing information which amounted to betrayal. The borderline between these two was a shady one, and 'ambiguity' in economic calculations and daily life has been seen by many as the defining characteristic of civilian adaptation to the German presence.

Any such shorthand has to encompass the irruptions of sudden events into the daily routine. They were no less a part of the everyday history of the Occupation. The trauma of national defeat brought widespread anger, fear and confusion: it translated in a minority of lives into hardened positions of collaboration or resistance; but even among the majority, ambiguity or a cautious waiting on events (*attentisme*) could change at any moment into a decisive course of action. Choices between acceptance and refusal, between collaboration and resistance, were often provoked by unexpected

factors. The definitions of both collaboration and resistance are plural ones, and covered single acts as well as persistent activity. The introspective rhythms of life in urban neighbourhoods, villages and small towns, accentuated an awareness of outsiders which forced crucial choices. Denunciations make up a vast history of their own, but the dramatic context of the Occupation also made saying nothing into an act of huge benefit to resistance. Jean-Paul Sartre tried to capture the Occupation in existentialist language as a period without a foreseeable future and cut off from the past, a constant present when everything was contingent, giving people a heightened sense of choice, which he equated with freedom.[1] Others could only see the Occupation in terms of constraint.

The occupiers

Under the Armistice conditions the Germans controlled the industries of the Nord and Pas-de-Calais through direct rule from Brussels which cut off these *départements* from the rest of occupied France. General Karl Niehoff, an epitome of the clinical Prussian officer, was given command in Lille. His tough rule and instant repression of dissent earned him promotion to command of the Vichy zone after November 1942. Alsace and Lorraine were not mentioned in the Armistice but were simply annexed by Germany and handed over to the rule of Gauleiters Robert Wagner in Alsace and Joseph Bürckel in Lorraine, the populations subjected to nazification, repression and massive mobilization into the German army and workforce. The large occupied zone, comprising the north and west of the country, contained most of France's industrial and agricultural wealth and the majority of the population. Paris was the seat of the German military administration under the pragmatic General Otto von Stülpnagel. Huge swastikas were hung from the buildings in the Place de la Concorde and the streets were covered with German signs, a model for the *Feldcommandantur* of every large town. Maximum humiliation of the local population was the desired effect. The German army could not easily believe that they had the whole of France at their feet: Hitler and Goering had few thoughts of what to do with the Occupation beyond exploiting it economically in revenge for the Treaty of Versailles.

Officers were billeted on the population and the costs of Occupation were set at the astronomical figure of 20 million marks per day, which took 55 per cent of French government revenue, with the franc forcefully devalued by 20 per cent. From the outset the demarcation line provided sites for identity checks, deliberately blocking French movement and the

flow of goods. The south was forced to keep the millions of refugees for over two months while the German authorities established an efficient presence in all parts of the occupied zone. The relative sufficiency of food that the Germans provided in the first few weeks allowed them to appear organized and caring. Many of the shocked population acknowledged that they were polite ('les allemands sont corrects') and that they paid individually in shops and restaurants.

Individual involvement with the German occupiers was largely evaluated within local terms, creating huge differences across the country in the degree to which social and intimate mixing with the Germans was tolerated. Most communities experienced some local curiosity for the Germans who arrived in their midst, and there were individuals, trades, professions or cultural interests who favoured various forms of accommodation. Motivations were complex, and variables existed on the German side also. The first Resistance novel published clandestinely, *Le Silence de la mer* by Vercors, was a recognition that an individual German billeted on a family could be musical and refined, embracing French culture, but the novel ended with a devastating realization by that German himself, Werner von Ebrennac, that he was insignificant in the rapacious reality of the Nazi Occupation. The importance of events over the four years was to expose local behaviour, by both French and Germans, to increasingly polarized expectations and judgements. Only local histories have been able to do full justice to this.

The German occupiers set out to make their own lives in France sophisticated and agreeable. They went to French night-clubs, races and cultural sites. Their military bands played in the town squares. In bulk they took anything they needed. By 1943 Germany was taking 40 per cent of France's total industrial output, including 80 per cent of its vehicle production. Goods and services derived from France were roughly equivalent to a quarter of Germany's gross national product. French firms and labour were requisitioned, and in 1943 over 600,000 men were drafted to work in Germany. Protected industries were designated by Albert Speer to serve German needs, particularly in bauxite and aluminium. Through the Todt organization workers were deployed to construct military installations and build vast portions of the Atlantic wall along the coast from the Netherlands to Spain. With 1.6 million prisoners of war initially lost to German camps, including well over 65,000 indigenous troops from the colonies, a huge French and colonial workforce was effectively held hostage to ensure French neutrality, at the very least, in the escalating war.

Political and ideological pressure followed on the heels of economic. The Gestapo established its presence in the winter of 1941–2. General Karl

Oberg was invested as its head by Heydrich in April 1942, but already Nazi propaganda and cultural control had been assured by the Propaganda-Abteilung, bitterly sweetened by the Francophile German ambassador to defeated France, Otto Abetz, who alternately encouraged and distanced the French neophytes of the Nazi New Order, many of whom he had known in the pre-war Comité France-Allemagne. German censorship watched over their fascist-style rallies and antisemitic journals, looking for any sign of a French military recovery but otherwise allowing them to fight among themselves for the spoils of collaboration. In contrast, 2,000 French book titles and 850 authors and translators were banned in constantly updated lists of Jewish and left-wing writers. Cinemas were strictly, but often ineffectively, controlled.

Hostages were seized in the northern towns in the first days of Occupation, to ensure the obedience of the population. They were released, but the threat of rearrest remained. On the first assassinations of German personnel in the autumn of 1941, waves of hostages were taken, and thirty or fifty shot for every German killed. With shootings and arbitrary deportations, the Germans moved from being essentially economic predators into a rhythm of repression which replaced any residual respect in the population with fear. Brutal arrests in the night became a stock image of Nazi Occupation in the main towns, sudden disappearance a widening reality of the population's experience.

In November 1942 an increasingly harsh and ideological German Occupation was extended to the whole of France in response to the Allied landings in North Africa. It neutralized many of the differences of place, while creating others. It was preceded four months earlier by the horrific round-up of Jews in both zones and their deportation via French internment and transit camps to the Nazi death camps in the east. Resistance was met with arrests, execution, torture and deportation.

The German terror in outlying places was never universal. Local histories of even the last phases of Occupation reveal German military commanders still concerned with managing rather than terrifying the population. Real-life von Ebrennacs existed in many places, officers and ordinary soldiers making generous and intimate relations with local people, not only women. Photographs, letters and oral memoirs point to the depth of many of these relationships. In Saint-Affrique in the Aveyron, German officers turned a blind eye in mid-1944 to sales of goods in a Protestant bazaar, the proceeds of which they knew were going to the Resistance maquis. But they, and others like them elsewhere, could not affect the Nazi ideology of racial victimization and the recourse to wholesale destruction. The final dominant

image of the occupiers in 1944 was of mass killings by heavily armed, mobile, SS units, as German repression spread to reprisals on whole villages.

2. *Opportunities in defeat*

The impact of Pétain's gift of himself to France registered on an epic scale and entered instantly into folklore. His cult ascended to heights unknown since the romantic image of Napoleon Bonaparte, captured in the poems of Hugo and Béranger. Pierre Laval, Pétain's unlikely deputy and nominated heir, alternated gestures of insolence towards the 'Maréchal' with obsequious reminders that no one had known such personal power since Louis XIV.

Pétain and Laval both saw opportunities in defeat, Pétain for a moral regeneration of France and an authoritarian state, Laval for recognition from Germany which would give France a bargaining power under Occupation. Their ideas and policies interwove, clashed and co-existed.

Pétain and the National Revolution

History was the force which Pétain summoned to judge him. It was a gratuitous summons: he rode high above the gritty details of recent history in which he had moved from a military role to become a right-wing figurehead, appointed Minister of Defence in Gaston Doumergue's conservative government of 1934, when he made known his enthusiasm for rescuing the nation's youth from the clutches of left-wing teachers. Not only Gustave Hervé's campaign,[2] but also Wladimir d'Ormesson in *Le Figaro* in 1936 called for his elevation to a providential role at the head of the nation. As a friendly ambassador to Franco's nationalist Spain in 1939 Pétain was suspect to the left, but he was not widely seen as anti-republican. He claimed to be above politics, a claim which strongly influenced popular and political response to his broadcast call on 25 June for a new France. On 10 July 1940 the National Assembly, elected four years earlier as the Popular Front parliament, met in the elegant casino of Vichy. The assembled politicians, minus the banned Communists, voted overwhelmingly, by 569 votes to eighty, to give Pétain full powers to bring in a new constitution.

The Republic was discarded, arguments for its primacy lost in the clamour for authoritarian decisiveness and for a national unity which party politics had long been accused of destroying. It was a revengeful nationalist state, the État Français, which took its place. Charles Maurras, alter ego of French politics since the Dreyfus Affair, finally saw the Republic collapse

as he had persistently predicted. In the following twelve months Pétain toured the southern towns to a rapturous welcome, captured as a saint's progress in the adulatory prose of René Benjamin's little pocket-book, *Le Maréchal et son peuple*.

Sales of Pétain's portrait and posters brought his white moustache, upright military bearing and clear blue eyes into millions of homes, schools, churches, offices, shop windows and public spaces, and earned over 16 million francs for the national welfare fund (*secours national*) destined as priority to the families of the 1.5 million prisoners of war. The huge statistics give some indication of the dimensions of the Pétain cult and the issues affected. The symbiosis of parental leadership from the top and distressed expressions of need from below created one of the most extraordinary living legends of the twentieth century. In the conjuncture of military defeat, civilian dislocation and enemy Occupation, Pétain's speeches found the good, warm values and words which people desperately wanted to hear.

The cult was shaped by the contingency of the moment but drew on a traditional Christian culture of sacrifice and martyrdom. Pétain was not a model Catholic but he used the language of atonement and called for a moral crusade. He demanded the dedication of discipleship. A catchy youth anthem, 'Maréchal, nous-voilà', was composed to be sung as a hymn in schools and youth movements, pledging young people to serve the Maréchal as his children. The infantilism went further. Pétain's broadcasts transmitted an aura of all-knowing, patriarchal wisdom which relieved the people of the burden of thinking for themselves. They were called on to follow and obey, and Pétain admonished dissent firstly with the sadness of a disappointed father and then with the rigour of an authoritarian ruler. Regressive dependency on the leadership of Pétain was the collective pathology which marked the history of France from June 1940 for at least a year, and in many sections of society considerably longer.

There was realism too. Realism in the National Assembly in mid-July 1940 acknowledged the close presence of German troops on the demarcation line which ran through Moulins just north of Vichy; an embittered realism pointed to the 1,297 sailors killed by the British at Mers el-Kébir as the sign of French isolation; the very real casualties of the war, the stipulations of the Armistice and the absence of so many prisoners restrained any thoughts of renewing the conflict on French soil, while the economic reality was one of utter dependence on the Germans to release energy and facilities for the recovery of industry and trade. Pétain's First World War reputation was one of realism: he had forecast a defensive, not a mobile war and had adjusted military strategy to that end in 1916. He

had been closer to the men of the trenches than other generals, a sign of both his humanity and the realism required to sustain a total war. It was in such ways that the 'victor of Verdun' was remembered, and now adulated.

Ideas of revival were not an obvious concomitant of realism, but they co-existed in Pétain's response to 1940. While his speeches favoured an acceptance of the facts, they also called for regeneration. The defeat was seized as an ideological opportunity. Four days before his 17 June broadcast, Pétain had stated that a French rebirth (*renaissance*) would be the fruit of the current suffering. He blamed the defeat on the individualism fostered by the Third Republic which, he stated, had brought decadence, hedonism and national decline.

A bundle of decrees after 10 July set up the État Français, soon known simply as the Vichy regime. There was no President. Pétain took the title of Chef, a leadership role which could be replicated at all levels of a hierarchical society. Pétain was head of both state and government; Laval was appointed as his Vice-Premier. Special leadership schools, notably the École des Cadres at Uriage outside Grenoble, were created to produce young male leaders (*chefs*) and inculcate the military and moral qualities necessary to spearhead a National Revolution.

The left-wing connotations of 'revolution' were countered by the adjective 'national', but Pétain in private preferred the word 'renovation'. This was autonomous policy-making, not the enforced concurrence of a satellite state. First came decrees in the summer and autumn of 1940 which chiselled away at the rights of Jews, culminating in two statutes, one on 3 October and the second on 2 June 1941, reducing them to pariah status by exclusion from state employment, administration and politics, and from any job in industry, finance and trade dependent on public subsidies. Deeply rooted in the antisemitism which went back to the Dreyfus Affair and beyond, the statutes broke with all republican precedent by excluding people from citizenship on the basis of 'race'. All Jews were affected, whether recent immigrants or long-established French. They were defined in Vichy propaganda as unworthy of state protection. Specifically, they were made into scapegoats for the misery of the civilian flight (*exode*) and the humiliation of the defeat. The legislation, finally amounting to fifty laws and decrees against the Jews, was underpinned by popular prejudice. Protest against the two major statutes was minimal, though the French Jewish Consistory protested officially. Its president, Jacques Helbronner, who knew Pétain from the First World War, wrote to him in July 1941 expressing the fidelity of French Jews (*les Français israélites*) while denouncing the 'vile passions of . . . hatred and jealousy' which had 'spread from racist doctrines abroad into France'.[3]

There were other declared outsiders: Communists, already outlawed by Daladier after the Nazi-Soviet pact, and Freemasons, sacked by Vichy from all state positions, particularly teaching, even though the Freemasonic lodges saw the writing on the wall and disbanded themselves. Left-wing mayors and councils of *communes* with a population of over 2,000 were evicted and replaced by appointed local notables. Very early in the life of Vichy a special court was established in the nearby town of Riom to try the republican leaders, and in particular Léon Blum, deemed responsible for the defeat and proclaimed by Pétain as guilty, prejudging any legal process. All trade-union federations were dissolved, and the discourse of class conflict replaced by that of an organic society.

The definition of internal enemies was not a once-only statement. It led to a web of official organizations and specialist bodies which pursued exclusion and furthered its ideological basis. The cult of Pétain made service on these bodies a matter of personal enthusiasm and dedication. The conservative Catholic deputy Xavier Vallat had fully internalized the teaching of Maurras that antisemitism was a 'rational' response to the 'logic' of Jewish difference. In *La Seule France* of 1941 Maurras repeated his routine argument that 'factually speaking' Jews could never be French and that exclusion was only a *raison d'état* which, he argued, had nothing to do with 'racism'. With this spurious reasoning Vallat took the lead in the Commissariat of Jewish Affairs set up by Vichy on 29 March 1941. He was not pro-German: his nationalism was uppermost, and as the German presence polarized France more radically he was replaced in April 1942 by the fanatical antisemite Darquier de Pellepoix, who had spent three months in prison in 1939 for articles of racial hatred. He joined the ethnology professor Georges Montandon, whose research into facial typology was at the forefront of the twisted science on which racism was built, and who boasted that the Nazis had copied his ideas. At the heart of the Commissariat, Montandon decided in contested cases who was a Jew.

Vichy as a regime of exclusion cut deeply across the claims of Pétain to have unified the country at its lowest point of morale. The emphasis on unity found its main social expression in working for the absent prisoners of war, work dedicated to Pétain in the sending of parcels and letters and family care. In the name of the state Pétain sent Georges Scapini, president of the association of blinded veterans, to liaise with the German authorities on conditions in the *stalags* and *oflags*, and where possible to secure repatriations. At all levels the work was a massive enterprise, and it was impossible for anyone to miss its moral, mobilizing force. By contrast the National Revolution radically divided society. Its exclusions were the vis-

ceral thrust of its high-sounding principles, summarized in a deluge of propaganda. The masthead trilogy 'Travail, Famille, Patrie', borrowed from the Croix-de-Feu, replaced the republican 'Liberté, Fraternité, Égalité'. The *francisque*, the battle-axe of the ancient Franks, was adopted as an emblem, and awarded by Vichy as a state honour. Colour images of folkloric richness were disseminated as political icons, conveying a world of family and children, artisan crafts and rural simplicity. With epigrammatic phrases taken from Pétain's speeches, the authorized press preached the goodness of the land and soil 'which never lies' (*la terre qui ne ment pas*), and the 'heroic patience' of the peasant. The aim was a 'return to the land' (*retour à la terre*). State backing was given for the ruralist idyll which had emerged as a response to urban society after the First World War. This elaborate iconography had its roots in the writings of Barrès and Péguy, and its own discourse of renewal (*regain*) which borrowed from, and attracted, Jean Giono. It was anchored firmly in the French romance of a mythologized past, now seen to be exemplified by the virtues of Pétain, the soldier-leader with a peasant family background.

Propaganda for the National Revolution excluded all mention of the German Occupation, which was not seen as either a constraint or a contradiction to the plans for national renewal. The problems this met with were soon exposed in the structure created in December 1940 to implement the new ruralism, the national Peasant Corporation (*Corporation paysanne*). It was the fulfilment of ideas from Louis Salleron and Jacques Le Roy Ladurie in the 1930s, who had variously attempted to work through the professional agricultural body UNSA to produce a corporate unity of all peasants. They were less activist and idealistic than Henri Dorgères, and closer to Pierre Caziot, nominated as Vichy's first Minister of Agriculture, whose lifelong ambition was to restore the primacy of the family farm. Dorgères was an immediate disciple of Pétain, but his robust influence had weakened by 1940 and it was the more considered doctrinaires of a peasant economy who managed the Corporation. Flattered by Vichy's interest and Pétain's patronage, rural communities expected economic benefits, improved resources including artificial fertilizer and greater mechanization, a priority release of rural prisoners of war and a light hand in government inspections, taxation and price control.

This agenda could not be disconnected from the extortions of the German occupiers, who took 15 per cent of French agricultural produce. Nor could it be met to peasant satisfaction while the Vichy Ministry of Provisions, with hungry towns to be fed, increasingly resorted to enforced requisitions from farmers at low prices. In reaction, peasant initiatives went into ways

of withholding or bartering their goods on the ubiquitous black market. By 1942 the workings of the Corporation were marginalized by the extent of direct government intervention to control illegal trafficking of food. The idyll had gone. The reports of prefects repeatedly bemoaned the 'incurable egoism of the peasantry'.

The peasant demand for more labour was partially met by the National Revolution's mobilization of male youth. Cohorts of young men aged twenty, called up for military service in June 1940 and numbering roughly 100,000, were overtaken by the defeat. Severely disoriented, they were pulled together by Vichy into the Chantiers de la Jeunesse, youth work-camps designed with a mix of the moral codes of scouting and a dose of economic urgency, replacing rural prisoners of war in autumn harvests and forestry work. The leader, General de la Porte du Theil, brought to the Chantiers a flamboyant flavour of ancient Gaul with his flowing warrior moustache and infectious optimism. By January 1941 an eight-month ser-vice in the Chantiers was established in the unoccupied zone as an obligation for all male youths, and by 1944 some 400,000 had passed through the camps. The Chantiers were banned by the Germans from the occupied zone, suspected, wrongly as it soon appeared, of training a supplementary army.

There was a further, but voluntary, grouping of young men from ages sixteen to thirty into the Compagnons de France, yet again a response to social dislocation, compounded by the initial unemployment which fol-lowed the defeat. Inspired by the artisan tradition of *compagnonnage*, with its code of solidarity, the Compagnons provided over 32,000 recruits with scouting skills and a basic apprenticeship in various trades which bred an attitude of truculent anti-bourgeois independence, worrying to the social conservatives at Vichy. The young leader from February 1941, Guillaume de Tournemire, appointed for his reputation as a disciple of Lyautey, developed links with the Resistance and went into hiding in the autumn of 1943. The Compagnons were disbanded early in 1944.

No equivalent state organization for women was created by Vichy, but the imperatives of family and motherhood were central to Vichy's doctrines and social policies. The National Revolution was heavily gendered. The busts of Marianne, female symbol of the Republic, were removed from town halls. The bust or face of Pétain took their place. Archetypal masculinity was hardly exemplified by an old, childless man and a defeated, powerless army, but the cult of Pétain turned this round, and the ideas of rebirth focused on virile male organizations with military values and the male peasant guiding the plough, with the moral base of society secured by the family as

'naturally' organic and hierarchical. In this reasserted world of male power, woman's place was as mother in the home (*la femme au foyer*), her allotted role in the rebirth of France one of procreation and family care. Daladier's family code of 1939 had already set this agenda, and there was little to distinguish Vichy's family policies from the natalist priorities which had gained in credibility as the pre-war crisis deepened. The defeat was widely seen to underline the demographic lessons of 'too few children'. Motherhood was reasserted as a national duty, reinforced by new state provisions for pre- and post-natal care and a law of 15 February 1942 making abortion a capital offence, under which one woman and one man were guillotined in 1943 and a further fourteen condemned to life imprisonment, among scores of other punishments.[4] In December 1942 a law was passed against adultery, with particular penalties for the wives of prisoners of war. The annual Mothers' Day (*Fête des mères*) was elevated into a community and national festival.

The world of work, first in the Vichy trilogy, was the last to be structured by the National Revolution. It was not until 26 October 1941 that a long-gestated work charter (*Charte du travail*) was published by the Ministry of Labour and Industrial Production, headed by René Belin, once the socialist leader of the postworkers' union, and for a while in the mid-1930s deputy leader of the CGT. Subsequently he had moved away from a syndicalism based on class struggle towards the corporative and planning ideas of the Belgian socialist Henri de Man, which Belin developed with conviction in the review *Syndicats*. More pacifist than Jouhaux, he resigned from the CGT in May 1940, and was considered by Pierre Laval to be the obvious figurehead from the labour movement to reconstruct industrial relations. Belin's own proposals would have kept a degree of leverage for the workers, but he failed to carry this at government level and the eventual charter put the firm at the centre, with single corporate unions of management and workforce, weighted in favour of state control and the employers, with no right to strike, no federal structure or access to collective bargaining. It remained a largely paper reconstruction.

Evolution of attitudes towards the Germans within all the bodies created by Vichy negated the pull of its doctrines away from the context of the ongoing war and Occupation. Huge shifts of focus marked the history of the Légion Française des Combattants, the body created and chosen to promote the cult of Pétain and the central Vichy tenets. Open to combatants from both wars, and seeking to unify the multitude of existing ex-combatant organizations, the Légion's instant popularity reflected the universal appeal of Pétain. Banned from the occupied zone, its members flocked to serve

Pétain, swearing an oath of allegiance to the Marshal, and forming uniformed guards of honour on his tours of the south. At its height it reached a membership of 1.2 million, including 350,000 in overseas France (*outre-mer*).

Within a year the enthusiasm for parades and propaganda dwindled. The war had not ended and Vichy had openly embarked on collaboration with the occupiers. Perception of the Légion as the political arm of the Vichy state or the embryo of a fascist-style party brought a gradual, and then precipitate, drop in membership. Its ideological role was accentuated by Pétain's agreement to open its ranks to all enthusiasts for the National Revolution. By mid-winter 1941–2 the vanguard realized that the Légion was losing its bite. A more militant section, the Service d'Ordre Légionnaire (SOL), was formed, led by Joseph Darnand, much-decorated war hero, passionate follower of Pétain and local head of the Légion in Nice and the Alpes-Maritimes. It dedicated itself to crushing dissent and hunting down those excluded by Vichy. It vaunted its methods of repression. For many ex-combatants, fearful of Darnand's direction, continued membership of the Légion and national regeneration were now a contradiction in terms.

Setting up collaboration

Counterpoint, complement, antidote to Pétain's moral ascendancy, Pierre Laval was an arch-negotiator, a driver of hard bargains, a pacifist with no respect for the military pomp of Vichy, a career politician without party and with no residue of democratic principle. His skill as a barrister; his pre-1914 socialism followed by a rupture with the party and a move to independence; his advocacy in the courts for syndicalists and those labelled as defeatists in 1914–18; his means to a personal fortune through property deals and the purchase of local newspapers, printing and radio; all earned him his reputation as a horse-dealer (*maquignon*), at home in the small-town bargaining of his native Auvergne. His foreign policy initiatives in the 1930s included ambiguous triumphs of negotiation with Mussolini and Stalin. He advocated similar overtures to Hitler. The Occupation brought Laval the opportunity to barter directly with Germany and the challenge to find ways of redressing some of the imbalance of power.

Unhampered ideology took the National Revolution forward. The road to impress the occupiers was more sinuous. Laval let it be known that he would have struck a better deal had he been involved in negotiating the Armistice. An activist with no time for the climate of national mourning, he strenuously cultivated the goodwill of Otto Abetz, who arrived in Paris

in early August 1940. Laval did not offer Germany a military commitment, but he unilaterally handed over to Germany the French interests in the Bohr copper mines in Yugoslavia and surrendered to the occupiers the Belgian gold reserves entrusted to France. Short-term concessions with an eye for long-term gain, they expressed Laval's confidence that Nazi Germany would defeat Britain and dictate the future of Europe. His goal was a privileged footing for France at the start of this new era, and en route a more flexible set of Armistice conditions as a prelude to peace. There was a logic here which was not lost on Pétain, who independently was sending discreet envoys to Berlin. On 11 October he expressed his hopes that Germany would be generous in victory and give France the opportunity to respond to a peace based on collaboration, which he offered to all France's neighbours.

A suddenly arranged meeting between Hitler and Pétain brought the possible meanings of collaboration to full public notice. The meeting, on 24 October 1940, took place in Hitler's railway carriage at the station of Montoire north of Tours. Laval had met Hitler two days before at the same venue, and Pétain agreed to make the journey on the 24th despite misgivings within his entourage at Vichy. Little of substance was either discussed or agreed, but Montoire immediately became a symbol of intent. Pétain was photographed shaking hands with Hitler and on 30 October he explained in a pungent, self-justifying broadcast that he had 'entered on the path of collaboration' (*la voie de la collaboration*). It was the context Pétain gave to that collaboration which set the new tone: it was 'with honour' and in the interests of keeping France united, but also in the framework of 'the new European order'. It was yet another broadcast in which Pétain found phrases which immediately shaped public opinion, emphasizing the immense power of radio at a time when people were hanging on every word of communication. People understood that a two-way collaboration was the government's goal, and that concessions by the Germans might well follow. But this time there was no consensus of gratitude and devotion. Prefects reported the first signs of disquiet. The word 'collaboration' had become a strategic concept: it entered political discourse and debate. It was no longer just a technical word for day-to-day adjustments to the exigencies of Occupation.

Pétain's broadcast made the word into a test of loyalty to himself, but also to French unity. He had praise for the 'heroism of French sailors' and the 'loyalty of indigenous colonial people', a reference to the failure of de Gaulle's Free French to land at Dakar in Senegal on 23 September 1940, despite the backing of a sizeable contingent of the British fleet. Repulsed

by fire from the colonial authorities in Senegal, the Dakar operation was portrayed by the Vichy press as a military defeat for de Gaulle, branded as a traitor determined to divide the French against themselves. It played into the hands of Vichy. Much of Vichy propaganda and Laval's diplomatic activity had been to show that Vichy France still had its empire intact. Both Pétain and Laval downplayed the support for de Gaulle given in August by the black Governor of Chad, Félix Éboué, which started the secession of Equatorial Africa to the Free French. If collaboration was a question of hard bartering as Laval anticipated, the empire was a vital strength.

Was Laval solely responsible for Montoire? Was Pétain manipulated into the idea of collaboration? These public questions appeared answered when Laval was summarily dismissed and arrested by Pétain on 13 December 1940. It was a palace coup, plotted by those at Vichy who resented Laval's arrogance and the autonomy of his negotiations with Abetz, pursued through Laval's chosen representative in Paris, Fernand de Brinon, notorious as the first French journalist to have interviewed Hitler in 1933 and co-founder of the Comité France-Allemagne. Laval's release was secured by German pressure, but not his reinstatement. The event confirmed the distinction in people's minds between Pétain and his government. First there had been Pétain: only secondly was there Vichy. The tenacity of the Pétain cult diverted people's doubts away from the Marshal and on to his ministers. In fact, Pétain did not go on to sack de Brinon, nor did he cease to promote state collaboration. In February 1941 he appointed Admiral François Darlan, one of the original plotters of 13 December, as Vice-Premier. It looked like the pursuance of the backlash against Laval, but Darlan had moved towards Laval's position that a German victory in the war was inevitable. He decided to restart the process of negotiation towards a two-way settlement.

The sixty-year-old Darlan, a distinguished naval officer in the First World War, had been head of the navy under Léon Blum who saw him as a safe republican. His accession to power under Vichy was testament to the dynamic political impact of Mers el-Kébir. His latent hostility to Britain's naval supremacy spiralled into a bitter anglophobia and a conviction that Britain was determined to lay its hands on the vulnerable French empire. He was won over to the anti-republicanism of Pétain, and disagreed with Laval more on the form of his negotiations with Germany than with their substance. For a year until April 1942 Darlan set the agenda of Vichy, holding several Ministries at once, including Foreign Affairs, Information, and for several months the Ministry of the Interior.

After Dakar the Germans authorized an increase in the size of the French

North African army. It was the first clear sign that Germany was prepared to recognize that French and German interests in Africa might be reciprocal. Montoire had been an encouragement to Laval and became a precedent for Darlan. He gained his own meeting with Hitler at Berchtesgaden on 11 May 1941 after agreeing that Germany could use airbases in Syria, still under French mandate, for their planned attack on British forces in Iraq. Sensing his opportunity for extracting concessions, Darlan returned to thrash out a reciprocity agreement with Abetz, known as the Paris Protocols, though there is little evidence that Hitler favoured a two-way deal. In Vichy General Weygand voiced cogent opposition. The Protocols came to nothing, but their potential made them a highpoint of voluntary state collaboration. Britain was permanently alienated from Vichy by Darlan's Syrian policy: British military support for the Free French and de Gaulle intensified. In November Pétain dismissed General Weygand, after pressure from Abetz. Prefects' reports underlined the growing public cynicism that the collaboration announced at Montoire would ever yield any tangible benefits. In principle it was increasingly rejected as its meaning grew in complexity after Hitler's invasion of Soviet Russia on 22 June 1941.

Collaboration diversifies

The Nazi-Soviet pact had frustrated the crusading ideology against Communism which permeated all aspects of the National Revolution. The launch of Hitler's war against Stalin unleashed the crusade. Vichy repackaged collaboration in liberational wrapping, 'liberating civilization from Communism'. It was the substance of Laval's gamble when Pétain recalled him to run the government in April 1942. On 22 June 1942, the anniversary of the invasion, Laval told the nation that he wished for German victory (*'Je souhaite la victoire allemande . . .'*) because otherwise Bolshevism would install itself everywhere ('. . . *parce que sans elle le bolchévisme demain s'installera partout.*') The shock of the first words of the declaration obliterated the reason given. The negative public response, almost universal, warned Vichy personnel throughout the country of how much had changed since Montoire. Developments in the war and the growth of resistance in France account for most of this change, but there was radical evolution in the history of state collaboration also.

Out of power, Laval had deepened his contacts with Abetz and sampled the strength of the political movements which strutted their collaborationist colours in occupied Paris. Laval's past took him towards the ex-Socialist Marcel Déat, arrested with him on 13 December, who created his version

of a 'single party' in February 1941, the Rassemblement National Populaire (RNP). Déat's main rival, Jacques Doriot, seemed better placed to promote the fascism of his Parti Populaire Français (PPF) and declared himself a fervent partisan of Pétain. Hitler's invasion of Russia propelled Doriot into Nazi uniform as a leader of the Légion des Volontaires Français contre le Bolchévisme (LVF) which recruited with flamboyant noise, but limited success, to send some 4,000 French volunteers to the eastern front on the crusade against Bolshevism. On the LVF's honorary committee were Cardinal Baudrillart, rector of the Catholic Institute in Paris, and the poet and journalist Abel Bonnard, member of the Académie Française, who became Minister of Education at Laval's return to power. Déat and Laval were both shot at and wounded at one of the LVF's meetings by a young nationalist, Paul Collette, opposed to collaboration.

Laval's connections with the Paris pro-German groups illustrated the blurred line between 'collaboration' as an official strategy of accommodation and 'collaborationism' as ideological commitment. In May 1942 the Nazi organizer of labour, Fritz Sauckel, demanded 250,000 workers from France. Laval responded with a scheme, announced in his broadcast of 22 June, to achieve the return (*la relève*) of prisoners of war in exchange for French workers who volunteered to go to Germany, an idea which went back to Georges Scapini in 1940. On the same day a shadowy duplicate of the LVF, the Légion Tricolore, was launched in the Vichy zone under Jacques Benoist-Méchin.

The *relève* scheme failed to secure the number of specialist workers Sauckel had demanded, despite the moral and patriotic exhortations of Vichy in posters persuading male workers to see themselves as heroic ambassadors of French quality, with wives pictured as pressing them to earn more money in Germany for the sake of the family. The scheme was toughened by forms of random compulsion in the autumn of 1942. Sauckel's pressure increased, and grew to demands for regular cohorts of 200,000 workers or more. Vichy responded with the sharply defined Service du Travail Obligatoire (STO) on 16 February 1943. The obligation to submit for labour service in Germany focused particularly on all male twenty-year-olds, replacing the pre-war conscription for military service and subordinating the Chantiers de la Jeunesse, whose current contingent was made immediately available for Germany. The law was heavily but erratically policed. Women were also enlisted for compulsory work but mostly close to their homes, without the obligation of service in Germany.

By mid-1943 Laval's framework of collaboration had changed. He saw in Sauckel's demands the growing labour and military needs of a Germany

which was no longer certain to win the war. His zest for bargaining returned, even while he fell more and more into collaborationism by authorizing deportation of Jews and repression of resistance. Sauckel experienced him as an opponent rather than a collaborator, and complained to Hitler that Laval was doing everything to limit and even thwart the workings of the STO. Over 600,000 workers were conscripted for Germany, but there was substance to Sauckel's perception of Laval's policy, once it became clear to Vichy that the STO had occasioned the biggest climate of revolt among the population since the Occupation had begun. Laval began to rein in its recruitment drive, promising an amnesty to the hundreds of thousands who had contrived to escape the STO. To local prefects he developed his argument that collaboration was now even more a vital balancing device for shielding the French against the imposition of direct rule by a Nazi *Gauleiter*, such as Sauckel.

Intensified persecution of the Jews

Of all the opportunities seized in defeat, the persecution of the Jews by French antisemites was the one which took collaboration irrevocably towards the inhumanity of Nazism. Vichy followed its two statutes on the Jews with state collusion in the theft, confiscation and sale of Jewish property and businesses. The government took part in the 'Aryanization' programme imposed by the Germans in the occupied zone, and extended it into the south to make sure that the legal agents and the economic beneficiaries were non-Jewish French. The campaign of legal harassment and spoliation of the Jews proceeded with the tacit collusion of Pétain. The most ignominious scenario of the Occupation unrolled: competition between Vichy and the Germans for pride of place in the legalistic victimization of the Jews. By the end of the Occupation over 40,000 Jewish firms and undertakings had been appropriated, and most had been sold to complicit and avaricious French interests.

After the invasion of Russia the Germans accelerated the persecution. The close inter-meanings of anti-Communism and antisemitism found Vichy not far behind. The total Jewish population of France was roughly 300,000, half of whom were refugees or recent immigrants, already under attack by the xenophobic movements of the 1930s. The internment of many Austrian and German Jewish refugees at the outbreak of war was justified as necessary measures against enemy aliens, and a form of moral justification accompanied the expansion of camps across the southern zone, into which foreign Jews of any origin were herded in 1941.

As early as September 1940 Vichy was running over forty-five camps in both zones for men, women and children, variously listed as foreigners, Jews, political prisoners and moral 'undesirables'. A Nazi concentration camp was created at Struthof in the *commune* of Natzweiler in Alsace, and the Germans also administered the camp at Compiègne in the Oise as a transit camp for political prisoners. Elsewhere it was Vichy administration which filled Gurs, Rivesaltes, Le Vernet and other internment camps near the Pyrenees with Jewish foreigners, replacing the Spanish republicans. Many of the original internees, both Spanish and German, were allowed to opt for emigration to Mexico or were moved to forestry workcamps, supervised by Vichy's Foreign Labour unit, from which many escaped. On 15 March 1942 Vichy authorities discussed the possibility of deporting all Romany gypsies. They decided against. A special camp constructed at Saliers near Arles in the Camargue was the alternative. The internees survived the total occupation of the southern zone.

Les Milles in the Bouches-du-Rhône was first a place for Jews from Marseille waiting to emigrate and then yet another site of Jewish internment. Close to Paris, camps in the Loiret at Pithiviers and Beaune-la-Rolande were linked to the camp in a half-completed housing estate at Drancy, in the north-east Parisian suburbs. It was first used by the Daladier government to intern Communists in the crackdown after the Nazi-Soviet pact, and subsequently by the Germans for British prisoners of war. Mass arrests of Jews instigated by the Germans and carried out by the French police began in May 1941. In August, over 4,000 Jews were arbitrarily seized in a vicious operation mostly in the 11th *arrondissement* of Paris. They were sent to Drancy. It began the horrendous history of Drancy as a transit camp, administered for the Germans by the French prefecture of the Seine until 1943.

Conditions of incarceration varied: they were hard in the women's camp at Rieucros in the Lozère, designated for political and moral 'subversives', but also squalid, cruel and disease-ridden in Gurs and Drancy. For the foreign Jews the petty rituals of humiliation by French guards, and the physical indignities, were the extension of the hunt for Jewish refugees carried out by the gendarmerie, an integral part of a census of all Jews decreed by Vichy in June and July 1941. Scores of officials in each *département* meticulously compiled mountains of details, a bureaucratic substructure for all subsequent victimization. No other authority in Nazi-occupied Western Europe gathered as much information for antisemitic purposes with such autonomy of aims and methods.

It was a Vichy precept that collaboration with the Germans should not

decrease the domain of independent French activity. Laval in particular sought to increase autonomy by anticipating German demands and suggesting a specifically French way of meeting them. In this light Vichy did not agree to the German insistence that Jews wear a yellow star, a regulation imposed on all Jews in the occupied zone in May and June 1942, but countered with its own policy in December 1942 to stamp every Jewish identity card with the word 'Jew'. The independence was increasingly illusory. In the winter of 1941–2 Vichy's autonomous legalism, discrimination and internment had been overtaken by the secret Nazi decision to eliminate the Jews. Vichy was not informed. There was no comparable 'final solution' in Vichy's own antisemitic agenda: no policy document of mass murder has been found in the Vichy archives. The Germans hid their intentions behind the cynical fable of providing work and settlement in the east, to which Jews would be transported by rail. Of this Vichy was informed.

Pierre Laval and the Vichy police chief, René Bousquet, grasped it as yet another opportunity: to empty the camps of foreign Jews. It was presumed by Vichy officials that expulsion or resettlement of the Jews was still a coherent German policy. On the night of 22 October 1940 the Germans had shunted a trainload of 6,000 Jews from the German Rhineland into Lyon station, an act which Laval, having just met Hitler at Montoire, personally resented. On his return to office in 1942 he welcomed the chance to send the Jews back across the frontier, though with no interest in their eventual destination. He and Bousquet offered to facilitate deportations from the south, surprising Theodor Danneker who had organized the first convoy from the occupied zone to Auschwitz on 27 March 1942. Bousquet provided Laval with information on the planned deportations from meetings with Karl Oberg. Bousquet had his own agenda: to extract from Oberg a greater degree of independent activity for the French police. In early July 1942 he offered Oberg a display of his police capacity in a massive round-up of foreign Jews in Paris, far greater than the arrests of 1941.

On 16 and 17 July 1942 some 9,000 French police arrested 12,884 Jews and herded them into a sports stadium, the Vélodrome d'Hiver (Vél. d'Hiv), in the 15th *arrondissement* before transfer to Drancy. Over 7,000, including 4,000 children, were kept inside the stadium for five days, in insufferable heat due to a scorching sun, with little or no water and food, and no sanitation, the children forced into terrible squalor through dysentery and diarrhoea. The images of suffering were relayed outside by a few of the police who were sickened by their actions. A few others had managed to warn some of the targeted Jews in advance. The majority obeyed orders. The target for deportation had been twice as high as the numbers seized.

Because of the shortfall, the youngest children, unwanted by the Germans and separated from their parents into the camps of the Loiret, were finally sent to be deported from Drancy, seven-year-olds trailing their younger brothers or sisters by the hand in pitiful scenes of fear and distress. Each convoy was escorted to the frontier by thirty-four gendarmes. The Germans agreed that the rest of the numbers would be made up from the southern zone. It was the opportunity which Laval and Bousquet had sought. The destination from Drancy was undeclared. Laval absorbed and spread the German fable. In Drancy the children imagined a rustic village called Pitchipoï, taken from a popular Polish song. It became a symbol of last hope. On the issue of deporting the youngest children Laval declared that 'they must all go'. Keeping the family together was Vichy policy.

Bousquet was rewarded by Oberg with an agreement on 4 August 1942 which boosted the weaponry and the freedom of French police operations against the Resistance, and relieved them of the burden of choosing hostages on German demand. In exchange Bousquet pledged greater sharing of information on active revolt and armed resistance. The deportations of Jews from the unoccupied zone began at the end of August. Trainloads taken from the camps, 7,000 in the first wave, repeated the appalling spectacle of frightened and bewildered people dehumanized by the brutality of the process and treated as mere numbers by the French authorities determined to satisfy the obsessional Nazi planning. The occupation of the southern zone gave more opportunities for German and French co-operation. In the Bouches-du-Rhône the head of the local police, Maurice Rodellec du Porzic, a Breton aristocrat who despised the Germans, nevertheless made sure that convoys from Les Milles were full, and organized co-operation with forces from the SS in the round-up of Jews in Marseille and the demolition of the Old Port in January 1943, acts of 'moral cleansing' according to Bousquet and Oberg.

The deportations, round-ups (*rafles*) and arrests of Jews continued all over France until shortly before the Liberation. Over 14,000 were deported in the last eight months, totalling in two and a half years 75,721 Jewish men, women and children, according to statistics from German records made official in post-war France. Only 2,567 survived the death camps.[5] At least another 4,000 died in the French camps or were executed in France.

The question of whether or not the Vichy authorities knew the real destination and horrendous fate of the Jews they willingly helped to deport is part of the 'Who knew what?' history of the Holocaust.[6] Information on the mass killings came in mid-1942 through the Red Cross and Swiss Protestant pastors. The Protestant leader in France, Pastor Marc Boegner,

confronted Laval with the news of massacres on 9 September 1942, but Laval stuck to the German line. Earlier, on the BBC French programme of 1 July, Jean Marin broadcast evidence of the killing of 700,000 Jews in Poland, 'simply because they were Jews' and went on to describe the German use of mobile gas chambers 'which even in Germany are known as the Hitler chambers'.[7] Boasts about a 'final reckoning for the Jews' were made in the antisemitic press in Paris as early as February 1942, and regularly throughout the rest of the year. Those who accompanied the brutal convoys to the frontiers can have had little doubt that further inhumanity awaited the Jews at whatever their destination. Laval, Bousquet, Pétain and other senior Vichy officials neither asked what happened to the convoys nor showed any signs of caring. Nor had there been any public demonstrations against the two years of victimization which laid the ground for the deportations.

The brutality of the deportations of 1942 did, however, trigger strong individual protests, widening and deepening resistance both by non-Jews and Jews themselves. Protecting Jews was a major feature in the history of certain localities under the Occupation. The deportations shattered the illusions of safety fostered in French Jewish circles by their trust in Pétain, epitomized by Jacques Helbronner. In November 1943 he and his wife were deported. They did not survive. It was the foreign Jews who figured most prominently in the convoys: they comprised over 56,000 of those deported. The Nazi authorities did not accelerate the deportation of French Jews with the same rigour. Laval claimed credit for this: he was, he told Pastor Boegner, sending foreigners as a prophylactic measure to protect the French. It was Vichy's defence, increasingly rejected on human grounds in the fifty years after the war. No calculated bartering was offered as a justification for Vichy's early acts of legalistic persecution and internment.

A plural Vichy

Symbolized by the bedroom-slipper image, the fads, gossip and introspection of the spa, the government at Vichy looked incurably archaic and makeshift in July 1940. Once established, it attempted to exude vitality and permanence and made a virtue of its provincial site. Its attraction to the 'old guard' but also to the 'new order', in Robert Paxton's classic formula of 1972, gave it plurality from the start.[8] Different potentials were discerned in Vichy, even as Pétain and Laval differed in ways of using the defeat. Vichy was not monolithic.

Within a few months it was clear that it had attracted experts and

technocrats who had little of the reactionary baggage of the Maurrassian ideologues, and who had already formed groups and centres of research as part of the 'nonconformist' passion in the 1930s for creating new forms of work and leisure which would fashion a more modern, efficent and rounded 'homme nouveau' (new man). Their plans for modernization stood to prosper without the obstacles of parliament, party politics and trade unions. They thrived on the opportunities presented by the neutrality of France, the aura of regeneration, and the tension between collaboration and resistance. Their history moves between commitment to Vichy and ambiguity. The all-powerful state was a potential brake, but it was also a malleable partner, or a body which closed a blind eye. Vichy was both a specific chapter in the history of interventionist government in the twentieth century, and at the same time a space in which certain individuals and specialized bodies, intent on rationalizing society in their own way, enjoyed the free hand they had demanded in the inter-war years.

The technocrat Jean Bichelonne, star graduate of the École Polytechnique, and François Lehideux, epitome of private finance and a senior manager of Renault, gave bite to some of the Comités d'Organisation (CO), set up by Belin and Bichelonne in August 1940 to restructure each sector of the economy. Both men were only thirty-six in 1940, and their approach favoured dynamic technical expertise and a rationalization of labour and production. Lehideux, responsible for the CO of car and cycle production, was given the oversight in 1941-2 of all national resources, a role in which he took the first steps in the state planning of the economy (*planification*).

As part of his oversight Lehideux directed his CO to handle the connection of Renault to the occupiers, which made Renault the producer of 29 per cent of the lorries sold to the Germans, while the company became a leader in the application of Vichy's labour charter, including a corporate programme of social welfare and housing, active in its claims to have the interests of the workers as its priority. Renault's commitment to the rationalization of production intensified within the straitened economic conditions of the Occupation.

Bichelonne, who had an astonishing head for figures, was an economic expert at the Armistice negotiations and continued to co-ordinate and organize both production and labour, adapting them to ways of meeting the demands of Sauckel and co-operating with Albert Speer in creating the protected industries inside France. No amount of expertise could mask the penury of resources, the reality of economic *dis*organization, and the splits in the COs and industry over both collaboration and resistance.

Alexis Carrel, medical specialist and Nobel prizewinner, ran a Founda-

tion from 1940 to 1944 of scientists, engineers, economists and eugenicists, to study human problems and improve the quality of 'civilized man in the totality of his corporal, social and racial activities'.[9] An academic venue throughout the Occupation for obsessive demographers and natalists, including Alfred Sauvy and Fernand Boverat, it fostered the illusion that Vichy would promote a higher level of mental hygiene and social efficiency.

State initiative in leisure activities centred on the 'mission' given by Pétain to the international tennis champion from the Basque region, Jean Borotra, to raise the sporting prowess and moral fibre of the nation's youth. A passionate admirer of the 'fair play' he saw in British amateur sport, he was joined by Jean-Jacques Chevallier, a law professor and a national athletics champion of the early 1920s. Borotra's department of sport within the Youth Ministry saw far more success than most Vichy enterprises, bringing athletics and swimming in particular into the mainstream of people's lives, and nurturing physical education. The emphasis was on amateur participation and competition, continuing in some close detail the initiatives of Léo Lagrange, who was killed on the front in the Aisne in June 1940. The debt to Lagrange was acknowledged by Borotra, forming a thematic link of state provision between Vichy and the Popular Front. Borotra's sporting Vichy was as specific as any, ending with his attempt to leave for England in November 1942 and his arrest and deportation by the Germans. He survived at Itter near Innsbruck, where other celebrity French hostages, including Paul Reynaud and Édouard Daladier, were held.

Emmanuel Mounier's involvement in Vichy did not last as long. The nonconformist Catholic intellectual sensed an opening for his personalist ideas in the spiritually charged atmosphere of Pétainism. Against the advice of many of his closest colleagues he restarted his journal *Esprit* in November 1940 in Lyon. To those who disagreed with him it looked like acceptance of Vichy policies and dogma. It was never that, but it came close, and its willingness to explore the possibilities of open expression bitterly divided the journal's core readership. By July 1941, repeatedly censored for independent thought, it ceased publication. Mounier was relieved that the ambiguity was over. The openness that he had imagined to exist in the organic ideals of the National Revolution was a potential Vichy which never materialized.

Mounier was one of very many who moved into a Vichy of their own intellectual construction, discovered rigidity, and moved away. Brief encounters with Vichy were as much the norm as the total commitment which the cult of Pétain demanded. Prefects in the winter of 1941–2 signalled an unmistakable decline in the popularity of the regime. After less

than a year and a half, the majority of the public considered it with hostility. Vichy's collaboration failed to carry conviction as a patriotic or effective response to the Occupation. A number of prefects called for new initiatives. It was not precisely Laval's return that they had in mind, nor his speech of 22 June 1942. Administrative confidence ebbed continuously.

The trial of Third Republic leaders at Riom had already been a farcical failure for the early Vichy and Pétain: Léon Blum turned the accusations on their head and the Germans demanded an end to the proceedings in April 1942, angry that the court had allowed speeches which rehearsed the enemy status of Germany.

The total occupation of the south in November 1942 reignited the issues of war. The French fleet in Toulon harbour scuttled itself rather than fall into German hands. The Armistice Army was dissolved. Admiral Darlan was by chance in North Africa and conceded a ceasefire to the Americans. His presence and that of General Giraud helped Pétainist officers in the African Army to adjust to re-entering the war on the Allied side, but on 24 December 1942 Darlan was assassinated in a plot which had unacknowledged British connections. At Vichy, Jean Borotra and others tried to persuade Pétain to leave France, without success. The Marshal, less and less able to conceal failings of concentration, fell back into periods of morose withdrawal. Pétain's revivalist Vichy had gone. Laval's tactical Vichy was dominant. Pétain as a national icon was heavily tarnished, yet almost four years after coming to power, he was greeted by crowds as a symbol of French endurance when he visited occupied Paris for the first and only time on 26 April 1944. He went there to acknowledge the death of over 600 Parisians in a severe Allied bombing raid six days before.

The Vichy of November 1942 to August 1944 was no more a single entity than in 1940–42. Ambiguities at local level in the face of mounting German demands on the one hand and a more structured and pervasive resistance on the other, produced a multifractured administration in which bluff and a readiness to play a double-game at all levels drove committed regional police chiefs like Marty in Montpellier, and certain prefects, to distraction. The rationale of collaboration as a barrier against Communism was dramatically cast in powerful, biting prose by Philippe Henriot, a devout Catholic and pungent broadcaster throughout 1943 on Radio-Vichy. A regular contributor to the Paris-based collaborationist pages of *Gringoire* and *Je suis partout*, he developed a radio talent which made him Vichy's most powerful communicator to the general public. He alone was responsible for whatever fidelity remained among Vichy personnel in 1944, even as the cause of Vichy was visibly in terminal collapse. He skilfully

attacked the idea that France could be liberated by the Allies: he reiterated his belief as a catechism of fact that an Allied landing could only end in a further defeat for France and submission to a Stalinist Europe. He created and played on fears that the Resistance was nothing more than rapacious Bolshevik terror. As a populist, his error was to join the Milice, mirror of the German Gestapo, which was regarded with repugnance and fear by most local Vichy authorities and never had any widespread public support.

The blackshirted Milice Française evolved in January 1943 from Joseph Darnand's activism within the Service d'Ordre Légionnaire (SOL). Laval supported its creation, worried that the police, even strengthened by special Mobile Reserve Groups (GMR), would not be able to protect German personnel and operations in France. Bousquet's agreement with Oberg placed Vichy law and order at the fighting front against the Resistance. As the foremost instrument of repression, infiltration and torture, the Milice at its height counted on some 35,000 volunteers, only a minority of whom were actively mobilized as an élite military unit (*franc-garde*). Youths who joined were assured exemption from labour service in Germany: it appealed to members of the inter-war fascist leagues, to ultra-Catholics, and to wealthy young royalists who, thirty years before, would have been the first recruits to the Camelots du Roi. Its intellectual theorist, Francis Bout de l'An, envisaged the Milice as the core of a totalitarian takeover of every state apparatus. Henriot joined in March 1943 and was photographed repeatedly in his black shirt. Darnand, the head of the Milice, also joined the Waffen SS in July 1943 with its pledge of allegiance to Hitler. He continued to proclaim his personal loyalty to Pétain and to the policies of early Vichy.

Towards the end of 1943 Pétain tried to sack Laval for the second time, but was outmanoeuvred. The two leading personalities of Vichy had contested supremacy from the start. Defiantly, Laval installed Henriot and Darnand in the government in January 1944, giving Darnand complete control over all policing, armed with special courts martial to expedite the repression of resistance. Marcel Déat was pressed into the government by German pressure in March. The collaborationism of Paris was joined to that of Vichy.

The Vichy of the Milice was a veritable police state. It was the violent reassertion of a failed National Revolution. It was comparable to any European fascism. It tied itself into the pathologies of Nazism. There had been separate roots and aims and there were separate histories, but in the activities of the Milice and the Gestapo there was a shared dénouement.

12

Occupied France (2). Resistance and Liberation, 1940–1944

1. *Individual refusal and dissent*

Refusal preceded resistance and revolt. A scattering of isolated individuals, unknown to one another, refused to accept the ceasefire announced by Pétain. Even earlier, as the German army was still encountering fighting units on its way south, a handful of individuals disobeyed a German prohibition placed on the burial of black soldiers. The first curfews were defied by a very few in the occupied zone to assist the families of those taken hostage. There was no co-ordination in these and other gestures of refusal, later seen as the seeds of resistance: typewritten protests handed out in the streets, clenched fists raised to express anti-fascism, and actions to mislead and annoy (*narguer*) the German occupiers in the streets and cafés. In private, several diaries, printed subsequently, expressed refusal and anger. Jean Guéhenno, writer and diarist, had nothing but contempt for Pétain. When the Germans withdrew from Clermont-Ferrand after the Armistice, his diary contained the terse lines: 'The Marshal can now make his entry. His bed, left by the Oberkommandant, is ready . . . No need to change the sheets.'[1]

Guéhenno later published some of his diary in the clandestine series of Éditions de Minuit, and called it *Dans la prison*. The metaphor of prison to describe the enclosed world after the Armistice was explicit among many of those who refused to accept the situation. In the different annexed or occupied zones, curfews were imposed by the German authorities enforcing confinement; in the unoccupied zone there was the moral weight of Pétainism. Breaking out, lifting the weight, dispersing the climate of penitence, battling against the anglophobia after Mers el-Kébir, turning round the vindictiveness of Vichy in order to accuse Pétain and Laval of capitulation, all these impulses among a very small minority in the summer of 1940 lay behind refusal and dissent.

The makeshift prisoner-of-war camps within France gave literal meaning to the metaphor. Escape from the camps was decisive action, but converting

it into further refusal was the choice of only a few of those who evaded the transit to Germany. The career officer Captain Henri Frenay was one; the academics François de Menthon and Pierre-Henri Teitgen two among others. Frenay's military mind was no less fertile than de Gaulle's. In late July 1940, with no equivalent access to radio waves, he elaborated a comparable vision of continuing the war, or rather restarting it through intelligence services and a secret army, the first *armée secrète* to be envisaged by a serving officer. Frenay was not critical of Pétain, nor of Vichy ideology, but the continuing influence of a close woman friend since 1935, the left-wing Anglophile Bertie Albrecht, reinforced his resolution to find alternatives to the submission and inactivity enforced on the Armistice Army. Another close parallel to de Gaulle within France was General Cochet, a senior airforce officer, who instructed his unit at the Armistice to continue the war by any possible means, including dissimulation. Cochet firmly believed that Pétain would be a bulwark against Germany. In the autumn he openly released a number of tracts entitled *Tour d'Horizon*, using the word 'resistance' to signify the action of refusal, not outlining an organization. Nevertheless, small spontaneous groups, inspired by his tracts, formed in Marseille and Lyon at the end of the year, without any initial knowledge of each other. They included journalists as well as demobilized military personnel, kicking their heels, and a few still attached to the Foreign Legion.

As everywhere, the question was what exactly to do. In fact, taking a position, contacting and informing others, were in themselves actions, and from the start risked arrest in the occupied zone, where Cochet would have had none of the initial freedom he had in the south. Subterfuge in the Vichy zone was seen to be advisable: in the north it was essential. Common to both zones were the good works and care for prisoners of war sanctioned by Pétain. They provided incomparable cover for transgressive action. A young ethnologist, Germaine Tillion, returned in June 1940 from fieldwork in Algeria to what she described as a deathly-silent Paris, like 'Pompei after the eruption'. She contacted Colonel Paul Hauet and together they installed an office representing indigenous soldiers from the colonies, behind which they tracked down colonial prisoners of war and helped some of them to escape and cross the demarcation line.[2] Bertie Albrecht, partner in Frenay's initiatives and a feminist proponent of birth control, improbably found work in the new climate of Vichy as a social worker in women's work and unemployment, a cover for her pro-British and dissident activity, extended by her work for prisoners in Lyon. Frenay was initially covered by his attachment to the intelligence services at Vichy, the 2e Bureau.

Submission was refused by individuals for reasons which they later gave as moral, military or political, all three grounds underlined as patriotism, at a time when the concept was virtually monopolized by Pétain. Only biographies can do justice to the individuals involved. They were too diffuse a minority to allow any sociological or even political generalization. Separately their acts created resistance: it was a wealth of initiatives from below, from women as well as men. Within France there was no blueprint imposed from above, no single organization to join. There were plans and often far-reaching visions. There was reflex response. A haphazard encounter was frequently the defining moment. Most early actions were improvised, though there were precedents to which some individuals looked. Marcel Lebon, the affluent owner of a gas and electricity company, cited the precedent of a clandestine paper in occupied Belgium, *La Libre Belgique*, during the First World War. He recommended the production of a similar newspaper to his young friend Philippe Viannay, studying to be a philosophy academic, who came to him after the defeat for ideas on what could be done. Viannay met up with Robert Salmon, another escaped prisoner of war awarded the Croix de Guerre for bravery, and an equally young Parisian librarian, Hélène Mordkovitch (later Hélène Viannay) who forced Viannay to decide what he intended to do. They took Lebon's idea and started to prepare what eventually emerged as the newspaper *Défense de la France*. There was no military intent of any kind. 'It was a moral act,' said Viannay.[3]

Moral, ethical, high-principled, spiritual, these were words synonymous with the leadership cult of Pétain. The decision to wrest them away from the climate of submission, from the whole of the authorized media, from the hierarchy of the Catholic Church and the social influence of local notables, was the sort of decision which made the first acts of refusal, in the words of Jean Cassou, art historian and early resister, 'un refus absurde'. Its absurdity, however, was the mark of its freedom. It was possibly less absurd, though more dangerous, in Paris, where Pétainism carried a more muted moral force than in the south. Cassou himself started with tracts of his own before joining friends from the Paris ethnological museum, the Musée de l'Homme, who had been engaged in producing a clandestine paper called simply *Résistance*, the first to use the word as a title. The duplicator in the basement of the humanist museum had been used for anti-fascist and Popular Front tracts in the 1930s by the founder and director, Paul Rivet. It was put to immediate use in July 1940, to duplicate advice offered by a 54-year-old socialist, Jean Texcier, in *Conseils à l'occupé* on how not to compromise with the Germans. Paul Rivet, the Russian-born

Boris Vildé, and other museum colleagues were joined by art historian Agnès Humbert and writer Claude Aveline, and the first number of *Résistance* emerged in mid-December 1940, eight months before *Défense de la France*, although the decisions to publish were taken at similar times. In Marseille, the academics de Menthon and Teitgen launched *Liberté* in November, with a strong moral justification for refusal, quoting both Foch and Pétain from the First World War.

Arguments of principle were the essence of refusal outlined in the earliest tracts. Going beyond that, several individuals decided that the provision of factual information, not available in the authorized press, would make an even stronger case, and would carry its own conviction. Journalists had avidly followed the government from Paris to Bordeaux and on to Vichy: many were uprooted as their papers were relocated to the southern zone. All papers were subject to censorship. The rationale for alternative news was not difficult to make, and a long tradition of fringe and sectarian papers sold or distributed on the streets had been one of the criteria of a free press since the late nineteenth century. Clandestine publication was the obvious route back into that freedom. It was a factual *Bulletin d'information et de propagande* that Henri Frenay and a military colleague Robert Guédon launched in early 1941, following the pioneer tracts of General Cochet. It drew on Swiss radio and press, easily accessible in Lyon, as well as the BBC from London which had already been a vital source of information for *Résistance* in Paris.

In the occupied zones one source of military information was very much at hand: the German presence itself. The occupied populations were observers of the Germans at the very least, whatever else was imposed on them: it was again a few individuals who decided to make this role active. The fiery reaction of a fervent nationalist farmer, Louis de la Bardonnie, an avid reader of *L'Action française* in the inter-war years, was to break with the position adopted by Charles Maurras and defy the defeat. The demarcation line was close to his village in the Dordogne, and he and a few others set out to inform London of detailed German troop movements, and ships coming in and out of Bordeaux. His first envoy routes were amateur and chaotic, but the intelligence eventually arrived, carried by a 71-year-old priest. The Germans had earmarked Brittany as a key to the control of the Atlantic. The British needed regular and reliable information on the Breton ports and others on the Atlantic coast. As early as the summer of 1940 Marcel Hévin created the core of an information network in Nantes. In the Côtes-d'Armor Claude Robinet-Rivière infiltrated the semaphore station of Bilfot, close to Paimpol, from which he stole a detailed plan of coastal

defences and transmitted it to London, before arriving there himself in January 1942.

Crossing in person to England was a spontaneous act of defiance among communities in the islands and ports of Brittany. From the Île de Sein, fishermen went in their boats to volunteer for the Free French almost before the movement was launched. From Lorient, the Breton-born Gilbert Renault left a business career in films and travelled to join de Gaulle, arriving on 28 June 1940. With the *nom de guerre* of Rémy, he returned to organize Louis de la Bardonnie's group, and small knots elsewhere, into the intelligence network Confrérie Notre-Dame (CND). Jeanne Bohec, a chemistry student from Brest, crossed immediately to London: three and a half years later she was parachuted back to instruct resistance groups in sabotage. Getting to England was far from simple: there were individuals who tried to swim across the Channel and were swept back. Others set off on their own to cross the Pyrenees and got lost or were arrested by the Spanish police. Initially, small French vessels putting into British harbours met an officious reception, and there are many accounts of French arrivals treated as irksome refugees rather than as volunteers to the Allied cause. Nor was leaving France an obvious patriotic case to make, given the treasonous reputation attached to the exiles (*émigrés*) who rallied in Coblentz in 1792 to fight against the Revolution. It was determination in 1940 to stay in France and do something which explains why so many of the acts of refusal had an ambiguous relationship to Pétain himself. By comparison with crossing to England, belief that Pétain must really be in touch with the Allies was an easy path to follow, if only for a few months.

2. Collective defiance

Free French (1)

In London, Charles de Gaulle's individual refusal did announce a collective movement to which others could rally. Churchill accepted de Gaulle on 28 June 1940 as the leader of those who rallied to 'la France libre', and on 7 August the financial and military backing of the British government assured a future for the Free French army, navy and airforce as co-belligerents. De Gaulle's first twelve speeches and appeals on the BBC in June and July, relayed direct to France, rallied few military leaders of status and experience, and no senior administrators or politicians. By mid-August he had assembled under his command only an embryo force of some 2,000, with 140 officers. The Dakar fiasco (see Chapter 11) might have ended his

challenge, but Churchill's loyalty, and the compensation of gaining the support of French Equatorial Africa, kept the movement growing. It was a confident de Gaulle who issued a declaration from Brazzaville in the French Congo on 27 October stating that the Vichy regime was unconstitutional and subject to the Germans, and that he himself was now directing the war policy of France at the head of an Imperial Defence Committee. It was a ringing response to the Montoire meeting of Pétain and Hitler. With this declaration, de Gaulle's initiative expanded to one of political autonomy, though his material dependency on Britain would deepen continuously. His claim to national legitimacy was as defiant as his original 'Appel' of 18 June but far more extravagant in its pretensions. In de Gaulle's terms the Free French were not to be dismissed as exiles: they were the very embodiment of France. It was a massively ambitious claim at the height of Pétain's power and Vichy's nationalist agenda.

De Gaulle's credentials for asserting such a national role were not strong, beyond his name, which Churchill romantically associated with the feats of ancient Gaul, and his first 'Appel', which rapidly assumed 'historic' dimensions. It helped also that he was unusually tall and imposing: once met he was not easily forgotten. He was born in Lille in 1890 and graduated through the military academy of Saint-Cyr to serve in the First World War as an infantry officer. A 'French Who's Who' published by government services in London in November 1943 and marked 'Confidential', stressed his three citations on promotion to Captain in 1915, his five attempts to escape from a prisoner-of-war camp after capture at Douaumont in 1916, his post-war military career initially under the wing of Pétain, his command of the 4th armoured division in May 1940 as a Brigade General and his distinguished actions at Laon and Abbeville, before being called from the front to be Under-Secretary for Defence to Reynaud. He was presented in this way as a purely military figure, with nothing to suggest a future of political or national leadership. There is no mention of his writings between the wars. A study of his *Vers l'armée de métier* of 1934, which set out the arguments for a professional, highly mobile army, would have indicated his capacity for bold ideas and his huge self-belief.

For over two years de Gaulle's hold on Allied commitment to the Free French was precarious. His obduracy in any matter touching on his independence and his resilient claim to represent France made relations with the Allied leaders fractious at best. President Roosevelt, in particular, decided he was insufferable and did everything to exclude him. The stories of policy and personality clashes were typified by de Gaulle's reported statement that Churchill shouted when he was in the wrong, whereas he, de Gaulle,

shouted when he was right, with the consequence that they were always shouting at each other. It was in a gossip-heavy vein that squabbles among the Free French were retailed among the 6,000 French residents in the London area, most of whom rejected de Gaulle as an upstart. It needed their belief in Pétain to ebb, and the realization of Vichy's collaboration to grow, before de Gaulle's headquarters at Carlton Gardens was socially recognized.

Something of the disputed nature of his claim to personify French defiance is rendered by the indifference shown to him by the French journal launched in London, *La France Libre*, under the aegis of André Labarthe, with literary and political features by a wealth of French writers in exile, including the political scientist Raymond Aron. The journal's first number on 15 November 1940, which sold 10,000 copies instantly, contained an article on 'The Capitulation' of June, with the words, 'Alas! There was no one to say to the French with authority, "The fight must go on".'[4] It was a deliberate omission of de Gaulle's 'Appel', a calculated slight by Labarthe who had started working for Carlton Gardens but had broken with de Gaulle in August.

Little, or nothing, was known in France of de Gaulle's career or personality. His 'Appel' was heard by very few. As his name and the existence of the Free French filtered through, it was not for who he was but for what he symbolized. Gradually the effect of his persuasive broadcasts and the French programmes on the BBC transformed him into a recognized leader. 'Only a soldier', wrote Léon Blum, 'could set out with such force and authority what our simple duties were, simple as the cry of our conscience.'[5] De Gaulle's was the first national reputation to be made entirely by radio, even as Pétain's cult was taken into the realms of mythology by radio broadcasts. In both cases radio reflected a democratic or populist conception of leadership as a status to be confirmed by the people's direct response, but unlike Radio-Vichy, and still more Radio-Paris, the BBC put independent voices and the 'right to know' at the forefront of its policy. The BBC broadcasts in French, known collectively as 'Ici Londres', and remembered principally for Maurice Schumann's voice on the programme 'Honneur et Patrie' and Jacques Duchesne's on 'Les Français parlent aux Français', set the agenda in 1940–41, but by 1943 they were taking much of their lead from resistance activity inside France.

The first collective action organized by Carlton Gardens through the BBC was for 1 January 1941. The French population were called on to leave the streets empty between three and four o'clock in the afternoon. The response was limited but noticeable, a minor psychological success,

which emboldened far more ambitious projects of public demonstration in the next three years. The graffiti outbreak of V signs for Victory and the Free French cross of Lorraine was largely inspired by radio promptings, and it was important to the 'Ici Londres' campaigns that individual letters from France, arriving unexpectedly by ordinary post from the southern zone, were full of defiant responses and praise for the broadcasts, not least for their musical diversions, contrasting with the diet of martial music imposed by Radio-Paris.

A demonstration, manifesto, strike

The calendar of traditional holidays (14 July, 1 May) and of remembrance (11 November) had an activating dynamic of its own, with or without radio encouragement. The arrest by the Germans of the physicist Paul Langevin, a popular professor at the Collège de France in Paris who made no secret of his left-wing views and anti-fascism, prompted his students to use the cover of 11 November 1940 for a protest march to the Arc de Triomphe. Numbers ran into hundreds on what was intended as a reminder of Germany's defeat in 1918, much to the offended surprise of the German authorities, who had banned all ceremonies in advance. They violently broke up the demonstration, injuring many. French police were called in to make arrests, but a few helped students escape into the métro. A number of student demonstrators, both male and female, were seized, and Vichy was forced ignominiously to bring them to trial early in 1941. A pattern was set for public holiday protests, which by 1942 flowed into the undercurrent of resistance, as increasing numbers in the large towns of the south took to the streets. It was a form of collective defiance, whether for more food and fuel, or generally to assert national identity, which the Vichy authorities were unable, and sometimes unwilling, to curb.

In response to Vichy's dissolution of trade unions, a collective manifesto from twelve trade unionists was published openly on 15 November 1940 in Paris and distributed across both zones. It was drawn up by Christian Pineau, a 36-year-old with a potential career in banking, who had thrown himself into the militant ranks of the CGT and, in his own words, 'was considered in my family and among my friends as a traitor to my class'.[6] Pineau brought together unionists from the socialist stream of the CGT and from the Catholic confederation, the CFTC. Only Communist militants were omitted, due to continued suspicion of the Nazi-Soviet pact. The 'Manifesto of the Twelve' could be read as a forthright, but not subversive, restatement of trade union principles, or as a wider commitment to freedom

and human rights beyond the purely syndicalist realm, recalling in its language the anti-fascist statements issued by the CGT in 1934–6. The German authorities paid it little attention, but René Belin in Vichy was outraged at what he interpreted as a direct attack on his authority. Within a fortnight this led the group of twelve, under cover of an economic study committee, to launch the first number of a clandestine paper, *Libération*, edited by Pineau. It appeared every fortnight until the Liberation itself, Jean Texcier succeeding Pineau on his departure for London in February 1942.

By the spring of 1941, after a winter of food shortages, high prices, stagnant wages and longer hours, the miners of the Nord and Pas-de-Calais decided on open defiance of the mining companies and moved from go-slow protests to a full strike. It broke out on 27 May 1941, the first major strike of occupied France, and inside the tightest of zones. Like the Manifesto of the Twelve, it has been seen either as a traditional form of trade-union assertion or as a collective defiance of the German Occupation. In the event it was both, and grew more boldly anti-German as General Niehoff declared that arrests by the French or Germans would be followed by five years of hard labour. By 3 June over 100,000 miners were on strike and women were active *en masse* at the picket lines. The climate of violence lasted for ten days. Arrests numbered 450, and 244 were deported to Germany a few weeks later.

What became known locally as the 'great popular strike' revealed a significant shift of policy within the Communist Party, whose militants in the banned mineworkers' union co-ordinated the action. Until May 1941 the illegal PCF was intent on reconstructing its party cells, contacting members, adhering to the 'imperial war' propaganda of the Nazi-Soviet pact, suppressing its pre-war anti-fascist rhetoric, and distributing its huge range of clandestine publications. This meant *L'Humanité* above all, but in the area of the strike a different version of *L'Enchaîné* for each of the *départements*. The centralized PCF press rarely addressed the fact of the Occupation and carried no call for active opposition to the German presence. On the other hand it was clear in its refusal of Pétain and its rejection of Vichy ideology. The regime's antisemitism was condemned by a Marseille edition of *L'Humanité* in October 1940, and it was local variations of emphasis and substance which conveyed something of the disparities and disarray within the party at grass-roots level.

L'Enchaîné in the Pas-de-Calais, an area of strong Anglophile sentiment and veterans from the International Brigades, had marked its dissident identity with a report on the student demonstration of 11 November in Paris, ignored by the main Communist press. By the end of May 1941 the

PCF's dogmatic avoidance of the Occupation was barely intact as collective policy. There was a desperate need to reconnect the party with the population at large. It launched the first tentative moves towards a unifying 'Front National' (FN) aimed at party members and non-Communists in both major zones. The moves coincided with the miners' greater militancy, allowing tracts to emerge locally attacking the exactions of the occupiers, although officially the party stuck to its line and disclaimed anything in the strike beyond purely trade-union demands.

The German invasion of the Soviet Union less than three weeks after the height of the strike obliterated the confusion and the blatant *mauvaise foi* of the long twenty-one months of the Nazi-Soviet pact. The PCF's immediate commitment to all forms of action against the Germans, its apparent seamless continuity of anti-fascism, was as if the pact had never been.

3. Basic structures of resistance

Detailing these early refusals and collective defiance might suggest that protest was widespread in 1940–41. This would be a false conclusion, given the very small numbers of people involved, but it would accurately indicate the diversity of activity that was undertaken, and the range of attitudes towards Pétain. By the winter of 1941 there were enough groups for the dissidence to be referred to as 'the Resistance', built from the early initiatives, and thriving on diversity. At the same time, the groups largely ceased to harbour illusions about Pétain and firmly added collaboration to the Occupation as the target of resistance propaganda and action. By 1942 there were movements and networks of resistance across the whole country to which people could be recruited, and although it still represented only a minority of the population, resistance was enacted at so many levels that the differences between vanguard and infrastructure, and between military and civil, are ones of shading and nuance: they are not distinct categories. From mid-1943, mainly because of the huge civil impact of forced labour service in Germany (STO) and developments in the war, it is possible to talk not just of movements (*mouvements*) of resistance, but also of a resistance tendency or climate (*mouvance*) which continued to spread throughout 1944, though it never entirely displaced the ambiguities of waiting on events (*attentisme*) until the Liberation was imminent.

As the Resistance took shape and structured itself, its needs were constantly redefined, affecting the kinds of jobs, people and places that were

deliberately drawn into its widening circle. Leader-figures with imagination, people known locally as 'resourceful', opinion-makers, journalists and printers are high on the definition of early resisters: soon it was railway workers, town-hall clerks with access to official stamps, garage mechanics, teachers and parish priests, café and restaurant proprietors, hoteliers, and anyone with a permit to travel, who were actively sought after. Finally, there was a need for peasant providers, mountain and forest guides, medical personnel, workers with access to explosives, and military expertise of all kinds. Something of the arbitrary, *ad hoc* nature of early refusals and defiance disappeared, though improvisation and creativity remained.

The psychology of obstinacy and individualism was high at the start. It never lost its place, but it was joined by a far less demonstrative range of personal qualities: a capacity for secrecy, for carrying out orders, for holding down a legal job as cover, for infiltration and subversion, for support, liaison and endurance. Resistance used what have been called 'weapons of the weak,'[7] such as silence, dissimulation and sabotage, and it occupied all the spaces of freedom left in the margins of constraint. It practised forms of military intelligence, engineered networks of escape, and moved into guerrilla warfare. It was both original and traditional in its forms of revolt. It explored all the avenues of illegality. It became an alternative society, a parallel universe. It never questioned its own legitimacy, though its methods and goals were always in dispute. It would be better to talk about 'resistances' (*les résistances*) in the plural, but this should not undervalue the common aim of liberation, which brought people of contrasting backgrounds and ideas together, however specific their time, place and form of resistance.

There was no photo-fit resister, no ideal type, no model. Throughout the Resistance (and throughout this chapter) the unqualified word 'resister' could stand for man, woman, adult, youth; Catholic, Protestant, Jew, non-believer; a French person or foreigner. Resisters were constantly surprised to find who their contacts and co-resisters were. In oral histories after the war they spoke of pride in diversity, trust in difference, and a readiness to work side by side with people of all kinds.

The activity undertaken by women outmanoeuvred Vichy and German police alike. Individual women were among the originators of several movements and networks: their achievements became nationally celebrated. At local level women created vital infrastructures of care, supply and communication. In the armed maquis period of 1943–4 they were everywhere as liaison agents, able to travel alone or together without raising immediate suspicion. They passed through barriers more easily; they used shopping

bags, children's satchels, prams even, to convey tracts, arms and ammunition; they used or simulated pregnancy to escape being searched. Gender attributes were turned to subversion, and few women resisters regarded this as subordinate to male activity. Most speak of an equality in resistance that was keenly felt at the time. There was a distribution and sharing of danger, inventiveness and skills which revolutionized the individual lives of men and women, even where the roles were gender-specific in predictable ways.

The presence of foreigners, refugees and immigrants in all aspects of resistance was exemplified by Polish miners in the north-east, Spanish republican fighters principally, but not solely, in the south-west, Italian anti-fascists across the south, refugee anti-Nazi Germans in the maquis, Jews creating their own resistance impetus as well as integrating with non-specific movements of all kinds, and Eastern European immigrants in the mainly Communist-organized urban groups. Neither Vichy radio and press nor that of the occupiers easily admitted the presence of resistance. When they did so it was to suggest that it was a ragbag of international criminals and terrorists. Joining a maquis band in the Cévennes in 1944, the young Jean-Pierre Chabrol found himself alongside Spanish and Eastern Europeans and commented that it was exactly the kind of internationalist grouping that Vichy had vilified. For him it was the quintessence of resistance.

Divisions are not hard to find in resistance history: they were there in approach and strategy, politics and command. But the mix of gender, class, nationality and belief pervaded the whole. It was structural to the nature of resistance, not incidental.

Movements and networks

Demobilized as an intelligence naval officer on 11 July 1940, the talented, aristocratic, aesthete journalist and writer Emmanuel d'Astier de la Vigerie looked for some way of expressing his frustration. Sickened by the atmosphere of abject submission, he envisaged himself and the friends he re-encountered on the Mediterranean coast as a last column of defiance, a 'Dernière Colonne', giving the term an inversionary twist from the negative connotations of a treacherous 'fifth column'. Its subversive intent was nevertheless its *raison d'être*, and it was as conspirators in an unformulated venture that de la Vigerie, a young history teacher, Lucie Samuel (later known as Lucie Aubrac), and the university philosopher Jean Cavaillès headed a small group in Clermont-Ferrand where the University of Strasbourg had been evacuated. Cavaillès was yet another escaped prisoner of

war, as determined as Frenay to find a way of actively continuing the war. They were unanimous in rejecting Pétain, and from the start Lucie Samuel saw their activity as necessarily directed against Vichy, the tangible authority in the *zone libre*, as well as against the German occupiers in the north.

The group was a movement of activists. Not until later, after failures to spark popular support for their activities of fly-posting, provocative agitation and distribution of tracts, did they decide that coherence and impact would only come from production of a regular clandestine newspaper. They dropped the name 'Dernière Colonne' and began to call their group 'Libération', issuing the first number of *Libération*, with a run of 10,000, from Clermont-Ferrand in July 1941. There were now two papers and two movements called Libération, north and south, started independently. In the south the movement preceded the paper; in the north it was the other way round. Either way, it was clear that clandestine papers generated and sustained recruitment. For reasons similar to the 'Dernière Colonne', a heterogeneous group of ex-Radicals, ex-Communists and liberal Catholics in Lyon in November 1940 initially called themselves 'France-Liberté' before launching their own clandestine paper, *Le Franc-Tireur*, in December 1941, the name finally taken by the group to emphasize its hard-hitting independence. Under the leadership of Jean-Pierre Lévy, a Jewish refugee from Strasbourg, whose business contacts brought in other Alsace refugees, the movement attracted Yves Farge among several journalists from the authorized local paper, *Le Progrès de Lyon*, whose offices were already a hub of dissidence.

When Henri Frenay's and Bertie Albrecht's movement combined with the *Liberté* group of de Menthon and Teitgen, the result, in December 1941, was the newspaper *Combat*, edited first by the liberal Catholic Georges Bidault and later by the left-wing engineer Claude Bourdet. It fronted a movement of the same name. The early acts of refusal and Frenay's projects for a secret army and intelligence gave Combat a maturity of organization and a sense of its own future, which led to difficult negotiations with the centralizing agents sent into France by de Gaulle in 1942–3. The creation of small knots of activists, called 'Groupes francs', registered the potential of an Armée Secrète (AS) in towns across the south, mainly in attacks with explosives on the homes and businesses of well-known collaborators. No less important was the co-ordinated practice of infiltrating Vichy's administration, local post offices, police stations and municipal government, a practice common to all resistance movements, but given the task within Combat of forming future administrators, through the Noyautage des Administrations Publiques, simply referred to as 'le NAP'.

Separate secret networks (*réseaux*) of intelligence and escape were the other main structure of resistance action, without any public expression through tracts or newpapers. The networks were financed and organized by the British secret services (MI6 and MI9) or by de Gaulle's own military intelligence under a 29-year-old officer from the Norwegian campaign, Captain André Dewavrin, known to resistance history as Colonel Passy. They carried out all forms of military intelligence against the Germans and Vichy, but sustained individual links, as indeed Frenay had, with Vichy's 2e Bureau. Research long after the war revealed that Vichy's counter-espionage continued throughout the Occupation to arrest German personnel for spying, suggesting there was more military independence at Vichy than is often credited.[8] It remains unclear to what extent this constituted resistance, but there is no such ambivalence attached to the activities of Rémy's CND, nor to the network Alliance known as the 'Arche de Noé' (Noah's Ark), attached to the British secret services, nor to the network Jade-Fitzroy, under first British and then Free French control.

Personalities with strong anti-Communist or Action Française backgrounds were prominent in both Alliance and Jade-Fitzroy, but their individualistic passion for subterranean action took them into Allied service despite the pull of Pétain. The significance of their right-wing connections meant that recruiting was initially among like-minded personnel in the Armistice Army or in Pétain's Légion Française. The 31-year-old Marie-Madeleine Méric (later Fourcade) took over Alliance after the arrest of its originator, Georges Loustaunau-Lacau, with whom she had worked in anti-Communist activity before the war, and it was she who furnished animal code-names for its agents, earning the network its nickname of 'Noah's Ark' and a considerable reputation within German counter-intelligence. The only woman to head a resistance network, she numbered Alliance at some 3,000 agents, who created intelligence and escape routes across the frontiers, with radio and Lysander aircraft connections to London. The human losses of all the networks to betrayal and German counter-measures were huge, underlining the danger of radio transmissions which could be quickly traced, and the shadowy world of double agents.

The sympathy for the British in the Nord and Pas-de-Calais made a fertile recruiting ground for the escape network of 'Pat O'Leary', code-name for the Belgian army doctor Albert Guérisse, working for the British secret services. Between the summer of 1941 and the end of 1943 his rapidly expanding network secured the escape of Allied servicemen across the various zones and into Spain. A rare photograph in the local history of the region shows three British airmen with the family of Maître Havet who hid

them at Lumbres in the Pas-de-Calais before their successful escape back to Britain.[9] The notary and his daughter both died in deportation. Over the whole period of Occupation some 3,000 Allied airmen were helped to escape through numerous networks, each with their rural and urban safehouses and frontier guides.

Yet a further parallel development brought men and women agents into France from the British SOE (Special Operations Executive), created specifically to carry out sabotage and to organize and train military units in German-occupied Europe. From 1941 in a steadily expanding number, they brought technical expertise, leadership, money and radio contact. One section (RF) worked closely with de Gaulle and Passy, and the other section (F) recruited and operated independently, to de Gaulle's permanent vexation. F section, under Major Maurice Buckmaster, set up over 100 circuits in France in which the hand-picked agents, smuggled or dropped into the country, recruited and trained substantial groups of resisters for military action determined by local circumstances and overall Allied strategy. About a quarter of the main body of agents were killed or died in deportation. They were adamant that they were not spies but special forces, a regular form of irregular warfare. Their creative role in inspiring effective resistance and securing drops of arms and ammunition is legendary.

4. Politics and ideology of resistance

Irregular, deviant, marginal, alternative: many of the early resisters were well aware of their maverick image. By contrast, their presumption was that they embodied the only defensible form of patriotism. Beneath this claim there were personal, professional, local and political reasons why people became angry or bold enough to try to do something, and these different reasons gave resistance its permanent individuality. It remained widely transgressive. What occurred in 1941–2 was the strengthening of collective voices and organized structures, and with them came an insistent presence of political and ideological issues. At one level these issues were familiar: at another and more significant level they were new and challenging. The familiar issue was the question of how resistance related to party politics and vice versa. The new issues were the internal relationship of resistance movements to one another, the politics of leadership and loyalty, aims, tactics and strategy. From this new set of issues, heavily conditioned by the pressures of the immediate situation rather than political doctrine or precedent, a form of ideology or *esprit* emerged.

Communists

One of the alter egos of pre-war politics was a suspicion of all political parties. Whether or not this amounted to willing their abolition, or merely blaming them for anything negative in life, the defeat of June 1940 precipitated their downfall in an unprecedented crisis, interpreted by Pétain and Laval as the bankruptcy of parliamentary democracy. No political party, as a coherent voice, presented itself as the party of resistance to the German presence or the dissolution of parliament. The majority of the eighty parliamentarians who voted against full powers for Pétain were Socialists, but the party as a whole was deeply split. It was partly reconstituted during 1941 by Daniel Mayer and J.-Pierre Bloch, with Léon Blum's support from his Vichy prison. It took its new shape as the Comité d'Action Socialiste (CAS), dedicated to resistance action, but not claiming itself as a separate resistance organization. The Radical Party and all parties of the right disappeared from view.

On the Communist left, acceptance of the Nazi-Soviet pact had demolished the anti-fascist politics of the PCF: the defeat and German Occupation did not restore them. Twelve months later, the German invasion of the Soviet Union did. The PCF, which had not disintegrated in its enforced illegality, now presented itself as the party personifying anti-German resistance, which some individual Communists had launched locally, against party directives, but which had been initiated almost in its entirety by non-Communist groups and individuals, both inside and outside France. Although early resisters instantly arraigned the PCF for its hypocrisy, they knew that an organized Communist resistance would be effective, much as they continued to suspect its motives. In the chronology of resistance, June 1941 was neither early nor late. Many individuals of all political persuasions, or none, took the first steps of resistance in their localities well after that date. Where the PCF had been early was in its rejection of the politics of Pétain and Vichy. It was this political record, and its methods of survival as a clandestine party, which guaranteed that its collective shift into anti-German action would make it a major player in the new realm of resistance politics and ideology.

It was quickly apparent what this might involve. In its new-found enthusiasm for action, the PCF justified the killing of German personnel, claiming that their individual presence as occupiers was a continuous act of war. This definition of the active enemy, which sanctioned the killing of a junior naval officer at Barbès métro station on 21 August 1941 by the Communist metalworker Pierre Georges (known later as Colonel Fabien), and

subsequent killings in Lille, Nantes and Bordeaux, reopened the German dossier of 1914 against civilians accused of *franc-tireur* sniping and assassination on the invasion of Belgium and northern France. In 1941 the German response was in the open. A decree emanating from Hitler through General Keitel on 16 September stated that in general 'the death of a German soldier should be met by the execution of 50 to 100 Communists as seems fit'.[10] Pierre Pucheu, the Vichy Minister of the Interior, and Joseph Barthélemy, Minister of Justice, provided a retrospective law making imprisoned Communists, many arrested a year earlier, liable to the death penalty, and set up a special judicial section to choose the hostages to be shot by the Germans.

The ninety-eight hostages shot on 22–23 October, twenty-seven of them at Châteaubriant in the Loire-Atlantique, provoked a broadcast from General de Gaulle on the 'savagery' of the Germans and on the hostages as martyrs, but with the argument that although it was 'both right and natural that Germans should be killed by Frenchmen ... my orders to those in occupied territory are, for the moment, not to kill Germans, for the good reason that it is too easy for the enemy to retaliate by murdering our combatant men and women, now temporarily disarmed'.[11]

It was the beginning of the debate within all resistance circles about the limits of direct action both as a moral and tactical issue, but also as a political question of leadership and command. The killing at Nantes was badly received by the local community, and the PCF was criticized for having its own agenda which would alienate people from resistance. By the end of the year it was forced to accept that individual assassinations were counter-productive. At the same time the German reprisals on hostages who had no part in the attacks began to radicalize resistance activity within the party and well outside it. On 15 December 1941, a further ninety-two hostages were shot in Paris, including Gabriel Péri, the well-known Communist deputy for Seine-et-Oise, writer and expert on foreign affairs, who was arrested by French police in May and subsequently turned over to the Germans. His name became synonymous with martyrdom, with powerful evocative effect, captured poignantly in Paul Éluard's poem listing words which carried a life-force, to which he added the name of Péri.[12]

In February 1942 the PCF united their activist groups into a single paramilitary organization, the Francs-Tireurs et Partisans Français (FTPF), making the language of irregular combat the keyword. Before that there had been youth 'battalions' under Albert Ouzoulias in the Paris region which had started sabotage operations. The FTP (as they were normally known), led by Charles Tillon, recruited volunteers in all the main towns,

creating particularly effective urban guerrilla squads of anti-fascist immigrant workers whose rights had been defended by the party in its pre-war organization, the Main-d'œuvre Immigrée (MOI). By mid-1942 a number of leaders from the non-Communist movements had begun an escalating series of visits and reports to and from London. It was apparent that Free French recognition of the width of resistance within France was essential, and that the politics of resistance had to come to terms with the high profile of Communist activity, not least in the success of the outstretched hand of its Front National (FN) to talented non-Communist leaders. De Gaulle had his own good reasons for bringing London and all of resistance in France more closely together.

Free French (2)

The different challenges to de Gaulle's presumptive assertions of authority were, on the face of it, well capable either of replacing him with another leader or of forcing him to accept a far more subaltern role in all issues affecting France. That he survived all British, American and internal Free French attempts to displace him registers his astonishing political ability, which was both the obstinate passion of a personal vision of France and just enough flexibility to ensure his retention of control. From each bruising encounter he emerged apparently weakened but effectively strengthened.

From within the Free French there was the challenge of Admiral Muselier, the first Naval Commander of the Free French fleet. Muselier, senior in rank to de Gaulle, initially accepted his leadership. With a father from Lorraine, he used the cross of Lorraine to distinguish his ships from those of Vichy, an emblem subsequently adopted by de Gaulle for the whole movement. In December 1941 Muselier led the Free French occupation of the islands of Saint-Pierre and Miquelon, France's oldest and smallest colony off the Canada coast, provoking fierce American displeasure, but he failed in at least two bids to unseat de Gaulle, despite some British connivance.

The British challenge was never made into a showdown, and over the four years there was more tacit support from Churchill at moments of crisis than outright hostility. But British policy in most matters affecting the French empire ignored de Gaulle's sensibilities. He railed against the decision to send Vichy forces in Syria back to France after the country had been secured by British, Australian and Free French action in July 1941, and insisted that they be allowed to opt for the Free French movement. Some 6,000 did, but many more returned to France. In May 1942 the British took the naval base of Diego-Suarez in Madagascar to forestall a

possible attack by the Japanese. The Free French were not consulted and de Gaulle strenuously protested at the British negotiations with Vichy personnel in the island. Later in the year the whole island, taken by the British, was handed over to the authority of the Free French.

Early in June 1942 a few thousand Free French forces under General Koenig successfully defended the fort of Bir Hakeim in the Libyan desert against a German and Italian attack. The victory was erected into the symbol of the Free French at war, with a new title for the movement: la France Combattante (the Fighting French). But in November 1942 de Gaulle was again not consulted, nor allotted a role, in the pivotal American-British landings in North Africa.

The indignity to de Gaulle was all the greater because during 1942 he had responded positively to the rich mosaic of resistance inside France. Pierre Brossolette, the Socialist radio-journalist of the late 1930s, a severe opponent of Munich, joined the Musée de l'Homme journal *Résistance* as editor, just as the group was decimated by German arrests. He was put in touch with Rémy's CND, and with Libération-Nord, made a fact-finding trip into the Vichy zone, reporting in April 1942 to the Free French in London. De Gaulle and Passy instantly estimated Brossolette's knowledge of internal resistance as vital to the Free French movement. He was not the only envoy from France. Jean Moulin, Prefect in Chartres in June 1940, had not abandoned his post to join the *exode*. Beaten up by the German army for recalcitrance, he had tried to cut his throat, but survived and returned to his job as the Germans settled in the town. Vichy sacked him and he went back to his roots in the south, making contact with the resistance movements in the Vichy zone. He took his inside information across the Pyrenees, reaching London in October 1941 as the most notable civilian figure to have rallied to de Gaulle. He was parachuted back into France in January 1942 with money and technical material for the three main movements in the south, Combat, Libération (Sud) and Franc-Tireur.

Barely a month after Moulin's departure from London, the Socialist Christian Pineau arrived at de Gaulle's headquarters with news of Libération-Nord, and took back from France the first open acceptance by de Gaulle of the political aims of resistance, secured by Pineau despite de Gaulle's dominantly military outlook. Pineau had to accept that de Gaulle condemned the abdication by the Third Republic in 1940 in the same sentence as the capitulation of Vichy, but in the final draft of the declaration there was also a forthright dedication by de Gaulle to restoring internal freedoms in France. He promised the election of a National Assembly 'by all men and all women', his first and binding commitment to female suf-

frage, and the creation of social security. The declaration was published in the clandestine press at the end of June 1942 and contained the rhetorical words: 'Even as the French people are uniting for victory they are gathering together for a revolution.'[13]

By using the left-wing term in this context de Gaulle not only marked himself as the protagonist of a revolution quite unlike that of Vichy, but also demonstrated the insubstantial nature of the rumours that he had a dictatorship of his own in mind. At the same time the term was clearly open to varied interpretation. It was widely noted that he had spoken for 'the French people', and the declaration did much to prosper Jean Moulin's negotiations with the three movements in the south. Moulin's personal charisma, the money he dispensed and the practicality of his mission allowed the three movements to unite in their diversity in January 1943 as the Mouvements Unis de la Résistance (MUR). It was the first, partial, unification of resistance within France, recognizing de Gaulle as leader, and seeking to turn the loose groupings of its Armée Secrète (AS) into an effective shadow army. The AS was increasingly described as a 'Gaullist' force within France

Moulin moved through France as 'Rex' and then 'Max', undetected until June 1943, in a myriad of train journeys, secret rendezvous in parks and labyrinthine alleys, a scarf hiding the scar on his neck, his brown felt hat pulled down over his eyes, and to his contacts the very epitome of the underground agent, elusive, authoritative and decisive. As de Gaulle's personal envoy his mission was to create the unity necessary for a genuinely national resistance. He accurately measured the significance of Communist activism which brought volunteers with no links to the PCF into both the Front National and the FTP across both zones. He recognized it as the pull of action and tight organization. Moulin recommended to de Gaulle that the Communists should be integrated into both political and military structures of resistance. In January 1943 Fernand Grenier, a representative of the PCF and the FTP, who had won back Saint-Denis in 1937 from Jacques Doriot, arrived in London. He had earlier escaped from Châteaubriant and had met Rémy who acted as intermediary between Gaullist resistance and the party. He arrived with the party's mandate to create effective relationships with the Free French.

The explicit snub to de Gaulle by the American and British military in North Africa faced him with an inferior role to the more senior General Giraud, whose dramatic escape in April 1942 from the fortress of Königstein in Saxony and return to Vichy was followed by his move to Algeria, after a murky American assurance that he would be given

command of the French forces in North Africa, numbering over 230,000. By comparison, the 50,000 of the Fighting French seemed insignificant to the Americans. Darlan's assassination cleared the way for the promise to Giraud to be honoured. It was President Roosevelt's determined attempt to marginalize the independent and rebarbative leader of the Free French. De Gaulle needed every piece of evidence that he, and not Giraud, could speak for France. To promote his national claims, he decided that resistance representatives of all the political parties connected to resistance, including the Communists, should be recognized in the projected Conseil National de la Résistance (CNR). The CNR, with oversight of resistance both north and south, was the climax of Jean Moulin's mission. He was caught at Caluire in the suburbs of Lyon on 21 June 1943 and died on the way to deportation after atrocious torture at the hands of Klaus Barbie, the Gestapo chief in Lyon.

The CNR was launched, with de Gaulle named as national leader of the Resistance, and after a period of uneasy shared leadership with Giraud in North Africa he defied the Americans. He comprehensively outmanoeuvred Giraud, who had none of his political agility. On 30 May 1943 de Gaulle moved his headquarters to Algiers, technically an integral part of France, forming a Comité Français de Libération Nationale (CFLN) to administer the liberated territories and co-ordinate military action. It was only one step away from facing Vichy with a rival government, no longer 'in exile'. Party politicians from non-Communist parties were brought into the CFLN in November, and a provisional Consultative Assembly created. In April 1944 two Communists were integrated into the CFLN and on 3 June the Committee assumed the functions and legitimacy of a Provisional Government of the French Republic. In retrospect it seemed an evolutionary process. In reality it was one of fractures and disputes. A dialectic between old parties and new resistance was just one of the dynamics.

Resistance 'esprit'

Because it was a matter of choice and not conscription, resistance had to create its national image from the actions and ideas of a minority. Because it was not the product of a *union sacrée* of party politics it had to formulate its own galvanizing ethic. Pierre Brossolette, writing in the Socialist paper *Le Populaire* at the end of 1938, had opposed the 'spirit of Munich' with the 'spirit of resistance'. It was a state of mind (*un état d'esprit*) that he believed was essential to rescue France from 'the most sensational capitulation in our history'.[14] He carried this belief into his dissident activity in

1940. Different activating and ethical words attached to resistance became common coinage in the clandestine press, with a resonance which not only recalled Péguy's celebration of *mystique* over *politique* but captured the sense that there was a tangible resistance ideology.

The ideas of resistance which went towards the making of an ideology were partly a reworking of republican and revolutionary concepts of liberty and justice, complete with a new edition in 1942 of *Le Père Duchesne*, Hébert's paper of 1793, which had been re-created in the revolution of 1848 and the Paris Commune of 1871. They were partly a rebirth of the patriotic 'gun-behind-the-door' mentality of barricades and revolt, with the re-emergence of Communard language in the paper *L'Insurgé* and the recurrence of words of voluntary and independent combat: *franc-tireur* and *groupe franc*.

In a more general sense they developed as a form of left-wing humanism, and appeared throughout the clandestine press in imagistic language which pictured resistance as a defence of human values threatened with extinction by the unacceptable forces of darkness. Yet as a symptom of the way in which resistance was built on disobedience, dissent, refusal and trans-gression, even the metaphor of darkness was given its own inversionary meaning. The acceptance of working underground, at night, in secrecy, in the shadows, challenged the imposed darkness of the Nazi Occupation.

The concept of midnight was given this classic ambiguity in the very title chosen by Pierre de Lescure and Jean Bruller (known as Vercors) for their clandestine literary venture: the Éditions de Minuit. Created early in 1942, the small, deluxe volumes of essays, novels and poetry were the symbol of everything that resistance set out to achieve. They were explicitly not an avant-garde venture attempting to mark an esoteric style or form. In one of the novels, *Les Amants d'Avignon* by Elsa Triolet, written in February 1943, the belief of the Éditions in resistance as an *esprit* that could be sensed in others as well as communicated, was expressed in the recognition by the Parisian heroine Juliette that she felt at home in a peasant farm in the mountains. She 'would never have believed that she could find a language in common with peasants'. But she also discovered that not all peasants were like this particular family.[15] A common bond across cultural and social frontiers, that linked some but not all, tied together the minority ideology of the Resistance.

Many of the properties of this shared mentality were set out by the religious authors of the *Cahiers du témoignage chrétien* in their first clan-destine number of November 1941. It comprised an essay by the Jesuit dissident, père Fessard, and was published by his co-Jesuit père Chaillet,

who ran a Catholic and Protestant circle in Lyon which provided active help for victimized Jews. In the essay addressed to France, they warned that 'its soul was in danger' from the spread of rancorous antisemitism, and the compromises with Nazism accepted by Pétain and Vichy. This was no sectarian definition of the soul, but one which corresponded to the broad humanitarian conscience which motivated their actions of resistance. The brutal deportations of the summer of 1942 forced other religious voices into the open. The Protestant Pastor Boegner had protested to Laval in person. He was joined by public protests from a small but significant minority of the Catholic hierarchy. The Archbishop of Toulouse, Mgr Saliège, made respect for humanity incumbent on all people in his letter to be read out at the end of August in the churches of his diocese: 'Jews are men and women. Foreigners are men and women. You cannot treat these men, these women, these mothers and fathers in any way you like. They are part of the human race . . .'[16] The words of Saliège and the graphic protest of Mgr Théas, Bishop of Montauban, were not conceived as truisms but as contestation, to confront the perpetrators and shock an indifferent majority.

Insistent on choice and commitment, there was nevertheless an aspect of resistance ideology which many resistance writers derived from necessity and logic. Both the philosopher Jean Cavaillès at the origin of Libération-Sud, and the moralist writer Albert Camus who wrote for *Combat*, argued that the unacceptable could not logically be accepted, whether seen by Cavaillès as the Nazi persecution of rational philosophy, or by Camus, in his *Lettres à un ami allemand* of 1943, as the stark inhumanity of Nazism. To declare resistance to be logically necessary did not demean choice. It gave it an added intellectual rigour, but it also located the *esprit* and ideology of resistance in the experience of necessity, the need to act forced not only by verbal logic but by the logic of situation and events. In 1943–4 the response to necessity pervaded the developments in resistance.

5. Home and fighting fronts
Culture of the outlaw?

The vivid distinctions between home and fighting fronts, which shaped perceptions and behaviour in the First World War, disappeared under the Occupation. There was either no fighting front at all or it was everywhere, wherever the enemy was located. The home front was reimagined by Pétain as families at home working for the prisoners of war: it was progressively

recuperated as a vital part of the infrastructure of resistance. In the spring of 1943 the home took off in significance. The German occupation of the southern zone in the previous November had spread the location of the occupiers into towns previously shielded from the Wehrmacht and the Gestapo. The STO law of 16 February 1943, enforcing compulsory labour in Germany, lit a civil fuse which burnt into all corners of society. It was not that resistance exploded into action overnight, or that it became a majority phenomenon, but rather that levels of civil disobedience rose dramatically.

The necessity to make a choice affecting young lives was starkly universal. Parish priests, schoolteachers, doctors and company managers were expected to advise young workers on whether or not to submit to the STO. In the early months the focus of the law was so precise that effective alternatives to compliance were hard to find, but prefects of rural *départements* protested against the numbers demanded and urban areas reported administrative chaos. In Marseille only 486 out of 866 convoked for 1 April presented themselves. Of these, 250 were exempted, many through medical collusion. Violent scenes of parental protest marked the train departures in many towns. Busloads of rural workers designated for the STO, guarded by a single gendarme, emptied progressively at every corner of the road. The word for those who refused, *réfractaire*, entered a discourse of revolt which openly confronted the Vichy notables and clerics who preached compliance as a patriotic and selfless duty. By the summer a major fault-line in society had opened up. Escaping as a *réfractaire* was covered by a multitude of ruses. There was a shortfall of 3,000 reported in the Breton Côtes-du-Nord alone, and rumours of hundreds roaming the Breton countryside were echoed across the south. Farms hid and absorbed individual *réfractaires* as welcome labour in the harvest months. Much of the rural gendarmerie was locally complicit.

The STO was a forcing-house of resistance. The movements in the south, recently unified into the MUR, were taken by surprise. Young men disappeared of their own accord into the *maquis*, the term, commonly used in Corsica, for dense and stunted mountain undergrowth. Within little more than a month, 'taking to the *maquis*' was a common phrase, followed quickly by a shift in meaning to indicate not just the terrain but bands of men living in the wild, either merely hiding, or forming units of resistance (maquis). Fired by news of *réfractaires* in the mountains of the Haute-Savoie, Maurice Schumann paid homage on 18 March 1943 to the 'Légion des Montagnes' in his BBC programme, implying a Savoyard rising. He was instantly rebuked in London, and his intimations of revolt were indeed

premature, but he had accurately caught the sense that a new phase of resistance had opened.

The shelter of Jews had already brought some rural areas into the orbit of resistance. The Protestant village of Le Chambon-sur-Lignon in the Haute-Loire and the surrounding Vivarais plateau adapted an existing culture of hospitality to create shelter and safety for at least 600 Jewish children, providing a battery of false papers and escape networks to Switzerland organized by the local pastors and the Protestant relief organization CIMADE in which Madeleine Barot, already known for her commitment to the victims of Vichy internment at Gurs, exemplified humanitarian resistance. In the larger area of the Protestant Cévennes further to the south some 800 Jews were concealed with equal readiness. It was later estimated that the number of Jews hidden from persecution in the two areas amounted to 2.5 per cent of the local population, and that if this had been the response of French society as a whole, the number hidden could have reached a million, over three times the total population of Jews in France.[17]

In a scattering of places a few handfuls of refugees and resisters had set up camps of refuge in the winter of 1942-3, dependent on the locality for food and protection. Due to the STO the number of makeshift camps grew haphazardly but steadily in 1943. The Vichy hunt for Jews and all those on the run, labelled by Vichy as outlaws (*hors-la-loi*), necessitated further decisions by peasant families not just about individuals but about embryo maquis groups which formed in their vicinity. The subterfuge of women who answered the door to the police had already protected resisters in the towns: the need for deception spread to the countryside. Police reports repeatedly end with the conclusion, 'Enquiries at the house led nowhere.' The 'woman at the doorway', outwitting even the most determined searches, was an unsung resistance role, as vital to the creation of active maquis groups as to the survival of those who merely wanted to hide.

The percentage of *réfractaires* who opted for active resistance and set up or joined a maquis varied across the south from as little as 3 per cent to over 50 per cent. What was important was the development of a culture of the outlaw in specific localities, urban and rural. It was strikingly present in some areas, such as the Cévennes in the south and the Côtes-du-Nord in Brittany: it was strikingly absent in many other areas, such as the Haute-Saône, where the maquis were accused of acts of banditry, and outsiders on the run were not welcomed by the local population. Nowhere was there a lack of local concern over the impact of armed bands in the vicinity: people divided sharply over the spiral of violence and the reality of reprisals that ensued. Both acceptance and fears of armed resistance (*la lutte armée*)

make the history of the maquis not just one of men in the woods, but of the communities that supported or rejected them.

Even as the early resistance movements in the towns were edging towards forms of unity in early 1943, the fresh initiatives in the countryside, as dispersed as those of 1940–41, needed urgent organization. Both the Gaullist Armée Secrète (AS) and the Communist FTP created their own maquis units, but individual maquis leaders, such as Jean-Jacques Chapou in the Lot and Henri Romans-Petit in the Ain, kept a tight hold on survival tactics and local strategic decisions. They decided where to blow up railways or ambush German convoys, and whether or not to stage raids on police stations and prisons, and on food, tobacco and clothing depots. Very few leaders of the FTP maquis were army officers: most had a civilian background. There were more in the AS, but guerrilla activity did not come easily to conventional military personnel. Most units remained small and mobile. From being the hunted, the resistance outlaws became the hunters, tracking down collaborators and threatening Vichy authority. There were parts of the Massif Central, the Savoyard Alps, the interior of Brittany, the forests of the Corrèze and the Dordogne, the Montagne Noire on the edge of the Tarn, the plateaux of the Isère and the Drôme, and the hills of the Cévennes, where Vichy administrators were unable to go, and where mayors began resigning, a potent sign of the growing climate (*mouvance*) of resistance.

The rising of resisters in Corsica on 9 September 1943, and the liberation of the island in early October raised the profile of resistance everywhere. The Corsican armed bands were mostly attached to the Front National with its Communist core. The occupying force of 80,000 Italians had been pulled out after Italy's armistice with the Allies earlier in September, not before a few skirmishes with a much smaller German force. Both de Gaulle and Giraud had representatives in the island and conflicting ideas on the timing of a landing. Giraud had his way, endorsed the uprising, and took overall command of a force from North Africa which harried the German troops into a corner of the island. The Germans withdrew from Bastia on 4 October, most of the island already liberated by maquis action.

The liberation of Corsica provided two distinct models for the AS and FTP maquis. The PCF on the mainland celebrated the Corsican rising and issued detailed plans for a national insurrection based on the barricade tradition of urban revolt to which the FTP maquis would bring support. Their maquis groups mostly kept close to the towns, in contact with urban FTP units. The Gaullist AS maquis, on the other hand, stayed further out in the hills and focused mainly on actions which would build up a sizeable

military force to co-ordinate with landings by conventional forces. *Jour-J* (D-Day) was a watchword from October 1943 onwards. An Allied landing (*débarquement*) was expected at any moment, to the point where its failure to happen throughout another long winter and the spring of 1944 became a tired joke.

War re-engaged

For months on end in 1942–3 the BBC and aerial tracts warned the French population that the Allies needed to bomb railways, aerodromes, ports and factories in France. With every bombing raid the Vichy and German radio accused the British and Americans of inhumanity and crimes of war. Few people heard the German protests with anything less than cynicism, but direct experience of the bombing was different. On 3 March 1942 a two-hour raid on the Renault factories at Boulogne-Billancourt to the south-west of Paris killed 620 and wounded 1,500. On 15 January 1943 the Breton port of Lorient received its first huge bombing raid, causing sixty-five deaths. The population of 40,000 were told by the BBC to evacuate the town. Seven more raids followed in close succession, making the town uninhabitable. All the surrounding villages were hit. Saint-Nazaire was equally destroyed, creating a further 40,000 refugees. In March bombs killed 274 in Rennes, the Breton inland capital, and a further 195 were killed in May. In the Lille area of the Nord and Pas-de Calais 554 civilians were killed in the little town of Portel near Boulogne in September. These are only a very few of the raids in 1942–3 and a fraction of the deaths, which reached over 50,000 by the Liberation. The Allied landings of 1944 in Normandy and Provence were preceded by the most intensive destruction: in Marseille alone on 27 May 1944 a raid was estimated to have killed 1,900 people and wounded a further 1,300.

Maurice Schumann, in his evening broadcast from London after the Renault raid of 1942, found words of explanation and tragedy, but also words of helplessness which echoed through France: '. . . and now we are reduced to the most atrocious fate: to be killed without killing back, to be killed by friends without being able to kill our enemies'.[18] The ambiguity expressed by the affected population could not be disguised. People tried to explain to themselves and others the frequent errors of targeting and apparently wanton destruction, and it was widely noted in prefectoral reports that anger did not substantially reduce support for the Allies. The Resistance in all its forms tried to harness the anger and turn helplessness into action. Gratitude to Allied aircrew making dangerous night flights into

the depths of France to drop arms and agents was repeatedly registered in resistance discourse. At the same time every group of resistance, including the British SOE agents, recommended to London the merits of sabotage over bombing.

The opportunity supplied by STO to recruit saboteurs and train combatants for the armed struggle was seized by the Resistance, however marginal the first results were in the perspective of the whole war. By the end of the year Vichy had advertised an amnesty for *réfractaires* if they gave themselves up, and many did so. The seasons had their own chronology, the summer months of 1943 producing a crop of camps in the hills and forests when living in the wild was comparatively easy, the winter of 1943–4 a retrenchment and a drift back into the towns and villages in the teeth of the bitter weather. In fact the winter months were the making of the maquis. Villagers in certain areas adopted the maquisards as their own: the structures of shelter, food, liaison and medical assistance were strengthened.

Specific regional traditions of independence, of revolt against central authority, came into play. These were mostly but not all within the republican canon of historical memory. One of the exceptions was the high valley south of Thônes in the Haute-Savoie where the cultural memory was of rebelliousness against Jacobin centralism at the time of the Revolution. An AS school for maquis leaders was created here in the village of Manigod at the height of winter. At the end of January 1944, with the snow still deep, an ascent of 465 maquisards on to the plateau of Glières was mounted from all the local valleys, with active support from the villages. An Allied parachute drop of arms and ammunition on to the plateau made them exactly the Alpine force prematurely celebrated on the BBC a year earlier. But there was no Allied or resistance strategy for what should happen next. Encircled and bombarded from the air, the Glières maquisards were defeated in late March in pitched battles with German troops, the Milice and other Vichy mobile police, which made up a vastly superior force.

Glières, nevertheless, sent out a resounding message that war had been actively re-engaged by the Resistance on the French mainland. The message on tactics was more ambivalent. Most FTP units and many AS groups stood by their belief in mobile guerrilla activity, avoiding pitched encounters. They intensified their actions. Volunteers substantially increased. In contrast, some resistance leaders argued that large concentrations of maquisards were possible, and they set out to secure a commitment from the Allies to provide reinforcements as well as heavier weapons of artillery. In expectation of such commitment resistance groups in the Auvergne planned for a mass mobilization in the Massif Central. It was launched in late May,

and when *Jour-J* (D-Day) was finally announced on 6 June 1944, a force of several thousand was already in place on Mont Mouchet in the Margeride mountains south of Clermont-Ferrand. There were rumours that de Gaulle would be parachuted in and that Allied troops would hop from one mountain maquis to another in a 'grasshopper' military movement behind German lines.

Further east, the maquis leaders on the vast pre-Alpine Vercors plateau, stretching across the inveterate republican areas of the Isère and the Drôme, believed that a 'Mountain Plan' of reinforcements had been agreed in London. By mid-July over 4,000 maquisards were encamped on the plateau in a self-styled Republic of the Vercors, a title taken to symbolize the liberation of at least a part of French territory. In the Margeride equivalent signs proclaimed that 'Free France begins here' ('Ici commence la France libre').

The Allied landings in Normandy on 6 June activated, energized and justified the armed resistance, which had gradually been organized since February as the Forces Françaises de l'Intérieur (FFI) under the overall command of General Koenig. Co-ordinated plans to immobilize railways, telephone lines and electrical power in all regions adjacent to Normandy were put into effect, while the mobilizations at Mont Mouchet and in the Vercors independently tied down heavy numbers of German forces, though in both cases the operations were defeated by German counter-attacks. In the south-west a maquis concentration in the Montagne Noire on the edge of the Tarn also kept German troops engaged, while the more mobile autonomous units harassed German troops moving towards Normandy, and proliferated raids on Vichy depots, material and personnel. As Vichy crumbled internally, the German counter-offensive, aided by the Vichy Milice, was based on the definition of all active resistance as terrorism. Savage reprisals on local villagers followed any ambush action. The scale of the reprisals had been horrifically announced on 1 April at Ascq in the suburbs of Lille, after resisters had set off an explosion which stopped a German train. It was not derailed and there were no German casualties, but elements of the SS Division Hitlerjugend seized all men between fifteen and fifty close to the station at Ascq and massacred eighty-six, including twenty-three railway workers.

On 9 June at Tulle in the Corrèze after FTP attacks, the SS Division Das Reich seized men at random and publicly hanged ninety-nine from the town's balconies. On the following day the Division's Der Führer regiment moved into the *commune* of Oradour-sur-Glane to the north-west of Limoges, wrongly believing it to contain a depot of maquis arms. They

rounded up the inhabitants and massacred 642 of them, setting the bodies and the whole village on fire. Atrocities decimated the areas of confrontation in the Margeride and the Vercors, where no Allied reinforcements arrived as had been hoped or expected. The Margeride maquis dispersed, but suffered heavy losses at la Truyère, preceded by German reprisals on the village of Ruynes on the edge of Mont Mouchet, where twenty-six villagers were shot. At Vassieux in the Vercors, gliders were seen approaching on 21 July and were momentarily thought to be the Allies, before the German markings were seen. Desperate fighting followed on the plateau. Over 600 maquisards died in action and more than 200 villagers were killed in reprisals. The wounded were discovered in the Grotte de la Luire and killed. Those looking after them were shot or deported.

The armed re-engagements had elements of civil war, with the Milice and the maquis giving no quarter to each other. In letters opened by Vichy, it is evident that maquis raids on agricultural goods, and individual murders of Vichy sympathizers, clearly caused hostility in public opinion. But the parallel with divided Spain in the 1930s was never a close one, the increasingly large minority of people involved in the different layers of resistance isolating the Milice and collaborators as a very small fraction of the population. In what was later referred to as a local or 'wild' purge of collaborators (*épuration sauvage*) it was mainly people accused of belonging to the Milice or suspected of betrayals and other pro-German activity who were sought out and killed.

Retribution and the settling of local scores was rife in these 'civil war killings', and the broadcasts of Henriot, assassinated by resisters on 28 June, had reflected, as well as provoked, fears of a full-scale civil war. But the fears were mostly of German reprisals, which made people eager to escape conflict in their vicinity. Anger against resistance was located in areas where actions heedlessly endangered the local population, or were perpetrated with little strategic rationale, and memories of the armed struggle continued to be polarized after the war. Conversely, the German atrocities hardened the horror and the hatred of the occupiers and spurred tens of thousands of new recruits into the last stages of uprising and conflict. The many who could still be called *attentistes* were not so much waiting for liberation as willing it forward.

6. Liberation: end and beginning

Arms and the state

The Allied landings in Normandy on 6 June 1944 and the fierce and protracted battles in the region brought a devastating, but this time a liberating, war back to the north of France. Over two months later, on 15 August, American and French landings in Provence led to liberations through the Rhône valley and in the Alps. General Eisenhower recognized the enthusiasm of the population in each town liberated by the Americans and British and acknowledged the contribution of the Resistance by stating that it was worth fifteen divisions. Such an estimate mainly reflected the resistance actions in and around the Normandy region, to which resisters added the achievement of liberating the Savoyard Alps in advance of the Allied armies, and most of the south-west and centre of France as the Germans retreated. The Eisenhower calculation was much quoted and debated after the war, but there have been few historians who settle for measuring resistance purely in military terms: most stress its moral, political and cultural impact over four years, far from easily quantified. The process of liberation did, however, focus on the first open appearances of resistance groups and leaders in military formation, after the defeat or evacuation of German troops, and on 22 September the 152nd anniversary of the battle of Valmy in 1792 was seized by the FFI and much of the resistance press as the moment to recognize the comparable achievements of a patriotic army in 1944.

In tense urban action or in relaxed celebration, the population saw resistance groups emerge everywhere at the liberation of the immediate locality. The focus on General de Gaulle arriving in Normandy was of the same nature as the interest in FFI units arriving in liberated towns in the south, a curiosity to see who these figures of resistance were, and spontaneous festivity at their appearance. De Gaulle and a small entourage landed on 14 June, a week after the Allied forces on D-Day, and celebrated liberation in Bayeux, where the depth of the popular welcome and de Gaulle's acceptance by the notables of the town finalized his claim to represent liberated France. In America a month later, de Gaulle was finally greeted with respect. Roosevelt scaled down his opposition, and the Allies conceded legitimacy to the Provisional Government on 12 July 1944, well before the liberation of Paris. The official Allied proclamation was made on 23 October. Plans for an Allied occupation of France were put to one side, though not immediately rescinded.

The differences from place to place in the nature and timing of liberation

added yet another huge diversity of experience to those of the defeat and the Occupation. The liberation of Paris was as complex and specific as anywhere. Hub of collaborationists, scene of the mass round-ups of Jews, centre of the Gestapo, its suburban industries bombed by the Allies, its poorer population barely subsisting in the long winters, its capital status in abeyance and much of its intelligentsia dispersed in the Vichy zone, its night-time rhythms geared to catching the last train (*le dernier métro*) before the curfew, Paris, full of German officers eating well, was equally the Paris of active resistance, not least that of Communist immigrant workers in the FTP–MOI. Led by the Armenian Missak Manouchian, they staged over forty armed attacks on German material and personnel in late 1943 before being betrayed, tortured and shot. The Germans condemned them as foreign and Jewish killers on a dramatic red poster (*l'affiche rouge*), which failed to undermine public sympathy. Paris as the international cradle of revolution re-emerged into consciousness.

The city's liberation was planned by the CNR and the strong groups of FTP brought into the unified FFI under the Communist leader Colonel Rol-Tanguy, but improvisation was its essence in mid-August 1944. Strikes, popular insurrection and barricades, the crucial revolt of the Paris police, and the street fighting of the FFI, who numbered 35,000, preceded the arrival of the Second Armoured Division under General Philippe Leclerc, designated several months earlier by de Gaulle as the French force to liberate Paris. Only at the last moment did he secure the agreement of the Allied command for Leclerc to make the crucial detour from the front. Leclerc's and Rol-Tanguy's forces combined in actions which consolidated the city's insurrection. The German military governor, General von Chol- titz, retaliated with strength to cover retreat, but disobeyed Hitler's com- mand to destroy the city. He signed the surrender on 25 August 1944, the symbolic moment of the Liberation, made epic and contentious by de Gaulle's heralded arrival and his installation at the Ministry of War. He put this government destination first, before agreeing to meet the CNR at the Hôtel de Ville, headquarters of the Parisian resistance. His speech there heightened the emotion of the day's events. He celebrated Paris 'liberated by her own people . . . and the armies of France . . .'. He did not proclaim the Republic, which he stated had never ceased to exist. Over 900 FFI and nearly 600 civilians were killed in the liberation of Paris. Over 500 FFI were killed shortly after, contributing to the lightning advance of the Allies once they reached the region of the Nord and Pas-de-Calais. The citadel in Lille was taken unexpectedly by resisters just before the British forces entered the town to a tumultuous welcome on 3 September.

It was feat of arms and the primacy of the state which de Gaulle represented on 26 August in Paris when he descended the Champs-Élysées in a victory parade which was both a symbolic and real declaration of legitimacy. De Gaulle in the name of France had continued the war in 1940, had prosecuted it for four years, had won over substantial parts of the empire, assimilated the internal resistance, and was now installing his military and political presence. The France of de Gaulle presented itself as the unbroken state, the enduring Republic. By contrast, Vichy had carried out no feat of arms and had capitulated in the war. Pétain and Laval were still in power in mid-June as de Gaulle nominated his first Commissaire of the Republic in Bayeux, but the case against Vichy had become a consensus among resisters, both internal and external. Vichy was seen as the rupture, the illegitimate state. De Gaulle claimed that it had never spoken for France and could not do so now. It was regarded as irrelevant, and its last contortions were simply ignored.

In their own ways Pétain and Laval both believed they should mediate the terms and future of post-Liberation France: they started futile manœuvres to this end, while Déat and the pro-German lobby of collaborationists sought to throw France into the war against the 'invading' Allies. Vichy had already decisively declared its own war on armed resistance on 2 May 1944 when Darnand's assistant Raymond-Clemoz circulated the prefects instructing them to hand over all information on all groups of dissidents to the German authorities. No distinction was made between any kind of resistance group or maquis. The Milice was Vichy 'at war' in 1944, but in mid-August the Germans decided to take Vichy with them in retreat. Laval and Pétain were forcibly removed to Germany, ending their Vichy days at another improbable site, the castle of Sigmaringen overlooking the Danube. The collaborationists, Darnand, Déat, Doriot, de Brinon and Luchaire went to Germany more willingly, acting out their fantasies in a charade of ideological and impotent invective.

Replacing Vichy had been meticulously planned ever since de Gaulle's first contacts with the internal resistance. Liberation Committees, representing a cross-section of political parties and social interests sympathetic to resistance, were theoretically in place for each of the *départements* in early 1944 if not before. Still more centralizing were the replacements for Vichy's regional prefects, the Commissaires of the Republic, appointed well in advance by the Provisional Government. The untroubled assumption of power by most of the Commissaires pointed to the vision and decisiveness behind the reconstruction of the republican state. They held the promise of a unified resistance, which was still in effect diverse and often divided. Yet

despite the divisions, administrative order in most places was not so much imposed as assumed, the touchstone of commitment to running a country still at war, decimated and impoverished by the Occupation and the struggles for liberation. It was expected that de Gaulle's Jacobin-style centralism would also reflect the revolutionary ideals which he had himself promoted in his declaration of June 1942.

Liberational beginning

The collective exaltation and happiness which accompanied Liberation, the dancing in the streets, the flowers strewn in the path of resisters, the focus on youth, the humiliation of collaborators and Pétainists, the power exercised by previously unknown individuals, momentarily turned society upside down. The days between the end of German–Vichy rule and the embedding of the Provisional Government seemed like time in suspension, a period of several days at least in which boundaries of behaviour, and frontiers of class and status, were crossed. It was later given geophysical properties, like crossing the equator, or metaphorical ones of carnival in its revolutionary mode. Inversionary power was evident in bands of armed youths, formed loosely into patriotic militias (*milices patriotiques*) who briefly administered order or sanctioned disorder, stopping people at will and hunting down collaborators, real or suspected, as prey. It was also evident in uniformed women marching as part of the urban FFI and *groupes francs*, as caught in the photographs of Julia Pirotte in Marseille. Contradictions were everywhere. Celebrations were both carefree and laden with anxiety. Liberation as a beginning divided those who saw the moment of liberation itself as the opportunity for change from those who cautioned the need to wait for the new government, the end of the war, the return of prisoners and deportees, and the first post-war elections.

Marianne, symbol of the Republic, was pictured in Paul Colin's iconic poster of August 1944 as standing in front of an execution post, her body bloodied and martyred, one stigmatized hand shielding her eyes as she looks into the glare of the future, the other pushing back the recent past. The light of a new beginning, the dawn of a new France, were figures of speech common to the clandestine press as it published its first open editions. There was a universalism in the images, which marked them as different from the purely left-wing expectations of the Popular Front, or the right-wing ideology of the Révolution Nationale. People expressed the need to take the future into their own hands, unlike the submissive self-denial behind the cult of Pétain.

De Gaulle endorsed the universalism, but was adamant that power should not slip into the streets or fall to a sectarian political group. He had no time for the anarchic or carnivalesque. He obscured resistance as a minority phenomenon, making it the achievement of the whole nation (*la nation résistante*) and stressing the military over the political. He was intolerant of local demands and insisted on the national needs of the moment. He nullified the diversity of resistance. On his tour of the liberated regions his usual greeting was to ask resisters their military rank. He was dismissive of reputations built up in raids and sabotage, and silent when forced to share the company of ordinary maquisards. Toulouse had been one of the centres where the local FFI under the young Serge Ravanel, and other resistance elements, called for the radical social charter of the CNR to be implemented. De Gaulle visited the town on 16 September. Head to head, Ravanel said he found himself 'facing a man who refused to listen. He had come to establish order.'[19]

The Communist Party played its own role in preserving order. It rejected the Liberation as a revolutionary moment, the second time it had refused to sanction revolution in ten years. Both times have to be seen in the light of Stalin's two calls for a broad-based alignment, first in pursuit of anti-fascism in 1934 and then to ensure support for the continuing war in 1944. The response to both instructions saw the party at its most appealing to new recruits who were not steeped in loyalty to the Soviet Union, but who saw in Communism an active pursuit of social change and justice. Acceptance of the Nazi-Soviet pact lay between these two periods as the most forceful reminder of the party's craven trust in Stalin. The thousands of volunteers who joined the FTP in 1943–4 knew little if anything of how close the party had come to self-destruction in 1939–41. At the Liberation they did not force the party's hand and demand a political revolution, but locally they constituted most of the pressure for implementing the CNR Charter adopted on 15 March 1944.

By far the most ambitious project to emerge from the Resistance, the Charter of the Conseil National de la Résistance (CNR) gave substance to the 'revolution' for which de Gaulle in 1942 had declared that the people were gathering. Its social aims included structural change to produce worker participation in management, the nationalization of leading industrial and financial companies, and the full implementation of a state system of social welfare. There was also the proposal for equal rights for all colonial citizens, though without a commitment to decolonization. As a body the CNR had slipped away from de Gaulle after the death of Jean Moulin. Its leadership was assumed by a representative of the internal

resistance, initially the Christian Democrat resister Georges Bidault of Combat, and the Charter envisaged the continuation of the CNR as a political and social force after the Liberation. This expectation made it appear to de Gaulle as a potential threat. He refused the CNR a role in the reconstruction of the state, but this did not signal his rejection of all elements of the Charter. Looking backwards as well as forwards, both he and the CNR Charter had declared that all collaborators would be punished.

Retribution and closure

Of all the expectations of liberation, a systematic purge (*épuration*) of collaborators was seen as essential for any new beginning. The threat of a purge had been carried by most of the clandestine press from as early as 1941, and intensified after the occupation of the southern zone. For local communities the focus was on collaboration at the individual level, and in the course of 1943–4 collaborators who chose to work for the German police or in any of the collaborationist political groups were sent small black coffins or black-edged warnings, and their homes and official buildings daubed with swastikas. The ferocity of the re-engaged war saw many of the threats carried out, some 5,000–6,000 executions during the armed struggle already mentioned, and a further 3,000 at the time of the local liberations, when the intensity of summary justice depended entirely on the local context in which power was exercised. In some places flimsy pretexts were the basis for the settling of personal or political scores, though almost everywhere the local collaborators were well known, and passions were inflamed by first-hand accounts of the extent of German atrocities and new revelations of the tortures inflicted by the Milice. Only during September did special courts appointed by the Provisional Government begin to replace the *ad hoc* military sessions of the local FFI which had continued to dispense 'civil-war' justice and vengeance as part of the bitter struggle against the Occupation and those who had collaborated with the occupiers.

Retribution invaded every sphere. The labyrinths of collaboration and the number of those victimized by both Germans and Vichy meant it would never be otherwise. Among the many borders crossed during the Occupation, that of public and private was as significant as any. In arriving at a definition of collaboration, all social relations with Germans, whether at musical soirées or in cafés and bars, were interpreted as public acts. A mature woman and a German who fell discreetly in love, or a young girl arm-in-arm with a German soldier, were seen not as private persons but as symbolic of occupied and occupier. Some communities allowed them their

own space, and an approach to behaviour of any kind under the Occupation, whether sexual, commercial, social or political, has to recognize the local variables in what was thought acceptable.[20] In the heightened sensibilities of Occupation it was often stated that people were aware of everything. It was the basis on which neighbourhood information flourished. Letters sent to the Vichy and German police, denouncing neighbours or rivals, ran into tens of thousands, most penned from jealousy and personal resentment. The authorities investigated a mere fraction. But at the Liberation everyone believed they knew who had written the letters. There was the same open knowledge of conspicuous profiteers, even though small-time buying on the black market was tacitly condoned.

The ubiquity of the most noted public revenge at the local liberations was gender-specific. Women accused of intimate relations with the enemy were subjected to a public shearing of their hair, shaving of their heads, and in many places enforced nakedness and exposure to crowds of jeering onlookers. The shearing was an archaic, ritual punishment of women by men, most often connected with the repression of female adultery. The photographs taken in numerous places of this display of retribution do not hide the presence of women in the crowds urging on the acts of humiliation, nor do written records deny the depth of anger expressed by both men and women at the material advantages which lovers of German soldiers were accused of having enjoyed. It is estimated that some 20,000 head shearings took place at or after the Liberation, all over France, only thirty-five to fifty of which are recorded as punishments on men. The greatest density was in areas such as the coastal region of northern Brittany, and the industrial centres of the Oise to the north of Paris, where there were strong concentrations of German personnel employing local people.[21] Probably less than 50 per cent of the women sheared (*femmes tondues*) were specifically convicted of sexual relations, but it was this reason which assumed a form of universality, even when their collaboration had been for economic or political motives. Women working for the Germans were assumed to have only sexual motivations.

It was not this assumption, but the public nature of the punishment, which left feelings among some resisters of a shameful episode, one best forgotten and not quantified. Liberation Committees in some areas questioned the bestial nature of the events, while still condemning the women who chose collusion with the enemy. There were admissions that blatant injustices occurred, and the practice was discouraged, though not everywhere. A few localized shearings, alongside other 'community violence' and 'neighbourhood purges', still took place at the end of the war in May 1945

and when the prisoners of war and deportees returned from Germany.[22] Only forty years later were the shearings fully researched and the events widely interpreted as the sexual reassertion of male dominance.

Hesitations in the *épuration* as a whole marked the post-Liberation period, and there were constant requests from local Liberation Committees for the administrative purge to be intensified. It was felt that police, judges, civil servants and industrialists were being handled leniently by the courts. There was agreement in liberated France that Vichy collaboration should be judged severely. It was Vichy as an internal government that still divided a few loyalties, and residual respect for Pétain even more. The major trials had to wait until Germany was defeated. The final rites of closure were delayed, the new beginnings also. It was an ongoing war and a long and difficult winter that the successful Resistance immediately inherited.

13

Ending War . . . Not in Indo-China or Algeria, 1944–1962

1. The meanings and sequel of Occupation and Liberation

Turning round defeat

At the height of the Pétain cult, at a school in the old ducal town of Uzès in the Gard, the young Évelyne Sullerot, aged sixteen, was instructed to raise the flag in honour of Joan of Arc and Marshal Pétain: 'I went to the flagpole in the centre of the schoolyard before all the students and teachers and shouted, "Joan of Arc drove the enemy from France. When Marshal Pétain does that I will raise the flag, but not before." Two hours later the gendarmes came and arrested me.'[1] The Vichy instruction to schools to compare Pétain and Joan of Arc provoked a number of similar incidents. History teacher Lucie Samuel (Aubrac) encouraged her pupils in Lyon to mock its absurdity, while at the Vichy leadership school at Uriage the aristocratic director Pierre Dunoyer de Segonzac was convinced by mid-1942 that the studies of Joan of Arc promoted at the school led logically to resistance. He became a maquis leader in the south-west.

The heritage derived from Joan of Arc, recuperated by the Resistance but initally claimed by Vichy, was of patriotic resilience. It was the basis of Pétain's appeal. The euphoria which greeted Pétain in 1940 was one of gratitude that he had rescued France from the depths of despair: he was seen to turn the situation round. The resisters inside France, and the Free French outside, turned round not only defeat but also the patriotism attached to Pétain. Resistance as an initial fight to recuperate words and consciousness began the reversal of defeat. Gestures like that of Évelyne Sullerot, the weapons of the weak, the culture of the outlaw and the military mobilization of volunteers were threads in the complex weave of internal resistance which kept a minority France effectively at war.

At the Liberation the military focus was dominant. The FFI numbered roughly 100,000 before the Normandy landings, a figure which was only

the military tip of resistance, its bulk still lying in a wealth of civilian structures, and in actions by those who never carried a gun or set up an ambush. In the conflicts which accompanied and followed *Jour-J* (D-Day) the FFI numbers rose to over 400,000, of whom a third joined the regular armies under de Gaulle to pursue the war into Alsace and Germany, and others were left to encircle the Atlantic ports. Many were judged by the regular army to be too young, or too anarchic, for conscription. By the end of 1944 the Provisional Government had an army of over a million, with a surfeit of officers, many of them contemptuous of the FFI and their leaders.

It was noted as symbolic of the turn from defeat to victory that French forces in February and March 1945 were at last fighting forward from the site of the Maginot Line. By 20 March the French frontier had been cleared by the Allies. The First French Army, led by General de Lattre de Tassigny, which had landed with the Americans in Provence on 15 August 1944, advanced across the Rhine and into Wurtemburg, and it was de Lattre who represented France as one of the Allied signatories of victory at the final German surrender. Despite further American distrust of de Gaulle, nine French divisions occupied the south of Germany and the west of Austria. News of the German surrender brought the immediate capitulation of the Atlantic ports. The whole territory of France was liberated. France gained recognition as one of the victorious Allies, and was allotted its zone of occupation in Germany, though it was not a full equal to Britain, the USA and the USSR in the 'Grand Alliance' which planned post-war Europe at Yalta in February 1945. Excluded from Yalta, de Gaulle had nevertheless seen his astonishing claim of 18 June 1940 vindicated by Allied forces and by resistance inside and outside France: the war had not been lost. The defeat of 1940 had been retrieved.

The human costs of the war from 1939 to 1945 and the four years of Occupation were estimated to total 600,000 deaths: 210,000 in the regular armies and the forces of the Free French and the internal FFI, but also Alsace-Lorrainers forcefully conscripted to fight for the Germans; 150,000 civilians, of whom 60,000 died under bombings by both Allied and German planes; and 240,000 deaths in German camps and work places, encompassing over 73,000 Jews, 60,000 political deportees for acts of resistance, 40,000 prisoners of war and 40,000 workers. The whole history of resistance cut across the categories of civilian and military, as did the deaths within the German camps.

Trials

The special Liberation Courts set up by the Provisional Government to carry out the purge of collaborators in legal fashion mostly put an end to the disorder of the summary executions, though a few were perpetrated in 1945. The legality of the courts still left unresolved the question of how justice could be adequately met if the definition of collaboration was decided by members of the Resistance. The pressures for making the collaborators pay grew exponentially with the difficulties of life experienced after the Liberation. Disillusionment set in at many levels, making for personal animosity and a culture of blame.

Given these factors, it was not surprising that roughly 350,000 accusations of collaboration were made to the courts, but the surprise in the other direction was that less than half were taken up, and that death sentences were pronounced in only 4 per cent of the cases judged. Just under three-quarters of these were commuted by de Gaulle, and the figure of those executed was officially given in 1948 as 791, to which must be added a further 769 from the military tribunals which were the first attempt to bring a semblance of legality to the local purges.[2] In total, including the 8,000–9000 killed during the period of armed conflict and liberations, about 10,500 were executed at different stages by the forces of resistance.

Refusing asylum in Switzerland, Marshal Pétain returned from Germany and appeared before the superior level of the special courts, the High Court of Justice, on 23 July 1945. He declared that he had been a shield, protecting the French people. He then denounced the court as unconstitutional, refusing to answer any questions. The evidence of Laval, who had hoped for asylum in Spain, did not help Pétain's cause, since he insisted that all his actions had been endorsed by the Marshal as head of government. Pétain was found guilty and condemned to death, with the recommendation, accepted readily by de Gaulle, that it should be commuted to permanent detention. He died in 1951, aged ninety-five, on the Île d'Yeu off the coast of the Vendée. Laval's own trial brought no credit to the courts: he was prevented from setting out the defence he had prepared, and was shot on 15 October 1945 after he had tried to commit suicide. Joseph Darnand and Fernand de Brinon were also executed. Doriot had died in an accident in Germany, and Déat was hidden by a religious order in Italy until his death in 1955. The antisemitic Darquier de Pellepoix escaped to Spain, and some of the other prominent figures who carried out the deportation of the Jews were only brought to trial in the last two decades of the century.

Several trials of journalists, broadcasters and writers whom the nihilist

Lucien Rebatet proudly called the 'Academy of Collaboration' in Paris demonstrated the crucial role that words and ideology had played in the taking of sides for or against the Nazi new order. Nihilism, antisemitism and fascist idealism had filled the pages of *Je suis partout*, *Gringoire* and *Aujourd'hui* among many other Paris publications. It was said that people bought them to light their fires since they were thicker than the clandestine press. The role they played in the vilification of Jews and the Resistance, as well as conservative Vichy, was designed to be inflammatory. Robert Brasillach's ecstasy at youthful fascist vitality and the German presence was thought by some Resistance intellectuals not to deserve the death penalty, and they pleaded for clemency, but his sentence was not commuted, nor was that of the newspaper owner Jean Luchaire and the pro-German radio voice Jean-Hérold Paquis. Henriot had already been assassinated.

The administrative and economic purges were placed in the hands of commissions which looked at tens of thousands of dossiers over two years or more. Prison sentences or national degradation were the most common punishments, affecting over 100,000 people, and a further indeterminate number of around 25,000 were sacked. Of all the aspects of the purge it was leniency towards the police, judges and collaborators in industry that was most commonly rebuked, especially among those in the trade unions and the more radical local Liberation Committees, pressing the need for an economic democracy heralded by the CNR Charter. In mitigation, the Provisional Government asserted the priority of re-establishing law and order and meeting the demands of economic reconstruction. The popularity of the PCF, swollen to a membership of 380,000 by January 1945, had paradoxical effects: it both increased the pressure for a wider purge and at the same time helped the government on the road to reconstruction and productivity (see Chapter 14).

Narratives

The return of prisoners of war and deportees in the last half of May 1945 was marked by civic receptions, speeches which rehearsed local versions of the Occupation, and the exchange of experiences. The historical accounts offered at the return, together with those at the Liberation and in the course of the official trials, created a set of powerful narratives, with legitimizing force.

In the first place Vichy and all it stood for was not only declared illegitimate and treasonous but was deemed to have played a puppet role in German-occupied Europe. No analysis of its freedom of manoeuvre, its

revivalist intentions or its initial public support was undertaken: if its inheritance was examined at all it was in terms of the fascist leagues of the 1930s and the reactionary anti-republicanism of Charles Maurras, who was condemned to permanent detention and national degradation in January 1945. When he exclaimed that the judgement was 'the revenge of Dreyfus' it was not just a sign of his unyielding historical perspectives. It was also a tacit recognition that the court had used his own ideology against him: he was judged to be a representative not of the 'true France' but of 'anti-France'. The moral, social and cultural aims of Vichy, as well as its attitudes to the Germans, were thus effectively excluded from national history. They were not officially labelled 'un-French', but that is the direction in which the narrative led.

Secondly, there was a unifying narrative of national suffering. It was there in the words of people welcoming home the prisoners and deportees. Setting out their own Occupation experiences in comparison, there was a tendency to say 'we also suffered in France', an understandable reference to the repression, bombings and reprisals, but a more contentious one when it exhibited a fixation on the scarcity of food. Faced with this narrative, many of the returning deportees, and especially the few Jewish survivors, found it difficult to get people to listen to the horrors of the German camps: Simone Jacob (later Simone Veil, see Chapter 17), said she felt forced into silence on her return from Ravensbrück. It was the same incomprehension which men from the trenches in the First World War had encountered when returning home, but in 1945 the image of the 'martyred Marianne', as in Paul Colin's Liberation poster, was a potent source of general legitimacy. Identity with that martyrdom was widely claimed in public and private during the events of 1944–5 and justified subsequently. Its indiscriminate nature was bound to unravel, provoking cynicism towards the spurious claimants and suspicion of the entire narrative.

Thirdly and most centrally, the premise for excluding Vichy lay in the all-pervading resistance narrative. Resistance had every reason to establish itself as the sole heir in the 1940s to the republican and patriotic tradition from the Revolution onwards. The epic resistance narrative formed postwar national identity: it created a sense of unity and it was formed in continuity with the consensual history of 'the republic at war'. A seamless mantle covering the *poilus* of 1914–18, the Free French and the FFI, Clemenceau and de Gaulle, it included the Pétain of Verdun, but self-evidently not the Pétain of 1940–44.

Resistance as the national identity made it difficult for the diversity of the Occupation to emerge in collective accounts and memory. Nuances in

collaboration, the reasons for *attentisme*, the experiences of the majority who were involved in neither collaboration nor resistance, and finally the disparate origins, aims, motivations and practices of resistance itself, were eclipsed.

The unifying role of this resistance narrative subordinated its component parts. The vital contribution of refugees and immigrants, Spanish, Poles, Italians and anti-fascist Germans and Central Europeans, was sidelined by the need for national reaffirmation. More insidiously, many of the uncomfortable sides of resistance, including the raids on depots, businesses and banks, seen by many as banditry, were wrongly attributed solely to foreigners. Spanish guerrilla fighters from the republican exile and diaspora in the south were conspicuous in the armed struggle against overwhelming German superiority, but their contribution to the Liberation of France was obscured by the ease with which they were dubbed in many areas as social bandits with irresponsible hopes of going on to liberate Spain from Franco.

The downplay of immigrants and exiles in the Resistance revealed the reactionary and exclusive side of the resistance narrative. It emerged in the Nationality Code drawn up by the Provisional Government on 19 October 1945 which reproduced categories from the xenophobic climate of 1938, and in many ways hardened the criteria for naturalization of foreigners, with 'failure to assimilate' written for the first time into legislation as a reason for exclusion. Here was a covert continuity from Vichy in the reliance on Georges Mauco and other demographers, whose pre-war categories of immigrants most likely, and least likely, to assimilate had found favour in Vichy, for overtly racist reasons.[3] The theme of nationality foregrounds the extent to which the Resistance was transgressive yet also nostalgic, how it looked towards Liberation but also restoration, how it created new identities and yet reinvigorated old ones. It points to the paradox of frontiers broken and frontiers re-established. The prevalence of those re-established after the war obscures for almost two decades the nature of those that had been broken. Foreign names of exiles and refugees in the Resistance disappeared; military and political modes of resistance obscured civil dissent; the centre and the top occluded the periphery and the bottom. Jacobin centralism was reaffirmed.

The multiple role of women in the Resistance was subordinated, in this case by a dominant male account and by women themselves who described their own activities as 'natural', suggesting misleadingly that no choice was involved. Men paid tribute to women but often as 'anonymous helpers'. The right to be considered a resister was substantially restricted by the term 'combatant' which was the criterion used for official resistance recognition

after the war. As a result only a very small proportion of the cards of Combattant Volontaire de la Résistance (CVR) were allotted to women by the mostly all-male commissions set up in each *département*. Similarly, at the highest level of the Ordre de la Libération, only six women were honoured with the order, compared to over 1,035 men. Every resistance movement was required to close its record with a brief official history and figures of membership. Women were rarely numbered as more than 12 per cent, a percentage which was accepted as accurate partly because it corresponded to that of women 'activist' members of the PCF in 1946, the party most noted for its female representation.[4] It was a conventional political meaning of 'activism': it did no justice to the much larger percentage of women in the informal infrastructures of resistance.

Recognition of rural resistance suffered no less from generalized assumptions. Judgements on the passive or 'self-seeking' nature of the peasantry were common coinage, while regional and local identities, and specificities of local action, were neglected in the pressure for national unity. For over twenty years after the war, attempts to examine the place of ruralism, regionalism or peasant culture in the history of resistance were met with a blanket association of all three with Vichy. Urban certainties permeated the narrative.

When it came to the resumption of elections and the creation of a Fourth Republic to which resistance manifestos had mostly pointed, the main resistance narrative, for all its success in creating a national identity, was unable to sustain a united political party. A group of resisters, including Henri Frenay, who believed that their combined activity had transcended the old divisions between republican left and right, between anticlericals and Catholics, and between secular socialism and Christian socialism, created the Union Démocratique et Socialiste de la Résistance (UDSR) in June 1945. One of its immediate goals was to keep the Communist Party from retreating back into sectarian isolationism but at the same time to stop it from becoming politically dominant. It had a broad-based humanistic aim, but within a few months it was clear that the UDSR had failed to become a pivotal new form of republican politics.

The failure of the UDSR marked the absence of party political thinking within the resistance narrative. Party political élites re-emerged together with political rivalries. The Communist Party claimed that 75,000 Communists had been shot (*fusillés*) for resistance. The number was an exaggeration but it was not necessary to insist on it for the party to attract members and votes as *le parti des fusillés* (the martyred party). Other parties shared or disputed the achievements of resistance. A single, monolithic resistance

party had never appeared likely to succeed. While certain aspects of resistance history were elevated to open up a new France, others were closed down or marginalized. By the late 1940s the two rival political monopolists of the resistance narrative, de Gaulle and the PCF, had fashioned the richly diffused history of resistance into simple mobilizing myths. Before that, the newly minted national identity stamped itself not only with the seal of republican legitimacy but also with the legacy of empire.

2. The larger France

The question of empire received little exposure at the Liberation, not least because consensus opinion on the benefits and necessity of empire rang with praises for the early support given to the Free French by black leaders in Equatorial Africa, the value of Brazzaville as de Gaulle's African headquarters and the identification of the Provisional Government and Assembly with Algiers.

The continuity of French presence as colonies moved from Vichy control into the realm of the Free French was one of both French governors and indigenous élites. In Senegal the African political leaders, epitomized by the black poet Léopold Senghor and Lamine Gueye, were vocal in their French republicanism. In Martinique where the Vichy governor, Vice-Admiral Georges Robert, was punitive and unpopular, creole and black Martinicans supported the Free French minority amongst the white population in forcing his deposition in June 1943, accepting de Gaulle as a symbol of a beneficent and reforming France. In Indo-China, however, Vichy's weakness allowed the Governor, Vice-Admiral Decoux, to negotiate a form of protection from all-powerful Japan, which turned rapidly into subservience. Japanese troops took over the ports and airfields and finally deposed Decoux in March 1945, allowing Bao Dai as Emperor of Annam to head a quasi-independent Vietnamese state, alongside other puppet royalist regimes in the area. The victorious resistance in France was determined to pursue the war against Japan. There was no real doubt in the Provisional Government that this should involve the restoration of French authority in Indo-China, contested since May 1941 by the Communist League for the Independence of Vietnam (Viet Minh) under its leader Ho Chi Minh, whose resilience in his cause was no less than that of de Gaulle's.

The vision of a fully restored France at the Liberation was inseparable from the positive evaluation of all pre-war colonial resources. There was both evolution and continuity from the imperial assumptions of 1931,

evident in the African conference called at Brazzaville by the Provisional Government in late January 1944, at which Henri Laurentie in the colonial commissariat set out ideals of wider citizenship for indigenous populations, and constitutional reforms which would create a form of federalism of associated peoples. De Gaulle's opening speech acknowledged that the war had seen attitudes evolve and that France would proceed towards 'structural imperial reform', and he glorified the 'immortal talent (*génie*)' of France as a nation for raising people under its flag 'to heights of dignity and fraternity'. But he stopped short of imagining decolonization. The Brazzaville conference was a missed chance for a serious debate on independence. After the Liberation, de Gaulle appeared to go further: he spoke at a press conference of bringing colonial peoples to the point of 'administering their own affairs and later to govern themselves'.[5]

The aim of self-government had long been the agenda of nationalist movements within the colonies. De Gaulle and the Provisional Government could be interpreted as merely limping behind these nationalist initiatives. It would be more accurate to emphasize that the resistance recovery of 'one France' encompassed the recovery of the 'larger France' stretching across continents. The war had forged multiple new strands of French consciousness among indigenous leaders as well as liberational projects. Their expressions of loyalty to the Free French encouraged the Provisional Government to value the colonies as necessary for the ultimate recovery of world status and power. A virtue was made out of the far-flung unity of purpose that this envisaged. To this end, de Gaulle and his ministers agreed that colonial reform should be accelerated but at the same time rejected indigenous nationalism. The ambiguities of this position allowed events to provoke regressive responses from liberated and resistance France.

Independence denied

Celebrations in France at the end of the war on 8 May 1945 were a pale shadow of the festivities at the Liberation, following a hard winter of shortages and the lowering of expectations. The 'day the war ended' never rivalled 11 November 1918 in public consciousness. What took place in towns and villages on 8 May 1945 was soon largely forgotten. This was not the case at Sétif in Algeria.

Sétif was a town of some 32,000 inhabitants in the hills of Kabylia, south-west of Constantine. Thousands of Algerians joined the victory parade with placards denouncing both fascism and colonialism: there were shouts of 'Free Messali Hadj' and 'Independence for Algeria'. The celebra-

tions became a riot. Zina Haraigue, later imprisoned in La Roquette in Paris as a militant Algerian nationalist, was an eleven-year-old at the time who accompanied her brother to watch the parade. She saw a young Algerian unfurl a nationalist flag, prompting the police to open fire on the crowd. Bodies fell everywhere and for eight days all Algerians were confined to their houses, unable to go out for food or water. It was, she said, at that moment that nationalism became rooted in the population. Her memory is of arbitrary police repression of a nationalist demonstration.[6] The memories of Europeans in the regions of Sétif and Guelma were, on the contrary, of an unprovoked revolt on a festive day and the brutal killing of 80–100 Europeans. Almost all accounts now agree on the bloodiness of the revolt but also that the French reprisals that followed, orchestrated by General Duval, exceeded everything in brutality and ferocity. Algerians were shot indiscriminately, villages were bombed from the air or shelled from the sea. French military officials eventually acknowledged that between 10,000 and 15,000 Algerians were killed in the wake of Sétif. Algerian estimates have never been less than 45,000. The reprisals were authorized by the government of de Gaulle. They set out to crush all ideas of Algerian liberation, even as the liberation of France continued as the proud reference point for French identity in the post-war world. Of all the events on 8 May 1945 it was the one most deliberately occluded and forgotten, except among Algerians.

In Morocco and Tunisia, attempts by nationalist movements in 1943–4 to turn the war to their own account had already been met with harsh, though less indiscriminate, French repression. In Madagascar revolts broke out in March 1947, several months after the formation of the Mouvement Démocratique de la Rénovation Malgache (MDRM), a nationalist party which proposed that Madagascar be transformed into an independent state but still associated with France. The authorities of the newly formed Fourth Republic rejected the proposal. The rebellion was started by other secret nationalist groups, who perpetrated individual killings of over 150 Europeans, but the MDRM was held responsible and its leaders arrested, including the three representatives to the French parliament, Ravoahangy, Rabemananjara and Raseta, all of whom had condemned the rebellion and urged moderation on their members. Arrests were accompanied by an inhumane military repression under General Garbay which turned to massacre across vast areas of the island and combined with extreme deprivation to kill an estimated 100,000 Madagascans, a number admitted and then withdrawn by French authorities in 1949. The final statistics of the massacre remained unknown, but its extreme cruelty was publicly denounced during

the MDRM trials in 1948 by defenders of the Madagascan people, notably the barrister Pierre Stibbe and the ex-Resistance editor of *Combat*, Claude Bourdet.[7] General Garbay was transferred to Tunisia where he was empowered to pursue his methods of repression.

By the time of the Madagascan massacre the Constituent Assembly had replaced the dominating concept of Empire with the associative French Union, whose preamble in October 1946 stressed that it was 'formed by France and overseas countries (*pays d'outre-mer*) and based on equality of rights and obligations without distinction of race or religion'. Consistent with the limited precepts of the Brazzaville conference, no concession was made to the mounting tide of independence. A complex amalgam of local assemblies elected by male and female suffrage were joined to various levels of representation in the French parliament. The ancient colonies of Martinique, Guadeloupe and Guyane in the Caribbean and Réunion in the Indian Ocean east of Madagascar were made full *départements* of France. The Martinican poet Aimé Césaire, who had formed the black cultural movement of *négritude* in the 1930s with his older fellow-poet Senghor from Senegal, was elected as a Communist to the Constituent Assembly and was the parliamentary *rapporteur* for the bill of 1946 which effected the transition. He remained mayor of Fort-de-France in Martinique and deputy for over forty years, though he left the PCF in 1956. His anti-colonial *Discours sur le colonialisme*, published in 1950, asserted a distinctive racial and cultural identity for the colonized, and his influence was profound on the later liberational and revolutionary theories of the Martinican psychoanalyst Frantz Fanon, who joined the Free French and fought with them in Morocco, Algeria and France, gaining the Croix de Guerre. The involvement of black notables in the constitutional changes of 1946 bore out the promises that all indigenous adults in the overseas countries would be citizens of the French Union, but French rule by decree in the colonial territories was not abandoned.

In 1947 a special statute for Algeria outlined several long-overdue reforms and announced how citizenship would change the status of Muslims, but unequal political weighting of Europeans and Algerians was perpetuated by two separate electoral colleges. With the Algerian population nearing 8 million and the European just over 1 million, each European vote carried at least seven times more weight than the equivalent cast by an Algerian.

As late as 1953 the doughty Gaullist and liberal colonial administrator General Catroux summarized the state of the French Union with optimism. The omens, he concluded, were good, and he added, 'despite Indo-China'.[8] The omens were, in fact, quite the opposite. The post-war republic, adamant

in its assertion of world status and blind to the anachronisms of its imperial power, had stumbled into the first of two of the most shameful wars of the twentieth century.

3. The war of Indo-China, 1946–1954

The surrender of Japan on 2 September 1945 created a power vacuum that Ho Chi Minh was ideally placed to exploit. In Hanoi, the ageing, fragile but wiry 55-year-old Communist leader, survivor of prisons and repression, proclaimed independence and announced the creation of the Democratic Republic of Vietnam. It was both a coup d'état and a popular revolution. The Vietnamese had never accepted French colonial domination as permanent. Combined with a literacy drive in the villages, measures to prevent the spread of famine were enacted by Ho Chi Minh. The results were impressive and the penetration of the Viet Minh into rural areas intensified, accompanied in the north by the elimination of rival nationalist leaders.

In Paris de Gaulle brushed aside all talk of Ho Chi Minh's Vietnam republic and reasserted the primacy of French sovereignty. On 5 October General Leclerc arrived in Saigon to lead an expeditionary force of 31,000 well-armed troops, with a mission to rid the country of 'terrorists and brigands'. The Viet Minh forces were poorly equipped but were steadily organized into an efficient fighting force by a former history teacher, Vo Nguyen Giap. They began to fall back into the fastness of the hills, perfecting the art of guerrilla tactics. The French Communist Party, firmly represented in de Gaulle's government, was pulled in contrary directions. It called for negotiations with Ho Chi Minh but did not endorse independence. Public opinion polls in France showed strong support for continued French rule throughout Indo-China.

The war, initally known in official parlance as a campaign of pacification, was almost averted in 1946. After de Gaulle's sudden resignation in January, the tripartite government of Socialists, Communists and Christian Democrats agreed to negotiate with Ho Chi Minh. Leclerc had progressed to the centre of Vietnam, and the French High Commissioner, Admiral Thierry d'Argenlieu, had parried the Viet Minh republic with the recognition of the Annamite emperor Bao Dai as a republican figurehead in Saigon. On 6 March Ho Chi Minh, in a move which was criticized by many of his supporters as appeasement, met the French envoy Jean Saintenay in Hanoi. Twelve days later he was photographed holding a champagne glass alongside General Leclerc. In early June he arrived in France, where his

charm, his ready reference to the French classics and his frail physique won him wide public sympathy and the sobriquet 'Oncle Ho'. A supportive France–Vietnam Association brought together a wide range of personalities including Emmanuel Mounier, Paul Rivet, Pablo Picasso, François Mauriac, Maurice Schumann and Benoît Frachon. It even appeared as if Ho had accepted the French Union.

The formal negotiations broke down at Fontainebleau in July 1946. The diehard French lobby in Saigon was adamant that there should be no concessions to the Viet Minh. The talks were sabotaged by this unseen presence. Ho Chi Minh left France empty-handed. Like the Brazzaville conference of 1944, it was another missed opportunity. Events in November and December brought unremitting war. From Saigon, General Valluy, already planning an assault on the north, used a tense incident in the port of Haiphong to order Colonel Debès to carry out a full-scale repression of the region. Its central thrust on 23 November was a savage aerial bombardment of Haiphong and its population. General Morlière, in command in Hanoi, had favoured conciliation. He was bypassed by Valluy, who made the decisions and controlled the news. Like the reprisals at Sétif, the punitive raids which killed 15,000–20,000 were barely mentioned by the French press, who had no journalists in place. In Paris, Georges Bidault, ex-leader of the resistance CNR, who held the Foreign Ministry in a sequence of governments from 1944 to 1948, reaffirmed his commitment to French Indo-China in every ministerial meeting, insisting that France 'would defend its presence there by every means'.[9]

If the bombardment was a merciless strategy to force the Viet Minh into the open, it succeeded immediately but failed badly in the long term. On 19 December 1946 extreme elements in the Viet Minh declared their hand with a murderous assault on French *quartiers* in Hanoi, but at the same time the bulk of the Viet Minh dissolved further into the countryside. The war of Indo-China was declared from the air on French terms, but it was fought over eight years on terms and ground dictated by the local knowledge of the Viet Minh and the support they received from the grass roots.

It was not until a year after the Haiphong–Hanoi escalation that the war began to be seriously disputed in France. Over a quarter of the French electorate were regularly voting Communist, and their internal politics drew them into the global ideological conflict of the Cold War. Communist ministers left the tripartite government in May 1947 and moved into permanent opposition. Among anti-Communists the endearment of 'Uncle Ho' was swept away in the vortex of ideology, giving way to the demonization of the Viet Minh and its leader. On the other hand, the Communist Party

(PCF) rediscovered its anti-colonial panache and vigour of the late 1920s. The victory of Mao Tse-tung in China in 1949 brought Chinese aid to Ho Chi Minh, and when the acclaimed Liberation hero General de Lattre de Tassigny was sent in 1950 to raise the depressed morale of the French troops and relaunch offensives, he was soon in receipt of substantial aid from America. Indo-China, to which most French opinion seemed perversely indifferent, replaced Korea as the key site of ideological warfare in the Far East.

The numbers raised to fight the Viet Minh exceeded 560,000 by 1952, drawn principally from within Vietnam, secondly from Africa and North Africa, and only thirdly from France. The French troops, which never numbered more than 70,000, were volunteers, and the recruitment posters advertised in luxuriant colours the lure of a tropical adventure as a heroic sequel to the battles of liberation within Europe: 'Yesterday Strasbourg, tomorrow Saigon'. The absence of conscripts kept the war in the margins of people's consciousness, but it was never popular. No majority of opinion expressed itself clearly in favour of military action, but nor was there any majority concern for negotiation or withdrawal until late in 1953. Lassitude, inflexibility and paralysis fed on the certainties of ideological conviction. Positions were adopted and handed down from government to government without reconsideration. The new Christian Democratic Party (MRP) produced the most resolute belligerents in government, led by Georges Bidault, while the Socialists, although conscious of the war's growing unpopularity, continued to vote the war credits. It took the hard reasoning of Pierre Mendès France from outside the two main government parties to galvanize a non-Communist opposition and bring the republic to its senses, but not before the most catastrophic military defeat. Early in 1954 a vast strategic ploy to stem the Viet Minh and bar their route to Laos was enacted by General Navarre at Dien Bien Phu, an interior enclave fortified to give it the reputation of a tropical Verdun. The plan was a disaster. Outmanoeuvred by Giap's massive mobilization, the troops under General de Castries were encircled and the air routes cut. It was the biggest pitched battle in French colonial history. On 7 May 1954, after an eighty-day siege and the loss of sector after sector, Dien Bien Phu fell to the liberation army of the Viet Minh. Over 1,500 defenders from the élite of the French forces had been killed in the siege: a further 10,000 were taken prisoner. The shock reverberated through French politics. It should have averted any further colonial conflict. It failed to do so.

Explaining the war. Context and meaning

Even after the fall of Dien Bien Phu, Georges Bidault, who had consistently refused all contact with Ho Chi Minh, insisted on proposing a peace plan which took no account of the realities of the situation. His record of stubborn refusal earned him praise from the right-wing press, *L'Aurore, Paris-Match* and *Le Figaro*, which had defended the French presence throughout and now honoured the French dead as martyrs in an anti-Communist crusade. There was irony in this homage. At no point had the right in or outside parliament been prepared to argue for the increase in taxation needed for a more adequate financing of the war. Colonial economic interests were not well served by the war: exports from Indo-China, including rubber, fell severely; the Bank of Indo-China moved investments out of the area; by 1954 it was American aid that accounted for over three-quarters of the war's budget. On the political left and centre-left, Socialists and the MRP perpetuated the war but never gave it priority. Increasingly criticized by their own supporters, they were unable to explain why 'pacification' was not working, although the bitter complaint from the demoralized French forces was that nobody at home really cared anyway. For the Communist *L'Humanité* it was 'the dirty war': for the liberal *Le Monde* in 1950 the war was already 'absurd'.

The Radical Pierre Mendès France, sharply critical of the war, was backed by the new political weekly, *L'Express*, launched in May 1953. On 7 November 1953 it carried an article which described the Viet Minh not as a band of rebels but as a 'nation at war'. This perspective finally prevailed in June 1954. Bidault had conspicuously failed; Mendès France promised to deliver peace within a month of taking office. He succeeded. At Geneva on 21 July Vietnam was divided at the 17th parallel, leaving Ho Chi Minh's Republic sovereign in the north, and affirming independent states in Cambodia, Laos and South Vietnam. Russian pressure secured Ho's agreement to the partition of Vietnam on the assurance of elections in 1956 to decide the fate of the whole. These assurances were never honoured by Saigon. The independent states left the French Union, whose associative ideals for the Far East were in tatters. The good sense and incisive conduct of Mendès France made him a distinctive and individual figure within the Republic, but brought accusations of betrayal and antisemitic abuse against him as a Jew from resurgent movements on the extreme right.

In January 1955 the figures of French casualties were carried in the *Journal officiel*. Over 20,000 from France were killed or missing, 11,300 from the Foreign Legion, 15,200 from Africa and North Africa and 45,600

from the armies raised in Vietnam. The toll was much higher among the Viet Minh and its popular base. It is now estimated that in the war as a whole the civil and military dead totalled between 400,000 and 500,000. Inhumanity and atrocities were not confined to one side or any one area: inhumane conditions for prisoners were rife; brainwashing was employed by the Viet Minh and allegations of torture were brought against the French. To the mental and physical scars of the combatants was added an incredulity in France that the war could have been protracted over eight years, seemingly without direction or hope. It still provokes disbelief.

Explanations were advanced: the French Union carried the hopes of regaining national grandeur lost in 1940; the French army needed its own victories; the Cold War produced an ideological imbroglio from which there was no easy escape; the sapping nature of guerrilla combat did not make for headline news; the beginning of economic boom and the burning questions of Europe kept eyes away from the Far East. These all made their mark in subsequent accounts. More recently, emphasis has been given to a cultural reluctance of the French public to relinquish an exotic romance of the East, symbolized by the replica of Angkor Wat in 1931 and enriched by an abundance of novels and films.[10] But underpinning all the reasons for perpetuating the war was the continued belief in the civilizing mission of colonialism. In *Le Figaro* on 3 January 1950 the conservative political geographer André Siegfried articulated the opposition to decolonization in terms which brought the two concepts of the West together: 'It is not just the status of colonialism which is at issue but the destiny of the white race, and with it that of Western civilization of which it is the guarantee, the only guarantee.' There was no high-level recognition that this very equation of the white race with civilization was no longer an acceptable alibi for the forceful occupation of other lands and the subjugation of their people. Decolonization was discussed at ministerial sessions but it was not seen as a necessity for the peoples of the French empire. It was all too easily interpreted as a rebuff for French republicanism and enlightenment, and, within the paradigms of the Cold War, a defeat for the West.

The moral and cultural critique of colonialism came only from a minority of voices or from the colonies themselves. A non-Communist exposure of the wrongs perpetrated on indigenous people was carried in the liberal Catholic pages of *Témoignage chrétien* and the intellectual review *Esprit*. The presence of many well-known Catholics in the movement 'France–Maghreb' marked a new level of co-operation between secular and religious critics of colonialism. Behind the movement lay the new weekly, *France-Observateur*, launched in 1950, which expressed the long-held

anti-imperialist views of Gilles Martinet, Roger Stéphane and Claude Bourdet, while *Le Monde* with its 'neutral' stance between West and East, and Jean-Jacques Servan-Schreiber and Françoise Giroud in *L'Express*, attacked the Indo-China War as a failure of statecraft and political vision. The tightrope act for voices on the left was to oppose Western imperialism without being dismissed as an agent of Moscow. It was not easy to do so.

From 1947 the lead given by the PCF to action against colonialism was a dynamic one. Though scorned by Trotskyists and anarchists as merely a mouthpiece of Stalinism, the PCF attracted more fellow-travellers and intellectual support for its denunciation of the 'dirty war' in Indo-China than for any other cause in the long history of East–West tension. The Young Communists and the recently created Mouvement de la Paix organized demonstrations, petitions and tracts; dockers held up the transport of arms and troops from the ports. This tactic tapped into the recent history of resistance units who had dislocated German and Vichy movement under the Occupation, but in the post-war context it provoked accusations of treasonous sabotage. Police were quick to move against outbreaks of 'anti-national activities' after the violent Communist-led strikes of November–December 1947 which had raised the spectre of revolution or even civil war on the model of Greece (see next chapter).

The clampdown on those seen as saboteurs brought public attention to Henri Martin, a 23-year-old naval worker in Toulon, who distributed his own writings on the injustices towards the Indo-Chinese which he had seen at first hand between 1945 and 1947. Arrested on 13 May 1950 and accused of fomenting mutiny and desertion on the aircraft carrier *Dixmude*, he was acquitted of sabotage but then rearrested and condemned to five years' imprisonment for the distribution of tracts 'harmful to the national interest'. It was a symbolic case. Martin had joined the Francs-Tireurs et Partisans (FTP) in 1943 and had participated in the liberation of Bourges: he had enrolled in the Communist Party but was not considered a militant. It was in his letters home as a soldier in Indo-China, well before the PCF had broken with the government consensus, that he had first expressed his anger at the military repression he was ordered to carry out. In his defence at Toulon he argued that 'those who fought against the criminal orders of Vichy are not considered as traitors'. His case was taken up by thirty-three barristers who protested to the President of the Republic, Vincent Auriol, at the enormity of the sentence, and by Jean-Paul Sartre, Jacques Prévert, Vercors and a string of other writers and journalists associated with the Resistance.[11] In a precise way the Henri Martin affair resonated with ques-

tions of conscience that the governments and army leaders of the Fourth Republic progressively exacerbated.

4. *The Algerian war, 1954–1962*

Moroccan and Tunisian independence, but 'Algeria is different'

The Saigon camarilla of European interests had its equivalents in the protectorates of Morocco and Tunisia. In Rabat French officials clung on to their direct administration against the determination of the Sultan, Mohammed Ben Youssef, to gain French agreement to his political emancipation. A plot to depose the Sultan was hatched in France and Rabat by military leaders Generals Juin and Guillaume, working closely with the 'French Presence' group in Morocco and the schismatic pasha of Marrakesh, El Glaoui, who engineered the appointment of his protégé, Moulay Arafa, as the new Imam. On 20 August 1953 Guillaume arrested the Sultan and deported him to Madagascar, giving Arafa a puppet status. The Foreign Minister, Bidault, overtaken by events, meekly acquiesced. For two years, unrest and disturbances, violent killings and protests became the norm of Moroccan politics. The leader of the Istiqlal (Independence) Party, Mohammed Hassan Ouazzini, who had already spent nine years in a French gaol, nevertheless proposed a new treaty between Morocco and France which would guarantee the interests of the French population in return for the restoration of the Sultan. In *France-Observateur*, Roger Stéphane emphasized the eminent rationality of Istiqlal's proposal. By the end of 1954 the absurdity and the illegality of the French exclusion of the Sultan was obvious to all except those ideologically committed to European dominance at any price.

In Tunis the new French Resident in 1952, Jean de Hautecloque, turned against the liberalism of his predecessor, banned the Nationalist Neo-Destour conference and empowered General Garbay of Madagascan notoriety to crush the protest strikes that ensued, killing over 200 Tunisian civilians. The independence movements in both Morocco and Tunisia were buttressed from Cairo by the Arab League's support for the North African Liberation Committee, set up in January 1948 by the mythological figure from the 1920s, Abd el-Krim, and the leader of Tunisian nationalism Habib Bourguiba. Their expectations turned towards the United Nations. France was now under constant international pressure to relax its colonial hold over North Africa.

Mendès France rescued the situation in Tunisia shortly after bringing an

end to the war in Indo-China. In a much-publicized visit to the Tunisian Bey in Carthage in July 1954 he declared that France was preparing to give sovereignty back to the Tunisian people. He confronted the outrage of the colonists and their support on the political right, and set up a transfer of power to a Tunisian government which would include Bourguiba's nationalists. In August his measures received the support of parliament. Following the Geneva peace settlement, this turn by Mendès France to negotiated decolonization set a successful precedent for his Radical successor as Prime Minister, Edgar Faure, who brought the Sultan back to Morocco and signed an agreement with him on 6 November 1955. By 1956 both Tunisia and Morocco were independent.

It was during General Garbay's repressive military authority in Tunisia that *Témoignage chrétien* published an account entitled 'The Tunisian Drama'. The carefully documented article was unequivocal in its analysis of colonial violence. Firstly it described the riots provoked by the banning of the Neo-Destour movement in vivid terms: 'At Moknine three French policemen were killed and atrociously mutilated . . . Colonel Durand was assassinated by a small group of frenzied rioters: this fine soldier was one of the most respected French people in Tunisia.' But the article went on to argue that it was the French themselves who were responsible for this violence due to broken promises and their own military brutality.[12] This theme of the 'mirror image' of colonial violence runs throughout the 1950s. It was argued in Tunisia by Bourguiba and in Morocco by the Istiqlal Party who set out the years of French massacres and repression in *Les Cahiers du Maroc*.[13] It was argued by Messali Hadj, but in France there were very few indeed to see its relevance to Algeria. Algeria was held to be different.

On 1 November 1954 the self-declared Front de Libération Nationale (FLN) and its Armée de Libération Nationale (ALN) announced an armed struggle for Algerian independence with co-ordinated acts of violence against French buildings and personnel in all parts of Algeria, most effectively in the mountainous region of the Aurès, south of Constantine. In France no national credence was given to the insurgents, and their demands were summarily dismissed. The attack on a civilian bus in the Gorges de Tighanimine, which resulted in the death of a French teacher, Guy Monnerot, and the severe wounding of his wife, was portrayed as the epitome of cowardly terrorism in the French press. Mendès France, conscious that he had reversed the downward spiral of the Fourth Republic's colonial policy, was insistent that Algeria was not a colonial issue. To parliamentary acclaim he announced that secession from the metropole was unacceptable. The government department in charge was not the Colonial nor the Foreign

Office but the Ministry of the Interior, held by François Mitterrand. His declaration that 'Algeria is France' set the parameters of discussion. It became apparent that both Mendès France and Mitterrand had seen the settlement of Indo-China as the prerequisite for consolidating a more restricted French power within Europe and Africa. They spoke for a consensus of politicians and public which defined France as reaching 'from the Channel to the Sahara' and which, among French *colons*, imaged the Mediterranean running through France 'as the Seine runs through Paris'. In 1957 Mitterrand went on to denounce the previous 'politics of force' in Hanoi, Saigon, Rabat and Tunis: in contrast he outlined the prospects for a French community from Flanders to the Congo, structured as a voluntary federation of autonomous states and territories, with French Algeria at its heart. He defied the vagaries of the future by stating in delphic terms that 'without Africa there would be no history of France in the twenty-first century'.[14]

The difference which was held to particularize Algeria was not just the 124 years of occupation, nor its political integration as three *départements*, but the deeply cultivated sense of permanent rights among the 1.2 million Europeans who had arrived as outsiders but who had made themselves the insiders in a land which they defined, and experienced, as their own. Their description as *colons* was increasingly taken to indicate the rich settlers and the political élite, or the cultural tradition of the 'Algerianists' with their claims to the inheritance of ancient Rome. More generally the Europeans became known as *pieds-noirs*, a term with no certain origin but held to refer to the black boots worn by the early European soldiers and settlers. They saw the irruption of the FLN as no more than banditry, its demands no more than extortion, its national claims fraudulent.

The *pieds-noirs* claimed to inhabit a peaceful and fruitful province of France with a mixture of religions and races which coalesced into a unitary Frenchness within the republican cultural tradition. In the months after the emergence of the FLN, the information service of the Governor General in Algiers, with an implicit reference to apartheid in South Africa, sent pamphlets to the mainland stressing that there was no segregation in Algeria: 'Europeans and Muslims can live in the same blocks of flats, go to the same schools, use the same hospitals, work in the same factories and go to the same entertainments.' The pamphlets were addressed to people in France who were 'ignorant and prejudiced' and who had never been to Algeria or 'studied the facts'.[15] Far from homogeneous in occupation or wealth, many of the Europeans were small traders or artisans and were proud to have struggled hard merely to reach a standard of living equal to the average on the mainland. Those who worked small farms were privileged compared

to the Algerian *fellahs* (peasantry) but showed little of the conspicuous consumption and easy lifestyle of the rich landowners and the urban bourgeoisie, whose leafy *quartiers* most clearly epitomized the French municipal culture projected as the essence of civilization.

Since 1935 there had been a new cultural vanguard among the Europeans of Algeria, the École d'Alger, which denounced the Algerianist claim to Roman pedigree as an élite and tyrannical myth. In its place the writers Gabriel Audisio and Albert Camus proposed a more expansive culture in which the lives of colonizers and colonized were fused in the lyrical nature of the Mediterranean. Camus came from a working-class background in Algeria and his first essays were celebrations of nature and basic human existence which he later strived to protect against the divisiveness of both French colonialism and Algerian nationalism. Where the Algerianists had preached domination, the École d'Alger advocated harmony, and it was this more inclusive ideology which revitalized the conviction among liberal colonialists that the Mediterranean was not a frontier between nations but a shared site of cultural unity.

The mainland French who went to Algeria and 'studied the facts' did not all arrive at identical conclusions about the health of the Franco-Algerian link. Both Jacques Soustelle and Germaine Tillion were ethnologists, with eminent research careers in the 1930s, Soustelle in Mexico and Tillion in the Aurès in Algeria. Both had a distinguished record in the Resistance. Soustelle was one of the first to rally to de Gaulle and remained fervently loyal to him after the war. Tillion was one of the earliest resisters in the Musée de l'Homme group: she survived deportation to Ravensbrück and returned to her work in Algeria in 1955, where Soustelle had just been nominated to the post of Governor General. Both believed that Algeria and France were inextricably linked, but whereas Tillion moved back into the world of impoverished Algerians, Soustelle became increasingly involved in the economic potential of the Sahara. His lectures and writings eloquently promoted the recently discovered gas and oil fields which he advertised as a lucrative future for French Algeria by the year 2000, and he also stressed how the Sahara thrived on the French suppression of slavery and the greater security of the nomadic caravans.[16] Germaine Tillion's new work was in social centres for the Algerian poor and in 1956 she coined the term *clochardisation* to describe the process by which Algerians had become vagrants and down-and-outs (*clochards*) alongside the modernizing French economy. Adopted as a fact, the term was used by apologists of French Algeria to highlight the need for more modernization, and by opponents to decry the structural inequalities produced by colonialism.

Soustelle arrived not just as an ethnologist but also as the choice of Mendès France, and on both counts was initially greeted with reserve by the wealthy *colons*. He proclaimed his intention to respect equality of citizenship and the different communities which gave Algeria its distinct cultural personality, but he made it clear that his aim was to integrate that personality more completely into French republicanism. His integrationism was predicated on the firm belief that Algeria had no national identity of its own, and his information service never tired of quoting the Algerian moderate Ferhat Abbas who had stated in 1936 that a separate Algerian nation did not exist historically. What the pamphlets from Algiers did not add was that Ferhat Abbas went over to the insurgent nationalism of the FLN during 1955.

The paths of Soustelle and Tillion had converged in early 1955 but within a year had dramatically separated. Informed understanding of French Algeria was advanced by Soustelle to justify heavy repression of the revolts. His political reactions rapidly merged with those of the *colons* and during his governor-generalship a state of emergency was declared for Algeria, suspending civil liberties. He considered his overtures to assimilationist Algerian opinion unproductive and he fell back on military and police intimidation as the norm of authority. By contrast, an inside understanding of Algerian society made Tillion a moderating voice in the growing inhumanity of the war.[17] She represented the liberal humanist tradition of professional involvement in the colonies which had given many French women, as well as men, a significant career, and although she did not openly support the movement for Algerian independence she was one of the very few authority figures to gain the respect of imprisoned Algerians. She did everything to try to stop arbitrary executions and the institutionalization of murder and torture by the French, while also securing a brief suspension in mid-1957 to the murder of Europeans by the FLN.

Algerian revolt: means and motivation

The salient fact which nullified the French claims that Algeria was a province of France was precisely the failure to have created a viable French culture and society amongst the indigenous population. After over a century and a quarter of occupation the general level of acculturation of the Arabs and Berbers was no more than superficial, and in the countryside mostly non-existent. The failure was evident in figures which pointed to 85 per cent illiteracy among Algerians. Only one Algerian boy in every five went to primary school and only one girl in sixteen. European schoolteachers

were gaining Algerian respect, as were doctors who had halved the Algerian mortality rate in fifty years, but both were operating within a caste system in which Europeans held all the reins of industry and commerce, monopolized the professions and had so dislocated the balance of town and country that a mass of uprooted, landless peasants were heaped on each other in urban shacks, veritable ghettos which nurtured loathing for the *pieds-noirs* and in direct consequence provoked a steadily rising fear close to psychosis within the dominant French culture.

The resilience of traditional customs and beliefs in the countryside and even in the shanty towns meant that there really was comparison between the alienation of the Algerians from French rule and that of the Vietnamese. The French colonial discourse allowed pre-colonial Algeria a past but no history. Only with French conquest was its history seen to begin. Algerian nationalists and anti-colonialists within France demanded the restoration to Algerians of their own indigenous history together with a future of independence. Whatever the analysis of 'difference' and whatever the declarations of politicians, Algeria was a colonial issue.

Messali Hadj had been the most rigorously insistent voice in calling for Algerian independence. Influenced initially by the French Communist Party, though mutual suspicion followed later, he was the uncontested leader of Algerian immigrants in France throughout the inter-war period, open to the cultural heritage of both Islam and Republican France, and regularly imprisoned for his dedication to the liberation of Algeria. He was at the hub of all oppositional politics in Algeria. The movements associated with his name and ideas culminated after the massacre of Sétif in the Mouvement pour le Triomphe des Libertés Démocratiques (MLTD). It attracted young, politically active Algerians who were increasingly aware that all attempts to reform the power relationship of France and Algeria would founder on the intransigence of the *colons*. A paramilitary Special Organization (OS) created in 1947 was decimated by arrests three years later, and splits on policy and strategy were increasingly common within the MLTD. By 1954 Hadj was embroiled in political arguments with the Central Committee who accused him of dictatorial tendencies, but with the fall of Dien Bien Phu and the accelerating crises in Morocco and Tunisia more and more voices were demanding military action and an end to political wrangling.

Out of a maelstrom of ideas, personalities, groups and sub-groups emerged the Front de Libération Nationale (FLN) and its army (ALN), secretly structured in different rural locations during 1954 by six activists co-ordinated by Mohammed Boudiaf, leader of the OS in Constantine and ill with tuberculosis, and backed by three prominent leaders who

were operating from Cairo, Ahmed Ben Bella, Hocine Aït-Ahmed and Mohammed Khider. Hadj himself, still under constant police surveillance, was bypassed by the FLN whose aim was to engage in immediate military action and dispense with the decades of political manoeuvring. The actions of 1 November 1954 cut across the labyrinthine paths towards reform and set up an armed liberational struggle in the name of the Algerian nation.

The FLN owed as much to the precedent of European resistance against Nazism and the guerrilla strategy of the Viet Minh as to the populist tradition of Algerian nationalism. It derived its concept of a separate Algerian nation not only from Hadj but also from the Muslim intellectuals (*oulémas*) and went well beyond the moderate political claims of Ferhat Abbas and his Union Démocratique du Manifeste Algérien (UDMA). In France the FLN was stigmatized by many as yet another outbreak of international Communism, but it was in no way an offspring of the Algerian Communist Party (PCA), which responded negatively to the revolts of 1 November. Ultimately the FLN portrayed itself as a popular Islamic movement but it was also secular and modernizing, with strong links to the Jacobin tradition of authoritarian revolution. It brooked no opposition and eliminated all rivals. Initially it was no more than the sum of its actions, a series of armed revolts to which the other Algerian movements reacted with suspicion, fearing another Sétif-style backlash.

The notion that a single Algerian people had launched a united armed struggle was always a mythic construction by the FLN itself, and yet by 1956 most of the political rivals of 1954, including the *oulémas*, had joined the FLN or been subsumed as the rebellion intensified. The major exception was Hadj and his numerous supporters, many still loyal from the late 1920s, who re-formed into the Mouvement National Algérien (MNA) and were caught in a brutal fratricidal conflict within the Algerian cause, tragically affecting thousands of Algerians in both North Africa and metropolitan France.

The in-fighting between the FLN and the MNA was particularly heavy in France, claiming 4,000 victims, while in Algeria a paroxysm of killings by the ALN targeted entire villages deemed to be Messalist, such as Mélouza on the edge of Kabylia where 300 villagers were massacred in May–June 1957. This internalized terror was a calculated weapon against anyone suspected by the FLN of betraying its struggle. It was merciless in its elimination of Algerians known as *harkis*, those recruited by the French army and police, whose numbers were estimated by the French as 200,000, more than twice the number of ALN fighters (*moudjahidine*). Their reasons for not rebelling were complex: some had been in a position to benefit from

the basic social and educational opportunities provided by the French; some were pulled in contrary directions by the feud between the FLN and the Messalists; some came from villages and families, victims of early and arbitrary ALN violence; many believed that the French would look after them. This picture of disunity has been accentuated by many historians as a way of demythologizing the unified-nation and single-party discourse of the FLN. The FLN never represented the whole of Algerian society, but there was a logic of united action which fuelled the Algerian struggle for independence, and which brought Arabs and Berbers, town and country, peasants and urban workers into a combined, if pluralistic, cause.

The nature of the struggle had a gender dynamic, resulting in unprecedented departures of women from their cloistered lives to set up widespread provisioning of the *moudjahidine*. Some 2,000 women became maquisardes in the hills, mostly as nurses and carers but also in some cases bearing arms, while in urban guerrilla activity, notably during the battle of Algiers in 1957, women were responsible for carrying out the majority of the bomb attacks aimed at the European community. Their inversionary actions, either using traditional clothing and veils for hiding weapons and tracts, or playing the decoy role of available sexual object, were accurately stressed in 1966 in *The Battle of Algiers* by Gillo Pontecorvo, the most atmospheric and forceful film on the war, which is still mistaken for a newsreel documentary. Something of the commitment of the struggle was expressed by Zohra Drif, from a bourgeois Algerian family, who volunteered in 1956: 'They suggested', she said, 'that I worked with the families of prisoners, but I wanted to participate directly in armed conflict. I thought I would only be used as a nurse or secretary in the maquis; I wanted to work with a terrorist group, here in Algiers.' She became one of the leading organizers when French troops cut off the Casbah from the rest of Algiers and no men could leave. Women had more freedom of passage: 'We were well aware of our weakness, but we had the irresistible conviction that all the paratroops of the world could do nothing against us.'[18]

'La guerre sans nom'

The deepening commitment of Algerians to the national struggle was not clearly perceived by the French authorities, who harboured the illusion that significant regions of Algeria could be rallied to the continuation of French rule by a combination of pyschological pressure, schemes of privileged integration and firm repression of terrorist activity. Soustelle was at the origin of this multipronged strategy, his general ethnological expertise

reflected locally in the Kabylia by that of another ethnologist, Jean Servier, who believed that certain villages belonging to the proud Ifflissen people with their long Berber traditions and mistrust of the Arabs were ripe for active recruitment. The Kabylia was seen as the kernel of Algeria and a key zone in the operations against the rebels. It was the link between Algiers and Constantine and its mountains dominated the rich agricultural plain of the European *colons*. Much of the ethnology employed in setting up the integration schemes was anachronistic: the information that the area was not committed to the FLN was largely incorrect, and the secret formation of a 'counter-maquis' code-named Oiseau Bleu was no less fantastical than Maeterlinck's fairy tale from which it appears to have derived its name. It turned to farcical disaster when the carefully groomed recruits turned the arms they had been given against their French commanders, ambushed them close to the village of Iguer n'Salem on 1 October 1956 and escaped to the mountains with the local inhabitants. Angry and humiliated, the French unit set fire to the abandoned village, and the 'integration' strategy was replaced by one of reprisals. Those who had fled to the forest of Adrar, a traditional place of refuge, were unable to survive the heavy bombing and artillery fire.[19] The FLN was the only victor: it had sabotaged the counter-insurgency plan and its army gained hundreds of new volunteers as the French repression interned scores of villagers in guarded camps and made everyday life into a nightmare of arrests and arbitrary shootings.

None of this desperate army activity made the headlines in France. Under the state of emergency declared in April 1955, the French public heard little beyond the shocking accounts of murder and mutilation of Europeans by the Muslim fighters. As in Indo-China, it was thought that pacification adequately described the aim of the French forces, increased from 60,00 in 1954 to 200,000 two years later. But troops recalled from the reserve were aware that this was more than a law-and-order exercise. Protests at points of mobilization and embarkation were hushed up by an intrusive censorship, but legislative elections in January 1956 gave voice to disquiet, and a Socialist victory led to a government under Guy Mollet which appeared ready to reconsider the whole Algerian campaign. Mollet turned to General Catroux, who was identified with reconciliation in Morocco, and went in person to Algiers on 6 February 1956 to announce his new, conciliatory line. He was met by nothing short of a threatened coup by *pied-noir* activists, gathered in Algiers at the head of an angry European mob who paraded their deep emotional attachment to Algeria, demanded an intensified repression of the FLN and no reforms until the terror had been defeated.

Mollet was both shaken and moved by his reception, which recalled the passion of the Paris riots of 6 February twenty-two years before. He conceded immediately and reversed his policy. Catroux was withdrawn and the tough Robert Lacoste, ignorant of Algeria but responsive to strong patriotic gestures, was nominated in his place. Mollet was given sweeping special powers by a huge parliamentary majority, including an ambivalent Communist Party which condemned the demonstration in Algiers as 'fascist' but voted the powers none the less. Young conscripts on national service were sent to Algeria, doubling the number of troops to 400,000, and the Socialist Lacoste was given virtual *carte blanche* to resort to wholesale internment and violent house-to-house combing operations. Ironically Mollet's Minister for France *d'outre-mer*, Gaston Defferre, Socialist mayor of Marseille, simultaneously gained the backing of the Chamber for a project giving Madagascar and black Africa extended self-government under French-appointed governors, a notable step towards decolonization. His liberalizing law of June 1956 applied to all parts of France *d'outre-mer*, bringing representative hopes to repressed indigenous groups such as the Melanesians in New Caledonia. But again, Algeria was different. In July 1957 Mollet's special powers were extended to France: Algerian immigrants were viewed as potential enemy aliens and FLN suspects were confined in special centres. Under Mollet the reality of war was there for everyone to see, but the word was withheld. The government refused to call it a war: it remained a *guerre sans nom*.

The depth of the war's inhumanity was reached in 1957. Following a spate of FLN terror bombings in Algiers, the Tenth Paratroop Division under General Jacques Massu arrived in January to track down the local FLN networks. Confined to the jumble of narrow streets and impoverished dwellings of the Casbah, the FLN leaders and activists were ruthlessly combed out by counter-resistance tactics, based on the systematic use of torture, mainly electric shocks to feet, throat and genitals, administered to naked bodies flat on a table, with the head covered to avoid recognition of the torturers.[20] The parallel to Nazi tactics during the Occupation was no deterrent to the French perpetrators. Their justification was the same as the Gestapo's chilling logic and calculation: Massu argued that torture was the only way to unmask an unidentified enemy. In response the FLN extended its urban terror, planting bombs in cafés, clubs and restaurants full of young Europeans. The bloody battle of Algiers lasted over eight months until all the FLN of the Casbah were dead or arrested. The French victory was pyrrhic at best. The moral cost still continues to mount in an unending sequence of memoirs and histories by Algerians and French, exposing the

ugly facts of torture and rape which subsequent French governments of the twentieth century never fully admitted. Torture in the Algerian war was institutionalized by the French army: it was not an exception, and ministerial appointees of Guy Mollet's government were shown by the historian Pierre Vidal-Naquet to have authorized its practice.[21] Guy Mollet denied all knowledge of it; General de Gaulle knew of it but kept silent. André Malraux recognized officially on 24 June 1958 that torture had been used in Algeria, and announced its cessation. It did not stop.

Among those in France deeply concerned at events in Algeria, the evidence of torture was appalling confirmation of the judgement made as early as November 1955 by an Action Committee against the war in North Africa: 'This war is shameful. We have no right to impose on our soldiers methods that we ourselves condemned ten years ago.' It was signed by a wide range of well-known personalities identified with the Resistance, and by numerous younger intellectuals, and justifiably claimed to be the widest expression of similar opinion since the Anti-fascist Vigilance Committee of 1934 and the constellation of Dreyfusards at the time of the Affair. Many had already taken a stand against the Indo-China war, and the same newspapers and journals, *Témoignage chrétien*, *Esprit*, *L'Express*, *France-Observateur*, *Le Monde* and *L'Humanité*, were at the forefront with articles which exposed the descent of French authorities, army and police into atrocities against the Algerians.

Protests escalated in 1957–8, heavily censored and often unknown until many years later. Claude Bourdet had arraigned the police and army for Gestapo methods in *France-Observateur* in January 1955; Pierre-Henri Simon's *Contre la torture* in 1957 was a humanist rejection of torture by a liberal Catholic author who was conspicuously not a partisan of Algerian independence. He did not give his sources, but in contrast Vidal-Naquet fully documented his accusation that a young Algerian mathematician, Maurice Audin, had been tortured to death. It was published in May 1958 as *L'Affaire Audin* by Éditions de Minuit, the iconic Resistance publishing house, and its details caused a storm. It became revered as the symbolic revelation of French democracy in crisis, alongside *La Question* by Henri Alleg who had been arrested shortly after Audin. An Audin Committee was formed and Jean-Paul Sartre made the crimes of the war a focal issue of the leading left-wing review, *Les Temps modernes*. The fullest dossier, vividly describing the types of torture, naming the army torturers and listing the victims, was compiled by the Audin Committee and the Ligue des Droits de l'Homme in September 1958 and was prefaced with the statement that the Algerians had also perpetrated brutal atrocities which needed to be

condemned. 'Nevertheless,' it went on, 'we have concentrated on the acts of French soldiers and officers because they are acting in the name of the French nation.'[22]

The anti-war movements which mushroomed after the battle of Algiers expressed anger at the traumatic predicament of young French conscripts, whose fear in the face of guerrilla warfare and the mutilations practised by Algerians in certain areas of the fighting was compounded by their moral disarray at the everyday acts of brutality by the French army to which they themselves became accustomed. In seven years almost 2.7 million soldiers crossed from France to fight in Algeria, many returning after their period of service with accounts which severely undermined the official line. It was the involvement of raw twenty-year-olds in this savage war without a name which finally tipped public opinion against it, and made French withdrawal from Algeria a necessity. But this was not without the threat of civil war, the turn to General de Gaulle to resolve the most severe national crisis since 1940 and the unlamented collapse of the Fourth Republic.

The national and international drama of the war

In April 1955 FLN representatives attended the Bandung conference in Indonesia which marked the arrival of Third World countries in international politics. The ideological impetus given by the conference to liberational movements across the world cannot be exaggerated. Sheltered and supported by General Nasser in Egypt, the FLN missed no opportunity to claim Third World status, to play on the international repercussions of the Cold War and exploit the instability of Western influence in the Middle East. In contrast the French authorities, while insisting that Algeria was an internal matter, committed a series of blunders which alienated international opinion. On 22 October 1956 a Moroccan plane carrying the FLN leaders Ben Bella, Boudiaf, Aït-Ahmed and Khider from Rabat to Tunis was re-routed by the pilot under instructions from the French military command and flown to Algiers. The rebel leaders were arrested and despite the outcry from Morocco and Tunisia the illegal hijack was condoned by Guy Mollet. At exactly the same time Mollet's government was preparing a military operation with Israel and Britain against General Nasser, who had nationalized the Suez Canal in July.

The determination to attack Egypt was largely punitive, in response to Nasser's support for the FLN, though also ideological in the sense that the ministers most closely identified with the Algerian war denounced him as an agent of Soviet Communism. The *casus belli* was reinforced by images of

the Egyptian leader as an antisemitic dictator who should not be appeased. Protecting the young Israeli nation, laying the ghosts of Vichy's persecution of the Jews and righting the mistakes of Munich were high among the motivations for the Suez operation, but the composite reasoning lacked overall credibility and the campaign, launched on 1 November, was scandalously over-secretive, under-co-ordinated and unsure of its ultimate objectives. The United Nations, the USSR and most significantly the USA condemned the action, and the invaders were forced to withdraw after less than a week as hostile British public opinion as well as international opprobrium undermined the rationale of the whole expedition. The French public was not so critical, and the Mollet government even gained a certain parliamentary kudos from the event, but in North Africa there was derision, and within the FLN a surge of confidence.

Neither the hijack nor the Suez affair produced the guilt which followed a French raid on the Tunisian village of Sakhiet Sidi Youssef on 8 February 1958. Accused by Lacoste of harbouring the ALN, the village was bombed from the air and destroyed. Seventy villagers were killed, many of them children. The parallel with the Nazi bombing of Guernica was immediately drawn by international opinion, universally horrified. The atrocity of Sakhiet alienated world opinion more than any previous event in the war. Within France confidence in the government's handling of the war slumped both inside and outside parliament. A downward spiral of shame, mistrust and inter-party recriminations paralysed the political system for over two months. The right feared a sell-out in Algeria, forced by American 'good offices' imposed on France by international pressure. Prime Ministers came and went and President Coty finally decided he would have to appoint Pierre Pflimlin, known to be in favour of negotiations with the FLN and totally unacceptable to the *pieds-noirs*. The date for his investiture was 13 May 1958.

Early in the morning a violent and angry crowd of *pieds-noirs* assembled in Algiers, inflamed by the news that three soldiers had just been executed by the FLN. They took the government buildings by assault, and established revolutionary credentials by acclaiming a Committee of Public Safety led by General Massu. Algiers confronted Paris. Pflimlin was defiantly invested by parliament, but yet again there was a clear echo of 6 February 1934: like Daladier, Pflimlin was forced to yield to the event. It was clear the army would not put down the Algiers revolt. On 15 May the name of General de Gaulle was put forward by army leaders and he declared himself ready to assume the responsibilities of power, neither praising nor condemning Massu and the insurgents but carefully stressing his respect for republican

government. To the army and the European rebels in Algeria the appointment of de Gaulle as Prime Minister was the favoured solution. In Paris it became apparent that he was the only solution to what was clearly a terminal crisis of the regime.

On 1 June General de Gaulle, the political leader most identified with opposition to the Fourth Republic, came formally out of retirement and was invested as Premier. Now the echo was of Pétain in June 1940. De Gaulle was adamant that a new constitution had to be devised, but contrary to Pétain he never ceased to talk in republican terms. His proposals for a new Republic, the Fifth, were overwhelmingly endorsed by referendum on 28 September. The 'Yes' vote of almost 80 per cent was interpreted by some as giving retrospective legitimacy to the revolt of 13 May, but this was always inaccurate. What it really entailed was a massive belief that de Gaulle could rescue the whole Algerian crisis.

The repercussions revealed the extent to which French opinion about Algeria had polarized since Mollet's shock encounter with *pied-noir* intransigence in 1956 and the deployment of national servicemen in active combat. In opinion polls there was still little support for Algerian independence, but there was a significant demand for negotiations, supported by 53 per cent in 1957 and 71 per cent in 1959. Still more, a vocal ideological front denounced what was perceived as a fascist threat from the *pieds-noirs* and the army leaders in Algiers. The argument for French Algeria began to look less and less like the optimistic vision of the future that Mitterrand had outlined and more and more like a doctrinaire crusade of the extreme right. It was indicative that Mitterrand and Mendès France were both to be found among the 300,000 demonstrators who marched to the Place de la République on 28 May to register their refusal of a 'fascist' takeover from Algiers.

The wealthy *colons* and the majority of the *pieds-noirs* were prepared to threaten civil war to protect the Algeria they had created. Alongside them the French army officers deployed against the FLN had a practical reason for defending the aims of the *putsch*. Many were still moderating repression with inducements to the Algerian people through constructive modernization projects. The officers knew that the goal of integration depended on Muslim confidence that the French were going to remain in Algeria. Their brief was to convince villagers that this was the case. In many areas officers herded Algerians to the polls on 28 September, giving them only 'Yes' ballot papers in the referendum, and most enforced a 'Yes' vote on the contingent of soldiers under their command. For many of the conscripts, just turned twenty-one, it was their first experience of the democratic process. They favoured de Gaulle, but the farce of the vote alienated many

from their officers.[23] A new alterity began to operate within the ordinary ranks of the army in Algeria. The image of the 'other' was predominantly that of the Algerian, stereotyped racially as savage, dirty and lazy: but emerging now was a political 'other', the *pieds-noirs*, the *colons* and the officers who were increasingly seen as undemocratic, privileged and fanatical. Some of the officers who had fought in Indo-China were seen by the conscripts as psychologically damaged by the defeat: their zealous determination to succeed in Algeria made their motives suspect to those whose main concern was to get home as soon as possible. The events of 1958 accelerated the disenchantment of many conscripts. Behind their enthusiasm for de Gaulle was a belief that he would end the brutalizing war quickly; this was quite different from the ideology of 13 May which was to keep Algeria French, whatever the costs.

The ambivalent legacy of resistance

The legendary status of de Gaulle in the nation's history from 1940 to 1945 and the expectations on his return accentuated the significance of the German Occupation and the Resistance in people's attitudes to the Algerian war. Parallels, contrasts and comparisons were drawn at every turn of events. What clearly emerged was the relativity of personality and politics: the polarity between colonial apologist Bidault and anti-colonialist Bourdet was symptomatic of a political diaspora of ex-resisters: they could be found on all sides of the conflict. The resistance ideal was fragmented but was still a vital point of reference. A few hundred French men and women worked secretly for the FLN within France. Their smuggling of money raised for the war from Algerian immigrants led them to be named *porteurs de valises* (suitcase carriers). High among their motivations was the memory or experience of resistance against the Germans, couched in terms of the fight for freedom, the very cause which they believed the FLN embodied.[24] If the defence of this cause involved acts of civil disobedience, then that too had its precedent in the acts of illegality undertaken by resisters in the name of patriotism and a higher form of justice. When Francis Jeanson created a clandestine network of *porteurs de valises* in 1957, and when the public campaign against the use of torture exploded in 1958–9, it seemed logical to all those involved that the resistance tradition would be aligned against the perpetrators of repression in Algeria. De Gaulle's arrival on the scene opened up other aspects of the resistance legacy, not least the primacy of national interest, the 'certaine idée de la France' to which the insurgents of 13 May appealed.

Initially de Gaulle identified with the lobby which had brought him to power: Soustelle was appointed as Minister of Information and he confirmed General Raoul Salan, who had authorized Massu's Committee of Public Safety and put forward de Gaulle's name, as political and military supremo in Algeria. Everything indicated that de Gaulle would seek to integrate Algeria through a combination of military action and economic concessions and his supporters were sure he would succeed where the Fourth Republic had failed. But the militants of French Algeria were watching his every turn of phrase, and when he made signs in October 1958 that he envisaged more of a partnership between Algeria and France, there were rumblings of discontent among the *pieds-noirs* and the army leaders. On 19 September the FLN had set up a Provisional Government of the Algerian Republic under Ferhat Abbas, and refused all talk of a ceasefire or a peace with honour. They were not speaking from a position of military strength, having suffered major reversals, but their political cause was attracting increasing international support and de Gaulle was acutely aware of the resulting damage to French prestige. From December 1958 and throughout the following year his policy moved sharply towards political negotiation, but to free his hands completely he had to remove the army out of politics. Salan was withdrawn and Massu forced to abandon his political role. It seems certain that only de Gaulle as military leader could have brought the army to heel, but it was not without dramatic consequences.

The turning point was signalled by de Gaulle on 16 September 1959. He affirmed Algeria's right to self-determination once there was a cessation of the fighting. The gauntlet was picked up instantly in France with the formation round Bidault and the Algerian deputies of a Rassemblement pour l'Algérie Française. In January 1960 Massu declared that the army no longer backed de Gaulle and called on the *colons* to set up paramilitary organizations which he would arm. He was recalled at once, but the trail of powder had been lit. Barricades went up in Algiers on 24 January in defence of French Algeria. De Gaulle responded by condemning the FLN and the French activists in Algiers in equal measure but also giving assurances to the *pied-noir* community that the links between Algeria and France would not be severed.

It was enough to defuse the revolt, but intractable lines of conflict had been drawn. Soustelle was excluded from government at the beginning of February and joined Bidault in consolidating all those in French politics who responded to the die-hard slogan of 'Algérie Française'. The FLN, sensing its ultimate power, intensified its tactics of terror against both Europeans and their Muslim recruits. De Gaulle's policy of a ceasefire

followed by a compromise settlement was consistently rejected by the FLN, and his political realism took him gradually towards an acceptance of its failure, confirmed by a television broadcast on 4 November 1960 in which he finally acknowledged that the future lay with an Algerian Republic. He submitted his changed perspective to a further public referendum, receiving a majority of over 75 per cent on 8 January 1961 in favour of negotiations on this basis.

In the vanguard of support for the FLN, the Jeanson network of *porteurs de valises* had extended its subversive activities alongside a more public campaign to encourage conscripts to defy the draft. The network was infiltrated by the police, and those arrested were brought before a military tribunal in Paris in September 1960, accused of aiding terrorism. They based their defence on the right established by de Gaulle on 18 June 1940 and the internal Resistance to rebel against an unjust order: 'Of course . . .,' said Micheline Pouteau, one of those who received a ten-year sentence, 'we used the texts of de Gaulle against him . . .'[25]

In the vanguard of Algérie Française a civil and military coup was hatched in the winter of 1960–61 by the newly formed Organisation de l'Armée Secrète (OAS), with Salan at the centre. Its name invoked the actions and heroism of the Armée Secrète of the Resistance: Colonel Godard, an ex-maquisard of the Vercors, was in charge of information. Meanwhile de Gaulle, the embodiment of the *nation résistante*, tacked his way towards a peace initiative to re-establish French credibility. The claim by all sides to the inheritance of the Resistance was a measure of the struggle for legitimacy.

The bitter end

There was no relief to the horrors of the war during 1961. The OAS declared that the French army, in major part loyal to de Gaulle's change of direction, was no less its enemy than the FLN. Adapting ALN and Viet Minh tactics to its own ends, the OAS was made effective by several officers associated with psychological warfare and the battle of Algiers. Generals Challe, Zeller, Jouhaud and Salan led a further political *putsch* on 22 April 1961, stepped up reprisals against the FLN, and mobilized the anger of the European population against what they saw as de Gaulle's treachery, the treason of FLN supporters within France and the decadence of a left-wing intelligentsia. The ideological trappings of racial superiority, right-wing nationalism and anti-Communism led some to invoke Vichy and Pétainism as the 'true' resistance against the forces of national disintegration. For its

part the ALN increased its attacks on Europeans and pursued the liquidation of all those who served the interests of the French.

The theory of mirror violence was carried to new heights by Frantz Fanon, the Martinican psychoanalyst whose escalating commitment to anti-colonialism had made him the intellectual representative of the FLN's Provisional Government and one of the editors in Tunis of the FLN paper *El Moudjahid*. Following a close psychological study of the war, banned by the French government, he produced a revolutionary treatise which justified black liberational violence against the inherent white violence of colonial rule, published as *Les Damnés de la terre* (*The Wretched of the Earth*) in 1961. It became the classic vindication of the Algerian cause and a permanent indictment of colonialism, more unyielding than the writings of Fanon's teacher Césaire. In 1961 it gave a powerful twist to the spiral of ideology.

So too did the extension of OAS violence into metropolitan France. The last stand of Algérie Française was bombs planted in Paris and the threat of a paratroop invasion of the mainland. De Gaulle in person and the household of André Malraux were targets of assassination attempts, while the unpredictability of the bomb blasts made civilians into random victims. Bidault and some eighty political followers argued the case for the OAS within parliament. Supported internationally by apartheid South Africa and Salazar's Portugal, the OAS kept the birthright of French Algerians to the fore, but as a political defence of colonial privilege it badly miscalculated majority public opinion, which for the first time began to face the stark facts that decolonization was a reality, that it had been mishandled over two decades and that the whole process had become a severe national defeat. Anti-colonial protests were in the ascendant, vitalized by the Manifesto of 121 prominent writers, actors and intellectuals issued on 6 September 1960 in support of the Jeanson network and affirming the 'right to refuse to take up arms in Algeria'. The swing in opinion was both cause and effect of de Gaulle's mounting concessions to the FLN, capped in September 1961 by the cession to Algeria of sovereignty over the oil and gas fields in the Sahara.

De Gaulle's shifts of policy did not mean that the new Fifth Republic was sympathetic to demonstrations of Algerian opinion within France. Still legally French, the 350,000 Algerians living in France were the object of arrests and internment and were controlled by curfew instructions which were of dubious legality. On 17 October 1961 a peaceful protest against these controls and in solidarity with the FLN brought thousands of Algerian men, women and children in a festive mood on to the streets of Paris. They

were brutally broken up by the forces of order under the authority of Maurice Papon, ex-Vichy administrator in Bordeaux and ex-Prefect of Constantine in Algeria, who was now Prefect of the Paris police. In an operation which was later compared to the herding of Jews into the Vélodrome d'Hiver in 1942, the police penned 11,500 Algerian men overnight into the Palais des Sports, detaining over 1,000 for several weeks and releasing the others only slowly. In the night's action the police killed or made away with an unknown number of Algerians, and the appearance of bodies floating in the Seine over the following days led to some estimates that as many as 200 were murdered.

Pogrom or massacre, the facts of the night were suppressed, although Bourdet challenged Papon to respond to the accusation that at least fifty Algerians had been killed in the actual courtyard of the Préfecture de Police. There was no reply. Papon's trial in 1997–8 for complicity in the deportation of Jews from Bordeaux in 1942 spurred the Jospin government into releasing archives relating to 17 October 1961, and in February 1999 there was the first admission by an official of the state that excessive violence had been used by the police, but how many had secretly been killed remained obscured by the years of official denial or silence, begun by the government of de Gaulle.

In 1962 the paratroops of the OAS did not descend, but the police were responsible for yet more deaths in Paris, when a Communist-organized protest on 8 February against the OAS bombings was driven backwards by baton charges in which eight people, three of them women and one a young child, were crushed to death trying to escape the beatings at the entrance to the métro station of Charonne. The adult dead were mostly ordinary French Communists, and the political and public outcry against these French deaths at Charonne contrasts starkly with the absence of any major public protest against the deaths of Algerians on 17 October 1961. Mention of police killings at a demonstration in the final stages of the Algerian war was always taken to mean Charonne, a permanent memorial site in the history of the PCF, which had increasingly opposed the repression in Algeria but had not taken the strong pro-independence line that it had argued for the Viet Minh.

The burial of the Charonne dead in the cemetery of Père Lachaise was the occasion for hundreds of thousands from the political and trade-union left to show opposition to the war, shortly before de Gaulle and the FLN signed a ceasefire at Évian-les-Bains in the Haute-Savoie on 18 March, approved by 90 per cent of the electorate on 8 April. In Algiers the OAS replied to Évian with a general strike of Europeans and insurrectional

defiance in the *quartier* of Bab el-Oued, which eventually exposed a civilian demonstration of *pieds-noirs* to the mercy of the French army who fired on the crowd, killing forty-six. In utter despair the *pieds-noirs* left their homes in their thousands, eventually reaching over 800,000 after the declaration of Algerian independence on 1 July 1962. Some fled to Israel and Spain, but 80 per cent of them made their way to the south of France, forming their own communities in exile, embittered at betrayal and defiantly proud of their past.

Separate, and far more vulnerable, were the Algerian *harkis* who had identified with the French, less than half of whom managed to reach the mainland. In Narbonne and other areas of the south they were housed in disused internment camps which themselves became ghetto communities, deliberately isolated by the French authorities from the rest of society which knew little and cared less about their existence. Used in the first years of the war to exemplify the policy of integration, they were now victims of social ostracism and a mix of racial and political contempt. Within Algeria they were despised as collaborators, hunted down by the FLN and killed. The numbers executed at the end of the war were estimated by Jean Lacouture, after an investigation for *Le Monde* in October 1962, to have exceeded 10,000, although French army sources put the total Muslim victims of the FLN throughout the war at over six times that number.[26] This higher estimate has to be considered in relation to the army's underestimate of the number of Algerians killed by the French, in combat or in reprisals, which it totalled at 141,000, whereas the FLN produced figures of at least a million, figures which officially entered the national Algerian history of the revolutionary and liberational struggle. Other, demographic, accounts have varied between 200,000 and 500,000 as a total of all Algerian losses in the war, a ratio of deaths to population none the less equivalent to the terrible figures for France during the First World War. No doubt surrounds the deaths suffered by the French army in combat or as a result of accidents, which were established as 24,614, with civilian losses among the European population between 4,000 and 4,500.[27] The OAS killed 2,700 people, 2,400 of them Muslims.

The disputed statistics and the exodus of the *pieds-noirs* were two of several highly charged issues which perpetuated conflict over the war, influencing the political landscape and the perceptions of the 1940s resistance generation by the youth of the 1960s. The professional soldiers, national servicemen and reservists who died in the fighting were not commemorated on war memorials, nor did they receive the accolade of 'morts pour la France'. Interviews by historians, and the bitter accounts in the

1990 film by Bertrand Tavernier, *La Guerre sans nom,* have registered the historical limbo of the soldiers. It was not until mid-1999 that the word *guerre* was officially established for the events of 1954–62. Already certain *communes* whose politics were mainly on the right had insisted on recognition of the French who died in Algeria: but in 2000 this was still a contested political gesture. Legitimation for the OAS was collectively established in much of *pied-noir* memory and was periodically rehearsed by extreme right-wing movements throughout the rest of the century. The presence of ex-resisters among them confirmed the fragmentation of the Resistance as a force in post-1945 politics.

A new resistance

A new resistance, however, had been born and was vindicated by the liberation of Algeria. An independent politics of human rights succeeded where the main parties of the left had failed. 'A man has disappeared' was the simple headline of the first pamphlet on Maurice Audin, with his photograph underneath. That a French campaign and a committee should be set up to find what had happened to a virtually unknown Algerian was a potent symbol in itself. To go further and accuse the state of torturing Algerians when the French public had been horrified by the press images of European bodies appallingly mutilated by the ALN, marked a decisive break with national sentiment. Opposition movements were the stock-in-trade of French politics, but the Jeanson network, the Audin Committee and the intellectuals who signed the Manifesto of 121 did not constitute themselves as new political parties but represented the rights of those that successive governments claimed to have integrated into French culture and had then repudiated as the brutal enemy. Resistance to the Algerian war was the proclamation of the necessity of dissidence within France against unacceptable government policies. It assimilated Third Worldism and the liberational movements within the colonies into the existing tradition of resistance dating from the German Occupation. Its power was that of words, information and independent enquiry. Its innovation was to challenge the dominant belief in a unitary Frenchness and its civilizing mission. It was a landmark in the discovery and the defence of cultural and ethnic difference.

The *porteurs de valises* were the first component of this resistance and their commitment to the FLN an extreme version of 'seeing the war from the other side'. They sparked no strikes and little sabotage and they persuaded very few conscripts to desert. They were clandestine but did not

take up arms in the hills nor organize international brigades to fight in Algeria. Many other critics of the war parted company with them over atrocities committed by the FLN. The young historian Pierre Vidal-Naquet argued at the time that the strength of the anti-torture campaign was that it condemned the abuse of human rights on all sides.[28] As partisans of the FLN, therefore, the *porteurs de valises* have never gained the legitimacy that might have been expected. And yet Benjamin Stora, eminent historian of Algeria, could reasonably conclude, 'A handful of *porteurs de valises* awoke the French and European left, raised the question of state terrorism . . . and faced the problem of new relationships between the West and the Third World.'[29]

As for the role of government in the ending of the war, de Gaulle's shifting policies were viewed alternatively as premeditated or as a realistic politics of response. The nature of his return to power and his enlarged authority as President provoked charges of Bonapartism, autocracy and even fascism. In the massive consensus on the Évian proposals there were people on the left who abstained in the vote of 8 April 1962 or who wrote, 'Yes to peace, No to de Gaulle'. On the extreme right for several years de Gaulle continued to be the object of assassination attempts by an OAS whose leaders were sentenced to imprisonment or exile, but which continued a shadowy existence. Bidault was stripped of his parliamentary immunity but was allowed to leave for Portugal and Brazil; Soustelle went into exile; Salan was imprisoned. A pardon for members of the OAS was signed by de Gaulle in June 1968 and a series of political amnesties followed. There was no national recognition of the inhumanities of French rule and repression, but nor was there any attempt to gild the loss of Algeria. At Évian in 1962 there was only one victor, the FLN, but de Gaulle emerged as a decolonizer. Given the political objectives of 13 May 1958, this was the most unexpected outcome of the war.

14

The Chequered Imperative of Change, 1940s–1958

1. The urgency of social change

In 1945 the difficult emergence of French society from yet another decimating war with Germany was also an awakening to the urgency of social change. It was no longer a political option but a national necessity. After the First World War, nostalgia among the privileged sections of society for an imagined pre-war *belle époque* of tradition and stability had reasserted the hold of social conservatism, which continued to be dominant in the inter-war years. The Popular Front reforms had broken the mould, but the backlash under Daladier followed by Vichy's social policies had re-established the dominance of traditionalism. In 1945 the urgency for change involved coming to terms with the social implications not just of the Second World War but also, finally, of the First.

Programmes of social change were not without their own elements of tradition, nor was social change itself a united and coherent programme. For over twenty years two forces for change had been pitted, often violently, against each other. On the one hand, the labour movement, identified with the expectations of socialism, Communism and anarcho-syndicalism, had heralded social change for so long that it was imbued with its own ritualistic traditions of protest, strikes and class conflict. On the other hand, there was a rival vision of social change from employers who exalted the market economy and a rationalized system of industrial production, identified largely with American innovations. Productivist bravura promised to change the dynamics of industry and outmanoeuvre class conflict with the mass effects of market-based capitalism. It was referred to simply as 'modernization' but it also had its traditions, in this case the age-old economics of labour exploitation. Despite the fascination of some industrialists and technocrats with improving workers' conditions as well as their productivity, and despite the interest of Jouhaux and some other CGT leaders in the possibilities of harnessing technological change in the interests of the

workers, these two forces in the inter-war years represented stark alterna-tives in their understanding of the present and their images of the future.

And yet, for nearly three years after the Liberation, productivism had the backing of the CGT and the Communist Party in what was probably as singular a conjuncture as any in the social history of twentieth-century France.

Productivism

Vichy had placed work at the front of its triad of national values, 'Travail, Famille, Patrie'. Recovering 'travail' from Vichy was the agenda of clan-destine trade-union activity throughout the Occupation. The aim was to restore the historic discourse of the labour movement with its stress on the right to work and the rights of workers. But in the crisis of continuing shortages and with the need for rapid reconstruction, something of the moral urgency of Vichy's call to work was repackaged in the immediate post-Liberation period. A third of the active population were registered as workers (*travailleurs*), and it was to these, and to peasant farmers, that the exhortations from the Provisional Government and Assembly, and notably from the Communist Party, were addressed in the name of resistance and patriotism, demanding a battle for production as the necessary complement and sequel to the successful battle against the Germans and Vichy.

'We are building a brighter tomorrow' ran the pamphlet produced by the Union de la Jeunesse Républicaine de France late in 1945. It claimed 300,000 members from a constellation of Communist and affiliated youth movements, and extolled the way in which young men and women were rebuilding Caen, Le Havre, Royan and Digne and were everywhere in the vanguard of the national battle for production and reconstruction. It was self-consciously modern in its call for voting at eighteen, its recognition of the bravery of young women in the Resistance 'equal to that of young men', and its support for mixed youth organizations with contingent provision for 'girls whose parents do not permit such intermingling'. It was committed to secular education but made no reference to political ideology or class conflict. For two and a half years it was symptomatic of the high profile given by the PCF to pragmatic politics, and it was coupled with a propa-ganda salvo to reassure small farmers, boost their productivity and secure a rapid improvement of food supplies to the towns. Overtures from the party to peasants, calling for improved market prices for their products, the defence of peasant property, free loans to young farmers and an end to the exploitation of share-cropping, convey something of the rural as well

as urban roots of Communist resistance and the drive at the Liberation to produce a wide-ranging package of social change.

Extolling production meant extolling practices at work which had long been unacceptable within the trade-union movement. The irony of Communists issuing instructions and moral lectures which echoed those of productivist employers was not lost on the workers themselves, but their protests were blunted by their own belief in the PCF as the vanguard of the proletariat and as *le parti des fusillés* during the German Occupation.

Miners, in particular, were exposed to the force of the productivist drive. An imagery of pit-heads, slag-heaps and mining cottages took on an epic, heroic quality. Nationalization of the northern mines in May 1946 was followed by a special statute for miners which elevated them above all other comparable workers and led to an assurance of a lifetime's social security with medical care and improved housing. Maurice Thorez, both as leader of the PCF and as government minister, stepped up the pace of exhortation after telling miners in July 1945 that 'producing ever more coal is your highest duty as workers and as Frenchmen'.[1] Productivity was further promoted by the PCF and the CGT as the way to defend the nationalized industry. By July 1946 the output of coal was back to pre-war levels.

Nationalization and welfare, 1944–1946

The context to this singular campaign for productivity was a forthright resistance programme of nationalizations, greater democracy at the workplace and universal welfare legislation. De Gaulle, after visiting the liberated north in September 1944, accepted that the prime industrial riches of the nation should be administered by the state. The whole programme expressed the ideals of the Conseil National de la Résistance (CNR) whose charter the Socialists (SFIO), Communists (PCF) and the new alignment of Christian Democrats (MRP) endorsed in their election manifestos throughout 1945–6; and both nationalization and welfare carried the CGT seal of approval and that of the Christian-based trade unions, the CFTC.

The programme was dubbed at once the French 'New Deal', and it consolidated a larger consensus of opinion behind it than any previous project of social change in the twentieth century. The wave of nationalizations in 1945 gave the state direct or indirect control not just over the coal-mines of the Nord and Pas-de-Calais but also the industries of gas and electricity, the airlines which became Air France, the aircraft engines of Gnôme et Rhône, the automobile industry of Renault, the Banque de France, the four main deposit banks and much of the insurance business.

Municipal pressure brought the Paris buses into the public domain, and there were experiments of workers in management through requisitions of the Berliet trucks in Lyon, the coal-mines of Alès on the fringe of the Cévennes, the Fouga metalworks in the Languedoc town of Béziers and prominent companies in Marseille. In these southern towns the initiatives were taken by the Commissaires de la République in sympathy with local resistance ideals and objectives, but the new structures which they authorized were short-lived, and permanent workers' control in these requisitioned local industries was not secured.

There was, in fact, no single model of nationalization, but the public company which took over Renault rapidly became a byword in productivist drive and efficiency. Under the dynamic leadership of Pierre Lefaucheux, who was born in 1898 in the same year as the Renault factory itself, the launching of the immediately popular Renault 4 CV in October 1946 gave nationalization a positive imprint. It reinforced the high level of public support for state initiatives, already well entrenched in state education and the running of the railway network, the SNCF, as a public service. The patterns of Jacobin centralism, Napoleonic *étatisme* and Jules Ferry's use of the state to revolutionize education all re-emerged in the social programme of post-1945, but the acceptance of state control was not uncritical: it was balanced by an insistence that degrees of representation should be assigned to workers or personnel and also to user groups. Private ownership was severely dented by these reforms, but ultimate authority in business and industry remained at the top, and the creation of a state academy for the training of administrators, the École Nationale d'Administration (ENA), underscored the post-war commitment to management as an élite profession.

Welfare provision, central to resistance ideals, was announced in December 1944 and October 1945, with subsequent amendments and extensions. It improved working people's lives in basic ways which had long been demanded by the labour movement. Compulsory contributions by all wage-earners and employers brought a measure of social security to all those in work, with payments for unemployment, illness, accident and death, and old-age pensions at roughly 20 per cent of working wages. Maternity benefits and child allowances were increased and expanded. Unemployment contributions were managed directly by the state, but the rest of the welfare system was controlled by administrators elected indirectly by the contributors, bringing together public provision and democracy in a consensus form which proved remarkably stable and effective. The impact of the CNR charter, together with ideas from over a century of social reformers,

ensured that individual contributions were wage-related but payments were common to all. Opposition to compulsory contributions did not, however, disappear in the face of social idealism: it remained high on the political agenda of groups who represented small business, peasant farming and the retail trade.

The voice of the *patronat* was muted throughout. Faced with the moral assertiveness of a left-wing majority which claimed the patriotic inheritance of the Resistance, the employers who formed the Conseil National du Patronat Français (CNPF) in June 1946 were strictly on the defensive. The CNPF's choice of its first president signified its acceptance of the post-war social mood. Georges Villiers, head of a medium-sized metal-working business, had been appointed by Vichy as mayor of Lyon to replace Édouard Herriot, but had become closely involved in resistance activities and had been deported by the Gestapo to Dachau. As a distinguished ex-resister, and blatantly not one of the largest industrial magnates, he was to lead the CNPF for twenty years.[2] His role was to rehabilitate the reputation of employers, heavily tarnished by over-identification with Pétain and variously accused of collaboration. He immediately found ways of adjusting to the new primacy of the state, not just in nationalizations and social welfare but also in economic planning, an adjustment made easier by the flexibility of Jean Monnet, the architect of post-war planning, whose pro-American policy secured the injection of capital into French industry through Marshall aid.

Originally from a family of brandy merchants at the centre of production in the small south-west town of Cognac, Jean Monnet was the epitome of the widely travelled and cosmopolitan expert. He had been economic co-ordinator with Britain during the First World War, consultant on modernization in China in 1933, negotiator with the USA for aviation rearmament in 1938–9, Vice-President of the British Supply Council in Washington in 1940, and adviser on liaisons with Roosevelt first to Giraud and then to de Gaulle and the Provisional Government. It was a testimony to Monnet's unique skills and experience, and to de Gaulle's rarely remembered capacity for the unpredictable, that the General did not hold Monnet's British–USA–Giraud connections against him. In December 1945 de Gaulle appointed him to head a planning commissariat to re-equip and modernize the French economy. Working with a team of specialists and political representatives, including Communists, Monnet drew up a five-year plan, firstly to get production back to the level of 1929 and then to surpass it by 25 per cent. It was by co-operation with Monnet's plan that the *patronat* moulded itself to the changed social realities.

No political upbeat

Women voted for the first time in municipal elections in April–May 1945 and in legislative elections in October, but women's suffrage was so long overdue that for many voters the milestone caused less excitement than had been anticipated. Newspapers carried patronizing articles on the need to educate women into the technicalities of politics, and there was an un-subtle subtext that women in politics should look after 'women's issues'. In the circumstances, however, these issues, defined in the press as food, family and health, were regarded as central to the urgent social needs which dominated public concern. This was forcibly recognized by the thirty-three women who were elected to the Constituent Assembly in October 1945, making up 5.6 per cent of the deputies. Most had been prominent in the Resistance. Seventeen were members of the PCF, nine of the MRP, and six of the Socialist Party (SFIO). Twenty-three of them were still there in the first National Assembly of the Fourth Republic from 1946 to 1951. They were the visible face of women resisters in politics, drawing attention to gender by their frequent cross-party references to the nature of women's resistance which had involved the struggle to find food for men and children at the same time as fighting the occupiers and Vichy. The relevance of this to the hardship of 1944–6 was explicit: so too their arguments on behalf of war widows and women working outside the home to keep their families fed. The women deputies' emphasis on these areas of concern and experi-ence appeared to accept the notion of 'women's issues' while at the same time challenging the limited language and focus of conventional party politics, and the definition of heroism in the war, as in peacetime. 'It's a lot easier,' argued Francine Lefebvre, 'to accomplish one outstanding act than to carry on fighting day after day with the same difficulties.'[3]

A strong case can be made that this gender-specific discourse was in tune with the priorities of the time, in a way that constitutional niceties, for all their necessity, appeared not to be. Whatever the precise reasons, the shortcomings of party politics as they configured the new Republic be-came one of the main causes of public discontent between 1944 and 1946. Any broad brush-strokes to depict the two years after the Liberation will capture the fact that voices were raised from every corner in favour of active political initiatives, and yet little enthusiasm was generated for the political process of elections and constitutional policy-formation at party level. Some explanation can be sought in the general absence of party politics in the clandestine press, where the motivations towards resist-ance lay in general principles on the one hand, and local objectives on the

other. There was also a sense of predictability in the constitutional outcome.

The failure of a united resistance party to survive underlined the near-consensus that all the existing parties of the left were justifiably the inheritors of the Resistance, particularly after the formation of the new party of Christian Democrats, the Mouvement Républicain Populaire (MRP), launched by resisters Georges Bidault, Pierre-Henri Teitgen, François de Menthon and Maurice Schumann in November 1944. The eventual placing of the MRP deputies in the Assembly measured the force of the Resistance in swinging the centre of political gravity to the left. Catholics replaced the Radicals as the main left-of-centre party, bringing consternation to old-style anticlericals. The Resistance marked the integration of Catholics into the politics of the Republic, despite the continued estrangement of the Church hierarchy which, with notable exceptions, remained tainted by Vichy. Nevertheless, Catholics sitting next to Socialists in the Chamber suggested that the world had really turned upside down. Or had it? There was agreement that the Third Republic could not be resuscitated, but party political debate appeared to many to narrow to the point where it looked predictable and familiar. It was regarded as repetitious and trivial by much of the public. For different reasons it increasingly irritated de Gaulle, whose identification with 'the resistance of the whole nation' (*la nation résistante*) and his grand rhetoric of national unity, world status and strong executive power grew more insistent as the interplay of the parliamentary parties intensified. On 20 January 1946 he abruptly resigned.

It was later claimed by de Gaulle's supporters that his departure revealed the unpopular and rudderless nature of the nascent Fourth Republic, but this was not really the case. The tripartite co-operation of the three largest blocks of deputies elected to the Constituent Assembly in October 1945, Communists, MRP and Socialists, worked effectively throughout 1946 to underpin the restructuring of society and determine the future of planning. This was a major historical achievement, even though the irony of the post-Liberation years deepened. The massively popular social changes took place against a backdrop of growing apathy about the nature of the new Republic. The intricate issues involved in launching the constitution and the four consultations of the electorate in 1946 enthused very few in the country at large. The rapid repetition of referenda and elections seemed increasingly irrelevant to a population struggling to feed itself.

Mounting inflation in the two years after the Liberation reduced the purchasing power of wages by 30 per cent. Food and household necessities were in acutely short supply and the situation appeared never to improve.

Monnet's plan was taking shape but was not put into effect until 1947, and no take-off in the production of consumer goods was visible, political sights being fixed on relaunching coal and heavy industry.

Cynicism about the economy was universal, and the illegal market (*marché noir*), masked by collusion at all levels, was probably more rampant and more exploitative than under the Occupation. Yves Farge, an eminent resister leader under cover as a journalist on *Le Progrès de Lyon*, Commissaire de la République for the Lyon area, and Minister of Provisions in mid-1946, waged a high-profile campaign against criminal stockists and traffickers whom he exposed in *Le Pain de la corruption* in 1947, accusing them of keeping prices extortionately high and creating the depths of poverty experienced in both town and country. Other ex-resisters such as Jacques Debû-Bridel, who had co-launched the Éditions de Minuit, equally blamed the *marché noir* but also argued that the highly controlled and centralized economy of the post-Liberation period had facilitated the ubiquitous corruption of what he called 'le gang'.[4]

The grudging voters, consulted in a referendum on 5 May 1946, rejected, by a slight majority, the Communist and Socialist plan for an all-powerful single Chamber, and voted more substantially on 13 October for an MRP compromise under which there would be an advisory second Chamber called not a Senate but a Conseil de la République. The Fourth Republic was finally given shape. Present in the making of both majorities was a fear that an unchecked Chamber of Deputies would give too much power to the popular PCF. In fact what checked the party were disagreements within the Tripartite pact which flared into open division in the spring of 1947. By then the PCF had 183 deputies from 28.2 per cent of the votes cast in the elections on 10 November 1946. The MRP was the second largest party with 167 deputies (25.9 per cent) and the Socialists third with 105 (17.8 per cent). The right was still tarred with the ignominy of Vichy.

Since well before the Liberation the PCF had done what it refused to do in 1936 at the time of the Popular Front. It accepted ministerial posts and responsibility under non-Communist leadership. The CGT, which Communists dominated after the Liberation, embraced productivism. Neither policy could avoid considerable disillusion at the grass roots of Communist and trade-union activity. In the mining industry a growing minority of voices in the pits objected that nationalization was centralized and bureaucratic: it was not the cherished ideal of 'mines run by miners'. There was escalating resentment at the reintroduction of piecework, of payment by results, of competition between and within pits, and of bonuses for foremen of the productive shifts. The working week steadily increased

from forty hours to forty-five. Calls grew for the Communist deputies to exercise their strength in numbers and insist on a more social politics of government, to relieve poverty, increase wages and control prices. It was this crescendo of Communist opinion throughout 1946 which led Socialist and MRP partners in Tripartism to mark their distance from the PCF. The broad left-wing majority began seriously to divide within itself.

2. Polarization and the Cold War

The reconfiguration of politics

The Cold War swept in from the East and the West. It also came from within. Politics in 1947 were reconfigured for a plethora of reasons. Punitive policy in Madagascar and the intensification of the Indo-China war exacerbated the tensions within Tripartism. Five Communists were members of the government which was bent on holding Madagascan politicians responsible for the island's revolt, and adamant on repressing the Communist movement of Ho Chi Minh. The PCF deputies abstained from voting further war credits on 22 March 1947, even though the Communist ministers voted reluctantly in favour. Their growing discomfort was expressed some three weeks later when they staged a walk-out from a government meeting on the Madagascan issue. A strike at Renault for increased wages on 25 April was at first condemned by the CGT and the PCF as instigated by 'Trotskyist provocateurs', but its popularity forced them to change direction and back its demands. This was precisely the shift of policy at the top of the PCF in response to pressures from below which the Socialists and the MRP had anticipated. The Socialist Prime Minister, Paul Ramadier, decided to force the Communists, both ministers and deputies, to decide the future of Tripartism at a vote of confidence in the Chamber. All Communists voted against the government, and Ramadier dismissed their ministers on 4 May. It was the end of over three years of innovative, reforming co-operation between the left-wing political inheritors of the Resistance. That inheritance was now to be bitterly disputed, not just on the left, but between the left and a new incarnation of Gaullists.

It took General de Gaulle less than a year to decide that he could not stay out of politics. A dress-rehearsal speech was staged in Bayeux on 16 June 1946, the second anniversary of the Norman town's liberation where de Gaulle had first been proclaimed the hero-liberator of the nation. The place was a potent symbol; the speech a reaffirmation of his constitutional vision for France: an independent head of state, elected by a broad

college and wielding full executive power, separated from two counter-balancing legislative Chambers. The autocratic tone of the speech was a miscalculation: if anything, it pushed his previous allies within the MRP into a more urgent compromise to protect the power of the legislature. This only reinforced his dire predictions for the Fourth Republic.

De Gaulle's full return was messianic. In a series of speeches in April 1947 he announced that he was to lead a Rassemblement du Peuple Français (RPF) and he appealed to all those who cared about the common good (*le salut commun*) to join him, over and above their political affiliations. His contempt for the constitutional settlement of 1946 was total; his doomsday image was of France unable to protect itself against the hegemonic ambitions of Soviet Russia abroad and the PCF at home. His appeal replicated that of 18 June 1940 from London, but immediate critics on the left heard also the echo of Pétain's self-projection as saviour of the nation.

There was, however, no external danger in 1947: the enemies of the RPF were all internal. De Gaulle re-entered politics with a populist agenda and set himself overtly against the entire left-wing majority. Within a year the RPF claimed it had more than a million adherents, undoubtedly more than double the reality, but in the municipal elections of October 1947 it registered itself across the country as the acceptable face of the right, dramatically taking Paris, Marseille and Bordeaux. Its success continued into the 1951 legislative elections: it won 21.6 per cent of the vote and 117 seats, second only to the PCF. The core support came from the self-employed middle classes, small traders, white-collar workers and peasant proprietors, notably in the northern half of the country. The RPF in theory and rhetoric reanimated the flame of de Gaulle's resistance. In reality it reformulated the ideology of nationalism which had been no less divisive in the inter-war years than the politics of the Marxist left.

Nationalism on the right and Communism on the left now re-created familiar roles as the two main oppositional forces to governments in which Socialists, the MRP, Radicals and others made up a series of revolving cabinets and constituted what was known as the Third Force. But the Gaullist epic from 1940 to 1944 gave the nationalism of the RPF a maverick quality which defied easy comparisons with right-wing predecessors. It was not the inheritor of the reactionary right which had welcomed Vichy. Die-hard Pétainists never forgave de Gaulle, nor did many of the followers of Giraud, and although the RPF was fervently anti-Communist, de Gaulle was widely blamed by the old right for having given the Communists a taste of government. Nor was the PCF of 1947 a facsimile of the marginal oppositional party of much of the inter-war period. It boldly disputed with

Gaullists the control of the resistance narrative, and it embodied the ideas and aspirations of over a quarter of all voters, mostly from the industrial centres, but numerous also within rural *communes* of the south. The Cold War hardened its ideology, but initially sharpened its appeal.

Insurrection?

American aid to Europe through the Marshall Plan, announced in June 1947 and accepted by the French government, was linked to President Truman's doctrine of containing Communism. A meeting of European Communist Parties in Poland in October 1947 was part of the Soviet response. The PCF was obliged to reformulate an anti-American, anti-capitalist and anti-colonial policy which would firmly break with the three years of co-operation with the Socialists and the MRP and would back the policies of the newly created Cominform. The reconfiguration of politics was inseparable from the Cold War scenario, but in many ways it made sense of the inherent tensions in post-Liberation France. Such was the level of unrest among trade-union militants that the return of the PCF to opposition was all that was needed to give political bite to pent-up industrial protest.

On 12 November the death of a young worker, Vincent Voulant, in clashes with the police in Marseille brought a stoppage to the area's port activity, metal industry and building work. By 15 November the strikes had spread to the mining industry of the Nord and Pas-de-Calais and two days later to Renault, Citroën and other metal industries in the Paris suburbs. In the south the tinderbox in Marseille lit a trail of incidents which flared to Lyon, Saint-Étienne, Nice, Perpignan, Béziers and Montpellier, with local Communist leaders of the CGT unions in the vanguard of organization. The demands were for an end to the incessant rise in prices and the decline in the standard of living. Workers had made sacrifices for productivity: their attitudes were now tough and unyielding. Occupation of factories and public buildings, sabotage and collective violence spread fiercely to other industrial centres. It was almost exactly the kind of political and social revolt that had been mistakenly expected from Communists at the Liberation. At moments it looked not only like the delayed insurrection from 1944 but still more the revolution for which militants had confidently joined the PCF in the inter-war years.

Municipal transport systems and the main rail network were effectively disrupted by strike action to which were added strategies of sabotage developed during the Resistance. René Clément's memorable film *La*

Bataille du rail in 1946 had extolled the heroism of railway resistance which had made the *cheminots* into martyrs at the hands of the Germans. In 1947 similar tactics were used but circumstances had changed. On the night of 2 December the Paris–Lille postal train was derailed near Arras. Sixteen people were killed and over thirty injured. The sabotage was aimed at suspected manoeuvres of armed police. The outcry in the press and the National Assembly chimed with that of the country at large: this time the saboteurs were not national heroes. Public sensitivity to the strikers' demands had marked the outbreak of the strikes: during early December it turned to criticism and hostility. But the violence was reciprocal. On 4 December two demonstrators were shot by police and military in a struggle for the railway station at Valence in the Rhône valley: a third died later. Injuries were serious on both sides. So too were injuries widely incurred in bitter fighting between strikers and non-strikers. Observers noted the absence of carnival humour, games and role-play so prevalent in 1936. The movement of 1947 was more specific to certain areas, many of them places where local and autonomous Communist activity had been strong during the Resistance. In the public service sector the support was fitful, but a sizeable minority of primary-school teachers took strike action, especially in the south.

Apogee of Communism

The daily organ of the PCF, *L'Humanité*, promoted the strikes with a campaign which claimed 2 million strikers by the end of November and considerable rural support from the peasantry. But Thorez did not have Stalinist authority to create an insurrection, still less a revolution. France was not in the Soviet sphere of influence and the word he brought back at the end of November 1947 from a meeting with Stalin in Moscow was to widen the anti-American front by any means possible. If this meant links with management across the factory floor they should have precedence over class conflict. The Cold War was given primacy over revolutionary strikes.[5]

By 7 December the movement was fragmenting, though strong bastions remained in the ports, the mines and the metalworking industries. Two days later the CGT strike committee called for a return to work. It was staged as a tactical closure, ending what was claimed by the strikers as a significant victory, in the sense that the labour movement had shown its ability to fight. Marseille was the setting for the last, as the first, casualty: on 9 December Sylvain Bettini, a young builder, died of injuries inflicted by the police the previous night.

The end of the strikes was willed by the Communist Party, but from the government's perspective it was claimed as a victory for Jules Moch, the Socialist Minister of the Interior who co-ordinated the state's counter-offensive, purging Communists from the new mobile republican police, the CRS, and re-establishing order by armed repression and retaliation. An ex-resistance volunteer in the Free French, Moch had been a member of Blum's team at the Matignon agreements in 1936, and was a deputy for Montpellier in the Hérault, one of the *départements* most affected by the strikes. His report a year later acknowledged that there had been no discernible revolutionary planning by the PCF, though he alerted the governments of the Third Force to the party's insurrectionary potential. Like Clemenceau exactly forty years before, Moch as strike-breaker became legendary, hated on one side, revered on the other. In defiance of Moch, the southern Communist deputy Raoul Calas broke into the 1907 song of revolt and mutiny before being forcibly expelled from the Chamber. A year later in October 1948 Moch reaffirmed his reputation by military intervention in the mines to suppress a widespread strike of 15,000 miners against a continued fall in real wages. Tanks and armoured cars spear-headed a brutal incursion into the mining communities. In Alès in the Gard a young worker, Marc Chaptal, was killed by the CRS, who were sent by Moch 'to protect the population' and who fired on a crowd of miners and their families. In an impassioned speech to the Chamber, the Communist deputy Gabriel Roucaute defied Moch to go and ask the people of Alès: 'Whose liberty was threatened by whom?'[6]

The prolonged year of social conflict, 1947–8, followed three years of political co-operation, reform and restructuring, though the tensions between the parties of the left were never far from the surface, tensions which many accepted as inevitable and were reflected in the post-war fractures within the labour movement after its show of unity during the Resistance. In the course of two years after the Liberation the Catholic unions (CFTC) debated how closely to adhere to their Catholic legacy while preferring independence from the CGT even at the expense of marginalization within the industrial working class. In 1946 the reformist wing of CGT, identified with the career of Léon Jouhaux and grouped around the publication *Force ouvrière*, marked its own opposition to the increasing Communist dominance at the top of the main confederation. The strikes of 1947 were less the cause of the final rupture between the two rival tendencies in the CGT than the occasion for their disagree-ments to be recognized openly. In December 1947 the reformists led by Robert Bothereau carried Jouhaux with them and resigned from the CGT's

leadership. They formed the CGT-FO (Force Ouvrière) in the spring of 1948. The break affirmed the division of trade-union institutions along ideological lines. The small CFTC remained critical of the fundamental doctrine of class conflict within the CGT; the reformists of Force Ouvrière (FO) made a feature of their anti-Communism, and the majority CGT claimed to encompass the vast bulk of the working class in its Communist revivalism. The united anti-fascism of the 1930s was no longer an urgent political necessity and the emotional ties of the shared Resistance had loosened.

One of the many glimpses of alternative pathways for the left is shown in the diary notes of Édouard Morin, a Catholic, resister, and trade unionist in the Burgundy complex of Le Creusot, centre of the Schneider family's industrial empire. In August 1940, at the age of forty-three, he started *Volny*, his own clandestine paper with its borrowed Polish title meaning 'free'. He bitterly criticized what he called 'official Catholicism' for its pro-Pétain sympathies. His 'nonconformism' continued after the Liberation when he worked tirelessly for a trade-union synthesis of social Catholicism and socialism, but this did not prevent him from agreeing with the CFTC's refusal to entertain a merger with the CGT in October 1944. Even at that early date, '... despite the trust that we had, by and large, in ordinary Communists ... we felt that the CGT was too much a vassal of the PCF, whose allegiance to Moscow threatened a form of unified syndicalism in which our Christian and French dimensions would be lost.' As an alternative he expressed his hopes that Catholic democrats would merge with the democratic Socialists of the SFIO to create a French Labour party, but he was disillusioned by what he called 'the absence of a socialist economic perspective' within the MRP which he had initially joined with enthusiasm.[7]

The Cold War was blamed by many for blowing away the residue of left-wing unity which they had felt was the only way forward at the Liberation. For those trying to sustain the governments of the Third Force this was their reading of political events in the latter years of the 1940s. But the perspective of the militant strikers in 1947 was radically different. For them, the PCF had finally moved into the oppositional role which, they argued, it should have adopted at the Liberation. They now saw it as preparing for revolution: 'Without any doubt,' wrote the PCF philosopher Roger Garaudy in 1950, 'the twentieth century will go down in history as the century of the victory of Communism.'[8] It turned out to be poor prophecy but at the time it was revealing of the Communist euphoria which was such a force in intellectual opinion. The PCF was seen to have cut new oppositional teeth on a period of violent conflict and to have thrown itself

into the millenarian future projected by Marxist-Leninist theory. The strikes expressed a certain revolutionary idealism in parts of France; the Cold War promoted the values of Soviet Communism worldwide. For whichever reason, or both, the PCF in the immediate post-war years attracted more intellectuals than at any period since its inception in 1920.

It continued to proclaim itself as the party of resistance, which it reinvented as a movement against 'the excesses of capitalism, encroaching daily through American money and influence'.[9] Catholic worker-priests were drawn into its orbit by its sheer presence in the factories. In 1953 Pope Pius XII, responsive to the Cold War, closed the seminary in France in which the worker-priests were formed and in 1954 ruled that they were a scandal in the Church: their factory work and involvement with Communism was condemned. Few took the route away from the Church but those who felt abandoned by Rome, like Jean-Marie Huret, worker-priest in Le Havre, found room to manoeuvre under Benoît Frachon's leadership of the CGT without adhering to the party.[10]

The oppositional PCF, main political scourge of the government's 'dirty' war in Indo-China, ensured that the governments of the Fourth Republic, like those of the Third since 1920, continued to have 'enemies to the left' as well as to the right, the situation that Gambetta had warned against. It also kept alive an internationalist perspective in its refusal to accept the nation as an organizing principle of political theory and practice, even though its internationalism was persistently revealed as Soviet-dependent.

Intellectuals and commitment

It was less the political opposition of the PCF than its monopoly of working-class loyalty that attracted intellectuals into becoming *compagnons de route* (fellow travellers), prepared to give the party the benefit of the doubt rather than be accused of anti-Communism and run the risk of losing touch with the historic role they ascribed to the proletariat.

The question of intellectual integrity posed by Julien Benda in 1927 was given a fundamental twist by Jean-Paul Sartre in 1947 in his *Qu'est-ce que la littérature?* (*What is Literature?*) in which he set out to show that literature, and the novelist in particular, was of necessity communicating a perspective on the world. In this sense all literature, he argued, is implicitly committed, but necessity should be turned into an explicit commitment to improving the world. The choice that this involved would be an existentialist one, through which writers would actively create themselves and rise above the contingencies of existence. Sartre's argument was grounded in

his existentialist philosophy and in his own commitment to anti-fascism and resistance after he had escaped from a prisoner-of-war camp in 1941. Being committed (*engagé*) in Sartre's terms was imprinted with left-wing meanings of freedom and liberation, even though he claimed that the theory of committed literature was not, of itself, politically prescriptive. It was nevertheless closely identified with the Marxist critique of the bourgeois intellectual advanced by Nizan, his exact contemporary and friend. Nizan's Communist beliefs were severely shaken when the Communist Party accepted the Nazi-Soviet pact in 1939. To his friends he expressed his acute sense of betrayal. Less than a year later he died, aged thirty-five, on the front near Dunkirk. Sartre never ceased to see him as a paradigm of the committed writer.

The monthly journal started by Sartre in 1945 with the novelist and philosophy teacher Simone de Beauvoir, the philosopher Maurice Merleau-Ponty and the political scientist Raymond Aron took the title *Les Temps modernes* as a measure of its contemporary commitment. It developed the intellectual influence of Marxist and other revolutionary thought and was open to independent young critics and writers. Its essays were the existentialist voice of the Resistance, but were also advanced as a comradely alternative to the voice of the PCF. It did not submit to party orthodoxy, but was intent on avoiding anti-Communism. The fragility of this position was given fictional form in Simone de Beauvoir's novel *Les Mandarins* of 1954, in which Resistance intellectuals grapple with each other and themselves over whether or not to speak out over the revelations of the slave labour camps in the Soviet Union. One of the lead characters, Robert, confesses to the intransigence of the situation after the clarity of the Resistance: 'An intellectual no longer has any role to play . . . Oh, you can amuse yourself stringing words together like you string pearls, being careful not to say anything. But even that's dangerous.'[11] The danger was not just of falling into what Benda had defined as intellectual betrayal, but the opposite, the danger of being called a traitor to the political cause. Sartrean commitment could not escape from this dilemma.

The very real argument over the existence of the Stalinist camps was one of the issues which fractured the unity of purpose behind *Les Temps modernes*. The revelations came most dramatically in Victor Kravchenko's account of why he had sought political asylum in the USA. His memoir, *I Chose Freedom*, was translated into French in 1947 and attacked as American propaganda by Communist writers who dominated the Resistance literary journal, *Lettres françaises*. The polarization of the Cold War was prefigured in the conflict over Kravchenko. In 1948 Sartre tried and failed

1. Humanist and Dreyfusard, Jean Jaurès united the socialists in 1905. His social idealism echoed down the century. Portrait by Nadar.

2. Denied the vote, women featured prominently in a wide variety of street activism. 'Champagne or death' reads one of the placards of wine-growers from vineyards near Bar-sur-Aube in 1911 demanding the *appellation* of 'champagne' for their wines.

3. Mobilization, 1914. Reservists with their army-issue kitbags step out into Paris from the Gare du Nord.

4. Images of war. A trench 'somewhere in France' photographed to show African troops mounting guard.

5. Images of war. The mass of bones of men killed at the Battle of Verdun.

6. The victors. Clemenceau takes off his hat to the crowd after signing the Treaty of Versailles, followed by Woodrow Wilson and Lloyd George (*right*).

7. High point of jazz *à la française*. The Quintet of the Hot Club de France, starring Django Reinhardt on guitar (*centre*) and Stephane Grappelli on violin.

8. Veteran memory. Marshal Pétain, Minister of War, joins *anciens combattants* at Meaux in 1934 to commemorate the twentieth anniversary of the Battle of the Marne.

9. Dilemmas of peace. Léon Blum at a peace rally in September 1936. Apparently relaxed, he faced opposition within the Popular Front to his pact for non-intervention in the Spanish Civil War.

10. A decade of refugees. Spanish Republicans arriving at Bayonne from the Basque area of Santander, taken by the Francoist rebels at the end of August 1937.

11. The civilian experience of defeat. Millions fled with their belongings along the roads under a hot sun, desperately heading south to escape the Nazi invasion of 1940.

12. Occupied France. Crossing the demarcation line, even on a daily basis, was anything but routine.

13. Grass-roots Resistance. A triumphant maquis unit from the village of Kersaint, near Brest.

14. Acts of retribution. One of the many women whose heads were shaved at the Liberation: 'Caused her husband to be shot' runs the accusation.

15. Albert Camus, winner of the Nobel Prize for literature, moralist and philosopher of revolt, critical of the pro-Communist sympathies of Sartre and de Beauvoir.

16. Simone de Beauvoir, novelist, autobiographer, campaigner for sexual equality, famed for her stress on the construction of gender in *Le Deuxieme sexe*.

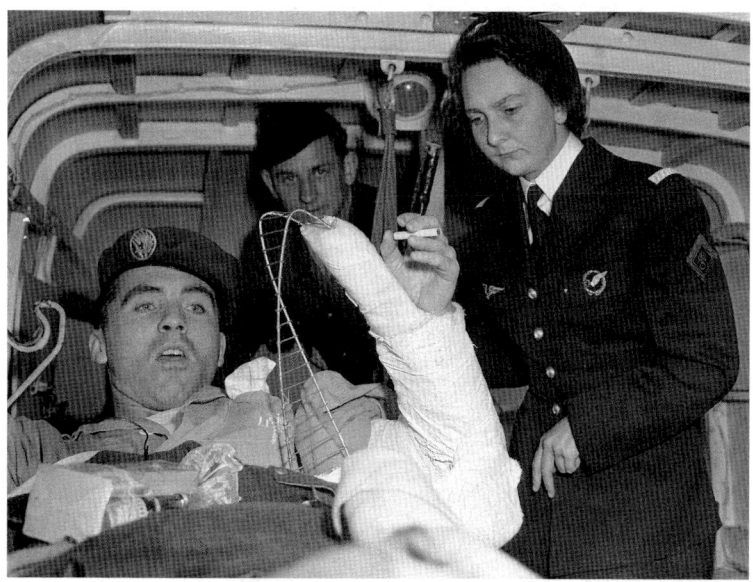

17. Backdrop to intellectual politics: the war in Indo-China. Known as the 'Angel of Dien-Bien-Phu', Geneviève de Galard Terraube brings back the last French wounded after the decisive victory of the Viet Minh.

18. De Gaulle with Konrad Adenauer saluting the Bonn crowds in a gesture of Franco-German friendship within the new Europe, 1962.

19. Algerians celebrate their country's independence, 1962.

20. The strategy of *grandeur*. De Gaulle in person supervising atomic tests at Mururoa, Polynesia, accompanied by Alain Peyrefitte, Minister for research and atomic issues (*left*).

21. Technological boom. Prototype of the Franco-British supersonic Concorde at Toulouse, 1967. After 50,000 flights the Concorde service was finally grounded in 2003 after one burst into flames on take-off from Roissy in 2000.

22. May 1968. Casualty of street clashes.

23. May 1968. Occupation of the Renault factory of Boulogne-Billancourt.

24. Simone Veil, survivor of the Holocaust, right-of-centre deputy, reformer of the abortion law, President of the European Parliament in 1979. Constantly voted the most respected politician of her generation.

25. Catherine Deneuve, star of *Belle de jour* (1967), signatory of the abortion manifesto of 1971, model for the bust of Marianne in 1985, TV face of Chanel, Saint-Laurent, and privatized shares in the Suez bank.

26. A *bidonville* (shanty town) still in existence in 1973 in the Parisian suburb of Nanterre.

27. Persistent civil and racial violence in New Caledonia. Kanak women approach armoured police to give evidence after the killing of ten Kanak militants in December 1984.

28. The Gaullist inheritance. Jacques Chirac establishes his hold over the Gaullist party in 1975, in the shadow of de Gaulle and Pompidou.

29. Re-asserted alignment at the heart of Europe. President Mitterrand (*left*) and Chancellor Kohl at Verdun in September 1984.

30. Secularism in schools and the *foulard* issue. Two girls wearing Muslim headscarves arriving at their school in Lille in 1994.

31. Jean-Marie Le Pen, leader of the Front National, celebrates his candidature for the Presidency in April 2002.

32. Architect of the 35-hour week. Socialist Martine Aubry, epitome of the 'plural left', voting in the election which made her mayor of Lille in 2001.

33. Rejection of Le Pen. 'No to racism', 'France at half mast' ('*en berne*'), and a pun on FN ('*F. Haine*') among banners in Nice at the Presidential run-off in 2002.

to create a political space for himself and others who were pulled in both directions by the issue, forming the short-lived Rassemblement Démocratique Révolutionnaire (RDR), while Raymond Aron, the political analyst on *La France Libre* in London during the war, opted squarely against Communist 'mystification'. He had already broken his liaison with Sartre by choosing to throw his support behind de Gaulle's RPF. In his prescient essay of 1948, *Le Grand schisme*, Aron depicted the rupture between East and West as an impossible peace but an improbable war between two irreconcilable systems of thought. In the mid-1950s he turned Marx's description of religion as the opiate of the people against Marxists themselves, with an exposure of their ideology as *L'Opium des intellectuels* (1955).

Sartre's choice not to fall into anti-Communism was mirrored in the decisions made by the Catholic personalist philosopher Emmanuel Mounier. His misconceived decision to publish *Esprit* in the early days of Vichy was put into context by his subsequent imprisonment by the regime and his overt identification with resistance. Shortly after the Liberation, in December 1944, Mounier restarted *Esprit*. His credentials as the young sage advising other Christian resisters in Lyon gave him a post-war moral authority among Catholics equal to that of the novelist François Mauriac. Open to writers of any faith or none, *Esprit* represented the pluralism of ideas within Catholicism and the width of the humanism engendered by the Resistance. No less than Sartre, Mounier felt that anti-Communism was a trap: he pioneered Catholic co-operation with the PCF, convinced that a wide-based programme to tackle the inequalities created by capitalist society demanded constructive forms of partnership with the party. His indulgence towards the PCF was not, however, unquestioning: *Esprit* carried articles in December 1949 from ex-resisters Jean Cassou and Vercors critical of Stalin's attacks on Tito, and Mounier defended the articles in the face of Communist protests. Whether or not this was the start of a different phase in his relationships with the PCF has engrossed Mounier experts ever since. He died suddenly of a heart attack in 1950.

Commitment to overthrowing the structures of capitalism was assumed as a necessity in Simone de Beauvoir's intellectual analysis of women in society. To wildly contrasting reactions she published *Le Deuxième sexe* (*The Second Sex*) in 1949, made up of two volumes, with some chapters aired in *Les Temps modernes*. Immediate sales of each volume reached over 20,000 in a week. They were one telling pointer to its phenomenal success. The admiration, outrage, scorn, anger and defensiveness the book provoked were the more indicative sign of the epic status it was to achieve. De Beauvoir was made instantly famous by the thrust of her existentialist

argument that 'woman' is an identity which is either constructed or created: 'On ne naît pas femme, on le devient' ('One is not born a woman, but becomes a woman'). It was a compendious theory of woman's gender, with copious quotes from literary sources, and a scorching review of the 'myths' of femininity which made women into 'the other' in their relationships with men. The chapter on motherhood began with a section on abortion. She appeared in much of the text not to be writing as a woman but about women, as if from the outside: it was the mark of her profession as a philosopher among philosophers, equal to her male colleagues and as determined as they to demonstrate the 'objectivity' of the Marxist tenet that liberation of women was dependent on the achievement of socialism. The book accepted as given that it was bourgeois ideology which constructed the humiliations of marriage, maternity, housework and the host of 'eternal feminine' ruses imposed on, but also adopted by, women to massage the superiority assumed by men. Equality of the sexes was the only answer: social revolution its prerequisite.

De Beauvoir had no feminist lineage: the idea of writing on women did not come from years of political involvement in women's causes. Her own individualist lifestyle among avant-garde intellectuals was said to reflect revolt against her comfortable, narrow upbringing, but in many ways she never lost the early expectation of ease. She chose to study philosophy at the highest level; she chose to be a writer; to engage in a heterodox partnership with Sartre, without marriage and without children. She chose a café-centred existence in Saint-Germain-des-Prés; equal involvement in running *Les Temps modernes*; a passionate relationship with the American writer Nelson Algren; sympathy with the PCF, and fuller involvement in its politics as the Cold War sharpened. The choices were her commitment to creating her individual identity with its assertiveness and anxieties. Writing *Le Deuxième sexe* displayed her identity even if she did not offer herself as its subject.

Savage criticisms greeted *Le Deuxième sexe*. It was put on the Catholic index of banned books; François Mauriac and Albert Camus both refuted its central arguments; the graphic pages on women's physiology and sexuality were regarded as scandalous or pornographic by newpapers which upheld the social taboos on the representation of sex. There was little sympathy from columns written by Communists; insults and mocking reactions came from all sides. Yet the book was quickly regarded as a watershed in the analysis of women's and men's relationship within modern society, the gender predicament central to the contemporary human condition. It was in a direct line from Malraux as well as Marx and Engels. It was also

open to being read and re-read in a plurality of ways. It moved in and out of feminist, and Marxist, theory for the rest of the century and beyond.

De Beauvoir's and Sartre's closest phase of identity with the PCF was in the four years after 1952. From being part of a heterogeneous collection of 'revolutionary' intellectuals, they came to head a much narrower group at the centre of *Les Temps modernes*, casting the Soviet Union and the PCF as a force for peace against American Cold War positions and against the colonial wars waged by successive Fourth Republic governments. In these crucial years Sartre and Albert Camus, dual intellectual leaders at the Liberation, moved radically apart. Camus in *L'Homme révolté (The Rebel)*, published in 1951, distinguished his category of revolt from the theory of historical determinism, giving his image of the rebel a freedom and moral strength protected from the totalitarian tendencies within Marxism. Merleau-Ponty distanced himself from Sartre by questioning the active nature of Sartre's 'commitment' once Sartre appeared to have surrendered his freedom of choice through sectarian attachment to the PCF.

Intellectuals committed to the PCF interpreted revelations of Stalinist tyranny as anti-Communist propaganda until heads could no longer be buried in the sand. Ritual denial of Soviet methods became patently absurd with the brutal suppression of the Hungarian revolution in 1956. In the face of this overwhelming evidence of Soviet realities, which the PCF continued to refute, Sartre and de Beauvoir closed their affair with the party. It had involved intellectual blindness and *mauvaise foi* in the protracted avoidance of Stalinist crimes against humanity, but was motivated by a passionate faith in both the historical necessity of the Soviet experiment and the ultimate triumph of the proletariat. This widespread faith in the post-war years marked the high point of Marxist-Leninist commitment in France. The image of the PCF as the powerful embodiment of Marxism, as the *parti des fusillés*, but also as the cultural hub of working people's lives, enabled persuasive intellectual voices to formulate their identity with the Communist cause as rational and pragmatic.

At all levels of everyday life the party was solidly implanted in working-class communities: its elected officials were dedicated to structuring union activity, leisure-time, youth movements and holidays. Memories of their first childhood encounters with the countryside or the sea through PCF *colonies de vacances* kept adults after the war keen that their children should benefit equally from party organizations. The PCF's very solidity through countless affiliations brought it an aura of power, but in contrast its rootedness also encouraged bureaucracy, conservative structures and inertia. Stalinism, incorporated into party practices, made all political

dissent abstract and disloyal to the concrete cause of proletariat and party. Liberal and libertarian intellectuals had condemned Stalinist crimes from the start, but a fundamental left-wing critique of the party's rigid theory and practice posed little serious rivalry to the PCF at the grass roots until alternative readings of Marx and a surge in libertarianism created a New Left in the 1960s. Even then, critics were well aware that the PCF had not only survived as an ideological monolith but was still a massively popular force.

3. Peace: the European alternative

Schuman and Monnet

As after the First World War, ideas of change were intertwined with fertile ideas of international peace emerging directly from the experience of war, in this case from anti-fascism, the Resistance and the hopes of the Liberation. At first the humanist vision of a federal Europe struggled to be heard in the patriotic glow of Gaullism and the social emergency of shortages and inflation. If anything, the Cold War freed the European vision from its pre-war moorings in grand ideals and small committees and gave it a new and, for the first time, national momentum. This became evident in 1948. In August, Communists created their international peace organization, the Mouvement de la Paix, crusading against the American atomic bomb and Western colonialism. Both Irène and Jean-Frédéric Joliot-Curie, were prominent peace campaigners, winners of the Nobel Prize for Chemistry, and Jean-Frédéric was made president of the Mouvement de la Paix. His affiliation to the PCF was the reason given for his dismissal in 1950 from the French atomic energy commission to which he had been nominated in 1946. By this time the deepening East–West crisis, epitomized in the Communist seizure of power in Czechoslovakia and the *de facto* separation of East from West Germany, had prompted the MRP leaders of the government to contribute strongly to plans for the military consolidation of Western Europe which led to the North Atlantic Treaty Organization (NATO) in 1949.

With the Mouvement de la Paix campaigning vigorously against NATO, the government targeted Joliot-Curie as unsafe. The incident symbolized the extent to which the Cold War ensnared all movements for peace. Visions of Europe indicated a possible way out, and if not an independent military line, at least a degree of autonomy under the American shield, in which caution towards America could be voiced without incurring accusations

of Communist sympathies. But Europe would mean integrating post-war Germany into new patterns of security. What role should West Germany be allowed?

Speakers at a non-political congress at the Cirque d'Hiver on 22 May 1949 reminded the assembled artists, intellectuals and public figures that peace was more than a solution to international conflict: it was also a permanent rejection of racism and fascism. With the artist Marc Chagall as president of honour, the Mouvement Contre le Racisme et l'Antisémitisme et pour la Paix (MRAP) had been created four months before. This first congress of the MRAP heard the testimony of Régine Prochover, aged thirteen, who spoke poignantly as a child of Jewish victims of the Nazis, and the delegates called attention to the reappearance of *Der Stürmer* and the dangers of German rearmament. An MRAP tract of 1953 repeated the warnings, and listed the worrying number of racist publications within France. The anxiety of MRAP members at the possible resurgence of the German industrial-military complex was shared by many organizations emanating from the Resistance, though it was precisely among notable ex-resisters such as Georges Bidault and René Pleven that the ideas of a federal Europe, including Germany, were most creative. They believed fundamentally in European peace even as they prosecuted colonial war.

The exception to the resistance background was Robert Schuman. Born in Lorraine in 1886, Schuman was German until he was thirty, becoming French in 1918. His dual culture opened up a political career as a moderate Catholic deputy for the Moselle, a strong defender of the specificity of the border region. He voted full powers to Pétain but was imprisoned by the Germans from whom he escaped in 1942, crossing into the southern zone without ever committing himself to resistance. A mild suspect at the Liberation, he was easily cleared and became central to MRP politics and government from 1946 until 1952. He was Prime Minister in 1947 and strongly behind Jules Moch's repression of striking workers. As such he confronted the visceral hostility of the Communist left, where his German origin was levelled against him. In fact it was his experience on the edge of two nations that made him responsive to Europeanism, turning his liminal position between France and Germany into a central one in Western Europe.

Monnet was his economic mentor, whose projects for a common regulation of French and German coal and steel echoed farsighted proposals of visionaries in the 1920s who had talked of bringing the German industrial furnace of the Saar and Ruhr under permanent international control. After the Second World War the laboratory for similar European ideas was the Council of Europe created at Strasbourg in 1949. But it was Schuman's

own decision as Foreign Minister from 1948 to 1952 to portray the Cold War and the conundrum of Germany's role as the propitious moment for a new epoch in Western Europe. In May 1950 he proposed the creation of a European Coal and Steel Community (ECSC). It was a sensational initiative: not a further round of hopeful bilateral treaties between France and Germany, but a common economic authority over the powerhouse of Germany's two World Wars.

The Schuman plan gave the governments of the Third Force a watershed role in twentieth-century French and European history. It faced the opposition of Communists and the CGT who decried it as anti-Soviet and a threat to world peace; it was denounced by the Gaullist RPF as supranational; it was rejected by the iron and steel producers in the employers' federation, the CNPF, who feared a loss of profitable cartels of their own, but it was made finally viable in employer circles by the clear success of the Monnet five-year plan and the weight of the nationalized industries, major consumers of steel, who welcomed the principle of open access. Schuman built on his close understanding with the Socialist Paul-Henri Spaak of Belgium, and the Catholic democrats Konrad Adenauer of West Germany and Alcide de Gasperi of Italy. Their confidence and resolve carried the project to completion. In Paris on 18 April 1951 France, Germany, Italy, Belgium, Netherlands and Luxembourg (the Six) signed into the ECSC. A common market in coal and steel operated in these six countries from 1953. Britain stayed out, fearful for its own nationalized coal and steel industries.

The EDC affair

Economic integration was conceptualized by Schuman as the new democracy, crossing the divisions of Europe which he labelled anachronistic. Economics would lead to common military and political authorities, he believed, and a democratic assembly should be elected, but not as a way of sapping nationality, rather as a means of assuring the modernization, security and survival of the nation-state.[12] In this he was both a visionary and yet anchored in his own time. The nation continued to be the focus of expectations and there was a majority of public opinion against military integration if it meant rearming Germany. The outbreak of the Korean war brought security issues to a head. René Pleven was Prime Minister in 1950. An ex-resister in the Free French, he had surprised de Gaulle by not joining his RPF. Deeply respectful of the parliamentary regime and the British model in particular, Pleven was pragmatic and conciliatory, though convinced by the escalation of the Cold War of the need to rearm France and

Western Europe. On Monnet's advice he proposed a European Defence Community (EDC) which would include Germany, and he returned to this project in December 1951. The proposal divided the country at every level. As the MRAP tract of 1953 specified, the image of a remilitarized Germany was a very particular threat. Pleven argued that it was precisely within the structure of a European Community that Germany would be contained, and that Western Europe and Schuman's Coal and Steel Community would only be secure if Germany was part of the EDC. For entirely different reasons, the Communists and the RPF made the elections of 1951 into a unrestrained attack on the EDC. Their disparate but linked campaign did not prevent the first post-war liberal-conservative Premier, Antoine Pinay, from signing a treaty to establish the EDC in May 1952. It remained for the Chamber to ratify it.

For two years the EDC hypnotized the public, with debate reaching a passionate crescendo in 1954. Commentators talked of a nation's politics poisoned by inflamed opinions, of a new Dreyfus Affair, of permanent rifts between friends and families. Into the balance were thrown the disasters of the Indo-China war, over which Pleven presided as Minister of Defence, publicly booed at the Arc de Triomphe in April 1954. Mendès France became Premier and brought the catastrophic war to an end, but he did so with a view to strengthening the French Union in North Africa. This colonial retrenchment and search for elusive national grandeur in a France from the Channel to the Sahara seemed to many quite incompatible with the EDC. Mendès France did not put his authority or his government on the line, and the EDC was definitively rejected by the Chamber on 30 August 1954 by 319 votes to 264. The 'Marseillaise' broke out spontaneously amongst the opposition, both Gaullists and Communists. Their unholy alliance seemed a final ironic climax, but it was not the end of the story. The EDC was dead, but in the Paris agreements of October West Germany was brought into NATO and its sovereignty established: the government of Mendès France accepted that this would involve the re-emergence of a German army.

The project for the EDC had envisaged greater European political integration. This was now put on hold. A plan for a general common economic market among the Six took its place, with the democratic institution of a parliament in Strasbourg, an administrative commission in Brussels, a European court of justice and three overarching structures: a European economic community (EEC), a European community of atomic energy (Euratom) and the existing community for coal and steel. Formulated in the Treaty of Rome, signed on 25 March 1957, this relaunch of economic

Europeanism envisaged that certain executive decisions would be taken by the Commission in Brussels, but ultimate power still lay with the Council of Ministers of the Six, in which the question of a veto would ensure that national sovereignty was never absent from the agenda.

The Chamber gave its prior approval to the Common Market in late January 1957, two weeks after General Massu had been made responsible for crushing the FLN networks in Algiers, with a strategy of repression which included the systematic use of torture. The Socialist Premier Guy Mollet set his hand to both the infamy of the battle of Algiers and the imaginative clauses of the Treaty of Rome. From Monnet and Schuman to Mollet the European alternative grew into a revolutionary reconstruction of Western European economics and international relationships, and internally it underlined a radical reorientation of politics. At no time did it embrace decolonization in Algeria. The obsession for colonial permanence first in Indo-China and then in North Africa became an offence against the very human values which post-war governments claimed to embody. The obsession was grounded in the essentialist image of France as a country with a civilizing imperial mission, which was proudly reaffirmed at the Liberation and not seriously questioned until the racism and brutality of colonial rule in Algeria could no longer be ignored. By contrast, the search for a permanent European peace through European structures was visionary. The co-existence of narrow intransigence in Algeria and breadth of vision in Europe made the 1950s a decade of major paradox. This was reflected by contrasts between movement and immobility at almost every level of society and politics. Nevertheless, the chequered mosaic of change, whatever the inconsistencies within it, created a France which, by the mid-1960s, was fundamentally different from the France of the 1930s in a way that the 1930s had not been from the early years of the century.

4. Economic boom, political fall-out

Expansion and growth

Paris-Match, the illustrated magazine which came to symbolize modernity in post-war France, was launched in March 1949. Rationing was ended in the same year. The images in *Paris-Match* of audiences at the cinema laughing at Jacques Tati's comic nostalgia for the 'French way of life' in *Jour de fête*, and of couples at weekend dances in provincial *guingettes* (café-dance halls) and at urban clubs of be-pop and jazz, heralded the year as the rebirth of *joie de vivre* and consumer spending.[13] Within the next

twenty-five years it popularized a new press-button world of household appliances, the freedoms of family motoring and a surge of confidence in the future, evident in the dramatic rise in the number of births and fall in the mortality rate from 1946 onwards, and a new commodity market for those under twenty years old who represented a third of the population. From pre-war figures of 9,000 nursery classes (*écoles maternelles*) the number rose to 30,000 by the mid-1950s. By the beginning of the 1960s an atmosphere of social well-being based on high employment levels, a 40 per cent rise in real wages and a 47 per cent rise in consumption was widely held to signify the triumphs of what in effect was the third and most revolutionary industrial revolution in France, the first dating back to the mid-nineteenth century and the second to the early years of the twentieth.

Three politicians disputed the financial policy which was variously described as facilitating or impeding the economic take-off. The first two presented de Gaulle with conflicting arguments in the post-Liberation crisis of acute shortages and inflation. Pierre Mendès France, born in 1907, Radical deputy for the Eure at the age of twenty-five, persecuted as a Jew under Vichy, escapee from prison, reunited with his airforce squadron in the Free French, Minister of National Economy in 1944–5, told de Gaulle that he could only defeat inflation by a severe restriction of the money supply. He set out a programme which would call in all banknotes in circulation, freeze bank loans and control all prices and wages. In the inter-war years as a young follower of Jaurès, he had worked out schemes for socializing the Republic, for modernizing the nation's finances and redistributing income. His byword was rigour. René Pleven, born in Rennes in 1901, a Catholic industrialist but with a secular outlook, pre-war colleague of Jean Monnet, volunteer for the Free French, Minister of Finance in 1944–5, was not against state control of finances but argued that it was preferable to keep public confidence and resort to loans rather than coercion. De Gaulle accepted Pleven's advice; Mendès France resigned and for the rest of his volatile career remained convinced that de Gaulle had consigned France to permanent and damaging inflationary pressures. Pleven's own solid conviction earned him the nickname of 'the Breton menhir'. He was twice Prime Minister between 1950 and 1952, during the first Monnet plan, when Marshall aid from America financed the massive investments which put French heavy industry back into substantial growth and expansion. But inflation was not curbed. It was higher than in Britain, Germany and Italy.

Antoine Pinay was the third. Born in 1891 to a family of straw hat-makers in the Rhône, he gained a reputation as 'the man with the hat and the

wise head of a voter'. The first politician from the centre-right to lead a government under the Fourth Republic, he was the unexpected choice of President Vincent Auriol in March 1952 and swiftly established himself as a post-war Poincaré, by a range of transparent fiscal manoeuvres to strengthen the franc, including a loan with low interest but guaranteed against the price of gold. As inflation slowed and purchasing power was restored, Pinay's prudence was elevated by *Le Figaro* to the status of rare common sense and by *Paris-Match* to the miraculous. As mayor since 1929 of the small *commune* of Saint-Chamond in the Rhône, he had stood against the Popular Front in 1936 and defeated a Communist in the second round, before moving on to become a senator, and voting full powers to Pétain in 1940. Astonishingly, it was this economic liberal and moderate conservative who alleviated the economic struggle for millions of wage-earners whose battle against ever-rising prices undermined their positive experience of the massive post-war social changes. From 1952 to 1958 the purchasing power of metalworkers, for example, rose by 20 per cent, though it was still below that of 1938.[14]

The boom could initially be seen as reconstruction, restoring industrial growth to pre-war levels, and this was achieved and substantially passed under the first Monnet plan from 1947 to 1952. The second plan (1953–7) was expansionist and aimed at exceeding all previous growth rates with a target of 25 per cent increase in production. Again the success was spectacu-lar. Annual growth increased to roughly 6 per cent. The distribution of high productivity was uneven across the whole of the country, but the national result was a staggering 50 per cent increase in industrial output in the mid seven years of the 1950s. No less uneven was the restoration of purchasing power. Pauperization did not disappear and the rural exodus to the towns was described as a process of selection by depth of deprivation and despair as well as by sense of opportunity. Henri Groués, known by his Resistance name as abbé Pierre, seized a microphone of Radio Luxembourg in February 1954 to make a dramatic appeal for help in confronting the problem of the homeless. Thousands were migrating from the countryside with nowhere to go but the streets in a bitterly cold winter. People responded with blankets, clothes and money. Abbé Pierre and his organization, the Compagnons d'Emmaüs, changed the public perception of the tramp sleeping rough under the bridges of Paris. He began forty years of direct action which made him a popular and idiosyncratic public conscience in the consumer society.

The expansion of the pre-1914 decade and the growth of the 1920s were both dwarfed by these years of boom which were prolonged until the oil

crisis of 1974, representing an expansive thirty years popularized by the celebrant of economic productivity and mechanization, Jean Fourastié, as 'les trente glorieuses'.[15] By 1959 it was observed by an outside analyst that France had the highest *per capita* consumption in Europe.[16]

The proliferation of popular magazines was a symptom and symbol of expansion, providing seductive images of public and private consumption in health, hygiene, housing, home modernization, transport, culture and leisure. By 1958 11 million homes had radio sets and by 1960 almost a quarter of all homes had a refrigerator (*frigo*) and a washing machine, a threefold increase since 1954. In *Elle*, *Marie-Claire* and *Marie-France*, the 'modern housewife' was portrayed as the fulfilled and contented woman, and the 'ideal woman' as a creative housewife. Manuals written in the 1920s by Paulette Bernège and reproduced in new editions brought the language of rationalization and Taylorism into the home. Labour-saving timetables for household work were laid out in domestic science courses taught to girls at school where 'a gendered division of household work was always assumed'.[17] Modernity in the home was preached and sold to women as freedom from drudgery, giving time for reading, self-improvement, play with the children and preparation for the return of the husband in the evening. The universalism of this image was integral to the commodity market. Product advertising obscured the treble burden of outside work, household work and low income under which the majority of women lived. It took for granted that deprivation and discontent would ultimately give a powerful impetus to consumerism.

The *frigo* and formica were held to epitomize American styles of life in a way that gas cookers, radio sets and cars were not: the Renault Frégate of 1951, hailed as the most American of all French cars and advertised by Maurice Chevalier, failed to impress compared to the runaway success of the Citroën 2 CV, the Renault 4 and, for ultimate mass-produced elegance, the Citroën Déesse of 1955.[18] It was Renault which in February 1956 inaugurated a third week of paid holidays, the first increase since the Popular Front, immediately adopted for all workers. After the summer holidays of 1956 it was noted that reminiscences about cars and camping almost eclipsed the invasion of Suez and the revolution in Hungary. Passive public reaction to both events caused critics of consumerism to grow steadily at the end of the decade, denouncing a new 'bread and circuses' for the workers, a new 'opiate of the people'. The debate about moderniz-ation and Americanism was now one about everyday life and the pace of social and domestic change. Whatever the product, the mechanization in and outside the home signified the domestication of the machine age,

previously defined in a mixture of fantasy, awe and fear as belonging to industry, war and science fiction.

Political anti-Americanism: pigeons and Poujade

Largely an obsession of intellectual and technocratic circles in the inter-war years, the arguments about Americanism involved a plethora of issues and experience throughout the second half of the century. The sheer diffusion and paradoxes of anti-Americanism make it one of the richest and most complex cultural themes of the whole century. In the 1950s and 1960s it appeared in multiple roles in grass-roots political action. Before the success of Pinay's financial policies was fully apparent, his reputation for shrewd calculation was made in outmanoeuvring Communist anti-Americanism. On 28 May 1952 police broke up a forceful demonstration in Paris against the visit of the American Commander of Allied Forces in Europe, General Ridgway, accused by the PCF of backing germ warfare in Korea. Violent clashes between police and demonstrators caused one death and led to the arrest of several notable Communists, including the editor of *L'Humanité*. Jacques Duclos was found with pigeons in the back of his car and was farcically accused of using them as a carriers to communicate directly with Moscow. His arrest should have acutely embarrassed Pinay's government, but it was the PCF who lost face, unable to respond by a successful campaign to secure his immediate release, even though it was popularly accepted that the pigeons were 'due to be eaten *aux petits pois*'. This was not another Henri Martin affair where moral certainty and anti-colonial fervour galvanized widespread indignation.[19] The government was determined to humiliate Communist leadership and counteract its anti-American bravura. By the time Duclos was freed in July, it had succeeded: significant damage had been done to party self-esteem at the grass roots, even though Duclos was vindicated by the Paris Appeal Court and tried to regain the initiative by circulating his prison experiences with poems by Aragon and Éluard, a bid to mobilize wartime sentiment.

The carrier-pigeon affair was used by the authorities to debase an ideological demonstration of Communist and working-class anti-Americanism. A year later in the market town of Saint-Céré in the Lot, a local newsagent, Pierre Poujade, began a political movement of shopkeepers and small traders which invested a taxation protest with anti-American sentiment and raised it to a maverick ideological level, with echoes of all rural protests from the wine-growers of 1907 to the Greenshirts of Dorgères, and more than a hint of fascism.

It was Pinay's 'wise' management of the economy which ironically triggered a sense of crisis among shopkeepers who would otherwise have registered as keen defenders of his policies. Pinay received backing from small and medium employers, but his halt to runaway inflation rebounded on the profits of the shopkeepers and small producers for whom scarcity and high prices at the Liberation had ensured a minor boom. By 1954 there were over 1.3 million small shops, staffed by almost 2.3 million people, many of them owners working over twelve hours a day. With strong economic growth in the 1950s, modernization of industry, a quickened rural exodus into the large towns and increasing demand for mass-produced goods, the retailers of small towns and villages faced declining receipts and higher outgoings. The complex system of direct and indirect taxes hit small commerce harder than wage-earners. Widely suspected of falsifying their accounts, dairy retailers in particular suffered from a poor public image. Known in popular parlance as 'les BOF' (*beurre*, *œufs*, *fromage*), they had been accused of milking the rationing system and creaming profits under the Occupation, a view given comic credence in the merciless satire by Jean Dutourd, *Au bon beurre* (1952).

Poujade, however, stood for all small shopkeepers. The youngest of seven children, whose Maurrassian father had died in 1928 when Pierre was eight, he had fly-posted for Jacques Doriot's PPF against the Popular Front and had served as a team leader in Vichy's Compagnons de France, but left France in November 1942 and reached Morocco after a brief period in a Spanish prison. He joined the French airforce in North Africa where he met his wife Yvette, a nurse from a *pied-noir* family. Poujade moved within Gaullist and Giraudist circles in Algeria before the Liberation, and in 1953 had been recently elected on to Saint-Céré's municipal council under the Gaullist RPF label. Angry at the exactions of tax inspectors, whom he saw as the intrusive mercenaries of Parisian politicians, and convinced that American-style chainstores, such as Félix Potin, were a form of foreign domination, he forged an alliance with a local Communist under the slogan 'Unite or go under'. Their campaign took off as fast as the retail branches of the new commerce which they opposed in the name of 'la vieille France', and in November 1953 the Union de Défense des Commerçants et Artisans (UDCA) was created, without a coherent political programme but with an ideology immediately dubbed *poujadisme*, a potent example of Péguy's notional *mystique*.

As the campaign rolled out from the Lot across the real and mythic landscape of rural traditions it gathered momentum from an inchoate sense that the taxation issue for small-scale commerce epitomized all that was

wrong with American-inspired modernization in France. The clash of traditions was one of symbols: the French *coq* against the American eagle; the cry of 'cocorico' defying 'Coca-Cola'. When Mendès France launched a campaign against the staggering human costs of alcoholism and preached the virtues of drinking milk, Poujade countered as the defender of the *vignerons* and the symbolic values of red wine. A degree of Communist support ensured extra popularity in the early stages, but this was largely forfeited when Poujade took the first national congress of the UDCA in 1954 to Algiers, where it embraced the interests of the white *commerçants* within the wider colonial cause of French Algeria. Shades of Doriot's PPF, which had also been strong in French Algeria, were further darkened by Poujade's language of antisemitism and the reinvention in the movement's newspaper, *Fraternité française*, of the contemptuous Maurrassian term for foreigners, *métèques*. The strength of Poujadism was its popular and populist refusal to meet either the tax bill or the tax collectors, but it surrendered to the all too familiar ideological pattern evident in the inter-war years. It tried to legitimize xenophobia as basic patriotism. Poujade as an iconic 'Pierrot' attempted to personify that independent streak of Gallic and republican defiance associated with Vercingétorix, Joan of Arc and the *poilus* of Verdun. He had experience of working as a docker before opening his shop and played on his workerist image.[20]

In January 1955 the movement amassed a demonstration in Paris of some 100,000–250,000 supporters with the intention of facing down the gamut of internal enemies which Poujade had identified. The ever-fresh memory of the *ligues* and 6 February 1934 was galvanized by strident media coverage, but there was no desire among the Poujadists for a similar anti-parliamentary riot. The government of Edgar Faure parried with a promise to suspend recent tightening of the tax laws, but refused to concede any further. A legal charge against Poujade for tax evasion was pursued. At the same time the economic circumstances which had spurred Poujadism went into reverse. A demand-led economy began to see prices start to rise again and by the end of 1955 some of the crisis language had gone out of the Poujadist propaganda. Nevertheless the movement had sufficient mystique to persuade 2.5 million voters to give it fifty-two seats in the January 1956 elections. It was a democratic sensation, though once in the Chamber the poverty of the Poujadist political programme was harshly revealed. Popular support quickly ebbed; Poujadist deputies broke up as a bloc, many returning to the Gaullist flag, and some, like the young deputy for Paris 1er, Jean-Marie Le Pen, finding more satisfaction in volunteering for paratroop action against the Algerian FLN. *Poujadisme* as a form of

protest against change took on a pejorative and reactionary connotation. For its ideological supporters, however, it remained a heroic attempt to defend the interests of a traditional France: 'If, despite everything,' wrote J. Lesieur for the far-right publication *Défense de l'Occident*, 'the joint forces of capitalism and Communism contrive to keep our people on their knees, at least we will have done our duty.'[21]

Rural transformation

Pierre Poujade, even at the height of his popularity, was unable to counteract growing public contentment at the effects of economic expansion. He drew vivid attention to the threat it posed to traditional structures and values, and gave voice to those who lamented the costs of an accelerated pace of life. But Poujadism failed to reach beyond its own small-trader interests, and those who confused it with the multiple strands of rural expression in the 1950s severely misrepresented the complex realities of social and economic reaction to change in the countryside. There was no single dramatic moment of change and much of it was evolutionary, but whatever the terminology, the years which gave Poujade his political entry, and yet confirmed the longevity of economic growth, were also the years in which transformation in the countryside occurred at bewildering speed: by the mid-1960s it would be called a rural revolution. It had long been predicted, and its causes had been bitterly contested in the first half of the century, but the pace of its happening took much of rural society by surprise. Anxiety was accompanied by adaptation. A sense of inevitability gave a fatalistic tone to gestures of protest.

From 1901 to 1962 the rural population declined from just under 60 per cent of the total to just under 40 per cent. Whereas initially the rural exodus featured those who were not owners of their land, by the 1950s it was not only the most marginal who were leaving but also peasant proprietors and the local lawyers, traders and doctors whose clientèle was rapidly declining. Railway stations, post offices and schools were equally affected. The number of agricultural units, which mostly meant peasant farms, diminished by 40 per cent between 1948 and 1973, while the revolutionary pace of change was marked by the withdrawal of 400,000 farmers from agriculture during the short eight-year period from 1955 to 1963. The obverse of this decline was the huge rise in productivity due to mechanization, symbolized by the increase in tractors from 121,500 in 1949 to 967,600 in 1963. The yield of wheat and other cereals almost doubled during the 1950s, as did that of milk and meat, while the vineyards produced 25 per cent more wine.

Ephraïm Grenadou, a peasant proprietor with 100 hectares at Saint-Loup in the cereal-growing plain of the Beauce close to Chartres, emerged in his spoken memoirs of 1966 as a prime example of the beneficiaries of mechanization. He waited several months for a replacement for his ancient pre-war Fordson tractor, but once it arrived it heralded a period of swift change in the 1950s, a consolidation of smallholdings into larger units at Saint-Loup and mechanization which allowed him to reduce the number of his hired hands. In 1946 he joined a co-operative to share a threshing machine and in 1950 he bought his second Lanz tractor. By the early 1960s he could comment with satisfaction, 'Now it's machines that do the hard labour rather than men.' One of his sons-in-law started at agricultural college and would become a 'cultivateur' rather than a 'paysan'. At much the same time Henri Mendras was researching his treatise on innovation in agriculture, published in 1967 and entitled provocatively *La Fin des paysans*, but what Grenadou suggests is that peasant ways of life still carried their own justification: his crops were cereals but he kept two cows because he could not imagine having to go to his neighbour for milk, and market days were more affluent but culturally unchanged.[22]

And yet agrarian income in the 1950s, as a percentage of gross national income, sharply declined: industrialization reaped most of the benefits of investment under the Monnet plan. Agricultural prices could not compete with the rising wages of urban industry which continued to fuel the rural exodus. Discrepancy across the countryside saw the large cereal and dairy farms of the north and east grow steadily more mechanized and more wealthy, while the smaller farmers of the south faced at worst extinction and at best poverty amidst national plenty, with the Tarn, Haute-Garonne, Landes, Ariège, Hautes-Pyrénées, Lot, Corrèze, Lozère, Ardèche, Hautes-Alpes and Savoie severely disadvantaged. Experts in 1956 began to allude to the 'two agricultures of France'. Half of the peasant population in 1958 was still living at no more than a bare subsistence level, and a year of low wine prices in 1953 provoked the *viticulteurs* of the Midi to unleash their most active protest since 1907, using tractor blockades to inflict chaos on the main roads, a new and effective tactic which spread to small meat producers in the regions of central France.

The answers to individual peasant hardship were seen by politicians to lie in cheap loans to young farmers and government subsidies, both of which were increasingly available during the mid-1950s, but also in co-operative mechanization, praised by Grenadou, one of the few lasting successes of the Liberation provision for small-scale agriculture. Sharing a tractor and a threshing machine, at the very least, enabled some smaller farms in the

south to survive. But what became increasingly apparent was that serious political thought about rural France was not seen as necessary by the governments which embodied the resistance tradition in the Fourth Republic. With the notable exception of François Tanguy-Prigent at the Liberation, no Minister of Agriculture spoke directly from experience of peasant life, and the unthinking ideological equation of the peasantry with Vichy survived as a more powerful political reference than the experience of rural support for the maquis. When the Socialist Guy Mollet became Prime Minister in 1956 he downgraded agriculture's ministerial status, subordinating it to the Minister of Finance. The massive transformation was happening, therefore, without any concept of structural change. It seemed as if rural France was expected to retain its distinctive culture and vitality while submitting to the most rapid loss of peasant population for over a century. Grenadou's memoirs indicate his own fidelity to this culture, and if his experience was more generally shared, it was due to initiatives by a younger generation of farmers who propelled agriculture into taking charge of its own revolution in the early 1960s and secured the necessary structural reforms from the state.

The oustanding issue: decolonization

The ultimate paradox of economic boom and political collapse in the 1950s left the decade with not just an ambivalent reputation but also one which highlights the curious asymmetry of social and political developments characteristic of much of French history in the twentieth century. Theoretically the politics of high productivity and low unemployment should have been ones of confidence and stability, but even before the crisis year of 1958 there had been twenty-two different governments since 1945, the shortest lasting less than a week and the longest no more than fifteen months. De Gaulle demonized party politics, and blamed the constitution of 1946 for giving final power to a fractured Chamber of Deputies, in which coalitions to unseat the government could easily be formed on the slightest of pretexts. Authority, de Gaulle insisted, should rest with the executive and not the legislative. Even among the proponents of parliamentary rule, for whom debate and choice were the name of the democratic game, there were critics of the Fourth Republic who berated the inability of politicians to settle for a stable dialectic between government and opposition.

In a positive sense the multiparty system registered the multiplicity of political viewpoints within France: the fracturing began well before the Chamber debates, and could be said to reflect the intense politicization of

French life, and the determination of groups and group interests to mould parties and elect deputies with exactly their own nuance of ideas and policies. As can be seen from the success of economic planning (*planification*) and the impressive industrial and agricultural revolutions, ministerial instability did not paralyse the workings of society, which were carried forward by a strong civil administration and efficient public services, while twenty out of the twenty-two governments recycled a nucleus of ministers from the non-Communist left and the centre, so there was more continuity over twelve years than polarized change. In this respect both the Gaullists and the Communists who lay outside the system were a threat to stability. In a negative sense, however, the merry-go-round of governments registered the inflexibility of political discourse and practice: no one could agree for long enough to enable coherent coalitions to survive for more than a few months.

What sent the system into free-fall was the space left for self-destructive ideology. The long-term failure of the Liberation and the Fourth Republic was the failure to produce a determined post-war set of policies which would have stopped the Republic from lurching into a repressive ideology of archaic imperialism. Europeanism showed that political thinking could break with traditional confines, but the vision did not extend to colonial policy. In a document of 1950, Socialist voices for a free, united Europe argued that it would only be viable if its resources included those of the colonies.[23] The governments representing the democratic inheritance of the Resistance failed to see the need to translate the cultural humanism of resistance into colonial independence abroad. It was the other legacy of resistance, its moral and patriotic ascendancy and its Jacobin sense of a unitary mission, which determined the colonial decisions of governments within the Fourth Republic. It was this ideological inflexibility, not that of the party system, which brought down the Fourth Republic. It gave the *colons* in Algeria the belief that their show of nationalist defiance against Mollet on 6 February 1956 would find a popular echo within France.

It did. Mollet himself changed course, and the 'savage war of peace' intensified. As detailed in the previous chapter, the pressures of those who identified with Algérie Française both in Algeria and in France led to the recall of General de Gaulle to power and his abolition of the Fourth Republic. That almost 80 per cent of the electorate should endorse the constitution of the Fifth Republic, which gave France the powerful executive that de Gaulle had always claimed was necessary, suggests that the Fourth Republic was indeed the unloved regime (*la mal aimée*) which historians have repeatedly described. Had Mendès France shown the same

grasp of realities over Algeria as he had over Indo-China, he might have formed a decolonizing movement within the Chamber which would have confronted the *colons* in 1954 if not earlier: he certainly had the conviction that the emergence of the Third World was the most important fact in post-war history. Had Mollet stood firm and extended the logic of the Defferre law of June 1956 from Equatorial Africa to Algeria, might there have been a chance for negotiation with the FLN? In either case, would conciliation towards the Algerians in 1954 or 1956 have met the determined opposition of de Gaulle as an extra-parliamentary force defending the Frenchness of Algeria, and would this have led to an even bigger political crisis?

These are only three of the many speculative attempts to suggest an alternative history for the Fourth Republic, but it is notable that in any such shuffling of the cards the game always returns to the colonial issue. The Fourth Republic collapsed not because its governments changed so often but because it failed to decolonize in Algeria. De Gaulle, brought back to solve the Algerian crisis, also failed in the short term as he continued to back the French presence in Algeria which allowed the entrenched forces of Algérie Française to dig in more deeply, but within mainland France the expectations of his recall were so high that he was ensured of a majority support for any policy which would end the war. He opted for realism and not the ideology of French Algeria with which he was identified and which had brought his return to power. Léon Blum did the same in 1936 when he argued that the victory of the Popular Front was not the Marxist revolution of which he had been a prophet. They both believed they had avoided civil war, and they both brought politics into line with the country's needs. In the 1930s France desperately needed social reforms. In the 1950s the desperate need was for decolonization.

15

De Gaulle's Ascendancy, 1950s–1968

1. De Gaulle and Gaullism

A few days after the rebellion in Algiers of 13 May 1958, General de Gaulle was photographed in his extensive garden in the village of Colombey-les-Deux-Églises saluting a fly-past of French planes which had formed the shape of the Croix de Lorraine in the sky overhead. His arms were outstretched in a V for Victory, his ritual gesture from the war years.[1] By the end of the month he had accepted President Coty's invitation to form a government and on 1 June he became premier of the Fourth Republic which he was determined to abolish. It was agreed that he should have the freedom to design a new constitution. On 4 September, the anniversary of the proclamation of the Third Republic in 1870, he came to the Place de la République in Paris to deliver a major speech, against the backdrop of the allegorical monument to the Republic draped in a huge V, this time a grandiose symbol not just of Victory but also of the Roman V for the imminent Fifth Republic. Had the Gauls possessed a similar sign de Gaulle might have used it: it was perhaps sufficient that on 19 July the appropriately named Charly Gaul won the 1958 Tour de France, a coincidence which might have been suspect had the champion climber been French and not from Luxembourg. It was none the less seen as an omen. Gestures, rituals, symbols, omens and history became keywords in 1958: it was four years since the first volume of de Gaulle's *Mémoires de guerre* had appeared, and the opening sentence, probably the most quoted first line of the century, was already common coinage: 'Toute ma vie, je me suis fait une certaine idée de la France' ('All my life I have had a certain idea of France').[2]

The 300,000 of the political left who had signalled opposition on 28 May, who suspected a conspiracy between General de Gaulle and the rebellion in Algiers, and who talked of a coup d'état, made free with their historical allusions to Napoleon III's coup of 2 December 1851 which overthrew the Second Republic. The more recent event on everyone's minds, the right-

wing riot of 6 February 1934, was vividly recalled, as was the persistent belief that a fascist Fifth Column had prepared Pétain's accession to power in June 1940. Among events beyond France it was the army rebellion of Franco and his invasion of the Spanish mainland in July 1936 that seemed suddenly most relevant. As if in anticipation, the liberal Catholic Edmond Michelet, one of the earliest resisters, survivor of Dachau and a fervent supporter of de Gaulle, wrote at the end of 1957 that only de Gaulle could avert 'the civil war which is threatening to spread from Algeria to the mainland'. De Gaulle alone, he continued, could keep a reconciled Algeria within France 'with the consent of all Algerians', and he concluded: 'It was the Resistance which enabled our nation to emerge victorious from a foreign war, which realists declared was irremediably lost.'[3] Michelet was a member of de Gaulle's first cabinet of 1958. But how parallel was 1958 to the war years? Who exactly was de Gaulle expected to resist?

The year was one of endless such questioning and historical references, not all of them tendentious. It was clear that de Gaulle in his memoirs self-consciously cast himself as a providential leader of a France whose destiny was marked out to be exceptional, but far less quoted was the sentence: 'I feel instinctively that Providence has created France for complete successes or exemplary misfortunes.'[4] This streak of fatalistic melancholy in de Gaulle was known to his supporters in the RPF who had seen him despair of any political gain in 1953 and retire to write his memoirs, but many of them had expressed the conviction that he would return. There was a sense of inevitability when he did so.

De Gaulle appeared to present himself only in terms of principles. It was in such terms that he recommended his new constitution to the voters on 28 September. In a heightened atmosphere of destiny the electoral college specified in the constitution made him President of the Fifth Republic at the end of December. On 8 January 1959 he took up residence in the Élysée. All commentators, in France and abroad, were conscious that a new era of politics had begun. Few cast de Gaulle as a pragmatist, still less as an opportunist, but his initial policy towards Algeria seemed improvised from speech to speech. Delphic utterances and a prodigal scattering of platitudes kept most commentators guessing and encouraged a disparity of expectations. While the French *colons* expected unremitting support and unsurprisingly voted 'Oui' to the new constitution, a majority of the Socialist Party also voted 'Oui' but expected major initiatives on France overseas. In the constitutional proposals de Gaulle promised a new structure for the colonies, a federated Community. The Socialist Gaston Defferre saw in this an extension of his own initiative of 1956, and one which would assure

self-government for the colonies. His expectation turned out to be a sound one. De Gaulle's first substantial tour overseas was to Madagascar and Equatorial Africa. He went full of principles but also with promises.

Decolonization

De Gaulle arrived in Brazzaville on 23 August 1958 in stifling heat. He reviewed the assembled troops on the tarmac and was welcomed by an immense enthusiastic crowd on the route from the airport. The mayor of Brazzaville, abbé Fulbert Youlou, gave him the key to the town in the Faubourg of Poto-Poto, before a visit to 'De Gaulle House' on the banks of the Congo, headquarters of the Free French in 1943. The glittering festivities continued before 3,000 guests in the evening, and the following day de Gaulle met the local administrators to encourage them in their work, and then proceeded to the Félix-Éboué stadium for his main speech. He started with personal memories of 'these historic sites' and praised France for its African achievements which he said he would not repudiate and which would not be devalued by 'certain demagogic denunciations of imperialism in general'. His peroration ended: 'When one is a man and a free man [un homme libre] one has no right to conceal it . . . I have spoken. You have heard me. Africans will choose.'[5] The choice he offered was clear: either self-government within the Community proposed by the new constitution, or secession from it. Africans would vote with the French at the end of September.

The same grand principles and the same message had been delivered in Tananarive in Madagascar two days before. The warmth of de Gaulle's reception suggested widespread trust among Madagascans. In September all but one of the African colonies voted for the Community. Guinea was the exception. Led by Sékou Touré, it registered a vote for secession and complete independence. De Gaulle's integrity was at stake. He did not withdraw his promise of choice, but he intransigently refused to recognize the new state. Support for Guinea came from other countries: it did not collapse without French tutelage, and de Gaulle was forced to concede. Within two years Guinea was followed by the others who had initially chosen the Community. By 1960 all the African colonies from Madagascar to Senegal had chosen independence and separate representation in the United Nations. De Gaulle's hurt pride over Guinea suggests that he did not envisage that secession would be the consequence of his promises, but he had done more than any previous head of state to give such an impetus to self-rule.

The African tour itself was a model of the political method which shaped de Gaulle's Presidency of the Fifth Republic: identification with the place and its history, protocol and receptions, speeches to enunciate principles, exhortations, but no bargaining or discussion, and no space given for *cahiers de doléances*, the time-honoured presentation of local grievances. The pattern was followed within France when he toured the provinces. It was followed, too, in Algeria, and for the first time the *colons* did not hear the constant reiteration of previous governments, that Algeria was different. De Gaulle, on 13 July 1958, referred to Algeria's special place in his planned Community, but when he used the word 'exceptional' it was to describe the history of France, not that of any group, faction, interest or area within it. Slowly and haltingly, over the course of four years, in the name of France, he extended to Algerians the choice that he had given to the African colonies.

It is not easy to see who else might have achieved the same result. De Gaulle's military and resistance prestige was certainly the key factor in keeping the bulk of the army away from the generals' *putsch* of 1961. Thereafter, the French dissidents and rebels in Algiers were the kind of faction that de Gaulle, as President, refused to tolerate. His own factious role in creating the RPF in 1947 was occluded.

It was in the welcoming speech by Léopold Senghor in Dakar on 13 December 1959 that the role of de Gaulle as decolonizer was most openly celebrated, with a subtle touch of irony. With references to French history which cleverly outflanked de Gaulle's own selective sense of the past, the Senegalese writer and political leader praised de Gaulle for fidelity to the French Revolution and the Rights of Man in liberating 'whole peoples and not just individuals'. It was not a heritage claimed openly by de Gaulle.[6] In stark contrast, his role as decolonizer was openly ridiculed in Tunisia in July 1961. The port of Bizerta had remained in French hands after Tunisian independence in 1956. The President of Tunisia, Habib Bourguiba, applied diplomatic pressure for French evacuation. Anti-French demonstrations turned to riots in 1961 to which the French replied with devastating air strikes which killed over 1,000 Tunisians. 'À bas de Gaulle' was scrawled everywhere on ruined buildings. The Communist paper, *L'Humanité*, was not alone in blaming the bloody reprisals on the role allowed to angry French paratroopers, determined to avenge so many colonial humiliations, and the paper's special envoy, Madeleine Riffaud, vividly reported the stench of corpses piled high in the streets.[7] De Gaulle defended the legality of the French position to UN delegates, but in October 1963 France evacuated Bizerta.

Throughout the remainder of the decade de Gaulle ran a well-concealed

African policy from within the Élysée entrusted to the mysterious Jacques Foccart, who kept a careful eye on the possibilities for influencing the new African rulers in a system of clientelism. Decolonization more widely was incomplete. It was limited by the retention of those colonies in which independence movements were never more than a minority. The 'old' colonies of Martinique, Guadeloupe, Réunion, Guyane and Saint-Pierre and Miquelon retained the status of *départements d'outre-mer* (DOM), with the same rights as metropolitan *départements*, while the far-flung smaller lands of Polynesia, New Caledonia and the Comores remained *territoires d'outre-mer* (TOM), with more indirect representation in French politics and a repressive residue of colonialist attitudes. Publicly, a monetary zone of the franc, including all the ex-colonies in Africa, enabled French commerce and investment to operate in what was quickly dubbed neo-imperialism on the one hand and economic aid on the other. It underpinned the continuation of a francophone area of global dimensions. More specifically the Saharan oil, though owned by the new Algeria, continued to be exploited by French oil companies. Over 50 per cent of the oil extracted was exported to France, reinforcing Algeria's tight dependence on French economic involvement. New Algeria and France cobbled together a working relationship which lasted until 1971 when President Boumédienne, asserting Third World rights, nationalized the assets of the French oil companies. Four years of icy Franco-Algerian relationships ensued, a phenomenon which, to the surprise of most commentators, had not followed the ending of the war in 1962.

Power and legitimacy

The Fifth Republic at its inception was identified entirely with de Gaulle and the Gaullists. It had none of the philosophical roots of republicanism at the start of the century, no co-identity with reason and *laïcité*, no pantheon of revolutionary martyrs, heroes and heroines, no imagery of liberty on the barricades. The Fifth Republic's discourse under de Gaulle was of a republic represented as the nation. It admitted few affiliations with the republican ideology of the traditional left, although de Gaulle proclaimed his respect for Gambetta and Clemenceau. The pre-history of the nation was one which de Gaulle traced back to the resistance of both Vercingétorix and the Gauls against the Romans, and to the Merovingian dynasty founded by Clovis at the end of the fifth century. Its most reiterated pedigree, however, was in the history of Gaullist resistance, with the *appel* of 18 June 1940 as the prime signifier of moral authority.

The constitution set up a Presidential regime which broke fundamentally with the tradition of parliamentary rule: the power of the President, elected for seven years, would now be independent of both parliament and government. Elections to the Presidency could no longer be according to Clemenceau's old adage that parliament should 'vote for the stupidest', which had ensured compliant and easy-going Presidents for most of the century, pictured like René Coty dressed informally and playing billiards, whose personalities were judged by members of the public on their resemblance to their own. As a young man, de Gaulle had been indelibly marked by the debates about the nature of France which animated the Dreyfus Affair and intensified during the nationalist revival in the early years of the century. At the time he was attracted to the arguments of Charles Maurras that the nation could only reproduce the grandeur of the past by restoring the monarchy, and once he accepted that France had to remain a republic it was on the basis that it should be a Presidential state. This model of authority was the cornerstone of what was widely called 'de Gaulle's republic'.

Legitimacy was initially created by the legendary status of de Gaulle's war years, but it was immediately and constantly reinforced by de Gaulle's use of the referendum, which elevated popular sovereignty to the same mythic level and replaced the primacy of parliamentary authority. By such means, every Presidential action by de Gaulle after 1958 and every referendum conferred further legitimacy. He elevated Ernest Renan's famous statement into practical politics: 'The existence of a nation is an everyday plebiscite'.[8] De Gaulle's nation-republic was self-legitimating, both by the presence of de Gaulle himself and by public acceptability, creating its own philosophical myth of President and people united in *rassemblement*, the word promoted by de Gaulle as the antonym to *parti*, the symbol of division. His V for Victory gesture ended most of his public speeches: it was now an all-encompassing movement of the arms to enfold the 'Français, Françaises' ritually addressed.

Within a year of de Gaulle's Presidency his singular status and the style of his public performance had swept political comment into a mould where everything related to his person. Aged seventy in 1960, de Gaulle was one year younger than the Eiffel Tower. It was a gift to the cartoonists. Both were caricatured as 'a giraffe with elephant's feet'. The Eiffel Tower, 'a giant paperweight on a corner of Paris to prevent it from being blown away in the night', was also providentially designed, said one Parisian wit, as a house for de Gaulle in which he could 'bring himself fully to attention without knocking his head on the ceiling'.[9] A wickedly perceptive essay by

Jean-François Revel, called *Le Style du Général*, was one of the first to observe that his frequent references to the 'universe' and the 'whole world' suggested an intimate relationship with the cosmos, while his omniscience was cultivated by saying 'Yes, I know' and 'I am not surprised' to any statement of problems or anxieties.[10]

On 22 August 1962 de Gaulle narrowly escaped assassination when his car was riddled with bullets at le Petit-Clamart in the south-west suburbs of Paris. The ambush was planned by a group led by Colonel Bastien-Thiry code-named 'Didier' acting in the cause of Algérie Française. It was Didier's seventh attempt over several weeks. Aged thirty-five with three young daughters, Bastien-Thiry, a researcher in the Air Ministry and a keen Gaullist until 1959, made no attempt to hide or escape abroad. In March 1963 he was executed by firing squad. Much of the press condemned Bastien-Thiry's action but criticized the execution. There were comparisons with Raoul Villain, the assassin of Jean Jaurès. He had killed and was acquitted. Bastien-Thiry had failed to kill and was executed. But, it was noted, he made repeated references to de Gaulle as head of an unlawful state, 'un État de fait'. His attack was therefore held to be against the state, and it was for this that he was shot.[11] It refuelled arguments about the permanence and nature of the regime, with a widespread conclusion, underlined by Guy Mollet and Pierre Mendès France in the Chamber, that the Fifth Republic was, in fact, separable from the person of de Gaulle. This gave it greater legitimacy beyond the ranks of the Gaullists.

The approach of 1964, the twentieth anniversary of the Liberation, focused attention on the legacy of the Resistance. The claim by the leaders of the OAS that they were in the true patriotic line of the Resistance was treated with revulsion at the congress of the National Federation of Deportees, Internees, Resisters and Patriots in May 1962. Speakers made it a criterion of the resistance tradition that it should withstand the pull of Algérie Française, and on this basis de Gaulle was elevated still higher as the ultimate resistance symbol. School textbooks on the war written after 1958 increasingly referred to *la nation résistante*, a Gaullist abstraction which obscured both Vichy's collaboration and the minority status of resistance, but Communist histories and publications for a general public continued successfully to dispute this orthodoxy with their alternative construction of the PCF as the martyred party of resistance, *le parti des fusillés*. Locally-based resistance organizations preserved a much more diffuse and individualized account of resistance activity, which some localities felt de Gaulle had never really understood or valorized. The twentieth anniversary was an opportunity to promote the merits of one or another of these

traditions. With a sure touch which surprised all politicians, de Gaulle had made André Malraux his Minister of Culture and thereby appropriated the writer's anti-fascist and universalist humanism of the 1930s. On 19 December 1964, together with Malraux, de Gaulle staged the transfer of Jean Moulin's ashes to the Panthéon. It was a spectacular theatrical and propaganda coup: Moulin, emissary of de Gaulle, hero and martyr, respected by Gaullist and Communist resisters alike, was an irreproachable choice for republican canonization. No one denied this. The consensus of national opinion was widely noted: so too was the significance of the Panthéon, burial place of republican icons. The choice of Moulin and the Panthéon extended the resistance and republican legitimacy of both de Gaulle and the Fifth Republic.[12]

The nation reimagined

De Gaulle was too much of a historian to claim that France was 'naturally' great, whatever his belief in providence. Too often, he believed, the people had been misled into choices which discredited the nation: these were the 'malheurs exemplaires' to which he referred at the start of his memoirs, and by which he meant periods in French history such as the 'decline' of France under Vichy and then again under the rule of political parties in the Fourth Republic. In both cases the 'rise' of France, which he and Gaullist writers of the 1950s believed invariably followed decline, were associated precisely with his own career.[13]

In all his references to national achievements de Gaulle perpetuated the paternalism of right-wing nationalists: it was not explicitly the infantilizing father–child relationship promoted by Pétain, but a state–people dualism in which the state had to lead the people. The pursuit of the greatness of France through foreign policy was overtly undertaken by de Gaulle in the decade after 1958, providing the clearest expression of the way in which he reimagined the nation.

The Europeanism of Schuman and Monnet was never intended to demote the nation, though it envisaged a steady escalation of European integration which would constrain the power of the state. De Gaulle ruled this out as supranationalism well before he returned to power. With even more vehemence he denounced any residue of the dependence on Britain and America which he had increasingly resented during the war. His assertion of French independence within and across the ideological division of East and West was symbolized by the testing of the first French atomic bomb in 1960 and his refusal to sign the nuclear test-ban treaty in 1963. It was at

the start of that year, on 14 January, that he vetoed Britain's entry into the European Common Market, on the basis that Britain was too subordinate to the USA. In the same month he signed a Franco-German Friendship Treaty with Chancellor Adenauer, with whom relations had been strained at the start of the decade. The two elderly men who had lived through the two wars made this treaty a historic end to a century of Franco-German conflict. It promised a powerful nucleus of co-operation at the heart of Europe, and set up institutional and youth exchange which fostered Europeanism independent of the vagaries of political relations between the two states. Adenauer retired at the end of 1963 and his successors had to deal with de Gaulle's persistent insensitivity to their points of view. Germany was never the buttress for de Gaulle's anti-Americanism that he had hoped for. But the treaty was a milestone of reconciliation in the twentieth century.

At the time of the Cuban missile crisis of 1962 de Gaulle was as critical of the USSR as any other Western leader, but with the Soviet threat withdrawn he came to see the USA as a permanently more dominating force, and he openly sought to counter this by referring to the Soviet Union as Russia and reviving the special Franco-Russian relationship of the era before 1914. It was an individualist manoeuvre, cobbled together from his never-forgotten altercations with Roosevelt, his respect for the Soviet Union's part in the war and a realization that Russia's pro-Arab policy would coincide with his reorientation of France towards the Arab states after the Evian settlement with Algeria. At a very local level the pro-Russian policy had been anticipated in Dijon in March 1960 by the mayor and deputy, Canon Kir, when Nikita Khrushchev visited France at de Gaulle's invitation and selected Dijon as one of the provincial towns on his tour. Canon Kir was aged eighty-four: he was not a Communist but had been promoting Stalingrad as a twin town, in recognition of Soviet Russia's epic resistance against Nazi Germany. The government feared that Kir, a virulent opponent of the Algerian war and as spontaneous a character as Khrushchev, would use the opportunity to criticize de Gaulle for not having withdrawn the French army from Algeria. The papacy was even more concerned to prevent a priest from welcoming an atheistic Communist. Kir reluctantly ceded to Church and state pressure and remained 'confined' to an agricultural college during the visit. Crowds outside shouted 'Libérez Chanoine Kir' and later in the year Kir and Khrushchev did meet and Dijon did become twinned with Stalingrad.[14] The visit, and de Gaulle's pro-Russian sentiments, inspired a highly disparate range of sympathetic and contrary press coverage, no less of a mix than the 'kir' of blackcurrant liqueur (*cassis*) and white wine to which the eminent canon had given his name.

De Gaulle's autonomous, nationalist angle on all issues confounded the expectations of President Kennedy whose offer of Polaris missiles was rejected by de Gaulle. He antagonized US strategists and hawks in the Far East when he recognized Communist China in 1964, visited Cambodia in 1966 and persistently held America responsible for the war in Vietnam. His withdrawal from NATO in the same year finalized his diplomacy of military independence, though at no point in the decade did he allow anyone to harbour the illusion that he was an advocate of Communism.

To much of American and British opinion there was little logic in de Gaulle's foreign policy beyond the obstreperous promotion of policies which advertised the autonomy of France without affecting the structural realities of a bipolar world. This judgement vastly underestimated the effect that his personalized vision of the world had on those groups in the West and the Third World who were looking for a way of denouncing American hegemony without ceasing to denounce in equal terms its apparent alternative, the neo-Stalinist Communism of Khrushchev and Brezhnev. De Gaulle showed that there was a pathway across and beyond the Cold War divide, even if the reimagined *grandeur* of France was a regression to the archaic primacy of nationalism. His foreign policies received majority backing in opinion polls until 1967 when he reversed French policy in the Middle East by rejecting Israel's justification for the Six Day War, and flouted Canadian sensibilities by saluting French separatists with 'Vive le Québec Libre'. At this juncture, for the first time, de Gaulle appeared to a majority of the French to be improvising irresponsibly.

De Gaulle's tortuous, or at least sinuous, path of foreign policy initiatives led to unpredictable conjunctures of interests. The PCF approved of de Gaulle's anti-Americanism and his moves to create an understanding with Khrushchev; nationalists and right-wing independents endorsed his insistence that Europe could only be a Europe of sovereign nations; pro-Europeans saw his moment of close relationship with Adenauer as a strengthening of European autonomy in the world; the pressure groups speaking for Muslim immigrants from North Africa welcomed his pro-Arab position in 1967. Conversely, all these policies had substantial detractors within France and still more outside.

His policy statements at the time of the Six Day War in the Middle East in June 1967 indicated not only his readiness to reinterpret national interests, but still more his capacity for offending sensibilities with an ill-considered turn of phrase, a weakness largely obscured by the reputation of his epic broadcasts during the war and the literary skills of his memoirs. Confronting the rapid escalation of enmity between Israel and

the surrounding Arab states, de Gaulle warned that he would not condone an attack by any side and banned arms sales to the region, an embargo which would clearly prejudice Israel, a major buyer of military material from France. When Israel launched its action de Gaulle's threatened condemnation followed. Public opinion was more accepting of Israel's pre-emptive strike, though the rapidity of the Israeli advance, the instant defeat of Egypt and the issue of Israeli annexations provoked a more divided public response. The possibility that Russia and America would be drawn into a Third World War passed, but dire predictions were common in the press that the Middle East was engaged on a new 'Hundred Years War' in the region. It was with a similar historical sweep that de Gaulle addressed a press conference on 27 November 1967 and chose to review Israel's action with a reference to the Jews as 'un peuple d'élite, sûr de lui-même et dominateur' ('an elite people, self-confident and dominating').

The words were particularly offensive to those who had kept their reactions to Israel's policy separate from their own Jewish origins. The pro-Gaullist intellectual Raymond Aron spoke for many when he castigated de Gaulle for the gratuitous adjectives used to define Jews generically, which, he argued, would be eagerly received by antisemites in France 'as authorization to speak out and use the same language as before the great massacre', the language of Charles Maurras and Édouard Drumont.[15] Aron's placing of de Gaulle's words in the context of the Holocaust and the Dreyfus Affair was met with the President's repeated denials of any antisemitic intent. He defended his statement as a positive tribute to the Jews, but he had clumsily situated the Six Day War in the most contentious of perspectives. There were few more sensitive areas of identity. From 1967 an increasingly assertive Jewish voice was present, determined that the Holocaust and the acts of French antisemitism should be at the forefront of national consciousness. The necessity for confronting the repression of collective memory was intensified.

Not all of de Gaulle's foreign policy was original, though its expression was distinctively shaped by his discourse of principle. The French nuclear deterrent and the provision of nuclear energy were inherited directly from the Fourth Republic he despised. It was in 1956 that the Chamber endorsed an independent nuclear programme after Félix Gaillard had initiated a five-year plan of nuclear research in 1952, and Mendès France in 1954 had overseen preparations for both the manufacture and future testing of an A-bomb. De Gaulle, nevertheless, made a nuclear force his own personal priority, showering it with resources, urging Third World countries to welcome it as a sign of French commitment to non-alignment and advocat-

ing it ceaselessly as 'a service to the balance of the world'.[16] Having personally promoted the Muroroa site close to the island communities of Polynesia, he travelled there to witness an explosion in September 1966. In the mid-1950s he had visited New Caledonia, where he had spoken at the capital Nouméa of the need for greater freedom for the islanders under French tutelage. His regime's enthusiasm for atomic testing led to the opposite, a reduction of the liberal dispositions assured by the Defferre law of June 1956. French control over the important nickel mines of the island was reinforced in 1969. De Gaulle personally harried experts to speed up a thermonuclear sequel to the A-bomb tests. As a result, the H-bombs were ready in 1968 and the first two were exploded in August. The threat of global proliferation and damage to the people and environment of the South Pacific were never seen by de Gaulle to countermand the national prestige of an independent nuclear strike force (*force de frappe*). Nor were the dissenting voices within France as numerous as those of the British and European nuclear disarmament movements.

Political stasis and a new left

The subordination of parliament and the reliance on experts and technocrats were the twin aspects of de Gaulle's personal ascendancy which attracted most analysis by social scientists. He did not attempt to destroy party politics altogether: the government was still expected to carry a majority in the Chamber. A new Gaullist party, the Union pour la Nouvelle République (UNR), was formed immediately after the referendum of September 1958. Jacques Soustelle's ambitions to use the UNR for the cause of Algérie Française were checked from the outset, and although the new party and its associated groups gained the largest number of seats in the elections in November, de Gaulle did not confine himself to politicians in his choice of ministers. André Malraux was neither a deputy nor a member of the UNR but as Minister of Culture became de Gaulle's leading political emissary within France; Georges Pompidou, key adviser to de Gaulle in the RPF, but from 1952 a financial director within the Rothschild group, was called back as an expert and in April 1962 was appointed Prime Minister. Maurice Couve de Murville, ambassador in Italy for de Gaulle's Provisional Government in 1945, and subsequently in Washington and Bonn under the Fourth Republic, was taken from the highest level of the diplomatic corps and made Minister of Foreign Affairs in 1958. He kept this post for a decade, trimming his Europeanism to de Gaulle's volatile decisions but nevertheless ensuring that France took a lead in developing the European Common Agricultural Policy.

The President's own entourage at the Élysée acted as a secondary cabinet, though many saw it as the primary one. Made up of high-ranking civil servants and de Gaulle's long-standing counsellors, it provided the information for the President's reception of foreign heads of state, for his provincial tours, his regular talks to the press and his broadcasts on the state-controlled radio and television. De Gaulle's promotion of his idea of France on personal tours and in the media was ritualized and patronizing: it was an expression of his belief that the people preferred to be addressed and informed in this way rather than through debates and discussions in parliament. In between elections politicians were relatively stranded from the electorate. In the first four years, parliament was prevented from discussing the President's manoeuvres over Algeria, and, as the frustrated opposition to his style of government grew increasingly vocal within the Chamber, de Gaulle found still more ways of gaining public endorsement through referenda. It was to spike the guns of the politicians in 1962 that he decided that there should be a referendum on his proposal for electing the President by popular suffrage. It was a calculated relaunch of the 1958 constitution into a fully Presidential mode and the opportunity for a vote of confidence in de Gaulle's form of government. On 28 October 1962 it gained the support of 61.75 per cent of the votes cast, but this was less than 50 per cent of the electorate. For a moment it looked as if de Gaulle had failed to keep the majority backing of 1958, but in the legislative elections which followed in November, the UNR eclipsed all political rivals and decimated the opposition who had urged a 'No' vote at the referendum. The advocates of a return to parliamentary rule were apparently crushed by de Gaulle's diarchy of state and people.

The unfolding of politics in the Fifth Republic was, in fact, far more complex than this simple Yes/No vote implied. That the scene had radically changed since the height of the 1950s was undoubted. On the right, the rump of Poujadists had dispersed in 1958, and the UNR, faithful to de Gaulle's notion of *rassemblement*, refused to label itself either left or right, though commentators situated it on the centre-right once it had lost the proponents of Algérie Française who moved into visceral opposition to de Gaulle. On the left the Communist Party was criticized by supporters of the FLN for its initial ambivalence towards the cause of Algerian independence. Despite its unrepentant Stalinism it gained in oppositional stature by its refusal to vote 'Oui' to de Gaulle in 1958. The killing of demonstrators at the Charonne métro on 8 February 1962 gave the party good reason to accentuate its history of victimization at the hands of the state.[17] An estimated million people attended the funeral cortège on 13 February on its

way to the cemetery of Père Lachaise. The PCF saw itself and was seen by de Gaulle as rigidly opposed to his regime, but its rigidity was undermined by the appeal of de Gaulle's independent foreign policy and his open espousal of East–West détente. In elections the party kept 20 per cent of the vote, a 5 per cent decline from the 1950s. On 12 July 1964 Maurice Thorez died suddenly on his way to holiday in the Crimea. To the end he was fondly respected as the voice of both party and proletariat, but he had already given way to his successor, Waldeck Rochet, by trade a market gardener in the Saône-et-Loire, and deputy in 1958 for Saint-Denis, the PCF stronghold in the northern suburbs of Paris. As leader, Waldeck Rochet began to move the party inconsistently away from Stalinism, opening up the possibility of wider left-wing alliances. Ideological debates within the party were no longer so routinely manipulated.

On the centre-left the MRP were as discomfited by their support for de Gaulle in 1958 as were the Socialists (SFIO) under Guy Mollet. Both these pillars of Fourth Republic politics reinforced the structures of the Fifth, but suffered a severe identity crisis in the face of de Gaulle's dismissive arrogance towards parliament. The MRP began to disintegrate and only found a little continuity in joining other non-Gaullist liberals in the centre, while the SFIO began to regain some confidence as de Gaulle's solutions to the Algerian war stumbled on into the 1960s and his style alienated increasing numbers within the Chamber.

Mollet's backing for de Gaulle in 1958 had not, however, carried the whole SFIO. An ideological split took the left of the party into the political terrain already mapped out by the resistance to the Algerian war and the denunciation of torture, a loose grouping of committed intellectuals and politicians who aimed to revitalize a non-communist Marxism and at the same time pragmatically modernize the party of Jaurès and Léon Blum. In April 1960 the breakaway section finally formed the Parti Socialiste Unifié (PSU), promoted in the high-quality pages of *France-Observateur*, edited by Claude Bourdet and Gilles Martinet with a moral prerogative formed in the heat of anti-colonialism. In July 1958, a young dissident from Communism, Serge Mallet, writing in Sartre's review *Les Temps modernes*, predicted that the Gaullist regime would be a neo-capitalist enterprise based on the state, technology and a consumer-led market, and that only a similarly modernized socialism, which took on board the facts of economic growth, would stand any chance of opposing it. The classic Marxist conviction that capitalism was failing and was incapable of renewal was challenged at its very core by this analysis, to which many of the PSU subscribed. In theoretical terms it made the PSU the first coherent political expression of

a new left, which nurtured its socialist humanism in readings of early Marx, and its opposition to the Communist Party in the host of post-war writings which had denounced Stalinism as a tragic or criminal parody of socialism.

The PSU diagnosed a lack of creative thought within the SFIO, but was less unified in its alternatives than its name suggested. The moral idealism in the language of the resistance veteran Claude Bourdet seemed to sit uncomfortably with the discourse of formulating an efficient counter-plan and technology advanced by the young Michel Rocard. Its range of positions, however, recommended it to the minority trade-union movement, the CFTC, which discarded its Christian label in 1964 and voted to become the Confédération Française Démocratique du Travail (CFDT), representing a depth of membership among skilled and white-collar workers. A rump of the confederation continued with its religious perspectives. Even more indicative of the new left was the support for the PSU of the national student union (UNEF), which emerged as a force of opinion against the war in Algeria, passionately opposing the drafting to Algeria of young men on military service.

No one in 1962 predicted that François Mitterrand would emerge as the strongest candidate of the left to oppose de Gaulle at the Presidential polls in 1965. Aged forty-nine, Mitterrand was six years younger than his prestigious Socialist rival Gaston Defferre, mayor of Marseille. Mitterrand was leader of a small political grouping with origins in the Resistance, and a friend and ministerial colleague of Mendès France. In 1964 he set out his denunciation of de Gaulle's regime in *Le Coup d'état permanent*. It was a forthright rejection of the whole Gaullist system, against which he sought to re-create a republican front, which took the title of Fédération de la Gauche Démocratique et Socialiste (FGDS). His relative isolation from the main political parties gave him unexpected credibility and he gained the support of both the PCF and the SFIO in the second round of the election. De Gaulle was humiliated by failing to gain an outright majority in the first round of the popular vote he had initiated, and though elected in the second he had to live with the fact that Mitterrand gained 45.5 per cent of the vote, and that the contest, featuring Presidential candidates on television for the first time, had polarized into political left against right, exactly what his creation of the Fifth Republic had set out to transcend.

De Gaulle swept the board in the traditional bastions of the right in Alsace-Lorraine, the west and the extreme south-west, but also clearly appealed to voters in the northern parts of France which had most benefited from economic growth. The political centre-ground was redefined by the candidacy of Jean Lecanuet, aged forty-five, democrat and European, who

scored 15.5 per cent in the first round. He projected an image of youth and modernity yet ironically he attracted a sheaf of votes from elderly peasant farmers, protesting at the impact of modernizing rural policies backed by Debré and the Minister of Agriculture, Edgard Pisani. Mitterrand took over some 40 per cent of Lecanuet's support in the second round, and scored heavily in the traditional left-voting areas of the rural Languedoc from the Gard to the Gers, in the industrial Pas-de-Calais, in his own *département* of the Nièvre and across the left-wing areas of the northern Massif Central from the Allier to the Haute-Vienne and the Corrèze. If the Presidential constitution was no longer rejected by the opposition, de Gaulle's personal standing was badly dented. Momentarily, familiar political speculation re-entered public discourse, but the stasis between President and parliament was not affected. As de Gaulle showed no awareness that his autocratic manner might be a fault, it seemed to many that political vitality could exist only outside the conventional parameters of politics.

The new generation of farmers

Early in the morning of 28 July 1962, the popular screen actor Jean Gabin was woken by a posse of 700 local farmers at Bonnefoi in the Normandy *département* of the Orne. The number testified to Gabin's national reputation. With exaggerated respect they told him they could no longer tolerate his accumulation of farms and farmland in the area. In Jean Renoir's classic anti-war film *La Grande illusion* of 1937 Gabin's role as an escaping prisoner of war in Germany had involved a vignette love affair with a young German woman, running her farm after the death of her husband at the front. Gabin, identified mostly with urban themes, is seen to adapt quickly to farm work. Over twenty years later, off screen, he developed a passion for stock-breeding. He bought a string of farms in rich dairy land, compensating the tenant farmers but replacing them with his own managers and hired farm hands. The protests germinated for months before breaking into the open. Whatever his film-star status, he was held to be an urban predator, a *cumulard* (accumulator), moving in on peasant territory. Given the extent of the rural exodus and the transformation of agriculture in the 1950s, the incident's notoriety might seem to owe everything to public interest in Gabin, but in fact it was seen to reveal the confidence of a new generation of farmers, who took hold of the rural changes and turned them to their advantage.

The main farmers' union, the FNSEA (Fédération Nationale des Syndicats d'Exploitants Agricoles), had its own organization of young farmers

in which the Catholic influence was strong. Dating from the inter-war years, the Jeunesse Agricole Chrétienne (JAC) had appeared to throw itself irrevocably into the service of Vichy and Pétain, but had shifted towards resistance activity as the Chantiers de la Jeunesse were targeted increasingly for labour service in Germany. The political reflexes of the Jacistes were attuned to shifts of circumstance and by the end of the 1950s they had moved from a purely religious presence in the countryside to a more formative role, using technical training centres established after the war, and inspired by an energetic young farmer, René Colson, from an area of small farms in the Haute-Marne. Colson died young in 1951, but he had carried several influential chaplains of the movement into new ways of constituting a powerful farming lobby among peasants with farms of moderate size. The tractor revolution was fully assimilated, and with mechanization assured the Jacistes preached a professionalism of young farmers to take advantage of the productive opportunities of the late 1950s. A national voice was created within the union's youth organization, relaunched as the CNJA (Cercle National des Jeunes Agriculteurs) in 1956, with a visionary young stock-farmer from the Puy-de-Dôme, Michel Debatisse, at its head, and an assertive monthly paper, *Jeunes agriculteurs*. Debatisse saw clearly that peasant farmers faced either a buyout or decline unless they could stabilize their land-holdings, apply the latest agricultural technology, and influence the government. The means of influence would be syndical not party-political, though he leaned more to the political left than his elders in the corporatist FNSEA.

The ideas of the young farmers were revolutionary in the sense that they aimed less at guaranteed high prices for their produce than at structural change to the access to land, whether through inheritance, buying and selling or accumulation, providing it stayed as a viable holding within the peasant farming community. After an initial period of laissez-faire agricultural policy, the Gaullist government of Michel Debré and the Minister of Agriculture Edgard Pisani agreed to a set of proposals which would provide exactly this viability. Initiated in 1960, they were accelerated by a year of peasant violence in 1961, sparked by young farmers who feared the government might change its mind. The focal riot was at Morlaix in Brittany, a region where the Jaciste farmers were well organized and had experience of guerrilla tactics in the Algerian war. Serious rural insurrection was threatened as the action leapt to the Massif Central and the Midi. Concessions from the government included promises of immediate legislation to enact the laws proposed in 1960. Pisani's name was attached to a charter which gave wide-reaching powers to regional land societies, SAFER

(Sociétés d'Aménagement Foncier et d'Établissement Rural), to buy land as it became available and sell or lease it to well-qualified and 'progressive' farmers. Producers' co-operatives were strengthened, and in many areas, notably Brittany, they were the marketing outlet for hundreds of medium-sized farms which would otherwise have disappeared.

By the end of the 1960s the Communist Party was comparing the success-ful young farmers to the kulaks in Soviet history. Prosperous through technology, concentration of resources and initiative, they thrived, argued the PCF, at the expense of the smaller peasantry and through collusion with government agencies. In response the young farmers saw the PCF and the Socialist Party as irrelevant to their revolution which equipped a peasant-based agriculture to survive the recession of the oil crises in the 1970s, and to prosper from the European Common Agricultural Policy (CAP). The drive to ever more productivity and the separation of agriculture from rural planning as a whole were hallmarks of the modernization under the CAP. Agriculture was categorized into production networks or sectors (*filières*) such as cereals, viticulture, stock-farming, fruit-growing or dairy products, and the intensified productivism in each sector often took place regardless of local considerations or in conflict with rural needs. Town and country planning (*aménagement du territoire*) was still in its infancy and tended to accept that the countryside and agriculture were synonymous. It was nevertheless an essential part of the rural revolution that repopulation of certain rural areas, particularly areas close to the large towns, was first recognized in the late 1960s. Over the following three decades the expan-sion in the number of new rural dwellers with no involvement in agriculture would force rural policy to be reconsidered.

For the moment, the needs of ex-farmers were recognized. A social fund was part of the Pisani charter and indemnities were paid to elderly farmers willing to sell their land to the younger generation. In fifteen years under the provisions of 1960–62 almost a third of the nation's farming land was made available. The rural transformation had become a revolution in land availability and usage. For many analysts of rural society it was the pro-fessional drive of the younger generation which carried the most impact. The much-heralded 'end of the peasantry' could be rephrased as 'the re-invention of the peasantry as a profession'. The culture of working one's own land had not been surrendered, but productivism ruled.

2. *Two phrases: marrying the century; dependent participation*

On 14 June 1960, in one of his most effective speeches, full of imagery, General de Gaulle called on France to accept contemporary realities and face the loss of empire. Whatever the nostalgic appeal of 'gentle oil lamps and the navy under sail', old France 'must be transformed into a new country and must marry its epoch'.[18] Throughout the 1960s the mobilizing phrase was repeated as the factual achievement of de Gaulle's republic, that France had indeed married its century. The second phrase, 'dependent participation', came from the sociologist Alain Touraine, professor at the University of Nanterre: 'A man is alienated when his only relationship to the social and cultural directions of his society is the one the ruling class accords him . . . cancelling out social conflict by creating dependent participation.'[19]

De Gaulle had few socio-economic ideas outside the need for healthy public finances, a strong national economy and social well-being, and the mark of his interest was in the experts he appointed and the pressure he then exerted for his expectations to be met. Alain Touraine had positive views of the student and worker revolt of May 1968, and behind this sympathetic reaction lay an acute perception of the shape of society. Both phrases addressed the nature of change brought about during the 1960s. The epigram from de Gaulle was celebratory. Touraine's concept pointed to ambivalence.

Marrying the century

De Gaulle did not personally manage the economy as he managed foreign policy and the image of the French nation. Yet almost his first significant appointment in 1958 was of Antoine Pinay as Finance Minister, told to end the parlous state of public finances and the high level of debt and inflation inherited from the Fourth Republic. The expert added to Pinay's team was Jacques Rueff, the famed financial adviser to Poincaré. Rueff pushed Pinay into accepting stronger measures than he had himself planned: severe cuts in public expenditure including social security, devaluation of the franc and its replacement by a 'new franc' equal to 100 old ones to bring it close to the level of the German mark and the Swiss franc. The 'nouveau franc' was taken to symbolize a new France, although people continued to calculate in 'anciens francs' for years to come, especially in land and property transactions. At the same time the European common

market came into operation among the six nations, with some adjustment of tariffs in 1959, a 50 per cent reduction on 1 January 1962, and full abolition in July 1968.

French expansion continued to reflect and outpace the phenomenon of international economic growth in the 1950s. The impetus given to firms to compete across Europe, and the investment facilitated by the big banks of Suez and Paribas and the financial houses of Schneider and Rothschild, led to spectacular mergers of major companies, the decline of uncompetitive firms, an overall growth rate second only to Japan's in the industrialized world, and the continued concentration of agricultural land into fewer and more profitable farms. The supermarket took custom from the small grocery shop, to hydro-electricity was added nuclear power, and coal was increasingly replaced by oil. A vertiginous rise in the size of suburbs in Paris and in towns such as Caen, Amiens, Orléans, Reims, Dijon, Toulouse, Grenoble and Montpellier was signalled in the acronyms ZUP, ZAC and ZI indicating zones for priority urbanization, development and industrialization. It was the golden age of managers and technocrats, trained in ENA and the other *grandes écoles*, of medium to large firms employing 200–500 workers, and of architects and builders of the towering geometrical blocks of flats, known as HLM, 'housing at moderate rents', symbolized by the vast new dormitory town of Sarcelles in the north of Paris. The huge population increase over thirty years was due to more births, fewer deaths, the 'repatriation' to France of 800,000 *pieds-noirs* in 1962 and the continued labour incentives for immigrants from Spain, Portugal and North Africa to come to France and settle with their families. From 40.5 million in 1946 the population of France grew to 52.6 million in 1975. The expansion of the tertiary sector registered the vast proliferation of new opportunities. Health and education services, office work, banking and insurance, administration, transport and commerce provided at least three-quarters of the new jobs created in the 1960s and established the central thrust of the commodity drive within the economy, as well as the gendering of clerical and secretarial work as female employment. Life expectancy for men leapt from 61.9 years in 1946–50 to 69.1 in 1975 and for women from 67.4 years to 77. In literal terms de Gaulle was determined that it should be a golden age: in the second half of the decade France massively converted money into gold, building up reserves which overtook the UK and put sterling and even the American dollar under pressure.

Extending and intensifying the changes of the 1950s, those of the Gaullist years were seen as closing an over-long era in which France had been

typified by small producers and subsistence farmers, by market fears and protectionist reflexes, and by urbanization without industrialization. In 1954 peasant farmers were 26.7 per cent of the active population, many facing imminent decline. By 1975 they were under 10 per cent, but mainly viable and frequently prosperous. Jean Fourastié imaged the new society by portraying two villages, one called Madère, undeveloped and hanging on desperately to the past, and the other Cessac, developed, confident and affluent, only then to reveal that they were his names for the same village, Douelle on the river Lot, at different dates, 1946 and 1975. It was his effective device for calling the two ends of the period 'les deux France'.[20] De Gaulle's metaphor of marriage had made a similar claim, that France had finally come to terms with the century. The claim was widely endorsed. It was also open to the charge that there had been, and still were, quite different opinions on the kind of century that people wanted it to be.

Participation and dependency

In December 1962 Renault announced that its workers would receive a fourth week of paid holidays per year. The rest of industry followed. The annual summer departure from the big towns had its microcosm in the urban exodus at the end of the week. The leisure phenomenon of 'le weekend' was as much a symbol of the changing society as any other indicator. So too were the 14,000 deaths on the road in 1967 or the 2.5 million accidents at work reported in 1968. Measuring exactly what was happening to society in the 1960s reinforced the post-war proliferation of instant statistics and opinion polls. It was noted that the recurrent average rise in household expenditure of 4.5 per cent per year was the most indicative of all statistics, especially when coupled with the information that transport and leisure, health and housing were the key sectors of escalating consumption. It enabled social commentators to argue that it was neither the Gaullist regime nor 'the market' as an abstract economic force that was the prime mover, but rather the insatiable appetite of the public for more commodities. Critics argued that it was the reverse: ever more commodities needing and creating the consumers. Whichever way round, a consumer society based on consent was claimed by the government. Participation became de Gaulle's key social theme. Yet opinion polls of the decade failed to register a comparable sense of growing contentment.

The evidence of participation was manifest. Equally evident, though less analysed, was dependency. Coupled together, argued Touraine, they equalled alienation, the situation in which people became dependent by

participating, apparently making their own decisions but in reality unable to determine for themselves the shape and content of their lives. The young rural workers who migrated to the towns in their hundreds of thousands 'participated' in the rapid urbanization, yet they were utterly 'dependent' on the jobs, housing and training provided. Only a fraction of the professional training courses that were needed were in operation, and the hostels for the young were full of archaic restrictions. Participation in moving into the new suburban housing estates was massive, but there was no urban strategy to bring work and leisure to the places where people now lived. The concrete housing units were impersonal and soulless. They were, in both senses of the word, blocks. The most ambivalent participation was in the purchase and enjoyment of a television set. It could, and did, open horizons: it could, and did, increase dependency.

Solid sociological research during the *trente glorieuses* showed that most people had benefited from the new opportunities and affluence, but also tried to explain why some had not. The landless agricultural labourers, numbering 600,000 in 1968, were the lowest beneficiaries, since the minimum agricultural wage (SMAG) lagged well behind the industrial minimum (SMIG). Regional and gender bias accounted for flagrant pay disparities. The Parisian male worker gained 50 per cent more than the male worker of the Limousin, who in turn gained 50 per cent more than the female worker of the same provincial area. Among the extensive changes in land ownership and the upward mobility of commercially astute farmers, there were huge tracts of cultivated land in the south and the Massif Central which were deemed unprofitable. They reverted to wilderness, and farms in these areas just disappeared. Long before Fourastié's portrait of the transformed village, Laurence Wylie, the American social historian of the villages of Roussillon, west of Avignon in the Vaucluse, and Chanzeau, close to Angers in Maine-et-Loire, revisited his sites of detailed research and found that Jacques Baudot in Roussillon had moved from scepticism about the future in 1950 to embracing consumption and exuding optimism in 1960. He now had 'a new car, a tractor, and a television set, all of them bought on the installment plan'. It signified a major shift in rural attitude towards credit, and Wylie added, 'By 1960 it was obvious that people who had prospered were not those who held back but those who took risks.'[21]

These explanations suggest that reasons for inequality in the benefits of growth can be found at all levels of society, but the concept of 'dependent participation' went further. It identified the fact that people who benefited could also feel trapped, and that this, as well as inequality, was the key to the later events of the decade.

3. The search for self-management

Despite his rhetoric of independence in foreign policy, at home Charles de Gaulle's refusal to embark on political discussion signified his regime's reluctance to consult or to enable people to manage their own lives. Checks and controls increasingly frustrated a wide range of groups within de Gaulle's Republic. The regime's authoritarianism was more random than coherent, but in the mid-1960s increasing groups of people began to declare that control was the essence of Gaullist ideology. De Gaulle's republic reproduced in a more extreme form the recurrent paradox of France in the twentieth century: a society which was highly differentiated and full of independent ideas and actions, yet one in which difference and self-management (*autogestion*) were suspect and denied. This was evident within several distinct areas of social activity.

Regional interests

Involvement of people at local level in resistance against German Occupation and Vichy was formally acknowledged after the war by the recognition of notable resistance sites (*hauts-lieux de la résistance*). Regional pride in the Resistance led to embryonic organizations for the development of regional interests, created democratically as part of economic reconstruction. Conscious that the national economic recovery was uneven and that the bulk of growth was in the Parisian region, small committees in the provinces pursued the study of regional recovery, acting in Brittany, for example, as centres of cultural and economic initiatives, with members of industry and commerce, doctors, teachers and engineers alongside representatives of the peasantry and the trade unions. A geographer, Michel Phlipponneau, was on the Breton committee and showed in his history of the grass-roots movements that their collective point of reference was the searing analysis by a more senior geographer, J.-F. Gravier, entitled *Paris et le désert français*, published in 1947 and immediately accepted throughout France as the definitive study of regional decay and neglect. By 1952 there were sufficient of these regional groups for a conference to meet at Reims, and in December 1954 their consultative role was formally endorsed by government.[22] Under Mendès France the first tentative steps were taken towards establishing regional economies which moved outside the bureaucratic limits of the *département*, and in 1956 twenty-two regions were designated. For the first time since 1790, wrote Gravier, 'from Picardy to

Provence, from Alsace to Aquitaine, from Brittany to Franche-Comté, the deep and age-old realities were recognized and proclaimed after a long exile'.[23]

The identification of regionalism with the ideology of Vichy, and earlier in the century with Barrès and Maurras, militated heavily against these initiatives throughout the Fourth Republic. A profound Jacobin suspicion among the parties of the political left towards any form of regionalism undermined the regional committees but did not entirely stop their activity. The advent of de Gaulle and his choice of Premier in 1958, Michel Debré, brought another genre of political centralism to power. Debré was a fierce opponent of any form of regional autonomy. In his memoirs he stated that his firm intention was 'to nationalize the regions, not to regionalize the nation'.[24] At the end of 1959 his government declared that the extent of coal-mining was surplus to national energy requirements and that certain mines would be run down. Decazeville in the Aveyron was initially targeted. There was no discussion or consultation with the miners. The first dismissal notices arrived in December 1961, provoking a strike which became a symbolic act of regional defiance. On 1 January 1962, 230 mayors in the Aveyron resigned, and by the end of the month a regional escalation of protest reawakened memories of the 1907 revolt of the *vignerons*. On 22 January representatives of organizations from seventeen neighbouring *départements* assembled in Rodez and declared that defeat for the miners 'would sound the death-knell of the underdeveloped regions'.[25] The government refused to back down and a return to work was decided by the trade unions at the end of February, the whole conflict leaving bitterness and a sense of betrayal widespread across the south. The regional passion it had aroused was central to the consolidation of a left-wing Occitan movement which had its own poets such as Max Allier, and its emotional roots in the Resistance and the pre-war anti-fascism of Charles Camproux. From the Decazeville strike onwards there was an improbable convergence of libertarian activists and social conservatives on the issue of regional identities and autonomy. It was one of the first indications that issue politics could play havoc with conventional political alignments. A 'new' regionalism moved in a leftward direction.

The sweeping Gaullist success in the 1962 elections enabled the government of Pompidou to bypass the democratic initiatives in the regions and superimpose its own form of regionalism through the creation of regional prefects in 1964, armed with commissions for regional economic development under the town and country planning authority introduced in 1963, a high-profile new area of central administration, creating new jobs in the

west to compensate for the rate of rural exodus, distributing money and contracts to the regions and watching carefully how it was spent. Known by its acronym DATAR, it aimed at creating a regional balance so that no region was disproportionately failing to benefit from economic growth.[26] The fifth national plan for 1965–70 was the first to be regionalized, establishing a ring of towns round Paris where local economic development would reverse the trend of commuting into the capital; new towns were launched close to Rouen, Lille, Lyon and Marseille, and the idea of regional metropolitan centres was created to ensure a dispersal of the urban economy to balance the dominance of Paris. Less obviously geared to local development were the national parks, first instituted in 1960 and concentrating on the conservation of nature, but widely seen within some of the designated areas as subordinating the needs of agriculture to the new god of tourism.

Within the government there was no more concern for devolved discussion and politics than for parliamentary debate and, as Gravier objected, there was no democratic base to these bodies, however much of an economic incentive they deployed.[27] Both before and after the events of 1968, Robert Lafont, a university professor at Montpellier and the promoter of a socialist-oriented Occitanism, decried the economy imposed from Paris as one of capitalist standardization and uniformity, in short as internal colonization.[28] Not all regional figures saw it so negatively or as so imposed. The enterprising power of 'pan-Celtic visionary' Alexis Gouvernnec in Brittany lay in persuading central government to fund his project for a deep-water port in Roscoff, from which Brittany Ferries, a parallel local initiative, would eventually and successfully operate.[29] From the Gaullist perspective central planning was enlightened planning: regional development in the 1960s, like André Malraux's cultural development through the Maisons de la Culture, was aimed at bringing local and national figures together in joint projects, mostly decided according to criteria from above. Malraux's brief for the Maisons was to replicate the achievement of Jules Ferry's educational reforms; giving everybody access to a national high culture, professionally presented. When he opened the fifth Maison in Amiens in 1966 he expressed his wish that within ten years 'the hideous word Province' would cease to exist in France.[30] The transparency of central authority over the direction of culture and economic planning in the regions was claimed by de Gaulle as a necessary element in his national *rassemblement*. He believed that the people, summoned to yet another referendum, would endorse this vision, but by 1969 his credibility in this major area of social policy had gone.

The centralism at the heart of Gaullist polity was largely seen as the

reason for a relocation of regionalist ideas from political right to left. Theoretical investment in the regions as sites of autonomous culture also tipped towards a more left-wing connotation during the 1960s. Under de Gaulle criticisms of a consumer-led, market-driven, commodity culture came more from left-leaning sources than from old-style traditionalists. In 1964 the words of the committed singer and composer Jean Ferrat, warning the children of his Ardèche mountains against the allure of 'formica and the movies' were emblematic of the opposition located within the left to American packaged culture and a readiness in student and bohemian circles to look for authenticity in the regions.[31] The warm, satirical songs of Georges Brassens, the Mediterranean poet-singer, born in the fishing port of Sète in the Hérault, brought this authenticity together with anarchic humour and a strong musical Midi accent. Much of the *chanson* tradition associated with the songs and voices of Charles Trenet, Édith Piaf, Yves Montand, Juliette Greco, Serge Reggiani, Georges Brassens, Jacques Brel and Léo Ferré gained a mythical status in the 1960s as a bastion of French musical culture against the incursion of American and British pop. By itself this iconic status was more Parisian-based than regional, but its defiant identity was easily interwoven by individuals into the independent culture of the new regionalism.

'Bidonvilles'

The forced displacement of whole villages during the Algerian war was the main reason given by male Algerian immigrants in France for the arrival of their families on the mainland: 'It was just as well', said one, 'for my wife and children to come and join me as be shunted about under military guard to who knows where. It was the lesser evil.' He was speaking as one of some 10,000 Algerians who created a semblance of home and community among the rats, mud, rags and misery of one of the *bidonvilles* (shanty towns) in Nanterre in the north-west suburbs of Paris.[32] The *bidonville*, meaning literally 'a town of jerry cans' and 'a mockery of a town', grew by accretions throughout the 1950s on land close to the industries and impoverished housing of already overcrowded suburbs. Café owners or proprietors of cheap hostels provided makeshift accommodation for the increasing numbers of immigrants, and were the first to throw together planks and corrugated tin on adjoining land to meet the demand for somewhere to sleep. Their exploitation of need gave them the derogatory title of 'marchands de sommeil' and their profit-seeking role in the creation of the *bidonvilles* was crucial. The shacks started to spread across waste land

and turned into an agglomeration of self-owned huts, with no running water and no sewerage, for which Algerian workers paid anything from half to a whole year's wages. They declared it was an improvement on the mattresses laid out in dingy cellars in which they had lived on arrival. At the very least it was a sign of their desire to manage their own lives.

Symptom of the booming, unregulated labour market, the mass influx of male workers from the Maghreb (Algeria, Morocco and Tunisia), followed by their families, had not been foreseen when immigration was planned after the Liberation. De Gaulle and the Provisional Government respected the advice of ethnicity expert Georges Mauco, despite the fact that he had been dubiously involved with Jacques Doriot's PPF at the outbreak of war and had elaborated racial arguments for a hierarchy of preferred foreigners, with 'Arabs' at the bottom of the scale.[33] On the one hand, the experts wanted to boost the population with European immigrant families; on the other, the urgent needs of reconstruction demanded unskilled male workers from the Maghreb. In 1947 unrestricted freedom of movement between Algeria and France was established and residence on the mainland was not dependent on obtaining work. Male workers were expected, but there would be no discrimination against women or their children. Within the next twenty years the economic boom, the upturn in the French birth rate, the decline in immigrants from most of Europe except Portugal, and finally the effects of the Algerian war, radically altered the situation. By the 1960s Algerians in France were no longer just the male labourers of reconstruction but a rapidly growing underclass of families that fuelled the expanding economy, looking for the jobs that no one else wanted, and living mostly in poverty and degradation. Between 1946 and 1975 immigrants from the Maghreb grew from 2.3 per cent of foreigners in France to 32.3 per cent, and Algerian numbers from 22,000 in 1946 to 805,000 in 1982.[34]

The *bidonvilles* of Paris, Lyon and Marseille were the shameful public face of immigrant deprivation, tolerated by the increasingly affluent society of the 1960s. They were not confined to Algerians. A *bidonville* in Saint-Denis which moved to La Courneuve in 1961 was the home of Portuguese and Spanish workers, living in shacks and discarded buses and caravans, with water from a standpipe and no sanitation. The influx of Portuguese families in the 1960s exceeded for a decade that of the Algerians. Beside and beyond the shanty towns were the hostels tightly run by some companies for their workers, and the accommodation provided from 1956 onwards by the SONOCOTRA, the national society for the construction of workers' housing. Initially formed to set up lodgings for male Algerians, the SONO-COTRA hostels for all immigrants left no space for private life and refused

the inhabitants any autonomy. Privacy and independence were even reduced during the Gaullist years, as the state rigidly set out to increase control over its poorest workers, thought to be a potential social danger if given any opportunity of running their own lives. To go to a *bidonville* represented for many a life of comparative freedom, whatever the conditions. It was in these makeshift communities that cultural and religious practices from North Africa were re-established, and indigenous trades and skills perpetuated.

In the 1970s the shanty towns were gradually replaced by vast HLM high-rise blocks, and immediately a certain nostalgia among ex-inhabitants of the *bidonvilles* alternated with warnings against romanticization. Theft, disease, violence and cheating were endemic. The women initially preferred the shacks to the virtual imprisonment of the hostels, but also acknowledged that they were debased by abuse and promiscuity. Fire was a constant hazard, although the victims were sometimes rehoused in improved accommodation. It was also a preoccupation: inhabitants frequently dreamed of setting fire to all the filth and misery, but would not risk their families' lives.[35]

At the height of de Gaulle's republic over 75,000 were registered as living in *bidonvilles*, probably little more than a third of the real number. They were condemned to gradual clearance by a government decision in 1964, but even as their destruction began it was clear just how far the *bidonvilles* were a form of social control: the police were content to see the families from the Maghreb corralled into distinct areas, even if there was no official policy of ghettoization. If, for some, they did represent a form of autonomy, for most of the inhabitants they were a mockery of a town and of freedom. The *bidonville* contained no avenues of social mobility.

Independence and the cinema

It was accepted that the harnessing of André Malraux's cultural reputation was a perfect illustration of de Gaulle's opportunism, but also of his ability to merge symbols of liberation and authority. Malraux was his plenipotentiary in cultural circles, the instigator of the Maisons de la Culture, the authority behind the cleaning of Paris public buildings and monuments, the state patron who commissioned Marc Chagall to paint the ceiling of the Paris Opéra and allowed the Mona Lisa (*La Joconde*) to travel to New York and the Venus de Milo to Japan for major exhibitions. During the 1960s Malraux's revolutionary pedigree from the 1930s was overlaid with the authoritarian style and expectations of de Gaulle's regime. His Ministry

watched magisterially over cultural institutions and personnel, and in early 1968 he intervened in the running of the Cinémathèque Française, founded in 1936 and allotted regular government money since the war. He sacked the co-founder and director, Henri Langlois, for unorthodox administrative methods. It brought de Gaulle's republic into direct confrontation with the élite of the cinema, the sector of culture which had long represented a distinctive French identity, inheritor of the avant-garde role played by modernism in the *belle époque* and the 1920s.

The cinema as art and industry had been an immediate beneficiary of the national discourse with which de Gaulle returned to power in 1958. As a counterbalance to the all-pervasiveness of American cinema it was granted financial support at the box office, known as the *avance sur recettes* system, by which the advance subsidies were only repaid once the film's receipts were assured. It enabled young film-makers to get started and was a source of stability much exploited by a *nouvelle vague* (New Wave) of directors, labelled as such by Françoise Giroud of the weekly magazine *L'Express*. The New Wave was never a coherent movement: there was no membership or manifesto, though it had a collective origin in the years 1958–60. The leading luminaries, all young critics and directors (*cinéastes*), were François Truffaut, Jean-Luc Godard, Jacques Rivette, Eric Rohmer and Claude Chabrol, whose theoretical approach filled the pages of the journal *Cahiers du cinéma*. It was here that François Truffaut led a critical reaction against the studio-centred quality cinema of the 1950s, phrasing his critique with such aggression that he was banned from the Cannes Film Festival in 1958. His proposals were for a cinema in which the emphasis would be on the director as an individualist *auteur* (author), with a free style which might involve, according to different directors, a stress on location shooting, jump-cuts, improvised dialogue and a consciousness of film as a system of signs or personal signatures. His first feature film, *Les Quatre cent coups*, based partly on his own adolescent experience of reform school, scooped the Director's Prize at Cannes in 1959, a much-commented reversal of Truffaut's relationship with the festival, and in close competition with Godard's first feature, *À Bout de souffle*, and another first from Alain Resnais, *Hiroshima mon amour*. The output of the New Wave directors exercised no monopoly, but the existence of a group of innovative pioneers with their own distinctive style, treating certain distinctive Hollywood directors, notably Alfred Hitchcock, as formative *auteurs*, brought international eminence to French cinema and film theory throughout the 1960s and well beyond.

The New Wave was grounded in the retrospective film showings by

Langlois at the Cinémathèque, and Langlois was given guru eminence by *cinéastes* for his seasons dedicated to single directors, his compendious recovery of films from the silent era, his eclectic taste and openness to untried innovation. As an administrator he spurned organizational warnings from the Ministry of Culture and asserted the Cinémathèque's independence from other archival institutions. Relationships with the government finally broke down in February 1968, but his removal by Malraux galvanized film-makers and connoisseurs into a campaign of agitation and protest. Truffaut was keen for it not to be seen as oppositional politics, and part of his success was to recruit film critics in papers which buttressed the regime. Malraux was forced to give way. Langlois and his staff were reinstated in April, although the government subsidy was withdrawn. It had mushroomed into a symbolic conflict over self-government. A number of students for whom cinema had become the critical culture of self-expression joined the film directors to defend the Cinémathèque. The campaign set out to protect a specific area of cinematic autonomy. Yet in less than a month the Langlois affair was given a quite different perspective as an advance tremor of a widespread cultural eruption.

Youth and universities

A film made by Bertrand Blier about youth in 1963 decided on a shock title, *Hitler, connais pas!* (*Hitler, Don't Know Him!*). It confirmed the prevalent view among many older citizens that young people born since the war were spoilt and had no sense of history. With the massive demographic change since the war, there were many more elderly people to make this judgement and hundreds of thousands more children and students to be judged. University student figures alone rocketed from 202,062 in 1959–60 to 615,300 in 1969–70. De Gaulle's Ministry of Education opened several new faculties in Paris, including one at Nanterre alongside the *bidonvilles*, and in the provinces a dozen new universities were created. References to youth became obligatory in official speeches and publications. Leather-jacketed youths (*blousons noirs*), aggressively pugilistic in suburbs and small towns, were unthinkingly dismissed as louts (*voyous*), and the teenage pop fans of Johnny Hallyday and Sylvie Vartan raised adult eyebrows, but broadly youth activity was embraced as a pertinent sign of French social renaissance since the war. It was not as visibly and audibly provocative as youth cultures in Britain and the USA.

A 56-page booklet on the government's policies towards youth was exported abroad in June 1965 through the cultural attachés, and took

pleasure in telling the Americans and the British, who were already worried about 'juvenile delinquents' and 'dropouts' in the 1950s, that France had it all in hand. A thriving market for the young in clothes, music, sport, entertainment and transport provided the salient facts: the booklet proudly stated that one in seven young men and one in eight young women owned a car before they were twenty, and that 43 per cent of university students found part-time employment alongside their studies.[36] The inference was clear: the mark of the social integration of youth was their participation in consumerism and paid work. The sociologist Edgar Morin, subtle analyst of social transformation at both village level and throughout the Western world, provided a radically different interpretation. Early in the 1960s he saw contemporary youth as forming a generational class, a 'bioclass', determined on emancipating itself through its difference, its alterity, but at the same time demanding the rights of adults, presaging what he later called a kind of 1789 revolution of adolescents.[37]

In 1967 there was a noticeable slowing of the economy. From July to the following May the national unemployment figures almost doubled from 270,000 to 470,000. They had been negligible since 1945. The sudden rise was a shock, and there was widespread anxiety among those with little social protection. An element of insecurity infused the confident self-image of young workers and gave a cutting edge to any protest in which they were involved. University students were not immune from the effects of the slowdown, not least because Christian Fouchet as Minister of Education had introduced more selectivity and a higher failure rate during the three years of student courses. The image of the unemployed or unemployable student makes a side entry into student literature in 1967–8. It was a minor subtext of the main student agenda which was increasingly to contest the archaic inflexibility of authority. Participants in the massive overcrowding of lecture rooms, libraries, halls of residence (*cités universitaires*) and refectories, they were increasingly located in overspill faculties built too fast on suburban sites with few or no leisure facilities. Once enrolled, they were dependent on structures of teaching, administration and discipline which took no account of the social and cultural changes which were blatantly apparent in the wider society.

Student campaigns to be treated as sexual and political adults found easy targets in sexually segregated halls of residence and puerile restrictions on self-expression. Politicized groups were denied the freedom to distribute information on the Vietnam war, the Cuban revolution, the Cultural Revolution of Mao Tse-tung, and the civil rights movement in the USA. Political splinter groups established a sectarian existence, equally critical of the

control exercised by the dominant political parties as by the university authorities. Solidarity Vietnam committees, denouncing the Americans, proliferated in universities and lycées. The Communist student organization (UEC) was the most prone to internal dissent, leading to a series of purges by the party and the formation of counter-groups, notably the Jeunesse Communiste Révolutionnaire (JCR), whose passion for a more revolutionary ideology was dismissed by Communist elders as 'adventurism'. In October 1966 hundreds of JCR militants attended a demonstration in Liège against American imperialism. It brought the name of Rudi Dutschke and the German socialist student grouping (SDS) to the fore, a small group which organized violent protests at the visit of the pro-American Shah of Iran to Germany in June 1967, during which a student, Benno Ohnesorg, was killed by police. Twenty thousand students demonstrated solidarity at his funeral.

Violence as a strategy divided students among themselves. Secession and splintering became the norm. The pursuit of assertive student action through specific ideological groupings was the clearest expression of the supreme value attached to self-management. Only a small minority of students were involved, but it was an expanding and increasingly vocal minority, each group producing its own tracts and news-sheets. Collectively, alongside the PSU, they made up *les gauchistes*, with a vanguard dubbed *les enragés*. The mainstream press carried few references to the student world, but with the agitation caused by the economic downturn in 1967, the surveillance of the police was watchful. On 7 March 1968 police intelligence warned of student violence spreading from Germany, and pinpointed the 'intention of German student leader, Rudi Dutschke, to organize revolutionary groups of students and implant his *"revolution"* in all countries of Western Europe'.[38] It was symptomatic of the government belief that trouble, if any, would come from outside.

16

May–June 1968

1. Revolt

In 1965 a supplement to *Droit et liberté*, the journal of the anti-racist MRAP, gave a picture of the extreme right which made it appear ready at any moment to launch an attack on the republic. The MRAP's target was the career and opinions of Jean-Louis Tixier-Vignancour, the powerful advocate at the Court of Appeal and deputy for Orthez in the Pyrénées-Atlantiques, who had defended the OAS in general and the persons of General Salan and Bastien-Thiry in particular. A member of Action Française in the 1930s, propagandist for Vichy, supporter in 1952 of the neo-fascist journal of Maurice Bardèche, *Défense de l'Occident*, and passionate advocate of French Algeria, Tixier-Vignancour stood for the extreme right in the Presidential elections of 1965, winning just over 5 per cent of the vote. The supplement also listed the activities of Jean-Marie Le Pen, a close associate of Tixier-Vignancour in Poujadist and Algérie Française campaigns and a member of Occident in 1964, whom the MRAP accused of peddling records of songs from the Third Reich and Pétain speeches.[1]

The networks of the extreme right were under constant police surveillance after 1961. If any revolt against de Gaulle's republic was expected by state intelligence it was from the disinherited activists of the OAS. But the campaign of Tixier-Vignancour did not bring disorder, and the Gaullist regime in the mid-1960s seemed secure and firmly rooted in public acceptance. Nor was the PCF seen as a force for political revolt: its structures were firmly embedded in the status quo. Alongside it the CGT still represented the everyday critique of capitalism at the workplace, and in 1963 it collaborated with the CFTC in heading a successful and popular national strike by miners, which effaced the climbdown at Decazeville a year earlier. It was seen as a model trade-union victory, but it did not destabilize government economic policy. In the four years that followed, the CGT 'days of action' showed that the unions were working to a formula to maximize

workers' benefits, not to overthrow the system. The insurrectionary potential of the CGT was rehearsed at delegates' meetings but it was increasingly a discourse of the past.

Strikes in 1967 rekindled some of the old fire, inflamed by the return of unemployment as an issue. At Besançon in February workers at Rhodiacéta, making artificial fibres and textiles, occupied the factory, and the strike spread to Rhodia plants in Lyon and Péage-de-Roussillon in the Rhône valley. At the Berliet truck works in Lyon, workers' action provoked a lockout, and in Lorraine miners threatened by the run-down of the industry occupied surface buildings throughout April. Saint-Nazaire was paralysed on 11 April by a solidarity strike for the naval dockyard workers, who pursued a long campaign for wage parity with Parisians and job security, and in the autumn there were battles with the police in Le Mans. Violent confrontations at Caen during the winter were headed by metalworkers from the Saviem plant who fought a running battle with police on 26 January 1968. Two days later some 15,000 workers in Caen were on strike. It was the most serious labour dispute that the region had known, spreading to Fougères and further west to Redon in Brittany. In all three towns it was the fighting with police which reached the headlines, revealing the lead taken by young workers, often in defiance of union instructions. The strikes ended mostly in failure or compromises, unsatisfactory to the militant workers. The *patronat* showed itself to be resourceful and determined, meeting demonstrations with lockouts and refusing to negotiate under threat of violence. University students at Caen collected 2,000 francs for the workers, but that only appeared relevant in retrospect.

May '68: students

At the time it seemed as if the events of May 1968 came from nowhere. As a revolt it was so unfamiliar and innovative that a precise definition was elusive, and still largely remains so.

A libertarian wave of student protests, demanding the right to political activity and male access to female halls of residence, solidified into a political movement in the impersonal, functional corridors of Nanterre. The movement took the date as its name, an early sign of the importance of the immediate present in the events. It was 22 March. Fire-bomb attacks in Paris on the Chase Manhattan Bank and American Express had led to the arrest of five students, three of them from lycée Vietnam committees, and one, Xavier Langlade, from Nanterre. The Nanterre movement condemned the arrests. On the back page of its *Bulletin du 22-Mars* instructions were

417

printed on how to make a 'Molotov cocktail' (petrol bomb). It was a flawed recipe but explosively provocative. The police rose to the bait. The student held to be responsible, Daniel Cohn-Bendit, born in France of German parents, was arrested on 27 April. The Movement of 22 March replied with the occupation of administrative rooms and a lecture hall in which it projected a film on the revolutionary Che Guevara, whose death in Bolivia in November 1967 had added martyrdom to the romance of his bearded portrait, aesthetic and political icon for hundreds of student followers. The Dean of the Faculty, Pierre Grappin, appointed for his liberal attitudes, decided the situation was running out of control. On 2 May he closed the campus for a second time in three months, and called in the police. On the same day right-wing students of the nationalist movement Occident attacked left-wing targets in the Latin Quarter in Paris, a familiar battle of ideological militants which had already caused the police to intervene at the University of Toulouse on 25 April.

The political geography of the Latin Quarter was one of educational buildings, cafés, bookshops and meeting places, each with its own ideological orientation. A century of high student density in the 5th and 6th *arrondissements* of Paris made the territorial battle one which dated back to the Popular Front and beyond that to the Dreyfus Affair. Much had changed since the eras of Péguy and Léon Blum, most importantly the demise of the nationalist strongholds. Even the military École Polytechnique on the slopes leading up to the Panthéon had been infiltrated by the left-wing student union, UNEF, which had its headquarters in the neighbouring rue Soufflot. This was at right angles to the rue d'Ulm, where the liberal atmosphere of the École Normale Supérieure had made it a veritable headquarters of the tightly-knit ideological groups who had broken with the Communist Party. The Sorbonne was the centre of the university and of the *quartier*. On Friday, 3 May the UNEF and the Movement of 22 March organized a protest in its courtyard against the closing of Nanterre. It drew only about 300 students and a second demonstration was mooted for Monday when Cohn-Bendit and others were due to appear before a disciplinary hearing. The rumour that Occident were returning stopped the protesters from disbanding. They decided not to move but to fight it out, spearheaded by UNEF's *service d'ordre*, armed with chair legs and iron bars. The mobile police had arrived in the Latin Quarter, through a growing crowd of students arriving from all parts of the *quartier*. The university Rector, Jean Roche, contacted the new Minister of Education, Alain Peyrefitte, and instructed the police to clear the Sorbonne courtyard. It was perhaps the single most important moment in the first chain of events, immediately

registered by students as a political and cultural offensive, a crossing of symbolic frontiers. It was followed by the arrest of protesters even though they had agreed to leave. The packed police vans had to force their way through angry and jeering students outside the Sorbonne, triggering the confrontation which initially appeared to have been avoided. Stone-throwing, visceral and comic abuse, but above all the density of students surrounding the vans made up an unco-ordinated and impromptu student riot. Tear gas and the seizure of individuals were the police response: police files indicate that 574 arrests were made 'including 179 minors, 45 women and 58 foreigners' and featuring Daniel Cohn-Bendit, Alain Krivine of the Jeunesse Communiste Révolutionnaire (JCR) and Jacques Sauvegeot of UNEF.[2]

The police sealed off the Sorbonne, but they had been taken by surprise at the numbers and violence of the students. Nor had the students been prepared for what happened. By Monday, 6 May, positions had hardened. UNEF called an all-out student strike, demanding the withdrawal of the police, the release of students and recognition of student grievances. The police sharpened tactics and armed themselves more effectively. The university authorities insisted on discipline and then vacillated; the Minister of Education condemned the strike as illegal, told the police to stay in the Sorbonne, and dismissed the activists as rabble. The Prime Minister, Georges Pompidou, was on a visit to Iran and Afghanistan. De Gaulle was silent.

The nature of the revolt, violence and repression which spiralled in and out of control from 6 May was prefigured in the events of the Friday. The *gauchiste* groups took the initiative, with anarchist, Trotskyist and Maoist ideas manifest in verbal arguments and physical action. Individuals emerged with bravura. The 23-year-old anarchic Cohn-Bendit, with his tousled red hair, already fixed in police reports as 'le rouge', had the political brilliance and repartee which made brazen insolence towards authority into the street-wise language of the mass of students; the handsome Jacques Sauvegeot, twenty-five, epitomized the romantic young rebel; the tall, calm Trotskyist Alain Krivine, twenty-seven, gave the JCR a reputation for tight organization, and to these was added the passion of the round-faced Alain Geismar, twenty-nine, the National Secretary of the university teachers' union which threw its weight behind the student demands. The number of demonstrators on 6 May, swollen by lycée students to some 60,000, exceeded expectations. Indiscriminate use of truncheons and tear gas by the police in the most violent clashes since the Algerian war was recorded on camera and swept public opinion on 8 May into sympathy for the students.

Before an opinion poll registered the extent of this sympathy, the Communist Party in *L'Humanité* branded the students as pampered provocateurs playing into the government's hands, and scorned the activist movements as insignificant little groups, *groupuscules*. By contrast the minority trade union movement, CFDT, had openly backed the student strike. After the poll, and as the revolt spread to university towns across the whole of France, the PCF appeared increasingly out of touch. 'We are all *groupuscules*' was the ironic chant of thousands of massed students with banners of local demands and the universal 'Libérez nos camarades', replicated in Strasbourg, Lyon, Toulouse, Nantes, Rennes, Rouen, Le Mans, Grenoble, Dijon, Marseille and Aix-en-Provence, Bordeaux, Clermont-Ferrand, Lille, Besançon and many smaller towns. Hundreds of lycées across France were on strike, many of them occupied by their students.

Paris-centred media coverage was spurned no less in Paris than elsewhere as a false localization of the conflict. Yet on the night of 10–11 May paving stones (*pavés*) were dug up in the rue Gay-Lussac, the rue d'Ulm and the small streets behind the Panthéon, trees were felled, cars turned over, and barricades constructed for the first time since the liberation of Paris, echoing the famous Parisian revolutions of the nineteenth century. The riot police (CRS) were ordered to avoid clashes with the lycée students, and were thus held back as the barricades were constructed, but at 2 a.m. orders were given to move on to the offensive against stones, bottles and home-made petrol bombs. It was a full military repression without live bullets, but with the stronger CS type of tear gas which burns on exposure to water, and with sorties off the streets to drag students out of cafés and staircases. The battle of 'the night of the barricades' left the police with a pyrrhic victory, cafés in debris, devastated streets and squares littered with smouldering cars and buses, and public opinion in disbelief. Only the barest mention of the night's battles had been permitted on state-controlled television and radio. Newspapers carried it all.

May '68: students, workers, artists

Reactions to the 'night of the barricades' revealed a number of solidarity movements between students and young workers, particularly in Brittany where an incipient unity between individual workers in the fishing industry, certain Breton regionalists and students had been visible as early as 8 May. In Bordeaux, Dijon and Lyon among many other centres, young trade unionists from the CFDT joined with students, and in Marseille on Saturday 11 May, students and workers joined in a major demonstration on the

Canebière, with the mayor, Gaston Defferre, in attendance, caught by the camera close to a student banner proclaiming 'De Gaulle, assassin'. False rumours that more than three students had already been killed by the police had given an extra ferocity to the fighting on the night of the 10th, and it was precisely the severity of the repression that forced the Communist Party to end its isolation from the events. Trade unionists from both the CFDT and the CGT met with the students of UNEF and teachers' unions on 11 May and launched a joint call for a national day of strikes and demonstrations on Monday the 13th, the tenth anniversary of the coup that had brought de Gaulle to power. 'Dix ans ça suffit' ('Ten years, that's enough') and 'Bon anniversaire, mon général' were among the hundreds of defiant slogans painted on to huge banners over the weekend.

Pompidou, returning from Afghanistan on 11 May, read the signs clearly. He had decided on the way back from Kabul that the government should capitulate to the basic student demand to withdraw the police from the Sorbonne. De Gaulle acceded, not least because neither he nor the rest of the government had any alternative policy, or, in fact, any policy at all. Pompidou went further and gave a pledge on television that the arrests would be reconsidered and he expressed his 'profound sympathy' for the students. The police were told to evacuate the Latin Quarter. It defused the violence for more than a week; it may even have stopped student ideas for a paramilitary assault on the CRS. But it failed to halt the momentum of the revolt, now with good reasons to be triumphal.

On the morning of the 13th the students streamed back into the Sorbonne, hoisted red flags and opened it to the people. The Censier university annexe was occupied and became the nerve-centre of co-ordination with universities across the country, many already in the process of being occupied in preparation for the day of action. Such was the enthusiasm of the response on 13 May that towns which had barely been touched by any other event since the Liberation saw marches of workers, students and teachers. The surging demonstrations were estimated everywhere as vast, headed by 600,000 in Paris. The revolt was national, with its motivation, energy and cultural creativity provided by an exuberant younger generation, now as vocal in factories and public services as in universities. Strikes broke out everywhere with the spontaneity and self-confidence of the workforce pushing a hesitant CGT officialdom into following the lead from below. The CFDT needed no such prodding, but rallied to the qualitative nature of the strikes, with a stress on human relationships at work and ideals of self-management.

De Gaulle left for a state visit to Romania on the 14th, a departure which

was read as a sign of indifference. It was the day that Nantes workers at the Sud-Aviation plant occupied their workshops and locked the director in his office, a pattern of collective assertion and disrespect for authority which spontaneously affirmed itself throughout the country. Renault factories followed in the next two days, giving the lead to metalworkers, shipyards, transport and mining. By 17 May air traffic was at a standstill, matched by the railways a day later. Métro lines, bus stations and post offices were occupied. Within a week people either had no intention of going to work or were unable to do so. At their zenith the strikers were estimated at between 7 and 10 million. No one missed the fact that this was the biggest general strike in French history.

Comparisons with the occupations of the Popular Front recorded similar scenes of *joie de vivre*, but without the attendant fear of management reprisals. Where 1936 had affected mainly private industries, 1968 extended to the nationalized sector, commerce, public administration and services. In the second week, when strikes at Michelin and Peugeot continued the galloping proliferation throughout industry, the news was carried by radio journalists who had occupied the state-controlled ORTF and called for free and objective broadcasting. Of all the occupations it was this action that conveyed to the widest public the message of revolt in May '68. Authoritarian control and tutelage were no longer acceptable. De Gaulle, returning from Romania, called it *la chienlit* (chaos and havoc) with the word's unmistakable reference to bed-soiling. Student inversion followed instantly: posters and graffiti mocked de Gaulle with the reply that he was the havoc, '*la chienlit, c'est lui!*'.

The Rabelaisian wit of the student revolt was joined to design images of ingenuity and simplicity in an outpouring of production centred on the occupied Beaux-Arts faculty in Paris. Renamed 'Atelier Populaire' (people's workshop), its prints furnished immediate décor to student occupations and to the public discussions launched by Parisian students at the Odéon national theatre, situated opposite the Senate and occupied provocatively on 15 May. Throughout the country, musicians, actors and artists occupied theatres and cultural centres and expressed their art in the streets. Theatre, library and museum staff formed collectives. It was not only a protest against what they deemed to be the 'official' or 'bourgeois' culture of Malraux's Maisons, but also a demoting of the work of art as rarefied object in favour of the act of creativity. Jack Lang's international festival of university theatre, launched in Nancy in 1963, had been a notable forerunner. François Borella of the local PSU, to which Lang belonged, had welcomed it with the statement that 'Culture is participation in the act

of creation not the act of consumption'.[3] The zest, idealism, dreams and creativity of the revolt ultimately prompted the defender of political reason, Raymond Aron, to use the dismissive metaphor of a 'psychodrama' in his diagnosis of May. It captured the make-believe quality of many of the ideas but was wide of the mark as a useful definition. Ironically, Aron too was involved in play: he played down the perspectives on history and the social seriousness of May '68.

May '68: whose history?

The students in revolt were unrelenting in their scorn for established reputations: the dominant theme was resistance against unacceptable authority, including the authority of history. History was suspect for its mythology of greatness and success. The student events were a revolution of the present: they were not seen as a preparation of the future nor as an outcome of the past. History was reimagined from the perspective of the downtrodden, and the past was invoked as a way of drawing attention to politics in the present. The students appropriated the history they needed and used it as metaphor: 1968 was not only the tenth anniversary of de Gaulle's republic, it was also fifty years since the end of the First World War. The mutineers at the front in 1917 had bleated like sheep as a mockery of the submissive and sacrificial role they were expected to play: graffiti in 1968 denounced the war as 'la guerre des moutons', and posters portrayed herds of sheep to epitomize 'normal' society under the Gaullist regime. The Second World War provided the students with references to fascist brutality, most overtly in the slogan 'CRS-SS' chanted against the riot police. Victims of fascism were celebrated. On 22 May the government refused Cohn-Bendit re-entry into France after a visit to Germany, declaring him an undesirable alien. Ten thousand students marched through Paris in protest, chanting, 'We are all German Jews.' State propaganda was exposed. Broadcasting was pictured as 'His Master's Voice'. A powerful poster image of May was the dark silhouette of a towering, historical de Gaulle, his hand over the mouth of a youth, with the words 'Sois jeune et tais-toi' ('Be young and shut up'). Still more iconoclastic was the Cross of Lorraine represented as a double-headed screw twisted into the brain.

Not all politicized youths in 1968 were *gauchiste* rebels: the paper *Aspects de la France* (*AF*), which was a cover for the banned Action Française (AF), recruited among students during May, as did the other extreme right-wing movement, Occident. But the vast bulk of students in the university and lycée occupations identified with the *gauchiste* idea of

liberation through spontaneity and revolt. Identification with historical figures of revolt was highly selective. The renowned resisters of the Second World War, and especially de Gaulle, the Gaullists and the Communist Party, were stripped of their legitimacy because they were seen by students to have abandoned the practice of revolt. This attitude to history was rejected by political realists as naive: it was resented by veteran campaigners for change as ungenerous, and it was diagnosed by watchful liberals as dangerous in the primacy it gave to action, a primacy to which fascist movements had subscribed. More than a few university professors felt the uncomfortable presence of force and irrationalism in the contempt with which students mocked their attitudes and ideas. But it was also acknowledged that there was reason within the student revolt, a reason which stripped away many of the irrationalities of tradition, convention and authority, even while it left others, notably male dominance, in place.

The product of the ambivalent state of Western societies as half-archaic and half-modern, May '68 was part of an international revolt of youth, and not just another example of *les guerres franco-françaises*. The youth accused their parents' generation of inability to meet the needs of decolonization. They took on the role of an avant-garde intelligentsia in protest at the failures of post-war society to grapple with the perceived dangers of a commodity culture. In 1959 the sociologist Edgar Morin was one of several intellectuals who drew attention to the 'atrophy' of a rationalized, modernized society in which there was 'no real communication with others' and widespread 'alienation in a world of objects and appearances'.[4] Morin found the students of 1968 powerfully articulate in their refusal to accept this alienation. The modernization to which the rebellious youth objected was one which, they insisted, forced people to work more and more competitively, with crippling stress, for benefits decided for them by advertising and the capitalist market. There was a puritanism in this attack which conflicted with the hedonism of many of the most effective student tracts and posters, a paradox quickly used by critics to ridicule the serious pretensions of May.

Whatever the genre of protest, whether libertarian, sectarian, romantic, cerebral, puritan or hedonistic, parts of the world were turned upside down: it was a spring awakening, a carnivalesque revolution, disrespectful, creative and wickedly observant. It was anti-consumerist, but devoured every tract and publication; it was self-advertising in its universal graffiti; it was writing on the wall, yet another omen in a decade of signs. It was anti-possession, but conquered its own space in the streets and occupied buildings. In its distillation of existentialism, anarchism and socialism, it was a final twist

of the modernist, ideological spiral which had conditioned all French politics since the 1920s. Later it would be seen by persuasive critics as forcibly individualistic and relativist, heralding the atomization of politics and the arrival of post-modernism.[5]

May '68: the strikes

In contrast to the student revolt, the strikes which paralysed the whole country in their unprecedented range and solidarity were more easily defined and recognizable. They thrived initially on the wave of public sympathy for the students and were radically affected by the exuberance and spontaneity of younger workers, but their aims and methods remained largely conventional, and were safe enough to attract the active support of immigrant workers who had good reasons to be wary of an involvement in revolutionary *gauchiste* ideology. Immigrants who were deemed by the government to be politically subversive met with instant deportation, yet substantial numbers were evident in the strikes and accompanying demonstrations, particularly in the car industry.[6] The Communist leadership of the CGT did everything possible to direct and control the strikers and to emphasize the social gulf between industrial workers and middle-class students.

This gulf did exist. There was a convergence of student and worker revolt but no fusion. Students who marched from Paris to the occupied Renault works at Boulogne-Billancourt on 17 May with expectations of unity were dismayed that the CGT kept the factory gates closed to them, in contrast to the receptivity of the CFDT sections within the workforce. In other industrial centres the gulf was partially bridged: there was student–worker co-operation at Sud-Aviation in Nantes, at Rhodia in Besançon, at the CSF company in Brest, and at the Renault works of Cléon in the Seine valley south of Rouen. Influence was often reciprocal: at the huge Lyon lorry factory the workers' rearrangement of the 'Berliet' sign to read 'Liberté' was in pure carnivalesque mode, while students' involvement in picketing or in the strike committees which distributed food from sympathetic peasants was an acceptance of trade-union organization.

The contested area of interchange between students and workers was self-management (*autogestion*). The student occupations had pushed it to the top of the agenda, but only in very few cases did the factory occupations embark on action which envisaged taking control of the means of production. Movement in the direction of greater democracy by limiting the arbitrary powers of the *patronat* was rife among the strikers, but beyond

that it was rumours rather than realities of workers' control which thrived, the best example being the 'myth' of *autogestion* at the electronic factory of CSF in Brest which employed over 1,000 technicians and workers, both male and female, making radar equipment for the army. The CFDT, the dominant union there, had given far more attention to ideas of *autogestion* than the CGT, but the Brest occupation never elaborated the plans for workers' control which the media attributed to it.[7] At most it looked at areas of possible co-management, and even this exceeded the norms of occupations run by the CGT, which concentrated on substantial wage increases alongside improvements in conditions of work and the rights to union activity at the workplace. This kept the strikes within the bounds of familiar industrial conflict, but at the same time the significant role of the educational, consumer, arts and communication sectors in the whole social revolt of May enabled certain sociologists, notably Alain Touraine, to argue with some conviction that society had entered a post-industrial stage.[8]

In the week of 20-24 May the number of student and worker demonstrations redoubled in intensity across the whole of the country, with a return to Parisian violence and barricades. The strikes created a heat of expectation in the big cities which was easily inflamed. On 24 May de Gaulle tried to calm the situation by announcing a referendum on his keyword '*participation*', but his radio broadcast was perceived as a lamentable failure of understanding and he was immediately bypassed by renewed fighting on the streets of Paris and the clearest evidence to date that a sizeable minority of peasants and agricultural workers was involved in movements of strike and protest. The weekend of 25-26 May saw festivities throughout the occupations, dances, football matches, the projection of films in the factories and theatrical co-operation between strikers and the local Maisons de la Culture, the flagships of André Malraux's renovation of cultural activity in the ten years of de Gaulle's republic. By now the strikes were affecting supermarkets and chainstores, petrol stations and depots, telephone exchanges and post offices, refuse collections and all transport. It was in this mood of celebratory defiance that the strikers received news on Monday, 27 May that Pompidou had secured agreements, at a meeting in the rue de Grenelle between the trade unions and the *patronat*, which offered a 35 per cent increase in the minimum wage, a 10 per cent wage increase throughout industry in two stages, half-pay for days on strike and specific concessions to union representation at the workplace, subject to ratification by the management. There was no reference to the structural changes which the CFDT had urged on industrial relations. The CGT in its sense of triumph misread the strikers' mood as

lamentably as de Gaulle. Its Secretary-General, Georges Séguy, was jeered by Renault workers, whose rejection of the Grenelle agreements as seriously inadequate was indicative of striker opinion almost everywhere. The occupations continued. Younger workers were conspicuous in their determination to step up the pace of revolt, though it was less than clear exactly what qualitative changes in industry they were prepared to fight for. It was more a case that the strikers had reached an unprecedented level of confidence that only a creative political initiative would be able to equal.

2. Counter-events: June '68

The outbreak of revolutionary ideas and action in the midst of economic affluence had taken everyone by surprise, not least the leaders of the political opposition on the left of the Chamber. On 27–28 May they tried to put themselves at the helm of the revolt. At a mass demonstration at the Charléty stadium in Paris, PSU speakers took the platform; in corridor politics François Mitterrand put forward Pierre Mendès France as a potential leader, and in L'Humanité the Communist Party called for a government of the people. But no decisive challenge to de Gaulle resulted. Politics were, ironically, the Achilles heel of a passionately political revolt. There was no agreement on a single left-wing candidate for power nor a purposeful coalition of parties. The ideological groupuscules were either divided over a political outcome or gave little thought to the seizure of power, concentrating more on the insurgent tactics of their action committees (comités d'action). Cohn-Bendit, inspirational in his anarchist contempt for authority, had no aspirations for personal rule, nor did the other student and academic leaders. Even in Nantes where the central strike committee appeared to have taken over the municipality and the prefect had lost all control, there was a reluctance to pursue a takeover of power while there were hesitations in Paris. De Gaulle was nevertheless sufficiently pessimistic and confused by his loss of touch to fly secretly to Germany on 29 May to seek advice from General Massu. It is clear that he contemplated resignation, and his unexplained absence for almost a day caused panic in government circles. He returned obviously strengthened. His self-assurance as the providential figure in a national crisis was rekindled. In a broadcast on 30 May he accused the Communist Party of conspiring to take power, dissolved the National Assembly and called for immediate new elections.

The effect was dramatic. In the evening Gaullists organized a mass demonstration down the Champs-Élysées. With Malraux, François Mauriac

and Michel Debré at the head of de Gaulle's faithful followers, a forest of hands raised in victory signs, and military medals copiously on display, it rivalled all the demonstrations of the past month in spontaneity, size and fervour. The Gaullist march was the clearest sign that the events of May, and in particular the widespread strikes, were finally taken seriously by the conservative majority in the country as a revolutionary threat. The march was a counter-revolutionary *coup de théâtre*. Students and strikers were unable to counteract its popular impact. The *gauchiste* revolutionaries found themselves increasingly isolated; general student involvement in the revolt started to subside; the strikes and factory occupations, deprived of any vigorous CGT support after the Grenelle agreements, flickered and flared but were mostly called off by mid-June, at which time the student occupiers of the Odéon and the Sorbonne were removed by the police. De Gaulle flaunted the virtues of his social recipe of 'participation' and in elections at the end of the month the Gaullists, now under the fighting label of Union for the Defence of the Republic (UDR), were overwhelmingly re-elected to power, with a gain of ninety-three seats. For the first time in the Fifth Republic a single party had an absolute majority. The Communist Party and the Federation of the Left both lost over half of their deputies. This could not have been predicted in mid-May.

Initially in the first week of June a partial return to work by some strikers had hardened the struggle elsewhere. At the Renault works at Flins-sur-Seine to the north-west of Paris over 1,000 CRS police evicted the occupying workers on the night of 5 June and protected the buildings by charging at the strikers and supportive students with a ferocity which had not been seen at industrial workplaces during May. Running battles in the surrounding fields cut off small groups on the banks of the river. On 10 June Gilles Tautin, a lycée member of a *groupuscule*, aged seventeen, drowned as he escaped the severe baton attacks. His death provoked a final surge of student demonstrations in Paris, Toulouse and Lyon, but preventive police tactics enforced dispersion. Clear signs of significant student withdrawal from revolt were only interrupted by an angry presence at the funeral of Tautin on 15 June. Two workers, P. Beylot and H. Blanchet, died on 11 June in some of the fiercest fighting between workers and CRS at the Peugeot factories of Sochaux-Montbéliard to the north-east of Besançon, from where a number of students joined the workers in constructing barricades close to the factories. Across the country a number of acts of defiance and posters calling for 'struggle to the end' were still in evidence at the end of June and into July, but the familiar patterns of work, and of summer holidays, were widely re-established. Those who talked of

a return to normality, however, more than often elicited the response that nothing would ever be the same again. The disillusioned took refuge in accusing the Communists and the CGT of sabotaging the revolt. More widely they mocked de Gaulle's recipe for participation as 'we participate, they profit' or 'we participate, they examine'. Given the creativity with which graffiti took over the walls, there was much truth in the wry conclusion of many political students that 'We had stormed the word but not the Bastille'.

In self-defence the leaders of the PCF and the CGT denied that there had ever been a revolutionary situation, and argued that had the student rebels been workers they would have met heavy fire-power from the police rather than baton charges and tear gas. It remained a much-quoted fact that those who died as a direct or indirect result of all the confrontations numbered fewer than ten, of whom one was a member of the police in Lyon and three were students, though all three student deaths were in June and none in May. The injured, however, ran into figures of over 1,000, and the deportation of immigrant workers officially reached 150 though some estimates were six times higher.[9] That all numbers are still uncertain and the social impact incalculable testifies to the extraordinary range and nature of the May revolt. It affected areas of life untouched by any other civil disturbances throughout the century, and its social and cultural ideals did not disappear with the success of the counter-events in June.

De Gaulle's last crisis

Despite the huge rally of support for de Gaulle in person on 30 May, it was Georges Pompidou, and not de Gaulle, who was largely seen to have held his nerve during the revolt. Many credited him as the only voice of government. To everyone's surprise Pompidou was replaced as Prime Minister after the elections by the Foreign Secretary Maurice Couve de Murville. Pompidou had told the President that he wished to stand down, but his reasons for doing so appeared superficial at best. De Gaulle made no serious attempt to dissuade him. To the country at large and to many of the newly elected UDR deputies de Gaulle appeared ungrateful, or disturbed by Pompidou's popularity, although others pointed out that Pompidou had been in power for several years when the May revolt broke out and had to bear much of the responsibility. It was a rupture which rapidly deepened. Pompidou disagreed either publicly or in private with almost every decision taken by de Gaulle in the next nine months, although there was no other consistency in the positions that they adopted. Pompidou

had been flexible enough to make concessions to both students and workers during May, but it was de Gaulle after the elections who promoted a more radical version of 'participation' in both education and industry which Pompidou opposed in the name of conservative caution and the interests of the *patronat*. They clashed over the franc which de Gaulle refused to devalue in November when most of the business world confidently expected him to do so, and at the personal level they exuded a mutual mistrust.

Few people fully understood de Gaulle's policy or motivations in the wake of the May revolt, with the exception of his decision that an urgent reform of the universities should be undertaken. The new Minister of Education, Edgar Faure, proposed reforms which would introduce participation of the different echelons of teachers, administrators and students in faculty management, and would give each university more autonomy to develop new departures in the map of learning, including greater interdisciplinarity. The UDR majority accepted the proposals out of loyalty to de Gaulle, but their reservations revealed several overlapping layers of hostility and a barely repressed criticism that the President had given in to the *gauchistes*. There was more open UDR opposition towards de Gaulle's readiness for participation within industry, but he did not press this particular programme, opting instead for public consultation on a plan for greater regional powers and a major reform of the Senate which would remove its legislative functions while increasing its representation of social, economic and cultural interests. The two constitutional measures were connected by de Gaulle's populist vision of linking the President more directly to the disparate forces of society and reducing the role of parliament. From any other angle the two were quite separate areas of policy. De Gaulle was widely advised to keep them apart, not least because the new regional structures he envisaged would be far more popular than the more arbitrary changes to the Senate. He refused this advice and insisted on a linked referendum, declaring that he would resign if defeated.

The proposals went to the people on 27 April 1969. Initial opinion polls suggested that de Gaulle would receive the 'Oui' to which he was accustomed, but at the end of a contested campaign there was a late swing of opinion. The result was just over 53 per cent 'Non' and 47 per cent 'Oui'. Three-quarters of the *départements* recorded a negative vote and in terms of the regions only in Alsace, parts of Brittany and the Vendée, areas which had voted regularly to the right throughout the century, did the support for de Gaulle register itself strongly. It was clearly a popular defeat, which put the June election successes into a more ambivalent light. De Gaulle immediately acknowledged the defeat from his home in Colombey-

les-Deux-Églises where he and Madame de Gaulle had voted. Just after midnight the words of his resignation were carried by Agence France-Presse: 'I am ceasing to exercise my functions as President of the Republic. This decision takes effect at noon today.'

The 'Non' was more than the rejection of a specific package. Within the negative vote there was the knowledge that Pompidou had already declared he was prepared to stand for President should de Gaulle resign: there was also rejection of de Gaulle's continued indictment of Israel; there was anger when he pardoned the Algérie Française conspirator General Salan in June 1968 and allowed Georges Bidault and Jacques Soustelle back into the country; there was a neo-Poujadist wave of resentment among small traders in 1968–9 at the lack of economic and financial protection, and there was, finally, the legacy of May '68 and its rejection of de Gaulle's personal rule. Every morning on the radio de Gaulle's media representative had warned that chaos would ensue if de Gaulle was defeated. The 'Non' vote challenged the prophets of chaos. There was no chaos and no crisis at his resignation, only a consciousness that this time de Gaulle would not return.

PART THREE

Issues of Identity,
1960s–2000s

Introduction to Part Three

May 1968, end or beginning? It was end and beginning.

In terms of revolutionary politics and the Parisian barricade tradition it was an end, and within a year it was also the end of de Gaulle's personal rule. His resignation on 28 April 1969 was widely interpreted as the delayed shock of May '68. The final 'Non' vote in the referendum was symptomatic of an underlying loss of public confidence in his method of government, which the June elections of 1968 temporarily obscured.

The May revolt in all its creative expression displayed the extent to which the ideological terrain of anti-capitalism, on which the policies of the left and syndicalism had been built since the beginning of the century, was now actively occupied by small splinter groups. They accused the PCF and the Socialist Party as well as the CGT of abandoning the revolutionary heritage of socialism. Whether the mainstream parties of the left should deny this fact or seek a new identity gave the Communists and the Socialists a decade of urgent rethinking.

The revolt of May 1968 also brought about the final disintegration of the archaic ideological opposition to social change which had limped on in the ranks of the political right throughout the 1950s and had sheltered behind the authoritarian rule and nationalism of de Gaulle in the 1960s.

The era of 1968, known as *les années '68*, more often refers to the years which followed 1968 than to those of the sixties which went before. In the history of feminism, in the growth of immigrant consciousness, in the place of youth in society, in many aspects of education and culture, and in attitudes to France's recent history, May '68 was a beginning.

The insights of Michel Crozier in 1971 into the blocked nature of society did not decide on end or beginning, but they carried the imperative that the conflict of 1968 should be an end if French society was ever going to modernize itself.[1] His work propelled the take-off in analyses which reached

their height over ten years later in the public debate on the positives and negatives of French 'exceptionalism'.

Crozier was far from the first who articulated the exceptional role accredited to the republican state in the twentieth century, a role which de Gaulle amplified in his own particular nationalist way. Crozier's book showed just how far this exceptionalism had created more and more bureaucracy which was seen to be necessary because, he argued, the French avoided face-to-face negotiation. The 'blocked society' was the result of this failure, and conflict was seen as the only way forward, in its extreme form resulting in *les guerres franco-françaises*.

The critics of exceptionalism gain in confidence from the early 1970s onwards. Opposition to a *dirigiste* state is fuelled by the economic pressures of neo-liberalism and the market. Pressures for a more consensual and less conflictual society are evident under President Giscard d'Estaing. It is also argued by some that the anarchic drive of May '68 facilitated the break-up of exceptionalism, by giving primacy to individuality.

Proponents of state initiative stage an astonishing recovery in 1981, but within a few years the reversals of the Mitterrand Presidency herald what was widely assumed to be the 'end of exceptionalism'. Sixteen years later this was not so obviously the case. Both the retreat and the resilience of the state bring crises of identity. They would not be so pre-eminent if they did not arise just as insistently from the challenges of cultural diversity and immigration, of Europeanism, and of globalization.

Ideology does not disappear, nor is there an absence of passionate commitment. But the anxiety and cynicism over party politics seemed to suggest that a politicized society could no longer be taken for granted. Of all identity issues this posed the most searching questions for government and voters alike. Crucially, issues of identity involve the issue of 'identity with' as well as 'identity of'. The accent on choice in the 1990s forced an answer to the question 'Who or what do you identify with?' When this was articulated it was apparent that clarity of choice and identification, of cause and affiliation had not been abandoned. Social movements outside formal politics were seen to create many of the most obstinate, and most innovative, political identities of the *fin-de-siècle* and early years of the twenty-first century.

17

Whose New Society?, 1960s–1979

1. The era of '68 ('les années '68')

How were the events of 1968 to be interpreted? In the years that immediately followed, four currents of meaning dominated a host of others. They interconnected and fed off each other, creating the possibility of ambivalent judgements which grew in complexity as the revolt and strikes of May were reanalysed at every anniversary.

The four currents of meaning at the time can be presented in any order.

The meaning most widely assimilated was that May 1968 had administered a massive and timely shock to a society which, under Gaullism, had become ossified and archaic or was in grave danger of becoming so. In 1971 Michel Crozier's diagnosis of a 'blocked society' gave a permanence to this reading of France in the 1960s which has survived endless reinterpretations.

Secondly, the strikes were registered as a considerable, if not total, success in terms of wages, conditions of work and union recognition. The CGT claimed most of the credit, but confidence was particularly high in the minority trade-union confederation, the CFDT, which had backed ideas of worker self-management.

Thirdly, there was the Gaullist electoral triumph of June in a highly charged atmosphere, which stopped in its tracks any possibility of a political revolution: the revolutionary discourse of the students was rejected by popular vote.

And fourthly, there was a growing focus on the way in which the French Communist Party leadership had been challenged, not only by the student leaders, by the spontaneity of the strikes and the backlash of Gaullism, but also by the brutal ending to the Prague Spring: the PCF was seriously diminished in stature and was seen to have lost its post-war credibility.

These four meanings, or various combinations of them, informed a series

of sequels and adjustments which richly coloured a period of six to seven years. In the longer term May, as both revolt and strikes, was held to be self-contradictory: there was an anarchic thrust which promoted individualism, and a collective thrust which promoted community solutions and buttressed the public sector. In the shorter term, however, the symbiosis of these two was held to be the creative essence of those who both revolted and went on strike, and it was replicated widely in the years immediately following, subtitled *les années '68*.

The explosion of sexual politics

On 5 April 1971 the weekly *Le Nouvel Observateur* published a manifesto signed by 343 women demanding freedom of abortion. It began: 'A million women, every year, undergo an abortion in France . . . in dangerous conditions . . . and are forced to remain silent . . .' And then came the shock of the manifesto: 'I declare that I am one of them. I declare that I have had an abortion.' Readers looked immediately to see who was among the 343, and found the writers Simone de Beauvoir, Marguerite Duras and Françoise Sagan, and the film stars Catherine Deneuve, Jeanne Moreau and Delphine Seyrig among other well-known women in the public eye. It was a journalistic coup, but also an act of political courage, rivalling the critical stance taken on the Algerian war by the paper's forerunner, *France-Observateur*, for which Roger Stéphane, Robert Barrat and Claude Bourdet had been sentenced to prison. In theory *Le Nouvel Observateur* in 1971 ran an equal risk of prosecution, as did the women signatories, since theirs was an admission of illegality under the law of 1920 which had criminalized abortion and was still in force.

The head-on confrontation of the Manifesto with the authority of the state bore all the hallmarks of May '68. The origins of its rebelliousness lay precisely in the feminist consciousness which had been expressive but sidelined during the May events, in which women had been assigned, or had assumed, mainly supportive roles. This consciousness pushed itself to the centre of social confrontation in 1970. As it did so, the substance and style of feminist agitation announced a new sense of liberation.

Thousands of women activists during May had contributed no less than their male counterparts to student solidarity in the face of police repression, but they, no less than the men, were influenced by various forms of socialist ideology which subordinated gender issues to those of class. Much of student discussion after the legalization of contraception in 1967 revolved round the question not of women's own sexuality but of women's sexual

availability to men. Passion for revolt and for making love appeared inter-changeable in some of the slogans of May, but the sexual nuances as well as the demands for open access to halls of residence were clearly male-inspired. The dramatic silk-screened silhouette from the Atelier Popu-laire of a young woman with her skirt swirling, throwing a cobblestone, carried the caption, 'La beauté est dans la rue' ('Beauty is in the street'). It was conventional in its representation, despite the insurrectionary content and the double meaning of the caption. News photographs during both the revolt and the strikes testified to the numbers of women involved, an involvement celebrated by feminists Annie Zelensky and Jacqueline Feld-man in pamphlets which underlined the active presence of women, but berated the fact that '. . . during these decisive days no woman has appeared as spokesperson in the general meetings, on the radio, on the television . . .' They concluded: 'The society that will be built must give all women equality of opportunity with men.'[1]

It was the shift from this political terrain to the sexuality issues explicit in the Manifesto of the 343 which marked the radical turn in the feminist movement. Within two years, the recognition that the May events, viewed in gender terms, had been remarkably conservative, gave feminism a new combative edge. Women liberationists in the USA had already reformulated feminist action to denounce patriarchy and target the exploitation of women's bodies. In August 1970 they called for a women's strike to include household work and conjugal sex. In Paris, nine women met at the Arc de Triomphe on 26 August to depose a wreath on the tomb of the Unknown Soldier, with a message reading, 'Even more unknown than the soldier: his wife'. Despite the arrests which followed and the presence of invited journalists, this symbolic gesture against male oppression was not exten-sively reported. In October, however, the concepts of 'patriarchy as the enemy' and 'the personal as political' were projected on to a wider public screen by a special issue on women's liberation by the review *Partisans*. It effectively launched what was already being called the Mouvement de Libération des Femmes (MLF), with 1970 proclaimed as 'Year Zero'.

The MLF's visible campaign to highlight sexual oppression sharpened the impact of feminism in the same way that street activism by female suffragists had done in the earlier years of the century. Votes had been demanded by Hubertine Auclert and others as a right: women's control of their own bodies was demanded by the MLF as an equal right. The two issues in their different contexts had a similar capacity to inspire single-minded commitment. With the Manifesto of the 343, the focus sharpened still further on the issue of abortion. Eight of the nine women who had

placed the wreath on 26 August signed the Manifesto: Catherine Bernheim, Monique Bourroux, Christine Delphy, Emmanuelle de Lesseps, Christiane Rochefort, Jeanine Sert, Monique Wittig and Annie Zelensky. There was controversy within the MLF about using an established periodical, but Simone de Beauvoir's support for the initiative by the two *Nouvel Observateur* journalists, Delphy and Zelensky, precipitated the publication. A decade or more of shifting private perspectives on matters of the body and sexuality had led a substantial element of French opinion to accept that the issues were indeed public ones. This began to dispel the air of secrecy about sexual matters in which even the assertive Family Planning Movement of Madame Weill-Hallé had been forced to operate, to the point of holding its international conference on abortion in 1966 behind closed doors.

Illegal abortion, legitimate protest: the issue forced its way over the next three years into prime-time politics. Prosecution did not follow the Manifesto but Simone de Beauvoir and the lawyer Gisèle Halimi formed an organization to defend the women just in case. Called 'Choisir', it fed on the coupling of choice and liberation which had marked resistance against Nazism and movements of decolonization. Halimi seized on the case of Marie-Claire Chevalier, a seventeen-year-old prosecuted in 1972 for having an abortion after being forced to have sex. Preparing her defence, Halimi declared, was itself a defiantly political act. The outcome was a complete justification for the MLF. The tribunal at Bobigny released the accused. It was the first judicial departure from the law of 1920, and Marie-Claire received the support of several mainstream journalists, including Françoise Giroud of the weekly *L'Express*. Feminist encouragement for women to go abroad for abortions led to an estimated 36,000 annual journeys by 1974, but in questionnaires on the issue it emerged just how far the costs for this option put it outside the reach of working-class women. Acknowledgement of this social injustice was voiced across the middle ground of party politics, while the whole of the political left in 1974 pledged itself to reform of the law. Feminism was accused by its detractors of inventing sexual politics: what it had successfully done was to bring them visibly into the open.

A new society?

The radical turn taken by feminism in the early 1970s was undoubtedly influenced by May 1968, but in its own right it was as symptomatic of revolt against a blocked society as the May events themselves. A whole range of ideas and activity marked *les années '68*, aimed at unblocking

society. Much of it ran parallel to the events of May 1968 rather than being a direct result. Zelensky and Feldman in their Sorbonne pamphlets had referred to 'the society that will be built', while the trade unionists of the CFDT had campaigned during the strikes under the slogan of 'A new society'. Alain Touraine opened his 1969 book on *La Société post-industrielle* with the sentence, 'A new type of society is now being formed', a reference to changes which had begun well before the 1968 events. There is no doubt that the concept of a new society was floating in the air throughout the last years of the 1960s. Much of its easy passage into people's consciousness was due to their perception of the changes brought to their own lives by consumerism and the staggering growth in the nation's productivity. Such perceptions were often tinged with regret at the passing of familiar patterns of life, but newspapers, weekly magazines and television swept people along in a choreography of affluence, and for many it was precisely the plethora of material goods which constituted a new society. At the heart of the change was the transformation of France from rural to urban, whose drama had been given an apocalyptic note by Henri Mendras with his 'end of the peasantry' in 1967. By 1988 he concluded that the mid-1960s were the start of the key twenty years in which a widely perceived 'Second French Revolution' occurred, one which finally ended not only the identification of France with its rural economy but also the attitudes and behaviour which had typified a traditional society.[2] The crisis in the Catholic Church was symptomatic: not only an accelerated decline in church attendance and baptisms, but also a sharp fall, amounting almost to a collapse by 1979, in the number of ordinations into the clergy. To the recurrent May slogan 'Changer la vie' there was the obvious rejoinder that life in France was already in the process of momentous change, regardless of the student revolt.

The Gaullist victory of June 1968 seemed at the time to be exactly that kind of rejoinder. But this was where May '68, stripped of its revolutionary discourse, spoke for more people than the electoral results of June suggested. The pace of material change and the decline of traditional social attitudes had not been matched by corresponding changes to underlying social structures. A growing acceptance that certain structures would have to be modernized mitigated the conservatism of the June results. De Gaulle belatedly came to share some of that acceptance though he was always more interested in manipulating political rather than social structures. His dramatic failure to carry his last political referendum should not, however, obscure the priority he gave to university reforms under Edgar Faure. De Gaulle's successor as President, Georges Pompidou, made the

transformation of social relations his major theme in the Presidential elections of 1969, which he won with ease, though he was known to be wary of committing himself. Refusing to say 'Oui' or 'Non' to de Gaulle's last referendum, he had been nicknamed '*Non*pidou or Pompid*oui*'.

It was therefore both expected and yet something of a surprise when Pompidou's first Prime Minister, the 54-year-old Jacques Chaban-Delmas, confronted the National Assembly on 16 September 1969 with ambitious ideas for a 'New Society', apparently purloining the phrase from the syndicalists of the CFDT. Deputy and mayor of Bordeaux, Chaban-Delmas had been a loyal colleague of de Gaulle in wartime resistance and all post-war politics. Known in his fiefdom as the 'Duke of Aquitaine', he had developed an interactive style of discussion with allies and opponents alike, and was well versed in negotiating for regional interests against the bureaucracy of the state. Accepting the role of Premier in June, he announced that he would seek to resolve conflict and would build a mutually supportive society, notably bringing trade unions and management together in a system of dialogue. Some form of profit-sharing for workers, and the presence of trade union officials on company sites, were two measures foreshadowed in the Grenelle agreements of May 1968 on which he 'set great value'. The gauge of his commitment to the 'New Society' was that he placed the reforming Jacques Delors in charge, an expert within the state's economic planning department who had focused on the social effects of industrialization.

Delors took the opportunity to work with a co-operative majority within the *patronat* (CNPF), headed by François Ceyrac, on a programme to update the training needed by workers in an increasingly technological society. In the immediate wake of the Grenelle agreements the employers showed few of the revengeful tactics adopted thirty years before, after the gains of the Popular Front. The government was able to index the minimum wage to growth in the economy, and to negotiate an increase in the number of workers on monthly salary payments. Aware that in a blocked society the two polarized sides of industry resorted to conflict as a ritual, Chaban-Delmas and Delors attempted to break this cycle by promoting contract and negotiation. And yet every move in that direction revealed the entrenched number of ways in which conflict was actively provoked, not just by unions but by employers. Still the highest source of resentment was the increased pressure exerted by employers on assembly-line workers, known since the inter-war years as *ouvriers spécialisés* (OS), among whom women and immigrants were the most vulnerable. With growth and high productivity unaffected by the events of 1968, it seemed to certain single-minded

employers that conflict was a risk worth taking in the interests of spiralling profit. Well represented in the Gaullist majority, they encouraged President Pompidou to moderate the radical tone of the government's programme. Pompidou had been personally critical of the idealistic terms in which Chaban-Delmas had announced his 'new society' and after three years he decided to rein in his Prime Minister. He took advantage of flimsy press accusations that Chaban-Delmas had evaded income tax and replaced him in July 1972 by the overtly conservative Pierre Messmer. The move appeared to be an abrupt step backwards, but in several post-mortems on the aims of Chaban-Delmas it seemed not unreasonable to ask, 'Whose new society was it anyway?'

Aubervilliers

In his first speech as Premier, Chaban-Delmas specifically drew attention to 'the hard conditions of life' endured by immigrant workers. He promised improvements. The visible scandal of *bidonville* existence had been partially tackled in some parts of suburban Paris while in others it had merely been dispersed into older rat-infested shacks and disused factories which served as hostels. In the depths of winter there was no means of heat other than bodies huddled together. During the night of 1 January 1970 five African workers died of asphyxiation from fumes produced by a makeshift fire in one such hostel in Aubervilliers, in the northern industrial suburbs of Paris. The press made it headline news. It was the first shocking image of the new year, of the new decade and of the 'new society', a horrific and symbolic drama of social deprivation. Ten days later a Portuguese family were found dead from fumes in their single room in Grenoble. Journalists vied with one another in references to the novels of Zola and Dickens, but more significantly they produced detailed reports on the immigrants' appalling accommodation and called for those responsible to be exposed and punished. Racketeering landlords and employers were denounced as slave-traders, and Chaban-Delmas made it a priority to visit Aubervilliers in person. He acknowledged that the conditions were 'indescribable'.

No other single event so instantly drew the attention of politicians and public to the levels of squalor within the affluent 'new' society. The Prime Minister promised yet again to eradicate the *bidonvilles* as part of his social programme, setting 1972 as the target.

Intense media debates followed the further acknowledgement by Chaban-Delmas that 'without the 3 million foreigners who reside in our midst' the economy would be severely weakened and that therefore 'there was no

question of stopping immigration'. Instead there was to be a controlled system of labour contracts and negotiated quotas, symptomatic of the new government's stress on dialogue. Sartre and the Algerian writer Kateb Yacine called for a far more fundamental criticism of the double standards of society and Michel Rocard spoke for the PSU in setting the scandal of Aubervilliers within the logic of capitalism which 'only a general mobilization of workers could defy'.[3] Red flags were prominent at the Africans' funeral and there were militant occupations of immigrant hostels in conflict with landlords and police. There had been an immigrant presence in the strikes of May 1968: the Aubervilliers deaths radicalized their protests and brought more immigrant involvement in *gauchiste* activity.

The coverage given to the Aubervilliers fire, no less than the feminist Manifesto of the 343, vividly demonstrated the place of *les années '68* in the history of twentieth-century France. In both cases there was a readiness by public opinion to see the issues in terms of unacceptable failures of society. The criminalization of abortion and the scandal of immigrant housing were seen to be anachronisms which could not be justified in a modern society. Arguments about modernization had revolved since the 1920s round issues of technology, the pace of industrial change and the role of economic planning. Social theorists and industrial entrepreneurs had dominated the first debates, followed by arguments among state planners and apostles of an unrestricted market. Rationalization of production had clashed with traditional rhythms of work, while a mix of individual employers, engineers and trade unionists attempted to bridge the two with ideas of enlightened factory conditions and an emphasis on work-satisfaction. For most of public opinion during the boom years the pursuit of economic progress still set the agenda for the future, but by the end of the 1960s it no longer monopolized the concept of modernity. It was challenged by a whole range of social reformers with claims that modern society should be judged and defined, not by its progress towards rationalized production but by its readiness to promote social and human rights which cut across differences of class, sex and ethnic origins. Such a criterion recalled the way in which Jaurès had qualified the meaning of republicanism in his Albi speech of 1903: modernity, like republicanism, had to be a social and human concept if it was not to result in more injustice rather than less.

Housing, as much as any issue in this period, exposed the ambivalence of modernity and the growing complexity of social protest in the wake of 1968. In the face of slum conditions, revealed in all their inhumanity by the fire at Aubervilliers, both local and national government had posed an answer in subsidized new apartment blocks (HLMs) and out-of-town

estates (ZACs) providing often more than 10,000 new homes at a time in constructions of mind-numbing uniformity. Sooner or later immigrants from the condemned hostels would be moved to these cheap, functional units of mass housing. The density and height of the huge residential constructions had already transformed urban skylines in the 1960s and it was considered a mark of the Fifth Republic's unbroken pact with modernization that the housing stock was still growing at twice the rate of the population in the six years following 1968. But was this merely the substitution of one form of social inhumanity for another? The students of 1968 and local protest groups of the early 1970s were convinced that it was. Their posters showed bloated developers reaping urban areas like fields of corn, driving huge mechanical binders which bundled everything, including old houses and streets, into lines of regimented concrete blocks. These protests at the anonymity of the new 'modern' housing appeared to be put into perspective by the desperate need of immigrants for the basic heating and amenities which the modern blocks provided. On the one hand, guilt in government circles at the public shame of Aubervilliers reinforced the move towards more mass housing. On the other, a more militant anger at the dehumanization suffered by immigrants fed into the protests against the soulless character of much urban life and development.

Lip and Larzac

Social confrontation had taken on new meanings in May 1968. The spontaneity and creativity of the student movement, and much of the strike action by younger workers, did not conform to the conventional rituals of trade-union protest. The eventual acceptance of the Grenelle agreements brought the labour force back into familiar territory and notched up a major victory for the CGT, but the radicalization of protest was far from extinguished. On the contrary, a new ritual of radical confrontation was confirmed. Using 1968 as model and inspiration, it was geared to ideas of autonomy (*autogestion*) and featured the grass roots (*la base*) as the motive force of social action. It spawned movements, groups, committees, collectives and self-management, not political parties, unions, soviets or democratic centralism. What made it of more than fringe interest after 1968 was its appearance in a wide diversity of work situations, in banks, supermarkets, the postal service and a range of agricultural action. It affected even the factories of the industrial giants: at Renault in Le Mans in 1970 machine operatives rebelled against Taylorism, and in 1973 workers at the aluminium plant of Pechiney in Noguères near Pau in the south-west shut

down the electrolysis process. Speaking for the *patronat* in July 1973, François Ceyrac warned against 'a certain tendency to radicalization', indicting skilled workers for acting without any concern for the firm's productivity or for union directives, and for turning their backs on conciliation, the very agenda of the social project launched by Chaban-Delmas and Delors. His warning was issued as the extraordinary conflict at the watchmaking factory of Lip in Besançon-Palente moved into its fourth month.

By the end of 1973 Lip had become shorthand for what many perceived as a new era in industrial action. 'Tomorrow,' wrote François-Henri de Virieu, 'people will refer to pre-Lip, just as we say pre-war.'[4] Watchmaking at Besançon dated from the late eighteenth century, introduced by a Swiss political refugee, Laurent Mégevand. In 1867 Emmanuel Lipmann created a workshop with ten watchmakers which in 1931 became the company Lip, employing 350. The modern factory at Besançon-Palente dated from 1960, with 1,200 employees by the end of the decade. Lip was a household name in French timekeeping, but from 1970 was in severe financial difficulties and was dependent on the Swiss company Ébauches who were sold a controlling portion of its capital by the company director Fred Lip, descendant of the Lipmanns and an individualistic *patron* 'capable of inventing the watch of the future, but incapable of selling the watch of today'.[5] Swiss money was not made available to relaunch Lip into prosperity, and in April Jacques Saintesprit, who had succeeded Fred Lip in 1971, declared the company bankrupt and resigned. The workforce argued that the company was productive and was capable of being saved. They refused the redundancy payments, protected the existing stock and continued production and marketing, defying the courts. Evicted by the police from Palente in August, they set up an alternative workshop in a nearby gymnasium and continued to pay out wages and to negotiate with the official mediator. In the first six months they sent delegations to enthusiastic, supportive meetings and demonstrations across the country, with a high point on 29 September 1973, when 100,000 supporters from across France and abroad marched into Besançon through driving rain.

The protracted survival of Lip was described by a fascinated media as an affair, an epic, a romance, an irrelevance, an absurdity, an embarrassment, a turning-point in economic democracy and 'the real '68 of the workers'. Charles Piaget, Catholic, socialist, local PSU candidate and long-term offical of the CFDT at the core of the workforce, claimed the direct heritage of 1968 in his account of Lip, borrowing the student slogan 'l'imagination au pouvoir'. Testimonies of the workers themselves, recorded by Piaget,

include one by sixty-year-old, Russian-born Ludmilla Kita who travelled to Brittany to represent Lip at an action committee of Algerians, Tunisians and Moroccans, 'des garçons sensationnels', to discuss the immigrant experience of being sacked. 'It was a great meeting,' she said, 'and they came down here to support us. We think we're not racist, but it's embedded in the individual . . . It's already a form of racism not to accept that people think or live differently from us.'[6] Hers and other voices emphasize the human as well as economic and political dimensions of the action at Lip. It was what made their arguments central to any discussion of 'Whose new society?'

The Prime Minister, Messmer, called the Lip affair 'finished' when it still had months to run, while Pompidou on 27 September 1973 uncomfortably defended the government's incapacity in the conflict. He accepted that there had been errors in the way the company had been run, and promised to review the law on bankruptcies to provide better protection for workers. François Ceyrac, for the *patronat*, wondered whether getting excited for a whole summer over Lip showed the French as far too weak-minded.

In the same summer a heterogeneous assembly of protesters met with peasant sheep farmers on the plateau (*causse*) of Larzac in the southern Massif Central between Millau and Lodève. Protests were against a vast extension of the Larzac army training camp on to even more pasture belonging to the peasants, whose livelihood and way of life were seen to count for little in the government's military plans for the area. The main production centres of Roquefort cheese were not directly threatened, but suppliers from the plateau's highest pastures faced displacement by tanks. One hundred and three farmers had formed a defensive Community and had gathered at Rodez in July 1972 in a demonstration which brought committed support from a number of Larzac committees, quickly formed by anti-militarists such as the young José Bové who had refused military service in Bordeaux. With his wife, Alice, he backed the leader of Paysans Travailleurs, Bernard Lambert, in calling for a Larzac assembly in 1973. Lip workers were there. So too were feminists, conscientious objectors, regionalists, *gauchistes*, members of the PSU and early ecologists. The attachment to Larzac, to the shepherds and to the simple life of the plateau cut across the myriad of ideological nuances which distinguished the protesters from each other. For post-war Occitanists, Larzac was a campaign which both expressed and tested their new radical identity.

Sheep had figured in May '68 as a metaphor for the *poilus* of 1914–18 (*la guerre des moutons*) or, satirically, as images of 'normality' to which de Gaulle called the country to return. On Larzac they stood for

self-determination and local autonomy. The peasant farmers vowed in solidarity never to give up their land or sell to the military. The government vacillated. Every year throughout the rest of the 1970s the farmers' determination was ritualistically reaffirmed to the thousands of sympathizers who came to discover the unknown stretches of the *causses* and assure the peasants of their support.

The Larzac peasants and the workers at Lip etched themselves into the national consciousness. By their action they were transformed from social victims into subjects asserting control of their own lives. It was a theme central to May 1968 which spread in a scattered way throughout French society, with specific political alignments formed in response to every social issue. It was a widening of democracy and a dispersion of politics away from the centre. It represented an acute challenge to national political leaders and parties who were faced with the repeated statement that something significant had changed. There was an urgent sense that 1968 had been a watershed and that politics were now either post-May or, by contrast, post-June.

Politics post-May

Almost a consensus judgement on May '68 was that student politics, and *gauchisme* generally, meant splintered politics, and splintered meant weak. From the point of view of the small, militant groups it seemed very different. They saw weakness in the caution of the established left-wing parties and leaders, and strength in their own dedication to revolt. In the immediate years that followed, the most robust of the *gauchiste* movements thrived on the status they had achieved, initiated new activists into social struggles and sustained their production of newspapers and pamphlets. But the mainstream parties of the left also fed on May '68: they reassessed their strategy and embarked on a substantial realignment. The survival of splinter groups and the mainstream reappraisals gave left-wing politics in *les années '68* a vigour and volatility which contributed still further to the 'unblocking' of society.

The small Marxist groups which had flourished in May as a direct challenge to the Stalinist pedigree of the Communist Party encouraged their followers with the idea that 1968 in French revolutionary history would be similar to the place of 1905 in Russia: a successful revolution would follow as in 1917. Trotskyists were particularly active and optimistic, especially those writing and distributing the weekly papers *Lutte ouvrière*, which represented a current of revolutionary thought and action since the

late 1930s, and the more recent *Rouge*, the organ of the Ligue Communiste led by Alain Krivine, Daniel Ben Saïd and Henri Weber. To their dogged recruitment of workers at factory gates, the placing of 'red moles' within the factories and their involvement in strikes and picketing they added a small but dedicated minority presence at all elections, including the Presidentials where Krivine in 1969 and 1974, and Arlette Laguiller in 1974 and subsequently, put forward Trotskyist programmes of revolutionary anti-capitalism.

Paradoxically, many of the political inheritors of the student revolt accepted individually that France was an affluent democracy quite unlike Russia in 1917 or the South America of Che Guevara in the 1960s. It was highly improbable that French workers would pick up machine-guns and storm a Parisian Winter Palace, or that peasants would become armed bands in the hills, however recent the memory of the maquisards. It was a fantasy that Maoism would transfer itself from China to France. The burning question of how to deepen and diversify the revolutionary struggle after 1968 might therefore have seemed sterile and hopelessly anachronistic, had it not been for the wide range of specific socio-political issues which enabled ideologies to be honed and energies to be focused. Maoist hopes of a violent proletarian revolution, still visible in the propaganda of the group known as the Gauche Prolétarienne, were given the face of realism in social agitation and 'revolutionary' methods of enquiry, such as their exposure of prison conditions. In this practical and controversial drive for suppressed information, the work of the radical thinker and pioneer historian of prisons, madness and sexuality, Michel Foucault, was closely associated. Professor at the ancient Collège de France, a humanist foundation from the sixteenth century, and eventually located on a site next to the Sorbonne in Paris, Foucault combined political and social activism with his hugely influential dissection of the authoritative body and discourse of power. He persistently called for the voices of those silenced by power to be heard.

Wresting 'knowledge as power' away from the structures of authority gave a democratic purpose to the marginal groups which proliferated in and after May 1968. Aubervilliers, Lip and Larzac, protests at nuclear power stations on the Breton coast, agitation against authority in factories, prisons, schools and universities, even the dawn vigils in 1971 against the demolition of the iron and glass Baltard buildings at the old Parisian market of Les Halles, all reinvigorated both the theoretical understanding of power and an awareness of alternatives. Whether or not they accepted the term *gauchiste*, whether they were Marxist-inspired or anarchist-oriented, the

fragmented extreme left in *les années '68* sustained a volatile mix of ideological dogma and pragmatic, issue-based politics. Prepared for revolutionary violence and illegality even when not openly practising it, they were
defiantly outside 'the system'.

Those on the inside, and still the majority voice of the left, hesitated,
reflected and negotiated for four years after May before finally producing
a blueprint for a single set of policies. On 27 June 1972 the Socialist and
Communist Parties signed up to a Common Programme for Government,
testament to the delayed but creative impact of May, though it was ham-
mered out in the wake of disaster at the polls in both 1968 and 1969. The
Socialists experienced electoral marginality when their candidate for the
Presidency in 1969, the uncharismatic Gaston Defferre, received only 5 per
cent of the vote and was pushed closely by the PSU candidate, Michel
Rocard. Even together they could not begin to mount a Socialist challenge
to Pompidou, nor could the Communist leader Jacques Duclos, even though
his 21.5 per cent of the vote demonstrated that the strikes of 1968 had
sustained a significant Communist presence at national level. This visible
presence enabled *L'Humanité* to continue to play down the *gauchiste*
initiative in the May events, but it could not stop the gathering conviction
that the party was neither the voice of radical youth nor that of political
revolution.

Since the war the PCF had regularly rallied a quarter of the electorate;
through the CGT it spoke for the majority of organized labour, while its
Cold War offensive after 1947 had attracted an intelligentsia which sought
an ideological alternative to the dominating Americanism of the West. Yet
by the 1960s the conservatism of its structures and the dogmatism of its
pro-Soviet idolatry were undermining its very credibility as the party of
change and revolution. May 1968 exposed its deeply ingrained contradictions. Intellectual defections accelerated with the final smothering of the
Prague Spring under the satellite conformity of Gustáv Husák, and in
the post-May scramble to show who had learned most from the events the
PCF faced the recognition that it would never obtain power in France
on its own. After 1969 it moved ambivalently but successfully towards
agreement with the Socialists, a strategy which maximized the reformism
which the leaders knew was their only real strength, though this was not
the language in which they could openly express it. The impact of May was
such that any new programme had to claim that it would transform society.
Georges Marchais, the party's deputy leader, adjusted the rhetoric of revolution and in 1972 presented the Common Programme as one 'of profound
change' whose implementation 'would constitute a form of transition

towards socialism'. It was, he wrote, 'progressive, innovative and realistic'.[7]

Realism, and yet ambivalence, marked the converging path of the Social-ists also. The humiliation of 1969 showed that Defferre was incapable of being a national figurehead, however strong his control of Marseille, while François Mitterrand from outside the party talked up his 1965 score against de Gaulle and proposed to recruit socialists at the grass roots, despite his total lack of background in the socialist movement. Bitterly fragmented at two messy party conferences in 1969, the SFIO nevertheless managed to signal a new departure with a change of name to the Parti Socialiste (PS) and a new leader, Alain Savary, a dedicated decolonizer with an eminent record in the Free French, who was elected after the resignation of the long-term fixture, Guy Mollet. Two years later and after multiple shifts of position, François Mitterrand decided to consummate his *pas de deux* with the party and stepped inside to claim the leadership. He did so by proposing a modernization of the party and a move away from theological Marxism, yet he committed himself to anti-capitalism and to humanist socialism and gave a high profile to getting the left into power, for which an alliance with the PCF would be a necessary strategy. On 16 June 1971, in a tightly fought contest at the party conference at Épinay in the northern suburbs of Paris, he replaced Savary as leader. His proposals and his election were seen by his close associates as an assurance that the Socialists had finally recognized the full import of the demand for change in May 1968. The new manifesto of the party made this explicit in March 1972 by promising to give the process of nationalization and state planning an ambitious range of democratic structures based on decentralization and self-management.

There was no discourse of *autogestion* in the PCF nor would they endorse the Socialists' pro-Europeanism and respect for the Atlantic alliance, but the editors of the Common Programme minimized the disagreements and focused on socio-economic policies and on radical new forms of democracy. Commitment to a broad range of nationalizations involving more than twelve leading companies together with increased workers' representation in running all public concerns made it more recognizably socialist than any previous unified programme of the left, including the agreements which led to the Popular Front and the Resistance Charter of 1944. In the title to the first section of the agreed document, the words 'Changer la vie' clearly proclaimed the cultural heritage of May, though there was no hint of the anti-materialist ideas which so many of the student groups had favoured. Raising the purchasing power of wage-earners was the very first aim of the Common Programme.

It appeared to many that the Socialists had made the most concessions

in the negotiations, but within two years it was evident that they were also reaping most of the rewards and that only an alliance dominated by the PS had the potential of winning power for the left, a potential underlined in the 1973 elections when the PS and left Radicals secured almost thirty more seats than the PCF, while in 1974 Mitterrand was very nearly elected President of France. In the same year significant individuals from both the CFDT and the PSU joined or rejoined the PS, including Michel Rocard. This widened and rejuvenated the party's appeal. By contrast, the Communist Party's turn to reformism appeared to signal a loss of identity, rather than the creation of a new one. It was unable to recapture its cherished role as a political vanguard. The flair for change on the left was increasingly identified with forces beyond and outside the PCF.

Politics post-June. The death of de Gaulle

Given the panic among Gaullists during May 1968, it was astonishing that they had emerged so strengthened in June. Pompidou was the leader who had remained relatively calm, but it was de Gaulle who finally reasserted his authority and found a resounding popular echo. His resignation a year later ended almost three decades of personality politics, but while he was still at Colombey-les-Deux-Églises, or discovering his mother's family roots in Ireland, or making a carefully selective visit to Spain and General Franco, there was only muted public debate about the future of Gaullism. To André Malraux in December 1969 he appeared to compare himself to Don Quixote, and other intimate friends found significance in every utterance. He continued with his memoirs, still possessing a remarkable memory and finding in his retirement 'a serenity touched with sadness'.[8] On 9 November 1970 a blood vessel broke in his stomach. He died within two and a half hours.

He was buried on 12 November in a simple grave in Colombey-les-Deux-Églises. In respect of his wishes made in 1952 and never altered, there was no national funeral, no music and no speeches. He wanted only his family, close friends, Compagnons de la Résistance and local councillors to be individually invited to the village burial, but he added that men and women of France and of other countries would be welcome if they wished to be there, in silence. Special trains brought some 40,000 mourners to the small *commune* of some 400 inhabitants. On the same day the world's leaders gathered to pay homage in Notre-Dame. Two simultaneous ceremonies: the prestigious one in Paris without de Gaulle's body. It was the start of endless tributes to an individualistic, paradoxical career, which in the first

years of the twenty-first century still bolster his hold on public estimation. Repeatedly General de Gaulle is placed at the head of opinion polls on greatness in French history.

But what of the Gaullism that survived its leader? Which of de Gaulle's contradictory achievements and characteristics was it to embody? The newly elected Socialist leader at the time, Alain Savary, was one of the few political figures to be at Colombey for the funeral. He was there as a close wartime colleague, a Gaullist in Resistance terms but far from a Gaullist in terms of the RPF in the 1950s or the politics of 'de Gaulle's Republic'. It was loyalty not to one but to all three periods of de Gaulle's political life that marked out what can be called Gaullist fundamentalism, jealously guarding his memory in special associations and establishing an Institut Charles de Gaulle in Paris to enshrine his life's work: military, political and literary. Such studied devotion prompted many commentators to declare that Gaullism was inseparable from de Gaulle himself, but others saw themes in his politics which could be developed, manipulated or even changed by subsequent leaders in a Gaullist tradition. This wider definition made Gaullism less of an ideology than an identity: it would continue to register as a flexible but highly principled form of nationalism, a science of Presidential government, loyalty to the Fifth Republic, a notion of independence and prosperity as preconditions of national *grandeur*, and a specific set of historical legacies headed by 18 June 1940.

In foreign policy de Gaulle had been strikingly idiosyncratic, not least in his use of absence and veto within Europe. Pompidou as his successor looked to a more stable relationship between France and the rest of Europe, for which enlargement of the European Economic Community appeared essential, a step formally ratified on 22 January 1972 when Britain, Ireland and Denmark joined the EEC. Internally, de Gaulle had either avoided pressing social issues or undertaken change by hierarchical decision. Bureaucratic centralization had flourished. Civil servants had been appointed as ministers. Parliament had been bypassed. Raymond Aron had no doubt in 1969 that Gaullism had 'considerably worsened the structural defects in French society'.[9] The 'New Society' of Chaban-Delmas sought to redress this negative legacy and soon collided with the fundamentalists in the Gaullist UDR as well as individual *patrons*. The modernizing effects of the boom in the 1960s, which Chaban-Delmas and Pompidou both promoted, had brought the Gaullists votes from certain prosperous *communes* in areas which had traditionally voted Radical or Socialist, but this 'opening to the left' was regarded with grave suspicion by those Gaullists who represented more static or economically backward societies. Pompidou's

decision to replace his Prime Minister asserted a recognizably Gaullist form of Presidential authority, but it was later than the critics had wanted and Pompidou was seen to have dithered. He was more assertive in the pursuit of his own industrial policy of company mergers and intensive growth, notably in telecommunications, aeronautics, computer technology and nuclear energy. In this, as in his enthusiasm for property ventures on the Mediterranean coast and projects of urban redevelopment, Pompidou's readiness to use the state to promote and back major private initiatives had created a particular pattern of modernization which, under de Gaulle's Presidency, could be labelled Gaullist, but was in no way either monopolized by Gaullism or tied to de Gaulle's legacy.[10] It did, however, depend on the continuation of the boom years in which the third period of Gaullism had flourished. In 1973 the boom faltered and in 1974 it collapsed.

How Georges Pompidou might have permanently inflected the meaning of Gaullism is speculative. Suffering from a rare blood condition, whose effects became visible and publicly known in 1973, he died on 2 April 1974, aged only sixty-two. De Gaulle had still been President at seventy-eight: Pompidou, the obvious successor, had seemed young in comparison. In the last months of 1973 his physical deterioration had been dramatic but there was no younger Gaullist primed as Dauphin. A sense of drift and disintegration pervaded government circles and sapped the confidence of the Gaullist majority in the Chamber, despite its re-election at the polls in June. Conscious of the revival of the left with its Common Programme, and mindful of Mitterrand's showing in 1965, the Gaullists decided, with no unanimity and little sense of direction, that Jacques Chaban-Delmas had the width of appeal to succeed as Presidential candidate. The electorate disagreed, and elected the independent Finance Minister, Valéry Giscard d'Estaing. Less than four years after de Gaulle's death, Gaullism failed to retain the Élysée. It was no longer de Gaulle's Republic, but the inheritors of June 1968 were still in control.

'Après-Gaullisme'

On 21 February 1966 *L'Express* carried the headline 'Birth of a Dauphin'. Giscard d'Estaing, Finance Minister to de Gaulle from 1962 to 1965, had just emerged impressively from a television interview. He was young, informally aristocratic in manner, but he was certainly no Dauphin. His theme was the nature of government and society after de Gaulle but the 'après-Gaullisme' of his agenda was also a criticism of de Gaulle himself. In 1967 he objected to de Gaulle's 'solitary exercise of power' and in 1969

he openly declared he would vote against de Gaulle's referendum. He had formed the group known as Independent Republicans in the Chamber, which buttressed the Gaullist majority but looked to an eventual constellation of Europeanism, technology and economic liberalism in the centre of the political spectrum. Pompidou's Presidential promise to open Gaullism to a wider political horizon and to work for an enlarged Europe brought Giscard back into government. He held the Finance Ministry throughout Pompidou's Presidency. Technocrat, economist, deputy for Clermont-Ferrand and mayor of the nearby Auvergne *commune* of Chamalières, Giscard was forty-eight when he decided to bid for the Élysée.

It was the first fully media-conscious Presidential campaign. However ambivalent Giscard's own relationships with Gaullism, his self-presentation was conspicuously 'après-Gaulliste'. Gone was the heavy, authoritarian presence of an untouchable figurehead, so easily caricatured in May 1968. In its place were colourful family posters, smiling accessibility and the harnessed glamour of television. Giscard's campaign themes reflected those of Pompidou in 1969, but he expressed them with a disarming mix of ageless sagacity and youthful candour which outmanoeuvred the other inheritors of June '68 and attracted the support of the unpredictable Jacques Chirac, Pompidou's protégé and his last Minister of the Interior, who gambled that Giscard would best preserve the legacy of Gaullism. Against Mitterrand in the second round Giscard exploited the polarity between Gaullism and Communism which had been the keynote of the June victory, but he also used his facility with economic facts and figures to obtain a slight but discernible advantage in a ground-breaking television debate with Mitterrand, watched by an audience of 25 million.

In the event, Giscard defeated Mitterrand on 19 May 1974 by only a narrow margin, with 50.8 per cent of the votes cast in a record poll, against Mitterrand's 49.19 per cent. The split was seen by some as the clearest dichotomy of right and left since the war, and was therefore pre-Gaullist, if de Gaulle as President was held to have substantially crossed the right–left divide. But more important than the patterns of voting left or right, which showed a remarkable tenacity at local level, it was the rival bids for change in a post-Gaullist era which really marked the difference between the two candidates. Mitterrand played on the solidarity and electability of a revived left, with its agreed Common Programme. Despite overtures to the centre and to disillusioned Gaullists, Mitterrand projected himself as a determined left-wing candidate in his promises of change. Giscard, by contrast, muddied the waters between left and right by his vision of a liberal reforming centre. It was regarded by the opposition as an opportunistic

tactic, but to the surprise of the left and the dismay of much of the right, Giscard converted his campaign into policies.

The '68 era: a final twist

Twelve years before her defence of Marie-Claire Chevalier in the key abortion issue of 1972, the barrister Gisèle Halimi was one of the lawyers who had argued the case of Djamila Boupacha, a young FLN woman being tortured by the French army in an Algerian prison. Halimi made the inhumanity of her treatment public, but it was widely understood that it was the tenacity of Simone Veil that was critical in securing her removal from the hands of the OAS. Simone Veil (née Jacob), survivor of Ravensbrück, had defied the gender prejudices in the higher echelons of the law and had qualified for the magistrature, opened to women after the war. An expert on women's prisons and prison reform, Veil was entrusted in 1959 with the dossiers of FLN prisoners by Edmond Michelet, ex-Resistance deportee and Minister of Justice. He acted on the advice of Germaine Tillion, the ethnographer still working in Algeria and herself a noted survivor of Ravensbrück. This grouping of individuals, highly sensitive to human rights, did not have a specifically feminist agenda, but with Halimi and also Simone de Beauvoir involved, they were particularly conscious of the torture perpetrated on women. Fourteen years later, in 1974, Simone Veil was made Minister of Health by President Giscard d'Estaing, which he followed shortly after by creating a state secretariat of women's affairs (*condition féminine*) headed by Françoise Giroud, the co-founder of the weekly *L'Express*, and a surprise appointment, given her friendship with Pierre Mendès France and her support for Mitterrand in the Presidential elections. Giscard was exercising his power of recruitment outside the norms of party politics. He endorsed Giroud's statement that women were marginalized and that this should cease, even if it meant concessions on issues largely associated with the left. In the government led by Jacques Chirac, Simone Veil's in-tray contained the dossier on abortion, a priority in the radical feminist campaigns of the MLF.

Simone Veil made waves by being the first woman in the Fifth Republic to become a full minister. She caused a storm by carrying through the legalization of voluntary abortion (IVG – *interruption volontaire de grossesse*). Women who could demonstrate distress would have access to legal abortion in the first ten weeks of pregnancy. Giscard and Chirac were solid in their support, but only the votes of the Socialists and Communists allowed the bill to pass into law, initially for five years, but adopted perma-

nently in 1979. Catholic and familial groups who expressed fundamental opposition on religious and moral grounds found it impossible to understand why a President from a wealthy Catholic family, for whom they had voted as the conservative candidate, and a minister who had no personal liking for abortion, should condone what they saw as the taking of life. Giscard for his part expressed a determination to modernize society, and the motives of Simone Veil were ones of order, justice and humanity: 'We can no longer shut our eyes to the 300,000 abortions which every year mutilate the women of this land . . .' The chaos and scandal of dangerous, illegal practices had to give way, she claimed, to a law which could be realistically applied, both to dissuade and protect those who sought and provided abortion. She ended her speech to the National Assembly on a strong note of confidence in the younger generation, 'brought up by ourselves in a different way than we had been'.[11]

Radical legislation, sexual politics on the floor of the Chamber, a feminist campaign brought to fruition, an appeal to youth, and all stemming from a Presidency which had been thought to represent the right against the reforming left in the elections. There was clearly a new political identity here. The Veil law was only the most controversial of a whole raft of reforms which, in July 1974 lowered the age of majority from twenty-one to eighteen, in August broke up the monolith radio and television network (ORTF) and established key areas of independence from government control, in December authorized the open sale of contraceptives and made them refundable in certain cases through national health insurance, and in June 1975 permitted divorce by mutual consent. All these items had been on the May '68 agenda. They were now the programme of the centre.

Nothing is immutable

This twist given to *les années '68* was codified by Giscard in 1976 in a little book which he entitled *Démocratie française*. He rehearsed two years of reforming measures, stressing also a selective lowering of the retirement age, a 63 per cent increase in the old age pension, the introduction of ecology into all large-scale planning and more humane prison conditions. The old ideologies, Marxism and traditional liberalism, were, he argued, anachronistic and were being replaced by a new democracy and social unity axed round 'a large expanding amorphous central group' in society and politics: 'Hard-working, but far-sighted, ambitious but capable of generosity, numerous but individualistic, it really resembles nothing except itself, and, I should add, it is typically French in its characteristics and way of

life.'[12] Pluralism and freedom were his key concepts and were seen as moulding the ambience of the decade. They extended to that rarefied realm of cooking, *haute cuisine*.

The 1970s saw high cuisine's refusal to be defined purely in immutable terms. The changing profile of gastronomy was underlined when the controversial chef Paul Bocuse received the Légion d'Honneur from President Giscard on 25 February 1975. His skill in reinventing the cuisine of the Lyon area became proverbial, as did his own creations, not least his black truffle soup and his lobster Meursault which he served in his family restaurant at Collonges on the Saône just outside Lyon. He became a roving ambassador for French cooking. At the time he was seen as a militant convert to the *nouvelle cuisine* launched in 1972 by two food critics, Henri Gault and Christian Millau, promoting authentic and simple cooking and insisting on the freshness and natural harmony of all ingredients. It was a movement not only against processed food but also against the heavy and fattening dishes which, they said, were pushing the French to resemble Michelin's inflatable Bibendum.

The *nouvelle cuisine* was scorned by traditionalists as ideological asceticism, the substitution of philosophy for cooking. The decoration of Bocuse by Giscard inflamed the gastronomic battle, which mirrored to some extent the clash before 1914 between the 'futurist' dishes of Jules Maincave and the legendary cuisine of Auguste Escoffier, who was decorated by Édouard Herriot. The battle convinced neither side, although Bocuse later distanced himself from what he deemed to be the excesses of the new. But few chefs after the clash in 1975 eschewed originality or avoided public celebrity. The reputation of the chef as artist or philosopher was constantly renewed. The creation of new dishes continued, no less than the annual controversy over the stars awarded by the rival food guides.

By the end of the decade and prompted by the tenth anniversary of 1968, influential voices were arguing that Giscardism was not a twist to the legacy of May, but a direct consequence of the very individualism of the student revolt. This was, itself, an anachronism, a reading of history backwards. It was a symptom of a movement in language and concepts that would be universally visible by the end of the 1980s, but was already discernible in Giscard's *Démocratie française*: the recuperation of 'freedom' from an almost exclusive identity with the political left, to serve as a keyword of the liberal, market economy. Giscard himself did not interpret May '68 as a thrust in this direction, but those who did so, either mischievously or seriously, interpreted the libertarian ideas and images of the students as a blanket endorsement of all *liberté*, regardless of who was claiming freedom

and for what ends. The distortion of May 1968 that this involved fuelled a controversy which, in the early twenty-first century, is sustained with as much intellectual vitality as ever.[13]

Contesting liberation

In the canon of republican imagery it was difficult to imagine Delacroix's classic depiction of 'Liberté' being replaced by an icon of free trade. In the canon of Fifth Republican legitimacy it was no easier to imagine the inheritance of 1944 being contested. De Gaulle's special relationship with the Resistance and the Liberation had filtered into the historical blood of the Fifth Republic, and it was not to be contaminated by other liberational narratives. Guardian of his own history as symbolic, de Gaulle made Resistance and Liberation into a fixture in the history of the whole nation. The sacrilege of May 1968 was that it asked whether this carefully nurtured history was no longer liberational but repressive. How the Presidents who followed de Gaulle would deal with this challenge was not imagined to be a major problem until the first cinema showings of a documentary film on the Occupation in April 1971. The Pompidou and Giscard Presidencies, whatever the nature of their *après-Gaullisme*, were imbricated with the layers of heritage identified with de Gaulle. The film revealed that the heritage was full of traps for the unwary. Fidelity to de Gaulle's image of a 'resistance nation' was at stake.

The powerfully insistent documentary, *Le Chagrin et la pitié (The Sorrow and the Pity)*, was made by Marcel Ophuls for television in 1969. With his talented cinema-director father Max Ophuls, Marcel had escaped from the invading Germans over the Pyrenees. The family had already fled from the Nazis in Germany in 1933 and had taken French nationality, with a change of name from Oppenheimer. Set in Clermont-Ferrand, the four and a half hours of the documentary were strongly pro-Resistance but left no doubt that France had not been *la nation résistante* that de Gaulle had projected. Using oral history from carefully constructed interviews with a range of people from the peasant Grave brothers to the aristocratic collaborationist Christian de la Mazière, Ophuls concentrated on representing the conflict of French against French, leaving de Gaulle and much of the resistance contribution to the war against Germany in the margins of his story. The implication was that the history of resistance, and notably the Free French, was either too well known to need repeating, or had become a suffocating force, stifling other approaches and other voices.

Influential individuals, including Simone Veil, who spoke either for the

deportees or for 'the Resistance', accused the film of giving a negative picture of the period and recommended that it should not be shown on television. Its formal brilliance was recognized but its content was labelled as unbalanced, as if it purported to be not just one film about the Occupation but a definitive account. As a result, the broadcasting authorities in the state-monopolized ORTF refused to buy the rights, denying it a TV screening throughout the whole of the 1970s. Its outlet had to be a more limited one. For over a year in 1971–2 it played to full houses in small cinemas, and a generation of young researchers, influenced, like Ophuls himself, by the anti-authoritarian ideas of May '68, gave it iconic status in the posing of new questions about Vichy, collaboration and resistance. There was no rehabilitation of Pétain in the film, but rather an innovative and probing account of the different motivations and extent of collaboration. It announced a massive shift away from the Gaullist image of the war and Occupation.

It seemed that Pompidou might have reason to overrule the ORTF's ban when he was quoted in an American article in August 1971 as detesting all the fuss and panoply of resistance medals and decorations.[14] Instead he kept a discreet silence on the fate of the film while trying to remain loyal, less to the heroic image of the Resistance than to a Presidential spirit of national reconciliation, also identified with de Gaulle. In this vein he became embroiled in the murky case of Paul Touvier, who had been a leader of the Milice in the Lyon area. Like Philippe Henriot, Touvier was a prominent Catholic: as a *milicien* he had hounded resisters. He was sentenced to death twice after the Liberation for crimes which included the killing of Victor Basch, an elderly philosopher, Dreyfusard and activist in the Ligue des Droits de l'Homme, who was murdered with his wife Hélène by the Milice in January 1944. Touvier escaped execution and imprisonment by remaining hidden by various Catholic convents and institutions until his death sentence lapsed after twenty years. He emerged to deny any killing or torture and to claim the restoration of his property and freedom. In November 1971 Pompidou discreetly gave him the Presidential pardon necessary for his civil claims to succeed. The news could not be hidden from the localities most affected by Touvier's repressive violence, and Pompidou was forced to defend his decision in the face of angry demonstrations by resistance organizations. He did so in September 1972 by appealing for old wounds to be healed, for a veil to be drawn and for the French 'to forget' the times when they hated each other and tore one another apart.

Ophuls was widely credited with opening a can of worms. Pompidou's pardon of a prominent collaborator seemed to many to confirm that the

authorities were manipulating history and were not facing up to the past. Giscard as President found it no easier to escape suspicion. His brand of political negotiation appeared to some to resemble fascism in its attempt to create a populist synthesis of right and left. It was not that Giscard was accused of fascist intentions, but 1974 was the thirtieth anniversary of the Liberation, and the first such celebration of the Resistance since the death of de Gaulle. It was known that Giscard, aged eighteen at the time, had probably distributed tracts for the Resistance in Paris, had certainly enlisted in the French army at the Liberation, and was decorated with the Croix de Guerre. But his father had been a militant member of the Croix-de-Feu, and both Giscard's parents had been staunch Pétainists. His 'après-Gaullisme' was under close scrutiny for any departure from the resistance tradition or any rehabilitation of Pétain. Film critics in the *Cahiers du cinéma* in 1975 discerned a climate of tolerance for fascist and Vichy themes, notably interpreting Louis Malle's sensitive *Lacombe Lucien* in this way, which they attributed to a shift under Giscard away from Gaullist and resistance ascendancy. In May 1975 Giscard decided that France should no longer celebrate victory over Germany on 8 May. A year later he spoke at the sixtieth anniversary of Verdun, ending a eulogy of Pétain's leadership in 1916 with what seemed a mitigation of Pétain's role in 1940–44, when 'enfeebled by age, he was associated with the failures and misfortunes which afflicted France'. Giscard suggested that the enduring memory of Pétain should be that held by the *poilus* of Verdun. The derisive headline of the left-wing *Rouge* on the following day was 'Maréchal, me voici!'

Sinister to some, but unsurprising and explicable to others, Giscard's post-Gaullism in this respect had a plurality of contexts: de Gaulle's own request that Pétain should be remembered as the great general of the First World War; the need to cement a strong, forward-looking relationship with Germany in Europe; and a consciousness that the legendary reputation of Gaullist resistance, or alternatively of Communist resistance, was in relative decline among the younger generation.

Other liberations

In 1973 there was a provocative shift on the margins of the media. A new daily paper was launched with the title *Libération*. It had nothing to do, said the widow of Emmanuel d'Astier, with the *Libération* founded by her husband under the Occupation, which ran until 1964. The new paper was the creation of Jean-Paul Sartre, Serge July and a collective of journalists of varying *gauchiste* tendencies. It set out to be independent and sacrilegious; it

refused to finance itself through advertisements; it gave free space to personal messages; it represented the creativity of form and ideas which had burst to the surface in May '68; it was global in coverage and viscerally anti-colonial and anti-Communist; it featured revolutionary graphics, scatological cartoons and taboo sexual subjects.

Its title was not accidental. This was the liberation of subjugated voices, central to the discourse of protest which had widened over the years since the campaign against torture in Algeria. It was pungently in revolt, and always out of pocket. It was internally divided on several crucial issues of opinion such as the Yom Kippur war of October 1973. This prompted it to define its central aim as 'giving the most accurate information available, unsullied by a political line or economic interests'. By 1977 it was selling only some 30,000 copies, but *Libération*, later referred to intimately as '*Libé*', had nevertheless survived. Still more, it had shifted the parameters of what constituted news.

As *Libération* moved into its anarchic stride, it was indicative of the multiple waves of left-wing opinion which battered the defensive walls of Soviet Communism and the PCF. Shortly after President Giscard's election, the translation of *The Gulag Archipelago* by the exiled Russian author Alexander Solzhenitsyn almost obliterated all other political discussion in the thirtieth anniversary year of the Liberation. It was a tactical embarrassment to the political leaders of the renewed Socialist Party in their promotion of the Common Programme with the Communists, but its impact on young political intellectuals reared on Marxism but independent of the PCF was systemic. For an individualized collection of writers eventually known as the *nouveaux philosophes* (new philosophers) the need was clear: nothing short of a full liberation of thought from the totalitarian Communist system terrifyingly exposed. Best-selling publications by André Glucksmann, Claude Lefort, Jean-François Revel and Bernard-Henri Lévy propelled them to a celebrity status in the press and on television, where they were fêted as thinkers who had finally brought political philosophy down to earth.

Their success provoked Régis Debray, the once-revolutionary comrade of Che Guevara, to mourn the final age of the intellectual, self-sacrificed on the altar of media stardom. 'Every prosperous thinker', wrote Debray in 1979 in his own best-seller, 'is hanging out a sign with letters of gold saying, "I am just an elementary popular thinker."'[15] It was a caustic judgement on the individuals targeted and heavily debated as the funeral oration on the role of the intellectual in France, but at its core lay the realization that the sting of intellectual conflict had been drawn once Marx-

ist philosophers began *en bloc* to renounce their earlier beliefs. As they did so it was not only a question of 'paradise lost' but of acute awareness that the liberal Raymond Aron had carried many of their ideas thirty years before in his analysis of the Cold War and his subsequent attack on Marxism as 'the opium of the intellectuals'. They also had their predecessors in the pages of *Esprit*, which acknowledged their significance in a special edition of September 1976 on 'Revolution and totalitarianism'. The *nouveaux philosophes* captured a media eager for the strands of a liberational anti-Communist theory to be pulled together.

The imperatives of liberation on the ground were evoked in Corsica in 1976 by a Front of National Liberation (FLNC). Since the war a complex system of clientelism had kept the island in a state of tutelage to the clans which disputed its politics. Favours and obligations were the interwoven tissues of Corsican society. Votes were dependent on services rendered. Political parties existed but it was the family and the locality which determined where loyalties lay. The system was not entirely rigid. Money injected through the state began to modernize expectations and introduce a fluidity in the services that could be demanded. A regional action plan for Corsica had operated since 1957, rationalized into more co-ordinated state initiatives in 1966. Groups pursuing regional autonomy were both at odds with the financial control exerted by clientelism and yet implicated in the system. Poverty was acute in the outlying streets of Bastia in the north, and it was violence there and in the tourist centre of Aléria further down the east coast that brought the 'Corsican problem' into the headlines. In August 1975 three members of the mobile police were killed in clashes with regional activists.

Within a year the FLNC was created, dedicated to achieving independence through secret organization and armed actions. It defied right or left categorization. Over the next twenty years attacks and explosions became almost everyday news, the rationale of the targets often escaping the closest of political observers. It was estimated by national polls that the nationalists were never more than a minority of under 10 per cent, that they were mostly young, that they were fractured by internal rivalries, and that their ability to deter mainland and foreign tourists greatly exceeded their numerical strength. It was repeatedly stressed in the press that most Corsicans were outraged at the violence, but the temptation to dismiss it as archaic banditry missed its distorted reflection of the island's clientelist politics.

Active decolonizers in the columns of *Libération* could reach no agreement on Corsica's nationalism and the violence of the FLNC. They showed only passingly a more united front on the person and programme of the

Iranian religious leader, Ayatollah Khomeiny. Eminent political exile, granted asylum in France, Khomeiny's venerable presence and white-bearded image had much the same width of support as Ho Chi Minh had briefly enjoyed in 1946. The Iranian revolution in 1978–9 against the Shah of Iran and his pro-Western modernization forced the flight of the Shah and brought the triumphant return of the Ayatollah. He was acclaimed by the *gauchiste* left as a liberational figure, but soon after his installation in Iran, cartoons in *Libération* identified his Islamic fundamentalism with the subjugation of women. Even before the Ayatollah's departure from France, *Le Monde* had signalled the significance of fundamentalism in the revolution, but the complexities of Islam were as yet barely known or seriously discussed in French society. It was the image of its declared adversary, the Americanized West, which led the discussion. The initial sympathy of left-wing decolonizers for the departing Ayatollah owed as much to ideas of 'liberating' France from American economic models as restructuring Iran and Islam.

2. *Enter the economy (centre stage)*

The prevalence of ideas and politics stemming from May or June '68 was superseded in the mid-1970s by the prevalence of 'the economy'. This was not just a response to the economic down-turn precipitated by the first oil crisis of late 1973; it was a change of language, discourse and priorities. The economy becomes a personified character, occupying centre stage and given an all-pervading role in political history which it had never occupied before. Its prevalence could well be seen as an inversionary Marxism, the dominant voice of materialist thought stripped of its social and political agenda, or more simply over the following two decades as the strident voice of the market with its presumptions of reason and historical validation. Its other incursions to the centre of history had included different guises such as the strong or ailing franc, the price of agricultural goods or the rationalization of industry. In its previous most dominant presence as *la crise* (depression) of the early 1930s it had shared the lead with the conflict of ideologies, but it was not until the return of *la crise* in 1974, as recession, down-turn or end of the boom years, that the new discourse of economic primacy began to register. It was reflected in the stress on profitability, the advanced science of marketing and the increasing reference to labour costs as part of investment strategy, an area of human resources rather than human relations. The economy was the focus of daily attention, dressed in

increasingly elaborate trappings of analysis and indices. But there was still a marked element of puppetry about its performance. The strings were being pulled. 'We still have much to accomplish,' wrote Giscard d'Estaing in 1976, 'if we are to ensure that society is really master of its economic evolution.'[16] Over seven years he alternatively tightened and loosened the strings. They were not always visible: increasingly the economy was attributed a life of its own.

End of the boom years

The stoical pessimism of 'what goes up must come down' was missing from *les années '68*. The high expectations nurtured by the prosperity curve of the 1950s and 1960s were key factors in the response of both government and public to the first signs that the boom might be faltering. Pompidou was alarmed by President Nixon's decision in August 1971 to detach the dollar from gold, but only in later years was it realized how much of a trigger this had been to financial instability and inflation in the West. Pompidou was said to have talked about the prospects of an 'end of growth' during 1972, but without a sense of imminent crisis. The cutback in crude oil production decided by the Arab states in October 1973 as a response to Western sympathies for Israel in the Yom Kippur war sounded a much clearer note of alarm. Pompidou, like de Gaulle in 1967, controversially backed the Egyptian cause, but this provided no special economic relief: Israel's planes and armaments derived in many cases from France. Of all the industrialized nations Japan and France were the most dependent on the imports of oil. As prices per barrel quadrupled, businesses, private and public, increased the price of goods, recouping their losses from the customer. The inflation rate soared to over 15 per cent, from the slowly escalating rate of 6 per cent in the first years of the decade. It was the rapidity of the rise rather than the level itself which was staggering. The impact of the oil bill was likened by some in business to the incidence of reparations on the German economy after 1919. The *patronat* reported that 1974 was the most severe industrial recession since the Liberation, a language of crisis which marked the extent to which the boom years had come to seem normal and permanent.

Giscard's Presidency inherited the high inflationary trend, but also the expectation that it would be temporary. It became an acknowledged crisis with a rash of lay-offs and redundancies which doubled the unemployment figures in 1974–5 from 500,000 to a million, particularly affecting workers in the heavily industrialized regions of the east and south-east. It was the

index of industrial production which most clearly signalled the slow-down. From 1962 to 1974 it had increased by 100 per cent. In the decade following 1974 the progression was only 10 per cent. This was comparatively registered as stagnation but unlike the crisis of the 1930s it was accompanied by persistent inflation. The bewildering phenomenon was nicknamed *stagflation*. It threw economic theory into turmoil. As government measures to reduce demand attempted to curb inflation, companies cut their costs and forced more workers into redundancy. Conversely, when unemployment was tackled by a package to stimulate industrial growth, demand for goods increased and with it the rate of inflation. The limits of this stop-go policy were acknowledged in 1976, although for those in work the standard of living continued to improve, wages just kept ahead of prices and exports were comparatively buoyant. But inflation and unemployment remained obstinately stuck in the headlines, affecting certain sections of society acutely.

The immigrant workforce was instantly the object of press and political attention. There was no departure from the 1930s here. By 1976 the net inflow of immigrants, who had been brought in to provide unskilled manual labour in the boom years, was stopped. Well before the recession, articles in *Le Monde* warned against the outbursts of racism directed against Arab workers and families after Algeria nationalized its oil production in 1971. In Lyon in particular, fights and abuse escalated throughout the year, reflecting the extent of racial segregation effectively in place on which the Prefect and several mayors of suburban *communes* insisted, banning new migrant settlements in certain *quartiers*. Daniel Mayer of the Ligue des Droits de l'Homme denounced the racist extremism, but as the first government measures to restrict conditions of immigrant entry and settlement began to bite, and the recession loomed, serious incidents of racial intolerance broke out across the south. With the lurch upwards of unemployment in 1973, it was a short step from racial abuse to a form of argument which cloaked discrimination in statistics. It could be heard at all levels. In February 1976 the Prime Minister, Jacques Chirac, stated on television that a country with 900,000 unemployed but 2 million immigrants was not a country where unemployment was insoluble.[17]

Away from the economy, Giscard was locked in bitter political rivalry with Chirac over who represented the parliamentary majority. It gave the President ample personal reason to replace him, but it was Chirac who resigned in August 1976 and a year later became the first elected mayor of Paris, defeating Giscard's nominee. As Prime Minister he was replaced, but not by another politician. Giscard announced that Raymond Barre was the

best economist in the land and appointed him as both Premier and Minister of Economy and Finance. The 52-year-old Barre was a career academic who had been a recent vice-president of the European Commission: he had an elevated reputation in confined European circles as shrewd and pragmatic. He had been brought into politics as Minister for Foreign Trade in January. He was dropped into the Matignon from above, barely familiar with parliament and scarcely known to the public: an economic *deus ex machina*.

Face to face with the recalcitrant economy, Barre prescribed stability of the franc and a rigorous assault on inflation. It spelt austerity. Adaptation was equated with radical modernization and reduction of labour costs, with the word 'restructuring' indicating a policy of profitability above all other considerations. His plan was deeply unpopular with those whose jobs were most threatened: he was accused of turning the knife in the wounds of unemployment. The franc held steady on the foreign exchanges and exports continued to prosper, although Barre's negative public image seemed likely to endanger the government's majority in the 1978 elections. Within the opposition the electoral partnership of Socialists and Communists broke down as the PCF tried to stop its gradual decline by sticking with its own candidates, but within the Gaullist and allied electorate there were still dominant fears that a victory for the left would give power to the Communists. The government was comfortably returned, with the centre party loyal to Giscard outscoring Chirac's Gaullists in the first round. Barre and Giscard were confident enough to readdress the economy. They abolished price controls, even of bread – the daily *baguette* – and released an economic liberalism which Giscard had previously kept in check. It had, however, always been there: the sentence qualifying his aim of social control over the economy ran: 'In a pluralist society this attempt to regulate the economy presupposes competition and a free market.'[18]

The state and market forces

Ten years after de Gaulle's resignation, Valéry Giscard d'Estaing did not pretend to embody France personally in the way that de Gaulle had done, and with Chirac in his Paris fief playing the part of a Gaullist *frondeur*, it was less and less clear whether anyone on the right or centre-right would effect a special relationship with the nation. Giscard, however, did articulate a particular understanding of the state. He did so first in his easy rapport with technocrats for whom he was both model and colleague and second in the pragmatic mix of free market and state control which was still evident

even after the policy shift to economic liberalism in the last years of the decade.

The extent of state intervention, or *dirigisme*, in the running of society and the economy continued to express the Jacobin and Napoleonic traditions of state power (*étatisme*) evident in the Third and Fourth Republics, to which had been added the mystique of the national plan (*le plan*) from Monnet onwards and the nationalist centralism of de Gaulle's regime. At the heart of government, Daladier in 1938, Pétain in 1940 and de Gaulle in the 1960s had all replaced politicians with technocrats from the Civil Service and industry. Giscard promoted a formidable range of technocracy, capped by the status of the *énarques*, graduates of the Parisian École Nationale d'Administration (ENA), situated in Saint-Germain-des-Prés, of which Giscard himself and his new rival Chirac, were both graduates. ENA monopolized recruitment and training of the highest-placed administrators in government and increasingly in big business. Their unity of aims and methods was something of a myth, but it was one which the élite themselves did not set out to dispel. It certainly did not amount to a conspiracy. Their political tendencies were not monolithic: from the early 1970s opinion polls place the *énarques* to the left of the average voter and with a penchant for the upwardly mobile Parti Socialiste (PS). Giscard's own ideal of centre politics was also attractive, but it was essentially the openings afforded by the running of the economy that gave the technocrats their conspicuous power.

The *esprit de corps* of the technocrats was a cultural structure and a buttress of the state. It was expressed in the élite and prestigious national bodies (*grands corps*) which administered the country's finances (Inspection des Finances to which Giscard had belonged), its mining engineering (Corps des Mines) and its infrastructure of bridges, canals, roads and railways (Corps des Ponts et Chaussées). The technocrats dominated the special committees created by Giscard to stimulate economic development, controlling the distribution of state funds and subsidies, negotiating contracts with fellow members of the élite at the heart of industry. Renault, synonym of post-war nationalization and profitability, was not protected from competition within France, a huge state loan permitted the merger between privately owned Peugeot and Citroën, and other sponsored mergers in chemicals, tyres, electronics and nuclear energy continued initiatives taken under Pompidou. They fulfilled an explicit Giscardian policy of grooming at least one French firm in every leading industrial sector to compete internationally, a policy which dated back to 1969 and owed much to the carefully defined roles ascribed to the state and to the market by the theories

of the mining specialist Lionel Stoleru, whom Giscard regularly consulted. In 1976 he brought him into the government with responsibility for relationships with manual workers, an irony not missed by the labour movement who held the technocrats responsible for the unemployment which increasingly followed the restructuring of industry.

The history of planning diversified as it became an essential ingredient in company policy. There was a steady recruitment of technocrats into the private sphere. The significance of the national body that produced the five-year plans noticeably decreased with the government recourse to stop-go policies, and was merely theoretical under Barre. Some industrial success stories continued, however, to be associated with prescient state planning. The belated but huge expansion of the telephone industry after 1976 was attributed to Giscard's insistence that individual access to a telephone was a national priority, while the state funds for the air industry were finally seen to reap a major reward with the growing profitability of the Airbus by the end of the 1970s, compensating for the disappointing sales of the aesthetic phenomenon Concorde. The railways continued to prosper under state management, as did the arms and military aircraft giant Dassault, heavily subsidized by the state. The accelerated commitment to nuclear power as an urgent adaptation to the oil crisis of the early 1970s was seen by supporters and protesters alike as emblematic of *dirigisme*. Larger and more effective nuclear power stations were sited and built in rapid progression. The state responsiveness to shifts in nuclear technology took the industry into a deal in the early 1970s with the American company Westinghouse to develop its pressurized water reactors, and under Giscard to build a fast-breeder reactor, the Superphénix, with significant export potential, but alarming ecological implications according to protesters. Controversially, the extent of nuclear energy symbolized French industrial resilience when the second oil crisis broke in 1979.

On the debit side of industry the Giscardian state did not interfere as hundreds of individual firms moved from ailing to failing. Bankruptcies spiralled after 1974, increasing by 70 per cent with the severe social conse-quence of lost jobs, but the policy of Giscard and Barre became even more explicit: star companies (*vedettes*) were to be actively sought out and subsidized by the state, lame ducks (*canards boiteux*) were not. It was different when catastrophic decline affected a whole sector and region: steel and northern Lorraine. Manufacturing industry was struggling everywhere, inside and outside France, and its workforce fell by almost 9 per cent from 1974 to 1979. In heavy industry deficits in the steel sector were not new and even in times of buoyant demand from manufacturers the state had

subsidized production of the two industrial groups, Sacilor and Usinor, which had emerged from the family businesses of the steel magnates (*maîtres des forges*). In 1974 demand fell and prices crashed as the first oil crisis hit the steel industry and its 150,000 workers harder than most. Productivity by 1977 was 30 per cent below that of Germany, with labour costs correspondingly higher. Partial rescue and retraining schemes were funded by the state in the mid-1970s, and a certain diversification into new employment was achieved in the less stricken areas. In 1978 Barre virtually took over the industry with a renewal package of 3 billion francs, the appointment of state managers and the absorption of the industry's debts, all dependent on the closure of several steel mills and job losses of over 20,000, the majority of which would be in Lorraine. The violent protests which this provoked at Denain in the Nord and at Longwy in Lorraine caused the government to increase payments for redundancies and pensions, to intensify retraining, and to manipulate Renault and Peugeot-Citroën into investing in the region. Barre's plan for steel, like the government's *dirigisme* in the nuclear industry, kept the state as a reduced but still vital player within the new script of economic liberalism.

Place and identity

Across the length and breadth of France, in Toulouse or Metz, Grenoble or Rennes, there was a shift of emphasis in French history which was only fully grasped by the end of the century but was already visible in the 1970s. Individuals and groups began to relate their social and political causes more consciously to place. To varying extent they had always done so, but for most of the twentieth century the importance of place had been over-shadowed by the identities of class, religion, party alignment and ideology, the pull of national factors such as republicanism, education and patriotism, and the effects of a modernizing economy. Some of these were diminished in the last thirty years of the century, some were strengthened, none disappeared. The significance of place gave them sites of expression. The two World Wars and the Occupation had made specific localities into household names: Vercors, Glières, Ascq, Oradour. The archetype was Verdun. Paris was never absent. In the last quarter of the century, however, the focus on place began to redefine familiar social movements and signal new ones. As it did so it drew attention to the historic role of place in the formation of identity and memory.

Economic explanation of this shift highlights the importance of the growth years, especially in the late 1960s. Despite the central block on

political devolution, the collective self-confidence of regions, towns and villages grew commensurate with their share in the economic boom and stability, marked especially by full employment. The circulating tourism of the French discovering France provoked more overt signs of local identities, history and culture. Pompidou put the regions more firmly on the national map in 1972, with a collection of functional measures to advance development, planning and identity, although the stress still lay firmly on region as space rather than region as institution. The rural exodus and urban expansion began to be accompanied in small but significant ways by movement in the other direction. Secondary homes away from the big towns increasingly involved a reidentification with localities remembered from childhood or recovered from the mists of ancestry. Skills and enterprise found profitable opportunities in the provincial towns. Paris was no longer the only focus for high aspirations.

The recession with its confusing increase in both prices and unemployment did not reverse this movement of local self-awareness. If anything, it intensified it. It vastly increased the demand for a louder, more democratic local voice. In areas of prolonged decline, local consciousness of an industrial sector which had moulded the life of a region for generations was heightened by its accelerated collapse. Companies who cut their workforce were called to local account. The national government, arraigned in the 1960s by regionalists for internal colonization, was now, as during the Occupation and immediate post-war years, accused of neglect. In prosperous areas, thirty years of boom meant that much more was now at stake. Local identities were formed not only through growth but by strategies for sustaining development: local pressure increased on politicians with multiple mandates of mayor, deputy and minister; big entrepreneurs on a small stage now had everything to protect or lose; the state's vaunted pursuit of regional economic development was on trial; mandarin technocrats were expected to have the answers to regional disparities or give way to local competence.

Enforced redundancies increasingly focused on place. Close to maritime imports of iron ore, the steel plant at Dunkerque in the north and the new works at Fos-sur-Mer near Marseille in the south remained relatively productive. By contrast, the crisis of the steelworks in Lorraine, the region identified with Joan of Arc and Verdun, brought the area of Metz-Thionville-Longwy to national prominence. Longwy, invaded by union officials and journalists, was seen as the epitome of years of company neglect in the face of the changing industry. Its depressing image of blight and decay and its threat of a serious workers' revolt kept it on the surface

of politics throughout 1978–80. It forced Barre to increase retraining opportunities in the locality. On the union side too, local needs impacted on policy. Despite the angry marches of massed steelworkers on an industry-wide basis, organized mainly by the CGT, it was argued by Jacques Ché-rèque of the CFDT metalworkers' union that the way forward for the workers lay less in the escalation of traditional actions of this kind than in union negotiations for different employment and the rejuvenation of the region.[19] In Marseille an academic enquiry in 1979 into the motivation and needs of workers in industrial wastelands of closed factories asked at the outset, 'Are not the workers' demonstrations for employment also a search for regional identity?'[20] For almost three years from 1975, in an echo of Lip, women shirt-makers of CIP (Confection Industrielle du Pas-de-Calais) pursued their work with an occupation of their workshop day and night in defiance of the company's attempt at closure, defying the stigma still attached to the wives of miners who continued to work once they were married, even though men's unemployment in the area had gathered pace with the cumulative contraction of mining. The focus on the women's struggle in Haisnes, Houdain, Nœux-les-Mines and Hazebrouck in the mining basin of Zola's *Germinal* tied together a conscious feminism and the heritage of place.

Ecology emerged as an activist issue through place. The campaign for the sheep farmers of Larzac was seminal. Tenacious village protest at the loss of their valley to the dam and reservoir of Naussac in the Lozère was dubbed by *Libération* as a second Larzac. Later in the decade the opposition to nuclear power stations and secret chemical experiments was deeply formative, but also divisive as some ecologists refused to make common cause with anti-state anarchists while others saw a functional merging of parallel protests. The explosion in Italy of a chemical plant at Seveso in July 1976 and the devastating release of poisonous dioxin sensitized the whole issue of pollution in France at a time of record drought in the south. Violence brought Malville on the Rhône, east of Lyon, on to the front pages at the end of July 1977 as riot police forcefully protected the Super-phénix against over 30,000 protesters from France, Germany, Britain and elsewhere. In neighbouring villages opinion was divided between opposition to the reactor and recrimination against young German activists accused of a 'second occupation' of the village of Morestel. In the rain, mud and tear gas, a French teacher, Vital Michalon, died and a local man lost a leg in clashes with police, five of whom were numbered among the 100 wounded.

In 1979 the site was Plogoff. An active core of Breton regionalists and

ecological protesters backed the local mayor and villagers of Plogoff in Finistère who persistently refused to accept a giant nuclear power station on the coast, conflicting with the government, the state electricity company (EDF) and pro-nuclear Finistère councillors who pursued the project and argued the case of national energy but also the regional one of economic benefit. The debate over Plogoff brought a far more pluralist definition of regional identity. Fault-lines within the regions were visible. Yet for two years Plogoff was the destination for what the press called a significant new genre of political and social movement, prepared for the violence which erupted at the projected site in battles with police in 1980, but mostly recruiting non-violent activists with no party affiliation. It was noted that they expected to take their children with them to the marches and demonstrations which were European in their composition, and global, as well as local, in their reference.

Just how far Europe was imagined as a significant place and identity in the 1970s is more problematic. From the Treaty of Rome onwards, ideas of a supranational Europe clashed with preferences for a Europe which would be little more than a loose organization of nation-states. In the margins there was also the less developed idea of a Europe made up of regions. The European regional fund, created in 1975, made much more possible the outflanking of the state by shrewd economic intervention at regional level. Caught between Europe and the regions, nationalists could envisage that the very unity of France was threatened. But far and away the most conscious idea of Europe as place and identity turned on the historic realignment with Germany, which overshadowed its pivotal role between West and East and its perceived difference from America. Giscard constructed multiple levels of Franco-German partnership, symbolized by his personal rapport with fellow financial technocrat Chancellor Helmut Schmidt; he favoured a further enlargement of the European Community (EEC) to Greece, Spain and Portugal, and he and Schmidt steered the creation of a European Monetary System through the EEC in 1979, announcing the creation of a nominally common European currency, the Ecu, as a necessary corollary of a single European market.

Agriculture and Europe were almost interchangeable topics in the 1970s. Less afflicted than industry by the first oil crisis, farmers were able to exploit the enlarged European market to a point where the rich potential of agriculture was referred to as France's 'green oil'. The European Common Agricultural Policy (CAP), first introduced in 1962, had led to higher prices and widespread subsidies for farm produce, fragmenting the rural dissatisfaction of the Poujade era and enormously benefiting the bigger

producers, especially the cereal and sugar beet farmers of the north and Île-de-France areas. In many respects the CAP, as the most explicit achievement of integrated Europeanism, can be said to have 'rescued' national French agriculture. The income gap between the rural and urban sectors narrowed. On their own the agricultural interests could not have exerted the equivalent power in parliament or government. Europe and the CAP did it for them.[21] The dwindling numbers of those working the land and the emphasis on particular sectors and exports also increased the self-awareness among farmers of their strengths and weaknesses. Within most regional agriculture there were micro-regions, each one distinct from the next only a few kilometres away. From 1972 to 1974 Jacques Chirac, deputy for the Corrèze and Minister of Agriculture, made his career by listening to the specific needs of different peasant interests as the Radical Henri Queuille had done in the inter-war years. Giscard's regime provided grants for qualified young farmers setting up on their own, with rates adjusted to the types of terrain and produce.

Almost all the European opportunities of the 1970s encouraged the further stratification of agriculture and gave priority to cereal production with its high profile in international trade. From 1975 the Lomé Convention opened certain African countries to European agriculture on favoured terms, and lucrative markets were expanded in Japan, South Korea, Taiwan and Indonesia. French grain made profits from periodic poor harvests in Russia, the USA and Canada. Oil-producing countries with money to spend were attracted to French food, with Breton chicken much sought after by the Arab states. The overall result was a selective boom in French agricultural trade within and outside Europe, still with the internal protection of the CAP. By 1981 France was second to the USA as a world exporter of foodstuffs.

In terms of negative perceptions, Europe brought a new level of control as well as opportunity to the French countryside, and much of the reality of the EEC in the 1970s and 1980s was registered by struggling rural producers as imposition, not least when ideas of favouring tourism over agriculture were put forward by planners in the name of regional development, aimed at phasing out terraced smallholdings in the lower Alps, Massif Central and Pyrenees, and areas of cheap wine in Languedoc, Roussillon and Provence. In these rural sectors it was common to find Europe equated purely with Brussels as the place from which centralizing bureaucrats were seen to launch attacks on long-standing patterns of local identity. In this discourse Europe took the place of Paris as the unheeding, central power.

The tendency at government level was to talk about France and Europe

in general terms, missing the growing insistence on locality. When de Gaulle mentioned Europe it was usually in rhetorical counterpoint, to foreground the national identity of France. Pompidou discarded de Gaulle's static formulations, and when Giscard talked of Europe it was to further Pompidou's awareness of Europe's potential for the whole of France. In May 1976 he made a media-oriented and responsive visit to the USA, but on return and over the following few years he repeatedly affirmed his resolve to construct a strong European identity, *une personnalité européenne*. With Schmidt he endorsed the idea of direct suffrage for the European Parliament, and in 1979 the first of these elections gave some indication of the extent to which Europe could stir public passions. Jacques Chirac appointed himself as true heir to de Gaulle's nationalism and set out his campaign by attacking the Giscardian list of candidates, headed by Simone Veil, as 'the foreign party' (*le parti de l'étranger*). This xenophobic jibe did not make inroads into majority perceptions of Europe, which remained relatively positive, nor did it affect the popularity of Simon Veil, whose pro-European list comfortably led the rest of the field. There was only a 60 per cent turn-out: it was almost twice as high as the vote in Britain, but 5 per cent lower than in West Germany.

It was assumed that the 40 per cent abstentions and spoilt votes indicated indifference to Europe. What was confirmed by more accurate opinion polls was that the range of hostility to Europeanism crossed the parliamentary frontiers of majority and opposition, from fervent nationalists on the right to Communists on the left, and that many local economic interests, rural and industrial, felt unrepresented by the mainstream parties. Enthusiasm for Europe, both as place and ideal, equally fragmented politics. It complicated the main dialectic between the Giscardians and the Socialists: a European commitment defined them both. In all other ways, as the campaign for the Presidential elections took off as early as 1979, it was difference which marked the two sides and divided opinion polls. 'Whose society?' was now equally 'Whose economy?' and indeed 'Whose Europe?'.

18

Ideological Rupture and Retreat, 1970s–1984

1. The return of politics: the contest for President, 1981

Personalities and programmes

The metaphor of the post-Gaullist 1970s, of President Giscard d'Estaing's whole approach to politics, was *décrispation* (the easing of relationships), a call to relax the political muscles which had been braced in permanent tension throughout the century, or, indeed, as far as the historical eye could see. Conflict in politics, whether ritualized as barricades against repression, left against right, strikers against employers, or youth against authority, was under scrutiny. Was it the only way for people to resolve their differences? What about encounters across political divides? A sympathetic interview in the weekly *L'Express* in May 1980 allowed Giscard to elaborate on his understanding of the centre ground in politics, but his initial appeal for political détente met a crisp retort from the interviewer: 'But isn't politics inevitably a conflict?' Giscard consented but added that ideological debate should not be allowed to tear the social fabric apart. Meetings of political opponents, he claimed, should happen but never do: 'There is a systematic refusal to consider the right of others to hold views different from your own.' He had taken this as a challenge and had set out to practise a more relaxed style of Presidential government: 'I see more people and have more open and varied discussions than any of my predecessors.'[1]

This was more than an individual style of Presidency. Giscard's apparently impromptu visits to ordinary homes, and the meals he shared round recognizably typical family tables, were as media-directed as any of his Presidential activities, and they enshrined a confidence that his display of approachable centre politics linked to economic liberalism came as close to the common sense and the common interests of the public as any political leader could do. In February 1978 he took the initiative in creating a coalition of centre parties, the UDF (Union pour la Démocratie Française), its name intentionally recalling the title of his book, *Démocratie française*,

published two years earlier. The repeated stress on the Frenchness of the democracy proposed in both book and coalition did not diminish the extent to which Giscard had moved his Presidential discourse away from the nationalist rhetoric of de Gaulle. His Europeanism above all was a quest for a new, less nationalist, identity for France, in tune with his liberal economics. But he ascribed to his political and economic ideas the moral authority of national consensus, and in this respect he was no less Gaullist than de Gaulle himself. He believed, with good reason, that the public had no wish to see the radical confrontations of 1968 return, and that political frontiers had been crossed by the social reforms over which he had presided, but he underestimated the degree to which, in the context of recession and rising unemployment, his economic liberalism and austerity measures were seen as an aggressive political programme, ideologically driven.

Against Giscard's presumption of his Presidency as consensual, the opposition of the left, disunited and bickering since 1977, proposed to varying degrees an open ideological break with capitalism. At the same time, personal and political opposition came from within the parliamentary majority in the figure of Jacques Chirac, mayor of Paris since 1977 and creator late in 1976 of the RPR (Rassemblement pour la République), the new label for the powerful Gaullist bloc in the Assembly. Even as the economy held the stage, the clash of these three major tendencies, left, centre and Gaullist, marked the return of politics, literally with a vengeance.

Two years before the scheduled Presidential elections of 1981, public opinion polls sounded out the popularity of potential candidates and found the incumbent Giscard well ahead. His lead reflected the surprising success of the governing majority in the 1978 elections, and his prospects further improved with the triumph of Simone Veil's positive Europeanism in the European elections of 1979. Elected President of the European Parliament, she was repeatedly voted the most respected politician in France, perhaps the nearest to achieving consensual popularity, and undoubtedly Giscard's main asset. Locating ideas and discussion away from economics, she embodied an image of Europe and of politics which appealed to those with human and social priorities, a realm of policy-making in which all the candidates for 1981 found themselves fighting for ascendancy.

It was the quality of life which dominated the campaign. Neither Giscard nor Chirac argued that it should be left to market forces. Giscard's advocacy of economic liberalism never lost touch with his record of social reformism. Jacques Chirac in his writings of 1978, *La Lueur de l'espérance*, set out his 'conservative liberalism'. He endorsed the ideas of the classical economists that the economy had its own laws, and left to these it would prosper and

be able to promise the 'luxury of social generosity', but he was against the simplistic isolation of the economy from social ends. With obligatory quotes from de Gaulle, he sought to outflank Giscard by reinvigorating the concept of participation, joining with others 'who have sought a third way between capitalism and bureaucratic socialism for more than a century', and proposing a diffusion of property and capital among wage earners to give them 'social responsibility'. It was only this, he concluded, which would avoid what he called the anarchy of *autogestion* and the bureaucratic tyranny of Marxist collectivism.[2]

The socialist theory behind the left's anti-capitalism was discounted by Chirac as a historical failure, and Annie Kriegel in the majority's most widely read newspaper, *Le Figaro*, went further on the day after the 1978 elections to state that the 'union of the left failed because the left does not exist, either theoretically, ideologically or politically'. Shrewd historian and vehement critic of the Communist Party, Kriegel reached this stark conclusion by arguing that the Socialists were still reformists and the Communists were still wedded to Leninism. Nothing, in other words, had changed since the Congress of Tours in 1920, on which she had written extensively. Logically, she claimed, while these differences were fundamentally unresolved there could be no 'politics of the left' and therefore no 'left', and in the accompanying cartoon Mitterrand's red rosebush lies felled by the sickle (and hammer) of Marchais while Giscard walks off with Marianne.[3]

As a prediction for 1981 this looked comfortable enough throughout the two years that followed the failure of the disunited left in 1978. But contrary to most expectations the Common Programme of 1972 was not forgotten. The Communists and Socialists continued their in-fighting but the anti-capitalist drive of the Programme, with the targets of nationalization clearly specified, was not abandoned by Mitterrand, even though the Communist leader, Georges Marchais, restated his party's orthodoxy by approving the Soviet invasion of Afghanistan in December 1979 and appearing on Russian television a month later. This flew in the face of the moral damage caused to the PCF by the revelations of Solzhenitsyn. Although the party dropped its commitment to the 'dictatorship of the proletariat' in 1976, there was a constant haemorrhage of young membership throughout the 1970s, but the rising unemployment figures kept the ideal of nationalized industry and finance relatively intact from the taint of Stalinism: France had its own tradition of state control and intervention. As the recession caused increasing deprivation it was not difficult for both Communists and Socialists to argue in their own ways that the nationalization of major companies and

banks would enable the state to create more jobs and channel investment to social ends. The anti-capitalism of the Common Programme was, to this extent, loosened from its sectarian ties and made to seem more functional in the immediate crisis. This did not deceive the growing number of intellectuals with a left-wing past, whose denunciation of Communist totalitarianism, whether Stalinist or Maoist, made it impossible for them to accept Mitterrand's reasons for remaining in touch with the PCF.

There was, of course, far more than anti-capitalism behind Mitterrand's leadership of the Parti Socialiste (PS). There were the reasons why he was there in the first place. Both positively and negatively François Mitterrand was a paradigm politician of the post-war years, who emerged relatively unscathed from his close identification with the Fourth Republic, from the political indecisions of 1968 and from years of dallying on the edge of the Socialist Party. In the press there was much about his conservative, Catholic upbringing in the Charente, little about his student involvement in the Croix-de-Feu during the Popular Front period, and even less about his employment by Vichy before his turn to resistance. Ambiguity, coldness and cynicism were noted even by his friends, but there were shafts of crystallizing clarity which gave him a cutting edge of decisiveness. One such was his decision to do battle with the all-powerful de Gaulle of 1965; another was his displacement of Savary at the head of the new PS; a third was his resolute conviction that the Communist Party could be used and outmanoeuvred in a loose partnership. The calculation was that tactically a Socialist leader would eventually benefit from Communist votes in the second round of the Presidential election, while mutual suspicion between the parties would allow the PS to keep its identity intact.

A fourth sign of leadership was his intuition that culture could be mobilized for the 1981 campaign. Intellectual, writer and connoisseur of philosophy, history and the arts, Mitterrand deployed a political and cultural agility in the 1970s which had no equals. Nicknamed 'le Florentin' in the 1950s for intrigues thought to be the hallmark of Renaissance Florence, Mitterrand was actively courted in the 1970s for his patronage, well before he secured the Socialist nomination. He was not averse to other people's charm or manipulation, only to rivalry. He harnessed the cultural inventiveness of the idealistic Jack Lang; he watched the clever, popular, competitive Michel Rocard like a hawk.

Rocard consistently outpaced Mitterrand in opinion polls as the most acceptable Socialist candidate, although he promised the party in 1979 to stand down if Mitterrand gained its nomination. His attraction to the wider public lay in his claim to be more modern, less state-oriented and more

open to decentralization than Mitterrand. His PSU background kept him distanced from the Communists and closer to a social economy of co-operatives and mutualities which promised a reduction of state bureaucracy and a growth of *autogestion*. Rocard's social economy was not a rejection of market forces. He argued that the global role of the market as economic regulator could not be avoided, although socialists had ways of humanizing and socializing its operation. Within the party, however, Rocard was kept in a minority by Mitterrand's tactical alliance with the more Marxist group round Jean-Pierre Chevènement. Rocard did indeed withdraw when Mitterrand was nominated in January 1981, and his marginalization in the events of the year was later seen as a watershed by those who estimated that the party had lost the chance to accept the 'realistic' arguments of Rocard that anti-capitalism was a dead end. At the time it was Mitterrand's embrace of an energetic state socialism that set pulses racing and promised a future of radical change.

Culture, and world horizons

It was a huge cultural moment, recognized throughout France and the world: Jean-Paul Sartre died on 15 April 1980, aged seventy-five. In his last years the deterioration of his sight, which had always relied on one eye, forced him to stop writing and made him first a frail and then a sad shadow of his former self. One of his final public appearances was in 1979 on a deputation to President Giscard to express concern for the Vietnamese boat-people. He was photographed shaking hands with his long-term contemporary and opposite, Raymond Aron. It was noted by Sartre's critics that victims of Communism had not always been his first concern, and that he had sympathized with Soviet Russia in the early 1950s, before the shock of Hungary in 1956. Both opponents and followers stressed that he had endorsed Fanon's arguments for revolutionary black violence in the struggles for liberation and had later accepted the student violence of May 1968. His death induced a long introspection on the decline of the universalist intellectual in French public life. Raised by Serge July in *Libéra-tion* to the height of Voltaire and Hugo, Sartre was mourned in an emotional funeral procession which overflowed the cemetery of Montparnasse, a final street demonstration by those who had shared his campaigns against state torture in Algeria and other abuses of power. Aron asked in *L'Express* whether he should be seen as a utopian or a millenarian, and decided he would best be remembered as 'a moralist lost in the jungle of politics'. There were already many lesser cultural figures caught in the political

thicket of the Presidential elections: inevitably it was asked which candidate Sartre would have voted for.

The widest assumption was that it would have been Mitterrand, although Giscard was seen to be personally moved by Sartre's death. The need for intellectual support and world horizons was high on Mitterrand's priorities. He sought it by promoting culture and liberational causes, with key associates Jack Lang and Régis Debray, both identified with the ideas of May 1968. After a torrid financial time in charge of the Théâtre National Populaire (TNP) in Paris, Jack Lang had entered politics in 1977 as an independent Parisian councillor on the Socialist list, a response to Mitterrand's interest in his creative combination of university theatre, politics and internationalism at Nancy in the 1960s. Lang saw the potential of making the Socialist Party into the patron of culture, to wrest culture from its conventional bourgeois connotations and not least to outbid Michel Guy, Giscard's Culture Minister who had sacked him from the TNP. In 1979 Lang was appointed by Mitterrand as cultural delegate to the PS. For the European elections he brought Willy Brandt and Melina Mercouri as guests to a mass concert at the Trocadéro, aimed at youth and attracting an audience of 300,000. In 1980 he organized a campaign to protect European national cinemas against American domination, and in March 1981 an eye-catching symposium of science and culture at UNESCO with Mitterrand at its centre.

It was to Lang's Nancy that Mitterrand had come in May 1977 to inaugurate a museum in memory of Salvador Allende, the socialist President of Chile murdered in 1973 in the military *putsch* of General Pinochet. He was accompanied by Allende's widow and by Régis Debray, intellectual, novelist, guerrilla compagnon of Che Guevara in Bolivia and prisoner there for three years from 1967. Debray and Mitterrand had already travelled together to Mexico where they had met Gabriel García Márquez and Allende's two daughters. Mitterrand promised that if he came to power he would sever diplomatic relations with Chile, an abrasive hostage to fortune which gained him support from many *gauchistes* and confirmed his refusal of Giscard's *décrispation*.

It is difficult to adjudge what impact Mitterrand's culture and foreign causes would have made on the election had Giscard's reputation not been tarnished by scandal in Africa. In contrast to his sure handling of European affairs and Franco-German friendship, Giscard was vulnerable to the complexities of post-colonial Africa. His military interventions were concerned to stabilize established authorities against rivals, and in Zaïre, initially at the request of General Mobutu, they were successful, dramatically so at

Kolwezi in 1978. They resembled neo-colonialism more acutely in the Chad after a humiliating period of force and bargaining to rescue a French ethnologist Françoise Claustre: only the payment of a huge ransom secured her liberation. Over 1,000 French troops and ten Jaguar strike planes sent to the region in 1978 were forced to withdraw completely from the ex-colony in May 1980. In a separate entanglement Giscard was forced to back the overthrow of President Jean-Bedel Bokassa of the Central African Republic, whose dictatorship had become steadily more florid and imperious throughout the 1970s, culminating in a massacre of schoolchildren at Bangui in April 1979. The evicted Bokassa turned on the French President and released information that he had given him a package of diamonds when Giscard had been Minister of Finance under Pompidou. The satirical paper, *Le Canard enchaîné*, published evidence of the gift, valued at a million francs, on 10 October 1979, beginning a press round on Giscard in Africa, portrayed as a lover of big-game hunting and recipient of lavish hospitality. Much of it was parody, but the ludic side of politics was inflated by the ridicule and speculations, none of which Giscard deigned to answer. The scandal refused to go away: diamonds, it was quipped, were for ever.

Polarity and result

The comparative economic information which confronted voters in the two rounds on 26 April and 10 May 1981 suggested that since the second oil crisis of 1979 the franc had held up well against other European currencies despite its fall against the dollar, and that the pace of rising unemployment had been considerably less than in Britain and slower even than in Germany. But critical opinion, focused on the blighted areas of recession and the growing social gulf between those in and out of work, was far more affected by the high cost of living, and the disastrous effect of industrial cutbacks on dependent economic sectors. The acute unpopularity of Raymond Barre which continued throughout 1980 was a force in the electoral equation, and Giscard tried to maintain a dignified distance from his Prime Minister by optimistic speeches about the future. Like all the candidates, he acknowledged that unemployment was the most profound issue at stake but predicted that renewed growth would stimulate the labour market. Both Marchais and Mitterrand made specific, but different, promises that they would create thousands of new jobs in the public sector.

In the first round there were two major surprises. Marchais obtained scarcely more than 15 per cent of the vote, a loss of a 1.5 million votes compared to the Communist score of 1978: he trailed well behind

Mitterrand's 25.8 per cent. Giscard, too, polled less than expected, out-running Chirac by 10 per cent and heading the poll, but less than 3 per cent ahead of Mitterrand. Among the minority candidates, it was ecology that made most impact, with Brice Lalonde attracting over a million supporters of 'green' policies. It would be vital where these votes were transferred in round two, though far more questions were asked about possible abstentions by either Communists or Gaullists or both.

In the event, the confrontation on 10 May between Giscard and Mitterrand was not sabotaged by abstention on either side, nor was the result the repeat of 1974 that had seemed inevitable less than a few weeks before. After twenty-three years of continuous office the Gaullist and post-Gaullist hold on power was broken. Mitterrand was elected. Winning over 51 per cent of the vote, he became President of a Republic whose Gaullist construction he had denounced in 1964 as a 'permanent coup d'état'. His victory was a political sensation. Instantly Jack Lang brought musical equipment in abundance to the Place de la Bastille. Celebrations went on all night, not only in Paris and not only in predictable left-wing areas. Refuse collectors in the morning found empty champagne bottles in what they described as 'many surprising places'.

Mitterrand had said that he would dissolve the National Assembly and call new elections if he came to power. He promptly did so. His success in May brought a quite astonishing victory for the Socialists in June. Taken together, the Socialists and Communists lost 1.7 million of the votes cast for Mitterrand, but support for the outgoing majority fell by over 3.5 million and they retained only 157 seats out of their previous 286. By contrast the number of Socialist seats leapt from 117 to 288, an absolute majority in the Chamber which would not be numerically dependent on the support of the Communists whose seats were halved from eighty-eight to forty-four, wildly exaggerating the actual loss of votes, but continuing their visible decline as the major party of the left.

Pursuing the analysis of a fractured left by Annie Kriegel in 1978, many commentators stressed that the two elections of 1981 were less a victory of the left than the triumph of Mitterrand as personality and the Socialists as a newly recharged party of white-collar workers and professionals in the public sector. At the same time the fractures among those who voted for Giscard were held to be responsible for their dramatic loss of power and the absence of a decisive right-wing identity. Such interpretations were prescient in their emphasis on the fragmentation of politics, but they failed to register the widespread sense that Giscard in the last years of his Presidency had become steadily more identified as a non-consensual figure,

someone less of the centre than of the right (*de droite*), precipitating a consolidation of otherwise diverse opponents who had no difficulty in describing themselves as on the left (*de gauche*). Just as attitudes for and against the Popular Front in 1936 had been experienced by many as a re-run of the epic clash between republicans and clericals at the start of the century, so the contest between Giscard and Mitterrand was articulated by large sections of the public with references to the classic encounters of left and right in the 1930s. On the right there were fears of a Communist takeover on the back of a victory for Mitterrand which closely echoed those of 1936: for the left the nature of Giscard's and Barre's policies displayed the same indifference to the poor and unemployed that had been attributed to the *patronat* at the time of the great depression.

The heightened sense of left–right polarities in 1981 was at once anachronistic and contemporary. Mitterrand's manifesto, his '110 Propositions', reached back into the depths of left-wing consciousness across the century, but its grounding in the perceptions of the moment gave it a dialectic of its own. There was a sense that the left had found a revitalized socialist voice in its commitment to investment of state funds in public ownership. The antithesis was the sense that the right had adopted a newly dominant persona of liberal economics and market forces. Recast and reanimated, the left–right split of 1981 reached beyond economics into new, and old, areas of social conflict. So too did fragmentation; and so too did the pursuit of consensus. It was very much a sign of the times that *Le Nouvel Observateur* between the Mitterrand victory and the June elections carried the words: 'The left now occupy the territory of which Giscard dreamed: the centre.' It was one of countless reappraisals of political identity which characterize the last twenty years of the century.

2. Socialism in power: promise and problems

National elections, unsurprisingly, encourage national perspectives. Two decisive elections in two months made it easy to imagine that France could defeat the recession in its own way. The fact that the USA under Reagan and Britain under Thatcher were taking the opposite path was not considered a disqualification for Mitterrand's promise to 'break the discourse of private gain'. The new majority rejected arguments that the economy should be independent of politics: there was a pervasive confidence that an alternative mind-set would produce effective solutions. Jack Lang, appointed as Minister of Culture in the first Socialist government under Pierre Mauroy, had

already promised that at the bicentenary of the French Revolution in 1989 he would project a France 'animated by revolution'. He began on 21 May 1981 by orchestrating Mitterrand's investiture and the President's symbolic visit to the tombs of Jean Jaurès and Jean Moulin in the Panthéon, clutching a red rose. Gestural in words as in spectacle, Lang declared over a year later that on 10 May 1981 'the French had crossed the frontier from darkness into light'.[4]

'Changer la vie'

It was a massive programme of change that the new government undertook in 1981–2. Nothing less was expected. Pierre Mauroy, aged fifty-three, a teacher by training, Socialist mayor of Lille since 1973 with a solid, reassuring northern image, led a government which included Communists for the first time since May 1947, though they were given only four ministerial roles away from the hub of economic and political decision-making. It was what Mitterrand had promised, but there was irony in their inclusion, given the Communists' worst electoral showing since the war. Their presence accentuated the common readiness of the left to carry through its much-heralded 'rupture with capitalism'.

The most pressing commitment was to reflate the economy and create jobs. Over 8 billion francs were immediately pumped into family allowances, housing benefits, old-age pensions and the minimum wage, raising their levels significantly, while subsidies were provided for firms who took on more labour. By the end of September 1981 the government had its programme of nationalizations ready for legislation, a process which took a further five months of intricate constitutional negotiations before the bill became law on 11 February 1982. Nothing had shaken the belief expressed in the Common Programme of 1972 that further state control of major industrial companies, banks and insurance would 'break the grip of private profit' and by 1981 the recession was severe enough for nationalizations to be a popular agenda. On the one hand, state technocracy exercised through the Civil Service had been at the heart of the dysfunctional blocked society, diagnosed in *les années '68*. On the other, there was the long tradition of state initiatives and authority, which the anarchic thrust of students in 1968 had challenged but not destroyed. The state's welfare and educational provision, and its structural base in citizenship, still enjoyed respect and fostered expectation. This positive view of the state was mobilized in 1982 for the vast addition to state ownership of five major industrial companies, thirty-six banks and two financial houses (Suez and Paribas), along with

the purchase of majority holdings in other key industries. It could be seen as a functional strategy of crisis-management, but its doctrinal *élan* pointed to its long socialist pedigree, rooted in 1936 and beyond. A more consensual heritage lay in the nationalizations of 1945 which had not been rescinded by either de Gaulle or Giscard, and which featured the success story of Renault and the state ownership of the most widely used banks, the Banque Nationale de Paris, the Société Générale and the Crédit Lyonnais.

Industrial giants of glass production (Saint-Gobain), electronics (Thomson-Brandt) chemicals (Rhône-Poulenc), metals (Pechiney-Ugine-Kuhlmann), and electricity (Compagnie Générale d'Électricité) were added to the troubled steel producers (Usinor and Sacilor), all taken over fully by the state. Majority purchase of Dassault and Matra took the state further into the arms, aircraft and space sectors, and among the thirty-six banks there was a host of names, such as Worms and Rothschild, which had echoed down the years in ideological debate.

The election slogan of 1936, 'Make the rich pay', had resurfaced in 1981, and to that end the government introduced a 3 per cent wealth tax. On the other hand it acknowledged the right of nationalized companies and their shareholders to indemnity payments, and on top of these there were sub-stantial company debts to be regulated. It was soon estimated that the buyouts had cost over 43 billion francs. The reflationary intent behind such huge public expenditure was quickly dubbed 'Keynesianism in one country'. It referred equally to the increases in welfare payments and allowances, which Nicole Questiaux, the Minister of Social Security, believed France could and should afford. After wide consultation of trade unions and management, the retirement age was reduced on 4 February 1983 to sixty, bringing a revolution in individual and family lives. In retrospect it was seen as the most enduring improvement to the quality of life and the undisputed social success of the early Mitterrand years.

Continuity from the Popular Front of 1936 was underlined in three further ways: by the extension of annual paid holidays (*congés payés*) from four to five weeks; by the combative reassertion by Jean Auroux, Minister of Labour, of workers' rights to trade-union representation on company premises; and by the discussion on how much to reduce the forty-hour working week, fractured by the question, 'With or without loss of pay?'. Mitterrand himself insisted that a week of thirty-nine hours should be immediately enacted, without loss of earnings.

Presidential command was exercised sparingly in proportion to the sheer volume of legislation undertaken. Most resonant were Mitterrand's decisions, soon after his election, to reprieve Larzac from the threat of

military occupation and Plogoff from nuclear development, a recognition that the local campaigns had been nationally effective, striking chords of sympathy for regional interests which the Socialists composed into a major, if low-key, programme of decentralization. A sweeping change in local authority structures was initiated. The executive power of prefects, except in policing, was decentralized to the presidents and committees of the elected local councils, at *commune*, *département* and regional level. Local budgets were to be controlled by the localities themselves, and the regions gained power over key aspects of town and country planning. The changes were enacted piecemeal over more than a decade, and although boundaries of competence between regions and *départements* were often unclear, and many local decisions still had to pass through Paris, the programme was widely accepted as one of necessity and good sense. In a pre-election speech in Brittany Mitterrand had endorsed 'the right to be different' (*droit à la différence*), soon to become the most controversial slogan in a still dominantly unicultural France. The context of his speech was regionalism, not cultural diversity in general, and once elected he kept a wary eye on anything which would weaken the state, but in the Socialist programme of decentralization there was a qualitative change of tone from that of previous governments. Cultural specificities were more openly recognized, and links with Jack Lang's Ministry of Culture were evident in the stimulus, for example, given to regional cinema by a commission headed by Jean-Denis Bredin.

The cultural and economic institution of the family farm was approached with new interest by the Socialist Minister of Agriculture, Édith Cresson. Conscious of the hold that the big cereal producers had over the main farming representatives within the Fédération Nationale des Syndicats d'Exploitants Agricoles (FNSEA), she set out to elevate the role of the peasant producers in smaller farms. New structures were envisaged for production and marketing of fruit, milk, vegetables, pigs and poultry, the struggling sectors of French regional agriculture. Underpinned by the misogyny of male farmers who regarded Cresson's appointment as a sign that the Socialists were not taking agriculture seriously, the FNSEA resented being sidelined. Their leader, François Guillaume, brought the countryside to Paris on 23 March 1982 in the form of 100,000 protesting farmers, complete with tractors. After a decade of relative prosperity they accused the government of increasing the costs of production, and called also for pressure on Britain to stop its obstruction of European prices fixed by the Common Agricultural Policy (CAP). Cresson persevered in her tactics: they were seen, even by many of the family farmers, as divisive. She was replaced in 1983 by Michel Rocard.

Rights

The humanitarian drive of the Socialist reforms was marked by the abolition
of the death penalty on 18 September 1981, finally bringing France into
line with the rest of Western Europe, and by an active policy to normalize
the situation of immigrant workers. Mitterrand's repeated invocation
of human rights (*les droits de l'homme*) during his candidacy had been
matched by visits to immigrant hostels. Alone among the leading candidates
to suggest that settled immigrants might well be given voting rights in local
elections, he was welcomed with optimism by pro-immigrant and anti-racist
organizations. The positive reputation of the Communist Party and Georges
Marchais in immigrant matters had been tarnished by extensive media
coverage of the 'bulldozer affair' at Vitry-sur-Seine to the south-east of
Paris at the end of December 1980, when the local Communist municipality
was accused of stopping the transfer of Malian workers to a hostel in Vitry
by a partial demolition of the building. Counter-accusations were thrown
back at the right-wing mayor of neighbouring Saint-Maur-des-Fossés for
his role in the transfer, but the taunts of xenophobia levelled at the PCF
were sufficiently damaging for the party to stage an autocriticism on the
issue after the 1981 elections, leading to a full endorsement of the government's new legislation.

The measures on immigration suppressed the incentives to repatriation
introduced by Lionel Stoleru under Giscard in 1977 and introduced equal
rights of association, permitting immigrant membership of trade unions
and political parties. Still further, illegal immigrants were offered the possibility to declare themselves and take out residence and work permits:
130,000 did so. There was no attempt to reverse the ban of 1974 on
further immigration: the measures were directed at those already in place,
humanizing their lives. Hundreds, and soon thousands, of local associations
were launched to pursue the welfare, leisure and cultural interests of people
of immigrant origin. Many of these received subsidies from the immigrants'
original countries, notably Portugal, enabling the parent languages to be
studied, but public funding from the French Ministry of Social Affairs was
also critical to their success. A new visibility and confidence of immigrants
were evident. Media coverage of widespread strikes across the whole automobile industry from 1981 to 1984 brought a close-up of immigrant protests. In the Renault works at Flins and Billancourt, workers of recent
immigrant origin constituted over 50 per cent of the workforce, and over
70 per cent at the Citroën plant at Aulnay and the Talbot works at Poissy.
Unable to escape from the ironic category of 'specialized workers' (OS –

ouvriers spécialisés) they were confined to alienating, repetitive functions on the assembly line and were effectively barred from further training and promotion. The strike in early summer 1982 at the repressive plant at Aulnay in the Saint-Denis area north of Paris, where Moroccan workers were subject to constant humiliation, brought major concessions from the management. In a different climate a year and a half later the strike at Talbot-Poissy left a bitter after-taste among the OS workers, who rejected trade union negotiations and occupied the factory in pursuit of their claims.

The brief for radical change saw the creation of a public Broadcasting Authority (Haute Autorité de la Communication Audiovisuelle), finally removing direct government control of radio and television, and embracing a future diversity between public and private in all areas of audio-visual communications, including a musical galaxy of independent local radio stations, restricted only by frequency and radius. In essence, if not entirely in realization, this was what the technicians and broadcasters of the ORTF had been striking for in 1968. Reforms during the 1970s had only partially answered their case against control and intrusion. By the time the new bill was passed at the end of July 1982, there was a discernible ebbing of popular support for the Socialist government: in this context, the freedom given to broadcasting was acknowledged as a significant surrender of political power.

The historic creation of the first full Ministry of Women's Rights under Yvette Roudy was no less indicative of radical intentions. Still further, a woman, Édith Cresson, had been appointed Minister of Agriculture, upsetting assumed gender roles at their core, and a third senior appointment of a woman minister put Nicole Questiaux at the head of Social Security. Mitterrand had promised Roudy her role and title in 1978 should he and the PS ever come to power: it was more combative than the title held by Françoise Giroud under Giscard, limited to 'women's condition'. Roudy had stood firmly by majority party decisions against breakaway feminist tendencies, but her own political feminism was not in doubt: her secretariat within the party had published a summary of Socialist aims for women's rights, which featured women as 'les émigrées de l'intérieur', in line with feminist discourse on women's exclusion.

Publications backed by the Ministry spread the ideas of Olympe de Gouges, adopted name of Marie Gouze, whose feminism in the late eighteenth century and criticisms of Robespierre and Marat led to her death at the guillotine in 1793, accused of being an 'unnatural woman' who 'wanted to be a man of state'. Her career and her 'Declaration of the Rights of Woman and Citizen' in 1791 were positioned by feminists of the 1970s

and 1980s as a central text of sexual equality, at the same time as anti-racist groups placed racial equality at the heart of civil society. This two-pronged elaboration of 'rights' vastly increased the parameters of the Socialist 'changement', moving it well outside the sphere of economics and creating binding links with long-established organizations of civil liberties.

Roudy's Ministry was put squarely on the political map by Mitterrand on International Women's Day, 8 March 1982, with the announcement of seventeen measures to achieve women's 'autonomy, equality and dignity', and it was Roudy's successful piloting of a bill on sexual equality at the workplace (*égalité professionnelle*) in July 1983 which gave her Ministry real bite in working practices. Recalcitrant firms found their own ways of avoiding the bill's insistence on equal opportunities, training and pay, but Ministry officials showed tenacity in carrying the bill to business and industry, stressing its modernizing and enabling features and giving pro-active aid to firms preparing their 'equality plans'.[5] Consultation centres, created in over 100 towns, spread knowledge of women's rights, and the Ministry sponsored the visibility of contraception in a publicity drive, reaching millions for the first time through television. Roudy later claimed over 70 per cent public support for the Ministry's actions, and when Chirac abolished it on coming to power in 1986, this was seen by many women as confirmation that it had been disturbingly effective.

In a more private way the decriminalization of homosexuality marked an equally effective modernization of attitudes. Carried through in 1982, it rescinded the Vichy and Gaullist laws which had marked out the practising homosexual as a 'scourge' in society, against whom the forces of 'civiliz-ation' were called on to struggle.[6] Vichy had criminalized any homosexual practice involving youths up to the age of twenty-one, and after the war reformers struggled to obtain a lower age of consent. On the political left Sartre had used homosexuality as a metaphor for the attraction which had motivated collaboration during the Occupation, and there had been little public or left-wing protest at the continued severity of punishment for homosexual acts, reimposed in 1945 and reinforced in 1960, in both cases under the auspices of de Gaulle.

The homosexuality of well-known writers, from Gide to Montherlant, Cocteau and Mauriac, barely affected the climate of ignorance and silence within which the repressive laws operated, although the humanist and literary life of the élite homosexual club and journal *Arcadie*, nurtured by André Baudry, achieved a relatively privileged tolerance by public authori-ties. In the radicalization of sexual politics in *les années '68*, a Homosexual and Revolutionary Front geared itself to action in 1971, no less hostile to

the norms of patriarchy and moral convention than the feminism which broke the taboos about abortion. The permissive and commercialized attitudes towards sex during the 1970s featured the first homosexual nightclubs and bars, discreetly known to the international gay community. By 1982 a Gay Pride march was possible in Paris as the punitive laws were withdrawn, and in 1983 the journal *Homophonies* gave space to a pioneer look at acceptance of gay and lesbian couples, a perspective on sexuality and patterns of social behaviour which gradually over fifteen years, and then rapidly, etched itself into public consciousness.

Rigour and disenchantment

The politics of the Socialist vision in 1981 lacked nothing in self-belief. The government declared it was in tune with a widespread popular desire for something different: inertia, said more than one columnist, was now on the side of the fundamental change (*le changement*) envisaged originally at the Liberation. Every government department had an agenda of political action. Above all, the economy was held to be at the disposition of political will and direction. It was not that economics were treated lightly, but rather that the wing of the Socialist Party urging restraint, identified with Michel Rocard, was given a fringe position. This was equally apparent in the placing of Jacques Delors within the cabinet. Delors had been an integral part of the 'new society' of Chaban-Delmas in 1969; he had made a much publicized turn to the Socialist Party in 1974, and with Mitterrand's backing became a European deputy in 1979. Appointed Minister of the Economy and Finance by Pierre Mauroy, Delors was nevertheless placed low in the cabinet hierarchy. The ambivalence of his position became evident in the autumn of 1981 when the predicted disapproval of the financial markets forced a devaluation of the franc. Opposition from business and finance had always been anticipated: their exercise of power over Herriot in 1925 and Blum in 1936 was embedded in the folklore of the left. Yet financial viability was also an issue within the government and Delors had cautioned against excessive public expenditure. He followed the devaluation with renewed calls for financial rigour, viewing with dismay the inexorable rise of the budget deficit for 1982.

It was by borrowing that the government's measures would be initially funded, in the expectation of a renewal of growth and an upward curve in jobs and markets. Everything turned on the success of reflation, but also on the flexibility of the European Monetary System to sustain a franc under relentless pressure. Delors pointed to his desperate efforts to preserve a

European footing and an international outlook. They contrasted with the growing readiness of Jean-Pierre Chevènement as Minister of Research, Technology and Industry to argue that only by quitting the European system and protecting French industry from economic liberalism would the Socialist 'rupture' succeed.

The substantial returns from reflation did not materialize. More money improved the lives of thousands living on the edge of poverty, but also boosted inflation and imports: the budget of Laurent Fabius careered further into the red, and the trade deficit plumbed record depths. The number of unemployed did not drop. In a year from March 1981 it grew by over 300,000. In May 1982 it broke the 2 million mark, considered inconceivable a year earlier. The dramatic decline of the franc against the dollar recalled its weakness after each of the two World Wars. Political fallout was evident in cantonal elections in March when the opposition celebrated a partial return from the ignominy of 1981. Faced with a second devaluation in June, Delors argued that if the economy could not be made to turn round by political will, then financial rigour had to be applied to stop the country sliding into a currency free-fall. Pierre Mauroy was sensitive to his arguments of working within European monetary constraints and agreed to impose a price and wage freeze. It brought a temporary slowing of the unemployment rate, but as a political retreat it could not be camouflaged. Angry trade unionists argued that Delors was not reflecting the hostility of the financial markets, but encouraging it. Chevènement continued to imagine a solution beyond the constraints.

Mitterrand's victory as President had been at the origin of the expectations of 1981. He had personally announced the huge programme of Socialist change. In the face of financial resistance to the changes, people increasingly asked what kind of socialist he would now prove to be. He had to provide an answer in March 1983. Hard-fought municipal elections, with a high turnout of voters, revoked the national verdict of 1981 and gave a majority to the right with over 53 per cent of the vote in the medium-sized towns, and 58 per cent in towns with a population of more than 100,000. Jacques Chirac's triumph in Paris was total, his list of candidates succeeding in every *arrondissement* in the city, although in Marseille the Socialists just held on to the power base of the Minister of the Interior, Gaston Defferre, whose name was successfully identified with the measures of decentralization. Elsewhere, major Socialist and Communist losses confirmed popular uncertainty about the left's declared break with capitalism. The mood was registered by most of the press as disenchantment. After a week of hesitations and a third devaluation Mitterrand decided that policy

should move towards Delors. The 'rupture' was put into reverse. A Delors austerity plan was launched, with a severe curbing of public expenditure: it tacitly accepted the criticisms of international finance. With calculated irony, Raymond Barre said that he found much of it to his liking. He too had favoured a strong franc. From 1983 it became almost a Socialist obsession, keeping the franc strong within the European Monetary System, keeping inflation low and relying more and more on trade within Europe to stimulate economic growth and bring down unemployment. Trade with European partners did increase, noticeably. But more jobs did not follow.

Within the year Pierre Mauroy's reshuffled government embarked on restructuring the nationalized shipyards, coal-mines, steelworks and car industry, cutting the workforce and rescaling output to meet lower demand. Severe job losses seemed only the most obvious human cost of this process of rationalization: it was the planned closure of a way of life for whole towns and villages over the next five to ten years which brought embittered cries of betrayal. The restructuring indicated even more clearly than the austerity measures that the old-style Socialist, Pierre Mauroy, was in effect if not in word adopting the practices for which the left had so roundly condemned the Giscard–Barre regime. Mitterrand, impressed by a visit to Silicon Valley and envisaging France as the spearhead of an electronic future for Europe, made the theme of modernization explicit in 1984. It had already been used by Rocard in agriculture, in the realization that neither the government nor Europe could afford to continue subsidizing surplus produce. In the name of modernization he signalled that production quotas proposed from Brussels would have to be accepted by the farming industry, especially for milk, though he was wary enough not to announce any grand projects of agricultural restructuring. Mechanization and productivity gains in agriculture needed little window-dressing: in the statistics for 1983 it was estimated that over five times more people were now fed by the average farmer's output than in 1960.

Mauroy, having endorsed the ideological reversal, resigned in July 1984. Mitterrand appointed his own protégé of the 1970s, the young ENA graduate Laurent Fabius, who had built a rapid political career in Rouen and was Budget Minister in 1981. From his own deficit budgeting and ideas of leaving the European Monetary System he had veered round to the financial rigour of Jacques Delors, whose influence on the new direction of the Socialist government was profound, before he moved away from French politics and accepted the Presidency of the European Commission from January 1985.

Salvaging innovation

At thirty-seven Fabius was the youngest-ever Prime Minister in French republican history. His very adherence to the Socialist Party in the 1970s, instead of Giscard's UDF, had promoted the image of the PS as the up-and-coming, modern party, attractive to young, well-heeled graduates from ENA looking for a political career. Modernization in social and political terms had been a potent theme of *le changement*: its different ideological connotations when applied to financial, economic and industrial policy made it a difficult concept for Mitterrand to sell to stalwarts of the left, but it proved popular with the wider public. In pursuit of modernization, Fabius was even prepared to lower taxes and to risk further unemployment for long-term gains from a leaner, more technological and competitive industry in international markets. No Communists were in the government. It was a wholesale rethinking of the economic policy of 1981.

The about-turn of March 1983, continued in the anti-inflationary measures of the Fabius government from 1984 to 1986, raised endless barbed questions about the identity of the Socialists in power and the meaning of Mitterrand's Presidency. The only logic in the *volte-face* was a paradoxical one which stressed the primacy of politics at the very moment that the economy appeared to have forced the President's hand. With a mixture of unhurried response and survivalist agility, Mitterrand gave the impression of carefully measuring the extent of political adjustment that was necessary. From the political will of a triumphalist state socialism, the emphasis was moved to the shifting political needs of the day. The 'rupture' had not carried the people. Mitterrand appeared responsive to this political message, although his popularity slumped badly. It was the start of his highly ambivalent Presidential image as the wily democrat, adaptable to political exigency, cynic and realist by turns, slipping easily into realpolitik but not without a touch of nostalgia for the socialist experiment he had abandoned.

Fabius was credited with something approaching a salvage operation. His youth encouraged talk of 'the Fabius effect' as the economy showed a moderate improvement due to control of inflation and a fall in oil prices. An upturn in purchasing power for those in work contrasted with growing discontent at the pressure on wages and the continued rise in unemployment. The trumpeted successes of Reaganite economics in the USA provided a backdrop to the Socialist retreat in France. The powerful discourse of international market forces, marginalized in the expectations of 1981, was given increasing credibility in the mainstream political press and was

reflected in the Prime Minister's new identity for the government. If some ideological commitment to socialism remained it was not associated with Fabius, and the move of the PCF and the CGT into active opposition underlined the final collapse of the Common Programme of 1972, already consigned to atavistic memory only. The tenth anniversary of Pompidou's death was the occasion for a nostalgic poll in *L'Express*, revealing a dramatic decline in the sense of well-being since the last days of the *trente glorieuses*. In the following year a cautious business optimism returned, though in macro-economic terms the state was still heavily in debt and growth was minimal. If Fabius was mockingly dubbed by the right as 'the acceptable face of socialism', meaning that he was not socialist at all, the irony was not lost on those who drew attention to the new poverty on the streets in the visible increase in begging and homelessness: this was the unacceptable face of austerity.

It was several years before the shifts from Mauroy to Fabius were put into a longer French perspective. At the time the emphasis was on retreat from the attempted 'rupture' of 1981, on the failure of the experiment. The rigour of Delors was seen by those who approved as a return to economic realism. But the modernization equated with Fabius had innovative rhythms of its own, echoing those of the Giscard–Barre years, and setting up a counterpoint to all the various forms of state control, planning and central-ism by which the economy had been directed from the Liberation through to, and including, the rupture of 1981. Under Fabius there was a discernible cession of powers from the state to the market. It remains a question of opinion as to whether this was envisaged as a major shift of policy by Fabius and Mitterrand or whether they stumbled into it through necessity.

Mitterrand repeatedly told the press that he regretted nothing about 1981–2 and that he was still a convinced socialist. He was adept at talking to young people, pointing to the numerous schemes to retrain workers or to launch job programmes for the young unemployed. They were decried by *L'Humanité* as a mere safety net for a relaunched capitalism, but despite a clash of workers with police at Ivry in June 1985 and a series of strikes during the year, affecting the docks, railways, urban transport, the car and aircraft industries and naval shipyards, industrial disputes only underlined the progressive decline of CGT membership and the weakness of a work-force in the context of over 2.3 million unemployed. The speed with which the Socialists had abandoned their ambitions of 1981 encouraged a new level of scepticism about party politics in general, which spilled over into doubts about all long-established political and social institutions. More and more people found ways of expressing themselves through issues rather

than party or union commitment. There was an upbeat here as well as disillusion and fear.

3. Issue politics

Private schooling ('l'école libre')

The political left might have escaped some of the disillusion of the electorate if Mitterrand's '110 Propositions' had not been presented as if they were a fulfilment of all that was progressive in the twentieth century. It was only when the momentum of 1981 began to go into reverse that their full intent became clear. Among the propositions was a promise to produce a 'single public sector of national education, unified and secular (*laïque*)' which would put nineteenth-century state education back on track by absorbing private, dominantly Catholic, schooling (*l'école libre*). Since the Michel Debré law of 1959, private schools had been subsidized by the state on condition that they would teach at least a common curriculum. It had been a working compromise between *catholique* and *laïque*, but the pressure groups for a fully secular education continued to see in the expanding private sector, which catered for 16 per cent of schoolchildren, a focus of social privilege and a threat to the *laïcité* of the state. In the course of 1983 the Education Minister, Alain Savary, much respected for his Free French past and his negotiating skills in the creation of the new Socialist Party, first brought more student representation on to university committees in a bill on higher education, and then endeavoured to frame an acceptable bill on state and private education which would relieve the worst fears of the Catholic schools and yet appease the more militant secular voices in the Chamber.

Demonstrations in support of *l'école libre* in Bordeaux, Lyon, Rennes and Lille culminated in a gathering of over 550,000 at Versailles on 4 March 1984, to which the supporters of state education replied with rallies across the country on 25 April. Mauroy and Mitterrand tacked between different sets of reservations and amendments and the bill began to slip out of Savary's grasp. Nothing prepared them for the dénouement of the public campaign. On 24 June, just a week after the opposition list of Simone Veil had carried the European elections, Catholic organizations brought between 1 and 2 million partisans of private education from all parts of France to Paris, to stage the biggest protest demonstration that the capital had ever seen. Traditional dress from the provinces gave festive backing to regional flags, and for twelve hours banner after banner proclaiming 'Vive

l'école libre' converged on the Place de la Bastille, vestigial terrain of the political left. It was a public opinion coup of sensational breadth and depth, judged by *Le Monde* in retrospect to be a turning point in the first septennate of François Mitterrand.[7]

It shocked by its size, but even more by its monopoly of claims to freedom, facing down the Jacobinism of the ardent secularists who had shown little concern for the nuances of the original Savary bill. The self-assurance of the demonstration presented an image of individual liberties riding high against the state. While *Le Figaro* hailed the rally as historic, it was equally its acute sense of opportunity which struck the press. A vulnerable Mitterrand withdrew the bill, causing the resignation not only of Savary but also of Pierre Mauroy, whose deep unpopularity by June 1984 was the inverse of the confidence placed in him three years before.

Party politics were represented in the campaigns, Chirac conspicuous in the ranks of the *école libre*, and the Socialist Party secretary, Lionel Jospin, in those of the *action laïque*. In *Libération* the marchers of 24 June were described as a newly emergent phenomenon, a 'people of the right', but there was much analysis of the amorphous and even divergent political loyalties that could be found among the proponents of private education. Parental and teaching pressure groups lay behind both sides, and within the dispute over state or private, Catholic or secular, questions about education as a whole were at issue, reflecting several years of public anxiety about its form and content and a disparate concern about overcrowding on the one hand and selective intake on the other. Educational passions could have been expressed on the streets at any time, but the context of the government's reversal of its economic programme in 1983–4 was all-important. State control, as seen from any direction, was in retreat, while individual and sectional freedoms grew visibly in stature. Mitterrand's reaction showed how susceptible he was to this parade of rights and liberties. What made it a turning point was that it confirmed Mitterrand in his Presidental shift from political programming to political response. He moved towards a search for consensus. His main challenge, and arguably his identifying characteristic as President, was the manipulation of this new direction in his politics so that it appeared positive and not merely reactive.

Ecology

Mitterrand's response to the *école libre* march was a concession to the opposition and not an attempt to assimilate private education into his own political framework, whatever commentators made of his own childhood

experience of Catholic schooling. As such the response differed radically from the sympathetic gestures to issue politics represented by his reprieve of Larzac and Plogoff. As with the *ligues* which had impacted on French politics from the Dreyfus Affair to the end of the 1930s, issue politics in the last third of the twentieth century reflected both the politicization of society and a refusal to leave the issues to the established political parties. They made fragmentation of politics into a virtue and flourished on any rise in the unpopularity of politicians. Ecological campaigners had made their mark in this way, by their pluralism and independence during the 1970s.

Several distinct groups disputed the leadership of the ecologist-Green movement, the oldest being the Amis de la Terre (Friends of the Earth) founded in 1970 by local activists with a national figurehead in Brice Lalonde. The Amis disapproved of the decision by the Verts-Parti Écologiste, which was strongest in Paris and the Alsace region, to use the word 'party' with its conventional significance, but they continued to stand in elections as a broad-based Confederation which looked for ways of making a distinctive political impact. In the Presidential campaign of 1974 René Dumont stood as an ecologist, gaining only 1.3 per cent of the votes, but despite such marginalization at the polls, the ideas of the ecologists attracted public support throughout the crisis on the Breton coasts in 1978 caused by the oil pollution from the *Amoco Cadiz*. Issue politics were of that conjunctural nature. The sympathy shown by Mitterrand for the issues of Larzac and Plogoff was an overture to the ecologists, carrying the expectation that they would rally to the left in the second round of elections. This was disputed by many ecologist candidates during the municipal elections of 1983 who saw the pull of the left as a trap to marginalize ecological issues by assimilation. Their slogan 'Neither left nor right but forwards' proclaimed their dedication to autonomy, but they could not convince the public that their policies were coherently distinctive.

The heterogeneous ecologists and the small structured party, the Verts (Greens), formed in 1984, campaigned on decentralization, but that was identified in the public mind with the Socialist achievements of 1981–2. Other issues such as Third World sympathies in foreign policy and work-sharing and urban parks at home were insufficient to make up a forceful programme. Observers suggested that Mitterrand's bold gesture to the anti-nuclear lobby at Plogoff had paradoxically been followed by a growing public acceptance of nuclear power. Together, these factors in the early 1980s deprived ecologists of a single headline-catching issue. Their total municipal support even marked a decline from 1977, particularly in the larger towns.

The Soviet catastrophe of Chernobyl in 1986 spilt over into politics across the world. The Verts were quickly responsive, but the internal quarrels among the different strands of political ecology failed to abate. Their commitment to grass-roots democracy entailed a dysfunctional suspicion of all leadership. It was not until their conference at Lille in November 1993 that the Verts abandoned their non-aligned policy and began electoral negotiations with the Socialist left. The search for an effective left alliance brought Dominique Voynet to the head of the party. Aged thirty-five in 1993, trained in medicine as an anaesthetist, dedicated to family planning, a Green municipal councillor for Dole in the Jura since 1989, and a left-wing founder member of the Verts, Voynet combined ecology with feminism and succeeded in talking of the Verts as a naturally plural movement without weakening her bargaining power. Pulling the Greens definitively to the left took Voynet and the party into the framework of orthodox politics. Much of its membership, drawn from naturalists and ecologists, Third Worldists, pacifists, humanists, dissidents from the PCF and fractions of the left, still favoured the adrenaline of issue politics and the mechanisms of autonomy.

Feminism

In the aftermath of Simone Veil's abortion law of 1974 the absence of a comparable motivating campaign was felt acutely among feminists, although the law had to defeat a resurgent opposition in 1979 when it was renewed. As an issue it had almost defined the women's movement in public opinion, and its resonance in the media was not easily replicated. The tenth anniversary of the Veil law in 1984 induced a round of feminist self-assessments, not all celebratory but not all racked, as some commentators asserted, with the anguish of decline and fragmentation. Women were much photographed on the *école libre* march, especially in regional costume, but the old taunt by inter-war Radicals that women were vassals of the parish priest no longer had any political currency. In 1980 the Académie Française finally surrendered its all-male pretensions by electing the first woman, the novelist Marguerite Yourcenar, who took the opportunity to point to other women who ought to have been elected before her. Yet the myth of women's vassal status under male supremacy, effectively exposed in Colette Audry's *Collection Femme* in the 1960s, was still a referent in public rhetoric, whenever issues of sexual equality were raised.

The tenacious deconstructing of that myth and the provision of in-depth resources on women's rights brought the women's movement few headlines but caused a seismic shift within the all-important sphere of information.

Looking back in 1984 over ten years of activity in Marseille, Jeanne Mazel outlined the battles won by the pioneer Centre of Feminist Orientation, Documentation and Information (CODIF) which she had founded from her base in adult education. Her preface to a catalogue of CODIF's holdings starts with the centre's inauguration by the Socialist mayor, Gaston Defferre, but there is no implication that she identified feminism with any political party nor that she claimed any culmination of the women's movement in the Ministry of Women's Rights set up by the Socialists in 1981. The question of political alignment was as deeply contentious for feminists as for ecologists. It had come to a head in 1978.

Apart from Simone Veil and Françoise Giroud, it was Arlette Laguiller who made women in politics a talking point in 1974, less because of the 600,000 votes she received as a Presidential candidate than for her visibility on television, where she spoke for oppressed workers in the name of the Trotskyist group, Lutte Ouvrière (LO). Aged thirty-four, a typist in the Crédit Lyonnais, she was dubbed by the press as a smiling, female Saint-Just, denouncing injustices in the workplace. In the sexual politics of the LO, the choice of a woman as national representative was no accident: it was a forceful decision that women's oppression should be stressed, though within the Marxist dialectic of the class struggle.

In the sexual politics of feminism, however, Arlette Laguiller was controversial. Should feminists represent political parties or act autonomously? The legislative elections of 1978 brought this issue to a head within the mainstream left. In both the Communist (PCF) and the Socialist (PS) Parties, feminist tendencies were treated as divisive because they might encourage other social groups to claim special status. To this they replied that they were not just 'any social group' but 50 per cent of citizens: 'Un homme sur deux est une femme.' The vexed question in the PS was the gender imbalance in the selection of candidates, with the feminist tendency pressing for parity (*parité*) for women, but only offered a small quota by the majority at party conferences, a majority which included the votes of those Socialist women who opted for party consensus as the most effective route to women in power.

It was to these women, Yvette Roudy at their head, that Mitterrand would turn, but Presidential appointments were a well-charted exercise of power, as Giscard had shown in 1974. It was doubted by Choisir, the vanguard group formed over the abortion issue, whether any such appointments from above would change political structures to accommodate feminism. Choisir took the autonomous route and put up forty-three candidates of its own in 1978, with Gisèle Halimi to the fore, though without any success.

Arlette Laguiller stood again for President in 1981 and marginally improved her vote, higher than the score of de Gaulle's ex-Prime Minister, Michel Debré, and well ahead of two other women candidates, Marie-France Garaud, who had been one of Pompidou's most eminent advisers, and Huguette Bouchardeau, leader of the women's section in the PSU. After the June elections, women made up less than 6 per cent of the Chamber of Deputies, an increase of under 2 per cent since 1978. A renewed feminist scepticism with political structures set in, which fuelled criticism of Roudy's Ministry, particularly in 1983–4 when Mitterrand looked to the family for a consensual area of policy and encouraged a campaign to increase the birth rate. Feminists committed to working in local refuges for battered women had welcomed the Ministry's support and subsidies, but criticized its silence in the face of the President's rhetoric.

The Socialist ideological retreat from 1981 was interpreted by much of the press as a sign that confrontational feminism also had run its course. Roudy's Ministry was seen to have brought the political visibility of women to a minor crescendo: contraception and legalized abortion had already whittled away the Catholic-inspired, but conventional, equation of woman with mother, which had allowed public archivists since the nineteenth century to catalogue women under 'family'. Employment opportunities for women in the new technology, matched by government scholarships for girls in science, brought modernization and the Fabius effect into feminist debates.

In this greater pluralism of gender-related politics, divisions on the issue of women's political assimilation intensified. A greater diversity of feminist theory was evident at conferences, with the axis of interest shifting away from the dominant concern for universalism and 'equality' towards the reinvigorated concept of 'difference', drawing on the theories of the practising psychoanalyst Luce Irigaray, the writings of Hélène Cixous who had founded the Centre d'Études Féminines in 1977, and the linguistic research of Julia Kristeva whose work on subjectivity in literature and history encouraged feminists to talk about the singularity of women.

The plurality of ideas and strategies was variably registered as a strength or a weakness. Simone de Beauvoir died on 14 April 1986, aged seventy-eight. In the six years since Sartre's death she had published their correspondence, and much of the huge media coverage of her death was directed towards the details of their relationship. Her famed parity with male contemporaries such as Paul Nizan, Sartre himself and Raymond Aron was shown to have given *Le Deuxième sexe* the intellectual prestige which feminists the world over celebrated in their extensive tributes, recognizing

it as the most persuasive theoretical voice arguing for a gender-free society.

Followers and critics argued about the meaning de Beauvoir gave to women as 'other' in *Le Deuxième sexe*, and within the conflicting strands of feminism in the 1980s it was her symbolic status as an egalitarian and universalist that was most at issue. In the early 1970s she had reconsidered the core of revolutionary thinking in her epic study, and declared to *Le Nouvel Observateur* that women could no longer depend on a socialist revolution for their emancipation, and that they should 'take their destiny in their own hands'.[8] It was a public way of declaring herself a feminist, embattled for equality. Shortly before she died she yet again rejected feminists who argued for a theory of 'difference', one of whom, Antoinette Fouque, used a small corner of the twelve obituary pages in *Libération* to claim that de Beauvoir had personified feminism of the twentieth century, whereas the twenty-first century, only fifteen years away, called for a recognition of pluralism and the 'fertile differences . . . which start with gender'.[9] Challenging as this was, other feminists stressed the danger in dating Simone de Beauvoir in this way, as if the battles for sexual equality were over. The danger was apparent when Jacques Chirac, who had just become Prime Minister in March 1986, saluted her memory in terms of marking a point in history, judging that her death underlined the end of an era. He had already decided that a Ministry of Women's Rights was no longer necessary.

Multi-ethnicity and 'les Beurs'

Many leading feminists were engaged in the promotion of racial equality. Simone de Beauvoir and Huguette Bouchardeau were among signatories of the intellectual manifesto against the expulsion of immigrants in 1980–81 entitled, 'No to a France of apartheid!' In 1983 Françoise Gaspard, who had pressured the Socialist Party on parity for women, was prominent as the ex-Socialist mayor of Dreux in the launch of the 'Marche des Beurs'. Bouchardeau joined it at Amiens.

The march from town to town across France was staged by young people of immigrant North African origin from October to December 1983. It ended in Paris where marchers were warmly received by President Mitterrand. Initiated in Lyon, the march for equality and against racism, labelled by the press as the 'Marche des Beurs', took the marches of Gandhi and Martin Luther King as models: peaceful, educative manifestations of racial visibility, asserting rights and equality. The word 'Beur' had emerged in the 1970s within the second generation of immigrants from the Maghreb (mainly Algeria, Morocco and Tunisia). It was an assertion of identity, a

backslang corruption of the pejorative term 'Arabe'. Projected in 1981 by Radio Beur, one of the first new radio stations legalized by the Socialist government, the youthful Beur culture had entered politics through struggle against deportations in the Stoleru era. A hunger strike in Lyon in April 1981, co-organized with the immigrant communities by Catholic priest Christian Delorme and Protestant pastor Jean Costil, caught the public's imagination and forced Raymond Barre to suspend the planned expulsions. The march for equality, confronting the racism of the Front National, stepped up the momentum and was chronicled from day to day by one of the marchers, Bouzid Kara, who registered, to his own surprise, the multiracial welcome across the country. His account, *La Marche*, became one of a wealth of texts, films, strip cartoons (*bandes dessinées*), musical and theatrical events which expressed the cultural politics of difference and equality in the mid-1980s.

The initial surge of popular sympathy for Beur equality and presence reflected the enthusiasm in 1981 for an expansive and inclusive cultural identity for modern France. The march allowed the Beurs to be seen as a youthful distillation of two cultures, eager for integration into French society but bringing their own infusion of Maghrebi origin. Its success led much of public opinion to give a positive meaning to interbreeding, *le métissage*, recast as a creative mix of races and cultures through a consciousness of past and present French origins in all parts of Europe and the Mediterranean. Over 700 artists, intellectuals and political personalities backed the march with a statement indicating the ethnic pluralism of France. The popular youth slogan, 'We are all *métis*' echoed the inclusive student slogans of 1968, and in 1984 *Le Nouvel Observateur* imagined the future as one of 'la France multiculturelle'.[10] It was a vision and use of words which became the most bitterly contested issue in the last two decades of the century and well beyond.

The difficulty of restaging a first-time success, and an index of the rapidly changing political context, was the weaker effect a year later of 'Convergence 84', a second 'march', this time on mopeds, of five groups starting from Toulouse, Marseille, Brest, Strasbourg and Lille which encountered less enthusiasm, partly because of internal dissensions in its aims of bringing all ethnic minorities together, without any buttressing by French religious or political organizations. It contrasted with the instant media impact of SOS-Racisme, founded in November 1984 by a group of *gauchistes* headed by Harlem Désir, Julien Dray and Didier François, with the express policy of mobilizing action against the racism of the extreme right. Adding to the pressure of the Ligue des Droits de l'Homme dating from the Dreyfus

Affair, and the pro-peace movement against racism and antisemitism (MRAP), born in the Occupation and reconstituted after the war, the runaway success of SOS-Racisme was Désir's anti-racist slogan 'Touche pas à mon pote' ('Hands off my mate'). It was carried on an outstretched, hand-shaped badge which sold in millions, mostly to French supporters not only of anti-racism but of *métissage*.

Harlem Désir, a philosophy student in Paris and the son of two teachers, grew up in a working-class suburb of Paris, Bagneux; his father was from Martinique and his mother from Alsace. His name was as evocative of his cause as de Gaulle's had been in 1940. Aged twenty-five, he was politically astute and articulate. 'Pote' as pal, mate, buddy, entered popular mythology as a new social construct, a street-level version of *fraternité* and citizenship. It was the invention of tradition, imaged by Désir as 'La Concorde des potes', a multi-ethnic sociability between 'blacks, whites, Beurs, Auvergnats, Vietnamese, Bretons, Africans, Maghrebis, Jews, Muslims, Catholics . . .' brought together on 15 June 1985 in a concert of over 300,000 in the Place de la Concorde, subsidized heavily by Jack Lang as Minister of Culture.[11]

The speed with which SOS-Racisme attracted influential backing within the political establishment made it suspect to currents within the Beur movement who had celebrated the Beur march but were tightening their identity in the face of rising harassment by police and hostile neighbours in the densely populated blocks of housing which kept violence in the suburbs constantly in the news. Product of the optimism of 1981, often provocatively assertive, but forced to become a tough response to local racists, the Beur movement developed an inner pluralism through its identity with place and the freedom of association guaranteed by Socialist legislation. The original quality of films made by Beur directors, depicting the reality and inter-personal dramas of immigrant lives, allowed a new, initially marginal, genre, *le cinéma beur*, to gain representative status within the canon of national cinema. In 1985 Mehdi Charef won the coveted Jean Vigo prize for his first film, *Le Thé au harem d'Archimède*, a study of day-to-day realities in an HLM estate, including the unemployment of youths from both French and immigrant origins. It was premièred hard on the heels of Adelkrim Bahloul's *Le Thé à la menthe*, and was followed by Rachid Bouchareb's *Bâton rouge* of 1986, all three creating scenarios of survivalist ingenuity and giving identity to immigrants as individuals in their own right.

Each town produced its own distinctive Beur groups, among a range of immigrant organizations, and every locality its own music, slang and styles, undermining the national impact of a conference of immigrant youth called

in Lyon in June 1984. As with the activities of the *groupuscules* in May 1968 and in the 1970s, the lack of political unity was both strength and weakness. It gave individual purpose to local groups, but even as SOS-Racisme consolidated, the Beur movement became more dispersed, and a second newly created anti-racist organization, France-Plus, found itself critical of the all-encompassing aims of Harlem Désir. Led by Arezki Dahmani, France-Plus was launched early in 1985, with a more restricted goal of mobilizing young people of Maghrebi origin to take part in local politics and make their democratic voice heard. Always smaller than SOS-Racisme, it nevertheless succeeded in gaining several hundred town council seats for Maghrebi candidates in March 1989. After that date the influence of both organizations declined, and the meaning of 'Beur' lost the optimistic ring of the mid-1980s, however much the festival of the bicentenary tried to revive it.

Law and order

The positive image of 'les Beurs', SOS-Racisme, France-Plus and *le cinéma beur* was in direct confrontation with virulent sections of public opinion and the media which searched avidly for connections between any social violence and the immigrant community. Blurring all distinctions between fact and fantasy, the equivalence of immigrant youth and criminality was taken for granted by growing numbers of people, estimated by a poll of 1984 to constitute 26 per cent of the population, even though 70 per cent regularly linked delinquency more rationally to the high rate of youth unemployment.

In the last year of Giscard's Presidency, the Garde des Sceaux, Alain Peyrefitte, brought in a law and order bill entitled 'Sécurité et Liberté', which tightened the penal control of youths convicted of delinquency. A popular essayist with a strong moral sense of what was 'wrong' with French society (*Le Mal français*, 1976), Peyrefitte was a Gaullist deputy for Provins and the minister who had successfully overseen the repatriation of the French minority (*pieds-noirs*) from Algeria in 1962. The law and order issue was an amalgam of different experiences and fears, easily exploited. The pattern of youth violence in the 1970s had been perceived to move from Saturday-night fights to an American-style rivalry of armed gangs, and from the street into the schools. This was the context of the Peyrefitte law, but there was also the explosion outside the Jewish synagogue of the rue Copernic in Paris on 3 October 1980 which killed four passers-by and injured twenty. Raymond Barre's ill-chosen phrase deploring the death of 'innocent French', as if the Jews who were targeted were different, was

widely judged to be more than just a straw in the wind. The question of national and ethnic identity became more and more inseparable from issues of personal and social safety.

Peyrefitte's bill of 1980, attacked by the left, was revised by the Socialists in power, but within a year of the elections a government commission on delinquency published evidence showing the prevalence of anxiety about law and order in the big towns, including the worries of thirty-six Socialist or Communist mayors. From 1983 Peyrefitte chaired the editorial board of *Le Figaro*, the most influential right-wing daily, which in the mid-1970s had joined the populist *Minute* and *France-Soir* in regularly asserting an immigrant connection with delinquency. *Minute* in 1976 headlined Sully-sur-Loire as a town living in fear of immigrants after the murder of a French youth by an Algerian, while *France-Soir* had identified hooliganism closely with North Africans. After 1981 fear in society rapidly became a stock issue in the opposition press once the Socialists had carried through the abolition of the death penalty and the reforms regularizing illegal immigrants. The rising curve of fear fed on television coverage in April 1983 suggesting a typology of delinquency among immigrant youth and social violence among immigrant car workers. It culminated in *Le Figaro* on 12 November 1984 with a front-page article stating that the whole of France was gripped with fear after a series of murders of elderly women in Paris, for which the police could find no suspect. The paper pointed to the density of immigrants in the areas where the murders had occurred, but it was the generalized headline, 'La France a peur', which caused a sensation.

Here was an inversion of the language of locality which had characterized social movements in the 1970s and had emphasized the specificity of place. A number of sociological studies underlined the dubious role of television and newspapers in promoting mass identification with dramatic issues specific to a locality, and alerted people to the irrationality of a generalized social fear. At the same time they argued that a factual basis in certain localities could not be denied, such as the mindless vandalism in Lyon perpetrated in the 'hot' summer of 1981, when ethnic minority youths staged nocturnal 'rodeos' against cars and property. The huge complex of Les Minguettes in Vénissieux, a suburb of Lyon, was deemed to be a hub of violence between ethnic minorities and the police. Opinion polls and official statistics both reflected and nurtured the ease with which such local news could provoke a national fear. The first national poll to ask questions linking social disorder to immigration was in 1973. Ten years later it was an obsessive media and polling issue to which the march of the Beurs was essentially addressed.

National fears about safety hooked on to a protest demonstration to the Ministry of Justice by Parisian police in June 1983 after the death of two of their colleagues. The fears were stridently present in the municipal elections of 1983, and again in the European elections of 1984, reflecting the disorientation of a society in the face of multiple political changes followed by major political retreat. The fear was further politicized by Chirac in July 1984 when he denounced the government for permitting an influx of illegal immigrants 'of the worst quality', and by *Figaro Magazine* which labelled Marseille in 1986 as the national capital of fear and violence where 65 per cent of thefts and aggression were attributed to North Africans. Well before this, the issue had become the lifeblood of the Front National.

The issue of the extreme right

The word everywhere in the press was 'apotheosis'. The extreme right movement, the Front National (FN), personified by Jean-Marie Le Pen, monopolized the headlines by gaining ten seats in the European elections of 1984. The hyperbole of the word given to Le Pen's success, and the astonishment at his ultimate accession to national status after forty years of political trafficking at the margins, were symptomatic of the media's reaction. At the grass roots, among the exuberant militants of the FN, there was no such surprise. The first successful bid for national recognition had been in the municipal elections and by-elections of 1983, notably in the industrial town of Dreux to the north of Chartres, where unemployment was rife and where the FN candidate Jean-Pierre Stirbois took advantage of a pact with the right to become assistant mayor. Now, in 1984, its substantial breakthrough took it to just under 11 per cent of the vote, representing over 2.2 million voters, the highest poll for a comparable movement since the shock of Poujadism in 1956, in which Le Pen had played his own individualist role. In the early 1980s he was still appealing to forces of resentment among white-collar workers, self-employed and shopkeepers, but by 1984 his appeal was more consciously directed at the unemployed as well as those fearful of social violence. His ideology was variously labelled national-populism, neo-fascism, or simply LePenism. It thrived on savaging the Gaullist right as well as the left.

In the walled crusader town of Aigues-Mortes in Provence a 40-year-old convert to Le Pen, Alain Champ, stood for the cantonal elections in 1985, convinced that the left had triumphed in 1981 because the right had grown soft and weak. Only Le Pen, he believed, was capable of sweeping the left

from power. It was an analysis shared by Alain Jamet, aged 50, who had campaigned in Languedoc-Roussillon alongside Le Pen for Poujadism, Algérie Française, and Tixier-Vignancour, and who described Giscard, Barre and Chirac contemptuously as 'men of the left'. César Pelet, a local councillor in the rosé wine area of the Hérault, argued that France had grown rotten since the conflict in Algeria, and its leaders weak. He blamed immigrants entirely for the escalation of local crime and warned that sooner or later society would crack. In his town of Lunel he claimed fifty FN activists, all of them manual workers like himself. In Marseille a personnel director in industry, Paul-Yves Perche, had left Gaullism for the FN because of Algeria, and declared that getting rid of 500,000 immigrants for a start 'would solve a lot of our problems'. L'Express collected these and other FN opinions in March 1985. The social derivation of the FN militants, from labourers to consultant engineers, and the repeated emphasis on immigration, underlined the populist inroads of Le Pen. By the mid-1980s as Mitterrand was looking towards consensus politics, Le Pen claimed a consensus on his version of national identity, built on the opposition of 'French' and 'immigrant'. His demagogic flamboyance lionized Joan of Arc, French Algeria, and Marshal Pétain.

Access to television at each election gave the Breton-born Le Pen regular opportunity to make himself a talking-point in the media. His party political broadcast of 16 October 1985 was thought to have reached over 6 million households. Intellectuals began to see him as symptomatic of a severe identity crisis not only in politics but in France as a whole. The Front National made racism central to its populist anger against insecurity and unemployment, mounting a cultural offensive in the xenophobic tradition of Maurras and Action Française. By 1984 it was apparent not only that it was successful at exploiting fear as an issue in society, but that other parties were being forced to work out strategies for dealing with its appeal. The 'apotheosis of Jean-Marie Le Pen' was an acknowledgement that the extreme right had become an issue for the whole of French politics. Mitterrand's tactics in the run-up to the elections of 1986 confirmed, but also exploited, this fact.

19

Pressures for Consensus, 1980s–1993

1. Swing to the right, but . . .

Culture: monumental and diversified

During the mid-1980s people at all levels of society began to state openly that political identities, values and certainties were slipping from their grasp. Complexity and contradiction were perceived as invading areas of thought and opinion which had once seemed clearly defined. The polarizations of 1981 had given way to compromise. Strange bedfellows took the place of traditional allies: opposites ran together in tandem. A Socialist government advocating the exact opposite of its original policies was the epitome of contradiction. Taking stock of what was happening, columnists in the media repeatedly alluded to the decline and fragmentation of politics or the emergence of consensus. But new constellations of ideas created their own dynamic. Consensus could be experienced as innovative as well as bland. Jack Lang, Minister of Culture, successfully created new identities at the very time when confusion about the Socialists was at its height. To his critics his policies were so riven with contradictions that he was dismissed as the Minister of 'anything goes'. But an overwhelming consensus of public opinion approved and welcomed his initiatives, even as the Socialists headed for what everyone predicted would be a crushing defeat in the elections of 1986. Culture, unlike employment, was successfully delivered. Still further, it was radically diversified.

Why a Ministry of Culture should be so representative of both challenge and consensus in the 1980s leads not just to Jack Lang himself but more widely to the multiple meanings of culture in the last quarter of the century. Activists in 1968 had claimed that the cultural was political. Among committed students it was argued that everything came within the political: class, gender, race, youth, region, media, as well as culture. They were redefining politics as the total or universal phenomenon that Hegel had mapped out for history. This convergence of all aspects of life into politics

was resisted by most of the political professionals, whether politicians, political analysts or political historians. Despite 1968, a fairly narrow definition of politics as 'party politics' was perpetuated in much of popular discourse. But among certain influential thinkers there was a readiness to suggest that it was not politics but culture within which all these different realms of thought and action should be located, and that the original equation made more sense when it was inverted to claim that the political was in fact cultural.

Michel de Certeau, whose death in 1986 gave prominence to his inter-disciplinary legacy, had been involved in the 1970s with the research unit of the Ministry of Culture and had given culture a plurality of meanings, including the creative acts of everyday life which rarely end up as works of art. The sociologist Pierre Bourdieu, projecting the spirit of 1968, intro-duced the concept of 'culture capital' to designate the knowledge, skills, style and taste by which one class or social group dominated another, while within ethnology and anthropology the response to the diaspora of ethnic minorities in a post-colonial world brought increasing stress on culture as patterns of custom and behaviour, central to human relations and indeed human rights. Jack Lang and his Ministry came to symbolize this essential ubiquity of culture at its most accessible.

Culture as a powerful force for change, festival as a form of social engagement, people's creativity as democracy in action, cultural difference as the rich plurality of society – all these propositions gave direction to Lang's cultural policy, which he never tired of stating was also economic enterprise. It was internationally polemical in its use of anti-American sentiments; it was liberational in its embrace of Third World cultures, but it was also monumental in its support for Mitterrand's grand architectural projects, announced shortly after the 1981 election landslide.

Governments since de Gaulle's creation of a Ministry of Cultural Affairs in 1959 had tried to realize Malraux's ambition that the Fifth Republic should create universal culture as the Third had created universal education. By this Malraux meant universal access to what his Ministry defined as 'the major works of humanity, and particularly of France'. Patronage of new art projects was secondary. The Maisons de la Culture were launched, but neither Malraux nor de Gaulle commissioned outstanding works of architecture by which their concepts of culture or, indeed, of the French nation would be remembered, although the freedom given to property developers and the construction of tower blocks associated Gaullism nega-tively with what was indignantly called the 'massacre of Paris'. Pompidou's interest in modern art centred on his project for a Museum of the Twentieth

Century in the heart of Paris, though he died before the brave new world
of contemporary architecture rose in the rue Beaubourg in Paris, a hugely
imaginative structure of glass and coloured tubes, named after Pompidou
but nicknamed 'le monstre'. Diagonally across its main face, people could
ride the moving escalators and watch the cityscape gradually unfold, a
comparable delight, said Parisians, to a Sunday morning walking slowly
backwards up the steps to Montmartre. Inaugurated in 1977, it was already
the most controversial modern building in Paris, but it was also immensely
popular, not least as the focus for Picasso-famed *saltimbanques* among the
contemporary street entertainers.

The publicity created by the Pompidou Centre alerted innovative architects to the potential of Paris as a cultural site, an emphasis which Giscard
encouraged in a bid to reverse the slide of the city into alienating blocks of
offices. He initiated the transformation of the Gare d'Orsay into a museum
of nineteenth-century art and set up other cultural projects, one for a
complex of buildings celebrating science and industry at the old abattoirs
of La Villette in the north of Paris, and another dedicated to the culture of
the Arab world, a diplomatic act of recognition bringing financial contributions from nineteen Arab states at the time of the first oil crisis. Mitterrand adapted and completed these projects and significantly advanced the
'princely' role of the President as cultural patron. Alongside a new era for
socialism Mitterrand promised the restoration of Paris to world cultural
renown, the two aims galvanized by the approaching bicentenary of the
Revolution. A universal exhibition was envisaged, and just as the Eiffel
Tower had crowned the centenary of 1889, major new architectural projects (*les grands travaux*) were launched for the bicentenary, including the
revitalization of the east end of Paris with an opera house in the Place de
la Bastille and a new Finance Ministry, moved from the Louvre out to
Bercy. Within the park of La Villette there would also be a Cité de la
Musique. The Louvre was to be fully reclaimed as a museum, and its
courtyard entry transformed by a glass pyramid designed by the Sino-
American Ieoh Ming Pei. The eye would be drawn from the *pyramide*
westwards through the Arc de Triomphe to the distant modern development
at La Défense, now to be given a massive square arch designed by the
Danish architect Otto von Spreckelsen.

International architects, controversial aesthetics, Presidential ambitions,
none would have had an easy ride without the tacit collaboration of the
first of the new mayors of Paris, Mitterrand's political opposite Jacques
Chirac. In one of the surprising political convergences of the mid-1980s
Chirac found that his own aims for Paris could be made to coincide with

those of Mitterrand, with the exception of the proposed exhibition for 1989, which he rejected as too politically angled and too national in its historic function to justify a huge financial investment by Paris. Mitterrand, again surprisingly, dropped the proposal, leaving 1989 to be celebrated with festivities only, although it was expected that the Louvre *pyramide* would be completed in time to act as a technological and cultural showcase for Mitterrand and Lang's image of contemporary France.

As the Socialist mission of 1981 went into reverse, the cultural mission of *les grands travaux* might have faded also, especially after the rout of the left in Paris in 1983 and the defeat of the Socialists in 1986. Mitterrand's vision, however, remained fixed; cultural professionals, such as the vanguard musician Pierre Boulez, shared much of the detailed planning of the Cité de la Musique, and Lang took delight in defending the controversial Louvre *pyramide*, relishing the opposition from his old antagonist and predecessor, Michel Guy, who argued along with thousands of others that it offended the uniform aesthetics of the Louvre. Lang's interest lay in its transparent and universal classicism, however much, or perhaps because, it offended uniformity. It was the quest for innovation and challenge which marked his whole Ministry.

Cultural boundaries were continually crossed. For 21 June 1982, with his colleagues Christian Dupavillon and Maurice Fleuret, Lang planned and carried through the first nationwide Fête de la Musique, following the realization that one in every two young people played some sort of musical instrument. Scepticism in much of the media heralded this Ministry-inspired outbreak of professional and amateur music into streets, squares and courtyards across the country on the longest day of summer, instantly named *le jour le plus Lang*. Its success, and the spontaneity of response, blocked the centres of provincial towns with musicians of all talents or none, a musical festivity 'without precedent in French history', as celebrated by *Libération*.[1] Repeated each year, the spread of live music brought Lang popularity, but more significantly it took him into an eclectic involvement with music of all styles, into both its performance and its reproduction on record and disk, into the cultural impact of new radio and television channels and the economic marketing of musical taste. The recognition of flagrant youth preference for American pop music, *le rock*, brought compromise and further innovation from the Ministry, including subsidized pop festivals at Rennes and Bourges, a new performance centre, Le Zénith, in Paris and the promotion of compact disks as an integral part of the modernization programme of Laurent Fabius.

By contrast Lang set himself against the proliferation of the video market

which threatened the cinemas, and in particular the French film industry. He attempted, with little success, to use the European Community to restrict the dominance of American films, but his campaign created an ambivalent form of nationalistic preference for French cultural products, which on the one hand resisted the pull of market economics in the name of cultural diversity, and on the other came dangerously close to giving succour to the forces of xenophobia, the complete antithesis to his internationalism. It was therefore of overt cultural significance that Lang should see his role as one of fervent supporter and sponsor of the anti-racist concert organized in the Place de la Concorde by Harlem Désir on 15 June 1985. It was consistent with his passion for bringing ethnic minority cultures and liberational politics together and giving them prominence as acts of creativity. In reaction he faced accusations of subsiding cultures indiscriminately. As the year of the bicentenary neared, opinions for and against Jack Lang fed into the *fin-de-siècle* discord over French cultural identity and multiculturalism.

Damage limitation

On every index of success the cultural record of Mitterrand and Lang scored highly in the opinion polls. Two-thirds of French opinion backed *les grands travaux* and corresponding municipal initiatives for new projects and heritage work in the large provincial towns. Popular agreement that Mitterrand and Lang were raising the cultural prestige of the nation acted as a consensus brake on the runaway disillusionment of the electorate with Socialist policies. For the Fabius government much of the last year before the elections of March 1986 was one of damage limitation in the economic and employment spheres in the hope that the positive and consensus aspects of Mitterrand's Presidency would rescue the Socialists from total disaster at the polls. It was therefore particularly irritating for the Fabius 'effect' when one of those consensus areas ran into scandal of the government's own making: the affair of the *Rainbow Warrior*.

The consensus area in question was nuclear policy. Nothing radical was promised in this area in 1981, no *changement* away from the nuclear defence which had been the linchpin of de Gaulle's bid for world status in the 1960s. Ecologists and anti-nuclear campaigners, with the mud of Malville still fresh on their boots, demanded an end to nuclear tests at Mururoa and Fangatofa, but Mitterrand had been brought round to nuclear defence in 1978 by Charles Hernu, a long-standing friend from their days of opposition to the coup d'état of 13 May 1958 which had ended the Fourth Republic. Hernu was appointed Minister of Defence in 1981 and in the

next five years spread his own good relations with the military into Socialist ranks which had previously flirted with anti-militarism and nuclear protests. Much was said about his quiet skill in 'reconciling' the PS to the nation's army and creating a cross-party understanding on defence. Nuclear protests were the province of a dwindling minority but there was sufficient concern about the effect of nuclear testing on the Polynesian islanders for the media to respond to news on 10 July 1985 of two explosions which sank the Greenpeace protest ship, *Rainbow Warrior*, in the port of Auckland in New Zealand, with the loss of a Greenpeace photographer's life.

The French public knew little or nothing about the Greenpeace movement or its campaign to disrupt French nuclear activities, so there was some surprise when the New Zealand authorities arrested two French citizens, Alain Maffart and Dominique Prieur, masquerading under false passports as a Swiss married couple, and accused them of complicity in the destruction of the ship. Investigative journalists on *Le Monde* probed the identities of the two, revealing layers of mystery and suspicion leading back to the French Secret Services. The Fabius government began by denying all involvement in the affair, only to retract the denials and issue defensive or dismissive statements throughout the summer, culminating in Mitterrand's directive to the army on 18 August stressing the legitimacy of force to prevent any unauthorized access to French waters in the nuclear-testing zone. This was not an admission of guilt in the sinking of the *Rainbow Warrior*, although the inconsistencies emanating from official circles told their own story. On 22 September Laurent Fabius admitted in a tense television statement that French agents had indeed sunk the Greenpeace ship, acting 'on order'. Whose order? remained a talking point within and outside government, but Charles Hernu was forced to resign, many thought as a scapegoat, although his authorization to the Secret Services to destroy the *Rainbow Warrior* was later demonstrated. At the time the affair did him little further harm. He was comfortably re-elected for Villeurbanne outside Lyon in 1986. Long before that, the two agents were found guilty in New Zealand and the affair brought more world focus on the environmental threat to the Polynesian atolls. Greenpeace emerged strengthened in the numbers and self-belief of its supporters, but there was no immediate change to French nuclear policy. It was not until seven years later in 1992 that Mitterrand agreed to suspend nuclear testing.

No rash of accusations followed the *Rainbow Warrior* affair although Mitterrand and his government were seen as shifty once the cover-up started to unravel. There was some denunciation of state terror, but not by the public at large, nor by the political right. The parliamentary opposition

was only indignant at the government's bungling of the operation. There was terrorism within France which made a quite different impact. At the time of the war in Lebanon in 1982 antisemitic atrocities killed six in the rue des Rosiers in Paris; attacks by Armenians at Orly airport in 1983 killed eight and wounded over fifty; a range of murderous attacks in 1982–3 were attributed to the international terrorist Carlos; six deaths and fifty wounded at Marseille railway station were claimed in December 1983 by an 'Arab organization of armed struggle'; two assassinations of prominent figures, General René Audran of the Ministry of Defence and Georges Besse, President of Renault, were claimed by the revolutionary group Action Directe in January 1985 and November 1986; attacks were staged by sympathizers with 'Arab political prisoners' in big stores including Galéries Lafayette and Au Printemps in the winter of 1985–6, and the same group was held responsible for bombs which exploded in the popular bookshop of Gilbert Jeune and in the central branch of FNAC-Sports in February 1986.

Tabulating differently motivated terrorism in this way is dubious short-hand history: it was a staple of media summaries as the elections of 1986 approached and passed. A climate of insecurity was sustained throughout the mid to last years of the 1980s. Scrambled indiscriminately with anti-immigrant prejudices, it was called by the extreme right a consensus of fear. This was nine-tenths polemic but none the less effective. The humane and liberal attitudes of Robert Badinter, the Socialist Minister of Justice whose Russian-born father had died in Auschwitz, were increasingly execrated not just by the Front National but also by the Gaullists. He became an object of hatred in doctrinaire 'law and order' circles, together with his philosopher wife, Élisabeth Badinter, whose ideas on the social construction of maternal 'instinct' were attacked as morally subversive. Mitterrand made no concession to the vituperative campaign against his Minister but he was aware of how close the mainstream opposition and the FN had become on the issue. It provided one more justification for the turn to proportional representation for the legislative elections as an overt attempt to weaken the combined right by forcing them to divide against one another.

It could not be denied that this was central to damage limitation. Proportional representation had figured in Mitterrand's manifesto of 1981 and had been variously applied to local and regional elections. With opinion polls continuously pointing to the victory of the right, a decision to adopt it for the elections of 1986 was taken in April 1985, causing the resignation of Michel Rocard from the government. He argued that its predictable result would be seats for the Front National (FN), as already seen from the proportional system of the European elections of 1984. The probability of

such an outcome was not disclaimed by Mitterrand nor by the Minister of the Interior, Pierre Joxe, who officially introduced the new system. The corollary of successful bids by the FN was expected to be fewer seats for the mainstream opposition, a calculation which was widely denounced as cynical. It was also seen as the climax of Mitterrand's long-term strategy of first using and then discarding the electoral alliance with the Communists. The PCF, like the PS, would have its own list.

Chirac in power: redefining freedom

The overall result of the elections on 18 March 1986 followed predictions. Victory went to the combined forces of the main opposition, Chirac's RPR and the centrist UDF which had formed a loose pact to operate together in government. It was more a question of the Socialists having lost the electorate's confidence than of the opposition gaining it. On the left, the difficulty in deciphering what the Socialist Party actually stood for jostled with a commitment to its modernizing shift after 1983, and its loss of over 6 per cent of the vote compared to the 38 per cent obtained in the first round in 1981 was not in statistical terms a catastrophe. It was still the largest single party in the Chamber. In contrast, the confirmation of the Communist decline was stark, the vote for the PCF falling to 9.7 per cent compared to its regular score of over 20 per cent, achieved as recently as 1978. Its vote put it only just ahead of the Front National, and each party was allotted thirty-five seats. The humiliation for Georges Marchais was only equalled by the jubilation of Jean-Marie Le Pen, who quickly posed as the representative of the unemployed as well as the 'true French'.

For the first time in the history of the Fifth Republic an elected President was faced with a hostile elected parliamentary majority. Much discussed in advance, this potential predicament had sharply divided opinion. Would the Republic be able to function? It would be in the President's power to call for new elections. Would Mitterrand do this? It would be possible for a right-wing majority to refuse to create a government. Would their leaders do this? According to public opinion polls Raymond Barre was the favourite to head the opposition to the Socialists, but well before the elections he made it a point of constitutional principle that he could not co-habit with a hostile President. Chirac, however, had decided, partly on the advice of Pompidou's colleague and close friend Édouard Balladur, that such scruples would be a misreading of the constitution. So too had Mitterrand, whose advent to the Presidency in 1981 had been a sign that the Fifth Republic was

adaptable to change. He offered Chirac the Premiership. Chirac accepted. Co-habitation began.

The 53-year-old Parisian Jacques Chirac returned to the Hôtel Matignon almost ten years after his first term as Premier under President Giscard d'Estaing from 1974 to 1976. He was proud of the fact that he had resigned and not been dismissed, and that he had outwitted Giscard in the subsequent elections for Paris. He brought with him a decade of deals and initiatives as mayor of Paris and a reputation for opportunism, speed of decision in matters of tactics, lack of ideological dogma but also of consistency, and little concern for long-term strategy. Youthful volatility had taken him to a spell on a cargo boat in defiance of his father, followed by family reconciliation, graduation at ENA, interest in de Gaulle's RPF at the end of the 1940s, a quick experience of selling the Communist *L'Humanité-Dimanche* in 1952, a year at Harvard Business School and a hitch-hiking tour of the USA in 1953, marriage to Bernadette de Courcel of the notable Gaullist family, a romantic notion of giving up everything for a military career in North Africa, a firm commitment in 1958 to Gaullism, and finally an opening into the government circles of Georges Pompidou who became his mentor and political patron and whose staff affably named the young Chirac 'the bulldozer'.

In the mid-1980s the Gaullist movement that Chirac had turned into the RPR still had to nurture de Gaulle's legacy, but the old Gaullist barons such as Michel Debré and Jacques Chaban-Delmas, whom Chirac had refused to support in 1974, had been reconciled or distanced, and the RPR had robustly thrown itself into the 'game of party politics' that de Gaulle had abhorred. It had its own political clubs of young intellectuals, including the Club 89 established by Chirac's closest colleagues, Alain Juppé and Michel Aurillac, its central administration and political bureau, and a relationship with its members which was wryly but not inaccurately compared to the democratic centralism of the Communist Party. It had put down provincial roots among small and middle-sized business communities, the PME (*petites et moyennes entreprises*), but in reaction to the failure of the Socialist 'rupture' of 1981 it moved closer to the large business interests of the *patronat*. With the eclipse of Giscard it unapologetically adopted the liberal economics of the loose coalition of parties in the UDF, while retaining a nominal commitment to de Gaulle's social doctrine of participation.

Mayor of Paris and now Premier of France, Chirac's target was openly the Presidential elections scheduled for May 1988. The consensus backing for the Fifth Republic as a permanent constitution made it essential for every party to have a viable Presidential candidate. In 1985 Mitterrand's

popularity rating was at its lowest, Rocard was ready to set out his considerable claims after resigning from the government of Fabius, Raymond Barre was widely tipped as the safest representative of the centre-right, Le Pen was boasting that his dramatic ascent made him the only nationalist fit for the Élysée, and there was Giscard, reduced to an outsider but re-entering politics at local and regional levels. Chirac in power was in a hurry to make his case. His haste, confidence and the experience of bargaining with Mitterrand over *les grands travaux* mark his Premiership as one of dynamic retaliation against the *changement* of 1981, and yet also as one of certain continuities with Fabius, and eventually caution. 'The bulldozer' was quick to demolish: it took longer to build.

The demolition of the Socialist experiment hinged on pushing back the role of the state by rapid and extensive privatizations, prioritizing market forces and empowering the public to exercise consumer choice as shareholders in the companies floated on the stock exchange. Ideological reversal was paramount, even though much of the ideology of 1981 had already been reversed by the Socialists themselves. Chirac made still more room for what both sides called revenge: he abolished the Ministry of Women's Rights, cancelled the wealth tax, attacked the Savary bill on higher education, gave his Minister of the Interior, Charles Pasqua, the opportunity to formulate an anti-immigrant policy and a new code of nationality, and re-established the two-round majority system for parliamentary elections. In the Polynesian islands of New Caledonia where violence over the independence campaign of the indigenous, but minority, Melanesians or Kanaks had reached a crisis of violence and repression in 1984, the government of Chirac took on the forces of independence as a law and order issue.

This assertive agenda reinvigorated political conflict. The confusion of the mid-1980s and the creeping sense that consensus would sap politics of its lifeblood appeared to have been premature. And yet within the programme of the right there was a newly confident belief that consensus on economic policy was not only desired by the electorate but an inevitability. The unrestricted operation of market forces began to be paraded as almost the sole touchstone of common sense, and of freedom.

Chirac had already redefined Gaullism in the late 1970s as pragmatism in politics. As the indices evaluating the economy increasingly pointed to international competitiveness as the decisive missing ingredient, so the conviction within the RPR grew that French companies were shackled by government, even by government investment in research. The keyword of pragmatism was replaced by freedom. Discussion documents from the party pointed to 'crossroads of freedom' and summarized the party's ideas as

'free and responsible'. Delegates to conferences on business and freedom slipped into the normative expression of 'free enterprise'. The concept was everywhere and not merely borrowed from Reagan's America or Thatcher's Britain. It was said by its protagonists to have gained a primacy in French discourse through everyday reaction to Socialism in power. The Chirac government appropriated the frustrated liberational vocabulary of the left and appealed to the public to celebrate an economic freedom which would line their pockets and create the new jobs which had proved so elusive.

Sixty-five companies, nationalized post-war and in 1981–2, were to be privatized over five years, and all firms were given more autonomy and flexibility in the creation of part-time and contract labour. In a wholesale assault on public expenditure, government investment in research was severely cut in 1986, though it was raised in 1987; the running of prisons and municipal services was opened to the private sector, and landlords were given freedom to set their rents. Residual state interest in television and radio was largely replaced by commercial interests with the promise of a greater freedom of communication. François Léotard, the new Minister of Culture, stated that he 'wished to return television to the French people'.[2]

The thrust of Chirac's programme was parried by Mitterrand, but not deflected. The President saw an opportunity of playing the consensus card of national interest against his impetuous Prime Minister and used the *fête nationale* of 14 July 1986 to announce his refusal to allow privatizations by government order alone, forcing the proposals to be submitted to parliamentary procedures. The sale of companies would also have to ensure that there were no takeovers from abroad. The measures were held up, but only by a few weeks, and the first complete sale of a major nationalized company, the glass and paper manufacturers Saint-Gobain, was quickly oversubscribed in November on the stock market. It was followed in 1987 by an equal rush to buy shares in the finance group Paribas, and only slightly less demand for the electricity giant CGE and the media group Agence Havas, alongside banks including Indosuez, the Crédit Commercial and the Société Générale. Companies on the projected list saw many of their managers replaced by new government appointments.

Under Fabius the nationalized industries had accumulated a good deal of autonomy, and the first to be sold had already turned losses into profits, making them highly marketable. The Socialists accused Chirac and his Economic Minister, Édouard Balladur, of selling these national assets too cheaply, enriching a 'hard core' (*noyau dur*) of big investors. In reply Balladur pointed to the hard core as necessary for stable management and countered Mitterrand's caution by emphasizing the need to attract foreign

as well as home investors. By August 1987 it was estimated that some 5 million new shareholders had been attracted to the market, most of whom made substantial gains in the first flurry of buying and selling. There was government confidence that this would revolutionize the pattern of saving in society and create a buoyant enthusiasm for popular capitalism: the risks of investment appeared low, with rates on the Paris Bourse rising since 1983, and inflation no longer an issue.

The international crash of the stock market in mid-October 1987 was a severe corrective. As the value of shares tumbled the huge privatization programme was stopped in its tracks. The government backed away from its commitment with an alacrity which prompted critics to say that it was not only Socialists who had second thoughts. The whole new direction of economic policy was not, however, about to be changed. Chirac's halt at the end of 1987 was in no way comparable to the Socialist turn-round in 1983. It was circumstantial: the underlying ideology of market forces was untouched. By 1988 the number of individual shareholders had increased sixfold in two years to over 7 million. The market was creating its own political infrastructure.

Focus on exclusion

The film star Catherine Deneuve advertising the sale of Indosuez shares on television was one lasting image of the liberal economy. The clown and variety artist Coluche (Michel Colucci) opening restaurants for the down-and-outs was another. He was killed, aged forty-two, in a road accident in November 1986, and mourned as 'Saint Colucci', leaving behind the memory of his joky but bitter parodies of contemporary society at Presidential elections, and his string of *restaurants du cœur*. He launched them during the premiership of Fabius and they were much photographed in the winter of 1986–7, but even before his initiative the issue of the 'new poor' was beginning to affect all levels of social concern, from government departments to individual philanthropists, passing through trade unions, churches and the voluntary organizations of aid.

The new forms of poverty were ones inextricably linked to unemployment which grew steadily worse under the Socialist *changement*, under the subsequent austerity and restructuring, and under the liberalization programme of Chirac and Balladur. There were isolated months when a fall was registered, but by the end of 1986 over 10.5 per cent of the active population were without a job. From 1981 to 1988 more than 900,000 swelled the unemployed to a peak of over 2.6 million in March 1987, a

figure marginally below the average for the twelve nations of the European Community, but well above West Germany and slightly above the UK. Millions of households told a story of particular desperation among those leaving school and young adults: two out of every five unemployed were under twenty-six, one of the highest youth rates among the advanced industrialized countries. For low-qualified young women finding work was particularly hard, and among the youth of North African immigrants more than one in every three were without work.

Various imaginative, and several counter-productive, job-creation schemes were introduced by successive governments, creating on the edge of unemployment an area of precarious or limited work, and new levels of low pay, but going some way to redress the worst situations. From the community-style work introduced under Fabius by Michel Delebarre, to the schemes favoured by Chirac for subsidizing employers willing to take on the unemployed, the emphasis was on *insertion* or *réinsertion*, the preparation and (re)training for the job market. The words indicated a form of socialization for unemployed youth, or a process of social rehabilitation for the long-term unemployed. Integration into the workforce was seen as necessary for social inclusion or full citizenship. The obverse was exclusion. The 'new poor' were defined in terms of exclusion, and because it was clear that unemployment could be due to social, ethnic and cultural reasons and not just economic ones, the concept of exclusion also signified disqualification and discrimination, moving the notion of poverty away from purely economic destitution, and addressing its social and cultural dimensions. Why immigrant youth? Why underqualified women? Why one region and not another? The focus on exclusion raised all such issues.

At the same time, focus on the excluded, *les exclus*, raised fears and hostility as well as concern and sympathy. Questions about the efficacy of unemployment benefit, job-creation schemes, special training and early retirements were repeatedly posed as annual figures marked the huge escalation of their costs to the state, leaping from 2 billion francs in 1975 to over 40 billion in 1990. From the opposite perspective the damage of unemployment to national wealth was calculated in terms of lost taxation, consumption and production, and as no government appeared to find an answer, unemployment became the new 'question sociale' comparable in relative terms to the social problems associated with industrialization at the end of the nineteenth century.

Chirac's government, no less than that of Mauroy in 1981, believed that its ideological offensive would bring down unemployment. It was a sign of the special nature of the problem that an emergency plan to create jobs for

the young unemployed was announced in July 1986. Its estimated cost to the state was 4.5 billion francs, offset by the sale of nationalized companies but none the less an exception to Chirac's assault on public expenditure. More consonant with neo-liberal ideology was the legislation, also in July, to abolish the administrative control exercised by official work inspectorates over redundancies. The *patronat* had constantly opposed these controls as bureaucratic interference, restricting company initiative and restructuring. The decision provoked a more concerted opposition of the left and trade unions than the bills for privatization. Government action to give companies more flexibility in creating low-paid, part-time jobs, favoured by the Employment Minister Philippe Séguin, shifted power to the employers still further. The themes of flexibility and deregulation fleshed out the government's new definition of freedom and promised an impact on exclusion through a more profitable economy bringing growth and jobs. Public opinion was drawn into the pace of Chirac's changes: they expected the impact to be rapid. This did not happen. Month by month through to the spring of 1987 the figures for redundancies and unemployment grew worse. The government began to caress the image of the long term.

Liberalizing the economy, it emerged in 1986, did not mean liberalizing society. Distinguishing the two was the mark of neo-liberalism. Charles Pasqua, Minister of the Interior, made that clear. He typified a brand of tough but pragmatic, right-wing politicians with successful business careers that commentators saw rising in the upper echelons of the RPR at the expense of graduates from ENA and the other *grandes écoles*. His commitment to the Resistance at the age of fifteen and his Corsican family background added to a reputation for rugged action. In 1986 he aimed to outbid Le Pen by regulations to reduce the number of immigrants and a bill to curb rights to French nationality. The initial Socialist measures of 1981 to integrate clandestine immigrants had not led to an open-door policy, but this was not how the FN represented the issue. Nor did Pasqua, who moved immediately to restrict access to residence permits and to return illegal immigrants to their country of origin. Under cover of night on 18 October 1986, 101 illegal immigrants from Mali were bundled on to a charter plane and returned to Bamako. The act was exclusion in its most literal sense. Opinion divided radically. A month later Pasqua's proposals for a nationality bill deepened the issue. Children born in France to non-French parents who had been born abroad would no longer automatically have French nationality on gaining their maturity: they would have to apply for it. Civil rights organizations and SOS-Racisme argued that it would mean eighteen-year-olds living in a limbo of nationality, provoking discrimination

in the community. Religious opinion was alarmed. Mitterrand announced his opposition. Focus on exclusion in all its senses intensified. The bill was intensely debated in the media but was overtaken by events.

The diametrical play of the Chirac agenda against the Socialist programme of 1981 informed the policy not only of Pasqua but also of Alain Devaquet, the minister responsible for research and higher education, avid connoisseur of de Gaulle's memoirs. He set out to repeal Savary's extension of university democracy and restore power on the governing councils to the professoriat. Going beyond this retaliatory brief, he also proposed to give universities more autonomy in setting fees, awarding their own degrees and selecting students. The fear created by the visible evidence of youth unemployment made higher education a necessity for those in the last year of the lycées. Once at university, students saw it as vital to survive into at least the second year and obtain qualifications which carried a national status. They saw Devaquet as preparing universities for privatization, favouring inequality and selection through fees, and they turned the government's ideology of freedom on its head. Demonstrations in favour of free and equal access to universities erupted.

The sudden outbreak, size and extent of the massed protests surprised everybody. There had been endless talk of the 'unpolitical student generation' after *les années '68*, but on 27 November 1986 hundreds of thousands of students and lycée pupils took to the streets across the country. Schools and faculties were brought to a standstill for over three weeks. *Beurs* from the lycées were prominent, protesting equally at the nationality bill under consideration. Inter-ethnic solidarity against exclusion was a key element in the campaign. Coluche and his *restos du cœur* were an inspiration. Scepticism about politics was general: there were no divisive *groupuscules* as in 1968. The range of views which would previously have split the student body into segments were mobilized into collective action through a process of co-ordination. Where ideology was discerned it was attributed to the government and its supporters. 'It's the small minority of students in favour of the bill who are the hyper-political ones,' said one student in Marseille. 'It's they who have made it a political issue.'[3]

Mitterrand identified himself clearly with the protesters. Alain Devaquet, a professor himself, keen to show his rhetorical skills, was surprised to find himself matched on a Europe 1 broadcast by a student, Isabelle Thomas, who instantly became an icon of the movement. Charles Pasqua blundered into ordering defiant policing of the second huge march on 4 December in Paris. As it was dispersing on the night of the 5th, a young French student of Moroccan origin, Malik Oussekine, died under repeated truncheon

blows from the police. It was never established whether he was a demon-
strator or not. Devaquet immediately resigned. On 8 December Chirac
withdrew the Devaquet bill. Pasqua's proposals on nationality were also
halted and then submitted to a commission of experts. It amounted to
postponement.

2. . . . a Republic of post-socialism?

Mitterrand was drawn to the moral and altruistic tone of the pupil–student
movement. Its sense of engagement but absence of ideology made it particularly attractive to a President in search of a consensus policy with a combative edge. He made another foray a month later. With unemployment and
redundancies still rising, but with the high-profile privatization sales well
advanced, a long, bitter strike broke out on the railways on 18 December.
Spreading spontaneously from the Gare du Nord among train drivers across
most of the SNCF network, it was sustained over the Christmas holidays
and reached the Paris métro, the suburban lines and some electricity
workers at a time of severe wintry weather in January. Other public sector
workers stopped work. Chirac firmly condemned the strikes. The trade
unions were not the initiators, but eventually took control from the self-
organizing railway workers, and it was the leader of the CFDT, Edmond
Maire, who prompted a return to work. The strikes for more pay and job
security had less public support than the pupil–student movement but
Mitterrand sympathized with railway strikers at Brégançon in Provence on
New Year's Day 1987. Was this a more ideological commitment? He had,
after all, referred several times to the fact that he was still a socialist.

It was less ideology than political calculation. The confrontations over
education and nationality weakened Chirac's image as the Premier with a
pragmatic message. In the sustained feud of co-habitation, Mitterrand
emerged as more responsive: he had already marked out this territory in
accepting the policy reversals of 1983 and responding to the *école libre*
campaign of 1984. In promoting his own pragmatism still further it was
essential for Mitterrand that sections of the public and the media should
perceive that it was Chirac, Pasqua and Devaquet who were the ideologues.
On the other hand, a President who overcultivated balance and response
would lose the support of the Socialist Party and its voters. Sympathy for the
railway strikers kept Mitterrand's pragmatic image well short of political
neutrality.

An emphasis on calculation and response cannot be avoided in any

assessment of Mitterrand. But it is more than an entry into one person's political personality: it is a way into what was widely seen as the endgame of political ideology, played out in the decade of 1983 to 1993.

Presidentials and after: more redefinitions

Co-habitation necessitated a politics of calculation: Chirac knew this as well as Mitterrand. Neither could afford a breakdown in the system for which either one might be held responsible. As the Presidentials and the bicentenary approached, and the space and time given to them in the media escalated, co-habitation itself was deemed to be symptomatic of ideological restraint. Mitterrand had a head-start over Chirac: he had restrained his own zeal and the ideologues of his party since 1983. By mid-1987 he was deemed to be well practised in the art of both reversal and moderation. It was not unattractive to the public. Opinion polls began to place Mitterrand favourably should he decide to run as the Socialist candidate for a second term. This marginalized Rocard.

They also indicated that Mitterrand would defeat Chirac, and when Raymond Barre's support began to recede Mitterrand decided to stand, though he waited until 22 March 1988 to make his decision public. In April 1987 Jean-Marie Le Pen had easily obtained the nominations which he had failed to secure in 1981, and in May of the same year the Communists put forward André Lajoinie, the leader of the parliamentary group but not of the party. Another prominent Communist, Pierre Juquin, effectively left the party in October 1987 to stand for a renovation of the left, attracting support from the PSU and from a number of *gauchistes* who were not committed to Arlette Laguiller, candidate for the third time as representative of the Trotskyist *Lutte ouvrière*. A fervent anti-nuclear campaigner, Antoine Waechter, stood for the ecologists.

Well before making his decision, Mitterrand used his media opportunity of 14 July 1987 to tell the public that since 1986 his duty as President had taken precedence over his own convictions, but not to the point where 'essential values' might have been compromised, a scenario which, he added, had not arisen. The implication was either that Chirac had agreed on essentials or that Mitterrand had already outplayed his Prime Minister in the area of unspecified values which lay beyond or behind conviction. Very late in the campaign he made it clear that these essential values did not extend to renationalizing the privatized companies. He would leave them in private hands. It was heralded as final evidence that the Socialist ideology of 1981 had been abandoned. By 1988 this occasioned no surprise.

It was seen by relatively few as a betrayal. The challenge for the mainstream left, as indeed for Mitterrand himself, was to redefine what of fundamental substance remained. Over the next five years it proved elusive.

Redefinition was universal in the late 1980s. Both right and left repackaged their conflictual policies as consensus. On the right, in consonance with Chirac's promotion of the liberal economy as the touchstone of freedom, there was a wealth of political writing which claimed an unbroken heritage of liberalism and individualism in French history, whether distantly in Alexis de Tocqueville, in the inter-war essays of Alain, acknowledged philosopher of the Radical Party, or more recently in the independent voice of Raymond Aron, best known to the wider public for his dismissal of May 1968 as a psychodrama. The twentieth anniversary of the May events fell in the weeks of the Presidential election, and in a series of broadcast discussions and newspaper articles the one interpretation most vehemently debated was the redefinition of May '68 as the herald of a post-modern society. In 1983 *L'Ère du vide*, the first book by Gilles Lipovetsky, a 39-year-old philosopher teaching in Grenoble, portrayed an unstoppable culture of individualism under the collective rhetoric of the student revolt, which, he argued, later turned to narcissism. He re-evaluated the carnivalesque inversions of 1968 and subsequent years as essentially hyper-individualistic and narcissistic, stripped of any serious liberational content. Ranging across American ideas from the intellectual analysis of Daniel Bell to the films of Woody Allen, it gave backing to claims that the imperative of individualism had become an irresistible post-modern and post-egalitarian force in contemporary society, even among its apparent opponents. Young proponents of a 'new right' celebrated the admiration for America identified with Alain Juppé and many others in the government. Appropriating the libertarian slogan of May '68, they claimed that in the USA '*tout est possible*'.

Mitterrand's own redefinition was contained in an open campaign letter addressed to the French people, in which balanced judgement and sagacity took the place of 'Changer la vie'. Committed to the struggle against exclusion, its overture to 'La France Unie' and ethnic integration was enacted in rallies featuring a *beur* pop group, wittily called 'Carte de Séjour' (residence permit), and the disarming evocation of 'Douce France' sung by Charles Trenet. In bitter exchanges, Chirac attacked Mitterrand for favouring voting rights for immigrants in local elections, even though he himself had shown sympathy for the idea in 1979, while Mitterrand stuck to his long-term policy as a democratic necessity and castigated Chirac's campaign for pandering to the extremists of the Front National. In the first round of the election Mitterrand emerged as the clear front-runner with 34

per cent of the vote, but he had been sparing with details of what he would or would not do, and had put the onus on Chirac, who came second with 19.9 per cent, to justify his record in government. In fact Chirac's manifesto looked more to the future, promising a decade of national revival through free enterprise. Both Chirac and Mitterrand edged towards addressing the question of whether or not France was locked into economic decline, a possibility which they denied but which made the electorate unusually cautious.

Voters themselves, normally ready to defend their political choice, were worried that the economy seemed to defy all political persuasions. There were some upward signs of growth by the time of the election, though during 1987 French industrial products were shown to be less competitive in the international markets than at any time since 1969. Unemployment receded slightly from its high point in March 1987, and Chirac was credited by the leaders of the *patronat* (CNPF) for having started a process which would enable companies to expand and create more jobs, but they bemoaned half-measures in liberalizing the economy. In July 1987 the Vice-President of the CNPF called for more vigour from the government. He scornfully told *Le Monde* that there was only one consensus in France and that was to do nothing.

On the extreme right Le Pen excoriated mainstream politics, and redefined economic recession as social decadence which, he insisted, allowed North African immigrants to imperil the lives of French people and take their jobs. His support in the first round exceeded all poll predictions, bringing him over 14 per cent of the vote, with peaks of 28 per cent in Marseille and almost as high in Nice and Toulon. He attracted over 4.3 million voters, more than double those who voted for the Communist André Lajoinie (6.7 per cent). These two results alone emphasized the extent to which the landscape of French politics had been radically redrawn. In terms of public credibility the PCF had not experienced such marginalization since the Nazi-Soviet pact of 1939, even if many of the reasons lay outside France in the disintegration of international Communism.

The public had consistently seen Raymond Barre as the most practical and competent candidate, but despite being more popular than Chirac among the younger age groups he had no equivalent of the RPR organization behind him and failed to translate his professorial manner into personal charisma, receiving only 18.5 per cent of the vote. Mitterrand duly won a comfortable victory over Chirac in the second round of voting on 8 May by 54 per cent to 46 per cent. The 72-year-old President returned to the Élysée as a force for unification and no longer the ideological Socialist

of 1981. Confident, chastened, realistic and wily, Mitterrand had redefined himself to the point where he decided to nominate his political rival and alter ego, Michel Rocard, as Prime Minister. Legislative elections were announced for early June. His personal dislike for Rocard, thoroughly reciprocated, was subordinated to his calculation that Rocard was best placed to enable the PS to return to government, in the slipstream of his own Presidential success.

The parliamentary results justified Mitterrand's calculation by the narrowest of margins. Record abstentions stole the headlines: there was voting fatigue, but also ambivalence among centrist voters who had supported Mitterrand, who had no wish to support the PS, but could not bring themselves to vote for the RPR and UDF who once again formed an electoral alliance. The effects of a return to two rounds of voting made the rest of the news. The Front National secured majority backing for only one seat (in the Var). The PCF, by contrast, held on to twenty-seven of its traditional bastions, well down on the forty-four it held in 1981, the last time that two rounds had been used, but enough for *L'Humanité* to assure its readers that the party was the only left-wing force in the new Chamber. Neither the Socialists on the one hand, nor the combination of the RPR and UDF on the other, commanded an absolute majority, but if some ministerial posts were offered to the UDF, Rocard judged that he could continue to form a viable government. Three members of the UDF accepted, fewer than Rocard had hoped, but enough to avoid the votes of the centre going against him, enough even to suggest that Mitterrand and Rocard's government together firmly occupied the centre ground of French politics.

De Gaulle's Republic and the *après-Gaulliste* Republic, followed by the socialist Republic of 1981, might now have become the Republic of post-socialism (*après-socialisme*). It was never labelled as such, the preference being either for no label at all or for a personification of the whole of 1981–1995 as 'Mitterrand's Republic' or *les années Mitterrand*. Yet it was the notion of an aftermath of socialism, and reflections on the meaning of consensus, that dominated the comments on the elections of 1988. Mitterrand had been elected as more of a national leader than the Gaullist Chirac. His monarchical style strongly echoed de Gaulle and allowed him to represent continuity within the Fifth Republic. The Socialist Party had invested in his success and had taken on his national image which broke the monopoly that Gaullist figureheads had exercised since 1958. There was no longer one party which could claim to be the 'party of government'. The culture of government had diversified across a broad centre of the political spectrum. This was reflected in Mitterrand's vague electoral slogan of

ouverture (opening) and Rocard's actual overtures to the centre deputies of the UDF. But going beyond the mechanisms of coalition government, it was clear to many that the consensus of 1988 sprang more from social and cultural developments than from political agreement or expediency.

With the bicentenary imminent, the sociologist Henri Mendras published *La Seconde Révolution française* in 1988 in which he traced the transformations of class in the twentieth century in order to highlight the contemporary dominance of a 'centre constellation' in society. Like Bourdieu, Mendras referred to patterns of taste as evidence of the centre's shared social behaviour, citing the informal ritual of the outdoor barbecue: it reversed all the modes of the bourgeois ritual dinner, giving the appearance of spontaneity and disorder but in fact being thoroughly well organized. Many of the social categories included in his constellation made a parallel appearance in the influential trilogy of essays, *La République du centre*, by François Furet, Jacques Julliard and Pierre Rosanvallon. Writing his part of the book soon after the elections, Jacques Julliard, editorialist of *Le Nouvel Observateur* and historian, pointed to 'a heterogeneous tissue of private and public business directors, the upper ranks of public employees, politicians, intellectuals, artists, personnel of the press, television and advertising . . .' who formed what he called a 'super-élite'. He had high hopes that this social matrix of consensus would restore a sense of purpose to a political world which had become 'insignificant'.[4]

Everyone noted that Mitterrand's re-election in 1988 was greeted by a small rise in the stock market, a polar opposite to the dramatic fall which had been the response of the Bourse in 1981. A measure of how far Mitterrand had travelled in seven years, this was also an indication that a wary cohesion between the mainstream left and the world of finance and business had taken the place of inveterate hostility, yet another strand in the making of a centre consensus. The *patronat* had adapted itself to the Auroux laws of 1982, which had increased the expectation that the two sides of industry would negotiate, and there was no pressure to repeal them under Chirac. Contractual negotiations at company level between employers and unions became more common in the mid-1980s as the Socialists began to favour restructuring and labour flexibility within industry. By 1986 the employers' organization (CNPF) had good reason to see the state under Mitterrand as broadly sympathetic to its interests.

In these social perspectives the 'centre' existed outside politics, and the mark of realism in politics was seen as a readiness to pursue policies which reflected the values of the centre constellation, élite or consensus. Were these values the same as the 'essential values' evoked by Mitterrand in

1987? It appeared that they were. They made up a rough area of agreement on the ideas of a unified nation within an increasingly integrated Europe, economic modernization and social inclusion, that Mitterrand in 1988 appeared to embody. What had been rejected by this consensus was the state-run economy proposed in 1981 and the social exclusion which Chirac and Pasqua had exacerbated in 1986–7. The centre values were variously summarized but amounted to three paradigms: competitiveness but not to the point of exclusion: social inclusiveness but not to the point of stifling bureaucracy: modernization but not to the point of surrendering French distinctiveness.

Bicentenary

One public expression of consensus lay in the pressing demands for a unifying celebration of the bicentenary in 1989. François Furet, an ex-Communist who had become the leading revisionist historian of the French Revolution, carried conviction in 1978 when he argued that the Terror of 1793–4 demonstrated the kinship of revolution to tyranny.[5] His reinterpretation, and others very similar, gave sustenance to those increasingly critical of the Marxist historiography of the Revolution, and although they did not end the emotive sympathies of the political left for 1789, they were seen to discredit the continuous use of the French Revolution as justification for conflict. The *ouverture* theme of Mitterrand's Presidency made it invidious to celebrate 200 years of class struggle, violence or ideology. The liberal turn of the Fabius and Rocard governments, no less than the decline of the Communist Party, severely curtailed the impact of Jack Lang's 1981 promise to show a France 'animated by revolution'. The planners of the bicentenary could not afford to be divisive.

In fact, a gamut of historical interpretations of the Revolution made for unity and inclusion. In the first place, as Furet rhetorically asked of French people in 1988, 'Who isn't a republican?'[6] Secondly, the understanding of 1789 as a rural as well as an urban revolution kept town and country together. For decades in the twentieth century the rural exodus had intensified a social superiority which identified reason as essentially urban. By the late 1980s this had not entirely disappeared, but popular forms of ecology were joined to new waves of ruralism which made inroads into rational thinking about the quality of life. This was not an upsurge of reactionary politics or Vichy's 'retour à la terre' but formed part of the centre consensus, already evident to demographers in a population drift of the middle classes into *la France profonde*, to cultural analysts in the strength of regional

revival, and to sociologists of urban taste in the growing preference for *produits régionaux*. Thirdly, and most significantly for the immediate politics of the bicentenary, there was the identification of 1789 with the *Déclaration des droits de l'homme et du citoyen*. Updated by feminism and by anti-racism, civil and human rights constituted an assertively modern theme, accenting the necessity of cultural and racial inclusion and widening the revolutionary message of social justice from a conflictual project into a consensual one. Only Le Pen and the FN rejected such an emphasis as unacceptable.

The concern to use the bicentenary to mount a showpiece of ethnic inclusion finally overshadowed other political agendas. The highlight of the Paris festivities on 14 July 1989 showed what a rich vein of entertainment had been opened up by Jack Lang's musical fêtes and the SOS-Racisme concerts of the mid-1980s. Themes of multi-ethnicity, *métissage* and musical diversity were choreographed by the artist and director Jean-Paul Goude, variously labelled as maverick, iconoclast and guru of TV and poster advertising. The result was a flamboyantly spectacular and eccentric musical parade, ballet and theatrical display running the length of the Champs-Élysées. The decision to invite the African-American operatic diva Jessye Norman to sing the 'Marseillaise' in the Place de la Concorde was not the least of the symbolic gestures of the event. Goude projected a French Revolution transposed as world culture and celebrated as ethnic sounds in what he called the 'revolution of modern times': the era of communication.

It was the turn of France in 1989 to host the meeting of G7, the leaders of the seven richest industrialized nations. Mitterrand decided to hold it in Paris at the height of the bicentenary. It was the incongruity of a summit of international wealth invited to watch a multi-ethnic cultural extravaganza which gave an extra edge to taunts of hypocrisy and neo-colonialism levelled at the festivities. Mitterrand made no secret of his belief that French prestige should be on display, and he met disapproval by stressing the obligation of G7 to address the poverty and exclusion of the Third World. Other criticisms were levelled at the consensus as much as at Mitterrand or Jean-Paul Goude. The influence of Guy Debord's analysis of 'a society of spectacle' was at its height in the Presidential election year and during the bicentenary. Dating from 1967, Debord's contempt for a commodity-obsessed society which reduced everyone to mere spectators was one widespread intellectual theme which needed no redefinition at the end of the 1980s. It both influenced and defied Jack Lang's cultural policies, supportive of their popular involvement while insistent that festivals themselves had become commodities. The consensus-driven pursuit of productivity,

key to Rocard's and Mitterrand's regime after 1988, kept Debord's ideas in active minority circulation. Less esoteric was the analysis from voices in many of the regions that Paris had once again mounted a celebration of centralized power: the depiction of the Fédérés of the Revolution in Goude's planned parade was dismissed in advance by the Breton cultural organization Dastum as eliminating all regional specificity. In most local areas the tradition of *bals populaires* on the night of 13 July was kept, enabling *L'Humanité* and its regional variations to restate the people's role at the heart of republican ideology with 'The Revolution continues', its headline on 15 July. The paper called for the elimination of inequalities. It denounced the G7 summit in Paris as a scandal.

3. Identity in Europe and beyond

In his 1988 election letter to the French people, Mitterrand told them that their future lay in Europe. This was as much his intended direction for the consensus as the inclusive republicanism of the bicentenary. It had not been the priority of Mitterrand in 1981, when the most radical foreign policy statements of his first year in power envisaged a selective 'Third Worldism' as an ideological necessity, including help to insurgents in El Salvador and the Sandinista government in Nicaragua, and talk of a firm break with Pinochet's Chile. This appeared assertively anti-capitalist and anti-American, and in reply the US authorities made no secret of their opinion that Communist ministers in an allied government, and Régis Debray as Mitterrand's adviser, were pushing the new President into dangerous areas. No break with Chile was made, to the disappointment of many on the left, but the arms deliveries to Nicaragua kept Franco-American relations cool for two years, although Mitterrand was not far behind Ronald Reagan in backing the British expedition to recover the Falklands in 1982, against most of the French press and much of the Socialist Party which labelled Margaret Thatcher's naval task-force as neo-imperialist. Mitterrand justified his decision by arguing that European solidarity came before everything else, and this position could be interpreted as the first clear sign of a shift of gear in Mitterrand's long-standing Europeanism. It was at a time when the forced devaluations of the franc were straining Socialist attitudes towards the Exchange Rate Mechanism: the left of the party, identified with Chevènement, was staking out the possibility of France leaving the European monetary system and pursuing its anti-capitalist programme alone. Mitterrand rejected this line as part of his backing for an about-turn

in economic policy, and it was evident from 1983 onwards that he was looking to Europe for a reorientation of purpose. This acceleration in his Europeanism was just as much of a salvaging operation as the internal austerity and restructuring. It was a pragmatic search for a leading role in Europe, initially a Europe still locked into the Cold War.

Working within Europe had allowed French agriculture to be modernized without the massive social breakdown many had predicted in the 1950s. The subsidies provided by the Common Agricultural Policy had protected the prosperity of the peasant farmers who had harnessed the rural revolution: they brought relative affluence for the owners of the big farms who dominated the internal European markets. French governments had also used Europe successfully to contain post-war Germany and make containment into partnership, and thirdly they had found Europe flexible enough to allow the French state to continue its interventionism in the economy, to maintain a considerable degree of protection for French industry as well as agriculture, and to resolve social conflict by concessions to industrial and agricultural protests. On all the evidence of recent history, Europe was clearly the pathway to relaunching a socialist Presidency in the name of national interest, and Mitterrand had no personal difficulty in taking it.

It was certainly not a socialist Europe with which Mitterrand became identified in the decade of intensive European negotiating that ensued. Nor was it a neutralist one in terms of defence and security. The nuclear *force de frappe* was nurtured by Mitterrand as an independent deterrent, but he had no Gaullist illusion that it could be substituted for NATO or replace the American alliance. Mitterrand, mistrustful of the USSR throughout his career, identified with the wave of intellectual hostility towards Soviet Russia occasioned by the Gulag revelations and capped by the Soviet aggression in Afghanistan. Facing down the Soviet intention to site short-range missiles on the frontiers with Western Europe, Mitterrand journeyed to Bonn in January 1983 to address the German Bundestag and state in uncompromising terms that the European and German response should be to permit American Pershing II missiles on West German soil. The speech affirmed Mitterrand's complete independence of the Communists in the French government, mollified the USA, and began a close, if chequered, European partnership with the conservative German Chancellor Helmut Kohl. If he journeyed to Moscow in 1984 it was partly because he willingly travelled far more than his predecessors, but he yielded to pressure from the French press that he should use the occasion to intercede for the freedom of the Soviet dissident Andrei Sakharov and his wife. In 1986 he developed constructive relations with Mikhail Gorbachev, in the interests of renewing

détente and not in any clairvoyant sense anticipating the fall of the Berlin Wall or the collapse of Communism.

By the time of his re-election, Mitterrand's pragmatic involvement in European policy-making had helped resolve the question of Britain's payments to the Community budget and had facilitated the stages of a Single Act in 1985–6, revising the Treaty of Rome and setting up one common interior market for the expanded European Community (EC), to come into effect at the end of 1992. Greece had joined in 1981 and Spain and Portugal in 1986 and it was agreed by the Twelve to move towards majority voting in the Council of Ministers and to involve the European Parliament more directly in the decisions of the Commission. Greater democracy and more integrated structures in the EC were the mark not only of Mitterrand's own preference but emphatically those of his close friend and Foreign Minister, Roland Dumas, and the Presidential adviser on European affairs Élisabeth Guigou, an ENA graduate recruited by Jacques Delors, with experience as financial attachée at the London embassy. Her commitment to Europe recalled that of Louise Weiss in the Briand years of the late 1920s. The theme of Franco-German entente at the centre of a peaceful Europe was made more prominent by the fiftieth anniversary of the outbreak of war in 1939, and still more urgent by the dramatic fall of the Berlin Wall on 9 November 1989, raising the prospects of German reunification, for which Mitterrand was as unprepared as the rest of Western Europe. If there was to be a 'new' Germany, then fears of its possible independence urged French Europhiles to anchor it even more firmly in the European Community.

Guigou found Mitterrand extremely wary of an outbreak of German nationalism in the unknown territory of the post-Soviet world: his residual fears from the era of Franco-German wars were a sombre antidote to the general exuberance among Europeans which she herself shared. The explosion of a contemporary wave of revolutions unexpectedly made the year of 1989 far more than the parochial French bicentenary at which Mitterrand had been the genial host. His disarray at the epic and rapid turn of events was evident in his fumbling diplomacy on a curiosity visit to Berlin soon after the fall of the Wall, when Kohl clearly resented Mitterrand's initial reluctance to envisage a reunited Germany. Their mutual mission and respect nevertheless survived. Kohl was determined that the institutional steps towards a more unified Europe should still proceed; Mitterrand made it his priority. Containing a potentially resurgent Germany was one of the implicit French subtexts of the treaty reached by the European leaders at Maastricht in December 1991 and signed two

months later. It fulfilled Mitterrand's explicit dedication to continue the work of Jean Monnet at the transfer of his ashes to the Panthéon in November 1988.

Iraq

The calculated decision to back America at the crucial military stage of the Gulf crisis of 1990–91 gave Mitterrand reason to be confident of consensus in his command of foreign policy. Following Iraq's invasion of Kuwait in August 1990, the violation of the French ambassador's residence there on 15 September caused Mitterrand to step up support for the American-led alliance, which he signalled by sending the aircraft carrier *Clemenceau* surely but slowly to the Gulf. French troops numbering just under 10,000 under the command of General Michel Roquejoffre were sent to Saudi Arabia even as Mitterrand intensified his commitment to a peaceful solution through the United Nations which would involve Saddam Hussein's unconditional withdrawal from Kuwait. His peace initiatives, which much of the American and British press scorned as duplicitous, showed sensitivity to the multiple strands of history and policy linking France to Iraq, not least the considerable reputation of Saddam Hussein as an exponent of Jacobin-style secularism and modernity, enhanced during the fratricidal Iraq–Iran war of the 1980s. Oil had come to France from Iraq at cheaper prices than elsewhere in the 1970s and defence contracts between France and Iraq, including Exocet missiles and Mirage fighters, had deepened the commercial involvement. The enthusiasm for Saddam Hussein's regime was high in the North African Maghreb, which was the focus of over 80 per cent of French investment and trade with Arab states, and much of the opinion among the 3 million or more Muslims in France reflected this.

Rooted further in the past was the ambivalence of French policy towards the Arab and Berber world. Repressive and benighted in Algeria, it had a more enlightened image in the Middle East, and was well poised to respond to offers of friendship from Saddam Hussein after the relative failures of Britain as the mandatory authority and Iraq's moves away from direct Soviet influence. For years, French diplomatic efforts had been directed towards setting up an international peace conference on the whole Middle East, and Mitterrand continued to hope until the last minute that Saddam Hussein would accept such an offer as a way of withdrawing from Kuwait. He stated consistently that France had no intention of contributing to any conquest of Iraq. Backed by the parliamentary opposition of the UDF and RPR, he was clearly wary of a substantial rebellion from within the Socialist

Party. He made no attempt to win round the Communist Party (PCF), but did try to keep his own Minister of Defence, Jean-Pierre Chevènement, in line with his dual diplomacy. Chevènement's sympathy for an association of Franco-Iraqi friendship was publicized by *Le Canard enchaîné*, and his resignation on 29 January 1991 cleared the way for Mitterrand and Rocard to present a united government front. The obduracy of Saddam Hussein did the rest, and public opinion consolidated behind French intervention. It was never Mitterrand's war in the sense of a moral or political crusade. The length of time given to negotiations before troops were finally deployed convinced many doubters that pathways to peace had been adequately explored.

The vocal anti-war movement staged impressive demonstrations across the country on 12 January 1991. They showed that hostility to American liberal economics, to its cultural imperialism and oil interests could still ignite memories of the 1960s Vietnam protests, and that pro-Arab and Muslim sympathies had continued from the years of struggle against Algérie Française. Such grand narratives of the decolonization period brought Pierre Vidal-Naquet into the movement, but only at the start. As Saddam Hussein revealed his dictatorial and expansionist pathology, Vidal-Naquet and several other left-wing intellectuals moved with public opinion into condemnation of the Iraqi leader. Significantly, there was a wish by a majority of the Muslims in France not to take sides, though they feared public misunderstanding and victimization whatever their position. In fact there was widespread positive comment on the absence of violent Muslim reactions which many people had expected. There was also constant reference to the inchoate political nature of the anti-war movement, sections of which often demonstrated apart. The PCF found a voluble second wind after its battering in the polls; the Trotskyists led by Alain Krivine had their own section, Chevènement spoke for many dissident Socialists, Antoine Waechter carried his Greens into the cause. Unexpectedly Jean-Marie Le Pen declared that he too was against the war, causing defections from the FN, but he was obstinate in his populist gamble that French involvement would be seen as irresponsible blundering into an essentially inter-Arab affair. His presence in the anti-war camp was acutely discomfiting for the majority of the protesters.

Issue by issue people from across the political spectrum were crossing traditional alignments. Newspapers and television were held to be more formative of opinion on these issues than political parties. Positions for and against American policy and influence filled the pages of the weekly magazines, side by side with the commodity advertisements which imposed

their own subliminal grid of material culture. Mitterrand had ended the reflex anti-Americanism of the Fifth Republic identified with de Gaulle. On this issue he carried majority support. It gave him assurance that he could equally well depend on a similar majority to endorse his moves within Europe.

Maastricht. Yugoslavia in parenthesis

Accompanying Germany into the brave new world of Maastricht and the post-Cold War era was Mitterrand's third persona as President, after his first as socialist idealist and his second as the consensus pragmatist. From the first to the second was a mutation. The third was not. But it needed all his energy to persuade the French people that the Maastricht Treaty was the historic and irreversible event that he claimed, and that it both fulfilled the previous fifty years and heralded the next fifty to come. It stood, in his words, at the mid-point of a century of Europeanism, and he announced that it would be put to a referendum, set for Sunday, 20 September 1992. It seemed a perfect opportunity not only to ratify his own European initiatives but also to revive the flagging political fortunes of a quarrelsome and unpopular Socialist Party, by underlining the deep internal divisions over Europe which ravaged the opposition of the Gaullist RPR.

The aspect of Maastricht taken least seriously by the French public was the notion of a common EC foreign policy. The sheer indecision and camouflaged divisions within the Community over the Balkan crisis made it impossible to imagine the Big Three, Germany, France and Britain, agreeing to one foreign-policy voice. Mitterrand did not choose to be the mediator with Serbia, after Slovenia and Croatia had broken away in June 1991: it was assumed that he would be. Fulfilling the role brought him into conflict with Helmut Kohl and his Foreign Minister Hans-Dietrich Genscher, eager for the EC to recognize the breakaway republics. Mitterrand reluctantly agreed in January 1992, still highly cautious about the spread of nationalisms and the breakup of the old world order in the wake of the Soviet collapse. He rescued himself on one symbolic occasion from the next two years of European paralysis over the Balkan fratricide. On 28 June 1992, anniversary of the assassination of the Archduke Franz Ferdinand in 1914, he flew into the besieged and devastated city of Sarajevo, to meet people in the street and promise them a French airlift of supplies. The European press, surprised at his lack of consultation with other EC leaders, nevertheless hailed it as a *beau geste*, humanitarian, courageous and timely. It was more than a gesture: it was an initiative. Tentative steps

towards a European military intervention did not measure up to this one moment. Mitterrand came to accept the overwhelming evidence of Serbian aggression, but countering it continued to seem beyond decisive action. As an issue in French opinion it stayed in parenthesis. It was the EC's inability to act without the USA which created diffuse frustrations in opinion and remained in the collective memory.

Throughout the summer of 1992 French people took and retook their positions less on Yugoslavia than on the central creation at Maastricht of a European Union and a single currency, designed to replace national currencies in January 1999 in all EC countries where economic convergence had occurred. As the date of the referendum approached, a safe 'Yes' vote predicted in opinion polls in June turned into a possible 'No' vote at the end of August. The country was scoured for signs of political, social or geographical coherence in voting intentions. The conclusion was that the issue divided friends and communities far more radically than the Gulf war: it evoked the mealtime family fights caused by the Dreyfus Affair a century before. Tables were metaphorically or literally overturned. Among the political parties only the National Front and the Communist Party were said to be internally united, both declaring a firm 'No' for diametrically different reasons, the FN in the interests of exclusive nationalism and the PCF in pursuance of international anti-capitalism. The three main parties ranged themselves with varying commitment on the 'Yes' platform, but minorities within them made visceral thrusts against the treaty. From the Gaullist RPR two prominent ex-Ministers, Charles Pasqua and Philippe Séguin, led the 'No' campaign with vigour and an acute sense of timing, arguing for a Europe true to de Gaulle's conception of a loose confederation of nation states. From the solidly pro-European UDF, a quixotic individual Philippe de Villiers broke away to form an anti-Maastricht 'fight for values' which he claimed to personify as deputy for the old counter-revolutionary Vendée. From the Socialist Party Jean-Pierre Chevènement created a min- ority 'Citizens' movement' designed to fight the treaty in the name of social justice.

Chirac declared in favour, but was openly discomfited by the Gaullist orthodoxy claimed by Séguin and Pasqua; Giscard was a dedicated sup- porter, and Mitterrand was compelled to throw the full weight of the Presidency behind the treaty at the very time when he was also forced to undergo an operation for cancer of the prostate, nine days before the referendum. He had known for many years about his condition, but it had been kept from public knowledge, so that the sudden news added an acute extra mix of personality and politics to the highly charged atmosphere. In

Bordeaux, to which *Libération* went to sample the last-minute campaigns, a statue of a European Marianne was unveiled to the strains of Beethoven's 'Ode to Joy', while individual 'No' voices in the street urged others not to vote for a Europe run by the banks and big business. Wine was copiously offered and consumed on both sides. The daily *Var Matin* in the Saint-Tropez area, like many local papers, gave space to the opinions of every sector of society as well as those of the political parties and judged on 4 September that Maastricht was considered by most people as *the* question of the *fin-de-siècle*. In the locality only the anarchist federation of the Var called for a boycott of the vote, describing the whole debate as 'a smokescreen, hiding people from reality'.[7] The vitality of the campaign and media coverage could be seen as yet another justification of issue politics. It was the first time that the public had been fully consulted on moves towards European integration which had always been decided from above. The result was minutely analysed. The treaty was endorsed by the slenderest majority: by 50.8 per cent of the votes cast in metropolitan France, and just over 51 per cent in all.

National interest had been the crux of the issue, and the site of vituperative disagreement. For many 'Yes' voters the point of closer integration was to make Europe a powerful united player on the world stage, competing on equal terms with America with a resultant opening of markets and new cultural horizons, but they mostly added that only through such a Europe would French national products and culture prosper and expand. A positive endorsement was deemed necessary for national reasons, not just European ones. The nationalist declarations of the National Front, with Philippe de Villiers not far behind, argued the complete opposite. Only a 'No' vote would protect French interests from foreign predators and prevent France from becoming part of a homogenized, characterless world dominated ultimately by American goods and culture. The neo-Gaullism of Séguin and Pasqua urged voters to embrace some of the wider world vision but without any cession of national independence.

Causes beyond 'the national interest' were no less involved. Human rights campaigners and SOS-Racisme identified an integrated Europe with humanitarian progress. The regions were split. In many of the regions economic hardship determined a 'No' vote as in Nord–Pas-de-Calais, Provence and Corsica, whereas Bretons, although they divided locally over whether or not their agriculture was protected by Europe, eventually gave Maastricht a firm approval. The ecologists, who had registered something of an electoral breakthrough in the regional elections of March 1992 with more than 14 per cent of the vote overall, were made up of several rival

groups. Two of the leaders, Brice Lalonde and Antoine Waechter, saw hope for ecology in a bolder Europe, while a third, Dominique Voynet, threw herself into a 'No' campaign with arguments close to those of the left-wing citizens' movement of Jean-Pierre Chevènement. Syndicalists in the CGT campaigned for the Communist Party's 'No', but the CFDT welcomed Maastricht because of its clauses on workers' rights to which extra attention had been drawn by the refusal of the Conservative government in Britain to accept them.

Before Maastricht, it was the Common Agricultural Policy (CAP) which had notably symbolized European integration. Its predicament in 1992 was intensely discussed. Quotas had been gradually introduced in the mid- to late 1980s as the first sign that the CAP had to be reformed and could not guarantee endless farming subsidies. The price of cereals dropped and the reform was increasingly resented by farmers. A related rise of anti-Americanism was also noticeable in rural areas as American agriculture used the free trade promoted by the Uruguay round of negotiations on tariffs (GATT) to dump cheap produce in Europe while continuing protection of its own internal markets. Jacques Delors, writing in *Ouest-France* and other regional papers in 1987 on behalf of the European Commission, argued that quotas were the best way of protecting French agriculture, but he negotiated a slower run-down of CAP subsidies. François Guillaume, leader of the farming lobby, was made Minister of Agriculture under Chirac from 1986 to 1988, and he was expected to reverse reforms of the CAP. He failed to work out a strategy for adapting agriculture to the new pressures of international competition and was eventually held to have betrayed much of the farming community. There was no clear consensus on the type of productive unit to prioritize: farmers were united only in their determination not to be reduced to mere custodians of the countryside. By 1992 the changes in the CAP and the effects of American imports seemed to many peasant farmers to threaten this fate, and the 'No' vote was correspondingly widespread in rural areas. It was the culmination of over a year of physical agitation by peasant producers which had made any ministerial visit to the countryside into a local skirmish. The argument from Third Worldists that the CAP protected French and European agriculture to the detriment of products from and within the poorest countries of Africa was barely heard.

Almost at once the meaning given to the outcome by those who had voted 'Yes' was that half of the country was prepared to go forward and the other half was defensively clinging to an outmoded France. The 'No' votes were categorized as a kaleidoscope of whirling pieces, including unemployment, threats to small farms and loss of sovereignty, whereas the

'Yes' voters credited themselves with a more unified perspective. There was talk of a new France in a new Europe, hinting at the *après-socialiste* identity that Mitterrand had envisaged since 1983. He himself chose to say that there were no victors and no vanquished, hoping in the recognition of different perspectives to sustain a sense of national unity. He received little credit for this: it was seen as a confession of disappointment at the narrowness of the result. But at one level it was exactly what the Maastricht vote indicated. As already foreshadowed in the period of *après-Gaullisme*, the question of 'Whose society?' had also become 'Whose Europe?' and Maastricht was a climactic point in the history of both these questions, revealing not a single identity but the multiple identities in France which were no longer clearly attached to political parties nor even to the dominant political cleavage of the twentieth century, left and right. Maastricht also confirmed the notion of the circulation of élites, already widely discussed in the 1980s. The 'Yes' vote signalled a cross-party Europhile élite with just sufficient popular depth to win a national referendum. How they would distribute their votes in the next ten years across a largely unreconstructed political spectrum was impossible to forecast. In the short run the result did not benefit the Socialists or raise the standing of Mitterrand.

4. *'The end of ideology' and 'The limits of consensus'*

However people experienced the bicentenary year, the debate about its symbolic content was either refuelled or eclipsed by the historic events in Russia and Eastern Europe, the fall of the Berlin Wall, and the release of Nelson Mandela in South Africa. The repression of Chinese students in Tiananmen Square in June 1989, a month before the festivities, had already given an urgency to the world message at the centre of the celebration. A significant place was given in Goude's parade to the cause of the dissidents in Beijing, but there was no mistaking the sense in the West that the Chinese oligarchy had intensified its ideological hold. Elsewhere, the discourse of 'end' was dominant, starting as it had done internally with the intellectual decline of Marxism, the reversal of the 1981 *changement* and the shift to a liberal economy. The 'end of ideology' reached millenarian heights with the collapse of Soviet Communism, and awareness of the approaching 'end' of the millennium was thought to have brought extra focus on the debate over Maastricht. At the same time, the existence of a centre consensus in France gave weight to the concept of an 'end of French exceptionalism' (*la fin de l'exception française*).

Subtitle of the 1988 book on *La République du centre* by Furet, Julliard and Rosanvallon, and without a question mark, the 'end of French exceptionalism' had been in evidence, they claimed, for some twenty years in the gradual and then rapid demise of Jacobin concepts of the state, and the elimination of the paradigm conflicts which had originated in the Revolution, most obviously the internecine struggle between the Catholic Church and anticlericalism. They argued that both inside and outside France, the Revolution and the Jacobin state had been elevated after 1789 into ideological models, giving France an exceptional status in modern democracies. Furet approvingly summarized the 'end' of this exceptionalism in words which guaranteed the permanence of his analysis in French controversy: 'French citizens now argue over the distribution of national wealth and no longer over the legacy of national history. In giving up its stakes in the Revolution, French politics has lost its theatrical dimension.'[8]

Theatre of the absurd, theatre of spectacle had been two of many metaphors lifted from culture to describe French politics. Theatre of the Jacobin state, theatre of the Revolution were now being used to describe a French political culture which was perceived to be on the point of disappearing. Like stock characters from the *commedia dell'arte*, typologies derived from the conflicts of the Revolution had long been the leading players in politics, none more celebrated than the interventionist state, to which French society looked for solutions as to some theatrical *deus ex machina*. Michel Crozier had focused on the state in his 1971 diagnosis of the 'blocked society' of the 1960s. He argued that ritual patterns of conflict and excessive bureaucracy were the main symptoms of blockage. The primacy of the state (*étatisme*) was at the centre of French exceptionalism, overriding the conflicts which society seemed incapable of resolving through the democratic political process. The republican state carried so much credibility because it was seen as having preceded 'society', in the modern sense of the word.

Only in the period after de Gaulle did *étatisme* start to come under intense criticism from modernizers and liberals, though inevitably the state with all its power had to be the agent to transform itself. The 'new society' as proposed by Chaban-Delmas and Giscard d'Estaing, and the call for political *décrispation* could be seen as forerunners of the 'civil society' declared by Mitterrand and Rocard in 1988, which incorporated a self-regulating system of political alternatives and no longer saw democratic opposition as a threat to the republican regime. It was impossible to imagine de Gaulle co-habiting with the political opposition. Mitterrand had done so. The republic did not disintegrate. Furet and his two co-authors plausibly concluded that the Jacobin state which brooked no opposition had therefore

ceased to be a model. It could also be argued that its moral highground had been irretrievably lost in the 'savage wars of peace' in Indo-China and Algeria. In addition, its economic role was now severely restricted by the acceptance of the values of the international market. From all perspectives it appeared that France at the end of the 1980s had ceased to be a special case.

The 'end of French exceptionalism' as it was initially presented was hastened not only by the 'centre constellation' and the liberal economy, but also by the decline of nationalism as a traditional reflex, and of Gaullism as its main embodiment, particularly among the younger generation since 1968. Mitterrand's language of *ouverture* encouraged the concept of universal human rights as transcending national differences. The ubiquity of this concept was one of the conscious paradoxes of the 'national' celebrations of the bicentenary. Previously it had been French universalism stemming from the Enlightenment and the Revolution which had claimed to transcend other lands and cultures. The universalism of human rights on display in Goude's parade was one to which France, like any other democracy, was theoretically subject.

In the parallel debate on the 'end of ideology' it was acknowledged that the continued existence of the French Communist Party (PCF) was an anomaly, but how far there was any vitality in its ideology was less clear. Beset with numerical decline on all fronts, and the loss of youth and intellectual support, it was still essentially the party that Thorez had moulded and that Marchais had kept within the Soviet-led vision of Marxist-Leninist orthodoxy. It remained a forceful social presence in its working-class heartlands, but it was less the party line on major issues than the party culture at local meetings that kept older members singing the 'Internationale'. Nationally it lost far more than it gained by its participation in the Socialist governments of 1981–4, and the departure of its ministers could not eradicate the memory of its involvement in the first stages of austerity and economic liberalization. Squeezing the workers in the interest of economic recovery was impossible to sell to stalwarts of the CGT, though many of these were fast disappearing with the decline of heavy industry. Syndicalized labour in the CGT halved in the 1980s to little more than 10 per cent of the workforce, dropping still further by the early 1990s, one of the lowest levels in Europe. The circulation of its main newspaper, *La Vie ouvrière*, dropped by half between 1979 and 1985. At the Presidential election of 1988 PCF ideology was strained when it appeared that substantial sections of the working class voted for Le Pen rather than Lajoinie, notably in the Var and the Bouches-du-Rhône. Among dock workers in Marseille, and

the maritime workforce of Toulon and La Ciotat, unemployment and anti-immigrant prejudice were both high. The FN exploited both facts: the PCF was unable to disentangle them. The ideological belief in the historical role and virtues of the proletariat was badly scarred.

The virulence of racism and integral nationalism in the Front National showed far more clearly that ideology in France was far from dead. What was significant, however, was that Le Pen and the FN featured more in the debate about the 'limits of consensus' than in discussions of ideology, an indication that for many people only Marxism was considered to be ideological, and racism was explained as either circumstantial, due to unemployment and fears about security, or natural, harking back to the ideas of the late nineteenth century on the supposed inequality of races.

In the seven years of Mitterrand's second term, the 'limits of consensus' were seen to lie in a disillusionment with mainstream politics, in the crises of identity which gripped all the main parties, in the scandals of political corruption which stole more and more of the headlines, in the disaster of the Socialist Party at the elections of 1993, and finally in the erosion of trust in President Mitterrand without any balancing enthusiasm for his rival Chirac. It was frequently observed that it was a curious consensus that had so little public investment. In this light Le Pen's racist ideology often escaped scrutiny, and the FN was held to be an extreme symptom of a general political *malaise*.

The difficulties encountered by the governments of 1988–93 in dealing with both racism and social inequalities illustrated the perceived limits of consensus. The statistics of 1991 showed an unemployed total of 2.8 million, and those of 1992 registered 400,000 homeless, 2.5 million badly housed and 200,000 households overwhelmed by debt. In the winter of 1992–3 the unemployed figure reached 3 million. This was after four and a half years of three different Socialist Prime Ministers who cobbled together varying coalitions of votes to carry the Chamber, and who represented non-ideological government, producing serious identity problems at PS conferences, but also within the parties of the right who could not make their political specificity clearly felt. The cross-party similarities over the Gulf war and Maastricht were a case in point. The public repeatedly referred to a lack of difference in policies between government and opposition, and by 1993 almost half of the electorate was voting for parties outside the mainstream or not at all, abstentions becoming a serious comment on France's 'unexceptional' democracy.

Frustration to disrepute

Rocard's main innovation was the introduction in October 1988 of a guaranteed minimum income (the RMI) for the most deprived, taken up by over half a million households by 1991. The RMI was launched as a consensus initiative, foreshadowed in Mitterrand's election campaign, but even as it was approved by all main parties in the Chamber, at local level a stigma was attached to the beneficiaries by many potential employers, and its availability to immigrant families was bitterly attacked by the FN. Nevertheless its place in Rocard's ambitions to promote social cohesion was an important one. It helped the extremely poor, but did not serve as the way into a job (*insertion*) to the extent that Rocard had hoped. The upturn in the international economic climate which had started in 1987 continued for two years and brought increased industrial production, a rise in incomes and the creation of new jobs, but only a slight fall in unemployment figures. Disappointing as this was, Rocard did not resort to a flurry of extra legislation. Economically he continued the Socialist aversion to devaluation of the franc which had started after the forced devaluations of 1982–3. A strong franc (*le franc fort*) kept inflation low but also involved a macro-economic policy of contraction. Little was done by the government to stimulate economic growth. Increasingly the operation of the market was expected to have that effect and it was not easy for any economist, of left or right, to say with conviction why growth in France was so elusive. Politically Rocard reduced government bills to a minimum, believing that the measures he did enact would have more impact, and he fulfilled Giscard's mid-1970s call for more political consultation.

There was no attempt to reverse everything passed under Chirac, and opinion polls initially gave him credit for designing a method of non-conflictual government, treating each issue on its merits. The stultifying right-left split over the spiral of violence in New Caledonia called for new vision, to which Rocard notably responded. His compromise of 1989 promised a referendum in ten years on a timetable for self-government, and meanwhile greater social benefit for the indigenous Melanesians (Kanaks) from metropolitan subsidies and the profits of the nickel trade. It was the inflated market price of nickel which had brought a boom in the early 1970s for the well-established settlers from Europe and incomers from other areas of the South Pacific, whose numerical and economic strength sustained a majority vote in the island against the rural Kanaks. Rocard's pacification and promises provided reasons for optimism on all sides of what had become a murderous conflict of claims and interests. Some of the

injustices as well as the hopes created by colonial settlement were seen to be addressed.

Despite this considerable success, it was the limitations of Rocard's method which received most comment by the end of 1990. His Premiership was dogged by repeated public sector strikes which grew more demanding as growth in the economy once more slipped backwards in 1990 and fears of unemployment spread even further across society. The economic Minister Pierre Bérégovoy, nicknamed 'Pinay of the left', kept a tight budget, and held down government expenditure, showing little deviation from the Chirac years. Amongst the public, the cult of individualism allied to consumerism had created a volatile climate of expectations with peaks of spending and troughs of indebtedness. Rocard's careful method seemed an antidote to this volatility, and yet the ups and downs in his dealings with the nurses, prison officers, postal workers, civil servants, gendarmes, transport workers, peasant farmers and lycée pupils, all of whom made claims on public funds and stretched government tolerance, seemed to exacerbate a febrile climate of uncertainty. His readiness to try to defuse each strike, sometimes by providing the requested extra money and some-times not, created confusion; his complicated tax scheme to meet spiralling Social Security costs was understood by nobody and resented even by those who were not affected. For all his realism and moderation, he created an aura of unfinished projects, of an inability to deal with the underlying social problems. There was no cutting edge of reform: consensus seemed a blunt instrument. The Minister for Europe, Édith Cresson, resigned in October 1990, complaining of the government's lack of leadership in promoting French and European interests in competition with Japan. Mitterrand grew increasingly inept at covering up his dislike of Rocard and in May 1991, shortly after the end of the Gulf war, he asked Rocard to resign. By all accounts it was a curt dismissal.

Neither of Rocard's successors dissipated the public's frustration with the Socialist-led consensus. Neither found a way to reduce unemployment. But Mitterrand's choice of Édith Cresson to replace Rocard was in itself just the kind of bold initiative that politics appeared to lack. She was the first woman in French republican history to be head of government. It was eleven years since the first woman, the novelist Marguerite Yourcenar, had been elected to the Académie Française. The two events were both hailed in their respective times as a symbolic gender revolution, the end of a male monopoly. Both women were the object of media and public attention, but there was no pressure on Yourcenar to do anything further to justify her election. Cresson in power was forced continuously to justify herself, with

everyone hyperconscious that she was a woman. The gender revolution in Cresson's case was anything but complete: the raised eyebrows at her appointment within male political and administrative circles damaged her prospects of success, and the gendered criticisms which she received showed just how far the institutional bastion was still largely intact. She was referred to by a UDF deputy as the monarchical Mitterrand's favourite, a Madame de Pompadour, and although this was not the overt accusation of most politicians or administrators, she was seen by the higher echelons of the Civil Service as 'unprofessional' in her manner and her dealings, and was berated on the one hand for intemperate individuality, and on the other for a weak dependence on Mitterrand. The male leaders of the various tendencies in the Socialist Party were said to be humiliated by her appointment. The conclusion was quickly reached across the political spectrum that she could not be trusted with important matters of state, or even minor matters of etiquette. She was replaced after eleven months by Pierre Bérégovoy, the Economic Minister, with whom she was constantly in friction, and it will probably never be clear just how far her considerable mistakes and ill-chosen language were responsible for her failure or whether she was always expected to fail and given little credit for any consistency in her politics.

Édith Cresson had shown in her ministerial career since 1981 a consistent readiness to confront the hierarchies, first the big agricultural producers and then the ultra-liberals in international trade, and finally the economic power of Japan to which she felt France had offered no resistance. Her conflict with Bérégovoy was over her preference for small and medium-sized businesses, while her plan to relocate many of the main centres of public administration away from Paris, including the prestigious ENA, met the rooted outrage of the mandarins. She knew that she ruffled feathers, and she mostly did so intentionally. It was not seen as strength of purpose, but as indiscretion, weakness and vulgarity. Unaligned with any of the rival tendencies within the Socialist Party, she was always exposed as an individual voice, which allowed critics to step up their accusations of personal and political fragility. There was evidence from other Socialists to conclude that she was trapped (*piégée*) whichever way she moved, simply by being there in the first place.[9] She was given most credibility by heads of business who registered her fight for their interests at international level, but neither opinion polls nor elections favoured her hold on the Premiership.

The Socialists lost badly in the regional and cantonal elections of March 1992: in the Île-de-France, the region which includes Paris, they fell from over 28 per cent of the vote to under 15 per cent and were forced into third place by the Front National. Only two regions remained in Socialist hands,

the Limousin and the Nord – Pas-de-Calais: the opposition succeeded in all the other twenty regions. The precipitate slide of the Socialists was universally seen as giving Mitterrand good reason to dismiss Cresson. He did so on 2 April 1992. She herself felt personally betrayed by the President. In turn, people of immigrant origin felt personally betrayed by Édith Cresson: she had talked wildly of chartering special planes to return illegal immigrants to their countries of origin. 'We won't fly Air Cresson' featured on placards in a mass anti-racist demonstration on 25 January 1992 at which the Socialist contingent was humiliated.

Rocard does too little; Cresson meddles and commits inexcusable gaffes; Mitterrand only barely carries the Maastricht Treaty. The backdrop to these negative assessments was a shifting tableau of scandal which prompted a serious decline in the public persona of politics and politicians. The pressures of co-habitation were largely thought to have caused an increase in political corruptibility. In November 1987 an editorial by Jean Daniel in *Le Nouvel Observateur* started with mock enjoyment of the spectacle of old inter-French battles rejoined, as all sides of the political scene charged each other with corruption. He then rehearsed the more serious view that co-habitation had been imposed on the political class by public opinion. As the Presidential election approached consensus was too tame: enmities needed to be recharged.[10] The vogue for investigative journalism did the rest. The search for corrupt or rotten (*pourri*) elements in politics was a comparatively easy one. The historical references were mostly to the *pourriture* of the Stavisky era of the early 1930s, and it was the same wheels of local or corporate power, fraudulent accounting and political cover which were once again seen to be turning. Leading politicians were invariably long-standing mayors of towns which handled huge sums of public money; the circles of top administrators overlapped public service and private business; all political parties needed money, and membership was dwindling. Practices to secure public contracts in an increasingly free and competitive market were sharp.

There were also blunders in the public realm for which someone had to be seen to be responsible. It was the tragedy of haemophiliacs who were given HIV-infected blood in 1985 which brought the issue of public responsibility into the realm of political scandal. AIDS was first revealed to the French public in 1982, after its discovery a year earlier, but it was not at once that the virus could be detected in stocks of blood. By early 1985 a reliable American test was available, but for several months the authorities of the national blood transfusion service waited for a French product and meanwhile continued to use and sell blood knowing that it might be

contaminated. It took seven years, and over 250 deaths from the infected blood, before three doctors and directors of the public service were brought to trial in 1992 and found guilty. The prison sentences were deemed by much of the press to be inadequate and the case was highly publicized, all the more when one of the convicted doctors, Jacques Roux, insisted on the political responsibility of government ministers at the time.

Two ex-Ministers of Social Affairs and Health, Georgina Dufoix and Edmond Hervé, were thrown into the press headlines, along with the ex-Prime Minister Laurent Fabius, and all three were formally accused of failure to help those at risk. The affair went to the dusty processes of the High Court of Justice, barely used since 1930. Fabius was eager to clear his name. The court's report shortly before the general elections of 1993 fell back on technical grounds that the passage of time carried political immunity. Nobody was satisfied. At the same time the current Prime Minister, Pierre Bérégovoy, was accused by the satirical paper *Le Canard enchaîné* of having received an interest-free loan of a million francs in 1986 from Patrice-Roger Pelat, a close business friend of Mitterrand who had been seriously charged in 1989 with insider-trading in take-over deals by the aluminium company Pechiney. Bérégovoy protested his innocence of any corruption, but despite several comparable accusations of fraud and deception against politicians on the right of the Chamber, it was the series of 'affairs' involving the Socialists in power that registered most with the electorate. The close Maastricht result had done nothing to boost either Bérégovoy, Mitterrand or the PS. The whiff of yet more scandal turned certain defeat to disaster. The Socialists were routed at the elections in March 1993, retaining only sixty-seven seats out of their previous 276. No commentator at the time, and no historian since, could miss the sense of 'ending' which ensued. The evicted Prime Minister, Pierre Bérégovoy, one of the rare self-taught workers who reached the top of the Socialist Party, mayor of Nevers and director of Mitterrand's electoral campaign in 1988, felt an acute sense of personal isolation and responsibility for the defeat. He shot himself on 1 May 1993.

The limits of consensus were starkly revealed in the shocked analysis and moralizing that followed. Mitterrand was still President, angry at the role of the press in hounding Bérégovoy, bruised by Maastricht, suffering noticeably from his cancer, but determined on staying to face another round of co-habitation. For many people the time-honoured conflict of political ideas and ideologies had been reduced to a messy fight over position and influence with all its accusations and scandals. Political programmes faced consistent public contempt as banal or even irrelevant.

Such profound mistrust of the political process did not reduce the passion stirred by the formidable problems nor indeed the possibilities of the last decade of the century, identified chiefly with the challenges of market forces and ethnic diversity. The intensity of divisions over the Gulf War and Maastricht did not fit a cynical image of declining political involvement. Was it not more accurate to say that the sites of involvement had been relocated and that political persuasion was in search of more relevant structures? In terms of fundamentals people asked whether anything was ever new in politics. However 'unexceptional' or consensual politics had become, had it really lost its theatricality? A local decision at a school in Creil in the Oise on 3 October 1989 to forbid three Muslim girls from wearing a headscarf (*foulard*) in class, on the basis that it breached the axioms of secular education, provoked a struggle over fundamental principles which forcefully engaged people's passions and prejudices. In the same month the mayor of Montfermeil in Seine-Saint-Denis provoked both outrage and support when he refused to register children of immigrant origin at the municipal nursery school (*école maternelle*). It was evident that questions of exceptionalism and ideology were very much alive.

20

The Challenge of Plurality, 1990s–2000s (I)

The self-consciousness of French politics and history was not exhausted by the introspection of the bicentenary. It was soon clear that the 'end-of-exceptionalism' debate had only just started. Throughout the last decade of the century and the first years of the new millennium, with political power oscillating between left and right, two major themes assured a continuous anxiety about national identity: issues of difference, and the pressures of the worldwide market. Both themes kept arguments about the role of the state and the concept of a unitary national culture at the centre of social and political conflict. The themes had common structural layers, the most impacted being the persistence of high unemployment which affected almost every subject of public concern, from youth culture in the towns to the pace of privatization.

Even as the two themes threw issues of the state into even sharper relief they revealed the multiple images of deregulation. Free-marketeers had no copyright on the word. They promoted deregulation in order to reduce the public sphere in all aspects of business. In contrast there were social movements inside and outside the mainstream of politics which sought to deregulate state machinery in order to expand and democratize the public sphere. 'Liberal' and 'libertarian' had always been split stems from the same root. 'State' and 'public' had the same ambiguous relationship to each other.

I. Issues of difference

In the six years following the head-teacher's action at Creil, the symbolism of the Islamic headscarf (*foulard*) on the one hand and exclusion from school on the other precipitated judgements of high significance. In autumn 1993 in the small lakeside town of Nantua in the Jura mountains, two sisters, Fouzia and Fatima Aoukili, were sent home from the Xavier-Bichat

college for wearing their Islamic headscarves in defiance of instructions from their physical education teacher. The case reached the Conseil d'État in 1995, as the Creil exclusions had done in 1989, and this time the exclusion was justified in view of the 'serious threat' to orderly school conduct, not least by the girls' father who organized protests at the school gates. Even as the Conseil d'État reached its verdict, a book of interviews with girls who persisted in wearing the headscarf to school suggested that their main motivation was to establish their female identity. The reviewer in *Le Monde*, while recognizing the book's new empirical material and its break with stereotypes, criticized the authors, Françoise Gaspard and Farhad Khosrokhavar, as naive in minimizing the influence of Islamic organizations. The debate on the headscarf, the reviewer concluded, was not only about preferences within French society but also about a complex international context.[1]

In Montfermeil to the east of the industrial Parisian suburb of Saint-Denis, the mayor's refusal to admit more 'foreign' children to the *école maternelle* in 1989 focused attention on the densely populated high-rise estate, Les Bosquets, where unemployment levels ran at 25 per cent, and over 80 per cent of the 9,000 inhabitants were estimated to be of immigrant origin. The mayor, Pierre Bernard, represented the loose right-wing coalition which in 1983 defeated the Communists who had dominated in the area since the 1930s. His personal version of Catholic nationalism was projected on to the national stage through an association assertively entitled 'France debout' which signalled an upright (*debout*), pugnacious concept of Frenchness, replicating the populism of the Front National without any formal connection. Bernard had already tried to control access to the local primary school, and had battled with Harlem Désir of SOS-Racisme on television. His action was rejected by the Bishop of Saint-Denis and the local priest of Les Bosquets, but staunchly supported by a neighbouring priest, père Éory, whose ideas were rooted in belligerent anti-Communism. Within two years of the mayor's action, 'France debout' had spread to over 130 town halls in small and medium towns as far apart as Beaucaire in the Gard, with its hydro-electric installations on the Rhône, and the metal-working town of Haumont in the Nord.

The *foulard* incidents at Creil, Nantua and elsewhere, and the populist racism exemplified in Montfermeil, were not technically linked, but between them they raised most of the issues about minorities of immigrant origin that had been simmering in the 1980s; they revealed an undergrowth of social exclusion which threatened to entangle all main areas of public policy; they animated popular attitudes in ways which were as often socially

positive as negative; they displayed the fragility of any consensus on national identity; and they sparked a fissiparous debate on the cultural criteria used to shape the nature and contours of politics. The essential references went back to the early twentieth century and beyond.

Headscarves, secularism, Islam, gender

Danielle Mitterrand, wife of the President, and Lionel Jospin, Education Minister, were among the first to censure the exclusions at Creil in 1989, both suggesting that state education should be secure enough in its secularism to cope with expressions of religious difference, even, in Jospin's words, to 'welcome the *foulard*'. Speaking as if to an end-of-exceptionalism script, he told *Le Nouvel Observateur* that secularism (*laïcité*) no longer needed to be conflictual: 'Society has moved on: now it is plural.'[2] Within days, as incidents extended to other schools across the country, every possible angle of *laïcité* was explored, with Jules Ferry and Émile Combes the obligatory points of reference, and Aristide Briand, the historic conciliator, quoted as the model for those calling for compromise. Timidly, Rocard supported Jospin, and Mitterrand belatedly did the same. Jack Lang as Minister of Culture remained true to the mosaic of cultures displayed in the bicentenary, and Harlem Désir spoke for SOS-Racisme and endorsed a flexible secularism. But nobody who presumed that humanism was ranged on the side of the excluded girls could ignore the humanist defence of rigid secularism mounted against any form of religious intrusion into the school system. Passionate secularists emerged with strong anticlerical allusions. They saw no reason to discriminate in favour of Muslim practices when a century of struggle against Christian clericalism had defined the secular nature of the Republic in the separation of Church and state in 1905. They vehemently argued that the state should impose conformity to the secular ideal. Among the Socialists, Laurent Fabius and Jean-Pierre Chevènement, renowned for their economic disagreements since 1983, came together against the *foulard* in schools. So too did Yvette Roudy and Pierre Mauroy, and from the opposition Jacques Chirac, Giscard d'Estaing, Charles Pasqua and Alain Juppé. France-Plus, the parallel movement to SOS-Racisme, condemned the wearing of all religious insignia in schools, including the *foulard*. While most Greens were prepared to accept the headscarf, Antoine Waechter, often called the most ideological ecologist, was not. Nor was Arlette Laguiller, the visible Trotskyist at Presidential elections.

Intellectuals ranged openly and vociferously on both sides of the debate, with slogans drawn from all internal conflicts which had divided the French

among themselves (*les guerres franco-françaises*) from the Revolution onwards. The Conseil d'État was asked to pronounce, and it did so on 27 November 1989, with what many saw as a wise degree of Delphic imprecision. The wearing of religious items in the classroom was judged to be acceptable provided it was not ostentatious or conflictual. On this basis the girls at Creil were judged not to have offended, and the exclusion in 1990 of five girls from a college in Montfermeil for wearing headscarves was also ruled unacceptable, but the return of the political right to power in 1993 and the number of incidents such as those at Nantua brought a tougher circular from a new Minister of Education, François Bayrou, who had initially accepted the *foulard*. Changing his mind, and holding Islamic fundamentalism responsible, his circular to schools in 1994 banned the wearing of the Islamic headscarf in the classroom, which he now considered to be ostentatious in itself and a proselytizing act, regardless of individual motivation.

As a catalyst for differences within French opinion, the headscarf issue was raised to mythic proportions. Each public opinion poll was history in the making as representation. What did the *foulard* represent? What kind of sign was the act of exclusion? Meanings proliferated. It was quickly apparent that this was not a simple debate over the parameters of secularism. Gender arguments were crucially asserted on both sides, widening the possibilities for a crossing of loyalties. The feminist lawyer Gisèle Halimi, previously at one with the aims of SOS-Racisme, broke publicly with the movement on the issue. Together with other feminists in the 'equal rights' tradition she saw the *foulard* as imposed by Islamic patriarchy, enforcing the submissiveness of women. In Algeria in the early 1990s more and more women who dressed in a 'Western' way were the victims of assault by religious fundamentalists. Each case made news in France. On the other hand it was not forgotten by Maghrebi women in France that the French as colonizers in North Africa had committed their own gendered assaults, unveiling women in public squares as a punishment, particularly at the height of the Algerian war. Feminists who prioritized difference, found evidence of autonomous decision among the girls who wore the headscarf at school. For some it was even a defiance of their own family. The sociological study by Gaspard and Khosrokhavar went further down this route, prepared to interpret the wearing of the *foulard* by certain Muslim girls as a sign of taking control over their own bodies against the expected norms of Western exposure.

Gender perspectives had always cast a sardonic light on secularism, and nobody could forget that secular Radicals in the inter-war years had refused women the vote on the conviction that women were the unpaid agents of

the local priest. The presumed inseparability of women and religion no longer had any mileage in debates about women and Catholicism, but it re-emerged in the 1990s in replica assumptions about women and Islam. Despite overwhelming evidence from opinion polls that the majority of Muslim women and certainly the vast majority of Muslim girls were not intent on challenging secularism in state schools, there was a widespread refusal among secularists to credit them with any independence, either from the family patriarch or the local Imam. Many feminists were able to reject this resurgence of gendered assumptions and yet argue the necessity for secularism and the cause of liberation among women in Islamic communities. Others argued that the headscarf was a question of women's choice, even though many Muslim girls, besieged by researchers, stated that secular norms at school relieved them of need to choose. It was noted that the Muslim mother was both a mediator of Muslim tradition and a guarantor of her children's integration into secular schooling. It was to be expected that some Muslim girls would register the pull in both directions.

As Islamic belief became the second largest religion in France, regular polls suggested that there was only scattered interest amongst Muslim youth for any fundamentalist Islamic position, even after the immensely popular return in 1979 of the Ayatollah Khomeiny to Iran from his exile in France, and the effect on Muslims worldwide of the subsequent Iranian theocracy. Islam in France was barely a structured organization and Imams were mostly in favour of close relations with the civil authorities and co-existence with Christian and Jewish practices. The Gulf war provided an opportunity, and some argued a reason, for violent pro-Arab protest. It did not materialize. An Islamic backlash in Maghrebi communities was also predicted when the Algerian government suspended its democratic process in January 1992, depriving the Front Islamique du Salut (FIS) of the opportunity to win the second round of national elections. Forced into illegality, the FIS was accused increasingly of acts of terror, met by the repression of the Algerian government and army in a horrific, undeclared civil war.

In France the Islamic fundamentalism which did develop was confined to a small minority among the 3 million nominal Muslims, whose patterns of behaviour and belief were no less diverse than those of nominal Catholics: they were just more exposed to public scrutiny, fears and misconceptions. The fears had been volubly expressed in opposition to the building of new mosques, starting at Mantes-la-Jolie, fifty kilometres to the west of Paris, where a mosque was built in the years 1978–81 with the agreement of the Socialist mayor but in the teeth of a fierce anti-Arab campaign which pictured Mantes as a potential Mecca bringing 'hordes of Muslims' to the

town. In 1982 a bomb completely destroyed the newly built mosque at Romans in the Drôme. The *foulard* affair shifted attention from local religious centres to the nerve-centre of national acculturation: the state school. By 1995, in response to events in Algeria, even SOS-Racisme had inverted its position. The liberal *Le Monde* and the libertarian *Libération* had tried to situate the *foulard* debate in the widest cultural context: they too explained the hardening of public attitudes over six years by both an irrational and rational fear of Islamic fundamentalism.

Official Catholics were asked throughout the debate to give their opinion. With few exceptions their reaction marked the extent to which a secular state and secularism in schools had become assimilated into Catholic attitudes, ninety years after the bitter conflicts over *laïcité* at the turn of the century. Most Catholic opinion on the first incidents at Creil in 1989 advised against any intemperate response in either direction. By 1994, duplicating Bayrou's evolution, Catholic officials were clearer in their public acceptance of the need for secular uniformity in the schools. Mgr Lustiger, conservative Cardinal-Archbishop of Paris, declared that there should be no exceptions to *laïcité* in state education: he expected that Islam, given time, would come to the same position. Meanwhile, he said, the state should not exceed its role and interfere with the religious life and practices of Muslims, providing they were not a threat to law and order.

Secularism as a point of principle in public opinion was boosted early in 1994 in an issue which had nothing to do with headscarves, but everything to do with republican education. On 16 January demonstrators from all over France, estimated by the organizers at close to a million, marched through Paris to protect secular schooling (*l'école laïque*). The new government of the right under Édouard Balladur had set out to amend the Falloux law of 15 March 1850, the historic compromise of the nineteenth century which had established the freedom of education demanded by the Catholic Church, but had set a limit to the financial support the religious schools could receive from the local authority. A bill, hustled through the Chamber in December 1993 by François Bayrou, removed this restriction and opened the door to unlimited public subsidy of private schools. Mitterrand had already refused to back any change to the *loi Falloux*, particularly one that would reignite educational conflicts. The government believed it had a sufficient right-wing mandate from the election to carry it through, but the critical change was ruled unacceptable by the Constitutional Council. This was known on 13 January 1994, but the march, already planned, went ahead. It mirrored the *école libre* march of ten years before, which had broken all records of organized public demonstrations and to which

Mitterrand and the Socialists had conceded. This time it was the government of the right which backed down.

Not everyone on the *école laïque* march agreed about the *foulard* but the numbers of demonstrators involved suggested that the debates over *laïcité* induced by the Creil exclusions had reawoken old passions on the secular-clerical issue which the ill-timed reform of the Falloux law further enflamed. Yet the the *foulard* affair also prompted forward-thinking. The Catholic Church showed that it had internalized the separation of spheres: the state with its secular rights; religions with their own freedoms of expression. There was a rapid public education on the beliefs, the practices and the plurality of Muslim communities, and Jospin gave a positive lead in the consolidation of an updated secularism. Simone Veil was equally construc-tive in 1994, appointing young Muslim women in the Parisian area as mediators between schools and Muslim families. *Libération* interviewed them under assumed names in December 1994. Their aim was to convince, not to constrain. They pointed to ways in which Islamic fundamentalism could become a comforting refuge in the most conflictual suburbs, and wearing the *foulard* a defiance against the educational failings imputed to Muslims by a hostile environment. The mediators helped Muslim girls to try new forms of socializing, and teachers to acknowledge that exclusion might force Muslims into the very separatism that the secularists feared. The serious weekly press carried in-depth enquiries into the attitudes of young people towards different religious customs. Many of these revealed an indifference towards the differences which divided older generations. This could not be called apathy: there was a majority rejection of any fundamentalism, which many defined to include dogmatic secularism.

The negative impact of the affair was that a minority of all ages used the issue to sharpen their social anger. The variables depended on housing, locality, deprivation and the degree of social bitterness already in evidence. In many areas the protracted affair was both cause and effect of exacerbated racial tensions. It was located within a much more envenomed conflict over identity.

Codes of nationality

The immediate political impact of the incidents at Creil and Montfermeil appeared to be the victory of the Front National (FN) candidate, Marie-France Stirbois, at the legislative by-election at Dreux on 3 December 1989. The renewal of a special relationship of the Stirbois family, the FN and Dreux, first established in 1983, was hailed by Jean-Marie Le Pen as a

national trend. On the same day the FN defeated the Socialists in a canton of Salon-en-Provence, run by Socialists for over fifty years, and almost took another local seat in Marseille. For the next four years the FN was rampant in its ideological confidence, leading the local party leader in Marseille to predict that the FN could easily come second in the Presidential election of 1995 and take the Presidency in the second round.[3] Anti-immigrant attitudes were acknowledged to have determined this surge in support for the FN, precipitating an increasingly defensive reaction from the troubled Socialist governments that limped on until 1993. The Socialist policy from Rocard to Bérégovoy was one of integration, and not the 'right to be different' (*droit à la différence*) on which SOS-Racisme had made its pact with the Socialists in the mid-1980s in colourful celebrations of diversity. Cultural difference was now a concept increasingly trumpeted by the Front National, not as a right but as a danger.

A scaffolding of terms indicating the threat of different cultures, and the alien nature of 'the other', the outsider and the foreigner, propped up the ideology of the FN as it had done the ideology of Maurras, Action Française and Vichy. Maghrebis were held to be the invaders of French civilization as Jews had been earlier in the century, though Jean-Marie Le Pen did not miss any opportunity to deliver an antisemitic thrust. When pressed by foreign journalists he fell back, as Maurras had done, on a manipulation of facts and figures and a defence of traditional Frenchness which he denied was racist. The Front National differed, however, from Action Française in the degree of its working-class support in specific areas and the political plausibility of Jean-Marie Le Pen himself. The literary and philosophical writings of Maurras provided a useful backdrop for the publications of the FN. Its monthly *Le Choc* echoed the emphasis on 'true France' and the devotion to the national heritage of Clovis, Charlemagne, Saint Louis and Joan of Arc, all, it claimed, dethroned from their heroic place in history by the new gods in the Panthéon in Paris which had become 'nothing more than the burial chamber of the left and extreme left . . . an annexe to the Ligue des Droits de l'Homme'. State schools were attacked as cradles of un-French values, and anti-racist students dismissed as '*beurs* on the binge' or just as 'Jewish students'.[4] The fact that Maurras was born in Martigues and that neighbouring Vitrolles, Salon and Marseille had become strongholds of the FN was coincidental, partly ironic and yet significant. Maurras inveighed against the industrialization of his Provençal *pays*; the FN flourished in what industrialized Provence had become, exploiting crisis and decline, the competition for jobs, the influx of immigrant labour and the conflicts generated in areas of urban deprivation.

Many of the dockers in Marseille who were regularly quoted as both members of the Communist CGT and supporters of the FN had themselves been immigrants from Spain, Italy and elsewhere in Europe, and had turned against the newest arrivals from North Africa. In 1991 the image of a tall mosque promised in Marseille since 1920, but still not even started, was an emblem in popular polemic of the threat believed to be posed by the 80,000 Muslims in the city. Mainstream parties of the centre and right in the area attempted to outflank the FN by backing a policy of quotas or 'zero' immigration. They were buttressed by the headlines given to key words used by Chirac and Giscard d'Estaing in 1991. In June Jacques Chirac, speaking in Orléans, conjured up the anger of an imaginary French worker, resident in a high-rise block, at being neighbour to a man 'with three or four wives, and some twenty children who gets 50,000 francs from Social Security without having to work. Add to that the noise and the smell ... (*le bruit et l'odeur* ...)' It was the most-quoted speech of the time, shocking to many of Chirac's own party, but not in Marseille or Montfermeil. Giscard d'Estaing rivalled the controversy with an article in *Le Figaro Magazine* of 21 September entitled 'Immigration or invasion?'. It was another sign that the extreme right was setting the agenda, and that major figures in politics were unwilling to avoid the pull of its language.

The subject of 'immigration', as normatively defined in French journalism and academic research, covered not only the arrival of foreigners but all aspects of relationships between settled communities of immigrant origin and the rest of French society, including the means of integration. The subject of nationality was technically separate. In the early 1990s at least a million of the 4 million immigrants born abroad had taken French nationality, while the 5 million second and third generations of immigrant origin who were born in France were automatically entitled to French nationality at the age of maturity, and had family backgrounds as diverse as Italy, Spain and Portugal, Eastern Europe, the Maghreb, sub-Saharan Africa and East Asia. There were estimated to be a further 5 million French who had at least one immigrant grandparent. Being foreign was therefore not the status of the vast majority of those of immigrant origin. The actual percentage of foreigners in France in 1990 (6.35 per cent) was slightly less than that of 1931 (6.58 per cent). The change stressed in every media coverage was in the percentage increase of North Africans among those of all immigrant origins. Most calculations put them at around 40 per cent by the 1990s from under 5 per cent in the 1940s, while the humanitarian policy of allowing families to 'regroup' in France after the official suspension of immigration in 1974 had significantly increased the Maghrebi presence in

all aspects of French society. Over twenty years the number of Maghrebi women came to be almost equal to that of their male counterparts who had been recruited to work in France.

The language of the extreme right insisted that 'foreign' was 'realistically' defined less by nationality status than by visible and behavioural difference. Maurras had invented a nationalist 'logic' according to which Jews could never be French. The FN propagated a similar casuistry against those of Maghrebi origin. It drew on the readiness of state commissions before, during and after the Second World War to rate immigrants in terms of their potential to be 'assimilated'. Those from North Africa always came last. Georges Mauco had given academic status to this categorization, and his findings, steeped in devious science, were still quoted forty years later. Its racist core would have been more transparent had the issue of cultural integration not been central to the language, the concepts and the expectations of French society as a whole. The unitary tradition of French culture, mediated by education and other cultural vectors, was the backdrop to conflicts over immigration and nationality. On the one hand it informed the processes of social integration. On the other hand the FN used it to legitimize exclusion.

There had been thick layers of multicultural discourse sandwiched in the policy statements of Lang's Ministry of Culture. With the perceived 'end of French exceptionalism' it might have been presumed that the notion of a unitary culture would go the same way. On the contrary, its resilience into the last decade of the century was, in all senses, exceptional. In the early 1990s the consensus on integration into a unitary culture gave multiculturalism a negative image, redolent of fractured societies such as Lebanon and the internecine communalism of Southern Asia. Integration (*intégration*) was diametrically opposed to any form of fundamentalism (*intégrisme*) and it was precisely Islamic fundamentalism which was feared as the inevitable beneficiary of multiculturalism. A reluctance to talk of 'ethnic minorities' for fear of weakening the drive to integration limited the perception of difference but strengthened the sense of one society. The challenge for the consensus was to allow diversity and to harmonize difference within the unitary culture: the many politicians, teachers and administrators determined to do this displayed their confidence in the republican tradition and at the same time their profound distance from the FN. Adept as he was in adjusting his rhetoric to the politics of the moment, Le Pen effectively scorned integration as a false solution. A return of all Maghrebi immigrants to North Africa was the FN's cultural and political remedy. It stood little chance of becoming a consensus policy, but in 1993 there was

a majority in the Chamber that favoured two steps towards it: 'zero' tolerance for illegal immigrants and a tightening of access, both to France and to French citizenship. Charles Pasqua returned to the Ministry of the Interior to resurrect his nationality bill of 1986, as altered by the Commission to which it had been hurriedly sent. A new nationality code was passed in June 1993.

The rump of Socialist and Communist deputies who had survived the electoral rout voted solidly against the new code. They registered opposition to its authoritarian origin and its potential for racial discrimination, but in fact the disagreement in the Chamber was not intense. The new code did not remove the right of French nationality from children born in France whose parents had been born abroad, but it did adopt Pasqua's change of procedure: the children would have to make a formal request for nationality between the ages of eighteen and twenty-one. In the climate of 1993–4 this did not seem as hostile to those of immigrant origin as it had done in 1986. There were many who argued that it would concentrate teenage minds on the benefits of citizenship and facilitate integration, but further measures to complicate and delay the arrival of the family of a legal immigrant, and the intensification of random identity checks in areas of ethnic diversity, convinced human rights organizations that integration would suffer. Any violence perpetrated by those of Maghrebi origin provoked populist demands that the retention of nationality should be subject to continuous good behaviour, but this line of argument was ruled unconstitutional. Simone Veil as Minister of Social Affairs had much to do in curbing the zealotry of deputies with racist inclinations. She did not have to deal with the FN in the Chamber. Marie-France Stirbois had lost her seat at Dreux in the 1993 elections and the FN had failed to gain any others, though it had 12.5 per cent of the votes, more than in 1988, but less than in the regional elections of 1992.

Pasqua enjoyed his reputation as the strong defender of police integrity when the police were accused of racism: he legalized unrestricted identity checks, car searches and summary internment in his crackdown on suspected Islamic terrorism and illegal immigration, which he often merged into one category in his 'straight talking'. He gained popular notoriety for putting security before individual freedoms but his fidelity to Gaullism made this acceptable to a broader right, who saw his policies as reducing the appeal of Le Pen. He had little time for Balladur and Simone Veil, and over Maastricht he had lost his close relationship with Chirac. In 1994 he looked an outside candidate for the Presidential elections. His name became synonymous with a toughness that was easily generalized into ways of

running not only the police and security but also business, the economy and foreign policy. In the event it was Chirac who became President, and Alain Juppé Prime Minister, in 1995. Pasqua was not reappointed, but it was the Pasqua methods that Lionel Jospin had in mind when he unexpectedly became Premier at the head of a plural left government in 1997 and promised to break with 'a style of power which the French people are no longer willing to tolerate'. The style did change. Not all Pasqua's policies were repudiated but the essential Pasqua element in the Nationality Code was deleted in Élisabeth Guigou's recoding of 4 March 1998. Children born in France to parents born elsewhere would not have to apply for French nationality. It was granted to them automatically at the age of eighteen, or earlier if requested.

A crisis of national identity?

Throughout the four years from headscarves at Creil to Pasqua as Minister of the Interior, it was repeatedly affirmed in the media that there was a crisis of national identity. Sequel to the introspection which accompanied co-habitation and the bicentenary, fanned by the winds of scandal which debilitated politics, and articulated in the divisions over the Gulf war and Maastricht, the crisis was on every page of the *foulard* debate. It was held to be closely related to the effect of post-industrialism on lives and communities, but the precise relationship of social dislocation to issues of national identity was not easily measured: nor was the impact of a more global consciousness, common to other Western societies in the 1990s.

At the time of the 1993 elections there was eager media research into specific regions and communities looking for different angles on national identity. The million ex-colonial French from Algeria (*pieds-noirs*) were interviewed extensively across the south for their views thirty years after their enforced repatriation to France. Many called themselves 'exiles', backed the Front National, paraded French nostalgia and anger for an empire 'abandoned by de Gaulle', and took pride in their derivation from a 'white' Mediterranean mix which included Sicilians, Maltese, Spanish, Sardinians and Italians. Their difficulties of accepting their own 'integration' into the Gaullist 1960s had left many of them with an experience of 'difference', but they denied that the concept applied to themselves. They projected it outwards on to Maghrebi immigrants. The FN election slogan to which they rallied was 'We're well at home' ('*Bien chez nous*'), meaning that people of Maghrebi immigrant origin were not. The other 'exiles' from Algeria, the Algerian *harkis* who had fought for the French against the

FLN, were even more in a world of their own: trebly exiled, from Algeria, from French society, and from Maghrebi communities. They lived a segregated, poverty-stricken existence in the Midi towns. The very few journalists alerting the public to details of the *harkis* repeated the obvious rhetorical question: 'What unitary national identity could they possibly share?'

Much of the media coverage created a certainty that the crisis was due to 'immigrant' riots and disorders in overcrowded working-class estates on the periphery (*la banlieue*) of Paris and other large towns, a style of reporting in which 'immigrant' carried the same racial meaning as popularized by the FN. Police in the deprived suburbs encouraged victims of theft, burglary and stolen cars to agree that their unseen attackers were 'probably Maghrebis', swelling the statistics of 'immigrant' crime. The representation of these suburbs in the public imagination from the late 1970s onwards was rigorously studied by serious journalism, revealing deep-lying causes of disorder in economic deprivation and social frustration erupting in youthful revolt which transcended differences in ethnic origin. Nevertheless the fear grew in the 1990s that the suburbs were turning into 'immigrant ghettos' and 'no-go' areas, and that French towns were becoming racially divided on the scale of certain American cities. It fuelled an alarmist style of crisis reporting, exemplified by the illustrated *Paris-Match* in its coverage of riots in the Lyon suburb of Vaulx-en-Velin in October 1990 and Sartrouville to the west of Paris in April 1991.

Much of the allusion to America came from a different direction, not from a climate of crisis but from positive assertion by Maghrebi youth themselves, with claims that their Moroccan, Algerian or Tunisian origin was less formative than the black culture which had spread from America in the 1980s in the music of 'rap', the narrative musical story-telling of 'hip-hop', and the graffiti-style of 'tagging' which had little to do with *intégrisme*. If there was a national identity crisis in these critical years of the early 1990s it has to be assessed partly as confusion on how to react to French youths of immigrant origin who had developed a musical language and a street art which was popular and aggressive in its difference. Recurrent in the pages of *Libération*, this mix of Maghrebi-French-American affirmation was construed in many other influential media as a visible and vocal refusal of Frenchness rather than as a dissident subculture, capable of counter-attack and inversion of nationalist propaganda. Turning the FN concept of 'invasion' on its head, the successful Marseille rap group IAM, which claimed Africa as the birthplace of humanity, denounced the French racists as the real invaders.

Few people disagreed with the fact that certain outer-city housing estates

were problematic and that tensions erupted without pretext into violence. But no perspective had a monopoly of realism. In 1995 a 27-year-old screen actor turned director, Mathieu Kassovitz, made *La Haine*, immediately recognized as the first film to capture the violent, funny, tragic, angry, bored, racist mix of the *banlieue*. There had been others, such as *Hexagone* in 1994 by Malik Chibane, but all were eclipsed by Kassovitz, whose three youths, white Jewish, black and *beur*, in running skirmishes with the police, shocked and entertained with images which marked the decade as powerfully as the reality they conveyed. Influenced by rap and claiming the *banlieue* as his own social milieu, Kassovitz denied any romantic or revolutionary aim. Most critics commented on the racial mixing (*métissage*) of the youths and saw it as a study of alienated youth seeking identity in a violent, lawless environment, in the teeth of excessive police brutality. The film was well received by the media and won the Best Director prize at the Cannes Film Festival of 1995. Government representatives commended its documentary veracity.

There was realism but no clear answers in *La Haine*. The necessity for youths of the *banlieue* themselves to work out solutions, after another outbreak of senseless killings in northern Paris in the spring of 1999, motivated an urgent campaign and movement calling itself 'Stop la Violence!'. Insisting on dialogue and justice, the multiracial movement of young people from several different suburbs was as harsh as *La Haine* in its accusations against the police, and, like Kassovitz, did not concentrate solely on racial issues. It knew the complexity of its terrain from the inside, and spoke its language: it had echoes of SOS-Racisme fifteen years before, but its first year of support was slight by comparison. It spread patchily to Marseille, Lyon and Lille; it was taken up by *Nova* magazine and faced criticism of being a media stunt; it was backed by Élisabeth Guigou and Lionel Jospin of the plural left government. Its potential lay in its origins. It demanded from its own communities a closure of violence; it demanded from the state an active commitment to inclusion.

'Stop la Violence!' as a slogan challenged the twenty-first century: it rang backwards across the twentieth. On 14 May 1990, 200,000 demonstrators, including Michel Rocard, Jacques Chirac and President Mitterrand, had marched in Paris in protest at a resurgence of antisemitism. Four days before, perpetrators had violently desecrated ancient Jewish graves, daubing them with antisemitic slogans and Nazi swastikas. The cemetery was in Carpentras in the Vaucluse, close to the areas of FN influence in the south. The desecration was clearly designed to salute the fiftieth anniversary of the German invasion of 10 May 1940. The extreme right was known to be

responsible, proved beyond doubt later in the decade. Against the background of a series of trials for crimes against humanity and the multiple engagement of journalists and academics with Vichy and collaboration (see Chapter 21), racism and anti-racism were prominent in issues of national identity as they had been fifty years before under Vichy and 100 years before in the Dreyfus Affair. People in the 1990s were made to be acutely conscious of memory and history. The importance of recurring syndromes and sites of memory (*lieux de mémoire*) was reaffirmed throughout the last decade of the century. It was seen by some as a *fin-de-siècle* obsession with the past. On the contrary, others argued, it had urgent contemporary relevance for the ways in which difference in French society was still being perceived.

Associations and social movements

An informal 'university of the citizen' began to exist in Marseille in 1992. Three years later its initiator, Jo Ros, told the self-help street magazine, *La Rue*, how it had originated in workers' memories of a naval shipyard at Port-de-Bouc which had closed down in 1966. Professional social workers in run-down parts of the city used memories as a starting point for collective expression and activity, leading to projects on school experience, local housing, health and policing. Civil and civic awareness spread. The potential of citizenship was explored in a network of groups: Ros underlined the discrepancy between this potential and the role ascribed to the citizen by the state authorities. Confronting this discrepancy first at Mantes-la-Jolie and then in the volatile Parisian *banlieue* of Saint-Denis, a much-respected social innovator, Suzanne Rosenberg, created teams from the public officials who had daily contact with the people of the huge estates: postal workers, teachers, police. She said she had to avoid the trap of creating a local mafia but argued from a successful record that public policy should originate from the grass-roots officials who were geographically and sociologically part of the community.

The proposal that the state should participate in the projects of citizens, rather than the other way round, was a variant on the ideas of the 1968 era. The state had been rejected by many of the movements of *les années '68*, but in the 1990s the call from social innovators was for its 'modernization'. This was not the language of liberal economics but of people seeking to invert the hierarchies of authority. They perceived the crisis in the towns as one of outmoded state structures and unbending norms of policy formation. It was a form of deregulation that they proposed: a flexibility

of the state apparatus to allow the flow of ideas and decisions from below. Working over many years in deprived areas they had already begun to change the state's reliance on its own hierarchy. When Édith Cresson was Premier in 1991 she appointed Kofi Yamgnane, born in Togo in West Africa, as a junior Minister for Integration, and then came Simone Veil's outreach through appointed Muslim mediators. The ripple effect was positive. At the grass roots by mid-1995 over 1,000 women of immigrant origin had been recruited as voluntary links with their own communities, given the title of *femmes-relais*. One such, Maria-Iva Gomez from the Cap-Vert islands in the Atlantic, west of Senegal, was an interface in the rough estates in the northern part of Amiens, bringing officials and local people together. The norms of authority in the town were perpetuated by the flow of money from the state downwards: the mayor and UDF deputy in 1995, Gilles de Robien, looked for an urban Marshall Plan of massive aid. He said that he dreamed of spending millions to create a multipurpose social and leisure centre in the deprived area, to convince the people there that they had not been forgotten. In 1996 a bill in his name introduced tax concessions for firms prepared to cut the working hours of their staff so that jobs could be preserved or new ones created. It met with some success. He was seen locally as an innovative politician working from the top, whose initiatives did not invalidate the social innovators who worked from the ground upwards.[5]

The fiftieth anniversary of worker-priests was celebrated in 1993. Almost 600 still remained active in French society, working among the excluded and the unemployed. At the end of the 1960s after the second Vatican Council a degree of reauthorization enabled them to relaunch their work and writing, highly influential on liberational theology in South America. By 1993 the site of their action was no longer the factory but the *banlieue*. Their past was still occluded in official Church histories, but they were recognized by secular innovators as a singular example of what unorthodox social action could achieve. So too was the 81-year-old abbé Pierre, in the news in 1994 with the publication of his *Testament*. Still in the vanguard of empowering the homeless, whose numbers were officially registered as over 200,000, including those in makeshift accommodation, he had kept the freedom to regulate his own social mission, the Compagnons d'Emmaüs. Analysed by Roland Barthes for his studied image as a latter-day messianic pilgrim complete with beard, cloak and staff, the abbé Pierre was for many the exemplar of protest, quixotic but effective. The Bishop of Évreux, Mgr Jacques Gaillot, was equally celebrated for his outspoken identification with the deprived and excluded, whether homeless, unemployed, immigrants or AIDS victims. He dissociated himself from the defence of private schools

in 1984 and roundly criticized Pasqua's nationality code in 1986. De-nounced by right-wing Catholics as irresponsible, and rebuked by Mgr Lustiger of Paris, he made close alliances with the anti-racist movements, but did not create a new movement of his own. The papacy decided in January 1985 that he was a political liability and removed him from his post. Angry demonstrations against the decision showed the depth of his following among lay Catholics. With references to the papal proscription of the Sillon in 1910, almost a century of internal Catholic conflict over social and political issues was telescoped into 'for or against' Mgr Gaillot.

The voluntary bodies and the hundreds of associations and social move-ments registered in the 1990s questioned the pessimism that civil society was relapsing into self-regard and isolated individualism. Many in the mould of SOS-Racisme were clear alternatives to traditional political par-ties, and were promoters of issue politics, demonstrations and direct action, but most were local, low-profile bodies, empowering different sections of diffuse communities. Many could just as easily be described as cultural movements, expressing a way of life otherwise unrepresented. At moments of racial tension, there was a focus on the new associations legalized in 1981, enabling people of immigrant origin such as Nanas Beurs, composed of young Maghrebi women, to find a voice. There was a richness of women's associations among sub-Saharan Africans from Mali, Senegal, the Ivory Coast and Cameroon living mainly in outer Paris and the Normandy towns of Le Havre and Rouen. Qualifying for official registration, and still more for a grant from the Social Fund, involved collective encounters with the state, valued as a first step towards integration, but it would miss much of these African women's purpose if their groups were seen solely in terms of their position vis-à-vis the state. Crucially the associations acted also as family and gender mediators between women's demands for individuality and their own cultural background.

Without papers

The republican right to demonstrate needed no extra impetus, but the new associations needed the tradition of collective protest. The two came together at numerous local and some notable national protests, but it was a dramatic choice of action in 1996 by immigrants without associative status and without residence papers (*sans-papiers*) that drew attention to difference and integration at the same time. On 18 March a substantial body of 300 *sans-papiers* occupied the church of Saint-Ambroise in the 11th *arrondissement* of Paris. Mostly African, and originating largely from

Mali, they included eighty women, one of whom, Madjiguène Cissé from Senegal, took a prominent role in the demand for legalization of the tens of thousands living irregularly over several years in France.[6] The government of Alain Juppé, the first of the new Chirac Presidency, kept to the policy rarely suspended by any government since the mid-1980s, of evicting immigrants without papers, even if they had arrived with legitimate expectations of family reunification. Expelled from the church, but finding a series of shelters, some of the protesters were flown back to Mali, while others staged regular demonstrations outside the Élysée or started hunger strikes. Brutal proposals by a parliamentary commission to cut off medical treatment to all *sans-papiers* and expel their children from school were a disaster for the government, alienating much of public opinion. Many of the children in question had been born in France, and even under the Pasqua law were technically French. The televised violence of police in August, dragging African women and men out of yet another refuge in the church of Saint-Bernard in Paris brought indignation to a climax, marked by a popular demonstration of sympathy at the Place de la République.

The left-wing government headed by the Socialist Lionel Jospin in 1997 was expected to announce a significant change of attitude. In fact it was a 'generous but firm' policy towards the *sans-papiers* that was set out by the new Minister of the Interior, Jean-Pierre Chevènement. He did not repeat the general offer of legalization made in 1981 but started a more individual scrutiny of the 142,000 demands. For over 40 per cent this led to rejection, and in the face of more protests, divisions arose in the governing coalition, the Greens calling for a general amnesty but Chevènement and Jospin replying that it would be irresponsible to signal that the door to illegal entry was open. Chevènement's bill in April 1998 reinforced the need for legality and a rigorous process of application, but softened many of the regulations surrounding residence and family regrouping. Madjiguène Cissé discerned a utilitarian aspect to the policy: it makes it 'easier for intellectuals, doctors, people whom France needs, to get a visa and come and live in France. But for the others the repressive laws have been upheld.'[7]

Without work

The *sans-papiers* militants were an effective vanguard. French politics and culture might both be defined by the status given to vanguards. Even as the cult of opinion polls signified the importance of counting heads there was still the expectation that any idea or movement worth consideration would have its own vanguard, however small, which would be taken as representa-

tive of a general principle. It was therefore something of an anomaly that people were surprised at the existence of a vanguard movement of the unemployed (*chômeurs*). The sociologist Pierre Bourdieu called it a 'social miracle'. Speaking at the occupation of the École Normale Supérieure in Paris by the Movement of the Unemployed on 17 January 1998, he said that 'the first conquest of the movement is the movement itself, its very existence. It pulls the unemployed, and with them all insecure workers, whose numbers increase daily, out of invisibility, isolation, silence, in short, out of non-existence.'[8] Like many of the collective innovations of the 1990s the movement was consciously different, questioning the limitations of trade union practice and enlarging the compass of labour politics. Ten years after the Beur march, the tactic of 'visibility' marches converging on Paris from various starting points around the country was reinvented by groups of unemployed in 1994.

The campaign of *chômeurs* reached European dimensions in 1997 and the movement occupied public buildings and social security offices to keep in the news. Some of the activists co-operated with campaigns by the homeless and movements against racism. From the start, the campaigners were split over the issue of autonomy, certain pioneers arguing that public impact would depend on bringing workers and workless together. The established trade unions were unenthusiastic about the movement: their coolness was the reason for Bourdieu's remarks. As the traditional embodiment of labour, they were reluctant to agree that a separate organization and strategy were necessary. The CGT made room for the movement's representatives in a limited way, but the CFDT leadership of the mid-1990s had abandoned its militancy of the 1970s and deplored the confrontational activism of new, autonomous unions, whose existence it deemed as divisive. Nevertheless, the occupation tactics in January 1998, co-ordinated across the country, gained the support of Dominique Voynet, leader of the Greens and Minister of the Environment in Jospin's government. A fellow minister, Claude Allègre in Education, was also responsive, calling the movement 'a cry which must be heard'. Martine Aubry, Minister of Employment and Social Affairs, whose initiatives for creating jobs were the highlight of the Jospin government, labelled the tactics excessive and unnecessary, but she did not ignore the movement altogether. Evidence that 70 per cent of public opinion were sympathetic to the occupations, and 78 per cent of the population were, or had been, closely acquainted with at least one unemployed person, made negotiation with the vanguard leaders essential.[9] The net result of activist pressure was to widen the process of policy-formation on unemployment, at least until 2002.

2. *Market highways*

Balladur's route

Following the runaway electoral success of the right (UDF and RPR) in 1993, it was Georges Pompidou's loyal political colleague and friend, the 64-year-old Édouard Balladur, who was appointed as Premier in co-habitation with President Mitterrand. His father, of Turkish origin, had been naturalized in 1926, three years before Balladur's birth in Smyrna and the family's move to Marseille. As he gave time for Pasqua's new code of nationality early in the life of his government, public rumours spread, with no foundation, that he was really of ancient Provençal lineage, a small sign in a forest of signifiers of the importance of 'origin' in the climate of 1993. He showed none of the intemperate haste that Chirac had displayed on coming to power in 1986, but was none the less proud of his record in shaping the privatizations which had marked the Chirac government, a policy he was determined to pursue. Chirac's horizon was now the Presidential campaign looming in 1995: the division of roles in 1993 suited both RPR politicians.

Balladur's self-controlled manner had a ponderous authority which matched the composure of Mitterrand. Frictions between them were mostly avoided. It was apparent after a year that this was due to Balladur's combination of economic consistency, by which he ruled out alternatives, and social inconsistency which saw him yield repeatedly to public protest.

Mitterrand had appeared to exclude a return to privatizations in his Presidential manifesto of 1988, but in fact several partial sales of nationalized assets had been initiated under Balladur's Socialist predecessors, with the aim of reducing the budget deficit, swollen every month by the escalating costs, human as well as financial, of unemployment. The pressure on the franc was Balladur's first concern. He considered the possibilities of opting out of the European Monetary System, but chose a route which allowed the franc to float within the system, made more flexible with hurried European agreement when the system was close to collapse in July. Balladur's success in achieving this adjustment astonished both French and co-Europeans. Accompanied by a curb on government spending he kept inflation extremely low. A new government loan was created with a bond bringing 6 per cent guaranteed interest: it was immediately popular. Financial confidence was regained, and at the same time the privatization of the Banque Nationale de Paris (BNP) and the chemical industries of Rhône-Poulenc were heavily subscribed. In 1994 public opinion polls

reflected the government's confidence that privatizations were no longer a bone of contention in French politics. Over 3 million individuals bought shares in the sale of the oil company Elf-Aquitaine. There was even a partial privatization of Renault in November. Sustaining industry across the board, however, was quite another matter. Recession in France in 1993 was more serious than in any other year since 1945. Stable prosperity within the competitive international economy was still eluding French industry and business.

Balladur resisted calls from within the RPR to break free of European restrictions and give priority to reflationary, pro-employment measures. Initiated by the anti-Maastricht voice in the RPR, Philippe Séguin, aspects of this counter-policy appealed to those who criticized Balladur's leaden style as insufficiently dynamic, though he held on to a generally favourable public opinion. No other government had found an answer to the absence of sustained growth, or even a way of explaining it. Balladur stuck to his belief that financial stability, a continued programme of privatization and the co-efficient pursuit of restructuring would soon bring rewards, though few expected these to permeate through society in the short term. He made some concessions to reflation, with taxation cuts for households announced for 1994, and a sizeable money injection to create more jobs in the building industry, but he rejected the wholesale return to protectionism demanded out of desperation by most of the 12 per cent unemployed, officially totalling 3,290,000 in December 1993 and growing still further to a record peak of 3.42 million in the following month. Exports, however, picked up in 1994. A stabilization of the number of unemployed, followed by a very gradual decline, was evident in 1994–5. It was greeted by Balladur and much of public opinion as the beginning of the recovery he had promised. It seemed nothing more than a mirage to those surviving on the supplementary benefit (RMI) introduced by Rocard and used as a barometer of social exclusion. From half a million their numbers had almost doubled by December 1994.

The Balladur path to recovery did not lead radically away from all government intervention (*dirigisme*) or protectionism. While the Socialist governments and Mitterrand himself were identified with *dirigisme* as a means of protecting both labour and certain key industries, the governments of the right were expected to run down state intervention with liberal *élan*, accelerating the end of French 'exceptionalism'. Privatization was billed in this way, as the fervent embrace of market forces. What was more important, however, was the nature of the privatizations. Chirac and Balladur in 1986–7 had reserved controlling shares in the major privatized industries

for a 'hard core' of chosen corporate investors. This perpetuated government involvement, protected French firms from passing substantially into ownership outside the European Community, and gave added power to the Finance Minister, as did decisions on the price to be set, often well below the market value of the company. In 1993 Balladur opened up more of each privatization to European investment, but some potential foreign investors were wary of the state's continuing role: the problem of state 'interference' was given as the reason by the Norwegian-based Volvo for declining a merger with Renault.

Nor did Balladur's route avoid embarrassing U-turns, notably over the restructuring of Air France where the government demanded sweeping measures, including 4,000 job losses in two years. The strike this provoked in October 1993 brought air transport to a standstill. Balladur stood firm and then climbed down. His manoeuvre was repeated in 1994 and not only over the *loi Falloux* (see above). He conceded to widespread protests of young workers, students and trade unions and withdrew a plan to allow employers to take on young labour below the level of the minimum wage (SMIC), and his government was forced into putting pressure on the European Commission to set minimum prices for imported fish in order to protect the French fishing industry.

Erupting in Brittany with a strike of fishermen (*marins-pêcheurs*) on 1 February 1994, the storm over fishing was dramatic and violent. A traditional industry and community, hit by international competition, undercut by imports which forced down prices, faced with higher costs and the need to modernize equipment, saw its livelihood in sharp decline. On 4 February, after attacking several import depots, thousands of angry protesters from the Breton fishing ports moved on to the regional capital, Rennes, to coincide with a visit of Balladur and attendant ministers. Clashes with police degenerated into street battles. Barricades went up in the main squares. By the early hours of 5 February the historic seventeenth-century Palais de Justice, seat of the old Breton *parlement*, was on fire, the exact cause unknown. The profound public shock was articulated by the mayor, Edmond Hervé, on 7 February: he registered a regional loss and sadness, but also repudiated the violence, criticized the inadequate policing, and, in his first words, expressed sympathy for the legitimate grievances of the fishing community.[10]

Government intervention secured some respite for the *marins-pêcheurs* and injected more finance, but the European Commission did not provide the degree of protection they were demanding. In all these successive confrontations Balladur appeared inured to adjustment and retreat, which

could be read as a form of pragmatism. It fashioned French liberal economics in a specific mould, keeping France on the market highway but with a lane of its own. It was obviously important that jostling for an acceptable economic policy which could win the voters at the Presidential elections of 1995 was a constant constraint, or incentive.

GATT and agriculture

The end of the Cold War and the Maastricht decision for European economic integration were watersheds in economic policy in France. They complicated and accelerated the hard bargaining over world trade begun at Punta del Este in 1986, known as the Uruguay round within the General Agreement on Tariffs and Trade (GATT). A pervasive belief that liberal triumphalism, identified with America, was poised for a final assault on all remaining vestiges of protectionism across the world sharpened both expectations and defensive reflexes in France. For several years French negotiators encamped behind protection of both agriculture and audio-visual products, the two areas most at risk from American dominance. The round was stalled. But the end of Soviet Communism and the push from a post-Maastricht Europe towards international competitiveness gave an extra edge to the cause of free trade: Jacques Delors and the European Commission showed untrammelled enthusiasm for this latest and most ambitious of the GATT negotiations. By 1993 a consciousness in France that the Uruguay round would have to be concluded if uncertainties were not to protract the recession was spiced by the sense of opportunity on the one hand and apprehension on the other. The arms industry, headed by Dassault, and international transport, communications and services, featuring Airbus, France-Télécom and Thomson Electronics, were among the enthusiasts for a GATT agreement. European industry would be stronger if it was restructured to compete internationally, but so too would the whole French economy if the government used the bargaining process skilfully. It was a question of keeping a sufficient degree of protection to prevent violent rural protests.

The initiative and professionalism of the young farmers of the early 1960s were mirrored twenty years later by those who adapted to the vastly expanded food-processing industry. Brittany was quoted everywhere as the success story. At least a million of Brittany's rural population, and half of the peasantry, had left the region over the century, but three-quarters of the farmers who remained were the mechanized, market-oriented younger generation. Already in 1980 Brittany, with 6 per cent of the nation's

cultivated land, accounted for 11 per cent of its agricultural wealth. Five of the ten largest butter companies were in Brittany, which produced 20 per cent of the country's milk supply. One reason why Brittany voted in favour of Maastricht was that the co-operatives and food-processing plants were finely attuned to a widening market. But keeping abreast of technology and mechanization was largely achieved on credit. The debts which accrued across the rural sector made all farmers vulnerable to shifts in culinary habits and patterns of shopping which determined the market as critically as competition from abroad. Frozen food and hypermarkets set much of the agricultural agenda. Fast-food restaurants and chains were beginning to dictate urban eating habits.

By the 1990s no more than a third of agricultural income came from sales of raw produce. Food-processing took its own profits and controlled much of the pricing of agricultural products, and the farming scene was further complicated by over-production of staple commodities, notably butter and potatoes, but also affecting all vegetables, fruit and wine as competition from southern Europe continued to fuel the productivist drive which had been the secret of French agricultural success since the 1950s. It was now more a recipe for disaster. Quotas were meant to stem the 'food mountains' but they were slow in doing so. The generic answer to over-production within Europe was quality over quantity. The wine industry was quick to adapt, not least because consumption of inferior wines dropped dramatically with the diversity of taste and the challenge of beer in the last twenty years of the century. The French governments and European directives induced large-scale uprooting of vineyards where there was little chance of reaching the standard mark of quality (*appellation contrôlée*). Nevertheless in wine as in other foodstuffs the lure of undercutting international rivals by sheer quantity was still a factor in agricultural thinking. It was here that direct competition with American produce prolonged the acrimony of the Uruguay round. The two largest competitors in the West were openly disputing a protected access to the world's food markets.

There were glaring contradictions in the US position, not least the record of protection afforded to their own farmers, parallel to the benefits which accrued to French farmers from the European Common Agricultural Policy (CAP). Room was found in these comparable systems to negotiate varying degrees of continued agricultural protection which would meet rural pressures on both sides of the Atlantic, and yet accept the expanding principle of open markets. Mitterrand was the continuity factor in forming a defensive French policy, and the new Foreign Minister in the Balladur government, Alain Juppé, was as willing to protect French farming interests as his

immediate Socialist predecessors. Balladur's commitment to international free trade and his relative freedom from the rural pressure groups shifted policy towards compromise. With all participants pressing for a speedy resolution, and Jacques Delors expressing European impatience with the French 'Maginot mentality', the Uruguay round finally produced an agreement in December 1993 for a selective and gradual reduction of agricultural protection, affecting both Europe and America, but Balladur assured parliament that not a single hectare of fallow land would be imposed on farmers as a result. Positively it was argued that French agricultural products, already accounting for almost a third of French exports, would benefit from increased access to the US and wider markets. The GATT process was handed on to a new body, the World Trade Organization (WTO), to take effect in January 1995. By then the dubious benefit of free trade for the poorest Third World countries and for traditional forms of agriculture within Europe put the GATT agreement into a new dimension of economic, and moral, dispute.

Cultural products

As part of the GATT package, audio-visual products were exempted from the free trade formula. An outright success for French and European negotiators, the protection of European culture (*l'exception culturelle*), backed strongly by Mitterrand, was elevated to an epic resistance story against the all-invasive American cinema. There were almost universal headlines that French cultural heritage had been preserved and that aesthetic quality had been rescued from the quantitative, materialist ethic. The concept of a definable national identity appeared to have found expression and relief in cultural resilience. The relief was palpable.

In cinema, the protection of French films went back to 1946 when negotiations between France and the USA stipulated a percentage of weeks in which French film screenings would be guaranteed. Immediately following the Liberation there had been a danger that all screens would be monopolized by the strength and popularity of Hollywood products. Film distribution was controlled almost exclusively by American companies. Successful demonstrations by film-makers, actors and technicians in the winter of 1947–8 extended the number of protected weeks for French films to five in any three months. The Cannes Film Festival, planned in 1936 but only launched after the war, was a further guarantor that critical prominence would be given to French and European films. In the 1960s and 1970s the reputation of new French cinema was so high, and its popular products

sufficiently successful, that 50 per cent of films screened in 1980 were French and 31 per cent American. Within a decade the ratio had been turned on its head and American cinema was close to claiming 60 per cent of screen time. The prolonged debate over the GATT negotiations was one registering crisis in the French film industry.

Most directly, the reprieve of audio-visual products rewarded Jack Lang for years of campaigning for the maintenance of a quota system to protect the French cinema both as art and as industry. French film was acknowledged to be the most consistent quality competitor to American cinema in Europe. Lang had conceded as early as 1984 that France was also the European country in which American films were most popular, successful and influential among serious film critics and directors. Despite this ambivalence and Lang's acceptance of American-derived pop and rock music, he was one clear voice for protection. But he was far from an unchallenged representative of French cultural identity.

Lang's intention to mobilize all aspects of creativity regardless of class, ethnic origin or belief, exposed him to the scorn of those who argued that French thought and culture was singular and universalist and who accused Lang of opening the door inside France to cultural pluralism. Intellectual polemicist Alain Finkielkraut had put himself forward in 1987 as the scourge of those who were open to the ways in which sociology, anthropology and politics had made culture a relative term, and in 1990 he was critical of a Ministry of Culture survey of French cultural practices which included leisure pursuits, eating out and holidays.[11] The plurality of ideas about culture did not convince the universalists that national identity should adapt itself to cultural relativism, still less to multiculturalism. As the GATT negotiations filtered into public consciousness it was possible to be in favour of protecting the French audio-visual industry but also of cultural relativism. It was equally possible to define French culture in a universalist way and yet favour economic liberalism. The multiple cross-overs of opinion suggested that national identity could no longer be found to reside unambiguously in culture, if indeed it had ever done so.

'Culture is not a commodity' was one of the slogans dating back to 1968 which drew comfort from the GATT agreement. It was less a statement of fact than a commitment to culture as creativity and expression, at individual or collective level. But it was also an attempt to create parameters for economic liberalism. As the impact of the international market economy led to the globalization of goods and services, the argument about what is and what is not a commodity intensified and broadened. It animated people in education, health and justice as much as those in the realm of culture,

however defined. It had already primed much of the debate about French television, subaltern to the cultural eminence of the cinema.

The Socialist law of 29 July 1982 proclaimed that the citizen had a right to audio-visual communication that was 'free and plural'. It was freedom from political control, but the law also effectively opened television to the private sector. In 1985 Mitterrand overturned forty years of government policy by allowing the launch of two commercial channels, La Cinq and TV6, funded by advertising (*publicité*). His aim was to outmanoeuvre the right and liberalize television in his own way. Disbelief among Socialists was rife. The franchise of La Cinq was allotted to a group co-organized by the Italian media tycoon, Silvio Berlusconi, notorious for his contempt towards Italian cinema and his promotion of television as a commodity game-show. Jack Lang, opposing Mitterrand on this issue, deplored everything about the new channel, but ultimately gave his unwilling consent to the President's initiative, amidst talk of a sabotage of the national culture. The earlier launch of Canal Plus in 1984 had introduced the new era in television with private money and part-private management of its subscription-based programmes, but no revenue from *publicité*. The notion of television as a public service was uneasily perpetuated, with the monopoly of transmission in state hands. The Chirac government ended the monopoly in 1986 and spectacularly went even further and privatized one of the major public channels, TFI. Mitterrand was heavily critical but unable to affect the sale. The Socialists swung the pendulum back to public service after 1988, and in 1992 created a Franco-German cultural channel, Arte. State influence in the world of audio-visual communication was reasserted, and was only modified, not abolished, under Balladur.

Each change in the control of programming in television sparked controversy. Accusations of scandal and corruption were endemic, but while attention was riveted on the question of management and ownership, and how to keep quotas of French programmes at 60 per cent, the power of commercial television as a cultural vector grew through the popularity of imported American programmes and the creative verve of its advertising. Opinion polls suggested that the programmes, images and sounds of the market highway were irresistible. It was for this reason that many of those who had been concerned over forty years to promote high culture and high quality in television argued at the time of the GATT negotiations that the cultural pass had already been sold by Mitterrand in the mid-1980s: there was little left to protect.

Pessimism or élitism, this judgement gave insight into the culture and national identity issues encoded in the debates about free trade and protection.

Mitterrand at several junctures enforced a state presence in the development of audio-visual communication, and was compared by some to de Gaulle in his determination to have a broadcasting system at his disposal, though not exclusively so. He himself inaugurated a francophone satellite channel, TV5, designed to represent France abroad. Yet the cultural exception that was celebrated in 1993 was essentially the French cinema, elevated to an emblem of the nation. Mitterrand's personal journey to attend the Lille opening of Claude Berri's film *Germinal*, based on Zola's realist novel of a coal-mining community, was interpreted as a part-socialist, part-romantic, but mostly national gesture. Television did not hold the same cultural or emblematic status. The imbalance was an update of the 1950s distinction between the 'French' car and the 'American' fridge.

Deregulation and the job market

The GATT agreement was not the only route into the international economy. Privatization had been another; restructuring of industry in the mid-1980s preceded it and was pursued by every succeeding government. It was even claimed that the welfare state had eased access into the global market, providing a safety net for the casualties of change. Confidence in liberal economics drove the governments of right and left to adapt to globalization and determine the rules of the game, or more precisely which rules to abandon. Deregulation in the economy was everywhere in demand. Flexibility in the financial markets made the funding of business a competitive area of its own with a marketing strategy which constantly questioned the need to rely on the state for funds, loans and contracts. Government agencies and administrative élites had always intervened to encourage business mergers and create 'leading' national companies. As they propelled nationalized firms into buying shares in other companies and high-profile restructuring, they were increasingly met by managerial claims for more liberalization, and by the workforce for more protection. The tension created by this pull in contrary directions is the shorthand history of the 1990s and the early years of the twenty-first century.

By the time the dust from the GATT conflicts had settled, it was clear that employment raised issues of state intervention closer to the electorate's concerns than either agriculture or audio-visual products. The statistics of unemployment barely changed as Mitterrand was succeeded by Chirac, Balladur by Juppé and Juppé by Jospin: the figures stayed obstinately high, even as France began to move out of recession in 1997 and firms entered the market highway with mounting success.

The European single market and the GATT agreement were premised on the deregulation of international markets. Open competition was to be the model for business: it was assumed too that states would become competitive in creating a free economic space with a flexible labour market in which companies from inside and outside the country could operate, promising lower prices, more choice to consumers and an expansion of jobs. Business sights were being rapidly focused on opportunities outside Europe. An influential report from the Senate finance commission in June 1993 in the name of Jean Arthuis, a considered advocate of liberalism, warned that one result would be 'delocalization' of business and industry, as firms moved from one country to another in pursuit of cheaper labour. This possibility was nervously watched by governments and the media, and interpreted by the trade unions as a threat to keep labour costs low in France. Three years later in 1996 talk was equally about a doomsday approach to globalization by Viviane Forrester in a book entitled *L'Horreur économique* which pictured a form of dictatorship of economics over politics.[12] It was seen by some as another variation on the 'end of exceptionalism', and it fed public despair that the state was powerless to protect labour. It was Chirac's first full year as President and Juppé's as Premier and by December the unemployment figures, even in the government's new calculations, were still above 3 million, or over 12 per cent of the active population.

The reality of political power, however, was much more complex than a generalized horror scenario suggested. Regulation of employment was not progressively abandoned. From the late 1970s projects of partial protection had been advanced by different governments with inconsistent effect. Flexibility did occur, and was significant in the world of small and medium business: part-time working and short-term contracts, especially for women, mushroomed from the late 1980s onwards. The service sector continued to expand until it employed two-thirds of the active population by the end of the century. Temporary work agencies grew to be one of the most prominent features in the business landscape, not least as major employers, and from 1991 to 1995 there was a 15 per cent growth in the proportion of the country's workforce employed abroad. But market incentives to uproot business completely in pursuit of low-cost labour were countered by state-financed inducements to stay. As a potent sign of attitudes, the morality of a French firm's employment policies outside the country was publicly questioned in February 1997 when Renault pulled out of Vilvorde in Brussels with the loss of 3,000 jobs. Chirac was forced by the degree of outrage and the imminence of European-wide strikes to declare that he was shocked by the way it had happened. Such public

concern for the ethics of the international economy kept the issue of regulation alive. It did not appear to affect inward investment which reached as high as 35 per cent of French stock-market capital in 1997. Labour was judged to be relatively expensive in France, but a skilled workforce was a major compensation. State provision of retraining and reskilling had been a constant feature since the de-industrialization of the late 1970s.

Even party politics still carried enough conviction to inject life into state regulation under Chirac's Presidency. The sensational upturn in Socialist fortunes in 1997, four years after apparent obliteration, brought Lionel Jospin to power in a year when official international statistics confirmed France as significantly tenacious in its protection of labour. Jospin and his Minister of Employment, Martine Aubry, challenged the inevitability of state withdrawal from the economic sphere. Aubry introduced a plan for youth employment, with contracts for five years funded to 80 per cent by the state, and she echoed Léon Blum's Popular Front legislation with two ambitious bills to reduce the working week. She aimed to bring it down to thirty-five hours, to take effect at the start of the new century. The target of the youth project was 150,000 new jobs in the first year, and if this was only two-thirds achieved its psychological impact outstripped the statistics.

Martine Aubry was a graduate of ENA, and had been assistant to Jean Auroux in the formulation of the 'Auroux laws' on workers' rights at the workplace, passed in 1982. She was the daughter of Jacques Delors. Her project for a 35-hour week was a multipronged policy not only for new jobs but also for a new work–life balance for all workers. The practicalities of the scheme involved a process of consultation between government, unions and employers, often at local level, which recognized the plurality of interests in society and the need for each sector to negotiate, rather than dictate, its economic position. For many it became an innovative experience in industrial relations. Aubry's heritage of ideas included the social engineering and idealism of the inter-war years, and the rationale behind the lowering of the retirement age in 1983. The project had historical depth and cultural resonance. It had long formed part of the ecology platform, and was backed by the Communists and CGT provided there was no loss of pay; Mitterrand had decreed a reduction to thirty-nine hours; the aim of his first government in 1981 had been to move eventually to thirty-five; influential Catholic voices urged firms to experiment with job-sharing, and throughout the 1980s and early 1990s various ideas for a shorter week and job creation had regularly been aired, not just by the left.

To employers looking for deregulation of labour, the proposal to regulate the hours of paid work was a step backwards, though there was some

ambivalence within the *patronat* due to the moderate success of Gilles de Robien's bill, already mentioned above, to reward businesses which reduced their working week in order to employ more staff. It was estimated that its system of tax incentives had already produced an extra 45,000 jobs and saved even more. The bruising confrontation over the Aubry bills came from their insistence that cutting the 39-hour week to thirty-five would not entail a cut in wages. Without this stipulation the trade unions would have opposed the project from the start, the CGT wholeheartedly and the CFDT with more reluctance. As it was, the 'thirty-nine hours' pay for thirty-five hours' work' allowed the project to be resisted by employers as counter-productive. Alain Madelin, leader of the liberal right in the Chamber, spoke for much of the business world by declaring on France 2 in January 1998 that the 35-hour week would drag both wages and the economy down-wards.[13]

Negotiations at sectoral level had to begin from this level of disagreement. Deals were struck with certain firms on an annual calculation of hours rather than a weekly one, and the time was continously extended by the government for firms of different sizes to adapt to the regulations. The process of bargaining at local level was given new bite and relevance. But in the complexity of the issues, the bills as general policy and as social improvement became increasingly ambiguous: they were still a matter of rebarbative confrontation and economic controversy at the Presidential elections in 2002 and beyond. President Chirac's campaign for re-election claimed that the 35-hour week had been introduced by the Jospin government 'unilaterally', even though he had previously shown signs of readiness to work with the proposals. His greater assertiveness on the issue reflected the growing demand from employers for labour flexibility. The initial enthusiasm of the public for the shorter working week had not disappeared, but it had cooled. The government calculation that over a quarter of a million jobs had been created by 2001 was thought to be exaggerated, and yet Aubry's employment policies emerged in opinion polls as having played a positive role in creating a distinctive mix of state intervention and liberal economics as the old century ended and the new one began.

21

Political Oscillation, 1990s–2000s (2)

1. Mitterrand to Chirac, Juppé to Jospin

Outgoing President

In the final year of Mitterrand's second term two major reports to the Balladur government outlined projects to connect every household to the information superhighway by the year 2015. Rapidly overtaken themselves by the speed of change, the reports looked back to the head-start that the Minitel system of the 1980s had given France. The Mitterrand years would be noted at least for the paradox of a President deeply and elegantly steeped in philosophy and literature and frequently likened to a nineteenth-century connoisseur, and yet identified with the take-off in information technology. There had been little foretaste of this in the 1981 poster for his election campaign, with the slogan 'The quiet force' ('*La force tranquille*') set against a village church and rural landscape, but for his earlier Presidential election against de Gaulle in 1965 there had been a pylon, set in a flat ploughed field with an industrial backing of smoking power-stations and the caption: 'A young President for a modern France'. As 1994–5 became increasingly bitter for the 78-year-old President, his identity with technological change was reduced by many to the mere fact that he had been in power when it happened. His opening of the Channel Tunnel on 6 May 1994 in company with the British Queen Elizabeth was given as an example. The tunnel was the fulfilment of a futurist engineering dream dating back over 200 years and was hailed as a historic and symbolic event in the modernization of Europe. It was not ascribed to Mitterrand. Nor, on the debit side, were the finances of Eurotunnel, deplored for the 80 billion-franc debt they carried, leaving at least ten years before the shareholders would see any benefit.

Mitterrand represented a modern France but he was not seen to personify the term 'modernization', increasingly monopolized by the partisans of a liberal economy. They claimed he too often obstructed it, or had sullied it

by abuse of personal power. Both perspectives concentrated on the running scandal of the Crédit Lyonnais, the leading deposit bank, whose massive losses were attributed to the prodigal policy of Jean-Yves Haberer, appointed head of the bank in 1988 by Finance Minister Bérégovoy with Mitterrand's full approval. Setting itself up as a model of deregulation and state protection combined, it numbered among its disasters unregulated loans to Bernard Tapie, the extrovert and popular owner of the Marseille Olympique football club and a friend of Mitterrand, who was brought into Bérégovoy's government as Minister of Urban Affairs (Ministre de la Ville) in 1992, convinced he had the creative drive for a renaissance of the *banlieues*. Almost immediately indicted for misuse of company money, Tapie was never out of the scandal pages, the journalists revealing the fortune he had made through the Crédit Lyonnais and investigating Mitterrand's promotion of Tapie's political populism in a grouping called Radical Energy, thought to be able to defeat Le Pen in his Mediterranean stronghold. Both affairs, the bank and Tapie, came to a head in 1996 after Mitterrand's death, but already in 1994 Haberer was sacked from the Crédit National after being moved from the Crédit Lyonnais, and Tapie was arrested at dawn on 29 June to face charges of fraud and tax evasion. He had just been elected to the European Parliament. There was intense speculation on the precise patronage bestowed on Bernard Tapie. Guilt by association with a questionable entourage was levelled recurrently against Mitterrand.

Rwanda and Vichy

On 6 April 1994 in the African 'land of a thousand hills', a plane carrying the Hutu President of Rwanda, Juvénal Habyarimana, and the President of neighbouring Burundi, Cyprien Ntaryamira, was shot down as it was about to land at Kigali. Both Presidents were killed. Rwanda, a small densely populated country in the Great Lakes area of Africa, bordering on Zaïre, had been colonized by Germany in 1898 and administered by Belgium as a mandated territory after the First World War. Independent since 1962, its land, politics and heritage were violently disputed by the Tutsi and Hutu peoples, whose rivalry was ascribed as much to colonial obsession with institutionalizing tribalism as to the ingrained folk-myths of the origin of the Tutsis in Egypt and their subjugation of the Hutus. By the early 1990s French military investment in the Hutu-dominated republic made Mitterrand and the French Foreign Office, along with Belgium, the United Nations, America and Britain, blind to the extent of the genocidal plans

prepared by Hutu extremists in Kigali who refused to accept the precarious peace agreements reached within the country at Arusha in August 1993. No faction admitted responsibility for shooting down the Presidential plane. It was used to spark the genocide of over 800,000 Tutsi men, women and children in under three months, an orgy of killing, orchestrated by Hutu Radio, which also victimized moderate Hutus who had lived and inter-married with Tutsis and who tried to protect them.

The inactivity of the international community in the face of the genocide in Rwanda appeared particularly inexplicable when French troops and contingents from francophone African countries provided protection to the Hutus in the south-west of the country at the end of June, as the extremists abandoned the capital Kigali to incoming Tutsi forces. It was this apparent bias in their delayed intervention that attracted the condemnation of Paul Kagame, the Tutsi leader who established an authoritarian rule in Rwanda in July. Exactly what the French role was, before and during the genocide, provoked steadily increasing debate and acrimony. The tangled complexity of the murderous civil war, the abrupt reduction of UN forces on 21 April, the failure of any country to intervene, all left crucial facts buried or disputed and guilt randomly apportioned, to which was added the desperate crisis of 'the largest dislocation of people that the Red Cross had seen in its seventy-five years of Federated existence'.[1]

Suspicion of French motivation in Rwanda did not specifically implicate Mitterrand in 1994. It was his association with Vichy which surprisingly resurfaced during the year with wounding effect. Some of the facts of his Vichy career, including the award of the Vichy medal, the *francisque*, had been aired at the time of his Presidential contest with de Gaulle in 1965. His move into resistance in 1943 had been sufficient to guarantee his political integrity, and his close working life with Pierre Mendès France secured him an unimpeachable republican reputation. In the autumn of 1994 Pierre Péan, journalist and historian, raised new doubts in his study of Mitterrand's early political years, based on long interviews with the President. Called *Une Jeunesse française, François Mitterrand 1934–1947*, its title suggested that Mitterrand's youth was typical of any other French beginnings.[2] That was where the irony lay. Péan showed the Vichy episode to have been longer, and Mitterrand's right-wing youth to have had more fervour than had been imagined. He forced people to ask questions about the President's involvement in the ideology of Vichy. How much of the shameful history of collaboration had he known, or accepted?

These questions had not been pursued in 1965. Thirty years later, the context of Holocaust memory and the trials for crimes against humanity

of Klaus Barbie and Paul Touvier (see Chapter 22) exerted a quite different level of pressure. Mitterrand's post-war relationship with René Bousquet, Vichy chief of police, was thrown yet again into the headlines. Bousquet was assassinated on 8 June 1993, just before he was finally to stand trial, accused of responsibility for the French role in the round-up of Jews in July 1942 into the Vélodrome d'Hiver (Vél. d'Hiv). For several years Mitterrand had shielded Bousquet from prosecution on the legal basis that the case brought against him in 1949 had been withdrawn, and on the general grounds of 'not reopening the wounds of the past'. After Péan it was even more noted that Bousquet had used the influential paper *La Dépêche du Midi* to help Mitterrand's campaign in 1965, and was still entertained in Presidential circles in the mid-1980s until the evidence against him could no longer be ignored by the Élysée.

Mitterrand as President had reacted to antisemitic outrages, from the rue des Rosiers bombs of 1982 to the desecration of Jewish graves in 1990, with a depth of humanity which no one disputed. He had no antisemitism to hide. He was the first President to attend the ceremony remembering Vél. d'Hiv on its fiftieth anniversary on 16 July 1992, and he then decided that it should be a national day of remembrance, but he would not publicly accept the responsibility of the French nation, on the basis that Vichy had not been a legitimate state. His refusal was seen as particular obstinacy in the face of young opinion, whose right to make judgements about the Occupation period he seemed to resent. Péan was making no accusations of guilt, yet Mitterrand, visibly ill and frail, decided to appear on television to talk about what he had said to the journalist, greatly extending the publicity already given to the book. His repetition of many of the facts was soberly received, but opened even more questions about what he had known at the time. The public disquiet gave Mitterrand's reputation a further downward twist. His closest allies acknowledged it with dismay and sadness. He was not a popular President in his last year.

Incoming President and Premier

Speculation on his successor in the elections due in April–May 1995 eased the pressure on Mitterrand. It was far from certain that it would be another right–left conflict as it had been in 1981 and 1988. The in-fighting in the Socialist Party (PS) had become repetitive and sterile, holding the interest of careerists and masochists only. Such optimism as there was went towards Jacques Delors: he was entreated to leave his European stage and was front-runner in the polls, but could not be persuaded to stand. Lionel Jospin

was the ultimate choice of the PS. He emanated integrity, had ceased to be an ally of Mitterrand, and carried the aura of the lecture room with him, but his didactic presence was given little hope by the media. The barely known Communist leader, Robert Hue, jovial in appearance and undogmatic, was seen as a lightweight. On the right, the entente between Balladur and Chirac collapsed. Balladur saw the chance of capitalizing on his Premiership and decided to stand. Chirac, the expected candidate of the RPR, mixed accusations of betrayal by Balladur with a populist campaign promising to heal the fractures of society. He gradually outpointed his rival. When it was decided by the RPR and UDF, more by default than by intent, that they should both stand, it was with the confidence that they would be first and second in the opening round, such was the parlous state of the left.

Jean-Marie Le Pen set his Front National supporters directly against Chirac, and in the event his 15 per cent in the first round on 23 April 1995 came from more working-class voters than in 1988, after a campaign which was less raucous than in previous elections. There was talk of Le Pen 'maturing' as a politician. The surprise was Balladur's poor showing, only 3.5 per cent beyond Le Pen, and over two points below Chirac. Astonishingly, Jospin led the field with just over 23 per cent, a long way ahead of Hue (8.6 per cent) who kept just three points ahead of Arlette Laguiller, the hardened Trotskyist campaigner who received over 5 per cent of the vote for the first time in her four Presidential appearances. The Green, Dominique Voynet, failed to reach the 5 per cent which would have given ecologists more of the bargaining power they were beginning to exert on the left.

The victory in the second round for Jacques Chirac (52.6 per cent) was only momentarily in doubt, but Jospin's 47.3 per cent signalled a recovery for the left which gave the contest unexpected political bite. Much of the considerable anger expressed by the electorate was against the whole political class. Jospin, feuding with Chirac on television or in their radically contrasting tours of the country, reawoke some of the emotion of an ideological left–right conflict. A breakdown in the broadly defined economic consensus was thought unlikely, and the sense of decay in Mitterrand's last year made it difficult for the left to demand that Chirac's reputation for sharp business practice as mayor of Paris should be investigated. But Chirac's ideological fervour of 1986 was a recent memory and some major gesture of his political pedigree was anticipated. On 13 June the new President announced that nuclear testing would be resumed, ending Mitterrand's moratorium of 1992. If anything forcefully reminded people

that Chirac was the first Gaullist President for twenty-one years, this was it.

It was difficult to imagine the President devising a more contemptuous gesture towards world opinion. The insensitivity to the South Pacific islanders provoked the burning of the French flag on Bastille Day in countless locations around the world. In France over half the population declared themselves against the resumptions, reeling under the impact of such impassioned worldwide anti-nuclear protests. This was another side of globalized consciousness. Mitterrand and the Socialist governments had not nurtured a nuclear disarmament movement, but in the ten years following the *Rainbow Warrior* scandal, humanitarian and ecological movements had flourished within issue politics. Chirac embodied the anachronistic government belief, shared no less by Mitterrand, that French arms trade and defence policies were a purely French affair. To his surprise he was forced to explain his decision to the European Parliament and to allow European observers at the underground tests. In January 1996 he conceded that they would be the final tests before signing up to an international policy of disarmament.

Defence analysts were quick to argue that Chirac's nuclear tests within an overall policy of de-escalation were less hypocrisy than a reminder to Europe and the USA of French capability in the post-Cold War era. Mitterrand had also kept French bargaining power at the forefront of defence negotiations. In 1988 he had been the first French President since 1966 to attend a NATO summit. He had pursued the development of a European military force while admitting to dependence on American hegemony. The crisis in Yugoslavia had revealed how many urgent issues could fall between these two positions and Chirac maintained he was keen to move the balancing act forward. The Dayton accords on Bosnia brought Europe and the USA together in November 1995, and to promote more realism in military planning Chirac announced in February 1996 a massive cut in the defence budget over five years, and the end of national service by 2001. The conscripted army was to be replaced by a much-reduced professional one. It had been the young de Gaulle's early project, set out in *Vers l'armée de métier* (1934) but de Gaulle had not made it his policy in the 1960s. In making this historic change to the republican tradition of a citizen army, Chirac was more in tune with contemporary thinking than the nuclear decision had indicated.

Far more of a reversal of Mitterrand's position was Chirac's acceptance on 16 July 1995 of French involvement in the deportations of Jews under Vichy. On Vél. d'Hiv day, Chirac admitted that the French state had assisted

the Nazi occupier. It was an official apology: 'France,' he declared, had 'committed the irreparable'. He spoke for most people: their reactions were positive. Mitterrand, it was widely felt, should have taken the opportunity to say the same.

Badly, or well, as Chirac's first gestures were received, judgement by the public was mostly reserved until it was clear how he would handle the social discontent volubly expressed during the election. During the summer of 1995 economic growth stalled and the rate of unemployment increased. On 26 October Chirac told the country that the first policy adopted by Juppé's government of mixing restraint with stimulus had not shown results, and he would turn to tight fiscal control, reducing the budget deficit with a new economy drive to meet European convergence targets under the Maastricht Treaty. Juppé resigned but was immediately reappointed and in mid-November set out a plan for a complete overhaul of the social security budget, through severe cuts in public expenditure and reforms to family allowances. Special pension arrangements for state employees (*fonctionnaires*) were to be revised. The 'Juppé plan' was launched as an explosive plan for modernization of the state apparatus, and explicitly used reports prepared for previous Socialist governments. It expressed the liberal orthodoxy that growth and new jobs in a competitive market were dependent on cutting the national costs of the welfare state. The money and stock markets approved: Juppé also received the public support of Nicole Notat, leader of the CFDT unions, who argued to a hostile grass roots that modernization was necessary. The other union federations were opposed, not all with equal vehemence.

A day's strike of *fonctionnaires* in the post office, electricity, gas and transport, was staged on 10 October 1995 in protest at a freeze on wages for the following year: at the same time students at Rouen University began a strike against education cuts, followed gradually by students elsewhere. The Juppé plan and a reorganization of state funding for the railways over four years decided railway and other public service workers to start a much more serious action at the end of November. It spread to all public transport. Within days trains, buses, métro and trams were at a standstill. To expressions of surprise from all sections of the media, the strikes and accompanying demonstrations became the biggest and most popular movement of social protest since May 1968, and was seen by many to outdistance its famous predecessor by its inclusiveness of all social issues. On 25 November, for example, over 30,000 women staged a demonstration in Paris, organized by the combined associations defending abortion and contraception (CADAC), which attacked not only globalization practices but also religious

fundamentalism as dangerous for women's employment, freedom and social equality. Equally effective in the grass-roots organization were the new trade unions, such as Solidaires, Unitaires, Démocratiques (SUD), comprising dissidents largely from the CFDT, disillusioned by the shift from the radicalism of the 1970s. The very low membership of the big confederations, dipping below 10 per cent of workers, renewed autonomous ideas and methods of a more confrontational syndicalism at the workplace which scorned officialdom and bureaucracy in the labour movement. It revelled in the cross-society activism of the strikes.

With the Christmas break looming, Juppé and Chirac were forced to retreat on the railway reorganization and the revised pension schemes, though much of the Juppé plan for social security was not withdrawn. With concessions won, transport began to return to normal, though the tramworkers in Marseille held out into January to achieve their demands. Over the New Year supporters of the strikes exchanged their stories of how they had got to work, revealing the extent to which cars had been amicably shared, and the pleasures of cycling and walking rediscovered. In immediate retrospect, what was new was not the balance sheet of victories for workers or government, but the claims from a significant number of strikers, intellectuals and sympathetic public that this was an epic moment in the defence of the welfare state and its most vulnerable citizens against globalization and the liberal market. Disputing this, other intellectuals and much of the media argued the benefits of modernization, and analysed the protests as a conservative defence of sectional interests.

The sociologist of education, class and culture, Pierre Bourdieu, went further than most in his rejection of the ideology behind the plans of Chirac and Juppé. In public meetings and in motions taken to the CGT he decried the globalizing economy as the destruction of a civilization which was based on public service, a 'civilization of republican equality of rights: rights to education, to health, culture, research, art, and, above all, work'.[3] Demonstrations, nationwide, by 500,000 to a million or more on a series of days throughout December 1995, carried banners in similar apocalyptic vein. Yet Bourdieu found many fellow social experts against him. Alain Touraine, who had perceived the start of post-industrialism earlier than most, and Pierre Rosanvallon, one of the three who had set up the 'end of exceptionalism' debate, were among the academics and intellectuals who backed Nicole Notat's 'realism' in her stand against the older and the newer unions.

Death of Mitterrand

Shortly after the weeks of social turbulence came the news on 8 January 1996 that François Mitterrand had died. The ideological conviction of the protesters and their critics throughout the long autumn primed the response to his death. The euphoria and promise of the socialist *changement* in 1981 had never been entirely dissipated. It re-emerged in the emotional crowds across the country on 10 January 1996 who carried red roses to remember Mitterrand and the day fifteen years before when, said one mourner in Paris, 'We felt that we had stormed the Bastille.'[4] Universally admired for his courage in fighting his cancer, Mitterrand was buried at Jarnac, the village of his birth in the Charente, which had never quite reciprocated the fondness that Mitterrand felt for it. Chirac rose to the opportunity to show his own responsiveness, and paid generous homage to Mitterrand's ideals of social justice, humanism and the cause of Europe. Borrowing de Gaulle's choice of words about France, he said that Mitterrand had 'married his century', but meaning less a pact with modernity than the sheer range of his contribution to the history of the twentieth century, and the plenitude of life, private and public, rural and urban, cultural and political, that he had represented.

Contradictions featured in every obituary: by themselves they justify a pluralistic approach to France and the French since 1900. By holding his own court Mitterrand descended into abuse of personal power, yet at the nodal point of the state he had adjusted the Republic to the sharing of political power within France and potentially within Europe. He had continued to call himself a socialist and he kept friends and enemies by saying so. As his legacy was summarized even before he died, he was blamed, or credited, by both sides for the passions displayed in the autumn conflicts of 1995. On the one hand he had not allowed the state to wither away, so the public sphere still had passionate defenders. On the other hand he had not, in his last twelve years of power, dismissed the rationale of economic liberalism and the significance of private enterprise.

Mitterrand's conversion to the regime of the Fifth Republic took him to a form of parental leadership in which he was sometimes called *dieu* ('god'), not always with irony, but more often *tonton*, a child's pet name for 'uncle' which did not convey an infantilism of the public in the way that Pétain's cult of fatherhood had done. It was more a recognition that he had adopted a beneficent aura of authority. He understood that de Gaulle as President had personified his own political ideology: de Gaulle had been the figure-head, a heroic expression of ideas which were bigger than mere policies.

Mitterrand as President cultivated much the same romantic image: in 1981 he was seen as personifying the socialism which had been given a new political life under his leadership in the 1970s. This cult of the leader was the basis on which the many comparisons between the two Presidents were made. But unlike General de Gaulle, Mitterrand left no creed in his own name, no Mitterrandism equivalent to Gaullism, nor even a reinvention of socialism which could express his fourteen years as President.

After 1983 he came to prioritize consensus over ideology. He contributed to the 'end-of-ideology' climate of the late 1980s with an emphasis on inclusive republicanism, rather than any attempt to give socialism a new definition. His personal antipathy to Michel Rocard was decisive in this decision, since Rocard's career was directed towards the redefining of social-ism. In the last seven years Mitterrand played a leading role at the heart of consensus but even as the major player he could not divert the downward spiral of the Socialists in power and with it the image of his Presidency. Calling himself 'a socialist' to the end was a misleading summary of the ambiguities of his political journey. It is reasonable to say that he embodied the greater complexity of politics at the end of the century: it is also possible to judge that he failed to give a viable and ethical meaning to a 'post-socialism' that was well within his grasp.

Majority reversed

The everyday paradox of co-habitation that linked François Mitterrand to Jacques Chirac gave the new President a way of ending his speech of homage. Just over a year later Chirac unintentionally reproduced the same pattern. On 21 April 1997 he dissolved the National Assembly and announced new elections, a year before they were due. The surprise was total. There was no national crisis: the majority behind Juppé's government had not disintegrated. Chirac had no new policy and no new Premier to propose, merely a wish to capitalize on a rare moment of upbeat for an unpopular government and discover a 'new élan'. It was not a recognized reason for dissolution. It turned to disaster for Chirac, Juppé and the right. The Socialists constructed a left-wing alliance and captured power, four years after the PS appeared in terminal decay. Chirac was forced into co-habitation, His miscalculation appeared as incompetence. His loss of a parliamentary majority in two years was much faster than Mitterrand's in five.

Alain Juppé, the fifty-year-old talented meritocrat, was described as Chirac's younger shadow, given the years of their close association in both

Parisian and national government. Deputy for Paris since 1986, he had been Chirac's first choice in 1995, preferred to the alienated Balladur and the volatile Séguin. Nicknamed 'Amstrad' for his high intelligence, Juppé made few friends and kept his colleagues at a cold distance. His dramatic defeat in 1997 looked logical in the light of two years described by even the sympathetic press as ones of constant setbacks without any clear respite.

During the social protests and 'great strike' at the end of 1995 Juppé appeared to look on disdainfully. He made concessions but retained the government's commitment to cutting public expenditure. In 1996 his government failed to achieve its promised reduction in taxes and the expected revival of consumer spending; both Juppé and the President were tarnished by accusations of housing corruption and channelling public money to the RPR in Chirac's time as mayor of Paris; there was no fall in the unemployment figures which rose by a further 87,000 over twelve months; the public was repelled by police violence in evicting the *sans-papiers* in August (see Chapter 20); a lorry drivers' strike led to the blockage of roads in November; yet more scandal enveloped the municipal government of Paris and Chirac's successor as mayor, Jean Tiberi; all seriously diminished public confidence in Chirac and contrived to make the arrogant but vulnerable Juppé the most unpopular Prime Minister for twenty-five years. Nevertheless the decision of the inseparable Chirac and Juppé to stage a dissolution in April 1997 was at one brief moment when opinion seemed more positive and when, looking forward, they knew that their policies for the scheduled election year of 1998 would be perilous. They had brought the budget deficit down through continued privatizations which included the end of the state's historic control of Renault. France was on line to meet the Maastricht requirements for entry into the single currency, but a further year of stringent budgeting was held by Juppé to be necessary. What appeared as an impetuous dissolution, therefore, had a certain rational basis. Few predictions envisaged a left-wing victory. It was only when Juppé faced defeat after the first round that the decision was judged a sensational political blunder.

The oscillation to a Socialist-led government, with Jospin at its head, gave commentators good cause to conclude that it was now the political right which had lost its identity and rationale. In 1993 it had been the left. The process of the right's defeat was analysed as a similar slide into scandal, internal conflict and ineptitude. In the first round the parliamentary right polled its lowest percentage of the vote since 1958. A high level of abstentions could be blamed, but the second round was only marginally more successful. The combined right lost 217 of its 465 seats: the patchwork left

moved from 99 to 320, giving it a majority which had been considered unlikely for a decade at least. The Greens for the first time entered parliament with eight seats, while the Communist Party continued to defy the necrologists with thirty-seven. The Front National reached its highest percentage in legislative elections with almost 15 per cent in the first round, but ultimately secured only one deputy, elected in the bitterly divided Mediterranean port of Toulon.

Yet again Le Pen reserved his most contemptuous propaganda for the mainstream right. He still claimed that he would replace the inheritance of Gaullism with his exclusive form of nationalism. A mark of the inroads made by fears of immigration was notched in Juppé's government by his Minister of the Interior, Jean-Louis Debré. He moved, as Pasqua had done, into FN ideological territory with a bill in February 1997 to toughen controls. He added an obligation for anyone who gave accommodation to a foreigner to inform the local authorities when he or she left. The mockery and indignation which greeted this improbable measure were articulated in high-profile demonstrations of artists, writers, film-makers and trade unionists. The invasive clause disappeared, though the bill itself was passed. A subsequent opinion poll suggested that a majority of three to two accepted the tougher controls. Evidence from the two rounds of the election was inconclusive on whether the bill had diminished the appeal of the FN or legitimized anti-immigrant sentiment more generally.

From a patchwork of parties Jospin formed a government coalition dubbed the 'plural left' (la gauche plurielle). It included Jean-Pierre Chevènement from the Socialist group who had formed the Citizens' Movement (MDC), Dominique Voynet for the Greens and three Communists. When Juppé had re-formed his government in November 1995 he sacked eight of the twelve women ministers whom he had nominated a few months earlier. It was seen as a retrograde step. The Socialists decided on positive discrimination at the election, earmarking 30 per cent of their candidatures for women, and Jospin started with eight women ministers, two in prime positions, Martine Aubry in Employment and Élisabeth Guigou as the government's legal head (garde des sceaux). Dominique Voynet was Minister of the Environment; a Communist, Michèle Demessine, was appointed to Tourism and another, Marie-George Buffet, became a popular Minister of Youth and Sport. There was little equivalence to the idealism of 1981, but the Jospin government quickly showed that it had a notion of what post-socialism could mean. To add a further twist to the dissolution calamity for the right, the economy marked a decisive return towards growth. A plural left began to take credit for better unemployment figures

and for the steady move out of a series of recessions which had scarred and moulded politics for over twenty years.

2. *A viable post-socialism*

The plural left

Lionel Jospin, born in 1937 to a socialist and Protestant family in Meudon in the south-west suburbs of Paris, chose to teach economics at university level instead of entering the foreign service for which his ENA studies had prepared him. Briefly drawn towards Trotskyism as a student and then attached to the PSU, he was rapidly promoted within the Socialist Party which he joined aged thirty-four, rising to become its First Secretary in 1981 when Mitterrand was elected to the Presidency and Jospin to a parliamentary seat for Paris. In 1988 he transferred to the more socialist terrain of the Haute-Garonne, but in 1993 lost his seat in the rout of the left. His ministerial experience was in Education under Rocard and Cresson, but neither as minister nor as local figure did he create a political reputation for himself. It was as a party politician that he was seen to excel. He incarnated a moderately traditional socialism against the slippage of Fabius and Rocard into the consensus centre. His bitter ten-year feud with Fabius lost him the patronage of Mitterrand, but his resilience in the party led to his nomination as the Presidential candidate in 1995 and Premier in 1997. He was surprisingly effective. His sincerity was noted by every commentator, together with his rigorous concern for social justice. He presented as rather pedantic and easily exasperated, though the verve of his campaign led people to discover a more engaging personality. He handled most encounters with other politicians and journalists firmly and with competence, and was seen by public opinion to be a coherent communicator, reliably in touch and in control.

Jospin's creation of the plural left government carried his party's enthusiastic support, including the approval of Rocard and Fabius. It was a level of unity unknown to the PS for well over a decade. For partners on the left he relied on the permanence of the shift within the Communist Party to the relative pragmatism of Robert Hue, reinforced by the PCF's loss of direction under Georges Marchais. Tired, ill and an obvious handicap to his party, Marchais had withdrawn from the leadership in 1994. He died in November 1997. Robert Hue, working-class by background, a nurse by profession, and never a figure in international Communism, assured Jospin of the Communists' total solidarity. Dominique Voynet had stood as the

ecology candidate in the Presidential elections of 1995, rewarded by less than 3.5 per cent of the vote, but she could not speak as easily for all the ecologists, whose fractious existence had declined into self-parody in 1995, with some fifteen different groupings. She led the most structured of these, the Verts (Greens) in overtures to the Socialists which the PS reciprocated, leaving her main rivals Antoine Waechter and Brice Lalonde at the head of their groups to pursue chequered careers, Waechter dedicated to political autonomy and Lalonde moving to the right and backing Jacques Chirac. In 1997, when over a fifth of all candidates featured ecological issues, Brice Lalonde, the senior ecological politician, could secure only 7 per cent of the vote at Saint-Malo in Brittany, compared to Dominique's Voynet's first-round score of 31 per cent in her native Jura, where she campaigned against the environmental costs of widening the Rhine–Rhône canal.

Jospin's awareness, both intellectual and personal, of where the left had come from, how it had been transformed in office under Mitterrand, and how it had lost support and credibility, made him determined to recover at the very least a functional *raison d'être* and at best a new meaning. It made him a conscious creator of post-socialism, more often labelled social democracy *à la française*, left-wing realism (*réalisme de gauche*), or in his own words 'modern socialism'.[5] His readiness to disseminate power throughout his government was ascribed by some to his Protestant background, though he himself had no religious beliefs. In his book of 1991, entitled *L'Invention du possible*, he observed that democracies in Protestant countries tended to relativize power rather than elevate it to something sacred. It was an observation that others came to make about Jospin.

He was not content to be a passive spectator to the liberal economy, but intended to synchronize it with political goals and make the market work for social ends. Without reasserting the Keynesian idealism of 1981, he made it clear that the state would provide the money and intervention that was necessary. Regulation of capitalist enterprise was back on the government agenda, but with the aim of creating an alliance between the state and the market. Jospin's ability in both theory and practice was quickly recognized by the *patronat* (CNPF) which re-formed itself in 1998 into the Mouvement des Entreprises de France (MEDEF) in order to combat his proposals more effectively. In the absence of a coherent parliamentary right, the MEDEF was the surrogate opposition, particularly in resistance to the blanket application of the 35-hour week. It was helped by a conservative Senate and by certain constitutional rulings which restricted Martine Aubry's range of legislation.

The Jospin formula for post-socialism brought together the left-wing

parties but also drew on the vitality of those issue politics which were geared to creating a more equitable society. It did not deny the constraint of international market forces, nor of Maastricht for which Jospin had voted with a cautious *oui*, but established that there was more viability for socialist-based ideals within the constraints than had seemed possible at the time of the 'end of ideology' in Mitterrand's second term. Forming the plural left was a creative political act which had eluded Mitterrand in his second term. Making it cohere was the initial success of the government. Promises made in the election campaign to the Greens were kept, including the abandonment of the Superphénix fast-breeder reactor at Creys-Malville and the plans for the Rhine–Rhône canal. Bills to tackle poverty involved redistributive budgets canvassed by the Communists, raising the minimum wage (SMIC) above the level of inflation, as indeed Juppé had done, but also increasing the guaranteed minimum income (SMI) and weighting tax cuts to benefit the lower-income groups and the small to medium-sized businesses.

Unemployment was confronted as a problem which could be resolved. It was with this certainty that Martine Aubry embarked on her job-creation projects for youth, and the legislation for a 35-hour week (see Chapter 20). Health cover was made free for the very poor, so that no one fell outside the system, a universalism which extended the compass of human rights, long demanded by poverty action groups. The argument that a higher basic wage, and more money at the lower end of the social scale, would help stimulate the economy and lead to more jobs, was pitted against the liberal economic argument that jobs would be lost if flexibility of labour and wages was restricted. The idea that government regulation could widen choice and provide economic stimulus was at the heart of the plural left's challenge to the liberal economy. It was a distinctive bid to recuperate the concept of freedom.

There were two favourable contexts to this challenge.

Firstly, the election year turned into one of renewed economic growth, with even higher promise for 1998, based mainly on rising exports and the confidence shown by foreign companies to expand into France, putting it at the head of European countries for attracting outside investment. This was not affected by Jospin's less stringent measures for meeting the conditions for European Monetary Union (EMU). It was, however, dependent on market perception that the plural left had no wish to reverse the macro-economic consensus inherited by Chirac from Mitterrand and established over fourteen years from Delors and Fabius to Juppé, via Chirac, Rocard and Balladur. If 1997 was a surprise return of the left to power, it was not

the kind of surprise that elicited a financial backlash as in 1936 and 1981.

Secondly, the fratricidal state of the recent right-wing majority gave the plural left several years of security. The disarray expressed itself in conflict between Chirac's entourage in the RPR and Philippe Séguin, who took over the leadership, while the parties making up the liberal conservative centre (UDF) split apart, with the ultra-liberal marketeer Alain Madelin taking his Liberal Democrats out of the loose grouping altogether. The RPR councillors who had run Paris since the late 1970s quarrelled bitterly and publicly over their own scandals and personalities. In the regional elections of March 1998 the region with Paris at its centre, the Île-de-France, lost its habitual right-wing majority to a left-wing list, and the feuding within the capital created the imminent possibility of losing Paris itself to the left, a possibility which became reality in the spring of 2001.

The casting influence wielded by the Front National in eight of the twenty-two regions fragmented the right still further. Presidents of the regional councils mostly resigned rather than accept an agreement with the extreme right, but in four of the regions, Picardie, Bourgogne, Rhône-Alpes and Languedoc-Roussillon, the support of the FN was not repudiated, and in Rhône-Alpes, Charles Millon, ex-Defence Minister under Juppé, fought against a subsequent judicial exclusion by forming a break-away party, called simply La Droite. It came to nothing, but the harm done in all these regions to the moral standing of the right was glaring. A year later after fighting the European elections on a nationalist programme, Charles Pasqua confirmed a more substantial rift within the RPR by forming his own party, the Rassemblement pour la France (RPF), a ponderous echo of de Gaulle's RPF (Rassemblement du Peuple Français) which marked the most sectarian phase of de Gaulle's long political career. Pasqua's move was a schismatic Gaullist thrust at Chirac, the Gaullist inheritor.

Enjoying the economic upturn and the right's discomfort, the plural left allowed bargaining to operate within its parliamentary majority, and difference to co-exist within the government. Both the sequel to the *sans-papiers* protests, and the reaction to the activist unemployed (see Chapter 20) split the government without disabling it. Disagreement and paradox were more readily recognized as norms of government, reflecting the relativism within life and culture at the end of the century, a worrying loss of direction for some but a stimulating 'post-modern' condition for others. Paradox was enshrined at the top of the system in the fact of political co-habitation of Chirac and Jospin, and there was a general sense at the base of society that groups stressing difference, paramount in the history of the 1990s, were more inventive, and often more secure, in fighting their

corner during the Jospin years than they had previously been. Jospin's 'modern socialism', characterized initially by clarity of intent, did not immediately fall apart when its ambiguity became more pronounced. If it challenged the constraints it also accepted certain parameters for action. Paradox and ambiguity could have made the plural left, and Jospin himself, suspect to almost everybody. In a period of recession they might well have done. In the context of growth, public opinion remained relatively positive.

Universalism and the 'right to indifference'

The Jospin government was acutely conscious that the regime of the plural left would conclude the twentieth century. Its legislative programme was intense, its reforms carrying a singular quality of addressing issues which could not be allowed to continue unresolved into a new century. In particular it played the modernizing card with aplomb in creating rights for homosexual couples through legislation known as the PACS, passed in November 1999, and in tackling the widely felt need for a bill establishing gender parity (*parité*) in politics. The two issues were connected by the government's initiative in both instances and not by any innate similarity, though comparisons of a theoretical and constitutional nature were made between the two.

The growing impact of social movements of all kinds in the 1990s, with their dual relationship to private lives on the one hand and the public domain on the other, posed the issue of difference in a multitude of ways. Particular causes and special interests were increasingly promoted by an expansive media and by the spread of information technology, but what gave the multiplicity of social activism its historical importance in the last years of the century was its effect on universalism, the central pillar of republican ideology. Within the universal human rights guaranteed to the individual citizen since 1789 by the republican constitution, and elaborated by subsequent law, there was no theoretical place for difference. Constitutionally, a French citizen was the same as any other French citizen, regardless of differences of sex, class, religion and race, to all of which the law respecting citizenship was 'indifferent'. The citizen of the 1990s was often said to have 'a right to this indifference'. Citizenship was not defined in subsections such as 'white French' and 'black French' or 'male French' and 'female French'. It was theoretically no more divisible than the concept of French culture, though in practice divisiveness and discrimination were rampant, creating or accentuating difference in areas where indifference ought to have been assured.

The difference between the sexes and the different colours of skin were the most basic of the differences to which universalism was theoretically indifferent, but palpably failing in its effectiveness. The Jospin government removed the divisive 'opting-in' clause for children born in France of immigrant origin, attached by Pasqua to the code of nationality (see Chapter 20). But the question for social movements campaigning for women's equality with men, as for those combating racial discrimination, was how far to continue emphasizing difference in order to raise awareness of the failings of universalism. The question for homosexual couples was at an even less advanced stage: it was how to get to the very point where they could begin to claim a 'right to indifference'.

The PACS

After over a year of fierce campaigns for and against a pact of union for either homosexual or heterosexual couples, the passing of the Pacte Civil de Solidarité (PACS) brought two new words into current French discourse: *pacs* and *pacsé*, moving towards the words 'marriage' and 'married'. Shortly after the legislation, *Le Monde* of 28–29 November 1999 featured a front-page Plantu cartoon of a mayoral official outside a town hall waving goodbye to a newly contracted couple lovingly driving off and trailing old tins inscribed with the words, written in English, 'Just pacsed'. The adjoining article carried the personal stories of the first '*pacsés*'. Plantu, by punning on the English 'Just married' sign, gave an international romance to the new words, or, in the eyes of opponents of the scheme, a foreign quality. The debate about the PACS was in turn whimsical in its post-modernism and yet heated and intensely moral, signifying the resilience of competing grand narratives built on fundamental principles.

The attention given to the Lesbian and Gay Pride march of June 1996 in Paris, estimated at 100,000, spoke eloquently for the public education effected by various gay social movements from the 1980s onwards, eliciting support from SOS-Racisme, the Greens and the Citizens' Movement. Different possible packages for achieving legal rights for gay couples were proposed, made urgent by the number of AIDS victims in France, as high as anywhere in Europe in the 1980s or even higher. A stable gay relationship carried no legal recognition, and gay partners were excluded from the welfare and inheritance rights for couples when one of them fell ill or died. The strain of care, the pain of loss, compounded by the social injustice, compelled the government to make welfare concessions in 1993, but they were hedged with qualifications which continued to treat the gay couple as

essentially different. It was the universalist 'right to indifference' which took over in 1997. The PACS proposal emerged in February 1998, the Socialists brought it to parliament, and a series of rejections, amendments and resubmissions followed. As a pact available to all couples, regardless of their sex or sexuality, it impinged on the territory of conventional marriage. It raised the imminent probability that the tradition of marriage would be extended to gay couples as the next, logical step in a Republic ostensibly governed by reason.

Opposition from Catholic and other family organizations impressed wavering opinion by a large demonstration in January 1999. Undecided Socialists in parliament made a point by abstention at certain moments; the political right was almost unanimously critical, and particular passion against the PACS was voiced in the key November debate by the UDF deputy Christine Boutin, President of the Right to Life organization, mainly known for its campaigns against abortion. She argued that homosexuals excluded themselves, and that no advanced civilization had accepted that normative laws for everyone could be based on exceptions.[6] In the final vote, however, the plural left carried the bill, and the PACS became effective from 15 November 1999. The end product was not the opening up of marriage but a universally applicable contract giving couples of the same sex, or opposite sex, equal rights in law. There was a flurry of requests for information, but no immediate public rush for *pacsé* status.

Within days of the PACS law, the tempo of moral change was further quickened: Ségolène Royal, the Minister for Schools, announced on 26 November that she would allow school nurses to prescribe the day-after contraception bill to pupils in severe distress. Five million copies of a pocket-guide to contraception would be distributed to secondary-school teenagers. It would openly educate on sexuality between male and female, and the means to 'safe sex', and parents would be told why this was being done publicly and not left purely to family guidance. No such state education on homosexual practices was proposed, but the PACS was immediately recognized as a watershed. Homosexual couples had secured a constitutional 'right to indifference', and with the increasing presence of gay themes and personalities in entertainment and the media, homosexuality began to be seen as a variant form of sexuality and not automatically as deviant.

3. Pursuit of equilibrium

It was widely remarked that despite the numerous initiatives of the plural left in power Lionel Jospin was not seen, even by his critics, as an ideologist forcing the pace. If anything he was seen as someone avoiding collisions rather than provoking them. Jospin was analysed incessantly by the press as an escapologist, refusing to be trapped by situation or doctrine, escaping the consequence of mistakes by admitting his failures, rescuing contradictions in his government's policies by frequent reference to the plurality of life and politics. Critics and admirers used the same images of pendulum, weather vane or rocking toy: knocked sideways, he seemed always to return to his feet. He himself promoted equilibrium.

There was little doubt in the first two years of his Premiership that he was popular in a considered and judicious way. Public opinion seemed to have internalized the benefits of having a left-wing government and a right-wing President: co-habitation itself was interpreted as a productive balance, rather than a sterile conflict, though the conflictual problems grew steadily in the first two years of the new century, changing people's reading of co-habitation. At the start it was seen as a guarantor of negotiation, and with the left plural in form and the right fragmented, any viable policy would be as a result of different elements coming together for a specific purpose. Issue politics, associated with pressures outside the parliamentary system, could be said to have invaded the workings of the Republic at its centre. There was one outstanding example of negotiated consensus on a fundamental issue, once associated with pressure-group activity at its height: the equal access of women and men to elected political office.

Parity

The demand for equality between the sexes had been at the heart of the women's liberation movement (MLF) of the 1960s and 1970s. As a feminist orthodoxy it was rivalled by issues of sexual difference coming from within feminism. A fragmentation of feminist theory and practice resulted, compounded in the 1990s by a move among many younger feminists away from women-only organizations towards a mix (*mixité*) of women and men in gender politics. When Édith Cresson was made the first woman Prime Minister of the Republic, it was widely observed that women constituted almost 53 per cent of the electorate but only just over 5 per cent of representatives in elected assemblies. In almost fifty years since universal

suffrage there had been no increase in women's relative position. Seen as nothing short of scandalous for an 'enlightened' and 'universalist' Republic, the percentage of women in parliament (6 per cent) put France next to bottom in Europe and no higher than seventieth in the world at large.

The Greens were the first to write equality of access into their party statutes in 1988; the Council of Europe circulated the concept of parity (*parité*) in the bicentenary year of the Revolution; Michel Rocard implemented it in his list for the European elections in 1994. In 1992 a much-quoted twist in the republican trilogy by Françoise Gaspard, Claude Servan-Schreiber and Anne Le Gall made their book hugely influential: *Au pouvoir, citoyennes! Liberté, égalité, parité*. Equally motivating was the commitment of women's organizations to parity, expressed at the Beijing World Congress of Women in 1995. Nothing impeded the progress of *parité* in gaining majority support in public opinion polls. A string of bills and proposals from various political sources in the 1990s suggested different ways of making it law. *Le Monde* in 1993 published a manifesto of 577 (288 men and 289 women) in favour of parity. It was intended as a model: there were 577 seats in the Chamber. Jacques Chirac on election to the Presidency established a research body to look into parity, which presented a report headed by the feminist lawyer Gisèle Halimi in January 1997. Halimi was as well known as any feminist activist. A further ten prominent women from across the political spectrum also signed a manifesto for parity, published in *L'Express* in early June 1996. They included Simone Veil and Monique Pelletier on the mainstream right, Yvette Roudy and Édith Cresson on the left.

The problem was the universalist constitution of the Republic. Already an attempt in 1982 by the Socialist government to set same-sex quotas for municipal elections had been ruled as unconstitutional. Jospin made it clear that there would have to be a change in the constitution. In barely two years, with astonishing rapidity, this was achieved by a broad consensus of left and right on 28 June 1999. Articles 3 and 4 were changed to say that the law favoured equal access for women and men to elected office: political parties were enjoined to make it happen. The word *parité* was not used, but the concept had been accepted, and for the first time men and women were specified in the constitution. A year later on 6 June 2000 an electoral law laid down ways in which parity would be implemented, and the results were first seen at the municipal elections of 2001. The number of women councillors increased dramatically to over 47 per cent in *communes* with a population of more than 3,500, though movement towards equality at the important career level of mayor was barely visible. Less than one in ten

mayors was a woman. Only four of the biggest towns had a woman mayor, Lille, Caen, Strasbourg and Aix-en-Provence.

The end of the century was observed as one reason for the speed of the constitutional change. It was seen to give focus and urgency: the Republic of the twenty-first century could not remain identified with its sorry record on women in politics. The vote in 1999 was transformative: it made France the first country to specify equal political access in its constitution. There was a huge majority behind the momentous change, but no absence of emotion or reason in the argument. A number of feminists stood out by opposing the move, not because they were against equality, but because they believed the Republic should not start to abandon its universalist constitution. Citizens, they argued, would be 'trapped' in their biological difference by being specified as men and women; the universalist principle should be expected to ensure equality. Clearly it had failed, but the principle itself was hailed by the purists as the only defence against the eventual fragmentation of the Republic into categories of citizens. Arcane as some of the debate became, the crux for most feminists was balancing a major social victory with yet more evidence of the fragmentation of feminist theory. Did it help or hinder the cause of feminism if women (and men) were specified in this way? Was it the triumph of egalitarian feminism, or of feminists who emphasized difference? Élisabeth Badinter made the universalist arguments her own and Robert Badinter opposed the constitutional change in the Senate. Among those they confronted were Sylviane Agacinski and her spouse, Prime Minister Jospin. Polarity on the issue was dramatized in the media as the duel of these two symbolic left-wing couples, preserving a sense of conflict within the plural left at a moment of rare political unity within the Republic as a whole.

'La vie en bleu'

Unity had been the headline theme a year previously. On the night of 12 July 1998 at the new Stade de France at Saint-Denis in Paris, the French football team won the World Cup. Disbelief and delight made it an astonishing occasion. Spontaneous street festivities had followed the semi-final victory over Croatia, and a national celebration was planned in the Champs-Élysées, whatever the outcome of the final. Few, if any, predicted a victory, yet the French (*les bleus*) beat the favourites Brazil by three goals to nil. The colour everywhere was blue, and the pun on 'la vie en rose', the ultimate twentieth-century image of happiness, could not be resisted. 'La vie en bleu' was expressed in festivities across the country,

which many compared to the spontaneous celebrations at the Liberation in 1944. Every detail of the players was promoted as news. Zinédine Zidane, nicknamed 'Zizou', from La Castellane in northern Marseille, son of Algerians, scored the first two goals, and Emmanuel Petit, born in Dieppe, the third. Other players had overseas origins in Guadeloupe, Ghana, Senegal and Armenia, and the outlying regions within France were well represented. If the shirts were blue with the emblematic *bleu-blanc-rouge* tricolour stripe, it was the multiracial *black-blanc-beur* of the players that provided columnists with an unmissable opportunity to interpret the victory in terms of a plural national identity. It was not a passing indulgence.

Le Monde on the day of the match carried a range of popular opinion on the racial mix of players, and headed the article, 'If the mix works in football, it can work in the street'. The statement made by a grocer, Abdella-tif, in the Paris suburb of Poissy, was typical of the positive attitudes presented: 'This team: it's modern France!'. Inside and outside France the victory was given social as well as symbolic significance. Repeatedly in interviews members of the public said that it carried more hope for race relations than any recent policy measures. It was widely assumed that it would force the Front National on to the defensive. Two years before, Le Pen had refused to accept that players whom he deemed to be foreign could possibly represent France, and he had criticized members of the national team for not appearing to know the words of the 'Marseillaise'.

In face of the national unity behind the World Cup, Le Pen took the opposite position, protesting that the FN had always accepted that persons of different race and religion could become French citizens providing they shared a love of France and served its interests. He went further and claimed that the team's patriotism indicated its 'Le Penization' and that the enthusiasm of French citizens for the competitiveness of the cup showed an acceptance of the FN's policy of 'national confrontation'. The casuistry of this reaction provoked scorn and contempt in most of the press, but Le Pen's emphasis on the unifying patriotism of the team was, on the surface, not far removed from the dominant motif in the media. 'Playing together' emerged as the acceptable metaphor for racial and social integration. Alain Peyrefitte, initiator of measures on law and order in the last government of Giscard d'Estaing's Presidency, wrote in *Le Figaro* that France as a nation, like France as a football team, could only succeed as a unity. He labelled the achievement at the Stade de France as a lesson in ensemble playing. The lesson was repeated in 2000 when the French team went on to win the European Cup. More and more people mixed metaphors linking football to social or political behaviour.

Despite his rhetorical efforts, Le Pen did not recuperate the World Cup victory for the FN's exclusive nationalism, but it was not so obvious that the FN was weakened. In the municipal elections of 1995 they had won control of Toulon, Marignane and Orange. To these they added Vitrolles in the Bouches-du-Rhône in February 1997, while in the regional elections of March 1998 the FN confirmed its local solidity with 15.27 per cent of the vote. These cumulative results galvanized opponents into more effective organization, featuring artists, writers and academics who had been censored by intolerant FN councils as subversive. Anti-racist and anti-FN fronts raised public consciousness of the threat posed, not only by Le Pen's demagogic appeal but also by his cool second-in-command, Bruno Mégret, whose fief was Marignane, the airport *commune* of Marseille.

By 1998 Mégret had his own distinctive tactic of making openings to the mainstream right, the opposite of Le Pen's strategy. A government-sponsored survey emerged shortly before the World Cup, with figures suggesting that over a third of the population were prepared to call themselves racist, though other statistics in the report moderated the impact of this finding. The World Cup victory occurred precisely at the point when racist ideas in France were officially recognized to be commonplace. Mégret's overtures to a wider conservative electorate prospered, and by the beginning of 1999 he was poised to challenge for the leadership of the FN. Le Pen was relatively sidelined by a one-year loss of civil rights after conviction for assault during the elections of 1997 on Annette Meulvast-Bergeal, the Socialist mayor of Mantes-la-Jolie. Despite Le Pen's disadvantage, Mégret's take-over failed. He formed his own tendency, calling it the Mouvement National Républicain (MNR). The FN had split into two.

Le Pen's flamboyance; Mégret's calculation; the consciousness-raising of the anti-racist organizations; the *black-blanc-beur* euphoria of the World Cup, and the unity theme of the media; all put race and racism into the everyday domain. When the FN split into two, this was also commonplace. Most French political movements divided at some point. It was not necessarily a sign of terminal decline.

Food and agriculture. Return to the 'pays'

If there was one animated topic of conversation, apart from unemployment, which outstripped football in 1998–9, it was the state of food. Statistics in the early 1990s showed that at least 3 million jobs existed in food-processing and associated networks, employing some 12 per cent of the working population. In a language of standardization, packaging and

freezers, the doom-laden writing on the wall proclaimed the decline of fresh food and traditional French cuisine. People's changing eating habits, the attraction, or scourge, of fast food, worries about food hygiene, and the crisis of mad cow disease (BSE) brought consumers and agriculture into a frenetic mix of fears and vested interests.

The plural left inherited the mad cow crisis. It had erupted when the British government declared in March 1996 that there might be a link between the bovine sickness and recent human deaths from a variant of the incurable Creutzfeldt-Jacob brain disease (v-CJD). In a decade since 1986, over 170,000 British cattle had contracted BSE. It was an epidemic. France had fewer than thirty. On the news from London, beef exports from Britain were immediately banned by the EU, but it emerged that illegal, contaminated animal feed was continuing to be used in small quantities throughout France. Crisis became panic and the consumption of all beef fell dramatically. Dairy farming was damaged to a lesser extent, but in the enforced slaughter of affected herds not even prized Salers and Charolais cattle were spared. State indemnity to farmers was set at 100 per cent, and support was given by the government for the toughest of measures, reinforced by the impetus given to public-health issues by the trial in March 1999 of Fabius, Dufoix and Hervé for the HIV-infected blood scandal of 1985.[7] When the EU decided in 1998 that the ban on British beef should be lifted from August 1999, the government initially refused to do so. It could point to the same popular support as there was for the European ban on imports of hormone-fed meat from America.

Food scares made rural policy into a prime area of political activity at all levels, from the re-emerging unit of the local *pays* to the European Commission in Brussels. The *pays* was an area sometimes defined as one of the 713 micro-agricultural regions recognized by the Ministry of Agriculture, but more often it was identified locally by its social and cultural specificity, such as the *pays bigouden* in Brittany, setting of Pierre-Jakez Hélias's memoirs of Breton local culture, or the Argonne region on the edge of Champagne and Lorraine, site of the battle of Valmy in 1792 and likened to the classic area of Thermopylae in ancient Greece. Officially at the end of the century there were 94 *pays* recognized by Prefectoral order, and a further 149 waiting for recognition.[8]

On all sides of the political and social spectrum there had been moves to sustain local and regional traditions. Entrepreneurs in choice regional products, and restaurants offering the distinctive cuisine of a local *pays*, had been marketing tradition with growing success since the 1970s and the controversy over the *nouvelle cuisine*. The lifestyle of the élite, regardless

of political orientation, promoted this flourishing market. Adoption of regionalism as a Socialist programme in 1981 had allowed the mainstream left to challenge the right on awareness of provincial customs and identities. Building on Mitterrand's reprieve of Larzac, government planning in the 1980s began to re-establish the identity of the small locality within the larger region, bringing some co-operation from fringe elements of the left, whose criticism of the state in *les années '68* was localized in defence of threatened peasant and artisan culture. Associations of ramblers helped to restore local routes of the annual transhumance of sheep between low and high pastures, resurrecting the accompanying festivals in the Vercors, the Cévennes and the Pyrenees. Market competition for labels of guaranteed local quality (*AOC, Appellation d'Origine Contrôlée*) in wine, cheese and other products intensified as exports expanded. The campaigns for conservation and rural planning were stiffened by new concepts of rural heritage and the impact of ecology. Demographic shifts provided an underlying dynamic. During the 1980s the repopulation of sought-after rural areas by people from the towns had little to do with agriculture: the countryside was definable in other terms.

Collectively these changes and initiatives 'reinvented' rural France, or rather confirmed its diversity, even when many of the identities attributed to the diverse cultures and regions were seen by rooted local opinion to be imposed by urban-based authorities. It was a distinguishing feature of the 1990s that government saw urban and rural space as increasingly interlinked, giving planning an integrated and integrating function.

The plural left's commitment to greater social justice overlapped with its environmental ideals and made it theoretically receptive to local demands for 'a better deal' in the countryside. It could not avoid the growing rural anxiety about local identity within an expanding European Union (EU) which controlled agricultural policy. The EU was intent on reducing still further the subsidies to French agriculture. Reduction of subsidies was clearly linked to the furthering of world free trade, at the heart of the GATT agenda, but the changes to the Common Agricultural Policy (CAP) proposed in 1992 also attempted to shift French farmers away from intensive productivism. From being the motor of French agricultural prosperity, productivism was now criticized as endangering the balance of rural life.

The plural left was faced with a difficult choice by the European directives. In the interests of the small and medium producers it could remonstrate against the reduction of subsidies. This would secure the support of the main federation of agricultural interests (FNSEA) who were looking to President Chirac to protect French agriculture against European

cutbacks. On the other hand it could support the reduction of productivism and the moves to greater rural equilibrium, which would lose the sympathy of the FNSEA, the majority of whose members were still attached to pursuing productivity, independent of other rural concerns.

Through policies initiated by Dominique Voynet, the Green Minister of the Environment and Planning, and Jean Glavany, the Minister of Agriculture, the government accepted the need for cutbacks in the CAP, and identified itself with rural equilibrium. Voynet incurred the immediate enmity of the hunting lobby, the active voice of 1.4 million hunters. They mounted repeated demonstrations against EU restrictions on types of hunting and the length of the season, and attacked Voynet in person, physically threatening her in July 1999 in the streets of Dole in her own *pays*, the Jura. They had supporters across the whole range of political parties, including the left, sufficient to block many of the restrictions when it came to a vote, and in 1999 they fought the European elections as the hunting, fishing, nature and traditions list (*Chasse, pêche, nature et traditions*), securing 1.2 million votes and six seats in the European Parliament.

Aiming to keep mainstream agriculture and the hunters relatively pacified, the government nevertheless took issue with the FNSEA in a report of 1999 accusing the agricultural industry of large-scale pollution of the environment. The separation of agriculture from other countryside interests had been criticized progressively in the 1980s: it was finally accepted by governments and the European Union in the 1990s as untenable. From his own perspective, a law from Charles Pasqua had already moved rural planning towards a concern for the local *pays*. Pasqua as Minister of Planning in 1995 sought to bolster his nationalist drive by consolidating the grass roots. He brought the *pays* closer to the centre of development policy, not just in a romantic echo of Barrès (see Chapter 3) but in the Gaullist sense of recognizing the *pays* as a constituent part of the French nation, which the state should promote and protect. Dominique Voynet and Jean Glavany used the opportunity of a new orientation law of 1999 to introduce the concept of a 'multifunctional agriculture', and to accelerate the process of incorporating farmers into policies of sustainable rural development. The *pays* was central to the strategy. Financial incentives were increased to farmers prepared to sign a contract to work for the equilibrium of agriculture and the local environment, both natural and social.

The 'mal-bouffe'

The EU ban on hormone-fed meat rankled with the USA to the point where retaliation was threatened. In 1998 the USA drew up a list of quality European foods that would be subject to a 100 per cent import surtax if the ban continued. The list included Roquefort cheese made from the milk of ewes in the upland *pays* within the Aveyron, from pastures including the plateau of Larzac. Some 3,300 workers were employed in the production of Roquefort in the region.

Action by Jose Bové and the sheep-rearing 'commandos of Millau' brought a whole new dimension to the interwoven issues of food, agriculture, trade and rurality. In peak summer holiday period, on 12 August 1999, he led a raid on the fast-food McDonalds under construction at Millau in the Aveyron. They dismantled parts of the building, drove them by tractor through the town in carnival style and deposited them on the steps of the subprefecture. The symbolism was clear. Bové specified that 'McDo' stood for hormone beef and the competitive neo-liberal world market. He denounced the recourse to fast food as *la mal-bouffe* ('bad eating'), an effectively pungent phrase with which Bové challenged the world of standardized food, supermarkets and multinationals. The Millau action was carried out in the name of the Confédération Paysanne (CP), formed as a left-wing breakaway from the FNSEA in 1987 by small producers and family farmers who sought to give a renewed economic and social identity to 'the peasant'. Assertively a simple *paysan*, Bové had proved himself in his identity with the sheep farmers against the army presence on Larzac (see Chapter 17). With his *bandito* moustache, and plain-speaking, humorous pugnacity, he wielded a whole Roquefort cheese on meeting the press. He was given instant notoriety across the world, linked with the cause of small farmers in the USA, Europe, India and Brazil, from all of whom he received messages of solidarity.

From his local Aveyron base and spells in prison, Bové fronted an international defence of peasant farmers against the pressures of a neo-liberal market that he, like Pierre Bourdieu, believed had been mythologized as irreversible. He outlined an alternative world structure for agriculture in which poorer communities in developing countries, as well as those in the West, would be able to protect themselves from 'corporate globalization'. He generalized outrageously about food, but not about countries. He refused to be typed as a nationalist or an anti-American. He presented himself, with the President of the CP, François Dufour, as a rural syndicalist, defending his own *pays*. In millennium year, looking to the future, he

and Dufour spread the rallying cry that 'the world is not a commodity' (*le monde n'est pas une marchandise*). With the individualist René Riesel, a student militant from 1968, he agitated effectively against genetically modified crops.[9]

In the face of the media barrage after Millau, Jospin and Chirac kept Bové at a distance, but both eventually met him; the Greens signalled their backing; Charles Pasqua considered him favourably; the local Aveyron magistrates and *Le Figaro* in Paris condemned him as a vandal, and the FNSEA leaders deplored his action, though in Languedoc-Roussillon local members of the federation were supportive. For several weeks any agricultural protest, and there were many from sections of the FNSEA, fed the Millau story, due to indiscriminate attribution of all rural action to the CP. This made nonsense of the gulf between the CP and the FNSEA, but it reflected the ease with which coverage of rural protest slipped into the topical category of 'anti-globalization'.

The congress of the World Trade Organization (WTO) at Seattle was scheduled for the end of November 1999, its agenda to pursue the 'millennium round' of talks on world trade. Pre-Seattle marches against 'neo-liberal' globalization occurred in over thirty towns. All featured banners supporting Bové. The need to find ways of describing an acceptable globalization had already invaded government speeches in September when Bové emerged from his first spell in prison. The emphasis from Jospin was yet again on equilibrium and the necessity to pursue 'just causes' with 'reasonable means'. He described as just the need 'to balance the rewards in agriculture between producer and distributor' and the need 'to attend to the quality of food products'. He underlined the importance of the WTO in 'regulating' world trade. On the eve of going to Seattle, François Huwart, Secretary of State for Foreign Trade, told an interviewer from *La Voix du Nord* that the aim of Seattle must be to 'humanize globalization'.[10]

Balance in Corsica

It was not just the 200th anniversary of Napoleon's coup d'état of 18 Brumaire that brought Corsica to the forefront of politics in 1999. As the best-known Corsican, Napoleon was a problem for contemporary Corsican nationalists. His Jacobinism was exactly the inheritance that was disputed in the 'île de beauté'. Inhabited by fewer than 270,000 people, only a third of whom were registered as 'active', the island had little industry apart from food-processing and a faltering agriculture. Most of the population worked in administration or in what was called its 'monoculture', tourism.

Its regional standing with its own Assembly was changed in 1991 to that of a 'territory' with individual status and more autonomy, a move sanctioned by the Socialist government of Michel Rocard and his Minister of the Interior, Pierre Joxe. It was preceded by a parliamentary discussion on 'the Corsican people' which had led to a constitutional decision against the use of the term as fracturing the unity of the nation. It was similarly decided by the Conseil d'État that the Council of Europe's charter of 1992 on maintaining and developing regional languages could not be signed by France, since 'the language of the Republic is French'. A plurality of official languages was repeatedly rejected by governments and the national media as unworkable, though the voluntary study of the main regional languages within France had been encouraged since 1981 (Occitan, Breton, Basque, Catalan, Flemish, Alsatian, Corsican). In September 1998 Lionel Jospin declared that he would favour signing the charter, provoking an avalanche of quips about judicial procedures in Basque and tax forms in Breton. The 'Jospin Republic' that might emerge was caricatured as a modern tower of Babel.

Jospin's initiative on the language issue came in a year which had opened dramatically with the assassination of the Prefect of Corsica, Claude Erignac, on 6 February 1998. The hunt for the elusive killers was accompanied by outrage from Chirac and Jospin downwards at this ultimate challenge of the Corsican nationalists to the presence on the island of the French Republic. The Minister of the Interior, Jean-Pierre Chevènement, had almost universal support in measures to crack down on Corsican nationalism in all its aspects, reinforcing his own reputation as a force in the government for unitary republicanism. It became yet another dissonance within the plural left. Jospin's commitment to equilibrium gradually took him on a divergent course towards meeting Corsican nationalism half-way, though he insisted that negotiation on 'the Corsican problem' could not proceed without a cessation of violence.

In elections to the Corsican Assembly in March 1999, the nationalist and regionalist vote increased to almost 25 per cent, including the 10.4 per cent scored by the party urging independence, Corsica Nazione. In the polarized climate of the elections it meant that over three-quarters of voters were in favour of remaining in the Republic, a clear majority emphasized in newspaper coverage of Corsica at the opening of the new century. By then Jospin had made his first move in opening a wide debate on Corsica's constitutional future. It was known that as secretary to the PS in May 1996 he had not ruled out a statute giving Corsica autonomous powers within the Republic, and although far more cautious in his language on an official visit to the

island in September 1999, he was greeted in parts of Corsica by crowds urging him to follow through his earlier devolutionary thoughts. This seemed unlikely when two large bombs exploded at administrative locations in Ajaccio on 25 November. The explosions raised images in the press of terrorism on a massive scale, but they also divided Corsican nationalists among themselves at a time when the non-violent route was raising expectations. Despite the heightened tension, on 13 December 1999 Jospin brought all sides of the island's political life to Paris for a round-table meeting. Yves Stella, mayor of a *commune* of Cap Corse, hailed it as 'a historic negotiation in its recognition of the equality of all participants'.[11] They included the nationalists Jean-Guy Talamoni and Paul Quastania of Corsica Nazione who declared themselves ready to respect the workings of democracy.

Jospin's idea of a round table was backed by the President of the Corsican Assembly, leader of the mainstream right in the island, José Rossi. He had said after the November bombs that it was a matter of urgency to establish a climate of confidence between Paris and Corsica. A long process of discussion aimed at a balance of powers was Jospin's public formula, but the sense that a form of autonomy might be Jospin's private preference proved unacceptable to Chevènement, who left the government on 23 August 2000, fortified by an opinion poll among Corsicans a few days earlier which registered 13 per cent for independence and 80 per cent for staying within France.

Figures which suggested that the votes in March 1999 for nationalists and regionalists had accurately reflected the incidence of unemployment and poverty on the island kept the social dimension of the 'Corsican problem' at the head of Jospin's considerations. The unresolved debate saw a wealth of evidence pointing to the resilient ability of notables in the island to benefit from the huge amounts of state money pumped into the island over many decades, shared out or fought for on the basis of the clientelist system, a veritable 'blocked' situation or society whose violence could not be understood purely by reference to an archaic vendetta culture.[12] It was a new political configuration that Jospin was pursuing, to produce a less divided Corsican society.

'The state can't do everything'

Corsica seemed an intractable site for a new state initiative. The nature of its society was presumed by many to limit the power of any government project. It would not have surprised public opinion if Jospin had acknowl-

edged on a visit to the island that 'the state can't do everything'. These were his words in a television broadcast on 13 September 1999, but not on the subject of Corsica. They referred to cuts in the workforce announced on the 8th by Michelin, the vast tyre and rubber industry in Clermont-Ferrand. Was it naïvety that made the young Édouard Michelin announce a cut of 7,500 jobs over three years at the same time as detailing the company's considerable profits? Was it Jospin's naïve miscalculation to comment on France 2 that not everything could be expected of the state? Naïvety or plain talking, the two sets of words which created the 'Michelin affair' of autumn 1999 accentuated divisions over the function of the state. They gave the Communist leader Robert Hue an opportunity to assert his party's identity within the plural left. With the backdrop of unemployment still a fixture in all policy-making, Hue challenged Jospin and the Socialists to show solidarity against Michelin with a trade-union and left-wing demonstration. He set the date for 16 October and said that the PS should either get on board where they belonged or miss the boat altogether. The Minister of Employment, Martine Aubry, as well as Jospin, was clearly targeted. She and the PS general secretary, François Hollande, tried to minimize the impact of Jospin's words by repeating their commitment to penalizing firms who sacked workers when they were clearly in profit, and Jospin reaffirmed his own belief in the necessity of state intervention to combat unemployment.

No less than the Communist Party, the employers' federation, MEDEF, made their identity clear. Capitalizing on Jospin's 'admission', the MEDEF launched the idea of a separate social constitution for France. United in its October meeting against the 35-hour week, it proposed that such a constitution would free the social sphere from state intervention, initially in respect to the needs and aspirations of workers, and the possibilities and constraints of companies. The result would be that social contracts of all kinds would be negotiated freely, beyond the reach of the government. In essence the MEDEF stated that the identity of the Republic based on the state's role in society had already been recast and should be reformulated still further.

As an outcome of liberal economic thinking the MEDEF proposal carried no surprises. It was the timing, looking again at the nature of the Republic in the new century, which caught people's attention. It caused members of the plural left to say that the real Jospin should stand up. Would it be the Socialist Jospin who would develop an even fuller government agenda in social and employment policy, or Jospin the Presidential candidate who would extend his search for equilibrium across the nation to appease

the employers? In Clermont-Ferrand all positions for and against the words of Michelin and Jospin were aired. Most agreed that Jospin would be unable to sit on the fence, but it was no secret that Jospin had his eye on succeeding President Chirac in 2002 and this would require an elaboration of the balancing act he personified, to appeal to a width of opinion that would register him as more of a national figure than Chirac, capable of representing the whole nation as well as the interventionist, or non-interventionist, state.

He had reasons to be hopeful. As ferocious and unprecedented storms battered the whole of France at the very end of December 1999, causing more than seventy deaths and making sixty *départements* into catastrophe zones, the last opinion polls of the century still expressed over 60 per cent satisfaction with Lionel Jospin. After three years in power, this too was almost unprecedented.

Presidential front-runners: Jospin and Chirac, or . . .

In the first months of the millennium year Lionel Jospin reinforced his reputation as a leader ready to pacify discontents raised by his own government policies. He finally acknowledged that his friend Claude Allègre had been a public-relations disaster in his three years as Minister of Education, alienating teachers, pupils and parents in equal measure by his intemperate language and his campaign against what he saw as the over-protected, over-staffed and self-serving world of secondary education. Allègre, appointed by Jospin in 1997 at the age of sixty, was an international geophysicist, with a distinguished career in research, but with no experience of schoolteaching, though he had been Jospin's own second-in-command at the Ministry of Education in 1988–92. Allègre's proposals for reducing the influence of teaching unions and removing 'the fat' from educational structures and practices were advanced with barbed remarks on the 'privileged' status of teachers and their 'long holidays', appealing to those who enjoyed any assault on the world of *fonctionnaires* and the public sector. As a result his positive aim of opening education to the world of business and enterprise and providing pupils from poor backgrounds with financial incentives was lost in the acrid disputes which he provoked. Not without a touch of self-criticism, Jospin replaced Allègre in March 2000 with Jack Lang, brought in as a peacemaker, a replay of 1992 when Lang was appointed to replace Jospin himself, to calm students and jettison Jospin's controversial plans for university reform.

The year 2000, with its infinite retrospection and parallel anticipation,

alerted people to the norm of contrary directions. Almost inevitably comparisons multiplied stressing the two or more faces of Jospin and the growing convergence of apparent opposites, Jospin and Chirac, especially on macro-economic policy. On 25 May, the third anniversary of Jospin's access to power, *L'Express* portrayed him as 'Janus Jospin'. Ambivalence, it suggested, or the search for synthesis, had been elevated by Jospin to an art equivalent to that of the chef who adjusts the mayonnaise with the merest drop of oil or the deftest movement of the whisk. But, continued the article, Jospin was in the process of moving on to the offensive as a skilful political animal, confident that he could outmanoeuvre Chirac in his bid for the Presidency. He had already overtaken Chirac with his advance commitment to a five-year Presidency in place of the seven-year term introduced by de Gaulle. Chirac could not claim any credit for the change which he was equally ready to promote. It passed easily through the National Assembly in June and was ratified three months later by a referendum, referred to as the most boring event of any millennium. A mere 30.2 per cent of the electorate bothered to vote.

The alignment of future Presidential terms with those of the legislature carried the expectation that voters would produce a parliamentary majority and a President of the same political hue, reducing the risk of co-habitation and clashes of policy between President and Premier. Seeing co-habitation as dysfunctional rivalry became more widespread as Jospin continued to invade the policy spheres of the President. In February 2000 he used an official visit to Israel to denounce the Lebanese Hezbollah as a terrorist organization, leaving Chirac confronted with the diplomatic anger of the Lebanon. He interpreted the French turn for the Presidency of the European Union in 2000 as an opportunity to outplay Chirac on the same stage. Gradually both press and public began to tire of the political jousts between the two, a fatigue which did not favour Jospin nor indicate an upsurge of support for the President.

Chirac continued to be plagued by accusations of involvement in corrupt practices when he was mayor of Paris. Repeated rumours and testimonies associated him with the appropriation of funds allocated for municipal purposes and their diversion into the hands of the Gaullist party, the RPR. In December 2000 the President claimed he was being victimized by judicial innuendo in what had become nothing less than a public spectacle. He denied all charges of corruption and invoked Presidential immunity from prosecution and from the obligation to give evidence. In January 2001 the full details of the corruption in the oil giant company Elf-Aquitaine emerged, but in this case it was close colleagues and friends of Mitterrand who were

indicted. Roland Dumas, twice Foreign Minister under Mitterrand, was accused of misuse of public money and sentenced to thirty months in prison, with two years suspended. Later in 2003 on appeal he was found blameworthy but not criminally culpable, but in 2001 his responsibility, and Mitterrand's too, for corrupt practices in the relationship of government to big business, made repeated headlines, intensifying public cynicism towards the exercise of power by both left and right. Thwarted opponents of Chirac urged the electorate to act as surrogate judge by voting against the Parisian RPR in 2001 and Chirac in person in 2002.

Paris did indeed fall to the left, but apart from the symbolism of victories for the Socialist Bertrand Delanoë in Paris and Gérard Colomb in Lyon, the municipal elections of March 2001 did not begin to live up to the hopes of Jospin or the Socialist Party. The Greens' 12 per cent, however, appeared to denote a movement of public opinion towards ecological issues, just as the poor showing of the Communists in their previous urban strongholds underlined the permanent realignment of the left. That the Greens were already the second force in the *gauche plurielle* had been the conclusion drawn from the European elections of June 1999, when, led by the resurgent European deputy Daniel Cohn-Bendit, they had scored more highly than the PCF under Robert Hue. The media were half intrigued and half dismissive at the transformation of 'Danny-le-rouge' from the anarchist student hero of 1968 into the Green sage of 1999, a shift which had taken place within the German political scene before Cohn-Bendit's return to France. Jokes proliferated: 'How do you know that Danny Cohn-Bendit is German? Because he invades France every thirty years.' He himself acknowledged that he was still a political romantic at the edges, but argued that the dream of a united Europe was the most rational of contemporary aspirations.

The left was still plural in 2001, despite the secession of Chevènement, but the support for the Greens, along with the rising tide of abstentions at all elections, could be interpreted as one of the multiple signs of disinterest in mainstream party politics. It was evident that the popularity and democratic vision of the openly gay Bertrand Delanoë in Paris reflected the diversification of political formation and practice. Co-ordination around single issues had come to structure movements and attitudes to the point where it could no longer be assumed that party allegiance would be manifest at critical moments. Issues relating to the quality of life, such as lowering petrol pollution in Paris and creating new spaces for exercise and relaxation, brought as much support to Delanoë as the Socialist indictment of RPR corruption at the Hôtel de Ville.

Issue politics, notably attitudes to Europe, diversified the political right

just as dramatically. Standing on a platform of 'French sovereignty' against European integration, Charles Pasqua and Philippe de Villiers ran a list for the 1999 elections which outscored the official pro-Europe RPR list headed by Nicolas Sarkozy, the 44-year-old mayor of Neuilly-sur-Seine. Sarkozy reached the party leadership despite having backed Balladur in 1995 against Chirac, but the disarray of the RPR was evident in the fractious relationship between Sarkozy and Chirac which was seen as the most newsworthy saga in the politics of personality over the following five years and beyond.

The combination of protest votes and the fragmentation of politics allowed the extreme Front National to maintain its pressure and exude a grass-roots optimism despite its internal division of 1999. Jean-Marie Le Pen made a feature of his Presidential ambitions for 2002, gaining credibility through his populist denunciation of Jospin and Chirac as 'indistinguishable' and equally guilty of surrendering France to Brussels. He chose the cross-party issue of street and neighbourhood violence on which to focus his campaign. It was one on which the plural left was acutely vulnerable. Jospin had tried to mediate between a tough crack-down on violent gangs of youths urged by Chevènement and the long-term measures of social integration preferred by Martine Aubry and Élisabeth Guigou. Accounts of violence and fears for personal safety filled the pages of the opposition press. Nobody could miss the frequency with which people in the *banlieues*, interviewed on television, represented the insecurity of their property and lives in terms of race and immigration.

As the number of aspiring candidates for the Presidential elections escalated to reach sixteen, commentators reflected on the equal performance of both Chirac and Jospin, neither of whom had either a heroic or charismatic appeal. Trust in both their capacities to represent France was registered in a sequence of polls at the end of 2001 after the 11 September terrorist attacks on the USA. Chirac drew slightly ahead of Jospin in the climate of anxiety which put pressure on state authorities to demonstrate reassurance. He was visibly active in the months after the attacks, making highly publicized visits to the provinces where he emphasized that the law-and-order issues of personal and national *sécurité* were central to his campaign, criticizing the *gauche plurielle* for its lack of solutions to localized criminality. If this was Chirac's gesture towards social fears at large, Jospin tried to reassure critics of a different kind by stating that his programme was 'not a socialist one'.

... the totally unpredicted

On the eve of the first ballot on 16 April 2002 Chirac and Jospin still led the polls, but it was unclear who might come third: François Bayrou representing the rump of the Christian Democrats, Jean-Pierre Chevène-ment at the head of his Citizens' Movement, the Green candidate Noël Mamère, Jean-Marie Le Pen, or even Arlette Laguiller in her fifth contest for President and still representing the Trotskyist Party Lutte Ouvrière.

The result stupefied pollsters and population alike. The turn-out was just over 71 per cent, the lowest in any first round of a Presidential election in the Fifth Republic. Chirac headed the poll with 5.6 million votes, representing just under one in five of those who voted. It was far from a ringing endorsement of his Presidency. But it was Le Pen's result which shocked the whole of France and Europe. He came second with 4.8 million votes (16.8 per cent), forcing Jospin into the humiliation of third place, 200,000 votes behind the Front National leader. Le Pen had the showdown with Gaullism that he had always envisaged.

Jospin's elimination from the Presidential race was not predicted at any point during the campaign. Nor was the position achieved by Jean-Marie Le Pen. In the first national vote of the twenty-first century, the populist who for fifty years had denounced 'French decadence', 'betrayal of the Empire' and 'abandonment of the nation to immigration and Europe', had defeated the sitting Prime Minister whose five-year premiership had notched some of the highest opinion ratings of the Fifth Republic. Civil and social fears had been more effective as mobilizing agents behind Le Pen than the raft of social and civil reforms behind Jospin. An electoral system designed to allow all parties and personalities a representative place in the first round had achieved exactly that. More people expressed a first choice for Jean-Marie Le Pen than for Lionel Jospin.

All the statistics of self-confessed racism in society, gathered over the previous ten years, were seen as starkly relevant, though the most repeated analysis of Le Pen's support was of levels of local frustration at violence, vandalism and disorder. Le Pen was voted into first position in thirty-five *départements*, and achieved a minimum of 10 per cent support across the whole of the country outside Paris. His appeal was more apparent among male than female voters. It was in areas of the Mediterranean, the Rhône valley and Alsace-Lorraine that his count rose to 30 per cent and above, featuring the long-standing bitterness of former settlers in Algeria, the incidence of racial confrontations and the fall-out from de-industrialization. The Jospin government had redistributed income to lower wage earners

through changes in income tax, and unemployment had been reduced from 12.5 per cent in 1997 to just under 10 per cent in 2001. The achievements were impressive. But locally the pressure on jobs was still a foremost influence on opinion, and in Alsace-Lorraine and the south-east its effect continued to feed the search for those who could be held responsible, a catchment area of blame in which families and workers of immigrant origin were bitterly resented, despite the fact that youth unemployment remained highest among those of Maghrebi descent.

Le Pen's success in maximizing support in his ideological sphere was compared to Jospin's failure to do the same in his own. Across the spectrum of those with socialist views, disillusion with Jospin's drift into compromises with liberal economics had led many to vote for his left-wing rivals, without counting the possible effects. The predicted Jospin–Chirac contest had been taken for granted. Its apparent inevitability accounted partly for the number of voters who stayed away and partly for those who wanted to protest against the political establishment by whatever vote seemed appropriate. The erosion of mainstream party politics was paramount.

Le Pen against Chirac: democratic nerves were strained to respond to this unexpected confrontation. It was the first time since the Algérie Française *putsch* of 1961 or the Vichy regime of 1940–44 that the extreme right had appeared so menacing. Le Pen had his emotional and ideological roots in both. His party rival, Bruno Mégret, had secured a further 667,000 votes. Together their potential appeared formidable. Lycée pupils, too young to vote, demonstrated with posters asking their parents' generation, 'How did you allow fascism to re-emerge?' Huge anti-Le Pen marches filled the streets. Repeating the tactics of 1968, tens of thousands of people carried banners through Paris and Marseille saying, 'We are all children of immigrants'.[13] Distant memories of the anti-fascist vigour of the 1930s were rekindled. The cry of 'The Republic in danger' was echoed by Chirac's and Jospin's supporters alike. With expressive political misgivings, the Socialists called on all the followers of the plural left to vote for Chirac despite their antagonism. They rose to the occasion, many declaring on their way to the polls that they would use gloves 'to keep their hands clean' and were voting purely to defeat the FN leader. As evidence of a positive involvement in national politics, participation in the second round was demanded of the whole electorate. Abstentions were not seen as an option. A vibrant statement of national preference was called for by the whole of the media and political world, inside and outside France.

On 5 May 2002, in a markedly higher turn-out, 82 per cent of the voters combined to vote against Le Pen. His 18 per cent fell far short of his

illusions. The landslide result was celebrated by Chirac with promises to respect the range of opinion evident in his vote. It was greeted by most of the press, with occasional references to *les bleus* of 1998, as a reassuring victory for the Republic, 'playing together'. *Libération* gave its whole front page to the expression of relief, '*ouf*'. The result lessened but did not remove the disquiet about politics which the first ballot had induced. Jospin deepened the disarray of the Socialists by resigning from the leadership and from politics altogether, a self-denial which was read by the public as more than an admission of his failures as a personality. The whole of the *gauche plurielle* suffered, and the apparent viability of post-socialism was questioned.

By contrast the mainstream right was galvanized by the threat of Le Pen into recognizing the necessity of unity. Chirac looked for an acceptable compromise Prime Minister and appointed Jean-Pierre Raffarin, a provincially-based politician from the Poitou-Charentes area with known regional sensibilities who had been a low-profile Minister for Small and Medium Businesses under Juppé. An electoral coalition on the right was sealed to give the re-elected Chirac a majority in parliament. Calling itself the Union pour la Majorité Présidentielle (UMP), it secured an absolute victory for the right in the elections of early June, at which another heavy bout of abstention regained attention as a comment on a damaged political process. Le Pen's surprise success in the first round of the Presidentials failed to translate into any seats for the FN: to that extent the April result was put into perspective. The highlight of the new government for much of the press was the appointment of Nicolas Sarkozy to the key post of Minister of the Interior, charged with the pressing issues of *sécurité*. His energetic pursuit of effective solutions and focused policing was deemed a success within the course of a year. It kept the political prophets in business, assessing the prospect of an inner challenger to President Chirac in 2007.

The oscillation between right and left had once again been dramatic. The emphatic overturn of one by the other in 1997 and 2002 was viewed either as a sign of a new kind of political discretion or alternatively as a loss of principle and meaning in politics. Whatever the conclusion, it furthered divisions on how the underlying identity of France should be interpreted. There was no shortage of context to the debate.

22

Memory and Identity,
1990s–2000s (3)

1. Memory and judgement

The martyred village of Oradour-sur-Glane, site of the massacre by SS troops on 10 June 1944, was declared a historic monument in 1946, its ruins to be left in perpetuity. It stood for the 'martyrdom of France' under the German Occupation and came to assume a symbolic status for all massacres of the Second World War. A place of pilgrimage, and with thousands of other visitors who merely stumbled on the site, its affective symbolism deepened steadily over the years. Ideas emerged that it should house a war crimes centre among the ruins. These plans came to fruition in July 1999 when President Chirac opened a 'Centre de la Mémoire' created for the nation by Jean-Jacques Fouché in a spacious crypt at the heart of Oradour.

Memory in the locality had never been detached from judgement. Fourteen of the surviving SS troops who perpetrated the massacre had been from Alsace. They were found, tried in Bordeaux in early 1953 and sentenced for their part in the crime, but in Alsace they were seen as victims, not as perpetrators, men forced into the German army after the annexation of the province in 1940. Contingents amounting to 160,000 men had been conscripted by Nazi Germany from Alsace and Lorraine and were known as the *malgré-nous* ('against our will'). Over 40,000 of them died in the war. Associations of the *malgré-nous* opposed the entire Bordeaux trial, and in Strasbourg vocal demonstrations protested against what they saw as the demonization of their province. The trial was increasingly reported as one symbolic community, the martyred Oradour, against another, the hostage region of Alsace-Lorraine.

The government intervened at the last moment of the trial with an amnesty for all those who had been 'forcibly incorporated into the German armies'.[1] Only the Communist Party in parliament voted wholly against the bill. Resentment on the two sides died hard. Covering the opening of

the centre in 1999, *Le Monde* reported the comments of the mayor of Strasbourg who stated that Franco-German reconciliation had occurred some five years after the war, but that it had taken fifty-four years for a dialogue to be opened between the Limousin and Alsace.

Charles de Gaulle regretted the divisiveness of the Bordeaux trial, and as President after 1958 continued the promotion of national unity to which he had given priority in 1944, and Georges Pompidou in 1972 suggested that France should try to forget (*oublier*) the times when the French hated each other. The theme of dialogue was embraced by Giscard d'Estaing. It was in the interests of asserting a consensual national history that Mitterrand refused to acknowledge that the nation state should carry responsibility for the round-up of Jews at the Vélodrome d'Hiver. In his eyes, as in those of de Gaulle, Vichy had no legitimacy. It was effectively obliterated as a national regime.

President Chirac in 1995 reversed Mitterrand's refusal. In the years since de Gaulle it was not that reconciliation had been sidelined but that the act of forgetting, encouraged by Pompidou, had been judged by informed opinion to be regressive and morally unacceptable. The only way forward was discerned to be through memory. By the early 1990s a duty to remember (*devoir de mémoire*) was widely established, initially related primarily to memory of the Holocaust (Shoah). It came to represent a mentality towards past and present of unpredictable potential. The stakes are still high for those who seek to channel or control it.

In the last third of the century an active national memory was acknowledged to be a necessity. It was neither neutral nor innocent. It could carry exculpation or recrimination. Collective memory was distinguished from individual memory, public from private. Memory and commemoration were shown to be distinct from each other. From psychoanalysts to historians, the process of memory was linked to recovery of the repressed, to facing trauma at personal or national level, to therapeutic and cathartic outcomes. Memory and witness became almost interchangeable concepts in law and history. Both in courtrooms and conferences, it proved easier to handle the concept of memory than the content of memories. A readiness emerged in certain quarters to equate memory with truth. The memory boom had its parallel in the commodity boom. At many levels memory itself became a commodity.

Why all this happened was explained by reference to the momentous social changes in the forty years after the war and the impact of internationalization which appeared to threaten national identity. At the same time greater decentralization and renewed vitality in the regions brought

an affirmation of local identity, registered in an outcrop of regional claims to their own distinctive heritage (*patrimoine*). In 1979 a department of *patrimoine* was created within the Ministry of Culture, and 1980 was chosen as heritage year. High-budget films led by Claude Berri's evocative remake of Marcel Pagnol's Provençal saga *Jean de Florette* and *Manon des Sources* in 1986 began a decade or more of heritage cinema, hugely successful at the box office and mixing nostalgia and memory of the past into a palette of regional colour which did not seem exploitative. In 1992 the singer Charles Aznavour rescued the heritage of café and cabaret songs, mostly of the inter-war years, when the collection made by the famed music publisher Raoul Breton came up for sale. Songs of Mistinguett, Tino Rossi, Maurice Chevalier, Charles Trenet, Édith Piaf, Jean Gabin, Fernandel and many others were purchased by Aznavour as an explicit conservation of French *patrimoine*.

Memory was boosted as a defence against standardization and the obliteration of old ways of life. Everywhere the memory boom was related not only to tradition but also to democratization and emancipation. Not only authorities were interviewed: the lived experiences of specific groups and communities were sought. Recording a memory allowed new and marginalized identities to be asserted. Older creative work featuring memory was rediscovered. The cinema of Alain Resnais was quoted as one among many subtle precedents. In 1959 Resnais explored the power of traumatic memory in his highly literary and innovative film *Hiroshima mon amour*, relating a love story between a French film actress and a Japanese man she meets when filming in Hiroshima. The relationship against the backdrop of the obliterated city reactivates her memory of a previous love with a German soldier under the Occupation in her home town of Nevers on the Loire in the *département* of the Nièvre. With interwoven fragments Resnais evokes the trauma of her German lover's death, her humiliation as a *femme tondue* and her subsequent breakdown. His sensitivity to memory was reprised in his splintered film of 1963, *Muriel*, set against the background of the Algerian war. Three years later he featured Yves Montand in *La Guerre est finie*, a study of the ambivalent presence of the past in the lives of Spanish republicans still in exile thirty years after the Civil War.

The primacy given to memory in the cinema of Resnais was forerunner of its universal obligation assumed in the 1980s. The *devoir de mémoire* strengthened challenges to a national history which had occluded or denied vital aspects of the past. It was in this respect that the rival Gaullist and Communist accounts of the Occupation were both deconstructed. At the harshest level they were declared to be travesties of a complex past, and at

a more nuanced level they were seen as post-war myths, which had a mobilizing or unifying function at the time but were no longer sustainable.

Reliance on individual memories in *Le Chagrin et la pitié* (see Chapter 17) set a precedent for the public reconstruction of the history of the Occupation. In the realm of academic research its impetus towards a focus on collaboration was reinforced in 1973 by the French edition of Robert Paxton's *Vichy France. Old Guard and New Order*. The American historian used archives, mostly from Germany, and did not solicit oral memories, but his careful argument that Vichy's collaboration and its National Revolution were two parts of a whole, and that neither part was imposed by the Germans, inspired fresh archival research and prompted yet more public debate through testimony and opinion. Amidst acute controversy, leading French historians found Paxton's interpretation to be not only sensational but accurate. Together with the Ophuls documentary, the 'Paxtonian Revolution' of the early 1970s 'broke the mirror' of post-war representation of the Occupation. Film and book were critical moments in the history of representation and memory of Vichy, analysed in epic form in 1987 as 'the Vichy syndrome' by the young French historian Henry Rousso.[2]

The revelations of the extent of wartime collaboration and the role of Vichy in the deportation of the Jews kept pace with the international resurgence of Jewish testimony and the compulsive questions asked by the post-war generation about the Nazi concentration camps. The need to know was pursued in France by Serge and Beate Klarsfeld, determined hunters of surviving Nazi officials and meticulous compilers of the facts of the Holocaust. In 1964 the National Assembly accepted the special status accorded by post-war international law to 'crimes against humanity', prosecution of which would be unaffected by the lapse of time. To most people this meant specifically the genocide of the Jews. Serge Klarsfeld's Jewish father of Romanian origin had been gassed at Auschwitz in August 1944, but it was Beate, a German Protestant, who initially made most of the running with denunciations of the Nazi past of notables still in positions of influence in post-war Germany. In 1978 the Klarsfelds compiled their *Mémorial de la déportation des juifs de France*, and in 1983–5 Serge Klarsfeld published two volumes on the role of Vichy in the Final Solution, entitled *Vichy-Auschwitz*. Their work listed all the convoys to the death camps and established the foreign origin of two-thirds of the deportees. For the first time the French public were fully confronted with the personal identity of the Jews who had been killed: whole families were cited with their individual names. From thirty to forty years after the Liberation the

documents gave a solid base to the remembered details of French involvement in the deportations. They gave memory its moral authority. In Annette Wieviorka's term France entered the 'era of the witness'.[3]

The published details of the Nazi death camps did not go unchallenged. They were countered in 1978 by a spate of bogus scholarship from a literature lecturer in Lyon, Robert Faurisson, who denied the realities of the Holocaust, and by an interview in *L'Express* carried out in Madrid with Darquier de Pellepoix, Vichy's second head of the Commissariat of Jewish Affairs. Darquier had been condemned to death *in absentia* in 1947 and was believed to have died somewhere in exile. More than any other single happening, Darquier's statement to *L'Express* that gas in Auschwitz was used only for killing lice shocked the majority of opinion into realizing the extent to which the past could be distorted. Holocaust denial, a minor industry in itself, filled the journals of the extreme right. Darquier died in Spain two years after his interview. Faurisson was convicted in July 1981 of racist defamation, but the court ruled itself incompetent to judge on how the past should be represented.

The return of the repressed

In the midst of the fall-out from the Darquier interview, a little book was compiled by a Jewish child psychiatrist, Claudine Vegh, which illustrated the growing imperatives of individual memory. She presented a number of personal memories from Jews who had survived the deportations as children, due to their parents' desperate and impromptu decisions to entrust them to others. The title expressed the anguish in the memory of the children: *Je ne lui ai pas dit au revoir* (I didn't even say goodbye). Most of the parents died in the camps. The survivors, no longer children, mainly found that releasing their memories was painful but healing. The book, wrote Bruno Bettelheim in the Postface, 'was a hugely important step'. It countered the process of denial and repression, enabling the children of the genocide to grieve for their parents and 'finally to live a normal life'.[4]

The name most clearly linked to the deportation of children was that of the Gestapo chief in occupied Lyon, Klaus Barbie. He had escaped the post-war trials of Nazi war criminals and had made his way to South America where he lived an opportunist life of some notoriety under an assumed name. He was located there by Beate and Serge Klarsfeld. Known among ex-resisters as 'the butcher of Lyon', he was execrated in public memory for the murderous torture of Jean Moulin. The Klarsfelds and others focused on Barbie's brutal seizure of forty-four Jewish children

between the ages of three and thirteen, who were peacefully sheltered in the remote Alpine village of Izieu. He had personally insisted that they should be deported. They were taken to Auschwitz. None survived. His repressive actions in the Lyon area accounted for the deportation of 600 civilians, including 200 Jews, and over 6,000 killed or disappeared. The local Vichy Milice and Paul Touvier in particular had collaborated with him in civilian murders, and were held responsible for the massacre of seven Jewish hostages in the Rhône *commune* of Rillieux-la-Pape.

The terrier-like pursuit of both the German Barbie in his Bolivian refuge and the French Touvier after his pardon by President Pompidou marked the determination of numerous individuals to see justice done for crimes against humanity perpetrated on French soil, regardless of national origin. Attempts to extend the definition to crimes perpetrated by the French in the Algerian war ensured the libertarian barrister Jacques Vergès a constant byline in the story of Barbie's extradition process. The seventy-year-old Barbie was finally brought to France in 1983 and his trial opened in Lyon in 1987. Jacques Vergès perversely opted to be Barbie's defence lawyer, declaring his intention to use the trial to expose the crimes of ex-resisters in Algeria.

Public opinion was deeply divided on whether Vergès should or should not succeed. There was virtual unanimity against Barbie, and it was expected that conclusive evidence on the person who had betrayed Jean Moulin would emerge. The court ruled otherwise. Until almost the end it insisted that the repression and torturing of resisters by the German occupier fell into the category of crimes of war, for which Barbie had been judged *in absentia* after the war. The lapse of time put them well outside its jurisdiction. Ex-resisters were denied the stage they had expected, and Vergès was baulked of opportunities to turn his accusation against them. Barbie refused to acknowledge the court and was absent from the third day. He was found guilty of crimes against humanity and sentenced to life imprisonment. He died in prison in 1991.

The significance of the trial was that it concentrated on Barbie's inhumanity towards the Jewish children of Izieu and his role as a calculating perpetrator of genocide. Towards the end, the court allowed certain crimes against the Resistance to fall within the generic category of crimes against humanity, so that his treatment of resisters was not entirely neglected. But the substance of the trial inverted the post-war priorities given to the sufferings of the Resistance, lifting the genocide of the Jews into historical prominence in the reconstruction of national memory. It gave justification for proceedings to be opened against René Bousquet for his responsibility

in the round-up of the Vélodrome d'Hiver, and made the prosecution of Paul Touvier a logical necessity. The trial of one of Bousquet's representatives, Jean Leguay, would have served as a bridge. For his oversight of deportations he was the first French person to be indicted for crimes against humanity, but he died in 1989 before the trial could take place. As recounted in the previous chapter, Mitterrand's protective arm kept Bousquet away from his pursuers, but not from a lone assassin.

Touvier had returned to his refuge in Catholic sanctuaries, but was finally seized in 1989 in Nice. A first decision in 1992 by three Paris judges was that he had no case to answer. They argued that the delineation of crimes against humanity in the Barbie trial presupposed that the perpetrator should be implementing a 'hegemonic ideology'. Nazi Germany had such an ideology: Vichy, they decided, did not. Touvier was free to go. Widespread incredulity at this judgement enforced an appeal. The status of Vichy was put to one side and Touvier was recalled for trial in Versailles. In April 1994 he was convicted and imprisoned for the Rillieux-la-Pape killings. He died two years later.

The context of Chirac's apology on behalf of France in 1995 was therefore both the Vél.d'Hiv commemoration itself and the legal acknowledgement that crimes against humanity had been committed throughout the Occupation. The sequence of indictments and trials had recovered the actions of certain French individuals which had been omitted from national history, but the Vichy regime itself had escaped responsibility. The courts from Barbie to Touvier had left it to history to interpret Vichy. This separation of spheres did not, however, recognize the extent to which historians were assuming roles as public arbiters not only of historical truth and falsehood, but also of national culpability.

The media fanned and flattered historical research as a process of criminal detection. Access to historical archives was deemed by television and the press to be access to proof. Such proof would rule in matters of disputed national memory, and it was precisely national memory which was increasingly on trial. The indictment in 1997 of a local Vichy official, Maurice Papon, for crimes against humanity amounted to the long-delayed trial of Vichy for more than treason. Families of deported Jews were among the civil plaintiffs: their memories were heard. Historians were invited to 'testify' on the history of the period.

The trial of the 87-year-old Papon lasted for six months from October 1997 to April 1998. He was accused, as Secretary-General to the Gironde prefecture under Vichy, of knowingly deporting Jews from the Bordeaux region to their death, in convoys during July 1942 and after. In the course

of the trial his subsequent role as Prefect of Police in Paris at the time of the killings of Algerians on 17 October 1961 came under close scrutiny, not in the court but in the national media, and particularly in the memories of those for whom the conflicts over Algeria were their initiation to political commitment.

It was *Le Canard enchaîné* in May 1981 which had made Papon's Vichy past into news. By then his public career in the high echelons of administration and politics had reached ministerial level as he was appointed by Giscard d'Estaing and Raymond Barre as Budget Minister. Had the Barre austerity programme been less controversial, he might not have been featured by the satirical, but also investigative, journal. Even then, it was not difficult for Papon to demonstrate a resistance record in the Bordeaux area in 1943–4, which many local ex-resisters claimed had offset his rigorous service to Vichy.

Ambiguity characterized the whole of the trial. The verdict was both conviction and acquittal. Papon was sentenced to ten years in prison for complicity in crimes against humanity, but found not guilty of knowing that the Jews were going to their death. Complicity, like the post-war verdicts of collaboration and collusion, was the final judgement in the twentieth century on Vichy. The regime's role in the deportations of 1942 emerged as criminal, but also complex. People were left wondering whether Vichy would have been judged more severely had René Bousquet ever come to trial, or if more attention had been given to the Vichy statutes on the Jews. Just before the trial, the Catholic Church chose the fifty-seventh anniversary of the first Jewish statute to apologize for the hierarchy's compromising role in Vichy. It came a month after the Pope's apology for the massacre of Protestants on St Bartholomew's Day in 1572. The two apologies launched the three years of public confession and reconciliation designated by the Church, leading up to the jubilee of 2000.

A broad acceptance of the legal and historical judgement on Papon was registered in opinion polls, but arguments that the court had been the wrong forum, or Papon the wrong target, and that justice, memory and history had all been poorly served by the trial kept specialist opinion fractured. Despite this, a feeling of resolution in public opinion was widely noted.

The long-repressed issue of Algerian deaths on 17 October 1961, the subplot of the Papon affair, prompted Jospin's government to authorize an early release of archives relevant to the event, while Papon unsuccessfully sued the historian Jean-Luc Einaudi for libel in his assertion that a massacre had occurred under Papon's orders. This had been Einaudi's conclusion in

his substantial analysis of 1991, reiterated in the press during and after the trial. Asked by *Le Monde* on the anniversary of the event, 'What is Papon's responsibility for the death of more than 200 Algerians in October 1961?', Einaudi replied, 'It is direct, personal, overwhelming'.[5] The libel court did not endorse Einaudi's precise accusations but in the summary of its reasons for rejecting Papon's libel plea it was the first official body since 1961 to acknowledge that extreme police violence on that night had occurred.

The peaceful demonstration of 17 October had been remembered on its thirtieth anniversary in 1991 in a march of over 10,000 under banners asserting that Algerians too had a 'right to memory'. The question of whether a 'massacre' had ensued surfaced again in the following year's commemorations of the end of the Algerian war, and was a point of comparison when the massacres of Sétif were recalled on their fiftieth anniversary on 8 May 1995. After Papon's trial, two enquiries into the released archives found Papon to have covered up the number of deaths, but calculated figures were still at variance with one another and with the entrenched memory of the communities affected.[6]

The testimonies which came thick and fast from the Barbie trial onwards made it clear that the polarities in recent history were still starkly remembered. In 2000 the repression of state torture during the Algerian war was brought to full public consciousness. Military admission to torture and summary executions, the first to make the headlines from high-ranking officers, came from Generals Jacques Massu and Paul Aussaresses, both ninety-two, who had been in key positions in the battle of Algiers in 1957. Massu's description of his actions to break the FLN contained his regrets over the institutional use of practices which he now said should be formally admitted and condemned. The government officials, he said, knew exactly what was happening, but to round out the context he recalled the reciprocal horrors inflicted by the FLN on both French and fellow Algerians. The admission of Aussaresses, on the contrary, carried no apology. He stated to *Le Monde*, 'Torture gave me no pleasure . . . but if forced to relive it . . . I would do the same thing again because I believe one could not have done otherwise.'[7] He published his memoirs in 2001 and in the following January he and his publishers were taken to court by human rights organizations. They were found guilty and fined for 'complicity in apologies for war crimes'. In protest at the verdict, which was seen as one on the whole Algérie Française heritage, an elderly military man in the court broke into a defiant rendering of the 'Marseillaise'. It was the memory entrusted to *Le Monde* in June 2000 by the FLN militant Louisette Ighil-Ahriz of the torture inflicted on her in August 1957 that began this particular recovery

of the repressed. Motivations for memory were as diffuse as the experiences recalled. She wanted to track down the doctor who had intervened and saved her life.

From the memories of war, resistance, deportations, Algeria and torture, the ethnologist Germaine Tillion emerged in the press in 2000 as an all-encompassing icon, one year older than the generals whose practices of torture she had denounced in 1957. An ex-resister and survivor of Ravensbrück, she testified for her own mother and the other women who were killed there: representative of dialogue in Algeria, she had interceded for the victims of each side (see Chapters 12 and 13). At ninety-three she was portrayed as a woman who had modified the representation of history, an unclassifiable protagonist whose memory was morally combative and reconciliatory, exactly the two dimensions most valued at the end of the century. Among those who interpreted her successive irruptions into national history as emblematic was the prolific intellectual writer Tzvetan Todorov, a student visitor from Bulgaria in 1963 who stayed to become a leading theoretician of language and culture in the footsteps of Roland Barthes. He found in Tillion a memory which was exemplary: '. . . she appears to us today . . . as the living incarnation of the best of the century'.[8]

A composite memory

Maximizing honesty about the past, but at the same time minimizing the splintering effect of memory, preoccupied groups of intellectuals, politicians, journalists, and experts of all kinds from the 'end of exceptionalism' debates onwards. The reinvention of a collective purpose was at the heart of Jospin's plural left: ten years before it had been the essence of a massive enterprise led by Pierre Nora, an innovative historian of ideas. In 1980, the year of Sartre's death, he had stated that the era of the intellectual as a committed prophet was over, replaced by the need for enlightened understanding of the present through study of the past. Collective memory was the link that needed to be understood.

Entitled *Les Lieux de mémoire* (sites, or realms, of memory), Nora's project gave structure and meaning to the outcrop of memory, and inspired a generation of historians to research recurrent historical syndromes. Undertaken in the early 1980s and lasting over a decade, the project set out to show that a history can be written of memory itself. This was achieved by the study of sites, realms and traditions of national life which carry a symbolic status and are depositories of national memory. The vast range of topics included the *tricolore* and the 'Marseillaise', Verdun, the

Louvre, the names of streets, the civil code, proverbs, songs, Alsace as frontier and the idea of *patrimoine* (heritage) itself. Nora's conviction was that collective memory had once been an internalized, everyday process: it was now reliant on the external stimulus of commemoration. He traced the permanence but also the evolution of *lieux de mémoire* across the changing landscapes of history and memory.

The seven volumes became more and more encyclopedic over the years of publication: they became a monument to monuments, a symbol of symbols, telling people where and how their history was given body and their collective memory shaped. The Socialist Culture Minister, Jack Lang, was enthusiastic about the very concept of the enterprise; the title became common coinage, and the project was recognized as a phenomenon in its own right. The indication of sites which did not have to be either geographical or material, but could be ways of cooking, or the symbolism of the conventional small cup of black coffee, had a liberating effect on cultural history. A focus, a fixation even, on the past as seen through this wide lens was acknowledged by many to be a compensation for the loss of grand political narratives which led towards the future. But it was the effect on memory, history and identity in the present which was the project's singular strength.

Nora grouped his sites into ones symbolic of the *République*, the *Nation*, and what he called *les France*. This plural subtitle to the last three volumes, which came out in 1992, appeared to demonstrate a readiness to look at a diverse range of collective memories. A few years before, in 1986, the eminent 83-year-old historian Fernand Braudel had added to the identity introspection of the 1980s with a much-anticipated book called *L'Identité de la France*. Steeped in the structural and long-term approaches of the *Annales* school, he was a brilliant maker of historical and geographical mosaics. He started with the concept 'that the name of France is diversity'. It was more than conceptual: 'Nothing is gained by talking theoretically about French diversity. You have to see it with your own eyes, delight in its colours and smells, touch it with your hands, eat and drink it in an authentic *auberge*.'[9] Braudel placed himself squarely among those for whom the identity of France lay in the ways in which its diverse geography, customs and continuity had been moulded into a vast cornucopia of riches. Were the last three volumes of *Les Lieux de mémoire* to echo Braudel's celebratory approach?

Nora began his presentation of *les France* with defiance of Braudel's diversity theme. In terms of memory, he stated, 'the name of France is not diversity but division'.[10] It was a range of dualities which his plural title

initially explored. It looked not only at the constant replay of politics in its classic form of left and right, but also at the way the collective memory shaped regional diversity into the duality of 'Paris and provinces', while ethnic and cultural diversity was rendered as 'French and foreigners'. Nora did not minimize the importance of division, but by encompassing the divisions of the past into a shared collective memory, he added his weight to those seeking a resolution to *les guerres franco-françaises*.

Diversity or duality, both are recognized as parts of a whole. The journey undertaken by Nora and his many colleagues through a multitude of sites reached a similar destination to Braudel's road through diversity. Whether that destination was called unity in diversity or collective *lieux de mémoire*, a composite was achieved.

The end of the bipolar world of Soviet Russia and the West gave added momentum to the revision of polarities in the history of the republic. The bicentenary of 1989 was the obvious opportunity. In anticipation, the weekly magazine *L'Événement du jeudi* seized on the Presidential elections of 1988 as a rationale for listing all the dates ending in 8 which had formed a collective republican history through Franco-French conflicts. Obligatory inclusions were: May–June 1968, the end of the Fourth Republic in 1958, class conflict in 1948, divisions over Munich in 1938, Clemenceau against the strikers in 1908, the February revolution of 1848 and the crucial challenges to the monarchy in 1788 which had triggered the Revolution of the following year. The editors happily agreed that this was only a device for a discursive ramble through history, but, they argued, the theme of *les guerres franco-françaises* was real enough to merit a prolonged analysis. Was it necessary to perpetuate such divisions? Were they a national pathology? Introducing the theme, the historian Michel Winock argued inclusively that 'these divisions, deep and recurrent, are also our wealth. We are always a duality: we are ourselves and we are the other.' His conclusion was that moderating voices of tolerance and freedom could also be heard in all the opinion polls which registered division. It was clearly with these voices, later exemplified by Germaine Tillion, that he identified himself and the underlying 'unity' of France.[11]

Memorialization transformed

The emphasis on memory had not been purely about the past: it galvanized people into creating new ways in which the present might be remembered in the future. Memorialization itself was often a collective act of reorientation, suggesting that identities should evolve. It is memory as a creative process

which emerges most strongly from the events and introspection at the end of the century.

At Péronne, in the valley of the Somme east of Amiens, the process was at its most radical. The small market town of Péronne had been the German headquarters at the time of the first Battle of the Somme in 1916. In 1992 a highly original museum and research centre on the First World War was opened there as a result of initiatives from the *département* of the Somme and a team of historians from Britain, France and Germany, headed by Jay Winter from Cambridge. It was the first of its kind to attempt an exhibition and history of the war as a shared experience of the different nationalities, a multinational resolution to the most nationalist of wars. Its coined name, 'Historial de la Grande Guerre', inscribed history and memorial as one; its funding was French but its rationale and academic resources were international; its shift of focus away from Verdun re-educated the French public into the multiple locations of the war and the huge losses sustained in the Somme; its reflective focus on the lives and deaths of ordinary people at war, on the mundane objects of the war, and on the war's place in the memory of families, reinforced the move towards a cultural history of wars and their aftermath.[12]

In the Normandy town of Caen, totally rebuilt from its obliteration in 1944, the opportunity was seized in the 1980s to project a new collective identity within the fast-growing memorialization of the Resistance and the Second World War. Its new museum in 1988 was given the role of re-education for peace, a 'Mémorial pour la Paix'. By its very title it rapidly assumed national and international significance. Influenced by its approach, many local Resistance museums tried to situate their exhibits in a reflective context, looking outwards for wider and more inclusive themes.

One such example was the Resistance museum opened in 1990 at the famous Provençal site of Fontaine-de-Vaucluse, where the Italian poet and humanist Petrarch made his home in the fourteenth century. Its express purpose was to transmit a collective sense of *liberté* grounded in the United Nations charter of human rights. The museum created a process of dialogue among schoolchildren on varying expressions of freedom, from the Resistance through to the concepts of *liberté* within the global market and, conversely, among those who challenge globalization. The exhibitions and discussions pursue the aim of 'building together citizenship and solidarity in the world'.

2. *Shifting patterns of identity*

Against those who decried an identity loss in the last part of the twentieth century and the first years of the twenty-first the argument was made that national identity was an ongoing process, a constant re-forming of new and existing patterns in national life. The range of memory was matched by the patterns of diversity increasingly representative of society and politics. Projecting the nation at the millennium, the organizers of celebrations in 2000 made a virtue out of both the single identity of France and its multiple constituent identities. A national picnic scheduled for 14 July, on check tablecloths laid on the meridian from the north to the south, was a bold manifestation of a decision from the top, utterly dependent on local and individual identification from below. Objects and rites of passage were always going to predominate, and there were many of them to evoke the theme of temporal and technological transition. Most reliant on diffused creativity was the idea of millennium gates or arches, designed at the local level as symbolic entry points into towns and *communes*. There was anxiety that the symbolism would be banal: it was 'unity and diversity' on a grand scale and it was criticized for representing something ideal and abstract rather than facing the real problems of discordance within the national community. But seen historically, the millennium projects were a declaration that the combative mentality in France, summed up in the archetypal reaction, '*je suis contre*' ('I'm against'), had been played out in the twentieth century and had been replaced by something more ambivalent, an acceptance of the interplay of opposites, or simply a recognition of the multiple patterns within a single kaleidoscope. The appeal of the kaleidoscope as a metaphor was that its patterns could be shaken.

A volatile identity in Europe

The prospect of European enlargement in the early part of the new century caused Jacques Delors to state in January 2000: 'The Europe of 15 member states has failed to face the divisive and quarrelsome issue of what project we will have in common when we are 30. Even now, what is common to the 15?'[13] Closely allied to this question was the fundamental problem of how to make the citizenship of Europe, proclaimed at Maastricht, into a reality, when Europe was still seen by most people as an external authority. After a 53 per cent abstention in the European elections of 1999, public opinion in 2000, the year of French presidency of the EU, expressed major-

ity discontent at the functioning of democracy in the Union and anxiety about the effects of enlargement.

In the minds of many, both issues raised the possibility that the economic primacy of the market, when extended to countries of Eastern Europe, and potentially Turkey, would relegate the political vision of a united Europe to the lost causes of the twentieth century. It was conceivable that only a version of the Gaullist 'Europe of nations' would survive, nuanced by the close partnership between France and Germany. Each of the two countries was the main trading partner of the other, and to this extent economics was thought to structure a reciprocal Franco-German perspective, even though the partnership in 2000 was stuttering at best. The new German Socialist-led government of Gerhard Schröder flexed the independency of United Germany and seized on opportunities to advance Germany's own needs and agenda without the sanction of the French. In reaction, Jospin's policy towards an integrated Europe looked increasingly cautious.

Discussions on the effects of enlargement emphasized the elusiveness of a single political outcome. To interpret monetary union as the vanguard of political union was still possible, and the choice of 'Euro' as the name of the currency was symbolic for some, though for many it expressed no political inevitability. In 2001, after two years' adaptation to the new 'integrating' currency, 29 per cent of French people thought regularly of themselves as European, 28 per cent never did, and 42 per cent not often.[14] The Socialists within the plural left remained in theory committed to constructing a Europe whose social politics would resist the dominant ideology (*pensée unique*) of the the neo-liberal economy, but Jospin's Government was seen to give away in practice what it resisted in theory. From a marked return of growth in 1997–2000, the French economy slowed down in 2001, and the downward curve of unemployment tipped once again upwards. Anxiety at the spiralling cost of public services and administration, which accounted for over a quarter of all jobs and 51 per cent of the country's GDP (gross domestic product), 3 per cent higher than Germany's and 11 per cent higher than Britain's, forced the government into conceding privatizations. Concession in this direction was not the political message that the plural left had intended other social democracies in Europe to hear. It had a strong bearing on the outcome of the elections of 2002.

In May 2000 Jospin set out the aims of the French period of EU presidency in a pragmatic way. They revolved round the social needs of full employment and economic growth, greater citizen involvement, a stronger voice in world affairs, and a European defence capability. Jospin was keen to signal an end to European indecision over military deployment, nakedly

revealed during the merciless wars which marked the breakup of Yugoslavia in the early 1990s. In contrast he interpreted the French and European response to the Kosovan crisis of 1999 as one of greater decisiveness. The repressive ferocity of President Milosovic of Serbia against the Kosovan independence movement in 1998–9 exposed the incapacity of the EU by itself to mount an effective reply. It was the leadership of the USA, yet again, which provided the dynamic counter-measures. President Clinton took the initiative to launch NATO forces into air strikes against the Serb dictator. The move propelled the French executive into positive support for military action. Jospin and Chirac committed the French airforce to the NATO offensive, and Jospin justified it with a speech on 26 March 1999, setting out his image of a Europe committed to fight for human rights in Kosovo. Against the opposition of the Communist Party, the Front National and the nationalism of Charles Pasqua, the combined rhetoric of Jospin and Chirac rebutted the charge of submissiveness to US military power, and turned the debate into one about European military potential. As the details of Serb inhumanity proliferated and the plight of the Kosovan refugees intensified, the consensus between Premier and President led to initiatives for ground troops to take over from the aerial bombardment. The indictment of Milosovic for crimes against humanity, the first charge in history against a head of government still exercising power, was described by Chirac as a great step forward in creating a universal moral conscience.

The process of cautious pragmatism sketched by Jospin in 2000 was shaken in June by the German Foreign Minister Joschka Fischer who raised the stakes of European federalism. He rejected the immobilism which had crept into the process of integration, and his call for a major political leap forward echoed the questioning of Delors in January. On a visit to Berlin, Chirac responded with his own vision of an integrated future. It looked like political leadership, but during the French presidency of the EU he fell back on arrogant tactics which alienated the smaller members of the Union and uncomfortably recalled the personal style of de Gaulle. By the end of the year, after the Nice summit of the EU in September, the indignant criticism of Chirac's tactics from outside France alternated with comments on the lack of focus in French policy towards treaty reform and political integration. Tracing a constant theme in French Europeanism since de Gaulle, it was possible to conclude that France had always preferred the process of inter-governmental decision-making, leaving the French nation free, in post-Gaullist terms, to express its own distinctive identity.

The patterns of Europeanism were forcefully shaken yet again in 2003. A revived Franco-German partnership suddenly threw itself into a world

role. President Chirac and Chancellor Schröder refused to countenance the US-British war against Iraq, launched by President George W. Bush and Prime Minister Tony Blair with the backing of the Spanish Prime Minister, José María Aznar. Chirac insisted that there could be no international legality to a 'preventive' war against Iraq without the specific and final sanction of the United Nations. The Foreign Minister in the Raffarin government, Dominique de Villepin, put forward the French position with elegant conviction, to which a majority of assembled national representatives in the UN responded with unusual applause. George W. Bush and Tony Blair persisted, in the name of their two nations, and called for a coalition to back the invasion.

People in each country made their own voices heard. In France, there was massive solidarity behind opposition to the US–British assertion of the right to invade. Across Europe most Muslims denounced the war, and found themselves alongside millions of non-Muslim Europeans. The Franco-German position was dismissed by the White House as the obstinacy of an 'old Europe', and in response a majority of French newspapers and TV channels inverted the negative phrase to indicate positive pride in the capacity of 'old Europeans' to face up to the USA in world affairs. Anxiety at possible economic consequences acted as a counterweight to rampant anti-Americanism, but the issue produced dramatic citizen support for the expressions of peace from an 'inner Europe'. Tony Blair's insistence that Saddam Hussein had weapons of mass destruction at the ready and had already failed to meet successive UN demands was met by detailed French reasons urging caution and a more protracted search by the UN weapons inspectors. The disagreements were fundamental and precluded any united policy by the European Union as a whole. The damage to Europeanism was thought to be incalculable.

The Iraq crisis gave an irritable edge to the process of EU enlargement to twenty-five members. There was no less discomfort over the repeated question of national budgets within the Eurozone after both Germany and France exceeded the deficit limits imposed by the convergence criteria on all countries embracing the common currency. The implication that there was a binding restriction which the larger nations were able to break with impunity threw the central economic policies of the EU into confusion. The turbulence coincided with proposals for a European Constitution drawn up by a Convention which had been open to all European institutions and had staged a notably wide-ranging intellectual and political debate. The final recommendations were presented publicly in 2003 by the ex-President of France, Valéry Giscard d'Estaing, who had presided over the workings of

the Convention. In Giscard's own mind there was a direct line between the proposals and the integrated Europe that he and many other Europeanists had eagerly promoted, but he was obliged by the fragility of EU relationships in the wake of the Iraq war to point out that the Constitution would, for the most part, merely formalize existing structures and clarify practice.

After months of angular negotiation and compromise the Constitution was endorsed by the European Council of Ministers on 18 June 2004, subject to ratification by the twenty-five constituent countries, nine of which, including Britain, had already decided to put it to a vote by referendum. Chirac stood initially by his adamant rejection of calls for a referendum in France but finally conceded. It was acknowledged that the outcome would be unpredictable. The possibility that a 'no' vote would be entered by many previous pro-Europeans was considered to be high. The pressure to restore the Eurozone budgetary regulations provided extra rationale for major cuts by the Raffarin government in public expenditure. After reductions in the budget for research in 2003 the government took the decision in 2004 to tackle the huge debt in the national funding of the health service. It had been a major expectation in Jospin's call for a radically 'social' character to the enlarged Europe that integration would facilitate state provision of universal health care. Under Raffarin and Sarkozy this expectation disappeared. The market necessity they ascribed to public expenditure cuts and the restructuring of health care perpetuated the challenge of liberal economists since the late 1970s to the legacy of an interventionist state. The identity sought by France within Europe had long become inseparable from attitudes to the global market economy. Reaction to these interlocking and volatile areas of policy conditioned the assessment of an eventual vote on the European Constitution: it also continued to extend the political dimensions of social protest and discord, underlining the plurality of identities within the contemporary understanding of Frenchness.

France, multilayered and multiform . . .

From the fifteenth century onwards, apprentices, mainly from the building trades, made a *tour de France* to learn different aspects of their trade from local skills and methods. The traditions and rituals of their guilds (*compagnonnages*) survived into the twentieth century, and after the Second World War hostels known as *maisons du compagnonnage* were revitalized to house travelling workers. Acts of murderous rivalry within the guilds, dating from the wars of religion, had disappeared, but the memory was

more about these rival traditions than the visits paid to different parts of France.

The cycling Tour de France, whose centenary was celebrated in 2003, canonized rivalry at the Olympian levels which had re-entered international sport through the vision of Pierre de Coubertin in 1896. The Tour which started in 1903 had a conflictual origin. In 1900 two industrialists protested at the support given by the sports paper *Le Vélo* to Alfred Dreyfus. They launched a rival paper, *L'Auto*, and it was to boost its image and income that the editor Henri Desgrange created the race whose itinerary was to be a tour of the whole of France. The business competitiveness of its origin and the combative politics behind *L'Auto* gave the race an uneasy ride in the early years: in certain areas cyclists were attacked and nails strewn on the roads. Within the race, competition was individual at the start, and the winner in 1903 and 1904 was Maurice Garin, the first of many French 'giants of the road' who became national heroes of the Tour. As its popularity expanded, so did the international origin of the riders and the wearers of the leader's yellow jersey (*maillot jaune*). Desgrange introduced national teams in 1929.

The feats of endurance made the cycling Tour into an emblem of suffering, with images of religious intensity. The legends were of the riders and their rivalry, of the gruelling mountain climbs, the tactics of the teams and the ruthlessness of the backers. As the centenary approached in 2003 the focus for Tour connoisseurs had not changed, but the promotion of towns and villages through which the race passed had progressively made the Tour into a window for local products and festivities. Its international appeal and the successive victories of the American Lance Armstrong took away any French parochialism in the centenary celebrations, while its commercial imperative and its drug scandals caused wry comments on the whole event as representative of the contemporary era. But as a singular national event with a diversity of local sites and layers of meaning it personified the millennium themes of 2000.

The temptation in 2003 to use the phenomenon of the Tour de France as a paradigm of French identity, both single-minded and multiform at the same time, was hard to resist. More anxious conclusions about national identity, reached at the turn of the century, noted the progressive disappearance of specific institutions which might at earlier moments in the previous 100 years have been seen as typically French. For its first publication in 2000 *Le Monde* carried a cartoon by Plantu of a seated stereotype of a capitalist, replete with large cigar, balancing the five minuscule leaders of the *gauche plurielle* on his knee and telling them, 'Fine. I've listened to you. Now I'll tell you what plural capitalism is!' The accompanying article listed

the French companies, household names for most of the century, which had merged with foreign-based firms or had been taken over: the financial house of Paribas, the chemical and pharmaceutical Rhône-Poulenc, the scandal-ridden oil giant Elf, the aeronautic industry Aerospatiale, and the cigarette and matches company Seita.

The merger of Seita was related against a backdrop of 400 years since the French diplomat Jean Nicot first introduced tobacco into France and from whom the word nicotine derived. 'Never have mergers and acquisitions been so numerous as in 1999,' ran the subheadings. 'The historic ties of these companies with different French regions, have been loosened.' By contrast, other French firms such as Renault and Total were said to be pursuing their own conquest of the globe. Dispersion and redistribution of the economy was the theme of the article, concluding with the statement that France in 2000 had only one dimension: the world. This dimension as a new pattern of identity begged the question of loss or gain, but the article accepted that a global French economy now had its own independent existence.[15]

The thrust of such an article was towards identities in the plural and towards the process of identity-creation. Such a process was the aim of the Ministry of Agriculture in 2000 in its campaign to promote rural heritage: it marked a clear break with imposition from above by asking local associations to articulate what for them constituted their heritage. Such an open-ended agenda favoured the creative exercise of social imagination (*l'imaginaire social*) as a projection of local self-image. The result was a boost to the discovery or reinvention of tradition. Popular books produced on the different localities (*pays* or *terroirs*) insisted that there was no definition of a *terroir* without consideration of culture in its widest ethnological sense of customs, rituals and legends, whether the folklore of sorcery in the region of Berry south of Paris, or the importance of the *estaminet* (local bar) in the everyday culture of the Nord–Pas-de-Calais.

The plural identities within France were multiplied by the constituent cultures of the Départements and Territoires d'Outre-mer (DOM-TOM), grouped together under one ministry for administrative purposes. Lionel Jospin was conscious that he had outscored Jacques Chirac in votes from the DOM-TOM in the Presidential elections of 1995, and as Prime Minister after 1997 he was ready to look at new constitutional settlements in the *outre-mer*, as in Corsica, reinforcing ideas of devolution. The ordinary people he met on journeys to the *outre-mer*, however, were less preoccupied than the local politicians with issues of the constitution. Almost everywhere they raised economic and social questions. In Réunion ideas of making it into two *départements* were rejected by 57 per cent of the population as

irrelevant to the real problems of the island, while nearly 75 per cent backed state intervention in local affairs because they accused the locally elected officials of not fulfilling their role.[16] The plural left responded with an increase in the 2000 budget for the DOM-TOM of 13.6 per cent, compared with the average increase in the rest of the budget of 0.9 per cent, and Jospin backed down at the first sign of trade-union dispute from tackling the privileged salaries of DOM-TOM *fonctionnaires* which had always been set at a higher rate than the equivalent in metropolitan France.

The responsiveness of the Jospin government to these outlying regions was a further sign that the plural left intended all constituent identities to be updated. It created a climate of optimism that racial and gender stereotypes were capable of being transformed, even if the dire effects of exclusion and racial conflict were all too visible in certain urban areas. Against all optimists the xenophobia orchestrated by the extreme right appeared to force itself into any contemporary definition of French political and social identity. Yet against this evidence, journalism and academic research provided constant examples of ways in which new forms of cultural identity were being actively imagined. The living strength of French culture within and outside the *outre-mer* had been formally promoted by the creation in 1970 at Niamey in the Niger of a francophone organization, the Agence de la Coopération Culturelle et Technique (ACCT). Léopold Senghor of Senegal was among its most enthusiastic promoters and was widely seen to be the re-animator of the very concept of *francophonie* in geographical as well as linguistic terms. Some fifty-two countries took membership of the ACCT, some with only a mere fraction of French speakers.

By the end of the century, and even more so at the time of the Iraq war in 2003, the fact and idea of *francophonie* was being increasingly invoked in French politics and diplomacy. It was promoted as a rival or bulwark against Anglo-Saxon-American culture, food, language and world power. But it was not dependent on the international clash of values and interests. Although the primary status of the French language was declining, the worldwide impact of the consciousness of French culture confirmed a movement of identity-creation not just from mainland France outwards, but equally from French-speaking areas back into France. It was no longer dominated by the one-way influence of empire. Born in French-speaking Rwanda, Jean-Marie Rurangwa, a writer and teacher of French, published his essay on the genocide of 1994 under the rubric of *devoir de mémoire*.[17] The significance of the memory-boom and the search for cultural legacies throughout the French-speaking world brought the century full circle to Henri Bergson's pre-1914 insights into the relativity of memory. The cul-

tural identities within *francophonie* were no less relative even when used as a source of national pride and assertion.

From Marcel Pagnol's original scripts for his Marseillais film trilogy *Marius*, *Fanny* and *César* in the early 1930s, to Renoir's Popular Front films, to the treatments of gender in the films of Godard and Agnès Varda, to the heritage films of the 1980s and 1990s, regional, class and gender identities were given distinctive images assimilated by audiences as part of French diversity. The *cinéma beur* extended the exploration of what was now French. Three films made in the mid-1990s by directors of Maghrebi origin, *Bye Bye* by Karim Dridi, *Krim* by Ahmed Bouchaala and *Douce France* by Malik Chibane gave a deeper identity to their first- and second-generation Maghrebi-French characters while accentuating the specific settings of Marseille, Lyon and the Saint-Denis suburb of Paris. Pluralizing the ethnic representation of ex-Maghrebi communities through different approaches and localities, with different observations about their integration or lack of it, was as significant in identity-creation as the original expression of a *beur* cultural consciousness. The class, gender, regional and ethnic images of France registered a multiformity of cultures.

. . . but not 'multicultural'?

Looking back over the twentieth century through the lens of diversity, it was not absurd in the early years of the twenty-first to discern an evolution, however slow and fractured, of a multicultural society. The very concept was as central to discussions of national identity as any raised by the memory-boom. But the wider use of the word 'culture' which affected historical narrative and analysis was not matched by a flexible use of the term 'multiculturalism'. The very concept of 'multiculturalism' indicated the negative side of difference. Its synonym was not diversity but disintegration. It was used interchangeably with the word *communautarisme* to indicate the threat of separate and exclusive communities, as promoted by apartheid or fundamentalist religious ideologies. For years South Africa and then Lebanon (*Liban*) were cited as prime examples of permanently fissured states. It was to avoid *libanisation* that the unitary Republic was seen as protective of a single national community.

The opponents of separate constitutions for Corsica and the overseas communities were not themselves unified, but Jacques Attali's column in *L'Express* in July 2000 spoke for many: he argued that major elements of the economy, social rights, Civil Service powers, conceptions of justice and systems of defence have been 'privatized, regionalized, Europeanized'. Only

the 'very heart of national identity' was left, 'the sentiment of belonging to one community with one destiny, speaking the same language' and this would be under attack if Corsica was given a special status. Other regions, he argued, would demand the same: 'The effect of this escalating desire for difference would be ravaging.' Regionalization would join with globalization in destroying state institutions: it would be 'the end of French exceptionalism which has protected our country for over a thousand years from the worst enemy of democracy, the dictatorship of minorities. At the very best France would be transformed into a large Belgium, or at worst, a small Russia.'[18]

The designation of 'minorities' in the debate on multiculturalism was not reserved specifically for regions or ethnic groups, but it invariably signified religious denominations. In an issue of the history journal *Vingtième Siècle* in 2000 on 'Religions of Europe', the emphasis was placed on the shift of religion from institutions to individuals. Martine Cohen judged that integration of Jews in France was so well established that individual Jews experienced just the same problems as Catholics and Protestants in conveying difference should they wish to do so, and added that the 'legitimacy of diversity must be assured not just within the Jewish world but in society as a whole, to allow individuals to compose and recompose their identities throughout their lives'. In the same issue Danièle Hervieu-Léger, writing on Islam in France, pointed to its polycentric nature, diffused from separate mosques, radios, schools, newspapers and associations, all with their own definitions of authentic Islam. She concluded that secularism, always in conflict with religion as an institution, should be able to accommodate to individualized religion.[19]

Individualism and diversity were the keywords in all the millennium discussions of identity. The state would gain strength from both. But references in 2000 to state secularism and its enlightenment tradition were undiminished. The words of Ferdinand Buisson in Tunis in 1903 (see Chapter 1) echoed down the century, and they were still revered as visionary words of reason. Much had perceptibly changed in the context of the arguments, but the basic positions were clearly recognizable, except that the consensus behind secularism was much wider at the start of the twenty-first century than it had been in 1903. Education remained the main vector of a unifying culture, and schools remained the main site of conflict over any ideology or separatist behaviour perceived as a disintegrating force. In the long-running saga of pupils wearing the Islamic headscarf, the Chirac–Raffarin government and the National Assembly in 2004 passed the first formal ban on the wearing of all religious signs and clothes in state schools. The target was explicitly the Muslim *foulard*, though the ban extended to Jewish

skull-caps and the wearing of overt Christian crosses. Over the course of 100 years, the determination to preserve a secular republican state had not significantly weakened. Clericalism, in whatever form, was still 'the enemy'.

The government in power in 2004 was one of the conservative centre right, not one of the Radical left as it had been in 1903. In itself this was a significant reflection of changes over 100 years: where the political left had been the centre of hostility to the presence of Catholicism in state education, the political right was now the democratic centre of hostility to Islamic intrusion into the state classroom. In terms of the century's history of France and the French the very notion of a unitary republican identity had ceased to be the monopoly of one particular political tradition. It was scattered across the political spectrum, located just as much in the post-Gaullist right as on the plural left.

More widely, oppositional politics had become demanding or disputing areas of reform within the Republic. They were no longer the sites of conflictual ideologies designed to overthrow the regime. The first cohesion round the Third Republic in 1914–18 had solidified into a permanent one behind the Fifth Republic in the last three decades of the century. As France became, in Jospin's words, 'a plural society' or, in Braudel's words, the synonym of diversity, the Republic as state retained its unitary identity. France did not proclaim itself as a multicultural state. Diversity was acknowledged: difference that implied incompatibility was not.

It is the resilience of a unitary state within a multiform and multilayered society that constitutes the singularity of France since 1900. Its distinctiveness lies in what is objectively a paradox, especially to outsiders. Subjectively, however, it can seem coherent. Accusations of intolerance aimed at the unitary state have been met by reminders of how many people had fought for inclusiveness throughout the century, and how the very strength of the republican identity had attracted a vast range of artists and intellectuals, refugees and immigrants. There is a robust history of the unitary state in the twentieth century which is one of humanity, nurturing secularism, promoting social and cultural diversity and integrating difference.

One outstanding symbol among many is the high profile achieved by the Institut du Monde Arabe (Institute of the Arab World) in Paris, housed since 1987 in Jean Nouvel's contemporary building of exceptional elegance. It represents the internationalism of state-funded research, dialogue and cross-cultural exchange in which the legacy of generations of French involvement in Arab and Islamic history and culture stands as a corrective to the negative images of Arab-French relations which capture the headlines. In 2003 the autobiography of one of the outstanding modern histori-

ans of Algeria, Benjamin Stora, born in Constantine in Algeria in 1950, traced his academic and political journey from the smoke-filled rooms of the extreme left in 1968. He and his family had left Algeria with the other exiled settlers in 1962, his father permanently unable to understand what had happened to the belief in Algérie Française. What Stora missed from his origins was the sociability of the south, which he contrasted with his experience of the cold individualism of the mainland until he discovered the community of the barricades in May 1968. By 2004 he had come to epitomize the strength of a pluralist historical perspective, alongside the FLN combatant and historian Mohammed Harbi, who was imprisoned by his own independent Algeria from 1965 to 1968 and exiled to France in 1973 to become a respected Paris-based historian of the contemporary Algerian world.

Both writers put Algerians back at the centre of their own history without any romanticization, while objectively assessing all aspects of the French and European presence in North Africa, a tradition with roots in the oriental scholarship of Jacques Berque, translator of the Koran, and the *longue durée* Mediterranean history of Fernand Braudel. Assessing the legacy of the French empire in this tradition acknowledges the forceful dialectic of two powerful cultures. There is no triumphalism or historical fatalism involved.

The temptation of the unitary state to insist on its universalist values with rigidity and arrogance has been resisted from within the integrated societies of France overseas. Poet and politician Aimé Césaire, speaking for France *outre-mer*, interpreted inclusion as the right to difference. It was not only in the early days of the Socialist government of 1981 that *droit à la différence* appeared to make sense of the existence of minority interests and values. Attali's definition of democracy did not command universal agreement in the century. Like Léopold Senghor in Senegal, Césaire in Martinique extolled a black culture which defied obliteration within the republican identity of metropolitan France. Both challenged the negative inference given to multiculturalism.

At all points of the history of France and the French since 1900 there is need to ask what place the cruder forms of nationalism have secured in the promotion of a unitary state. The spiral of ideology in the 1930s and 1940s acted as no less of a warning of intolerance than the divided communities of the Lebanon. At the start of the twenty-first century, the continued infiltration of Front National ideas into democratic politics, and the mixed social nature of its support, led some commentators to define the FN as essentially an opportunist party of protest. If this was perceived to be its nature at certain points, the bulk of its history expressed an unapologetic

renewal of the extreme nationalism which had earlier characterized Pétainism and Vichy and which collective memory in the 1980s and 1990s had sought to confront.

In the hands of the Front National the unitary culture became first and foremost a tool of exclusion. Its policies in the elections of 2002 prioritized the fears of citizens victimized by lawlessness and the insecurity of streets and urban estates. Yet in its action and campaigning, in its propaganda and its theories, it made victims of immigrants and Maghrebi youth. In response, young urban Muslims found self-protection and pride in their own groups: they began to form what Farhad Khosrokhavar in 1997 called the 'Islam of youth', tending towards the separate cultural communities which the unitary state and culture set out to resist. He defined them less in terms of their heritage than as constructed communities in the immediate context of racism, deprivation, unemployment and discrimination.[20] In such urban groups Muslim youths sought to valorize the exclusion forced upon them as a sign of their own identity. The spread of the FN across class and locality had reactivated the spiral of ideology. In the propaganda of Le Pen, a common humanity and a plural society were denied. It was this discordance which was seen by many in France and outside to nullify the unity and diversity theme announced at the millennium celebrations of the Republic, though it also increased its moral imperative.

Responsibility for exclusion far outran the extent of the FN's influence. Republican authorities of all political persuasions carried responsibility for failures to integrate housing and remove the stigma attached to 'sink' estates and life in the *banlieues*. Social investigations in 2003–4 into poverty-ridden and high-unemployment estates such as Val-Fourré in the Seine valley some fifty miles from Paris, or the Petit Bard in Montpellier, revealed the total alienation of their inhabitants from the meaning and benefits of citizenship. They declared themselves the forgotten people, the unrecognized and the unrepresented, accusing the state of institutional racism. In July 2004, across a wire mesh outside the Petit Bard, protesters of Moroccan origin stretched a sign saying 'Stop urban apartheid'. A fire in one of the lifts had caused the death of a young resident and made numerous families homeless. An angry march by over 1,000 residents pushed the event into the media and forced the government into allocating extra money, but not before the fires at Auber-villiers and Grenoble in 1970 had been recalled. At Val-Fourré references to images in the Kassovitz film of 1995, *La Haine*, were recurrent, but none of the compensating lightness of tone was discernible. The downward cycle of poverty, exclusion, violence and crime had left people without hope for either recognition or justice. An aura of permanency pervaded the desperation.

In the context of this acute dispossession, the plurality of social movements which had mushroomed since the 1980s expressed the vigour of new forms of political inclusion and identity. Alongside the autonomous trade unions whose co-ordinated action gave a new character to the public sector strikes of 1995, the movement ATTAC formed its acronym in a demand for a new tax on financial transactions to provide citizen support.[21] Launched in 1998, its ideas had been nurtured in *Le Monde diplomatique*, a monthly which specialized in critical articles against the global liberal economy, bought by more than 200,000 in France, and reaching readers across the world. Within five years ATTAC's membership of 28,000 made it a formidable presence in issue politics, as were the activist groups which continued to agitate and campaign for those without papers, without jobs or without homes. A growing insistence that a globalism of social values and human rights faced the globalism of the market made for a revival of political theory to incorporate the new voices. The generic aim of social inclusion featured Jean Jaurès in its lineage, but the vocabulary of social and economic transformation had moved towards the recognition and creation of identities which cross class, gender and race.

In the context and effects of political diversification and the loss of old certainties, a recognizably 'permanent' France, with its multilayers and its multiforms, was nevertheless evoked by the press of the year 2000 as a vibrant and positive entity. Articles reminded people of the richness of culture created by cinema, intellectual life, avant-garde art, fashion design, sport, music and even the tradition of dissident politics.

Images of a collective identity by which France was widely known proliferated: the knots of *pétanque* players in sun-filtered squares in the south; the epic flair of the national rugby XV in beating New Zealand in the semi-final of the rugby World Cup of 1999, dubbed as the 'match of the century'; the timeless *chansonnier* tradition of melancholy and love in Jacques Prévert's and Joseph Kosma's *Les Feuilles mortes* as sung by Juliette Greco or Yves Montand; the ritual tours of megaliths and menhirs in the Carnac region of Brittany; school parties visiting the battlefield cemeteries of the First World War; photographs of women with their bicycles at checkpoints of the demarcation line in Occupied France; the indefinable tastes of gastronomic creations, such as Marc Menaud's *cromesquis* at Vézelay, for which epicureans made their pilgrimages; the singing of political songs from the Commune of 1871 accompanied by the accordion in the narrowly climbing rue Mouffetard in Paris; the arc-lamps (*lamparos*) on the prow of flat-bottomed boats fishing at night on the shallow coastal lakes of the Languedoc; the ritualized masks and inversions of the annual

celebration of *Carnaval* (Carnival); these typical images unapologetically evoked a reassuring Frenchness, a national community singular at its core and plural in its diversity.

Roots, if not nostalgia, were further accentuated in the recognition that the Airbus, the high-speed train (TGV), economic modernization, Europeanism and the global market had their own heritage in the century and had not been superimposed. Yet the controversial nature of globalization and the politics addressing ethnic origins and disparate cultures were also seen to perpetuate the conflictual history which many saw as the defining feature of the century that had just ended. In the light of so many internal divisions, any ideal type, any abstraction or personification of France could only be one of many. National biographers looked to eminent men and women eligible for the Panthéon; photographers emulating Henri Cartier-Bresson and Robert Doisneau looked at ordinary women, men and children in ordinary places, symbolized by the banks of a canal running through an industrial suburb, or a festive village wedding; the photography and discourse of provincial *terroirs*, pioneered in Daniel Boudinet's 1970s images of Alsace, distilled an essence of French rurality; rap and hip-hop musicians in Marseille personalized the street as *ma rue* (my street) at the heart of cultural assertion. Cohesion and conflict vied with each other for prominence. Memory, even collective memory, was unavoidably partial. Identities were made of this.

It is clear in the early years of the twenty-first century that the issues raised by the question of multiculturalism cannot be adequately discussed purely with regard to France and Frenchness. The European dimensions of the issue, greatly increased by enlargement of the EU, impose themselves. The making of a multicultural Europe is not a new process: diasporas of different peoples and the settlement of immigrants and refugees have happened before. They brought new cultures to Europe and to France. Only narrow nationalist historiographies occluded the impact they made on European, and French, identity. The challenge of creating a constitution for a still-expanding Europe involves a new awareness of the multiculturalism deemed essential for a larger community of equal citizens. No less than decolonization, this challenge has brought more pressure on the unitary French state, but it need not curb a discerning use of reason nor the contribution of its humanist tradition. In the Europe and world of the present, the struggles of people to be heard and included in the France of the twentieth century constitute a human and rational legacy for new, and old, forms of politics to carry forward.

Notes

INTRODUCTION

1. Stanley Hoffmann, Charles P. Kindleberger, Laurence Wylie, Jesse R. Pitts, Jean-Baptiste Duroselle and François Goguel, *In Search of France*, Cambridge, Mass., Harvard University Press, 1963.

PART ONE THE PRIMACY OF THE REPUBLIC, 1900S – 31

INTRODUCTION TO PART ONE

1. 'Une heure avec M. Julien Benda', *Les Nouvelles littéraires*, 23 May 1925, quoted in Michel Winock, *Le Siècle des intellectuels*, Paris, Seuil, 1997, p. 239.
2. Régis Debray, 'Êtes-vous démocrate ou républicain?', *Le Nouvel Observateur*, 30 November 1989, quoted in John Marks and Enda McCaffrey (eds.), *French Cultural Debates*, Melbourne, Monash University, 2001, p. 3.

CHAPTER I THE USE AND ABUSE OF REASON, 1900–1906

1. Ferdinand Buisson, 'Allocution au congrès de la ligue de l'enseignement', Tunis, April 1903, reprinted in *Cahiers laïques*, No. 30, November–December 1955, pp. 16–18.
2. Pierre-Jakez Hélias, *The Horse of Pride. Life in a Breton Village*, translated by June Guicharnaud, New Haven and London, Yale University Press, 1978, pp. 131–40.
3. Jean Jaurès, 'Discours à la jeunesse', Albi, 1903, reprinted in *Cahiers laïques*, No. 30, November–December 1955, pp. 4–11.
4. Quoted in Azzedine Haddour, *Colonial Myths: History and Narrative*, Manchester, Manchester University Press, 2000, p. 38.
5. Philip Dine, *French Rugby Football. A Cultural History*, Oxford, Berg, 2001, p. 34.

6. Hubertine Auclert, *Le Vote des femmes* (Paris, 1908), translated and quoted in Jennifer Waelti-Walters and Steven C. Hause (eds), *Feminisms of the Belle Époque*, Lincoln and London, University of Nebraska Press, 1994, p. 267.

7. Charles Sowerwine, *Sisters or Citizens? Women and socialism in France since 1876*, Cambridge, CUP, 1982, p. 113.

8. Georges Clemenceau, *La 'Justice' du sexe fort* (Paris, 1907), translated and quoted in Steven C. Hause with Anne R. Kenney, *Women's Suffrage and Social Politics in the French Third Republic*, Princeton, Princeton University Press, 1984, p. 16.

9. Quoted in Georges Dupeux, *French Society 1789–1970*, London, Methuen, 1976, pp. 185–6.

CHAPTER 2 NEW FORCES: SOCIALISM AND SYNDICALISM, 1900–1909

1. Patricia Hilden, *Working Women and Socialist Politics in France, 1880–1914. A regional study*, Oxford, Clarendon Press, 1986. The report by Marcelle Capy is quoted on p. 27.

2. Tony Judt, *Socialism in Provence, 1871–1914. A study in the origins of the modern French Left*, Cambridge, CUP, 1979.

3. Gérard Noiriel, *Les Ouvriers dans la société française, XIXe–XXe siècle*, Paris, Seuil, 1986, pp. 110–11.

CHAPTER 3 NEW FORCES: NATIONALISM AND PATRIOTISM, 1900–1914

1. Philip Nord, *Paris Shopkeepers and the Politics of Resentment*, Princeton, Princeton University Press, 1986.

2. Charles Péguy, *Cahiers de la Quinzaine*, 22 October 1905.

3. Quoted in Karen Offen, 'Exploring the Sexual Politics of Republican Nationalism', in Robert Tombs (ed.), *Nationhood and Nationalism in France*, London, HarperCollins, 1991, p. 200.

4. Quoted in Charles Sowerwine, *Sister or Citizens? Women and Socialism in France since 1876*, Cambridge, CUP 1982, p. 143.

CHAPTER 4 TOTAL WAR, 1914–1918

1. Henri Castex, *Verdun, années infernales. Lettres d'un soldat au front (août 1914–septembre 1916)*, Paris, Imago, 1996, pp. 47, 51. Captain Anatole Castex, the author of the letters, was killed on 6 September 1916 in the wood of Vaux-Chapitre close to Verdun.

2. ibid., p. 53.

3. Jean-Jacques Becker, *The Great War and the French People*, New York, St Martin's Press, 1986, p. 16.

4. Castex, *Verdun*, p. 50.

5. Yves Pourcher, *Les Jours de guerre. La vie des Français au jour le jour entre 1914 et 1918*, Paris, Plon, 1994, pp. 53–6.

6. Quoted in John Horne and Alan Kramer, 'German "Atrocities" and Franco-German Opinion, 1914: The Evidence of German Soldiers' Diaries', *Journal of Modern History*, Vol. 66, No. 1, 1994, pp. 1–33. See their ground-breaking *German Atrocities 1914. A History of Denial*, New Haven and London, Yale University Press, 2001.

7. *Les Carnets de guerre de Louis Barthas, tonnelier, 1914–1918*, Paris, La Découverte, 1997, pp. 67, 170, 211, 215.

8. *La Sainte-Biffe. Témoignages de survivants du 155e R.I.*, n.l., 1976, p. 140. Léon Sebelin was killed at Marie-Thérèse on 2 August 1915.

9. See John Horne, '"L'impôt du sang": Republican Rhetoric and Industrial Warfare in France, 1914–18', *Social History*, Vol. 14, No. 2, 1989, pp. 201–23.

10. Henri Barbusse, *Le Feu (Under Fire)*, translated by W. Fitzwater Wray, London, Dent, 1926, pp. 334–42.

11. Becker, *The Great War*, p. 63.

12. Quoted in Georges Lefranc, *Le Mouvement syndical sous la Troisième République*, Paris, Payot, 1967, p. 204.

13. *Mémoires d'outre-mer: les colonies et la Première Guerre Mondiale*, exhibition catalogue, Historial de la Grande Guerre, Péronne, 1996, pp. 30, 59.

14. Quote from Henri Lavedan in *L'Illustration*, taken from Becker, *The Great War*, p. 164.

15. Quoted in Christine Bard, *Les Filles de Marianne. Histoire des féminismes, 1914–1940*, Paris, Fayard, 1995, p. 105.

16. Barthas, *Carnets*, p. 422.

17. Hervé Jovelin, 'Poilu's Park (1914–1919), un parc d'attractions pour soldats sur le front', *Guerres Mondiales et Conflits Contemporains*, No. 183, October 1996, pp. 111–23.

18. Leonard V. Smith, 'Remobilizing the Citizen-soldier through the French Army Mutinies of 1917', in John Horne (ed.), *State, Society and Mobilization in Europe during the First World War*, Cambridge, CUP, 1997, p. 145.

19. Fédération Nationale des Syndicats d'Institutrices et d'Instituteurs Publics, Section de la Charente, *Les Instituteurs syndicalistes et la guerre*, Dignac, 1917.

20. Paper by Commandant Herscher, 12 July 1917, quoted in Anthony Adamthwaite, *Grandeur and Misery. France's bid for power in Europe 1914–1940*, London, Arnold, 1995, p. 37.

21. Quoted in John Horne, *Labour at War. France and Britain 1914–1918*, Oxford, OUP 1991, p. 211.

22. Quoted in *14–18: Mourir pour la Patrie*, Paris, Seuil, 1992, p. 272.

23. Barthas, *Carnets*, pp. 548–9.

CHAPTER 5 THE REPUBLIC AT WAR AND PEACE,
1914–1920S

1. From a reporter of the *Morning Post* who arrived in Lille on 14 December 1918, quoted in *14–18: Mourir pour la patrie*, Paris, Seuil, 1992, p. 251.

2. Pascale Verdier, *Les Instituteurs meusiens, témoins de l'occupation allemande 1914–1918*, Collection Meuse, Archives départementales, 1997. Jeanne Macquart's report is on pp. 97–111.

3. Jean-Yves Bonnard and Didier Guénaff, *La Première Guerre Mondiale dans l'Oise: Chiry-Ourscamp, commune martyre*, Chiry-Ourscamp, 1997.

4. *Les Carnets de guerre de Louis Barthas, tonnelier, 1914–1918*. Paris, La Découverte, 1997, p. 552.

5. Jay Winter, *Sites of Memory, Sites of Mourning. The Great War in European cultural history*, Cambridge, CUP, 1995, p. 26.

6. The suit was named after a Secretary of State to the War Ministry, who had introduced the idea. It was repudiated as being too obviously a kind of civilian uniform.

7. Antoine Prost, 'Verdun', in Pierre Nora (ed.), *Les Lieux de mémoire*, Part II, *La Nation*, Paris, Gallimard, 1986, Vol. 3, pp.111–41.

8. Jean-Louis Robert, 'The image of the profiteer', in Jay Winter and Jean-Louis Robert, *Capital Cities at War: Paris, London, Berlin, 1914–1919*, Cambridge, CUP, 1997, pp. 106–7.

9. Fernand Boverat, *Une Politique gouvernementale de natalité. Étude présentée, sur sa demande, à M. le Président du Conseil des Ministres par l'Alliance Nationale pour l'accroissement de la population française*, Paris, Alliance Nationale, 1924.

10. See Mary Louise Roberts, *Civilization without Sexes. Reconstructing Gender in Postwar France, 1917–1927*, Chicago, Chicago University Press, 1994.

11. Ephraïm Grenadou and Alain Prévost, *Grenadou, paysan français*, Paris, Seuil, 1966, pp. 133–4.

12. Quoted in Paul Smith, *Feminism and the Third Republic. Women's Political and Civil Rights in France, 1918–1945*, Oxford, Clarendon Press, 1996, p. 111.

13. *Le Désarmement général et l'armée de la défense*, Paris, Librairie Populaire (SFIO), 1922.

14. *Rapport de la commission chargée d'étudier la question 'A': rapprochement franco-allemand, rapprochement franco-russe, Société des Nations*, Neuilly-sur-Seine, Loge 'La Lumière', 1922; Pierre Parot, *Causerie*, Paris, Berland, 1932.

15. Christine Bard, *Les Filles de Marianne. Histoire des féminismes, 1914–1940*, Paris, Fayard, 1995, pp. 135–41; Siân Reynolds, *France Between the Wars. Gender and Politics*, London, Routledge, 1996, pp. 181–94.

16. Anthony Adamthwaite, *Grandeur and Misery. France's bid for power in Europe, 1914–1940*, London, Arnold, 1955, pp. 110–39.

CHAPTER 6 A DISTINCTIVE SOCIETY, 1920–1931

1. Eugen Weber, *Peasants into Frenchmen, 1870–1914*, London, Chatto & Windus, 1977.

2. William Kidd, *Les Monuments aux morts mosellans*, Metz, Éditions Serpenoise, 1999, pp. 37–9.

3. Quoted in David Assouline and Mehdi Lallaoui, *Un Siècle d'immigrations en France. De l'usine au maquis, 1919–1945*, Paris, Syros, 1996, p. 23.

4. ibid., p. 24.

5. Jacqueline Costa-Lascoux and Émile Temime, *Les Hommes de Renault-Billancourt. Mémoire ouvrière de l'Île Seguin, 1930–1992*, Paris, Autrement, 2004, p. 34.

6. Roger Magraw, *A History of the French Working Class. Vol. II, Workers and the Bourgeois Republic*, Oxford, Blackwell, 1992, p. 231. See also Gérard Noiriel, *Les Ouvriers dans la société française XIXe–XXe siècle*, Paris, Seuil, 1986, and *Longwy. Immigrés et prolétaires*, Paris, PUF, 1984.

7. Siân Reynolds, *France Between the Wars. Gender and Politics*, London, Routledge, 1996, pp. 102–5.

8. Laura Lee Downs, *Childhood in the Promised Land. Working-Class Movements and the Colonies de Vacances in France, 1880–1960*, Durham, Duke University Press, 2002, p. 272.

9. Hélène Desbrousses, *Le Mouvement des masses ouvrières en France entre les deux guerres d'après 'La Vie ouvrière'*, Paris, Centre de Sociologie Historique, 1975.

10. Patrick Barrau and René Bianco, *Le Théâtre social, 1900–1914. Un essai de culture ouvrière*, Marseille, Centre International de Recherches sur l'Anarchisme, 1976, pp. 41–5.

11. Quoted in David James Fisher, 'The Origins of the French Popular Theatre', *Journal of Contemporary History*, Vol. 12, 1977, p. 475.

12. *L'Illustration*, 18 May 1907, reproduced in the exhibition catalogue, *La Belle Époque*, Paris, Archives Nationales, 1972, Exhibit 269.

13. Quoted by G. Guilleminault, *Prélude à la Belle Époque*, Paris, Denoël, 1956, p. 106.

14. The term 'le Parmentier du jazz' came from the artist Francis Picabia, as quoted in Nadja Maillard, 'Le jazz dans la littérature française (1920–1940)', *Europe*, special issue on *Jazz et littérature*, No. 820–21, August–September 1997, p. 48.

15. See J. F. V. Keiger, *Raymond Poincaré*, Cambridge, CUP, 1997, pp. 312–44.

16. *Voyage en Algérie de M. Alexandre Millerand*, Algiers, République Française, 1922, p. 5.

17. 'Ne visitez pas l'Exposition coloniale', *Tracts Surréalistes*, Paris, Losfeld, 1980, Vol. 1, 1922–1939, pp. 194–5. The signatories included Éluard, Aragon, Breton, René Char, Yves Tanguy and Georges Sadoul.

18. Herman Lebovics, *True France. The Wars over Cultural Identity, 1900–1945*, Ithaca, Cornell University Press, 1992, pp. 110–21.

19. Quoted in Jean-François Sirinelli, *Intellectuels et passions françaises*, Paris, Gallimard, 1990, p. 103.

20. Quoted in Dominique Olivesi, 'Les instituteurs rouges des Alpes-Maritimes', *Les Cahiers de l'IHTP*, No. 26, March 1994, p. 147. The number is entitled *Intellectuels engagés d'une guerre à l'autre* and is edited by Nicole Racine and Michel Trebitsch.

21. Alison Murray, 'Le Tourisme Citroën au Sahara (1924–25)', *Vingtième Siècle*, No. 68, October–December 2000, pp. 95–107.

PART TWO THE SPIRAL OF IDEOLOGY, 1920S–1969

CHAPTER 7 MANIPULATING CRISIS, 1920S–1934

1. Henri Barbusse, *Manifeste aux intellectuels*, Paris, Écrivains Réunis, 1927, pp. 11–12, 43.

2. Jacques Maritain, *Primauté du spirituel*, Paris, Plon, 1927. See Jean-Louis Loubet del Bayle, *Les Non-conformistes des années 30: une tentative de renouvellement de la pensée politique française*, Paris, Seuil, 1969, p. 40.

3. Georges Bernanos, *Noël à la maison de France*, Paris, Éditions les Cahiers Libres, 1930, pp. 18, 21, 30.

4. Édouard Vaillant, *Opportunistes, Radicaux et Socialistes*, Paris, Publications de *La Femme socialiste*, 1930, avant-propos par Louise Saumoneau.

5. Albert Thibaudet, 'Réflexions sur la politique', *Nouvelle Revue Française*, April 1928, quoted and analysed by Martyn Cornick in his article 'Unity and Discord: The *Nouvelle Revue Française* and Intellectual Responses to Politics and Ideology in the 1930s', *Nottingham French Studies*, Special Number, Autumn–Winter 1992, pp. 1–15.

6. *Syndicalisme révolutionnaire et communisme. Les archives de Pierre Monatte, 1914–1924*, Paris, Maspero, 1968, pp. 407–13.

7. Étienne Fajon, *Ma vie s'appelle liberté*, Paris, Laffont, 1976, pp. 44–54.

8. See Tony Judt, *Marxism and the French Left. Studies on Labour and Politics in France, 1830–1981*, Oxford, Clarendon Press, 1986, pp. 115–68.

9. *Le Courrier français*, No. 2, 1938. Quoted in Pierre Milza, *Fascisme français. Passé et présent*, Paris, Flammarion, 1987, p. 133.

10. See, for example, Serge Berstein, *La France des années 30*, Paris, Colin, 1988, pp. 25–46.

11. Paul Reynaud, *Jeunesse, quelle France veux-tu?* Paris, Gallimard, 1936, p. 17.

12. Cover drawing, *L'Animateur des Temps Nouveaux*, 30 December 1932.

13. Christine Bard, *Les Filles de Marianne, Histoire des féminismes, 1914–1940*, Paris, Fayard, 1995, p. 313.

CHAPTER 8 CONFRONTATIONS, 1934–1936

1. Gilles Martinet, *Une Certaine idée de la gauche (1936–1997)*, Paris, Odile Jacob, 1997, pp. 15, 79.

2. *Je suis partout*, 5 February 1943.

3. Kevin Passmore, *From Liberalism to Fascism. The right in a French province, 1928–1939*, Cambridge, CUP, 1997, p. 218.

4. Quoted by Antoine Prost, 'Les manifestations du 12 février 1934 en province', in Jean Bouvier (ed.), *La France en mouvement, 1934–1938*, Seyssel, Champ Vallon, 1986, p. 27.

5. Antoine de Saint-Exupéry, *Terre des hommes* (1939), in *Oeuvres complètes*, Paris, Gallimard, 1994, Vol. 1, p.283.

6. Ephraïm Grenadou and Alain Prévost, *Grenadou, paysan français*, Paris, Seuil, 1966, p. 172.

7. The manifesto is reproduced by Nicole Racine-Furlaud, 'Antifascistes et pacifistes: le Comité de Vigilance des Intellectuels Antifascistes', in Anne Roche and Christian Tarting (eds), *Des Années Trente*, Paris, Éditions CNRS, 1985, pp. 58–9.

8. Robert Soucy, *French Fascism: The Second Wave, 1933–1939*, New Haven, Yale University Press, 1995, p. 108.

9. Passmore, *From Liberalism to Fascism*, pp. 229–36.

10. For a full analysis of the relationship between Dorgères and Le Roy Ladurie see Robert Paxton, *Le Temps des Chemises Vertes. Révoltes paysannes et fascisme rural, 1929–1939*, Paris, Seuil, 1996.

11. Henri Dorgères, *Au XXe siècle. Dix ans de jacquerie*, Paris, Scorpion, 1959, p. 107.

12. See the study of the Creuse, Corrèze, Dordogne and Haute-Vienne by Laird Boswell, *Rural Communism in France, 1920–1939*, Ithaca, Cornell University Press, 1998.

13. Danielle Tartakowsky, 'Stratégies de la rue 1934–1936', in Bouvier (ed.), *La France en mouvement*, p. 58.

14. The figures are all drawn from the standard work on the elections, Georges Dupeux, *Le Front Populaire et les élections de 1936*, Paris, Colin, 1959 pp. 125–40. Subsequent comments on the geographical strengths of the parties are also dependent on his analysis and maps, pp. 141–71.

15. Boswell, *Rural Communism*, pp. 236–9.

CHAPTER 9 POPULAR FRONT, 1936–1938

1. Noëlle Gérôme, 'Images de l'occupation de l'usine à gaz de Poitiers', in Jean Bouvier (ed.), *La France en mouvement, 1934–1938*, Seyssel, Champ Vallon, 1986, pp. 62–7.

2. Robert Capa, David Seymour 'Chim' and Georgette Elgey, *Front populaire*, Paris, Chêne-Magnum, 1976, p. 46.

3. David Berry, 'The other Popular Front: French anarchism and the Front Révolutionnaire', in Martin S. Alexander and Helen Graham (eds), *The French and Spanish Popular Fronts. Comparative Perspectives*, Cambridge, CUP, 1989, pp. 131–44.

4. See Léon Blum, *Pour être socialiste*, Paris, Éditions Socialistes, 1919.

5. Quoted in Charles Sowerwine, *Sisters or Citizens? Women and Socialism in France since 1876*, Cambridge, CUP, 1982, p. 133.

6. See Siân Reynolds, *France Between the Wars, Gender and politics*, London, Routledge, 1996, pp. 150–53, 159–62; Paul Smith, *Feminism and the Third Republic, Women's Political and Civil Rights in France, 1918–1945*, Oxford, Clarendon Press, 1996, pp. 101–2; Christine Bard, *Les Filles de Marianne, Histoire des Féminismes, 1914–1940*, Paris, Fayard, 1995, pp. 352–6.

7. Quoted by Vicki Caron, *Uneasy Asylum. France and the Jewish Refugee Crisis, 1933–1942*, Stanford, Stanford University Press, 1999, p. 129, an important source for all sections in this chapter on refugees.

8. *Les Oeuvres de plein air et de vacances*, Lille, Association des Maires du Nord et de l'Est, 1935; *Vacances: carnet de route*, Paris, JEC, 1936.

9. All issues of *congés payés* were meticulously presented in the first full study in 1939, Jean-Victor Parant, *Le Problème du tourisme populaire*, Paris, Pichon and Durand-Auzias, 1939.

10. See Julian Jackson, '*Le Temps des loisirs*: popular tourism and mass leisure in the vision of the Front Populaire', in Alexander and Graham (eds), *French and Spanish Popular Fronts*, pp. 226–39.

11. L.-O. Frossard, *Le Désert au village*, Paris, Gallimard, 1938 pp. 9, 11,39.

12. Shanny Peer, *France on Display. Peasants, Provincials and Folklore in the 1937 Paris World Fair*, Albany, State University of New York Press, 1998.

13. Theodore Zeldin, *France 1848–1945*, Oxford, Clarendon Press, 1977, Vol. 2, pp. 60–64; Solange and Christian Gras, *La Révolte des régions d'Europe occidentale de 1916 à nos jours*, Paris, PUF, 1982, p. 138.

14. Peer, *France on Display*, p. 97.

15. Jean Touchard, 'L'esprit des années trente', in *Tendances politiques dans la vie française depuis 1789*, Paris, Hachette, 1960; Jean-Louis Loubet del Bayle, *Les Non-conformistes des années 30*, Paris, Seuil, 1969; Aline Coutrot, *Un Courant de la pensée catholique: l'hebdomadaire 'Sept' (mars 1934–août 1937)*, Paris, Cerf, 1961.

16. See Jackie Clarke, 'Imagined productive communities: industrial rationalisation and cultural crisis in 1930s France', *Modern and Contemporary France*, Vol. 8, No.3, August 2000, pp. 345–57.

17. Quoted in Norman Ingram, *The Politics of Dissent: Pacifism in France 1919–1939*, Oxford, Clarendon Press, 1991, p. 274.

18. Rudolf Léonhard, *Confiance en Hitler? Autour d'une interview de M. Jean*

Goy, Paris, Comité Mondial des Femmes, 1935, Preface by Gabrielle Duchêne, p. 3.

19. Pierre Drieu la Rochelle, *Avec Doriot*, Paris, Gallimard, 1937, p. 20.

20. Kevin Passmore, *From Liberalism to Fascism, The right in a French province, 1928–1939*, Cambridge, CUP, 1997, p. 249.

21. La Rocque, *Le Mouvement Croix-de-Feu au secours de l'agriculture française*, n.l., n.d. [1935], p. 5.

22. See for example the Surrealist group's condemnation of the Moscow trials in tracts of 1936–7, *Tracts Surréalistes*, Paris, Losfeld, 1980, pp. 304–11.

23. Raymond Guyot, *Avec le Front Populaire allons au-devant de la vie!* Paris, Jeunesses Communistes, 1937.

24. See Marie-Monique Huss 'Pronatalism in the Inter-war Period in France', *Journal of Contemporary History*, Vol. 25, 1990, pp. 39–68.

25. *Le Bonnet Jaune, organe de combat contre l'invasion juive et la Franc-Maçonnerie*, Vol. 2, No. 2, March 1939.

26. Caron, *Uneasy Asylum*, p. 233.

CHAPTER 10 NOT ANOTHER WAR? SHATTERED ILLUSIONS, 1930S–1940

1. Quoted from Jean Giono, *Vivre libre. Lettre aux paysans sur la pauvreté et la paix*, Paris, Grasset, 1938, in Pierre de Boisdeffre, *Giono*, Paris, Gallimard, 1965, p. 118.

2. *L'Humanité*, 12 March 1938.

3. *Non! La guerre n'est pas fatale*, Paris, Comité de Vigilance des Intellectuels Antifascistes, 5 March 1936.

4. Quoted in Norman Ingram, *The Politics of Dissent. Pacifism in France 1919–1939*, Oxford, Clarendon Press, 1991, p. 225, to which this section is much indebted.

5. Quoted in Robert Zaretsky, *Nîmes at War. Religion, Politics, and Public Opinion in the Gard, 1938–1944*, University Park Pennsylvania, Penn State Press, 1995, p. 40.

6. Quoted in Jean-Pierre Azéma and François Bédarida (eds), *La France des années noires*, Paris, Seuil, Vol. 1, p. 53.

7. Quoted in Pierre Laborie, *L'Opinion française sous Vichy*, Paris, Seuil, 1990, p. 212.

8. Quoted in Julian Jackson, *The Fall of France. The Nazi Invasion of 1940*, Oxford, OUP, 2003, p. 93.

9. See Jean Vidalenc, *L'Exode de mai–juin 1940*, Paris, PUF, 1957.

10. Philippe Pétain, *Appels et messages*, Paris, Fasquelle, 1941, p. 15; Charles de Gaulle, *Mémoires de guerre. L'Appel 1940–1942*, Paris, Plon, 1954, p. 267.

CHAPTER 11 OCCUPIED FRANCE (1). VICHY AND COLLABORATION, 1940-1944

1. Jean-Paul Sartre, 'La République du silence' in *Situations, III*, Paris, Gallimard, 1949, p. 11. 'Never have we been more free than under the German Occupation . . . [because] every one of our actions had the weight of a commitment.'

2. See Chapter 9.

3. Quoted in Denis Peschanski, *Vichy 1940-1944. Contrôle et exclusion*, Paris, Éditions Complexe, 1997, p. 160.

4. Miranda Pollard, 'Vichy and Abortion: Policing the Body and the New Moral Order in Everyday Life', in Sarah Fishman, Laura Lee Downs, Ioannis Sinanoglou, Leonard V. Smith and Robert Zaretsky (eds), *France at War. Vichy and the Historians*, Oxford, Berg, 2000, pp. 191-204.

5. The figures were set out in every detail taken painstakingly from the German archives by Serge and Beate Klarsfeld. See Chapter 22.

6. Stéphane Courtois and Adam Rayski (eds), *Qui savait quoi? L'extermination des Juifs 1941-1945*, Paris, La Découverte, 1987.

7. *Ici Londres, 1940-1944. Les voix de la liberté*, Paris, La Documentation Française, 1975, Vol. 2, pp. 159-60.

8. Robert Paxton, *Vichy France: Old Guard and New Order, 1940-1944*, New York, Columbia University Press, 1972.

9. Quoted in Julian Jackson, *France, the Dark Years 1940-1944*, Oxford, OUP, 2001, p. 327.

CHAPTER 12 OCCUPIED FRANCE (2). RESISTANCE AND LIBERATION, 1940-1944

1. Jean Guéhenno, *Journal des années noires, 1940-1944*, Paris, Gallimard, 1947, p. 16.

2. Quoted and recounted in Nancy Wood, *Germaine Tillion, une femme-mémoire. D'une Algérie à l'autre*, Paris, Autrement, 2003, pp. 56-7.

3. Quoted by Olivier Wieviorka, *Une Certaine idée de la résistance: Défense de la France, 1940-1949*, Paris, Seuil, 1995, p. 26.

4. *La France Libre*, Vol. 1, No. 1, 15 November 1940, p. 23.

5. Quoted by Jean-Louis Crémieux-Brilhac in *Les Voix de la liberté. Ici Londres 1940-1944*, Paris, La Documentation Française, 1975, Vol. 1, p. xv.

6. Quoted in Alya Aglan, *La Résistance sacrifiée. Le mouvement 'Libération-Nord'*, Paris, Flammarion, 1999, p. 36.

7. The phrase is James C. Scott's. See his *Weapons of the Weak. Everyday Forms of Peasant Resistance*, New Haven, Yale University Press, 1985, especially pp. 28-47.

8. See Simon Kitson, *Vichy et la chasse aux espions nazis*, Paris, Antrement, 2005.

9. Étienne Dejonghe and Yves Maner, *Le Nord–Pas-de-Calais dans la main allemande, 1940–1944*, Lille, La Voix du Nord, 1999, p. 311.

10. Quoted in Denis Peschanski, *Vichy, 1940–1944, Contrôle et exclusion*, Paris, Éditions Complexe, 1997, p. 119.

11. *The Speeches of General de Gaulle*, Oxford, OUP, 1942, p. 87.

12. Paul Éluard, *Gabriel Péri*, 1944, in *Oeuvres complètes*, Paris, Gallimard, 1968, p. 1262. See also *Péguy Péri: deux voix françaises*, Paris, Éditions de Minuit, 1944.

13. *Déclaration du général de Gaulle publiée en France dans les journaux clandestins, le 23 juin 1942*, in Charles de Gaulle, *Mémoires de Guerre*, Vol. 1, *L'Appel, 1940–1942*, Paris, Plon, 1954, p. 678.

14. Quoted in Guillaume Piketty, *Pierre Brossolette. Un héros de la Résistance*, Paris, Odile Jacob, 1998, p. 123.

15. Laurent Daniel (Elsa Triolet), *Les Amants d'Avignon*, Paris, Éditions de Minuit, 1943, pp. 13, 17.

16. *Un Évêque français sous l'occupation. Extraits des messages de Mgr Saliège*, Toulouse, Éditions Ouvrières, 1945.

17. Michel Fabreguet in Pierre Bolle (ed.), *Le Plateau Vivarais-Lignon. Accueil et Résistance 1939–1944*, Le Chambon-sur-Lignon, Société d'Histoire de la Montagne, 1992, p. 140.

18. *Ici Londres, 1940–1944. Les voix de la liberté*, Paris, La Documentation Francaise, 1975, Vol. 2, p. 67.

19. Serge Ravanel, *L'Esprit de résistance*, Paris, Seuil, 1995, p. 15.

20. Robert Gildea, *Marianne in Chains. In Search of the German Occupation 1940–1945*, London, Macmillan, 2002, p. 13.

21. The most detailed, scholarly analysis is that of Fabrice Virgili, *La France 'virile'. Des femmes tondues à la libération*, Paris, Payot, 2000, pp. 59–84. The figures in this paragraph derive from his extensive research.

22. The two terms 'violences communautaires' and 'épuration de voisinage' are those used with great subtlety and originality by Luc Capdevila, *Les Bretons au lendemain de l'Occupation. Imaginaire et comportement d'une sortie de guerre 1944–1945*, Rennes, Presses Universitaires de Rennes, 1999, pp. 124–96.

CHAPTER 13 ENDING WAR . . . NOT IN INDO-CHINA OR ALGERIA, 1944–1962

1. Margaret Collins Weitz, *Sisters in the Resistance. How Women Fought to Free France, 1940–1945*, New York, John Wiley, 1995, p. 132.

2. The figures come from the most authoritative summary of the different official enquiries, and from research which was still proceeding at the end of the century: Henry Rousso, 'L'épuration, une histoire inachevée', *Vingtième Siècle*, No. 33, January–March, 1992, reproduced in Henry Rousso, *Vichy. L'événement, la mémoire, l'histoire*, Paris, Gallimard, 2001, pp. 489–552.

3. Karen Adler, *Jews and Gender in Liberation France*, Cambridge, CUP, 2003, pp. 106–43; Gérard Noiriel, *Les Origines républicaines de Vichy*, Paris, Hachette, 1999, pp. 276–9.

4. PCF figures quoted in Claire Andrieu, 'Les résistantes, perspectives de recherche', in Antoine Prost (ed.), *La Résistance, une histoire sociale*, Paris, Éditions de l'Atelier, 1997, p. 76.

5. The date was 25 October 1944. Quoted in Guy Pervillé, *De l'Empire français à la décolonisation*, Paris, Hachette, 1995, pp. 101–3.

6. Danièle Djamila Amrane-Minne, *Des femmes dans la guerre d'Algérie*, Paris, Karthala, 1994, pp. 165–6.

7. Pierre Stibbe, *Justice pour les Malgaches*, Paris, Seuil, 1954, pp. 19–44.

8. General Catroux, 'L'Union Française', *Politique étrangère*, Vol. 18, No. 4, September–October 1953, p. 266.

9. Minute of an inter-ministerial committee, 29 November 1946, cited by Alan Ruscio, *La Guerre française d'Indochine*, Paris, Éditions Complexe, 1992, p. 83.

10. See Nicola Cooper, 'Urban planning and architecture in colonial Indochina', *French Cultural Studies*, Vol. 11, No. 31, February 2000, pp. 75–99.

11. *L'Affaire Henri Martin*, Paris, Gallimard, 1953. The book has commentary by Jean-Paul Sartre and text from Hervé Bazin, Marc Beigbeder, Jean-Marie Domenach, Francis Jeanson, Michel Leiris, Jacques Madaule, Marcel Ner, Jean Painlevé, Roger Pinto, Jacques Prévert, Roland de Pury, Jean-Henri Roy, Vercors and Louis de Villefosse.

12. 'Le Drame Tunisien', *Cahiers du Témoignage chrétien*, No. XXXIV, 1952.

13. 'La Question marocaine: problème et solutions; le gouvernement français devant ses responsabilités', *Les Cahiers du Maroc*, No. 4, December 1954.

14. François Mitterrand, *Présence française et abandon*, Paris, Plon, 1957, p. 237.

15. *Algérie?* Algiers, Service de l'Information, 1955; *Le Destin de la France se joue en Algérie*, Algiers, Union Syndicale Algérienne d'Action Économique et Sociale, 1955.

16. Jacques Soustelle, *Le Sahara d'aujourd'hui et la France de l'an 2000*, Paris, Conférences des Ambassadeurs, No. 22, 1959.

17. See special issue of *Esprit*, No. 261, February 2000, subtitled 'Les Vies de Germaine Tillion. Résistance, Ravensbrück, Aurès, Algérie, le réseau du Musée de l'Homme, l'anthropologue et l'avilissement des femmes'.

18. Amrane-Minne, *Des femmes dans la guerre*, pp. 138,140.

19. Camille Lacoste-Dujardin, *Opération Oiseau bleu: des Kabyles, des ethnologues et la guerre d'Algérie*, Paris, La Découverte, 1997, pp. 42–92.

20. As documented in *Nous accusons . . . Dossier sur la torture et la répression en Algérie* compiled by the Ligue des Droits de l'Homme and other groupings, September 1958.

21. Pierre Vidal-Naquet, *La Raison d'État*, Paris, Éditions de Minuit, 1962; *Torture: Cancer of Democracy, France and Algeria 1954–62*, London, Penguin,

1963. The Penguin book was not published in French until nine years later as *La Torture dans la République*, Paris, Éditions de Minuit, 1972.

22. *Nous accusons . . . Dossier sur la torture et la répression en Algérie*. Sent to René Coty, President of the Republic and Charles de Gaulle, Prime Minister, on 12 September 1958, and seized immediately by the police.

23. Claire Mauss-Copeaux, *Appelés en Algérie. La parole confisquée*, Paris, Hachette, 1998, pp. 124-6.

24. Martin Evans, *The Memory of Resistance. French Opposition to the Algerian War (1954-1962)*, Oxford, Berg, 1997, pp. 31-72.

25. Ibid., p. 62. The interview with Micheline Pouteau was conducted in April 1989.

26. Jean Lacouture, *De Gaulle. The Ruler: 1945-1970*, London, Collins Harvill, 1991, p. 318; Benjamin Stora, *La Gangrène et l'oubli. La mémoire de la guerre d'Algérie*, Paris, La Découverte, 1991/1998, pp. 180-84.

27. Gilles Manceron and Hassan Remaoun, *D'une rive à l'autre. La guerre d'Algérie: de la mémoire à l'histoire*, Paris, Syros, 1993, pp. 155-6; Charles-Robert Ageron, 'Les pertes humaines de la guerre d'Algérie', in *La France en guerre d'Algérie*, Paris, BDIC, 1992, pp. 170-75.

28. Pierre Vidal-Naquet, *Face à la raison d'État. Un historien dans la guerre d'Algérie*, Paris, La Découverte, 1989, pp. 45-82; Charles-Robert Ageron (ed.), *L'Algérie des Français*, Paris, Seuil, 1993, p. 273.

29. Benjamin Stora, 'Guerre d'Algérie: le Vietnam français?', in Ageron (ed.), *L'Algérie des Français*, p. 326.

CHAPTER 14 THE CHEQUERED IMPERATIVE OF CHANGE, 1940S-1958

1. Quoted in Evelyne Desbois, Yves Jeanneau, Bruno Mattéi, *La Foi des charbonniers. Les mineurs dans la Bataille du charbon 1945-1947*, Paris, Maison des Sciences de l'Homme, 1986, p. 9.

2. Richard Vinen, *Bourgeois Politics in France, 1945-1951*, Cambridge, CUP, 1995, pp. 58-62.

3. Quoted in Hilary Footitt, 'The First Women *Députés*: "les 33 glorieuses"?', in H. R. Kedward and Nancy Wood (eds), *The Liberation of France. Image and Event*, Oxford, Berg, 1995, p. 133.

4. Quoted in Paul Sanders, *Histoire du marché noir*, Paris, Perrin, 2001, p. 319.

5. See Robert Mencherini, *Guerre froide, grèves rouges. Parti communiste, Stalinisme et luttes sociales en France: les grèves 'insurrectionnelles' de 1947-1948*, Paris, Syllèpse, 1998.

6. 'La guerre de Moch contre les mineurs', speech by Gabriel Roucaute, 17 November 1948, in the Chamber of Deputies.

7. Renée Bédarida (ed.), *Un Non-Conformiste chez Schneider: Édouard Morin*

(1897–1967). Journal, Paris, Éditions Ouvrières and Éditions du Témoignage Chrétien, 1984, pp. 75, 23–4.

8. Roger Garaudy, *Lettre à Emmanuel Mounier, homme d'Esprit*, Paris, Nouvelle Critique, 1950, p. 2.

9. Author's interview with Raoul Calas, Paris, 1969.

10. Quoted in 'Les prêtres oubliés', *Libération*, 27 September 1993, pp. 24–5.

11. Simone de Beauvoir, *The Mandarins*, translated by Leonard M. Friedman, London, Fontana, 1960, p. 540.

12. See Alan S. Milward's impressive argument in *The European Rescue of the Nation-State*, London, Routledge, 1992.

13. For the importance of *Jour de fête* as a defence of Frenchness against Americanism, see David Bellos, 'Tati and America: *Jour de fête* and the Blum-Byrnes Agreement of 1946', in *Modern and Contemporary France*, Vol. 10, No. 29, June 1999, pp. 145–59.

14. Michèle Luc, *La Lutte de classe et le système politique*, Paris, Éditions Culture Populaire, 1984, pp. 54–5.

15. Jean Fourastié, *Les Trente Glorieuses ou la Révolution invisible de 1946 à 1975*, Paris, Fayard, 1979.

16. J. Walter Thompson, 'France, Europe's Fastest-growing Market', Analysis produced as a small pamphlet, Paris, February 1959.

17. Claire Duchen, *Women's Rights and Women's Lives in France, 1944–1968*, London, Routledge, 1994, p. 68; see also her 'Occupation Housewife: the Domestic Ideal in 1950s France', *French Cultural Studies*, Vol. 2, No. 4, February 1991, pp. 1–11.

18. *Les Années 50: la vie quotidienne de 1950 à 1959*, Rennes, Ouest-France, 1996, pp. 40–41.

19. See Chapter 13.

20. Richard Vinen, *France, 1934–1970*, London, Macmillan, 1996, p. 108.

21. Défense de l'Occident, *Le Poujadisme*, Paris, Les Sept Couleurs, 1956, p. 113.

22. Ephraïm Grenadou and Alain Prévost, *Grenadou, paysan français*, Paris, 1966, pp. 225–53; Henri Mendras, *La Fin des paysans. Innovation et changement dans l'agriculture française*, Paris, Sédéis, 1967.

23. SFIO, *L'Heure de l'Europe*, Paris, 1950.

CHAPTER 15 DE GAULLE'S ASCENDANCY, 1950S–1968

1. *Histoire d'aujourd'hui, 1957–8*, Paris, Hachette/*Paris-Match*, 1958.

2. Charles de Gaulle, *Mémoires de guerre: L'Appel, 1940–1942*, Paris, Plon, 1954, p. 1.

3. Edmond Michelet, *Contre la guerre civile*, Paris, Plon-Tribune Libre, 1957, p. 104.

4. De Gaulle, *Mémoires de guerre*, p. 1.

5. *Voyage du Général de Gaulle à Madagascar et en Afrique Noire, août 1958*, Tananarive, 1958, p. 12.

6. *Réception du Général de Gaulle à l'Assemblée fédérale du Mali*, Dakar, 1959, p. 2.

7. Madeleine Riffaud, *Ce que j'ai vu à Bizerte*. The articles appeared in *L'Humanité* and *L'Humanité Dimanche* from 22 July to 2 August, and were republished together by *L'Humanité*, Paris, 1961.

8. Ernest Renan, *Qu'est-ce qu'une nation?*, Paris, Calmann-Lévy, 1882, p. 27.

9. Pierre Cadot, 'Tour Eiffel', in *Chansonniers 60*, Paris, Pierre Horay, 1960, pp. 102–4.

10. Jean-François Revel, *Le Style du Général*, Paris, Julliard, 1959, p. 22.

11. *Présence de Bastien-Tiry*, Paris, Éditions du Fuseau, 1963.

12. Maurice Agulhon, *De Gaulle. Histoire, symbole, mythe*, Paris, Plon, 2000, pp. 79–86.

13. Hugo Frey, 'Rebuilding France: Gaullist historiography, the rise-fall myth and French identity (1945–58)', in Stefan Berger, Mark Donovan and Kevin Passmore (eds), *Writing National Histories. Western Europe since 1800*, London, Routledge, 1999, pp. 205–16.

14. Jean-François Bazin, *Le Chanoine Kir et Nikita Krouchtchev*, Dijon, Bazin, 1976, pp. 1–26.

15. Quoted in Michel Winock, *Le Siècle des intellectuels*, Paris, Seuil, 1997, p. 696.

16. Charles de Gaulle, *Discours et messages*, Paris, Plon, 1970, Vol. III, p. 134.

17. See Chapter 13.

18. Quoted in Jean Touchard, *Le gaullisme, 1940–1969*, Paris, Seuil, 1978, p. 271.

19. Alain Touraine, *La Société post-industrielle*, Paris, Denoël, 1969, translated by Leonard F. X. Mayhew as *The Post-Industrial Society*, London, Wildwood House, 1974, p. 9.

20. Jean Fourastié, *Les Trente Glorieuses ou La Révolution invisible de 1946 à 1975*, Paris, Fayard, 1979, p. 21.

21. Laurence Wylie, 'Social Change at the Grass Roots', in Stanley Hoffmann et al., *In Search of France*, Cambridge, Mass., Harvard University Press, 1963, pp. 163–4.

22. Michel Phlipponneau, *La Gauche et les régions*, Paris, Calmann–Lévy, 1967, pp. 28–50.

23. J.-F. Gravier, *La Question régionale*, Paris, Flammarion, 1970, p. 64.

24. Michel Debré, *Trois Républiques pour une France. Mémoires*, Paris, Albin Michel, 1988, Vol. 2, *1946–1958, Agir*, p. 435.

25. Wylie, 'Social Change . . .', in Hoffmann et al., *In Search of France*, p. 226.

26. Délégation à l'Aménagement du Territoire et à l'Action Régionale (DATAR).

27. Gravier, *La Question régionale*, pp. 65–82.

28. Robert Lafont, 'Une restructuration de la France', *Le Monde*, 6 November 1968.

29. John Ardagh, *France in the 1980s*, London, Penguin, 1982, pp. 137–8.

30. Quoted in David L. Looseley, *The Politics of Fun. Cultural Policy and Debate in Contemporary France*, Oxford, Berg, 1995, p. 41.

31. Jean Ferrat, quoted in Jean-François Chanet, 'Terroirs et pays: mort et transfiguration', *Vingtième Siècle*, No. 69, January–March 2001, p. 68.

32. Abdelmalek Sayad, *Un Nanterre algérien, terre de bidonvilles*, Paris, Autrement, 1995, p. 36.

33. Karen Adler, *Jews and Gender in Liberation France*, Cambridge, CUP, 2003, pp. 120–23.

34. Alec G. Hargreaves, *Immigration, 'Race' and Ethnicity in Contemporary France*, London, Routledge, pp. 10–13.

35. Sayad, *Un Nanterre algérien*, pp. 76–124.

36. *France and the Rising Generation*, New York, Ambassade de France, 1965, pp. 3–7.

37. Edgar Morin, *L'Esprit du temps*, Paris, Grasset, 1962, pp. 205–21. See also his *Commune en France: la métamorphose de Plodémet*, Paris, Fayard, 1967.

38. Quoted from the archives of the Renseignements Généraux in *Le Nouvel Observateur*, 23–29 April 1998, p. 12.

CHAPTER 16 MAY–JUNE 1968

1. *Les Racistes contre la République*, Supplement to No. 247 of *Droit et liberté*, s.l., s.d.

2. Archives of the Renseignements Généraux, selected and reprinted in 'Mai 68: les archives secrètes de la police', *L'Express*, 19 March 1998, p 47.

3. Quoted in Mark Hunter, *Les Jours les plus Lang*, Paris, Odile Jacob, 1990, p. 46.

4. Edgar Morin, 'Sociologie d'un échec', *France-Observateur*, 5 November 1959, quoted in Henri Weber, *Que reste-t-il de mai 68? Essai sur les interprétations des 'événements'*, Paris, Seuil, 1998, p. 89. Weber's essay first appeared in 1988 as part of the twentieth anniversary of May 1968.

5. See Gilles Lipovetsky, *L'Ère du vide*, Paris, Gallimard, 1983.

6. For an early case-study of the nature of strike activity in 1968 with a chapter on immigrant strikers, see Danièle Kergoat, *Bulledor ou l'histoire d'une mobilisation ouvrière*, Seuil, 1973.

7. Vincent Porhel, 'L'Autogestion à la CSF de Brest', in G. Dreyfus-Armand et al. (eds), *Les Années '68: le temps de la contestation*, Paris, Éditions Complexe, 2000, pp. 379–97.

8. Alain Touraine, *La Société post-industrielle*, Paris, Denoël, 1969.

9. Daniel Gordon, 'Immigrants and the New Left in France, 1968–1971', D. Phil thesis, University of Sussex, 2001, pp. 182–90.

PART THREE ISSUES OF IDENTITY, 1960S–2000S

INTRODUCTION TO PART THREE

1. Michel Crozier, *La Société bloquée*, Paris, Seuil, 1971.

CHAPTER 17 WHOSE NEW SOCIETY?, 1960S–1979

1. Quoted in Claire Duchen, *Women's Rights and Women's Lives in France, 1944–1968*, London, Routledge, 1994, p. 199.
2. Henri Mendras, *La Fin des paysans* (see above, Chapter 14); *La Seconde Révolution française (1965–1984)*, Paris, Gallimard, 1988. Compare the diagnosis by John Ardagh of a France in radical transition: *The New French Revolution*, London, Secker & Warburg, 1968, re-edited for Penguin in 1970 as *The New France* and subsequently updated in 1982 for both Penguin and Secker & Warburg as *France in the 1980s*.
3. Yvan Gastaut, *L'Immigration et l'opinion en France sous la Ve République*, Paris, Seuil, 2000, pp. 52–66.
4. François-Henri de Virieu, *LIP. 100,000 montres sans patron*, Calmann-Lévy, 1973, p. 7.
5. Ibid., p. 17.
6. Charles Piaget, *LIP. Charles Piaget et les LIP racontent*, Stock, 1973, p. 121. The postface is by Michel Rocard.
7. *Programme commun de gouvernement du Parti Communiste Français et du Parti Socialiste*, Preface by Georges Marchais, Éditions Sociales, 1972, pp. 7, 36–9.
8. Léon Noël, quoted by Jean Lacouture, *De Gaulle. The Ruler, 1945–1970*, London, Harvill, 1991, pp. 585–7.
9. Raymond Aron, *The Elusive Revolution. Anatomy of a Student Revolt*, London, Pall Mall Press, 1969, p. 83.
10. See Jean Touchard, *Le gaullisme, 1940–1969*, Paris, Seuil, 1978, pp. 345–56.
11. Simone Veil, speech to the National Assembly on 26 November 1974, reproduced in Michel Sarazin, *Une Femme Simone Veil*, Robert Laffont, 1987, pp. 277–87.
12. Valéry Giscard d'Estaing, *Démocratie française*, Paris, Fayard, 1976, translated by Vincent Cronin as *Towards a New Democracy*, London, Collins, 1977, pp. 10–11, 46, 81.
13. See Kristin Ross, *May '68 and Its Afterlives*, Chicago, University of Chicago Press, 2002, and the essay review by Julian Bourg, 'Hello to all that: rescuing

May 1968', *French Cultural Studies*, Vol. 14, Pt 1, No. 40, February 2003, pp. 117–26.

14. The article was in the *New York Times Magazine*, and is quoted in Henry Rousso's epic analysis of the persistent presence of issues of the Occupation in post-war France, *Le Syndrome de Vichy, 1944–198 . . .*, Paris, Seuil, 1987, p. 129.

15. Régis Debray, *Le Pouvoir intellectuel en France*, Paris, Ramsey, 1979, translated by David Macey as *Teachers, Writers, Celebrities. The Intellectuals of Modern France*, London, Verso, 1981, p. 199.

16. Giscard d'Estaing, *Towards a New Democracy*, p. 99.

17. Quoted in Gastaut, *L'Immigration et l'opinion*, p. 302.

18. Giscard d'Estaing, *Towards a New Democracy*, p. 99.

19. *Libération*, 26 September, 1978.

20. Danielle Bleitrach and Alain Chenu, *L'Usine et la vie. Luttes régionales: Marseille et Fos*, Paris, Maspero, 1979, p. 6.

21. The concept of 'rescue' is from Alan S. Milward, *The European Rescue of the Nation-State*, London, Routledge, 1992, pp. 314–17.

CHAPTER 18 IDEOLOGICAL RUPTURE AND RETREAT, 1970S–1984

1. 'Giscard vu par Giscard', *L'Express*. 17 May 1980, p. 39. The interviewer was the journal's editor, Jean-François Revel.

2. Jacques Chirac, *Discours pour la France à l'heure du choix suivi de La Lueur de l'espérance*, Paris, Stock/Table Ronde, 1978 pp. 316–28.

3. *Le Figaro*, 20 March 1978, pp. 1–2.

4. Quoted in Mark Hunter, *Les Jours les plus Lang*, Paris, Odile Jacob, 1990, p. 126.

5. The Ministry's modernizing role is examined in Siân Reynolds, 'The French Ministry of Women's Rights 1981–86: modernization or marginalization?', in John Gaffney (ed.), *France and Modernization*, Avebury, 1988, pp. 149–68.

6. Words used by the Gaullist deputy Paul Mirguet in July 1960, quoted in Antony Copley, *Sexual Moralities in France, 1780–1980. New ideas on the family, divorce, and homosexuality. An essay on moral change*, London, Routledge, 1989, p. 216. See also Copley's perceptive analysis of his interview with Daniel Guérin, political activist, historian and homosexual, who died in 1988, ibid., pp. 181–97.

7. 'Bilan du septennat', *Le Monde. Dossiers et documents*, 1988, p. 18.

8. Quoted in Elizabeth Fallaize (ed.), *Simone de Beauvoir. A Critical Reader*, London, Routledge, 1998, p. 6.

9. *Libération*, 15 April 1986, p. 5.

10. *Le Nouvel Observateur*, 14 December 1984, quoted in Yvan Gastaut,

L'immigration et l'opinion, en France sous la Ve République, Paris, Seuil, 2000, p. 428.

11. Harlem Désir, *Touche pas à mon pote*, Paris, Grasset, 1985, p. 11.

CHAPTER 19 PRESSURES FOR CONSENSUS, 1980S–1993

1. Quoted in Mark Hunter, *Les Jours les plus Lang*, Paris, Odile Jacob, 1990, p. 148.
2. *Le Monde*, 12 December 1986, quoted in John Tuppen, *Chirac's France, 1986–88. Contemporary Issues in French Society*, London, Macmillan, 1991, p. 190.
3. *La Marseillaise*, 4 December 1986, p. 20.
4. Jacques Julliard, 'La Course au centre', in François Furet, Jacques Julliard and Pierre Rosanvallon, *La République du centre. La fin de l'exception française*, Paris, Calmann-Lévy, 1988, pp. 112, 129.
5. François Furet, *Penser la Révolution française*, Paris, Gallimard, 1978.
6. François Furet, 'La France unie', in Furet et al., *La République du centre*, p. 56.
7. *Var Matin*, 13 September 1992, p. 2.
8. Furet et al., *La République du centre*, p. 55.
9. Élisabeth Schemla, *Édith Cresson, la femme piégée*, Paris, Flammarion, 1993.
10. *Le Nouvel Observateur*, 6–12 November 1987. The cover headline was 'Tous pourris?'

CHAPTER 20 THE CHALLENGE OF PLURALITY, 1990S–2000S (I)

1. Françoise Gaspard and Farhad Khosrokhavar, *Le Foulard et la République*, Paris, La Découverte, 1995; *Le Monde*, 12–13 March 1995, p. 8. See also their earlier article in *Libération*, 8 December, 1994, p. 7, called 'L'Égalité des filles, avec ou sans voile'.
2. *Le Nouvel Observateur*, 26 October 1989, p. 38.
3. Maurice Gros, interviewed by David Levy for BBC *File on Four*, broadcast 6 August 1991. Unpublished script.
4. *Le Choc*, No. 1, December 1987, pp. 59–60; No. 3, February 1988, p. 21.
5. Material from 'Politique de la ville: recherche citoyens', *La Rue: le magazine contre l'exclusion*, No. 19, June 1995, pp. 22–3, 18–19, 14–15.
6. See the interview with her in 1999 by Jane Freedman and Carrie Tarr in their edited book, *Women, Immigration and Identities in France*, Oxford, Berg, 2000, pp. 29–38.
7. Ibid., pp. 37–8.
8. Pierre Bourdieu, *Contre-feux*, Liber-Raisons d'Agir, 1998, translated by

Richard Nice as *Acts of Resistance. Against the New Myths of Our Time*, Cambridge, Polity Press, 1998, pp. 88–9.

9. *Le Monde*, 17 January 1988, p. 7; *Libération*, 19 January 1998, p. 2.

10. 'Les journées des 4 et 5 février 94', *Le Rennais*, No. 242, March 1994, p. 3.

11. Cited and discussed in David Looseley, 'Cultural policy in the twenty-first century: issues, debates and discourse', *French Cultural Studies*, Vol. 10, Part 1, No. 28, February 1999, pp. 5–20. See also Michael Peters, 'Against Finkielkraut's *La Défaite de la pensée*: culture, post-modernism and education', *French Cultural Sudies*, Vol. 4, Part 2, No. 11, June 1993, pp. 91–106.

12. Quoted in Mairi Maclean and Susan Milner, 'France and Globalization', *Modern and Contemporary France*, Vol. 9, No. 3, August 2001, p. 285.

13. *Le Monde*, 6 January 1998, p. 6.

CHAPTER 21 POLITICAL OSCILLATION, 1990S–2000S (2)

1. Quoted in Michel Gaud (ed.), *La Tragédie du Rwanda*, Paris, Documentation Française, 1995, p. 12.

2. Paris, Fayard, 1994, 597 pp.

3. Pierre Bourdieu, *Contre-feux*, Liber-Raisons d'Agir, 1998, translated by Richard Nice as *Acts of Resistance, Against the New Myths of our Time*, Cambridge, Polity Press, 1998, p. 24, taken from a speech at the Gare de Lyon, Paris, in December 1995. Also quoted in René Mouriaux and Françoise Subileau, 'Les Grèves françaises de l'automne 1995: défense des acquis ou mouvement social?' *Modern and Contemporary France*, Vol. NS4, No. 3, 1996, p. 300.

4. *Libération*, 11 January 1996, p. 2.

5. Lionel Jospin, *Modern Socialism*, Fabian Society, 1999. Cited in Ben Clift, 'The political economy of the Jospin government', *Modern and Contemporary France*, Vol. 10, No. 3, August 2002, pp. 325–37.

6. Cécile Velu, 'Faut-il "pactiser" avec l'universalisme? A short history of the PACS', *Modern and Contemporary France*, Vol. 7. No. 4, November 1999, p. 439.

7. See Chapter 19. Laurent Fabius and Georgina Dufoix were acquitted; Edmond Hervé was found guilty of negligence but was not penalized.

8. Figures given by Jean-François Chanet in an appendix to his 'Terroirs et pays: mort et transfiguration?' *Vingtième Siècle*, No 69, January-March, 2001, pp. 61–81. For Hélias, *Le Cheval d'Orgueil (The Horse of Pride)*, see Chapter 1, n. 2.

9. José Bové and François Dufour, in interviews with Gilles Luneau, *Le Monde n'est pas une marchandise. Des paysans contre la malbouffe*, Paris, La Découverte, 2000. See the article by Jean-Philippe Martin 'José Bové, un activiste sans project?' *Modern and Contemporary France*, Vol. 11, No. 3, August 2003, pp. 307–21.

All the articles in this special edition of *M & CF* are excellent on the topic of tradition and modernity in rural France.

10. Jospin's words are quoted in *Le Monde*, 9 September 1999, p. 6; Huwart's in *La Voix du dimanche*, 28–29 November 1999, p. 22.

11. *Le Nouvel Observateur*, 23–29 December 1999, p. 34.

12. Jean-Louis Briquet, *La Tradition en mouvement. Clientélisme et politique en Corse*, Paris, Belin, 1997, p. 295.

13. *La Provence*, 28 April 2002, p. 16.

CHAPTER 22 MEMORY AND IDENTITY, 1990S–2000S (3)

1. Quoted in Sarah Farmer, *Martyred Village. Commemorating the 1944 Massacre at Oradour-sur-Glane*, Berkeley, University of California Press, 1999, p. 162, a path-breaking reconstruction of the trial and the place of Oradour in national memory. See also Jean-Jacques Fouché, 'Le Centre de la Mémoire d'Oradour' *Vingtième Siècle*, No. 73, January to March 2002, pp. 125–37.

2. 'Le miroir brisé (1971–1974)' is the title of Chapter 3 of Rousso, *Le Syndrome de Vichy*; see also Jean-Pierre Azéma, 'The Paxtonian Revolution', in Sarah Fishman et al. (eds), *France at War. Vichy and the Historians*, Oxford, Berg, 2000, pp. 13–20.

3. Annette Wieviorka, *L'Ère du témoin*, Paris, Plon, 1998.

4. Claudine Vegh, *Je ne lui ai pas dit au revoir. Des enfants de déportés parlent*, Paris, Gallimard, 1979, p. 209.

5. Jean-Luc Einaudi, *La Bataille de Paris, 17 octobre 1961*, Paris, Seuil, 1991; *Le Monde*, 17 October 1997, p. 10.

6. See Jim House, 'Antiracist memories: the case of 17 October 1961 in historical perspective', *Modern and Contemporary France*, Vol. 9, No. 3, August 2001, p. 364.

7. *Le Monde*, 23 November 2000, p. 11.

8. Quoted in Nancy Wood, *Germaine Tillion, une femme-mémoire. D'une Algérie à l'autre*, Paris, Autrement, 2003, p. 6. On Todorov and the 'exemplary' see Robert Zaretsky's chapter in Sarah Fishman et al. (eds), *France at War*, pp. 261–24.

9. Fernand Braudel, *L'Identité de la France. Espace et Histoire*, Paris, Arthaud-Flammarion, 1986, p. 40.

10. Pierre Nora (ed.), *Les Lieux de mémoire*. Part 3, Vol. 1, *Les France*, Paris, Gallimard, 1992, p. 35.

11. *L'Événement du jeudi*, No. 180, 14–20 April 1988, p. 53.

12. See the personal account by Jay Winter, 'Public history and the "Historial" project 1986–1998', in Sarah Blowen, Marion Demossier and Jeanne Picard (eds), *Recollections of France. Memories, Identities and Heritage in Contemporary France*, Oxford, Berghahn Books, 2000, pp. 52–67.

13. Quoted in *Libération*, 17 February 2000, p. 6.

14. Quoted in Gérard Mermet, *Francoscopie 2003*, Paris, Larousse, 2002, p. 265.

15. *Le Monde*, 1 January 2000, p. 14.

16. Public opinion statistics from *L'Express international*, 6 April 2000, p. 15.

17. Jean-Marie V. Rurangwa, *Rwanda. Écrire par devoir de mémoire. Le génocide des Tutsi expliqué à un étranger*, Lille, Fest' Africa, 2000.

18. *L'Express international*, 27 July 2000, p. 15.

19. Martine Cohen, 'Les Juifs de France. Modernité et identité', *Vingtième Siècle*, No. 66, April–June 2000, p. 106; Danièle Hervieu-Léger, 'Le Miroir de l'Islam en France', ibid., pp. 79–89.

20. Farhad Khosrokhavar, *L'Islam des jeunes*, Paris, Flammarion, 1997.

21. *Association pour une taxation des transactions financières pour l'aide aux citoyens et citoyennes (ATTAC)*. See the special edition of *Modern & Contemporary France*, Vol. 12, No. 1, February 2004, edited by Joanna Drugan, Jim House and Sarah Waters, and entitled 'New Voices in French Politics'.

Abbreviations and Glossary

ACCT Agence de la Coopération Culturelle et Technique (Agency for Cultural and Technical Cooperation). Francophone organization formed in 1970.

ACJF Association Catholique de la Jeunesse Française (Catholic Association of French Youth). A movement of Catholic Action initiated by the papacy in 1922.

ALN Armée de Libération Nationale (National Liberation Army). The armed organization of the Algerian FLN.

AOC Appellation d'Origine Contrôlée. Quality guarantee of origin for wine and foodstuffs.

ARAC Association Républicaine des Anciens Combattants (Republican Association of Veterans). A left-wing veterans' association, identified with Henri Barbusse, created during the First World War.

arrondissement Administrative district within a *département*. Paris is divided into twenty *arrondissements*.

AS Armée Secrète (Secret (Clandestine) Army). Armed Resistance organization inside France, envisaged initially by Henri Frenay. From 1942 it was the military side of the MUR under the leadership of General Delestraint.

BBC British Broadcasting Corporation.

BCRA Bureau Central de Renseignement et d'Action (Central Intelligence and Action Bureau). The secret service organization of the Free French, headed by Colonel Passy (André Dewavrin). (See also **SOE**, RF section.)

CADAC Coordination des Associations pour le Droit à l'Avortement et à la Contraception (Coordinated Associations for the Right to Abortion and Contraception). Formed in 1990 as an activist grouping to defend women's 'right to choose'.

CAP Common Agricultural Policy (Politique Agricole Commune, PAC). Developed from the late 1950s onwards by the EEC.

CFA Comité France–Allemagne (Franco-German Committee). Committee formed in 1935 to promote cultural and political interchange between France and Germany.

CFDT Confédération Française Démocratique du Travail (French Democratic Confederation of Labour). Trade-union movement formed from the CFTC

in 1964, emphasizing its democratic base rather than its previous religious association.

CFLN Comité Français de Libération Nationale (French Committee of National Liberation). Formed in Algiers in 1943, first under de Gaulle and Giraud, then under de Gaulle alone.

CFTC Confédération Française des Travailleurs Chrétiens (French Confederation of Christian Workers). Trade-union movement launched in 1919, largely Catholic-inspired but open to Protestant workers. Strong in Catholic industrial areas, but a minority within trade unionism. More than two-thirds of the movement agreed to change the name in 1964 to CFDT.

CGT Confédération Générale du Travail (General Confederation of Labour). Formed in 1895. The main trade-union body throughout the twentieth century.

CGTU Confédération Générale du Travail Unitaire (Unitary CGT). The trade-union body formed as a minority breakaway from the CGT in 1922 by revolutionary syndicalists, but soon organically linked to the Communist Party. Merged again with the CGT in 1936.

CND Confrérie Notre-Dame (Our Lady's Brotherhood). Clandestine name for a Resistance intelligence network in occupied France organized by Rémy (Gilbert Renault) within the BCRA.

CNFF Conseil National des Femmes Françaises (National Council of French Women). Federation of women's movements dating from 1900.

CNJA Cercle National des Jeunes Agriculteurs (National Circle of Young Farmers). The youth organization of the FNSEA, reformed in 1956.

CNPF Conseil National du Patronat Français (National Council of French Employers). Replaced previous employers' organizations in 1946. Often referred to simply as 'le patronat' (the employers).

CNR Conseil National de la Résistance (National Council of the Resistance). Formed by de Gaulle's envoy, Jean Moulin, in May 1943. Second president was Georges Bidault.

CO Comités d'Organisation (Organization Committees). Vichy committees set up in 1940 to restructure the economy.

CP Confédération Paysanne (Peasant Confederation). Left-wing breakaway in 1987 from the FNSEA to promote the interests of peasant farmers.

CRS Compagnies Républicaines de Sécurité (Republican Security Forces). Formed in 1944 from Resistance militias. Became the state security police, given the role of policing demonstrations and confronting strikes and riots, as in May 1968.

CVR Combattant Volontaire de la Résistance (Voluntary Resistance Combatant). The official name given to accredited Resisters after the Second World War.

DATAR Délégation à l'Aménagement du Territoire et à l'Action Régionale (Town and Country Planning and Regional Action). Created in 1963 to promote the development of towns and the economies of the regions. Vastly expanded in 1982 and subsequently.

département Main administrative division of France headed by a *préfet* (prefect). In 2000 there were currently ninety-five *départements* in metropolitan France, including two in Corsica. There were four *départements d'outre-mer* (see DOM).

député/e Elected deputy. Member of the Assemblée Nationale, also known as the Chambre des Députés (Chamber) which, together with the Sénat (Senate) makes up the Parlement Français (French parliament).

DOM Départements d'Outre-Mer. French Overseas *Départements* (in 2000: Guadeloupe, Martinique, Guyane, Réunion). (See also **TOM**.)

ECSC European Coal and Steel Community (Communauté Européenne du Charbon et de l'Acier, CECA). Created in 1951 by France, West Germany, Italy, Belgium, Holland and Luxembourg.

EDC European Defence Community (Communauté Européenne de Défense, CED). Controversial project of 1952, rejected by the National Assembly in 1954.

EDF Électricité de France (French National Electricity Company)

EEC European Economic Community (Communauté Économique Européenne, CEE). Formed by the Treaty of Rome in 1957 of the six nations of the ECSC. Known colloquially as the Common Market, and then as the European Community. In 1993 its enlarged membership (which included Britain) changed the name to EU.

EMU Economic and Monetary Union. Project for a common European currency.

ENA École Nationale d'Administration (National School of Administration). Created in 1945, as one of the *grandes écoles* (such as the École Polytechnique) to train government personnel, senior civil servants and state administrators. Graduates are known as *Énarques*.

EU European Union (Union Européenne). Name taken by the enlarged EEC in 1993 after the Treaty of Maastricht in 1992.

FFI Forces Françaises de l'Intérieur (French Forces of the Interior). The military forces of the Resistance inside France, formally unified in June 1944.

FGDS Fédération de la Gauche Démocrate et Socialiste (Federation of the Democratic and Socialist Left), formed in 1965 after François Mitterrand had announced his candidature for the Presidency.

FLN Front de Libération Nationale (National Liberation Front). Ultimately the leading movement for the liberation of Algeria, formed in 1954, with its army the ALN.

FLNC Front de Libération Nationale de la Corse (National Liberation Front of Corsica). Militant activist movement for Corsican independence created in 1976.

FN Front National (National Front). Extreme right-wing movement formed in 1972 and led by Jean-Marie Le Pen. Totally unconnected was the Resistance movement of 1941–4 called the Front National and organized by the clandestine Communist Party, but not limited to Communists only.

FNSEA Fédération Nationale des Syndicats d'Exploitants Agricoles (National Federation of Farmers' Unions).

FO Force Ouvrière (Workers' Force). Socialist-oriented trade-union confederation initially known as CGT-FO, formed in 1947–8 in a break from the main confederation, the CGT.

fonctionnaire State employee/ public administrator/civil servant/ government official.

FTPF Francs-Tireurs et Partisans Français (French Irregular Soldiers and Partisans). The Resistance fighters organized by the clandestine Communist Party. Most often known simply as the FTP.

GATT General Agreement on Tariffs and Trades.

GPRF Gouvernement Provisoire de la République Française (Provisional Government of the French Republic). Formed in 1944 under the leadership of General Charles de Gaulle.

HLM Habitation à Loyer Modéré (Low-rent housing). State or local council housing identified with big estates and blocks of flats.

ILO International Labour Organization created in 1919 by the Treaty of Versailles.

IVG Interruption Volontaire de Grossesse (Abortion).

JCR Jeunesse Communiste Révolutionnaire (Communist Revolutionary Youth). One of the extreme left Trotskyist groups prominent in 1968.

JOC Jeunesse Ouvrière Chrétienne (Young Christian Workers). Catholic-based organization for young workers dating from 1926. Also **JAC**, Jeunesse Agricole Chrétienne, a parallel organization for young agricultural workers.

laïcité Secularism, particularly in state education.

LFAJ Ligue Française des Auberges de la Jeunesse (League of French Youth Hostels). Catholic-based association for youth holidays, active from the late 1920s, founded by Marc Sangnier.

LICP Ligue Internationale des Combattants de la Paix (International League of Combatants for Peace). Pacifist movement launched in 1931 by Victor Méric.

LO Lutte Ouvrière (Workers' Struggle). The Trotskyist party for which Arlette Laguiller was a recurrent candidate at Presidential elections from 1974 to 2002.

LVF Légion des Volontaires Français contre le Bolchévisme (Legion of French Volunteers against Bolshevism). Volunteer unit recruited from August 1941 to fight with the German army against Soviet Russia.

MDC Mouvement des Citoyens (Citizens' Movement). Formed in 1992 by Jean-Pierre Chevènement, initally as an anti-Maastricht group within the Socialist Party.

MDRM Mouvement Démocratique de la Rénovation Malgache (Democratic Movement for Madagascan Revival). Nationalist movement in Madagascar.

MEDEF Mouvement des Entreprises de France (Movement of French Firms/ Businesses/Companies). The name taken by the employers' federation in 1998, succeeding the CNPF.

MLF Mouvement de Libération des Femmes (Women's Liberation Movement). Main movement for women's rights in the 1970s.

MLTD Mouvement pour le Triomphe des Libertés Démocratiques (Movement for Triumph of Democratic Freedoms). One of the Algerian nationalist movements prominent after the Second World War and associated with Messali Hadj.

MNA Mouvement National Algérien (National Algerian Movement). Created by supporters of Messali Hadj during the Algerian War.

MNR Mouvement National Républicain (National Republican Movement). The breakaway group from Le Pen's FN, formed in 1999 by Bruno Mégret.

MOI Main-d'œuvre Immigrée (Immigrant Labour). Communist-based organization for immigrant workers, formed during the 1930s and active in the Resistance.

MRAP Mouvement contre le Racisme et l'Antisémitisme et pour la Paix (Movement against Racism and Antisemitism and for Peace). Activist movement for human rights and peace created in 1949.

MRP Mouvement Républicain Populaire (People's Republican Movement). The Christian Democrat party formed after the Liberation of 1944 by leading members of the Resistance.

MUR Mouvements Unis de la Résistance (United Resistance Movements). Formed in January 1943 through the agency of Jean Moulin and comprising movements in the southern zone, Combat, Franc-Tireur, and Libération-Sud.

NAP Noyautage des Administrations Publiques (Infiltration of Public Administration). A Resistance organization of *fonctionnaires* carrying out acts of resistance while still in post.

NATO North Atlantic Treaty Organization, created in 1949.

OAS Organisation de l'Armée Secrète (Secret Army Organization). Armed vanguard of Algérie Française, which carried out acts of urban terror in mainland France in 1961–2 in an attempt to keep Algeria French.

ORTF Office de Radiodiffusion-Télévision Française (French Broadcasting Service).

OS Ouvrier Spécialisé (Specialized worker). Semi-skilled or unskilled worker. The term used for basic machine operatives and workers on a production line, particularly in car manufacturing.

OST Organisation Scientifique du Travail (scientific organization of labour). The name given to 'modernizing' and 'rationalized' practices in industry in the 1920s–30s.

PACS Pacte Civil de Solidarité (Civil Pact of Solidarity). Contract akin to marriage concluded between two persons of the same sex or different sex introduced by a law of 1999.

PCA Parti Communiste Algérien (Algerian Communist Party).

PCF Parti Communiste Français (French Communist Party). Formed at the Congress of Tours in 1920 by a majority from the SFIO who voted to join the Communist Third International.

PME Petites et Moyennes Entreprises (Small and medium-sized businesses).

PNB Parti Nationaliste Breton (Breton Nationalist Party). Party campaigning for Brittany's independence.

PPA Parti du Peuple Algérien (Party of the Algerian People). Formed by Messali Hadj in 1937.

PPF Parti Populaire Français (French People's Party). Extreme right-wing party formed by Jacques Doriot from 1936, often considered the main French fascist party of the 1930s.

PS Parti Socialiste (Socialist Party). The name gradually adopted by the SFIO between 1969 and 1971 with a major relaunch of the party as the PS when François Mitterrand became first secretary in 1971.

PSF Parti Social Français (French Social Party). The title adopted in 1936 by the nationalist movement of the Croix-de-Feu led by Colonel de la Rocque.

PSU Parti Socialiste Unifié (Unified Socialist Party). Created in 1960 mainly by socialists arguing for a 'modern socialism'. Michel Rocard was its leading voice from the mid-1960s until he joined the Presidential campaign of François Mitterrand in 1974.

RATP Régie Autonome des Transports Parisiens (Autonomous Authority of Paris Transport). Parisian buses and underground (métro).

RMI Revenu Minimum d'Insertion (Minimum income for social integration). The most basic social welfare payment needed for survival, introduced by the Rocard government in 1988.

RNP Rassemblement National Populaire (National People's Rally). Extreme right-wing and collaborationist party founded in February 1941 and led by Marcel Déat and Eugène Deloncle.

RPF Rassemblement du Peuple Français (Rally of the French People). General de Gaulle's political movement founded on his re-entry into politics in 1947. Also stands for Rassemblement pour la France, the political grouping formed by Charles Pasqua and Philippe de Villiers in 1999.

RPR Rassemblement pour la République (Rally for the Republic). The name taken in 1976 by the Gaullist political party led by Jacques Chirac, in a continuation from the Gaullist UNR of 1958 and the UDR of 1967. The RPR transformed itself into the UMP in 2002.

SFIO Section Française de l'Internationale Ouvrière (French Section of the Workers' International). The first united Socialist Party created in 1905 and led by Jean Jaurès. It was relaunched as the PS in 1971.

SGI Société Générale d'Immigration (General Immigration Society). Formed in 1924 to co-ordinate the employment of immigrant labour.

SIDA Syndrome immuno-déficitaire acquis (Acquired immune-deficiency syndrome, known as AIDS).

SMIC and SMIG Salaire Minimum Interprofessionnel de Croissance; Salaire Minimum Interprofessionnel Garanti (Guaranteed minimum wage). Also **SMAG**, Salaire Minimum Agricole Garanti, the guaranteed minimum wage in agriculture.

SNCF Société Nationale des Chemins de Fer (National Railway Company). Nationalized railway system which originated with take-overs of private companies by the Popular Front and thrived after the Second World War.

SOE Special Operations Executive. British special services unit during the Second World War, with F section working independently and RF section working in liaison with the BCRA.

SOL Service d'Ordre Légionnaire (Contingent for Legionary Order). Paramilitary vanguard section of the Vichy Légion Française des Combattants (French Veterans' Legion) created by Joseph Darnand in December 1941.

STO Service du Travail Obligatoire (Compulsory Labour Service). Vichy's forced labour service made obligatory by the law of 16 February 1943, and entailing labour in Germany for young men of military service age.

SUD Solidaires, Unitaires, Démocratiques (Solidarity, Unitary, Democratic). One of the new groupings of trade unions, originating in 1989 among postal workers.

TGV Train à Grande Vitesse (High-speed train). Dating from the early 1980s with the first line from Paris to Lyon.

TNP Théâtre National Populaire (National People's Theatre). State-run theatre dating from 1920.

TOM Territoires d'Outre-Mer (Overseas French Territories). Remaining colonial territories which are not *départements d'outre-mer* (see **DOM**).

TVA Taxe sur la Valeur Ajoutée (Value-added tax, known as VAT).

UDCA Union de Défense des Commerçants et Artisans (Union in Defence of Traders and Artisans). Movement launched in 1953 associated with the ideas and leadership of Pierre Poujade.

UDF Union pour la Démocratie Française (Union for French Democracy). Constellation of right-of-centre and centre parties created in 1978 by Giscard d'Estaing.

UDMA Union Démocratique du Manifeste Algérien (Democratic Union of the Algerian Manifesto). The Algerian political movement of Ferhat Abbas.

UDR Union des Démocrates pour la (Ve) République (Union of Democrats for the (Fifth) Republic). Sequel in 1967 to the Gaullist UNR.

UDSR Union Démocratique et Socialiste de la Résistance (Democratic and Socialist Union of the Resistance). Political party launched after the Liberation which attempted to unite the different strands of Resistance.

UEC Union des Étudiants Communistes (Communist Students' Union).

UF Union Fédérale (Federal Union). First World War veterans' association associated with the political left.

UFF Union des Femmes Françaises (Union of French Women). Women's organization in the last months of the Resistance and at the Liberation, close to the Communist Party.

UFSF Union Française pour le Suffrage des Femmes (French Union for Women's Suffrage). Active pressure group founded in 1909.

UGIF Union Générale des Israélites de France (General Union of French Jews). Created in Occupied France under the Vichy regime as a national council of Jewish affairs and social organizations.

UMP Union pour la Majorité Présidentielle (Union for a Presidential Majority); Union pour un Mouvement Populaire (Union for a People's Movement). The names assumed consecutively by the main right of centre parties, principally the Gaullist RPR, but also members of the UDF and liberal democrats, at the time of the Presidential elections of 2002.

UN United Nations (Organisation des Nations Unies, ONU)

UNC Union Nationale des Combattants (National Union of Veterans). First World War veterans' association associated with the political right.

UNEF Union Nationale des Étudiants Français (National Union of French Students).

UNR Union pour la Nouvelle République (Union for the New Republic). Political party formed mainly by Gaullists after the ratification of the Fifth Republic constitution in 1958.

UNSA Union Nationale des Syndicats Agricoles (National Union of Agricultural Syndicates). The main organization of agricultural interests in the 1930s and 1940s.

UPR Union Populaire et Républicaine (People's Republican Union). Catholic-based regional party in Alsace, influential in the 1930s.

WTO World Trade Organization.

ZAC, ZI, and ZUP Zone d'Aménagement Concerté (Urban development zone); Zone Industrielle (Industrial zone); Zone à Urbaniser en Priorité (Priority urban development zone). Urban and industrial development projects of the 1950s and 1960s.

Selected Further Reading

Note. Places of publication of University Presses are normally contained in the name of the Press. Abbreviations: CUP (Cambridge University Press, Cambridge); OUP (Oxford University Press, Oxford, which also publishes as the Clarendon Press, Oxford); PUF (Presses Universitaires de France, Paris); UCL (University College London). Yale University Press publishes principally in New Haven (USA) and Harvard University Press at Cambridge (USA). Unless specified otherwise the place of all other publications is London for books in English and Paris for books in French.

Abbreviations of periodicals: *M&CF* (*Modern and Contemporary France*); *FCS* (*French Cultural Studies*); *JMH* (*Journal of Modern History*)

General works covering all or a major part of the twentieth century

Established histories in English include:

Alfred Cobban, *A History of Modern France, Vol. 3: 1871–1962*, Penguin, 1965;

D. W. Brogan, *The Development of Modern France (1870–1939)*, Hamish Hamilton, 1940;

Theodore Zeldin, *France 1848–1945*, Clarendon Press, 1973–7, the classic and unrivalled study of French attitudes and passions in two volumes; note also his *The French*, Collins, 1983;

Maurice Larkin, *France since the Popular Front. Government and People, 1936–1986*, Clarendon Press, 1988, full of good material especially on economics;

Gordon Wright's 1960 survey, *France in Modern Times: From the Enlightenment to the Present*, New York, Norton, fourth edition, 1987;

James F. McMillan, *Twentieth Century France*, Edward Arnold, 1985/1992, succinct and much respected.

Recent histories in English:

Charles Sowerwine, *France since 1870: Culture, Politics and Society*, Basingstoke, Palgrave, 2001, an excellent history with wide gender and cultural range;

Robert Gildea, *France since 1945*, OUP, 1996, a perceptive history of the second

half of the century, conscious of the presence of the past, as evidenced in his wide-ranging *The Past in French History*, Yale University Press, 1994;

Martin Evans and Emmanuel Godin, *France 1815–2003*, Arnold, 2004, a well-organized, lively 'Modern history for Modern Languages';

Richard Vinen, *France, 1934–1970*, Macmillan, 1996, has many new perspectives.

Martin S. Alexander (ed.), *French History since Napoleon*, Arnold, 1999, has a number of excellent essays on aspects of society, economics and culture as well as politics.

The series from Éditions du Seuil entitled *Nouvelle histoire de la France contemporaine* has detailed volumes on the century split into seven parts. Note particularly:

Madeleine Rebérioux, *La République radicale? 1898–1914*, 1975;

Jean-Jacques Becker and Serge Berstein, *Victoire et frustrations, 1914–1929*, 1990;

Jean-Pierre Azéma, *De Munich à la Libération, 1938–1944*, 1979;

Jean-Pierre Rioux, *La France de la IVe République, 1944–1958*, 2 vols, 1980–83,

Jean-Jacques Becker with Pascal Ory, *Crises et alternances, 1974–2000*, 1998–2002.

At the end of the series there is a well-chosen volume of documents for each year of the century, Olivier Wieviorka and Christophe Prochasson, *La France du XXe siècle. Documents d'histoire*, 1994.

Cambridge University Press (CUP) has published English translations of these volumes in the textbook series entitled *The Cambridge History of Modern France*. They are strongly recommended.

Two well-organized French studies, with good material on the economy, foreign policy and decolonization:

Maurice Agulhon, André Nouschi and Ralph Schor, *La France de 1914 à 1940*, and *La France de 1940 à nos jours*, Nathan, 1993 and 1995.

Major essay of interpretation as discussed in the Introduction to this book: Stanley Hoffmann, Charles P. Kindleberger, Laurence Wylie, Jesse R. Pitts, Jean-Baptiste Duroselle and François Goguel, *In Search of France*, Harvard University Press, 1963, with the title of the London edition, *France: Change and Tradition*, Gollancz, 1963.

Social histories:

Georges Dupeux, *French Society 1789–1970*, Methuen, 1976;

Pierre Guillaume, *Histoire sociale de la France au XXe siècle*, Masson, 1993;

Maurice Parodi, Philippe Langevin, Jean-Pierre Oppenheim, Nadine Richez-Battesti, *La Question sociale en France depuis 1945*, Armand Colin, 2000;

Brilliant pioneering study of rural change, Gordon Wright, *Rural Revolution in France: The Peasantry in the Twentieth Century*, Stanford University Press, 1964;

Pierre Miquel, *La France et ses paysans. Une histoire du monde rural au XXe siècle*, L'Archipel, 2001;

Annie Moulin, *Peasantry and Society in France since 1789*, CUP, 1991;

René Mouriaux, *La CGT*, Seuil, 1982.

Political themes and traditions across the century:

Maurice Agulhon, *Les Métamorphoses de Marianne. L'imagerie et la symbolique républicaines de 1914 à nos jours*, Flammarion, 2001;

Sudhir Hazareesingh, *Political Traditions in Modern France*, OUP, 1994, a valuable survey of the Republican tradition among others, conveying the breadth of French political ideas;

Serge Berstein and Odile Rudelle (eds), *Le Modèle républicain*, PUF, 1992;

Kay Chadwick (ed.), *Catholicism, Politics and Society in Twentieth-century France*, Liverpool University Press, 2000;

Jean-François Sirinelli, *Histoire des droites en France*, 2 vols, Gallimard, 1992;

Nicholas Atkin and Frank Tallett (eds), *The Right in France, 1789–1997*, Tauris, 1998;

Peter Davies, *The Extreme Right in France 1789 to the Present. From de Maistre to Le Pen*, Routledge, 2002;

Richard Mayne, Douglas Johnson and Robert Tombs (eds), *Cross Channel Currents. 100 years of the Entente Cordiale*, Routledge, 2004, a centenary edition with articles by historians, journalists and politicians;

J. F. V. Keiger, *France and the World since 1970*, Arnold, 2001, excellent on the determinants in foreign policy;

Michael Scriven and Peter Wagstaff (eds), *War and Society in Twentieth-century France*, Oxford, Berg, 1991, includes an essay by Jean-Pierre Rioux on *La Guerre Franco-française* asking whether France is a society at war with itself.

Empire and immigration:

Charles-Robert Ageron with others, *Histoire de la France coloniale, 1914–1990*, Armand Colin, 1990 and his *Modern Algeria: A history from 1930 to the present*, Hurst, 1991;

Gérard Noiriel, *Le Creuset français. Histoire de l'immigration, XIXe–XXe siècles*, Seuil, 1988, a significant general survey of immigration, widely quoted;

Marianne Amar and Pierre Milza, *L'Immigration en France au XXe siècle*, Armand Colin, 1990;

Benjamin Stora, *Ils venaient d'Algérie: l'immigration algérienne en France, 1912–1992*, Fayard, 1992;

Neil MacMaster, *Colonial Migrants and Racism: Algerians in France, 1900–1962*, Macmillan, 1997;

Vincent Viet, *La France immigrée, 1914–1997*, Fayard, 1998;

M. Silverman, *Deconstructing the Nation: Immigration, Racism and Citizenship in Modern France*, Routledge, 1992;

Pierre Birnbaum, 'La France aux Français'. Histoire des haines nationalistes, Seuil, 1993.

Political and biographical dictionaries:

Jean-François Sirinelli (ed.), Dictionnaire historique de la vie politique française au XXe siècle, PUF, 1995, an excellent volume with long, detailed entries;

J. Thomas Ferenczi (ed.), La Politique en France. Dictionnaire historique de 1870 à nos jours, Larousse and Le Monde, 2004;

Michèle and Jean-Paul Cointet (eds), Dictionnaire historique de la France sous l'Occupation, Tallandier, 2000;

Bertram M. Gordon (ed.), Historical Dictionary of World War II France, Aldwych, 1998;

David Bell, Douglas Johnson and Peter Morris (eds), Biographical Dictionary of French Political Leaders since 1870, Harvester Wheatsheaf, 1990.

Cultural and intellectual histories:

Michel Winock, Le Siècle des intellectuels, Seuil, 1997;

Jean-François Sirinelli, Intellectuels et passions françaises, Gallimard, 1990;

Jeremy Jennings (ed.), Intellectuals in Twentieth-century France, Macmillan, 1993;

Pascale Goetschel and Emmanuelle Loyer, Histoire culturelle et intellectuelle de la France au XXe siècle, Armand Colin, 1994;

Peter France (ed.), The New Oxford Companion to Literature in French, Clarendon Press, 1995, essential, critical, informative and wide-ranging;

J. E. Flower, Literature and the Left in France, Macmillan, 1983;

Martyn Cornick, The Nouvelle Revue Française under Jean Paulhan, 1925–1940, Amsterdam, Rodopi, 1995, richly perceptive on the 'magnetic fields' of ideology;

Malcolm Cook (ed.), French Culture since 1945, Longman, 1993;

Ludovic Tournès, New Orleans sur Seine. Histoire du jazz en France, Fayard, 1999;

Jeffrey H. Jackson, 'Making enemies: jazz in inter-war Paris', FCS, Vol. 10, Part 2, No. 29, June 1999;

Matthew F. Jordan, 'How jazz got francisé: a case study in the ongoing construction of cultural identity', FCS, Vol. 13, Part 2, No. 38, June 2002;

Richard Cobb, Paris and Elsewhere. Selected writings edited and introduced by David Gilmour, John Murray, 1998, includes 'Maigret's Paris' and 'Brassai's Paris';

Charles Rearick, The French in Love and War: Popular Culture in the Era of the World Wars, Yale University Press, 1997;

Jean-Pierre Rioux and Jean-François Sirinelli, Histoire culturelle de la France: Vol. 4, Le Temps des masses: le vingtième siècle, Seuil, 1998;

Susan Hayward and Ginette Vincendeau (eds), French Film: texts and contexts, Routledge, second edition, 2000, analyses key films from 1931 to 1995;

Richard Holt, *Sport and Society in Modern France*, Macmillan, 1981;
Philip Dine, *French Rugby Football. A Cultural History*, Oxford, Berg, 2001.

PART ONE 1900s–1931

Politics and Society

The Dreyfus Affair and its aftermath:
The period is vividly treated in the last parts of Robert Tombs, *France 1814–1914*,
Longman, 1996; Roger Magraw, *France 1815–1914. The Bourgeois Century*,
Fontana, 1983; and R. D. Anderson, *France 1870–1914*, Routledge and Kegan
Paul, 1984;
William Fortescue, *The Third Republic in France, 1870–1940: Conflicts and
Continuities*, Routledge, 2000, contains a very useful selection of documents;
Douglas Johnson, *France and the Dreyfus Affair*, Blandford, 1966;
Eric Cahm, *The Dreyfus Affair in French Society and Politics*, Longman, 1996;
Richard Griffiths, *The Use of Abuse: the polemics of the Dreyfus Affair and its
aftermath*, Oxford, Berg, 1991;
Roger Shattuck, *The Banquet Years. The Arts in France, 1885–1918*, Faber and
Faber, 1955, reissued in 1969.

Church and State:
Maurice Larkin pioneered much of the work on the battle between the Church
and anticlericalism, *Church and State after the Dreyfus Affair: the separation
issue in France*, Macmillan, 1974, and *Religion, Politics and Preferment in
France since 1890: La Belle Époque and its legacy*, CUP, 1995.

Nationalisms:
Eugen Weber, *Action Française. Royalism and Reaction in Twentieth-century
France*, Stanford University Press, 1962;
Robert Soucy, *Fascism in France: the case of Maurice Barrès*, Berkeley, University
of California Press, 1972;
Zeev Sternhell, *The Birth of Fascist Ideology*, Princeton University Press, 1994;
Brian Jenkins, *Nationalism in France: Class and Nation since 1879*, Routledge,
1990, a perceptive and original thematic study.
Nelly Wilson, *Bernard Lazare. Antisemitism and the problem of Jewish identity
in late nineteenth-century France*, CUP, 1978;
Robert Tombs (ed.), *Nationhood and Nationalism in France*, Harper Collins,
1991;
J. F. V. Keiger, *Raymond Poincaré*, CUP, 1997.

The left from Radicals to anarchists:

D. R. Watson, *Georges Clemenceau. A political biography*, Eyre Methuen, 1974;

Jean-Baptiste Duroselle, *Clemenceau*, Fayard, 1988;

Tony Judt, *Socialism in Provence, 1871–1914. A study in the origins of the modern French Left*, CUP, 1979, a seminal book on Marxist ideas in the south;

Harvey Goldberg's account of the Socialist leader and Dreyfusard has stood the test of time, *The Life of Jean Jaurès*, Madison, Wisconsin University Press, 1962;

Annie Kriegel, *Aux origines du communisme français*, Flammarion, 1978;

Gérard Noiriel, *Les ouvriers dans la société française, XIXe–XXe siècle*, Seuil, 1986;

Georges Lefranc, *Le Mouvement syndical sous la Troisième République*, Payot, 1967;

Jean Sagnes, *Le Mouvement ouvrier en Languedoc*, Toulouse, Privat, 1980, gives the local background to the PCF, including the wine-growers' revolt;

Jean Maitron pioneered the detailed history of the labour movement in France, especially the anarchists, *Le Mouvement anarchiste en France*, 2 vols., Maspero, 1975;

David Berry, *A History of the French Anarchist Movement, 1917–1945*, Westport, Greenwood Press, 2002, is a modern history based on primary research.

Peasantry and rural France:

Eugen Weber, *Peasants into Frenchmen. The Modernization of Rural France 1870–1914*, Chatto and Windus, 1977, a massively impressive study;

Pierre-Jakez Hélias, *The Horse of Pride. Life in a Breton Village*, Yale University Press, 1978, full of atmosphere and insights into rural and regional life;

Ephraïm Grenadou interviewed by Alain Prévost, *Grenadou, paysan français*, Seuil, 1966, provided excellent material on his life and ideas as a peasant farmer.

Immigration:

David Assouline and Mehdi Lallaoui, *Un Siècle d'immigrations en France. De l'usine au maquis, 1919–1945*, Syros, 1996;

Note the books under **General works** above.

The First World War

Outbreak:

John F. V. Keiger, *France and the origins of the First World War*, Macmillan 1983, and his chapter on France in Keith Wilson (ed.), *Decisions for war 1914*, UCL Press, 1995;

Gerd Krumeich, *Armaments and Politics in France on the Eve of the First World War*, Oxford, Berg, 1984;

Douglas Porch, *The March to the Marne: The French Army, 1871–1914*, CUP, 1981;

Jean Rabaut, *Jaurès assassiné*, Éditions Complexe, 1984;

A respected short history of the war, Marc Ferro, *The Great War 1914–1918*, Routledge, 1973; note also the succinct history, Pierre Miquel, *La Grande Guerre*, Fayard, 1983.

Experiences:

The work of Jean-Jacques Becker has been influential on all following research. See notably his 1914. *Comment les Français sont entrés dans la guerre*, Fondation Nationale des Sciences Politiques, 1977, and *The Great War and the French People*, New York, St Martin's Press, 1986, essential reading for questions of war support and the home front.

At the founding of the international research centre at the Historial in Péronne the cultural approach of Jay Winter was central, brilliantly displayed in his *Sites of memory, sites of mourning. The Great War in European cultural history*, CUP, 1995; see also Jay Winter and Jean-Louis Robert, *Capital Cities at War: Paris, London, Berlin 1914–1919*, CUP, 1997.

Among those associated closely with the Historial, John Horne's understanding of the war experience in its many aspects is outstanding, most expressly evident in: John Horne and Alan Kramer, *German Atrocities 1914. A History of Denial*, Yale University Press, 2001, and John Horne (ed.), *State, society and mobilization in Europe during the First World War*, CUP, 1997, while the relationships of labour movements to the war are analysed in his earlier work, *Labour at War. France and Britain 1914–1918*, Clarendon Press, 1991.

The research of others equally important to the work at Péronne is further displayed in the new and illuminating approaches from Leonard V. Smith, Stéphane Audoin-Rouzeau and Annette Becker, *France and the Great War 1914–1918*, CUP, 2003, and Annette Becker's *War and Faith*, Oxford, Berg, 1998.

Note also the good set of essays, Patrick Fridenson (ed.), *The French Home Front, 1914–1918*, Oxford, Berg, 1992.

Day-to-day responses:

Louis Barthas, *Les Carnets de guerre de Louis Barthas, tonnelier, 1914–1918*, La Découverte, 1997, passionate, colourful, calculating;

Henri Castex, *Verdun, années infernales. Lettres d'un soldat au front (août 1914–septembre 1916)*, Imago, 1996;

Yves Pourcher, *Les Jours de guerre. La vie des Français au jour le jour entre 1914 et 1918*, Plon, 1994, full of little-known material;

Margaret H. Darrow, *French Women and the First World War. War Stories of the Home Front*, Oxford, Berg, 2000, personal and dramatic.

Colonial troops:

Mémoires d'outre-mer: les colonies et la Première Guerre Mondiale, Péronne, Historial de la Grande Guerre, 1996;

Claude Carlier and Guy Pedroncini (eds), *Les Troupes coloniales dans la Grande Guerre*, IHCC-Economica, 1997;

Ruth Harris, 'The "Child of the Barbarian": rape, race and nationalism in France during the First World War', *Past and Present*, Vol. 141, 1993;

Annabelle Melzer, 'Spectacles and Sexualities: The "Mise-en-Scène" of the "Tirailleur Sénégalais" on the Western Front, 1914–1920', in Billie Melman, *Borderlines: Genders and Identities in War and Peace, 1870–1930*, Routledge, 1998;

Tyler Stovall, 'The color line behind the lines: racial violence in France during the Great War', *American Historical Review*, June 1998;

and a fascinating article on the war and jazz in France in 1918, Colin Nettlebeck, 'Jazz at the Théâtre Graslin: a founding story', *FCS*, Vol. 11, Part 2, No. 32, June 2000.

Peacemaking, veterans and war memorials:

Alan Sharp, *The Versailles Settlement. Peacemaking in Paris, 1919*, Macmillan, 1991;

Antoine Prost, *In the Wake of War. 'Les Anciens Combattants' and French Society 1914–1939*, Oxford, Berg, 1992, a distillation of his detailed research into the veterans of the war first published as *Les Anciens combattants*, Presses de la Fondation Nationale des Sciences Politiques, 1977, 3 vols;

Jay Winter's *Sites of Memory* (see above under Experiences)

William Kidd, *Les Monuments aux morts mosellans*, Metz, Éditions Serpenoise, 1999, an imaginative regional study;

Frank Field on Barbusse, Drieu la Rochelle and Bernanos, *Three French Writers and the Great War. Studies in the rise of Communism and Fascism*, CUP, 1975.

Empire and foreign policy

Anthony Adamthwaite, *Grandeur and Misery. France's bid for power in Europe 1914–1940*, Arnold, 1995, has excellent insights;

Charles-Robert Ageron, one of the foremost writers on colonial France, made his reputation with *Les Algériens musulmans et la France, 1871–1919*, 2 vols., PUF, 1968; note also his *France coloniale ou parti colonial?*, PUF, 1978, and his *L'Anticolonialisme en France de 1871 à 1914*, PUF, 1973;

Tony Chafer and Amanda Sackur (eds), *Promoting the Colonial Idea: Propaganda and Visions of Empire in France*, Palgrave, 2002;

Martin Evans (ed.), *Empire and Culture. The French Experience, 1830–1940*, Palgrave, 2004, an interdisciplinary collection of stimulating essays;

Azzedine Haddour, *Colonial Myths: History and Narrative*, Manchester University Press, 2000, has a perceptive theoretical approach;

Peter Dunwoodie, *Writing French Algeria*, Clarendon Press, 1998, a major study of the literature, theories and self-image of the French in Algeria;

Benjamin Stora, *Histoire de l'Algérie coloniale, 1830–1954*, La Découverte, 1991, one of his many writings which have made him a renowned specialist on Algeria (see books on the Algerian war below).

Gender and sexuality in society and politics

The necessity of women's history:

Huguette Bouchardeau, *Pas d'histoire, les femmes*, Syros, 1977;

Michelle Perrot (ed.), *Une Histoire des femmes est-elle possible?*, Marseille, Rivages, 1984, translated as *Writing Women's History*, Oxford, Blackwell, 1992;

James F. McMillan, *Housewife or Harlot: The Place of Women in French Society, 1870–1940*, Brighton, Harvester, 1981, one of the very first modern studies;

Siân Reynolds, *France Between the Wars. Gender and Politics*, Routledge, 1996, already mentioned in the Preface to this book for its significance. Note also her earlier influential edited volume, *Women, State and Revolution. Essays on Power and Gender in Europe since 1789*, Brighton, Harvester, 1986.

Women's suffrage and politics:

Steven C. Hause with Anne R. Kenney, *Women's Suffrage and Social Politics in the French Third Republic*, Princeton University Press, 1984;

Jennifer Waelti-Walters and Steven C. Hause (eds), *Feminisms of the Belle Époque*, Lincoln, University of Nebraska Press, 1994;

Paul Smith, *Feminism and the Third Republic. Women's Political and Civil Rights in France, 1918–1945*, Clarendon Press, 1996;

Christine Bard, *Les Filles de Marianne. Histoire des féminismes, 1914–1940*, Fayard, 1995.

Women and the war:

Margaret Darrow in the section on the war above;

Françoise Thébaud, *La Femme au temps de la guerre de 14*, Stock, 1986.

Specific studies, all creating new areas of research:

Charles Sowerwine, *Sisters or Citizens? Women and socialism in France since 1876*, CUP, 1982;

Patricia Hilden, *Working Women and Socialist Politics in France, 1880–1914. A regional study*, Clarendon Press, 1986;

Laura Lee Downs, *Manufacturing Inequality: Gender Division in the French and*

British Metalworking Industries, 1914–1939, Ithaca, Cornell University Press, 1995;

Mary Louise Roberts, *Civilization without Sexes: Reconstructing Gender in Postwar France, 1917–1927,* Chicago University Press, 1994;

Marie-Monique Huss 'Pronatalism in the Inter-war Period in France', *Journal of Contemporary History,* Vol. 25, 1990;

Karen Offen, 'Body politics: women, work and the politics of motherhood in France, 1920–1950', in Gisela Bock and Pat Thane (eds), *Maternity and Gender Politics: women and the rise of the European welfare states, 1880s–1950s,* Routledge, 1991;

Antony Copley, *Sexual Moralities in France, 1780–1980: New ideas on the family, divorce, and homosexuality. An essay on moral change,* Routledge, 1989;

Carolyn J. Dean, *The Frail Social Body. Pornography, Homosexuality and Other Fantasies in Interwar France,* Berkeley, University of California Press, 2000.

PART TWO 1920s–1969

Economics and society in the inter-war years

Industrial relations and class:

Jacqueline Costa-Lascoux and Émile Temime, *Les Hommes de Renault-Billancourt. Mémoire ouvrière de l'île Seguin, 1930–1992,* Autrement, 2004;

Roger Magraw, *A History of the French Working Class. Vol. II, Workers and the Bourgeois Republic,* Oxford, Blackwell, 1992;

Gérard Noiriel, *Longwy. Immigrés et Prolétaires,* PUF, 1984;

Jackie Clarke, 'Imagined productive communities: industrial rationalization and cultural crisis in 1930s France', *M&CF,* Vol. 8, No. 3, August 2000, excellent on the anxieties about Fordism in France and the ideas of a new industrial order;

Laura Lee Downs, *Childhood in the Promised Land. Working-Class Movements and the Colonies de Vacances in France, 1880–1960,* Durham, Duke University Press, 2002, an original and penetrating study of holidays for workers' children.

Aspects of regionalism:

Shanny Peer, *France on Display. Peasants, Provincials and Folklore in the 1937 Paris World Fair,* Albany, State University of New York Press, 1998, a remarkable insight into the rural and regional thinking of the Popular Front;

Solange and Christian Gras, *La Révolte des régions d'Europe occidentale de 1916 à nos jours,* PUF, 1982;

Theodore Zeldin's *France* (see **General works** above).

The 1930s, ideology and politics

Vividly stimulating reading on the period:

Eugen Weber, *The Hollow Years. France in the 1930s*, Sinclair-Stevenson, 1995;

Herman Lebovics, *True France. The Wars over Cultural Identity, 1900–1945*, Ithaca, Cornell University Press, 1992, a scintillating study, not least on the Colonial Exhibition of 1931;

Tony Chafer and Amanda Sackur (eds), *French Colonial Empire and the Popular Front. Hope and Disillusion*, Macmillan, 1999, a set of excellent essays on a hitherto neglected topic;

Nicola Cooper, 'Urban planning and architecture in colonial Indochina', *FCS*, Vol. 11, No. 31, February 2000;

Jean-Louis Loubet del Bayle, *Les Non-conformistes des années 30: une tentative de renouvellement de la pensée politique française*, Seuil, 1969;

Tony Judt, *Marxism and the French Left. Studies on Labour and Politics in France 1830–1981*, Clarendon Press, 1986;

Romy Golan, *Modernity and Nostalgia. Art and politics in France between the wars*, Yale University Press, 1995, brilliant, challenging, controversial.

Personalities and politics:

Among the Left Book Club editions, Maurice Thorez, *France Today and the People's Front*, Gollancz, 1936, and for a study of the PCF leader see Philippe Robrieux, *Maurice Thorez, vie secrète et vie politique*, Fayard, 1975;

Gilles Martinet, *Une Certaine idée de la gauche (1936–1997)*, Odile Jacob, 1997;

Jean Lacouture, *Léon Blum*, Seuil, 1977, English version from Holmes & Meier, 1982;

Jacques Nobécourt, *Le Colonel de la Rocque (1885–1946) ou les pièges du nationalisme chrétien*, Fayard, 1996, a huge biographical study of the Croix-de-Feu leader.

The issue of 'right-wing nationalism or fascism?':

Robert Soucy's consecutive books on French fascism: *French Fascism: The First Wave, 1924–1933*, and *French Fascism: The Second Wave 1933–1939*, Yale University Press, 1986 and 1995;

Philippe Burrin, *La Dérive fasciste: Doriot, Déat, Bergery, 1933–1945*, Seuil, 1986;

Pierre Milza, *Fascisme français. Passé et présent*, Flammarion, 1987;

Zeev Sternhell, *Ni droite ni gauche. L'idéologie fasciste en France*, Seuil, 1983, translated as *Neither Right nor Left: Fascist ideology in France*, Princeton University Press, 1996, a highly controversial study.

The reactions to Sternhell are discussed in:

R. Wohl, 'French Fascism, both Right and Left: reflections on the Sternhell

controversy', *JMH*, Vol. 63, 1991, and indirectly by Robert Paxton, 'The Five Stages of Fascism', *JMH* Vol. 70, 1998;

Kevin Passmore is excellent on the nature of the radical and nationalist right, and displays the importance of local studies in his *From liberalism to fascism. The right in a French province, 1928–1939*, CUP, 1997;

On rural fascism see Robert Paxton's impressive research and analysis, *French Peasant Fascism: Henry Dorgères's Greenshirts and the crisis of French Agriculture*, OUP, 1997;

Communism in its local settings:

Laird Boswell, *Rural Communism in France, 1920–1939*, Ithaca, Cornell University Press, 1998;

Jacques Girault (ed.), *Sur l'implantation du parti communiste français dans l'entre-deux-guerres*, Éditions Sociales, 1977, particularly good on the PCF in the Parisian region.

The Popular Front:

Julian Jackson, *The Popular Front in France: defending democracy, 1934–38*, CUP, 1988, is essential reading for its multiple angles and perceptive interpretations. Note also his previous work, *The Politics of Depression in France, 1931–36*, CUP, 1985;

Jean Bouvier (ed.), *La France en mouvement, 1934–1938*, Seyssel, Champ Vallon, 1986;

Georges Dupeux, *Le Front Populaire et les élections de 1936*, Colin, 1959;

Jacques Kergoat, *La France du Front Populaire*, La Découverte, 1986;

Pascal Ory, *La Belle illusion: culture et politique sous le signe du Front Populaire*, Plon, 1994, is a richly rewarding interpretation of state and left-wing involvement in all aspects of culture;

Martin S. Alexander and Helen Graham (eds), *The French and Spanish Popular Fronts. Comparative Perspectives*, CUP, 1989, is a collection of excellent essays including Siân Reynolds on 'Women, men and the 1936 strikes in France', and note also her 'Women and the Popular Front: the case of the three women ministers', *French History*, Vol. 8, No. 2, 1994.

Refugees and asylum:

Geneviève Dreyfus-Armand, *L'Exil des républicains espagnols en France. De la Guerre civile à la mort de Franco*, Albin Michel, 1999, a massively impressive study of Spanish refugees;

Vicki Caron, *Uneasy Asylum. France and the Jewish Refugee Crisis, 1933–1942*, Stanford University Press, 1999, is equally impressive, and essential for the reactions to refugees from Central Europe.

Prospects of war, and the portents of ideologies:

Ralph Schor, *L'Antisémitisme en France pendant les années trente. Prélude à Vichy*, Éditions Complexe, 1992;

Gérard Noiriel, *Les origines républicaines de Vichy*, Hachette, 1999, particularly perceptive on links between aspects of republican France and those of Vichy;

Judith M. Hughes, *To the Maginot Line. The Politics of French Military Preparation in the 1920s*, Harvard University Press, 1971;

M. S. Alexander, *The Republic in Danger. General Maurice Gamelin and the politics of French defence, 1933–1940*, CUP, 1992;

Nicole Jordan, *The Popular Front and Central Europe: The dilemma of French impotence*, CUP, 1992;

P. M. H. Bell, *France and Britain, 1900–1940: entente and estrangement*, Longman, 1996;

Robert J. Young, *France and the Origins of the Second World War*, Macmillan, 1996, and his earlier important work, *In Command of France. French Foreign Policy and Military Planning, 1933–1940*, Harvard University Press, 1978;

Norman Ingram, *The Politics of Dissent: Pacifism in France 1919–1939*, Clarendon Press, 1991, a major study to which all subsequent work on peace in the inter-war years is indebted;

Louise Weiss, *Mémoires d'une Européenne*, Albin Michel, 1980.

Note that most books listed in **Part One** above under **Gender**, continue through to the Second World War.

Defeat, Occupation, Vichy and Collaboration

General on occupied France and Vichy:

Robert Paxton, *Vichy France: Old Guard and New Order 1940–1944*, New York, Columbia University Press, 1972, remains the watershed study, its significance and standing recognized in the essays in his honour, edited by Sarah Fishman, Laura Lee Downs, Ioannis Sinanoglou, Leonard V. Smith and Robert Zaretsky, *France at War. Vichy and the Historians*, Oxford, Berg, 2000;

Jean-Pierre Azéma and François Bédarida (eds), *La France des années noires*, 2 vols., Seuil, 1993, has readable and considered coverage of all aspects of the period;

Julian Jackson, *France, the Dark Years 1940–1944*, OUP, 2001, is a brilliant composite history, based on an enormous range of sources, and is essential reading; note also his lively study of the defeat, *The Fall of France. The Nazi Invasion of 1940*, OUP, 2003;

H. R. Kedward, *Occupied France. Collaboration and Resistance, 1940–1944*, Oxford, Blackwell, 1985, a short account;

Philippe Burrin, *La France à l'heure allemande*, Seuil, 1995, translated as *Living with Defeat. France under the German Occupation 1940–1944*, an influential study which explores the degrees of 'accommodation' to the German presence;

Marcel Ophuls, *Le Chagrin et la pitié*, the watershed documentary film, translated and published as *The Sorrow and the Pity*, New York, Outerbridge and Lazard, 1972;

Martin Thomas, *The French Empire at War, 1940–45*, Manchester University Press, 1998, a hugely valuable study of the war and response in the French colonies.

Pierre Laborie, *L'Opinion française sous Vichy*, Seuil, 1990;

Richard Vinen, *The politics of French business, 1936–1945*, CUP, 1991;

Richard Cobb, *French and Germans, Germans and French. A Personal Interpretation of France Under Two Occupations, 1914–1918, 1939–1944*, Hanover, University Press of New England, 1983;

Hanna Diamond, *Women and the Second World War in France, 1939–1948: Choices and Constraints*, Longman, 1999, invaluable, wide-ranging yet succinct, excellent use of oral history;

Claire Gorrara, *Women's Representations of the Occupation in post-68 France*, Macmillan, 1998, a perceptive study of women's writings and memoirs.

Richard Griffiths, *Marshal Pétain*, Constable, 1970, new edition 1995;

Marc Ferro, *Pétain*, Fayard, 1987;

Nicholas Atkin, *Pétain*, Longman, 1998, succinct, judicious and perceptive;

Geoffrey Warner, *Pierre Laval and the eclipse of France*, Eyre and Spottiswoode, 1968;

Jean-Paul Cointet, *Pierre Laval*, Fayard, 1993, a sound and reliable assessment.

Local and regional studies, essential for the diversity of reaction and experience:

Pierre Laborie, *Résistants, Vichyssois et autres: l'évolution de l'opinion et des comportements dans le Lot 1939 à 1944*, CNRS, 1980;

Étienne Dejonghe and Yves Maner, *Le Nord–Pas-de-Calais dans la main allemande, 1940–1944*, Lille, La Voix du Nord, 1999;

John F. Sweets, *Choices in Vichy France. The French under Nazi Occupation*, OUP, 1986, a model study on local divisions within Clermont-Ferrand;

Robert Zaretsky, *Nîmes at War. Religion, Politics, and Public Opinion in the Gard, 1938–1944*, University Park Pennsylvania, Penn State Press, 1995;

Robert Gildea, *Marianne in Chains. In Search of the German Occupation 1940–1945*, Macmillan, 2002, a penetrating study of the Loire valley, and very revealing on the ways in which daily life adapted to the Occupation;

Nicholas Atkin, *The Forgotten French. Exiles in the British Isles, 1940–44*, Manchester University Press, 2003, is a wholly original and fascinating study.

Collaboration:

Bertram M. Gordon, *Collaborationism in France during the Second World War*, Ithaca, Cornell University Press, 1980;

Michael Marrus and Robert Paxton, *Vichy France and the Jews*, New York, Basic Books, 1981, pursues the theme of Paxton's *Vichy France* (above) on the responsibility of Vichy;

Denis Peschanski, *Vichy 1940–1944. Contrôle et exclusion*, Éditions Complexe, 1997;

Stéphane Courtois and Adam Rayski (eds), *Qui savait quoi? L'extermination des Juifs 1941–1945*, La Découverte, 1987;

Paul Webster, *Pétain's Crime; The Full Story of French Collaboration in the Holocaust*, Macmillan, 1990;

Donna Ryan, *The Holocaust and the Jews of Marseille. The Enforcement of Anti-Semitic Policies in Vichy France*, Urbana, University of Illinois Press, 1996.

Special studies, all eminent in their field:

W. D. Halls, *The Youth of Vichy France*, OUP, 1981, and his *Politics, Society and Christianity in Vichy France*, Oxford, Berg, 1995;

Sarah Fishman's two highly original studies: *We Will Wait: Wives of French Prisoners of War*, Yale University Press, 1991, and *The Battle for Children: World War II, Youth Crime, and Juvenile Justice in Twentieth-Century France*, Harvard University Press, 2002;

John Hellman, *The Knight-Monks of Vichy France: Uriage, 1940–1944*, Montreal, McGill-Queen's University Press, 1993;

Miranda Pollard, *Reign of Virtue: Mobilizing Gender in Vichy France*, University of Chicago Press, 1998, showing the primacy of gendered politics in Vichy ideas and propaganda;

Simon Kitson, *Vichy et la chasse aux espions nazis*, Autrement, 2005, intriguing, bold and original study of intelligence activity under Vichy;

Paul Sanders, *Histoire du marché noir*, Perrin, 2001, a detailed account of the black market, inside and outside France.

Resistance and Liberation

Free French and SOE:

Charles de Gaulle, *Mémoires de guerre*, 3 vols., Plon, 1954–9, translated as *War Memoirs*, 3 vols, Weidenfeld and Nicolson, 1955–60;

Jean Lacouture, *De Gaulle: The Rebel, 1890–1944*, Collins Harvill, 1989;

Jean-Louis Crémieux-Brilhac (ed.), *Les Voix de la Liberté. Ici Londres 1940–1944*, La Documentation Française, 1975, 5 vols., gives all the broadcasts of the French Service of the BBC;

M. R. D. Foot, *SOE in France*, Her Majesty's Stationery Office, 1966, second edition, Frank Cass, 2004, still unrivalled and still riveting reading.

Inside France:

The material is vast and specific, though six major conferences on all aspects of resistance, called collectively, *La Résistance et les français*, took place in the 1990s, allowing the possibility that there will soon be a single eminent history of the whole, which will inevitably stress its diversity.

Good recent studies of Resistance movements and leaders:

Olivier Wieviorka, *Une Certaine idée de la résistance: Défense de la France, 1940–1949*, Seuil, 1995;

Alya Aglan, *La Résistance sacrifiée. Le mouvement 'Libération-Nord'*, Flammarion, 1999;

Guillaume Piketty, *Pierre Brossolette. Un héros de la Résistance*, Odile Jacob, 1998;

Daniel Cordier, *Jean Moulin. La République des catacombes*, Gallimard, 1999, the major volume on Moulin's resistance, capture and death, after several other massive volumes of text and documents on Jean Moulin by Cordier, published by JC Lattès from 1989;

A pre-eminent local study: Jean-Marie Guillon, *Le Var, la guerre, la résistance, 1939–1945*, Hemisud, 1994;

Adam Rayski, *Le Choix des juifs sous Vichy: entre soumission et résistance*, La Découverte, 1992;

After forty years, a tentative, but successful, attempt at a social breakdown of resistance: Antoine Prost (ed.), *La Résistance, une histoire sociale*, Éditions de l'Atelier, 1997;

Two studies by the current author concentrate on resistance in the south: H. R. Kedward, *Resistance in Vichy France. A Study of Ideas and Motivations in the Southern Zone, 1940–1942*, OUP, 1975, and *In Search of the Maquis. Rural Resistance in Southern France, 1942–1944*, Clarendon Press, 1993.

The study of women in the Resistance started often with single chapters and articles, of which one was seminal, Paula Schwartz, 'Partisanes and Gender Politics in Vichy France', *French Historical Studies*, Vol. 16, No. 1, 1989;

Books on women resisters now include: Margaret Collins Weitz, *Sisters in the Resistance. How Women Fought to Free France, 1940–1945*, New York, John Wiley, 1995, a vivid treatment of themes and personalities;

Lucie Aubrac, *Outwitting the Gestapo*, Lincoln, University of Nebraska Press, 1993, is a translation of her colourful memoir, *Ils partiront dans l'ivresse*, Seuil, 1984;

Rita Kramer, *Flames in the Field. The Story of Four SOE Agents in Occupied France*, Penguin, 1996, gives a powerful account of four women who died at the Natzweiler Concentration Camp in Alsace.

Liberation and purges (*épuration*):

For the shaving of women's heads at the Liberation see the definitive research by Fabrice Virgili, *La France 'virile'. Des femmes tondues à la libération*, Payot,

2000, translated as *Shorn Women. Gender and Punishment in Liberation France*, Oxford, Berg, 2002;

See also the interpretative study by Alain Brossat, *Les Tondues: un carnaval moche*, Manya, 1992;

The local context of the Liberation is established brilliantly by Luc Capdevila, *Les Bretons au lendemain de l'Occupation. Imaginaire et comportement d'une sortie de guerre 1944–1945*, Rennes, Presses Universitaires de Rennes, 1999;

Karen Adler, *Jews and Gender in Liberation France*, CUP, 2003, is a highly original angle on questions of change and continuity;

Hilary Footitt and John Simmonds, *France 1943–1945*, Leicester University Press, 1988;

Hilary Footitt, *War and Liberation in France: Living with the Liberators*, Palgrave, 2004, which sensitively examines how the French reacted to the liberating forces;

Margaret Higonnet, Jane Jenson, Sonya Michel and Margaret C. Weitz (eds), *Behind the Lines: gender and the two world wars*, Yale University Press, 1987, an important collection of articles, including Jane Jenson, 'The Liberation and new rights for French women' and Paula Schwartz, 'Redefining Resistance: women's activism in wartime France';

Andrew Shennan, *Rethinking France: Plans for Renewal, 1940–46*, OUP, 1989;

H. R. Kedward and Nancy Wood (eds), *The Liberation of France, Image and Event*, Oxford, Berg, 1995.

Fourth Republic and society

The translated volume in the Seuil and CUP series (see **General works** above) by Jean-Pierre Rioux, *The Fourth Republic, 1944–1958*, CUP, 1987, is outstanding;

The architect of planning, Jean Monnet, *Mémoires*, Fayard, 1976; and his biography by Eric Roussel, *Jean Monnet, 1888–1979*, Fayard, 1996.

Industrial workers and strikes:

Evelyne Desbois, Yves Jeanneau, Bruno Mattéi, *La foi des charbonniers. Les mineurs dans la Bataille du charbon 1945–1947*, Maison des sciences de l'homme, 1986;

Robert Mencherini, *Guerre froide, grèves rouges. Parti communiste, Stalinisme et luttes sociales en France: les grèves 'insurrectionnelles' de 1947–1948*, Syllepse, 1998;

Renée Bédarida (ed.), *Un Non-Conformiste chez Schneider: Édouard Morin (1897–1967). Journal*, Éditions Ouvrières and Éditions du Témoignage Chrétien, 1984.

Politics, business and boom years:

Richard Vinen, *Bourgeois Politics in France, 1945–1951*, CUP, 1995;

Alan S. Milward, *The European Rescue of the Nation-State*, Routledge, 1992;

Jean Fourastié, *Les Trente Glorieuses ou la Révolution invisible de 1946 à 1975*, Fayard, 1979;

Women after the Liberation:

Claire Duchen, *Women's Rights and Women's Lives in France, 1944–1968*, Routledge, 1994;

The second volume of Simone de Beauvoir's memoirs covers her intellectual development from the 1930s into the period of the Occupation, and her early relationship with Sartre, *La Force de l'âge*, Gallimard, 1960, translated as *The Prime of Life*, Penguin, 1965;

Elizabeth Fallaize (ed.), *Simone de Beauvoir. A Critical Reader*, Routledge, 1998.

Peasantry:

Henri Mendras, *La Fin des paysans. Innovation et changement dans l'agriculture française*, Sédéis, 1967;

Susan Carol Rogers, *Shaping Modern Times in Rural France. The Transformation and Reproduction of an Aveyronnais Community*, Princeton University Press, 1991.

Imperial wars and decolonization

Issues of decolonization:

Frantz Fanon, *Les Damnés de la terre*, Maspero, 1961, translated as *The Wretched of the Earth*, MacGibbon and Kee, 1965, the necessity and ideology of liberation;

Raymond F. Betts, *France and Decolonization 1900–1960*, Macmillan, 1991;

Guy Pervillé, *De l'Empire français à la décolonisation*, Hachette, 1995;

Charles-Robert Ageron, *La Décolonisation française*, Armand Colin, 1991;

Kristin Ross, *Fast Cars and Clean Bodies: decolonization and the reordering of French culture*, Cambridge (USA), MIT Press, 1995, stimulating and original approach.

Indo-China war:

Martin Shipway, *The Road to War: France and Vietnam, 1944–1947*, Oxford, Berghahn, 1996, crucial account of the origins;

Alan Ruscio, *La Guerre française d'Indochine*, Éditions Complexe, 1992;

Excellent collection of articles in Charles-Robert Ageron and Philippe Devillers (eds), 'Les guerres d'Indochine de 1945 à 1975', *Cahiers de l'Institut d'Histoire du Temps Présent*, No. 34, June 1996.

Algerian war:

Alistair Horne, *A Savage War of Peace: Algeria 1954–1962*, Macmillan, 1972, still a moving, perceptive and impressive history;

Jean-Pierre Rioux (ed.), *La Guerre d'Algérie et les français*, Fayard, 1990, comprehensive coverage;

Mohammed Harbi, *La Guerre commence en Algérie*, Éditions Complexe, 1984;

Benjamin Stora, *Messali Hadj, pionnier du nationalisme algérien, 1898–1974*, L'Harmattan, 1987;

Charles-Robert Ageron (ed.), *L'Algérie des Français*, Seuil, 1993, with chapters on terrorism in Algeria, the OAS and the *pieds-noirs*, and on the *Harkis*;

Irwin M. Wall, *France, United States and the Algerian War*, Berkeley, University of California Press, 2001.

The combatants: Danièle Djamila Amrane-Minne, *Des femmes dans la guerre d'Algérie*, Karthala, 1994; Martin S. Alexander, Martin Evans and J. F. V. Keiger (eds), *The Algerian War and the French Army, 1954–62. Experiences, Images, Testimonies*, Palgrave, 2002, starts with an excellent chapter on the 'War without a name' and the recovery of testimony;

Claire Mauss-Copeaux, *Appelés en Algérie. La parole confisquée*, Hachette, 1998;

Patrick Rotman and Bertrand Tavernier, *La guerre sans nom: les appelés d'Algérie*, Seuil, 1992;

Torture in Algeria:

Henri Alleg, *La Question*, Éditions de Minuit, 1958, and the revelations of Pierre Vidal-Naquet, *Torture: Cancer of Democracy, France and Algeria 1954–62*, Penguin, 1963, together with his autobiographical account, *Face à la raison d'État. Un historien dans la guerre d'Algérie*, La Découverte, 1989, and his account of *L'Affaire Audin*, Éditions de Minuit, 1989.

Resistance, memory and images:

Hervé Hamon and Patrick Rotman, *Les Porteurs de valises. La résistance française à la guerre d'Algérie*, Albin Michel, 1979, the pioneer and influential account;

Martin Evans, *The Memory of Resistance. French Opposition to the Algerian War (1954–1962)*, Oxford, Berg, 1997, an invaluable oral-based history, extending the meaning of resistance;

Jean-Pierre Rioux and Jean-François Sirinelli (eds), *La Guerre d'Algérie et les intellectuels français*, Éditions Complexe, 1991;

Benjamin Stora, *La Gangrène et l'oubli. La mémoire de la guerre d'Algérie*, La Découverte, 1991/1998, a vital contribution to the memory and identity themes of the 1980s and 1990s;

Gilles Manceron and Hassan Remaoun, *D'une rive à l'autre. La guerre d'Algérie: de la mémoire à l'histoire*, Syros, 1993, bringing French and Algerian perspectives together;

Nancy Wood, *Germaine Tillion, une femme-mémoire. D'une Algérie à l'autre*, Autrement, 2003, shrewd and important insights into a remarkable life;

Philip Dine, *Images of the Algerian War: French Fiction and Film, 1954–1962*, Clarendon Press, 1994, an excellent study.

De Gaulle and the Fifth Republic

De Gaulle and Gaullism:

Alexander Werth, *De Gaulle. A Political Biography*, Penguin, 1965;

Jean Lacouture, *De Gaulle. The Ruler: 1945–1970*, Collins Harvill, 1991;

Serge Berstein, *The Republic of De Gaulle, 1958–1969*, CUP, 1993;

Two concise biographical introductions: Andrew Shennan, *De Gaulle*, Longman, 1993, and Julian Jackson, *De Gaulle*, Sphere Books, 1990, revised for Haus Publishing 2003;

Maurice Agulhon, *De Gaulle. Histoire, symbole, mythe*, Plon, 2000;

Hugh Gough and John Horne (eds), *De Gaulle and Twentieth-Century France*, Edward Arnold, 1994;

Jean Touchard, *Le gaullisme 1940–1969*, Seuil, 1978;

J. Charlot, *The Gaullist Phenomenon: The Gaullist Movement in the Fifth Republic*, Allen and Unwin, 1971;

Odile Rudelle, *Mai 1958, de Gaulle et la République*, Plon, 1988;

Michel Debré, *Trois Républiques pour une France. Mémoires*, 2 vols., Albin Michel, 1988.

Nature of society:

Philip Williams and Martin Harrison, *Politics and Society in de Gaulle's Republic*, Longman, 1971, unerringly prescient on later approaches, with the subtitle of the first chapter, 'The Stalemate Society';

Stanley Hoffmann, *Decline or Renewal? France since the 1930s*, New York, Viking, 1974 edition, a collection of remarkable essays over eighteen years;

Michel Crozier, *La Société bloquée*, Seuil, 1971, translated as *The Stalled Society*, New York, Viking Press, 1973, the influential diagnosis of France between tradition and modernity, whose French title derived from Stanley Hoffmann's work;

John Ardagh encapsulated all the elements of France and the French which made up *The New France. A Society in Transition*, Penguin, 1970, a revised edition of his first account, *The New French Revolution*, Secker & Warburg, 1968;

Alain Touraine, *La Société post-industrielle*, Denoël, 1969, translated as *The Post-Industrial Society*, with its revealing subtitle, *Tomorrow's Social History: Classes, Conflicts and Culture in the Programmed Society*, Wildwood House, 1974.

Specific social studies:

Edgar Morin, *Commune en France: la métamorphose de Plodémet*, Fayard, 1967, translated as *Plodémet*, Penguin, 1971;

Laurence Wylie, *Village in the Vaucluse*, Harrap, 1961, immensely stimulating;

Abdelmalek Sayad, *Un Nanterre algérien, terre de bidonvilles*, Autrement, 1995.

1968

Patrick Seale and Maureen McConville, *French Revolution 1968*, Penguin, 1968, an instant and riveting account;

Charles Posner (ed.), *Reflections on the Revolution in France: 1968*, Penguin, 1970, showing the multifaceted nature of the events;

Raymond Aron, *La Révolution introuvable*, Fayard, 1968, translated as *The Elusive Revolution. Anatomy of a Student Revolt*, Pall Mall Press, 1969, an essential text in the immediate controversy about meaning;

Vladimir Fisera (ed.), *Writing on the Wall: France, May 1968*, Allison and Busby, 1978, full of ideas and interpretations;

Henri Weber, *Que reste-t-il de mai '68? Essai sur les interprétations des 'événements'*, Seuil, 1988/1998, a confrontation with the numerous theoretical perspectives;

G. Dreyfus-Armand, R. Frank, M.-F. Lévy and M. Zancarini-Fournel (eds), *Les Années '68: le temps de la contestation*, Éditions Complexe, 2000, an essential collection of articles, where hindsight and *parti pris* are taken for granted as main ingredients in the meanings given to 1968;

Claire Duchen, *Feminism in France from May 1968 to Mitterrand*, Routledge, 1986;

Peter Lennon, *Foreign Correspondent. Paris in the Sixties*, Picador, 1994, a personal insight into the decade from the *Guardian* correspondent;

David Caute, *Sixty-eight: The Year of the Barricades*, Paladin, 1988, gives wide context;

Two stimulating cultural studies:

Keith Reader with Khursheed Wadia, *The May 1968 Events in France: Reproductions and Interpretations*, Macmillan, 1993, and Margaret Atack, *May 68 in French Fiction and Film. Rethinking Society, Rethinking Representation*, OUP, 1999.

Political legacy is examined throughout the above books, but note also;

Jean-Pierre Le Goff, *May '68, l'héritage impossible*, La Découverte, 1998, a significant personal essay which mixes involvement and critique;

Kristin Ross, *May '68 and Its Afterlives*, University of Chicago Press, 2002, on ideological continuity into subsequent politics.

PART THREE. 1960s–2000s

Politics and society in the 1970s

Eric Roussel, *Georges Pompidou, 1911–1974*, J. C. Lattès, 1994;
Andrew Knapp, *Gaullism since de Gaulle*, Aldershot, Dartmouth Press, 1994;
Bernard Esambert, *Pompidou: capitaine d'industries*, Odile Jacob, 1994;
John Frears, *France in the Giscard Presidency*, Allen and Unwin, 1981.

The 'New France' is widely discerned during the 1960s (see **De Gaulle and the Fifth Republic** above) and important studies continue to analyse exactly what it means throughout the 1970s and 1980s (see also **The Mitterrand Years** below):
Henri Mendras, *La Seconde Révolution française (1965–1984)*, Gallimard, 1988, translated and adapted by Alistair Cole as *Social Change in Modern France. Towards a Cultural Anthropology of the Fifth Republic*, CUP, 1991;
D. L. Hanley, A. P. Kerr and N. H. Waites, *Contemporary France. Politics and Society since 1945*, Routledge & Kegan Paul, 1979;
Valéry Giscard d'Estaing's political project is outlined in his *Démocratie française*, Fayard, 1976, and for perceptive essays on Giscard and Giscardian policy-making, Vincent Wright (ed.), *Continuity and Change in France*, George Allen and Unwin, 1984;
Yvan Gastaut, *L'immigration et l'opinion en France sous la Ve République*, Seuil, 2000, gives comprehensive details of all reactions to immigration, and is a vital source for little-known conflicts and protests;
Michel Sarazin, *Une Femme Simone Veil*, Robert Laffont, 1987.

The Mitterrand Years

Jean Lacouture, *Mitterrand. Vol. I, Les risques de l'escalade*, Seuil, 1998, gives biographical background to 1981;
Pierre Péan, *Une Jeunesse française. François Mitterrand, 1934–1947*, Fayard, 1994, and his study of Mitterrand's last years, *Dernières volontés, derniers combats, dernières souffrances*, Plon, 2002;
Alistair Cole, *François Mitterrand. A study in political leadership*, Routledge, 1997;
J. Hayward (ed.), *De Gaulle to Mitterrand: presidential power in France*, Hurst, 1993;
D. S. Bell and Byron Criddle, *The French Socialist Party. The Emergence of a Party of Government*, Clarendon Press, second edition, 1988;
On different socialist currents, Gilles Martinet's memoir listed under **The 1930s** above;

Julius W. Friend, *The Long Presidency. France in the Mitterrand Years, 1981–1995*, Boulder, Westview Press, 1998;

Sudhir Hazareesingh, *Intellectuals and the French Communist Party. Disillusion and Decline*, Clarendon Press, 1991;

David L. Looseley, *The Politics of Fun. Cultural Policy and Debate in Contemporary France*, Oxford, Berg, 1995;

Mark Hunter, *Les Jours les plus Lang*, Odile Jacob, 1990;

Régis Debray, *Le Pouvoir intellectuel en France*, Ramsey, 1979, translated as *Teachers, Writers, Celebrities. The Intellectuals of Modern France*, Verso, 1981.

'End of exceptionalism':

A good contextual analysis of French politics since the war and an introduction to the debate, Nick Hewlett, *Modern French Politics. Analysing Conflict and Consensus since 1945*, Cambridge, Polity Press, 1998;

The basic text on this debate is François Furet, Jacques Julliard and Pierre Rosanvallon, *La République du centre. La fin de l'exception française*, Calmann-Lévy, 1988; and the debate is central to definitions of change and continuity, following the approach of Stanley Hoffmann and colleagues (see **General works** and **De Gaulle and the Fifth Republic** above): George Ross, Stanley Hoffmann, Sylvia Malzacher (eds), *The Mitterrand Experiment. Continuity and Change in Modern France*, Cambridge, Polity Press, 1987, and James F. Hollifield and George Ross (eds), *Searching for the New France*, Routledge, 1991;

Many other important and perceptive analyses of the 'New France':

Emmanuel Todd, *La Nouvelle France*, Seuil, 1988, translated as *Making of Modern France: ideology, politics and culture*, Oxford, Blackwell, 1991;

John Gaffney (ed.), *France and Modernization*, Avebury, 1988;

Gino Raymond (ed.), *France during the Socialist Years*, Aldershot, Dartmouth Press, 1994;

A. Daley (ed.), *The Mitterrand Era*, Macmillan, 1996;

Mairi Maclean (ed.), *The Mitterrand Years: Legacy and Evaluation*, Macmillan, 1998;

Gregory Flynn (ed.), *Remaking the Hexagon. The New France in the New Europe*, Boulder, Westview Press, 1995;

Tony Chafer and Brian Jenkins (eds), *France from the Cold War to the New World Order*, Macmillan, 1996.

Richard F. Kuisel, *Seducing the French: the dilemma of Americanization*, Berkeley, University of California Press, 1993;

Jack Hayward, *The State and the Market Economy: Industrial Patriotism and Economic Intervention in France*, Harvester Wheatsheaf, 1986.

Consensus and oscillation

John Tuppen, *Chirac's France, 1986–88. Contemporary Issues in French Society*, Macmillan, 1991;

John T. S. Keeler and Martin A. Schain (eds), *Chirac's Challenge. Liberalization, Europeanization, and Malaise in France*, Macmillan, 1996.

Anne Stevens provides a detailed and comprehensive guide to *The Government and Politics of France*, Macmillan, second edition 1996;

Élisabeth Schemla, *Édith Cresson, la femme piégée*, Flammarion, 1993;

Lionel Jospin, *Modern Socialism*, Fabian Society, 1999;

Ben Clift, 'The political economy of the Jospin government' *M&CF*, Vol. 10, No. 3, August 2002, an excellent special issue on 'The Jospin government 1997–2002'.

Social protests:

Pierre Bourdieu, *Contre-feux*, Liber-Raisons d'Agir, 1998, translated as *Acts of Resistance. Against the New Myths of our Time*, Cambridge, Polity Press, 1998;

René Mouriaux and Françoise Subileau, 'Les grèves françaises de l'automne 1995; défense des acquis ou mouvement social?' *M&CF*, Vol. NS4, No. 3, 1996;

José Bové and François Dufour, with Gilles Luneau, *Le Monde n'est pas une marchandise. Des paysans contre la malbouffe*, La Découverte, 2000;

Jean-Philippe Martin, 'José Bové, un activiste sans projet?', *M&CF*, Vol. 11, No. 3, August 2003, a stimulating special issue on 'Tradition and Modernity in Rural France'.

Plurality

Religious and racial diversity and conflict:

Alec G. Hargreaves, *Immigration, 'race' and ethnicity in contemporary France*, Routledge, 1995; and the excellent collection of essays edited by himself and Mark McKinney, *Post-Colonial Cultures in France*, Routledge, 1997;

Françoise Gaspard and Farhad Khosrokhavar, *Le Foulard et la République*, La Découverte, 1995, and Farhad Khosrokhavar, *L'Islam des jeunes*, Flammarion, 1997;

Jane Freedman and Carrie Tarr (eds), *Women, Immigration and Identities in France*, Oxford, Berg, 2000;

Martine Cohen, 'Les Juifs de France. Modernité et identité', *Vingtième Siècle*, No. 66, April–June 2000, and in the same issue, Danièle Hervieu-Léger, 'Le Miroir de l'Islam en France';

Benjamin Stora, *Le Transfert d'une mémoire. De l'Algérie française au racisme anti-arabe*, La Découverte, 1999;

Peter Davies, *The National Front in France: Ideology, Discourse and Power*, Routledge, 1999;

Michel Wieviorka, *La France raciste*, Seuil, 1992, an investigation into the racism of several towns, and his highly thoughtful discussion, *Une Société fragmentée? Le multiculturalisme en débat*, La Découverte, 1996.

Other diversities:

Cécile Velu, 'Faut-il "pactiser" avec l'universalisme? A short history of the PACS', *M&CF*, Vol. 7. No. 4, November 1999;

Jean-François Chanet, 'Terroirs et pays: mort et transfiguration?', *Vingtième Siècle*, No. 69, January–March, 2001;

Tzvetan Todorov, *L'Homme dépaysé*, Seuil, 1996, a personal essay on transculturation.

Films and film-makers:

Phil Powrie, *French Cinema in the 1980s. Nostalgia and the Crisis of Masculinity*, Clarendon Press, 1997, and his edited collection of essays, *French Cinema in the 1990s. Continuity and Difference*, OUP, 1999;

The series on French Film Directors, published by Manchester University Press, has many excellent studies, among which, Susan Hayward, *Luc Besson*, 1998, Carrie Tarr, *Diane Kurys*, 1999, Sue Harris, *Bertrand Blier*, 2001, and Hugo Frey, *Louis Malle*, 2004;

For the wider French-speaking cinema note the invaluable Lieve Spaas, *The Francophone Film. A Struggle for Identity*, Manchester University Press, 2000.

Memory and identity

Many of the following are specifically discussed in Chapter 22:

Fernand Braudel, *L'identité de la France. Espace et Histoire*, Arthaud-Flammarion, 1986, translated by Siân Reynolds as *The Identity of France, Vol. I, History and Environment*, Fontana, 1990;

Pierre Nora (ed.), *Les Lieux de mémoire*, 7 vols, Gallimard, 1984 to 1992, translated as *Realms of Memory: The Construction of the French Past*, 3 vols., New York, Columbia University Press, 1997;

Henry Rousso, *Le Syndrome de Vichy, 1944–198 . . .*, Seuil, 1987, translated as *The Vichy Syndrome: history and memory in France since 1944*, Cambridge (Mass.), Harvard University Press, 1991;

Sarah Farmer, *Martyred Village. Commemorating the 1944 Massacre at Oradour-sur-Glane*, Berkeley, University of California Press, 1999;

Jean-Jacques Fouché, 'Le Centre de la Mémoire d'Oradour', *Vingtième Siècle*, No. 73, January–March 2002;

Annette Wieviorka, *L'Ère du témoin*, Plon, 1998;

Claudine Vegh, *Je ne lui ai pas dit au revoir. Des enfants de déportés parlent*, Gallimard, 1979;

Jean-Luc Einaudi, *La Bataille de Paris, 17 octobre 1961*, Seuil, 1991;

Jim House, 'Antiracist memories: the case of 17 October 1961 in historical perspective', *M&CF*, Vol. 9, No. 3, August 2001;

Fanny Colonna (ed.), *Aurès/Algérie, 1954. Les fruits verts d'une révolution*, Autrement, 1994, memory and experience of Algerians;

Nancy Wood, *Vectors of Memory. Legacies of Trauma in Postwar Europe*, Oxford, Berg, 1999, and her essay among many excellent ones in Richard J. Golsan (ed.), *The Papon Affair. Memory and Justice on Trial*, Routledge, 2000;

Sarah Blowen, Marion Demossier and Jeanine Picard (eds), *Recollections of France. Memories, Identities and Heritage in Contemporary France*, Oxford, Berghahn, 2000;

On the question of identity within Europe an excellent anthology of approaches and ideas, Patrick Savidan (ed.), *La République ou l'Europe?*, Livre de Poche, 2004.

Contemporary France

Jill Forbes, Nick Hewlett and François Nectoux, *Contemporary France. Essays and Texts on Politics, Economics, and Society*, Longman, 1994, new edition 2001, well-selected texts in French, with accompanying essays;

Sheila Perry (ed.), *Aspects of Contemporary France*, Routledge, 1997, interpretative essays on institutions and socio-cultural identities;

J. E. Flower (ed.), *France Today*, Hodder and Stoughton, eighth edition, 2002;

Mairi Maclean and Susan Milner, 'France and Globalisation', *M&CF*, Vol. 9, No. 3, August 2001;

Special edition of *M&CF*, Vol. 12, No. 1, February 2004, edited by Joanna Drugan, Jim House and Sarah Waters, entitled 'New Voices in French Politics', points to today's and tomorrow's range of political involvement;

John Marks and Enda McCaffrey (eds), *French Cultural Debates*, Melbourne, Monash University, 2001, good theoretical approaches;

David Looseley, 'Cultural policy in the twenty-first century: issues, debates and discourse', *FCS*, Vol. 10, No. 28, February 1999, and his excellent *Popular Music in Contemporary France. Authenticity, Politics, Debate*, Oxford, Berg, 2003;

Michael Peters, 'Against Finkielkraut's *La Défaite de la pensée*: culture, postmodernism and education', *FCS*, Vol. 4, No. 11, June 1993;

Christopher Flood and Nick Hewlett (eds), *Currents in Contemporary French Intellectual Life*, Macmillan, 2000.

As clearly signalled on many pages of this book, it is essential to consult the journal *Modern and Contemporary France (M&CF)* for sustained excellence on all aspects of contemporary French society, politics and culture. *French Cultural Studies (FCS)* is central to the ever-increasing scope of cultural history, while *Vingtième Siècle* publishes new work of quality across the whole of the last 100 years. Equally vital: *French Historical Studies*, for example its special issue on 'Writing French Colonial Histories', edited by Alice L. Conklin and Julia Clancy-Smith, Vol. 27, No. 3, 2004; *French History; Le Mouvement Social; Guerres Mondiales et Conflits Contemporains; French Politics, Culture and Society*; and *Revue d'Histoire Moderne et Contemporaine*.

Index

For abbreviations please consult *Abbreviations and Glossary* pp. 671–8.

PENGUIN BOOKS

Published by the Penguin Group
Penguin Books Ltd, 80 Strand, London WC2R ORL, England
Penguin Group (USA) Inc., 375 Hudson Street, New York, New York 10014, USA
Penguin Group (Canada), 90 Eglinton Avenue East, Suite 700, Toronto, Ontario, Canada M4P 2Y3
(a division of Pearson Penguin Canada Inc.)
Penguin Ireland, 25 St Stephen's Green, Dublin 2, Ireland (a division of Penguin Books Ltd)
Penguin Group (Australia), 250 Camberwell Road, Camberwell, Victoria 3124, Australia
(a division of Pearson Australia Group Pty Ltd)
Penguin Books India Pvt Ltd, 11 Community Centre, Panchsheel Park, New Delhi – 110 017, India
Penguin Group (NZ), cnr Airborne and Rosedale Roads, Albany, Auckland 1310, New Zealand
(a division of Pearson New Zealand Ltd)
Penguin Books (South Africa) (Pty) Ltd, 24 Sturdee Avenue, Rosebank, Johannesburg 2196, South Africa

Penguin Books Ltd, Registered Offices: 80 Strand, London WC2R ORL, England

www.penguin.com

First published by Allen Lane 2005
Published in Penguin Books 2006
1

Copyright © H. R. Kedward, 2005
All rights reserved

The moral right of the author has been asserted

Typeset by Rowland Phototypesetting Ltd, Bury St Edmunds, Suffolk
Printed in England by Clays Ltd, St Ives plc

ISBN-13: 978-0-140-13095-9
ISBN-10: 0-140-13095-0

LA VIE EN BLEU

FRANCE AND THE FRENCH SINCE 1900

ROD KEDWARD

## Chapter One

BROKEN ARROW RANCH, SPRING 2011

The Young Family—

Father Neil, Mother Pegi,

Children Amber and Ben

I pulled back the plastic sticky tape from the cardboard box. Wrapping paper was on the ground around my feet. Ben watched from his chair, and Amber and Pegi sat around me. I carefully lifted the heavy weight out of the box. It was further wrapped in packing paper and then a final layer of some foamy quarter-inch-thick protective material. Then it was revealed: a locomotive switcher with handmade Lionel markings. Curiously, it was not a real Lionel. It must have been some kind of prototype. There was a white typewritten sheet in the box from Lenny Carparelli, one of the endless stream of Italian-Americans connected in one way or another to the history of Lionel, a company I still have a small share of. I read the sheet. The model was from General Models Corporation. It was a beautiful switcher, and it was indeed the prototype that Lionel had used to create its own model. As the letter pointed out, this happened back in the days before corporate lawsuits and trade secrets invaded every little area of creativity and design.

Pegi always gives me Lionel collectibles for holidays, and I now have a very extensive collection of rarities, all proudly displayed behind glass in a room with a giant train layout. It is not a normal train layout: The scenery is made up of redwood stumps for mountains and moss for grassy fields. The railroad has fallen on hard times. A drought has ensued. Track work, once accomplished by hardworking teams of Chinese laborers, has been left dormant. Now expensive, highly detailed Lionel steam engines from China traverse the tracks. My railroad is historic in its own way as the site of many electronic development programs where the Lionel command control and sound systems were conceived and built from scratch; then the prototypes were tested and the software was written, tested, rewritten, and retested. Heady stuff, this electronics development. It all started with Ben Young.

Ben was born a quadriplegic, and I was just getting back into trains at the time, reintroducing myself to a pastime I had enjoyed as a child. Sharing the building of the layout together was one of our happiest times. He was still in his little bassinet when the Chinese laborers originally laid the track, thousands of them toiling endless hours through the nights and days. He watched as we worked. Then, after months, it eventually came time to run the trains, and later I devised a switch system run by a big red button that he could work with his hand. It took a lot of effort, but it was very rewarding for him to see the cause and effect in action. Ben was empowered by this.

That was thirty-three years ago, though, and now I have the Windex out and I am cleaning the glass doors on the display shelves where my prized Lionel possessions are kept safe and sound for all to see. Not that anybody ever comes here. You could count the visitors on your hand. Which is unfortunate, considering the amount of care that has gone into the display. The display and lay-out create a Zen experience. They allow me to sift through the chaos, the songs, the people, and the feelings from my upbringing that still haunt me today. Not in a bad way, but not in an entirely good way, either. Months go by with boxes piled everywhere and trains derailed with dust gathering on them. Then, miraculously, I reappear and clean and organize, working with every little detail for hours on end, making it all run perfectly again. This seems to coincide with other creative processes.

I remember one day David Crosby and Graham Nash were vis-iting me at the train barn during the recording of *American Dream*, a lot of which we did on my ranch at Plywood Digital, a barn that was converted to a recording studio. We had a truck parked out-side full of recording equipment and were working on several new songs. We were all pretty excited about playing together again. Crosby had recently gotten straight, was recovering from his addic-tion to freebase, had just completed jail time he got for something having to do with a loaded weapon in Texas, and was still prone to taking naps between takes. His system was pretty much in shock, and he was doing the best he could because he loves the band and the music so much. There is no one I know who loves making music more than David Crosby. Graham Nash has been his best friend for years, through thick and thin, and they sing together in a way that shows the depth of their long relationship.

They met in the Hollies and the Byrds, two seminal bands in the history of rock and roll, and then came together with Stephen Stills to form Crosby, Stills & Nash around 1970. CSN's first record is a work of art. It defined a sound that has been imitated for years by other groups, some of which have enjoyed greater commercial success, but there can be no mistaking the groundbreaking nature of that first CSN album. Stephen played most of the music then, overdubbing all the parts during the night with Dallas Taylor, the drummer, and Graham. There was so much Stephen had wanted to do with Buffalo Springfield in the years just before—like producing, writing, and arranging harmonies, as well as playing more guitar—and CSN was his first opportunity to be really creative after the Springfield ended, and he went for it big-time. But more about that later . . .

Anyway, I saw David looking at one of my train rooms full of rolling stock and stealing a glance at Graham that said, *This guy is cuckoo. He's gone nuts. Look at this obsession.* I shrugged it off. I need it. For me it is a road back.

Anyway, now I'm polishing the glass on one of the display shelves that houses my collection. With the glass all cleaned and sparkling, I stand in the room alone and admire the beautiful Lionel models, all perfectly lined up in an order that only I understand.

I leave that building and walk about 150 feet over to Feelgood's Garage. Feelgood's is full of my amps, old Fenders mostly, but also some Magnatones, Marshalls, and the odd Gibson. I remember my first Fender amp: I got it as a gift from my mom. She always supported my music. It was a piggyback model that was on top of the speaker cabinet. Two ten-inch speakers delivered the whopping sound of the smallest piggyback amp Fender ever made. But to me it was HUGE. Before that I had an Ampeg Echo Twin. I used to dream about amps and stage setups in school, drawing diagrams and planning stage layouts. I didn't do real well in those classes.

Feelgood's has my cars, too. I have a thing for transportation. Cars, boats, trains. Traveling. I like moving. Once when I was walking along a street in LA at age twenty-two or twenty-three, I saw a place called Al Axelrod's. It was a car repair place. There was a red convertible's rear end poking out of the garage. I recognized it as a '53 or '54 Buick. When I was young, one of my dad's friends, the writer Robertson Davies, lived near us in Peterborough, Ontario. We used to go to his house every Christmas and play charades at a party. He had a bunch of daughters. Very exciting. Anyway, he also had a '54 Buick. It was brand-new and made a large impression on me, with its beautifully designed grille, taillights, and an overall shape that featured a kind of bump or ripple in the lines at about the midpoint, accentuated by a chrome strip that mirrored it. This ripple emanated from the rear wheel's circular well and was unique to Buicks.

So I went inside Al Axelrod's and saw my first Buick Skylark. It really blew my mind. Only about 1,690 of that model were ever made! It was custom chopped at the factory about the same time as GM introduced the Eldorado and the Corvette. I looked for a Skylark for years after that, and finally Jon McKeig found one in a body shop in Pleasanton, California. Jon was a Vietnam vet who was taking care of my cars. He was an excellent body and paint man. I had him do a job for me, and then I hired him to come and work for me taking care of the thirty-five cars I had acquired by then. All of them were wild designs. Mostly from the fifties; a lot of Cadillacs. I was not overly interested in their mechanical condition when I bought them, just wanted those unique shapes. (That turned out to have been a big mistake, because most of them didn't run well and took a lot of time and money to restore. It would have been better and less expensive to just get original cars in excellent condition.) Anyway, after years and years of collecting, I sold a lot of them and just kept the good ones. Most of them were right there in Feelgood's. The best in my collection is a 1953 Buick Skylark, the one that Jon found, body number one. The first one ever made. That is the Big Kahuna.

So here I am, writing at Feelgood's, looking at my cars and a conference table with a whiteboard. Tomorrow is a big meeting with Alex, a representative who works for Len Blavatnik, the new owner of WMG, my record company. The reason for the meeting is my new start-up company, PureTone. At least that's what we're calling it this week. It's very early, and we are still changing names. The company aims to rescue my art form, music, from the degradation in quality that I think is at the heart of the decline of music sales and ultimately music itself in popular culture. With the advent of the new online music retailers, such as iTunes, has come terrible quality. An MP3 has about five percent of the data that can be found in a PureTone master file, or even a vinyl record. I have an idea to build a portable player and online distribution model to present a quality alternative to MP3s with the convenience today's consumers demand. I want to bring the soul of the music industry and the technology of Silicon Valley together to create this new model using artists as the drivers. My goal is to restore an art form and protect the original art while serving the music lover.

Tomorrow is the big presentation day, and I am going over my approach, which has been guided by PureTone CEO candidate Mark Goldstein, a start-up specialist introduced to me by friends of mine from the Silicon Valley community. These friends of mine are brilliant and very successful. Unlike me, they have mastered the art of monetizing their ideas. I have big ideas and very little money to show for them. I'm not complaining, though. It's not the money that matters; it's doing things right and efficiently that is my goal. I just want to succeed at this so badly.

I dislike what has happened to the quality of the sound of music; there is little depth or feeling left, and people can't get what they need from listening to music anymore, so it is dying. That is my theory. Recording is my first love in the creative field (along with songwriting and music making), so this really cuts to the quick. I want to do something about it. So it is important that I get my thoughts together, impress this gentleman, and get some financial backing for this project, which will surely need it.

My Skylark is right here with me.

With Crazy Horse—left to right, Ralph Molina, Billy Talbot, Frank "Poncho" Sampedro—on Malibu Beach, 1975.

Chapter Two

California, 2011

N ot that it matters much, but recently I stopped smoking and drinking.

I am now the straightest I have ever been since I was eighteen. The big question for me at this point is whether I will be able to write songs this way. I haven't yet, and that is a big part of my life. Of course I am now sixty-five, so my writing may not be as easy-flowing as it once was, but on the other hand, I *am* writing this book. I'll check in with you on that later. We'll see how it goes.

My doctor said it would be good for me to stop smoking weed because he sees a sign of something developing in my brain, and I am listening to him. My dad was a great writer and he lost his cognizance to dementia at about age seventy-five, so I am wary of that. When I stopped smoking weed, I threw in drinking, too, because I had never stopped both simultaneously and I thought it might be nice to get to know myself again. When my daughter stopped drinking a few years ago, I was very impressed by the example she set for our family. I love life with my wife, Pegi, and the kids, and want to live as much of it as I can, but not as a burden to anyone.

Although I have not written any songs in a while, a few songs that mean a lot to me and may have shaped my songwriting are listed here: "Crazy Mama" by JJ Cale is a record I love. The song is true, simple, and direct, and the delivery is very natural. JJ's guitar playing is a huge influence on me. His touch is unspeakable. I am stunned by it. "Like a Rolling Stone" by Bob Dylan is as fresh as the first day I heard it—I can still remember that afternoon in Toronto. It changed my life. The poetry, attitude, and ambience of that piece are part of my makeup. I absorbed it. "Be My Baby" by the Ronettes has a sound I always will love. It is in my soul. Ronnie sings it so great. The groove, the beautifully resonant background vocals, the track: It is all one thing. Phil Spector is a genius. Jack Nitzsche is a genius. "Evergreen" by Roy Orbison is one of the most beautiful sentiments ever recorded. I can still hear Roy's voice and feel my girlfriend's love. "Four Strong Winds" by Ian & Sylvia speaks to me always. It occupies part of my heart. There is a feeling in it. I love the prairies, Canada, my life as a Canadian. Of course I love songwriting, so I know someday I will write again.

I also have been thinking about Crazy Horse. To me, that band is a vehicle to cosmic areas that I am unable to traverse with others. Some people have asked me why I play with them. They say, "Why do you play with Crazy Horse? They can't play." The answer is blowin' in the wind. I can go places with them. Pegi just recorded "I Don't Want to Talk About It," written by Danny Whitten, the original Crazy Horse guitar player and singer who's all over *Early Daze*, an album of songs from the beginning of Crazy Horse that I have been working on compiling recently. Danny was every bit the artist that I am, but he died of a heroin OD in the early seventies. Every time I hear Pegi sing that song, it makes me tremendously sad. She sings it so beautifully, phrasing it to break my heart. She does it justice. You can see I have some unfinished business there, reckoning with Danny.

I have been working on *Crazy Horse: The Early Daze* for a few months, collecting unreleased tracks that tell a story of the band that no others can tell. Crazy Horse, formed at the beginning of 1969 with myself, Danny Whitten, Ralph Molina, and Billy Talbot, is still together today, in 2011. I love working on this *Early Daze* record. It makes me feel good. I told Ralphie, Crazy Horse's drummer, about this and how cool it was. He remembered that there were a lot of things that never saw the light of day. Now they will. He was very excited. I just have to finish it. At least get it on the road to being done. I will have to be hands-on for that.

Danny's playing is all over those early tracks. I miss him still. He would have grown to be great, and we would have really made history with him. I have some regrets there, but *this* record will set some of it straight. After Danny's passing, I was devastated, but I was also booked on the road doing the Time Fades Away tour in 1973 with Jack Nitzsche, Kenny Buttrey, Tim Drummond, and Ben Keith. The tour went on. Danny was supposed to play in that band. Only Tim and I are left now.

Back to the Horse. In 1974, after Danny's death, Poncho Sampedro was introduced to me by Billy Talbot, our bass player, and we became Crazy Horse again with Poncho on guitar. It was a different band, great in a new way. To his credit, Poncho would not try to play anyone else's parts. He was Poncho. That was a really good attitude, and it enabled us to stay true to ourselves, pick up the pieces, and move on. So we did, with *Zuma*, *American Stars 'n Bars*, and *Rust Never Sleeps*. We are a great live band, and playing with Crazy Horse is transcendent for me. If I only had a few new songs . . . I need new to get there.

Redoing old songs doesn't work very well. New blood. That's what the Horse needs. So I have a plan: Crazy Horse at the White House. Get together on my ranch in the big White House, a sprawling ranch-style bungalow made of redwood, painted white, located in the redwoods on the Corte Madera Creek. It has been the center of music-related activity on the ranch since I purchased that part of the property in 1972. (This is not to be confused with the little White House, a small home for working folks on the old ranch back in the day that is now used to house visitors who may be working on musical projects.) The plan: Set up in there and record, leave the equipment at the ready for a year or so until we have a great record. Just keep playing and let the *muse* back into the fold. Gently now. No searching. No working. No trying. Just let the *spirit* come back in and don't be greedy. Be ready. That should put my straightness to the test.

I want to use our old tube recording console known as the Green Board (I think it is the best soundboard ever) and record 8-track on two-inch magnetic tape for the fattest analog sound possible. The Green Board is full of history. The Beach Boys' *Pet Sounds* and "Heroes and Villains," Cream's *Disraeli Gears*, the Monterey Pop Festival, and Wilson Pickett were all recorded through the Green Board. We will run Pro Tools digital alongside just to have the modern tools for fixing our mistakes, but I want that old tube sound. I love the tubes, with their chemical and gas reactions creating the sound. I think this will be fun and will work, and I am going to get that started today. I'll keep you posted.

I want to release this Crazy Horse recording as my first Pure-Tone release. That would really be cool. You know, the way people experience music today is so different from how it used to be. It's not the same part of the culture that it was. I think a lot of that has to do with the quality of the sound, so I am addressing that with PureTone. The music is not the problem. It's the sound.

Years ago, we always would listen to acetates (reference vinyls that can only be played a few times) and hear what we had done in the studio. That is how we listened. The feeling would be there immediately, and off we would go into the spirit world, listening, feeling, and absorbing the waves of sound. That was an amazing time. It is gone now, but we could get it back with a quality sound that is visceral.

Today music is presented as an entertainment medium, like a game, without the full audio quality. It's like a cool pastime or a toy, not like a message to the soul. So things have changed.

So I am making music again. That is the plan. Go for the music again. So here I go. It's always been good to me. I just want to feel it. I need to feel it in my body, sing lyrics that make me want to play my heart out in long instrumental passages that only the Horse can carry me on. I remember once in the studio we were recording and I caught Ralph's eye. He was in pure ecstasy just for a moment; we made visual contact, and I have never lost that feeling. It is like we felt the force of the Horse all at once! Now Ralph always says, "Don't look at me while I'm playing." I know why. He wants to not think about how he looks. He wants to play. So we ride together, but we also ride alone. Crazy Horse is an animal unto itself. Anyone who has witnessed a full-on barrage from the Horse knows that of which I speak.

When I think about music today, I am struck by the history of it all, how important that has become to the audience. Knowledge of the roots of rock and R&B is coveted. Tracks of that music will live forever. Those times were magic, and I know that they will never be lived again. I know that if I can bring them all back in their pristine glory with PureTone, it will be a revelation for music lovers today, to actually hear these songs the way they were with the original resonance, creating the feeling that moved a generation's hearts in the beginning. This is getting closer with every passing day . . .

I'm going back to the train barn to see if I can fix the derailment that ended my last visit. It should be easy. After that, I will let a little time pass and see what happens in there. Maybe take my computer with me and keep on writing this. That is the way I wrote the script for *Greendale*, by not stopping for anything. I just carried a pad with me and would write whenever something came to mind. At first I didn't know I was writing a story, just thought it was a bunch of songs that featured the same characters. Anyway, I'm going to pack this thing up and go over there.

It's summer now and the insects are all out. On the way to the train barn I notice that the swans who live in the lake in front of our house have no way to quickly make it back into the water if they are out walking and sense a bobcat, mountain lion, coyote, or other threat. We have lost a few birds lately, and this is something that needs to be taken care of.

Back at the railroad, the derailment was between two crossover track switches. That is where two mainlines now coincide. There used to be two mainlines at this location. Originally, Chinese laborers, working for the railroad, had built some beautifully intricate trestle bridges over a feeder track that passed under the original twin mainlines. When an earthquake shattered the ancient structure in the early eighties, the railroad, having fallen on hard times, was unable to finance the reconstruction. To get things moving again and recover lost revenue as quickly as possible, the mainlines were quickly consolidated into a temporary bridge that carried a new single mainline over the underlying feeder track that was still in use. This resulted in a congested location that was not originally planned for and has consequently become the site of more than one derailment and ensuing safety inspections.

It was not an easy task to fix the derailment, and took over five minutes. The two switches had to be placed into manual mode for the reassembly of the train after the derailed cars were re-railed. Once again, my expertise at re-railing by touch instead of vision— the result of many years' experience—saved a lot of time and got the railroad up and running before an official inspection was necessary. Having dodged that bullet, I sit down to continue my writing.

## Chapter Three

I have to tell you what happened at the meeting yesterday at Feelgood's.

The gentleman representing the new owner of WMG came by, and I took him and my partner Craig Kallman, CEO of Atlantic Records, for a ride in my 1978 Cadillac Eldorado to listen to PureTone. It was very important that the gentleman, Alex, understand what we were doing and advise his boss it would be a good idea to finance this endeavor, so I gave it my best. He got the difference in sound quality immediately, and I was very happy. So was Craig. This is important stuff. The making of musical history, repossessing our sound, and bringing it back to the masses. After all, improving the quality of life is the ultimate goal of technology.

With that in mind, I was demonstrating the Revealer, a feature that allows the listener to compare PureTone with lesser formats like CDs and MP3s. Suddenly, Craig was tapping my shoulder rather frantically. Looking up, I noticed I was on a collision course with another vehicle! I stopped just in time to avoid a head-on crash. It was my road and I was not expecting a visitor, but the lady driving the other car was the wife of the catering chef I had hired for this meeting, and she was bringing down some BBQ sauce. With that episode in the past, I regrouped and moved on with the demo.

Mark, our PureTone CEO candidate, had told me that as part of the demo I should show the video I had made of musicians riding in the PureTone Eldorado, listening and testifying to how they loved the sound of PureTone. Tom Petty, Mike D of the Beastie Boys, Flea of the Red Hot Chili Peppers, and Kid Rock were all in the video, along with Mumford & Sons and My Morning Jacket. They were all espousing the merits of PureTone, truly enthusiastic about the prospect of listeners actually hearing the same quality that the artists heard in the studio when the masters were recorded. Mark had told me to show Alex the video on the iPad—the same iPad I was using as the user interface to control the PureTone player. That would be the Silicon Valley way. And, after all, we are a Silicon Valley company, bringing artists' music and record companies together with the Cloud to save the sound of music. I deftly extracted the iPad from its holder, brought up the video, and played it back *from the middle*! Realizing my mistake, I took it back from Alex and got the main page up, returning the video to the top and starting again—only to realize that I had turned the sound off, mistaking the sound control for the control for the position of the video. Mr. Silicon Valley! Was I cool or what?

This demonstration was going nowhere, but I finally got it back on track. Thank God the video is very cool and makes a great point. Alex said he liked it a lot, and the whole idea seemed to be a hit. It will be the first of many episodes we plan on rolling out on Facebook just before the launch of PureTone, one video per day for over a month. What a demo! We still don't know what Alex is going to tell his boss: invest or pass? This is a heck of a business, this start-up thing. Not for the faint of heart.

It's the next day. I'm back at Feelgood's waiting for a three-o'clock meeting with our new partner, WMG, to get a grip on our PureTone plan going forward. The Skylark is looking good. I just got new license plates for it. They are old California plates I bought on eBay. Other cars in Feelgood's right now include a '47 Buick Roadmaster Estate Wagon woodie I brought to the ranch in 1970, a '54 Corvette I bought back in '74 (in which I first learned that Carrie, Zeke Young's mom, was pregnant), a '57 Eldorado Biarritz convertible that Pegi and I bought at the San Mateo County Fair Antique and Collector's Revival back in the day, and a '57 Jensen 541 I bought in Fort Lauderdale in 1975 while I was refitting the *WN Ragland*, my 1913 Baltic Trader, with my old buddy Roger Katz. Every car tells a story. They are all packed with good memories. My latest purchase, a 1963 Avanti, is in the shop getting ready to take up a residency in Feelgood's. Someday I hope to write a history of every car I have ever owned. Cars all have stories to tell.

I used to think that buying a car or a guitar was like buying someone's memories, feelings, and history. I would always get a song out of it. I will do anything to get a new song . . . An old car can take you new places. An old guitar, well, that's a whole other story.

The Green Board is sitting twenty feet away here in Feelgood's, looking like a museum piece. I want to bring it back to life—and myself with it. Sitting around here waiting for this meeting with all these things and stories attached to them, that's the way my life is. I'm a material guy it turns out, looking to unload in a way that helps everything get lighter.

Waiting is not my strength in most matters. I may be a very impatient person when I am focused on something I would like to see happen. I think things are moving along, but I can't play them like a guitar. That is obvious. Being a musician enables a person to bend the notes and express things that are inside you, no matter what. That is probably why I am so happy when I am playing music or making a record. I am very excited about using the Green Board to record this next album. I love the sound, and though I don't have even one song or idea at this point, I am looking forward to expressing something through music, anything. It is this process of getting away from music and doing other things that lets me stay really into music. I need relief from music so that I can appreciate it when I have the chance to partake. Just thinking about playing makes me feel more at home.

My friend Paul feels the same way. He loves music but has to get away from it to stay vital with it. It is certainly a balancing act. Paul and I are friends because we both knew and loved Linda, who I met first during Buffalo Springfield days. Linda was a wonderful girl and lady. Today we are in touch periodically and talk about music or whatever. I like Paul a lot. He played at the Bridge School Benefit for us a few years ago and was really great. He reminds me a little of a modern-day Charlie Chaplin, the way he moves and the attention he pays to his art.

Next week there will be a big meeting about Lincvolt, another project of mine that I have been working on for four years now, repowering a huge car to make it more energy efficient. Why? Because if I can do this with a big car, people will imagine what can be done with a small car. And people in this country are big. They have an urge to travel long distances—the roads in North America are long and beautiful. The scenery is God. Using a big car for an electric project resonates with the wandering spirit of America and brings attention to the cause, makes people talk about it—even if they think it's a dumb idea and go out of their way to say why it is, I am succeeding because people are talking about how they would do it better. How do we lose our dependence on fossil fuels? By not using them and doing it in dramatic ways that attract attention.

That is one reason the generator in Lincvolt runs on ethanol. Oh my God! *Ethanol?* I have heard so many bad things about this fuel. It uses food stock and takes away from the supply of food. No! There is a lot of misinformation about ethanol. Ethanol does not replace the food we are using. The amount of corn we are using for food has been the same for years. It is flatlining. We are using ethanol from corn, but it is not taking away from our food. It isn't taking away from our feed for animals, either. Ethanol suppliers like POET in South Dakota actually produce food for animals from the waste of ethanol production. I have gone another route with ethanol. Lincvolt uses cellulosic ethanol from biomass—and we have a lot of biomass on this continent. We could use it for something constructive.

Even Henry Ford was intrigued by the possibilities. The other day, when I was doing some research, I came upon a paper by Bill Kovarik, a Ph.D. who works at Radford University, called "Henry Ford, Charles Kettering, and the 'Fuel of the Future.'" Here's my version, partly derived from Kovarik's defining work. It's called "Lincvolt and the Ford Legacy."

> Back in the early 1900s, Henry Ford was thinking about the future and was receptive to building electric cars. As time passed, news reports had Ford's EV coming in 1915, then 1916. Details varied: It would cost somewhere between $500 and $750 (between $10,000 and $15,712 today) and would go somewhere between fifty and a hundred miles on a charge. Thomas Edison, Henry Ford's business partner and friend, divulged no details in an interview with Automobile Topics in May 1914. "Mr. Henry Ford is making plans for the tools, special machinery, factory buildings, and equipment for the production of this new electric," Edison said. "There is so much special work to be done that no date can be fixed now as to when the new electric can be put on the market. But Mr. Ford is working steadily on the details, and he knows his business so it will not be long."
> —Bill Kovarik

> We will never know how Henry Ford's vision of the future would have turned out if his dreams of biofuel-powered cars

had come true in the early twentieth century. What would it have been like if we had not powered our cars with gasoline? A classic Lincoln Continental convertible originally produced by Ford Motors in 1959 may just give us a glimpse. Repowered as a series hybrid with a 200KW prime mover and a Ford Hybrid 2.5L Atkinson engine, Lincvolt may be like Henry Ford's dream car. Lincvolt's Ford 2.5L is fueled by E 100 ethanol or E 85 ethanol from biomass. An A 123 battery pack stores the power for silent running around forty miles. The Lincvolt Continental Electro-Cruiser, built with American components, will be on the road in late 2012, making many aspects of Henry Ford's dream a reality.

The innovation will not end there. Building on the tradition of user-friendly technology, Lincvolt will feature the world's best-sounding audio system, PureTone. Taking full advantage of Cloud-based libraries of recordings by your favorite artists, Lincvolt will simply sound like no other car on earth. Lincvolt passengers will enjoy PureTone SQS (Studio-Quality Sound), making Lincvolt audio sound superior in quality and digital resolution to any music ever heard in a car.

Am I a dreamer or what? I write blog articles like this all the time, hoping I can make it happen one way or another. Now I have AVL, a prototype builder of electric cars for many automakers, building the electric drive train and controls, Paul Perrone of Perrone Robotics making it autonomous to help it gather even more attention, and Roy Brizio of Roy Brizio Street Rods building the final shape around this behemoth concept. A 1959 Lincoln Continental convertible is one of the largest cars ever built, measuring 19.5 feet overall and weighing about six thousand pounds with my modifications. It is smooth as glass and whisper quiet, runs about forty miles on a charge—about an average daily commute—and has unlimited mileage without stopping to recharge because of its ethanol-fueled generator system, the result of years of experimenting and failing with different approaches.

I did that experimenting, and it wasn't always fun. It sucked watching a tape of my electric car in a warehouse burning to the ground at three A.M. (more on that later). It hasn't been easy to do, but we just keep trying and knowing eventually a solution will rear its head. Many talented people have had to come together to show this could be done, and it is being built right now and on schedule for completion in 2012. Sometime I'll tell you a few other parts of that story, like the many times I had to go to Wichita, where the car was being repowered, and wait for something to happen that never really did happen. Or the two weeks my good friend Larry Johnson and I spent waiting around in Wichita, after taking a train from San Jose, having been assured by Johnathan Goodwin, the master mechanic hired to perform the repower, that Lincvolt was ready to roll out of Wichita as soon as we arrived. Yes, sometime I'll tell you . . .

It can be frustrating and it may stress relationships with family to the limit, and there is no guarantee of success or recognition of success. I don't know why I have to try these things and become so engrossed and obsessed with them. For sure music is a huge release from these types of projects.

At almost five, fishing on a bridge over the Pigeon River,
Omemee, Ontario, August 1950.

## Chapter Four

Ontario

My bedroom in Omemee was the home of my first train layout. It was an L-shaped layout my dad made for me, and I had a Marx train. The couplers were flat and fit together in a way that made them stay together, but if you tilted them one way the cars would come apart and disconnect. I still remember that layout well, so it made quite an impression on me. It was right across from my bed in the corner where I remember emptying my Christmas stocking at dawn to see what Santa had brought me and finding a great barnyard set with tiny horses, cows, and fences.

It was where I remember being when the doctor, Dr. Bill, came one day with his black bag and told my mom and dad something important out in the hallway. I was about five years old. My mommy was crying, and my daddy said, "Sure, Doc, right away. We'll go today." Then, after breakfast, I was taken to the car. It was hard for me to walk for some reason. I slept on the floor in the back of the car. My older brother, Bob, was there with me in the backseat, and Mommy and Daddy were in the front with Dr. Bill.

The next things I remember are this big metal table and the biggest needle I had ever seen. It turns out I was getting a lumbar puncture. That hurt like hell and scared me to death. I really think that was my first big trauma. Then there was a hospital bed and a nurse who always sang "Beautiful Brown Eyes" to me. Then I was trying to walk across the floor to my mommy from my daddy in a little room. My mommy had her hands open and said, "Come on, Neil!" So I went over to her in stiff little steps and everyone was happy. The whole thing took about a week, and then I was on my way home. My brother Bob remembers it this way:

In November of 1951, Neil was six. It was prior to that, I believe in the spring, that he contracted polio. Salk vaccine had not been invented. It was a very serious situation. It was obvious that his life was on the line. I could feel it from both my mother and father, but I knew it anyhow. He was taken to Sick Children's Hospital in Toronto in our car, a 1950 or '51 Monarch, with my father and Dr. Bill Earle, and Neil and me in the backseat. I think it was raining and dark. Neil was lying on a board on the floor. A lumbar puncture was done at the hospital and con-firmed he had polio. The treatment was lengthy but it worked and he survived. When he came home he had to learn to walk again. I remember him trying to get from one part of the living room to another by hanging on to furniture to keep his balance. He was unsure of what had happened with his battle with polio.

"I didn't die, did I?" he said. It was a serious question. There were two children across the street, one of whom may have contracted polio also. I believe their family name was Goddard. I spent a lot of time as a child in Omemee being quarantined because of diseases that caught Neil. There was polio and diphtheria, measles, and others. His health has always been an issue. Later, there was epilepsy. We both had to deal with that. I do not know why Neil has had to contend with all these things. Later in his life, vertebrae in his lower back had to be removed as a result of polio. He wore a brace for a long time and even toured in that condition, including his famous concert recording at Massey Hall in 1971, which so many people hold close.

Walking was hard for a while, and my back hurt. We had a quarantine sign on our house that said POLIOMYELITIS on it and warned people about not entering or something to that effect. No one wanted to be near me for a while. The neighborhood kids stayed away, and when they ran away up the street, I couldn't catch them. I remember not being very good at sports, and my back hurt when I was skating and leaning over, so my position as a goalie was in jeopardy on the rink. I couldn't skate that well, and the puck scared the hell out of me. I was not meant to play hockey—but my brother Bob was. He was great! He was so fast it was scary, and we went to his games for years, cheering him on. Then he gave up hockey and became a golfer full-time. Of course, it was summer when I got sick. I am just putting that together now.

We lived in a small Ontario town—OMEMEE, POPULATION 750, a sign at the outskirts of town said. That is where I remember

With my brother, Bob, and our mom, Rassy Young,
at Summit Golf & Country Club, Richmond Hill,
Ontario, circa 1958.

growing up the most. We had a house on the main street, which was Highway 7, and my dad's typewriter was upstairs in the attic. No one could go up there. Of course, I went up there to see why not. Daddy was always able to stop typing and talk to me. He called me Windy.

"What's on your mind, Windy?" he would ask.

Then I would tell him about the turtles in my sandbox or something along those lines. He was a writer, and that's what he did up there. That's all I knew at that point. He went up there every day and sat down and wrote on his typewriter. It was a big old Underwood with ribbon, a truly amazing machine that my dad loved. My mother used to edit for him, cleaning up his spelling and grammar, I suppose.

Now, here I am with my computer, sixty years later, finally following in my dad's footsteps. I am well prepared. It turns out he taught me everything I need to know, and it's just now that I have gotten around to using my training. He said, "Just write every day, and you'll be surprised what comes out."

He was a good dad. We spent a lot of good time together. For a while after my parents broke up, my mom was always badmouthing him, but I always knew he loved me. He stayed in Omemee when my mom and I moved to Winnipeg—I wish I had seen him more in my formative years. (What the hell is a formative year compared to a normal year? That is a ridiculous phrase. *Formative years.* I am striking that from my repertoire.) I really loved him, and he loved me. Once, years later, when I needed his sage advice, I told him about a big problem I was having, and he just kept staring forward in his chair. I realized he couldn't answer me. He was there and not there. That's when I saw it for the first time. Dementia, Alzheimer's, you can call it whatever you want. It's just a name. He was gone. His eyes and hair and face were all turning gray at once. He never answered. Once he told me he couldn't write anymore. He said he couldn't remember what he was writing about. I said, "Try poetry, it's short." He said that wouldn't work. Damn. That was at his farm.

The last time we were at the farm, we went for one of our many walks. We always took long walks in the forest together when I visited him, at the farm or anywhere. Once in Ireland, when he was living there, we went for a long walk on the heath, crossing fences and covering a lot of ground. But on that day when we were back on the farm walking, Daddy got lost. That really was the last walk we went on together. All good things must pass. Why? When he died in 2005, I cried like a baby at his funeral service. Completely lost it. Life.

With Elliot Roberts at the USA Film Festival, Dallas, 1973.

## Chapter Five

D
avid Briggs used to say, "Life is a shit sandwich. Eat it or starve." David was my producer. He worked on all of my good records, as he used to say. His records were the ones that invoked the memories of the artistry created by Roy Orbison. He always mentioned Roy to me at critical times, knowing I admired him and his unique voice and songs, his willingness to be different. David was hard to work with for many of us, but we all loved him because he was the best. "Be great or be gone" was another one of his favorite expressions. I could go on and on about each session I had with David, the drugs, the women, the booze, the rock and roll, the fights, the laughs—but not yet. I am sure this will all come out eventually as I meander through my experiences in this walk through life. He was also my best friend, then Larry Johnson, my filmmaking collaborator, was after David passed, and now Elliot Roberts is. Earlier in the scope of things, Elliot was my manager and the necessary strength in my dealings with others. Sometimes he was seen as a villain, sometimes as a savior.

Although unpopular at times with my musician friends, Elliot is consistently there for the art, there for the artist, protecting me from the sharks, while sometimes being accused of being a shark himself. Elliot is the friend I call every day at least five times, no matter what. We live through every deal together, every project. I am harder and harder for him to deal with as I get older and more certain of my opinions on business matters, but he still protects me from others and tries in vain to protect me from myself. I will do anything to get started on something. I will use my own money when I shouldn't just because I hate waiting. That may be why I have spent so much money and built so many things. I just like to do it myself. I hate waiting for approval, because I have my own Approve-o-Meter. It works like a charm.

I put in the money to do it myself and do whatever I need to do to get the money, promise that I will deliver a record and get advances, anything I can do to get the cash to make something happen the way I envision it. So I get into a lot of trouble, though I also get a lot of things done. I did it with Shakey Pictures' *Human Highway*, *Greendale*, the Lincvolt movie in progress, the PureTone videos in progress, *Journey Through the Past* (my first film), the Lincvolt construction and development, the Lionel TrainMaster Command Control development, the Lionel RailSounds development, the Lionel LEGACY Control System development, and probably some others I have forgotten. None of these things would have happened if I hadn't done them myself. No one believes in my ideas until I actually do them. I am never able to get backing for anything I want to do other than records because I am the only one with money who believes in them—and I don't do them to make money. I am entrepreneurial. I do them because I can see it before it happens. That is the good, the bad, and the ugly, all rolled up into one big ball.

Mostly now, though, Elliot is able to save me from myself. As I said, he is a true friend, and also one of the funniest people on the planet. We have at least one disagreement a day. Whatever deal he gets, I ask him for more. And mostly he gets more. I have learned that taking less is not that good. It's not the money; it's the respect. And the money.

We have to have control. We fight for it tooth and nail. My father-in-law, T. A. Morton, Pegi's dad, lived by the fifty-one percent rule. You need that much for control. I have tried to be true to that, but some ideas are just too big for me to carry by myself. I hate the fact that the PureTone idea is probably going to get out of my absolute control one day. I hate waiting for other people to okay what I want to do. Ideas are the driver. There is nothing worse than having a great idea and losing it because you can't control the process. Working with me must be hell under those circumstances. I don't feel bad about it, though. I know I work well with people who want to get things done.

I dislike firing people. Since my first high school garage band, I have had to make those decisions and have those conversations. Although I always was the leader, there were times when I have been a wimp and had others do my dirty work, but I have learned that is not the way. No one can do that and feel good. Honesty is the only thing that works. It hurts to be honest, but the muse has no conscience. If you do it for the music, you do it for the music, and everything else is secondary. Although that has been hard for me to learn, it is the best and really the only way to live through a life dedicated to the muse.

Sometimes I am in a groove and everything is going great with the band—and then I wake up one morning and its over. I can't say why, but it is definitely time for change. This change is not arbitrary or capricious. It is spawned from an underlying sense of what is needed to keep the creative process alive and thriving. Sometimes a smooth process heralds the approach of atrophy or death. So the change must be made, disruptive as it may be. Then the hard stuff starts. People have families, need money, have obligations, need security. Or everyone thought it was cool, and it was, but now it isn't. The muse says, "If it isn't totally great, then don't do it. Change."

"Be great or be gone." Thanks, David Briggs.

"Quality whether you want it or not." Thanks, Larry Johnson.

"How can I help you?" Thanks, Elliot.

These are my guys. Whether they are still breathing or not, they are in me, in my music, in everything I do. But there is a lot of damage. A lot of times, spontaneous change is seen as irresponsible, uncaring, and self-serving.

So what do I do now that I'm sixty-five? Retire? Nope. I can't stop moving long enough to do that. I am going to go to Hawaii tomorrow and will keep writing this. I love it there and I kind of decompress. Pegi is going to Hawaii, too, in a few days, but I can't wait that long to get over there. She has just made a great record and wants to finish up all the business around it before she joins me. But it won't be long and we'll be together again. I love that. She is my life partner. My confidante. I can tell her anything. After all these years together, I am still getting to know her. I would be an island without my ocean if we were not together in our hearts. I am the luckiest man on the planet to be able to go to Hawaii and rest for a while and wait for her to join me. Not that I really know how to rest like others do. Creative work and writing are relaxing to me.

Seeing my friends Marc and Greg and Lynne and Vicki over there will be fun, too. Greg and Vicki have the Napa Valley Wine Train, among many other things. Marc and Lynne have Salesforce .com, and Lynne has the Homes for the Holidays program. Pegi has the Bridge School and her career as a singer/songwriter. We all have our jobs. We are lucky as hell. Pegi and I have shared some really good times with these friends.

I wrote the song "Leia" for Marc and Lynne's little girl. Her name is Leia. (See how creative I am?) We were just hanging in the house one night, the six of us and Leia, and I went over and started playing the piano so she would come over and play it, too. She is musical. She came right over and started some jazzy stuff while I was playing a simple percussion part. Next thing I knew, I was writing the song in my head. Lynne loved the chorus or bridge . . . I don't know what it's called. It goes:

> *Old people watchin' with their eyes aglow*
> *Mother gently smiling as she watches the show*
> *Leia, Leia, Leia*

She is a little sweetheart.

Love is everywhere. Marc says, "There is a river of love." I'm holdin' on to that thought.

The Bridge School, started in 1986 by Pegi and two of her friends, Jim Forderer and Marilyn Buzolich, is dear to my heart. It is a school that teaches communication through technology to children who have severe speech and language challenges. Quite often these students have cerebral palsy like my son Ben.

Recently I was sitting at a Bridge School board retreat in San Mateo, California, and we were all talking about the future of the school. Later in the day the board broke for the evening, and I asked Bryan Bell, a board member, and Brian Morton, Pegi's brother who is also on our board, if they would like to go to a local toy store, Talbot's Toyland, with me.

I like to wind down at the toy store after Bridge meetings. It's kind of a habit. I used to always go with Larry Johnson back in the day. He was a board member, too. He was our technology guy. Larry really gave a lot to the Bridge School. It is immeasurable what he did. He took kids to hockey games, using my set of season tickets for the San Jose Sharks while I was on the road, and he would take Ben Young with him all the time, too.

Anyway, Bryan Bell followed me over to Talbot's to kill an hour before we had a Bridge School board dinner at a nearby restaurant. When we got there, I asked him to jump in my '78 Eldorado in the parking lot and listen to PureTone.

Afterward, we went into Talbot's Toyland, where a new Hudson steam locomotive was waiting for me. This was the first Chinese-built model of the venerable classic 5344 NYC Hudson first made by Lionel in the 1930s. This engine represented the pinnacle of Lionel's expertise at that time and was the flagship product for the first hundred years of the company. Now the trains are manufactured in China, and Lionel and I had packed in every feature known to man, and had almost introduced the next revolutionary feature unknown to man, but not quite. (It wasn't ready, so we left it out of this model.) I was pretty jacked about getting it and taking it back to the train layout after the Bridge retreat was over the next afternoon.

At Talbot's, I met Keith from the train department. He broke out the Hudson from its brown made-in-China box with the familiar orange Lionel box inside, then we put a piece of track on the counter and hooked up the Lionel LEGACY Command Control System to the track. The remote was on the counter, and Bryan commented on how cool it looked. I got a good feeling from that. A lot of love went into its design. It is a pretty cool-looking retro modern remote, kind of old, with levers and sliders as well as a rotary throttle, but it has a soft key grid. We put the Hudson out on the track where I tested it with the remote to make sure everything was working correctly. I got it going, and we listened to the incredible LEGACY RailSounds system, the smoke puffing perfectly synched with the chuffs while the wheels were turning, the bell swinging back and forth while it rang, the steam coming out of the whistle every time I blew it with varying intensity from the sprung slider on the remote.

Bryan was intrigued. It was the first time he had ever seen the Lionel LEGACY system in action, and this was a top-of-the-line steam locomotive with every available feature. I eagerly, as always, demonstrated the loading effect technique by applying the train brake and listening to the heaviness of the chuffs increasing against that added load. Those little engines have so much technology in them . . .

I am very proud of the work I did with Lionel. I was instrumental in creating a series that celebrated Lionel's history with a bunch of made-in-the-USA classics that we reissued with the new sound and command control systems I had developed and tested in California along with the first generation Lionel TrainMaster Command Control. I had paid for that development myself, and it was helping to save the company. These were the last Lionels built in the USA. All we had to sell was collectibility, and we did it really well in that instance. It was all we could do, and it kept us alive during an assault of brand-new Chinese-manufactured models from our competition.

Lionel made the move to China years ago to keep competitive with another American train maker who was kicking our ass with Chinese detail and low manufacturing costs. I became an owner of the company when that happened, because as the company was being sold, I was able to parlay my investment in technology development into ownership participation. It was sad. But we hung on with the Postwar Celebration Series and "celebrated" our way through our transition to Chinese manufacturing by making products in the USA. Although the competition eventually caught on, copied our sound, and developed a proprietary control system, we made it over to China just in time to avoid bankruptcy. So here we are today, still manufacturing in China. Another great American brand, no longer being made by Americans. What a story. It was either go to China or go out of business. That NYC Hudson engine was kicking ass in that little toy store.

The next thing model trains need to do is abandon modeling the sounds by user input and become real. The effort involved in pulling a load needs to be measured, and algorithms that used to be based on user input need to be newly based on the locomotive's effort measured to pull the load or perform the task. Then there is little to do but drive the train down the track, allowing it to measure its own efforts and trigger sound and smoke effects and speed changes to reflect the laboring that is being measured. That is the next step, the future of modeling, or at least part of the future. Everything is there now in the Lionel system to make this happen on a basic level, except a good measurement of the effort being put out by the locomotive model to pull its load. Not just some gross measurement like measuring the electric motor effort, but an electromechanical high-resolution capturing of each nuance of the laboring. That will be nirvana, and I will be celebrating my ass off when that happens! And it almost happened on that 5344 Hudson at Talbot's. Almost, but not quite.

From Talbot's we took off to the dinner with the Bridge board and walked down to the restaurant together. When we got there, the ladies from the board (Vicki Casella, Executive Director of the school, and Sarah Blackstone, an expert in the field of Augmentative and Alternative communication) were already having a little wine and winding down. I would have had a beer or something, but as I said, I quit drinking, and I really don't miss it that much. I had a cranberry and soda mix, which is what I like these days. Steve Atkinson, another board member, showed up and said he had just missed us at the toy store and people were all talking about the fact that I had just been there. (That is always surprising for me to hear and think about. I guess a grown man who happened to be famous geeking out with a train in a toy store with two other guys is somewhat interesting and could be seen as news.)

The next day we returned to the retreat and finished at about noon. We had to come up with a few concepts on how to ensure the Bridge School's future. I have been able to help with concert fund-raisers, but Pegi is the force behind the Bridge School. The catalyst. It was her idea. One day when Ben Young was young and we were looking for school placement, after a particularly depressing look at a local California classroom for the disabled, Pegi was near tears. She just blurted out, "Why don't we just call your friends and put on a concert to raise money and start a school? We could get Bruce Springsteen!" I just looked at her, dumbfounded by this audacious idea.

Because of his grace, Bruce did it and made our first concert a sellout. We started the school on those funds. Bruce Springsteen is the real thing. He was at the first big peak of his career, and his appearance was amazing on all levels. We also had super performances from Nils Lofgren, Tom Petty, Don Henley & Friends, Robin Williams, and an unannounced CSN. The Bridge School was born. And it all came from Pegi. Elliot and Marsha Vlasic have been booking the Bridge School benefits since the first one, choosing the artists to be invited and making sure they are all taken care of.

Bruce is still my friend. We don't talk much. We don't have to. He is great and in his own league. I am not him and he is not me. But we are on similar paths, writing and singing our kind of songs around the world, along with Bob and a few other singer/songwriters. It is a silent fraternity of sorts, occupying this space in people's souls with our music. Last year, I lost my right-hand man, the pedal steel guitarist Ben Keith. This year Bruce lost his right-hand man, the saxophonist Clarence Clemons. It's time for another talk; friends can help each other just by being there. Now both of us will look to our right and see a giant hole, a memory, the past and the future. I won't play with another steel player trying to re-create Ben's parts, and I know Bruce won't play with another sax man trying to play Clarence's. Those parts are not going to happen again. They already did. That takes away a lot out of our repertoires.

Bob Dylan doesn't have anyone like that, I don't think, although maybe it was once Mike Bloomfield—now there was a great guitar player. Bob is painting now, and Elliot—who once was Bob's manager, too—says he is a master. I'm not surprised. I'm sure Bob has the master's touch, whether he is painting from a photograph or a memory of something he has seen. He chooses his images. He has been doing that for a long time. His songs have known no bounds in their influence, and the folk process transfers well to painting. He may just be getting started. Like music, the world of art has its own rules to break.

With Pam Smith, at Falcon Lake, Manitoba, August 1964.

Chapter Six

Mort

At age eighteen, I purchased Mortimer Hearseburg, or Mort, a 1948 Buick hearse that was for sale from a local mortuary. I had seen an advertisement in the paper for the hearse and went to a place where several hearses were parked. I thought a hearse would be the ideal band vehicle, something that could finally replace my mother Rassy's car. We always spent a lot of time loading and unloading her small Ensign, an English car made by Standard Motors. It wasn't big enough for our band's gear, but we made it fit. I must mention here that Rassy was the biggest supporter of my musical endeavors and believed in me from the very beginning, offering her encouragement always. (By the way, her real name was Edna, but her daddy nicknamed her Rassy.) While we lived in Winnipeg, she had supplied her little car for all the Squires' gigs up to that time, allowed us to practice in the living room of our little flat, even lent me money to buy my instruments and amps when my dad wouldn't because of my terrible school grades. Once she took me over to a relative's house with my amp and guitar and had me play "Malagueña" for them because she thought I was so great. I didn't even know the song, but I loved to improvise on the chord changes, which I thought were genius.

She got really pissed when my dad did not help me buy my instruments. When my dad's book *Neil and Me* came out in 1984, she was incredulous beyond description! She would quote from the book and then say, "Oh, for God's sake, what a load of shit!" noting that he didn't have any relationship with me compared to her and had done nothing to support my musical life.

She never forgave him for leaving us. I did.

Anyway, when I arrived at the place where the hearse was supposed to be, behind a wire fence, there was a gated area where two identical hearses were parked. The only real difference between the two was that one had a blue interior and the other had a burgundy interior. The interiors I am referring to are the inside velvet trim in the back of the hearses. The exteriors were wild! They were at least eight inches taller in the hood than a normal Roadmaster, and they were very long. The wheelbase was 156 inches. The name *Flxible* was on the side of the front fender. Two 1948 Buick Roadmasters that had been custom-built as hearses! I loved them.

In the back there were really nice curtains and a headliner of plush velvet with pull-down shades, and there was a sliding divider window between the front and the back. There were rollers on the floor for moving the caskets easily in and out of the back through a gigantic rear door. What could be better than that? Perfect for rolling amps and PA in and out, sleeping and storing equipment, I thought to myself. The price was $125 for either one.

They were both in good running condition. (That was the thing about hearses; they were always in good shape because of what they were used for.) I made a choice. The blue interior was the best, so I took that one. Rassy paid the bill. Thank you, Mom! I couldn't believe my good fortune. I was high as a kite! At the first gig with Mort, I felt like the Squires had a new identity. The hearse was an amazing attention-getter, and that is what being in a band needs. When you get to a gig, you got to be cool. We were the coolest thing in town with Mort. No one else had anything like that. Nothing they had could touch it.

Of course, Pam Smith's dad was not so sure about it when I pulled up in front of their house in the residential area where they lived. The neighbors all thought that someone had died. Pam was my steady girlfriend, my first real love. We went together for about a year, maybe less, as I remember it, a long time for someone that age. I saw a recent picture of her a while back, and she still is beautiful today. She was wearing a flannel shirt in that photo that looked like the same kind I love to wear. Even after I left Winnipeg, my thoughts kept coming back to Pam, and occasionally I would send her long rambling letters, which she did not answer, probably not knowing what to say. Long and short of it is, she was my first real love, my first companion of that kind, someone I could talk to, and as with old friends there is always going to be a warm feeling there. Sending good thoughts to you, Pam.

Today I have a hearse identical to Mort, given to me by Taylor

Phelps's partner, who said Taylor wanted me to have it when he died. I drove Taylor to his funeral in it. That car is in *Year of the Horse*, a cool film about Crazy Horse that Jim Jarmusch did. That film is very special to me because it has my dad in it. I loved my dad, and during that time, I started to see that he was not himself. Once I left him on one floor of the hotel in Dublin where we were filming with Jim, and he got lost. That was unsettling. Despite what my mom said, I know he was a cool guy. He was always doing what he thought was right for me.

One beautiful morning in 1963 or '64, Mort was parked in front of our triplex at 1123 Grosvenor Avenue in Winnipeg. We packed up Mort with everything we needed, and then we headed southeast to Fort William, Ontario. It was our first big road trip, and our first nightclub gig was booked at the Flamingo Club. I was eighteen. I felt on top of the world. (Mort had a straight-eight and a three-speed manual transmission. Mort was a good runner, and to save gas I used to go into neutral on downgrades, not knowing that this practice was putting unnecessary strain on the drive train, which I would pay for later. Even in those days, I was very energy efficient! Of course, Mort was a giant vehicle like Lincvolt, so nothing has really changed.)

We made it to Fort William with no problems, and three wide-eyed kids were finally in the big time. When we got to the Flamingo Club—a brightly decorated, multilevel supper club with a dance floor and long bar known locally as the Flame—we were ready to play, doing three to five sets a night for the $325 weekly salary plus meals at night. The first night we were nervous, but we did fine.

We played six days a week. The money was great! It was the most money I had ever made at that point, and I was on top of the world. We lived at the YMCA for a small payment, so after food expenses we made a little bit of profit. There were three of us splitting it evenly. Bill Edmondson on drums and vocals, me on guitar, and Ken Koblun on bass. Ken, my school classmate and an original Squire from the very beginning, had been keeping a diary since our first gig.

The Flamingo eventually put us up at the Victoria Hotel, and I was writing a lot of songs for the gig there. We were going Jimmy Reed–style big-time because I loved Jimmy and knew that kind of music would be perfect for the club. I wrote a couple of R&B songs in that vein right away, "Find Another Shoulder" and "Hello Lonely Woman," at the hotel. I wrote a lot more then, too. One older song that was the same type of beat was resurrected. It was called "Ain't It the Truth." These tunes were all R&B-based and we did a good job on them. We did "Hi-Heel Sneakers" and "Walkin' the Dog" and countless others of that type as well. A lot of local musicians came to hear us there, and local DJ Ray Dee also came to the club to check us out. Ray later recorded us at the CJLX studios and booked us in the area. He was a great help to the Squires in Fort William, offering his leadership and advice.

We made friends with many of the local musicians, and they hung out with us. Danny Hortichuk of the Bonnevilles was just one of them, and I remember him as being a really good guy. Being from out of town was working for us big-time like I had hoped it would. There is nothing like having no preconceptions to live up to or down. Today my past is a huge thing. Everybody has an expectation of what I should do. There comes a time when these things start to get in one's way. Expectations can block the light. They can shadow the future, making it more difficult to be free-flowing and creative. I need to find that freedom again today if I want to fly.

Meanwhile, back at the Flamingo Club, we were doing "Farmer John" every night and tearing the place up with it. Writing songs at night and in the morning, playing multiple sets every evening at the club, I was living the life I loved and every day was a new opportunity. We were very successful there and got asked back with a raise to $350 per week. I woke up every morning with a clean slate. No expectations weighing over me, and no history binding me to the past.

At night, I had something else on my mind. I was looking at the used-car ads in the paper. Back in Winnipeg, I had spent some time sitting in a 1959 Cadillac convertible that belonged to my school friends Brian and Barry Blick's dad. He owned a TV station in Pembina, North Dakota, and used to drive back and forth between there and Winnipeg in this big Caddy. It was red with a red leather interior. The car made a big impression on me, so I used to sit in the YMCA in Fort William figuring out how long I would have to work gigs like the Flamingo Club until I had enough money to buy a car like that. I checked all the ads in the paper for similar cars and compared prices. I actually have one today, but it's all in pieces because the fellow who was going to rebuild it never did get around to putting it back together, for a variety of reasons. I may still get it done, though. It would be worth it just to get closure. Today that car is worth a fortune and it would cost more than

52

it's worth to put it back together. It would fit right in as part of Feelgood's.

This car used to run fine. It's too bad I had it dismantled to rebuild. You live and learn. David Briggs had named it Nanu the Lovesick Moose. It had an interesting feature where the windshield washer had so much pressure that it would overshoot the windshield altogether.

Here's a memory: Once we pulled up at a gas station in Nanu with the top down and there was a car full of really fine babes right beside us, filling up with gas and looking like a million bucks. They were gorgeous and looked like real fun-loving girls. Knowing exactly what would happen, Briggs said a big "Hi" to the girls and then hit the windshield washer button. Water squirted out of the jets right over the whole interior without touching it and landed on the trunk lid eight feet behind us. He had made his point: It was an impressive and grand display of male virility. David just sat there like nothing was happening. I was laughing so hard I couldn't stop. We had some really great times, David and I! That was only one of them! I am laughing my ass off right now just thinking of the fun we had! How lighthearted. That was when Nanu was in her prime. I have to get that car running again. What a wonderful thing that would be! That would make me tremendously happy.

One other time we were in Malibu driving down the Pacific Coast Highway in Nanu. We had a gram of coke with us, and Art Linson, who was David's friend and Nils Lofgren's manager and friend, was in the backseat. David and I were sitting in Nanu's bucket seats up front. We were cruising Malibu and feeling real good about life. A Malibu sheriff pulled up beside us and turned his lights on. He was pulling us over! When we stopped, he got out of his car and walked up to ours.

I rolled down my window and asked, "What's the problem? Is it against the law to drive a '59 Cadillac convertible in Malibu?"

He was taken aback by my question.

"This car was made for this town!" I said.

He shook his head, smiled at me, and said, "Just take it easy. Have a good evening."

We drove away. After holding our breaths for a minute, it dawned on us.

"I've never seen anything like that," said Briggs. "You just blew my fucking mind." Linson just stayed put in the backseat, shaking his head.

Sometimes timing is everything. There was ZERO thought process involved in that. I had absolutely no idea what I was saying or doing. It just came out. It was a spur-of-the-moment event. We drove away laughing, counting the minutes till we did another blast. Those were some big times, a long way from the Flamingo Club.

Chapter Seven

Why This Book Exists

Remember the goose that laid the golden egg? This book is all about that. This book will keep me off the stage (except for a few benefits—Farm Aid and the Bridge School) for over a year. I need to go away and replenish. This book is one thing that I am doing to stay off the stage. It all started when I broke my toe at the pool.

Back at the ranch, Pegi and I were having a great time with Amber and Ben up at the pool. The pool is up a hill behind the house. Anyway, we were up there and having a great time on July 3 celebrating Father's Day, because Amber had been in Montana at an art retreat and Pegi had been down in LA working on her new record on the real date. So now we were together and celebrating Father's Day and all was cool. That's when I stubbed my toe on a rock and broke it. My little toe!

So I have to slow down. That's why I am writing this book *now*.

Or maybe it's because I'm not smoking weed anymore. I am a lot more focused now. That's odd. On one hand, I am wondering whether I can write songs straight, and on the other hand, I am saying that because I am straight I am probably writing this book. Someone should take note of that for his or her own research on the subject of sobriety, but not me.

I am feeling very fashionable, even trendy, for having stopped smoking and drinking. I should be in *People* magazine or on *Entertainment Tonight*. I am missing a lot of exposure. (Actually, I cannot imagine anything further from my mind than doing that type of thing, thank God.)

I am no fun to watch TV with. I am constantly heckling and criticizing and making fun of it. I suppose I will be on TV *hawking* this book, though.

Jonathan Demme recently made another movie about one of my performances. This is the last one of a trilogy. It's really about life. It's a docu-music-entary, what was once clumsily called a rock-umentary. Promoting it, I could be on *Colbert*! Now that guy is really funny. Or Jon Stewart! Thank God for humor! Those guys are brilliant. I am always getting scared that I will be in the middle of some long-winded story and forget what I'm talking about and my secret that I am slowly losing my mind will be out. It is a real fear. Everyone will know! But that is not new. That is not a recent development. I have always been like that. That is what makes detecting the onset of early stages of dementia in me so difficult. Maybe there won't ever be any. Maybe it's all in my mind.

M y first band that worked a lot was called the Squires. We formed in the early sixties in Winnipeg, Manitoba, and were made up of Jack Harper on drums, Allan Bates on guitar, Ken Koblun on bass, and me. The band went through a lot of changes over the first years, but that was the starting lineup. We played high school dances, church dances, community clubs, and the odd outside gig on the back of a flatbed truck. Once we even played a wrestling match.

Those were the kinds of gigs we did in the beginning. We made very little money, sometimes as little as five dollars for the whole band. This was our beginning. We didn't know where we were going, but we were going. There were good and bad gigs, but they all added up. Eventually, the Squires started getting booked out of town, and we would travel fifty miles to make a gig. We had my mother's little Ensign packed so full that I could never see out the back when I was driving to the gigs. It's a wonder we weren't pulled over. We never were.

Ken's amp was homemade and it was a big wooden box that

provided a huge bottom sound for the bass. Eventually we had to cut it down because it was too big for the car. Ken drove that speaker with a Heathkit amp he purchased as a kit and built. We had the shoddiest equipment in the beginning. My guitar, a Gibson Les Paul Junior, was hard to keep in tune. I didn't know that the intonation could be adjusted, so it went on like that until I got my next guitar, a Gretsch Chet Atkins "Horseshoe," just like Randy Bachman's from the Silvertones and the one I played later in Buffalo Springfield. My first amp was an Ampeg Echo Twin, until I graduated to a Fender Tremolux, which was a really big deal for me: The Tremolux was the smallest of the piggybacks, but it was my first big amp.

There was also a band in town called the Galaxies. They had three huge Fenders, two Showmans, and a Band-Master. They were the coolest band as far as equipment went. Then there was the Silvertones; they had a Fender Concert amp and they got big. Randy Bachman played guitar in the Silvertones. They were the best musicians in town, and Ken Koblun from the Squires and I used to watch them all the time whenever we could. They played everywhere and got all the big gigs. They were simply the best.

Randy's playing was the inspiration for a lot of my sound. He had an echo sound he derived from using a tape recorder to get a slapback effect from a tape loop. That is achieved by recording the note and automatically playing it back a split second later. The split second later comes from a length of tape between the two magnetic heads: one records, one plays back. The delay is created by the distance between the two recording heads that is heard when the tape travels from one head to another.

Randy was very advanced, and his echo sounded just like Hank B. Marvin's of the Shadows whenever the Silvertones did one of their Shadows instrumentals. I would go to their gigs with Ken and we would just stand there transfixed. The Silvertones did not have a weak link. Their singer, Allan Kobel, was really great. Bob Ashley on piano was unreal. He could really rock and play anything from Floyd Cramer to Professor Longhair. Jimmy Kale, the bass player, was totally unreal, and he helped us a lot. We got Ken's first bass through Jimmy—he connected us to order it through Cam's Hardware, a local shop that sold some musical instruments. Cam's had a connection to Silvertone, the musical instrument and amplifier company, in the States, and Silvertone made a cool bass. Later, Jimmy would lend us his concert amp for recording and big gigs. He was a real good friend. Thanks, Jimmy!

Eventually, Jack Harper, an original member, was replaced by Ken Smyth as drummer. Allan Bates knew Ken from high school. That configuration of the Squires recorded "The Sultan" and "Aurora."

Allan eventually wanted to further his education and was replaced by Doug Campbell (who later quit because his mother didn't want him to take a chance on music). Doug was a genius and played lead guitar. I say he was a genius because he actually worked on his guitar, shaving the frets down and adjusting the intonation. He was able to create a "fuzz tone" by doing something inside his amp. He knew no boundaries. He was really impressive. Too bad he couldn't go with us when we took off, but that's the way it goes. He left a hole and I had to fill it myself, but I had learned a lot from Doug.

The Squires played my own songs and rock arrangements

of folk classics like "Oh, Susanna," "Tom Dooley," and "Clementine." We got that idea from the Thorns, another band that came through on the circuit. We learned their arrangement of "Oh, Susanna," and I developed a theme doing other old folk songs along that way, with new melodies and arrangements that rocked. Tim Rose, leader of the Thorns, was one of those credited with writing "Hey Joe," later made a big hit by Jimi Hendrix. The Thorns were really great. I don't know what happened to them. They should have been huge. But we know life has her ways. Nothing is obvious, and you never know what is going to happen. The Thorns and Danny and the Memories were great bands that could have been huge, but just disappeared. Who knows what is next or why it isn't?

The Squires eventually became the number-three or -four band in Winnipeg, and we got really good. We had the most original material of all the bands. I was writing a lot, because I always was thinking about music. First it was instrumentals, and then songs with words that I had to start singing. That set us apart. I knew that and I took advantage of it. Original music was the key to moving up. Doing covers was good for gigs, but I wanted other bands to be doing my songs. A few years later, the Guess Who (formerly Allan and the Silvertones) actually recorded one of my songs, "Flying on the Ground," fulfilling that dream. I was very happy about that. They did a great version.

Original songs were not found that often in the bands that competed with us in Winnipeg. I never had to try to write. I learned to be ready to write when an idea came into my head, whether it was in school or wherever. I learned to drop everything else and pay attention to the song I was hearing. The more I did that, the more songs I heard.

We also had a constantly changing lineup. We had Al Johnston on drums, then Bill Edmondson, who moved in across the street from me when he arrived from Montreal with his mom and grandma. He was a genuine rocker with all of the attitude required. I was a big believer in attitude; I think that set the Squires apart as well. Bill Edmondson played on "I'll Love You Forever" and "I Wonder," eventually recorded at CJLX in Fort William and produced by Ray Dee, the number-one Fort William disc jockey who adopted us when he heard us at that first Flamingo Club engagement. Bill ended up marrying the secretary from CKRC, where we had our first sessions in Winnipeg, and ultimately stopped playing with us because she missed him so much when we were out of town. There were many reasons why guys dropped out of the Squires, but I never did really get them. I was in for the long haul.

Then, just before we left Winnipeg for the last time, we got Bob Clark. Bob was game and traveled with us to Fort William. He was really cool, and we rehearsed in a room above his brother's store where he gave drum lessons. He and his older brother were mostly into jazz, and there was a big jazz scene in Winnipeg, but Bob was into playing rock and roll and liked where the Squires were going. Bob Clark was a fine musician. He was really into it. With Bob on drums, we really had the version of the Squires that could move out of town and be successful. Bob sang, and Ken was getting better at singing, too. I thought we were ready to go. As I mentioned, we packed up Mort and headed to Fort William.

List of Shows

A list of some of my early shows with the Squires,
from Ken Koblun's diary, 1963.

		963				Held 134
	St. Peter's Mission	N.22	45	11.25	-	12 - stared
40	St. Agnatus P.Y.O.	N.29	50	10	-	
	St. Marie C.Y.O (HOFNER)	D.6	45	2.25	=	
✓	Dauphin	D.13	125	28.75	=	mini 124 city
✓	Charleswood Coll.	D.20	60	12.00	-	
✓	St. Agnatus C.Y.O	1964 J.3	50	10	-	
45	Kelvin Hi	J.24	-	-	-	
	4th Dimension	J.25	0	-	-	
✓	Miles MacDonell Coll.	J.31	60	11.30	-	Jazz mon
✓	Glenwood C.C	F.1	57	11.25	-	
	4-D	F.5	0	-	-	
50	Paterson's Roadhouse	F.7	25	5.50	1	
	4-D	F.8	0	-	-	
✓	St. Pauls of the Apostil	F.9	50	10	-	
✓	Our Lady of Victory	F.14	50	10	-	
✓	Portage la Prairie	F.21	60	10	-	
55	McLeans United Church	F.22	16	4	-	
	4-D	F.29	-	-	-	
	Paterson's Roadhouse	M.7	25	5		
	Glenwood C.C	M.14	24.25	7.50	-	
	Paterson's	M.26	0	-	.	
✓ 60	Paterson's	M.28	50	9	1.	
	Inland Broadcasting	A.1	70	1 Recording		
	C.K.R.C	A.2				
	Crescentwood	A.3	40	10	-	
✓	Norberry C.C.	A.4	60	12.10	-	
✓ 65	St. Pauls of the Apostil	A.5	50	10	-	
Proctio chite '47 →	Paterson's (bill is paid)	A.11	55	5		
	Winiakwa C.C. (Aussie)	M.8	25	6.50		
	Grendell CC (twin)	M.15	4.35	3.87		
	Notre Dame Aud.	J.9	0	-	-	
70	Maple Leaf C.C.	J.12	40	6.25	.	
	Towers - T&C	J.15	-	-	-	
	Weston C.C	J.19	0	-	-	
	Brofeen	J.5	20	5	-	
No.1	Cellar	J.24	30	7.50		
80	Cellar	J.31	36	9		
last Paws	Towers T&C	A.6	0	-	.	Bass mon.

In Fort William, Ontario, a working-class port town at the head of the Great Lakes where the Squires first played the Flamingo Club and hit the big time, we stayed and settled in. We played the Flamingo a few more times and sent our tapes out to record companies. Nothing happened. One of them is a song about Pam, who I have mentioned before, a beautiful, soulful girl I met at Falcon Lake who was my first love, in a fantasy setting by the ocean, which of course I had never seen at the time. I called it "I'll Love You Forever." We used sound effects of waves. I thought it was really cool. Another song I had written, "I Wonder," was recorded at CJLX, too. Those tapes live in my archives now.

I was writing more, and the Squires played the Hootenanny at the Fourth Dimension Club, a local coffeehouse in town that had entertainment all week long; the Hoot was on Sunday or Monday nights. There were 4D clubs in Fort William, Winnipeg, and Regina, and they became known as the circuit. One of the acts that came in was called Two Guys from Boston—they were Joe Hutchinson and Eddie Mottau. They were really good. They sang together and had a 45 rpm record that they played for us called "Come on Betty Home." I loved that song. I was so impressed that they had a record.

One day they received some black ganja in the mail and they were ecstatic. I had no idea what it was, and still really don't know whether it was hash or weed, but it was something and they were happy as hell. I hadn't smoked either weed or hash at that time, and I didn't then.

Around then, the Beatles had "Ticket to Ride" out, and it was on the jukebox at the Fourth Dimension as well. "Come on Betty Home" and "Ticket to Ride" got a lot of play. Many bands and performers played the 4D circuit. Mostly they were from the States (as we call the United States up in Canada). I saw Lisa Kindred, Sonny Terry and Brownie McGhee, and Don McLean before he had his hits "American Pie" and "Vincent," plus a lot of other performers. Don was traveling in a Dodge van, and he had changed the letters *DODGE* to read *DOG*. These were the early days that left such a mark on me. I was always fascinated and impressed by these groups and artists. I was so envious of them for being from the States and on the road.

The next band to come in and play on the circuit was called the Company. There was a guy singing in that band who was really great. He played guitar and sang, and it sounded like he was a soul singer. You had to look at him to be sure he was white. His phrasing was amazing. I really noticed him. He walked up and introduced himself to me. His name was Steve Stills. We got along real well immediately. We struck up an instant friendship after he heard us playing at that Hootenanny. It was amazing to me that after hearing us play he was so impressed.

A great friendship rose up between Steve Stills and me that goes on to this day. Stephen is a genius. Like any genius, he is sometimes misunderstood, and I misunderstood him many times when we were young. Later on I came to recognize him and understand him better. When I left CSNY to do my own thing, I missed him. Although Crosby and Nash loved him and his music, I always felt they never completely got the point with him, and he became a little reclusive in his creativity because of that, in my opinion. No one really knows him like I do, though. He is my brother. We went through so much and learned from each other along the way, discovering our music and life at the same time. It was all so new to us, and we discovered it together, like brothers, and I don't think we are finished with that yet. The way we play off of each other, the joy of that, is something seldom found. I never felt that David and Graham had that same sense about him; of course, we were older friends and both lead guitar players who could play together in a way that made it hard for us to tell who was playing what. David and Graham did not have that with Stephen in the same way. I think I respect Stephen's talent and genius in a way that they don't. They see something else, and now they have spent a lot more time with him than I have. When I spend time with him today, I still see that original genius. I want the Buffalo Springfield to play yet again, with a drummer who can drive the band in a way that we have never really had, and that goes way back to Stephen's original problems with Dewey Martin, our first drummer. There is still more to do there and no reason not to do it.

Before the Company left Fort William, Stephen gave me an address on Thompson Street in New York's Greenwich Village, where I could find him if I ever went there. Then the Company left to go to Winnipeg, and the Squires stayed at a motel called Dinty's Motor Inn. We were able to live there for nothing in exchange for playing Saturday and Sunday afternoons at the Fourth Dimension Club. Gordie Crompton, "Dinty," owned the motel and the Fourth Dimension. After we finished at the Fourth Dimension we got some other gigs around town, but times were rough and we had little money. For a while, we lived on Spam and Ritz crackers we bought in a little liquor store across the street from the motel.

Eventually we got kicked out of Dinty's Motor Inn and moved to the YMCA. Then we started playing at a place called the Pancake House on Sunday afternoons. That was okay, but it didn't make us enough money to live.

We played a lot in Fort William until I left after a long period of doing that and moved on to Toronto. That was a very sudden move. Late one night I was hanging with a bunch of guys from local bands, some guys from the Bonnevilles and Terry Erickson, a bass player who also played good guitar. We were thinking of him becoming a Squire and had even taken some pictures together. I decided to drive Terry to Sault Ste. Marie in Mort. We jumped in the hearse and left. Just like that. Ken was back at the YMCA, so he missed the trip and was left behind. Bob Clark and the Bonnevilles came along with us. We took Terry's motorbike with us in the back of Mort.

We were about halfway there, near a town called Blind River, when we broke down. Mort's transmission was toast. We got towed to Bill's Garage, a harrowing experience with the hearse being towed backward, the rear tires in the air and me steering in reverse. After holding on for dear life at a high speed and terrified, we finally got to Bill's Garage in Blind River, Ontario. Bill said he could find us a part to fix the hearse and get us going. Several days later, we were still there and running out of money; we were living on roasted potatoes from the market. We hung out in an old junkyard/dump near the edge of town.

A graveyard was just across the gravel road from that dump.

We were a funky lot. The Bonnevilles hitched back to Fort William for a gig they had that weekend. Bob went with them. Realizing that Mort was gone, I thought being in Fort William without the hearse would be nowhere. It was a feeling. The hearse was part of the whole thing. The picture. The image. There is an intangible to a group and a persona. You can't lose that. If you do, you have to start again. I felt that Mort was a large part of my identity, so I took off with Terry to North Bay to see his dad and try to get some cash. I don't remember what happened to Terry's gig in Sault Ste. Marie, but I do remember that when we got to North Bay, we saw a lounge band, the Mandala, with a great guitarist named Domenic Troiano and George Olliver, a fantastic vocalist. Wow! Those guys were really cool; very slick and professional R&B. I eventually went back to North Bay later on to do a folk club as a solo, working out of Toronto, just before I met Bruce Palmer and Rick James and joined the Mynah Birds.

But anyway, back in North Bay, Terry's father, who was a policeman, had no cash for us. We were offered Kellogg's Corn Flakes and Scotch in the morning, though, followed by a Coke. That was how Terry started his day, with Coca-Cola. His dad was enjoying the Corn Flakes. There was no milk. That was something new to me, Coke in the morning, and I tried it for a while.

Eventually we headed south to Toronto to get some help from my dad. We were treated well, but it was a little stiff and uncomfortable around there and we didn't stay too long. I felt like we were in the way. My father had remarried, and I met my little sister, Astrid, and her mother (by the same name) there for the first time. Little Astrid was very young then, three or four years old, taking oboe lessons. I started exploring the Yorkville music scene, the Canadian equivalent of New York's Greenwich Village. I called Ken and Bob, and after some apologizing for blowing off our last gig in Fort William, I convinced them to come out and give Toronto a try.

That was really the end of the Squires, though. Ken, Bob, and I tried to put together something in Toronto, but it was not that easy to get a gig there. We rehearsed in the lobby of an old theater that my dad was able to arrange for us. He was supporting us, and that made me feel like he was behind us. I think when he saw me up close in Toronto he realized how serious I was.

There was not a lot of room for us to break in in Yorkville. It was nothing like Fort William, and times were tough. There were many bands, and the competition for gigs was great. A manager I had met, Marty Onrot, brought people by to listen to us, but no one really bit. We had Jim Ackroyd in the band for a while, and he was really good. He had played with the Galaxies, the number-two group back in Winnipeg, and we filled out a lot with Jim playing guitar. We did a song called "Casting Me Away," and it sounded great. But no one hired us. There was zero success, and we got no jobs. Bob eventually left the band and went back to Winnipeg. Ken and I tried a few different players, got a new drummer named Geordie McDonald, and did maybe one gig at a ski resort in Vermont. It was an audition gig, and they didn't take us.

We didn't succeed in taking Toronto by storm. It was a tough time. We were small fish in a big pond, had no reputation, and really there was nothing special about us in the big city. We were out of our league. We tried, auditioned, practiced, but nothing panned out. Ken and I were living in a rooming house on Huron Street near Yorkville Village, eating macaroni with wieners and beans that we cooked up in the communal kitchen in the house. There were maybe six or seven other rooms with tenants. It was bleak. I met a girl named Sandy Glick, and that was the high point. I had a friend. I skirted around drugs and parties. I escaped.

Perhaps Jack Harper and Ken Koblun are the Squires I remember the most, Jack because he is still in contact with updates on Winnipeg and is still in the Squires in spirit, and Ken because he was so much of a friend and always gave everything he had. Ken was really the heart of the Squires. He lived it with me and went through all the same changes I did.

The breakup with Ken and the Squires was one of the hardest things I can remember. I probably handled it very poorly and that's why it is hard for me to remember. Ken did well for a while, actually better than I did, playing with the Dirty Shames and a few others in the Toronto area. I tried playing some solo gigs and did one in North Bay and another in the city, and a guest shot at the New Gate of Cleve on Avenue Road when the headliner was sick.

I went down to New York for an audition at Elektra Records that Marty had set up, went to Greenwich Village, and met Richie Furay, who had been in a group with Stephen Stills before the Company and was living for a short time at the address Steve had given me on Thompson Street. Richie said Steve had gone to LA to start a band! I taught Richie "Nowadays Clancy Can't Even Sing," and then I did that demo session at Elektra Records that went badly. They had me set up in a tape storage room. I had my electric Gretsch to play and I ended up not using my amp because

I had a bad guitar cord. (I had dragged my amp all the way to New York; I still remember lugging it through Port Authority Bus Terminal. I asked someone for a hand with it, and he replied, "You're in the Big Apple now, kid—carry it yourself!") Anyway, I ended up doing the demo without it. I sucked. I flunked the audition. They didn't take me.

I told Richie to say hello to Stephen if he heard from him and headed back to Toronto. Richie then heard from Steve and went to LA to join in a band with him. Back in Toronto, eventually I sold my Gretsch and got an acoustic twelve-string. The Gretsch had a white case that had been signed by everyone I had met to that time, including Stephen, and I am sorry I sold it. I was out of money and I didn't know what else I could do. I wanted to give the acoustic solo thing a try in the Village (Yorkville). That Gretsch guitar and signed case is probably around somewhere. I sold it at a music store on Yonge Street, and of all the things that are out there of mine, that is the one I wish I still had. That was my first Gretsch, just like Randy Bachman's, but it was gone and I took my acoustic twelve-string to a few gigs and got some bad reviews. My first review dismissed my songs as full of clichés. They probably were! What's wrong with clichés? I thought I was pretty good, myself. I had an arrangement of "Oh Lonesome Me" that I really liked, and people laughed at it, thinking it was a parody or something. I used it on *After the Gold Rush*, and that worked.

Once I went down to Detroit to the Chessmate Club and tried to get a job, but that didn't happen. I did write a song on a napkin in the White Castle across the street called "The Old Laughing Lady." I stayed at Joni Mitchell's house with her and her husband,

Chuck, in Detroit while I was there. Eventually they left, and after one night sleeping in some girl's basement, to the amazement of her parents, I left one morning in a snowstorm and returned to Toronto. It was cold and I didn't have any warm clothes. That was a long trip.

It was rough in Toronto, and then I joined the Mynah Birds. I didn't know it at the time, but Ken actually took off down to LA and played with Stephen and Richie for a week while I was in the Mynah Birds. He didn't like it and came back to play with the group he was with, 3's a Crowd. He was doing a lot better than me at that point.

In Toronto I became acquainted with Bruce Palmer, who I think I met with some folkies at David Rea's flat in the Village. That is where I smoked my first weed. I got high and loved it instantly. The music sounded like God. We were all playing. David was an excellent acoustic guitarist who played with various folk acts like Ian & Sylvia and the Allen-Ward Trio as an accompanist. Bruce was just there hanging, and we became friends quickly.

He asked me to come and check out the Mynah Birds, who had just lost their lead guitarist. I joined the band and played my acoustic twelve-string with a pickup. It was pretty different. I really liked playing rock and roll again, and the Mynah Birds decided I was in. Eventually, the backer of the band, John Craig Eaton, bought more equipment for us, and that included a Rickenbacker electric for me to play. I missed my Gretsch, but we did a lot of gigs.

Ricky James Matthews, as he was called then, was our lead singer, and he was known as the Black Mick Jagger. He sang his ass off. Living with Rick in a basement apartment on Isabella, near Yorkville Village, I became introduced to other drugs. I was trying amphetamines and smoking a little hash. Looking back, I could have gone a lot deeper. Luckily I didn't get too far in the stronger drugs.

The band definitely rocked, and eventually we started doing some tunes Rick and I wrote together like "It's My Time." Mostly we did Stones covers in the beginning. I was so jacked on pills that once I jumped off a stage and pulled out my cord! That was a high school gig somewhere in Toronto. But we got good and landed a recording contract with Motown.

It was early 1966, and we headed down to Detroit and stayed in a big hotel, the Pontchartrain. While we were there I saw the Newbeats, the group that had a big hit, "Bread and Butter," going up the escalator. They all had dyed blond hair and matching powder-blue suits. I was very impressed. A real recording group, right in front of my eyes! I thought the sessions went great at Motown's Hitsville U.S.A., 2648 West Grand Boulevard. Smokey Robinson dropped in and was helping us, and some of the Four Tops would come in and back up our vocals, standing behind us as we sang. They made us sound cool. Everything was going great! It was just a big family feeling around Motown.

It was a very cool time and place. We even went to choreography school to learn how to move, and I'm sure we flunked, but they treated us well. They fitted us for clothes. We were on our way to the big time! And then Rick, who was a U.S. citizen, got busted for evading the draft for the Vietnam War. He was gone, just like that. It was over. Zip.

Then, two days later, Morley Shelman, who was our manager, OD'd on some heroin he had bought with our advance money. The cash was all gone, and so was our manager. We went back to Toronto and the band broke up. It was time to make a big move. That night I met with Bruce Palmer at a seedy little club on Avenue Road called the Cellar.

Driving Pocahontas, 1978.

## Chapter Nine

Playing with Fire

I made a film once, *Human Highway*, in which I burned four wooden Indians in a bonfire. It was a great scene in the movie, and it had a lasting effect on my life. One of the wooden Indians, the chief, had lived for a long time in the trees outside my beach house in Malibu, where Pegi and I were married in 1978. Sometime after the filming of that part of *Human Highway*, I went on the road in my bus and toured America. It was a 1973 Eagle bus we had fitted with wooden wings on the side and car tops, a Studebaker and a Hudson, on the top. The interior was all custom woodwork. It was a wild machine used prominently in the movie. I called her Pocahontas. Whenever I was asked about the bus, I would say, "Give a hippie too much money and anything can happen."

Now I'm going to relate to you three stories; I think you'll notice a pattern . . .

First story: In 1974, CSNY did a tour of North America and

actually made it to England to finish up at Wembley Stadium for a final show with Joni Mitchell, The Band, and Jesse Colin Young. Most of these big stadium shows were just no good. The technology was not there for the sound. It was all about the egos of everyone. The group was more into showboating than the music. It was a huge disappointment. Listening back to the tapes of Wembley, it is pretty obvious that we were either too high or just no good. I am saying too high. I know we were *really* good when we were at our best. I heard it and I felt it, but not on that tape.

When the big CSNY tour started in the United States, I leased a brand-new GMC mobile home and took it on the road. David Cline (aka Ranger Dave), Jim Mazzeo (aka Sandy Castle), and I were on board, along with my older son, Zeke Young. It was a journey to remember. The GMC was a poorly designed unit with double back wheels and front wheel drive, and every thousand miles or so the front tires would need to be replaced. We did not have that unit for very long. We ended up abandoning it and flying to somewhere near Cleveland, where we purchased a 1954 Cadillac limo for a few hundred bucks and tried to make that work. It did work well for a while, until it had problems, too. We had it fixed, and then Taylor Phelps came out to drive it home to California, where I had it restored.

Eventually we purchased a 1960s Flxible bus that worked pretty nicely for the rest of the tour. We named it Sam. At the same time, we purchased a 1973 Eagle bus that I saw on the road and planned on converting to a motor home. Mazzeo, an artist I knew, and I had been talking about ideas for that bus for months. When the project finally got under way, Mazzeo introduced me to a master woodworker/artist/designer, Roger Somers, who took on the job in Sausalito, right on the San Francisco Bay. Roger was the sort of character only Mazzeo could have found. He built, with the help of a mechanic named Bart Ehman, a motor home that was completely over-the-top. Work was done over the period of a year and a half in a boatyard.

No one who saw it in real life would ever forget it. This was simply the most outrageous bus in history. So over-the-top in every way that it should have ended up in the Smithsonian as a testimony to what might have happened if Ken Kesey was a millionaire and a sex addict.

Roger Somers named the bus Emily Flowers. Its interior features were all slanted toward being phallic or sexual in some way or other. All of the details reflected a highly tuned awareness of sexual pleasures in subtle and not-so-subtle ways. I was not aware of this aspect of what he was doing. It never occurred to me that the bus was being made for someone other than myself! Considering how shy I was sexually, I was very uncomfortable in the bus until I started to change a lot of these details and mellow it out. It took years to get it to that point. It was a lesson of sorts.

I liked the exterior of the bus, except for one decorative part that sort of resembled Medusa of Greek mythology to me. You may remember her as the woman with snakes for hair. I changed that design several times until it finally became a cow skull on a redwood bark background. Eventually, after years of refinement and simplification, the bus became a very comfortable place for me to be (although it was still outrageous, like a giant woodie with its wooden wings and car tops on top). We renamed it Pocahontas and toured around the country for years and years in it.

First Zeke Young, then Ben Young, took the position of shotgun and grooved away the miles with me, both of those boys having the time of their lives! I loved traveling on that bus with my boys, and they loved being on the road with me. Drivers came and went. David Cline, Jim Russell, Paul Williamson, Dave McCleod, and finally Joe McKenna, who was with us the longest time of all. Bigger motors, better brakes, new air conditioners, better generators; we kept upgrading, tour after tour, show after show. Just the memories of life on that bus could make a whole book. It had a shower where you could climb out the top through a skylight hatch and dry off on the roof or just hang out in the sun on a beautiful teak deck. Its kitchen was fully equipped so we could cook whatever we needed on the go. The beds were super comfortable, with one of them below the floor in a luggage bay. You entered that one through a hatch in the floor. Zeke loved sleeping there and looking out the round portholes that were on either end. The big bus was insulated with lead and was so quiet it was eerie. Pocahontas was so heavy she was nicknamed the "lead sled."

One day I was at the train barn and the phone rang. It was Joe McKenna. He was crying. "Oh God, Neil! I lost the bus. It burned to the ground. I just couldn't put it out. I'm so sorry, man! It's gone." He was on his way to the Pittsburgh area to have the bus worked on as part of its regular maintenance. He was calling from the side of the road on the Pennsylvania Turnpike, where that great bus met its demise. I would probably still be riding in it today had that not happened. The 12-volt system had caught on fire somehow, and it was unstoppable. I consoled Joe. "Don't worry, man. It's only a thing." It had been a good run. There was nothing more you could say, unless I write another book just about that bus.

We brought Pocahontas's remains back to the ranch and buried her in a eucalyptus grove, up on a ridge. We began building another bus right away and were able to use some of the interior pieces from Pocahontas that we salvaged. The whimsical wooden wings were gone, though. Two Buick Fastback car tops from 1947 replaced the original Studebaker and Hudson in topping off the new bus, a 1993 Eagle, which is bigger and has a lot of aluminum siding. While it doesn't run as smoothly as Pocahontas, it is equipped with a special lift and bedroom for Ben Young, our spiritual guide. There is a slight vibration in it that I always attribute to something I can't explain. It's not a good vibration, but it's not a particularly bad one, either.

Second story: At the end of our 1978 tour, when we returned in Pocahontas to Los Angeles to play the Forum, we noticed a lot of smoke in the sky. You could see it for miles. Wildfires were burning, and the fires were traveling fast. It was on TV. I made it to the Forum and performed my show with Crazy Horse. Afterward, the mood was upbeat until we got backstage. Something was off. It turns out our Malibu house burned to the ground during that performance. Nothing was left but the fireplace and a plaster mask of my face some girl had done after a wild night of partying at the Crazy Horse Saloon in Malibu.

And a third story: One weekend not long ago, Pegi and I were on our own little retreat in Desert Hot Springs, visiting one of our favorite places, Two Bunch Palms. It is a spa with a great hot springs that really is relaxing. We always try to stay in the Al Capone Suite. That is where the notorious gangster stayed when he was there a long time ago with one of his starlet sweethearts. Pictures of her are all around the place. There is a cracked mirror in the room with what appears to be a gunshot in it. The place has great vibes. Anyway, we were at the spa and this was one of the times we were unable to book the Capone Suite. Early in the morning, the phone rang. I picked it up. Ben Johnson, Larry's son, was on the other end of the line. "Oh my God! It's gone, Neil! The car has burnt to the ground. It's gone! Lincvolt is gone!"

We got on the Internet and watched it burning on the morning news. They didn't mention the car specifically, but I could see the taillights reflecting through the fire. They just reported that a warehouse in Belmont full of things owned by rock star Neil Young was burning and there were a lot of tapes and archival materials in the fire. We jumped on a plane and headed home to view the site firsthand.

A day or so later, I watched Lincvolt burn on a closed-circuit Internet camera that recorded the car 24/7. It was devastating. Three and a half years of work gone because one of the team had left it plugged in and forgot to go back and unplug it. It was not ready to be left plugged in to charge alone yet. It was still in development. That part of the system was untested. Operator error. I started to rebuild the car immediately (having a new regard for insurance that I had not had previously). The filming of the rebuild continues. This time it went forward with new people on the team. They are the best that the world has to offer.

With regard to the three fires, draw your own conclusions. Here are mine: I am betting three is the charm and we're done, what goes around comes around. I am gratified that the Great Spirit has chosen to make material examples. I am always in awe of Her power.

Chapter Ten

I suffered a temporary delusion. I thought I was the chosen one. Somehow I thought I could accomplish what no one else had been able to do. I wrote that phrase, *chosen one*, somewhere, and Pegi told me that was a wrong way to think about myself. She sure was right. It was ego-based. I was thinking it was all about me. Wrong. I thought I was the one who could solve the world's energy problems, just by persevering and following my dream.

I have sometimes become so infatuated by a goal that I can visualize myself doing unbelievable things. I learned about men who had powered cars on water, and met some very interesting garage mechanics and backroom scientists who shared both the dream and a lack of knowledge of physics. I thought these folks were brilliant, and backed them all the way. That was not to be. Maybe they are brilliant, but they weren't in their work with me.

I have made a lot of mistakes, and that was a big one—something is not so just because you believe in it and wish it to be so. What if it had worked? The planet would have been safer without the oil wars, cleaner without the pollution, but that was not to be. At least not yet. But I have faith in the human spirit and innovation, creativity and determination. Someone or some group will eventually figure it out.

The Lincvolt project has been my longest-running to date, and it is still a work in progress. In the beginning, Larry Johnson and I set out to make a movie about a couple of regular guys, with no experience, trying to repower the American Dream. We just kept moving, changing teams, and continuing. Then, with the sudden passing in 2010 of Larry, my co-conspirator, partner, and friend, coupled with the spectacular fire that almost completely destroyed the car, it seemed like all was lost.

Thankfully, Lincvolt was not destroyed. We rebuilt it. We added rear quarter panels and the deck from Miss Pegi, a 1958 Lincoln Continental that Pegi gave to me for my birthday to use for parts. Can you see why I love her so? That is part of life. Now it's part of the movie Larry's son Ben and I are finishing together. But Larry is bigger than that. His spirit will live forever in the films he has made and the people he has touched, in his children who now work alongside me with the same endless energy, optimism, can-do attitude, and brilliant minds. Our Lincvolt film will be finished, and our car will travel this country with Larry's spirit in it alongside me. That was the dream, and it will be the life.

Lincvolt will be clean, powerful, and sexy. This has to happen. It is going to. After four years looking at alternative fuels, I have learned a lot. Lincvolt's generation system will be powered by biomass when the car hits the road again. That is where the car's electric energy will originate. Look at all the waste we have in this country. We are number one. Biomass is everywhere. According to U.S. Department of Energy studies conducted by Argonne

National Laboratory of the University of Chicago, one of the benefits of cellulosic ethanol is that it reduces greenhouse gas emissions by eighty-five percent over reformulated gasoline. We need to change the way we get around. That is obvious. Checked the weather lately?

I am going down to São Paulo, Brazil, to speak at the SWU Festival. It is an environmental festival. SWU stands for "Starts with You." I hope I do a good job. Yes, it is scarier to do this than to play in front of thousands of people. I am cashing in some of my fame now to try to make a difference with it. What else is it good for? I have never really considered myself to be an activist. I just want to have a voice. You can call me whatever you want. Rock star? I have never really spoken in public before except once. It was at the SEMA (Specialty Equipment Market Association) show in Las Vegas, when we showed Lincvolt one week before the fire nearly destroyed it.

So as I said, I am going down there to São Paulo to speak and motivate young people to think about what they can do in their day-to-day lives to make a difference in the health of the planet. I guess that is one thing I can do now that is useful. I hope so. I want to do a good job, and I hope my part of the program is solid and constructive. It's a new ball game for me. I need to prepare. I can't just go down there and run off my mouth for half an hour. I can't just talk about the car. I need to go deeper. Into the conscience, the inner spaces where people can be empowered to do what they only have dreamed of doing before. Young people are prime candidates. They are wide open. Note to self: Prepare.

Chapter Eleven

L ast night I saw a movie about Conan O'Brien on cable. It was a documentary about his tour of America during the time between when he ended his network show and the start of his TBS show. This was a road movie, and it made me uncomfortable. I saw Conan, a friend of mine (I played on his last NBC show), on the road falling into every pothole it had. His people were doing their best, but they did not know what they were doing. The shows were not the problem. He was just not handled correctly. Nobody knew how to preserve and protect him on the road. The road is not easy under the best of circumstances.

There are a lot of things that can go wrong on the road. If you get sick, you still play, but people think you are losing your edge. If you have half a house, people don't feel that they are part of something. If you don't have a great crew, your shit doesn't sound right. If you don't have the best equipment, your show may not sound as great as the last one or the next one. If you have a reputation, it is on the line. If you forget what you are doing, it shows up on YouTube. If you remember what you are doing, it shows up on YouTube. If you do something new that isn't ready, or something old that you screw up, it is on YouTube. If snot comes out of your nose while you are playing the harmonica and slithers down the harmonica rack onto your T-shirt, it is on YouTube. If you say something stupid . . .

It is a lonely job out there performing. I have to do it because I always have. I probably always will. I love the music part. I like it when the sound is right and the audience is into it and the music is relevant. If one of those elements is missing, you are screwed. You are killing yourself slowly. You need all three elements. At this age, I think relevancy is the big challenge. With Crazy Horse, I need to perform new songs on the next tour for me to feel anything other than ancient history up close. So that is why we will record at the White House before we book anything. We need to be sure the new songs and music are ready and are meaningful to us. They are our ticket, our vehicle to the future, and without the new songs we are just reliving the past.

We need a real reason to believe in what we are doing. I hope it's there. It always has been, and we are all still breathing. There is a lot of love, a lot of baggage, and a lot to give. I think we will make it and it will be great. I will be so thankful if we have another shot at being great. There is nothing to prove, other than the fact that we still care enough to not just run through our hits and misses. We just want to give ourselves the opportunity to show our audience who we are. It is a very special thing we have, the way we play off of one another, the real deal. But it all comes from the songs, the images in our minds and hearts, the lyrics and the way they resonate. That is the fuel for the band. That is what will make the music relevant.

Poncho is my neighbor in Hawaii. When I get there, we will talk it over and I'll see if he is in. Ralphie is in already. If Poncho is in, I will talk to Billy next. Ralphie, Poncho, and Billy. Drums, guitar, and bass. I am looking forward to the whole trip. Recording, writing, playing, doing it straight. That will be new and different.

## Chapter Twelve

And Now, a Word from PureTone . . .

I t would be a historical moment for recorded sound if all of the recording companies would bring their labels together and agree on a concept for the good of music. Create the new gold standard. In trying to present PureTone to the leaders of all of the music groups—WMG, Universal, EMI, and Sony—I need to present an image. Here is an illustration I made to show what it is like to listen to different types of digital sound—if you are Jacques Cousteau!

I believe this accurately represents the experience! It is important to understand that we cannot descend much further in quality or we will hit rock bottom. Cloud music streaming will get very close to stirring up whatever sediment may be down there. Right now, we all live in a yellow submarine.

Music is now like a game. Turntable.fm, Spotify, and all the rest are the new radio. If someone likes a song or album they hear on the new radio, they would have a new option to purchase this music for listening. In my dream, the listening option would be PureTone—the new gold standard.

PureTone resolutions are 192 kHz and 384 kHz. Although 192 is here today, 384 is on the horizon, and both could be presented by PureTone in the future. PureTone is the best it can be in the digital realm, signed by the artist and certified to be studio master–quality recording.

Of all of the projects I have undertaken, this one most closely affects my music. Technology is supposed to make life better for everyone. That is its aim. This goes a long way toward doing that. There is a feature in the PureTone user interface called the Revealer. It enables you the listener to take a PureTone recording and instantly degrade it to CD or MP3 quality so you can show your friends why you listen to PureTone. This is a way to share the knowledge without the need for long philosophical and abstract discussions over what can be heard and felt and what the human ear cannot comprehend. There is no need for that discussion with the Revealer. It is true that I like this sound of music better than Apple's iTunes, but I think iTunes and the other MP3 dealers and the new streaming services that provide musical discovery play an important part in getting music out to listeners. The listeners can decide whether they would like the PureTone version of any particular recording. PureTone players play MP3s from iTunes, too, but they will sound better than the other players because of the digital-to-analog conversion at the heart of PureTone technology. It has to be better to play back the high resolution of PureTone masters, and so that helps MP3s sound a lot better, too. PureTone players will be portable, everywhere players, usable at home, in the car, or in your pocket with earphones. Additionally, PureTone home players could be bigger and better, with more memory and audiophile features galore for the extreme listener, but basic PureTone is for the masses, for music lovers. "Quality whether you want it or not," as Larry Johnson used to say.

With the Stray Gators in the barn at Broken Arrow Ranch, 1971. Left to right, Tim Drummond, Jack Nitzsche, me, Kenny Buttrey, Ben Keith.

Chapter Thirteen

I n 1970, when I was twenty-four years old, I visited Northern
California, and CSNY's road manager Leo Makota told me
about a piece of property that was available. I wanted to see it
right away. I was ready for a change from Los Angeles where I was
living and had seen this beautiful area of land from the airplane
on my trips to the Bay Area. Looking out the window, I saw rolling hills above the ocean with the grass a wheat color, looking
like velvet on the hillsides. In the canyons, redwoods had stood for
centuries.

There used to be an airline called PSA that had stewardesses
who dressed in short, short skirts and white go-go boots. That was
a great airline. You could fly between LA and San Francisco for
$9.95. Flights left every half hour. I flew up one day from LA, got
directions from Leo, and went down to see the property in the
Santa Cruz Mountains. I knew I liked the place even before I got
to it. It was on a long road through the forest, actually at the end
of the forest, where it opened up into pastureland and a breathtak-

ing view of the Pacific coast. I knew I couldn't get on the property, because there was no realtor involved yet. I loved the place, though I only got as far as the outside gate.

Later I found out that wasn't even the right place! The place Leo had pitched me was even farther down the road! The realtor and I made arrangements, and I went down there and saw the whole thing. A ranch foreman named Louis Avila was living on the property. He lived there with his wife, Clara. Louis gave me a ride around the ranch, all 140 acres' worth, in an old blue army jeep I still have today. The property had two lakes, two houses, and a beautiful old barn. It was owned by a couple of lawyers, Long and Lewis, and was called the Lazy Double L.

"How does a young fella like yourself have the money to buy a place like this?" Louis asked.

"Just lucky, I guess," I replied.

Later, while I was living there in my first months, I wrote the song "Old Man" about Louis. My dad thought it was written for him, and I never told him it wasn't, because songs are for whoever receives them. It was a beautiful place to live. I was absolutely in love with it. I decided to call it Broken Arrow Ranch.

Driving up north to the ranch from Southern California to move in to the house was a great trip. I had a '51 Willys Jeepster that I had purchased in Santa Ana, California. It had a top speed of only fifty-five miles per hour. Loaded with all of my worldly possessions, mostly gold records and musical instruments, I took off north from LA. I had been living in the Chateau Marmont hotel for a while because I had broken up with my first wife,

Susan, and it felt good to get on the road to start again in a new place. Johnny Barbata, CSNY drummer (and former member of the Turtles), wanted to live up north, too, and was going to look for a place, so he was riding with me. As we left LA, there was a fire burning on both sides of Highway 101. Through the smoke and flames we went heading to the future!

Behind me was Bruce's white 1958 Caddy limo. It took about eleven hours to reach the ranch. Late that night, on September 23, 1970, we reached the ranch. It smelled unreal, all the plants and the redwood forest; there was just something about that smell I loved. Home. It was the smell of home. I had finally made it.

As soon as I got there with my friends Johnny, Bruce, and Guillermo, who were going to live in the area too, we started tearing the house apart. It was just a little ranch house built on a lake in the fifties out of plywood siding, and it had some pretty cheesy interior features as well. We took down the cheap plasterboard paneling with phony wood grain that was on the old cabin walls. After a few days, we replaced it with beautiful redwood planks I picked out myself at the lumberyard. I went through stacks and stacks of twelve-inch-wide planks of rough-sawn A-grade redwood, choosing the ones with the most beautiful sap and grain. Maybe I took one out of every twelve. I loaded them carefully into the back of my '51 Willys pickup truck. When we got the redwood to the ranch and inside the house, we cut the planks carefully to length, choosing the exact grain detail we wanted to see on the wall, and then put them up. I chose every piece and placed each one carefully, taking my time to examine the grain, then deciding where to put it. These planks had a lot of sap in them and a unique grain. They were not the best grade for structure, but they were my favorite and I was using them only for a wall covering. Pegi and I still enjoy them in the living room today.

Since we also tore out the low ceiling and exposed the fir roofing and beams, I thought it would be a good idea to stain them with some teak espresso stain. I had learned about this stain because it was used in my first house in Topanga Canyon. That house also had redwood A-grade inside. Anyway, after a little application of the teak espresso stain, I decided it wasn't working. It was way too dark. I stopped right there. It is still there in one small corner of the living room. It makes me feel good to look at it because it reminds me of how innocent I was. I feel good just thinking about it. That was a really good time for me. I love new beginnings.

The house stayed basically like that for about eight years, until 1978, when Pegi and I were married. We expanded and built on a whole new wing that was designed to house the whole future family. It was four times the size of the original house, but even with all that room, who could have foreseen the arrival of Ben Young, our spastic, quadriplegic, nonverbal spiritual leader, with all of his special support equipment and his team of caregivers? So onward we went, designing a space for Ben and his crew . . .

If there is one thing I love almost as much as making music, it is building things. Houses, boats, cars, buildings of all kinds, control systems, sound playback systems, and model railroads have all been built and rebuilt either by me or people I have commissioned during my time on the planet. Why do the processes of people, artists, designers, and engineers involved in building or developing things fascinate me? I suppose it's because I am not sure if an idea will work when a project begins. This creativity is fascinating. I love to watch and try to guide what is happening, expanding the goals and reach of a project as it unfolds. Some people think that is the wrong way to do things, but I think it is the true way to discover. Each tangent offers new possibilities for exploration and discovery. A job is never truly finished. It just reaches a stage where it can be left on its own for a while.

Next to the ranch there was a place called Star Hill Academy. It was my neighbor Jimmy Wickett's place, and it was sort of a commune. (California communes, places where hippies lived together on the land, were popular in those times.) I heard about it, and one day I went over to see it. That's where I met Mazzeo. He was calling himself Sandy Castle at the time. A lot of people were living there in makeshift dwellings. One of the most interesting was Ken Whiting's tree house. Mazzeo took me over there. It was accessed by going out on a funky gondola type of thing, which was hanging from a steel cable between the tree and a building left behind by the loggers who had used Star Hill as their headquarters while they were harvesting the native redwood growth from the forest. Ken's tree was way down in a canyon, and the building was up on the rim of that canyon. So the cable extended straight out to Ken's house, about a hundred feet up in the big redwood tree. It was a straight shot. The canyon was full of big redwood trees, and Ken's house was in one of the biggest.

I was convinced to ride out on the cable car, which was actually just a sheet of metal hanging from some clothesline pulleys that ran along the cable out to the tree. I jumped on a little hesitantly to ride out. The sheet of metal plating hung from the cable, and away I went. I got almost all the way out there when the car stopped moving and started traveling backward toward the middle of the sagging cable. I hung out there in midair! Then Ken started pulling me in toward the tree with a safety rope that was part of the design. There were no railings on the metal sheet. They hadn't been added yet. Just wire connectors to the four corners. These connectors were joined at the top to a big clothesline wheel that was turning over the cable as the "car" moved along.

I began to notice some of the weaknesses in the overall design. It was important to stay in the middle of the metal plate and maintain good balance. People were cheering. Ken was pulling me in, and the car tilted more and more as I reached the tree. I realized when I arrived at the tree that I was the first person other than Ken who had used the cable car. It took a while for me to get up the nerve for the return trip. Getting in and out of the device was a difficult move from the tree. There was a beautiful girl up there with Ken who had climbed up the tree to get to the house. She was impressive. Her name could have been Sun Green, and she was part of the inspiration for Sun Green, the heroine of a film/album I did, *Greendale*, years later. Or maybe that is all in my mind, where my imagination has taken charge. That kind of thing can easily happen.

When I was buying my house in Topanga, Billy Talbot was already living nearby. He was in a place up Fernwood Pacific that he had rented from the music historian Michael Ochs, brother to the great songwriter Phil Ochs. That house was a small place farther up another side of the ridge from mine. It was smaller than what the previous renters needed, so they had moved out and Billy and his family—his wife, Susan, and baby son, Chris—moved in.

They had Chris's crib set up in a little room, and there was a really creepy painting on the wall above it. The painting was so creepy that Billy covered it with wood paneling. The previous renters had created it and left it there. It was only later that Billy realized the previous renters were Charlie Manson and a small group of girls.

Around the same time, just a bit later, I was visiting with Dennis Wilson, who I had met with Buffalo Springfield when we toured the South with the Beach Boys, doing three shows a day in different cities, leapfrogging across Florida. Dennis and I had become pretty good friends. I wanted to show him some songs I had written. At the time, Dennis had a nice place on Sunset Boulevard near Pacific Palisades—it had been Will Rogers's old compound, a single-story mansion with a huge pool and a great main room, a very gracious design I remember as being really impressive, with a huge front room featuring a magnificent old fireplace. I really appreciate the old Spanish architecture in the Los Angeles area because it is art and reflects the culture and the times of old Hollywood. Those must have been great days to live in.

Anyway, I went to visit Dennis there and found him living with three or four girls who were kind of distant. There was a detached quality about them all. They were not like the other girls I had met in Hollywood or Topanga, or anywhere else for that matter. He had picked them up hitchhiking. They had a pretty intense vibe and did not strike me as attractive. After a while, a guy showed up, picked up my guitar, and started playing a lot of songs on it. His name was Charlie. He was a friend of the girls and now of Dennis. His songs were off-the-cuff things he made up as he went along, and they were never the same twice in a row. Kind of like Dylan, but different because it was hard to glimpse a true message in them, but the songs were fascinating. He was quite good.

I asked him if he had a recording contract. He told me he didn't yet, but he wanted to make records. I told Mo Ostin at Reprise about him and recommended that Reprise check him out. Terry Melcher was a producer at that time who made some very influential hit records. Apparently Melcher had already been checking out Charlie and decided not to go for it.

Shortly afterward, the Sharon Tate–LaBianca murders happened, and Charlie Manson's name was suddenly known around the world. We couldn't believe we had played with him. Those grisly murders took place in Terry Melcher's recently vacated house. Sharon Tate was the new tenant who had just moved in.

## Chapter Fourteen

A Few Thoughts . . .

I have been told that MIT evolved from a train layout. If that were true, I could understand. Of course, that is not true—I believed it until I Googled it and learned the history—but it still made sense to me. Almost all technology can be found to have some roots in the science of railroading and real railroad operations. During development of what is now Lionel's system for control of action and sound on a model railroad, I became obsessed. There are so many ways to model the actions and sounds of a machine like a locomotive, it is endless—and the complexity involved is like a drug. For instance, every action has a sound and every sound has variables. Every sound variable needs an algorithm based on an action, and every action needs a variable control mechanism and a sensor to monitor its position or at least predict its position, possibly based on the positions of other related moving parts of the machine's systems. To me, this is a stimulant. I am fascinated by it, by all of the possibilities. Every sound needs to be recorded in such a way that it is variable by an algorithm based on the mechanical action or by the controller. You can see how I get hung up.

The end result is music.

I always leave these projects and go on to make music. A completely different part of my brain is used for music, and it feels like I am massaging my soul when I make music. The senses and the feelings evoked by the lyrics and melodies and execution of the instruments in cooperation and sympathetic reaction with other musicians is very similar, yet totally different from the act of building and creating. It's cosmic, dude. (Is this *Wayne's World* or what?)

L ife is exciting.

Jonathan Demme's new picture is the third concert film we have done together.

Jonathan shot a show I did up in Massey Hall (Toronto) and is really happy with it. It was the last show of my solo Le Noise tour. We also filmed in a '56 Ford Crown Victoria on the way to the theater from Omemee, my hometown, for about three hours, and he has intercut that with the concert. I'm giving a tour, from the driver's seat, of my old haunting grounds.

I love Demme. You know, he's made films like *Philadelphia*, *The Silence of the Lambs*, and *Stop Making Sense*. His energy is infectious. He is so positive, knowledgeable, and up about all aspects of a project; it makes him a complete pleasure to work with. He has now made a trilogy of performance films with me—and I am very honored. The guy is a G-man (G is for genius)! Anyway, Elliot and I

With Jonathan Demme at the WNYC studio in New York to talk about Neil Young Journeys, *2012.*

both know the most exciting time for any project is when it's done, when people are experiencing it for the first time, and it hasn't been released yet. It doesn't get better than that. Elliot will call me after he sees a screening and deadpan what a disaster it is and how we have to sue Jonathan. That is a great review. (We have our ways.)

Here in Hawaii, in the real world (ha!), Poncho Sampedro just graduated from a gardening course that taught him all about Korean microbiological gardening, where there are no chemical sprays and the earth takes care of itself. He is very high on that. We talked about it for a long time, and I can't wait to walk over to his house and see what he is up to. Even during Crazy Horse's most active years, Poncho worked on *The Tonight Show with Jay Leno* to keep his independence, live his own life, and have a constant income without relying on the group. He worked with Kevin Eubanks, the orchestra leader and a great guitarist, taking care of Kevin's equipment and helping him with his projects. He worked there right up until the Leno–Conan controversy and departed at that time to come with his cat, Kitty, to Hawaii, where he has a great place just up the road from Pegi and me. Kitty, who has been with Poncho a long time, has adapted well after a couple of months. Poncho is a unique person to know and make music with, and he has a big heart. Like everyone in Crazy Horse, his playing is very sympathetic to what he is hearing and feeling.

I love these long-term relationships. Poncho and I talked about doing a Crazy Horse thing again, and he is in. I am very happy about that. Next I will call Billy Talbot, our bass player, and we will talk as well. Billy is up in Zeona, South Dakota, with his wife, Karin, a lovely lady we have all known for a long time. They first hooked up during the *Greendale* sessions at Plywood Digital in 2002. Plywood Digital was right across the barnyard from an old Victorian house that Karin was living in, where she had raised her children with her husband, Larry Markegard, who had passed away a few years before. Larry was the foreman of my ranch for a good twenty-five years and was there long before I purchased that land. He and Karin came to California from the Midwest, settled down, and raised a family. It was a hard time for us all when Larry died in 1996, because everyone loved him so much. He was a really cool character and a very good man. Now it's Karin and Billy Talbot. Bless both their hearts for finding each other at this point in their lives. Billy had been pretty much a wild man most of the time up to then, and Karin was always such a sweetheart. I think that it is beautiful, although at first I couldn't believe it because Billy never seemed to settle. Billy finally did with Karin. Love.

Old Black and my amps, 2012.

Chapter Fifteen

Cars and Guitars

ank is my 1949 Cadillac convertible, baby blue with a tan top and blue leather seats. She is a beautiful car, named after Hank Williams, the great country music icon singer/songwriter. I first met Hank (the car) through an ad in the paper. I was down in Hollywood with Ben Keith and Rusty Kershaw, recording *On the Beach* in March of 1974. We were recording at Sunset Sound on Sunset. That place is still there today, and as a matter of fact that is where Pegi just made her new album, *Bracing for Impact*. It is also where we made "Expecting to Fly" with Jack Nitzsche and Bruce Botnick, the great engineer who did the Doors' albums with Paul Rothchild. Stephen Stills and I did "Rock & Roll Woman" and many other Buffalo Springfield tracks there. I recorded "I Believe in You" and "Oh Lonesome Me" with Crazy Horse there, too. It is a great place with lots of history for many of us. Today, it looks pretty similar in some ways, although it has grown to include the building next door, incorporated a little courtyard with a basketball hoop, and has a parking lot behind the studio. Stephen and I used to park our Cadillac right where the basketball hoop is while we were making *Buffalo Springfield Again*, but the rooms where music was/is played remain pretty much exactly the same. These old studios are so wonderful—imagine a building constructed so that music would sound good in it.

Anyway, I was there in 1974 with Ben and Rusty, and we were recording *On the Beach*. I picked up the paper and saw this ad. I was always in the habit of rewarding myself for doing a project and completing it. I would buy a car or something to celebrate and have a material memory of that time. (As I said before, I am a material guy.)

In December 1974, I took Pegi for our first date. I picked her up at her little cabin in the redwoods in Hank. Zeke Young, who was then about two, went along for the ride. She was living in a very small town called Loma Mar, about fifteen miles from the ranch. I had Zeke with me and thought we would all have a nice day together. We went on a cruise down the Pacific Coast Highway toward Santa Cruz. The beautiful blue Cadillac convertible in its element on an oceanside drive, we were just talking, taking in the sights, getting to know each other. Pegi, twenty-two years old, was a beautiful girl. I loved the way she smiled so brightly, and her blue eyes really caught my attention. I already knew there was something different about her and that I was feeling things that I hadn't felt before. We stopped in a little town called Davenport, but there was nothing going on there, just looking around. When we got back in the car, Zeke tried to bite her. I think he was anxious for all my attention, since he did not see me every day. I should have known that.

Zeke had a rough start in life, with his mom, Carrie Snodgress, and me breaking up right when he was just getting going. Zeke was born in 1972 with cerebral palsy and had to wear a brace on his foot. Like any other kid who was a bit different from others, Zeke Young was picked on by his peers, but he is a resilient and loving person, with a heart as big as life itself, and he has become a man I am so proud to call son. He is hardworking at his daily job, one he found at the Home Depot, where he started part-time and has stuck with it to become a full-time senior employee.

Zeke had gone to an audio recording school and learned all the technical theory behind recording. He used to work with me on my tours, recording my shows on a Pro Tools system. One day he came to me and said, "Daddy, I think I should get another job, because I need to be independent and you will not be doing this forever. I don't want to be relying on you for a job." I think any father would be really proud to hear those words from his son, and I was very impressed with Zeke.

Although he possesses a lot of varied talents, he has made a commitment to work every day for the security it brings. He is well respected at his job, and specializes in handling complaints, one of the hardest things to do. He does it with a smile. Everyone loves Zeke. His sense of humor is legendary. You don't get away with anything when he is around . . .

But back to Hank. When *Harvest Moon* came out in 1992, MTV was in full swing and the video age was upon us. We made a video for the song "Harvest Moon," and Hank is featured in the video. Larry and Karin are in it, too. (Larry is the guy in the video with the big white beard.) It is beautiful to watch them together.

Speaking of cars, during 1983, I was touring with a band called the Shocking Pinks. We had a lot of cars with us. The Pinks were a throwback to the days of old rock and roll. Every night we had a different Cadillac to leave the stadium in, and it was part of the show. At the last note of the last song, we would make a mad dash to the car with the cameras following us, then we would jump in the car and drive away while the crowd watched on a twenty-foot-high model of a portable TV that was onstage. We had this announcer, Dan Clear, who would be chasing us out of the venue, trying to get one last-minute interview. It was a lot of fun! The video is ridiculous! That was about when my record company sued me for making music "uncharacteristic of Neil Young." Point is, there were a lot of cars.

Old Black is my guitar. This is the guitar I have played on almost every Crazy Horse recording I have ever made. Black is a 1952 Gibson Les Paul model that I got in a trade with Jimmy Messina back in the days of Buffalo Springfield. Originally, Old Black must not have been black, but was most likely gold. Someone had refinished it and changed the color a long time ago. That was obvious to me when I first got Black in 1968, because by that time Black had aged tremendously—was well-worn, you might say. Someone, probably the same person who made Old Black black, had special chrome-plated metal pickup covers and pick guard made. All the original gold tops had cream-colored plastic pickups (at least they seemed plastic to me—maybe they were not, but they were definitely not steel). Black's pickups were shrouded with chrome steel covers. They were beautiful.

That is the way the guitar was when I recorded *Everybody Knows This Is Nowhere* with Crazy Horse. That was our first record, and I played Black on every track that called for an electric guitar. I had added a Bigsby tremolo arm, or wang bar as it was called, to the guitar at some point very early on. (Matter of fact, I think it came that way in the trade. I'm pretty sure the same work—the black paint, the chrome-plated metal pickup covers and pick guard, the Bigsby—were all done by the same person. Special bone inlay was also added, but most of that had fallen out by the time I got it from Jimmy.) Then I used it on "Southern Man" and "When You Dance" from *After the Gold Rush*.

Sometime after that I decided to get the pickup next to the bridge fixed so that it wouldn't hum. It hummed like hell when there was a transformer or weird wiring or lighting in a building, and you had to orient the guitar a certain way in space or the hum was as loud as the notes. I took it to a guitar shop down on Western Avenue in LA and dropped off the pickup to get it wound again; there was a procedure that supposedly fixed the problem. I'm glad I only gave them the pickup, because when I returned later to retrieve it, the store was gone. Not a trace. They left with my pickup! Shit! That sucked. What a bunch of assholes!

I was shocked. My guitar was damaged beyond anything I could have imagined. Later I replaced the stolen pickup with an old Gretsch pickup.

I was never really happy with that Gretsch pickup. It just didn't sing like it used to. I knew I had to change. Larry Cragg, a master guitar tech and old friend who traveled on the road with me taking care of my instruments from the mid-seventies until 2010, is a very conscientious character, taking wonderful care of my guitars and amps. He played countless parts in my stage shows as well, from "Grandpa" in *Greendale* to "Farmer John" in *Ragged Glory*. He always gives it everything he has, no matter what he does. One night in the early to middle seventies, Crazy Horse was playing a coliseum somewhere and Larry ran up to me very excited. He exclaimed, "I have found the perfect replacement for Old Black's pickup. It's a Firebird, and it screams." He was so excited. Larry was really into his work and was always trying to make things better. It really did scream, like a banshee, and I played it for years. It's still on Old Black today. Larry takes care of much of our equipment now from his shop at home, and spends a lot of time playing steel in bands around the area. He is happy to be a playing musician, and he plays with Pegi when she goes out on the road, too. It's great to know he is still there to help if we get in any real trouble with our equipment. Thanks, Larry!

"Like a Hurricane" is probably the best example of Old Black's tone, although if you listen too closely, it is all but ruined by all the mistakes and misfires in my playing. That was a memorable recording, though, for the feeling that comes out of our instrumental passages.

I always record every note played, whether it is a run-through or not, and the recording of "Like a Hurricane" is a great illustration of why I do that. When you do that, you catch everything. Most often the first time something is played is the defining moment. That is what I like to capture in my recordings. It is a strict rule that my engineers are there to record *everything*. The master recording I used for the final version of the track was the run-through when I was showing the Horse how the song went. That is why it just cuts on at the beginning. There was no beginning. There was no end. It is one of those performances you can never repeat; the cherry, the original expression of the song, the essence. We just kept wailing on those changes until we couldn't move anymore.

One night in late November 1975, I wrote the "Like a Hurricane" lyrics on a piece of newspaper in the back of Taylor Phelps's 1950 DeSoto Suburban, a huge car that we used to all go to bars in. Taylor was a great friend who lived on the mountain, and everybody loved him. He and Jim Russell were my buds back then. Jim was a cowboy who drove big machinery and was a really nice guy. In the mid-seventies, Jim and I hung out a lot and went to bars looking to get lucky. We had both recently broken up with our kids' moms, and Zeke and Jenny, our two kids, would be in the truck in the parking lot when we went into the bars for "Daddy's Boogie." There was an Alaskan Camper on the back of my new 1975 Dodge Power Wagon, Stretch Armstrong, and Zeke and Jenny used to hang in it while we were doing our thing.

As was our habit between bars, we had stopped at Skeggs Point Scenic Lookout on Skyline Boulevard up on the mountain to do a few lines of coke; I wrote "Hurricane" right there in the back of that giant old car. Then when I got home, I played the chords on this old Univox Stringman mounted in an old ornate pump-organ body set up in the living room. It was painted antique white, and I had gotten it from Dean Stockwell, the great actor and another friend of mine in Topanga. None of the original guts were left inside the thing, but it looked great and sounded like God with this psychedelic Univox Stringman inside it I had hooked up so that it was hammering and overdriving a Fender Deluxe. I played that damn thing through the night. I finished the melody in five minutes, but I was so jacked I couldn't stop playing.

A few months later at the Village in LA, I put on all the vocals as overdubs. I just had to hear that song finished. Crazy Horse had never sung it or even heard the words. It was just a rundown of the track, and it became the master recording of "Like a Hurricane."

Taylor didn't go bar cruising with Jim and me, though. It turned out he was gay. He was such a cool guy. I knew he had something else going on. Later, he started One Pass Video in San Francisco and became very successful. Then, when he suddenly retired and dropped out, I said, "Hey, man, why are you dropping out now? You are going to be a huge fucking success. You are a natural. You could produce movies."

He just looked at me and said, "I can't do it anymore. I have more important things to do now."

About a year or so later, maybe a little more, Taylor died of AIDS. At the time, AIDS was still a relatively new thing with a stigma attached to it. People were just starting to understand what it was. Son of a bitch. That was sad. I really miss him. He was one cool and funny and smart guy. What a drag. He was one in a million. Unique as hell. Taylor had the gift of gab. When CB radios were popular, he talked like he was on a CB all the time. "Breaker

breaker, come back?" He outfitted all of his vehicles with them. He was always trying new things. Once he took on the character of a paramedic and drove around the mountain in his Yukon, full of emergency medical stuff, talking on his CB. Then he bought a semitrailer tractor truck and drove that everywhere. He was a very likable and a one-of-a-kind character. Life again.

## Chapter Sixteen

As You Can Tell

I am getting aware of the fact that I keep writing and thinking about people who have died. I love living. I do not want to die for a long time because I am not ready. I suppose if I thought I was going to die, I could get ready given a period of time, but I am not sure about that. Some folks think that is not a good thing to think about. I envy the control they must have over their thinking processes.

As you can tell, if you are still with me, I don't have much control over that. I have only rewritten about one paragraph so far. There is no such thing as spell-check for life, though. There is a big wind blowing today, and I'm part of it. I want to make a difference, and above all, I want to be a good person from here on out. I can't change the past. Don't look back. Thanks, Bob. I needed that. "How many roads must a man walk down before you call him a man?"

Buffalo Springfield, Malibu, June 1966. Left to right, Stephen Stills, Richie Furay, Bruce Palmer, Dewey Martin, me.

## Chapter Seventeen

How many seas must a white dove sail before she sleeps in the sand?"

My first time hearing Bob Dylan was back in Winnipeg around 1963. I was trying to figure out how to get to the USA and had met some friends who had told me about a possible job working on the railroad. Following up on that, I visited one of them. They were all sitting around listening to a record I had never heard. Some guy was singing, playing harmonica and acoustic guitar. We were all listening now. Hanging on to the words he sang. There was something about that, the way it sounded. I thought it was folk music, but not like the folk music of the Kingston Trio. I started to hear more and more of Bob. One day he came over the speakers of my radio singing "How does it feel?" over and over. The lyrics pounded their way into my psyche, this new poetry rolling off his tongue.

He spoke for a lot of us without knowing it. I felt connected to him in a moment. That was in Toronto, '64 or '65. Bob left his mark.

I had to avoid listening to him for a long time in the late sixties and early seventies because I thought I would assimilate so much that I would suddenly be copying him. It was a conscious thing to avoid being too influenced. I am like a sponge in that when I like something, I become so influenced by it that I almost start to *be* it.

Eventually I was able to pick up the harmonica without thinking I was copying Bob, just influenced by him. Dylan's words are part of the landscape, like country names on a map. I have heard people try to sound like him, and it turns me off. People have tried to sound like me to the point that my dad thought "A Horse with No Name" was mine! (Hey, wait a minute! Was that me? Okay. Fine. I am back now. That was close!)

I am currently tired of my musical self. I have reached a point where I have OD'd. When this happens, it is temporary, but my capacity to enjoy music disappears totally. Everything I think of musically is a joke and I reject it completely. That is part of the process. It has happened a few times before. The last time was near the end of 2009; I finished that tour and had to stop. Too much of a good thing. Even other people's music turns me off when I am like this. It all sounds the same.

I did, however, hear a group called Givers on TV a few nights back, and they blew my mind. It was completely original! WOW! It sounded like they were in a complete other zone from the rest of music. "Land of a Thousand Dances" did the same thing to me when I heard Danny and the Memories do their version on YouTube. So I am not dead. Just sleeping. Hibernating, like music lovers who can't feel what they used to when they heard music because of the low sound quality. They are hibernating bears. They will come out of their caves only when the sound of music shines like the sun again.

Anyway, when I first heard Bob, back in '63, I was just getting used to being independent, looking for a reason to stay in Winnipeg and finding a reason to leave. It was very hard to get out of there. I went down to the railroad station and could not get a job. I thought workin' on the railroad would be a good way to get out of town and go to the USA. Then I found out I needed a work visa. I didn't think I could get a visa, because I didn't know what I was going down to the USA to do. What was I going to say, "I'm going to write songs and play my guitar"? No. There was an American who could already do that job; we were just talking about him. You have to be unique to get a visa. Do something no one else can do. I was stumped.

So I made up my mind that someday I was going to sneak in. It took a long time for that to happen. A few year later, in 1966, I was in Toronto, in the middle of the night, sitting in a funky after-hours dive called the Cellar. I was with Bruce Palmer, bass player for the group I was in at the time, called the Mynah Birds. The group had just broken up. Bruce and I were just sitting there, probably pretty stoned, and I asked Bruce if he wanted to go down to LA. I targeted LA because that was where all the music was happening. Bruce and I knew that. He said yes, so we sold all the band's equipment (even though it had been purchased for the Mynah Birds by the group's backer, John Craig Eaton) to buy a '53 Pontiac hearse. We loaded it up with three girls and another guy, all from Yorkville Village in Toronto. We immediately headed for Sault Ste. Marie, the most nondescript border crossing we could find.

With six lids of grass and a few musical instruments, we crossed the border. As we headed into the States, we were laughing our way into the promised land. The U.S. immigration guard asked us where we were going. We said, "Vancouver, but the roads are so much better down here, we are dipping south to use them." With a compliment like that, six wide-eyed kids made it through!

We headed straight south. The roads *were* better. We were surprised at how good they were. They were made of gray concrete with yellow lines down the middle, and made a slight *ba-bump* sound as we rolled along. These roads all were smooth and looked brand-new. Most of the highways in Canada were black asphalt with white lines, and they had bumps and places where they had been repaired. It was a very different sensation, riding on these roads.

Having heard about Route 66, we headed for it south of Chicago. We broke out a lid, rolled a couple of joints, and smoked them. Then we just drove. Next thing I knew we were down in Texas and got pulled over by a state trooper. Oh shit. He asked us for our draft cards. We told him we did not have draft cards because we were Canadian and we were just on our way to Vancouver but the roads were so good, etc. He took down our Ontario plate number, went back to his trooper patrol car, and we sat and waited. Miraculously, he told us to keep going and obey the signs. We were off on our way again.

The girls were driving me nuts. It's hard to say why. I don't remember. I was just very stressed. One of them drove occasionally, and I didn't like the way she treated the car. I thought for sure it would break down because of how she drove. We had to start putting oil in it. We knew only a little about caring for a car. I was exhausted from driving, not eating much, and really not feeling well. We got to Albuquerque and stopped there, took up residence at a crash pad some hippies we met turned us on to, and hung out and rested for a few days.

Looking back, maybe I had my first epileptic seizure there. I know we went to a hospital emergency room, but I don't recall much about what happened to me there. Afterward, I slept on a mattress on the floor of the house for a really long time, probably a couple of days. When I started coming around, Bruce and I decided two of the girls were stressing us out too much. Things were not harmonic. So we hatched a plan. Bruce and I, along with the one of the three girls we liked who was really nice and kind of lost, would get into the hearse in the middle of the night and leave the others at a folk club in town where they had been hanging out. We felt a lot better after we left them behind.

Traveling through some tremendously hot and dry country, the next thing I remember is coming down a really steep hill near San Bernardino. And then we got to LA. It was April 1, 1966.

There was a freeway exit called Juanita Street, and Bruce and I, thinking that was particularly funny, were saying "Juanita" with big Mexican accents over and over and laughing our asses off. *"Juaneeeeeta, Juaneeeeeta!"* We were really giddy with happiness at having finally made it to LA. Then, of course, we had to find Hollywood and 77 Sunset Strip! I had a picture in my mind of the TV show where Kookie used to park the cars. I was looking for that building. We drove through Hollywood looking, but the numbers were way too high. So we turned around and headed west on Sunset toward 77. Finally we got to the ocean—but no 77!

There we were at the Pacific Ocean! A trio of Canadian kids in an old hearse with Ontario plates, in a parking lot off the Pacific Coast Highway, looking at the sea. It was a little cold and foggy, but finally we were there. The sandy beach was right between where we were parked and the waves. We got out and walked across the sand to the shore, full of wonder. And I mean FULL of wonder! We forgot all about 77 Sunset Strip! Eventually we headed back up to Hollywood on Sunset Boulevard, reversing our tracks. When we got to Hollywood again, I saw the building! I saw 77 Sunset Strip, just like the TV show. But it was not really 77. It was some other number. That was one of my first lessons about Hollywood. The numbers are not always what you think they are.

A long time before, back in Winnipeg at the Fourth Dimension Club, I had met a singer named Danny Cox. He gave me his phone number to call him should we ever make it to LA. I called him. He was there. We went to his house off of Laurel Canyon and visited. We couldn't crash there. It was just a small place in the hills, but he fed us and let us take showers, and that felt real good. (Thanks, Danny.) So we slept in the hearse on a side street parallel to Laurel Canyon Boulevard. I remember that every time I pass by, and I have passed by a lot in the last forty-five years or so. We lived there for almost a week. We used the bathrooms at gas stations and restaurants. It was cool. We weren't scared. We were fascinated by the whole scene in Hollywood.

We spent our days looking for Steve Stills, who I knew was down there. Richie told me that Stephen was down in LA trying to put together a band. That was all I needed to know. I remembered Stephen from Fort William, four hundred miles southeast of Winnipeg, at the Fourth Dimension Club, where I had first heard him play in a band called the Company. We had talked about playing more together then.

Bruce and I went to the Trip, a cool club on the Sunset Strip where the Byrds played. We asked around. No one knew Stills. We visited a place called Huff's on Sunset. It was a hippie hangout. I had never seen so many hippies in my life! Where did they get all those cool clothes? Where did all these girls come from? They looked so cool and unreachable. They had tie-dyed dresses and T-shirts, so colorful and beautiful. It made me feel like I was from another planet, but I loved it. We made a living that week by giving hippies a ride between Huff's and Canter's, another cool hangout that was down on Fairfax. We charged about fifty cents a ride. (These hippies mostly were rich.) The girls were really something; I had never seen anything like it. I was completely in awe!

One day, Bruce and I were walking down Sunset toward a hotel, the Colonial West, we visited regularly that we gave people rides to and from, and we found a joint on the sidewalk. Of course, we smoked it right away and got so high, we were completely flying. What the hell kind of pot was that? It smelled really pungent. So we walked along toward this hotel. Some places you can just feel are havens for drug users, heavy drug users. These places have a feeling to them. I sensed the dark seed (which is a phrase I've stolen from Stephen and Kristin Stills's twelve-year-old son, Henry, who used it to describe a Disney movie). There was an opening on the strip that led to a parking lot that was surrounded by about three stories of rooms, so the place was kind of separated from everything else, like a fort. Musicians lived there along with drug dealers, actors, and rich hippies I suppose. It was a scene, and you could feel it instantly. Bruce and I had never experienced anything like this. It was all new to us.

We couldn't find Stills anywhere. Eventually we gave up on LA and decided to head north to San Francisco, where Flower Power was in full bloom, with Jefferson Airplane and Big Brother and the Holding Company. Human Be-Ins were happening in Golden Gate Park. Hippies were everywhere. We were on our way to Mecca! The Great Pilgrimage was about to begin!

We made our way along Sunset and got caught in a traffic jam. It had dawned on us that we may not have enough gas money to get to San Francisco, but we were working on a solution when we heard a voice shout, "Hey, Neil!!! Is that you?"

I looked around out the driver's window of the hearse. It was Stills! We got out and hugged right there on Sunset Boulevard in the middle of traffic. Horns were honking! To us it seemed like everybody was celebrating! Something was happening, but we didn't know what it was. It was fucking Buffalo Springfield, that's what it was.

Stills and Richie Furay were living at Barry Friedman's house on Fountain Avenue. Barry had a background in the circus and the entertainment business. He was a smart guy with a great musical sense. He was managing Stills and Furay, which is how I met him. Stills had convinced Richie to come to LA from New York because he had a group going. When Richie arrived, Stephen explained that the group was now Stephen and Richie!

Richie was a natural vocalist. They had been working on a vocal sound, and they were really great. They sang like birds together. They were doing "Nowadays Clancy Can't Even Sing" (which I had sung for Richie in New York when I was there doing a demo tape in December 1965), and they sang it really great. I sat in and added a little guitar and a high voice here and there. This was going to be good. We needed a drummer, and Barry had contacted the Dillards, a great vocal group with a guy named Dewey Martin on drums—just when they were changing to all acoustic. We tried him out and took him, although Stephen was not a hundred percent sure. Dewey was country and took a little speed, I think. He was moving right along.

But Stephen, who was a genius, had an amazing groove. He possessed his own sense of rhythm that was uncanny, like a clock but with a feel, never rushing or dragging. There was a rub between him and Dewey because Dewey tended to push the beat and rush sometimes. I had never been aware of that type of thing until I met Stephen and started to learn from what he was saying.

We went outside onto Fountain Avenue and saw a big steam-roller on the side of the road. BUFFALO SPRINGFIELD, read the sign on the side. What a great name for a band! Buffalo Springfield was born that day. We lived and practiced at Barry's house in West Hollywood. I slept in a little room with the band instruments. Every day we would go to Pioneer Chicken on Santa Monica Boulevard and have a meal. Barry gave us the money. We ate once a day. Stephen always had a cheeseburger with mayonnaise only. Good taste is timeless.

Chapter Eighteen

tephen and I recently talked about the Springfield and writing books. We talked about the future. About musicians and friends, about loyalty, about the difficult decisions in life around loyalty, loyalty to friends and loyalty to the muse, how sometimes there was conflict, where serving one meant not serving the other. This is a heavy subject, and we, as two old friends, treated it well. It has not been an easy part of life for either of us. I think most musicians would agree with that. Stephen and I have this great honesty about our relationship and get joy from telling each other observations from our past. The past is such a big place.

I have heard it said about me that I have a rep for being difficult to work with. My decisions are made with the music in mind. For instance, I like to play to an audience that is into it. I dislike people sitting in the front rows talking on cell phones. Of course, these people are sitting in the most expensive seats, the ones they get through ticket scalpers and other services that somehow corner the market on the seats. Capitalism collides with music in this area. It was not like that when I started. The people in the front were music freaks, the real music fans, who knew every song, every lyric, every piece of information about the band that they could find. They were stoked to be there in front of the stage, and they were ready to rock. So these cell phones and rich folks who can afford the big bucks for prime seating distract me from what I am doing and make me feel like I am on display in a museum. It is not good for the music, which a lot of times feeds on the energy of the crowd. There is a thing called "festival seating" where the area in front of the stage is without chairs. People can stand there. Only a certain amount of people can get into that area, and it is not more expensive. It is general admittance. First come, first served, as far as proximity to the stage goes. Medium ago, I decided to sell festival-seating tickets at all my indoor shows so people who really wanted to see the band could get up close and watch, moving freely. There is a financial hit involved with that, because those are generally the expensive seats and they are all gone with this type of presentation. I had to really be firm about it. When we got festival seating, the feeling at all of the shows was much better. The band and I really enjoyed that change. Things like that enable me to continue and enjoy playing with a band. Recently I was planning a tour and it was just being announced. Venues were already booked. At the last minute I checked to make sure it was still festival seating. It wasn't. Feeling that I had already established that as the way I liked to play indoor shows, I insisted on it again. All the deals had to be redone at the last minute. It was a very complicated thing to do. I, having already been through this once, was amazed that no one had remembered the way I liked festival seating. If that gives me a rep for being difficult to work with, I earned it.

Because Stephen and I have been friends for such a long time, and we were really young when we met, some of these things run deep. He is really my oldest friend, and confiding in him is easy, once we get started. There is nothing to hide between us. We talked about the love of playing together and being in the groove, and about the fact that we need to have solid support from musicians on our level everywhere on the stage. Festivals are where you need that kind of strength at the core. That is how you elevate the audience and take them with you. We both love doing that.

We talked about playing with Chad Cromwell and Rick Rosas on the Living with War tour around five years ago and how solid that was. It was perhaps the most overtly over-the-top group of songs I had ever written, but we did what we did and I don't feel bad about it. There was no attempt at an artfully crafted message. It was just a straight shot. Stephen was uncomfortable with the political nature, singing songs like "Let's Impeach the President" and "Living with War," which were written as if they were from a raving political maniac. Hey! Maybe it was art. Like someone standing on a soapbox in the park, I didn't waste any time on a melody. The message wasn't worth a carefully crafted one. Production, pretty melodies, and the like would have been a waste of time on that record. It was delivered in a cheap paper bag like something that came with no desire to decorate it. We discussed that. I told him I thought it was a worthy part of our history. It was uncomfortable at times and pushed the limit of what our audience could handle. I was more okay than he was with that. But we talked it through.

Niko Bolas was my co-producer on *Living with War*. I met Niko in 1986. He was the engineer at Record One, a studio in LA's

San Fernando Valley where we made a record called *Landing on Water*. I liked Niko right away. We worked fast and did a lot together over time. *This Note's for You* with the Bluenotes in the late eighties, *Freedom* with "Keep on Rockin' in the Free World" in 1989, and *Living with War, Chrome Dreams II,* and *Fork in the Road* in the 2000s. I always liked Niko and enjoy working with him. He and John Hanlon (*Ragged Glory*) are both guys I can relax with in the studio and be myself with, like I did with Briggs. They know they are not Briggs. No one is like Briggs. But they know who he was and respect him and his memory. He was a legend. They try to keep his feeling going on, and that helps me a lot.

As for *Living with War*, we probably won't be doing any more of those types of records, but we did that one. Buffalo Springfield was not that kind of band anyway, and I think that will be our band for the next big run, whenever and wherever that is.

So I spoke to my old friend Bruce and told him I was feeling it, his loss of Clarence. We talked for quite a while, and there is no need to go into what two old friends had to say to each other at this point, except to say that two old friends spoke to each other about their music, their muses, their partners in crime, their proof, their friendship, their souls, and their lives. Ben Keith was my Clarence Clemons. Clarence was Bruce's Ben Keith. When he died last year, it touched me to the core. I don't want to ever think of anyone else playing his parts or occupying his space. No one could. I can't do those songs again unless it's solo. So I told Bruce, "Waylon once looked at me and said, 'There's very few of us left.'" He liked that. I told him when he looked to his right I would be there. That's enough. I'm not talking about that anymore.

When music is your life, there is a key that gets you to the core. I am so grateful that I still have Crazy Horse, knock on wood. You see, they are my window to the cosmic world where the muse lives and breathes. I can find myself there and go to the special area of my soul where those songs graze like buffalo. The herd is still there, and the plains are endless. Just getting there is the key thing, and Crazy Horse is my way of getting there. That is the place where music lives in my soul. It is not youth, time, or age. I dream of playing those long jams and floating over the herd like a condor. I dream of the changing wind playing on my feathers, my brothers and sisters around me, silently telling their stories and sharing their spirits with the sky. They are my life. How often can a guy make a living doing that? Not that often is my guess, so I accept the extreme nature of my blessings and burdens, my gifts and messages, my children with their uniqueness, my wife with her endless beauty and renewal. Am I too cosmic about this? I think not, my friend. Do not doubt me in my sincerity, for it is that which has brought us to each other now.

## Chapter Nineteen

Hawaii 2011

Writing this book, there seems to be no end to the information flowing through me. There is always more waiting to come out, whereas songs are nowhere to be found at the moment. Since I have never written a book before and my father, who was a writer of books and taught me how to write many years ago, is gone, I am alone but am comforted by the eternal presence of my father and his old Underwood up in the attic. I am both down here and up there. Omemee was my town, and that's where the house was. That's where the attic is. Someday I want us to live on a lake up there in North Ontario for a while. I have been there visiting my brother. This is not the time for us to go there, though. Maybe it will never come, and that's all right, but I want to do it someday, and that is important to me. It is part of my Canadian self. I feel it stronger these days than in days past, yet I know it may not ever be, and I accept that I cannot have every dream come true at once. Life is too short for that.

Anyway, the word count on my computer is a marvel. Think of

counting the actual words one by one and keeping track. My dad would never do that. That's not going to happen with me, either. I am beginning to see that the rest of my life could conceivably be spent as an author, churning out books one after another to the endless interest of, say, fourteen people with Kindles. Seriously, though, this is a great way to live. No wonder my dad did this. There is no live performing, which I love to do as long as I don't *have* to do it, and writing could be just the ticket to a more relaxed life with fewer pressures and more time to enjoy with my family and friends—and paddleboarding!

I suppose that sounds like the end of something, but I look at it as the beginning. I'm even considering starting a second book titled *Cars and Dogs* because there is so much more to say than I could ever say in one book. There is a lot of room there for me to wander, which I am very fond of doing. Maybe it would be disruptive to put out two different books at once, one in hardcover and one in digital, both memoirs, since the book industry is on its heels from the tech revolution. Disruptive is good in technology. No matter how many books I write, I will eventually get to fiction. That is where I am going.

When I injured my toe, I was amazed. It didn't hurt that much after the first shock of stubbing it on a rock. The next day, however, it hurt like hell. I took a picture of it and sent it to my doctor, Dr. Rock Positano, in Manhattan. He sent me back an e-mail. "You broke it." That was his diagnosis.

Pegi thought I should get it checked and X-rayed, but of course I didn't do that because I was busy writing this book. I am not trying to make you feel guilty. I am always busy doing something. I am sure it's broken. It's nine days later and it still hurts. I have a special pair of sandals that Dr. Rock sent to me with a wrap to put on my toe to hold it in place. I haven't used the wrap yet, but the sandals are quite stylish so I wear them, and I will use the wrap very soon, Dr. Rock. (The sandals kind of have the Devo look! Booji Boy would love to wear these babies!)

As I've said, I think the toe has had a lot to do with the book. It was the catalyst to get me started. Art and medicine have come together in a whole new way. Neither one of them is recognizable in the novel configuration we find them in with this project. Now when I walk around every step is a loud *clop*. It is not a stealth thing. I am debating whether to wear them tonight to dinner next door at Greg and Vicki's. We will be having grass-fed beef. I will keep you posted, as you no doubt have noticed.

With sunset coming on I feel particularly good at this moment. The day has developed nicely and I met the Master Gardener at Poncho's. He really seemed to be a Master, walking around and smelling things in the garden, followed by his wife and some other Korean folks who were very nice and very interested in Poncho's plants. Poncho's plants look exceptionally healthy and strong to me, and he is using absolutely no chemicals on anything. He is watering a lot less and spraying some organic microbiological liquid very sparingly.

I did feel I was in the presence of a highly evolved being when the Master was around. He definitely has a wealth of knowledge I don't have. I was very impressed with all of them, him and his friends. One of them was Poncho's teacher, and she did a lot of translating for the Master during the visit. Poncho was very nervous to be around him, and he was very respectful. Poncho really loves gardening, and to have the Master visit his garden and property was a great honor. They covered every area of the property and gardens and made detailed comments on everything Poncho was doing. Poncho has all kinds of blends of "inputs," as they called them, that he has brewed himself on the property just from natural ingredients and a little vodka, beer, and rice. The Master and his friends smelled and tasted all of these bottles and containers of inputs and made comments to Poncho through translation on how he was doing with the blends. When you are in the presence of someone obviously more knowledgeable than you are, who is very gracious, speaks no English, and treats you with a lot of respect, you really feel it.

Toward the end of the visit, Poncho gave the Master one of his famous apple pies, and the Master gave Poncho a pat on the back in thanks and invited him to a special meeting they were having to discuss even more advanced gardening techniques. Later, after they all left, Poncho confided in me that he did not feel qualified to be at the meeting, and I assured him that the Master knew what he was doing. I am sure Poncho is qualified. He is a highly evolved being himself, meaning that he is sensitive to his surroundings and the life around him, whether it is plant, human, or otherwise.

We shared a piece of Poncho's apple pie, and I told Poncho about PureTone. Like all serious musicians, he is depressed by the quality of sound the people's music is delivered in today. That is the impression I have gotten from every musician I have met. Everyone. After he heard PureTone, Ben Bourdon, one of Ben Young's caregivers, asked me if I was making war on Apple. I said, "No. I'm waging heavy peace."

I see online streaming services like Rhapsody, Spotify, and Pandora as the new radio. Apple's iTunes is the new radio, too. The sound is highly compromised, but people can get whatever they want, whenever they want. There is a lot of value to that convenience, but it has created a huge void in quality that begs to be filled. Turntable.fm is a lot of fun and exposes music to the masses in a new way. This is all very good for music. The only thing missing is quality.

Sound is very complex. It is not enough to just be able to recognize a song and hear the melody. There is a significant amount more to music than that. Many young people have never heard what I have heard, and that was not the case when I was young. In the age of technology we have grown used to many things being convenient and easy. We have grown up in the age of convenience and expediency. Videos can be shared and viewed around the world, and so can music, just like any document. The only problem with this is music is not like that. It is a storm on the senses, weather for the soul, deeper than deep, wider than wide. It is more than what you see or hear. It is what you feel. That is missing in today's technology for music, although many things have come along to replace it and distract from its absence.

I will not rest until the impact has been made and PureTone or something like it is available worldwide to those who love music. This is the sound of the twenty-first century, the sound we are capable of delivering. It is music. It has been an art form denied. There is something new now. Music as it should be heard. The promise of digital fulfilled.

But I am a pain in the ass now. I can't go anywhere without the annoying sound of MP3s or some other source of bad sound grating on my nerves and affecting my conversations. Everywhere is an elevator with bad sounds. Like tea bags that were hit with boiling water and scalded into submission, and like coffee that has been bombed by a boiling pot, my mind has been assaulted and has become edgy by this phenomenon of bad sound. This used to be my life, music. So I need to find or create a solution. Let everyone live, including those who crave quality. Mostly so I stop ranting about it.

Living in Hawaii, with the horizon of the ocean meeting the sky, is soothing. There is a magical healing to the Big Island, and I love this life. How many places are there on earth that really are healing places? There must be countless ones where people each can find their own peace. I hope you find all of yours and I find the rest of mine. In this world it is truly awesome how lucky we are, yet we keep hurting the planet in ways nature could never have come up with, mostly in the name of progress and moneymaking. It is hard to not get angry and discouraged on a quest for the health of the planet. Countless obstacles have been erected to impede that progress. Many souls have felt the pain of defeat. Yet the spirit endures and people try to spread the word. Ways to grow food without damaging the earth, ways to consume without excess waste, ways to use waste for fuel. Ways to serve and preserve the health of the planet are all around us, yet we stumble and repeat our old habitual ways, ignoring that which is speaking to us so clearly, not seeing the signals and signs. Somehow can we break the cycle? Somewhere can we see the light? Will we be served as we have served the earth? Is there fear in that thought? Then why oh why do we sing the same song over and over? The song, the song, the song.

*Buffalo Springfield near my Laurel Canyon cabin, 1967. Left to right,
Dewey Martin, me, Richie Furay, Jim Fielder (replacing Bruce Palmer),
Stephen Stills.*

There was a thing in Hollywood in the sixties called Teen Fair. It took place near the corner of Sunset Boulevard and Vine Street across from what was then Wallich's Music City, an amazing store. Let me describe Wallich's for you: They sold all kinds of music there—45s, LPs, sheet music, books about music—and in a little shop upstairs guitars and other instruments were displayed. There were also listening booths where you could hear singles on headphones and see if you wanted to buy them. I spent a lot of time there. Of course, the place was crawling with flower children and beautiful hippie girls.

Anyway, like I said, upstairs at Wallich's there was a great guitar department. Martins, Gibsons, all manner of electric and very nice old acoustic guitars were there. This was around the time the Springfield was happening; we were playing at the Whisky a Go Go, about a mile down Sunset toward Beverly Hills. Stills and I went to Wallich's a lot and tried out Martins together. Stephen was fast becoming an excellent player and had surpassed me in his knowledge of voicings, and he was always playing rhythms naturally that blew my mind.

One day, I was there at Teen Fair with a few friends, looking around, taking in the sights, the sounds, the girls, the crowds, an overwhelming chaos of inputs, when the sky started to spin a little and I felt a bit sick to my stomach. I started to fall. The sky was getting dark and the sounds were all echoing, a hollow reverberation inside my head. Lying on my back on the pavement, I saw the faces looking down on me. It was like I had just been born, and I recognized no one. I didn't really even know my own name. I was hot and sweating.

"Neil, Neil! Are you okay? Are you all right?"

I didn't know the answer to that question, but I was becoming aware that my name was Neil and that I was in a crowd of people lying down somewhere. I did feel strangely reborn. On the other hand, I was being helped up and people were all dispersing and walking away. Someone must have taken me home, back to Barry's, and later I fell asleep, I guess.

From that moment on, for years, I lived in constant fear that it was going to happen again. I could feel it in my stomach, and then I would get really scared and withdrawn until it went away. I felt it onstage, I felt it in crowds, I felt it in grocery stores, this unreasonable anxiety all the time waiting in the wings to come out and envelop me. It had an effect. Eventually I could not even go to the Laurel Canyon Country Store, which was near my place, to buy food. There were too many aisles and too much produce, too many choices for me.

The Canyon Country Store was just two blocks from where I had been living in the hearse less than a year before. I now had a house/cabin at the top of Ridpath Avenue near Utica Drive, way up at the end of the road at the top of Laurel Canyon. It was a crazy place up there, with a main house, a garage, and a little cabin. The shingles were all curved and mystical like a witch's castle. Wonderful. I was renting a cabin at the top of a flight of stairs, maybe one to two hundred–plus steps. Below it, the garage was down on Utica, and a drummer, John Densmore of the Doors, lived there. The garage was constructed with the same mystical shingle work. An astrologer, Kiyo Hodel, was my landlord. She lived in the main house of the whole compound and was very cosmic. The little cabin was made of knotty pine, very rustic, and I loved it. I had a llama rug on the floor. A lot happened to me up there. I brought a lot of girls up there to my little shack and we had good times, although I was not very confident in myself and probably not an impressive lover to be sure. We could call it performance anxiety.

I was kind of lost in that area and worked on that for a long, long time. Learning how to open up and give myself to another person, learning the depths of intimacy as more than sex. It has become the journey of a lifetime, one of the great revelations. I never did get much advice from my father and growing up missed his presence to quite a degree. I'm uncomfortable talking about that, but I feel a lot better about myself now than I did in my earlier days.

One day Dennis Hopper, who Stephen had met through Peter Fonda, came and took some pictures of the Springfield behind my little cabin. It was very simple, with only two rooms, a bedroom and a bathroom, and a little add-on porch where I kept my fridge.

Who knows what I put in that fridge? It was certainly not much. I think I had a hot plate, too. I used it for pork and beans . . . probably.

Once, when I had been on the road for a week or so, I stopped on Sunset at the Whisky before going home to the cabin. I met the daughter of one of the Rat Pack there that night and brought her up to show her my place. She was very nice. We went back to the cabin late that night without me having a chance to get there first. Somehow I had closed my cat in there for a week. The cabin was full of cat shit! Wow! I've never seen a girl get out of anyplace faster than she did. I did not make a very good impression on her.

In that little cabin, I wrote "Mr. Soul," "Expecting to Fly," "Broken Arrow," and a few other songs. I would listen to acetates of the mixes with my friends often there, too. (Acetates were records that you could make fast and play only a few times before they wore out and lost their sound. They would make them to take home and listen to right after we cut a song at Gold Star Studios in a little room where a lathe was set up. I still remember that acetate smell. The acetate would go in a little record sleeve and a Gold Star label would be typed up and stuck on it. I heard the first Buffalo Springfield album for the first time on my KLH record player and speakers in that little room.) We would hang and play records for hours, sitting on the llama rug in front of the speakers, listening to tracks like "A Day in the Life" by the Beatles over and over. The sound was so good, you could never get enough of it. I really feel sorry for kids with their MP3s today who can't hear music the way we did then. What a bummer. I can't imagine that. It really bothers me.

Now, I didn't get this cabin until the Springfield was happening, months after my first episode at Teen Fair, but somehow we got around to the subject, so here we are. The Canyon Country Store was where I bought food. Not that I bought much food. I would go down there and stand in the parking lot, working up the nerve to go in, hoping I would not get anxious and paranoid and freak out, leaving whatever I had chosen to buy inside and bolting for the door. This anxious feeling was similar to a seizure feeling in my stomach, and I couldn't tell the difference, so I just panicked.

Somewhere along the line, our managers, Charlie Greene and Brian Stone, who we hired in 1966, set up an appointment for me with a doctor at UCLA Medical Center to do some tests. April Full, Greene and Stone's secretary, took me down there. First they stuck a bunch of things on my head and gave me a little liquid in a cup and told me to go in this dark room and lie down. Then they wired all the things up, and while I was lying there I could feel these little flashes. I still feel those today, kind of like little rushes of something, gusts of cosmic wind in my head. My hearing changes for an instant, and it's hard to describe. Anyway. I live with that, and it's nothing. But it is somehow related to the feeling I used to get going up and down steep hills in my car. After that test, which revealed nothing to my knowledge, I went back to April's house. April chose that moment to explain to me what turned a woman on, demonstrating what would be physically stimulating for me to do as an education for me to apply later in life, say five or ten minutes later at the most.

It was not long afterward that suddenly I realized I had the clap. There were a lot of hippie girls, and we saw them at the

Whisky all the time. After the show it was time to go to the International House of Pancakes on Sunset Boulevard. I remember those German pancakes. They were delicious. How much sugar can one person eat? After that we paired off and went back to our shacks for some fun. Anyway, I had the clap and I had to go to the clinic. The doctor said he wanted to draw some blood. I said okay. I was on a metal table. He drew my blood. I crashed and had another full-on seizure on the spot. The same feeling. The room spinning slowly, the echoes, the darkness creeping in, and finally the doctor and nurses trying to get me back on the table, shoving a piece of wood in my mouth so I wouldn't bite off my own tongue. Then remembering my name, starting over. Getting a grip on my identity, where I lived, etc. It would all come back in a semi-orderly fashion, like a reboot. Eventually, I had to take another test with Dr. Morton K. Rubenstein. I DO NOT RECOMMEND THIS TEST. It is barbaric. It was called a pneumoencephalogram.

Pneumoencephalography (sometimes abbreviated PEG) is a medical procedure in which most of the cerebrospinal fluid is drained from around the brain and replaced with air, oxygen, or helium to allow the structure of the brain to show up more clearly on an X-ray image. It is derived from ventriculography, an earlier and more primitive method where the air is injected through holes drilled in the skull.

The procedure was introduced in 1919 by the American neurosurgeon Walter Dandy.

Pneumoencephalography was performed extensively throughout the early twentieth century, but it was extremely painful. The test was generally not well tolerated by patients. Headaches and severe vomiting were common side effects. Replacement of the drained spinal fluid is by slow natural production, and therefore required recovery for as long as two to three months before normal fluid volumes were restored . . . Modern imaging techniques such as MRI and computed tomography have rendered pneumoencephalography obsolete. Today, pneumoencephalography is limited to the research field and is used under rare circumstances.

Thanks, Wiki.

It is the most painful thing I have ever been through. Pure torture, where they tie you into a big device, stick a needle in you, and inject radioactive dye into your spinal column. Then they track its progress through your brain. Of course, being man-made, it is flawed, and bubbles sometimes get in there with the radioactive dye. These fucking bubbles are the worst pain ever in the universe. I took a long time to recover from that shit, and they learned *nothing*. I am still pissed about that. Of course, medical professionals don't do that test anymore. It's too barbaric. I am even more pissed now to realize that they *knew* they were injecting gas into my brain, then they had the nerve to tell me some bubbles *might* have gotten in there with the dye. I am pissed. I am over it. None of these tests revealed any new information about my condition. There was no conclusion. The doctor's recommendations were that I not take any LSD. Prior to that I had never had a doctor recommend that I take LSD. I had never taken acid. I never wanted to, anyway. I hallucinate enough on my own and can't control that.

In my life I have had various health threats: polio, seizures, a brain aneurysm. None of these things has really changed me much, although it is hard to say for sure. These are events that are part of my life. They make me who I am. I am thankful for them. They are scary.

With Joni Mitchell, doing her song "Raised on Robbery"
at Studio Instrument Rentals in Los Angeles, where the album
Tonight's the Night *was recorded in 1973.*

Have you ever wondered what goes into writing a song? I wish I could tell you the exact ingredients, but there is nothing specific that comes to mind. It seems to me that songs are a product of experience and a cosmic alignment of circumstance. That is, who you are and how you feel at a certain time.

I have written a lot of songs. Some of them suck. Some of them are brilliant, and some are just okay. Those are all other people's opinions. To me, they are like children. They are born and raised and sent out into the world to fend for themselves. It's not an easy place to be, the world, for a song. You might find yourself on a tape in the garbage, or on a CD someone threw out, or you may even be in the bargain bin. You may be a forgotten song languishing on a vinyl record in the dump or, more hopefully, in an independent record store rack. In one of the worst cases, you may be relegated to being nothing more than another MP3 file with less than five percent of your original sound. However, someone had to create you, and that is our subject for now.

I have not written one song since I stopped smoking weed in January 2011, so we are currently in the midst of a great chemical experiment.

When I write a song, it starts with a feeling. I can hear something in my head or feel it in my heart. It may be that I just picked up the guitar and mindlessly started playing. That's the way a lot of songs begin. When you do that, you are not thinking. Thinking is the worst thing for writing a song. So you just start playing and something new comes out. Where does it come from? Who cares? Just keep it and go with it. That's what I do. I never judge it. I believe it. It came as a gift when I picked up my musical instrument and it came through me playing with the instrument. The chords and melody just appeared. Now is not the time for interrogation or analysis. Now is the time to get to know the song, not change it before you even know it. It is like a wild animal, a living thing. Be careful not to scare it away. That's my method, or one of my methods, at least.

I was just thinking that I am putting a lot of pressure on myself to write a song. That never works. Songs are like rabbits and they like to come out of their holes when you're not looking, so if you stand there waiting they will just burrow down and come out somewhere far away, a new place where you can't see them. So I feel like I am standing over a song hole. That will never result in success. The more we talk about this, the worse it will get. So that is why we are changing the subject.

The Black Queen is a 1947 Buick Roadmaster sedanette fast-back. Originally the Black Queen was found in Idaho in a church parking lot by a friend of mine who purchased it for $650. That was a great deal. I used this car exclusively during the recording of *Tonight's the Night*. This is a beautiful car that is out of Feelgood's right now, getting some work done on the transmission. *Tonight's the Night* is an LP that centers in on the lives and deaths of Bruce Berry and Danny Whitten. Both tragic deaths were drug-related. There was an epidemic of these events going on in the early seventies, and I was not interested in referring to it directly. I did not want to be specific. These were just my friends. Actually, *Tonight's the Night* centers in on the aftermath of those deaths. It is a wake of sorts.

Anyway, the *Tonight's the Night* sessions, recorded on the Green Board by David Briggs, were done at SIR, Studio Instrument Rentals. Jan Berry of Jan & Dean, the surf legends, was an owner of SIR and the older brother of Bruce, one of CSNY's roadies. So memorializing Bruce Berry, the little brother of Jan, at those sessions was particularly close to home. Danny Whitten, the original Crazy Horse guitarist and singer, was the spirit of the album, as was Bruce. The songs were all pretty down. Both Bruce and Danny had OD'd on heroin.

It was an LP recorded in audio vérité, if you will, while completely intoxicated on Jose Cuervo tequila. We would not start recording until midnight, when we were so fucked up we could hardly walk. One night Joni Mitchell came in and did "Raised on Robbery" in the most sexy and revealing version that song ever had. She still refuses to let me release it. I don't know what the hell she was thinking when she joined us and sang the song. It kicks ass. What the fuck was that about? It was funkier than anything she has ever cut. A total gem!

I drove to SIR and home from SIR in the Black Queen nightly. The album was risky and real. It was a real mess of a recording, with no respect given to technical issues, although it sounds like God when played loud, under the able production of David Briggs. The original roughs were never remixed to our satisfaction, and the album was held up for more than a year, and released after one or two other albums were already done. Zeke Young used to use the rough masters on his toy tape recorder, practicing threading, winding, and rewinding the tapes for when he would grow up and be a big-time recording engineer.

This album survived a memorable production cycle unparalleled in my history, from the great David Briggs to my three-year-old son Zeke, all having their way with those rough master tapes. Those original roughs were used in the final release.

Homegrown had been recorded and *On the Beach* had already been released when Ben Keith and I played the tapes one midnight in what is now known as the Belushi bungalow of Hollywood's Chateau Marmont Hotel for Rick Danko of The Band and some other musicians. Rick said after hearing *Homegrown* and then *Tonight's the Night*, "You ought to put THAT out! What the hell is THAT?" So we did. It was Rick Danko who brought it back. *Home-*

grown, which I think is a great album, is still unreleased to this day. (It will come out, though, and we are preparing it now.)

When I played *Tonight's the Night* for Mo Ostin and Lenny Waronker at Reprise, as was always my habit to do when I handed a record in, Mo asked, "Neil, are you sure you want to put THAT out? It is really rough, and it may not be received well." I said yes. He understood why, which makes him one of the greatest record men of all time, along with Ahmet Ertegun and Clive Davis. Then we got in the Black Queen and rode home to the ranch, at least a full year after *Tonight's the Night* had been originally recorded. The car was there for every event tied to that record. Every night after those sessions, we rode the Black Queen home to the Sunset Marquis on Alta Loma in Hollywood, weaving down Santa Monica Boulevard at three or four in the morning, completely wrecked on tequila, and we made it, so there is a God.

When I first went to Topanga, I still didn't have a California driver's license, because I was in the country illegally. I had no Social Security number. I had recently gone to Santa Ana and purchased the 1951 Willys Jeepster that I have told you about already.

One fine summer day Briggs and I were out by Mulholland Drive, cruising in the hills, smoking a joint. It was a nice sunny day and we were grooving with the top down. California really is beautiful if you've never been there. It's worth a visit for sure. Anyway,

The Black Queen leaving the Sunset Marquis Hotel parking garage en route to the Roxy nightclub to debut Tonight's the Night *live in West Hollywood, 1973.*

we were driving along, Briggs, Danny Tucker (another good To-panga friend), and I, when a cop went by going the other way. He turned around and started following us. Briggs reached into his pocket and slipped me his license.

The cop pulled us over and asked me for my driver's license, looked at it, looked at me, and said, "I'm going to have to cite you for no brake lights. Get that fixed."

"Thanks, Officer," I said as coolly as I could.

I was scared shitless. Something happened later where I fucked up and Briggs was left holding the bag. I am not sure exactly what it was or how it was resolved, but I do remember Briggs saying that I had to get those lights fixed so the cops wouldn't be coming after him . . . Anyway, that was just another Briggs story, and there are a million of 'em. Point is, Briggs and I were brothers. He saw that cop coming and just slipped me his wallet without saying a thing. He was my best friend. Nobody can take that away from me. I always try to pay him back in any way I can. When he died years later, I did exactly what he asked me to do after he was gone, just like he asked me to do, some personal things that I know he would not want me to share with you. They had to do with how he felt about some people and how they should be dealt with.

A s I said, I didn't have a California driver's license for a long time. I couldn't get one. I was illegal. I needed a green card. I couldn't even leave the country without a green card, because I would have to sneak back in if I did. Remember? The "United States has better roads" story?

Thank God capitalism saved me, and I was able to *buy* a green card. A real one! Through my lawyer! It took a long time to find the right lawyer in New York with the correct connections in the INS, but by the end of the sixties, I had a real green card! America is great, and capitalism rocks! Most folks don't know how hard it is to get one of those cards. An American could do the job I am doing. There are plenty of other guitar players. I don't really know how the lawyer did it, but it cost $5,000. I don't know if that was his fee or whether he did it for nothing and the money was paid to someone else. But it was capitalism at work, I can tell you that. I can't tell you how good it felt to be free in the USA without worrying about being deported at that time!

I felt so free when I got my first driver's license in California that I was floating on air! Not looking around for cops all the time, not hoping I didn't get stopped and busted, deported. I was one paranoid person before I got my license. That was two or three years of looking over my shoulder. FREEDOM ROCKS! Hey. Is that a song or what? I might be having a breakthrough moment . . .

Chapter Twenty-Two

A Note About Ronald Reagan

L et's have a word or two about Ronald Reagan, President of the United States of America. I don't know what you think of him, and it doesn't matter that much, really. What matters to me, though, is when people get an attitude about somebody and paint that person all one color.

I was sitting on my bus in New Orleans, backstage at a concert in the mid-eighties, recording what turned out to be *A Treasure*. We were playing music that I was getting sued for because it was deemed "uncharacteristic of Neil Young" by my new record company. My new record company was run by people who liked to get their way. Success was measured in sales. My first record for them, *Trans*, was a bit of a departure from what they expected. First off, the owner of the record company, David Geffen, listened to the record *Island in the Sun*, which I thought was done, and told me to do more. I wanted to get started on a good foot, so I added another dimension, vocoded (electronically synthesized) voices, that made it into *Trans*.

Logically to me that would have been my second record for them, but they didn't want the first record I gave them, which was a fucking great record. I knew it was a great record, but then I wouldn't have wanted to release it if I didn't like it. I was used to Mo Ostin, who understood art. My new record company wanted me to make a hit as big as *Harvest* and thought that I had ripped them off by not repeating myself and making them look like a great record company. I have never thought it was my job to make a record company look great. I thought it was the other way around. The record company has to recognize when something is a statement by the artist or whether it is commercial enough to be a hit and do a good job of presenting either option to maximize the release.

Not every record made by me is designed to be a hit. Some are expressions in an artist's life. They tried telling me what to do so they could have their hit. They told me they wanted rock and roll, so I gave them *Everybody's Rockin'* by Neil and the Shocking Pinks! Then they tried canceling my sessions and interrupting my creative flow to show me they meant business. Then, in their apparent frustration, not being able to have their own way, they decided I was purposefully making records that made them look like losers. Then they sued me for making records that were "uncharacteristic of Neil Young."

This, of course, made me look like a hero.

Anyway, in that climate, a pair of AP reporters came to my bus to interview me. I did quite a few interviews during that tour. Elliot had set up another one. These guys were supposed to be good. They came on the bus and started right off making derogatory remarks about Reagan. They were presumptuous; I could see they thought they had me all figured out. I was that hippie who wrote "Ohio" and "Southern Man" and sang with that group CSNY. The more they said to ingratiate themselves, the more I didn't like them. I asked them if they'd ever met Reagan. They hadn't. Neither had I, I reasoned. I told them I did not believe in painting someone with one brush, that there must be more to a person than that, and I liked Reagan for some things he had said. Reagan had talked about the need for communities to come together to help themselves in ways that I thought were reasonable, and I told them that I did not believe that he was the villain so many had painted him to be. Just because you don't believe in some things a man says does not make him a bad man. There is good to be found in most people.

I also said that the guy is the president, so *someone* must think he is all right. Not everyone is against him.

I could tell they weren't buying it. Reagan was an asshole as far as they were concerned. So they wrote a story that made it sound like I was some all-out Reagan supporter, and I heard about it everywhere I went. One of my peers, who I respect, was calling me a buffoon, saying I didn't know what I was talking about and raving away about Guatemala.

Since the moment I met those two AP jerks, I have been trying to straighten out what they said. What they said *I* said. So in the end, I hate interviews, although I still do them every once in a while. I want people to know what I am up to if it supports my music in some way and brings awareness that a new recording exists. Sometimes that is the only way to get it out there. That certainly was the case in the eighties, although I don't think it is now. Things are better now, because we have tools to get information out there, and if you're smart enough, you don't have to talk to two dickheads on a bus anymore. And that's all I have to say about Ronald Reagan.

Original Crazy Horse guitarist/vocalist Danny Whitten backstage at the Electric Factory in Philadelphia, where I performed with Crazy Horse, February 1970.

## Chapter Twenty-Three

D anny and the Memories was the band at the root of Crazy Horse. They were a vocal group with Danny Whitten, Ralphie, Billy, and a guy named Ben Rocco. When I recently saw their old video of "Land of a Thousand Dances" on YouTube, I realized that is truly the shit. You know, I looked at it maybe twenty times in a row. Even though Danny was amazing and he held the Horse together in the early days, I did not know how great Danny was until I saw this! The moves! What an amazing dancer he was. His presence on that performance is elevating! He is gone, and no one can change that. We will never see and hear where he was going. I am telling you, the world missed one of the greatest when Danny and the Memories did not have a NUMBER ONE smash record back in the day. They were so musical, with great harmonies, and Danny was a total knockout! I am so moved by this that it could make me cry at any time. This is one of those many times when words can't describe music.

Danny and the Memories eventually transformed into the Rockets; they were playing in this old house in Laurel Canyon, and I somehow connected with them while Buffalo Springfield was at the Whisky. We had a lot of pot jams in that house. Later on I saw Danny and the guys at somebody's house in Topanga. After that I asked if Danny, Billy, and Ralphie would play on a record with me. We did one day, practicing in my Topanga house, and it sounded great. I named the band Crazy Horse and away we went. The Rockets were still together, but this was a different deal.

At that time, I thought Danny was a great guitarist and singer. I had no idea *how* great, though. I just was too full of myself to see it. *Now* I see it clearly. I wish I could do that again, because more of Danny would be there.

I have made an *Early Daze* record of the Horse, and you can hear a different vocal of "Cinnamon Girl" featuring more of Danny. He was singing the high part, and it came through big-time. I changed it so I sang the high part and put that out. That was a big mistake. I fucked up. I did not know who Danny was. He was better than me. I didn't see it. I was strong, and maybe I helped destroy something sacred by not seeing it. He was never pissed off about it. It wasn't like that. I was young, and maybe I didn't know what I was doing. Some things you wish never happened. But we got what we got.

I never really saw him sing and move until I saw that "Land of a Thousand Dances" video. I could watch it over and over. I can't believe it. It's just one of those things. My heart aches for what happened to him. These memories are what make Crazy Horse great today. And now we don't have Briggs, either, for the next record, but we have the spirit and the heart to go on. And we have John Hanlon, taught by Briggs, to engineer this sucker. It will rock and cry. Please let's get to this before life comes knocking again.

So we are getting into this now. There may have to be more than one book. I read up on this sort of thing, and the worst thing you can have is a book that is too long. That doesn't help the publisher. There is a lot here to cover, and I have never done this before. Also, I am not interested in form for form's sake. So if you are having trouble reading this, give it to someone else. End of chapter.

## Chapter Twenty-Four

Pains

Along the way, I have encountered many doctors. One of my favorites is Dr. Petter Lindstrom, who was well-known for performing laminectomies. He came to me highly recommended and coincidentally was a former husband of Ingrid Bergman.

I had a double laminectomy by him in 1971.

But let me back up.

I had just signed with Reprise as a solo artist and got a big enough advance to buy my first house in Topanga Canyon. 611 Skyline Trail was all mine, a really wonderful redwood house built with a view of the whole canyon.

I used to go to the Canyon Kitchen every morning for breakfast. Susan Acevedo, the beautiful Sicilian hostess/owner, would bring me a one-eye and bacon. I got to look at Susan Acevedo every day at breakfast! Morning on the deck began with coffee overlooking the canyon, watching everything start to move below as the day unfolded. The scene in there was always stimulating, full of the color of the canyon, with the artists and other local characters, drug dealers and beautiful hippie girls, and I really enjoyed my breakfasts.

Eventually I met Tia, Susan's daughter. She was a cute little girl about five or six years old with a pretty little round face. Although Susan was a little older than I was, I found myself becoming more and more attracted to her. Eventually we fell in love. Susan introduced me to a lot of great artists in the canyon: Wallace Berman, Roland Diehl (who painted my first album cover), George Herms, Dean Stockwell, Russell Tamblyn, Kiel Martin, to name just a few. Susan was active in the Topanga Players, a local theater group, and I remember going to see George Herms's play *Egg of Night* and many other theater presentations there with her. She made all of my patchwork clothes, creating a style that spoke to the times, really the only time I was anywhere near fashionable. That was all Susan's doing, and it was so beautiful.

Susan and I were married in my new Topanga house, perched on the top of Skyline Trail, overlooking the canyon, and George Herms performed the ceremony. Our house was on a steep hill with the garage at the lowest point on a steep drive. One time Susan loaded my Mini Cooper with pies in the garage, preparing for a catering job she was doing with her company, Scuzzy Catering. Somehow after the pies were fully loaded, the emergency brake came loose and the Mini and its pies rolled down the hill and straight into the neighbor's garage, knocking out the support posts for his house. Pies were splattered all over the inside of the Mini. The neighbor, a gay man, was yelling at Susan, and she was going right back at him. It was quite a moment, full of expletives. Susan was quite a spirited lady, and I don't think the poor guy knew what he was in for!

Sadly, I was not mature enough to be a very good father to Tia, and I regret that I missed the boat there, but she sure was a sweet girl. Eventually Susan and I broke up. I don't think I was mature enough for her, either. The instant fame that came with *After the Gold Rush* and CSNY were too much for us. I have a lot of respect for Susan. She never asked for anything from me that was unreasonable, and she gave all she had to our short marriage. I was too young, and the pressures were too great for who I was at that time. The marriage lasted about a year. Sometimes I hear little tidbits about her, and I am always hoping she is doing well with her life. She was seen in Mexico recently and looking very good, was my last report. Love you, Susan. Thanks. You, too, Tia. Maybe we will meet again someday.

One day in early '70, still living in Topanga with Susan, I was working with a hoe in the brush on the hillside outside the house. I don't know what I was doing. I had thrown a portable TV off the deck and I could see it down there. I may have been preparing for a garden. Anyway, the next day I was in my car and I went to put my left foot on the clutch and my foot wouldn't come up. It just wouldn't move. So I went to a chiropractor Susan knew, and he did an adjustment on my back. After that my movement came back pretty much like it was before, but there was a little pain in my leg. That was the end of that.

In September of that year, Susan and I had split up and I was living on Broken Arrow Ranch, tearing my new house apart. At

Crosby's advice, I went to Berkeley to a hardwood dealer and saw some amazing huge slabs of California walnut. There were six big ones. I mean nine-footers, three feet wide and two to three inches thick. I bought them all and wanted to do the walls of my dining room with them. I was so excited that I tried to put them up myself. Doing that, I injured my back again. But the symptoms were worse: My leg didn't work, and it hurt all up and down the front. So I went to LA to see the doctor there that Elliot had, a Dr. Lipshutz. Walking through the airport to catch a plane to fly to LA was very painful, and I was sweating profusely when the sexy go-go stewardess brought me a Coke on PSA.

Things get blurry now in the memory department. I was told by the doctor to take Soma Compound (a muscle relaxant) and rest in bed so that the swelling would go down. There was no mention of surgery at that time, and I was thinking that if I just mellowed out while taking this Soma and stayed in the hospital bed they had moved into my room at the Chateau Marmont that everything would work itself out.

So there I was in the hospital bed at the Chateau, and it was there and then I first met Carrie Snodgress. After reading a story about her in *Newsweek* or *Time*, I had found her number and called her up, introducing myself and inviting her down to the Chateau. She was very attractive to me. What a way to meet. I was taking so much of the Soma Compound that I could hardly move. I liked her right away.

A few days after that, I returned to the ranch on doctor's orders to rest in a hospital bed that had been moved into my house there. Lying in bed, taking Soma at Broken Arrow, I found out that

Michelob and Soma Compound are a great combination—and eventually I landed in traction at Cedars-Sinai on Melrose Avenue back in LA. The doctors were hoping that traction would solve the problem and there would be no need for surgery.

Anyway, Cedars back then was an old hospital. I was in traction, with wires and weights pulling on my feet to relieve the pressure on discs in my back. (While I was there, I listened a lot to a cassette tape I had from the Cellar Door in Washington, D.C. It was a live tape I had recently recorded with Henry Lewy. It was real good, and I made some notes for an album, and I will eventually release a very cool record of those times. (Now, these years later, I am still finishing some things and looking for closure.) A lot of folks visited me in the hospital. I had friends from Hollywood, and some of them were beautiful ladies. I had a pretty good stay in that hospital!

When I finally got out and went home, I was wearing a back brace. It was still painful, but not too bad. Back at the ranch, I tried to walk up the hill behind my house toward the site of my new pool, but I couldn't make it. That really depressed me. Two weeks later, I went on the road across Canada with the brace. That was in early January.

I was corresponding with Carrie and writing songs. A lot of songs, like "Old Man," "Heart of Gold," "Needle and the Damage Done," and "Bad Fog of Loneliness." During that tour, I recorded at Massey Hall, and that came out as a record years later. Briggs was living in Toronto then and produced that. He had gone up there to live and had started a studio called Thunder Sound. The live Massey Hall record is David's live mix to 7.5 ips analog. You can see the brace and my hunkered-over posture in the Massey Hall video—which is actually a Stratford, Connecticut, picture from a few days earlier with Massey Hall's sound synched up. I used the sound from one place and the picture from another. "A cheap Hollywood trick," as Larry Johnson used to say.

I went on to Nashville at the end of the tour to do the Johnny Cash television show, which was new and really hot at the time. Bob Dylan had just done the first one, and everyone wanted to do it. James Taylor and Linda Ronstadt were doing the second show, and so was I. Everyone loved Johnny Cash; he was the real thing. The show was all about music, and it was cool, very real.

While I was there I met Elliot Mazer, the record producer, and we went into the studio to try some studio versions of all my new songs. Tim Drummond was there, and he put together a great band, with Kenny Buttrey, John Harris, Ben Keith, and another guitarist who played some tasty things like the harmonics on "Heart of Gold." This was a great-sounding band. James and Linda came in and added some vocals; James even played banjo on "Old Man." That session was a solid beginning for *Harvest*. Then, a few weeks later, I was in London and recorded "A Man Needs a Maid" and "There's a World" with the London Symphony Orchestra, produced and arranged by Jack Nitzsche. After hearing the playback in Glyn Johns's truck, where the pieces were recorded outside the Barking Town Hall, Jack said, "I think it's a bit overblown." We knew it was over-the-top, but we had done it and we loved it.

Later, when Carrie and I were seriously getting together and she was moving to the ranch, I wrote the rest of *Harvest*, and we went back to Nashville for another session. We did "Out on the

Weekend," "Journey Through the Past," and a few other ones, including "Harvest" itself. Then I asked the band to fly out to the ranch with Elliot Mazer to record a little in my barn. That was where we got "Alabama," "Are You Ready for the Country?" and "Words."

"Words" is the first song that reveals a little of my early doubts of being in a long-term relationship with Carrie. It was a new relationship. There were so many people around all the time, talking and talking, sitting in a circle smoking cigarettes in my living room. It had never been like that before. I am a very quiet and private person. The peace was going away. It was changing too fast. I remember actually jumping out the living room window onto the lawn to get out of there—I couldn't wait long enough to use the door! Words—too many of them, it seemed to me. I was young and not ready for what I had gotten myself into. I became paranoid and aware of mind games others were trying to play on me. I had never even thought of that before. That was how we did *Harvest*, in love in the beginning and with some doubts at the end.

The album was received well, and I suppose that was my commercial peak, at least my first and biggest one, although I didn't do the math. Some people liked it a lot and it was a big thing for them in their lives. It was for me. But my Crazy Horse fans were not knocked out. There is a line there. I suppose it matters to them, but it doesn't matter to me. I just like to make all kinds of music and do what is coming naturally to me. Nobody told me to make *Harvest*. No record company told me what to do until a lot later—and that didn't work.

But this was not the end of my back problem.

Eventually surgery was required. My left side was chronically weak from my childhood polio, and I was too active for the sort of long careful recovery that limited my movement for the rest of time without surgery.

I met with Dr. Lindstrom, who advised me that surgery was the only option and I should get ready to leave my pain behind. He came to see me in the hospital in San Francisco. He asked me how I was feeling, and I told him, "Not too good." Then he looked at me and said that after the surgery, he would come back and get me out of bed to walk around the room without the brace and the pain.

I said, "Really?"

He said, "Yes, but first we have to do the operation, and that will be tomorrow morning at six."

The next day I went to surgery. All I remember is lying on the gurney, the ceiling rolling by on my way to the operating room. And the next thing I knew, there he was, asking me to get up and walk around my room. I did it. He thanked me and said he would check in on me regularly for a few days and then I could go home. He was an amazing doctor. He told me to swim and exercise and do everything gently for a while. No football or hockey, he laughed. Then he made some graceful moves imitating a tennis player in slow motion. Nothing too fast, he said. Forty-two years later, I am still fine. Thank you, Dr. Lindstrom; what a gift.

Maybe the combination of Michelob and Soma was such that my thoughts were completely jumbled—and perhaps my love affair with Carrie was part of that process. I was never really happy during it, with the excessive amount of analysis and psychodrama that was spawned. And I have never been in that type of relationship before or after, so there is just something about my time with Carrie that I am unsettled about.

It is important for me to say that I initiated our relationship based on an article about her I read in *Newsweek* or *Time* and a beautiful picture the magazine ran. Falling in love from a picture in a magazine, however, is not a very calculated thing; nor are the effects of loneliness on one's decision making. It is a great thing to write a song about, though. I am just trying to make sense of the thought process and emotional landscape that resulted, and I suppose that would be a fruitless endeavor at this point, an emotional Band-Aid.

Carrie had a lot to give, but it didn't work with me for very long. I can take the blame for that. A lot of people were telling me that I had ruined her acting career by taking her to the seclusion of the ranch. That may be true. Because of Carrie, I have my wonderful son Zeke Young, who I love. So I would never change what happened. About eighteen months after *Harvest* was released, Carrie and I broke up and started sharing Zeke.

Chapter Twenty-Five

Religion

R eligion is not one of my high points. I really don't sub-
scribe to the stories surrounding each one, because they
are just stories, remembered by men. I do feel the Great
Spirit in all that is around me, and I am humbled. I do pray with
others if that is what they do. I don't judge them for that. That
is their way. I join them. Then I move on. The moon means a lot
to me, as does the forest. All things natural speak to me with a
rhythm that I feel. It is this that probably makes me a pagan.

I think pagans have taken a bad rap from Christians. I feel,
although I was not present when it started, that the Christians
were threatened by the pagan beliefs and lashed out at them, attacking them and striking them down as witchcraft or something
bad and evil. I suppose evil is necessary to justify the existence of
organized religion. It seems to be the focus of a lot of sermonizing and preaching.

There is no evil in the forest or the moon. Or if there is, I don't
see it. Somehow these things, the moon and the forest, move

through space or survive on their own. I read a book called *The Mists of Avalon* by Marion Zimmer Bradley, which retells the Arthurian legends from the perspective of the female characters, especially Morgan le Fay, who fought to save her Celtic culture from the encroaching Christianity. There is a lot in that book that I relate to personally. Being alive may just be part of God, but not all. The Great Spirit, as I like to call her, is in us all and in everything that lives or used to live, in everything that exists or used to exist. So I have no story to tell that proves anything, but I think it was Pegi who gave me that book.

Stories from Topanga

When I came to Topanga Canyon to live, I think I was still in Buffalo Springfield, but it was near the end. There was a lady, Linda Stevens, who was a friend of mine who put me up in her house. She knew both Stephen and me. It was 1968, because I remember during the time I was there at her house, my dad came down to cover the aftermath of the assassination of Robert Kennedy at the Ambassador Hotel in Los Angeles. My dad was working as a columnist for *The Globe and Mail* in Toronto, and the paper sent him down on special assignment.

I went into town to see him, and we hung for a few hours; then he went back to work. It was nice to see his face. That may have been the first time I saw him since I left Toronto two years before. We talked and may have shared a meal. He was just as shy as I am, so there wasn't a lot of heavy communication. Just being together and seeing each other was enough for both of us.

Anyway, it was pleasant living in Topanga with Linda and her daughter. My cats from Laurel Canyon were there. They were two orange kitties, and one of them was named Duck Egg and the other

Orange Julius, for the beverage. There were a lot of Orange Julius stands in LA at the time. Orange Julius was a mixture of OJ and an egg, whipped to a frothy liquid with some ice. It was pretty nourishing and quite good. I don't know what happened to that franchise. Now I have a distinct memory with a taste and smell, of no interest to anyone but me. It is a memory of that era that is unique to me because it has a taste associated with it, along with the smell of LA air at that time in history. It was sometime around then when I was busted for pot in Stills's house in Topanga. That house, which Stephen called the Old Topanga Ranch, was an old rock structure with a barn of sorts behind it. There were a lot of people there, and it was a big party. Eric Clapton was there with Stephen, and we were all smoking pot, which was odd because Stephen has never been a big pot smoker. Linda Stevens was there, and so was Susan Haffey, one of Stephen's girlfriends from his days hanging with Peter Tork (Thorkelson) of the Monkees.

I was in a bedroom by myself, not being very social at the time, because I probably had smoked too much weed and was paranoid. Things got pretty quiet, and Stephen suddenly came through the room I was in and went out the window! I am not sure he saw me there. The cops had come in, and everyone was arrested and taken to jail. We were all in the *LA Times* the next morning; it was a big deal because Clapton was a pretty famous musician already. I don't know how we got off, but it had something to do with our managers, Greene and Stone.

I recently spoke to Stephen about this, and he remembers it differently. He says we both were sitting on the bed together because we had smoked too much weed and were too paranoid, so we were talking each other down. We heard something change in the room where the party was. It got quiet. I bolted out there to see what was wrong. He heard what he thought was a cop's voice and reached out to stop me, but he caught air. I was gone. Stephen went out the window and went next door to call Ahmet Ertegun, our friend and the president of Atlantic, our record company, to get help from some lawyers, so he escaped and I got busted. Ahmet told him maybe his actions would be misunderstood by everyone else who got caught when he didn't. So he says he has reflected on that.

Soon after, but not for any reason connected to the bust, the Springfield broke up. The success and legendary impact of the Springfield was not really apparent at the time. We were beginning to go our separate ways. Everyone was moving out to Topanga from Hollywood. Topanga was like an art colony. Art was everywhere, and the place was crawling with musicians, rebel actors, and associated culture. A few months later, one morning I was walking into town to the Topanga Village Shopping Center. I was just walking along, and this army truck pulled along beside me. It looked like a personnel carrier or something. A couple of guys were in it wearing hippie/army clothes. They stopped and picked me up. I guess there was a kind of hippie camaraderie that existed then and is nowhere to be found in today's culture. They may have picked me up because I looked like "one of them"; I don't think I was hitchhiking.

We went to the Topanga Center, and I remember we liked one another, 'cause they invited me back to the place they were staying. One of them was named David Briggs. David took me back to their house, and it turned out to be the Old Topanga Ranch where Stephen had lived and we had been busted! David and his wife, Shannon, were living there. Briggs and I became great friends, and I immediately learned he was a record producer. He had just finished making a comedy record with Murray Roman and he was producing some of the guys from Spirit in a new band. He was wonderful to hang with, with an extensive and interesting vocabulary. (I had never heard the word *nomenclature* before.) We really got along well, and it was the beginning of a deep friendship that lasted many years. Not to mention the records we made together.

The Topanga Center was a real melting pot of hippie and art activity, a cultural center for art and music in the sixties. In the very center of the Center was the Canyon Kitchen, a small restaurant that served food all day but specialized in great breakfasts. That's where, as I mentioned, I first met Susan Acevedo, the proprietress I was soon to marry.

I remember once I was at Topanga Days, a fair that happened annually. A flatbed truck was parked in the parking lot with Canned Heat jammin' along at their peak on the back of the truck. Al Wilson was holding down the vocals. The whole band was classic. It didn't get any better than that. The bass player, Larry Taylor, was crazy good, holding down a huge groove. Later he played with Bob and was still masterful. That was so cool! What a great band! Next up there was Taj Mahal playing with Jesse Ed Davis right there in the Topanga Center on the back of that truck. I still remember Jesse Ed Davis, the amazing guitarist, with his Telecaster, so slinky and bad.

People were everywhere. Local art was on display. Artisans sold their wares. Lance Sterling, a leatherworker Susan knew and introduced me to, was often there with his gypsy wagon and female apprentices making leather sandals and bags. I still have my bag. I got it at that time and it goes everywhere with me; I think Susan gave it to me. That was a wonderful time in my life. All was good. I was about to start my solo career after the Springfield, which had been a long time coming. My need to make solo records was one of the big contributing factors to the breakup of Buffalo Springfield, along with a need to be more independent and sing more of my own songs. I had so many of them.

I had met Briggs, and we were planning my first solo record.

The songs were gathered from the past and the future, mostly dreams, nothing concrete; they were mostly created as vehicles for record-making, like "Here We Are in the Years," or personal expression and longing, such as "I've Been Waiting for You." Some of them were stream-of-consciousness, like "The Last Trip to Tulsa," with no preconceived thought behind them. They were just songs. There was no big pressure on me at that time to top anything I had already done. That came later. The sky was the limit. I had no idea what was coming my way.

One more note on this period.

Elliot Roberts, my manager, was planning my first solo tour and coffeehouse gigs. I first met Elliot with Joni Mitchell at Sunset Sound. I already knew Joni from Canada; Elliot was managing her now. He wanted to manage the Springfield, and had actually just started. He had accompanied us to a gig in San Diego we were playing with the Turtles and some other groups. The Turtles were at their peak. It was a huge show for us. I was sick in the hotel room with the flu and wanted something. Elliot was gone, playing golf with somebody. I decided at that moment he was never going to work as our manager and insisted we fire him. I was a spoiled brat! But what did I know? So we fired Elliot. The next week I quit the Springfield for good.

A few days later I called Elliot and asked him to manage me. Was I making sense or what? That is the weirdest sequence of events I can imagine. I was totally committed every step of the way and had no idea what I would be thinking the next day. This was *not* planned. I was just completely crazy and fluid, changing from day to day, adapting to my feelings and acting on them immediately. Much of what I did then is the foundation for where I am today.

He took me on. We got started, and he negotiated a great deal for me at Reprise Records, where I still record today. I am a Warner Brothers artist. Reprise is a Warner label. I will probably always be on Warner-Reprise as long as it exists. And Elliot will be representing me as long as we both live. That is the plan. It makes me sad to think this could all end, so I hope it doesn't. I love my life and the people around me. But as you know, nothing lasts forever. We know life, don't we? Maybe that is why people need religion (please see previous chapter). That might be it. I just might have figured it out.

## Chapter Twenty-Seven

And Now, Another Word from
Our Sponsor, PureTone

I t has come to my attention that a lot of the people we are reaching out to in the PureTone project are scared of Apple and what would happen to their businesses if we were to provoke Apple in some way. It is disconcerting to feel the fear in others that what I am trying to do would somehow provoke Apple into a destructive action against someone trying to serve a quality product. I have consistently reached out to try to assist Apple with true audio quality, and I have even shared my high-resolution masters with them so that they could show me what they could do with them to make their iPod sound great. I guess there would be an area of concern if what they think is great is not great in my opinion, yet they wanted to market it as studio quality or master quality while it contained only five percent of the data of some original hi-res digital recordings I and others have made.

In the end, the record companies have the power to control the quality that is served online. Online service has been problematic in that it actively or discreetly promotes trading and duplication of music. It is not offensive to me that the MP3-quality sound is traded around. It is, in my opinion, the new radio and serves a great purpose: making music lovers aware of the content that is out there to buy. If the consumers want it, let them take it, whatever quality they prefer. Ultimately, nothing can stop absolute quality from making a big comeback. The stage is well set. I believe in what I am trying to do and that good karma will come from it.

It is just a matter of time.

## Chapter Twenty-Eight

W hen Zeke Young was born on September 8, 1972, Carrie and I had been together for about a year and a half. We had been going to Lamaze classes for a few weeks and (mistakenly) felt pretty prepared. Our neighbor Beverly Oaks was going to be the midwife. Our doctor had told us everything was going to be fine, and we were gung-ho to do a natural childbirth.

On the ranch on the morning when Carrie's water broke, Bev said we should go to the hospital because she thought something was going wrong, or at least differently from what she expected. So we got in a car and headed down to the hospital, forty minutes away.

Zeke was born that day, and we needed forceps to help the delivery, so it was a good thing we followed Bev's advice. He was a beautiful baby boy, and I was as high as I have ever been in my life! What a feeling! We brought him home and put him in our little bed; then he graduated to a handmade cradle that one of our carpenter friends, Larry Christiani, had made especially for us.

As Zeke grew, we noticed that his right foot seemed extended and he could not straighten out his ankle. His right hand was also held in a different position from his left, and he did not have the same control of it. He was a cool kid, really happy and beautiful, and we were really young and innocent. We talked to doctors and sought advice on what might be happening and what to do. There was some strain developing between Carrie and me as the dream of an idyllic life with few responsibilities came shattering down around us. We knew we had to do something, and felt like we were running out of time, not knowing what was the matter with Zeke, not knowing it was a condition of life, not something that could be cured.

Eventually we got a brace for Zeke, and he started to get picked on by the other kids. This was the beginning of a rough time for him, and he lashed out at other kids and had a lot of anger that he was expressing. At the same time, Carrie and I were not doing well together. We were breaking up, and it was a nightmare. Not fights, but distance. Not screaming, but pain. Everything was coming apart.

Then I got a call from Carrie that Zeke had experienced a grand mal seizure. The doctor thought he might be epileptic or have some other condition. Eventually it was decided that Zeke had cerebral palsy.

Zeke was going from school to school, getting in trouble at all of them. He was living with me in Malibu on weekends, and one day he came home from playing with the other kids and had taken off his brace. His foot was bleeding from direct exposure to the asphalt on the road where they had been playing some game. I remember how I felt the unfairness of it all, that he had to contend with this and the other kids didn't, but now when I look at him, I admire him for the wonderful man he has grown up to be, handling himself so beautifully, and I feel very proud.

Sometimes he was with me and sometimes with his mom. Mostly he was with his mom. Somewhere along the line she did an interview with *People* magazine. They went to the house in Hancock Park, a beautiful old residential area, that I had bought for Carrie and Zeke, and took pictures, etc. The magazines love this kind of thing. So a big story came out that was all slanted and crazy, making me look like a villain. I have never talked to that magazine since and don't plan on it.

Pegi and I were together by then, and Zeke would come to visit us. He had to be a member of the "Clean Plate Club" to leave the table! We had a lot of love and structure in our home, and it was always that way with Pegi. That is the important thing. Zeke loved both Pegi and his mother.

Back and forth and back and forth he went between homes. That was our life until, in a great stroke, Carrie found a school in Idyllwild, California, that was specifically for kids who were having problems adjusting. Carrie and I placed Zeke in that school. Working together, we did something really good. There was a man there who ran the Morning Sky School, and his name was Jack Weaver. I went and met him, and he saw Zeke. I felt really good about what Carrie had found for us. Zeke came out of there a changed young man. They really helped him, and he attributes it all to Jack, who he loved. Jack unfortunately died a few years later of an asthma attack, or I am sure we would still be visiting him today just to keep in touch and tell him how much we loved him for what he did for our family. He was a saint.

Today, Zeke and I are very close.

With Zeke Young in a dinghy off the WN Ragland, *1978.*

Chapter Twenty-Nine

The surf is coming up. It has been quiet here in Hawaii for about five days, and just a minute ago a wave broke on the seawall and put a slight tremble in the ground. The rhythm of the ocean is such a gift, and this is the perfect place to enjoy it. I don't expect to have another ocean place as cool and cosmic as this one is in my lifetime, so I am eternally thankful for it now.

Back when I was living in Coconut Grove in Florida in the mid-seventies, there was a houseboat that I slept in that was owned by a lady named Heather. We were recording the Stills-Young Band's *Long May You Run* at Criteria Recording Studios, and it was quite a trip from the studio in Fort Lauderdale back to the Grove every night—and I was usually pretty high on the way home. I had a '57 Jensen 541 that I drove regularly to and from the studio.

Heather's houseboat was way out on the end of the docks. Every night after the studio, I would end up in the houseboat and Heather would be there, welcoming me back. She was really kind to me, and I always was happy to get back there. We had a good relationship. The water was right there, and it was soothing to rock in the boat as dawn came up on the bay.

The Grove was intoxicating, and I stayed there on and off for years. I had a suite in a local hotel called the Rangoon. There were a lot of high rollers in and out of the hotel all the time. Fred Neil, the great folksinger/songwriter who wrote "Everybody's Talkin'," which was eventually used in the movie *Midnight Cowboy*, was there hanging out at the dock a lot with some of his friends. (It is ironic to me that someone as seminal and influential as Freddy Neil would become more known for a movie song than the influence he had on a generation of musicians, including Stephen Stills, but that's the way it goes.)

The high rollers always seemed entertained by my comings and goings, like I was just some inexperienced kid. I did not feel that inexperienced. Eventually I bought my own boat in Fort Lauderdale and brought it back to the Grove. It was an old Trumpy yacht that I called *The Evening Coconut*. I was in the habit of taking it out for cruises, and I was known for sometimes crashing it into the dock. The engine kept failing on my approach. I had a lot of fun times on the *Coconut* and met a guy there in the Grove named Andre Prest.

He was charged with finding me a sailboat that I could buy and sail around the world. It seemed like a simple enough task, and soon we found the boat. It was in Saint Vincent and the Grenadines, on an island called Bequia. We went way down there and saw the boat. It was a huge Baltic Trader, and it needed some work on the deck. When I first saw the boat it was in a bay, looking like a dream. We needed to take a skiff out to it. Cruising out to get on board, we saw a lot of sharks in the water. I was very happy to get off the small boat and onto *Lilli*, as she was called then.

After the purchase, we sailed to Grenada and had some deck work done, Captain Andre Prest in command. The good captain had hired a first mate named Roger Katz. It turned out that Andre knew nothing about being captain of a boat or sailing, so quite soon it became obvious that Roger Katz was the de facto captain. We got the boat to Saint Thomas somehow, even though we were seasick. We sat at the dock with the generator running and choked out half of the marina.

I flew back from there to my ranch to do some recording, and they managed to get the *Lilli* back to Fort Lauderdale, where Captain Katz took over officially and took charge of the rebuild. We renamed her *WN Ragland* in honor of my grandfather, Bill Ragland, a southerner who came north to Winnipeg from South Carolina and started his family there, giving birth to my mother, Rassy, and her sisters, Snooky and Toots. Naming my boat after him felt good. We took her to Rogers Marina in Fort Lauderdale, and many dollars were put into rebuilding the boat over a year or so.

Zeke came out and visited us there at Rogers Marina while we were working on the boat. Ellen Talbot, a friend of Carrie's and the wife of Johnny Talbot, who was my roadie with Crazy Horse at the time, brought him to Fort Lauderdale from his mother's house. He was a child with two homes: my house wherever I was, and his mother's house wherever it was. He was about five years old and as cute as could be. He went to a Montessori-type school while he was there, which he got kicked out of for being too rowdy. He had his brace on and was pretty angry with the other kids. He was a real handful.

But when we were together he was just a happy, sweet little guy who I loved and who loved me. We used to go for rides in our yellow rubber dinghy that he loved tremendously. It had a Mercury outboard and really went fast. It had a steering wheel, and he loved that, too. We really had a great time together and both remember those times very fondly, racing up and down the New River in Fort Lauderdale. Those boat rides are some of our happiest early memories.

One of the scariest was when he fell in the river getting on *The Evening Coconut*. It was tied at a dock and was out of the water for hull repairs. Zeke was fearless, and one day he just tried to get on board from the dock himself, even though we were always around to guide him and told him to always be with someone. While I was at the work site, Zeke, with his heavy brace on, fell into the water. Dennis Buford, one of the shipwrights working on the boat, rescued Zeke! Thank you, Dennis! You probably saved my son's life!

A great tradition was payday. Every Friday we got together for some Jose Cuervo on *The Evening Coconut*, where Roger would hand out the checks to the shipbuilders, who were a motley crew just like us, and then we would go out partying. We eventually moved the *Ragland* to another place on the New River to get her finished and rigged with sails. So there she was in Fort Lauderdale on the New River, tied alongside an empty lot where the workers parked their cars and eventually I brought Pocahontas, my bus, to live in. I parked the bus right alongside the boat. At first, I slept on the boat in the construction zone of my cabin on my cot with sawdust everywhere, and then I moved to Pocahontas. It was fun.

On Valentine's Day I asked Pegi, who I was just beginning to hang out with, to come out and see my new boat. That was our first big outing, the first time we traveled together as a couple. We flew out to Fort Lauderdale together and stayed for a while. She was game, but obviously the place was not ready for us yet, with carpenters crawling all over the boat at seven A.M. This was a remarkably good time, full of memories of Pegi and me together, rebuilding this beautiful old boat and getting ready for the first sail. We had a crew of about thirty people working on the project, and as I've said, I always love that kind of thing, building things.

We went into Miami, Roger, Pegi, and I, to see a place called Stoneage Antiques. Stoneage was owned and run by Milton Stone, a great and unforgettable character, and it housed a rich collection of marine antiques and a host of other things, among them a beautiful classic nineteenth-century nine-foot Steinway grand piano I bought and shipped to the ranch. It was restored, and I still enjoy it today. I love things with memories attached. It's nice to think that it was one of the first times Pegi and I were together when I found that old piano, which is now restored and in our hallway. We also purchased a collection of wood from the dance floor of the Essex House hotel in New York City to use as bulkhead finish on the interior of the *WN Ragland*.

There is another part of the boat story. It is the hurt part, the emotional-impact part.

Sometime in 1973 before I bought the *Ragland*, the touring and constant womanizing finally caught up with me. I was growing further and further from Carrie. During the recording of *On the Beach* I did a song called "Motion Pictures." I did the recording with Ben Keith and Rusty Kershaw and we were all high on "honey slides," a little concoction that Rusty's wife, Julie, cooked up. Honey slides were made with grass and honey cooked together and stirred in a frying pan until a black gooey substance was left in the pan. A couple of spoonfuls of that and you would be laid-back into the middle of next week. The record was slow and dreamy, kind of underwater without bubbles.

> *Motion pictures on my TV screen,*
> *A home away from home, and I'm livin' in between*
> *But I hear some people have got their dream.*
> *I've got mine.*
>
> *I hear the mountains are doin' fine,*
> *Mornin' glory is on the vine,*
> *And the dew is fallin', the ducks are callin'.*
> *Yes, I've got mine.*
>
> *Well, all those people, they think they got it made*
> *But I wouldn't buy, sell, borrow or trade*

Anything I have to be like one of them.
I'd rather start all over again.

Well, all those headlines, they just bore me now
I'm deep inside myself, but I'll get out somehow,
And I'll stand before you, and I'll bring a smile to your eyes.
Motion pictures, motion pictures.

I asked Larry Johnson what he thought of it. He told me, "It scares me." Carrie was in Hawaii with Zeke at the time, and I was in the studio. When the recording was over, I drove Hank to the ranch and jumped on a plane to Maui. I was too late for one thing and just in time for another. When I got there, I went looking for Carrie at the Pioneer Hotel, where she was staying. I found out she was out on a sailboat with Zeke and a guy I had heard of, a friend of Crosby's, and she'd been gone for a number of days.

I realized right there that it was probably over, and went off the deep end, drinking a lot of tequila and drowning myself in sorrow. Of course, I was as guilty as hell myself, but that did not take away the pain. The thought that my family was irreparably harmed was inescapable. There were too many disconnects between Carrie and me, aside from the infidelities. I was so drunk that I went to the Chart House and played a solo set in front of a few tourists. Who knows? I was really getting the meaning of "What goes around, comes around."

In this frame of mind, I wrote about twenty songs I recorded in one form or another. Tapes of this are in a shambles, still being sorted out and readied for *The Archives Volume 2*. There was a lot of traveling around, soul-searching, and the like, crossing over to Europe and Canada and Hawaii, just moving for the sake of moving. That is when I started looking for a boat, my own boat. In some sort of balancing act inside my own head and heart, I decided to buy a boat and sail around the world, which never happened in the end. I did not sail around the world.

It was also around that time I first saw Pegi Morton. She was the hostess at Alex's, a bar/restaurant up on the mountain above the ranch. I first met Pegi in 1974. I loved her instantly, but was very nervous about repeating my past and not being able to hold the relationship together. I remember thinking Pegi would always be a beautiful girl, even when she was a hundred years old. Time passed. It was a different kind of love, infatuating like Carrie, but I felt this much deeper. Pegi's blue eyes are like crystals. They are so deep and true. Too good for me? In those eyes I saw myself and a life I hoped I would be able to hold together.

Time passed, and Pegi and I visited the boat a few times and made a few trips. On one of the early ones, Pegi was pregnant with Ben Young. We both got so seasick. We returned to California and the ranch. Then Ben Young was born on November 28, 1978, at Stanford Hospital in Palo Alto. He was premature, and we had to keep him in the hospital for a while. Pegi remembers the day after we got little Ben home—we took him on a blue-jeep ride in the pasture near our house. She had him all bundled up like the wonderful mother she is, and was so protective. We sat there in the sun for a while and took it all in.

Things had moved pretty fast with us, and we were reeling a

little. We were deeply in love. Our family was starting. We kept on moving with our young lives shortly afterward and took Ben Young with us everywhere. But pretty soon Pegi started noticing that Ben was not doing the things some other babies were doing. Pegi was wondering if something was wrong. She was young, and nothing had ever gone wrong in her life. People told us kids grow at different rates and do things at different times.

But as Ben reached six months old, we found ourselves sitting in a doctor's office. He glanced at us and offhandedly said, "Of course Ben has cerebral palsy."

I was in shock. I walked around in a fog for weeks. I couldn't fathom how I had fathered two children with a rare condition that was not supposed to be hereditary, with two different mothers. I was so angry and confused inside, projecting scenarios in my mind where people said something bad about Ben or Zeke and I would just attack them, going wild. Luckily that never did happen, but there was a root of instability inside me for a while. Although it mellowed with time, I carried that feeling around for years.

Eventually Pegi and I, wanting to have another child after Ben, went to see an expert on the subject. That was Pegi's idea. Always organized and methodical in her approach to problems, Pegi planned an approach to our dilemma with her very high intelligence. We both loved children but were a little gun-shy about having another, to say the least. After evaluating our situation and our children, the doctor told us that probably Zeke did not actually have CP—he likely had suffered a stroke in utero. The symptoms are very similar. Pegi and I weighed this information. To know someone like her and to make a decision about a subject as important as this with her was a gift beyond anything I have ever experienced. It was her idea, and she had guided us to this point. We made a decision together to go forward and have another child.

We tried being on the boat with Ben, but it was not in the cards. Ben was a handful, and neither Pegi nor I was truly a sailor. The boat went around the world more or less, but we didn't. That dream didn't come true. There was something more important to me than that: my family. My Pegi and Ben.

Zeke was coming to the ranch for weekends, and Pegi was becoming a strong mother figure for him, too, building a strong family foundation, stability, and security for the kids. So we would fly out and meet the *Ragland* at different locations around the world. Acapulco, Alaska, Panama, Bora-Bora, Papeete, Huahine, Mooréa, the Virgin Islands, the Bahamas—we did have some really good times! Now that Ben is so big, it is largely impossible for us to travel on the *Ragland* as a family, and we *are* a family, so we have been trying to sell her for a few years. Eventually it will happen, and that chapter will close. But these memories will live forever.

*Ben Young on my lap, David Myers, Pegi Young, and John Thompson
on the* Human Highway *set, 1980.*

## Chapter Thirty

A fter Ben Young was born, Pegi and I headed south to Los Angeles to begin filming *Human Highway* on a soundstage in Hollywood. I needed to do something besides music to keep fresh and have a musical perspective. Have you ever heard the expression "How can you miss me if I don't go away?" That expression defines why I do other things. I love the variety, and the projects are all interrelated anyway. There is no reason to just repeat oneself until further notice. When we got to LA, we set up house at a hotel we really liked at the time called L'Hermitage, not to be confused with my favorite hotel in Nashville, the Hermitage.

Like movies made a long time ago in Hollywood, we used sets that were made to look like the real world. That's how a storybook quality can be created, and I was trying to get that look. It's harder to do that storybook quality, if not impossible, when you use real-life scenes and go outdoors. The *Human Highway* concept was for us to film on an indoor set that looked like a corner gas station in a fictional place called Linear Valley. Megapolitan City was visible in the distance, and a nuclear power plant was about a mile away in the background. We had a set designed and constructed that had a train track and a train that passed by occasionally. The action focused on the folks at the gas station and attached café, which was a caboose.

Three waitresses, played by Geraldine Baron, Sally Kirkland, and Charlotte Stewart, worked in the café. The part of the café cook was played by Dennis Hopper. Dean Stockwell, codirecting with me, played the proprietor. I played Lionel, a very dorky (think Jerry Lewis) mechanic working at the station, and Russell Tamblyn played Fred, a friend of Lionel's who wanted a job. Pegi had a small part as a biker girl. David Myers was our director of photography, with Larry Johnson as assistant director and Jeanne Field in production. It was a sort of day-in-the-life concept, all taking place in one day, just a regular day, the day the earth suddenly ended in a world war. It was a comedy.

Every day we began with shooting the script we had come up with the night before. What a blast! We did some really crazy and fun things, riding bikes and using rear-screen projection—really old-time techniques. We came up with new wacky things to do every day. Some of the ideas were really old-school, and some of them were just plain dorky. There was a lot of improvising, and the set was very alive. It was purposefully made to look like a set, not real.

It was a big family, and we shot for six weeks. I financed the whole thing myself because we couldn't get anyone to back the way we were approaching the film. It was a typical Shakey Pictures production! It was a definite high point for Larry, David Myers, and me. Pegi brought Ben Young down to the set on occasion to share the fun, and we were all having such a great time.

After we finished shooting, the film went through several versions in editing. We had a screening in San Diego and passed out info cards for people to comment on the film. It was a disaster, but a really funny one. People were outraged that I was playing such a dorky character, and some were advising me that we bury the picture because it would kill my career. I took that positively—it was a good sign that my character was getting a strong reaction. I felt strangely good about it.

It was my feeling that the film was what I wanted it to be, but the main area of concern for me was a dream sequence that was not quite what I had intended. Several versions of the film were edited and one was even put out on Pioneer LaserDisc. I still like the first cut, the director's cut that I did, and today we are preparing it for a release as part of the Shakey Pictures collection on Netflix. I am going back in to edit and finalize that dream sequence when I get back to the mainland.

Larry's great talent in filmmaking was partly his ability to get emotions from the scene in the editing room. His touch would bring out the soul and magic. He did an edit on the bonfire scene at Puye in *Human Highway* that he cut to my song "Goin' Back." It was magical to me. I think it is the turning point in *Human Highway*, where you forget about everything else and become in the moment with the counterculture, the hippies, the artists, the Indians. Everything in the film revolves around that scene to me. That was Larry. He went into the editing room one day and came out with that. Sheer brilliance. On top of that, he was so positive and energized, keeping everyone on their toes and having fun. His energy was contagious.

When we lost Larry in 2010, he was working with Toshi Onuki on revising *Human Highway*. Toshi is a very creative and important part of the Shakey Pictures team, who spent years with Larry developing the archives. Larry was upset because a piece of film was missing, and he never did get to complete the high-resolution digital version before he died. He wanted to maintain the quality of David Myers's original film. I am less concerned with that than I am with content, although we will try to find the footage, and Toshi and I will hopefully get this done in a way that Larry would have liked once and for all.

It was a wild time. Devo and I were doing "Out of the Blue" in the studio and a lot of stuff from *Trans* on the radio, plus Devo's performance of "Worried Man," the Kingston Trio classic. There was a lot of Devo in *Human Highway*; they contributed three performances. Add to that some of the off-the-wall scoring things we did with Mark Mothersbaugh from Devo and I am sure we will have something very memorable for the sound track.

I will be excited to close the book on *Human Highway*. There is certainly a lot to do to pick up the pieces strewn around from this long life so far, but I have an excellent crew and am confident that we are up to it. Of course, time must be set aside to have fun.

Right near the end of filming at the soundstage, Pegi started having some headaches. They were really bad ones. She was in a lot of very intense pain. At this time I must confess to one of the worst low points I have had. Pegi was in the hospital and they were looking at her brain, giving her some tests to find out why she was having these terrible headaches. The shooting on set was finished for *Human Highway* and we were having a wrap party. I got stoned and way too high to be visiting her in the hospital, but I went anyway. She had been having a bad time there, and her mother was visiting her when I arrived stoned. Pegi knew it right away and threw me out of the room, seeing the shape I was in. I really let her down. She was always there for me, and I had blown a chance to be there for her. Her mother, of course, had no idea why Pegi threw me out. It was just very confusing for her and a real low point for me.

Anyway, we had some tests done and found out that Pegi had a disorder in the veins in her brain called an arteriovenous malformation (AVM), and pressure was building. These AVMs often go undetected until something catastrophic occurs, such as stroke or death. They are also very often inoperable because of their location in the brain. So we were lucky on both counts. It was decided that this area of her brain had to be operated on. Major brain surgery was performed at Stanford University Medical Center. They had to cut off all her beautiful blond hair. I remember her sitting upright in her bed like a little girl, wrapped in a white hospital gown, with her hair all gone. She looked so beautiful and so innocent. I was so scared that something might happen to her in the surgery. It was possible. The brain is a very risky thing to operate on. I tried to show Pegi that everything was going to be fine, but I was really scared. That Pegi might never be the same or might be greatly injured as a result of the operation was a fleeting thought. I quickly pushed it out of my mind. After I left the hospital, I went out with Briggs and got really stoned. When I went back to the hospital the next day, Pegi could see that I was all hungover. It must have been so disappointing for her. I had let her down again.

The time arrived for the surgery, and it was successfully performed. During recovery, which took quite a while, Pegi spoke very slowly; over a period of about three months her speech gradually returned to normal. She used to go out into the garden and sit there, pulling weeds and doing simple things, while the sun rose and set. I was always thinking how much I loved her and how I never wanted to lose her. I can still see her sitting in that garden like a little girl, with her hair so short. I wanted her to get her laugh back. And she did. Her laugh started coming back slowly, and it returned to its full glory in a few months. I was so happy. Day after day. Week after week. She came back. My Pegi and I have been through a lot of life together. I am so thankful for every day.

Whenever I think of Larry Johnson, I am always struck by the amount of time he dedicated to helping others have a good time. He was always doing things for other people. In his work with me, he made sure that everything was ready for me to contribute when I arrived at the scene. Materials were lined up. People were ready. Larry was always looking out for everyone—except Larry. When he started getting tired in the afternoon and needed to take a rest, I should have known something big was wrong, because he was taking time out for himself. If I had really noticed that fully, it would have registered loudly that something was amiss. Of course, I was preoccupied, as is my nature, and I often miss important things going on with others around me. I was focused on something that had to do with me, or one of my creations, which is also my nature. So I missed helping the one person who helped me when he needed it most. That is the nature of life, to learn lessons too late in some instances. People like me learn the hard way. Now I am looking out for these signs in my loved ones more than ever before.

I will never be as giving a person as Larry—at least it is highly unlikely because I am so possessed. But *never* is also a big word, and things do change. Maybe someday I will evolve to a place where I have some of the qualities Larry had. Even the people who got the wrong end of the stick loved Larry. If you offended Larry, you went straight to the penalty box, and it was not easy to get released. If a professional did not do a great job and failed to deliver quality when he was offered an opportunity, that person went straight to the box. If you were focused on something other than your responsibility to Larry and he had given you a good chance, off you went. Some people spent years in that box. Larry had his reasons. But everybody loved him, even those put in the box.

He had more women in more places than anyone I know.

They all loved him dearly and they all understood that there were others. This was not totally comfortable for him, but he would juggle and balance it like a magician. When we held a celebration of Larry's life, the women he loved were all there together, and his most recent girlfriend was snubbed by the others. Somehow that made sense. She had certainly not established herself as being on the same level as Larry's previous ladies; they all knew one another, but they didn't know her.

When we first met, Larry was with Jeanne Field. "Miss Field," as Larry used to call her, was a jewel of a person and still is today. We were all working on *Journey Through the Past* and having a big old time. Miss Field was doing production. Larry had us down in Asheville, North Carolina, interviewing an old black couple, Sandie and Levie, who were a part of his early life. They were recalling the slave days, and Larry was hanging on every word. The footage was beautiful. We have not used it yet.

I am sure it will hold some great meaning for me now. It was like that. Larry did things and much later you would discover why. He often joked about being a redneck cracker. He carried a white kerchief and dabbed the sweat on his forehead, playing the part of a gracious southern gentleman, tipping his hat to lady passersby. I am sure he is doing the same in heaven, or something a lot like heaven.

Larry Johnson editing Journey Through the Past
at the ranch, 1972.

## Chapter Thirty-One

Hawaii

The Big Island's volcano has been active for a long time. It started spewing ash that resulted in a heavy vog around five-plus years ago.

Vog looks like smog, but it isn't. It is natural pollution from the fires inside the earth. Our paradise looks really different now, and our eyes and lungs have started complaining to us. Recently, the vog was coming and going irregularly with the changing winds and unknown other factors contributing. As I write this today, I have been here on the island for six days, and the vog is not around. It looks a lot like it used to back in the day before the vog came, and there is an air of happiness because of this.

We have no control over these things, and they are a good reminder of our helplessness and insignificance in the grand scope of natural events. The vog does remind me of the stupid laws against burning wood in fireplaces in the city because it causes air pollution. Shit! That is ridiculous! These beautiful fireplaces were built in the homes and apartments of New York and San Francisco and all the other big cities with winter for a reason. Thank you for the state law in California forbidding the inclusion of fireplaces in any new homes. What a law! How about the cars? They would not be possible to outlaw because of the economic consequences, so let's go after fireplaces and their evil smoke! Thank you, lawmakers, for your perception and vision in this matter. You are an inspiration to us all.

I am an electric-car fanatic who loves big luxury cars. Lincvolt is in its fourth year now. I can't wait to ride down to LA in Lincvolt. That will be a complete blast. I plan on stopping and staying in my favorite bungalow in a Santa Barbara hotel and lighting a fire in the fireplace. I was just kidding about that law. There really is no law. I might have just made that up, because part of this book is from my memory and I have a big imagination. (News bulletin: In truth, there really *is* a law like that. I just learned about it.)

Anyway, the air is clear as a bell in Hawaii, and I am very happy! Just as there is no way to change the past, there is no way to predict the future. I am sure of that. I have just learned that the vog on the Big Island is about one fiftieth of what it was for the last few years. I am so thankful!

Of course, it could be back tomorrow.

My archive project is a multiedged sword. It is something I love doing, but it raises some questions about my motives in doing it. A writer accused me of building my archives just to further my own legend, whatever that is. I hope you don't believe that. What a shallow existence that would be! I remember reading that article saying that about me. It pissed me off. It's my life, and I am a collector. I collect everything: cars, trains, manuscripts, photographs, tape recordings, records, memories, and clothes, to name a few. The fact that I want to create a chronological history of my recordings and supporting work is proof positive that I am an incurable collector, confronted with an amazingly detailed array of creations that I have painstakingly rat-holed over the years.

Some of them are complete pieces of shit, but they have their place in my chronological obsession. There is nothing we can do about it. I have already done enough good and damage with this book to defeat any number of earlier theories about the order of things and how I should be acting. There is no reason for me to start worrying about what people think now; I have already been worrying for far too long, and it hasn't helped or changed a thing. I do enjoy writing, and I hope someone gets something interesting out of this book. I already have. Now, if I ever have to write a book that is not about me, I may be totally stumped and have writer's block. We will see. Writing is very convenient, has a low expense, and is a great way to pass the time. I highly recommend it to any old rocker who is out of cash and doesn't know what to do next. You could hire someone else to write it for you if you can't write yourself. That doesn't seem to matter. Just don't hire some sweaty hack who asks you questions for years and twists them into his own vision of what is right or wrong. Try to avoid doing that.

I just spoke to Billy Talbot and told him about the plan to use my ranch's White House for a Crazy Horse session, with John Hanlon and Mark Humphreys. Mark is our onstage monitor mixer and loves Crazy Horse. John Hanlon was trained by Briggs to record the sound a certain way and not explain what he is doing. (John talks quite a bit, and Briggs, after listening to him talk too much in the studio, taking up a lot of space in the air, coined the phrase, "Don't explain.") Billy is in. The forces of good are all converging for the rebirth of Crazy Horse in its next incarnation, basically the same as it always was except with more years behind it.

God, I miss Briggs.

It would be so great to be talking to him today. I would like to know what he thinks of the fact that I have not written a song since I stopped smoking. Smoking weed opened up the door for me, and I miss that part, especially when it comes to songs and music.

This is very important. Don't spook the Horse. That is very essential to the success of any ride. The Horse will head for the barn if it is spooked, and the music will continue but not have that magic that the Horse possesses. Any ride on the Horse must not have a destination. History has shown that the best way to spook the Horse is to tell it what to do or where to go or, even worse, how to get there. You must not speak directly to the Horse or ever look the Horse in the eyes until the ride is over and the Horse is secured in the barn. It is okay to talk to the Horse directly, but care must be taken to have respect for the muse when discussing anything with the Horse. The Horse and the muse are very good friends. Disrespect for the muse will piss off the Horse, and possibly vice versa, although that is hard to prove. The Horse has met no equal, although there undoubtedly is an equal to the Horse out there somewhere. The Horse knows this well and will not tolerate anyone who is overly complimentary to the point of excluding other friends of the muse in a misguided attempt to gain the Horse's favor. That is absolutely not the thing to do, as it makes the Horse think, and that has a bad effect generally. The Horse has a voracious appetite. The songs the Horse likes to consume are always heartfelt and do not need to have anything fancy associated with them. The Horse is very suspicious of tricks. Keeping these simple guidelines in place is always a good idea when approaching the Horse for any reason.

One day Bob Dylan called me, which was a surprise. He doesn't typically call. It was after Hurricane Katrina destroyed New Orleans and I had done some TV with many other artists to help raise funds for the victims. New Orleans music is sacred. I was playing on the Nashville Network, and he heard us do "Walking to New Orleans" and wanted to tell me what a good performance it was. That was really cool, and it meant a lot to me.

I was in New York doing something, walking on the street, and it was a real surprise to hear from him out of the blue. He was also pointing out what a cool hat I had on during the telecast and that I looked good. Bob is always looking sharp when he performs. Once, we had Bob and Elliot for dinner at the ranch house, and he and Pegi had a conversation about my look. "Comfy" was one word that came up! So I think I made a big advance there.

It is always a struggle for me to get dressed up to play with the Horse. It seems incongruous with the music to me for some reason. Who knows, possibly the next time we play it will be the "Clothes Horse."

My love for plaid shirts goes back a long way. Susan, my first wife, made all those cool patches I wore back in the day when even I was fashionable. The pants on the back cover of *After the Gold Rush* were Susan's work. She was very artistic and put so much of her love into it. She even made me a beautiful patchwork vest with a blue velvet back. She sewed the patches on with some strands of her own hair. After we broke up, I wanted to keep it carefully tucked away forever. It was beautiful. I wanted to always remember her by it. One day I came home and Carrie had taken it apart and used the patches to cover holes in a pair of my jeans that I never wore. That was pretty numbing. I am not sure I am over that. Clothes make the man.

Pegi Young, with Larry Johnson in the background. In partial view on the left is Eric Johnson; on the right is Keith Wissmar (both part of my team).

## Chapter Thirty-Two

I like bands for different reasons, and the reasons are not consistent.

Pearl Jam is a band I have a lot of respect for. Nirvana and Sonic Youth I feel the same way about. Mumford & Sons, My Morning Jacket, Wilco, Givers, and Foo Fighters are just some of my favorites. I respect bands that give me something of themselves that I can feel. ("Posing" bands turn me off, generally speaking.) It all has to do with a feeling I have about them. That is what music is to me, a feeling. It's similar with people, too.

In 1995, I went to Seattle to record with Pearl Jam, minus Eddie, just after I was inducted into the Rock and Roll Hall of Fame. I knew I had a small window to get a record done because of their availability and mine—and I like working like that. When I got there, I wrote a song every night in the hotel so I would always have new material for each session. I still sometimes think Briggs should have been involved, but he wasn't, because I thought at the time that he might be too abrasive a producer for PJ. We used their producer, Brendan O'Brien, who was a fast-moving guy and who played keys on some of the tunes. We just kept rolling along, and soon *Mirror Ball* was recorded. We did an impromptu gig in a Seattle nightspot where local bands played.

Pulling up outside the place, I noticed an alert-looking guy standing on the loading dock who seemed to be in a leadership role. Later, I met him and found out he was working for PJ as a road manager. We got along well, and my enduring relationship with Eric Johnson began. After that PJ was not working for a while, so Eric came with us and ultimately stayed. It was not a rocky change where I stole somebody, although I did steal him, I suppose. It just seemed so right we all just fell into it. Eric still has deep feelings for PJ, and if they needed him, he would be free to go. But I need someone like him to go with me and make sure I am secure when I travel.

Times have changed. I can't go to public airports like I used to. Now when I arrive at an airport, there are professional autograph people all over me. I don't know how the hell they know what I am doing seemingly before I do, but there they are, bugging me in the security line and at the curb.

It costs me to avoid them, but so be it. They bother me. They pose as real fans and try to make me feel guilty if I don't sign something. They are so obvious and deceptive, feeding on my love for my real fans. I think either the travel agency or the hotels notify the autograph hounds' representatives when I am coming to town.

Eric tries to filter through them to get to the real fans so I can sign for them. He tries to get me nice rooms when I stay somewhere, books a lot of charters, coordinates the ins and outs of my appearances. I have also used his artistic talents extensively. He played the Devil in my stage and film productions of *Greendale*. He was the Painter in *Trunk Show*. Eric is my go-to guy for everything on the road. He is the "artist in residence" on my tours, does all the associated design that I ask him to do, from T-shirts to programs, anything having to do with art. He is always drawing on napkins and leaving them behind. I grab them up and Pegi and I save them.

When our dog Bear was really old, Eric would carry him through hotel lobbies to get to the elevator so Bear's feet wouldn't slip on the polished marble floors. Eric calls ahead so everything is ready for Pegi and me when we arrive somewhere. We are not exposed in the lobby, waiting for anything. He is a great artist and a fine person. I am proud to call him my friend. Plus, he is one of the funniest people I have ever met, along with Elliot, of course, who is the master.

Graham Nash, Stephen Stills, David Crosby, and me,
with Elliot Roberts in the background, backstage before
a CSNY show in Denver, 1974.

## Chapter Thirty-Three

I n 1969, when I joined CSN and it became CSNY for a while, I was at an interesting point in my life. I was working with two bands at the same time, recording with Crazy Horse and rehearsing with CSNY. David, Stephen, and Graham had their own sound, and I was brought in by Ahmet and Stephen to add something else to the mix for live appearances, more rock and roll, I guess.

For a while at the beginning, there was a short debate among some about whether I should be included, i.e., whether to add my Y to CSN or not. Thankfully, that never became an issue. Elliot was there and everything worked out fine. Stephen and I were happy to be playing together again and picked up right where we had left off. CSN had a big hit with their first record—they sounded like a new car coming off the assembly line!—and I had *Everybody Knows This Is Nowhere* with Crazy Horse, which stayed on the charts for two years.

We rehearsed together at Stephen's house in Laurel Canyon, trying out different bass players, including Bruce Palmer. Bruce, who was great as usual, had gotten back into the States from Canada somehow, and Stephen and I were very high on playing with him again. He rehearsed with us for a couple of days and was totally on his game. Then he got busted for pot and deported again, just like that. That was one of the last times we ever played together, except for once on the ranch years later when I played with him and Dewey, experimenting with getting the Springfield back together.

So CSNY eventually settled on Greg Reeves on bass and went on the road, where we played the Greek Theatre in LA, Chicago's Auditorium Theatre, the Masonic Temple Theatre in Detroit, and of course, Woodstock. A funny thing happened at Woodstock. I didn't want cameras onstage distracting me while we were playing. I hated the showboating atmosphere that surrounded the filming and thought it distracted from our music. The music was between us and the audience, and anything that got in the way was taboo in my opinion. So if you listen carefully to the band's intro, they say "CSN"—they cut out the Y as payback. On the Woodstock record, Atlantic Records used a song of mine recorded months later at the Fillmore East in New York called "Sea of Madness." That was kind of misleading.

Getting to Woodstock was a lot of fun, though. I remember meeting Jimi Hendrix in a small airport and riding in a pickup truck with Melvin Belli, the famous lawyer, to the gig. We had to take a little charter plane to get close, and then they picked a few of us up and brought us in. CSN were already there. They were anxious to get there early.

There was, of course, a huge crowd, and it was a turning point in rock and roll history. It was so big, it was scary. No one could hear. I was really uncomfortable because everyone was very jacked.

There was one other festival worth mentioning: Altamont. Security onstage was provided by the Hells Angels Motorcycle Club, and there was only one murder at the show. Getting there, starting way in the back, we rode in through the whole crowd in a pickup truck. I was in the cab, and the guys were in the back. Stephen was yelling at the top of his voice, "Crosby, Stills, Nash, and Young!" in an effort to clear a path through the crowd to get to the stage. The pickup crawled along through the crowd. The yelling continued. I was trying to disappear into the glove compartment of the truck's dashboard. It was surreal, and Fellini should have been there to film it. We sucked at the performance. It was one of the worst-feeling gigs I can ever remember. What a monster cocaine-fueled ego trip! The music really sucked air.

I had a sick feeling during that show that I never have forgotten and thankfully have never felt again. I could feel the music dying. There were some really fine CSNY gigs, but they were not in big places, they were in concert halls where we could hear and the band focused on the music instead of superstardom. The live record 4 *Way Street* captures some of that. We had some really great musical moments, and Crosby's energy was the catalyst. He was so into it that it was infectious. Stephen and I would trade licks back and forth under his singing and Graham's harmony. Those were some sublime moments. Graham wrote some incredibly vivid songs that suited the harmonies beautifully. It was a great experience I wouldn't trade for anything, although it had its imperfections along the way, like everything else I have done.

One night in San Francisco in the fall of 1969, CSNY was recording the *Déjà Vu* album at Wally Heider/Filmways recording studio. We were playing "Helpless," and I had been going over it with Dallas Taylor, Greg Reeves, and Stephen for hours. Although it is a simple song, it requires laying back, which was not really in Dallas Taylor's musical vocabulary that night. I just kept doing it over and over, waiting for him to settle down on drums and stop playing accents and fills everywhere. It really was a case of wearing him out to the point where he would play it slowly, without pushing it, and without adding little riffs that meant nothing to the song. It was an arduous task.

Stephen played beautiful piano on the track while I sang it live. I was just starting to sing live in the studio; that was one of the first times. Greg, on bass, was always in the pocket, although he played a lot of notes, so getting everyone to relax and just support the song took a while. It got to be the wee hours, and after many tries, we finally got *the* take. It was worth it. In the end, everyone played a really good performance. Sometimes you just have to stay with it.

The next session, Stephen added a guitar with a volume pedal, and it was really a fine part. Graham stayed with us all night in the control room, adding his support on the night of the original session with Bill Halverson at the console. Graham always stayed no matter what. He was always there providing a steady hand and positive constructive vibe, even if he wasn't playing. He was making up background and chorus harmony parts as we recorded and was ready with ideas when it came time to overdub with Crosby the next day. Crosby always had great harmonies that he came up with on the spot.

For some reason I have a vivid memory of that group of sessions. One day after CSN had cut "Teach Your Children," which they sang perfectly without me, I was in the control room and Jerry Garcia came in and played a steel guitar part on it. It was actually on a regular guitar with a slide, as I remember it. He just sat down with it on his lap in the control room down under the speakers and put that part on. I remember that every time I hear that song, which is one of CSNY's greatest. I am proud to have my name on it, although I didn't play or sing a note.

While we were recording in San Francisco, I was staying at a motel called the Caravan Motor Inn just down the street. No one else was staying there but me. I don't really know where everyone else was. (Stephen was probably at a nicer place. He always finds nice places to stay. Nash had a house there already, I think, or was just moving in to one that he later renovated. I don't know where David was staying—he had a lot of friends—probably the Airplane House.) Anyway, I was at the Caravan and I had two pets in my room, Speedy and Harriet. They were bush babies, little primates, which I kept in the bathroom. That was really crazy, but I was alone and wanted some company. They were dirty, and I had to clean up after them every time I came home from a session. I wore a leather glove because when I caught them to put them in their cage they would bite me. Imagine coming home from recording "Helpless" at three o'clock in the morning and cleaning up after bush babies in my bathroom. Is that the life of a star or what? I was not really very social at that point, and some of my behaviors must have been curious at best.

One day I visited Butano Canyon near Pescadero, California, with Crosby. It was 1970, and our CSNY lighting director, Steve Cohen, was living in a place right at the end of Butano Canyon Road. Since it was the last house, there was nothing but canyon to see from the deck of the old redwood home. Most of the houses in this canyon had been constructed as summer residences and were old places built totally with redwood, featuring heat from great stone fireplaces made with stones right from the creek. It was a stunning place. Giant redwoods and the healthy creek running by made for a spectacular view.

Crosby had invited me up there to see the place and hang. Leo Makota, our road manager, was there, too. It was Leo, as I mentioned, who first directed me to what is now Broken Arrow Ranch. Cros really wanted to see me living up north. He loved it up there himself. Cros had also taken me to the Airplane House, where Jefferson Airplane lived. There I met Grace Slick, who was beautiful, sang great, was topless, and blew my mind. That was the first time I met her. The whole San Francisco scene was something I had never seen. It was overwhelming. I remember Paul Kantner driving Cros and me to the airport from the city in his Porsche, demonstrating that the airport was only twenty minutes from Haight-Ashbury now that Interstate 280 had been opened. I was scared shitless with Kantner driving that Porsche at astronomical speeds to demonstrate how easy it was to get there fast! I was really not used to any of this stuff. I was shaking when we got to the airport to get on PSA for $9.95 and be served by stewardesses in short shorts on our way back to LA. Holy shit. Was I green!

So anyway, we're in Butano Canyon at Steve and Leo's place, and the tragedy at Kent State had just happened. *Time* magazine had a picture of the girl, Allison Krause, after the National Guard had killed her and three other victims. We were looking at it together. She was lying there on some pavement with another student kneeling down looking at her, as I remember.

These people were our audience. That's exactly who we were playing for. It was our movement, our culture, our Woodstock generation. We were all one. It was a personal thing, the bond we held between the musicians and the people of the culture: hippies, students, flower children, call them what you will. We were all together.

The weight of that picture cut us to the quick. We had heard and seen the news on TV, but this picture was the first time we had to stop and reflect. It was different before the Internet, before social networking to say the least. So full of this feeling of disbelief and sadness. I picked up my guitar and started to play some chords and immediately wrote "Ohio"; *four dead in Ohio*. The next day, we went into the studio in LA and cut the song. Before a week had passed it was all over the radio. It was really fast for those times; really fast. All the stations played "Ohio." There was no censoring by programmers. Programming services were not even around; DJs

The Kent State shooting, 1970.

played whatever they wanted on the FM stations. We were underground on FM. There was no push-back for criticizing the government. This was America. Freedom of speech was taken very seriously in our era. We were speaking for our generation. We were speaking for ourselves. It rang true. The U.S. government has still not apologized to the families of the fallen four of Ohio.

The band has gotten together for other political causes over the years, and I enjoy it. It's always fun to hear the singing and feel the love and respect, and there is a lot of that. During the Iraq War, when CSNY went on the road singing the songs of my latest album, *Living with War*, and a collection of older songs that reflected politics and American life, we had a sense of the old purpose. But things had changed; we split our audience in half with that music rather than bringing it together. It was a sign of the times. We have been through a lot together: the Summer of Love, hell, distrust, and hurt. Life. When we play now our audience still feels it, like a candle that is flickering, like a sun that is setting. A fog is rolling in. It is really all of our lives together.

That was CSNY to me. The connection with our generation was profound, and we could feel it. I loved all those guys. A lot has changed since those innocent times. We are different today. We were not bound by chemistry the same way as the Springfield was. We were all friends, experiencing a phenomenon together.

Crosby was forever the catalyst, always intense, driving us further and further. Just looking in those eyes made me want to deliver from the heart. He so believed in what we were doing. Graham was the consummate professional, always there with his parts, cheering us on as we jammed, writing the songs we became best known for. Stephen, my brother, always the soulful, conflicted one, was battling unseen demons and many-colored beasts through the days and nights, contributing an edge that was unmistakable.

The combination of that energy all at once—with our audience!—that is what CSNY was to me at its best.

But then came the fame, the drugs, the money, houses, cars, and admirers; then the solo albums. I had to break away. I had so much to give, so many songs in me, so many ideas and sounds in my head. I had to do it. The band didn't break up; it just stopped. It did not regenerate itself. It stopped functioning, like it had a lapse or a heart attack or something. No new songs came forward from anyone. We were all doing our own things. We needed a reason to get together and a purpose behind our music. In the end, we became a celebration of ourselves, and there was no way to keep that going. It doesn't regenerate. We had a golden time, and then we lost our way. Be great or be gone.

In the aftermath of my breakup with Carrie, Crosby was a really good friend. He kept in touch with me throughout, and we had some really deep conversations about that. He was so supportive; I could not have asked for a better friend. He has since gone through hell and back, and written two books about it with his friend Carl Gottlieb. I would like to read a book that he wrote in his own words because he is masterful with language and very articulate.

When he started to take a dive it was terrible to see. There was nothing we could do to stop him. Once he came to my boat and broke out his pipe to smoke some freebase. He wanted to share some so I could see how it was. As we all sat around, he got it out and started his torch. Then he did it all by himself, forgetting what he was doing completely. That was my experience with freebase, and I came away with a bad impression. He and his wife, Jan, were both into it, but their deep love for each other eventually rescued them from it. They picked up the pieces and moved on with their lives, having a beautiful son and getting the blue sky back finally. They really pulled it out of the jaws of hell and took it back. I still remember "the mighty Cros" visiting the ranch in his van. That van was a rolling laboratory that made Jack Casady's briefcase look like chicken feed. Forget I said that! Was my mic on?

Larry Johnson, me, and David Briggs, playing pool at the ranch, 1978.

## Chapter Thirty-Four

Pegi and I were at the Hawaii house relaxing from something or other. Conan and Jay Leno were having their moment with NBC, and Conan had walked out on *The Tonight Show*, which turned into a political quagmire when Jay Leno decided he was not going to step down as he had said he would. Conan was left hanging. So Conan's last show was coming up and I was his musical guest. Eric Johnson had come over to Hawaii to fly with me on the United flight to LA that I was taking. When we arrived, he got off the plane and went to make sure everything was ready so I could go straight to a car and to the hotel. Then he came back and said, "I have got some really bad news; Larry Johnson has died." I took that in. Larry was a lifelong friend.

Elliot met us at the LA airport. We hugged. I was in a fog. Tim Foster, my old stage manager, was there, too. We hugged. What can you say? I called Pegi, who was crying like a baby. Larry had died in Ben Young's van. He just slipped behind the wheel to drive Ben to the Sharks' hockey game and let out a last breath. He was gone. Just like that. On the phone, Pegi cried and cried. All I wanted to do was go back to Hawaii and be with her.

I had to go to the hotel, where Dave Matthews and I sat together in my room, learning a song while the time passed. Conan's last show was the next day, and later that night, Dave Matthews and I were doing a thing together for the Haiti Relief Fund; we had to rehearse to get a grip on what we were performing together.

The next day was the Conan show. It was surreal. Conan's shows were always loose and fun. This one was different. As I was singing "Long May You Run," the TV audience must have thought I was singing it for Conan. I was singing it for Larry, too. I barely made it through that performance. I looked over at Conan, and he was watching me with his head in his hands. That guy really got screwed. But he is a survivor. I said good-bye and off we went to the Haiti benefit over in Hollywood. It was the same place we had done the 9/11 Tribute to Heroes, where I sang "Imagine." I think we did a good job. Someone said Kanye West had left a message there for me. I kept seeing Larry in the hallway outside my dressing room. I never got the message.

Pegi came home to California, and we met at the ranch. Pegi cried for six months. She grieved and grieved. Pegi and Larry were very close, and there was nothing I could do but hold her, comfort her, and feel my own thoughts. Life again. (You might notice I refer to my son Ben as Ben Young all the time. Larry always called his son Ben Johnson. I liked the pride with which he would say "Ben Johnson." It is a lingering memory of his great spirit.)

While it's true that Larry Johnson and David Briggs have perhaps played the major roles supporting my endeavors, the others who have worked at my side cannot be underestimated. I have been very lucky to know and create with all of them. Elliot and I are getting older now and can feel the passage of time, but the energy to do what we do is still very much alive. Ben Johnson, Larry's son, and Will Mitchell, who worked beside Larry, are still with me every day, carrying on the work. Hannah Johnson, Larry's daughter, is doing my photography archiving and the preservation/re-creation of manuscripts and art for my current projects. There is a lot of love and caring going on with our whole team. Toshi Onuki, who worked tirelessly with Larry and me, is still with me, helping with UX (user interface) design and film editing. Our work together is so rewarding. Mark Faulkner is editing film for videos in Larry's old Airstream, known affectionately as the "Upstream Airstream." Larry loved those Airstream trailers almost as much as he loved Quonset huts. So although something has been lost, something has been gained along the way, and I am grateful to be working and creating. The Shakey Pictures team lives on in the great space that Larry found and moved us into just before his untimely passing.

I am very proud of the people who have worked with me. Probably my "front of house" sound mixer Tim Mulligan, who has been with me the longest besides Elliot, has withstood the most of my changes in style and content, just riding it out with me. I can always count on Tim to come to the dressing room and tell me how we made out in a show, and not just the good shows. Dave Lohr has been right by Tim's side for years, providing feedback and quality care in tuning the sound in each venue where we play. Honesty, constructive criticism: those things are priceless in this game. I have always had excellent people with me; Joel Bernstein is another one. He is a great photographer and archivist who came along with me for years and tuned my instruments. Now he is working with Graham Nash and others doing a lot of archiving work. In the early years Joel took a lot of pictures that have been priceless in my *Archives* projects.

R ecently I visited my brother, Bob, in Ontario. I stayed in his house on the lake with him and his friend Vicky. Dave Toms was there with us, too. Dave is an old friend of me and my dad. We had a really good time together, and it gave me time to reflect on some of the changes in my life. Dave is a big Canadian guy with white hair. I gave him the name SnowBear to go with the character SnowBear in the continuation of the *Greendale* story. If we ever do that movie, Dave will play that part, I'm sure. He has been a traveling companion on the last couple of tours we have done with Lincvolt, sitting in Larry's old seat, and now plays in that story as well. Ben Johnson will be helping with that once I get home and can focus on it again.

Actually, Ben is the one who will be sitting in his dad's seat when we finally take our trip around the country in Lincvolt. Dave will be there, too. There are sure starting to be a lot of loose ends. When we lost Larry Johnson, we had a lot of balls in the air. Maybe too many.

Performing with Pegi at the 25th Annual Bridge School Benefit Concert at the Shoreline Ampitheatre, Mountain View, California, 2011.

## Chapter Thirty-Five

Dustin Cline and Ben Young are on their way here to Hawaii right now and should arrive in a few minutes from the mainland. Dustin, the son of David Cline, who was my road manager and sometime bus driver, was born just about the same time as Ben. He is now one of Ben's main caregivers and the Minister of Fun and Social Activities. Tony Rivera, "Uncle Tony," will be traveling with them as well. We have tried to always have a crew of two with Ben Young to make his comings and goings as safe, fun, and easy as possible, while also taking excellent care of him.

He is completely dependent on others now and is taking nourishment through a feeding tube in his stomach. That is something we implemented a year or so ago, and Ben has responded well, especially now that we prepare our own food for him that is fresh and organic. One of Ben Young's original caregivers, Anne Marie Holmes, a very sweet and kind English lady with an excellent sense of humor, has created some nourishing and healthy formulas for Ben. Rather than the canned formula most people like him would have to settle for, Ben is Mr. Gourmet. You are what you eat. And Ben Young is looking good.

Ben has seen a lot in his thirty-three years, including Larry Johnson's passing. We talk about Larry a lot, and Ben is often a part of the memories. Larry was an excellent friend for Ben, taking him everywhere and including him in everything he possibly could. Larry was one of Ben Young's strongest advocates for inclusion in every activity, no matter what logistics were involved.

Ben Young will be rolling up the sidewalk anytime now and into his room for an overhaul before we all take off to the Bamboo in Hawi for our traditional Sunday brunch with friends. Next week, the shift will change and Ben Bourdon will arrive. With him will be Marian Zemla, "Uncle Marian," the senior caregiver who has been with Ben for the longest (except for Anne Marie). Marian, a former practicing doctor from Poland, loves Ben Young very much. I suspect Ben is like a son to Marian and his wife, Teresa. Everyone on Ben's team is top-notch, and we are so blessed that we have this assistance. Pegi and Anne Marie are always looking to have someone "in the wings" so we are never short should something ever happen to one of the team members. Pegi is masterful at organizing this and seeing that Ben Young's staff is organized and running smoothly. That alone is a full-time job. How she does all of that and writes and records a brand-new record that is totally top-notch is incredible to me. She is finally living the dream she had when I first met her. Even with all of the great singers I have sung with, there is nothing like singing with Pegi.

Pegi and I with Ben and Amber at Willie Nelson's Pedernales Ranch, Spicewood, Texas, June 1984.

Chapter Thirty-Six

My daughter, Amber Jean Young, was born May 15, 1984. We brought her home to the ranch from the hospital in a baby-blue 1957 Chevy Bel Air wagon called the Mother Ship. She grew up relatively shy with others and showed a strong interest in art right away, painting first with one hand, then with the other, switching back and forth as she went. Her sense of color is so pleasing to me that I feel it in my heart every time I see one of her works. And now she has an MFA.

Rich with an artist's sentiment, Amber Young today is a beautiful young lady, making her way through life's guesswork and planning her future with grace, style, and conviction. Of course, she would never say that about herself. This is her father talking. I love her. She has been well raised by her mother, who has a natural sense for the art of mothering and nurturing. Amber's art is as complex as it is beautiful, and the textures and boldness she uses speak to me. I get a visceral feeling from her colors, just like great-sounding music gives me. What a pleasure to watch her develop her natural talent. She really wants to be an independent artist, making her way with her art and not asking for anything. Amber works at galleries in San Francisco and curates exhibitions.

Looking at the poster for my new Jonathan Demme movie, I am especially proud of my daughter Amber's art. She has done the titles, at Jonathan's request, and the result is so cool. In her strong personality, she is a combination of her mother and my mother, two of my favorite people, plus a little bit of me thrown in there for good measure, along with that indescribably original thing that is just totally her. She is a true original, having created houses built of Ben Young's feeding bags, tubes, and medical devices, heavy-duty construction vehicles made of felt, a wedding cake you can walk inside with beautiful felt roses adorning it, and countless works that hang on walls—works in wax, in paint, and in other mediums I can't adequately describe at the moment.

There is nothing on earth like the feeling of a parent for a child that has matured as Amber Young has. She is my pal, sometimes my confidante—although I am careful not to burden her unnecessarily—and my muse. Named after my granny Jean, an active musician who worked in the copper mines of Flin Flon, Manitoba, during the day, handing out the metal ID tags to the miners before they descended and collecting them back, hanging them on nails in the wall of a little shack, when they finished their shifts, thereby becoming the first to learn of a missing soul in the mine. Then she was partying into the night, singing and playing a barroom piano or producing and playing in the local theater productions she created. She is my daughter, Amber Jean Young. Over the years her mother and I have tried to do our best raising her, and now it is up to her. She is well equipped, soulful and talented, wise and idealistic, and comes fully loaded with the Young/Morton temperament.

I remember once we were having some problems, and she told me I was gone too much when she was growing up and I missed a lot of things. She was so true, so right. Of course I felt terrible, but that was the price I had to pay for my choices. I followed my music and missed her moments. Amber was very honest with me. Who could ask for more? She's my girl.

## Chapter Thirty-Seven

Another Word from PureTone . . .

I think a lot about the music business and how it is reinventing itself. Streaming services like Spotify make ALL music available free instantly or through a subscription and a cool, easy user interface. This is completely different from the way I started, but I am open to it because it gets music to the people in a way that works with today's expectations of the capabilities of technology.

The convenience is fantastic, with instant access to and discovery of the history of recorded sound, but you can't *feel* it like you used to. I don't want to complain and not have a suggestion about how to fix the problem—complaining without a solution is a waste of time. So I have developed a solution. It's just a matter of dealing in the business world and offering people a new way to make money that reintroduces ongoing quality into the equation. I know a way to combine streaming services and PureTone, while improving the sound of streams and making some tracks in playlists available instantly in PureTone-master quality.

I keep thinking about this all the time because I want to make a contribution that lasts. I know I am obsessive about it. Music is an art form compromised by technology; this is not what technology is supposed to do. Maybe the music I make now will not have a huge audience like it once did, and my time in the light may or may not have passed, but I can reach more people than I ever have by helping to bring all kinds of music to them in a way that is superior to anything that has ever been presented in the history of recorded sound. I think *great* digital sound is the future of music, and we are a few steps away from delivering it. It could happen really soon, and that would be a massive sea change for the art of recorded music.

*With book art director and friend Gary Burden,
on the beach in Malibu, 1975.*

## Chapter Thirty-Eight

My very first recording session was on July 23, 1963, at CKRC radio in Winnipeg. I was seventeen years old. Harry Taylor was the engineer behind the board, and Bob Bradburn was the producer, a CKRC DJ. The Squires were there to make a record! The first day we played all of our songs so we could hear how they sounded when recorded. It was very exciting, and I was really jacked up. Just before and just after the sessions, we played at the Crescentwood Community Centre and earned $35 the first night and $36 the second night. As you can tell, we were hot.

The CKRC studio had a pair of mono tape recorders, some EQ, some echo, and a control board. The mixing was done live. It was at this session that I first sang on tape. I had a couple of songs, one of which I called "I Wonder." It was the best one that I sang, but we decided, because I had a "different" voice, that the Squires would be an instrumental recording group. I knew that I had to work on my singing, and I knew I felt good when I sang. Those songs meant something to me. I had written several instrumentals that we were also playing.

The two tunes picked from the audition session were "The Sultan" and "Image in Blue." During the second session we practiced recording these, working on the arrangements. At that time it was decided that "Image in Blue" needed a name change so that Bob Bradburn could say the title at the end of the record in echo. "Aurora" was the new title. They thought of the title and had the idea. I was so young and eager, I didn't complain. I was just happy to be making a record. I did like that a prerecording of a gong was added to "The Sultan" to give it that special sultanesque, desert-tent vibe—we knew all about that in Winnipeg.

After a few long weeks of anticipation, the record was released on V Records, a local company that mainly did polkas but was just getting into rock and roll. We were very excited. Then the big moment came, and we heard "The Sultan" on the radio! I was in my mother's car with my bandmate Ken Koblun, driving somewhere. I felt so good. I am sure I was walking on air for weeks. The Squires were recording artists. My mother was telling everyone she knew. I could hear her on the phone calling all of her friends. She was my biggest fan!

There are a few of these 45 rpm singles available on eBay every once in a while now. I have one signed by the band that Jack Harper, our original drummer, gave to me. The Squires on that record were Ken Koblun on bass, Ken Smyth on drums, Allan Bates on guitar, and Neil Young on guitar. Unreal! Listening to this today, I can say we were pretty good. We needed better equipment, but we played well and it was a good instrumental. What a rush!

Although there was never any art for the Squires' 45, album covers are very important to me. They put a face on the nature of the project. I know albums are viewed as passé by some today, but I am an album artist and I am not ready to give up on my form. I think it has a future and a past. The album cover and liner notes reached out to the music lover, filling them with images and helping to illuminate the story behind the music, the feeling coming from the artist. My first album cover told a lot about me, without words.

I first met Gary Burden while shooting the CSNY cover for *Déjà Vu*, my initial album with CSN. Gary and I became good friends and we immediately worked together on the album cover for *After the Gold Rush*. I loved what he did with the photographs. Gary and I have been working together since that time, and I have done the great majority of my album art, my ads, and my songbooks with him. He is one of my closest compadres. Gary and his wife, Jenice, still work with me on every album cover. We are doing our life's work together.

One of my favorite album covers is *On the Beach*. Of course that was the name of a movie and I stole it for my record, but that doesn't matter. The idea for that cover came like a bolt from the blue. Gary and I traveled around getting all the pieces to put it together. We went to a junkyard in Santa Ana to get the tail fin and fender from a 1959 Cadillac, complete with taillights, and watched them cut it off a Cadillac for us; then we went to a patio supply place to get the umbrella and table. We picked up the bad polyester yellow jacket and white pants at a sleazy men's shop, where we watched a shoplifter getting caught red-handed and busted. Gary and I were stoned on some dynamite weed and stood dumbfounded, watching the bust unfold. This girl was screaming and kicking! Finally we grabbed a local LA paper to use as a prop. It had this amazing headline: SEN. BUCKLEY CALLS FOR NIXON TO RESIGN. Next we took the palm tree I had taken around the world on the Tonight's the Night tour. We then placed all of these pieces carefully in the sand at Santa Monica Beach. Then we shot it. Bob Seidemann was the photographer, the same one who took the famous Blind Faith cover shot of the naked young girl holding an airplane. We used the crazy pattern from the umbrella insides for the inside of the sleeve that held the vinyl recording. That was the creative process at work. We lived for that, Gary and I, and we still do.

Collaborating with Gary has been a joy over the years. We have really maintained a wonderful friendship to this day, no matter where we are on the planet. I hung with him a lot after my breakup with Susan and before I moved north to the ranch. Then I sold my Topanga house to him. A few years ago when Gary married Jenice Heo, an artist he met at Reprise Records, I was his best man.

When CDs came along, it was more of a challenge to present our art. The CD package was about twenty-five percent the size of an album. Everything had to be small. The lyrics were not legible without glasses for anyone over a certain age. So our whole palette was changed by the advent of the CD. Of course, the audio quality also took a dive, with a maximum of fifteen percent of the sound of

On the Beach *LP cover.*

a master, but if you don't know how I feel about that by now, you should put this book down. Go directly to your doctor's office and have your eyes and ears checked.

Now that online music has taken hold with Spotify, Rhapsody, and the other online services, art has become challenged again. Quality has taken another hit, and tactile album art has an unknown future at this point. Things are changing. I have faith that there is a place for tactile art like physical books and album covers and think that we will settle into something new but recognizable. I am not totally sure of this, though. I do think that the future for books is in over-the-top quality printing, paper, photography, and binding. The high price of that quality may enable the survival of the printed and bound hardcover book.

## Chapter Thirty-Nine

Meditations

I was out by the water looking at the shoreline. The waves came in. They receded. The water lapped on the coral when it rushed in, knocking the pieces of coral all around. The lighter pieces got jostled the most, and the pieces that were wedged into other pieces held on and just moved a little, although they got wet. This pattern continued for hours until the tide went out and the water level became lower, causing the waves to not come in as far and to not touch the little pieces of coral I had been watching. The coral pieces dried out and changed color in the sunlight or reflected a little in the moonlight. They were all there together: big ones, little ones, broken ones, ones that looked like little fish.

When the tide returns, it will be higher or lower than it was the last time it came in, and the little pieces will be jostled again. If the waves are particularly big, the coral pieces might get worn down or be broken into smaller pieces, eventually losing their shape completely. If the tide is gentle and the waves are small, very little will happen except to the smallest pieces of coral. It's hard to track the progress of every little piece, but it is predictable that they will eventually be worn down and disappear, to be replaced by other pieces.

This is an example of paganism to me, possibly Buddhism, one of the ways I learn to accept change through nature and the way of things. I am not looking for a story to explain this or a legend to believe in or a place to go where I can learn about this. I am already here. The horizon speaks to me in my time of need, sharing the ultimate story of the moment of change. I accept the horizon for what it is. This is my religion.

When I was a little boy in Omemee, my mom and dad took me to Sunday school. I don't remember much about it, but it didn't last long. I suspect my mom and dad grew tired of taking me down there to the church. My dad always said, "For what we are about to receive, may the Lord make us truly thankful. Amen," before each meal, generally followed by "Neil, get your elbows off the table." I don't even know what religious denomination my mom and dad were.

We had spaghetti a lot. It was really good with my dad's special sauce. Before he poured in the chili peppers, he used to heat it up in a big pot. OMG, it smelled great! Then he would add hamburger meat and let it simmer for hours, covered. Al dente was his preferred way to cook the noodles, and later I got pretty good at that.

My dad's spaghetti sauce recipe is framed and hanging in our kitchen today, back at the ranch. It is so faded that I can barely read it anymore, but it does have his original handwriting. Pegi has made it a few times, and it's great when she does. At least someone

SCOTT YOUNG'S SPAGHETTI RECIPE

Start with two pounds of minced lean beef ~~the best you can afford~~ *for each four servings*

(over medium hot)
Place this ~~in a large pot with~~ ~~the contents of a large can of~~ *a 20-oz can of* stewed ~~of fresh~~

tomatoes and ~~a~~ a 4-ounce can or two (depending on taste) of tomato

paste.   Add a tablespoon of salt, a half-teaspoon of black pepper,

(or more)   *honey,*
a tablespoon of curry power , a tablespoon of ~~sugar~~, a pinch of rose-

mary, a tablespoon of oregano or pre-mixed italian seasoning, a teaspoon *(or more)*

of cayenne pepper. Crush ~~two to four~~ *several* cloves of garlic in a garlic

press over the pot, and then scrape the crushed buds into the sauce

along with the juices. ~~Chop the inner stalks~~

Stir well with a long fork to make the meat break up into a sauce ~~without~~

lumps.
       4 or 5
Cut ~~five~~ medium sized onions (red italian or Bermuda preferred but
                                              Chop the leaf end of a head of celery
cooking onions okay) into the pot. ~~Wash a pound of mushrooms and~~
~~into smallish pieces, leaves & all, and~~
~~add without browning, unless you happen to be a nut on browning~~
                                                           holding celery & pepper strips,
~~mushrooms~~ (Cut a green pepper or two into long strips ~~and hold~~ ready

to add later. ~~Prepare~~ *Prepare mushrooms for very high heat cooking at end.*

When the mixture begins to simmer boldly, let it cook for a minimum
                                     20
of one hour, a maximum of two. About ~~twenty~~ minutes before you plan
        celery and
to serve, add the green pepper strips and one six or eight-ounce (or so)

smoked sausage for every intended serving (these only need time to heat

through). ~~I use Schneider's)~~
         pasta   the size called bucatini),
Cook the ~~spaghetti~~ itself (I use ~~Lancia~~), about one-quarter pound per
       no more than   (will
person) ~~about~~ 10 minutes after it begins to boil. (Drain) and place on

plates.   On top of each mound of spaghetti, place one sausage, ~~and~~
                        (+ (optional) mushrooms cooked very fast in butter.
generous portions of the meat sauce,) Your table also should have

grated parmesan or romano cheese; cold celery, radishes and dill pickles;
and a
~~the~~ small dish of ground red peppers for customers who like the sauce hotter.

My father Scott Young's spaghetti recipe.

is making it, and that feels good to me. I would like to taste that again. Once, when Crazy Horse was doing what we called the Northern California Coastal Bar Tour in 1975, my daddy was living on the ranch in the little red house and driving my 1950 Plymouth. He came down to the White House and cooked spaghetti for us all one night. His glasses were fogging up while he ate it! It was amazingly great, that meal. A real good memory!

Old memories are wonderful things and should be held on to as long as possible, shared with others, and embellished if need be. Whenever I go back to Canada, my heart is flooded with them— memories, that is. I look forward to seeing my brother, Bob, and Dave Toms up there in Peterborough when I go back for the premiere of Jonathan Demme's new documentary. It will be a great time. (Canadians say *great* a lot, in case you haven't noticed. I know. I have looked up many other words I could have used in the thesaurus, but that is not my style. I prefer to be boring and use the same words over and over, because that is more true to who I really am. That may not work for you if you pride yourself on your great vocabulary.)

Visiting my mom, Rassy Young, in Winnipeg, June 1968.

With my dad at the Riverboat club in Toronto, February 1969.

Chapter Forty

When I arrived back in Toronto from Blind River in the mid-sixties, I visited my dad. I had not seen him much in the few years since our family split up and I moved to Winnipeg with my mother at age twelve or so. He had never shown much interest in my music or supporting it, and he had constantly urged me to improve my grades at school before he would help me with my music in any way. So I was not surprised when he thought I should get a job to support myself while I was looking around for gigs in Yorkville Village, the place where artists and musicians and former beatniks hung out and did their thing.

I got a job at Coles Bookstore on Yonge Street and took a flat nearby at 88 Isabella Street so I could walk to work. I had a hot plate to cook on there. Beans mostly. My job at Coles was described as stock boy. I was the person putting price tags on all the books. I only lasted two weeks. I had no discipline and could not put anything ahead of my music. I spent the days wandering around the

Village, trying to meet other musicians and seeing if I could get a gig or a band going.

Number 88 Isabella Street was filthy, because I never cleaned anything. I was a little pig. But I did write a song called "The Ballad of Peggy Grover" up there. It was pretty good, but not too good. "Peggy Grover" was a play on words for Grover pegs, which were the best tuning pegs you could buy for a guitar.

The way the story goes,
she just ran out of clothes.
This world just wore the peg down.

Then I wrote a song called "Nowadays Clancy Can't Even Sing." That song had a little more depth and was more a stream of consciousness about how it felt to be in my body at the time.

Hey who's that stompin' all over my face?

I was beginning to feel like songwriting was what I was about more than anything else. I wrote a few more songs there and started playing them for people in the Village. Some people said they liked what I was doing.

Then one day I bailed on the flat without paying because I had no money for the rent. I went and slept on the floor at Vicky Taylor's flat above the Night Owl, a club on Avenue Road, just north of the Village. Vicky was a folksinger struggling in the Village, and her parents were paying for the apartment. She was an important part of the scene there with musicians and hippies. She was a magnet. Everybody knew her. She had long, straight, jet-black hair. We were all trying to make it somehow in the music scene. One of the LP records we listened to with Vicky, and I in particular loved, was by Bert Jansch. His singing and guitar playing were masterful. I never forgot that. I learned a lot from him. Vicky was a big fan of Bert, as well.

John Kay, who would later sing "Born to Be Wild" in Steppenwolf, also slept there on the floor in front of the fireplace. We burned anthracite in the fireplace, white coal. We both would be sleeping there, listening to records and crashing. He showed me some cool guitar stuff that helped me to define the way I played. He had been in the Sparrow, a local band that did well. They were really great and had a slippery lead guitar player, Dennis Edmonton. They were the Toronto sound, along with the Hawks, who later became The Band. The Toronto sound featured R&B-based rock, with a Roy Buchanan–influenced Fender Telecaster guitar playing style that Robbie Robertson and Dennis Edmonton, along with Domenic Troiano, were all great at.

One night after hearing me at a hootenanny, Chick Roberts of the Dirty Shames told me he really liked my song "Sugar Mountain"—that made me feel like I was somebody.

F olk clubs and the folk life were burning their way into my psyche. Back in the beginning in Winnipeg, I played with the Squires at a club called the Fourth Dimension. That was one of my first gigs. I was green as could be and played the Hootenanny every weekend, and I would watch the headliners: the Thorns, Sonny Terry and Brownie McGhee, the Dirty Shames, the Allen-Ward Trio, Chuck and Joni Mitchell (who I first met there), Don McLean, Danny Cox, Lisa Kindred, the list goes on and on . . . They came through regularly, a new act every week or couple of weeks.

Joni Mitchell also really loved my song "Sugar Mountain." Later, she wrote "The Circle Game" about "Sugar Mountain." It was a real feeling of recognition that Joni wrote her song to answer mine; I didn't even hear it until she had already been singing it for a year.

Meeting all of these people had an effect on me. I saw myself as a part of it all, the music scene, the writers and performers. I wanted to do just what they did, too—get in a truck after they finished their set and leave.

Eventually that is exactly what I did, taking the Squires to the Flamingo Club in Fort William, Ontario, where to my surprise I discovered *another* Fourth Dimension Club! We played there, too. There was a guy there who played a Fender Telecaster, and he played the shit out of it. He was better than most of the players I had ever heard. He had the Toronto sound, that string-bending Telecaster technique. I don't remember his name or much else about him. He was pretty straight-looking, with really short hair, kind of like a Kingston Trio look. He was there watching the Squires one night when we played "Farmer John." When the instrumental break came along in the song, I just went crazy on the guitar solo. I had just started to do that. One night it just happened, and now I was doing it all the time.

When the set was over, he came up to me.

"What the fuck was that?!" He exclaimed. "What the hell were you doing? I have never heard anything like that in my life! It was fucking great, man! Shit!"

I knew that while I was playing like that I was out of my mind. It felt right, but I don't know what it was. Every note was out of the blue! I went places I had never gone before with no fear. It made an impression on him, and me too. That was the beginning of something. I knew I was doing something that had just come out of me, not something I learned, but something that *was* me.

With David Geffen (left) and Elliot Roberts, at Lookout Management offices in West Hollywood, 1971.

## Chapter Forty-One

Friends for Life

My manager, Elliot Roberts, plays such a large part in everything I am doing that it makes more sense to say what *we* are doing! I speak with Elliot five times a day at least. Everything we do, we talk about. He advises me on every move I make. I am involved in a lot of things and I am capable of screwing every one of them up without even trying. That is why I consult with my Wise Counselor on every little thing.

We fight. We argue. We laugh. We cry.

There is something to long-term relationships and loyalty that you learn over time. There are pitfalls to avoid, grooves that become ruts that you need to climb out of, and relationships that sour for one reason or another that still have to be managed gracefully. Because I tend to avoid the confrontations and delivering bad news, I am not good at doing any of that. Elliot is. He knows how to communicate where I don't. That is why I am where I am now.

He has a cell phone as his instrument. He is tech savvy, but he is a people person, believing in face-to-face relationships and speaking relationships being at the core of any e-mail. He hardly ever writes an e-mail. He has to talk directly to people. Just as I wake up every day with a new idea, he wakes up every day with a new approach to solving the problems that arise with the projects I am already immersed in. There are a lot of them. This is our pattern.

As I've said, he is also one of the funniest people I have ever met. He is full of one-liners, and I love to hear him talk when he is on a roll. Oh my God, he blows people's minds with some of his insights and humorous comments. If there is a heavy meeting, he is the icebreaker. Let me tell you a typical Elliot story: We were having a meeting in an office in San Francisco. Our agents were there and we were talking about the future of our music system project, negotiating some fine points having to do with a lot of money and my control of the business. It was a little tense in the room. The negotiations continued. Elliot made some strong statements, and the other people there did, too. It was not an easy situation, but we all had a common goal. Elliot reminded everyone of that. Eventually we got what we needed. The room was still tense. Elliot looked his adversary squarely in the eye and said, "I just want you to know, we have no issues at all with your partner's drinking problem. It's really not a problem to us." There was a pause. Everyone started laughing uproariously! Elliot had brought the house down. His ability to move seamlessly from one mode to another is unbelievable.

Elliot navigates the rocky shoals of Respect. He is not perfect, and neither am I. If we shipwreck, we jump in the same lifeboat and row like hell. Thank you, Elliot.

Elliot and I have a long history with David Geffen. David started in the mailroom at William Morris, as did Elliot. David was a master of the deal, as was Elliot. David shaped a lot of things and was an artist himself. He played a deal like it was a Stradivarius. He was always on the phone in his office when we all started out together. He and Elliot were Geffen-Roberts, our managers. A superstar in his field, David was used to winning and expected to be successful at everything he did, and he was successful at *almost* everything he tried to do. His first foray into film was not a success, and I can't even remember what it was. That was a rarity, in that he did not succeed. Geffen Records was not the success I think he expected it to be. He had a lot of great artists on board and wanted to re-create Asylum Records, which was a total success, giving artists freedom. It was the ultimate label. The Eagles were one of the first acts. David's taste was great, having started with Laura Nyro, who we all loved as a great artist and unique presence, but Geffen Records never quite achieved the success he'd hoped to reach.

I think David's biggest failure was with me. I was happy to move to Geffen Records. Things had fallen off a bit at Reprise, and my last couple of records had not been that successful; that was not because of Reprise, it was because careers go up and down. Some records are hits and some are great but are not commercial. That's just how it is. Reprise did a fine job of presenting all of my records in a way that did them justice, even if they were not commercially successful. *Tonight's the Night* is a great example of that, as is *On the Beach*. They were not *Harvest*, but they were good representations of where I was at the time. I was really interested in communicating what I felt at the time, more interested in that than succeeding commercially, and it was in that spirit that I moved to Geffen Records.

I made a record called *Island in the Sun* about the planet Earth and invited David over to hear it at the house I had rented in Hawaii. He was not impressed with it and asked me to do something else. That was the first time that had ever happened to me. It was a good record, and I liked it. To accommodate David, I thought I would do a record that was a combination of that one and one that I was already hearing in my head to follow it up. The second one, *Trans*, was inspired by my son Ben and his communication challenges. Because of Ben's quadriplegia, he couldn't talk or communicate in a way that most people could understand, so I made a record where I sang through a machine and most people couldn't understand what I was saying, either.

I felt like it was art, an expression of something deeply personal. I called it *Trans*, meaning trying to get across from one world to another, being locked in a body without an intelligible voice, trying to communicate through the use of machines, computers, switches, and other devices. It was a very deep and inaccessible concept.

I had visions of a series of videos to support it. They were set in a hospital with a lot of scientists and doctors trying to unlock the secrets of a little being who had so much to say and no way to say it. *Trans* should have been just that group of songs, not a combination of those and some from *Island in the Sun*, which diluted it. There were a lot of robots and half humans in the video dreams. Even though I had ideas on how to do it inexpensively, Geffen Records would not fund those videos.

When *Trans*, my first record for Geffen, was not a commercial success, it was obviously because it was a weird record in the eyes of some of my listeners. I was singing through a vocoder about things they did not understand, and they could not see the characters I was doing because there were no videos to go with them. Geffen Records tried to present it like it was a hit record, using their publicity machine. But it was incomplete without the videos and should not have been overpresented. It should have been pushed subtly. I had different goals from my new record company. So the lesson from that is I should not have caved to Geffen in the first place. I should have put out *Island in the Sun* in its original form and then I should have done *Trans*, with more room for the *Trans* songs to establish themselves as a complete cohesive atmosphere. I had betrayed myself by not staying true to my art and following the muse.

After that, the Guy Who Was President of Geffen started telling me what to do. He told me to make a rock and roll record. So perhaps vindictively, I gave them a record called *Everybody's Rockin'* that was traditional old rock and roll, literally what he had asked me to do. I conveyed his misguided request into an expression by becoming an old-fashioned rocker. Of course, my literal interpretation was not what he had in mind. He wanted *Rust Never Sleeps*. I think the Guy Who Was President was under pressure to deliver big hits.

Then I made a record in Nashville called *Old Ways*. They didn't like it, either. I didn't put it out. Then I did another record in Nashville that I called *Old Ways* as well.

I liked it.

They hated it.

They released it, but buried it completely, just like my previous two records. They were not behind them, because they were not box-office hits.

I was not doing what I was told to do. And they sued me for making music "uncharacteristic of Neil Young." That was Geffen Records' biggest mistake, I think. The mistakes all started when I caved and didn't give them *Island in the Sun*. They wanted me to be commercially successful, and I wanted to be an artist expressing myself—those two goals are not always compatible. I was expecting the same artistic freedom that Geffen gave his Asylum Records artists, but Geffen Records wanted me to be a smash, selling millions of records. Most important, Geffen was not hands-on at Geffen Records. He had other people doing that. It showed.

The lawyers got in a pissing contest and made things much worse. It was egos and Hollywood nightmares. But it's over, and I still love David. He just let his record company make a big mistake with me and was disconnected from what was happening.

Some people think there must be bad blood between us. No. There isn't any. David is still one of my best friends, a very brilliant, generous, and caring man, doing so much for AIDS research and so much for the arts, as well as the Bridge School and countless other projects. We go back.

## Chapter Forty-Two

The Aloha Garage is part of our property in Hawaii. There is a red 1971 Cadillac Eldorado convertible in the Aloha Garage. It must be the only one on the island, maybe even the whole Hawaiian Islands! Given my history with cars, particularly Eldorado convertibles, you would have to agree that it is significant that that car was in the garage of the house Pegi found for us and was not known to us at the time of the purchase.

I think we may have found out about it on the list of things the owner was "throwing in" to the purchase. Anyway, there she sits. Really nice faded original red paint and beautifully worn red leather interior. When we fly over to the island, Tom and Nell, our caretakers, always bring the Eldorado out to meet the plane, and then Pegi and I drive back to the Aloha Garage, which takes around a half hour. It is so cool to see that car waiting in the middle of a bunch of SUVs at the airport!

As I sit here today, writing this book, I cannot help but wonder about the significance of that car and our big green lawn with the palm trees blowing in the wind, two of my biggest dreams, coming to me at the same time in the same place. Right now I am listening to the wind blowing and rustling through the palms, the sound of the ocean just feet away, and the sun is beginning to sink into the waves. I see that big green lawn and remember the crazy nights when I would be amped out of my mind on coke, just praying that someday I could find relief and just be in a place like this, with the elements all working together to caress my senses.

For a while that happened a lot. I was into the drug so much that I would end up having the same dream very often, just being there amped out of my mind, wondering if and when I would be able to sleep, wishing I were on an island with the big green lawn and the palm fronds rustling, feeling that gentle wind. It was a recurring dream then, and now it is a reality.

Marc Benioff and Greg McManus are our neighbors in Hawaii. Marc, founder of Salesforce.com, and Greg, who owns and operates the Napa Valley Wine Train, scooped me up to go to Kona and trip around Costco and Sports Authority for an afternoon. These two guys are my good friends, and I very much enjoy hanging out with them. Costco and Sports Authority are like cultural centers here on the Big Island. You might get a similar feeling from walking around in them for a few hours, looking at the displays, as you would in a big museum in some forgotten future.

We started off at Costco by mistakenly going in the OUT door and being redirected by a helpful associate. First the flat-screen TVs greeted us with their shiny displays mirroring all of the neon lights in the ceiling. I learned that some screens are less reflective and noted that for a future upgrade to our existing TV. I also noted all of the online services that are now available on standard television sets. Things are evolving at a rapid rate.

My first big purchase was a set of replacement brushes for my Sonicare toothbrush, a product I am very impressed with. I really needed those and had been wondering how to find them. We wandered on through aisles of myriad products before we reached the book department, where Marc purchased several books for his little daughter, Leia. She is a beautiful and bright child who calls me Uncle Neil and asks me where my guitar is. We made a note to look for a guitar for her, but only found ukuleles at Costco. A plan was made to locate a music store. There were no records for sale at Costco except for local Hawaiian. I was happy for the locals.

The food department was awesome, with organic chicken breasts, much to my surprise. I am very big on organic food and did not expect to see it in Costco. Further exploration led to a staggering variety of fruits and vegetables, meats, fish, and local foods. Endless rows of packaged goods dazzled the eye. A guy went by with his cart completely full of chips, overflowing with a wide variety of brands.

For a moment I remembered the mom-and-pop record stores of my youth and the little towns I had lived in with families running the stores and restaurants, gas stations, clothing stores, and bakeries. I felt pretty old for a moment. Then I regrouped and realized I was alive and should be thankful.

You can find anything at Costco. After about two hours of walking the aisles, we had finally made it to the checkout with my new Fisker.

Next, Sports Authority beckoned, and the guys made some purchases. I came up empty. Greg got a nice wearable camera. Eventually we made our way to a music store. I was excited to get a guitar for Leia. Oddly, the store was called Kona Bay Books, and was located in the industrial area at the end of a funky parking lot. It featured CDs and DVDs, new and used. The doors opened and we entered an expansive store of used books, literally hundreds of thousands of them, categorized alphabetically by type and author.

The aisles were huge, very, very long, with the books stacked on homemade wooden shelves. Marc was way down one aisle along the wall looking in a box on the floor marked with a big letter Y. There was my life's work, all my CDs thrown in a box on the floor.

"Here you are!" said Marc.

As he sifted through the CDs, I saw the titles flying by and had flashes of memory of each one. There were about thirty or forty different albums in the box. I felt suddenly very sad. All of these people had given up their CDs! The original vinyl versions all sounded much better than the CDs, but they were still important to me. I had spent so long making each one, pouring myself into it, making it sound great. Now they were all in this little box, shadows of their former selves. If someone wanted to hear one of my old records, it was either on CD or online. This store was closing in on me. I found an old Clive Cussler book I must have missed back in the day, bought it for $2.50, and headed for the door. That place had become very depressing. I was overwhelmed with the reality of what had happened to my lifetime's work.

Stopping at the checkout, I inquired, "Do you carry vinyl?"

"Oh no, there's no demand for that," said the young lady at the cash register.

Next was a health food store located next door. I was not

really comfortable in there for some reason, so I waited outside at a little plastic table and chair, looking at the parking lot surrounded by a barbed-wire fence. Greg came out and offered me some coconut water. I was down. I was actually tanking.

"That's what's supposed to happen!" Marc said later. "We go on that trip to screw with our minds. That much sensory input is going to overwhelm the subconscious. It's the best way to shock your system out of the Hawaii nirvana!"

I am fascinated by the power of nature.

When the great Pacific earthquake hit in the spring of 2011 and the resulting tsunami devastated Japan, I was wondering how our beach house would make out when the waves reached the Hawaiian coast. Like everyone else, I watched on TV and the Internet. Our neighbor Greg had set up a webcam so we could watch it live. We couldn't see much, but could tell that the water level fell and then rose a few feet at least. Actually, the water rose and went right under our house! It went around the back of our house first and then went right under, leaving some debris there and doing about $10,000 of damage to the property. It knocked a hole in a gate we had that opened up so we could walk out to the shore. That had to be repaired. Some appliances that were located under the house had to be replaced.

I wish I had been there to watch. I would have liked to stay on the property and see that. Of course, that would have been too dangerous, because no one was really sure how big of an event it was going to be. We were so lucky compared to our Japanese friends.

Katy Lowry, a beautiful young lady of about ninety who grew up in our house a long time ago, has some stories about the old days. She told us that the house was built with wood that was brought into the bay on little boats, dropped into the water, and floated ashore. She also pointed out to us that there used to be sand in front of the seawall where there is only water and lava now. The water has risen a remarkable amount since the 1920s, more than you would think when you compare to the statistics of how much the sea level has risen in the last one hundred years— quite a bit more. Katy also told us that when other tidal waves have come in the past, fish and eels have been found on the lawn behind our house.

We should invite Katy down for dinner sometime. (Pegi says she brings her own food in a Tupperware container.) There are more stories I would love to hear. We could have a great dinner and screen all of the old movies of the area that we have collected that show the old ways and original buildings, how everyone used to dress, the old fishing traditions, dirt roads, and overgrown areas. Time passes, and these events are a way to keep track, to keep the history moving. The older I get, the more important things like that are to me. We are living right on the edge. They would never let us build here now with the regulations that are in place. I would love to stand on the upper deck of the house and watch a tsunami happen sometime, but I am sure the authorities would insist on our leaving and going to a safe area.

Time, the great healer, also brings the future. No one knows what is going to happen, so it is scary and exciting. That is why every day is so valuable and every minute so precious. On-the-spot decisions on what to do next are abundant. Life is unpredictable. My neighbor Greg called to see if I wanted to fly to Maui with him this morning, and I said that I think I will stay because I am writing. Poncho is coming by at eleven for a visit. It takes Poncho a lot of preparation to leave his garden. He is a bit of a recluse. I don't want to miss that visit. The flight to Maui is appealing, though. It's just a short one. I have made my decision, but it is lingering, and I've gone over it a few times. Basically I don't want to leave this spot. I am here and grounded. That would change big-time if I were to fly to Maui.

Ben Young is out on the deck with his team, having breakfast through his tube. I wonder how that feels. He seems to be content with it, although I am having some trouble reconciling the fact that Ben does not get all the big tastes anymore. He used to love Milanos and milk after every evening dinner. It was a tradition. Sometimes we still give him a tiny taste, just for old times' sake. He is so accepting. It's a marvel. He is the most accepting human being I have ever met, and he is very happy. Not all the time, mind you; he has a flair for impatience if he is going somewhere and there is a delay. He just yells! You know he is pissed. There is no stopping him. More power to you, Ben Young!

We had to stop feeding Ben Young by mouth because his lungs have become compromised by all of the aspirating he does.

It's a complex thing, eating. The body does a lot of work to protect itself and keep food out of the lungs. Ben's body is not working like a normal body does. Ben and Dustin and Uncle Tony are out on the deck listening to tunes on the computer and grooving. Ben's next support team is incoming for a shift. Uncle Marian and Ben Bourdon arrive in Hawaii today from the mainland, and the switch takes place around twelve-thirty. Time marches on. Because of this support, Ben has a very full life and keeps moving around, doing things, seeing people, and going to events. I reflect on this. Life is good.

*My brother, Bob, holding a rifle, and me with a bow, Omemee,
Ontario, 1955.*

Chapter Forty-Three

B ack in Omemee, there is a grade school called the Scott Young Public School, named after my dad. The original town school, the one I went to for grades one and two, was down by the swamp or bog, as it was called back in the day. That school is gone now. My first teacher, Miss Lamb, used to pick me up by my chin whenever I was misbehaving or not heading in the right direction. My partner in crime back then was Henry Mason. He and I laughed a lot at the funny faces we all would make behind Miss Lamb's back. He was hysterical, as I remember. This was way before my dad became a famous Canadian writer.

I did take the family up to Ontario from California for the opening ceremonies of the Scott Young School in 1993, and that was quite an event. The ceremonies were held on the stage in the gym, doubling as an auditorium, as was the tradition with most schools in Canada. I think the choir sang "Helpless." There were a lot of talks about the past and the history of the old school by various speakers and local luminaries. Most notably to me, Miss Lamb was there.

My dad spoke. He was always comfortable in front of people and was relaxed and happy about the whole thing. He recognized a lot of people who were in the audience, and mentioned those who had passed away, and then made a joke about not talking too long and forgetting what he was saying. I am very proud of my dad. I remember having a good feeling that day. He was very eloquent, and everybody liked him.

The new school was right where the old baseball field and hockey rink used to be. That used to be right behind the Omemee train station, and ball games were regularly played there, which I attended. An old steam engine used to haul a passenger train through town twice a day when I was a kid, and we used to go back to the tracks about a half mile behind my house and put pennies on the rails to watch them get flattened by the train as it rumbled by. I would put my ear down on the rail so I could hear the train coming before I could see it. Once we heard the train, we would carefully place the coins on the rail and then wait for the big moment to arrive.

Recently my brother, Bob, and I took a walk along the track bed. It's a walking trail now, really beautiful. The rails are all gone. We crossed the old bridge where we used to play when we were kids, down by our boathouse where my dad kept his boat and outboard. The tracks, station, and train are all gone now. So are the boathouse and boat. But they live on in my mind, along with my mom and dad. Bob and I had a nice long walk that day and thoroughly enjoyed it, talking over memories of the old days when we were kids in Omemee and life was in front of us.

When I was about ten, my dad and I used to get up at six every Sunday morning and drive about five miles down Brock Road to the intersection with Highway 2, where the newspapers for my paper route were dropped. This was a weekly event that we shared. I really liked it. On the way back to the house, we would stop at about four houses on the way and I would deliver *The Globe and Mail*, which was the paper my dad wrote for, being careful not to wake the residents. Daddy had a daily column on the first page of the second section where he wrote human-interest stories. Every day he would write about a different subject, and I think he was very happy doing this job. He also was the host of *The Hot Stove League*, a TV program that ran between periods on *Hockey Night in Canada*, which was on every Saturday night across the country. Now that was a really big deal because, as you may have heard, hockey is the national game of Canada.

When we got back to our house, I would take the remaining papers and jump on my bike, riding through the rest of the route that took me about an hour and a half to complete. It was a rural area, and that meant not many customers over a large piece of ground. First I would ride away along the road and drop off papers at about ten houses. Every one had a long driveway, and a dog was usually present. I would carefully survey the situation and move in for the delivery, trying not to wake the dogs or the customers. I was pretty darn good at it.

At the end of the first part of the bike ride, I would arrive at the schoolhouse. This was an old rock building of two rooms with a creek running behind it. A potbellied stove heated each of the rooms. Grades one through four were in one room, with five through eight in the other room. Two teachers taught all the kids. Right in front of the school was the playground. We used to play baseball there, and home plate was right in front of the main door of the old schoolhouse. That schoolhouse was like something out of a history book, and it was about a hundred years old when I was there as a kid in the mid-1950s.

I went back there about thirty years ago and it was still there. When I checked again more recently, it was gone, removed to make room for the new wide road, I suppose. That was a depressing event, the day I saw it gone. The big trees that were on either side of home plate were gone, too. So was the little store and gas station that used to be on the corner next to the school.

The new modern school that I went to for grade five, four hundred yards up the 4th Concession Road, was gone. I went there when it was still brand-new, ran right into the glass door leaving class one day and got a concussion. Now it's all gone.

On that 4th Concession Road, past the new school, there were four more *Globe and Mail* customers, and the last one was the LaBrie family. That's where Marilyn LaBrie lived. There was a bridge crossing the creek at the bottom of the canyon near her house, and I crossed it on my bike every Sunday morning delivering the route. Sometimes I would walk Marilyn home after school, and one weekday afternoon, carrying her books home for her, I kissed Marilyn on the bridge. I think that was the first time I ever kissed a girl. What a thrill! Thank you, Miss Marilyn.

I didn't make much money on my route, but then again, I didn't need much money. Besides selling golf balls I had found to golfers on the course across the street, I had about fifty chickens in the henhouse that my neighbor Don Scott helped build. Like my son Ben Young's own organic egg business, my egg business was my largest source of income. Those were some lucky chickens, because Don had a glass business in Toronto, and my chicken house had a huge picture window looking out over the endless field behind it! Those lucky chickens had a great view.

Foxes were a big problem, though, and kept killing my chickens, so I slept on a cot out by the hen house in a pup tent, listening for the first sign of any problem (although I don't remember ever hearing anything or getting up to save the chickens. Probably just my presence out there was a great inhibitor). Anyway, every morning my dad would come to the back door of the house and whistle. He had a most shrill whistle! It was very loud, and it was quite impressive the way he could put two fingers in his mouth on his lips a certain way and make this amazingly cutting sound that carried for a very long way. Hearing that whistle, I would stick my skinny arm out of the tent, signaling that I was up and ready to feed the chickens. On the weekends, though, I would feed the chickens only after the paper route was delivered.

Anyway, when my route was delivered and I had ridden my bike up the driveway, parked it, and entered the house, I would go into the kitchen, where Daddy would be creating a batch of pancakes for breakfast. Every week he tried something new: banana, blueberry, strawberry, combinations, you name it. (Once he even tried orange, and we both agreed that didn't work.) Every week it was a surprise to get home and find out what he was creating. We would sit at the table and enjoy the pancakes together, just my dad and me—nobody else was up yet.

I hope I have given my kids something like that to remember. Those Sunday mornings with my dad were a real gift. I did that route for a few years, and then something happened. I think I was growing up and didn't notice it, but time passed. A lot of time.

## Chapter Forty-Four

In 2005, Pegi and I went to the Rock and Roll Hall of Fame ceremony in New York, where I was inducting Chrissie Hynde and the Pretenders, who we love. She is one rockin' woman. We had a great time there. I had been to the Hall of Fame ceremony a few times before. Once in 1995, when I was being inducted myself, Pegi and I had flown out with David Briggs and Bettina, his wife. On the flight out to NYC from San Francisco, we were smoking weed on the Warner Brothers plane, living it up and celebrating the occasion, when the captain came back and busted us. He was very upset. I guess they thought they might get high or something because they were breathing the same air.

Anyway, in 2005 when I got up at the hotel the morning after inducting Chrissie and the Pretenders, Pegi was down in the gym working out and I was talking with Amber, Topher White (her boyfriend at the time), and Ben Young in our suite, looking at the great view of Central Park. I noticed suddenly that I couldn't see very well. What appeared to be a shard of glass was in my vision, kind of like looking through a broken mirror. When I described it, everyone was alarmed. When I called the doctor, he told me to lie down and call him when it stopped. I went into the bedroom and lay down. Eventually it grew and blocked my eye before it went away. I had noticed that it was in both my eyes and did not go away when I closed one or the other. So it was in my brain. That was very disconcerting. I had a headache. I called Dr. Rock Positano, who was my New York doctor. He was referred by Marsha Vlasic, who had been my agent and a very close friend to Pegi and me for many years. Marsha booked all of my own shows and the Bridge School concerts, and her husband, Peter, often accompanied her to the performances.

After Dr. Rock arranged with experts in neurology, we went to the doctor's office, and he set me up with a neurosurgeon and scheduled some tests. They were magnetic imaging tests to look at the inside of my brain. Then I met the neurosurgeon, whose name was Dr. Dexter Sun; I liked him immediately because he was very focused and friendly.

A few days later, Pegi and I went to see him in his office to review the tests. We were waiting in a little room to view the images when the nurse came in and said the doctor would be right out. That was odd, because we were planning on going into the room to see him. He walked out to us with a handful of films. He put them up on a light board to look at. This was not normal, was my first thought. Pegi and I held hands. He explained the different parts of the brain and settled on an irregular-looking part of the image that resembled the state of Florida, hanging off the southeastern United States.

He said to us, "This is what I found. It is not an emergency right this instant, but we have to take this out of your brain as soon as we can. This is a very bad thing to have staying in there." He then showed me how it was like a balloon or tube that had expanded in one area but not burst, and that it had blown out again and again and again. Several times to be sure. He said the surgeon who could remove it for me was Dr. Yves Pierre Gobin, who would be back in New York in ten days.

Pegi and I left the office and went back to the hotel. We were scheduled to go to Canada, and I was supposed to do something at the Juno Awards in a couple of weeks. It was a huge thing in my home country, recognizing Canadian musical talent. I did not want to perform on TV or be under pressure and was feeling a little shocky. I was not told that I couldn't travel, just to take it easy.

I decided that waiting around a week in New York would be impossible for me. We booked studio time in Nashville when I decided that the best thing to do was make some music. I began writing an album of new music called *Prairie Wind*. I felt it would keep me occupied until I had to go into the hospital. I called Ben Keith, and he began rounding up all my friends to do a recording session; Ben always was the kingpin for my Tennessee recordings. Pegi and I flew to Nashville together.

In Nashville we set up at Masterlink recording studios, formerly Monument Records' recording studio, where Roy Orbison had recorded years before, and began recording with Chad Hailey and Rob Clarke. We stayed at the Hermitage, and I wrote whenever I wasn't in the studio recording. Pegi stayed with me the whole time. At one point, in the middle of the sessions, Pegi and I flew back to New York to meet the surgeon, Dr. Gobin, and he scheduled the operation for a week later. We returned to Nashville to complete the recording. I did a lot of eating and gained about ten pounds in the week we were there. We did the whole album except for one or two songs, and then Pegi and I flew back to New York for the operation.

News was getting out among my friends. Quincy Jones called at the hotel and comforted Pegi, having gone through the same thing himself. Bob Dylan sent me a thoughtful collection of gospel music I think I mentioned earlier; he really is quite a musicologist with a deep knowledge of the roots of popular song, and his gift, which was beautifully presented in a wooden box, struck me as very thoughtful—I really appreciated it. Willie Nelson called me the night before the operation and wished me well. It was reassuring to hear from these musical friends. I really appreciated that. Pegi was right by my side.

Anyway, the time was upon us. The day before the operation, the surgeon, Dr. Gobin, assured me that the procedure was something that had been done with no complications many times at this very hospital by himself and his team. Of course there always is risk. I signed the normal paperwork so Pegi would have all the authority she needed if it was called for, then we went to bed. When we woke up we went right to Admitting in the hospital at some very early hour of the morning. They came to get me and I said, "See you soon," to Pegi. We exchanged a deep look. I was then taken to a small room and sedated.

When I woke up it was all over. I was in recovery. My leg was secured so that I didn't move it and disturb the wound where they had gone in through my femoral artery and up to my brain, where several platinum coils (like tiny little Slinkies) were carefully placed in the aneurysm. They would attract scar tissue, which would fill the entire problem area and redirect the blood flow correctly from that moment on. I had to stay absolutely still for about forty-eight hours, but was then allowed to go back to the hotel and begin slowly resuming my normal life. I returned to the hotel, happy to be out of the hospital. Following doctor's orders, I took it easy. A lot had happened. I did not want to do much or be booked for anything where I had to be there. I was scared to think about going to Canada. We moved slowly. Pegi was with me all the time, and Marsha and Peter were in close contact with us. Marsha was a good friend to Pegi throughout this whole situation.

After a couple of days in the hotel, I was stable, and since Pegi had previously had brain surgery of her own, and since we knew we had the best team ever to look at her radiological results, we decided to get her checked out too. While she was doing that, I decided I needed to go for a little walk down to a restaurant we knew. I was going with Eric Johnson, Elliot, and his son Zack. It was my first time away from the hotel or Pegi. We left the hotel, moving slowly along near Madison Avenue, and were half a block down the sidewalk when I took one more step and felt a pop above my thigh. My leg got really hot. I noticed it was wet. My shoe was filling up with blood and my pants were soaked. I called to Eric and turned back toward the hotel. I was weak. He helped me walk. I tried to make it to the hotel, but started fading fast near the front door.

I eventually made it to the elevator with Eric's help. We were there waiting for the elevator. I'm so glad it didn't come! That would have been so wrong! I would have had to go up and come all the way back down to go to the hospital, wasting precious time. I collapsed right in the lobby, crumpling slowly downward until I was on my back, my blood running all over the floor.

Eric was right there. He had figured it out and was applying massive pressure to my leg where the wound was, holding back the flow of blood. The incision point in my artery had failed to hold. I do credit Eric, absolutely, with saving my life. No question about it. We stayed there for a while on the floor, waiting for the ambulance and paramedics. Eric was holding my leg in the air and pressing on the wound. The hotel was calling for help. Elliot called Pegi to say what had happened and that there was an ambulance coming to pick me up; Pegi, who was getting ready for a CT scan of her own brain, went straight to the hospital to meet me. After about ten minutes, certainly no more than that, the paramedics arrived. I was on a stretcher, moving into the ambulance, and one very bright and strong EMT guy was saying, "Neil, stay focused! Stay right here." I tried to say something funny, but nothing came out. "Dropping! Dropping!" someone's voice said.

Bright lights and a siren came on above my head. "Which one?" "Lenox Hill!" "Not close enough, which one?" We sped through New York City.

The one face kept saying, "Neil, talk to me. What's your name? Where are we?" I looked at him and tried to speak. Tried to tell a joke again. I was full of them. But nothing came out. "Okay, fluid is in, fluid is in!" "We got him." "How do you feel, Neil? What's up? What's your name?" "Stabilizing!" said a voice. Then one guy kept yelling, "Stay with me! Stay here. No sleeping. Stay here!"

Then I felt really cold and good. My body was vibrating wildly! I was freezing! They turned off the street and I was on the runway to Emergency. We stayed there for a few beats, then into Emergency. A nurse put warm blankets over me. One of the doctors on the original operating team was with me then. The team that did the operation! I was back there!

He said, "I got you, Neil. You will be fine, just don't move your leg." He was pressing right where Eric had been pressing. I was starting to get warm again, but I was still shaking uncontrollably. A nurse brought more warm blankets. I was moved to a bed in my own room overlooking the river and a huge bridge into Manhattan. I was sedated, and when I finally awoke, I was with a very nice and floaty old black lady nurse from South Carolina. She moved slowly around the room, seemingly on air. She was my angel guide.

"You are fine now," she said. "He doesn't want you yet, or He would have taken you."

It was dawn. Headlights were crossing the bridge in the fog like diamond water drops dripping from a hanging leaf, continually forming and falling; commuters heading to work. She continued floating around the room, telling me how fine this day was. I will never forget her. I may even see her again. Pegi had arranged for me to have extra night care so that I was never alone, both after the original procedure and this emergency. So it was Pegi who provided my guardian angel.

The original procedure was on the Monday after Easter Sunday, and we were scheduled to fly to Winnipeg at the end of the week for the Juno event. It was a big deal because I was from Winnipeg and the Junos had never been held there. We had been trying to be quiet about the medical situation, but after the disaster happened, realizing there was no way we could make the Juno ceremonies, we alerted the family to what was happening so they wouldn't read any sensationalized stuff and be scared. Then we put out a press release explaining why I wouldn't be there. The folks at the Canadian Consulate in New York City were kind enough to offer us an opportunity to watch the Junos on satellite at the residence, so we did.

## Chapter Forty-Five

With the Lincvolt project in its fourth year, I am becoming much more experienced and less idealistic about what is possible than I was at the outset, but I still have the feeling that Lincvolt can make a really strong point about what is possible. I am trying to make a luxury car that has the ability to be environmentally responsible. I am realistic about what people want in this country. Small cars will never be what *everyone* wants, so big cars and pickup trucks need to be environmentally friendly. That will make a big difference. The people who like luxury vehicles have the ability to pay for this innovation, and they will if it's available.

Granted, a 1959 Lincoln Continental convertible is not necessarily the answer, but it is a great way to draw attention to the possibilities for change in design of large luxury cars and trucks. This car draws a crowd wherever it goes. I write articles for the Lincvolt website we created to tell the ongoing story of the development (www.lincvolt.com). It has been a joy. The ups and downs have been many, and I have made my share of mistakes, but I love this idea. It is worth it to me. One article from the *Lincvolt Gazette* reads:

A Ghost from the Past

Lincvolt is a constantly evolving vehicle. We have just announced our new A123 Battery system, far superior in every respect to the previous battery pack. We have made many more changes in design and we will be announcing them as the weeks unfold. The work will be done in California, home of the greatest hot rods on earth, both in Northern California and Southern California. We will be telling you more about that, too.

Here at Lincvolt.com, you have seen Lincvolt at Brizio Street Rods in South San Francisco for the last couple of weeks. A bare metal body, painstakingly restored at Camilleri's in Sacramento, is now covered with primer and ready for the rebuild. What you can't see is that the suspension and parts of the power train have been put in place or prepared for placement under Lincvolt's massive and beautiful uni-body during the last weeks.

Lincvolt has been redesigned in and out. When all of the new components are installed and tested, as a final stage, an aerodynamic covering will shroud the underbody, reducing drag and allowing Lincvolt to cut through the air more efficiently than ever before at high speeds. We expect the undershrouding to have more of an effect the faster the car travels. These measurements will allow us to see how much energy is consumed for highway cruising. A typical 400–500 mile day at highway speeds of 70 mph or more on changing terrain is nothing for a Continental, so she has to be ready for that challenge. Many of the changes we are about to announce are designed to

make long trips at highway speeds a reality. This is what the
Ford Motor Company's Lincoln Continental was designed for,
not just arriving in style like a '50s dream. That is why Lincvolt
is destined to be a Continental Electro Cruiser like the world
has never seen, like a ghost from the past, arriving smoothly and
silently at every destination.

You can see the love I have for this project, this car. I am so into this that I sometimes wonder where all the energy to keep doing it is coming from. I am not exactly sure, but it feels so good! Basically I just love the car. The idea to do this just sprang to mind one day as I was looking at the car, knowing what a guzzler it was. Since I was a kid I have loved big cars. It's just in me. I wanted to do something. Try to make a difference somehow. I didn't care if I failed or not, I just wanted to try. Having no knowledge is sometimes exactly what is needed to find a solution, so I qualified. I have come to think that electric power generated from natural sources like wind and solar is the optimum solution, but we need something created domestically to keep the power flowing, a fuel from the United States that does not require wars.

The movie about Lincvolt's odyssey is a monster project. After four full years of work, we have time lapse of almost all of the projects in the various shops. There was some pretty flaky stuff happening in the beginning, and I was so enthusiastic about it all that I couldn't really see what was going on. Using water for fuel was one of those things. We spent a year plus on that. The guys I was working with believed it could happen. Light was finally shed. Then we moved out of Wichita back to California and eventually had our fire accident (or thermal runaway, as it is sometimes called) because one of our team made an error and left an untested system plugged in. It was a human error, not a fault of tested battery technology.

When the car burned to the ground, it gave us a good opportunity to start over with the insurance money. And when everyone saw I was not pausing, that I was continuing with the project and was doubling down to get it right, they all started helping me like never before. I am overwhelmed with the support we are getting from Ford Motors, AVL, A123 Systems, UQM, and Brizio Street Rods!

The movie, though, is a whole other thing.

Shakey Pictures has an epic on its hands! My favorite part by far is that first ride out to Wichita in the original car with Larry Johnson. We had such a great time! I am so glad to have that memory and a recording of it. It is a beautiful thing to have, and it makes me feel so happy! All of the footage surrounding the Wichita build may end up on the cutting-room floor, though. Looking back, it doesn't make me feel very good, because the task of building the car became so difficult. But I am going to go through it, pull out the gems, and tell the story. Johnathan Goodwin had great energy and enthusiasm for the car. He gave us a good "proof of concept" and proved an electric car with a generator was feasible, but we kept getting derailed by undisciplined process, lack of planning, and not enough attention to detail. He gave it everything he had.

Anyway, I became so emotionally involved, I was talking to the car. It got personal. The movie is going to be nuts. We did a lot of episodes in my junkyard at the ranch, recapping progress. The one we did after Larry passed is going to be hard to watch. There is a scene where Larry's son, Ben Johnson, and I are driving in the car and talking about how we are going to handle Larry's passing in the film. Ben is editing this with me and is the cinematographer as well, now that Larry is gone from our lives. Not really gone; just physically not here with us. There is a lot of reality in this project. It is a labor of love. We are in the editing process now, and Ben has made a portable editing room we can take anywhere. Just the sort of thing his father would have done. I am constantly amazed by Ben's uncanny ability to continue in his dad's footsteps while completely retaining his individuality. Writing this book and finishing this film with Ben Johnson are my two big goals right now.

Today I have zero interest in touring or playing music, but that is not a threat to me. It has happened before. The muse is out and about and no doubt visiting with someone else, making magic. A little more rest in Hawaii and I will be ready to dive back into the Lincvolt movie with Ben Johnson. What a journey of discovery that will be.

## Chapter Forty-Six

I became very interested in filmmaking around the time I was recording *Harvest*. I was looking for another outlet, and film had a lot to offer, especially when combined with music. I saw it as a logical extension of my work. My first movie, with Larry Johnson and David Myers, *Journey Through the Past*, was a wild and crazy experiment that showed no fear. Larry and I, along with David Myers and Frederic Underhill producing, fashioned this documentary/fantasy piece and completed it in 1972. It was a great experience and the birth of Shakey Pictures.

My favorite filmmaker was Jean-Luc Godard. I loved long un-interrupted shots that played out and told a story. I was not a big fan of fast cutting and preferred to not use dissolves. I learned so much from David Myers. He was a gifted cinematographer. I learned how one camera could cover a live event and provide every-thing the editor needed to cut a sequence, and I learned the virtues of a fixed lens in documentary filming. David's 5:9 lens is still my favorite tool to create a documentary. I was editing on a KEM Universal table, an electromechanical editing machine that was able to run three reels at the same time, and I was learning as I went along.

It was all new and very captivating. It was an incredible experience, an absorbing way to edit film, so creative and empowering to put the pictures and music together and create a whole new experience.

We started editing in my house, and when the ranch studio was finished being built, we moved over there and continued. It is impossible to explain what that movie, *Journey Through the Past*, is or what it means; you just need to see it to understand. It is not *Citizen Kane* or *Gone With the Wind*. (The reviewers made that pretty evident.) I am not a mainstream movie guy. But it was a *way* early music video long form, in some obscure ways. We were proud of it. I wish Larry Johnson was still around so we could continue our life's work together. I guess that's why they call it "life's work."

We began by going to the South and doing some filming in and around the Carolinas and then Nashville. I had released "Southern Man" and wanted some aerial footage to use with the guitar jamming instrumentals. There was a good CSNY version we had on film that I wanted to embellish. While we were in Nashville, we started traveling around doing documentary shoots. We did one in a junkyard and one at a barge launching. Anything was fair game. We went to a radio station and I did an interview with the DJ, and we shot that. It is interesting to see that episode today because it shows what radio used to be like when there were still real people involved. I mean when the DJs chose their own content to play as well as the top hits and weren't following a formula devised by a media marketing company that had been hired by the station. (There was a kid in the reception area, Gil Gilliam, who had a unique look because he had a liver problem and had grown up with it. He was very talented, energetic, and outgoing. I liked him immediately. He had a great look, attitude, and presence. We asked him to continue with us in the film and he did a great job.)

Back in California we shot an old car traveling through redwood country and followed it to an old gas station. We put together a cast of characters inside the station and did a scene there.

Though all of the scenes were interrelated, there was really no thread of continuity that was obvious. I came up with a story about a graduate from school who was dropped off in the desert by some characters: an Italian mafioso, a Catholic cardinal, and an army general. They had dropped off this beat-up and bloodied graduate kid they had in the trunk, still in his cap and gown, out in the desert, and when he got up and started walking, we followed him until he arrived at the Pacific Ocean via Las Vegas and a lot of other places. Gil, the kid we met in the radio station, showed up at the gas station's restaurant with a card shark and they were sharing a booth. There was also a preacher walking and dancing with a truck. He eventually showed up at the gas station, too. There was a guy walking on the beach with his truck and the truck was talking to him. By the time the graduate got to the beach, he was a junkie. He kept his kit in a Bible he carried around. He broke it out and started to shoot up. A bunch of riders in black robes and hoods came charging down the beach at him on their horses. There was a Bible-thumping revival.

No beginning. No real ending. This was Shakey Pictures in full bloom.

We loved it!

We had the most fun making it and had no fear. We had our first screening at the Fox Theatre in Redwood City, California.

Shakey Pictures has a very particular fan base. People yelled at me after we first screened it for an audience. A mother who brought her kid to the screening was very offended. I completely forgot about the rating thing; the film wasn't really appropriate for a small child. It didn't make the Oscars, either.

It can be safely said that *Journey Through the Past* was ahead of its time. Of course, I paid for it all myself. There was no one going to take a chance on a hippie with a list of ideas and some friends with cameras, even if they were classics like David Myers and Larry Johnson. It was a very cheap film to make.

*Backstage with Larry Johnson (Larry in blackface for a Rust Never Sleeps show)
and stage manager and friend Tim Foster, 1978.*

## Chapter Forty-Seven

Today I got another FedEx package from Gary Burden. Over the years I have received hundreds of these. Today's is a songbook proof for *Rust Never Sleeps*. These books just keep coming out. It seems like we have done this one before. This is a new edition with a new publisher, and we are doing it again. Looking through the Pegi Young and Joel Bernstein pictures, I remember how wonderful that 1978 Rust Never Sleeps tour really was!

It all started on the *WN Ragland*. We were in the Virgin Islands—Pegi, pregnant with Ben, Captain Roger Katz and his girlfriend, Suzanne (Pusette), David Cline and his girlfriend, Leslie Tellier, David Briggs and Connie Moskos, and some crew members, notably Reynoud Bos, our sailing Aussie doctor, and Joe Trailor, a sailor and shipbuilder who was now helping out crewing with us. We were down in the Grenadines, near Grenada, and had gone ashore in Saint George's to buy supplies. I picked up a school notebook, the kind with lines drawn on the pages. It was rough paper, like we used to have in the Canadian schools when I was a kid. It had a political leader on the cover, a prime minister probably. I suddenly came up with an idea for the next Crazy Horse tour!

It was going to be from the standpoint of a young boy dreaming. All the amps were huge and there was going to be a giant microphone. It was going to be like Tom Thumb in reverse. The roadies were all like Jawas from *Star Wars*! A cone-headed wizard was the lighting director, and some scientists in lab coats were the sound mixers. It was all like a hospital experiment, with the scientists appearing in lab coats during the performance taking notes on clipboards and the Jawa-cloaked roadies with their illuminated eyes raising and lowering amp cases over the top of the amps from the ceiling by pulling on ropes with pulleys.

A thunderstorm like Woodstock would have a "no rain" chant, and announcements about the bad acid that should not be taken would be played over the PA. The show started with "The Star-Spangled Banner" played by Jimi Hendrix as the roadies (Jawas) raised the big mic into position like the soldiers at Iwo Jima with the flag. It continued with things like that for about a hundred minutes.

I took the little Grenada notebook and drew charts with song titles, effects, action, lighting, sound cues, all in a sort of data-based sequence I had handwritten in this grade school book. When I showed this to Tim Foster, my stage manager, who loved doing things theatrically, he got really into it! He dove right in and explained to the crew that they would all be wearing these outfits and be onstage doing things throughout the show. I was not using actors; I was using my road crew: Larry Johnson as assistant director, his girlfriend, Miss Jeanne Field, as production, Briggs as onstage sound, Stephen Cohen as lighting director, Sal Trentino my amp tech, Joel Bernstein my tuner (and also a great photographer who took all the pictures)—everyone in the whole crew was involved! It was quite a shock when everyone showed up for a rehearsal at the Cow Palace in San Francisco and learned what we were doing and that we only had a couple of days to learn it.

The "roadeyes" (the Rust tour name for roadies) put on their black face and head racks holding the two battery-powered lights placed to shine as eyes under a giant hood. Crazy Horse had the music down and the crew knew the songs and instruments, but that was the easy part. The rest of it put everyone in a state of shock. Our first show was in a few days. We had all the costumes made and the props built. Tim Foster and Larry Johnson did a superb job making this concept happen. It was billed as "Rust Never Sleeps: A Concert Fantasy," and it was even stranger for the audience because my brand-new album, *Comes a Time*, had just been released.

Comes a Time had been a completely different type of music recorded in Nashville with a different band! At that time I was in the habit of performing all of my new songs live first, recording them that way, and then taking the audience out of the mixes. Then I released them as studio albums. Crazy Horse was great live, and that was the most fun way to do it.

Of course, that was before the Internet, and it's not realistic to work that way anymore. Any experiment I try onstage is thrown up on YouTube, where people who think they know what I should be doing start shooting holes in it before it's even finished. This is the single most daunting challenge the Internet has provided, along with all the good things. The stage used to be my lab, where I could experiment in front of a live audience and see how it reacted and—more important—how I felt while I was doing it. That is how I created and adjusted most of my best plays, tuning them by feel. I try to avoid reading about myself on the Web for that reason.

Now I try to work things out in private while I develop ideas. That way I have a chance to present the first time to a large audience, the way I envision it. Unfortunately that is not as adventuresome for me. The first couple of performances of *Rust Never Sleeps* were full of disasters, from things not working right to not working at all. If that was today, the rap on the show would have been so bad on the Net that the show would have been killed before it even was fully born. That's life!

Things change. *Rust Never Sleeps* was named Album of the Year that year by *Rolling Stone*. The production of the concert got some awards as well and was seen as bold at the least. That made Briggs and me feel pretty good. The movie we made of the concert is one of my favorites.

#	ACTION	EFX	LITES	ROAD EYES
1	~~SET UP~~ SET UP		FADE IN STAGE	BRING OUT MIC
2	" "	STAR SPANGLED BANNER	STAGE	IWO JIMA/MIC
3	SET UP PIANO	DAY IN THE LIFE	STAGE	LIFT ANVIL CASE STAIRWAY IN PLACE
4	NEIL WAKES UP		STAGE/FADE DELUXE	ROAD EYES SCATTER TO HIDDEN POSITIONS
5	SUGAR MTN 12 STR 6 AMP		STAGE/FADE DELUXE	RODIS STAY HID.
6	NEIL DOWN STAIRCASE		STAGE/FADE DELUXE	STAY HID
7	I AM A CHILD		STAGE	HID
8	COMES A TIME		STAGE	HID
9	ALREADY ONE		STAGE	HID
10	GOLD RUSH		STAGE/PIANO	HID
11	THRASHER		SPOT	HID
12	OUT OF THE BLUE		STAGE	HID

#	ACTION	EFX	LITES	ROAD EYES
13	NEIL IN SLEEPING BAG		STAGE	PEEKING ROUND AMPS
14		WOODSTOCK	FADE TO HALF	DRAG BAG OFF STAGE
15	SETUP AMPS STAGE PIANO DRUMS	WOODSTOCK	HOUSE TO HALF LITES	SETUP AMPS YDRUMS ENTER DR DECIBEL & CONE
16	SETUP	WOODSTOCK	STAGE	LIFT ROAD CASES DOWN DROP CATPNK
17	CHECK INSTRUMENTS	WOODSTOCK	STAGE	TUNE & CHECK INSTRUMENTS MAC ON ENTER CLONE
18	CHECK SOUND	WOODSTOCK	STAGE	DISROBE RODIS BECOME BAND
19	WHEN YOU DANCE		STAGE	SCATTER TO POSITIONS LEAVING DR DECIBEL CONE & CLONE
20	THE LONER		STAGE	
21	TUNE UP	TONE ON CUE	STAGE	BRING OUT TUNING FORK MAKE TONE LEAVE STAGE

Original performance notes and cues for
the Rust Never Sleeps tour, 1978.

#	ACTION	EFX	LITES	ROAD EYES
22	BRIGHT SUNNY DAY		STAGE	HID
23	WELFARE MOTHERS		STAGE	HID
24	COME ON BABY LETS GO DOWNTOWN		STAGE	HID
25	STORM	WOODSTOCK RAIN	BLACK WITH STROBE	BRING OUT 12 STRING
26	STORM ENDS	WOODSTOCK RAIN TONE	FADE IN SPOT CENTER STAGE	BRING IN & SET PIANO
27	NEEDLE & OUT DAMAGE DONE		SPOT	
28	LOTTA LOVE 12TH STRING		STAGE	
29	PIANO STRIKE		STAGE	ROAD EYES STRIKE PIANO

#	ACTION	EFX	LITES	ROAD EYES
30	SEDAN DELIVERY (BRING BACK)		STAGE	HID
31	POWDER FINGER		GROUP	HID
32	TUNING	TONE	STAGE	BRING OUT TUNING FORK MAKE TONE LEAVE STAGE
33	" "	SEAGULLS & WAVES	STAGE	HID
34	CORTEZ THE KILLER	FADE WAVES SEAGULLS	STAGE	STAY HID
35	CINNAMON GIRL		STAGE	KEEP HID BACKSTAGE PREP FOR HURRICANE
36	TUNE & SET UP HURRICANE	TONE	-STAGE	BRING OUT FORK ETC FLY IN STRING MAN BRING IN & SET FANS
37	HURRICANE		STAGE	OPERATE FANS
38	COMPANY BOW		STAGE	ON STAGE
39	APPLAUSE	WOODSTOCK BRIAN & JUB	STAGE	ON STAGE
40	BAND LEAVES OUT OF THE EYE		GROUP/STAGE	ON STAGE CHECK EQUIPMENT RAISE STEVE MAN

#	ACTION	EFX	LITES	ROAD EYES
41	BAND RETURNS	WOOD STOCK	STAGE + HOUSE	
42	OUT OF THE BLUE			
43	STRIKE		HOUSE LITES	1 ROADEYE PLAYS PIANO OTHERS TEAR DOWN
44	" "		" "	DROP ANVIL LATES

## Chapter Forty-Eight

It's better to burn out than to fade away.

John Lennon disagreed with that.

Kurt Cobain quoted it in his last letter.

People have asked me about that line since I first sang it in 1978. I wrote it referring to the rock and roll star, meaning that if you go while you are burning hottest, then that is how you are remembered, at the peak of your powers forever. That is rock and roll.

At sixty-five, it seems that I may not be at the peak of my rock and roll powers. But that is not for sure. The idea that I should have died earlier is not the point. There really is more to life than its charged peak, because other things continue to grow and develop long afterward, enriching and growing the spirit and soul.

I wrote that song right after the death of Elvis Presley, one of my childhood heroes, and sang it first for Bruce "BJ" (Baby John) Hines, part of the original Crazy Horse family. He was visiting the ranch for some reason, and I had just finished the song. It was written as an acoustic song. Rather reflective.

During the filming of *Human Highway* when I played it with Devo, Booji Boy sang it in his crib, pounding on a synthesizer. I played it on Old Black. I remember seeing the video of that, and the peace signs and doves on Old Black's strap played against the visual of Booji Boy, and the image created a feeling I can't describe. It was the feeling of the hippie generation and the new punk generation juxtaposed. Devo's influence and where they came from is something that I have never seen adequately described. They were true originals. It was just one of those moments.

That was the defining original rock version. Booji Boy added some new lyrics and sang, "It's better to burn out, 'cause rust never sleeps" or "than it is to rust." I'm not sure which. One of the Devo members later told me that there was a sign on a shop in Akron, Ohio, where Devo originated, that read RUST NEVER SLEEPS. It was a maintenance and rust-prevention service. As is the case with many of my songs, some of it came from real-life things other people said or did.

Another time that happened was on my bus with Poncho. We were cruising along in the mountains between Spokane and Seattle. Something about the Berlin Wall and the recent unrest was on TV. "Keep on rocking in the free world," said Poncho. I said, "What?" Then I wrote that whole song and we did it that night. Poncho thought he should have credit for that and told me years later he had always felt that way. Now he gets credited and paid whenever that song is involved.

It's part of the process. I just do what I do and keep my ears and eyes open. Things are happening all the time. You put it out there and shit happens. Yesterday we were on our way to the movies and I heard some guy pouring his heart out in some song on the radio. I said to Ben Bourdon, Ben Young's caregiver and friend, "That sounds like Jimmy Fallon doing me. What the heck does that mean?" It was funny. It really did sound like me. We laughed our asses off! Ben Young thought that was really hysterical. Fallon sounded like a twenty-year-old me. Maybe not as good. Maybe better.

How about that Jimmy Fallon? He is a classic. He does me so well, I don't have to bother anymore. He looks great, and I am an old guy who doesn't want to be on TV, so Jimmy has done all of my television performances for the last year or so. Thank you, Jimmy!

As an aside to you, the reader: Writing this has been a lot of fun so far, even the tough parts where I have lost some of my best friends. As we make our way through this experience and I grab some thoughts out of the bag while waiting patiently for ideas that come out of the blue, inevitably we are going to get to some of the longest run-on sentences in history, ending in places I may have been avoiding, but not if I can help it! Seriously, though, there are still quite a few boulders to climb out from under.

Formal portrait, sitting in the Big Chair at home in Topanga Canyon, with Danny Whitten behind me, while recording Everybody Knows This Is Nowhere, *1969.*

## Chapter Forty-Nine

I n August 1968, Briggs and I began making our first record to-gether, my first solo. This was a big thing to me. I was finally going to create my masterpiece. Buffalo Springfield was fine, but I was creatively frustrated, with a lot more to give. I think Ste-phen felt the same way about CSN. He had a lot of arranging and production concepts, just like I did, that he wanted to try; Greene and Stone's production of Buffalo Springfield had made us both in-terested in doing it ourselves. Just singing on some of the songs was not good enough for me anymore. I was writing every day. I picked up the guitar first thing in the morning and started right in. I was imagining arrangements and couldn't wait to get started recording. Looking back, I don't know why we didn't just do solo records and keep the Springfield together as well. That might have worked. Don't look back.

Elliot made a solo deal for me with Reprise, and David booked some time at Wally Heider Studios on Selma Avenue in Hollywood. A lot of great records had been made in that place. I really respected the Beach Boys, who had worked there quite a bit, and Wally Heider had an engineer named Frank Dimidio who had built some incredibly good-sounding recording equipment. The place was state-of-the-art, with 8-track tape machines and a Dimidio recording console, known in town as the Dimidio Board. George Grantham and Jim Messina were the rhythm section, and I was recording by overdubbing most of the other instruments. Soon Briggs discovered that I needed to drink some beer to do vocals. In those days I didn't sing live; I overdubbed. I was very unsure of my singing, especially after my previous experiences in the studio with Greene and Stone producing Buffalo Springfield.

They tried feeding me amphetamines to get me loosened up enough to sing "Burned" with the Springfield, a song I wrote about having a seizure. Now there is a hit song idea! I sang "Burned" for about four hours after it had been recorded, unable to stop. David Briggs suggested an Oly—Olympia Beer was my favorite. It loosened me up quite a bit, and I actually sang a song, "Last Trip to Tulsa," that was about ten minutes long, without overdubs. Once I got loose and in the groove I was fine, although it still sounded like me. Briggs always said my voice was good. It was unique, and that's what we needed to make it.

Briggs and I always had a good groove working together. For another recording session at Sunwest Recording Studios on Sunset Boulevard, Jack Nitzsche came in and did "The Old Laughing Lady" and "I've Loved Her So Long" from my first solo album with me. Later on, Briggs and I did some work there with Crazy Horse. Pat

Boone owned Sunwest. I bought some monitors from the studio that I still have today in my living room. They are totally antiques now.

There's a quote from Briggs that I want to share, which comes from an interview (that I asked him to do) with Jimmy McDonough for his book *Shakey*. Here it is:

> *I can teach you everything I know in an hour. Everything. That's how simple it is to make records. Nowadays, buddy, the technician is in control of the medium. They try to make out like it's black magic, or flyin' a spaceship. I can teach anybody on this planet how to fly the spaceship. If you look at the modern console, there'll be thirty knobs—high frequency, low frequency, mid-frequency, all notched in little tiny, tiny, teeny tiny degrees—and it's all bullshit. All this stuff doesn't matter, and you can't be intimidated. You just ignore it—all of it.*
>
> *I walk into studios with the biggest console known to mankind, and I ask for the schematic and say, "Can you patch from here to here and eliminate the ENTIRE board?" I just run it right into the tape machines. All the modern consoles, they're all made by hacks, they're not worth a shit, they sound terrible. None of it touches the old tube stuff—like the green board from Heider's. It has two tone controls—high end, low end and a pan knob—and that's it. I had great good fortune when I was a kid and started makin' records. I made 'em at Wally Heider's, Gold Star, so all the people that taught me were Frank Dimidio, Dave Gold, Stan Ross, Dean Jensen—these guys were the geniuses of the music business, still are.*

They taught me more about sound and how sound is made and the principles of doing it, and it's unshakably correct *what they said to me: You get a great sound at the source. Put the correct mike in front of the source, get it to the tape* the shortest possible route—*that's how you get a great sound. That's how you do it. All other ways are work. The biggest moment of my life—the one I haven't been able to get past ever, really—is 1961, when I first got to LA. I got invited to Radio Recorders to see Ray Charles, and I walk into the studio, and Ray's playin' all the piano parts with his left hand, reading a braille score with his right hand, singing the vocal* live *while a full orchestra played behind him. So I sat there and I watched. And I went,* "This *is how records are made. Put everybody in the fuckin' room and* off we go." *In those days everybody knew they had to go in, get their dick hard at the same time and deliver. And three hours later they walked out the fuckin' door with a record in their pocket, man.*

Of course, in those days they didn't have eight-, sixteen-, twenty-four-, forty-eight-, sixty-four-track recording, ad nauseam, to fuck people up, and that is what fucked up the recording business and the musicians of today, by the way—fucked 'em all up to where they'll never be the same, in my opinion. People realized they could do their part . . . later. *Play their part and* fix *it later. And with rock and roll, the more you think, the more you* stink.

It's very easy for people to forget what rock and roll really is. Look man, I'm forty-seven years old, *and I grew up in* Wyoming, *and I* stole *cars and drove* five hundred miles *to watch Little Richard, and I wanna tell you somethin'—when I saw this nigger come out in a gold suit, fuckin' hair flyin', and leap up onstage and come down on his piano bangin' and goin' fuckin' nuts in* Salt Lake City, *I went, "Hey man, I wanna be like* him. *This is what I want." Even* today *he's a scary dude. He's the real thing. Rock and roll is not sedate, not safe, has truly nothin' to do with money or anything. It's like wind, rain, fire— it's elemental. Fourteen-year-old kids, they don't think, they feel. Rock and roll is fire, man, FIRE. It's the* attitude. *It's thumbing your nose at the world.*

It's a load. It's such a load that it burns people out after a few years. Even the best of 'em burn out. People get old—they forget what it's like to be a kid, they're responsible, they're this and they're that. . . . You can't have it both ways. You're a rock and roller. Or you're not.

I wanna tell you somethin': Neil's never been insecure about anything in his fuckin' life. First among equals is Neil Young, and it's always *been that way. When Neil's got his ax in hand, it's like the Hulk. His aura becomes solid—he becomes eight feet tall, six feet wide. The only guy other than John Lennon who can actually go from folk to country to full orchestra. The only guy. I think when it's all written down, he will unquestionably stand in the top five that ever made rock and roll.*

During these recording sessions at Sunwest, my love affair with cars continued. I bought a 1934 Bentley close-coupled Mulliner Coupe that Briggs and I cruised in between the Hollywood studios and Topanga Canyon while we were recording. It had a lever on the floor that bypassed the muffler for high-speed efficiency that was really a cool feature for saving fuel. It was loud as hell. Briggs and I cruised home in that car every night after the sessions, grooving on the cutout muffler bypass and the hairy sound it made as we flew along the interstate and into Topanga Canyon's backroads.

When we finished our first record, Reprise had some new technology they wanted to try with us. It was called the Haeco-CSG system, a new way to produce albums. According to the good folks at Wikipedia:

> *The Haeco-CSG or Holzer Audio Engineering–Compatible Stereo Generator system is an analog electronic device and method developed by Howard Holzer, Chief Engineer at A&M Records in Hollywood, California. His company, Holzer Audio Engineering, developed the system in the 1960s during the years of transition from monaural to stereophonic popular music recording ... The idea behind Haeco-CSG was to create stereophonic vinyl LP records that when played on monaural equipment would allow the two-channel stereo mix to automatically "fold-down" properly to a single monaural channel . . . Generally speaking, Haeco-CSG has a degrading effect on the performance of both stereo and mono sounds processed through the system. The effect can vary substantially from one recording to another depending on the characteristics of the original unprocessed sound. The system "blurs" the focus of lead vocals and other sounds mixed to the center of a stereo recording. As bass frequencies are centered on most recordings, it also causes a*

*partial loss of low frequency information, making the resulting
sound somewhat "tinny."*

Holy shit!

This completely fucked up my first solo record, *Neil Young*, so
that it didn't sound anything like the mixes! What a beginning! My
first solo record release! My masterpiece! I was totally blown out,
being a technical freak of sorts even at that age. We went back in
the studio and, of course, overreacting, remixed a few tracks and
took the process off the other tracks. We should not have done any
more remixing.

Then the next version of the record (which was also called *Neil
Young*) was released with the changes. Unlike the first edition, it
had my name across the top of the album cover in big letters so
you could know it was a different edition. Some copies of the original made it into the marketplace, and they are collector's pieces
today.

Ultimately, the record was disappointing to myself and to my
fans. All the people who were really waiting for it went out and got
the bad version. That was a big learning experience.

I started thinking about how much fun it was to play with a band,
not be *in* a band, but play *with* a band, where I could direct the
music and interact with other musicians. I was tired of overdubbing. It's a lonely job. Since that first album, with few exceptions, I

have only done minor overdubs for color on some tracks, mostly just a chord here or there; the rest has been playing live with other musicians in the same room at the same time.

Singing live in the studio was the next big hurdle for me to overcome. I could visualize myself singing live in the studio like musicians used to do for the old records, where there was a real performance, not some contrived built-up creation, but a real piece of music. I began building confidence in my ability to sing and play with a band at the same time while recording. I was doing that live onstage, so I figured it shouldn't take too much to do it in the more analytical environment of the recording studio.

Soon after that first record, *Neil Young*, came out, I remember meeting Billy Talbot and Danny Whitten from the Rockets at the Topanga Center. As I have said before, I met the Rockets first in Hollywood at the Whisky and visited them a few times in their house on Laurel Canyon Boulevard while I was still in the Springfield. We visited with a friend of Billy's at a Topanga house. It was way across the canyon from mine, and it was visible from near my place. I always wondered what it was like inside because it was an incredible house on a beautiful piece of land, set aside from any other houses. It was pale yellow in color and was quite striking to me.

After we visited that cool house in Topanga, I asked if they would like to play with me and try some stuff out. I just wanted Danny, Billy, and Ralphie from the Rockets, though, because I was looking for a simple band sound. I invited them up to my house in Topanga, and we got together in the living room. We hit it off instantly, jamming just like we had many times in the Laurel Canyon late-night pot fests they had at their house.

That was all before music became a business, an industry, a commodity, or an asset for any of us. Music was more important than "making it." It seemed to be more down-to-earth to me, and I think that is why I was more relaxed hanging there with the Rockets at the Laurel Canyon house. It was so cool, with everyone sitting in a big circle talking and sharing songs together or playing solo. Music was our language. We passed the guitar like Native Americans passed the pipe. It really was our language of love, our shared interest, our common bond, our own. That is the feeling we shared with our audiences back then, too. We had a bond.

The Rockets had a lot of friends back then, including Robin Lane, a musician singer/songwriter. She was Danny's girlfriend, I remember. I was unaware of her history with Danny and the Memories, but I could tell this group of people had been friends for a good long time. I always felt so comfortable jamming over there with Danny, Billy, Ralphie, Robin, and their friends. There was a lot less pressure there than there was around the Buffalo Springfield scene. There were no big expectations. Just dreams.

A few weeks before the people who would found Crazy Horse (as yet unnamed), Danny, Billy, Ralphie, and me, got together in my Topanga living room, I had been sick with the flu, holed up in bed in the house. Susan was bringing me soup and good stuff, but I still felt like shit. I was delirious half the time and had an odd metallic taste in my mouth. It was peculiar. At the height of this sickness, I felt pretty high in a strange way.

I had a guitar in a case near the bed—probably too near the bed in the opinion of most of the women I had relationships with. I took it out and started playing; I had left it in a tuning I was fond of, D modal, with the E strings both tuned down to D. It provided a drone sound, sort of like a sitar, but not really. I played for a while and wrote "Cinnamon Girl." The lyrics were different from how the song eventually ended up, but all those changes happened right there, immediately, until the song was complete.

Then I took the guitar out of D modal and kept playing. At the time, there was a song in E minor on the radio that I liked, "Sunny" or something like that. I remembered hearing it in the drugstore at Fairfax and Sunset while I was shopping for something to ease the flu. The song kept looping in my head, endlessly, like some things do when I'm sick and maybe a little delirious. So I started playing it on the guitar, and then I changed the chords a bit—and it turned into "Down by the River." I was still feeling sick, but happy and high. It was a unique feeling. I had two brand-new songs! Totally different from the last album!

Then I started playing in A minor, one of my favorite keys. I had nothing to lose. I was on a roll. The music just flowed naturally that afternoon, and soon I had written "Cowgirl in the Sand." This was pretty unique, to write three songs in one sitting, and I am pretty sure that my semi-delirious state had a lot to do with that.

So there Billy, Ralphie, Danny, and I were in the Topanga house living room. It was all so easy, just like falling off a log. We played so well together. Simple, down-to-earth rock and roll. There is a cool picture of us all in that living room, grouped around a big

I wish to marry a cinnamon girl
I could be happy the rest of my life
With a cinnamon girl

Purple canaries that live in the air
That would be happy would offer pearl
We could be flying away from the world
With a cinnamon girl

I wish to marry a cinnamon girl
Purple canaries would fly through the air for
a cinnamon girl

Purple canarys that live in the air
Look at them flying

I want to marry a cinnamon girl. Purple canaries
that live in the air for a cinnamon girl.
I want to find a cinnamon girl, some one to
take me away from the world a cinnamon girl
your diamonds and rattle your pearls
Maybe I'll buy one and carry home for my cinnamon
girl

The original "Cinnamon Girl" lyrics, 1969.

chair Briggs and I had found at an antique shop in Echo Park and brought back to Topanga. The only thing wrong with that picture is the suit I had decided to wear. It was the suit I married Susan in. Should have left that one on the rack.

Anyway, I remember saying to the guys when we were playing "Cinnamon Girl," describing the modal instrumental theme that introduces the song, "It's like the Egyptians rolling giant stones up to a pyramid on logs. It's huge and it's moving. Unstoppable. Think Egyptians!" Soon we were in the studio recording those songs with Briggs at Heider's. It was massive. I was so freed by this music. I was happy as hell.

Somewhere along the line I had suggested the name Crazy Horse after the great Indian chief, and the guys liked it. Neil Young *with* Crazy Horse. Not *and*. There was a distinction there. I am not sure why I did that, but I liked it being different. I liked that I was *with* them. Like we were together, not separate.

The idea was that the Rockets would still continue on. We asked Bobby Notkoff to play violin on "Running Dry," and it was great. I think that was my first live vocal on an electric track; it is really different from all the other electric songs on that album. I know we all sang live on "Round and Round": Danny, Robin, and me. All gathered in a circle like at Laurel Canyon, singing and playing. The vocals are so great—Danny singing on the top, and Robin's rich voice on the bottom. Danny's soulful acoustic playing. Amazing. That whole album is so pure. I love that music. I love that old feeling of just the music. Nothing else mattered to us then. I can remember singing that song with them in the studio like it was this morning. There was no success, nothing to live up to, just love and music and life and youth. That was a happy time. That is Crazy Horse.

I n Cleveland, there used to be a little club called La Cave; Crazy Horse and I played one of our first gigs there. The club held about two hundred people, and we stayed in a funky hotel just a few blocks away. I was playing Old Black through my little Deluxe amp, and we all had these other little Fender amps, too. We sounded perfect for that size of room.

I remember doing Danny's "Look at All the Things." It's too bad that Danny didn't get to sing more of his own tunes back then. It must have been frustrating for him to be so great and not be heard completely. Everything he contributed had that special edge. We were really great and we knew it. We were playing for ourselves. I would go out and play five or six songs acoustic, and then the Horse would come out and we would rock the place. We never did "Cowgirl" and "Down by the River" in the same set. We saved the long jam songs for the end, and focused on the shorter songs in the beginning. Every set had one of Danny's songs.

When we were finished at La Cave, we went on to the Bitter End in New York for a week in the Village. While we were in New York we stayed at the Gorham Hotel. It was a funky, soulful place on West 55th Street (now closed), and I stayed there every time I was in New York for years afterward. Once I played Carnegie Hall solo and the set list was written on Gorham stationery and taped on the top of my guitar.

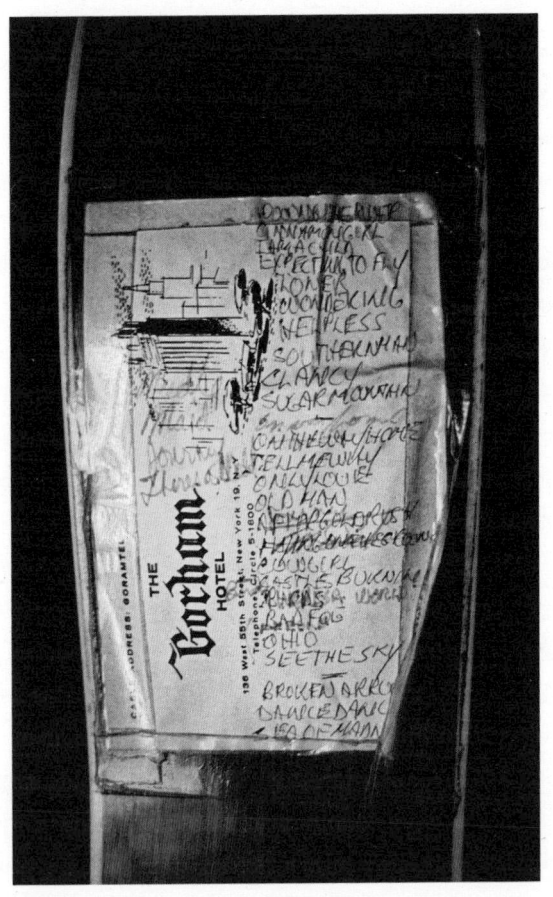

My set list taped to my Martin D-45 guitar
for a show at Carnegie Hall, 1970.

Anyway, the tour continued, and when Crazy Horse finally arrived in Providence, Rhode Island, we were playing down in the shipyards. I noticed when we arrived that there were a lot of slot machines in this club. I'm talkin' a *lot* of slot machines. A funny feeling was in the place. It was not like the other gigs. The owner was friendly enough, but nervous.

We set up our equipment and went out for something to eat. BJ was our roadie at the time and stayed back with the equipment. It was always necessary to watch the equipment in these gigs. We never left it alone. It was irreplaceable. We returned to play, and eventually people started showing up. This was a club with almost no chairs, maybe some around the edges with a few tables, basically a dancing kind of place, so people were standing around looking at the stage, which was not a stage. We set up on a riser, possibly six inches higher than the floor. At least it was a one-nighter, not a weeklong gig.

Night was falling, and the shipyards took on a different look, with the bright lights outside shining down on the decks of a few ships being serviced and loaded with cargo. There was no acoustic set. We just started playing, and soon the crowd was into it. During the second set, we were doing an extended version of "Cowgirl in the Sand" when a fight broke out on the floor. All hell broke loose, and people were leaving! The fight got really big. A lot of people were just beating up our audience. We just kept on playing. One of the cardinal rules of club gigs is KEEP PLAYING in a fight situation. Stopping is taboo. It was very surreal, playing this long jam while people were getting beat up all around us. We still don't know quite what happened that night in Providence, but it was clear that our audience had the shit beaten out of them by unknown thugs from somewhere else.

We packed up and left without getting paid. There was no money.

In mid-1970, on the last Crazy Horse tour with Danny, our final show was at the Santa Monica Civic. All of our friends were there, and it was a big success. We played great. We had also played the Fillmore East on that tour, and a performance series CD was recently released that documents our shows there. I am really happy that I recorded all of that and have something to show for it, because there was nothing like it in any of the Crazy Horse records made at that time.

One of my instruments, a very rare and valuable D'Angelico New Yorker guitar, was missing after that tour. It was never found. I'm not sure there was a connection, but I had a suspicion that one of our roadies had sold the guitar for drug money. I don't blame them, but junkies will do almost anything to score, and there were a few junkies with me. Danny was using heroin, and I didn't know it. Jack Nitzsche was playing piano with us on that tour. Bruce Berry was a roadie on that tour, too. So was BJ.

One day after that we had a group meeting at the Lookout Management offices in the Clear Thoughts Building. I made a big speech about the group not being able to go on if Danny was still using. It didn't feel right even as I was saying it, the wrong approach. Danny was hurt, the other guys were with me but uncomfortable. I hadn't learned how to deal with a dependency or addiction. It was a stupid thing to do and didn't solve anything. I think that was the last time the group played together for a long time. I went off with CSNY to San Francisco and recorded *Déjà Vu*.

When I returned to Topanga, Dean Stockwell came by the house with a screenplay called *After the Gold Rush*. He had cowritten it with Herb Berman and wanted to know if I could do the music for it. I read the screenplay and kept it around for a while. I was writing a lot of songs at the time, and some of them seemed like they would fit right in with this story. The song "After the Gold Rush" was written to go along with the story's main character as he carried the tree of life through Topanga Canyon to the ocean.

One day Dean brought an executive from Universal Studios to my house to meet me. It looked like the project was going to happen, and I thought it would really be a good movie. It was a little off-the-wall and not a normal type of Hollywood story. I was really into it. Apparently the studio wasn't, because nothing more ever happened.

I went on to record most of the album in the studio I had built in my house. Ralphie and Greg Reeves were the rhythm section, with Nils Lofgren mainly on piano and also on acoustic guitar on one song. Nils had come to LA after I met him in Washington playing a solo gig at the Cellar Door a month earlier. Nils was very young and had a lot of energy for the music. He came to LA to get started, and Briggs was going to produce him.

Nils, probably because he had no money, had walked to

Topanga from the airport, about fifteen miles. Greg Reeves had just done *Déjà Vu* with CSNY, and I put him together with Ralphie and Nils to see how it would go.

We had finished a lot of the recording when word came through Billy that Danny had cleaned up. He came out and we played "When You Dance I Can Really Love" with him, Billy, and Jack. Crazy Horse was back together again. We rerecorded a lot of the chorus vocals with Danny singing, and they were a lot better than what we had before. It was great having Danny back! It really made the record better, and it felt so good to play with Danny again. Jack, too! Jack's piano on that track is unreal. We were really soaring! But that was it for the original Crazy Horse with Danny and Jack.

## Chapter Fifty

In 2010, I decided to make a record with Daniel Lanois, a great record producer. I have always, with few exceptions, had a direct hand in the production of my own records. This is how I do things. When I started this studio recording with Daniel, though, I said to myself, *At this time I don't like participating in the production as much as I like writing songs and performing them. I just want to do that and leave the production to someone else.*

Daniel had always seemed interesting and creative to me, so I called him up and asked him to produce a record with me. I wanted to do a solo record. I could see myself doing a collection of new songs in the folk tradition, acoustic and live, similar to Bob's earliest recordings. He was interested. I had written a few new songs in Hawaii, so I was already started. It's very simple to write songs and play them, and I wanted to return to those roots.

We got together at Lanois's house in Silver Lake in Los Angeles and started. When I arrived there, I was very impressed with what he had going on. He had prepared a group of rooms for me to play in and set up the sounds in advance, even prepared some instruments for me to try. It was a very interesting way to start. He had really done his homework. Dan's team consisted of Mark Howard (engineer), Adam CK Vollick (cinematographer), and Margaret Marissen, a lovely Canadian lady who supplied hospitality and food. Keisha, who lived in Dan's guesthouse, also helped Margaret at the sessions. I don't want to forget to give credit to them for what they contributed to the recording. I also met my new guitar tech, Ian Galloway.

I told Dan I wanted to cut the album on the full moon and the days leading up to it every month until we were done. That's the way I like to do it. I noticed early on that a lot of my best recordings were cut on a full moon, and I started to make it a habit to schedule sessions around the moon cycles. It seems very natural to me.

For the first sessions I drove to LA with Eric Johnson in my old Cadillac Eldorado, a white '57 Biarritz convertible that is all original. The ride down was magnificent. Taking Highway 101, we carved our way along the California coast and inland, through Gilroy, Salinas, San Luis Obispo, Santa Barbara, to Ventura and into LA. That trip really opens up my head. Ben Keith and I had done that same ride many times. I checked into the Beverly Hills Hotel, into a bungalow with a nice fireplace and a peaceful vibe. There was a grand piano in the room as well. I felt very good. We started recording the next day. It took me a while to loosen up, and the first couple of things I tried we didn't end up using, but eventually we hit a groove and recorded "Love and War" and "Peaceful Valley Boulevard," two songs written in Hawaii, and an older song called "Hitchhiker" that I hadn't cut yet. The previous night I had added a couple of new verses and changed some words to make it more relevant to me now, and it was "a good 'un," as Ben used to say. I did that song on Old Black through some amps Daniel had set up, and it sounded rockin'!

When the moon started to wane, I returned to the ranch with Eric in the Eldorado. It had been a good start. I loved the low sound that Dan was triggering from my bass strings. He certainly had some ideas I had never used before. We went along for a couple of moons, and I went out on the road, doing a solo tour, using the effects Dan and Mark had crafted on my guitars while I was playing both electric and acoustic. I took my old pump organ, my grand piano from *Tonight's the Night* that Amber had painted, and my old *Gold Rush* piano that I had rented when I made that record, then loved so much that I purchased it. I was happy with the way the tour was developing.

We decided to do three-week runs throughout the year with that show and intersperse trips to LA to record at Dan's house. The house was actually a mansion from the thirties. I loved the architecture of the place. It was so Old Hollywood! It reminded me of the film era, with its spiral staircases and Mediterranean look; the beautifully designed windows and arches everywhere were pleasing to the eye. Dan was recording analog masters and using a digital recorder from Canada called RADAR. Things sounded good, and I was happy with how things were going. Dan told me that the analog masters were not working for mixing because we were doing so many dubs that were dropped into the digital. I was cool with that. I loved the dubs he was doing with Mark. It was very creative, and we were getting a quite unique sound. I assumed that the digital was recorded at the highest resolution.

In the midst of recording, Dan and Keisha were involved in a motorcycle accident; word at first was that Dan might not survive. I was devastated. I called the hospital and found out that the reports I had gotten were greatly exaggerated, although Dan did have some broken bones and was confined to a wheelchair for a couple of months. I got him hooked up with the best doctors, and they took good care of him and Keisha, who had suffered some broken bones in her arm.

When I first heard the news of the accident, I was thinking about Larry and Ben, both of whom had passed in the last year, and I was wondering whether I was jinxing people close to me. Thankfully that thought passed.

Dan recovered, we resumed, and when the album was done I loved it. It was a mixture of electric and acoustic solo performances with dubs. I called it *Le Noise*, after Dan. It was a French Canadian joke, a very English way of saying *Lanois*. I was doing a show that introduced a lot of the songs, and things were going great. I was very happy.

Recently, I got my very first Grammy for a track on *Le Noise* in the category of Best Rock Song. We also won Juno Awards in Canada for the record. That was a great honor. The whole team, Daniel Lanois, Mark Howard, Adam Vollick, Margaret Marissen, and myself, were all Canadians! It was a massive amount of fun.

There were some dark spots, though. When I put the master to one of the songs from *Le Noise* on my PureTone demo player, I noticed it did not have the same openness and fidelity as the other tracks. Checking with the studio, I had them analyze *Le Noise*'s "Walk with Me," the strange-sounding track. It was a low-resolution digital master! It was recorded several steps down from high resolution. I couldn't believe it! We checked with Mark, and he verified it. It was a complete surprise to me, and it sounded decidedly inferior to all of my other high-resolution masters. There is no extra work involved with making something high resolution. It is just a matter of having the correct equipment and pressing the right buttons. If that can happen to me, imagine how many other contemporary artists record at suboptimal resolution. In the future, those recordings will be seen as unfortunate.

After a few months, I decided to do one more leg of the Le Noise tour and film the last show with Jonathan Demme in Toronto's Massey Hall. It turned out to be a great night. Everyone was very happy because we had captured it. During a review of the digital files, we realized that the resolution was not full; it was a stepped-down quality, not the best it could be. My own team's excuses were not adequate, because I was not informed of the decision to go to a lesser quality. Lesser quality is so accepted as normal now that even I had used it unknowingly! I went back to Massey Hall and set up a PA system like the one I used at the show, played back the mixes through the PA, and rerecorded the house sound at the highest resolution. I did the best I could with a bad situation. It does sound great now. Thankfully, the PA mix was only one step down from the highest resolution, so when it resonated in the hall and was rerecorded at the highest level, a high-resolution hall sound was captured.

## Chapter Fifty-One

On the Road

In Feelgood's Garage there is a 1954 Corvette. I purchased this little car in a place called Old Time Cars on La Cienega Boulevard in LA. It's white with red interior, and when I purchased it in 1971, it was in very nice shape. Jon McKeig did a fine job at my old car barn bringing little details all the way back, fixing them as the years went by.

I was driving back to the ranch in it with Carrie in 1972 when she told me she was pregnant with Zeke. We were not getting married, because we had both decided not to. I think it was just something we weren't ready for, and of course, we knew nothing about the responsibilities of raising a kid. When we got to the ranch, she started to refer to the embryonic child as Goober. I was not particularly fond of that name. There were always a lot of her friends around the house during those days, and I was not particularly happy about that, either. It was like what my mother used to call a gab fest.

I just was overwhelmed and did not know how to deal. I was so young, even for my age. Confrontation was not big on the list of things I knew how to do—especially with women—so I didn't make a strong point about how uncomfortable I was with all these people around all the time. I really was happiest when things were quiet because I was not a very social kind of guy. Things never did fall into much of a groove with Carrie and me, so I have few memories to share. I guess I was not much of a partner. I was still adapting to lots of things, like this entourage of friends. That was not natural for me. I was happiest when I was with my musical cohorts, playing or touring. So that is the backdrop for our pregnancy period. It just seemed like another group encounter or something to me. Helluva guy I was. I was a fish out of water.

Traveling long distances in big cars is one of my favorite pastimes. There is really nothing that compares to the road. All of my days working with Lincvolt have been focused on the day when I would just get in the car and take off. Larry and I used to talk about that all the time. Of course I am sad that's not going to happen now, but I will do it with Ben Johnson. We will both do it for ourselves, but also because we wanted it so much for Larry. He will be with us every mile.

One afternoon, not long ago, I was making my way down to LA in the '78 Eldorado, listening to the PureTone system at loud volume on Interstate 5, making excellent time, when I noticed the fuel was low. I pulled into the next station, a Chevron with a convenience store, and fueled up, proudly remembering my zip code for the gas pump. I had Nina, Pegi's new dog, in the car. Nina is kind of like a poodle/pug/terrier mix, black and curly and soft. This was our first big trip together. Dad and Nina in the Eldorado for seven hours! She had water on the floor, and I had fed her at an In-N-Out Burger in Gilroy on the way. She was feelin' fine.

I left the AC on and had the engine running, but I locked the car as I went into the convenience store for water. It was 106 degrees. When I got back in the car she was ready for a walk, so we went over to the parking area and I let her out on some grass. She looked around and did nothing. After a while, we got back to the car and I noticed it was losing water from the radiator. I cruised around looking for a faucet and couldn't find one. In the whole complex I could not find water. I decided to keep going and find some water down the road at the next oasis.

Nina and I resumed our trip and headed south at about seventy-five miles per hour. I was looking for another exit for water, and we were about ten miles out when every alarm known to man started going off! The Eldo was talking to me. I turned off the AC right away and kept limping along at about forty-five miles per hour. No signs of an exit were forthcoming. The alarms kept flashing and buzzing. I decided to pull over and see what was up. There wasn't much room on the shoulder, and I was right on the side of the free-way with trucks roaring past at seventy miles an hour. The sun was high in the sky and it was really hot out there. Getting out, I left the windows down for a little ventilation. Nina got down on the floor. Raising the hood, I noticed it created a little shade, which I got into, although that was also where the engine heat was.

After a few minutes, I called Bruce Ferrario, my mechanic in South San Francisco, and told him what had happened. Bruce told me to wait for an hour before I tried to take the radiator cap off because it would be too hot and could scald me. Some folks I recognized from the last rest stop stopped and gave me some drinking water. That was kind of them. They said they knew Daniel Lanois and knew I had been recording at his home in the previous year. What a small world.

They also said they had seen fluid coming out from under my car at the area near where Nina had her little walk. I remembered a large puddle of dirty water about ten feet away from the car and I put it all together. I gave the fresh water to Nina and kept some for myself. She appeared uninterested in the water. About forty-five minutes remained until I could open the radiator and relieve the pressure, and it was really hot out there. I took off my shirt. Then I put it back on, fearing sunburn. I got out my wallet and called AAA. I finally got an operator and found out my card was expired. I told the operator that was not possible and to check further. I had all my cards out on the seat of the car, spread out everywhere. Cards from my whole life seemed to be appearing randomly from some source I was not aware of.

The heat was becoming quite intense, and the phone was losing its charge. For some reason it did not occur to me to charge the phone from the car. I waited for AAA to call back, but they didn't. I worried about the phone. Then I went through the procedure again to get someone on the phone. I finally did, and they discovered I was a "discontinued premier member." I told them to look further, and lo and behold! They discovered my card was *not* expired, though it would be in a month and a half. They informed me a truck was on the way. I stood in the shadow of the hood of the car. The heat would hit like a gust every time a semi went by, two feet away. A car pulled over in front of me and stopped about two hundred yards along the road. They sat there for a while. Then they took off farther down the road. I wondered who they were. Another truck flew by at about eighty! Credit cards and receipts went flying in all directions! One of the greatest collections of expired AAA cards ever known was lost. I was thinking to myself that this was the beginning of a seriously bad situation. I had a new awareness of heat stroke and the ramifications of that. I knew I was not thinking as clearly as I usually do. Nina had a credit card on top of her. She seemed unfazed.

Another half hour passed. Nina and I were beginning to get very uncomfortable. She was not moving, staying low, and panting a little. She would not drink water. A truck coming in the other direction crossed the median behind us, passed us, and pulled over in front of us. It was AAA. I had been sitting there a little over an hour. He backed up and got out of the truck, came back and told me I was a premier member so he could take me all the way to LA if I wanted. It was within the two-hundred-mile range.

Looking at my card further, he asked, "Are you Neil Young?"

I said, "Yes I am."

He asked, "Who is Cinnamon Girl?"

I told him he would meet her in LA—she was my wife and had the most beautiful eyes in the world.

He loaded the old Eldorado onto the back of the truck and chained it down. Nina and I climbed up into the cab. It was air-conditioned. We stopped somewhere near the Grapevine, a mammoth grade that climbs out of the valley. I got a sandwich at Subway and took Nina for a little walk. Along the way my mind drifted to dreaming about making that trip in Lincvolt someday, pulling into the hotel in LA silently, without a motor running, in a beautiful 1959 Lincoln Continental. I knew the dream was going to come true.

We got into LA at night, pulled up to Sunset Sound studios, where Pegi was recording, and just as I had promised, there was Cinnamon Girl, waiting by the curb.

*With Ben Keith at the Fox Theatre in Redwood City,
California, October 2007.*

## Chapter Fifty-Two

"Good 'Uns"

Today is one year from the day Long Grain died in 2010 at the age of seventy-three.

Ben "Long Grain" Keith was a close friend for forty years. I was cruising along in the bus with some of the boys, including my brother, Bob, and Dave Toms. The phone rang. It was Pegi crying and crying. I knew something was really wrong, so I went to the back of the bus with the phone. "It's Ben!" she cried. "Oh, I'm so sorry, Neil. He's gone."

I let out what Dave described as a primal scream. I was consoling her, thinking that she was talking about our Ben Young, when she finally said something that told me it was Ben Keith, Long Grain. I felt a sigh of relief, but then a different sadness came over me.

Long Grain was always there. He was such a friend, such a cohort. I could do anything if he was with me, any kind of music at all, and have a lot of fun at the same time. His death settled in on me. The giant bus rolled along over the Manitoba prairies.

It was time to call Heidi, Ben's beautiful daughter, the mother of a wonderful family that Long Grain loved. He was Grandpa. She answered. I told her and she cried. We talked and I comforted her as much as I could. I can never forget the feeling of that moment.

Ben was a wonderful man, gentle as the rain. The bus rolled on. He was a magical musician. It sank in and in. I realized right then that this was the end of an era. I could never play "Heart of Gold" or "Old Man" or any other songs from *Harvest* with anyone else on steel. That would not be right. I was so used to looking over and seeing him there, giving and giving. We spent so much time together.

Long Grain never understood why I would keep on mixing and mixing some of the records we made. "Let it go, Neil. It's a good 'un!" he would say as he walked out of the studio. "Call me if you are going to do any more." The bus kept rolling and the wheat fields floated by. Ben Keith was revered by all steel players as the original. His style was known around the world. He arranged horn sections, produced records, and played guitar, dobro, Autoharp, finger cymbals, piano, horns, and bass. He was a great singer. There will never be another like him. I still feel sad today that he is gone. He was taken too soon.

The silver bus rolled along, approaching the outskirts of the city of Winnipeg. He was not ready to go. I know he had accepted it in his heart, but he was not ready. Then we got to Winnipeg, which was the next show, and parked downtown near the theater. I went outside and sat in a little park on some grass behind the theater. I went inside. There it was, the stage I would walk out on, knowing I was more alone than I had ever been before. He was like a big brother to me, and he had been ill, but not *that* ill, I thought. I know his death could have been avoided with a doctor who was really on top of it. He had so much life in him. It was wrong. I played my way through that first show and did "Old Man" for Ben at the end. I looked over to my right and he was out there somewhere, but not next to me anymore.

In January of 1971, I was doing a solo tour of Canada and a few U.S. cities. It had started in Vancouver. Joni Mitchell sent me a hat she made for me. It was a beautiful knitted tuque with a seashell hanging on the front of it, made of wool in soft earth tones. I could feel the love in it. I wore it a lot on that tour. I was taking some Soma Compound to loosen up my back and drinking a little Michelob. My brace was with me everywhere I went, and I used to hurt a little at night and in the mornings from the slipped disc, but it wasn't too bad. The show in Vancouver went fine, and we flew to Edmonton or Regina after that. I remember the parking lot of the gig had all of the plugs for block heaters lined up on posts in front of the parking spaces so folks could plug in and not have their engines freeze up during the shows. Winnipeg was next, but my mother was down in Florida. She would have been there if she was in town, proud as could be and telling all of her friends. I met a girl named Nancy Eaton at the show there. She was one of the Eaton family, owners of a large chain of department stores across Canada.

(A relative of hers was the backer for the Mynah Birds when I played with them.) Nancy and I liked each other, had a good time, and planned to hook up again down the road.

Next came Toronto at Massey Hall. That was the biggest gig. It was a homecoming. When I walked out onstage, the place got really loud. It was a feeling like no other. It was where I had worked at Coles Bookstore, played at the Riverboat Hootenannies, lived on Isabella Street in my little flat writing songs, gone to school, experienced my mom and dad's breakup, bought records by Roy Orbison, delivered newspapers. It was a big moment in my life to be sure.

My dad was there for the first show, at six-thirty P.M., which was added because the originally scheduled show was sold out. I saw him and we chatted briefly. He said it was a lot different from the last time I had been in Toronto. Remembering the job at Coles and the little flat I had on Huron Street, eating macaroni for dinner every night, the uneasy feeling I had in his house when I first arrived in Toronto from the west, and the help he had given me finding a rehearsal space for my band, I agreed. It felt good to see him. It had been a long time. I played my heart out.

Briggs was living in Toronto at the time and had started a studio called Thunder Sound. He recorded the Massey Hall show. He thought this live show should have come out right away, and was disappointed and disagreed with my decision to instead put out *Harvest*—he thought it was not as good as the Massey Hall recording.

"It's great, Neil," Briggs said. "Put it out there." But that was not to be.

NOTICE

NEIL YOUNG

THE PRODUCER OF THE NEIL YOUNG CONCERT AT MASSEY HALL, TUESDAY, JANUARY 19 ANNOUNCES THAT THE 8:30 p.m. PERFORMANCE IS COMPLETELY SOLD OUT.

A 6:30 P.M. PERFORMANCE HAS BEEN ADDED TO THE CONCERT ON JANUARY 19.

THE ORIGINALLY PLANNED 8:30 PERFORMANCE HAS BEEN MOVED BACK TO 9:30. TICKET HOLDERS FOR THE 8:30 PERFORMANCE ARE ASKED TO USE THEIR TICKETS FOR THE 9:30 SHOW.

THE MAGNETIC PERFORMER JOHN HAMMOND WILL APPEAR AT BOTH THE 6:30 AND 9:30 SHOWS AS THE SPECIAL GUEST OF NEIL YOUNG.

TICKET PRICES: $6.00, 5.50, 4.50, 3.50
AVAILABLE AT: MASSEY HALL BOX OFFICE,
SAM THE RECORD MAN, YONGE ST.
ATTRACTIONS TICKET OFFICE, EATON'S COLLEGE
AND QUEEN STREET STORES.

MARTIN ONROT PRESENTS

NEIL YOUNG and **JOHN HAMMOND**

MASSEY HALL

Tues., Jan. 19

The 8:30 Show is to be performed at 9:30. The First Show is at 6:30

An announcement in the Toronto Star
of the added show at Massey Hall, 1971.

When I heard the show thirty-four years later while reviewing tapes for my archives performance series, I was a little shocked—I agreed with David. After listening, I felt his frustration. This was better than *Harvest*. It meant more. He was right. I had missed it. He understood it. David was usually right, and when I disagreed with him, I was usually wrong. Every time I go into the studio or onstage, he is missed.

After Toronto, I went on to the States, played in Stratford, Connecticut, at the Shakespeare Theatre, and ultimately to Nashville to play *The Johnny Cash Show* on TV. It was an opportunity to perform with my peers, but I felt I did not do as well there as I might have, for whatever reason. I played "Journey Through the Past" on piano. I'm really not that good on the piano. Maybe I should have done a different song, something where I played guitar. But something extraordinary came out of this trip.

While I was in Nashville, I wanted to do some recording. We met Elliot Mazer, a record producer who helped us get a session together. We went to a studio called Quadrafonic that he had recommended. He was going to record us. Elliot had a whole new group of musicians I had never met before waiting there.

We got Kenny Buttrey on drums; Kenny had played on many hits. Tim Drummond on bass had played with James Brown, JJ Cale, and Conway Twitty, among many others. Tim was responsible for finding the musicians, I found out later. There was a guitarist named Teddy Irwin. He played the beautiful harmonics on "Heart of Gold." John Harris was on piano. He was quite an original, obviously a genius live-wire player with an amazing touch. Then, as we started, a tall guy walked in and set up his steel. Ben Keith was his name. He was very quiet. As we started playing, I mentioned to Ben to just play some simple pads under certain sections to separate them and to also play some long, wide tones very spaciously, not like regular country-oriented licks. He made a few sounds and we talked some more.

"Ben," I said, "can you play the same note on a couple of strings and sort of phase them against each other instead of a chord?"

"Like this?" he replied, and played a long, deep, wide note that rang forever.

"Yes," I said. "That is definitely what we are looking for."

Then we recorded "Old Man" with the signature Ben Keith sound that went down in history. What a musician! Over the next few hours we played "Heart of Gold" and many other tracks that are on *Harvest*, and some that are not. "Journey Through the Past," in particular, is a great take that did not make it onto *Harvest*. (It is included in the *Harvest* section of the archives.)

Ben and I played together for forty great years, and I wouldn't trade that experience for anything on earth. I was so lucky to meet Ben and Tim and Kenny and John on that memorable day. Thanks, guys! What more can I say? I loved playing with you all.

This is a time for reflection. There is no time like the present.

As I sit here reflecting on my good fortune to have met these guys and made music with them, I miss them. I wish we were still together, and a lot of them are gone now. "There are very few of us left," as Waylon Jennings liked to say. "The mighty few," as Tim Drummond would say. What a great bass player and character Tim Drummond is! As deep as the sea! I just called him, and he told me I should have a mai tai for him. I didn't tell him I don't drink anymore. He still does. At least I can still talk to him.

Chapter Fifty-Three

Near the end of 2010, I did a leg of the Le Noise tour that dipped down to the Gulf of Mexico to play for the people who had been hit hard by the oil spill and Katrina. The economy down there had taken a tremendous hit. At the time, I thought it was the last leg of that tour. We lowered the price of the shows to an amount that let everyone come who there was room for. Johnny Tyson, an old friend of mine from many years back who is a music lover and a man who likes to do good things for people, followed us around with a semi of Tyson poultry products for the food banks.

The devastation from BP's Gulf oil spill disaster, plus Hurricane Katrina's aftermath, lingering for years, was an incredible load on those folks. I just wanted to go down there and help. I took Lincvolt, and after each show we would jump in the car and go. Ben Young, Zeke Young, Ben Johnson, Dave Toms, and I piled into Lincvolt with the top down and rode into the Gulf night. The warm air and gentle breezes make the Gulf area one of the most inviting places on earth. It was such a rush to cruise along the coast of the Gulf of Mexico in a big electric convertible with the laughter of friends and the wind in our hair! We were in the zone.

The shows were very close together, and it was easy to make it to the next motel or rendezvous area with the buses. Lincvolt would then ride in the semitrailer that we brought along. It doubled as a gym in the front and a garage for Lincvolt in the back.

We met with folks along the way who told us of the planes going out at night under cover of darkness to drop chemicals on the Gulf and disperse the deadly oil slick to the bottom, where it was out of human sight and, therefore, out of mind. These people were very upset at the deception being perpetrated by the media that everything was being cleaned up. Some of the coverage that actually reported the cover-up and night flights of dispersants dropped on the Gulf was indeed good, but a lot of coverage reporting that the Gulf was cleaned up was total fiction, according to the locals.

In Mobile, Alabama, we met a young man who would only tell his story if we filmed him from the neck down and didn't show his face. He was scared of recrimination. He told us how they were working on a fleet of boats paid by BP that had been working on cleaning up the spill for weeks, and suddenly had been given three days off. When they came back to work the oil slick was gone. Everyone working knew it had to have been dispersants from airplanes. Locals told us the planes flew over all night for three nights in a row. The oil was dispersed to the bottom, killing untold sea life.

A lot of folks were greatly intimidated by the oil power that controls so much of the area. People were down, frightened, yet strong. They are not going anywhere. This is their way of life, their roots and family history. Fishing families with four and five generations of history working the Gulf are not going easily. These things don't change.

The shows along the Gulf went great. I was so happy to play the casinos and smaller halls. Old theaters full of happy folks who I would likely never have played for were enjoying the night and the music, the togetherness and the moments of laughter and tears. You could see it in their faces.

Around the back of the venues after the show, people came to look at the old electric Lincoln, defying preconceptions of what a car like that could do. It silently glided out of the backstage lot, full of our family and friends, Ben Young being gently and easily held in the front seat by a giant Dave Toms, whose long white hair was streaming in the breeze, Zeke Young and Ben Johnson holding down the backseat. At nineteen and a half feet, Lincvolt can hold a lot of happiness.

We played Panama City, Clearwater, Hollywood, Biloxi, Mobile, Pensacola, then we headed north to Farm Aid in Milwaukee. Farm Aid was a departure from our normal shows on that tour because of the forty thousand people and a stadium, but it was a good 'un! It's all about the music. If the music soars and you feel good, then the show is good. If for whatever reason the music does not soar, then it is not a good show. There is no way to tell what it will be like. It's like the weather.

That short tour will always be one of my best road memories. Maybe it's because I had Zeke out there again! I'm looking forward to getting back out there with Lincvolt and the boys for another trip someday soon. Maybe I can get Amber to come next time, too. It really felt good to wind down from the show behind the wheel of that old convertible. I guess I was harkening back to the days when entertainers would travel in Cadillacs pulling trailers full of band equipment.

Only the headliners of the biggest shows could afford that back in those days. I wanted to be like them and just keep going to the next town. When I saw Roy Orbison in Winnipeg Municipal Auditorium around 1960, he had a big motor home; very impressive. Gene Pitney had a Cadillac and trailer. So did the Crickets, with Waylon and Sonny Curtis, when I saw them at Winnipeg Beach, sixty miles north of Winnipeg. Dick Clark's Cavalcade of Stars all rode in one bus when they played the Municipal Auditorium— eight artists and the band all in one bus with the master of ceremonies, Fabian!

Those were my glory days.

With Crazy Horse (Ralph Molina, me, Billy Talbot, Frank "Poncho" Sampedro), in a Copenhagen hotel room, March 1976.

## Chapter Fifty-Four

I n 1974, on the night Carrie's mom died, I woke up in bed at the ranch and I saw her head in the air screaming at the foot of my bed. It was a nightmare I will never forget.

Although Carrie and I had just broken up, I went to Chicago to help support her in her grieving and be with her family. There were rumors of some strange circumstances around her mother's death that would lead one to believe that it was very traumatic. It was investigated and concluded to be a carbon monoxide suicide in a garage. I was very uncomfortable, but I felt I should still be there with Carrie because she needed me. Zeke was back in California with a friend.

While I was there in Chicago, I called Ben Keith, who was in Nashville, and Crazy Horse in LA so that they could come and play with me at Chess Recording Studios, the historic Chicago studio where so many great blues records had been made. I had already played with Poncho once at Billy Talbot's house in Echo Park. Billy and his new, young wife, Laurie, had been there with a few kids.

We had played on the porch, and the music had echoed in the canyon outside. I guess that's why they named it Echo Park. Poncho had fit in real well, and we'd been able to jam on some cool stuff. I don't remember what we were playing, but it had a good sound. Poncho is Spanish, Billy is Italian, and Ralph is Portuguese; three Latins and a Canadian, I thought to myself. There was something sympathetic about the way we played together. It felt really fluid and hot, yet funky and solid.

When we all got to Chess Studios, we found it on the fifth floor of a big old brick building that really had a historic vibe. I felt I was in a hallowed place. It was funky and there was nothing high-class about it, like some of the studios we had played in Hollywood. It had everything it needed, though. We recorded one song, "Changing Highways," at that session. It was kind of an experiment with Poncho in the studio, and it went well. We rocked. Crazy Horse went back to LA.

After that session, I said good-bye to Carrie and her family, and Ben and I drove south to Nashville in the '59 Cadillac Eldorado I bought in Chicago—the as yet unnamed Nanu. That did not happen until Mr. Briggs first laid eyes on her and named her Nanu the Lovesick Moose. The car was really cool, and we had a good trip. It felt great to be on the road again; I was relieved to be free from all of the feelings around the death of Carrie's mom and the aftermath of my breakup with Carrie.

When we got to Nashville, we had a series of sessions with Levon Helm, then Karl Himmel, and, on one track, Kenny Buttrey on drums. Elliot Mazer was in the control room. Tim Drummond and Ben Keith were on all of the tracks. It felt really good. It was the beginning of an entire album I have held back, entitled *Homegrown*. I was making so much music then, it was hard to keep track of all of it and complete a record. The creative process was spinning slightly out of control because I had so much music to record. When *Homegrown* would normally have come out, I put out *Tonight's the Night* instead, because we all listened to both of them and *Tonight's the Night*, although almost two years old, just had to come out. I had delayed it originally, having felt it was not yet the right time for release, and also I had a sense that it needed something else added to it for perspective. I did find those tracks eventually, and then the record was complete. Now when I listen to it, I am not sure about that decision. Some things take a while to settle with me.

When I got to LA, I was soon in the Malibu groove. Briggs and I were up to our old tricks, having a lot of fun in the bars at night and lying around in the sun all day. I had rented a house on Broad Beach Road. Nanu became a regular on the Pacific Coast Highway (PCH). Ben had driven the car out from Nashville and brought it to LA. Nanu was the scene of many good times. There was a bar named the Crazy Horse Saloon in Malibu that we frequented. Poncho had a house on the PCH, and we hung out there, too. There were lots of girls and we were living the dream.

I kept writing, and when I wrote "Cortez the Killer" and "Hitchhiker," I called for the Horse to come and record. We decided on Briggs's Point Dume house with the Green Board as the ideal location. I lived a few miles north near Zuma Beach. Malibu, with the Crazy Horse Saloon, was a few miles south. It was a perfect situation for good times.

The album *Zuma* is the first album we made with Crazy Horse after Poncho joined the band. It's one of my favorites. The cover is by Mazzeo and came out of a conversation we had on a day trip from the ranch to Zuma. We set up a Green Board control room in Briggs's den. We played in the garage. One day Bob Dylan, who lived nearby, came along and sang a blues tune with us. On a break, Bob and I took a walk around the neighborhood, talking about the similarity in some of the paths we had each taken. It was the first time we had ever really talked. I liked him.

Back at Briggs's, we kept playing day after day and partying at night. We did the original "Powderfinger" and held it back. We did "Sedan Delivery" and held it back. My song "Born to Run" was recorded, left unfinished, and held back. "Ride My Llama" was completely finished and mixed and held back. We recorded a lot of tunes and held them back, but we released "Cortez," "Don't Cry No Tears," "Stupid Girl," and a bunch of other tracks on *Zuma*. It has a great feeling to it. Today I like listening to all of those tracks together in a compilation I call *Dume* that is in *The Archives Volume 2*. Those were some of the finest, most alive days of my life. I was getting past the lost relationship with Carrie, living the life with my best friends, making some good music, and starting to get a grip on something: an open future in my personal life and a new future with Crazy Horse after Danny.

Recently, I was in Point Dume visiting my producer friend Rick Rubin and told him about the sessions at David's old house; we went for a drive and could not locate it. It may have been torn down. It was a classic ranch-style house with wooden shutters around the windows. I saw a few others still around in the style of David's but couldn't find the one. Strangely, though, when Rick ordered some fish tacos to go for us at the local place located in the Dume Shopping Center, it turned out to be the same spot where Briggs and I used to eat breakfast every morning back in the day.

Chapter Fifty-Five

B ruce Palmer and I had been in LA for only six weeks when
Buffalo Springfield played at the Whisky a Go Go for the
first time. Buffalo Springfield had already done a hootenanny at the Troubadour, a club down on Santa Monica Boulevard
that showcased new talent all the time and had folk-oriented headliners playing weekly. That showcase had been set up by Dickie
Davis, our original road manager who worked the lights at the
Troubadour, and Barry Friedman, our manager who had put us up
and guided us through the first weeks of our existence. That gig got
the record companies interested in us and also got the attention of
some other managers.

All kinds of people got their start there. Sometimes ten acts
would be seen in one night, all of them looking for a break. It was
LA, and a lot of these acts made it. Just *getting* to LA was a big
thing, a launching spot to the big time. We had a one-night showcase along with a few other bands. It was an event because a lot of
people thought we were going to be the next big thing. We were
good that night, and though we were really nervous, it was obvious
to everyone that we had something. Stephen and Richie sang

incredibly well, and because of the diversity of musical roots, the band had a blend of music that was largely unknown at the time. It was kind of folk rock, but kind of country blues with a rock and roll edge. Richie's great voice and Bruce's unique Motown bass style brought depth. Dewey's smiling face behind the drums was both incongruous and appealing. It was Stephen's soulful vocals and phrasing that set us into another class.

Our guitar interplay was also something no one had ever heard. Stephen and I would play these intricate parts off of each other all the time that were largely improvised, and people could hear that it was spontaneous. It was exciting, and we were young and very alive. Everything started moving really fast.

Record companies, managers, everyone wanted to talk to us. Dickie Davis tried to handle the whole thing. He did the best he could and, as I mentioned earlier, we eventually ended up with Charlie Greene and Brian Stone, two guys from New York who had handled Sonny & Cher, as our managers. These guys were real hustlers. Before we met them, when they first came to LA from New York, they had actually set up an office on the Universal lot and were doing business there for six months before anyone at Universal realized they were there. Imagine that. They just walked in, set up an office, started using services, and lasted six months before they were caught. It was not long after that we first met them and we decided we liked them the best. They told us their story. They were also record producers, they said. They had a big Lincoln limousine and Joseph, their own driver. We were way too impressed by that limo.

They bought out Barry Friedman, who regrets it to this day,

and so do I. He was a musical guy with some knowledge of who we were. Losing him was a very big mistake. It was too late to back out of our agreement when we found out that Greene and Stone had never really produced a record. Still, with their connections, we were getting some major dates. We got a gig right away opening for the Byrds and played about a week of local California shows. We were playing with the Byrds! They were our heroes. It was so fast. I remember a show we played where the Byrds were pretty messed up. They were one of the biggest acts going, and that night we blew them away. It was obvious to us all that the Springfield was a force to be reckoned with.

Shortly after that, by chance Greene and Stone booked us into the Whisky to cover another band's night off—we ended up staying for six straight weeks without a break. We were building a following. We started opening for Hugh Masekela and then Johnny Rivers. Headliners came and went, but we stayed. We built our own fan base that kept returning every night. Mario Maglieri and Elmer Valentine ran the place and treated us like their own. Elmer was the boss. Mario was the doorman and floor manager. They were like fathers to all of us in the scene: the groupies, the bands, all of us. Mario still called me Skinny years later when I would drop in and say hello.

We were also recording our first album during that time. Greene and Stone had signed us to Atlantic, because they had connections there with Ahmet Ertegun through their success with Sonny & Cher. When we got the album down and mixed, we felt great. We had been there guiding the mixing process and everything. One day we were leaving to go on the road for a weekend, and we heard Greene and Stone had to go in and do a stereo mix. We had only done a mono. We were so unaware, so green! Stereo was the new big thing.

In one day they remixed the whole thing into stereo without us, and we only heard it when we got back to LA from our weekend tour.

We hated it.

The mixes sucked and didn't have the energy we felt in the studio or on the stage when we were playing live. That was what was missing. The sound was very thin, and the mix itself was terrible. Stephen and I were so disappointed. They released "Nowadays Clancy Can't Even Sing" as the first single, and that was a big mistake. It was way too weird to be a single. We had "Go and Say Goodbye" and "Do I Have to Come Right Out and Say It," either of which would have been a much better choice. But we went along with it. While I thought it was cool to have "Clancy" out there, I doubted whether it was commercial enough. But what did we know?

It bombed.

Riots were happening on the Strip. Hippies against the war, cops against the hippies. Stephen wrote "For What It's Worth" about the riots. It was a great message song of the times, with his signature vocal phrasing. We recorded it at Columbia with the help of Stan Ross, owner of Gold Star, because Gold Star was booked. Tom May was our Columbia engineer. Stan and Tom got us a decent sound. They got the drums right. Thankfully, Greene and Stone were not there producing. We had our first hit and rereleased the LP with that song on it. If you listen to that record now, you can hear the difference in tonal quality and production between "For What It's Worth" and the rest of the *Buffalo Springfield* album. We missed a good chance to remix the whole album right there and never even realized it.

Soon we were back at the Whisky, headlining on a Sunday night. We were recording artists now, and our fan base was exploding. We started to feel different and act different, but we were still just a bunch of green kids. That was our beginning, and we went on for a year and a half until we broke up. Bruce got busted a couple of times and was eventually deported. That was the beginning of the end for us.

Chemistry is the big thing in any group, and Bruce was the element that made us unique. His roots in R&B (that he got in Toronto playing in his first band, where he was the only white guy) were so important. Stephen and I loved Bruce. He was a complete original. He played like Motown, but he had an added flair that was totally Bruce. Everyone knew he was completely off the charts. A genius player. Musicians would just stand there slack-jawed, watching and listening to him play. After we lost him, we were never the same. It was the beginning of the end, right there. We had Jim Fielder on bass for a while, and he ended up with Blood, Sweat & Tears. Then we had Jim Messina, who we had met at Sunset Sound. But we could never find anyone like Bruce, and it was killing us slowly. Stephen became frustrated with the rhythm section problems and started cutting his songs with other guys, Buddy Miles on drums and Bobby West on bass among them.

When we used to play at the Whisky, Bruce and I would be back there with Dewey holding down a groove with our backs to the audience, lost in the music. That was magic. That is why Richie and Stephen sounded so great. They were singing on a rock-solid foundation that breathed and pulsed. We were so into the music back there that the girls in the audience could feel that pulse, and it drove them crazy. We didn't even realize what we were doing. The way Stephen and Richie sang their asses off, if we hadn't lost Bruce, the sky would have been the limit for Buffalo Springfield. But we did lose him. When he got busted for grass in a hotel in New York while we were playing a club there, he was instantly deported. Bruce was gone.

That was why the Springfield broke up. All the fighting was because we lost Bruce. If he had stayed in, we would probably still be together today (if we had all lived). Sure, I would have done some solo records, but with that sound there, I always would have come back to it. It is as simple as that. We broke up because we were broken. We were missing the essential ingredient, and all the momentum in the world could not replace it. People say we were great and ask why we ever broke up. That is why.

If you want to see the Springfield, the best representation of it is a Dick Clark production, *Where the Action Is*. On that show, you can see the real group. We were lip-synching, but that was what we looked like. Those were the finest times of Buffalo Springfield, and it never, ever got better. Without Bruce, that was all gone.

Our last gig was at the Long Beach Arena. We walked out and the place went nuts. Our fans knew this was the last time. We started playing and the crowd left their seats and rushed to the front of the stage. Some authority figure turned on the lights and walked out onstage, admonishing the crowd to sit down. He repeatedly said, "Buffalo Springfield will NOT play until you return to your seats."

Eventually we started to play again. It was a bittersweet moment. I was wearing my finest Buffalo Springfield fringe regalia, Stephen had on his great cowboy hat and suit. We all wore our finest. Without Bruce! It was like a funeral. We were just a little more than eighteen months old as a band. It was nobody's fault. We were just too young and we had made a lot of bad and inexperienced decisions, starting with losing Barry Friedman. But losing Bruce broke our heart.

Thank you, Buffalo Springfield. There will never be another. It's about chemistry. Love and chemistry.

## Chapter Fifty-Six

In Feelgood's there is a 1957 Jensen. It is a 541, one of just thirty-five ever made. In 1975, while I was down in Florida working on restoring the *WN Ragland* with Roger Katz and a bunch of shipbuilders and sailors, I found the Jensen in Fort Lauderdale in a little used-car place on Sunrise Boulevard. It was $2,750. I had never seen one before, and it was very beautiful. I needed a car. It was in original condition, faded red, well-worn, but nice. This was and is still my favorite combination; beautiful, original, and worn.

Its worst flaw was that the back window had been cracked from a falling coconut somewhere. It was a right-hand drive and had a unique little lever in the dash; if you pushed up, the horn honked, and if you pushed down, the brights would come on. Toggling it back and forth resulted in a classic European blasting-horn-and-flashing-lights combination effect. It also had been equipped with glasspacks. That meant it was loud as hell! I loved it and bought it the next day.

I drove it everywhere in Florida. Once I took it to West Palm Beach. I was feeling lonely and went lookin' around, found a little bar, and met a girl there who was playing pool. She had a white dress on. Playing pool with a white dress on blew my mind! She took me to the West Palm Beach Country Club the next day for breakfast, and I couldn't get out of there fast enough. I felt like a trophy. The Jensen got me back in a couple of hours of peaceful motoring along A1A, the Florida coast route. It is a beautiful highway along the Atlantic with motels that reminded me of going down there with my parents every winter from Omemee when I was a kid in the fifties. We went down to New Smyrna Beach every year for a few years. Daddy was working on books, and while he would write, Bob and I would go in the ocean. I went to school there for a couple of months for a few years in a row when I was about ten, because that was where my family was. No wonder I like to move. No wonder I love the South, especially Florida.

When I got back to the boat in Fort Lauderdale, I was always happy to see the progress and check in with Roger and the crew. On a Friday, after the traditional payday tequila, we headed out to the bars. Later that night I was driving the Jensen and got pulled over by the police. We were completely shit-faced! The car was full to capacity with drunken shipworkers. I explained that we were all good citizens who had been working hard all week and we were simply going to go and get some coffee. He let us off. Everyone in the car was amazed. So was I.

Later, after the *Ragland* was launched, Roger shipped the car back to California, and it was damaged along the way. I had to get it fixed. Afterward, they repainted the hood area that had been repaired. It was the European type of hood that lifted completely up, revealing the whole front end, wheels and everything. Now it was suddenly shiny red in the front. I was disappointed and missed the old faded look. We had to repaint the whole thing—Jon McKeig was great at mixing paint and finishing, and gave the whole car a faded look.

Today, it sits in Feelgood's in need of a big tune-up (at the very least). The horn/lights controller was broken when I left the car at a dealership to get something done. Some turkey got in the car and broke it with his knee. It has never been quite the same. I want to get it fixed, and that's what's happening now. I love that car. So does Pegi, because it's very sexy. Just seeing it in Feelgood's fills my heart with all good thoughts of an innocent time with really good friends.

A few meditations about success. Somewhere along the line it always comes up. Are you happy with what you have done? Have you been successful? I know I am thankful for the things I have been able to try. Success is hard to measure. If you have lots of cash, that doesn't make you successful—it makes you rich. (Even if you're like me and have lots of stuff and not much cash relatively, that doesn't make you a success; it only makes you materially rich.)

Success is a tough one for me to define. I have my failings to be sure, and I'm working on them all the time, except for when I forget or am so preoccupied that I'm not aware. These are my personal successes and failures, and they have nothing to do with money or possessions. My children are perhaps my biggest success, and I share that with Pegi, because without her, it would not be like that.

You may have noticed that a lot of my time is spent tying up loose ends, getting closure, and completing things. One early measure of success I set for myself was very material. Remember that red 1959 Cadillac convertible I sat in that was in my twin friends' garage in the early sixties while I was going to Kelvin High School? The one that was driven back and forth to a TV station in the States by their dad? Remember when I was in the YMCA in Fort William calculating how many months I would have to work at the Flamingo Club to earn enough money to buy that kind of car? Well, as fate turns out, I had it and I lost it and I still have it. The situation wears on me. It's not a big deal, but it isn't a success, nor is it a failure. You see, that car is the famous Nanu the Lovesick Moose! But there is much more to it than that.

One day in 1975, I was leaving my ranch. The long road out is very narrow; there is a very steep hill with twists and turns through redwood trees on either side of the road. As I was driving along, climbing slowly up the hill in Nanu, a Volkswagen came flying down the road between the trees and, seeing me, slammed on the brakes and slid directly into Nanu, scraping down the whole side of the car and destroying its side panels and the rare stainless molding that identified this Eldorado as a Biarritz. The driver of the Volkswagen, a teenage girl, was terrified. She was nearly hysterical, crying about the trouble she would be in with her parents for getting in another accident. She had been going way too fast and should not have slammed on her brakes. (That was the worst thing she could have done; she had plenty of room to stop or pass, but she panicked, hitting the brakes and locking them up, and slid downhill straight into poor old Nanu, the Innocent Convertible.)

I let the girl off the hook. I told her right there not to worry, I would take care of it and she should just go home, which she did. There was a place called Coachcraft in Scotts Valley, California, near Highway 17 between Santa Cruz and Walnut Creek. Nanu was taken there to be fixed around the third quarter of 1975. I asked the man in charge to do a perfect restoration of the car. "Make it museum quality," I said.

He took it down to bare metal in his shop and started to paint the chassis. At some point he decided he would like to work for me and complete the car while he was taking care of my whole collection. I liked Jon McKeig immediately; we were kindred spirits, so I hired him. He moved to the ranch and began taking care of my cars, maintaining and cleaning the building and the old autos, which had grown in number. He redid the entire building, which took a couple of years and was a beautiful work of art.

Jon's standards were very high, but so were his mechanics. (You don't have to read between the lines here.) Years went by. Anyway, to make a long story short, Nanu sat on the ranch for thirty odd years in the same condition, always next in line to be worked on, until one day Jon had to retire. It was just not feasible for me to have that many cars anymore, so I started selling them; I even sold the part of the ranch where the beautiful car barn Jon had built was. That was heartbreaking for Jon. We then constructed Feelgood's, where the cream of the crop of my old cars would stay. Today, there is also a warehouse in San Carlos, where

Nanu sits in pieces, patiently waiting to be reassembled. I have been told that Nanu is worth a fortune. I have also been told by Brizio Street Rods, the shop building Lincvolt, that to put Nanu back together again would probably cost around as much as she's worth. So when Lincvolt is finally done, I plan on starting one more job. If there is any money left in the Lincvolt fire insurance fund, I will use that cash to start reassembling Nanu the Lovesick Moose, completing my seventeen-year-old self's dream in one more giant step toward success.

Walking has always been good for me. I love to walk. Long walks on the ranch or over the lava in Hawaii are therapeutic and result in a clear head. Ben Keith and I used to walk the ranch together on a ridge every day for a couple of years. It is usually my preference to walk alone, but with Ben it was fine. One day Ben told me that he got winded starting where I start, so we began starting at the top of the first rise, rather than at the bottom. He was having a problem getting enough air. We adapted, and everything was fine. I miss him now on that walk.

For a year or more, I stopped the walking because my feet were hurting. At a doctor's advice, I tried wearing special inserts in my shoes, but they threw off my balance. Eventually I learned from various body workers on the Big Island, most notably a Feldenkrais practitioner there, that correct posture is very important and my bad posture was putting a lot of strain on the bottoms of my feet. It's amazing what you can learn when you step outside the realm of people who are selling you something and into the realm of people who treat the body, not the symptom.

Where the doctor had not helped me and the inserts were not working, the body workers' advice was the key to success. I took it to heart and solved the problem by working on my posture, which is a lot better now than it was. I was well on my way to being a stooped-over old guy. That did happen to my dad. That was my problem, and I solved it by changing my posture. After that, things were pretty good.

But I had another thing causing the problem, too. When I find something I like, I stick with it, sometimes for way too long. I had been wearing the same brand of hiking shoes for a long time. At first I loved them, but eventually I found that I had to get new ones more and more often. One day I went to a different store and got some real good leather boots instead of those hiking high-tops I had been getting for years. These new leather boots kick ass. No more problems. Now I have really good boots and can walk a long way again! Fantastic. Maybe I should call this book *The Shoe Chronicles*.

There *is* a reason why I am telling you so much about my shoes and my feet. Walking and all kinds of movement from one place to another are very important to me. It has always been my way to think about things while I walk. I am always going over ideas, songs, album running orders, all kinds of creative stuff, while I am walking. I love to walk. It soothes my soul. My mother always told me that my Grandpa Ragland would walk every day and he loved his walks. He lived a long time.

My favorite walk is still up on the ridge overlooking the ranch.

I walk about a mile and a half to two miles every time I go up there, and always feel better afterward, rain or shine. Nina goes with me now when I go. On the ridge, there is a place I walk to where two eucalyptus trees have grown together. One tree has a branch that reaches over to the other and grows right through its trunk. These two trees are permanently connected. I call them the Trees in Love. I walk to the Trees in Love and back home every time I get a chance.

Now, in Hawaii I like to paddleboard too. It does the same thing for me, I open up and start thinking about all kinds of ideas about music, life, my family, all matters personal. I take all of this to heart in my personal time of reflection.

*With David Briggs, backstage at the Roxy nightclub
in West Hollywood, 1973.*

## Chapter Fifty-Seven

Once, when Buffalo Springfield did a show in Albuquerque, I went for a ride in a rented car with Bruce Palmer and cruised the back roads around town. There was a road called the Old Indian Trail that ran along the edge of town and had a wonderful view of the mountains and the old Indian country on one side and the city of Albuquerque on the other.

As we were driving along we found an old roadside antique shop and stopped to check it out. Quite a selection of stuff was inside. There were a lot of old glass bottles and some old statues. The place had a vibe I really liked, and I spent a long time just walking around looking. I finally saw something in a corner I wanted: a bow and two arrows. The arrows were handmade, with iron tips that were jagged-edged and very sharp. They looked like hunting arrows. The arrows were long, very straight, and the tips were different on each one. The bow was very plain and I think it was lemonwood. At least that's what the old man at the shop said.

Anyway, the arrows had real feathers on the ends, tied with

twine that was neatly wound around the quills. They looked like authentic Indian arrows to me, although the iron tips were different. Maybe they were obtained from a white man, a trader. So I took them up to the counter and paid for them, along with an old Indian blanket I found, and when I got back to Laurel Canyon and my little cabin there, I stuck the arrows in the wall by throwing them at it and letting them stick.

I always took them with me whenever I moved to a new place, and I would again throw them at the wall and let them stick wherever they were.

They went to Malibu when Stephen found a house on Malibu Road and the Springfield lived there. I had a little separate place below the garage where we put up some paneling and a sliding glass door. It had an ocean view. A decorative llama rug was on my floor. A kerosene lamp was on my Monterey Spanish dresser. The arrows were stuck in the wall. When Bruce was allowed a second chance and returned to the USA with the help of lawyers, he got busted for the last time near that Malibu house, driving down the Pacific Coast Highway on acid without a license. That was really the beginning of the end for the Buffalo.

Later I moved to Topanga and stuck the arrows in the wall there in that house the same way, by throwing them at a wooden wall and letting them stick. Eventually, I packed the bow and arrows away in the back of my '51 Willys Jeepster and drove north on the 101 to move to my new ranch. When we were done renovating half of the living room, I leaned the bow up in the corner, threw the arrows at the wall, and left them right where they stuck for the first time. Every once in a while now, when Pegi and I move pictures around, we take the arrows down and I throw them at the wall again in a new place. They are still there for us to enjoy after all these years, whenever we return from our travels to our wonderful ranch home.

Of course, our little cabin has grown, and if you listen really closely on a misty morning, you can still hear little Amber's bare footsteps running gingerly down the long hall to the living room. At night, when a fire is flickering in the lava rock fireplace, you can see those time-aged and untreated redwood planks glowing in the warm reflection—pierced by two arrows from Albuquerque. I like to take a little bit of the past with me when I go to a new place, and those arrows really ground me. It's odd, but the way Pegi likes those arrows makes me feel like she knows me.

David Briggs's house in Topanga was known as Old To-panga Ranch and was hidden in the trees just off Old Topanga Canyon Road. I would visit David there, and we would listen to records and talk about the songs and records we were working on. There were a lot of good times.

On the weekends or at least on sunny days, we would all be outside around a fire pit or pitching horseshoes. Kirby, David's old friend from Wyoming, was there with us a lot, as was Shannon, David's wife and the mother of Lincoln Wyatt Briggs, David's son. LW, as he was called, was a great kid. Hannibal and Attila were David's two dogs, brown shorthaired hounds, who were always around in the living room somewhere. David produced a few records during this time with Spirit, Nils Lofgren, and Murray Roman, among others. Briggs is known to have driven several bands crazy with his temper and his rants about the inadequacies of certain musicians and bands. Subtlety was never David's thing, although he did work his magic in some pretty curious ways. His reputation grew and became legendary, and some musicians were actually scared of David.

David once said, "If you want to fight someone big, hit them first and run like hell!" He was fearless. But of all the records I made with David, what I most remember is his dedication to getting a great performance on tape at any cost. "Be great or be gone."

One time we traveled across the country from Key West to San Francisco together in Pocahontas. I was driving and David was navigating. When we got to the Rocky Mountains, we decided to give Independence Pass in Colorado a shot. It was about twelve thousand feet or so at the summit, and then it landed in Aspen on the other side. We were imagining all the starlets we would meet there, so we tried to take that two-lane road over the Rockies in a forty-foot-long bus. It was the wildest ride I have ever been on. When we got to the peak, there was a curve on the side of the mountain with a sheer drop down several thousand feet on the left side and a rock wall straight up on the right. The road was about fifteen feet wide at that point, less than two lanes, and slightly narrower than on a straightaway. I couldn't see around the curve because the rock wall was cutting down my angle. I swung the front end out over the line a bit to make it around the curve, when suddenly a car appeared coming the other way!

Quickly I turned away from it and simultaneously heard a

sickening scraping sound on the right-hand side of the bus where it had kissed the mountainside. We couldn't stop up there or anywhere, so we just kept going around the curve and down that road. We had peaked the summit and were on our way down into Aspen, and after about twenty minutes of driving we got to a place where we could pull the bus over and take a look. Holy shit! There was a gaping slash in the bus. The generator and the air-conditioning unit were both heavily damaged. We continued into Aspen and went for a series of beers. David was drinking Mexican coffees, a favorite of his, made of coffee and tequila.

When we exited the bar, we checked into a hotel to regroup. The next day we continued on toward California with no generator and no air-conditioning. A couple of days later we finally arrived at Alex's Bar on the mountain on Skyline Boulevard above the ranch, one of our old haunts. We went in, had dinner and a lot of alcohol. That was a trip to remember, but it was only one of the many experiences I shared with my good friend Mr. Briggs. I think I have time to tell you a few more, although I could never tell you all of them.

About twenty years later, in the mid-nineties, Briggs and I were making an album. I still call it an album because that is what I make. I don't make CDs or iTunes tracks. I make albums. That is just what I do. Call it what you like. I remember how I hated the shuffle feature on iTunes because it fucked up the running order I spent hours laboring over. Having tracks available independently and having the shuffle feature available sucks as far as I am concerned. Call me old-fashioned. I make albums and I want the songs to go together to create a feeling. I do those things on purpose. I don't want people cherry-picking the albums. I like to choose the singles. After all, it's my shit.

We were making an album at the Complex in LA that Briggs was producing with John Hanlon engineering. It was Crazy Horse, and it was cool. We were right into it. Briggs said at one point that this record was going to be Crazy Horse's Grammy. He was really into it then, and that surprised me. He never gave a shit about that in the past. Kurt Cobain had just committed suicide and left a note with my song quoted in it. "It's better to burn out than to fade away." He had been taking a lot of heat for canceling some shows. I, coincidentally, had been trying to reach him through our offices to tell him that I thought he was great and he should do exactly what he thought he should do and fuck everybody else. He was not just an entertainer; he was an artist and songwriter. There is a big difference. I knew him and recognized him for who he was. I wanted to talk to him. Tell him only to play when he felt like it. And that would be good enough. Be true.

So when he died and left that note, it struck a deep chord inside of me. It fucked with me. I wrote some music for that feeling: "Sleeps with Angels." David was right there with me because he knew. He knew the truth. At the end of that session, David did something highly unusual: He made a sort of declaration about the record and what we were doing. He did it on camera with Larry Johnson, who was there filming the sessions. I went back and revisited all that footage to see what the hell we were doing. I couldn't find that. I found a lot of other stuff. That is just one more loose end to finish up.

That was David's last album. He got sick after that. There was more recorded there than what we used. We missed something. I know it. He sleeps with angels.

There was a Crazy Horse tour, Ragged Glory, that Briggs and I did, with John Hanlon engineering, around 1990. I wrote a lot of songs in my car barn that were on that album. The car barn was a huge metal building with a gravel floor, and I set up my amps in there with a bunch of old cars. All my best shit. My Fender Deluxe with a Fender Reverb, my whizzer attached to it, my Magnatone feeding from that, and my Baldwin Exterminator feeding off of it, too. The fifties tweed Fender Deluxe I refer to is my original amp purchased from Sol Betnun Music on Larchmont Boulevard in LA in the sixties. That place was always full of old Fenders galore. I think it's gone now. I had that amp in my little Laurel Canyon cabin when I was in the Springfield. It had a fine sound. It sucked in a really good way when you turned it up to twelve! Yes! It goes to twelve! (Eat shit, Spiñal Tap!) At ten it is distorted and chunky but doesn't suck, at six it is nasty and edgy. At three it is just plain awful in a good way. The whizzer is something we built that turns the knobs manually so the signal doesn't get compromised. Any volume pot (controller) that's in the line fucks with the signal. The whizzer doesn't go in the line. It manually controls by rotating the master volume pot with a motor instead.

My Fender Reverb unit is from the fifties, too, maybe the early sixties. It has tubes and a spring reverb. It's very analog. If you rattle it, it makes a loud sound all by itself. It is a real effect. Not digital. Digital effects are trying to sound like this stuff. My Magnatone amp has a stereo vibrato. It takes a feed from inside the Deluxe at a point where the signal is least compromised and there is a boost to keep the level up. The Magnatone has a lot more balls than the Deluxe, but they are both run from my pedal board built by Johnny Foster, Tim's brother, attached with platinum switches built by Sal Trentino, the original tube amp guru. Thanks to Sal, I can bypass all that shit with one button if I don't want it, because it splits the signal, too. Thanks, Sal—rest in peace, my friend. (Of course, there's still that one platinum contact that the signal has to go through. If that was too techy for you, then you can just forget I said it, but it's staying right here in this book where it belongs.)

Anyway, back in 1990, I would go into my car barn with all this stuff and Old Black. I'd just started reviewing my archives, and I had recently heard some of my best shit, so I knew who I was and who I could be. I would come in every morning, smoke some weed, and start playing. Then the songs just came. *Ragged Glory*. The songs got written. We started recording and playing all the songs in a row two or three times a day for a week or two. No repeating. We'd just do a few sets a day. That was a cool way to make a record. No analyzing. Then at the end, we read our notes and went back and found the masters.

One day we were listening to tracks and we heard "Mansion on the Hill." It was a funky track, but it had the vibe. I asked David to play it one more time. David said to Hanlon, "All right then, let's hear it in all its ragged glory." That became the title. David had a way with words, an amazing vocabulary that he used poetically and to great effect always. So I finished the record, and we went out on tour with Sonic Youth and Social Distortion. Briggs went along, recording in an analog truck. We were a great bill; people got a real show. It rocked. I met Thurston Moore, and he told me about Nirvana, this great band, and how I should be taking them out, too, or at least hear them. Every night I would warm up backstage with Mike, my trainer, when Sonic Youth would come on, and they were fucking great. How original are they? Very. They would echo through the arena and sound like God. First, Social Distortion would come out cold and level the place. Then Sonic Youth! Then Crazy Horse! Because it was the Gulf War, we did an electric version of Bob's "Blowin' in the Wind." "How many times must the cannonballs fly?" It was just another great tour for the Horse . . .

One night in March of 1977, Linda Ronstadt and Nicolette Larson were in Malibu at Linda's house. I went over to see them and show them some songs I wanted to do with them for a new album. We made a cassette of the songs, and the two of them sang like birds. It was a thrill to be there with them. Everything was so easy. Unlike me, they always sang on pitch. It was like falling off a log for them. Linda has always been friendly to me and has helped me on quite a few records. *Harvest* was the first one of those. A few years later, I was very lucky to have Linda opening for me on the Time Fades Away tour. That was in 1973. She was dynamite. She got in trouble in Albuquerque for swearing onstage or something. I can't remember exactly what she did, but she caused an uproar.

I first saw Linda at the Troubadour in the sixties when she was with the Stone Poneys. She was great then, too. So young and beautiful! She blew everyone's mind with her big voice. Can you imagine sitting in the audience, seeing this girl walk up onstage, looking so amazing in her short shorts, and then hearing that huge voice? It was earth-shattering. She is always at the top of her game, but now Linda has become somewhat reclusive. She just dropped out to raise a family and live a "normal" life in the "real world." She used "real world" to describe me once. She told Nicolette not to get involved with me because I was "not living in the real world"! It didn't matter, though, because Nicolette and I did have a close relationship for a while. It didn't last for us, though. Life is like that.

Anyway, when I was getting to know Nicolette, she was at the ranch with Linda recording the songs I had shown the two of them in Malibu. (By the way, Linda was addicted to peanut butter at the time! Isn't that exactly the kind of interesting information you expect from a book like this?) That album, *American Stars 'n Bars*, we recorded in the White House with the Green Board, exactly like I want to do with Crazy Horse now. After we made that album, Nicolette came to Nashville and sang with me on the *Comes a Time* album. That is one of my best albums ever.

The tapes from *Comes a Time* were damaged en route to the mastering in New York, and I ended up purchasing all of the records that were pressed from those tapes, a couple hundred thousand of them, and remastered from a safety tape copy. All of the high frequency was missing from my master! I couldn't believe it when I got those dull test pressings and checked the master tape. It was severely damaged somehow. I don't know what happened

With Linda Ronstadt riding
at the Broken Arrow Ranch, 1977.

*With Nicolette Larson, Linda Ronstadt, and Crazy Horse,
during sessions for the* American Stars 'n Bars *album
at the Broken Arrow Ranch studio, 1977.*

to it. That was the last time I ever shipped a master anywhere. Now my guys hand carry.

The song "Comes a Time" is one of my all-time favorite recordings because it just has a great feeling. The song and the performance are a total mesh. Nicolette's singing is beautiful. I can see all the pictures. That is as close to a perfect recording as I ever have gotten. Karl Himmel laid down a unique groove on drums, and the band was locked in. Karl has the ability to play two grooves at once, which I have never heard anyone else do as well as he does. He is a completely unique musician. Chuck Cochran did the string arrangement. Rufus Thibodeaux played fiddle. JJ Cale played a guitar on it. Ben Keith played steel. Spooner Oldham played piano. There was a rhythm guitar section with six great guitarists all playing rhythm on old Martin acoustics. Everyone played and it was the country wall of sound, the Gone With the Wind Orchestra. What a sound!

Soon after I was so high on that orchestra that I did a free concert in Miami and took the whole group down there and played. But we didn't record it—I can't believe it. It must be the only thing I've ever done that I didn't record. I did "Sweet Home Alabama" at that show, and the folks loved it. (My own song "Alabama" richly deserved the shot Lynyrd Skynyrd gave me with their great record. I don't like my words when I listen to it today. They are accusatory and condescending, not fully thought out, and too easy to misconstrue.) We *did* record a rehearsal at the Musicians Union Hall in Nashville, and I have a tape of that from a room microphone for the archives. It was a golden moment.

In 1992, Linda's singing on the *Harvest Moon* album was beautiful, particularly on the title song. She really made that record what it is. She is a master. "Hangin' on a Limb" on the *Freedom* album is beautiful because Linda played such a part in it. She played such a part on all of those songs, and "Unknown Legend" was taken to new heights by her gifted arrangement and singing. When she came to Broken Arrow and sang on my records, she elevated everything she touched. I could never thank her enough. She never asks for anything, so I can't do any return favors for her. I am ready to anytime, though. She is like a sister to me, and I love her like that. So giving and selfless, just loving the music.

(Incidentally, I was playing really quiet on the *Harvest Moon* album because my ears were blown out from the *Weld* mixing. We mixed *Weld* twice because Billy Talbot and I were not happy with Briggs's mixes. We were wrong, and it was a waste of time. We should have used Briggs's work. Loud music hurt for a year after that. I still have and always will have tinnitus, ringing in the ears, from mixing too loud with low-quality digital sound. The resolution on those machines was nowhere near what we have available today. Tinnitus never goes away, but the pain does.)

Linda is now outside the pop music world, doing her thing. I don't know if there will ever be another singer who impacts me like she does. She is truly at the top of the class, along with Emmylou Harris and Nicolette. Some artists just have it. Like a painter who is great, you can't say why. I have been so fortunate to have these friends.

I find it unbelievable that Linda Ronstadt is not in the Rock and Roll Hall of Fame. There is something wrong with that. She should have been inducted a long time ago. I would be honored to induct her. Linda, Emmylou, Nicolette—these were beautiful ladies who gave to the music so selflessly. I have been truly blessed to make music with them all. The background chants by Linda and Nicolette on "Bite the Bullet" from *American Stars 'n Bars* will never fade from my mind. "Hold Back the Tears"—so rockin'! Linda has so much to give. In "Star of Bethlehem," the harmony of Emmylou and Ben Keith is so beautiful. So I have been lucky and life has gifted me. I know who I am and what I've been part of, but the music speaks when words can't. I will never forget those times.

These days, Pegi is singing her heart out about things that really matter to her, just like she dreamed of doing when she was so young. She is opening up her voice and her soul on her third recording, *Bracing for Impact*. It is really a true record; her songwriting is so focused and real. Her singing, so honest. More power to you, baby! I know we will have a lot more to look forward to!

With Mort and the Squires before moving from Winnipeg to Fort William, 1965. Left to right: Ken Koblun, me, and Bob Clark.

## Chapter Fifty-Eight

The Squires were ready to move. From August 8 through 14, 1965, we had a gig up in Churchill, Manitoba, on Hudson Bay. That was very far north, and it was a day-and-a-half-long train ride through Indian Territory. It was the farthest we had ever gone from Winnipeg, and we were excited. As the train rolled north, I remember seeing Indian villages by the tracks, teepees and little wooden and tin shacks side by side. The First Nation's people were in disarray, very poor, and their lives were brutal. Seeing and feeling that through the coach window was an experience I will never forget.

As the miles rolled by, characters of all kinds traveled on that train with us. When we finally got to Churchill, we found it a pretty desolate place, with a lot of trailers and some white buildings made of wood and concrete. They all looked the same to me. There were no trees there at all. The tallest bushes were so windblown that the branches all extended in only one direction, so the plants always looked like the wind was howling, even if it wasn't. And the people looked that way, too.

We stayed outside the hotel in one of the buildings during the day and ate at the hotel. There was a restaurant/supper club there, and we set up our gear. The crowd was pretty subdued until the weekend, and that was when people got rowdy. Nothing happened to us, but we could tell that it could have. We were too young to be playing in there, but they didn't know that.

One night the place was very rowdy, and suddenly the floor started moving! A polar bear was under the hotel! Some guys went out and shooed it away. Some shots were fired, and everything returned to normal. Another night during the week, an Indian guy was drunk and had left to walk home. He stopped and leaned on a telephone pole to rest, fell asleep, and died right there. Frozen to death. They found him in the morning, leaning on the pole, frozen solid. That place was not on the Squires' list of places to return to.

After the long trip back to Winnipeg, we got into Mort the hearse and took off to Fort William. I had written a few songs about Churchill on the train ride and updated the song "The Birds and the Bees" with lyrics about Churchill. It was a funny song. One of the updated lyrics was "A penguin I know, and a thing called snow." I don't remember the rest.

Whenever we went to a new place, I always thought that since we were from out of town, we would have a mystique about us and be more interesting than the other bands. That turned out to be true, and the Fort William days, when we were on the road, were among the best in the history of the Squires. We were headed for the big time at last.

The sky was the limit.

## Chapter Fifty-Nine

Life in LA

There was an apartment building called the Commodore Gardens on Orchid Avenue in Hollywood. It was there that I got my very first place to live in LA. The Springfield was playing the Whisky a Go Go, and I had some cash. Some girls who were real good friends of mine from the Whisky were living there. Their names were Donna Port and Vicki Cavaleri. I enjoyed their company. They had a girlfriend who was really nice who they were always trying to get me together with, but I wasn't ready for her at the time. We really hung out a lot.

They introduced me to the Commodore Gardens landlord, and I got my own apartment there. In an attempt to make it my own, I immediately broke all the rules and tacked up some matting on the walls that I had bought at Pier 1 Imports. I put a blue light-bulb in the fridge. It was an old fridge. I don't know what I ever put in it. Must have been Cokes and Twinkies. I wasn't into health food yet, that's for sure.

I wrote a lot of songs there for the Springfield, and it was an exciting time for me. "Flying on the Ground," "Do I Have to Come Right Out and Say It," and "Burned" were among the songs I wrote there. I was also dealing with my newly discovered seizure disorder, and come to think of it, I'm sure the food I was eating was not helping! We would come home from the International House of Pancakes on Sunset at about three A.M. after eating a bunch of German pancakes with sugar and lemon all over them. Those things were great because they reminded me of the pancakes I used to have back home in Canada, "rollers," we called them. Butter, sugar, and lemon juice, all rolled up and eaten like a hot dog. I did that almost every night after the Whisky, and we played that place for a long time and returned and did it over again night after night. We were the opening act for lots of stars.

We had lots of girls and lots of fun. I got a few sexually transmitted diseases and started to become aware that there was a responsibility connected to the decisions I was making. Breaking new ground, you might say. I visited the Hollywood Free Clinic a few times. That was a place by La Brea that had been set up that helped all the transient kids on Sunset to stay more or less clean and healthy. Those were simple days. Some of the support systems set up by the government actually worked for the people.

It was after that period at the Commodore Gardens that I got my next place up in Laurel Canyon. We were getting more successful. I had my own car, but no license because I was still an illegal alien and had no Social Security card. Driving my car was nerveracking for that reason. I was always worried about getting stopped by the cops. The first car I got was a '54 Packard ambulance. The next one was a '57 Corvette that I got with my share of the advance money from Atlantic Records, approximately twenty grand for the whole band, split many ways, when we signed with Ahmet Ertegun. Charlie Greene and Brian Stone retained most of that themselves.

Once during the height of tensions on Sunset, just before Stephen wrote his classic "For What It's Worth," I got stopped and put in jail for not having a license. My friend Freddy Brechtel, a singer without a band, was with me, and he took the car back to my place. I went to jail at the Hollywood substation, just down the hill from the Whisky. While I was in the cell, one of the officers called me a stinking hippie. He was wearing horn-rimmed glasses. Shooting back, I told him he looked like a grasshopper. He came in the cell and beat the shit out of me. Slamming my face and kicking me around on the floor. That was traumatizing.

The instances of that sort of thing were many in those days. Hippies were targets. Eventually Charlie and Brian got an attorney and I was out on bail, but I was even more scared of the cops after that. There was never any thought of pressing charges, because I didn't have a leg to stand on. No license. We felt lucky that I wasn't deported. They didn't realize I was an illegal alien. They weren't thorough, just brutal. I still cringe when I see a Hollywood sheriff's cruiser, even though I have been legal for a long time.

Once Stephen and I and the rest of the Springfield went to a beach near Point Dume to do a radio promotional event. You got airplay that way. KHJ was doing a promotion where the Big Kahuna was arriving from Hawaii in a canoe and giving out cash to KHJ listeners. KHJ Boss 93 was giving away big bucks, and Buffalo Springfield was going to be on the shore to greet the Big Kahuna when he arrived. It was live on the air, and we were all doing interviews. Soon a grass canoe with outriggers rounded the point and the Big Kahuna appeared! There were a lot of babes there, and Stephen and I were having a great time.

Later we met the Big Kahuna and found out his name was Chris. He sold us some of the best weed in Hollywood after that. It was called Kahuna grass. (Another name is sinsemilla, for "no seeds.") This was some really potent weed that all the bands were smoking. The Big Kahuna had delivered the mother lode. This went on for quite some time, and Kahuna grass is still legendary today in old LA musicians' circles. It used to make me so paranoid thinking that I was going to have a seizure that I had to stop smoking it. If you smoked a little, you wrote a song. If you smoked too much, then you were toast. That was the reputation it had with me.

## Chapter Sixty

Farm Aid 26 is coming up next week. I haven't played much lately. I don't have a musical direction at the moment, other than my wish to play with Crazy Horse and explore the territory, see the view. At times like these, I am at a loss. Gigs that come up on a time clock don't really work for the creative process and are a disturbance for the muse. That has nothing to do with my support for the farmers, a lifelong commitment. It has to do only with the muse. How can I play if I have no direction? It's not just a job you do.

Usually I do benefits in October. That way I can prepare myself, figure out what I will be doing, and play three or four benefits during that month. This Farm Aid is happening at an odd time of year, August. If I'm not on the road, I'm resting in August, and that rest is very important. After a long time off, playing one gig takes at least a month of mental preparation to get an idea of what I'm going to do, where I will be drawing from. I have less than a week left now to prepare. I need to start playing every day so my hands are ready with calluses on my fingers and I know the words and songs.

I'm going to do my best Bob Dylan imitation! I will go out there with an acoustic guitar and harmonica. No electric. This will be a folk approach, based on story songs with lots of words and verses. I will be like a ghost from the past, totally a throwback to another time. (It's funny; I call it a Bob Dylan imitation, but Bob never does it. It's what everyone would like to see him do, and he never does it. I suspect it would be too lonely and singular for him, no band to hang with or friends to see every day when he gets off the bus.)

So that is my plan. I will play a few new tunes that I did on the last tour—"Love and War," "Peaceful Valley Boulevard"—and do them differently, with a pushier groove and more harp playing with a straight acoustic rhythm instead of the more sensitive finger-picking and bass-reinforced *Le Noise* sound. I may revert to history with some story songs like "Powderfinger" and a few others, punctuated here and there with some more personal lyrics like "Sugar Mountain" and "Comes a Time." I will probably not play any other instruments, keeping it way simple and focused on the old-time folk music approach. Maybe I'll play "Vampire Blues," maybe not.

Basically I will come and go, just being myself in a really simple way. No bells and whistles at all. This is something I think I can do and make it work. I have been thinking about this for about three weeks and actually worrying about it. That is how a forty-minute set can take a month of preparation. It would take the same amount of preparation for me to do a whole tour.

B ecause someone had the rights to the name PureTone, we changed our name to Pono. It is Hawaiian for "righteous and good." We love our new name. Negotiations for the Pono project between Pono and WMG have been ongoing for about six weeks now, trying to settle on the details of the founding partners group. This process is distinctly different from most every other thing I have done in the past. My friend Marc Benioff told me that I need to remember what I'm in it for, saving the sound of music and rescuing an art form, and just focus on that. "Business is not like a song, Neil; there is no last note. It just keeps going on and on, and there is conflict almost constantly," he told me one night when I called asking for his advice.

The exercise is very frustrating.

He pointed out that I need to focus on what I *can* do, not what I *can't* do. I need to figure that one out for my own sake, because it's too wearing on me. I need to let it happen the way it will and not try to control every little part of it. Control is my way of ensuring that things go right, and if I don't have control, I worry that things are going to get away and not be done correctly. You know, the videos I have been making that showcase me playing Pono for musicians and music lovers are coming along so well, and I see the happiness on the faces of people who are hearing great sound and enjoying it, discovering that music can be much deeper an emotional experience than what they've grown used to recently. I feel this is so important, and it is so gratifying to watch all of these car interviews, some twenty-five now, as the editing continues on the ranch. The musicians and music lovers are of all ages, and they are all unified in their strong, supportive, and positive reactions. This is most positive and reaffirms what I believed in the beginning. I *should* be so happy to focus on that.

The goal is so great, and the success of this will be so gratifying. Yet everyone cautions me about the strength of Apple and iTunes. I think that no matter what, this project will force iTunes to be better and to improve quality at a faster pace. I just hope what Apple does is great enough, not some measured response that is hyped so much that the consumers feel they are getting the best when they are not.

The record companies are sort of held hostage in a weird way by the Internet's dominance in their industry. But because the record companies still hold the gold, their high-quality music masters, it's time for them to step up and take control of their own destiny. I realize the amount of cash Apple has far exceeds the amount of cash the United States of America has, and everyone is scared of that. But I think public opinion and social networking could win over money, just as it has upset the status quo in the Arab Spring and all of the other revolutions around the world organized through social networking. This is just another revolution. Quality sound can make a return and be reestablished for those who want the best. The best is just not available right now in a consumer-friendly way. The Sound Revolution could bring it back, if the cards the record companies hold are played. That is the big If. Will they have the balls to stand up and take care of the music?

These days it's all about closure of this and that for me. I have too many things to finish. How can I move on until I clean that slate? My film *Human Highway* is one of those things. It should be available to the public. Dean Stockwell and Russell Tamblyn, my old friends from Topanga Canyon, and Dennis Hopper, a good old friend, were in this movie with me, and we wrote the dialogue as we went along. It is the dorkiest damn movie ever and it walks a very fine line right on the edge of being too dorky. Some may say it falls over that line. The film was never put to rest to my satisfaction, and for the last ten years or so, Larry Johnson had been struggling, trying to find some pieces of that film that may be lost now. He was very occupied with getting the quality preserved for David Myers's legacy. Not that we don't have copies. We do. We have everything we need to edit together the film in a way I can rest well behind content-wise. When I finish something, I want it to be right, or as right as it can be.

As I mentioned, *Human Highway* is just one of those things. I am not Cecil B. DeMille. It is not a great commercial movie. But it has never reached its potential, so I have never been able to let it go. I have carried it with me all these years. It was released, bombed, and was buried before I even felt it was done. With Larry Johnson gone and David Myers gone and Dennis Hopper, too, I am left with this drive to finish. I went into the editing room on the ranch, which is actually in the train barn as fate would have it. (I love that I can leave the editing screens and walk around looking at the trains and work on some small detail of the layout or clean and polish some wheels while I work out some editing challenge in my head. That is so liberating. It is the combining of two different worlds in a good way for me.)

I asked Will Mitchell, Larry's and my right-hand man, for all of the existing Shakey Pictures' *Human Highway* footage to be brought to the editing room, and when it all arrived, I sat down with Toshi Onuki and we reviewed what we had. There were three separate versions of the film. One version, which was based on the original cut, the director's cut if you will, had last been worked on by Larry and Toshi. It was exactly what I was looking for. I asked to see it, and then I viewed it while taking notes. When it was all over, we took a little break and then went through the film, making corrections. It really got good when we made the changes. Humor is all about timing, and I have learned a lot about that in the thirty years since I first cut this picture. We had a hodgepodge of prints and qualities, but were able to cut together the story.

I now feel the picture is in its final shape, and I love it. It's not the greatest picture in the world, but it is my picture, and I love what it does. It moves me now like I always wanted it to. I think it might still get panned, but I don't care. I like it. That is what matters to me. Once the technical aspects are all pulled together and the final sound mix is done, I can rest knowing I have done my best. I hope it is what Larry would have wanted. That is a good feeling. Thank you, Larry. Thank you, David. Thanks, Dean and Russell. Thanks, Dennis. I love you guys. I'll show it to you when I see you.

When my studio album *Prairie Wind* was finished, I talked to Jonathan Demme about making a picture. We had discussed the idea a few times before but had no direction to go in. Now we did. We talked about the songs and the feeling on *Prairie Wind* for a long time, the musicians of Nashville, and the great history of country music. We talked about my home in Canada, my dad, my mom, my upbringing, my dad's hometown on the prairies, my dad's passing, my cousins singing under the direction of my uncle Bob, who was a great musician and my dad's brother; we talked a lot about those things. What it all boiled down to was an appearance at the Ryman Auditorium, home of the Grand Ole Opry in its heyday. We decided to do a performance that was a tribute to those times, to that heritage, while also showcasing *Prairie Wind* for the very first time. We were going to assemble a cast of the great musicians and singers who played on *Prairie Wind* and perform it live at the Ryman in front of an audience of Nashville folks on the night of the August full moon! It was a great plan, and we were very excited to get started.

One night in Nashville we were eating in the restaurant at the Hermitage Hotel. It's a wonderful place. We were enjoying some fine wine and talking about the picture. I'll never forget the look on Jonathan's face when I said I had invited the costume director down to meet him at the restaurant.

WHAT? You've chosen the costume director? (Jonathan's thought bubble!)

Jonathan Demme always chose his own costume directors! Of course I have the greatest respect for Director Demme's taste and knew he would love Manuel, who originated in Nudie's shop in Hollywood. Manuel was the man who made every country artist's clothing. He made Elvis's gold lamé suit. He made Dolly Parton's and Porter Wagoner's clothes. He was *the* man. And there he was, walking into the restaurant. He joined us. He was wearing a very cool shirt and looked like he was already in a movie. Accompanied by a young lady and a young man assistant, he sat down at the table and took a little sip of wine. Then he started talking. It was fascinating. He blew everyone's mind with his stories. Then Jonathan told him the whole concept for the show, describing the backdrop art, the Ole Opry atmosphere, the *Prairie Wind* songs and feelings, the ambience around the songs being written, my life-threatening situation at the time, the newness of the music, the audience itself, and the camera angles, and asked him what he wanted to do.

"Don't worry," Manuel said. "It will be perfect, like a dream you are having."

Manuel did not offer one detail. It was a moment to remember. Manuel was totally in control. Jonathan was seeing a living legend. This was a great moment.

We went on to make the movie, and it is something that will last a lifetime. We are all very proud of this film. We paid tribute to those who had come before and left an enduring document to the greatness of country music and the tradition of Nashville. My favorite shot is one taken from the back of the stage. You can see Emmylou Harris and me singing "This Old Guitar." It looks like it's from the forties, a perfect time capsule. And through beautiful camera work, lighting, and a great instrumental performance, we left a living picture of one of the greatest country music artists of all time, Ben Keith.

## Chapter Sixty-One

You may remember Nina. She is Pegi's new dog. All curly and soft, little Nina weighs about twenty-five pounds. She went through that broken-down Cadillac Eldorado episode with me out on Interstate 5 in the 106-degree heat. We bonded. Well, now Pegi is on the road with the Survivors, and I am at home with Nina. Nina sleeps at the foot of the bed whenever I am sleeping. It feels good to not be alone. Pegi calls quite regularly to tell me what to do with Nina in this case or that case, and that is always helpful.

Last night Nina was barking incessantly at something outside. I let her out and she just kept on barking. This is something that has just developed recently, and whenever I told Nina to stop barking, she would just ignore me completely. The barking just went on and on. I was beginning to get irritated with this development. Was this dog going to take over the whole house? She was really cute, but she was really LOUD, too. Once she started barking, she would never stop.

I tried yelling at her, "STOP BARKING, NINA!" in my biggest "man voice." It had no effect. I was getting pissed. Eventually, she got tired and stopped, but it had gone on for a long time. My always active imagination was now getting the best of me in a barrage of images and thoughts. I was starting to visualize a dog barking for the rest of time.

The next morning at about six, Nina and I got up and went out to the kitchen. I put on some water to boil and opened the door and we went outside. I stood there with her as she peed on the lawn. She went about her business, sniffing and carrying on in doglike fashion. Eventually, we returned inside and I made some tea. Sitting down at the computer to check my morning mail, I heard her growling softly, then more loudly, until it developed into a full-on bark. Nina was standing in the kitchen, barking! I sat there, digesting the situation. She continued her barking.

In an epiphany, I softly called her name and gave her my special little whistle that was just for her. She came over to me and I held her little head and in a very soft voice told her, "Nina, there is nothing out there. Just lie down here with me and chill out. Everything is fine. It's morning now, and it's all good. Just you and me right here, you on the floor and me with my morning mail." I patted her little head. She lay down on the floor at my feet and fell asleep. The dog is my new guru.

Drummers are very important to my music and the success of any band playing my music. Ralph Molina is the drummer in Crazy Horse, and his feel is a big part of that Crazy Horse sound. He is very sympathetic to improvisation and can quickly go with any flow change. That is really a key thing if you are playing a long jam or instrumental à la "Cowgirl in the Sand," "Down by the River," "Big Time," "Change Your Mind," "No Hidden Path," or "Rockin' in the Free World," to name just a few. Those songs require the drummer to listen to the subtle changes in guitar leads and rhythms, and follow with changes in the groove. Ralph is the best at that for me. Combining that with Billy Talbot's simplicity, soul, and aggression, Crazy Horse's rhythm section is solid as a rock.

Yet at the same time, Ralphie is extremely subtle and can express emotions beautifully in both a ballad and a laid-back song. He is completely unique, emotional, and driving at the same time. His flourishes with my feedback at the end of a long song are always right with me, as if he knows right where I am going. Fact is, we are going there together, feeling our way, and that really applies to all of Crazy Horse. That is what makes the Horse as great as it is, and as cosmic as it is. That is the Force of the Horse. Making the new albums, *Americana* and *Psychedelic Pill*, I have found that this cosmic force has increased, not diminished, with time.

Kenny Buttrey, on the other hand, is a finesse player with a master's touch on any song he plays. His grooves on *Harvest* are in the pocket, and yet so original at the same time. On drums, he just doesn't sound like anyone else. Kenny was a complete original who I was lucky to know and play with. His bass player was usually Tim Drummond, a master in his own right. The two of them together were just what my music needed. Tim Drummond also played with Karl T. Himmel on many of my recordings. They also played with JJ Cale on a lot of his early stuff, which just had that amazing groove. The International Harvesters' *A Treasure* is one of the best illustrations of the massive talent of Karl T. Himmel. Karl played on "Comes a Time" and "Four Strong Winds," as well as a lot of tracks on *Prairie Wind*. Karl's feel is so fluid and sensitive, and I still love playing with him today.

Chad Cromwell is a unique drummer, different from all the rest. He is very strong and steady, the most reliable. You can count on Chad to always be on the money. A band could hang on his groove because it never falters. His playing on *Prairie Wind* and with the Bluenotes is totally awesome. Equally at home in any genre from country to blues to rock, Chad is a very authoritative, consistent, and powerful drummer who just kicks ass. His drumming on "A Day in the Life" was amazing when I played it with him on my marathon tour with the Electric Band throughout the world in 2007 and 2009. He just rolled with the changes in that song, one of the most difficult and challenging songs for any band, including the Beatles, to play live. When Paul did it with us in Hyde Park at the end of our tour in London, I know he was impressed with how we took that song and delivered it live to the masses.

Chad also played "Words" from the *Harvest* album with its alternating time signatures on that tour. No one other than Buttrey could even play that song, but Chad took it by the horns and slapped it around. The groove with him and Rick Rosas on bass was so huge that we left the ground every night we played it. Save the original version, "Words" was played the best by Chad and that band. The first time I ever saw Rick and Chad playing was at Farm Aid one year with Joe Walsh. I loved the way they supported Joe. I asked them to play a little with me, and we did *Freedom*, the Bluenotes' *This Note's for You*; then we did *Living with War*, and most recently, the Electric Band's *Fork in the Road*. These were all wonderful groups, tours, and records. Rick is a pretty quiet guy until he starts telling jokes and getting funny; then he is hilarious. We've had some great bus rides. He's a slinky bass player with a lot of soul. I always enjoy playing with him and Chad, and we have a lot of fun together.

Dewey Martin of the Buffalo Springfield is possibly the fastest and lightest drummer I have ever heard or played with. His kick drum on "For What It's Worth" is what holds the whole thing together. Drummers are the heartbeat of a song, and it has to be good or you die. So yes, I have been lucky to play with all of these guys.

The Rock and Roll Hall of Fame is hallowed ground in my mind. Originally founded by Ahmet Ertegun, Bob Krasnow, Jann Wenner, and Jon Landau, the Hall was a great idea and an amazing place to imagine. Originally, it didn't really exist as a place, and that was fine. I supposed it was big, kind of like the silver lining around a cloud. Not something you could actually see or touch. It was the honor of a lifetime for me to be inducted. A dream come true.

All or most of my heroes were already in the Hall of Fame when I was inducted: Elvis, Little Richard, Jerry Lee Lewis, Chuck Berry—the pioneers and architects were all there. It is the biggest honor in rock and roll, and rock and roll is what it is.

When people got up to accept their inductions in the first few years, you could feel the energy. It was electric. It was their chance to say what they thought, their moment to be heard and be real. People spoke from the heart and said some outrageous things. You never knew what to expect. A few video cameras captured the moment. People spoke off the top of their heads or from a little sheet of paper. People cried and laughed and settled scores. A lot of them settled scores. There was a lot to say for some of them, and this was their best chance.

Some of these artists had not been active in years or had not had more than a moment in the light and certainly did not make a fortune in the music business. But they all had soul. Some did make a lot of money, of course, but the Hall was about the music, about rock and roll as a way of life. Phil Spector, Mike Love of the Beach Boys, and several others have made long speeches that covered things they needed to say and they had every right to say, and they exercised that right. It was amazing to hear their takes on life, how they had been done right or wrong, who they blamed for their problems and thanked for their victories on the road to the Hall. It was an honor to hear them talking to their peers, to the others who aspired to be like them, and to those who they felt had attained even higher ground than they themselves had.

My favorites spoke with no notes. Some cried. Some laughed. Some thanked. Some just lashed out at those who had screwed them out of royalties and security later in life. Rock and roll is no cakewalk. It was and is a shrewd and unforgiving business if you made some bad decisions about your representation when you were young. A lot of bad moves were made, particularly in the early days, as great as they were, and this was a chance to set it straight, and the inductees did, exercising their new power and rights as members of the hallowed Rock Hall.

Then the worst thing happened.

The founders decided to make the Rock and Roll Hall of Fame induction ceremony a TV show! VH1! What could be LESS rock and roll than VH1? Now a place that was beyond classification had been relegated to a VH1 show. Gone were the long speeches. Three minutes on TV was the new speech. Good-bye, long rambling diatribes. Teleprompters were now available. I made a lot of obscene comments in my speech and swore a lot about everyone involved, but in the end, I don't care to mention them here. They may know who they are, and they may not. People make mistakes. They probably don't know the difference.

It reminded me of the Lifetime Achievement Award the Grammys gave Frank Sinatra in New York one year. A recently successful artist came out and introduced Sinatra in a very long-winded oratory, and then Frank came out. He had just started talking when he was out of time. The band began to play and the introducing artist came back out and walked him off. Sinatra was definitely not finished speaking. I would have loved to hear him, but there was no time left. Frank looked confused and disappointed when he was escorted off. He was just getting started and couldn't believe he was cut short. That's TV. A rambling intro that was much longer than Frank's cut-short speech meant that time was up for one of the greatest legends ever in the history of music. That's life. It pissed me off. But sometimes it's better not to blow up at someone.

I can save that anger and emotion for my guitar playing. A Crazy Horse tour is just around the corner. I'll use it for fuel. I don't want to write some damning thing here about somebody and have to live with that for the rest of time. I don't think that would be a very good idea.

A lot of times things happen and you can't believe it. You walk around cursing under your breath and it really doesn't help. Life is too short. Things shake out. They really do. Take the dickhead record executive who came out to hear me once and went back to his Hollywood record company telling them the material wasn't ready to record. He really pissed me off. Who asked him? I never worked like that before, and I never will in the future. It's my music. But now I'm letting go of that. I might buy him a beer and tell him to drink it sometime, but that's about the extent of it now.

I don't drink anymore myself, I'm moving on. And that's not to say I won't drink again. I'm not making any promises, but I don't think I was a great drinker. Some folks are great drinkers; they drink and tell jokes and laugh their asses off, and they are funny as hell. We buried one of those last week. Life is just a big test, and if you try hard, you fail. If you don't try too hard and fail a little but have a good time, maybe that is success.

I've seen some really happy and content people in this life, and I am not one of them all the time, just some of the time, but I am thankful as hell for them and lonely for the old times and old friends. Not all the time, though. I'm really happy doing what I do, and what I'm doing now is trying like hell to rescue recorded sound so people can feel music again. That makes me happy because it's real, and if I succeed, I will have helped a lot of artists and music lovers achieve nirvana. Who knows where the feeling of sound went? It went so slowly and gradually that no one noticed but me and a few other narky old buzzards, as my daughter Amber lovingly calls me occasionally. But she was the one who heard Pono in my car after listening to MP3s her whole life and looked at me and asked, "What happened? How did that happen?" She knows why I am doing what I am doing. She is *them*, all of those young people who haven't felt the real sound of recorded music.

I am doing this for them, and me. Let's not forget me. I want to feel the sounds again like I did in the beginning, or even better now, because technology is supposed to improve life. Of course, you can't go back, but when I see a young person react to hearing Pono for the first time, well, that is good enough for me. Yes it is.

All I have to do now is navigate the waters of venture capital-ism, those treacherous shorelines of commerce, in the HMS *Pono*, a fine ship of significant age and worthiness, with a crew I barely know, but who seem to be committed to the great cause of deliver-ing the cargo to safe harbor in the Heart of Music. I can't tell you how scary this is. I have never been here before, on this vessel, in these waters, with the cargo on board. I seek counsel continuously from a wealth of friends who are experienced in carrying the cargo home to port. They have done this before me. But this is my cargo. I chose it myself, and it has gone undelivered for what seems like decades. How often I wake up at midnight full of questions. Am I alive? Yes.

I may have been asleep for forty years. It's hard to tell. Some people have pointed out to me how great I used to be when I wrote a bunch of songs, but I'm not sure they know what they are speaking about, or the subject, even. Why so pensive about the past? What can it say or do for you now? Nothing much, I fear. I used to wonder if people recognized me, and I was even worried if I thought they did because I didn't really need to be reminded what I was like or when something happened or if I met you once.

Perhaps I overstated that. Forty years is not an amount of time to ignore, though. I think I will have to use my time wisely and keep my thoughts straight if I am to succeed and deliver the cargo I so carefully have carried thus far to the outer reaches. Not that it's my only job or task. I have others, too. Sacred things that I need to protect from pain and hardship, like careless remarks on an open mind. I need to guard against that and honor the source of my feelings, not hide them in a blanket of doubt. My songs are hidden now, orphaned from their melodies and structure that once contained them. How am I, some forty years down the road, to deal with that past accomplishment? Cast it off? Relinquish it to the others who value it more? Was it me? Or who am I now that I cannot see or meet myself the way I was? That is not for me to know, because I am busy with new things now and have no time at all. I am very busy with all of this, and every day is shorter and I wake up earlier and go to sleep at a different time than before. I dream all the time at night, not like before, when I induced dreams in the waking hours to snatch them in their innocence and commit them to song and melody and words captured. Not now. It is not now for that. It is far over for that, I think. I am hoping for a revelation of dreams I can remember, but that is never the case with dreams, is it?

So now I am in the song machine gone awry. I wander the halls of straightness, not knowing how to hallucinate. Finally the course is clear and the sound of waves on rocks is fading. The fog is clearing and there is so much sea. An endless chorus of waves, melodies, refrains, and codas, cropping up and fading away, are a reminder of the duty at hand and the wasted moments. It is the time to gather this and make something of it, or it is not that time. There is no clue. Just the clear sound of the waves on the wood as the ship moves dutifully toward delivery of the cargo. I am on the deck now, at the wheel even, the wind in my hair, such as it is. And my hat is gone, blown away by the same wind that powers me on. The Heart of Music to be saved, delivered, moored, and off-loaded. This is my life, my dream, my moment in the wind. Escape me if you will, songs. Let yourselves go now. We approach safe harbor.

Chapter Sixty-Two

I t is 9:43 A.M. on the West Coast. I will hit the "Buy it now" button at exactly ten A.M.

My latest love affair is a 1961 Lincoln Continental with about fifty thousand miles on it. Very nice original condition with a few hot rod appointments, and not what I usually go for, but this car really caught my eye. I was looking for a Ford product to replace the Eldorado in the video series. One reason for this is the damage I did to the Eldorado that day on I-5 with little Nina.

The other reason is the real reason: For the same amount of money it would take to rebuild the engine in the Eldorado, I can purchase another Ford product. (Of course, I will rebuild the Eldorado anyway, so the money is not really a valid reason.) "Why is that so important?" you might ask. It is important to me because I will be taking Bill Ford, executive chairman of the Ford Motor Company, for a ride and letting him feel Pono. I really like Bill because he is a futurist, and not many people would actually believe how much of a visionary he is, since he is at the head of one of the oldest car-manufacturing companies in the world. He is taking a hard look at the future while he is here on earth. He is trying to understand where traffic will be in twenty years, what cars will be like, what people will need for transportation. He and Jim Farley, head of global marketing for Ford, have changed a lot of things.

Today's Ford cars are very different from yesterday's. They have evolved the interior and its features into many levels while using the same exterior with few changes from the top of the line to the entry level. That is really revolutionary. The quality is added inside. It's in the user experience inside the car. That is where the big difference is now. This enables a lot of money to be saved and put into the inside of the cars, where people are. So I want him to hear Pono in one of Ford's own cars. No car in the world has ever sounded that good, and I think he will hear that. Being me, I have chosen a 1961 Continental over a new Ford Focus, but I want to take the prototype system out of the Continental and put it in the Focus to show how easy that is as part of the demo I plan for Mr. Ford.

So I located this Continental and plan on buying it at ten A.M. PST, when the owner will put it up on eBay for a prearranged price, which is actually still a little too high. I go by feelings, and my feeling is that this is the right car, even though it is not standard stock, because it has nineteen-inch wheels and a new exhaust system resonating the original 430-cubic-inch V8, and I am paying for extras I don't really want. That said, it is rock and roll and worthy of the Pono feature. It is quite possibly the Hot Rod Lincoln you have heard so much about! The rest of the car is a really nice, near cherry original, beautiful in every respect, a true work of automotive history. I have looked at this car for almost two weeks in pictures, checking out each one and reading the description over and over. I trust the seller.

The car is in Canada, and I may go up there and get it next week and drive it home, stopping in Seattle on the way back to celebrate Pearl Jam's twentieth anniversary with them. Sounds like fun. 9:59 A.M.! Gotta go!

## Chapter Sixty-Three

In Kansas City for Farm Aid 26, I found myself strangely lightened, with all of the harsh business negotiations I am so unfamiliar with over for the moment and gone from my thoughts. I thought of myself as a breeze blowing through Kansas, not worried, not pensive at all. I saw my old friends in the Farm Aid family: Willie, John, Dave, Carolyn, Glenda, Corky, David, and a couple of new friends, Willie's talented son Lukas Nelson, and Jamey Johnson, a great singer/songwriter from Alabama who has landed in Nashville, I imagine temporarily. Jamey and Lukas are the new guard. Real country. Real good. No bullshit. They are not the only ones, but if they were, they could handle it.

Musicians like to check the stage and make sure everything is working before a show. Some groups let their crews do it. Some don't. If a band is running late, then the crew has to do it. If you sing, it's good to know that the monitor speakers onstage are right for your ears. Some singers today use in-ear monitors and listen to their voices pretty loud directly in their ears. I don't do this. I love to hear the sound of the hall, the echo off the walls, and the sound of the instruments onstage blending together. That is key for me if I'm going to improvise or get lost in the sound. I want to walk around the stage with my guitar, finding the sweet spot where I can hear everything in balance. That is key for me playing extended jams. In-ear phones are way too sterile and clinical for me. I have to hear the speakers and the amps and the hall sound.

The night before the Farm Aid show, I had a sound check and it was different. I sang the set I was planning on doing in the empty soccer stadium. I started with "Comes a Time." There was so much echo that I really couldn't hear too well, and the monitors sounded really harsh to my ears. I sang "Powderfinger," and it was too high for me to reach the notes that night. I hadn't really warmed up and it was hard to sing those high notes. I tried a few things and nothing really sounded too good, so I asked Mark Humphreys to just turn off the monitors completely, which not many musicians feel comfortable doing. All I could hear was echo now, just the sound of the stadium. I sang "Sugar Mountain." Actually it sounded good to my ears; notes just lasted forever. Nothing was abrasive. I tried my harmonica. It was like floating on air. The echo was amazing. I did "Peaceful Valley Boulevard" and then "Love and War." I tried out the harp in "Love and War." It worked, and the sound just floated out into the Missouri night.

So the next day at the show, when I was watching everyone play, adjusting their monitors all the time, trying to find a good sound and struggling, I used no monitors at all. I just didn't bother using any. I knew it was going to be cool. Just like a breeze blowing through Kansas. Everything sounded beautiful. I did an acoustic set and really enjoyed it. One guitar, one harmonica, and six songs were all I needed.

There was something about that set that still haunts me. I was ready for the echo. The sound was like I was in another world. Every note just hung there in space. I drew them out and felt them all lingering and fading. Somehow, just by myself, I had become so free that it was almost transcendent. The place was not that great of a venue, really. It had everything going against it until I stopped fighting it and dropped the onstage monitors. When I did that, it was like the gates of heaven swung open. I swear that sound was like being in a hallowed place. I was so free and unencumbered, really a very rare thing, very rare. Especially solo. "Golden," as Briggs used to say. I love it when it works. That echo was a gift from the gods.

Earlier in the day I had gone out for a walk around the grounds with Carolyn Mugar, Farm Aid's wonderfully dedicated executive director and a good friend, accompanied by some security people. They (security) were pretty subtle, and it all was good. I kept moving. I have learned how long I can stay in one place in that kind of situation: Not very long. I listened to the music playing from the stage as I walked around the concession area through the crowd, wondering how I would sound with just my guitar and harmonica. Pretty good, I thought to myself. Then I saw a guy with a really old and cool Neil Young and Crazy Horse T-shirt. He was lost in thought. I walked up to him, tapped him on the shoulder, and said, "Really nice shirt." He looked up and I caught his eye. Then I kept moving. People were beginning to notice me, and a little crowd was following me. We disappeared into an elevator and went back to the bus.

The Zen art of paddleboarding has been creeping up on me now for months. Recently my friend Rick Rubin, a great record producer, has taken up the pastime. Rick is quite Buddha-like, and to think of him on his paddleboard is a very harmonic vision. I went out this morning and only fell off five times, which I am feeling very good about. My knees were shaking as I stood for the first time and surveyed the great open expanse before me on the bay by our Hawaii home. I paddled for a long time until some disturbance in the force overtook my groove and I plummeted face-first into the welcoming sea. Doggedly, as in "like a dog," I climbed back on board with my beautiful Koa paddle resting on top of the deck. Then, on my knees, I resumed paddling until the nerve to stand assembled itself in my balance-challenged form. Suddenly I was up again and under way, gleefully rejoicing in my newly found existence as a man of the water. I approached a rock outcropping and had deftly avoided getting too close to it when a subtle swell rolled beneath me, completely throwing me off balance and into the welcoming sea again. The water was relatively calm, and the swell was a little like jelly when it came through. I vowed to be more aware and reasserted myself, standing once more with paddle in hand, looking out on the distant shoreline and feeling at one with the board.

The time had come to make a turn, an adjustment in course, and I was experimenting with this, first paddling on one side, then reversing the flow on the other side, making the craft unwieldy, and once again I found myself in the welcoming sea. On my knees,

I continued toward the launch point, thoroughly worn out and totally invigorated by my new experience.

This, I felt, was the beginning of a new chapter for me, the basis of a more broad understanding of my place in the universe. Perhaps I was taking it a little too seriously, but the bottom line is I had a great time out there. On this journey, my maiden voyage, I was accompanied throughout by my neighbor and friend Greg McManus on his paddleboard.

I told you before that Greg and his wife, Vicki, own and operate the Napa Valley Wine Train, which he repairs himself, among other feats of engineering. Previously Greg's engineering prowess had been demonstrated many times, notably in the design and implementation of a system he developed for getting Ben Young into the ocean via a system of wires and pulleys that was tied off on the shore to a tree and in the water to a big lava rock under the surface. The system was devised because carrying Ben into the water over lava rock was obviously a source of danger and concern. So, with this new idea, we would get Ben Young in a giant sling with pulleys on it connected to an overhead wire and let him glide down along the wire until he splashed into the water and the waiting arms of his dedicated support team, Dustin Cline and Marian Zemla. Of course, Ben Young was laughing his ass off all the time and having a wonderful water experience! (Since Ben had his feeding tube implanted, we have not been doing this sort of thing, but I am not so sure we need to stop it. We are getting familiar with the tube, and it's really quite stable. It just takes some serious getting used to. Ben should still have those ocean activities, and I see no reason to stop if it's safe.)

Although Ben will not be able to paddleboard with me, I know he will enjoy watching. He always likes sharing himself with us by watching, which is one of those gifts he has. He just enjoys what we're doing through our joy. He has become a master of that. Life is short and should be lived to the fullest. We will be trying to do everything we can to get back in the ocean again with Ben Young.

## Chapter Sixty-Four

So now I find myself rolling down a California two-lane high-way listening to the Pistol Annies' *Hell on Heels*, which I first heard on Rhapsody. The old fields and new factory farms fly by, the road full of cars I don't recognize, with young people behind the wheels talking excitedly about things of which I have only some understanding. A long grade approaches. My generator is cycled off and I'm running silent at about forty-five miles an hour. Visions of the future and past jostle for position in my coffee-soaked mind while the sun starts having its first warming moments. My windows are not as clean as they were when I started my journey, so I'll have to try to do something about that soon. I like looking and listening. The music is really good! I crank it up and lament the streaming quality, wanting to download the album from Pono as soon as I can so I can hear what they heard, but I love the songs. Finally I am hearing something that makes me feel good! I love the vibe these girls have! The way they talk about real things.

"Trailer for Rent" comes on and I strain to hear all the words, making a note in my mind to Google the lyrics as soon as I can.

The ones I can make out are really good, and the harmonies are just great. It's all about struggling with life at a young age, trying it out, discarding it, and grabbing for more. I love hearing this energy. I recognize it from my own youth, and it gives me faith in life and makes me feel. Feelings, once awakened, can take me anywhere, and they do. Now happy, now sad, reliving the past again.

I'm noticing the approaching grade as the generator cycles on and my speed holds at forty-five miles an hour. I am in my element, traveling past the small towns now on a side road that reminds me of the highways my family used to take when Daddy drove us down through Georgia to Florida every fall. Actually it is the same vintage of road, but it is seldom used now. That is all on the interstate a couple of miles away, running more or less parallel. This two-lane with the faded yellow line is soothing somehow, although the roughness of the surface harkens back to smoother times. Rolling down the side window, I feel the air rush in and smell the grass in the fields as they fly by. Life is good!

Now I notice a bad smell and it gets worse immediately. Up goes the window. Cresting a small hill I see the factory hog farm that is the source of the foulness. In a few minutes it is past and I am upwind. I try lowering the window again. Now the sweet smell of the fields returns as I see a few small family farms roll by. I love this road. I wonder how long that factory farm has been there and how the locals feel about it, what it would be like to live downwind. Damn, that music is good, something about her husband being a hunter and never being home, always out with his coonhounds. I realize that I am loving this music because it's talking about a life that I can't see, kind of a mirage from the back country of the South.

"Boys from the South" comes on and again I am taken by this music. It appears from nowhere as a new release on Rhapsody. No radio play. No hype announcement. Just real good country. I suddenly realize that things have changed so much that I might be getting lost. The old ways I know are losing ground. My way is fading. But I still feel. No one can take that away from me. It is a gift I still have and I want my own music to feel as alive and vibrant as what I am hearing now. Will that happen? Will I just be reliving my glory days when I record again? Will anybody hear it? Doubt enters the picture as I slow to thirty and cruise by a horseshoe-shaped complex on the side of the road. RETIREMENT MOTEL, reads a neon sign. The vacancy light is there, but I can't make out whether the sign is lit or not because the sun is hitting it.

I keep rolling along, and the grade has gradually started. I try to call home but the cell reception is gone for the moment. Checking the GPS, I decide to cross over a few miles and join the interstate to make the long climb. When I get to the big road, the pace is much faster, and I am cruising at seventy or seventy-five with the generator cycled on at maximum. Fuel is a bit low, and I start wondering if I'll be able to get E85 (85 percent ethanol, 15 percent gasoline) or if I will have to refuel with pure gasoline. This is a big grade, really long. The interstate seems to stretch for miles in a straight line as the fields and farms give way to a more barren landscape. "Loneliness has been good to me" is playing on my personal radio, where I hear songs before I write them, and I wonder if this is just another mirage I will forget or if this will become a real song. It has been a long time since I've written a song, and the visits from the muse seem to be lessened by something. I still keep my faith that the muse knows best and when I am ready the inspiration will be there. I am trying not to look too ready. I know that just invites false promise.

I pass a hitchhiker going the other way, on the other side of the big road. You don't often see those anymore, especially on the interstate. Glancing in my rearview mirror, I can't see him anymore, or maybe it was a her. I am sure I saw someone, but I know looking backward is not a good idea, so I abandon the thought and continue on my way up the grade. The big Lincoln holds steady at seventy-four miles per hour, displaying the legendary power that makes it a true Continental, even though it is totally electric at the prime mover. A soft whine comes through the rear set as the two hundred kilowatts does its work.

A lot of insects have met their demise and the windshield is even harder to see through than it was earlier, so I try to clean the glass with the wiper wash system. Initially it leaves some big streaks, so I keep pushing the button until I can see clearly again. The only clean area is where the wipers are. The rest is really pretty useless for anything other than windshield protection. Halfway up the grade, the road begins to turn and I see a fuel station. Taking the exit, I cruise into a modern fuel stop where there is no E85, so I fill up with gasoline. Using the towels and cleaning tool available there, I clean all the Lincoln's windows and even the headlights, as well as the front of the car, which is packed with dead insects, the victims of my passage. A few minutes later I return to the big road and the long climb. The summit is somewhere ahead.

Looking for another dose of that great music, I try to restart the Pistol Annies' *Hell on Heels* on Rhapsody, but there is not a clear enough signal to stream it. Cruising along, I see the pollution from LA lingering at the summit ahead and remember the first time I smelled LA air in 1966. It was new to me then, a smell I was unfamiliar with.

It wasn't bad, but it sure wasn't good. I was twenty years old at the time.

Walking in the forest for me is like going to church. It is my cathedral, and I haven't been doing that enough lately. With the cougars getting so close to our house recently (we found some cougar shit fifteen feet from the back door), I suppose I have become a little fearful of the forest. I'm going to have to let that go. I need to connect again. Walking the forest floor is one of the most spiritual things I can imagine. Just thinking about it now makes me wonder why I haven't been there in a couple of years. I used to take Ben Young into the forest all the time. We would fasten his chair into the old blue jeep and off we would go together. We both enjoyed it a lot.

Next time we're on the ranch we'll load up and go for a trip together. Just like old times. Rolling slowly down the old jeep road, giant redwoods surrounding us, Ben and I will see the God-rays streaming down through the trees and landing on the forest floor. The old jeep crawling along the pathway silently in low gear, effortless in its motion, creates just enough noise to warn the residents of our arrival, and that is the way. Every now and then we stop just to listen and smell the forest. The birds become silent, then slowly start their chirping, warbling, and finally, as if triggered by some unknown event, a jay cries a warning into the forest. All becomes quiet, and then the cycle begins again with a few warbles and chirps.

I have learned through walking with my dogs here that there is an unspoken law. Always send a warning. Never surprise the animal life in the forest. So walking along without the noise of the jeep, it is wise to whistle a little tune and give the creatures some kind of an idea that you are approaching their area. This gives them a chance to adjust and find a place to hide, so they can watch you from their position out of your view. It is wise to follow the rule of the forest.

Once I was walking with my dog Carl, a golden doodle, in the forest cathedral when I realized that he was not with me. I looked around and called softly. I heard a little yelp. Then I retraced my steps about a hundred feet back on the path around an outcropping on the canyon side and found Carl, just sitting there in the path. I called him softly again. He came forward and sat down about ten feet from me, indicating that he would not come closer. When I turned to continue up the path, beckoning him to follow, he let out a soft bark. Carl was a very quiet dog, and to hear him talk was unusual, yet there he was, sitting on the path, unmoving in his resolve. It was then I realized what Carl was telling me. We were trespassing. There was something ahead on the trail and we were not supposed to go there. He was warning me of the danger. When I felt that and grasped it, I immediately reversed course and headed back along the way I had come. Carl ran on ahead, happily wagging his tail.

Carl is gone now, and Nina is with us today, but I think that the same will hold true for her should she choose to go for a walk in the woods with me. So Nina, that is the plan. When Pegi and I return to the ranch, I will take you into the forest for a new experience and a little religion. You can be my guide. You will instinctively know the language. I am reticent to enter the forest without guidance. I will take you to my beautiful church, the place where I find myself.

I really need to do that now. I feel it. Something is missing.

I read on the blogs that legacy artists (i.e., artists with long histories and large catalogs) are just trying to hold on to what they have and keep their money. There is some blogging jerk out there who feels he can generalize his way to validity. I don't like being put into any group. This guy thinks he knows the motivations of artists like me. I am a legacy artist, like it or not; I have my history, for what it's worth. I love streaming. What a great replacement for radio! But radio used to pay mechanical royalties every time a song got played. It was a minuscule amount and artists were happy. Just because I would like to know the formula for artists getting paid by streaming services does not make me a greedy person. I have been trying to find out what the formula is for these services paying the artists/record companies, and you'd think I was trying to infiltrate the U.S. Mint. I get a letter asking me if I want to be "in or out" of streaming, with absolutely zero information with which to make my decision. Like I said, I am not trying to get rich here; I am trying to make an informed decision. It is my art, my creation, that is being served here, and I deserve to know.

Yet I have been told that the deals are so new that they are changing all the time, and my music is being streamed on multiple services in the meantime. That does not seem like good business to me. I'm wondering what the heck I should be thinking about when I make these decisions. There certainly is a lot more to music than technology, and the creative flow of songwriting does not revolve around a computer. I would like some answers.

My friend and manager, Elliot, is going to Warner Brothers today to find out what the deal is and get me a copy of it so I know what I and other artists are doing. Every artist everywhere deserves to know these things. It is the right of the artist. That does not make legacy artists and record companies greedy. Listen, I love the new technology. It fascinates me. Steve Jobs was a genius, and I was deeply saddened by his death. What a pioneer. His death marked the end of an era. I was so close to getting to talk with him in person about the future of music, after one or two telephone talks and a few e-mails, but now he is gone. I hope he knew what a wonderful thing he had accomplished, and I only wanted to help him make it better by bringing quality sound along with it. Thank you, Steve.

(As an aside here, I want to say that I have now learned the basis of the formulas for payment of streamed-music royalties, and they seem to be pretty fair. Remember, there are different formulas for different streaming services. Someone needs to explain these models to artists so they can feel good about the knowledge. Artists need a representative and a clear message. It's a brand-new way of dealing with the payment of royalties, and it has been carefully worked out so far, although there may be adjustments to the formulas as time goes by and everyone concerned begins to understand the impacts of these new models on their lives and businesses. Time will tell. This is the beginning. Some things will work, and some won't.)

Personally, from what I can see, I would hate to be in the position of dealing directly with the technology companies without a buffer if I was an artist, which I am. I would say neither legacy artists nor record companies are the buffoons some self-righteous music newbies have made them out to be. This is an evolving picture. It needs to be watched.

I have been clean now for seven months. That is a good long time. I still feel cravings. Maybe I'd like a beer, maybe a joint. I heard the Pistol Annies sing about reasons why they're broke and so who would invest in their future? One's drinkin', one's smokin', one's taking pills. Well, they are writing their asses off. I know that. I haven't written a song in more than half a year, and that is different for me. Of course I've written over ninety thousand words in this book, and that is different for me, too.

I always wrote when I was high before. Getting high is something I used to do to forget one world's realities and slip into the other world, the music world, where all the melodies and words come together in a thoughtless and random way like a gift. I always have said that thinking is the worst thing for music, and now I would like to know how to get back to music without getting high. Some people are probably saying I should get high and write more songs 'cause that works. My doctor does not think that is good for my brain.

My brain has a lot of something else in it that you can only see on an MRI. I don't know what it is or what it isn't, but I do know my dad's history. He was a writer and lost his mind to dementia. What the hell is that cloudy stuff in my brain? I wish I'd never seen that shit. Anyway, I have been advised to stop smoking grass, and I have. As a matter of fact, I've written this whole damn book straight. It certainly is a quandary.

Of course there are many reasons to be straight and many reasons to be stoned, but that doesn't solve anything. There are many reasons to live and die, too. Where is this headed? I'll be damned if I know, Hoss; some highway at the bottom of some hill? Tell me about it. I've been there. I can still see myself out on that road, ripping it up in some honky-tonk or tearing down some arena with the Horse, but when I occasionally see myself in the mirror, it just doesn't add up. Where are we headed with this? Beats the hell out of lookin' back, that's for sure. I'm not sure of what's real anymore, I can tell you that. The straighter I am, the more alert I am, the less I know myself and the harder it is to recognize myself. I need a little grounding in something and I am looking for it everywhere.

Cravings. Yes, I have 'em. And they are not insignificant, but then I imagine where that takes me and it scares the shit out of me. I have been with some of you for a real long time, and others of you don't have the foggiest notion what I am or what I stand for. I am possibly joining those legions myself. I am okay when I focus on something and stay with it; I may get abrasive and overbearing about it, but at least I'm busy. It's those other times that get me.

"It's Those Other Times": is that a song or what?

When will I put it together? How fucking loose do I have to get to put a song together again? Why not? Have you ever heard of transference? Am I taking on someone else's battles? Is that it? How the heck did I get to this place?

Now, in a few moments, I know this will pass and I will focus in on something a little easier. Maybe back on that highway, climbing that grade, burning that damn gas, heading for that pollution. Listening to "Bad Example" by the Pistol Annies. (Check that one out. Those girls can sing.)

When I was onstage at Farm Aid in Kansas City a couple of weeks ago, that was the realest I have been in a while. I was really happy to hear that echo. That's the closest to being high I've been in a long time. It *was* being high. I was so into that moment, and everything was so easy. I have to remember how the heck I got to that place. Why did that happen? What was the key? At least I know it happened and I was there. If I can bring that to the Horse when we get together in the White House, then I will be really happy. Farm Aid was a solitary experience, though; just me and my old guitar were playing. No other people. Except for the thousands of fans in the soccer stadium—I forgot about that.

When I started out I did a lot of acoustic solo playing and

found it to be quite liberating, if confining in that it meant jamming was more or less out of the question, while improvising was definitely easy and totally unencumbered. Dropping beats and bars is no problem when you're alone and is part of the folk process and storytelling freedom. All the while in my life I have been on these two separate paths, acoustic and electric music. Some people like one and some like the other. I like them both. Especially with the Horse, I have fans who could totally miss my acoustic solo stuff and not care at all, while fans of the acoustic solo appearances have little use for the Horse. I have often wondered why Bob, who was so great with just his guitar and harmonica, has never returned to that form since his first foray into band music with Barry Goldberg, Mike Bloomfield, later Al Kooper and the guys. That was great sound, but so was his solo acoustic stuff that defined a whole era. He has so rarely gone back, and that is notable. I don't know why. He plays a unique guitar and his harp playing is definitive. His storytelling is beyond my description, so why doesn't he do it? I guess I'll have to ask him someday.

I would really like to make a solo acoustic record at some point. You really have to have songs to pull that off. Usually when I do try to do that I end up with a band, because you can always hear a band playing songs when you write them, at least I can. In the studio with the Horse, though, you have to be real careful. Analysis is no good for the Horse. The Horse defines music without thought. The physical feeling of playing with the Horse is like nothing else. It leaves your brain wide open, like you can feel the wind blowing right through it. I am looking forward to that relief, that feeling.

Another thing about the Horse is that knowing the song structure before starting is important. There are no run-throughs. Generally the best feelings are the early takes. First or second takes, mostly. Whatever you think of the music I have made with Crazy Horse, those songs are the most transcendent experiences I have ever had with music. That has an immeasurable value to me, and I think it will still be there when we get together to record.

Of course, I have seldom played straight with the Horse.

With David Briggs, the night I was inducted into the
Rock and Roll Hall of Fame, New York, 1995.

## Chapter Sixty-Five

S omeday I would like to write a book, *The Life and Times of David Briggs*. I could research everyone he touched and really get to the bottom of some things about my mercurial, mysterious brother.

He was born Manning Philander Briggs on February 29, 1944, and grew up in Wyoming with family members who took care of him. His best friend was Kirby, and one day in the mid-sixties they up and went to LA to find their fortunes. Kirby became a grip, working in the movies, and Briggs became a record producer, eventually marrying a Wyoming girl, Shannon, and having a son, Lincoln Wyatt Briggs, in Topanga Canyon, which is where I met him. Shannon was a great girl, and he loved her. He was a wild man, and she loved him. Lincoln was a good boy, and I'm not sure how he is doing now, although I worry about him sometimes.

Briggs and I made my best records, the transcendent ones, the ones where I am closest to the Great Spirit. I say that because She visited me more often with Briggs than when I was with any other human being. Briggs and I had a way of getting to the place. We somehow knew the *way*. He was the most influential person on my music of anyone I've met. His guidance and friendship through the creation of countless pieces of music are one of the greatest gifts of my life, right up there with my wife's love and all of my children. I feel the loss. I feel the memories. I feel the weight of every mistake I made in our long relationship, the times he was right and I was wrong, the times I didn't use him to produce for the wrong reason, every battle we had. I feel the absence of his unbelievable energy for music, combined with mine. There is no replacement for that. It is one of life's little voids.

So there he was in his apartment in San Francisco with Bettina, his sweetheart. Barely standing and all crooked and bent over. Short in stature, this giant of a man, now resembling a tree with no leaves waiting for winter, was looking right at me. It was obvious he was dying from something and the process was well advanced. I was surprised at how far it had come in a short time, having only heard he was sick. It had been many months since we had worked together, and this was not the Briggs I remembered. Be that as it may, there he was, barely able to stand, which he did, for some reason I can't remember. He was in pain from an ailment, a mysterious ailment that may have visited him once earlier in life, in the seventies. At that time, he had disappeared for a few months and come back as if nothing had happened. There was a rumor of cancer and a hospital stay in Sacramento, but nothing was for sure. David was mysterious, and that is the end of that. Nobody knew what was really happening with David, ever. That is why a book on the subject might be worth a shot.

So now here we were with David's second big bout against whatever it was, and it had pretty well gotten him. He was taking a lot of morphine for the pain and looked terrible, although the spirit was still in his eyes, weak as it was.

"Do you have any advice for me on my music going forward?" I asked David.

"Just make sure to have as much of you in the recording as you can," he said. "Stay simple. No one gives a shit about anything else."

He told me to keep it simple and focused, have as much of my playing and singing as possible, and not to hide it with other things. Don't embellish it with other people I don't need or hide it in any way. Simple and focused. That is what I took away. He didn't exactly say that, but I got that message. I have failed to do that in some instances. "Be great or be gone," his famous phrase, echoes in my head. I have to remember that for sure. Damn.

So I left the apartment after a hug. It was devastating. He died a week later. He wanted to go. His body was all fucked up, and it was not easy. His tenacious spirit would not let him go.

The last time I saw Danny Whitten, it was late 1972 and he had come to play in the Stray Gators with Jack Nitzsche, Kenny Buttrey, Tim Drummond, Ben Keith, and me at the ranch. We were rehearsing for the first tour since my *Harvest* album had been released. The tour was my longest and biggest ever. I wanted the band to be able to play well live, and just as CSN wanted me for that, I wanted Danny in this band.

I had heard he was doing well, and had called him and invited him up. I went to pick him up at the airport and take him to the ranch. He wanted to stop at a liquor store and so we pulled over in Millbrae, a little town near the San Francisco airport. There was something weird about that. I really can't put my finger on what it was, but something happened at that stop. I wish I could describe it, but now I just have a feeling. I think it was because he didn't want me to go into the liquor store with him. Anyway, he reappeared and got back in the car and we headed up to the ranch, where I set him up in a little cabin on the ranch called the Red House.

Rehearsals started the next day, and I was excited. It was great to hear Danny singing and playing with these guys, but it didn't last long before he had to take a break and go back to the house. Eventually I started to see that he was still strung out. I'm pretty sure Jack knew right away, and maybe Tim knew, too. But no one was talking. After a few days of this, it was becoming obvious that Danny wouldn't be able to cut it. He wanted to. You could really see that. I had to let him go, and that was difficult. So I got him a ticket home and a ride to the airport. It was sad, but we had work to do to prepare for this huge tour that was already booked. It would have been great if Danny was with us, but that was not to be. We rehearsed without him and got started rebuilding the band.

That night Carrie and I were asleep in our little bedroom at the ranch house when the phone rang. It was the middle of the night, and Carrie got up to answer it. I fell back asleep. She woke me up.

"Danny has OD'd," she said. "That was the LA county coroner. He had the ranch phone number on a piece of paper in his wallet."

I lit a fire and sat there in my rocking chair. We lit a candle for him. It was as simple as that. I knew that what I had done may have been a catalyst in Danny's death, but I also knew that there was really nothing else I could have done. I can never really lose that feeling. I wasn't guilty, but I felt responsible in a way. It's part of what I do. Managing the band and taking care of the music is very painful at times. It's a sad story. A moment I will never forget, years I can never replace, music the world will never hear, all gone in the turning of a second.

One of the true greats, Tim Drummond is a musician at the highest level, and a very funny character, full of expressions like "You crack the whip and I'll make the trip," "We are the mighty few," "Been around like shit on a wagon wheel," and "Front row, white socks," to name just a few. He called me Rainy. As I have said before, he played with a lot of greats: Conway Twitty, James Brown, JJ Cale, Bob Dylan, and Jimmy Buffett come to mind. He had the big groove. He was sometimes known as The Moth by the crew because he was always in the edge of the spotlight when it was on me. I never minded that at all, because he was always watching my foot to see what I was doing with the beat. His playing on *Harvest* was wonderful, and he is responsible for putting that band together. Tim played with me in many bands over the years and was one of the very best.

Something happened to him when he broke up with his wife, Inez. He gave up music. He has been drinking a lot and is in a wheelchair now. The last time I saw Tim was in Nashville when I flew him there to be with me for a party celebrating the release of *A Treasure*, which is one of my favorite records of all time, featuring the International Harvesters with fiddler Rufus Thibodeaux, Spooner Oldham, Joe Allen, Karl T. Himmel, Hargus "Pig" Robbins, and Anthony "Sweet Pea" Crawford. Although Rufus had passed away, the rest of the band except for Pig was all there at the party, and it was fun to see everyone together again. *A Treasure*, titled by Ben Keith, was a record that had never come out before, a compilation of beautiful performances from the eighties by a seminal road band. Tim is one of the best I have ever known, right up there with Ben Keith. I wish he hadn't given up his music. Something in him just broke. And I miss playing with him and having him active. Thanks, Tim.

Jack Nitzsche was the composer-arranger who did the charts for Phil Spector's Wall of Sound. These masterpieces always had Jack's brilliant orchestrations as the major component or influence. In the back room at Gold Star Recording Studios in Hollywood, a few doors south from Hollywood Boulevard on Santa Monica Boulevard, there was a legendary echo chamber. The magical tones of this chamber adorned many, if not all, of the Wall of Sound records by the Righteous Brothers, the Ronettes, and the Crystals, to name just a few. These records are part of the history of rock and roll.

The Wall of Sound featured multiple players in the studio, many people all playing the same parts together, multiple tambourines, basses, and pianos, with string sections always in the same room at the same time. These sessions exemplified the spirit of music as I know and love it. It was a capture of the essence of many musical forces, musicians all playing their hearts out at the same time, following a chart, or a loosely preordained order, arranged by Jack. Of course, this was an analog recording, and the overtones were all universal and real. The Gold Star echo brought it all together into the Wall of Sound.

Imagine all of these people getting together in the room, setting up, and then Spector in the control room with Jack in the corner with his charts. Legendary. This was real music, mixed with that magical echo. Goose bumps were felt every night, at every session.

The echo chamber itself was somewhat of a secret. Stan Ross, the owner of Gold Star, would never let anyone see it. No one could go in there. Unlike today's little echo machines, this was a real echo chamber: A sound was fed into a speaker in the chamber from the control room, and a microphone placed in the chamber picked up that sound, with the added echo in the chamber, and sent it back to the control room, where it was remixed into the music according to how much of the effect was desired. The echo effect amount was varied by how loudly you sent the sound into the chamber and how much of it you remixed into the music. You could turn it up or down, change the treble and bass by EQing it, but you never, ever went in there and moved that speaker or messed with that microphone! That would be taboo! No way. It was already great, and the sound was magic. If someone were to change the placement of the microphones it would be disaster and the sound could be gone!

It was spooky, that sound. It was as real as it gets, not some adjustment on a digital device. The sound was different every time something resonated it. You could lose yourself just listening to the depth. It was true magic.

Outside the studio there was a little lounge for musicians where multicolored phones hung on the wall for several answering services to call in and book musicians for sessions at other studios. These phones were each dedicated lines to the different services. Musicians were always moving around town, going from studio to studio, with their cartage services delivering drum kits, stand-up basses, amplifiers, you name it. The services would set up drums or electric instruments so the musicians could just arrive and start playing. Many drummers had multiple sets, and guitar players had multiple amps. Vibraphones and harps were all rented from instrument rental services and delivered around town to multiple sessions, day in and day out.

Then, one day in the eighties, Stan Ross sold Gold Star. Those Wall of Sound days were gone, and it was real estate. Stan called me and asked me if I would like to buy the chamber. I said no. I regret that. I felt it would never be the same if it was moved. I think I was right, but now I'm haunted by that decision. The legendary chamber was an abandoned meat locker.

There was another great Hollywood chamber at Sunset Sound. It was there for a long time, until digital music arrived. Prince recorded exclusively at Sunset for a long time, and I heard he had the chamber made into a lounge. That may or may not be true. I hope it isn't. Anyway, Sunset Sound is where Jack and I recorded and mixed "Expecting to Fly" with Bruce Botnick, one of the most influential and accomplished recording engineers in the history of recorded sound. Jack and I spent weeks working on the chart for "Expecting to Fly" in his house in Coldwater Canyon.

I remember one night going down to the sheriff's office to help get Jack out of jail for drunk driving. I also remember one day when Jack was broke, Phil Spector gave him five grand. That was a shitload of cash in those days. Jack loved Phil because Phil was a genius with a big heart, even though he was crazy and very eccentric. Jack was not a businessman. He was a renaissance composer. His music, if ever collected in one place, would stand with the classics. "Expecting to Fly" was just one of his masterpieces, played by real people and captured on analog for the ages, at a time when no one anticipated what was going to happen to sound. We couldn't know that our beloved tones and recording techniques would be just part of the past, a forgotten art. When I made music that Jack didn't think was up to my potential, he hated me for it. Then he would forgive me and we would move on. Thankfully, that only happened a few times over the years. Jack was a genius. He taught me so much more than I can ever say.

A number of years later, the midnight call came again with a different name. Jack Nitzsche had OD'd in his little home studio in Hollywood. I sent twelve dozen red roses to the service and quite a few floral displays. It was completely over-the-top, but I heard it looked great at the ceremony and made the family feel good. I couldn't go. I was on the road. I didn't know what else to do, so I just sent flowers.

So yes, there has been a lot of loss. It is important to remember the times when life is in full bloom. Those are the moments that give us the faith to move through the darkness when it falls.

Videotaping Ben and Amber on a trip to New Zealand, 1987.

Chapter Sixty-Six

A lot has happened over the years. I am now a very successful musician with a lot of stuff and things of value. Music is a business. I have traveled a long way along life's pathway and have become somewhat of a hard person to work for, or with, because I set high standards and have lost some patience. The years have left a mark. Success has made it possible for me to form some bad habits, to lose respect for those I work with, to skirt certain responsibilities, and to make my own way in the world.

That said, now I am trying to find myself again and reconnect with the values I had in the beginning, find the love in the music with others again, return to the camaraderie that we all enjoyed back in the day, respect others, have empathy for them, be considerate, love myself again, and through that, be more true to myself and others, and above all, be deserving of Pegi. So yes, a lot has happened. I have a full plate, but I am up to the task, I think.

Changing the person one has evolved into is not a simple process, to be sure, but I know that with Pegi's love and support and my family close, I will be able to learn to reach out and live life in a more caring and conscious way. Maybe I have never been good at that, and that's why it's so hard to find it in myself. It may never have really been there. I may be starting from scratch. I've always been told that what I am doing is right. Maybe it isn't. Maybe just some of it is. I need to dig deep and discover some things along the way.

How do I avoid being short with those I love and respect? How do I try to make people feel good about what they are doing for and with me? How can I respect others' tastes while retaining my own? This is the knowledge I am searching for. I can remember so many times in my life when I have hurt others and hurt myself. I really need to find a way to change those patterns for good.

The Times They Are a-Changin' in the book world. I got an offer from my potential publisher today. Borders closed their local store yesterday and announced plans to close them all in the next couple of months. The bookstore culture is evaporating, though the online sales of books was not as great as anticipated.

A group of writers in our living room smoking their pipes and talking into the night was not uncommon to me growing up. Books have always been close to my life, with my father being an author and our family knowing so many writers as family friends. Now huge bookstore chains have closed their doors and liquidated their stock.

These changes would have blown my daddy's mind.

Just as the online social media revolution has brought on mammoth upheaval in the Arab world, it is bringing big change to the publishing world as well. In the new world order there will be an altered landscape, and it is exciting to be around to see it, even as it causes a sea change for the things I do for a living. I believe music and writing will always be around. They are not going anywhere. Actually, I think the full effects of this revolution are just beginning to be seen, and many more areas of world culture will be changed in unknown ways. I am glad I am a musician, and I am looking forward to making my next record with Crazy Horse. I'm not sure how many more albums I will make in the future, since they're not even called albums anymore, but I'm looking forward to finding out.

A long time ago, I started having little birthday parties at the ranch. These parties have become famous in our small community. Pegi and I love traditions, so I thought every year I would invite the children of our friends to a marshmallow roast on the shore of our pond. The pond is a beautiful place, with reeds all around it and an opening near our house that expands onto a huge lawn. It is the perfect place to watch the sunset and listen to the birds. I love the sounds of the red-winged blackbirds! Once while paddleboarding around the pond I was chased and led by a flock of these singing birds flitting about from the reeds behind me to the reeds ahead of me. It was a circular dance, me on my board and about fifty of these beautiful little red-winged blackbirds that I love so much going in a big arc around the edge of the pond.

Anyway, every year I would invite the kids and tell them they could bring their parents. Presents were always requested in a certain category. One year, presents were all requested to be "something from the ground." I got rocks and dirt and little pieces of wood, many of which still reside on my train layout, representing something in a different scale. Each year the presents were a little different, but always something the kids could find around for no money. Also, as part of the tradition, I would set a fire with fallen wood from around the ranch, and when I had it all ready, Pegi would come down and light it. That was always a great moment for us, as we watched the fire catch and begin another year together.

The years went by, and the little kids grew up. Soon they were in college and could not make it for one reason or another, so a new crop of kids came along, then the older kids started coming back. This went on for quite a long time and was a really beautiful feeling and memory. I would go out and gather sticks for the marshmallows and prepare them to be used around the fire by the kids, big and small, and we all would roast them together with the sun going down until we were there in the dark with the bonfire roaring away. It was really great. So one year I went out into the bush to get some sticks for the roast and found a great source. Every stick in the bush was the perfect size. Amazing! What a find! I was so lucky to locate these babies, and I gathered them all up, cut them carefully to length, and stored them by the unlit fire in preparation for the evening's activities. That night we had a wonderful time, planning and remembering the future and past. All was well in the world.

The next day, one of the guests came down with a rash. The day after that, everyone had it.

I went down to the doctor's office and all my friends were there! Some of them were so disfigured as to be unrecognizable. All of them had poison oak! Oh my God! What a feeling that was! I felt like a Canadian terrorist who had infiltrated this little community and poisoned all of the unsuspecting residents in a crime that was years in the making. No wonder those sticks were so different! I had to share that here because it is the single most embarrassing thing I have ever done. All those innocent kids got poison oak because of me! Every year it comes back to haunt me as everyone jokes about it mercilessly. I am not allowed to gather the sticks anymore. What a tradition.

With friends at the Broken Arrow Ranch, 1981. Left to right, standing: David Briggs, Ralph Molina, Larry Cragg, Steve Antoine, me, Jerry Napier; sitting: Tim Mulligan, Billy Talbot, Frank "Poncho" Sampedro, Sal Trentino. Crazy Horse and I were in the process of recording our album re·ac·tor *around this time.*

## Chapter Sixty-Seven

There is a song that I wrote in the middle of the night in front of my fireplace at the ranch that I think stands alone in its form and consciousness. It is a fairly long song that is pretty ambitious in a few ways. It was 1976. I recorded this song on a little Sony cassette player that had "Life is a shit sandwich. Eat it or starve" on a plastic strip label, applied by Briggs during the *Zuma* sessions right below the Sony brand marking. The door for the cassette opened right below the label so you saw it every time the cassette was inserted or removed.

Sitting on the floor late at night, I recorded in front of the fireplace with the cassette on the hearth, three feet from the fire, and you can hear the crackling and hissing of the fire as I played my old Martin guitar and sang "Will to Love," the story of a salmon swimming upstream. Laden with my own feelings of love and survival, the recording stands alone in my work for its audio vérité style, a live sketch of a massive production number with only the highlights presented, fragments of parts, the sound of the fire, the underwater sound created by vibrato.

> *It has often been my dream*
> *To live with one who wasn't there*
> *Like an ocean fish who swam upstream*
> *Through nets, by hooks, and hungry bears*
>
> *When the water grew less deep*
> *My fins were aching from the strain*
> *I'm swimming in my sleep*
> *I know I can't go back again.*

I was scheduled to fly to Miami to continue recording the Stills-Young album with Stephen in the morning; the flight was leaving very early and I had decided to just stay up all night and drive to the airport in time for the flight. I had some drugs, had written this song on a piece of paper, and had decided to sing it all the way through for the first time so I would have something to show Stephen and the band in Florida. I didn't listen back to it that night, I don't think. It was complex in that there were pieces that would have to be added later that I could not sing myself. It was layered, so I had to just sing little pieces of choruses and then go back to the verses and releases.

The cassette of that song was never played for those sessions. It was too sensitive and complex and wouldn't fit with the rest of the tracks on the album, so I saved it for later. Later came in a few weeks, when I was back in Malibu at my beach house, a beautiful little house I had purchased on Sea Level Drive, at the end of the road, right on the beach. The house was wonderful, a Cape Cod cottage that was totally overgrown with bougainvillea. The roof and outside walls were covered in vines, with flowers everywhere. It was a magnificent place that I loved dearly, situated right in a bunch of evergreen trees on the ocean. A big rock was in the water right in front of this house, and the beach went on for miles to the right with no other houses on the sand. They were all on the top of the cliff that started right past my little house. That was paradise. One of the most beautiful houses and locations I have ever seen. The actress Katharine Ross was living there when I bought the place, and I'm sure she was sad to have to leave.

Placed in the evergreens around the patio was an Indian chief with full headdress. That wooden Indian was a work of art. A few years later Pegi and I were married there, and Briggs was my best man. The house and patio, on two lots, were my pride and joy, and I wrote a lot of songs there.

So one evening, Briggs and I went up to Indigo Ranch to record. Indigo Ranch Studios was way up in one of the canyons above Malibu, at the end of its own road, with a beautiful canyon right outside the studio. The place was magnificent and had a great sound, with wonderful equipment that Briggs loved. The owner, Richard Kaplan, was really into his studio; he was an engineer himself, and kept it up really well. It was a perfect place, and David recorded me there a lot. We loved it and always enjoyed being there.

I had asked David to get me a lot of instruments, including drums, an electric bass, a vibraphone, some of my old amps including my Magnatone with the stereo vibrato, and a few other things. They were all there when we arrived. We always smoked some weed on the way up there and were feeling fine as we drove by The Band's Garth Hudson's place on the little dirt road, the last house before the studio, which was about a half mile farther. I realized there was no way I could sing the song again or perform it, and I never have since. I told David that I simply wanted to play back the cassette through the Magnatone with vibrato so it would sound like I was underwater at times during the song, when I was taking the point of view of the salmon. That was the first thing we did. Then I started layering on instruments, one at a time. The drugs began to flow and soon it was the middle of the night and we were still hard at it. I was sketching, not painting, the track. Instruments came and went, indicating their presence without the cumbersomeness of staying. I played some drums during one section, just following the muse. Then I sang all of the choruses, filling them in so that I was singing on top of myself, and added the releases as well.

Somewhere in the middle of that night, we did a mix. That was the perfect way to work. Get it all at once. Put it on tape and mix it immediately while the image is fresh. As the last chords died away, I felt Mr. Briggs's strong hands massaging my back as I sat in front of the console with my own head in my hands, my eyes closed and covered, just listening. The sound was cascading over me and all around me, and I was swimming in it. Our work was done. That memory is one of my favorite moments and is the perfect example of a great life with my friend David, who guided me and assisted me in every trip I decided to take through the world of music.

It was time to jump in Nanu for the slow ride home to dawn on Sea Level Drive, carefully avoiding any actions that would catch the sheriff's eye as he patrolled the Pacific Coast Highway in his cruiser.

## Chapter Sixty-Eight

The Continental climbs along up the grade with seemingly little effort, and the grade never seems to end. Traffic is thicker now, with more and more vehicles joining the procession. Six lanes wide, the big road winds and dips through the mountainous terrain, and I am a little lonely. For some reason the GPS is not functioning and Rhapsody is not getting enough signal to deliver another round of *Hell on Heels*, but everything else is going to plan as I glance in the rearview mirror and see myself looking back. I look really good somehow; maybe it's the light, but my face doesn't seem all lined with age. I actually feel great and eager to get to the city and see what's going on, but also strangely hungry. Thinking back over the last many hours, I remember the Retirement Motel, the small farms with their green grass, the stench of that factory farm I passed, and as I trace back through the day, which seems to have started a long time ago, I can't remember eating a thing or having a drink of water. Looking around the front seat, I don't see any bottled water or snacks. From where I am, I can't see the sun in the sky, although I can feel the heat on the convertible top. It must be noon or thereabouts. My mind is wandering to women I have met and loved, and when I come to Pegi, I feel really good, kind of complete in a way, like I really lucked out in the end, getting the best of the best.

I remember some of the dreams I've had where Ben Young is walking and talking, dreams that seem so real and vivid. The things he says are so natural, like he has always talked, and he exchanges a knowing glance with me as his mother makes an observation concerning the feelings she has had her whole life.

Family business is on the agenda, and reckoning with things is at hand. The meeting is set for tomorrow. Business people are flying in, and the pressure is mounting, or at least the anticipation. Perhaps we may not be able to keep everything we have and we may have to make some decisions and lighten our load. All of these houses, five on the ranch and three on the Hawaii property, may be too much for us to handle, and the moment has come to make choices. We have never looked forward to this, thinking that ultimately something might happen to help us avoid the inevitable, but here we are.

Brake lights line up in front of me and I slow to a crawl. Traffic is lined up for miles in the sweltering heat. I try rolling the window down to get a feel for the surroundings, and it's excruciatingly hot outside, with a lot of fumes. The Continental's generator cycles off and we are running on pure electric power, able to crawl at less than one mile an hour with total control, completely eliminating the stop-and-go actions of the older cars with their prime mover internal combustion engines. Thank God for the air-conditioning, which is still working.

The sound system comes on again with a glitch, somehow set to the Crystals' "Da Doo Ron Ron":

I met him on a Monday,
And my heart stood still . . .

What a great song, so simple and innocent. Somehow I am connected to a vintage radio show on Rhapsody, with a real DJ talking and old commercials. What a trip. Technology is amazing! It even sounds old. I remember that there is a café up here and decide to get off the interstate in a mile or two and take that two-lane road I remember to a little town Briggs and I used to visit, and get some food. That may give this traffic time to clear. After about twenty minutes of crawling along under five miles an hour, I finally arrive at the exit and discover it is closed. Looking about carefully, I spy an opening around the roadblock and decide to take a chance. There's nothing better to do, and the most that can happen is I will have to back up and lose some time. The Continental just fits!

Making it around the roadblock, I turn on the two-lane and find myself cruising along with no problem; the other direction was completely blocked, but this way is fine. How lucky can you get? This is the old road we used to take every time we made this trip back in the day. It's in pretty good shape really, and there is no traffic to speak of. A sixties car passes going the opposite direction, and I think to myself, *Wow, will they be bummed when they get to the interstate.*

It's very quiet out here, and I pull over at a place near a creek where I can just get a drink from the flowing water. Parking roadside, I get out and stretch my legs. I feel great! It's a beautiful day, and this road is just the kind I like. Now, watching my step on the rocks, I edge my way down to the creek, cupping my hands and scooping up some of the crystal-clear water. I love to drink this way; it's so refreshing. A couple of fish are visible in the pool in front of me, so I sit down on the shore to watch them for a while, remembering how I used to hang for hours near creeks in my boyhood, catching crawfish and chub and taking them back to my house in a little pail. Then I would store them in a little makeshift water scene I had created in one of my mother's old roasting pans with some water, sand, and rocks placed carefully to give a natural look. I used to stick little green grass plants in the sand and make believe they were trees. I feel so good here, I decide to just take a little nap.

I get back in the Continental and continue down the road to the café. Then I pull in and there's Larry Johnson's '57 Ford pickup in the parking lot. As I enter the little café, I see Larry and Briggs in the corner, drinking some coffee and having a late breakfast. I go right over and sit down with them. We don't say much. David says something about Kirby getting a job at one of the studios. Kirby is very good with his hands and can fix anything, plus he has a very friendly personality. We are happy for him. Larry has to make a call and gets up, heading for the pay phone in the corner. He asks us to get him another coffee when the waitress comes back. Briggs looks at me and asks what I've been doing.

Acknowledgments

I would like to thank all the people in this book and my next book. There can never be enough pages for you.

Photography Credits

He just wanted a decent book to read ...

Not too much to ask, is it? It was in 1935 when Allen Lane, Managing Director of Bodley Head Publishers, stood on a platform at Exeter railway station looking for something good to read on his journey back to London. His choice was limited to popular magazines and poor-quality paperbacks – the same choice faced every day by the vast majority of readers, few of whom could afford hardbacks. Lane's disappointment and subsequent anger at the range of books generally available led him to found a company – and change the world.

'We believed in the existence in this country of a vast reading public for intelligent books at a low price, and staked everything on it'
Sir Allen Lane, 1902–1970, founder of Penguin Books

The quality paperback had arrived – and not just in bookshops. Lane was adamant that his Penguins should appear in chain stores and tobacconists, and should cost no more than a packet of cigarettes.

Reading habits (and cigarette prices) have changed since 1935, but Penguin still believes in publishing the best books for everybody to enjoy. We still believe that good design costs no more than bad design, and we still believe that quality books published passionately and responsibly make the world a better place.

So wherever you see the little bird – whether it's on a piece of prize-winning literary fiction or a celebrity autobiography, political tour de force or historical masterpiece, a serial-killer thriller, reference book, world classic or a piece of pure escapism – you can bet that it represents the very best that the genre has to offer.

Whatever you like to read – trust Penguin.

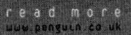